THE

CAMBRIDGE

MEDIEVAL HISTORY

VOLUME II

THE

CAMBRIDGE

MEDIEVAL HISTORY

VOLUME II

THE
CAMBRIDGE
MEDIEVAL HISTORY

PLANNED BY

J. B. BURY, M.A., F.B.A.

EDITED BY

H. M. GWATKIN, M.A.
J. P. WHITNEY, D.D.

VOLUME II

THE RISE OF THE SARACENS AND THE
FOUNDATION OF THE WESTERN EMPIRE

CAMBRIDGE UNIVERSITY PRESS

CAMBRIDGE

LONDON · NEW YORK · MELBOURNE

Published by the Syndics of the Cambridge University Press
The Pitt Building, Trumpington Street, Cambridge CB2 1RP
Bentley House, 200 Euston Road, London NW1 2DB
32 East 57th Street, New York, NY 10022, USA
296 Beaconsfield Parade, Middle Park, Melbourne 3206, Australia

ISBN 0 521 04533 9

First published 1913
Reprinted with corrections 1926
Reprinted 1936 1957 1964 1967 1976

Printed in Great Britain
at the
University Printing House, Cambridge
(Euan Phillips, University Printer)

PREFACE.

THE present volume of the *Cambridge Medieval History* covers the stormy period of about three hundred years from Justinian to Charles the Great inclusive. It is a time little known to the general reader, and even students of history in this country seldom turn their attention to any part of it but the Conversion of the English. Hence, English books are scarce—Dr Hodgkin's *Italy and her Invaders* is the brilliant exception which proves the rule—and the editors have had to rely more on foreign scholars than in the former volume. Some indeed of the chapters treat of subjects on which very little has ever been written in English, such as the Visigoths in Spain, the organisation of Imperial Italy and Africa, the Saracen invasions of Sicily and Italy, and the early history and expansion of the Slavs.

Professor Diehl begins with two chapters on Justinian, one dealing with the conquest of Africa and Italy by Belisarius and Narses, and the imperial restoration in the West, the other devoted to the administration in the East—the Empress Theodora and her influence, Justinian's buildings and diplomacy, and government civil and ecclesiastical. The city of Constantinople is reserved for the same writer in Volume IV. Dr Roby follows, with a general survey of Roman Law, of its history and growth, and of its completion by the legislation of Justinian. A survey of this kind has hardly been attempted since the famous forty-fourth chapter of Gibbon. Then Professor Pfister takes up the story of the Franks at the accession of Clovis, where he left it in the first volume, and traces the growth and decline of the Merovingian kingdom to the deposition of the last of the *rois fainéants*. He then follows it up with another chapter on the political and social institutions of Gaul in Merovingian times—the King, the Mayor of the Palace, the Bishop, the origin of the benefice, the state of literature and commerce. In the next chapter we turn with Dr Altamira to the Visigoths in Spain, and follow their stormy history from the defeat at Vouglé, through the Councils of Toledo, to the times of Count Julian and the Saracen Conquest, and to some further discussion of Gothic law. The next writer is Dr Hartmann, who traces the early history of the Lombards and their settlement in Italy, their conversion and the story of Theodelinda. After her come Rothari and Grimoald, and the great king Liutprand, and parallel with the main narrative is traced the history of the duchies of Friuli and Spoleto. So he comes to the conquests of Aistulf and the Frankish intervention, and then to the reign of Desiderius, under whom the Lombard power seemed to reach its height—and vanished in a moment at the touch of Charles the Great. The next section, also by Dr Hartmann, is on the Byzantine administration of Africa and Italy. Its special interest is the development of local powers in Italy—not only the Pontifical State, but Venice and other cities. We can see before the fall of the Byzantine power that Italy will be a land of cities. Then Archdeacon Hutton takes up the life of Gregory the Great. He has to tell of Gregory's administration and his measures for the defence of Rome from the Lombards, of his dealings with Emperor and Patriarch, of his relations with Brunhild and Theodelinda, and of his oversight of all the Western churches, reserving only the Mission to the English for a later chapter. Then Mr Norman Baynes gives a living picture of Justinian's successors—the unpractical Justin, the pedant Maurice, the crusader Heraclius, and of the tremendous vicissitudes of the Persian War, with Persians and Avars at one time besieging Constantinople, and Heraclius within two years winning the battle of Nineveh, and dictating peace from the heart of Media. The next three chapters are devoted to Islām. If this is the most brilliant part of Gibbon's narrative, it is also the part which more than almost any other needs revision in the light of later research. Professor Bevan begins with the life of Mahomet, and Dr Becker of Hamburg follows with the expansion of the Saracens. relating in one chapter their conquest of Syria and Egypt, the overthrow of Persia, and the rise and fall of the Umayyads. In another he traces their westward course through Africa and Egypt to Spain till their defeat at Tours, and then turns to the formation of Muslim kingdoms, their conquest of Sicily and their attacks on Italy to the coming of the Normans. Mr Brooks takes the successors of Heraclius to the coming of Leo the Isaurian. The chief topics of this chapter are the advance of the Arabs and their attacks on Constantinople, the history of the Monothelete Controversy, and the fall of the Heraclian dynasty. Dr Peisker takes us into a new region, describing the original country of the Slavs, their society and religion, and their modes of warfare. He then discusses their place in history, their relations to their German and Altaian conquerors, their spread on the German border and in the Balkan countries, and the new social conditions which prevailed when

Slav states became independent. Professor Camille Jullian's section on Keltic heathenism in Gaul goes back to the times of Caesar, but it coheres closely with Sir E. Anwyl's pages on Keltic heathenism in the British Isles. These are placed here rather than in the former volume for the purpose of bringing them into connexion not only with Germanic heathenism but with the Christianity which replaced them. Our material, not rich for Gaul, is scanty for Britain: it is only when we come to Germanic heathenism—the section taken by Miss Phillpotts—that we seem to see the living power of the religion. The next is an analogous chapter devoted to Christianity. Mr Warren first tells us the little that is known of Christianity in Roman Britain, then relates the story of its spread to Ireland and Scotland. In another section Mr Whitney traces first the conversion of the English from Augustine's landing through the reigns of Edwin and Oswald to the decisive victory at Winwaedfield, followed by the Synod of Whitby and the coming of Theodore. He then turns to Germany, where the story gathers round the names of Columbanus, Willibrord and Boniface, and stops short of Charles the Great's conversion of the Saxons by the sword. Mr Corbett takes up the history and institutions of the English from Edwin's time to the death of Offa. The thread of his narrative is the growth of Mercia— the ups and downs of its long struggle under Penda with Northumbria, the revolt under Wulfhere, and the formation of the commanding power wielded by Aethelbald and Offa. Its overthrow by Ecgbert belongs to the next volume. Mr Burr contributes a short chapter on the eventful reign of Pepin—a man whose fame is unduly eclipsed by that of the great Emperor who followed him. Its main lines are the change of dynasty, the intervention in Italy, the Donation, and the conquest of Aquitaine. Then Dr Gerhard Seeliger surveys the Conquests and Imperial Coronation of Charles the Great. He begins with the destruction of the Lombard kingdom, the precarious submission of Benevento and the settlement of Italian affairs: then come the disaster of Roncevalles and the gradual formation of the Spanish March. After this the annexation of Bavaria, the break-up of the Avars, and the long wars with Saxons and Danes. There remain the idea of the Empire, the events which led to the Coronation and its meaning, and Charles' relations to the Eastern Empire. Professor Vinogradoff then discusses the foundations of society and the origins of Feudalism. He describes the various forms of kinship, natural and artificial, the organisation of society, the growth of kingship, taxation, the *beneficium*, and the fusion of Roman and Germanic influences which resulted in Feudalism. Dr Seeliger returns to the legislation and administration of Charles the

Great. He marks the theocratic character of the Carlovingian State, and proceeds to describe the king and his court, the royal revenues, the military system, the assemblies, the legislation, the provincial officials, the *missi dominici*, and the failure of the central power, and of the Empire with it. Dr Foakes-Jackson concludes with a survey of the growth of the Papacy, chiefly from Gregory to Charles the Great—of its relations to the Empire and the Lombards, of its negotiations with the Franks, of the Frankish intervention and the beginnings of the Temporal Power, and of the circumstances and significance of the Imperial Coronation. He covers much the same period as Professor Seeliger, but he puts the Papacy instead of the Franks in the foreground of his picture.

We are indebted to our critics for many hints and some corrections, and we gratefully acknowledge their appreciation of the splendid work done by Dr Peisker and others of our valued contributors: but on one important question we are quite impenitent. The repetitions of which some of them complain are not due to any carelessness in editing, but to the deliberate belief of the Editors that some events may with advantage be related more than once by different writers in different connexions and from different points of view. Thus, to take an instance actually given, the sack of Rome by Gaiseric is a cardinal event in the history of the Vandals, and a cardinal event in that of the last days of the Empire in the West. In which chapter would they advise us to leave it out? Repetitions there must be, if individual chapters are not to be mutilated. Nor are we much concerned about occasional disagreements of our contributors, though we have sometimes indicated them in a note. Consistency is always a virtue in a single writer; not always in a composite work like this. We have often called the attention of one contributor to the fact that another is of a different opinion; but we see no advantage in endeavouring to conceal the fact that students of history do not always come to the same conclusions.

Our best thanks are due to Miss A. D. Greenwood for the laborious work of preparing the maps and the index: also to Professor Bevan for settling the orthography of unfamiliar Oriental names.

H. M. G.
J. P. W.

April 1913

TABLE OF CONTENTS.

CHAPTER I.

JUSTINIAN. THE IMPERIAL RESTORATION IN THE WEST.

By CHARLES DIEHL, Member of the Institute of France,
Professor at the University of Paris.

CHAPTER II.

JUSTINIAN'S GOVERNMENT IN THE EAST.

By Professor CHARLES DIEHL.

CHAPTER III.

ROMAN LAW.

By the late H. J. Roby, M.A., Hon. LL.D. Camb. and Edin., Hon. Fellow of St John's College, Cambridge.

CHAPTER IV.

GAUL UNDER THE MEROVINGIAN FRANKS.
NARRATIVE OF EVENTS.

By Dr Christian Pfister, Professor in the Faculty of Letters, of Paris.

CHAPTER V.

GAUL UNDER THE MEROVINGIAN FRANKS. INSTITUTIONS.

By Professor CHRISTIAN PFISTER.

CHAPTER VI.

SPAIN UNDER THE VISIGOTHS.

By Dr RAFAEL ALTAMIRA, Director-general of Primary Instruction (Ministry of Public Instruction); late Professor of Jurisprudence in the University of Oviedo.

CHAPTER VII.

ITALY UNDER THE LOMBARDS.

By the late Dr L. M. HARTMANN, Extraordinary Professor at the University of Vienna.

CHAPTER VIII.

(A) IMPERIAL ITALY AND AFRICA: ADMINISTRATION.

By the late Dr HARTMANN.

(B) GREGORY THE GREAT.

By the Very Rev. W. H. HUTTON, D.D., Dean of Winchester,
Hon. Fellow of St John's College, Oxford.

CHAPTER IX.

THE SUCCESSORS OF JUSTINIAN.

By NORMAN H. BAYNES, M.A. Oxon., Barrister-at-Law.

CHAPTER X.

MAHOMET AND ISLĀM.

By A. A. Bevan, M.A., Lord Almoner's Reader and Professor of Arabic in the University of Cambridge.

CHAPTER XI.

THE EXPANSION OF THE SARACENS—THE EAST.

By C. H. Becker, Professor of Oriental History in the Colonial Institute of Hamburg.

CHAPTER XII.

THE EXPANSION OF THE SARACENS (*continued*). AFRICA AND EUROPE.

By Professor BECKER.

CHAPTER XIII.

THE SUCCESSORS OF HERACLIUS TO 717.

By E. W. BROOKS, M.A., King's College, Cambridge.

CHAPTER XIV.

THE EXPANSION OF THE SLAVS.

By J. Peisker, Ph.D., Privatdocent and Librarian, Graz.

CHAPTER XV.

(A) KELTIC HEATHENISM IN GAUL.

By Camille Jullian, Professor of the College of France,
and Member of the Institute.

(B) CONVERSION OF THE TEUTONS.

By the Rev. J. P. Whitney, D.D., Dixie Professor of Ecclesiastical History.

(1) The English.

(2) Germany.

CHAPTER XVII.

ENGLAND (to c. 800) AND ENGLISH INSTITUTIONS.

By the late W. J. Corbett, M.A., Fellow of King's College, Cambridge.

CHAPTER XVIII.

THE CARLOVINGIAN REVOLUTION, AND FRANKISH INTERVENTION IN ITALY.

By G. L. Burr, Professor Emeritus of Modern History, Cornell University, Ithaca, N.Y.

CHAPTER XIX.

CONQUESTS AND IMPERIAL CORONATION OF CHARLES THE GREAT.

By the late Dr Gerhard Seeliger, Professor of Law in the University of Leipsic.

CHAPTER XX.

FOUNDATIONS OF SOCIETY (ORIGINS OF FEUDALISM).

By the late Sir PAUL VINOGRADOFF, Hon. D.C.L., F.B.A., Corpus Professor of Jurisprudence, Oxford.

CHAPTER XXI.

LEGISLATION AND ADMINISTRATION OF CHARLES THE GREAT.

By the late Dr GERHARD SEELIGER.

CHAPTER XXII.

THE PAPACY, TO CHARLES THE GREAT.

By the Rev. F. J. FOAKES-JACKSON, D.D., Fellow of Jesus College, Cambridge.

LIST OF BIBLIOGRAPHIES.

LIST OF MAPS

VOLUME II

(At end of book)

CHAPTER I.

JUSTINIAN.
THE IMPERIAL RESTORATION IN THE WEST.

I.

On 9 July 518 the Emperor Anastasius died, leaving nephews only as his heirs. The succession was therefore quite undecided. An obscure intrigue brought the Commander-in-Chief of the Guard, the *comes excubitorum* Justin, to the throne. This adventurer had found his way to Constantinople from the mountains of his native Illyricum in search of fortune, and now became, at the age of almost seventy years, the founder of a dynasty.

The position of the new prince did not lack difficulties. Ever since 484, when the schism of Acacius embroiled the Eastern Empire with the Papacy, incessant religious and political agitations had shaken the monarchy. Under pretence of defending the orthodox faith, the ambitious Vitalianus had risen against Anastasius several times, and proved a constant menace to the new sovereign, since he had made himself almost independent in his province of Thrace. The Monophysite party, on the other hand, which had been warmly supported by Anastasius, suspected the intentions of Justin, and upheld the family of its former protector against him. Placed between two difficulties, the Emperor found that he could rely neither on the army, whose allegiance was uncertain, nor on the disturbed capital, torn by the struggles of the Greens and Blues, nor yet on the discontented provinces, ruined as they were by war, and crushed under the weight of the taxes. He saw that nothing short of a new political direction could keep his government from foundering.

The part played by Justin himself in the new order of things was a subordinate one. He was a brave soldier, but almost completely lacking in comprehension of things beyond the battle-field. Quite uncultured, he could hardly read, still less write. Historians tell us that when he became Emperor, and was obliged to sign official documents, a plaque of wood was made for him, with holes cut in it corresponding to the letters of the imperial title. By means of these cracks the sovereign guided his halting hand. Having little acquaintance with the civil administration, ignorant of the intricacies of politics, diplomacy and theology, he would have been quite overwhelmed by his position, had he not had someone behind him, to help and guide him. This was his sister's son, Flavius Petrus Sabbatius Justinianus, known to us as Justinian.

Justinian, as well as his uncle, was born in Macedonia, in the village of Tauresium, near Skoplje. He was a peasant of the Latin race, and by no means a Slav as romantic traditions of a much later date affirm. To these traditions a value has long been assigned which they do not possess. Justinian went early to Constantinople by his uncle's request, and received a thoroughly Roman and Christian education in the schools of the capital. When, through a piece of good luck, Justin became Emperor, his nephew was about thirty-six years old; he was experienced in politics, his character was formed and his intellect matured. He was quite prepared for the position of coadjutor to the new Caesar, and immediately assumed it. The good will of his uncle brought him step by step nearer to the foot of the throne. He became in turn Count, *vir illustris*, patrician. He was Consul in 521, Commander-in-Chief of the troops which garrisoned the capital (*magister equitum et peditum praesentalis*), *nobilissimus*, and finally, in 527, Justin adopted him and associated him in the Empire itself. Under these various titles it was he who really governed in his uncle's name, while he waited until he should himself ascend the throne (1 August 527). Thus, during nearly half a century, from 518 to 565 Justinian's will guided the destinies of the Roman Empire in the East.

Of all the prominent men who fill the pages of history, few are more difficult to depict and understand than Justinian. Throughout his reign the testimony of contemporaries is abundant and ranges from the extreme of extravagant adulation to that of senseless invective, thus furnishing the most contradictory portrait that exists of any sovereign. From the unmeasured praise of the *Book of Edifices*, and the often foolish gossip of the *Secret History* it is by no means easy to arrive at the truth. Besides, it must not be forgotten that Justinian reigned for thirty-eight years, and died at the age of eighty-three; and that as he drew near the end of his reign, already too long, a growing slackness and lack of grip marked his last years. It is hardly fair to judge him by this period of decrepitude, when he almost seems to have outlived himself. However, this man, who left so deep an impress on the world of the sixth century, cannot lightly be passed by; and, after all, it is possible to estimate his character.

The official portrait is to be found in the mosaic of San Vitale in Ravenna, which dates from 547, though it obviously represents him as somewhat younger than he was. It gives us a good idea of Justinian's features. As to his moral attributes, contemporaries praise the simplicity of his manners, the friendliness of his address, the self-control which he exercised, specially over his violent temper, and, above all, the love of work which was one of his most characteristic traits. One of his courtiers nicknamed him "The Emperor who never sleeps," and in fact, early to rise, and late to retire, the Emperor claimed to know everything, examine everything and decide everything; and brought to this task a great love of order, a real care for good administration and an attention to minute detail which was unceasing. Above everything else, he strove to fill worthily the position of a king.

Endowed with an autocratic disposition, Justinian was naturally inclined to give his attention to all subjects, and to keep the direction of all affairs under his own control, whether they related to war or diplomacy, administration or theology. His imperial pride, increased by an almost childish vanity, led him to claim complete knowledge in every department. He was jealous of anyone who appeared to be sufficiently great or independent to question his decisions. Those who served him most faithfully were at all times liable to become the object of their master's suspicion, or of the libels to which he was always ready and glad to listen. During his whole life Justinian envied and distrusted the fame of Belisarius, and constantly permitted and even encouraged intrigues against that loyal general. Under an unyielding appearance, he hid a weak and vacillating soul. His moods were liable to sudden changes, rash passions and unexpected depression. His will was swayed by the decision and energy of those around him, by that of his wife Theodora, who, in the opinion of contemporaries, governed the Empire equally, or to a greater extent than he did, and by that of his minister John of Cappadocia, who dominated the prince for ten years by means of his bold cleverness. Naturally so weak a man changed with changing circumstances, and might become untrustworthy through deceit at one time, or cruel through fear at another. It followed that, as he was always in need of money—less for himself than for the needs of the State—he was troubled by no scruple as to the means by which he obtained it. Thus, in spite of his undoubted good qualities, his badly-balanced mind, his nature full of contrasts, his weak will, childish vanity, jealous disposition and fussy activity, make up a character of only mediocre quality. But, if his character was mediocre, Justinian's soul did not lack greatness. This Macedonian peasant, seated on the throne of the Caesars, was the successor and heir of the Roman Emperors. He was, to the world of the sixth century, the living representative of two great ideas, that of the Empire, and that of Christianity. This position he was determined to fill; and because he filled it, he was a great sovereign.

Few princes have realised the imperial dignity in a more marked degree than this parvenu, or have done more to maintain the ancient

Roman traditions. From the day when he first mounted the throne of Constantine, he claimed in its full extent the ancient Roman Empire. Sovereign of a State in which Latin was still the official tongue, and which was still styled the "Roman Empire" in official documents, Justinian was less a Byzantine than the last of the Roman Emperors. The most essential part of his imperial duty seemed to him to be the restoration of that Roman Empire whose fragments the barbarians had divided, and the recovery of those unwritten but historic rights over the lost West which his predecessors had so carefully maintained. The thought of the insignia of the Empire, symbols of supreme authority, which, since they had been stolen by Gaiseric in the sack of Rome had been held by the barbarians, inflicted an intolerable wound upon his pride, and he felt himself bound, with the help of God, to reconquer "the countries possessed by the ancient Romans, to the limits of the two oceans," to quote his own words.

Justinian considered himself the obvious overlord of the barbarian kings who had established themselves in Roman territory, and thought he could withdraw, if he wished, the delegated imperial authority which they held. This fact was the keystone of the arch of his foreign policy, while at the same time the imperial idea lent inspiration to his domestic government. The Roman Emperor was practically the law incarnate, the most perfect representative of absolute power that the world has known. This was Justinian's ideal. He was, according to Agathias the historian, "the first of the Byzantine Emperors to shew himself, by word and deed, the absolute master of the Romans." The State, the law, the religion; all hung on his sovereign will. In consequence of the necessary infallibility attaching to his imperial function, he desired equally to be lawgiver and conqueror, and to unite, as the Roman Emperors had done, the majesty of law to the lustre of arms. Anxious to wield the imperial power for the good of the Empire, he wished to be a reformer; and the mass of *Novellae* promulgated by him attests the trouble that he took to secure good administration. Desirous, furthermore, of surrounding the imperial position with every luxury, and of adorning it with all magnificence, he determined that the trappings of the monarchy should be dignified and splendid. He felt the need of resounding titles and pompous ceremonial, and counted the cost of nothing that might increase the splendour of his capital. St Sophia was the incomparable monument of this imperial pride.

But since the time of Constantine, the Roman Emperor could not claim to be heir of the Caesars only: he was also the champion of religion, and the supreme head of the Church. Justinian gladly received this part of his inheritance. Of a disposition naturally devout, and even superstitious, he had a taste for religious controversy, a considerable amount of theological knowledge, and a real talent for oratory. He therefore willingly gave his time to the consideration of matters relating to the Church. His decisions were as unhesitating on matters of dogma as on matters of law and reform, and he brought the same intolerant despotism to bear on church government as on everything else. But above all, as Emperor, he believed himself to be the man whom the Lord had specially chosen and prepared for the direction of human affairs, and over whom the divine protection would ever rest throughout his life. He considered himself to be the most faithful of servants to the God who aided him. If he made war, it was not simply in order to collect the lost provinces into the Roman Empire, but also to protect the Catholics from their enemies the Arian heretics, " persecutors of souls and bodies." His military undertakings had therefore something of the enthusiasm of a Crusade. Furthermore, one of the chief aims of his diplomacy was to lead the heathen peoples into the Christian fold. Missions were one of the most characteristic features of the Byzantine policy in the sixth century. By their means Justinian flattered himself, according to a contemporary, that he " indefinitely increased the extent of the Christian world." Thus the Emperor allied care for religion with every political action. If this pious ardour which consumed the prince had its dangers, in that it quickly led to intolerance and persecution, yet it was not without grandeur; since the progress of civilisation always follows evangelisation. As champion of God, as protector of the Church, and as ally and dictator to the Papacy, Justinian was the great representative of what has been called " Caesaropapism."

From the day when, under Justin's name, he originally undertook the government of the Empire, these ideas inspired Justinian's conduct. His first wish was to come to some agreement with Rome in order to end the schism. The announcement made to Pope Hormisdas, of the accession of the new sovereign, together with the embassy despatched soon afterwards to Italy to request that peace might be restored, made it clear to the pontifical court that they had but to formulate their requests in order to have them granted. The Roman legates proceeded to Constantinople, where because of Justinian's friendship they received a splendid welcome, and obtained all that they demanded. The Patriarch John with the greater number of Eastern prelates in his train signed the profession of orthodoxy brought by the papal envoys. The names of Acacius and other heretical patriarchs with those of the Emperors Zeno and Anastasius were effaced from the ecclesiastical diptychs. After this the Pope was able to congratulate Justinian upon his zeal for the peace of the Church, and the energy with which he sought to restore it. In consequence of the prince's attitude, and at the pressing request of the pontifical legates, who remained in the East for eighteen months, the dissentient Monophysites were vigorously persecuted throughout the Empire. In Syria the Patriarch Severus of Antioch was deposed and anathematised by the Synod of Tyre (518),

CH. I.

and more than fifty other bishops were soon afterwards chased from their sees. For three years (518–521) the persecution continued. The chief heretical meetings were scattered, the convents closed, the monks reduced to flight, imprisoned or massacred. However, the orthodox reaction lacked strength to attack Egypt, where the exiles found shelter, while the Monophysite agitation was secretly continuing to spread its propaganda in other parts of the East, and even in the capital itself. None the less, Rome had scored a decisive victory, and the new dynasty could celebrate a success which did much to establish it securely.

But it was not only religious zeal that moved Justinian. From this time he fully realised the political importance of an agreement with the Papacy. Without doubt the new government set itself, at any rate at first, to maintain friendly relations with the Ostrogothic kingdom of Italy. On 1 January 519 Theodoric's son-in-law and heir Eutharic became Consul as colleague of the Emperor Justin; and there was a constant interchange of ambassadors between Constantinople and Ravenna during the years that followed. From this moment, however, Justinian dreamed of the fall of the Ostrogothic power, and watched events in Italy with great attention.

In spite of the prudent toleration that Theodoric had always maintained, neither the senatorial aristocracy nor the Roman Church had forgotten their enmity towards a master obnoxious as a barbarian and an Arian. Naturally they turned their gaze ceaselessly upon Byzantium, where an orthodox prince was striving to restore the faith and to defend religion. In 524 Theodoric, exasperated by the intercourse which he suspected, had Boethius and Symmachus arrested and condemned to death, and furthermore in the following year sent Pope John on an embassy to Constantinople to protest against the Emperor's harsh measures towards those who would not conform. Justinian was ready to treat the matter in a way calculated to further his own ends. A solemn and triumphant reception was prepared for the pontiff in the capital. The Emperor, with the populace, sallied forth twelve miles to meet the first pope who had ever entered Constantinople. Sovereign honours were lavished upon him, and Justin desired to be reconsecrated by his hands. When on his return Theodoric, misdoubting the success of the embassy, arrested and imprisoned the unhappy John, who died miserably in his prison soon afterwards (18 May 526), no Italian could help comparing this heretical and persecuting prince with the pious *basileus* who reigned in the East. It followed that when death claimed Theodoric in his turn (Aug. 526) and when the regent Amalasuntha was involved in difficulties, the population of the peninsula was intoxicated by hope, and only waited an opportunity for changing their master, and eagerly cried out for a deliverer.

Meanwhile Justinian's domestic policy successfully overcame the obstacles which, one after another, threatened the security of the new government. Vitalianus was a rival not to be despised, and at first he was tactfully treated. He was given the title of *magister militum praesentalis* and became Consul in 520. He appeared to be all-powerful in the palace, and afterwards Justinian got rid of him by means of an assassin. The Greens were partisans of Anastasius. Against them the Emperor raised up for himself a devoted party amongst the Blues, to whom every privilege, and every opportunity to harm their foes was given throughout the Empire. Further, to please the mob of the capital, great largess was distributed. The imperial Consulate in 521 was unrivalled for the magnificence of its shows, which cost 288,000 *solidi*, more than £200,000 sterling to-day. In this way Justinian became popular amongst all classes in Byzantium, with the Church by his orthodoxy, with the senate by his flattery, and with the aristocracy and the populace. Feeling thus secure, he launched forth on his career. At this time his connexion with Theodora began, which ended in a somewhat scandalous marriage. Neither Justin nor Byzantium appear to have been much shocked by it. To please his nephew the Emperor conferred on his mistress the high dignity of patrician; he then, in order that the marriage might take place, abrogated the law by which alliances between senators and high officials and actresses were forbidden. When, in 527, Justinian was officially associated in the Empire, Theodora was crowned with him on Easter Day in the church of St Sophia, by the hands of the patriarch. When Justin died (1 Aug. 527), his nephew succeeded him without opposition. He was to reign over the Roman Empire in the East for nearly forty years (527–565), and to begin to realise the ambitious dreams which had long filled his soul.

II.

However, during the first years of his reign, before beginning to carry out the far-reaching plans which he had made, or even thinking of the reconstruction of the Roman Empire on its ancient plan, Justinian had to deal with numerous and serious difficulties.

The Persian war, stopped by the peace of 505, had again broken out in the last months of Justin's reign. The old king Kawad declared war, worried by the encroaching policy of Byzantium, and specially menaced by the increase of Roman influence during Justin's reign in the Caucasus region among the Lazi, the Iberians and even the Huns, and furthermore indignant at the attack that the imperialists attempted on Nisibis. The vassals of the two States were already at daggers drawn on the Syrian and Armenian frontiers, and in Mesopotamia open war was on the point of breaking out. To Justinian this was specially annoying, since it necessitated the mobilisation of the greater part of the Byzantine army under Belisarius, its most famous general, on the Asiatic frontier. The Emperor had only one care, which was not to proceed to extremities, and to end the war as soon as possible. Not realising, perhaps not wishing to realise, the greatness of the Eastern peril, and anxious only to free his hands for the conquest and liberation of the West, he shewed himself ready to make the largest concessions in order to heal the breach. In this way the peace of 532 was concluded, and gave to Justinian the disposition of his entire forces.

At home, other difficulties presented themselves. The special favour shewn by the government to the Blues, led to a dangerous agitation in the capital. Sure of imperial support the Blues took all possible licence against their adversaries without let or hindrance from police or justice. Thus injured, the Greens opposed violence to violence, and since they were still attached to the family of their old protector Anastasius, whose nephews Hypatius and Pompeius dwelt in Constantinople, their opposition soon took on a political and dynastic complexion. This resulted in a perilous state of unrest in the capital, still further aggravated by the deplorable condition of the public administration.

At the beginning of his reign Justinian had chosen as ministers Tribonian, nominated in 529 Quaestor of the Sacred Palace, and John of Cappadocia, invested in 531 with the high post of praetorian praefect in the East. The former was a remarkable man. An eminent jurist, and the greatest scholar of the day, he was unfortunately capable of any action for the sake of money, and as ready to sell justice as to amend the law. The latter was a skilful administrator, and a real statesman, but harsh, unscrupulous, greedy and cruel. Nothing could check him in his efforts to tear from the subjects the money needed for the Emperor's ceaseless expenditure, and although he won the favour of the prince by his great skill in finding resources, his harshness and exactions made him otherwise universally detested. Under such ministers, the officials in every rank of the government service thought only of imitating their chiefs. The rapacity of the government ruined the taxpayers, while the partiality of the administration of justice resulted in a general feeling of insecurity. Under the weight of these miseries the provinces, according to an official document, had become " quite uninhabitable." The country was depopulated, the fields deserted, and complaints poured into Constantinople from all sides against " the wickedness of the officials." An incessant stream of immigration brought a host of miserable folk to the capital, adding new elements of disorder and discontent to those already there. From these causes sprang, in January 532, the dangerous rising known as the Nika Riot, which shook Justinian's throne.

The Emperor was hissed at in the Circus (11 Jan. 532), and the disturbance spread beyond the boundaries of the hippodrome, and soon reached all quarters of the city. Greens and Blues made common cause against the hated government, and soon to the accompaniment of cries of *NIKA* (Victory) the crowd was tearing at the railings of the imperial palace, demanding the dismissal of the praefect of the city, and of the two hated ministers, Tribonian and John of Cappadocia. Justinian gave way, but too late. His apparent weakness only encouraged the mob, and the revolt became a revolution. The fires kindled by the rebels raged for three days, and destroyed the finest quarters of the capital. Justinian, almost destitute of means of defence, shut himself up in the palace without attempting to do anything, and the obvious result followed. As might have been expected, the mob proclaimed emperor Hypatius, the nephew of Anastasius, and, swelled by all malcontents, the insurrection became a definite political movement. "The Empire," wrote an eye-witness, "seemed on the verge of its fall." Justinian, in despair of curbing the riot which had continued for six days, lost his head, and thought of saving himself by flight. He had already ordered to load the imperial treasure in ships. It was then that Theodora rose in the Council, to recall to their duty the Emperor and ministers who were abandoning it. She said "When safety only remains in flight still I will not flee. Those who have worn the crown should not survive its fall. I will never live to see the day when I shall no longer be saluted as Empress. Flee if you wish, Caesar; you have money, the ships await you, the sea is unguarded. As for me, I stay. I hold with the old proverb which says that the purple is a good winding-sheet." This display of energy revived the courage of all. As soon as discord had been sown among the rebels by a lavish distribution of gold, Belisarius and Mundus with their barbarian mercenaries threw themselves on the crowd collected in the hippodrome. They gave no quarter, but continued their bloody work throughout the night (18 January). More than 30,000 corpses according to one computation, more than 50,000 according to other witnesses, flooded the arena with blood. Hypatius and Pompeius were arrested, and both executed the next morning. Other condemnations followed, and, thanks to the frightful bloodshed which ended this six days' battle, order was established once more in the capital, and thenceforth the imperial power became more absolute than ever.

In spite of every difficulty the imperial diplomacy never lost sight of any event that might further the accomplishment of Justinian's plans. Occurrences in the Vandal kingdom in Africa and the Ostrogothic kingdom in Italy were carefully watched for the profit of the Empire. In Africa, as in Italy, everything was in favour of the imperial restoration. The Roman people, governed by barbarian kings, had kept alive the memory of the Empire, and looked impatiently to Constantinople for a deliverer. According to Fustel de Coulanges "they persisted in regarding the Roman Empire as their supreme head; the distant power seemed to them to be an ancient and sacred authority, a kind of far-off providence, to be called upon as the last hope and consolation of the unfortunate." They felt still more keenly, perhaps, the misery of being ruled by heretical sovereigns. In Africa, where rigorous persecution of

Catholics had long been carried on, everyone hoped for the end of the "horrible secular captivity." In Italy, Theodoric's prolonged toleration had reconciled no one to him, and his ultimate severity exasperated his Roman subjects. A dumb agitation held sway in the West, and the coming of the Emperor's soldiers was eagerly awaited and desired. What is more surprising is that the barbarian kings themselves acknowledged the justice of the imperial claims. They also still reverenced the Empire whose lands they had divided, they thought of themselves as vassals of the *basileus*, received his commands with respect and bowed before his remonstrance. Hilderic, who had reigned over the Vandal kingdom since 523, was proud to proclaim himself the personal friend of Justinian. The two interchanged presents and embassies, and the Emperor's head replaced that of the king on the Vandal coinage. Amalasuntha, who had governed Italy since 526 in the name of her son Athalaric, made it her first care to recommend the youth of the new prince to Justinian's kindness: and the prince himself begged for the imperial favour the day after his accession. He recalled with pride the fact that his father had been adopted by Justin, and that he could therefore claim kinship with the *basileus*. So great was the prestige of the Roman Empire throughout the West that even the opponents of the imperial policy, such as Witigis or Totila, were willing to acknowledge themselves the Emperor's vassals.

Justinian realised this: he also realised the essential weakness of the barbarian kingdoms—their internal dissensions, and inability to make common cause against a foe. Therefore from the first he took up the position of their overlord, waiting until circumstances should furnish him with an opportunity for more active interference. This occurred, as far as Africa was concerned, in 531. At this time a domestic revolution substituted Gelimer, another descendant of Gaiseric, for the weakly Hilderic. Hilderic at once appealed to Byzantium, begging the Emperor to support the cause of his dethroned vassal. Byzantine diplomacy at once interfered in the haughtiest manner, demanding the restoration, or at any rate the liberation of the unhappy king, and evoking the decision of the dispute to the Emperor's court. Gelimer alone, perhaps, among the barbarian princes, recognised the fact that concessions, however large, would only postpone the inevitable struggle. Therefore he flatly refused the satisfaction required, and replied to the Byzantine demands by redoubled severity towards his political and religious enemies. The struggle had begun, and all was ready for the imperial restoration.

III.

Besides holding several trump cards, Justinian possessed another advantage in the redoubtable war machine constituted by the Byzantine army with its generals. The imperial army, in Justinian's time, was formed essentially of mercenaries, recruited from all the barbarians of the East and West. Huns, Gepids, Heruls, Vandals, Goths and Lombards, Antae and Slavs, Persians, Armenians, men from the Caucasus, Arabs from Syria, and Moors from Africa served in it side by side, glad to sell their services to an Emperor who paid well, or to attach themselves to the person of a celebrated general, to whom they would form the guard and staff (ὑπασπισταί). The greater number of these soldiers were mounted. Only the smallest part of the troops consisted of infantry which, being heavily equipped, was more notable for solidity than mobility. The cavalry, on the other hand, was excellent. Barbed with iron, armed with sword and lance, bow and quiver, the heavy regiments of Byzantine cuirassiers (*cataphracti*) were equally formed to break the enemy's ranks from a distance by a flight of arrows, or to carry all before them by the splendid dash of their charge. This cavalry generally sufficed to win battles, and the old regiments, proved as they were by a hundred fights, and matchless in bravery, made incomparable soldiers.

However, in spite of these qualities, the troops were not lacking in the faults inseparable from mercenary armies. Convinced that war should maintain war, and owning no fatherland, they pillaged mercilessly wherever they went. With an insatiable greed of gold, wine and women, and with thoughts always bent on plunder, they easily slipped the yoke of discipline, and imposed unheard-of conditions on their generals. Even treason was not below them, and more than one victory was lost by the defection of the troops on the field of battle, or their disorganisation in the rush for plunder. After a victory, things were still worse. Only anxious for leisure in which to enjoy their ill-gotten gains, they were deaf to entreaty, and the efforts of the generals to restore discipline frequently led to mutiny in the camp. The officers, of whom the greater number were barbarians, were not much more to be trusted than the men. They also were greedy, undisciplined and jealous of each other, always a willing prey to intrigue and treason.

Certainly the faulty organisation of the army explained some of these failings. The commissariat was badly arranged, pay generally in arrears, while the treasury officials and the generals sought, under various pretexts, to cheat the soldiers. Thus if the army was to be of any use, everything really depended on the Commander-in-Chief. Justinian had the good fortune to find excellent generals at the head of his armies; they were adored by the troops, and able, by a mixture of skilful energy and firm kindness, to keep them in hand and lead them where they wished. Such were the patrician Germanus, the Emperor's nephew, who commanded in turn in Thrace, Africa and Syria; Belisarius, the hero of the reign, conqueror of the Persians, Vandals and Ostrogoths of Africa and Italy, and the last resource of the Empire in every peril; and lastly the eunuch Narses, who concealed under a frail appearance

CH. I.

indomitable energy, prodigious activity and a strong will. He was a wonderful general, who completed the ruin of the Goths, and chased the Alemannic hordes from Italy.

The numerical force of the imperial armies must not be exaggerated. Belisarius had scarcely 15,000 men with which to destroy the Vandal kingdom, he had still less in his attack on the Ostrogothic realm, only 10,000 or 11,000; and altogether 25,000 to 30,000 sufficed to break down the Ostrogothic resistance. The weakness of this force added to the faulty organisation explains the interminable length of Justinian's wars, specially during the second half of the reign. It also illustrates the fundamental vice of the government, which was the perpetual disproportion between the end aimed at, and the means employed for its accomplishment. Lack of money always led to reduction of expenses and curtailment of effort.

However, when in 533 the chance of intervention in Africa presented itself, Justinian did not hesitate. Grave doubts as to the success of the distant enterprise were felt at court, and in the Council John of Cappadocia pointed out its many perils with a somewhat brutal clearness. Before this opposition, added to the critical condition of the treasury and the discontent of the soldiers, Justinian himself began to waver. On the other hand, the African bishops, surrounded as they were with the halo of martyrdom, revived the prince's flagging zeal and promised him victory. As soon as it became known that imperial intervention was probable, risings against the Vandal domination broke out in Tripolitana and Sardinia. Furthermore, Justinian could not hesitate long, because of the strength of the motives impelling him forward, his burning desire of conquest, and his absolute trust in the justice of his claims and in divine protection. He himself took the initiative in making the final decision, and events proved that in doing so he was wiser than his more prudent ministers.

The African campaign was equally rapid and triumphant. On 22 June 533 Belisarius embarked for the West. Ten thousand infantry, and from five to six thousand cavalry were shipped in five hundred transport-ships, manned by twenty thousand sailors. A fleet of war-ships (dromons) manned by two thousand oarsmen convoyed the expedition. The Vandals could offer little resistance to these forces. During the last hundred years they had lost in Africa the energy which had once made them invincible; and in spite of his boasted bravery, their king Gelimer proved himself, by his indecision, sensitiveness, lack of perseverance and want of will power, the worst possible leader for a nation in danger. The neutrality of the Ostrogoths, which Byzantine diplomacy had secured, gave Belisarius every chance of fair play. Early in September 533 he was able to disembark unhindered on the desert headland of Caput-Vada. He was well received by the African people, and marched on Carthage, while the imperial fleet turned back, skirting the coast in a northerly direction. On September 13 the battle of Decimum was fought, and shattered Gelimer's hopes by a single blow, while Carthage, the chief town and only fortress in Africa, fell into the conqueror's hands undefended. In vain the Vandal king recalled the forces which he had detached for service in Sardinia, and endeavoured to regain his capital. He was forced to raise the blockade, and on the day of Tricamarum (mid-Dec. 533) the Byzantine cavalry again overcame the impetuosity of the barbarians. This was the final and decisive defeat. All Gelimer's towns, his treasures and family fell in turn into Belisarius' hands. He himself, hemmed in in his retreat on Mt Pappua, was forced to surrender, on receiving a promise that his life should be spared, and that he should be honourably treated (March 534). In a few months, contrary to all expectations, a few cavalry regiments had destroyed Gaiseric's kingdom.

Justinian, always optimistic, considered the war at an end. He recalled Belisarius, who was decreed the honours of a triumph ; while he himself, somewhat arrogantly, assumed the titles of Vandalicus and Africanus. Furthermore he adorned the walls of the imperial palace with mosaics representing the events of the African war, and Gelimer paying homage to the Emperor and Theodora. He hastened to restore Roman institutions in the conquered province, but at this very moment the war broke out afresh. The Berber tribes had passively allowed the Vandals to be crushed ; now it was their turn to rise against the imperial authority. The patrician Solomon, who had succeeded Belisarius, energetically put down the revolt in Byzacena (534) but he was unable to break through the group of Aures in Numidia (535): and soon the discontented troops, dissatisfied with a general who was strict and demanded too much from them, broke into a serious mutiny (536). Belisarius was obliged to leave Sicily for Africa at once, and arrived just in time to save Carthage, and defeat the rebels in the plains of Membressa. To complete the pacification it was found necessary to appoint the Emperor's own nephew Germanus governor of Africa. After performing prodigies of courage, skill and energy, he succeeded at last in crushing out the insurrection (538). But four years had been lost in useless and exhausting struggles. Only then was the patrician Solomon, invested a second time with the rank of Governor-General, able to complete the pacification of the country (539). By a bold march he forced Iabdas, the strongest of the Berber princes and the great chief of the Aures, into submission. He overran Zab, Hodna and Mauretania Sitifensis, forcing the petty kings to acknowledge the imperial suzerainty. Under his beneficent rule (539–544) Africa once more experienced peace and security. His death occasioned another crisis. The revolted Berbers made common cause with the mutinous soldiers. A usurper Guntharic murdered Areobindus, the Governor-General, and proclaimed his own independence (546). Africa seemed on the point of slipping from the

Empire, and the fruits of Belisarius' victories were, to quote Procopius' phrase, "as completely annihilated as though they had never existed." This time again, the energy of a general, John Troglita, overcame the danger. After two years of warfare (546–548) he beat down the Berber resistance, and restored, permanently at last, the imperial authority.

After fifteen years of war and strife Africa once more took her place in the Roman Empire. Doubtless it was not the Africa that Rome had once possessed, and of which Justinian dreamed. It included Tripolitana, Byzacena, Proconsularis, Numidia, and Mauretania Sitifensis. The Byzantines also occupied Sardinia, Corsica and the Balearic Isles, all dependencies of the African government. But with the exception of several scattered places on the coast, of which the most important was the citadel of Septem (Ceuta) at the Pillars of Hercules, the whole of West Africa broke away from Justinian. Mauretania Caesariensis and Mauretania Tingitana always remained independent, joined to the Empire only by the loosest bond of vassalage. However, within these limited boundaries the work of the imperial restoration was not in vain. It is clear that Justinian's reign left a lasting impress on the lands drawn once more into the bosom of the monarchy.

The conquest of Africa by Belisarius furnished Justinian with a splendid base for operations in Italy, where he hoped to carry out his ambitious projects. As had been the case in Africa, circumstances provided him, in the nick of time, with a pretext for interference in the peninsula.

Amalasuntha, daughter of Theodoric, and regent for her young son Athalaric, had soon succeeded in arousing the discontent of her barbarian subjects by her Roman sympathies. Made uneasy by the growing opposition, she put herself into communication with the Court at Constantinople, begging of the imperial benevolence an asylum in the East should she need it. In return she offered all facilities for the fleet of Belisarius to revictual in Sicily in 533, and finally allowed herself to be persuaded to propose to Justinian the conquest of Italy (534). The death of the young Athalaric (October 534) further complicated the princess's position. In order to strengthen it, she made her cousin Theodahad her partner; but a few months later a national revolution, like that which had hurled Hilderic from the throne in Africa, deposed Theodoric's daughter. Amalasuntha was imprisoned by order of her co-regent, and soon afterwards assassinated (April 535). As had been the case in Africa, but even with increased imperiousness, the Byzantine diplomacy demanded satisfaction for the arrest of a princess allied to and protected by Justinian. Her death proved to be the wished-for *casus belli*.

As if to complete the remarkable parallelism presented by Italian and African affairs, Theodahad the Gothic king was, like Gelimer, impressionable, changeable, unsteady, unreliable, and, in addition, a coward. After the first military demonstrations he offered to Justinian's ambassador to cede Sicily to the Empire, to acknowledge himself as a vassal of Byzantium, and, soon afterwards, he proposed to abandon the whole of Italy in return for a title and a money settlement. Against such a foe Belisarius had no formidable task, specially as in view of the Ostrogothic war, Byzantine diplomacy had secured the Frankish alliance just as in the African war it had secured that of the Ostrogoths. From the end of 535, while a Byzantine army was concentrated in Dalmatia, Belisarius landed in Sicily, and occupied it, hardly needing to strike a blow. Theodahad was terrified, and "already feeling the fate of Gelimer about to descend on him" offered any concessions. Then, on hearing that Belisarius had been obliged to return to Africa, he once more plucked up courage, imprisoned the imperial ambassadors, and flung himself desperately into the struggle. Little good it did him. While one of Justinian's generals conquered Dalmatia, Belisarius crossed the Strait of Messina (May 536) and, greeted by the Italian people as a liberator, in turn seized Naples and occupied Rome unopposed (10 December 536). However, the Ostrogoths still possessed more energy than the Vandals. On the news of the first disasters, even before the fall of Rome, they dethroned the incapable Theodahad, and elected as king Witigis, one of the bravest of their warriors. With considerable skill the new king checked the march of the Franks by the cession of Provence; then, having united all his forces, he proceeded with 150,000 men to besiege Belisarius in Rome. For a whole year (March 537—March 538) he exhausted himself in vain efforts to take the Eternal City. Everything miscarried before the splendid energy of Belisarius. Meanwhile, another Roman army, which had landed at the beginning of 538 on the Adriatic coast, was occupying Picenum. Greek troops, at the request of the Archbishop of Milan, had made a descent on Liguria, and seized the great town of northern Italy. Witigis, in despair, decided to abandon Rome. The triumph of the imperialists seemed assured, and to finish it Justinian despatched another army under Narses into Italy. Unfortunately, Narses' instructions were not only to reinforce Belisarius, but also to spy upon him; and the misunderstanding between the two generals soon paralysed all operations. They confined themselves to saving Rimini, which was attacked by Witigis; but allowed the Goths to reconquer Milan, and Theudibert's Franks to pillage the valley of the Po on their own account. At last in 539 Justinian decided to recall Narses, and to leave to Belisarius alone the task of conducting the war. It was brought rapidly to a successful end. Pressed on every side, Witigis threw himself into Ravenna, and the imperialists besieged it (end of 539). For six months the Ostrogoths held out, counting on a diversion to be caused by the Persians in the East, the intervention of the

Lombards, and the defection of the Franks. When they saw themselves abandoned by all, they determined to negotiate with Justinian (May 540). The Emperor leaned towards conciliation and shewed himself inclined to allow Witigis to keep possession of Italy north of the Po. But for the first time in his life Belisarius refused to obey, and declared that he would never ratify the convention. He wished for complete victory, and hoped to destroy the Ostrogothic kingdom as completely as the Vandal. Then occurred a strange episode. The Goths suggested that the Byzantine general, whose valour they had proved, and whose independence they had just ascertained, should be their king, Witigis himself consenting to abdicate in his favour. Belisarius pretended to fall in with their plans in order to obtain the capitulation of Ravenna; then he threw off all disguise and declared that he had never worked for anyone but the Emperor.

Once more, as he had done in Africa, Justinian in his optimistic mind considered the war at an end. Proudly he assumed the title of Gothicus, recalled Belisarius, reduced the troops in occupation; and in the Ostrogothic kingdom, now transformed into a Roman province, he organised a system of purely civil administration. Once more the issue disappointed his anticipations. The Goths indeed soon recovered themselves. Scarcely had Belisarius gone, before they organised resistance to the north of the Po, and instead of Witigis (a prisoner of the Greeks) they chose Hildibad for king. The tactlessness of the Byzantine administration, which was both harsh and vexatious, still further aggravated the situation; and when, at the end of 541, the accession of the young and brilliant Totila gave the barbarians a prince equally remarkable for his chivalrous courage and unusual attractiveness, the work of the imperial restoration was undone in a few months. For eleven years Totila was able to hold at bay the whole force of the Empire, to reconquer the whole of Italy, and to ruin the reputation of Belisarius.

He passed the Po with only five thousand men. Central Italy was soon opened to him by the victories of Faenza and Mugillo. Then, while the disabled Byzantine generals shut themselves up in forts, without attempting any joint action, Totila skilfully moved towards Campania and southern Italy, where the provinces had suffered less from the war, and would consequently yield him supplies. Naples fell to him (543), and Otranto, where the imperialists revictualled, was besieged. At the same time Totila conciliated the Roman population by his political skill; he made war without pillaging the country, and his justice was proverbial. Justinian felt sure that no one except Belisarius was capable of dealing with this formidable foe. Therefore he was ordered back to Italy (544). Unfortunately there were just then so many calls on the Empire, from Africa, on the Danube, and from the Persian frontier, that the great effort needed in the peninsula was not forthcoming. The imperial general, bereft of money, and almost without an army, was practically powerless. Content with having thrown supplies into Otranto, he fortified himself in Ravenna and stayed there (545). Totila seized the posts by which communications were maintained between Ravenna and Rome, and finally invested the Eternal City, which Belisarius was unable to save when he finally roused himself from his inaction (17 December 546). Totila then tried to make peace with the Emperor, but Justinian obstinately refused to negotiate with a sovereign whom he held to be nothing but an usurper. Therefore the war went on. Belisarius did manage to recover Rome, evacuated by the Gothic king and emptied of its inhabitants, and clung to it successfully in spite of all Totila's hostile attacks (547). But the imperial army was scattered over the whole of Italy, and quite powerless; and reinforcements, when they did arrive from the East, could not prevent Totila from taking Perusia in the north and Rossano in the south. Belisarius, badly supported by his lieutenants, and driven to desperation, demanded to be recalled (548). When his request was granted he left Italy, where his glory had been so sadly tarnished. "God himself," wrote a contemporary, "fought for Totila and the Goths."

In fact, no resistance to them remained. Belisarius had been gone for less than a year when the imperialists were left with only four towns in the peninsula: Ravenna, Ancona, Otranto and Crotona. Soon afterwards the fleet which Totila had created conquered Sicily (550), Corsica, Sardinia (551), and ravaged Dalmatia, Corfu and Epirus (551). Meanwhile the fast ageing Justinian was absorbed in useless theological discussions, and forgot his province of Italy. "The whole West was in the hands of the barbarians," wrote Procopius. However, moved by the entreaties of the emigrant Italians who flocked to Byzantium, the Emperor recovered himself. He despatched a fleet to the West which forced Totila to evacuate Sicily, while a great army was mobilised under the direction of Germanus to reconquer Italy (550). The sudden death of the general hindered the operations, but Narses, appointed as his successor, carried them on with a long forgotten energy and decision. He boldly stated his conditions to the Emperor, and succeeded in wringing from him those supplies that had been doled out so meagrely to his predecessors. He obtained money, arms and soldiers, and soon commanded the largest army ever entrusted by Justinian to any of his generals, numbering probably from thirty to thirty-five thousand men. In the spring of 552 he attacked Italy from the north, moved on Ravenna, and from there made a bold push for the south in order to force Totila to a decisive engagement. He encountered the Goths in the Apennines at Taginae (May or June 552), not far from the site of Busta Gallorum where, Procopius tells us, Camillus repulsed the Gauls in ancient days. The Ostrogothic army was stricken with panic, and broke and fled as soon as the battle was joined; Totila was borne away in the rout, and perished in it. The Gothic State had received its death-blow.

The Byzantines could hardly believe that their formidable enemy was really overcome. They wanted to disinter his body to assure themselves of their good fortune; "and having gazed at it for a long time," wrote Procopius, "they felt satisfied that Italy was really conquered." It was in vain that the unhappy remnant of the Gothic people rallied under a new king, Teias, for a last desperate struggle. By degrees the whole of central Italy, including Rome itself, again passed into the hands of the Greeks. Finally Narses fought the last barbarian muster in Campania near the foot of Mt Vesuvius on the slopes of Monte Lettere (Mons Lactarius) early in 553. The battle lasted for two whole days, "a giants' combat" according to Procopius, desperate, implacable, epic. The flower of the Gothic army fell round their king, the remainder received honourable treatment from Narses, and permission to seek land amongst the other barbarians, where they would no longer be subjects of Justinian.

Italy had still to be cleared of the Franks. They had profited by what was happening, and had occupied part of Liguria, and almost the whole of the Venetian territory, had repulsed the imperialists of Verona after Taginae, and now claimed to inherit all the possessions of the Goths. In the middle of the year 553 two Alemannic chieftains, Leutharis and Bucelin, rushed on Italy, with seventy-five thousand barbarians, marking a trail from the north to the centre with blood and fire. Fortunately for Narses the remnant of the Ostrogoths thought submission to the Emperor better than submission to the Franks. Thanks to their help, the Greek general was able to crush the hordes of Bucelin near Capua (autumn of 554), while those of Leutharis, decimated by sickness, perished miserably on their retreat. In the following year peace was restored to Italy by the capitulation of Compsae, which had been the centre of Ostrogothic resistance in the south (555). Thus, after twenty years of warfare, Italy was once more drawn into the Roman Empire. Like Africa, her extent was not so great as it had been formerly, as the Italian praefecture. Without mentioning places like Brescia and Verona, where a handful of Goths held out till 563, neither Pannonia nor Rhaetia nor Noricum ever came under Justinian's rule again. The imperial province of Italy did not extend beyond the line of the Alps, but Justinian was none the less proud of having rescued it from "tyranny," and flattered himself on having restored to it 'perfect peace," likely to prove durable.

It might easily be imagined that Spain, conquered by the Visigoths, would be added to the Empire, after the reconquest of Africa and Italy. Here also, just at the right moment, circumstances arose which gave a pretext for Greek intervention. King Agila was a persecutor of

Catholics, and against him uprose an usurper Athanagild, who naturally sought help from the greatest orthodox ruler of the time. A Byzantine army and fleet were despatched to Spain, Agila was defeated, and in a few weeks the imperialists were in possession of the chief towns in the south-east of the peninsula, Carthagena, Malaga and Corduba. As soon as the Visigoths realised the danger in which they stood, they put an end to their domestic disagreements, and all parties joined in offering the crown to Athanagild (554). The new prince soon returned to face his former allies, and managed to prevent them from making much progress. However, the Byzantines were able to keep what they had already won, and the Empire congratulated itself on the acquisition of a Spanish province.

The imperial diplomacy was able to add successes of its own to the triumphs won by force of arms. The Frankish kings of Gaul had gladly received subsidies from Justinian, and had entered into an alliance with him, calling him *Lord* and *Father*, in token of their position as vassals. They proved themselves fickle and treacherous allies, and after Theudibert, King of Austrasia, had in 539 worked for himself in Italy, he formed the plan of overwhelming the Eastern Empire by a concerted attack of all the barbarian peoples. In spite of such occasional lapses, the prestige of Rome was undiminished in Gaul: Constantinople was regarded as the capital of the whole world, and in the distant Frankish churches, by the Pope's request, prayers were said by the clergy for the safety of the Roman Emperor. To his titles of Vandalicus and Gothicus Justinian now added those of Francicus, Alemannicus and Germanicus. He treated Theudibert as though he were the most submissive of lieutenants, and confided to him the work of converting the pagans ruled by him in Germany. It was the same with the Lombards. In 547 the Emperor gave them permission to settle in Pannonia and Noricum, and furnished them with subsidies in return for recruits. They were rewarded by receiving imperial support against their enemies the Gepidae; and Greek diplomacy was successful in keeping them faithful.

On the whole, in spite of certain sacrifices which had been wrung from the pride of the *basileus*, Justinian had realised his dream. It was thanks to his splendid and persistent ambition that the Empire could now boast the acquisition of Dalmatia, Italy, the whole of eastern Africa, south-east Spain, the islands of the western basin of the Mediterranean, Sicily, Corsica, Sardinia, and the Balearic Isles, which almost doubled its extent. The occupation of Septem carried the Emperor's authority to the Pillars of Hercules, and with the exception of those parts of the coast held by the Visigoths in Spain and Septimania and the Franks in Provence, the Mediterranean was once more a Roman lake. We have seen by what efforts these triumphs were bought, we shall see at what cost of suffering they were held. We must however maintain that by them Justinian had won for the Empire a great and incontestable increase of prestige and honour. In some respects it may have proved a misfortune that he had taken upon him the splendid but crushing heritage of Roman traditions and memories with the crown of the Caesars: none the less, none of his contemporaries realised that he had repudiated the obligations they entailed. His most savage detractors saw in his vast ambitions the real glory of his reign. Procopius wrote "The natural course for a high-souled Emperor to pursue, is to seek to enlarge the Empire, and make it more glorious."

IV.

Justinian's great object in accomplishing the imperial restoration in the West was to restore the exact counterpart of the ancient Roman Empire, by means of the revival of Roman institutions. The aim of the two great ordinances of April 534 was the restoration in Africa of that "perfect order" which seemed to the Emperor to be the index of true civilisation in any State. The Pragmatic Sanction of 554, while it completed the measures taken in 538 and 540, had the same object in Italy—to "give back to Rome Rome's privileges," according to the expression of a contemporary. By what appears at first sight to be a surprising anomaly, remarkably well illustrating however Justinian's disinclination to change any condition of the past he endeavoured to restore, the Emperor did not extend to the West any of the administrative reforms which he was compassing in the East at the same time.

In Africa, as in Italy, the principle on which the administrative re-organisation was carried out was that of maintaining the ancient separation between civil and military authority. At the head of the civil government of Africa was placed a praetorian praefect, having seven governors below him, bearing the titles of *consulares* or *praesides*, who administered the restored circumscriptions which had been established by the Roman Empire. The numerous offices in which Justinian, with his usual care for detail, minutely regulated the details of staff and salaries, helped the officials and assured the predominance of civil rule in the praefecture of Africa. It was the same in the reconstructed praefecture of Italy. From 535 a praetor was at the head of reconquered Sicily, after 538 a praetorian praefect was appointed in Italy, and the *régime* of civil administration was established the day after the capitulation of Ravenna. The reorganisation was carried out by the Pragmatic of 554. Under the praefect's high authority, assisted, as formerly, by the two *vicarii* of Rome and Italy, the civil officials governed the thirteen provinces into which the peninsula was still divided. Occasionally in practice political or military exigencies led to the concentration of all the authority in the same hands. In Africa Solomon and Germanus combined the functions and even the titles of praetorian praefect and *magister militum*. In Italy Narses was a real viceroy. These, however, were only exceptional deviations from the established principle, and only concerned the supreme government of the province. At the same time Justinian introduced the legislation that he had promulgated into the reconquered West. The financial administration was co-ordinated with the territorial. The ancient system of taxation, slightly modified elsewhere by the barbarians, was completely restored, and the supplies so raised were divided, as had formerly been the case, between the praefect's *arca* and the coffer of the *largitiones*. A *comes sacri patrimonii per Italiam* was appointed, and the imperial *logothetae* exacted with great harshness arrears of taxation, dating back to the time of the Gothic kings, from the country already ruined by warfare.

Thus Justinian meant to efface, with one stroke of the pen, anything that might recall the barbarian "tyranny." Contracts signed in the time of Totila, donations made by the barbarian kings, economic measures passed by them in favour of settlers and slaves, were all pronounced void, and the Pragmatic restored to the Roman proprietors all lands that they had held before the time of Totila. However, though he might shape the future, the Emperor was obliged to accept many existing facts. The newly-created praefecture of Africa corresponded to the Vandal kingdom, and included, as the Vandal kingdom had done, along with Africa, Sardinia and Corsica which the barbarians had torn from Italy. The Italian praefecture, already reduced by this arrangement, was further diminished by the loss of Dalmatia and Sicily, which formed a province by themselves. The Italian peninsula alone concerned the praefect of Italy.

The military administration was on the same lines as the civil, but very strictly separated from it. Responsible for the defence of the country, it was reconstructed on the Roman model, according to the minute instructions of the Emperor. Belisarius in Africa and Narses in Italy organised the frontier defence. Each province formed a great command, with a *magister militum* at its head; Africa, Italy and Spain comprised one each. Under the supreme command of these generals, who were Commanders-in-Chief of all the troops stationed in the province, dukes governed the military districts (*limites*) created along the whole length of the frontier. In Africa there were originally four, soon afterwards five (Tripolitana, Byzacena, Numidia and Mauretania), four also in Italy, along the Alpine frontier. Dukes were also installed in Sardinia and Sicily. In this group of military districts, troops of a special nature were stationed, the *limitanei* (borderers) formed on the model formerly invented in the Roman Empire, and partly restored by Anastasius. Recruited from the provincial population, specially on the frontier, these soldiers received concessions of land, and pay as well. In time of peace their duty was to cultivate the land they occupied, and to keep a sharp watch on the roads crossing the *limes*; in time of war they took up arms either to defend the post specially committed to their charge, or combined with similar troops to beat back the invader. In either case they might never leave the *limes*, as perpetual military service was the necessary condition of their tenure of land. These tenant-soldiers were empowered to marry, grouped in regiments commanded by tribunes, and stationed in the fortified towns and castles on the frontier. This kind of territorial army, organised by Justinian along all the borders of the Empire, enabled him to reduce the strength of the troops of the line, and keep them for big wars. A close-drawn net of fortresses supported this formation. In Africa, specially, where the Vandals had razed the fortifications of nearly all the towns, Justinian's lieutenants had an enormous task before them. No point was left undefended, and in Byzacena and Numidia several parallel lines of fortresses served to block all openings, cover all positions of strategic importance, and offer a refuge to the surrounding population in time of danger. A number of fortresses were built or restored from Tripolitana to the Pillars of Hercules, where stood Septem "that the whole world could not take," and from the Aures and Hodna to Tell. Even to-day North Africa abounds in the colossal ruins of Justinian's fortresses, and the hardly dismantled ramparts of Haidra, Beja, Madaura, Tebessa and Timgad, to cite no more, bear witness to the great effort by which, in a few years, Justinian restored the Roman system of defence. Furthermore, in following the example set by Rome, Justinian tried to incorporate in the imperial army the barbaric peoples dwelling on the outskirts of the Empire. These *gentiles* or *foederati* made a perpetual treaty with the Emperor, on receiving a promise of an annual subsidy (*annona*). They put their contingents at the disposal of the Roman dukes of the *limes*, and their chiefs received from the Emperor's hands a kind of investiture, as a sign of the Roman sovereignty, when they were given insignia to denote their command, and titles from the Byzantine hierarchy. Thus from the Syrtis to Mauretania there stretched a fringe of barbarian client princes, acknowledging themselves as vassals of the *basileus*, and called— *Mauri pacifici*. According to the expression of the African poet Corippus, "trembling before the arms and success of Rome, of their own accord they hastened to place themselves under the Roman yoke and laws."

By carrying out the great work of reorganisation in Africa and Italy, Justinian flattered himself that he had achieved the double object of restoring the "complete peace" in the West and "repairing the disasters" which war had heaped on the unhappy countries. It remains to be seen how far his optimism was justified, and to reckon the price paid by the inhabitants for the privilege of entering the Roman Empire once more.

In a celebrated passage of the *Secret History* Procopius has enumerated

all the misfortunes which the imperial restoration brought on Africa and
Italy. According to the historian the country was depopulated, the
provinces left undefended and badly governed, ruined further by financial
exactions, religious intolerance, and military insurrections, while five
million human lives were sacrificed in Africa, and still more in Italy.
These were the benefits conferred in the West by the " glorious reign of
Justinian." Although in crediting this account some allowance must be
made for oratorical exaggeration, yet it is certain that Africa and Italy
emerged from the many years of warfare to a great extent ruined, and
that a terrible economic and financial crisis accompanied the imperial
restoration. During many years Africa suffered all the horrors incident to Berber incursions, military revolts, destruction of the country
by sword and fire, and the murder and flight of the population. The
inevitable consequences of the struggle pressed no less hardly on Italy,
which underwent the horrors of long sieges, famine, massacre, disease,
the passage of the Goths, and the passage of imperialists, added to the
furious devastations of the Alemanni. The largest towns, such as
Naples, Milan, and specially Rome were almost devoid of inhabitants,
the depopulated country was uncultivated, and the large Italian proprietors were repaid for their devotion to Byzantium and their hostility
to Totila by total ruin.

The exactions of the soldiers added yet more wretchedness. By their
greed, insolence and depredations the imperialists made those whom they
declared free regret the barbarian domination. The new administration
added the harshest financial tyranny to the misery caused by the war.
Justinian was obliged to get money at any cost, and therefore the barely
conquered country was given over to the pitiless exactions of the agents
of the fisc. The provinces were not only expected to support unaided
the expense of the very complicated administration imposed on them by
Justinian, but were further obliged to send money to Constantinople for
the general needs of the monarchy. The imperial *logothetae* applied the
burdensome system of Roman taxes to the ruined countries without
making any allowance for the prevailing distress. They mercilessly
demanded arrears dating from the time of the Goths, falsified the
registers in order to increase the returns, and enriched themselves at the
expense of the taxpayer to such an extent that, according to a
contemporary writer, " nothing remained for the inhabitants but to die,
since they were bereft of all the necessities of life."

Desolate, helpless, brought to the lowest straits, the Western
provinces begged the Emperor to help them in their misery if he did
not wish, to quote the official document, " that they should be overcome
by the impossibility of paying their debts." Justinian heard this appeal.
Measures were taken in Africa to restore cultivation to the fields, the
country districts were repeopled, various works of public utility were
organised in the towns, ports were opened on the coasts, hydraulic

CH. L.

works were supported or repaired in the interior of the land, and new cities were founded in the wilds of the high Numidian plateau. Carthage itself, newly adorned with a palace, churches, splendid baths and fashionable squares, shewed the interest taken by the prince in his new provinces. The result of all this was a real prosperity. Similar measures were taken in Italy, either to tide over the crisis resulting from the mass of debts and give time to the debtors, or to alleviate in some degree the crushing burden of the taxes. At the same time the Emperor busied himself in the restoration of the great aristocracy which had been broken down by Totila, but to which he looked for the chief support of the new *régime*. For a similar reason he protected and enriched the Church, and set himself as in Africa by means of the development of public works to repair the evils of the war. Ravenna was beautified by such buildings as San Vitale and San Apollinare in Classe, and became a capital; Milan was raised from her ruins, Rome was put in possession of privileges likely to lead to an economic revival, and Naples became a great commercial port.

Unfortunately, in spite of Justinian's good intentions, the financial burden weighed too heavily upon a depopulated Italy to allow of any real revival. In the greater number of towns industry and commerce disappeared; lack of implements hindered the improvement of the land, and large uncultivated and desert tracts remained in the country. The middle classes tended more and more to disappear, at the same time that the aristocracy either became impoverished or left the country. Justinian exerted himself in vain to restore order and prosperity by promising to protect his new subjects from the well-known greed of his officials: the imperial restoration marked, at any rate in Italy, the beginning of a decadence which long darkened her history.

CHAPTER II.

JUSTINIAN'S GOVERNMENT IN THE EAST.

I.

At the time when Justinian was only heir-presumptive of the Empire, probably in the year 520, he met the lady who was to become the Empress Theodora. Daughter of one of the bear-keepers of the hippodrome, brought up by an indulgent mother amongst the society which frequented the purlieus of the circus, this young girl, beautiful, intelligent and witty—if we may believe the gossip of the *Secret History* —soon succeeded in charming and scandalising the capital. At the theatre where she appeared in *tableaux vivants* and pantomimes she ventured on the most audacious representations: in town she became famous for the follies of her entertainments, the boldness of her manners and the multitude of her lovers. Next she disappeared, and after a somewhat unlovely adventure she travelled through the East in a wretched manner for some time—according to contemporary gossip. She was seen at Alexandria, where she became known to several of the leaders of the Monophysite party, and returned—perhaps under their influence—to a more Christian and purer mode of life. She was again seen at Antioch, and then returned to Constantinople, matured and wiser. Then it was that she made a conquest of Justinian. She soon wielded the strongest influence over her lover: desperately in love, the prince could refuse nothing that his mistress requested. He heaped riches upon her, obtained for her the title of patrician, and became the humble minister of her hatred or her affection. Finally he wished to marry her legally, and was able to do so in 523, thanks to the complaisance of Justin. When, in April 527, Justinian was associated in the Empire Theodora shared the elevation and the triumph of her husband. She ascended the throne with him in August 527, and for twenty years the adventuress-Empress exercised a sovereign influence on the course of politics.

Theodora's name may still be read with that of the Emperor on the walls of churches and over the doors of castles of that date. Her picture makes a fellow to that of her imperial husband in the church of

San Vitale in Ravenna, and also in the mosaics which decorated the rooms of the Sacred Palace, for it was Justinian's wish to associate her with the military triumphs and the splendours of the reign. The grateful people raised statues to her as to Justinian, the officials also swore fidelity to her, for she was the Emperor's equal throughout her life, while ambassadors and foreign kings hastened to her to pay their respects and to gain her good will as well as that of the *basileus*. In deliberating on the most important occasions Justinian always took council of "the most honoured wife which God had given him," whom he loved to call "his sweetest charm," and contemporaries agree in declaring that she did not scruple to use the boundless influence which she possessed, and that her authority was equal to, if not greater than, that of her husband. Certainly this ambitious lady possessed many eminent qualities to justify the supreme authority which she wielded. She was a woman of unshaken courage, as she proved in the troublous time of the Nika rising, proud energy, masculine resolution, a determined and a clear mind, and a strong will by which she frequently overruled the vacillating Justinian. She undoubtedly combined defects and even vices with these qualities. She was domineering and harsh, she loved money and power. To keep the throne to which she had risen she would stoop to deceit, violence and cruelty; she was implacable in her dislikes, and inflexible towards those whom she hated. By means of a disgraceful intrigue she pitilessly destroyed the fortunes of John of Cappadocia, the all-powerful praetorian praefect, who dared for one moment to dispute her supremacy (541). She made Belisarius bitterly expiate his rare lapses into independence, and by the ascendancy which she gained over Antonina, the patrician's wife, she made him her humble and obedient servant. As passionate in her loves as in her hates, she advanced her favourites without scruple. Peter Barsymes was made praetorian praefect, Narses a general, Vigilius a pope, while she turned the imperial palace into a hotbed of incessant intrigues. Her influence was not always good—though the loungers of Constantinople have strangely lengthened the list of her cruelties and increased the number of her victims—but it was always powerful. Even when she was forced temporarily to give way before circumstances, her audacious and supple wit was always able to devise some startling retaliation. Wily and ambitious, she always aspired to have the last word—and she got it.

In the twenty years during which Theodora reigned she had a hand in everything; in politics, and in the Church; in the administration, she advised the reforms, and filled it with her *protégés*; in diplomacy, concerning which the Emperor never decided anything without her advice. She made and unmade popes and patriarchs, ministers and generals at her pleasure, not even fearing, when she considered it necessary, openly to thwart Justinian's wishes. She was the active help-mate to her husband in all important matters. In the legislative reform her feminism inspired the measures which dealt with divorce, adultery, the sanctity of the marriage-tie, and those meant to assist actresses and fallen women. In the government of the East her lucid and keen intelligence discovered and advised a policy more suited to the true interests of the State than that actually pursued, and if it had been carried out, it might have changed the course of history itself by making the Byzantine Empire stronger and more durable.

While Justinian, carried away by the grandeur of Roman traditions, rose to conceptions in turn magnificent and impossible, and dreamed of restoring the Empire of the Caesars and of inaugurating the reign of orthodoxy by reunion with Rome, Theodora, by birth an Oriental, and in other respects more far-seeing and acute than her husband, immediately turned her attention to the East. She had always sympathised with the Monophysites; even before she had become Empress she had willingly received them at the palace, and allowed them to draw on her credit. She admired their teachers, and loved the unpolished candour of their monks. She was not actuated by piety alone, for she had too much political instinct not to realise the importance of religious questions in a Christian State, and the peril attending indifference to them. But while Justinian, with the mind of a theologian, occupied himself with religious questions primarily for the empty pleasure of being able to dogmatise, Theodora, like all the great Byzantine Emperors, recognised the main features of political problems under the fleeting form of theological disagreements. She realised that the rich and flourishing provinces of Asia, Syria and Egypt really formed the mainstay of the Empire; and she felt that the religious differences by which the Oriental nations manifested their separatist tendencies threatened danger to the monarchy. Furthermore she saw the necessity for pacifying the growing discontent by means of opportune concessions and a wide toleration, and she forced the imperial policy to shape itself to this end; and carried with her the ever worried and vacillating Justinian, even so far as to brave the Papacy and protect the heretics. It is only fair to say that she foresaw the future more clearly and grasped the situation more accurately than did her imperial associate.

Before the advent of Justin's dynasty Anastasius' dreams of an ideal monarchy may have taken this form or something approaching it. He may have imagined an essentially Oriental Empire, having well-defended frontiers, a wise administration, sound finances and blessed with religious unity. To realise this last he would not have hesitated at a breach with Rome if it had become necessary. In spite of his efforts and good intentions Anastasius had not succeeded in realising his ideal. But it was right in principle and, thanks to Theodora, it inspired the policy of Justinian in the East. In this way the Empress made a great impression on her husband's government, and as soon as she died a decay set in which brought the glorious reign to a sad close.

CH. II.

II.

The imperial policy in the West had been essentially offensive. In the East, on the other hand, it was generally restricted to a defensive attitude. Justinian submitted to war or accepted it when offered rather than sought it, because he was anxious to preserve all his forces for Africa and Italy. Thus he maintained the safety of the monarchy in the East less by a series of great victories than by military arrangements combined with clever diplomatic action.

In Asia, Persia had been the perpetual enemy of the Romans for centuries. There was a ceaseless temptation to strife and a pretext for warfare in the coincidence of the two frontiers, and the rival influence which the two States exercised in Armenia in the Caucasus, and among the Arab tribes of the Syrian desert. The hundred years' peace concluded in 422 had certainly restored tranquillity for the rest of the fifth century, but hostilities had broken out afresh in the reign of Anastasius (502); and it was evident that the peace of 505 would only prove to be a truce, although Persia was torn by domestic discord, and had lost her prestige and strength, and her old king Kawad did not seek adventures. In proportion as Justinian profited by the relative weakness of his foes he attempted to bring more peoples into the relation of clients to Rome. Such were the populations of Lazica (the ancient Colchis), the tribes of Iberia and Georgia, and even the Sabirian Huns who occupied the celebrated defiles of the Caspian Gates at the foot of the Caucasus range on the boundary of the two Empires. With great skill Byzantine diplomacy, by spreading Christianity in those regions, had inclined the peoples to wish for the protection of the orthodox Emperor, and so had obtained possession of important strategic and commercial posts for Greek use. This policy of encroachment was bound to lead to a rupture, which came in 527, during the last months of Justin's reign.

The war however was neither very long nor disastrous. Neither of the two adversaries wanted to fight to the death. Kawad, who had taken up arms, was distracted by domestic difficulties and the task of assuring the succession of his son. Justinian wanted to disengage himself as soon as possible in order to have his hands free to deal with affairs in the West. Under these conditions the imperial army, which was of a good size, and well commanded by Belisarius, was able to snatch a signal victory at Dara in 530, the first victory won against Persia for many years. Another general was able to make considerable progress in Persian Armenia at the same time, but Justinian did not set himself seriously to profit by his successes. The next year a Persian invasion of Syria forced Belisarius to engage in and to lose the disastrous battle of Callinicum (531). Then, in spite of the fact that the Persians were besieging Martyropolis (531) and that a career of pillage had brought the Huns under the very walls of Antioch (December 531), the Great King troubled as little to push his advantages as the Emperor did to avenge his defeat. Negotiations were as important in this war as military operations. When therefore in September 531 the death of Kawad gave the throne to his son Chosroes I Anoushirvan, the new sovereign was preoccupied by the endeavour to consolidate his power at home, and willingly joined in the negotiations which ended in the conclusion of an "everlasting peace," in September 532. Justinian was delighted to end the war, and gave way on almost every point. He agreed to pay once more the annual subsidy which the Romans had handed over to the Persians to keep up the fortresses which defended the passes of the Caucasus against the Northern barbarians. This was a large sum of 110,000 pounds of gold, a thinly veiled form of tribute. He promised to move the residence of the Duke of Mesopotamia from Dara, the great fortress built by Anastasius in 507, to Constantina, which was further from the frontier; and he abandoned the protectorate over Iberia. In return the country of the Lazi remained within the sphere of Byzantine influence, and the Persians evacuated the fortresses in it.

But Chosroes was not the man to rest contented with these first successes. He was a young prince, ambitious, active and anxious for conquests. It was not without suspicion that he viewed the progress and success of the imperial ambition, for he knew that the longing for universal dominion might well form a menace to the Sassanid monarchy, as well as to the West. He therefore made use of the years which followed the peace of 532 to reconstruct his army, and when he saw what seemed to him a favourable opportunity, he resolutely began the war again (540). This happened when he discovered that the Roman frontier was stripped of troops, Armenia and the country of the Lazi discontented under Byzantine rule, and the Goths at bay after the Vandals were conquered. At the beginning of hostilities he threw himself on Syria, which he cruelly ravaged, and seized Antioch, which he completely ruined under the eyes of the helpless Roman generals. In vain Justinian sent the best generals against him, first Germanus and then Belisarius, hastily recalled from Italy at the beginning of 541. Their troops were not sufficient to defend the country effectively. In 541, Chosroes attacked Lazica, reduced Iberia and swept away the strong fortress of Petra, which Justinian had lately built to the south of Phasis. In 542 he ravaged Commagene; in 543 he made a demonstration on the Armenian frontier; and in 544 he again appeared in Mesopotamia which he ravaged cruelly, in spite of the heroic resistance of Edessa. Meanwhile the imperial troops did nothing: and the generals spent their time in intrigues instead of in fighting. The military prestige of Belisarius had made Chosroes give way for a brief space, but the general was absorbed in his domestic troubles, and let slip the time when he should have taken the offensive with vigour; and by so doing more or less justified the disgrace which soon overtook him through Theodora's ill-will (542). The only military enterprise undertaken in 543 by Justinian's army was the invasion of Persian Armenia, with more than 30,000 men, and it led to a great disaster. The Emperor was seriously concerned with events in Italy —Totila had just reconquered nearly the whole peninsula—and he was very lucky to be able to buy with gold a truce for five years, instead of a final peace (545). Thanks to the renewal of this convention in 551 and 552 the Asiatic provinces enjoyed tranquillity once more, though the war continued in Lazica for many years afterwards.

It was an easy matter for the diplomacy of the two Empires to win allies from amongst the belligerent tribes of the Caucasus, since their good faith was always an uncertain quantity. While the Lazi, who were discontented under the Persian tyranny, returned to Justinian in 549, other peoples who had formerly been within the Byzantine sphere of influence now attached themselves to Chosroes. Furthermore the war seemed unending in a country rendered almost impassable by mountains and forests. A struggle was maintained for several years over Petra. Taken by the Persians in 541, it was attacked in vain by the Byzantines in 549, and was only finally regained in 551. Other places were attacked and defended with equal tenacity. Justinian realised the importance of possessing a region which would enable him to deprive the Persians of an outlet on the Black Sea, and therefore he made unheard-of efforts to keep it. He concentrated as many as 50,000 men there in 552. Finally Chosroes saw the uselessness of the interminable strife; and the armistice of 555 was turned into a definite treaty in 561. Peace was declared for fifty years, and the Persians agreed to evacuate Lazica, where they knew that their power could hardly be maintained, since the people were enthusiastically Christian. But the Emperor's success was dearly bought. He bound himself to pay an annual tribute of 30,000 *aurei*, handing over the sum-total for the first seven years in advance. He promised for the future to discontinue any religious propaganda in the dominions of the Great King, in return for the extension of toleration to Christians in Persia. These concessions dealt a blow at Justinian's pride as an Emperor and a Christian. However, Lazica remained to him, and it was a considerable gain in the direction of securing the safety of the Empire. Still the treaty was intentionally so vague in some points that it contained the beginnings of many future difficulties.

While Roman Asia was cruelly suffering from these endless wars, the European provinces were not escaping. Although the shock of the great barbarian invasions had shaken the East much less than the West, a succession of barbarian peoples were settled north of the Danube. The Lombards, Heruls and Gepidae were on the west; Slavs and Bulgars, Antae and Huns on the lower reaches of the river, while behind them

lay the strong nation of Avars, still roving to the north of the Palus
Maeotis but gradually spreading themselves westward. The Empire
proved as attractive to these barbarians as to those who had invaded
the West. They had all one wish and one aim—some day to become
members of the rich and civilised commonwealth, whose towns were
fair, whose fields were fertile, and in which men received great treasures
and honour from the hand of the Emperor. Without doubt these
sentiments were largely inspired by greed of the splendid plunder that
the Roman territory offered to the enterprise of the barbarians, and if
their peaceful offers were declined they did not hesitate to keep their
vows by the use of force. Thus, at the end of the fifth century the
tribes had formed the habit of crossing the Danube periodically, either
in unnoticed driblets, or by sudden invasions, and certain groups were
legally settled on the south side of the river by the beginning of the
sixth century. The movement continued during the whole of Justinian's
reign.

From the beginning of his reign the Huns had appeared in Thrace
and the Antae in Illyricum; but they were repulsed with such energy
that, according to Malalas, "a great terror overcame the barbarian
nations." Soon however the resistance gave way. As had been the
case in Asia, the frontier was denuded of troops in consequence of the
expeditions to the West, and the boldness of the invaders increased.
In 534 the Slavs and Bulgars crossed the Danube, and the *magister
militum* of Thrace perished in the attempt to drive them back. In 538
the Huns invaded Scythia and Moesia, in 540 they went further and
ravaged Thrace, Illyricum and Greece as far as the Isthmus of Corinth.
One of their bands even penetrated to the environs of Constantinople,
and spread a terrible panic in the capital. In 546 there was another
Hunnish invasion, in 547 an attack from the Slavs who devastated
Illyricum as far as Dyrrachium, while the imperial generals did not even
dare to face them. In 551 a band of three thousand Slavs pillaged
Thrace and Illyricum and advanced as far as the Aegean Sea. In 552
the Slavs and Antae menaced Thessalonica and settled themselves on
Byzantine land as though they had conquered it. In 558 the Kotrigur
Huns pushed into Thrace, one of their bands reaching Thermopylae,
while another appeared under the walls of Constantinople, which was
only just saved by the courage of the old Belisarius. In 562 the
Huns reappeared. Then the insolent and menacing Avars became
prominent, on the very eve of Justinian's death. It is quite certain that
none of these incursions would have led to the permanent establishment
of a barbarian people within the limits of the Empire, as had happened
in the West, for the imperial generals were always finally successful in
hurling the swarms of invaders back over the Danube. At the same
time the incessant scourge could not fail to produce lamentable
consequences in the provinces which suffered from it. Procopius

estimates that more than 200,000 people were either slain or led captive during its course. He also compares the annually ravaged lands to the "Scythian deserts," and tells how the folk were forced to flee to the forests and mountains to avoid the outrages and atrocities which the barbarians would have inflicted upon them.

However, in Asia as in Europe, Justinian had taken wise and vigorous measures to secure the defence of his provinces, to give them, as he said, "peace and tranquillity," and to remove the "temptation to invade and ravage the countries where the Emperor's subjects dwelt" from the barbarians. With this object of efficiency in view he re-organised the great military commands which were created to guard the frontier. In Asia one general, the *magister militum* of the East, had commanded the enormous district reaching from the Black Sea to Egypt. This command was too large, and Justinian divided it, instituting *magistri militum* for Armenia and Mesopotamia. In Europe he added a *magister militum* of Moesia to those of Illyricum and Thrace. But above all, for the immediate defence of the frontier he organised all along the *limes* military districts commanded by *duces* and occupied by special troops, the *limitanei*. We have already seen how the duties and divisions of this formation were determined in Africa. The same system was extended to the whole Empire, and a large strip of military lands round its whole circumference assured the safety of the interior. Although several of these *limites* were in existence before the time of Justinian, he had the merit of organising and completing the whole system. Three *limites* were formed in Egypt, several commands were halved in Syria and on the Euphrates, and *duces* were established in Armenia, while others kept watch on the Danube, in Scythia, in the two Moesias and in Dacia. Thus the barbarians were again confronted with the opposing wall that used to be called "the monarchy's wrapper" (*praetentura imperii*).

Justinian also busied himself in building a continuous chain of fortresses along all the frontiers, as he had done in Africa. Rome had formerly been forced to undertake the immediate defence of the frontiers of the Empire in order to protect her territories. Justinian did more. Behind the first line of *castella*, and attached to them by a succession of stations, he built a series of large fortresses placed further apart, and more important. These served to strengthen the frontier castles, made a second barrier against invasion, and were a place of refuge for the inhabitants of the country. Thus the whole district was covered with strong castles. They were of unequal importance and strength, but they kept a watch on the enemy's territory, occupied points of strategic importance, barred the defiles, commanded the important routes, protected the safety of the towns and sheltered the rural population. They covered all the provinces with a close-meshed net of fortresses, a network through which it seemed impossible for the enemy to slip. It had taken only a few years for Justinian's resolution to raise or repair hundreds of fortresses, from the Danube to the Armenian mountains, and to the banks of the Euphrates. If ancient Roman posts were merely repaired at some points, while at others it was only necessary to complete buildings begun by Anastasius, yet the dazed admiration which contemporaries seem to have felt for this colossal work was justified, for Justinian gave unity to the whole system and displayed the greatest energy in carrying it out. According to Procopius, by it he truly " saved the monarchy."

In his *De Aedificiis* Procopius gives the detailed list of the countless buildings repaired or built by the Emperor's orders. Here it must suffice to notice the chief features of the work. On the Danube more than eighty castles were built or restored between the place where the Save enters that river and the Black Sea. Among them may be mentioned Singidunum (Belgrade), Octavum, Viminacium, Novae, further to the east Ratiaria, Augusta, Securisca, Durostorum (Silistria), Troesmis, and, on the left bank, the strongly fortified bridge of Lederata. These were for the most part ancient Roman citadels newly repaired. Justinian's original work consisted chiefly in the measures which he took to strengthen the rear. Hundreds of *castella* sprang up in Dacia, Dardania, and Moesia, further south in Epirus, Macedonia and Thrace. Thus there was a second and even a third line of defence. In Dardania alone, Justinian's native country, Procopius enumerates more than one hundred and fifty *castella* besides such great posts as Justiniana Prima, Sardica and Naissus. Fortifications were even constructed on the shore of the Sea of Marmora and the Archipelago. To protect Constantinople Anastasius had built the Long Wall in 512. It ran from the Sea of Marmora to Selymbria on the Black Sea. Similar long walls covered the Thracian Chersonesus, barred the passes of Thermopylae, and cut across the Isthmus of Corinth. Fortresses were also raised in Thessaly and northern Greece. Thus the whole of the Balkan peninsula formed a vast entrenched camp. On the side of the Euxine long walls protected the approaches to Cherson, and the strong castle of Petra Justiniana defended Lazica. Then several lines of fortresses were drawn up from Trebizond to the Euphrates. In Armenia there was Theodosiopolis (now Erzeroum), Kitharizon and Martyropolis; in Mesopotamia Amida, Constantina, Dara, called "the rampart of the Roman Empire," and another Theodosiopolis; Circesium was on the Euphrates and Zenobia and Palmyra on the borders of the desert. Added to these there were the intermediate *castella* which connected the big fortresses. A little to the rear, in the second line, were Satala, Coloneia, Nicopolis, Sebaste, Melitene, "the bulwark of Armenia," Edessa, Carrhae, Callinicum in Osrhoene, Sura, Hierapolis, Zeugma in the Euphrates district, and Antioch after the catastrophe of 540. These made a formidable field for warfare. It is certain that all these buildings do not date from Justinian's reign, but he must have the credit of combining them all into a sure and splendid defensive system.

Military methods alone were not employed for the defence of the Empire in the East. The imperial diplomacy was putting forth all its powers to that end, and displayed wonderful skill and ingenuity in the task. The Empire always possessed a great influence over the barbarians settled on the Roman frontiers. They were proud when their services and good faith won for them the approval of the *basileus*. They gladly placed their forces at his disposal when they received the annual subsidy (*annona*), and became the auxiliaries and vassals of the Empire, bearing the name of *foederati*. Their chiefs felt themselves honoured when they received the splendid insignia of their commands from the hands of the *basileus*. They gladly adorned themselves with titles culled from the hierarchy of the palace, and hastened to declare themselves to be "Slaves of the imperial Majesty." Constantinople and the Court dazzled their simple minds, they flocked there gladly, and it was easy for the Emperor by the mere splendour of their reception to impress them with a great idea of the strength of the monarchy. During the whole of Justinian's reign the Sacred Palace was filled with a never-ending succession of strange and barbaric sovereigns. Heruls, Huns, Gepidae, Avars, Saracens, Axumitae, Lazi, Iberians, men of every race and of every land, with their wives and children and their retinue in picturesque garments, filled the capital with a babel of all the tongues in the universe. They were loaded with honours, presents, and magnificent demonstrations of affection, and returned to their native wilds dazzled by the spectacle of the imperial majesty. Naturally they felt themselves only too happy to be allowed to serve this *basileus* who gave so warm a welcome to his faithful servitors, and recompensed them so generously.

Thus by the clever distribution of favours and money the Emperor was able to maintain a fringe of barbarian clients on all his frontiers. At the same time the authorities at Byzantium never forgot that the fickle and perfidious allies might prove to be dangerous servants because of their indiscipline, faithlessness and greed. The imperial diplomacy watched them with an eagle eye, skilfully treating them with a mixture of sternness and leniency; and endeavouring to render them harmless by the policy of setting them against each other, and fostering rivalry and hatred amongst them. Justinian maintained a possible rival to every barbarian king, he had always a hostile people waiting his word to descend on every other people. The Lombards menaced the Gepidae, the Utigurs the Kotrigurs, the Avars the Huns. Thus, as Agathias wrote, "so long as the barbarians destroyed each other, the Emperor was always victor without drawing his sword, no matter what was the end of the struggle." Formerly Rome had found the same methods necessary to govern the barbarians. Byzantium was able to add to the Roman traditions the influence which she wielded because of her propagation of Christianity. Her missionaries worked for the consolidation of the imperial power as effectively as her diplomatists. They opened a road for politicians, and prepared new territories for Byzantine influence and civilisation. Thanks to them conversions increased everywhere, from the plains of southern Russia to the Abyssinian plateau, and from the Caucasus Mountains to the oases of the Sahara.

By means of Christianity Byzantine influence spread beyond the boundaries of the Empire in Justinian's reign, and many were the peoples affected by it; Huns from the Cimmerian Bosphorus, Suanians, Abasgi, Apsilians from the Caucasus district, Alans, and Sabirian Huns, Tzani from the upper Euphrates, Arabs from Syria, Himyarites from Yemen, Nobadae and Blemmyes from the upper Nile, Berbers from the oases of the Sahara, and Heruls from Moesia.

By these means Justinian was able to checkmate his enemies. In the East he sought amongst the Sabirian Huns for allies against the Sassanid monarchy, because they could rush upon the Persian realm from the north. He also went to the Arabs of the Syrian desert because they might make useful diversions from the south, and he formed them into a unique State, under the *phylarchus* Harith the Ghassanid (531). Not content with this, he went yet further and made friends among the Arabs on the Yemen and in the Ethiopian kingdom of Axum. In the West he skilfully managed to sow discord amongst the tribes who crowded on the Danube frontier, checking the Bulgars by the Huns, the Huns by the Antae, and the Antae and Utigurs by the Avars. He scattered money and lands liberally amongst them all, loading their ambassadors with silken robes and golden chains, in return for which he only asked them to supply Byzantium with soldiers. In this way he settled the Lombards in Pannonia, the Heruls in Dacia, and the Kotrigur Huns in Thrace. He offered the Avars lands suitable for settlement on the Save, and similarly managed to procure a number of vassals on all the frontiers of the Empire. On the Danube there were the Heruls, Gepidae, Lombards, Huns and Antae; on the borders of Armenia the Lazi and Tzani; on the Syrian frontier the crowd of Arab tribes; in Africa the Berber inhabitants of Byzacena, Numidia and Mauretania.

Thus with wonderful skill Justinian exercised the difficult art of ruling barbarians, and he did it from the depth of his palace and capital. Contemporaries waxed eloquent in praise of the prudence, the fairness and delicacy displayed by the Emperor in carrying out this policy, and in celebrating that εὐβουλία by which, according to Menander, "he would have destroyed the barbarians without fighting if he had lived long enough." However this policy was not without its dangers. By displaying the riches of the Empire to the barbarians, and by lavishly distributing money and lands amongst them, their demands were naturally increased enormously, and their invasions provoked. Procopius very wisely observed that "once they had tasted Byzantine wealth it was impossible to keep them from it, or to make them forget the road to it." The obvious antidote for the dangers of this course of diplomacy was a strong military organisation. Procopius again wrote "there is no other way of compelling the barbarians to keep faith with Rome except by the fear of the imperial armies." Justinian understood this quite well. Unfortunately, in proportion as the West again absorbed the resources and attention of the Empire, lack of money led to the disorganisation of those military institutions which had been formed to protect the East. Corps of *limitanei* were disbanded, the fighting force of the troops of the line in Syria was diminished, strong positions were left undefended, often bereft of garrisons altogether, and Justinian's excellent network of fortresses no longer sufficed to keep out the barbarians. The Emperor seemed to prefer diplomatic action by itself to the practical military precautions that he had applied so actively at the beginning of his reign. He thought it more clever to buy off the invaders than to beat them by force of arms, he considered it cheaper to subsidise the barbarians than to maintain a large army on a war footing; he found it more agreeable to direct a subtle diplomacy than great military operations, and he never realised that the first result of his policy was to encourage the barbarians to return.

This was the fundamental defect of Justinian's foreign policy in the East. It rested on a skilful combination of military force and diplomacy. As long as the balance was maintained between these two elements equilibrium was secured, the end aimed at was attained, and the Empire was well defended and comparatively safe. But when this balance was upset, everything went wrong at once. The Slavs appeared at Hadrianople, the Huns under the walls of Constantinople, while the Avars assumed a threatening attitude and regions of the Balkans were terribly ravaged. Procopius was justified when he reproached Justinian with having "wasted the riches of the Empire in extravagant gifts to the barbarians," and in his assertion that the Emperor's rash generosity only incited them to return perpetually "to sell the peace for which they were always well paid." The historian goes on to explain that "after them came others, who made a double profit, from the rapine in which they indulged and from the money with which the liberality of the prince always furnished them. Thus the evil continued with no abatement, and there was no escape from the vicious circle."

This mistaken policy cost the Empire dear. Nevertheless, it was founded on a right principle, and some of the results which it produced were not to be despised, in connexion with the defence of territory, the development of commerce, or the spread of civilisation. Justinian's mistake—specially during the last years of his reign—lay in the fact that he carried the system to excess. When he allowed the army to become disorganised and fortresses to fall into ruin he bereft his diplomacy of the force that was necessary to support his plans. When he ceased to awe the barbarians he found himself at their mercy.

III.

The domestic government of the East took up as much of Justinian's attention as the defence of the territory. The urgent need for administrative reform in the midst of a serious religious crisis provided ample food for his anxiety.

In Byzantium the sale of public offices was an ancient custom, and this venality led to deplorable results. The governors expected to recoup themselves from the province for the expenses which they incurred in obtaining their posts, and to enrich themselves to as great an extent as possible while they held them. The other agents in so corrupt an administration only followed the governor's example, when they pillaged and crushed the district to their heart's content. The financial system was oppressive and exacting; justice was sold or partially administered, and deep misery and general insecurity was the natural result. The people left the country, the towns were emptied, the fields deserted, and agriculture abandoned. While those who were strong or rich enough to defend themselves managed to escape the exactions of the tax-collector, the great proprietors maintained troops of armed men in their pay, and ravaged the country, attacked people and seized land, sure of immunity from the magistrates. Everywhere murder, brigandage, agitation and risings abounded, and last and most serious result of all the disorders, the returns of the taxes from the exhausted provinces were but scanty. Justinian calculated that only one-third of the taxes imposed really reached the treasury, and the misery of the subjects destroyed the source of the public wealth. It will be easy to understand why the Emperor felt so much concern at affairs in the East, if we add that the laws abounded in contradictions, obscurities and useless prolixity, which gave rise to very long law-suits, and furnished an opportunity for the judges to give arbitrary decisions, or to decide matters to suit their own convenience.

Justinian, as we know, had the qualities that go to make a good administrator. He loved order, he had a sincere wish to do good work, and a real care for the well-being of his subjects. With an authoritative disposition and absolutist tendencies, he combined a taste for administrative centralisation. But above all, his vast projects left him incessantly in need of large sums of money. He saw that the best way to ensure the regularity of the returns was to protect those who paid from the functionaries who ruined them; and thus in furthering the well-being and quiet of his subjects the Emperor was also serving the best interests of the fisc. Moreover it satisfied Justinian's pride to maintain the tradition of the great Roman Emperors by being a reformer and legislator. For these various reasons from the time of his accession he undertook a double work. In order to give the Empire certain and unquestionable laws he had legislative monuments drawn up under Tribonian's direction, which are known as Justinian's Code (529), the Digest (533), the Institutes (533), and completed by the series of *Novellae* (534–565).

The details of Justinian's legislative work will be found in another chapter. All that is done here is to indicate their place in the reign as a whole and in the general policy of the Emperor. After the great crisis of the Nika riot had clearly shewn him the public discontent and the faults of the government, he promulgated the two great ordinances of April 535. By these two documents Justinian laid down the principles of his administrative reform and shewed his functionaries the new duties which he expected of them. The sale of offices was abolished. To take all pretext for exploiting the population from the governors, their salaries were raised, while their prestige was increased in order to remove from them the temptation to yield to the demands of powerful private persons. But before all things, the Emperor wished his agents to be scrupulously honest, and was always urging them to keep their "hands clean." He gave minute instructions to his magistrates, and bade them render the same justice to all, keep a watchful eye on the conduct of their subordinates, protect the subjects from all vexations, hinder the encroachments of the great, ensure the maintenance of order by frequent progresses, and govern, in fact, "paternally." But above all he bade them neglect nothing that might defend the interests of the fisc, and increase its resources. To pay in the taxes regularly was the first duty of a good officer, as the first duty of a taxpayer was to acquit himself regularly and completely of the whole sum due. Furthermore, to ensure the carrying out of his plans, Justinian requested the bishops to inspect the conduct of the magistrates; and he invited anyone who wished to make complaints to come to Constantinople, and lay his grievances at the feet of the sovereign.

During the years 535 and 536 a series of special measures was added to the general enactments. Their object was to strengthen the local government and to ensure obedience to the central power. In the fourth century the traditional method of conducting the administration was to multiply provincial districts, to complicate an endless hierarchy of officials and to separate civil and military authority. Justinian made a determined break in these pedantic traditions. He desired to simplify the administration, to have fewer provinces but to have them better organised. He also wished to diminish the number of officials, to give those that remained better salaries, and to make them stronger, and more dependent on the central government. To further this end he reduced the number of *circumscriptions*, by uniting couples of them or by grouping them more reasonably. He suppressed the useless *vicarii*, who had been intermediaries between the provincial governors and the praetorian praefect, and he reunited the civil and military authority in the hands of the same officials in a great number of provinces. He created *praetors* in Pisidia, Lycaonia, Pamphylia and Thrace; *counts* in Isauria, Phrygia Pacatiana, Galatia, Syria and Armenia; an administrative *moderator* in the Hellespont; a *proconsul* to govern Cappadocia. The Emperor adorned all these officials with the high-sounding title of *Justiniani*, and they united authority over the troops stationed in their circumscription to their competence in civil matters. This was a great innovation and was fraught with serious consequences in the administrative history of the Byzantine Empire.

The reorganisation of the judicial administration completed these useful measures. Justinian desired that justice should be administered with more speed and security in these provinces. In order to avoid the obstruction of business in the courts of the capital he made a series of courts of appeal midway between the court of the provincial governor and that of the praetorian praefect and the quaestor. Thus appeals were made easier and less burdensome to the subjects, and at the same time Constantinople was freed from the crowd of litigants who had flocked there, and who, since they were discontented and idle, were only too ready to join the ranks of thieves or agitators.

One of the great difficulties confronting the government was the police of the capital. *Praetors of the people* were instituted there in 535, to judge cases of theft, adultery, murder, and to repress disturbances. In 539 another magistrate, the *quaesitor*, was established, to rid the city of the crowd of provincials who obstructed it with no valid excuse. At the same time, probably owing to Theodora's initiative, the guardians of public morals were reorganised, and rigorous mandates were issued to check excessive gambling, impious blasphemy and the scandal caused by infamous persons who did not wait for night to hide their deeds. To those who had been driven to vice by need rather than choice protection was also given against the *lenones* who took advantage of them. The Empress' charity was exercised to provide a refuge for these unfortunate girls, in the convent of Repentance (μετάνοια) established by her wish in an old imperial palace on the Asiatic side of the Bosphorus. But above all the various factions were closely watched, the games in the circus were suppressed for several years, and the tranquillity of the capital was undisturbed for at least fifteen years.

This administrative work was completed by the great impetus which was given to the public works. In the instructions to his officials Justinian had commended to their attention the maintenance of roads, bridges, walls and aqueducts, and had promised large supplies for such purposes. In consequence new roads were everywhere made to facilitate

CH. II.

communication, wells and reservoirs were established along them so that caravans might be supplied with water; bridges spanned the rivers, and the course of the streams was controlled. Schemes were carried out in order to supply drinking-water to the great towns in the Empire, and many public baths were built. After the disaster of 540 Antioch was rebuilt with unheard-of luxury. It was plentifully supplied with aqueducts, sewers, baths, public squares, theatres, and in fact with "everything which testifies to the prosperity of a town." After the earthquakes of 551 and 554 the Syrian towns rose from their ruins more splendid than ever, thanks to Justinian's munificence. The Empire was covered with new cities built at the prince's wish, and bearing, to please him, the surname of "Justiniana." Tauresium, the modest village in which the Emperor was born, became a great city in this way with the name of Justiniana Prima. It was populous and prosperous, "truly worthy of a *basileus*." Constantinople, which had been partly destroyed by the fire of 532, was rebuilt with incomparable magnificence. The church of St Sophia was begun in 532 under the direction of Isidore of Miletus and Anthemius of Tralles, and finished in 537; the Sacred Palace with the *Chalce* vestibule was built in 538 and completely lined with mosaics and marbles, while the great throne-room or *Consistorium* was dazzling with the shimmer of precious metals. There were also the great square of the Augusteum, in the centre of which stood an equestrian statue of Justinian and which was surrounded on every side by splendid monuments; the long porticoes which stretched from the imperial residence to the forum of Constantine; the church of the Holy Apostles, begun by Theodora in 536 and completed in 550; and the numerous hostels and hospitals founded by Justinian and Theodora, together with palaces and basilicae; all these attested the luxurious taste and magnificent pride of the Emperor. To this day the splendid reservoirs of Jerebatan-Serai and Bin-bir-Direk (the thousand and one columns) shew the trouble that was taken to supply the capital with drinking-water; and the churches of St Irene, and SS. Sergius and Bacchus, above all St Sophia, that miracle of stability and boldness, of purity of line and brightness of colour, remain as incomparable witnesses to Justinian's grandeur[1].

A solid economic prosperity justified so many expensive splendours. In order to develop industry and commerce in his Empire Justinian gave great attention to economic questions. He set himself to free the Byzantine merchants from the tyranny of middlemen who had oppressed them and to open fresh fields for their enterprise. As a matter of fact, in the sixth century Byzantium did not obtain exotic commodities and precious materials for her luxury straight from the countries which produced them. The land routes by which the products of the

---

[1] A fuller account of the city will be given in Vol. IV.

Far East were brought to the Mediterranean from China through the oases of Sogdiana, and the sea routes by which precious stones, spices and silk were brought from Ceylon to the ports on the Persian Gulf, were in the hands of Persia. Persia not only guarded these routes jealously, but also regulated with special severity the exportation of silk, which was indispensable to the Byzantines. Justinian determined to remedy this state of things. In the Black Sea, the ports of the Crimea, Bosporus and Cherson made, with the south of Russia, a splendid district for barter; besides this Byzantium, situated at the mouth of the Black Sea, carried on a brisk trade with Lazica. But, from the Sea of Azof, as well as from Colchis, the Caspian could be reached, and then if a northerly direction were taken the oases of Sogdiana could be reached without crossing Persian territory. Another route offered itself more to the south. The Syrian and Egyptian merchants set out from Aila on the Gulf of Akabah to work the shores of the Red Sea, and then extended their operations as far as the ports of Himyar on the east, and the great Ethiopian port of Adoulis on the west. But Adoulis kept up widespread relations with the whole of the Asiatic East, and her ships, like those of the Arabs of Yemen, went as far as Ceylon, the great emporium for India. Thanks to these routes, Justinian thought that he could divert the trade of which the Persians had the monopoly from the usual routes. During 530 or 531 strange negotiations took place with the Himyarites and the Court of Axum, with the object of persuading those peoples to agree with the Emperor's plans, and to bring the products of the Far East straight to the Red Sea. The "King of Kings" of Axum readily agreed to do so; but the Persians had the upper hand in the Indian ports, and they would not allow themselves to be deprived of their profits. The peace therefore of 532 restored the transactions between the Empire and the Sassanid monarchy to their ordinary footing.

However, thanks to the importation of raw silk, which became once more regular, the Syrian manufactures were flourishing. The rupture with Persia in 540 brought about a grave crisis for them, and Justinian only made matters worse by the unwise measures which he took. In his excessive love of regulations he attempted to fix the price of raw silk, by a law which enforced a maximum price. He hoped thus to substitute a monopoly of the manufactures of the State for the ruined private industry. The Syrian industry was seriously injured by these measures. Luckily the cultivation of silk-worms did much to repair the disasters. The eggs of the worms were brought into the Empire from the country of Serinda by two missionaries, between 552 and 554. The silk industry soon recovered when raw material could be obtained more cheaply, although Byzantium was not successful in freeing herself completely from Persia.

On the whole, however, Byzantine commerce was flourishing. Alexandria was a splendid port, and grew rich by exporting corn, while her merchants travelled as far as the Indies. Syria found a market for her manufactures as far away as China. But above all, Constantinople, with her incomparable situation between Europe and Asia, was a wonderful mart, towards which, according to a contemporary, the ships of the world's commerce sailed, freighted with expectation. Her numerous industrial societies, and the active commerce in silver carried on there with wealthy bankers, increased her riches still further; and seeing the prosperity of his capital, Justinian was able, with his usual optimism, to congratulate himself on "having given another flower to the State by his splendid conceptions."

But in spite of the Emperor's good intentions, his administrative reform miscarried. From 535 until the end of the reign Justinian was constantly obliged to renew his ordinances, think out new measures and blame the zeal of his officials. In the great ordinance of 556 he was forced to repeat everything which he had laid down twenty years earlier. From the statements of the public documents themselves we learn that the peace continued to be disturbed, the officials continued to steal openly "in their shameful love of gain"; the soldiers continued to pillage, the financial administration was more oppressive than ever; while justice was slow, venal and corrupt, as it had been before the reform.

More and more Justinian needed money. He needed it for his wars of conquest, for his buildings, for the maintenance of his imperial luxury, and for the expenses of his policy with regard to the barbarians. Thus after having ordered that the subjects of the Empire should be treated leniently, and having declared that he would be content with the existing taxes, he was himself forced to create new dues, and to exact the returns with a merciless severity. Worse still, thanks to the financial distress against which he struggled, he was obliged to tolerate all the exactions of his officials. As long as money came to the treasury, no one troubled to enquire how it was obtained: and as it had been necessary to yield to the venality of the public offices, so the only course was to appear as blind to the dealings of the administration as to the sufferings of the subjects. Besides, a corrupt example was set in high quarters. John of Cappadocia, brutal and covetous as he was, speculating on everything, stealing from everyone, still maintained the Emperor's credit in a wonderful way until 541 "by his constant labours to increase the public revenue." Peter Barsymes who succeeded him in 543 was the prince's chief favourite until 559, in spite of his shameless traffic in the magistracies, and his scandalous speculation in corn, simply because he was able, in some degree, to supply money for all Justinian's needs. The provincial officials followed the lead of their chiefs, and even rivalled them in exactions and corruption, while the Emperor looked the other way. The financial tyranny had reached such a pitch by this time that a contemporary tells us that "a foreign invasion seemed less formidable to the taxpayers than the arrival of the officials of the fisc." The misery suffered was terrible enough to justify the sinister fact recorded by John Lydus, "The tax-gatherers could find no more money to take to the Emperor, because there were no people left to pay the taxes." Justinian's administrative system had woefully miscarried.

In common with all the Emperors who had occupied the throne of the Caesars since the time of Constantine, Justinian gave much attention to the Church, as much for political reasons as because of his zeal for orthodoxy. His autocratic disposition was unable to realise that anything could be exempt from the prince's inspection in a well-regulated monarchy. He claimed therefore to exercise his authority not only with regard to ecclesiastics—the greatest included—but further, when questions of discipline or dogma arose his word was never lacking. He wrote somewhere that "good order in the Church is the prop of the Empire." He spared nothing which might lead to this good order. Both Justinian's *Code* and the *Novellae* abound in laws dealing with the organisation of the clergy, the regulation of their moral life, the foundation and administration of religious houses, the government of ecclesiastical property and the control of the jurisdiction to which clerics were liable. During his whole reign Justinian claimed the right to appoint and dispossess bishops, to convoke and direct councils, to sanction their decisions, and to amend or abolish their canons. Since he enjoyed theological controversies, and had a real talent for conducting them, he was not deterred by pope, patriarchs and bishops, from setting himself up as a doctor of the Church, and as an interpreter of the Scriptures. In this capacity he drew up confessions of faith and hurled forth anathemas.

In exchange for the mastery which he assumed over it, he extended his special protection to the Church. A crowd of religious buildings, churches, convents and hospitals sprang up in every part of the Empire, thanks to the Emperor's generosity. Throughout the monarchy the bishops were encouraged to make use of the government's authority and resources to spread their faith as well as to suppress heresy. Justinian believed that the first duty of a sovereign was "to keep the pure Christian faith inviolate, and to defend the Catholic and Apostolic Church from any harm." He therefore employed the most severe measures against anyone who wished to injure or introduce changes into the unity of the Church. Religious intolerance was transformed into a public virtue.

From the beginning of his reign Justinian promulgated the severest laws against heretics in 527 and 528. They were excluded from holding any public office, and from the liberal professions. Their meetings were forbidden and their churches shut. They were even deprived of some of their civil rights, for the Emperor declared that it was only right that orthodox persons should have more privileges in society than heretics, for whom "to exist is sufficient." The pagans, Hellenes as they were called, were persecuted by the enforcement of these general rules; Justinian endeavoured, above all things, to deprive them of education, and he had the University of Athens closed in 529; at the same time ordering wholesale conversions.

Missions were frequently sent to the Monophysites of Asia by John, bishop of Ephesus, who called himself "the destroyer of idols and the hammer of the heathen" (542). Those sanctuaries which were not yet closed, that of Isis at Philae and that of Ammon in the oasis of Augila, were shut by force, and nothing remained of paganism but an amusement for a few men of leisure, or a form of political opposition in the shape of secret societies. The Jews fared no better, and the Samaritan revolt in 529 made their position still worse. Other sects which refused to conform, Manichaeans, Montanists, Arians and Donatists, were persecuted in the same way. Religious intolerance accompanied the imperial restoration in the West. In Africa, as in Italy, Arians were spoiled for the benefit of Catholics, their churches were destroyed or ruined, and their lands confiscated. The Monophysites alone profited by comparative toleration, because they engrossed more of Justinian's attention, since they were stronger and more numerous than the others.

Justinian had been thrown into the arms of Rome at the beginning of his reign, partly by the orthodox restoration effected by Justin, and partly by his own desire to maintain friendly relations with the Papacy; a desire due to political interests as well as to religious zeal. Resounding confessions of faith testified to the purity of his belief and his profound respect for Rome, while his measures against heretics proved the sincerity of his zeal. Justinian spared nothing in his efforts to conciliate the Roman Church, and we find inserted with evident satisfaction in Justinian's *Code* pontifical letters, which praise his efforts to maintain "the peace of the Church and the unity of religion," and assert that "nothing is finer than faith in the bosom of a prince."

However, if concord with Rome was a necessary condition of the establishment and maintenance of the imperial domination in the West, the Monophysites had to be reckoned with in the East. In spite of the persecutions of Justin's reign, they were still strong and numerous within the Empire. They were masters of Egypt, where the monks formed a fanatical and devoted army at the disposal of their patriarch. In Palestine, Syria, Mesopotamia, Osrhoene and Armenia they held important posts, and found protectors even in the capital itself; and their furious opposition to the Council of Chalcedon and the Roman doctrines was the more dangerous since under the guise of religion they displayed those separatist tendencies, which had long been hostile towards Constantinople in both Egypt and Syria. Justinian had to choose between the horns of a dilemma, between the restoration of political and moral unity in the East by the sacrifice of peace with

Rome—the course followed by Zeno and Anastasius, and advised by Theodora—and the maintenance of friendly relations with the West at the price of meeting the Eastern Monophysite opposition with force. Justin had pursued this policy and Justinian had carried it on. But now, placed as he was between the Pope and the Empress, he found a change of policy necessary. A middle course seemed fraught with least difficulty, so he tried to find a neutral position which would allow him to recede from the Council of Chalcedon sufficiently to satisfy the dissidents, and so, without sacrificing his orthodoxy, to extinguish an opposition which troubled the Emperor as much as the theologian. This was the fundamental idea underlying his religious policy, in spite of variations, hesitations and contradictions. Theodora suggested it to him, and it would have proved a fruitful conception if time had been allowed the Empress to finish her work; in any case it was an idea worthy of an Emperor.

From the time of his accession Justinian had busied himself in the attempt to find some common ground with the Monophysites. In 529 or 530, on Theodora's advice he recalled the fugitive or proscribed monks from exile, as a pledge of his good intentions. He invited to Constantinople Severus, the ex-patriarch of Antioch, for whom the Empress professed a passionate admiration, to seek with him for a way which might lead to an agreement. In 533 he arranged a conference in the capital "to restore unity," at which the heretics were to be treated with complete kindness and unalterable patience. Soon afterwards, in order to satisfy the Monophysites, he imposed on the orthodox clergy, after the theopaschite quarrel, a declaration of faith that has rightly been called "a new Henotikon." Further, he allowed the Monophysites complete liberty to spread their teaching, and not only in the capital but in the Sacred Palace itself heresy increased, thanks to the open protection of Theodora. When, in 535, the patriarchal throne became vacant, Epiphanius' successor was Anthemius, bishop of Trebizond, a prelate secretly attached to the Monophysite cause. Under the influence of Severus, who was in the capital, and a guest at the palace, the new patriarch pursued the policy approved by the religious leaders of the East, that is the same that Zeno and Anastasius had followed; while Theodora actively helped, and the Emperor gave a tacit consent.

But the orthodox position was restored by several events. In March 536 the energetic pope Agapetus came to Constantinople and boldly deposed Anthemius; the Council of Constantinople anathematised the heretics with no uncertain pronouncement soon after (May 536), while the apostolic legate Pelagius acquired in the following years considerable influence over Justinian. Towards the end of 537 persecution of the Monophysites broke out again: bonfires were lighted in Syria, Mesopotamia and Armenia, and it was boasted that heresy had been rooted out by severity and tortures. Even Egypt, the Monophysite stronghold, was not spared. The patriarch Theodosius, one of Theodora's *protégés*, was torn from his see, driven into exile (538) and replaced by a prelate fitted to inspire respect for orthodoxy by means of terror. Egypt bent under his iron hand. Even the monks accepted the Council of Chalcedon; and Justinian and Pelagius flattered themselves that they had beaten down heresy (540).

Although the Emperor returned to the Roman side in the dispute, he had no intention of giving up for that reason the supreme authority which he considered his due, even over the Papacy. Silverius, successor of Agapetus, had made the great mistake of allowing himself to be elected by Gothic influence just when Theodora wanted her favourite, the deacon Vigilius, to be elevated to the pontifical throne. Belisarius accepted the uncongenial task of paying off imperial grudges towards the new pope. In March 537 Silverius was arrested, deposed, and sent into exile on an imaginary charge of treason. Vigilius was unanimously elected in his place under pressure from Byzantium (29 March 537).

The Empress counted on her *protégé* to carry out her revenge for the repulse of 536. But once installed, Vigilius made delays, and in spite of Belisarius' summons to carry out his promises, finally refused to accomplish any of the plans expected of him. At the same time, Monophysitism was spreading in the East in spite of the severity of the edicts of 541 and 544. Justinian had taken what he thought to be the wise measure of assembling the heretical leaders in Constantinople, where they would be in his power, and under the eye of the police. But Theodora soon procured a return to court favour for the exiles. The Emperor willingly made use of their enthusiastic zeal, and sent them to convert the pagans of Nubia (540), to struggle with those of Asia Minor (542) and to establish Christianity amongst the Arabs of Syria (543). Theodora did still more. Thanks to her efforts Jacob Baradaeus, who had been secretly consecrated bishop of Edessa (543), was able to continue the work of reorganising the Monophysite Church throughout the East. Active and indefatigable, in spite of the harshness of the enraged police who dogged his track, he was able to reconstruct the scattered communities in Asia, Syria and Egypt, to give them bishops and even a leader in the patriarch whom he ordained at Antioch in 550. It was owing to him that a new Monophysite Church was founded in a few years, which took the name of its great founder, and henceforth called itself *Jacobite*.

This unexpected revival changed Justinian's plans once more. Again his old dream of unity seemed to him to be more than ever necessary for the safety of the State as well as for the good of the Church. Thus, when Theodore Askidas, bishop of Caesarea, drew his attention, among the writings approved by the Council of Chalcedon, to those of the three men Theodore of Mopsuestia, Theodoret of Cyrrhus, and Ibas of Edessa, as notoriously tainted with Nestorianism, he was easily persuaded that to condemn the Three Chapters would be to create an easy and orthodox way to dissipate the Monophysite distrust of the Council "renewed and purified." And since Pelagius was no longer there to counterbalance Theodora's influence, and as the heretics joyfully welcomed any scheme which injured the authority of Chalcedon, the Emperor pronounced the anathema against the Three Chapters by an edict of 543.

It was still necessary to obtain the adhesion of the Papacy; but this did not trouble the Emperor. It was essential to remove the pope from his Roman surroundings, which were hostile to the designs of the Greek theologians, and to put him in the Emperor's power. Therefore Vigilius was carried off from Rome in the midst of a display of the troops (November 545) and transported under escort to Sicily, whence he travelled slowly towards Constantinople. He arrived at the beginning of 547, and soon yielded to the importunities of the *basileus*, the energetic summons of Theodora, and the subtle entreaties of the court theologians. He promised "to set their minds at rest" by condemning the Three Chapters, and he published his *Judicatum* on Easter Eve 548. This, while formally maintaining the authority of the Canons of Chalcedon, condemned no less clearly the persons and writings of the three guilty doctors. This was Theodora's last triumph. When she died soon after (June 548) she could think that her highest hopes were realised, in the humiliation of the Apostolic See and the constant progress of the Monophysite Church.

When the news of these events at Constantinople spread to the West, there was a general protest against Vigilius' conduct in Africa, Dalmatia and Illyricum. Justinian was unmoved. By an imperial edict bearing the date of 551 he solemnly condemned the Three Chapters a second time, and set himself to overcome all opposition by the use of force. The most recalcitrant bishops in Africa were deposed, and the rest appeased by means of intrigues; and since Vigilius, alarmed at what he had done, insistently clamoured for an oecumenical council to settle the dispute, strong measures were taken against him. In the month of August 551 the church of St Peter in Hormisda, where he had taken refuge, was entered by a band of soldiers, who dragged the clerics composing the pontifical train from the sanctuary. Vigilius was clinging to the altar pillars; he was seized by the feet and the beard, and the ensuing struggle was so desperate that the altar was pulled over and fell, crushing the pope beneath it. At the sight of this dreadful occurrence the assembled crowd cried out in horror, and even the soldiers hesitated. The Praetor decided to beat a retreat; the plan had miscarried. But the pope was nothing more than the Emperor's prisoner. Surrounded by spies, fearing for his liberty, even for his life, Vigilius decided to flee. On a dark night (23 Dec. 551) he escaped from the Placidian Palace with a few faithful followers, and sought refuge in the church of

St Euphemia at Chalcedon, the same place where the Council had been held for which Vigilius was suffering martyrdom.

Justinian was afraid that he had gone too far: and he resumed negotiations. Not without difficulty nor without another attempt to use force, he persuaded the pontiff to return to Constantinople, and brought forward the idea of a Council once more. After various hindrances this great assembly, known as the Fifth Oecumenical Council, opened (5 May 553) in the church of St Sophia. A few African prelates, chosen with great care, were the only representatives of the West; the pope refused to take part in the debates, in spite of all entreaties: and while the Council accomplished its task, obedient to the Emperor's commands, he tried to make a pronouncement on the question in dispute on his own authority by the *Constitutum* of 14 May 553. While he completely abandoned the doctrines of Theodore of Mopsuestia, he refused to anathematise him, and shewed himself even more indulgent towards Ibas and Theodoret, saying that all Catholics should be contented with anything approved by the Council of Chalcedon. Unfortunately for Vigilius he had bound himself by frequent vows and by written and formal agreements to condemn the Three Chapters at Justinian's wish. At the Emperor's instigation the Council ignored the pontiff's recantation. To please the prince it even erased the name of Vigilius from the ecclesiastical diptychs; and then, the Three Chapters having been condemned in a long decree, the fathers separated, 2 June 553.

Violence was again used to enforce the decisions of the Council. Particular severity was used towards those clerics who had supported Vigilius in his resistance. They were exiled or imprisoned, so that the pontiff, deserted and worn out, and fearing that a successor to him would be appointed in newly-conquered Rome, gave way to the Emperor's wish and solemnly confirmed the condemnation of the Three Chapters by the *Constitutum* of February 554. The West however still persisted in its opposition. The authorities flattered themselves on having reduced the recalcitrants by floggings, imprisonment, exile and depositions. They were successful in Africa and Dalmatia, but in Italy there was a party amongst the bishops, led by the metropolitans of Milan and Aquileia, who flatly refused to remain in fellowship with a pope who "betrayed his trust" and "deserted the orthodox cause," and in spite of the efforts of the civil authorities to reduce the opposition, the schism lasted for more than a century.

The Papacy emerged from this long struggle cruelly humiliated. After Silverius, Vigilius had experienced in full measure the severity of the imperial absolutism. His successors, Pelagius (555) and John III (560), elected under pressure from Justinian's officials, were nothing more than humble servants of the *basileus*, in spite of all their struggles. Their authority was discredited in the entire West by the affair of the Three Chapters, shaken in Italy by the schism, and still further lessened by the privileges that the imperial benevolence granted to the church of Ravenna, since that town was the capital of reconquered Italy. By paying this price, by cruelly wounding the Catholic West, and recalling the Monophysites, Justinian hoped until his dying day that he had obtained the results which were the aim of his religious policy, and had restored peace to the East. "Anxious," wrote John of Ephesus, "to carry out the wishes of his dead wife in every detail," he increased the number of conferences and discussions after 548, in order to reconcile the Monophysites . while he had such a great wish to find some common ground with them that to satisfy them he slipped into heresy on the eve of his death. In an edict of 565 he declared his adherence to the doctrine of the *Incorrupticolae*, the most extreme of all the heretics, and as usual he used force against the prelates who made any resistance. Thus until the end of his life Justinian had consistently endeavoured to impose his will upon the Church, and to break down all opposition. Until the end of his life also he had sought to realise the ideal of unity which inspired and dominated the whole of his religious policy. But nothing came of his efforts; the Monophysites were never satisfied with the concessions made to them, and upon the whole this great theological undertaking, this display of rigour and arbitrariness, produced no results at all or results of a deplorable nature.

IV.

It remains to be seen what were the consequences of Justinian's government in the East, and what price he paid, specially during the last years of his reign, for this policy of great aims and mediocre or unskilful measures.

A secret defect existed in all Justinian's undertakings, which destroyed the sovereign's most magnificent projects, and ruined his best intentions. This was the disproportion between the end in view and the financial resources available to realise it. Enormous, in fact inexhaustible supplies were needed, for the drain on them was immense; to satisfy the needs of a truly imperial policy, to meet the cost of wars of conquest, to pay the troops, and for the construction of fortresses; to maintain the luxury of the Court and the expense of buildings, to support a complicated administration and to dispense large subsidies to the barbarians. When he ascended the throne Justinian had found in the treasury the sum of 320,000 pounds of gold, more than £14,400,000 sterling, which had been accumulated by the prudent economy of Anastasius. This reserve fund was exhausted in a few years, and henceforth for the rest of his long reign, the Emperor suffered from the worst of miseries, the lack of money. Without money the wars which had been entered upon with insufficient means dragged on interminably. Without money the unpaid army became disorganised and weak. Without money to maintain an effective force and provision the posts, the badly defended frontier gave way under the assault of the barbarians, and, to get rid of them, recourse was had to a ruinous diplomacy, which did not even protect the Empire against invasions. Without money the attempted administrative reform had to be abandoned, and the vices of an openly corrupt administration to be condoned. Without money the government was driven to strange expedients, often most unsuitable to its economic as to its financial policy. To meet expenses the burden of taxation was increased until it became almost intolerable; and as time passed, and the disproportion between the colossal aims of the imperial ambition and the condition of the financial resources of the monarchy became greater, the difficulty of overcoming the deficit led to even harsher measures. "The State," wrote Justinian in 552, "greatly enlarged by the divine mercy and led by this increase to make war on her barbaric neighbours, has never been in greater need of money than to-day." Justinian exercised all his ingenuity to find this money at any sacrifice, but in spite of real economies—amongst others the suppression of the consulship (541)—by which he tried to restore some proportion to the Empire's budget, the Emperor could never decide to curtail his luxury, or his building operations, while the money which had been collected with such difficulty was too often squandered to please favourites or upon whims. Therefore a terrible financial tyranny was established in the provinces, which effected the ruin of the West already overwhelmed by war, of the Balkan peninsula ravaged by barbarians, and of Asia fleeced by Chosroes. The time came when it was impossible to drag anything from these exhausted countries, and seeing the general misery, the growing discontent and the suspicions which increased every day, contemporaries asked, with a terrified stupor, "whither the wealth of Rome had vanished." Thus the end of the reign was strangely sad.

The death of Theodora (June 548), while it deprived the Emperor of a vigorous and faithful counsellor, dealt Justinian a blow from which he never recovered. Henceforth, as his age increased—he was 65 then— the defects of his character only became more prominent. His irresolution was more noticeable, while his theological mania was inflamed. He disregarded military matters, finding the direction of the wars which he had so dearly loved tiresome and useless; he cared more for the exercise of a diplomacy, often pitifully inadequate, than for the prestige of arms. Above all, he carried on everything with an ever-increasing carelessness. Leaving the trouble of finding money at any cost to his ministers, to Peter Barsymes the successor of John of Cappadocia, and to the quaestor Constantine, the successor of Tribonian, he gave himself up to religious quarrels, passing his nights in disputations with his bishops. As Corippus, a man not noted for severity towards princes, wrote "The old man no longer cared for anything; his spirit was in heaven."

Under these circumstances, everything was lost. The effective force of the army, which ought to have numbered 645,000 men, was reduced to 150,000 at the most in 555. No garrisons defended the ramparts of the dilapidated fortresses, " Even the barking of a watch-dog was not to be heard" wrote Agathias, somewhat brutally. Even the capital, inadequately protected by the wall of Anastasius, which was breached in a thousand places, only had a few regiments of the palatine guard— soldiers of no military worth—to defend it, and was at the mercy of a sudden attack. Added to this, successive invasions took place in Illyricum and Thrace; the Huns only just failed to take Constantinople in 558, while in 562 the Avars insolently demanded land and money from the Emperor.

Then there was the misery of earthquakes, in 551 in Palestine, Phoenicia and Mesopotamia, in 554 and 557 at Constantinople. It was in 556 that the scourge of famine came, and in 558 the plague, which desolated the capital during six months. Above all there was the increasing misery caused by the financial tyranny. During the last years of the reign the only supplies came from such expedients as the debasement of the coinage, forced loans and confiscations. The Blues and Greens again filled Byzantium with disturbances: in 553, 556, 559, 560, 561, 562 and 564 there were tumults in the streets, and incendiarism in the town. In the palace the indecision as to a successor led to continual intrigues: already the nephews of the *basileus* quarrelled over their heritage. There was even a conspiracy against the Emperor's life, and on this occasion Justinian's distrust caused the disgrace of Belisarius once more for a few weeks (562).

Thus when the Emperor died (November 565) at the age of 83 years, relief was felt throughout the Empire. In ending this account of Justinian's reign the grave Evagrius wrote, " Thus died this prince, after having filled the whole world with noise and troubles: and having since the end of his life received the wages of his misdeeds, he has gone to seek the justice which was his due before the judgment-seat of hell." He certainly left a formidable heritage to his successors, perils menacing all the frontiers, an exhausted Empire, in which the public authority was weakened in the provinces by the development of the great feudal estates, in the capital by the growth of a turbulent proletariat, susceptible to every panic and ready for every sedition. The monarchy had no strength with which to meet all these dangers. In a novel of Justin II promulgated the day after Justinian's death we read the following, word for word—" We found the treasury crushed by debts and reduced to the last degree of poverty, and the army so completely deprived of all necessaries that the State was exposed to the incessant invasions and insults of the barbarians."

It would, however, be unjust to judge the whole of Justinian's reign by the years of his decadence. Indeed, though every part of the work of the Byzantine Caesar is not equally worthy of praise it must not be forgotten that his intentions were generally good, and worthy of an Emperor. There is an undeniable grandeur in his wish to restore the Roman traditions in every branch of the government, to reconquer the lost provinces, and to recover the imperial suzerainty over the whole barbarian world. In his wish to efface the last trace of religious quarrels he shewed a pure feeling for the most vital interests of the monarchy. In the care which Justinian took to cover the frontiers with a continuous network of fortresses, there was a real wish to assure the security of his subjects; and this solicitude for the public good was shewn still more clearly in the efforts which he made to reform the administration of the State. Furthermore, it was not through vanity alone, or because of a puerile wish to attach his name to a work great enough to dazzle posterity, that Justinian undertook the legal reformation, or covered the capital and Empire with sumptuous buildings. In his attempt to simplify the law, and to make justice more rapid and certain, he undoubtedly had the intention of improving the condition of his subjects: and even in the impetus given to public works we can recognise a love of greatness, regrettable in its effects perhaps, but commendable all the same because of the thought which inspired it.

Certainly the execution of these projects often compared unfavourably with the grandiose conceptions which illuminated the dawn of Justinian's reign. But however hard upon the West the imperial restoration may have been, however useless the conquest of Africa and Italy may have been to the East, Justinian none the less gave the monarchy an unequalled prestige for the time being, and filled his contemporaries with admiration or terror. Whatever may have been the faults of his diplomacy, none the less by that adroit and supple combination of political negotiations and religious propaganda he laid down for his successors a line of conduct which gave force and duration to Byzantium during several centuries. And if his successes were dearly bought by the sufferings of the East and the widespread ruin caused by a despotic and cruel government, his reign has left an indelible mark in the history of civilisation. The Code and St Sophia assure eternity to the memory of Justinian.

CHAPTER III.

ROMAN LAW.

ROMAN LAW is not merely the law of an Italian Community which existed two thousand years ago, nor even the law of the Roman Empire. It was, with more or less modification from local customs and ecclesiastical authority, the only system of law throughout the Middle Ages, and was the foundation of the modern law of nearly all Europe. In our own island it became the foundation of the law of Scotland, and, besides general influence, supplied the framework of parts of the law of England, especially of marriage, wills, legacies and intestate succession to personalty. Through their original connexion with the Dutch, it forms a main portion of the law of South Africa, Ceylon and Guiana, and it has had considerable influence in the old French province of Louisiana. Its intrinsic merit is difficult to estimate, when there is no comparable system independent of its influence. But this may fairly be said: Roman Law was the product of many generations of a people trained to government and endowed with cultivated and practical intelligence. The area of its application became so wide and varied that local customs and peculiarities gradually dropped away, and it became law adapted not to one tribe or nation but to man generally. Moreover singular good fortune befell it at a critical time. When civilisation was in peril through the influx of savage nations, and an elaborate and complicated system of law might easily have sunk into oblivion, a reformer was found who by skilful and conservative measures stripped the law of much antiquated complexity, and made it capable of continued life and general use without any breach of its connexion with the past.

Sir Henry Maine has drawn attention to its influence as a system of reasoned thought on other subjects: "To Politics, to Moral Philosophy, to Theology it contributed modes of thought, courses of reasoning and a technical language. In the Western provinces of the Empire it supplied the only means of exactness of speech, and still more emphatically, the only means of exactness, subtlety and depth in thought."

Gibbon in his 44th Chapter has employed all his wit and wealth of allusion to give some interest to his brief history of Roman jurisprudence and to season for the lay palate the dry morsels of Roman Law. The present chapter makes no such pretension. It is confined to a notice of the antecedents and plan of Justinian's legislation, and a summary of those parts of it which are most connected with the general society of the period or afford some interest to an English reader from their resemblance or contrast to our own law. Unfortunately a concise and eclectic treatment cannot preserve much, if anything, of the logic and subtlety of a system of practical thought.

The sources of law under the early Emperors were Statutes (*leges*), rare after Tiberius; Senate's decrees (*senatus consulta*), which proposed by the Emperor took the place of Statutes; Edicts under the Emperor's own name; Decrees, *i.e.* his final decisions as judge on appeal; *Mandata*, instructions to provincial governors; *Rescripta*, answers on points of law submitted to him by judges or private persons; the praetor's edict as revised and consolidated by the lawyer Salvius Julianus at Hadrian's command and confirmed by a Senate's decree (this is generally called The Edict); and finally treatises on the various branches of law, which were composed, at any rate chiefly, by jurists authoritatively recognised, and which embodied the Common Law and practice of the Courts. By the middle of the third century A.D. the succession of great jurists came to an end, and, though their books, or rather the books written by the later of them, still continued in high practical authority, the only living source of law was the Emperor, whose utterances on law, in whatever shape whether oral or written, were called *constitutiones*. If written, they were by Leo's enactment (470) to bear the imperial autograph in purple ink.

Diocletian, who reformed the administration of the law as well as the general government of the Empire, issued many rescripts, some at least of which are preserved to us in Justinian's Codex, but few rescripts of later date are found. Thereafter new general law was made only by imperial edict, and the Emperor was the sole authoritative interpreter. Anyone attempting to obtain a rescript dispensing with Statute Law was (384) to be heavily fined and disgraced.

The imperial edicts were in epistolary form, and were published by being hung up in Rome and Constantinople and the larger provincial towns, and otherwise made known in their districts by the officers to whom they were addressed. There does not appear to have been any collection of Constitutions, issued to the public, until the *Codex Gregorianus* was made in the eastern part of the Empire. (*Codex* refers to the book-form as opposed to a roll.) This collection was the work probably of a man named Gregorius, about the end of the third century. In the course of the next century a supplement was made also in the Eastern Empire and called *Codex Hermogenianus*, probably the work of a man of that name. Both contained chiefly rescripts. A comparatively small part of both has survived in the later codes and in some imperfectly preserved legal compilations. During the fourth century, perhaps—as Mommsen thinks—in Constantine's time, but with later additions, a compilation was made in the West, of which we have fragments preserved in the Vatican Library. They contained both branches of law, extracts from the jurists Ulpian, Paul and Papinian, as well as Constitutions of the Emperors.

At length the need of an authoritative statement of laws in force was so strongly felt that the matter was taken up by government. Theodosius II, son of the Emperor Arcadius, having previously taken steps to organise public teaching in Constantinople, determined to meet the uncertainties of the law courts by giving imperial authority to certain text writers and by a new collection of the Statute Law. The books of the great lawyers, Papinian, Paul and Ulpian and of a pupil of Ulpian, Modestinus, were well known and in general use. Another lawyer rather earlier than these, of whom we really know nothing, except his name (and that is only a *praenomen*), Gaius, had written in the time of Marcus Antoninus in very clear style a manual, besides other works of a more advanced character. The excellence of this manual brought it into general use and secured for its author imperial recognition on a level with the lawyers first named. Another work in great general use was a brief summary of the law by Paul known under the name of *Pauli Sententiae*. All these lawyers were in the habit of citing the opinions of earlier lawyers and often inserting extracts from them in their own works. Theodosius (with Valentinian, then seven years old) in A.D. 426 addressed to the Senate of Rome an important and comprehensive Constitution, intended to put what may be called the Common Law of Rome on a surer footing. He confirmed all the writings of Papinian, Paul, Gaius, Ulpian and Modestinus, and added to them all the writers whose discussions and opinions were quoted by these lawyers, mentioning particularly Scaevola, Sabinus, Julian and Marcellus. The books of the five lawyers first named were no doubt in the hands of judges and advocates generally, but the books of the others would be comparatively rare, and a quotation from them would be open to considerable doubt. It might contain a wrong reading or an interpolation or even a forgery. Theodosius therefore directed that these older books should be admitted as authorities, only so far as they were confirmed by a comparison with manuscripts other than that produced by the advocate or other person alleging their authority.

But Theodosius went further. If the writers thus authoritatively recognised were found to differ in opinion, the judge was directed to follow the opinion of the majority, and if the numbers on each side were equal, to follow the side on which Papinian stood and disregard any notes of Paul or Ulpian contesting Papinian's opinion, but Paul's *Sententiae* were always to count. If Papinian's opinion was not there to decide between equal numbers of authorities, the judge must use his own discretion.

The great portion of law which had been set forth in text-books as reasonable and conformable to precedent and statute having thus been sanctioned, and rules given for its application, Theodosius turned his attention to the Statute Law itself. The jurists had in their various treatises taken account of the pertinent rescripts, edicts, etc., already issued and it was therefore only from the time when the series of authoritative jurists ended that the imperial constitutions required collecting. The books of Gregorius and Hermogenianus (*Codices Greg. et Herm.*) contained those issued down to Constantine's time, which was therefore taken as the starting-point for the additional collection. Theodosius in 429 appointed a Commission of eight, and in 435 another larger Commission of which Antiochus the praefect was named first with other officials and ex-officials of the Record and Chancellery departments and Apelles, a law professor, power being given to call other learned men to their aid. He instructed them, following the precedent of Gregory and Hermogenianus' books, to collect all the imperial Constitutions issued by Constantine and his successors which were either in the form of edicts or at least of general application, to arrange them in the order of time under the known heads of law, breaking up for this purpose laws dealing with several subjects, and while preserving the enacting words to omit all unnecessary preambles and declarations. When this is done and approved they are to proceed to review Gregory, Hermogenianus and this third book, and with the aid of the pertinent parts of the jurists' writings on each head of law to omit what was obsolete, remove all errors and ambiguities, and thus make a book which should " bear the name of the Emperor Theodosius and teach what should be followed and what avoided in life."

The Theodosian code, technically called, as Mommsen thinks, simply *Theodosianus*, was published in Constantinople 15 February 438 and transmitted to Rome at the end of the year. The consul at Rome holding the authentic copy in his hands, in the presence of the imperial commissioners, read to the Senate the order for its compilation, which was received with acclamation. We have an account of this proceeding with a record of the enthusiastic shouts of the senators and the number of times each was repeated, some 24 or 28 times. Exclusive authority was given to the code in all court-pleadings and court-documents from 1 January 439, the Emperor boasting that the code would banish a cloud of dusty volumes and disperse the legal darkness which drove people to consult lawyers; for the code would make clear the conditions of a valid gift, the way to sue out an inheritance, the frame of a stipulation and the mode of recovering a debt whether certain or uncertain in amount.

With the knowledge which we possess of the Vatican Fragments and the Digest and Code of Justinian, we might expect from the above description that the Theodosian Code would contain a selection from the juristic writings as well as the constitutions of a general character arranged under the several titles or heads of law. But the Code, which has in a large part (about two-thirds of Books i–v being lost) come down to us, contains no extracts from the jurists and no constitution earlier than Constantine. So that the exclusive authority which the

Emperor gave to his code can only be understood to relate to constitutions since Constantine, and he must have relied on the Gregorian and Hermogenian Codes for earlier constitutions still in force, and on the text-books of the lawyers, approved by his constitution of 426, for supplying the requisite details of practical law.

The Code of Theodosius was divided into sixteen books, each book having a number of titles and each title usually containing a number of constitutions or fragments of such. The order of subjects is similar to that of Justinian's Code with some exceptions. Private law is treated in Books ii–v, military matters in vii, crime in ix, revenue law in x and xi, municipal law in xii, official duties in i, and xiii–xv, and ecclesiastical matters in xvi. The names of the Emperors at the time of enactment and the date and the place either of framing or of publication were given with each constitution though they are not wholly preserved. Compared with Justinian's Code it contains a much larger proportion of administrative law and a much smaller proportion of ordinary private law. The Code remained in force in the East and in Italy until Justinian superseded it, though the traces of its use are few. In the West, in Spain, France and Lombard Italy, it remained in practical use for long, chiefly as part of the Code issued to the Visigoths by Alaric II in 506.

A number of constitutions issued by Theodosius and his successors after the Code and therefore called *Novellae* (*i.e.*, *leges*), "new laws," have come down to us—84 in number, the latest of which bearing the names of Leo and Anthemius was issued in 468. Of further legislation by Roman Emperors until Justinian we have only what he chose to retain in his Code.

After the Theodosian Code and before Justinian there were compiled and issued codes of laws for the Romans in Burgundy, for the Ostrogoth subjects in Italy, and for the Romans in the Visigothic kingdom in South France and in Spain; and we have evidence of other laws prevailing in the Eastern part of the Empire, before and after Justinian's time.

In Burgundy about the beginning of the sixth century King Gundobad issued a short code of laws for all his subjects whether Burgundian or Roman. A few subsequent constitutions by him or his successors have been appended to it. Somewhat later he issued a code for his Roman subjects, when suits lay between them only. This code is about half the length of the other but many of the headings of the chapters are the same. The matter is principally torts and crimes (*e.g.*, cattle-lifting), runaway slaves, succession, gifts, marriage, guardianship, process and some brief rules on other parts of the law. It appears to have been taken from the same sources as the *Lex Visigothorum* and the particular source is frequently named. But instead of simply repeating selected words of the source, it is rather an attempt at real codification. (The name *Papianus* often given to it arises probably from this Code having followed in the MSS. the *Lex Visigothorum* and the extract from Papinian which closes that having been taken as the commencement of this.   *Papianus* is a frequent mistake for *Papinianus*.)

For the kingdom of the Ostrogoths in Italy a code of laws was issued by Theodoric about A.D. 500. It is usually called *Edictum Theodorici*. The code is nearly the same length as the *Lex Romana Burgundionum* and much resembles it in character and sources, but does not name them. The contents are torts and crimes, especially attacks on landed possessions and cattle-lifting, successions, marriage, serfs, conduct of judges, process, etc. The first editor, Pithou, had two MSS. in 1578, but these have completely disappeared.

The *Lex Romana Visigothorum* is much more important than either of the above. It is a compilation promulgated by Alaric II for Roman citizens in Spain and part of Gaul in the twenty-second year of his reign, *i.e.*, A.D. 506. He states in an accompanying letter to Count Timotheus that it was compiled by skilled lawyers (*prudentes*) with the approval of bishops and nobles, to remove the obscurity and ambiguity of the laws and make a selection in one book which should be solely authoritative. No power of amending the law appears to have been given.

It contains a large number of constitutions from the Theodosian Code, omitting especially those which relate to administration rather than general law. Consequently there are few taken from Books vi, vii, xi–xiv. Some post-Theodosian Novels follow; then an abridgment of Gaius' Institutes, a good deal of Paul's *Sententiae*, a few extracts from the Gregorian and Hermogenian Codes and one extract from Papinian. A short interpretation is appended to all of these, except to Gaius and to most of Paul's Sentences, where interpretation is stated not to be required. The author and age of the interpretation are quite unknown. It sometimes gives a restatement of the text in other words, sometimes adds explanations. The selection of matters for the code shews the intention of giving both Statute and Common Law. The code was no longer authoritative law after Chindaswinth (642–653), but it was used in the schools and assisted largely in preserving Roman Law in the south and east of France till the twelfth century; and a tradition that it received confirmation from Charlemagne is possibly true. Our knowledge of Books ii–v of the Theodosian Code and of most of Paul's Sentences is due to this compilation, which in modern times has received the name of *Breviarium Alarici*.

In the lands on the eastern part of the Mediterranean—Syria, Mesopotamia, Persia, Arabia, Egypt and Armenia—a collection of laws, evidently translated from Greek, was used under the name of "Laws of Constantine, Theodosius and Leo," probably composed at the end of the fourth century and enlarged in the fifth, perhaps with later alterations from the Justinian laws. Versions of it in Arabic, Armenian and several in Syriac, differing in some degree from one another, have been lately published. The chief portion relates to family law, marriage, dowry, guardianship, slaves and inheritance, but obligations and procedure are also included. It is supposed to have been compiled for practical use in suits before the bishops and minor ecclesiastics. Differences between the law prevailing in the East and that in the West are sometimes mentioned, *e.g.*, that in the former the husband's marriage gift was only half the value of the wife's dowry. Other differences from the regular Roman Law of the time are the requirement of a written contract for marriage, the recognition of the possession (as in the Gospels) of wives and slaves by demons, punishment of a receiver of others' slaves or serfs by making him a slave or serf, prescription of 30 years for suits for debts, prohibition of purchase by creditor from debtor until the debt is paid, allowance of marriage with wife's sister or brother's widow if dispensation be obtained from the king, many peculiarities in intestate inheritance, privileges and endowments for the clergy, etc.

Justinian succeeded his uncle Justin in 527 and at once took up the task partially performed by Theodosius, and succeeded in completing it in a more thorough manner than might have been expected from the speed with which it was done. In 528 he appointed a commission of ten, eight being high officials and two practising lawyers, with instructions to put together the imperial constitutions contained in the books of Gregorius, Hermogenianus and Theodosius, and constitutions issued subsequently, to strike out or change what was obsolete or unnecessary or contradictory, and to arrange the constitutions retained and amended under suitable heads in order of time, so as to make one book, to be called by the Emperor's name, *Codex Justinianus.* The book compiled by the commission was sanctioned by the Emperor in 529, and it was ordered that no constitution should be quoted in the law courts except those contained in this book, and that no other wording should be recognised than as given there.

The next step was to deal with the mass of text-books and other legal literature, so far as it had been recognised by the courts and by the custom of old and new Rome. In 530 Tribonian, one of the members of the former commission for the code, was directed to choose the most suitable professors and practising lawyers, and with their aid in the imperial palace under his own superintendence to digest the mass of law outside the constitution into one whole, divided into fifty books and subordinate titles. All the authors were to be regarded as of equal rank : full power was given to strike out and amend as in the case of the constitutions : the text given in this book was to be the only authoritative one : it was to be written without any abbreviations ; and, while translation into Greek was allowed, no one was to write commentaries on it. This work, never attempted before and truly described by Justinian as enormously difficult, was " with the divine assistance " completed in

three years, Tribonian calculating that he had reduced nearly 2000
rolls containing more than 3,000,000 lines into a *Codex* of about
150,000 lines. Justinian called this book *Digesta* or *Pandectae* and
directed that it should take effect as law from 3 December 533. Its
somewhat irrational distribution into seven parts and fifty books was
probably due to a superstitious regard to the mysterious efficacy of
certain numbers. The really important division is into titles, of which
there are 432.

From reverence to the old lawyers, he directed that the name of the
writer and work from which an extract was taken should be placed at
the commencement of it, and he had a list of the works used placed
before the Digest. This list requires some correction. There were
used between 200 and 300 treatises of about 40 authors, some of the
treatises being very voluminous, so that over 1600 rolls were put
under contribution. Over 95 per cent. of the Digest was from books
written between the reigns of Trajan and Alexander Severus. Two
works by Ulpian supply about one-third of the Digest: sixteen works
by eight authors form nearly two-thirds: twice this number of books
supply four-fifths. From some treatises only a single extract was taken.
Tribonian's large library supplied many books not known even to the
learned. Many were read through without anything suitable for
extraction being found.

The plan which Tribonian devised appears to have been to divide
the commission into three parts and give each committee an appropriate
share of the books to be examined. Ulpian's and Paul's Commentaries
and other comprehensive works were taken as the fullest exposition of
current law and made the foundation. They were compared with one
another and with other treatises of the same subject-matter; antiquated
law and expressions were cut out or altered, contradictions removed,
and the appropriate passages extracted and arranged under the titles to
which they severally belonged. The titles were, as Justinian directed,
mainly such as appeared in the Praetor's Edict or in his own code. The
extracts made by the committee which had furnished the most matter for
the title were put first, and the others followed, with little or no attempt
to form an orderly exposition of the subject. What connexion of thought
between the extracts is found comes mainly from the treatise taken as
the foundation. There is no attempt at fusing the matter of text-books
and giving a scientific result, nor even of making a thorough and skilful
mosaic of the pieces extracted. The work under each title is simply the
result of taking strings of extracts from the selected treatises, arranging
them partly in one line and partly in parallel lines, and then as it were
squeezing them together so as to leave only what is practical, with no
more repetition than is requisite for clearness. This process done by
each committee would be to some extent repeated when the contributions
of the three committees came to be combined. For special reasons

occasionally this or that extract might be moved to some other place, sometimes to form an apt commencement for the title, in one case (Book **xx**, title 1) by way of honour to Papinian.

Justinian's work was thus not a codification, as we understand the word, but a consolidation of the law, both of the *jus* and the *leges*, as it may be called, of the Common and the Statute Law.   It was consolidation combined with amendment.   The removal of obsolete law and of consequent reference led necessarily to innumerable corrections both of substance and of wording.   Whatever criticism this mode of solving the problem may justly receive, it had two great merits.   It gave the Roman world within a short time a practical statement of the law in use, cleared of what was obsolete and disputable, full in detail, terse in expression, familiar in language and of unquestionable and exclusive authority. And it has preserved for the civilised world in all ages a large amount of the jurisprudence of the best trained Roman lawyers of the best age, which but for Tribonian would in all probability have been wholly lost.

But Tribonian was not satisfied with this achievement.   In preparing the Digest it was found desirable formally to repeal parts of the old law, and for this purpose fifty constitutions were issued.   On this and other accounts Justinian directed him with the aid of Dorotheus, a professor at Berytus, and of three eminent lawyers in the Courts at Constantinople to take the Code in hand, to insert the new matter, to omit what were repetitions, and thoroughly to revise the whole.   This second or revised Code is what we have.   It took effect from 29 December 534.   The earliest constitution in it is one of Hadrian's and there are few before Severus, the jurists' writings having embodied earlier ones so far as they were of general and permanent application.   Many rescripts of Diocletian are given, but none of subsequent Emperors.   Many constitutions are much abridged or altered from the form in which they appear in the Theodosian Code, which itself contained often only an abridgment of the originals.

A manual for students (the Institutes) founded largely on Gaius' Institutes (which have come down to us in a palimpsest luckily discovered at Verona by Niebuhr in 1816) was also sanctioned by Justinian, and took effect as law from the same day as the Digest.   An authoritative course of study was ordained at the same time, and law schools were sanctioned, but only in Constantinople, Rome and Berytus, those existing in Alexandria, Caesarea and elsewhere being suppressed, under the penalty for any teacher of a fine of 10 lbs. gold and banishment from the town.

Justinian did not end here his legislative activity, but issued from time to time, as cases brought before him or other circumstances suggested, new constitutions for the amendment of the law or regulation of the imperial or local administration.   Of these 174 are still extant, about half relating to administration and half to private law and procedure.　About forty deal with the law of the family and of succession to property on death.　Some are careful consolidations of the law on one subject, some are of miscellaneous content.　These constitutions with a few issued by his near successors are called *Novellae*, and as being the latest legislation supersede or amend some parts of the Digest, Code and Institutes, which with them form the *Corpus Juris*[1] as received by European nations.　Almost all are written in Greek, whereas very little Greek occurs in the Digest (chiefly in extracts from the third-century lawyer, Modestinus) and not much relatively in the Code.　An old Latin Version of many of the Novels, probably prepared in Justinian's lifetime, is often quoted by old lawyers under the name of *Authenticum*.　It is a significant fact that only eighteen of the Novels, and those almost wholly administrative, are dated after the year of Tribonian's death (546), though Justinian survived him nearly twenty years.　One may be sure that it was Tribonian who suggested and organised this great reform of the law, though no doubt it owed much also to the good sense and persistence of the Emperor.

It would not be practicable to give anything like an adequate summary of Justinian's law books within the limits which can be assigned to it in a general history.　His own Institutes contain an authoritative and readable account, which however on some matters, especially marriage and inheritance, requires correction from the Novels. But summary information may be given here on such topics as the position of slaves, freedmen and serfs; of the power of the head of a family; of marriage, divorce, and succession to property; of some leading principles of contract, of criminal law and of procedure.

In Rome the household comprised SLAVES as well as free men, and slaves gave occasion to a great deal of legal subtlety.　Theoretically they were only live chattels, without property or legal rights, absolutely at the disposal of their owner, who had full power of life and death over them.　But at all periods, more or less largely, theory was modified in practice, partly by natural feeling towards members of the same household, partly by public opinion.　Antoninus Pius, either from policy or philosophic pity, so far interfered between master and slave as to make it a criminal offence for a master to kill his own slave without cause, and he required one who treated his slave with intolerable cruelty to sell him on fair terms.　Constantine (319) went still further and directed any master who intentionally killed his slave with a club or stone or weapon or threw him to wild beasts or poisoned or burnt him to death to be charged with homicide.　But discipline was not to suffer, and therefore

---

[1] On a rough estimate the *Corpus Juris* would fill about four such volumes (of 800 pages) as this *History*: and of the four the Digest would fill more than half.　It is the Digest that comes nearest to the popular notion of Justinian's Code.

by another law (326) chaining or beating in the ordinary way of correction for offences, even if the slave died of it, was not to justify any inquiry into the master's intentions or to found any charge against him. Justinian in his Code reproduced only the former constitution, and retained in the Digest the duty imposed on the city praefect and provincial governors of hearing the complaints of slaves who had fled from cruelty, starvation or indecency, to the refuge of the Emperor's statues. To give such protection, said Antoninus (152), was required by the interests of masters, whose full command over their slaves should be maintained by moderate rule, sufficient supplies, and lawful tasks. On the other hand any offences of slaves which came under the animadversion of the State were visited with severer punishments than those of a freeman.

The economical position of slaves requires some notice also. In theory they were simply instruments of their master; what they acquired passed at once to him; they were not capable of having property of their own, he was responsible for them as he was for any other domestic animal that he kept. But in practice slaves were usually allowed to accumulate property out of their savings or from gifts, and the law by a fiction allowed them to use it in purchasing their own freedom. Such quasi-property was called their *peculium* (" petty stock "): it existed only so long as their master chose; he could withdraw it, but rarely did so, except for grave offences. But so long as it existed and his master gave him a free hand, a slave could trade with it and enter into all kinds of business transactions ostensibly for himself, but in the eye of the law for the master's account. He could not however give away anything, and he had no *locus standi* in court: he could sue and be sued only in the name of his master. If he was freed by his master when living, the *peculium* was deemed to accompany him, unless expressly withdrawn. But if he was freed by will or alienated, it did not pass with him unless expressly granted.

The law of persons was greatly simplified by Justinian's legislation. There were now only two classes of persons, slaves and freemen, though freemen were not all treated alike by the law. Besides some discrimination in favour of persons of high rank, freedmen and serfs were in a very inferior position.

FREEDMEN were manumitted slaves and retained traces of their former servile condition. In earlier times, besides the regular forms of manumission by a ceremony before the praetor or by last will, some legal effect used to be given to informal expressions of the master's will. The slave so informally emancipated became free in fact during his life, but his property on his death did not pass as a freeman's by will or to his relatives, but remained like a slave's *peculium* to his former master or master's representatives. Such half-freemen were called Latins as not being complete citizens. Justinian (531) allowed the informal acts which had this imperfect effect to confer in future full freedom, so that a letter to the slave subscribed by five persons as witnesses, or a declaration similarly witnessed or recorded in court, or the delivery to the slave before five witnesses of his master's documents of title, or the slave's attendance on the bier of the deceased master by his or the heir's direction, or the giving a female slave in marriage to a freeman with a dowry settled in writing, or addressing a slave in court as his son, were acts sufficient without further formality to make the slave a freedman or freedwoman. So also, by an edict of Claudius, ejection of a sick slave from the master's house without making provision for him, or prostitution of a female slave in breach of a condition of her purchase, forfeited the master's rights, and full freedom now ensued; and other cases of freedom by operation of law are mentioned. Further Justinian repealed the laws which required a master to be twenty years old before he could emancipate slaves by will, and restricted the number. Constantine confirmed (316) a custom of giving freedom in church before the priests and congregation, a record of the matter being signed by the former; and he allowed clerics to confer freedom on their slaves by any form of words without witnesses, the freedom to take effect on publication of the document at the master's death.

A freedman did not however by the act of manumission lose all trace of his former condition. He remained under limited control of his former master or owner, now patron, and patron's children. A patron could claim respect (*obsequium*), services, and the succession to some or all of his property at death if he left no children as heirs. From services he could be exempted by a special grant by the Emperor of the right of wearing gold rings, and by a like grant (*restitutio natalium*, "restoration of birth") from the patron's claim to his estate. Such grants were rarely made without the patron's consent. Justinian dispensed with the formality of special grants and made the removal of the patron's claim to services and inheritance follow of itself on a manumission. But unless the master then, or by way of trust in his will, made a declaration to that effect, this automatic grant did not exempt a freedman from the duty of due respect to his patron. He was punishable for using abusive language to him: he could not sue him or his children except by consent of the proper authority: and any suit which he brought had to shew formal respect by the complaints being couched in a mere statement of the facts without casting any imputation. Constantine allowed freedmen guilty of ingratitude or insolent conduct, even though not of a grave character, to be remitted into their patron's power. A patron in need could claim support (*alimenta*) from his freedman. Claims to the status of freeborn, when disputed, were reserved for the decision of the city praefect or governor: claims to the status of freedman were reserved likewise for the same high officials, or if the treasury was a party, then for the chief officer of that department.

SERFS though free were in some respects not far removed from slaves. They were found usually in country districts in the provinces, and were often included under the general term "cultivators" (*coloni*), which was also applied in republican and early imperial times to small farmers, who were freemen not only in law but in practice. The origin and history of this serfdom is not clear. It may very possibly have been developed on the example of Marcus Aurelius' settlement in Italy of numbers of the peoples conquered in the Marcomannic War, and possibly on the example of the German "Liten" (*laeti*), settled on the Gallic border. But besides conquered tribes retained in their own country or settled in other countries, voluntary contract under pressure of poverty and statutes against beggary probably added to the number. The maintenance of the land tax introduced by Diocletian made the retention of the cultivators on the several estates a necessity.

The characteristic of a serf was that he and his descendants were inseparably attached to the land, and as a rule to one particular farm, specified in the government census, and held under a lord. If this particular part of the lord's estate was over-supplied with cultivators, he might transfer serfs permanently to another part which was under-supplied, in accordance with the purpose of the institution—that of keeping the land under due cultivation and enabling it to bear taxes. But except in such a case the serfs could not be separated from the farm nor the farm from them. They were part of its permanent stock. If the lord sold a part of the land, he must convey with it a proportionate number of the serfs belonging. If a serf wandered or was stolen, or became a cleric without his lord's consent, he could, whatever was the social position to which he had attained, be reclaimed by his lord just as if he were a runaway slave. And for some offences, *e.g.* marrying a freewoman, he was liable by statute, like a slave, to chains or stripes. He was not admissible to the army, but as a free man he paid poll tax. He could sell the surplus produce of his farm, and his savings, called his *peculium*, were in a sort his property but were inalienable except in the way of trade; on his death, (*e.g.* as a monk) childless and intestate, they passed to his lord, but usually would pass to his children or other successors on his farm. He might (apparently) own land, and would be entered in the Register as its holder and be liable for the land tax, whereas the tax on the farm to which he was attached as a serf would usually be collected from the lord. A serf was bound to pay a rent to his lord but the rent was certain, usually a fixed portion of the produce but sometimes a sum of money. Against any attempt of the lord to increase the rent, he could bring the case into court, but on all other grounds he was disabled from suing his lord. The rent was called *canon* or *pensio*.

The union of serfs was held to be a marriage and accordingly the children were serfs, and even the children of a serf by a freewoman or a slave followed the condition of the father, until Justinian pressed by the analogy of the rule regarding slaves' unions, first made a serf's offspring by a slavewoman to be slave (530), and afterwards from the love of liberty made a serf's offspring by a freewoman to be free (533). He confirmed this again in 537 and 539, though, by the later law, he required the children, though free and retaining their property, to be permanently attached to the farm. Finally in 540, influenced by representations of the danger of thus depleting the land of its proper cultivators, he restored the old law and made the children serfs, without affecting the mother's status as a freewoman. His successors made such children personally free.

It was difficult for a serf to improve his status. Justinian abolished (c. 531) any claim to throw off serfdom by prescription, but allowed anyone who had been consecrated as a bishop to be free from serfdom as from slavery (546). Orthodoxy however was essential, and any serf who encouraged Donatist meetings on his land was to be beaten, and if he persisted was fined one-third of his *peculium*.

Serfs were sometimes called *originarii* from being in the class by birth; *censiti* from being enrolled in the census-register; usually *adscripti* or *adscripticii* from being enrolled as of a certain farm; *tributarii* from paying poll tax. Another term, *inquilini*, which appears in the Digest in the begining of the third century, and in earlier inscriptions, appears to denote a similar class, possibly serfs living in huts on the land and employed either as cultivators or herdsmen or otherwise. The clear recognition of serfs as half-free is seen chiefly in laws since Constantine. After Justinian there is little said of them.

PATRIA POTESTAS. The father (or grandfather) when regularly married, as head of the family (*paterfamilias*), had in early times absolute power over the other members whether sons or daughters. And his wife, if married by the ancient forms, ranked as a daughter. In imperial times this relation was largely modified. She remained outside her husband's family, who instead of taking her whole property, received only a dowry of which he was rather the accountable manager than the beneficial owner. The children unless emancipated had no property of their own, any more than slaves had. Whatever came to them, from any source, passed in strict law at once to the father, who could do what he liked with it. This "fatherly power" endured irrespectively of the age or social or political position of his sons and daughters. A man of full age, married, with children and occupying a high office was, unless formally emancipated, still under his father's power and had only a *peculium* like slaves. He could sue and be sued only in his father's name and in law for his father's account. Nor could he compel his father to emancipate him, and if emancipated himself he did not thereby carry his children with him, unless expressly included in the emancipation. If his father died, his children fell into his own power; if he died first, his children remained under his father's power. Loss of citizenship had the same effect as death.

Constantine in 319 made an important innovation. He enacted that the father's full right over what came to his children should be restricted to what came from himself or his relatives; and that in anything that came from their mother, the head of the family should have only the usufruct and the administration, but with no right of alienation or mortgage. If the children died, (it was enacted in 439) their property, apart from the usufruct, passed to their children, or, if there were none, to their father as next heir, not to the grandfather, who if alive would be enjoying the usufruct. When the head of the family emancipated a child, he lost the usufruct, but was authorised to take one-third of the property. Justinian (529) repealed this and gave instead to the father (or other head of the family) the right to retain one-half of the usufruct. Further this arrangement was made to apply not only to what came from the mother but (excepting, as we shall see, camp-*peculium*) to everything which the children acquired by their own labour or by gift or will from other than their father's relatives. The administration which accompanied the usufruct was not subject to any interference or impeachment by the children, who however were to be supported by their father. The father retained the usufruct, even if he married again.

Soldiers from the time of Augustus were privileged to treat as their own property, disposable as they chose in their life or by their will, all gains made while in the army and in connexion therewith, including gifts from comrades. Such acquisitions were called their *castrense-peculium*. On this analogy Constantine (326) granted the like privilege to the court officials (*palatini*), and later Emperors extended it to provincial governors, judicial assessors, advocates and others in the imperial service (which was often called *militia*); and eventually (472) to bishops, presbyters and deacons of the orthodox faith. Wills disposing of such *castrense*, or *quasi-castrense peculium*, were specially exempted from challenge by children or parents on the ground of failure in due regard. In case of intestacy, before Justinian altered the law in 543, the intestate's camp-*peculium* passed to the father as if, like any other *peculium*, it had been his all along.

As regards the persons of (free) children the father had the power and duty of correction and in early times presumably could sell or kill them, as he could slaves. But this right was rarely exercised, at least in historical times, though not until Constantine (319) was killing a son formally forbidden and ranked as parricide. Sale (with a right however of redemption) was possible only in case of a newly-born child, under pressure of extreme poverty. Exposure of a child, at least after the second century, made the parent liable to punishment. Exposed children of whatever class could not be brought up as slaves or serfs or freed, but were to be deemed freeborn and independent (529). Previously to this law of Justinian it was left to the bringer-up to make them slave or free at his choice.

The dissolution of the natural father's power over his children, whether in order to make the child independent (*sui juris*), or to give him by adoption into another's power, was in old times effected by a complicated ceremonial. This was abolished by Justinian (531), who substituted in the case of adoption a declaration before a competent magistrate, both parties being present, and, in the case of emancipation, either the like simple declaration, or, according to a law of Anastasius (502), if the son or daughter were of age and not present in court, a declaration, supported by a petition to the Emperor, with his grant of the prayer and the consent of the child, if not an infant.

By ADOPTION in older times a person passed under the fatherly power of one who was not his natural father. If he was not independent, he passed entirely from one family to another : his natural father no longer controlled him or was responsible for him, the son's acquisitions did not pass to him, nor had the son any right to his inheritance. The adoptive father stood in the natural father's place, and could retain or emancipate him. Justinian (530) altered this in all cases where the adopter was an outsider. The adopted person retained all his rights and position in his natural father's family, and simply acquired a right of succession to the adopter if he died intestate. But if the adopter was the grandfather or other ascendant either on the father's or mother's side, the effect of adoption remained as of old.

Adoption of a person who was *sui juris* was often called adrogation, and required a rescript from the Emperor. If the person to be adopted was under age (*impubes*), inquiry was made whether it was for his advantage, and the adopter had to give security to a public officer for restoration of all the adopted's property to his right heirs, if he died under age. If he emancipated him without lawful cause, or died, he was bound by a law of Antoninus Pius to leave him one-fourth part of his property, besides all that belonged to the adopted person himself. If a person adrogated had children, they passed with him under the power of the adopter. In all cases it was required that the adopter should be at least eighteen years older than the adopted.

GUARDIANSHIP. In the old law guardians (*tutores*) were required not only for young persons for a time, but for women throughout their life, though the authority they exercised was often nominal. Guardianship for women was criticised by Gaius as irrational, and it ceased probably before Constantine. By Justinian's time, guardianship affected only *impuberes*. He fixed the age for *puberes* at fourteen for males, twelve for females. Up to that age, if their father or other head of the family was dead, or if they were freed from his power, they required a guardian to authorise any legal act which was to bind them. Without such authority they could bind others but not themselves, the rule being that they could improve but could not impair their estate. After the age of puberty the law regarded them as capable of taking the responsibility of their own acts, but practically they had not the requisite knowledge and discretion. No one could deal safely with them, because of the risk of the contract or other business being rescinded, if the praetor found that it was equitable to do so. To meet this difficulty a *curator* was often appointed to guide young persons in the conclusion of particular business, and eventually was appointed to act regularly in matters of business until the ward became 25 years old. It was the analogy of madmen, etc. (mentioned below), which probably suggested this course. From the third century allowance of age (*venia aetatis*) could be obtained from the Emperor by youths of 20 years, women of 18, on evidence of fitness. Justinian however (529) restrained them from all sale or mortgage of land, unless specially authorised.

A guardian was appointed by the father's will. In default of such appointment, the mother or grandmother had the first claim by Justinian's latest legislation, and then the nearest male in order of succession to the inheritance. If such were disqualified, the praetor at Rome, the governors in the provinces, and if the estate was small, the town-defenders, made the appointment of both guardians and curators. Guardianship was regarded as a public office, and no one was excused from undertaking it, except for approved cause. Guardians and curators were liable for any loss caused by their act or neglect. They could not marry their wards, unless approved by the ward's father or by his will.

Mothers had been allowed (since 390) to act in these capacities for their own children, but by Justinian's final legislation, had to renounce the right of re-marriage and the benefit of the Velleian Senate's decree (see below). If they broke their promise, they incurred infamy and became incapable of inheriting from any but near relatives, besides losing part of their property.

Severus (195) prohibited all sale of a ward's land in the country or suburbs unless authorised by the father's will or by the praetor. A subsequent edict directed everything else to be sold and reduced into money. Later Emperors (326 and after) reversed this direction, and partly on the ground of probable attachment of the ward to the family house, and the utility of old family slaves, and partly from the difficulty of finding good investments, ordered all the property to be preserved, unless land had to be purchased or loans made in order to supply the ward's needs.

Madmen and spendthrifts, pronounced such by the praetor, were by the XII Tables under the care of their *agnates* (relatives through males) but in practice under a curator appointed by the praetor or provincial governor. So also a curator was appointed, without limit of age in the ward, for the demented, or deaf and dumb, or for persons incapacitated for business by chronic disease. The practice of making contracts by oral stipulation brought deaf and dumb into this category.

CH. III.

The protection of *minors*, mentioned above, was an interesting feature of Roman Law but must often have been very embarrassing in practice. Whatever business a minor had conducted, a sale, a purchase, a loan, a pledge, acceptance of an inheritance, agreement to an arbitration, etc., if it was shewn that he had been in any way deceived or overreached or had suffered from want of due vigilance, application might be made to the Court, to have the matter rescinded, provided he had not acted fraudulently and there was no other remedy. The Court heard the parties, and if it found the claim just, put the parties back, so far as possible, into their old positions. This was called *in integrum restitutio*. The application had to be made within (originally) one year after the minor's completing his twenty-fifth year, and would be rejected if after this age he had in any way approved his former act or default. Justinian extended the period to four years.

A similar reinstatement was sometimes granted to persons of full age, if it were shewn that they had suffered serious loss owing to absence on the public service, or to captivity, or fraud, or intimidation. Or the reverse might be the case : similar absence of others might have prevented plaintiff from bringing a suit or serving a notice within the proper time : reinstatement might then sometimes be obtained.

A person, who had been taken captive by the enemy and returned home with the intention of remaining, was held to re-enter at once into his old position, his affairs having been in the meantime in a state of suspense. This was called the law of *postliminium* (reverter). His own marriage was however dissolved by his captivity, as if he were dead, though his relation to his children was only suspended till it was known whether he would return.

Slaves and other chattels taken by the enemy, if brought back into Roman territory, similarly reverted to their former owners subject to any earlier claims which attached to them. Anyone who ransomed them from the enemy had a lien for the amount of the ransom.

MARRIAGE was often preceded by betrothal, that is by a solemn mutual promise. The consent of the parties was required, but, if the woman was under her father's power, she was presumed to agree to his act unless she plainly dissented. The age of seven was deemed necessary for consent. The restrictions on marriage applied to betrothal, and a betrothed person was for some purposes treated in law as if married. Betrothal was usually accompanied by gifts, as earnest from or on behalf of each party to the other. If the receiver died, the giver had a right to its return, unless a kiss had passed between them, when the half only could be recovered (336). Breach of the contract without good cause, such as lewd conduct, diversity of religion, etc., previously unknown to the other, at one time involved a penalty of fourfold (*i.e.*, the earnest and threefold its value), but in the fourth century this was remitted altogether, if the father or other ascendant of a girl, betrothed before she was ten years old, renounced the marriage, and in the fifth century (472) it was reduced generally to twofold. Delay for two years to fulfil the promise was a sufficient justification for the girl's marrying another.

Marriage in Roman Law is the union of life of man and woman for the purpose of having children as members of a family in the Roman Commonwealth. Both must be citizens of Rome or of a nation recognised for this status by the Romans; they must be of the age of puberty; if independent, must give their own consent, if not, their father must consent. *Nuptias non concubitus sed consensus facit* was the dominant rule of Roman Law. It was the avowed purpose of such a union and public recognition that distinguished marriage from concubinage. In earlier times the woman passed by one of several forms with all her property into the power (*manus*) of her husband and occupied the position of a daughter. Gradually a freer marriage was developed, by which the woman did not become part of her husband's family, but remained either under her father's power, or independent, and controlled, with the aid of a guardian for a time, her own property, except so far as she had given part as dowry. The ceremonials, which accompanied the old forms of marriage, gradually went out of use and had apparently ceased in or by the third century. The only external mark of marriage was then the woman's being led into her husband's house, and thus the paradoxical statement could be made that a woman could be married in the absence of her husband, but a husband could not be married in the absence of his wife. The settlement of a dowry grew to be, and was made by Justinian, a decisive characteristic of marriage, though its absence did not prevent a union otherwise legal and formed with the affection and intention of marriage from being such in the eye of the law.

Marriage, and of course also betrothal, could take place only between free persons, not of the same family, and not otherwise closely connected. The old law was reaffirmed by a constitution of Diocletian (295), which expressly forbad marriage of a man with his ascendants or descendants or aunt or sister or their descendants or with step-daughter, step-mother, daughter-in-law, mother-in-law or others forbidden by the law of old. A woman was forbidden to marry the corresponding relatives. Such marriages were incestuous. Relationship formed when one or both parties were slaves was equally a bar. Constantius (342) also forbad marriage with brother's daughter or grand-daughter and (in 355) marriage with brother's widow or wife's sister—a prohibition repeated in 415. The marriage of first cousins, forbidden with the approval of St Ambrose by Theodosius about 385, was relieved from extreme penalty (of fine) by his sons in 396, and expressly permitted in 405. Justinian (530) forbad marriage with a god-daughter. No change was made in the old law which permitted a step-son of one parent to marry a step-daughter of the other, and forbad the marriage of brothers and sisters by adoption so long only as they remained in the same family. Marriage with the daughter of a sister by adoption was legal.

Other prohibitions were based on considerations outside of the family tie. A guardian or curator was prohibited by Severus and later Emperors from marrying his ward, if under twenty-six years of age, either to himself or his son, unless special permission was obtained. Provincials were forbidden by Valentinian (*c.* 373) to marry barbarians under threat of capital punishment. Jews and Christians were forbidden by Theodosius (388) to intermarry, the act being punished as adultery. Justinian (530) " following the sacred canon " forbad presbyters, deacons, and sub-deacons to marry at all; if they did, their children were to be treated as born of incestuous connexion.

Senators and their descendants were forbidden by Augustus and by Marcus Aurelius to marry freed persons or actors or actresses or their children. Constantine (336) forbad any person of high rank or official position in towns to marry, whether after concubinage or not, freed women or actresses or stall-keepers or their daughters or others of low condition, mere poverty not being regarded as such (Valentinian 454). Justin, in consequence of his nephew Justinian's marriage with Theodora, removed this prohibition, if the woman had ceased to practise her profession, and gave to his law retrospective effect from his accession. Justinian relaxed the rule still further, and eventually (542) enabled all persons to marry any free woman, but in the case of dignitaries only by regular marriage settlement: others could marry either by settlement or by marital affection without settlement.

Forbidden marriages were declared to be no marriages, dowry and marriage gift were forfeited to the Crown, the children were not even to be deemed natural children; the parties were incapable of giving by will to any outsiders or to each other. Incestuous marriage, by Justinian's latest law (535), was punished by exile and forfeiture of all property, and in the case of persons of low rank by personal chastisement. Any children by a previous lawful marriage became independent, took their father's property and had to support him.

Dowry. A woman's dowry was a contribution from herself or her relatives or others to the expenses of the married life, placed under the charge and at the disposal of the husband, and, although theoretically his property, to be accounted for by him on the dissolution of the marriage to the donor or the wife. It presumed a lawful marriage: it could be given either before or after, but if given before it took effect only on marriage. It was governed by customary rules and often by special agreements consistent with its general principles. From the time of Constantine a betrothed husband's or wife's gift made in view of an intended marriage was revocable by the donor, if the donee or the wife's father was the cause of the marriage not taking place. And a gift from the husband, which was now a usual incident, was treated as balancing the dowry and gradually subjected to like treatment (468). As the dowry could be increased by the wife or others during the marriage (notwithstanding the rule against gifts between husband and wife), so also could the husband's antenuptial gift, and, if none such had been made, he was allowed to make one not exceeding the value of the dowry, and any agreements which had been made for a marriage settlement could be modified accordingly. The amount of the settlement could be reduced by mutual consent, unless there were children of the marriage, for which the settlement was made (527). Justinian enacted (529) that all agreements for the share to be taken by the wife in her husband's gift after his death were to apply to the share to be taken by the husband in the wife's dowry on her death, the larger share to be reduced to the smaller, and altered the phrase *ante nuptias donatio* to *propter nuptias donatio*, that it might fit the extended character (531). In 539 he enacted that the dowry and the marriage gift should be equal, and that in all cases of dissolution of the marriage, whether either party married again or not, the amount coming to him or her from the settlements of the marriage or former marriage should pass as property to the children of the marriage and only the usufruct to the parent; and that was to be subject to the support of the children. In 548 he enacted that either party abstaining from a second marriage should as a reward share with the children in the property of the dowry or nuptial gift, besides enjoying the usufruct of the whole: and further he required that the husband or his friends should (as in other cases of gift) record in court the amount of his marriage gift if over 500 *solidi* (about equal to £500) under penalty for omission of losing all share in the dowry.

A woman's claim for her dowry had since 529 (and still more since 539) precedence of almost all other claims on her husband's property; and if her husband was insolvent she could maintain her claim on the settled property even during his life against his creditors, and against her father or mother or other donor unless they had expressly stipulated for its return.

Any money or securities or other property which the wife had beside her dowry (*parapherna*) were not touched by any of these agreements or statutes, but remained entirely the property of the wife and subject to her claim and disposition. The fact was sometimes mentioned in the dowry deed, and the husband and his property were answerable for the *parapherna* so far as they were under his care. Justinian (530) allowed him to sue for them on his wife's behalf, and to use the interest for their joint purposes, but the capital he was to deal with according to her wish.

SECOND MARRIAGES were the subject of much change of opinion, in the minds of the Emperors at least, between Augustus and Justinian.

Under the former celibacy was not merely discouraged, but visited with the penalty of incapacity to take an inheritance or legacy, if the man was under sixty or the woman under fifty years of age. Constantine appears to have been the first to modify this legislation. No doubt the declension of the Roman population had ceased to have the importance which led to Augustus' stringent enactments, now that the Empire contained a wider field for supplying recruits for the army. And the Christian Church, coming by the fourth century to count the single life nobler than the married, and encouraging anchorite and monastic asceticism, looked on second marriages with increasing dislike and reprobation. The Emperors in the fourth century, though requiring the father's consent to the re-marriage of a woman under twenty-five years of age, and severe in condemnation and punishment of any woman who married again within ten months (in 381 extended to one year) from the death of her husband, in other cases interfered only to secure the interest of the children of the former marriage. Justinian dealt with the subject in 536 and 539. As regards any property derived from the former husband or wife the party marrying again, as already mentioned, retained only the usufruct, the children of the former marriage being entitled to the property in equal shares. As regards property not derived from the former partner, the party re-marrying was disabled from giving by dowry or otherwise or leaving to the second wife or husband more than the smallest share of it which any child of the former marriage would get. Under the law any excess was to be divided equally between the said children if not " ungrateful."

If property was left to a person on condition of his or her not marrying again, it used to be the practice to require an oath for the observance of the condition before the property was transferred. Justinian, in order to prevent frequent perjury and secure the execution of testator's intention, allowed the legatee, after a year for reflexion, to have a transfer of the bequest, or, if it be money, the payment of interest on it. Security had to be given, or at least an oath to be taken, by the recipient that he would, if the condition were broken, restore the property transferred with the profits or interest. His or her own property was tacitly pledged by the statute (536).

By second marriage a mother lost the right, which the law usually gave her, of educating her former children, and the guardianship, if she had it, and lost all dignities and privileges derived from her former husband.

DIVORCE. Until the year 542 marriage could be dissolved in the life of the parties by mutual consent without special cause and with only such consequences as were agreed between them. In that year Justinian forbad any such divorce except in order to lead a life of chastity. For breach of this law he enacted in 556 that both parties were to be sent into a monastery for the rest of their lives; of their property one-third was to be given to the monastery and two-thirds to their children: if there were no children, two-thirds to the monastery and one-third to their parents; if they had no ascendants alive, all to the monastery. If however husband and wife agreed to come together again, the penalties were not enforced: if one only was willing, he or she was freed.

Justinian's nephew, Justin, in 566 yielded to persistent complaints and restored the old law permitting divorce by mutual consent.

Divorce at the instance of one party only, called *repudium*, in old times was subject to no restraint, but in Augustus' time required seven witnesses to the declaration, which was made orally or in writing and delivered to the other party by declarant's freedman. Under the Emperors a dissolution of marriage without good ground was visited with penalties. Good ground was either incapacity on the part of the husband for a period of three years from marriage, or desire to lead a life of chastity, or captivity, combined with the other's ignorance for five years of the captive's being alive. In these cases, called by Justinian *divortium bona gratia*, the dowry is given back to the wife and the marriage gift to the husband, but no penalty is incurred. On the other hand for grave crime or offence either party may repudiate the other and gain both dowry and marriage gift. The offences as specified by Valentinian (449) were in the main the same in both cases, adultery, murder, enchantments, treason, sacrilege, grave-robbery, kidnapping, forgery, attacks on the other's life, or blows: also in the case of the man, cattle-lifting, brigandage or brigand-harbouring, associating with immodest women in presence of his wife: in the case of the woman, revelling with other men not belonging to her, without her husband's knowledge or consent, or against his will going to theatres or amphitheatres or horse races, or without good cause absenting herself from his bed. Justinian (535) added to the wife's offences wilful abortion, bathing with other men, and arranging a future marriage while still married.

By a later law (542) Justinian reduced the number of offences which would justify repudiation to six on the part of the wife, viz., conspiracy against the Empire or concealing such from her husband, proved adultery, attempt on the husband's life, banqueting or bathing with strange men without his consent, staying out of her own house except at her parents' house or with her husband's consent, visiting circus shows or theatres or amphitheatres without his knowledge and approval. On the part of the husband five offences only are to count: conspiracy against the Empire, attempt on his wife's life or neglect to avenge her, conniving at others' attempts on her chastity, charging her with adultery and failing to prove it, associating with other women in the house where his wife dwells or frequently consorting with another woman in the same town and persisting after several admonitions by his wife's parents or others. The regular penalty for the guilty person in such a case and for repudiation on other grounds than those sanctioned by the law was forfeiture of all the settled property to the innocent person, if there were no children, and if there were children, the innocent person was to have the usufruct and the children the property in remainder. In graver cases an additional amount from the other property of the delinquent equal to one-third of the dowry or nuptial gift forfeited, was to be so treated. Where the marriage was not accompanied by a settlement, the guilty party was to forfeit one-fourth of his or her property to the other. By the latest legislation (556) the penalty was to be as for dissolution merely by mutual consent.

If a husband beat his wife with whip or stick, the marriage was not dissoluble on that account, but he was to forfeit to her of his own property as much as was equal to one-third of the marriage gift.

As regards persons in military or other imperial service, Justinian eventually enacted (549) that death should not be presumed from absence of news however long, but if the wife hear of her husband's death she must inquire, and, if the authorities of the regiment swear to his death, she must wait a year before marrying again. Otherwise both husband and wife will be punished as adulterers.

CONCUBINAGE was a connexion not merely transitory or occasional but continuous, for the gratification of passion, not for the founding of a family of citizens. The children, if any, had no legal relation to their father any more than their mother had. And thus, the economical relations between the man and woman being in law those of independent persons, gifts were not barred in concubinage as they were in marriage. Such a connexion was a matter of social depreciation, but not subject to moral disapprobation if the man was unmarried. Foreigners and soldiers in the early Empire were rarely capable of contracting a regular Roman marriage (*matrimonium justum*), and a looser connexion became almost inevitable. By Romans in a higher class it was rarely formed except with a woman of inferior position, a slave or a freedwoman, and in such cases was thought more seemly than marriage. With freeborn women it was unusual, unless they followed some ignoble trade or profession or had otherwise lost esteem. Constantine and other Christian Emperors viewed it with strong disfavour, and discouraged it by refusing legal validity to all gifts and testamentary dispositions by the man in favour of the children of the connexion. On the other hand the conversion of concubinage into marriage and consequent legitimation of the children was encouraged, at first under Constantine, only when there were no legitimate children already and when the concubine was a freeborn woman. Marriage settlements having been executed, the children born before as well as any born after became legitimate, and (if they consented) subject to their father's power and alike eligible to his succession. After varied legislation eventually Justinian enacted in 539 that this should apply to freedwomen also and apply whether there were children before, legitimate or not, and whether others were born after or not. In the previous year he had provided that, where by the death of the mother or for other cause marriage was not feasible, the children might be legitimated on the father's application or in accordance with his will; and that a woman who, trusting to a man's oath on the Gospels or in church that he would regard her as his wife, had lived long with him and perhaps had children, could on proving the fact maintain her position against him and be entitled to the usufruct of a fourth of his estate, the children having the property; if there were three children she had the usufruct of a child's share. In 542 he provided that if a man in a public deed, or his own writing duly witnessed, or in his will called a child by a free woman his son without adding the epithet "natural," this sufficed to make him and his brothers legitimate and their mother a legitimate wife without further evidence.

As regards connexions with slave women Justinian in 539 enacted that they might be legitimatised by enfranchisement and marriage settlement, and the children of the connexion though born in slavery would thereby become free and legitimate. He had already in 531 provided that if a man having no wife has formed such a connexion and maintained it till his death, the woman and her children should become free after his death, if he did not make other disposition by his will.

Theodosius in 443 had introduced another mode of improving the condition of natural children. He authorised a father either in his life or by his will to present one or more of his natural children to the municipal council of his town to become a member of their body, and further authorised him to give or leave such children any amount of his property to support their rank and position; and similarly to give his natural daughters in marriage to members of the council. Those so presented were not allowed to decline the position, burdensome though it was. They succeeded to their father's intestate inheritance just as if they were legitimate, but had no claim to the inheritance of their father's relatives. Theodosius restricted this right to a father who had no legitimate children. Justinian (539) in confirming the law removed this restriction but limited such a natural son's share of the inheritance to the smallest amount which fell to any legitimate son.

The *jus liberorum* exempting from the disabilities imposed by the Papian law was acquired by natural as well as by legitimate children, and so also the reciprocal rights between mother and children of intestate inheritance given by the Tertullian and Orfitian Senates' decrees. The Papian law was abolished by Constantine (320).

Incestuous connexion was not tolerated as concubinage any more than as marriage. Children of such or other prohibited connexion were not capable of legitimation or of any claim on their parents, even for aliment.

CH. III.

WILLS. A will in Roman law was not a mere distribution of testator's property: it was the formal nomination of one or more persons to continue as it were his personality and succeed to the whole of his rights and obligations to men and gods. In early times the heir[1] had to perform the sacred rites of the family and to pay the debts, and if testator's property was not sufficient, he was still liable himself in full.

The power of making a will belonged to all free persons who were *sui juris* (*i.e.*, not under the power of their father or other ascendant), of the age of puberty, not mad at the time and not naturally quite deaf and dumb. Spendthrifts and persons in the enemy's power could not make a will, but a will made before interdiction or capture was good.

The procedure was simplified by Justinian, partly indeed by previous Emperors. Seven witnesses were required, all present at the same time and subscribing and sealing the written document containing the will. Neither woman nor child nor anyone in the power of testator nor slave nor deaf nor dumb nor mad nor spendthrift nor the heir named nor anyone in the heir's power nor one in whose power the heir was, is a good witness. There was no objection to legatees as witnesses. The testator must sign the will and acknowledge it as his will to the witnesses, but need not disclose its contents. If he cannot write, an eighth person must subscribe for him. If he is blind, there must be a notary (*tabellarius*) to write and subscribe the will, or at least an additional witness. If the will be written entirely by testator and he states this fact in the document, five witnesses suffice. Valentinian III (446) had allowed a holographic will to be valid even without witnesses. The will might be written on boards or paper or parchment: the material was unimportant. Nor need the will be written at all. An oral declaration by the testator of his will in the presence of seven witnesses was enough without further formality.

Justinian made a concession to country people in places where literates (*i.e.* persons able to read and write) were scarce. There must be at least five witnesses, literates if possible, one or two of whom if necessary might subscribe for the rest. In such wills the witnesses must however be informed who are appointed heirs, and must depose this on oath after testator's death.

Soldiers although in the power of their fathers were competent to make a will dealing with their separate estate (*castrense peculium*). If they were in actual service in camp or had not retired more than a year, their will was exempted from all formalities. This concession was begun by Julius Caesar and made permanent by Trajan in the most general terms: "Let my fellow soldiers make their testaments as they will and as they can, and let the bare will of the testator suffice for the division of

---

[1] The heir (*heres*) is concerned with both personalty and realty (Roman law drawing no such distinction), and (except for that) is fairly represented by the earliest form of English executor, who was entitled to take the residue.

his goods." It must however be definitely made and understood as a will and not be a mere casual remark in conversation. Such a will ceased to be valid after testator had left the service for a year; he must then make his will in the ordinary form. Words written on his shield or scabbard with his blood or scratched in the dust with his sword at the time of death in battle were allowed by Constantine as a soldier's will.

A will might be revoked not only by a second will duly made, but by cutting the threads which fastened the tablets or breaking the seals with that intention. If ten years have elapsed, a verbal declaration of revocation proved by three witnesses or made in court is enough. If a second will not duly made gave the inheritance to the persons who would be entitled on intestacy and the first will gave it to others not so entitled, the second will, if witnessed by five persons on oath, is to prevail (439).

CODICILS. An informal disposition of property was sometimes made by a testator's writing his desire in a note-book (*codicilli*). The practice was introduced with Augustus' approval and was confirmed by the great lawyer Labeo, in that he followed it himself. It was originally connected with *fideicommissa*. Codicils presupposed a will appointing an heir, and might be made more than once, before or after the will, but should be confirmed expressly or impliedly by the will, subsequently or by anticipatory clause. Even if no will followed, codicils were held good, if there was evidence of testator's not having retracted his intention, testator in such a case being deemed to have addressed his request to the heir *ab intestato*. Only by way of trust could an heir be appointed in codicils. Codicils required five witnesses who should subscribe the written document. Testator's subscription was not necessary if he had written the codicils himself. Oral codicils are mentioned.

It became a practice for a testator in making a formal will to insert a clause declaring that if for any cause the will should be found invalid as a will, *e.g.* by the heir's non-acceptance, he desired that it should pass as codicils. Any person claiming under the will had to elect whether he claimed as under a will or under codicils, and to declare his intention at the first. Parents however and children within the fourth degree were allowed after suing on it as a will and being unsuccessful to apply as for a trust, for they are regarded as claiming what is due, whereas outsiders are trying to secure a gain (424).

A testator could appoint as many heirs as he pleased. If no shares are mentioned, all take equally. If some heirs accept and others do not, those who accept take the whole among them, the shares being in the original proportions to each other. A testator may also provide for the contingency of the heir or heirs named not accepting, or dying, or otherwise failing to take, and substitute another or others on this contingency. And he could also appoint a substitute for a child in his power becoming heir but dying before he came of age (puberty). In

CH. III.

such a case the substitute becomes heir to the father, if the son does not become heir, and heir to the son, if the son has become heir but dies before puberty. Nor was a testator bound to appoint his son heir; he might disinherit him and yet appoint an heir to any property which came to his son from inheritance or gift from others. Justinian allowed a father to make a similar will for a son of full age who was demented.

If an heir is appointed on a condition, which at the time of testator's death it is impossible to fulfil, the condition goes for nothing and the appointment is absolute. But if the appointed heir is a son, the appointment is treated as bad, and the son being thus passed over, the will is null, and the son becomes heir on an intestacy. A condition which could be fulfilled but involved an illegal or immoral action was treated as impossible, Papinian laying down the principle that acts should be deemed impossible which do violence to dutiful affection, to fair repute, to respectful modesty, and generally which are opposed to good conduct.

A testator could make one of his slaves heir, if he also gave him his freedom. The slave then became heir of necessity, and this plan was sometimes adopted by a testator who was insolvent, in order that the disgrace of the estate being sold in bankruptcy might fall on him rather than on the testator. As compensation for this misfortune, the creditors were not allowed any right to be paid out of acquisitions made by him since testator's death.

Madmen, dumb, infants, posthumous, children under power, others' slaves, were capable of being heirs.

INHERITANCE. The position of an heir as a representative of the deceased was in many cases attended with much uncertainty and serious risk. His own estate was liable, if testator's was not sufficient, to pay the creditors. If more than one person was appointed heir, each was liable in proportion to his share as specified by testator, or, if no share was named, then in equal shares. Testator might give away from his heirs such parts of his property as he chose, and these legacies, unlike the heirship, carried no unexpressed burden with them: a legatee was a mere recipient of bounty, unless some condition was attached: he was a successor to testator's rights in a particular thing only.

In such circumstances the appointed heir or heirs could not prudently accept the inheritance until after careful inquiry into the solvency of the estate, and even then the emergence of some previously undiscovered debt might upset all his calculations and ruin him. Further, besides testator's debts, the heir is liable also to pay the legacies, and cannot prevent the loss to the estate of the slaves to whom testator may have given freedom by his will. Hence there might be further ground for hesitation in accepting the inheritance, and yet if no heir named accepts, the will becomes a dead letter, intestacy results and the legacies and freedoms fall to the ground.

The first-named difficulty was met very imperfectly by testator's fixing a period for the heir to make his decision (*cretio*); afterwards by statute (529) allowing an heir a year for deliberation without his losing the right, if he died before decision, of transmitting to his child or other successor his claim to the inheritance.   But a still more effective remedy was enacted in 531.   The heir was empowered, under suitable precautions for accuracy and after inviting the presence of creditors and legatees, to make an inventory and valuation of the assets of the deceased, and was then not bound to discharge debts and legacies beyond that total amount.   He need not distribute the value of the estate *pro rata* to the claimants, but (unless fully aware of the insufficiency of the estate) could pay them in the order of their application.   Then creditors who had any right or priority could proceed against any posterior to themselves who had received payment, or against holders of any property specifically pledged to them, and all creditors not satisfied could proceed against legatees who had been paid out of what turned out to be insufficient to cover the debts.   This provision for limiting the heir's liability was called " the benefit of an inventory," and heirs were thus no longer prevented from promptly accepting an inheritance which might turn out to be ruinous.

Further difficulty arose from legacies and freedoms left in the will. Testator's estate might be able to meet the debts, but if there were many or heavy charges for bequests, there might be nothing left to make it worth while for the heir to accept the inheritance, and the will might therefore be nullified.   Several attempts to meet this difficulty were made, but nothing effectual, until a *Lex Falcidia* was passed *c.* B.C. 40.   This law, as interpreted by the lawyers, allowed the heir or heirs, if necessary, to reduce the amount of each legacy by so much as would leave the heir or heirs collectively one-fourth of the inheritance in value, the value being taken as at the time of death after deducting the value of slaves freed, the debts, and funeral expenses.   If any legacies lapsed or other gain accrued to the heirs from the estate, this would be counted towards the Falcidian fourth (as it was called).   By this arrangement the heir was sure of getting something, if he accepted a solvent inheritance.   And as, if he refused, the will would drop and the legacies be lost, the legatees might be willing to accept possibly a further deduction to prevent intestacy.   The application of the Falcidian law had been so thoroughly worked out by the lawyers that Justinian seems to have found little occasion for further enactment, except (535) to provide for the presence of the legatees or their agents at taking the inventory, with power to put the heir on his oath and to examine the slaves by torture for the purpose of getting full information.   An heir neglecting to make an inventory was liable to creditors in full and could not use the Falcidian against the legatees.   In 544 Justinian directed that the Falcidian should not apply to any immovable which testator had expressly desired should not be alienated from his family, otherwise it might have now to be sold. In 535 he had directed the Falcidian not to be used, if testator had expressly so willed.

Differences in the form of legacies led to many legal discussions which Justinian settled by treating all the forms as having the same effect, and giving the legatee both a direct claim to the thing bequeathed and also a personal claim on the heir to transfer it. TRUSTS (*Fideicommissa*[1]) were another subject of complication. In or before the time of Augustus attempts were made by testators to leave their estates, or a legacy, to persons legally disqualified to take them (*e.g.*, foreigners, Latins, unmarried persons, women in some cases). In a trust the heir was not directed to transfer the estate or legacies but simply requested to do so. There was no legal compulsion, the heir could fulfil the testator's desire or not as he chose; if the property was transferred, it was as the act of the living heir and not therefore hampered by restrictions which affected gifts from the dead. Augustus, after much hesitation, treated such a desire as obligatory on the heir. Gradually such appeals to the honour and good faith of the heir became frequent and obtained full recognition and use. Advantage was eagerly taken of this untechnical language to get round many of the limitations of ordinary testamentary law; and if only an heir was duly appointed and entered on the inheritance, almost any dispositions, direct or contingent, present or future, might be made of the estate or part of it through him as a channel. Thus testator might secure the transfer of his estate or of a legacy in certain events from the person first made heir or legatee to another person. Or he might prevent his estate from being alienated from his family by requesting the successive holders to pass it on at their deaths to other members. And trusts might be imposed not only on named persons, but on the heir or heirs by intestacy, in case the will should not have regular validity. The Courts strove to give effect to the intentions of a testator however mildly or informally expressed, and to protect the trust against the heir. But the old difficulties then recurred: the heir might as easily be overburdened with trusts as with legacies, and if he did not think it worth while to enter on the inheritance, the will failed and the trust with it. It was thus found necessary (*c.* A.D. 70) to ensure

---

[1] The difference between an English trust and a Roman *fideicommissum* is rather in the practical object and working than in the conception. In both one person holds property under an obligation to give another the benefit of it, and ceases to hold it on the obligation being completely fulfilled. But a trustee has usually, as Morice points out, a continuous duty lasting some time according to the needs of the *cestui que trust*. A fiduciary usually has no duty other than the transference of the property to the fidei-commissary on the occurrence of a condition. Both can claim to be put to no expense, but a trustee does not benefit as a rule even (at any rate since the Intestates' Estate Act 1884) if the purpose cannot be executed. A fiduciary retains the property in such a case for his own account. A fiduciary heir could in any case claim under the Falcidian Law.

that any heir burdened with a trust should get some advantage out of it; and accordingly he was empowered, if he entered and accepted the liabilities, to retain one-fourth as by the Falcidian statute. Or if he suspected the estate to be insolvent, he might restore, as the phrase went, the inheritance altogether to the person favoured by the trust and be free from both risk and advantage. Otherwise he might indeed take his fourth, but would, as partial heir, be liable for his share of the heir's obligations. If however testator had directed him to retain a certain thing or a certain amount, which was equal in value at least to one-fourth of the inheritance, and restore the rest, he was regarded as a legatee and not in any way liable to the creditors of deceased's estate. The risk and difficulty attending heirs did not arise where a trust was imposed on a legatee; he was liable for no more than he received; and as the validity of the will was not at stake, there was no necessity for the law to bribe him to accept by a share of the gift.

Justinian swept away a mass of distinctions and perplexities by putting trusts and legacies in other respects on the same footing, giving legacies the flexibility of trusts and fortifying trusts with the legal character and effective suits belonging to legacies. The phraseology was held to be unimportant, the intention was to prevail. Not only the trust but the will and legacies might now be written in Greek.

When an oral trust was added to a written will, or the will itself was oral and contained a trust, and the regular number of witnesses had not been present on the occasion, Justinian enacted that if the heir denied the trust, the person claiming under it should, having first sworn to his own good faith, put the heir on his oath whether he had not heard the testator declare the trust: the heir's answer on oath was then decisive.

LEGITIM. The Statute of the XII Tables authorised, according to tradition, full effect to be given to a Roman's will for the disposal of his estate at his death. But a *paterfamilias* was expected to shew in the will that he had duly considered the claims of his children in his power, and especially of his sons, they being his natural representatives. He must either appoint them heirs or expressly disinherit them, whether they were sons by birth or by adoption and even if posthumous. In default of such express notice, the will was set aside. Others in his family, whether daughters or grandchildren by his sons, had either to be appointed heirs or to be disinherited, but general terms were sufficient, *e.g.*, "all others are disinherited." If no notice was taken of them, the will was partly broken, for the daughters and grandchildren were admitted to share with the appointed heirs. Justinian in 531 abolished the distinction in these matters between sons and daughters and between those in testator's power and those emancipated, and required express notice for all. The praetor had already in practice made the like amendments of the old civil law.

CH. III.   6—2

But disinheritance, as well as disregard, of his children imperilled the will. As next heirs on an intestacy they could complain to the Court that the will failed in the due regard which a sane man would shew to his children. This was the "plaint of an unduteous will" (*querela inofficiosi testamenti*). If complainant established his case, the will with all its legacies and gifts of freedom drops and intestacy results. To establish his case he has to prove three things: that his conduct did not justify disinheritance, that he did not get under the will (*e.g.*, by legacy) at least one-fourth of the share of the inheritance to which he would have been entitled under an intestacy, and that he had not in any way shewn an acceptance of the will as valid. Parents could in the same way complain of their children's wills, and brothers and sisters of the testator could complain of his will, if the heirs appointed were disreputable. An illegitimate child could complain of his mother's will. If complainant had judgment given against him, he lost anything given him by the will. An analogous complaint was allowed against excessive donations which unfairly diminished a child's or parent's claim.

The value of the estate is taken for this purpose as for the Falcidian fourth. Justinian in 528 enacted that if complainants had been left something but not enough, the deficiency could be supplied without otherwise upsetting the will, provided testator had not justly charged them with ingratitude. In 536 Justinian raised the share of the inheritance which would exclude the plaint to one-third, if there were four or fewer children, and to one-half if there were more than four, *i.e.* to one-third or one-half of what would be claimant's share on an intestacy. Thus supposing two children, each would now be entitled to one-sixth (instead of one-eighth) of the estate· if three children, to one-ninth: if five, to one-tenth, and so on. Such share is called "statutory portion" (*portio legitima*) and could be made up either by an adequate share of the inheritance, or by legacy, or through a trust, or by gift intended for the purpose or by dowry or nuptial gift or purchaseable office in the imperial service (*militia*), or a combination of such. This statutory portion becomes in French law "legitim," in German "Pflichttheil."

In 542 Justinian put the matter on a new footing by requiring children to be actually named as heirs in their father's or mother's or other ascendant's will, unless the will alleged as the cause of disherison "ingratitude" on one at least of certain grounds, and the heirs prove the charge to be true. These grounds are: laying hands on parents, gravely insulting them, accusation of crimes (other than crimes against the Emperor or the State), associating with practisers of evil acts, attempting parent's life by poison or otherwise, lying with step-mother or father's concubine, informing against parents to their serious cost, refusing, if a son, to be surety for an imprisoned parent, hindering his parents from making a will, associating with gladiators or actors against his parent's wish (unless his parent was such himself), refusing (if a daughter under twenty-five years of age) a marriage and dowry proposed by her parent, and preferring a shameful life, neglecting to free a parent from captivity, neglecting him if insane, refusing the Catholic faith. If ingratitude is charged and established, the will is good · if it is not established, the appointment of heirs made in the will is null, and all the children share the inheritance equally (subject to bringing any marriage settlement into hotchpotch), but legacies, trusts, freedoms and guardianships remain valid (subject of course to the Falcidian deduction).

Those who have no children are required to name their parents as heirs, unless on similar grounds (a reduced list is given) they can be justly omitted.

Having left to children (or parents) the due amount, a testator or testatrix can dispose of the residue at his or her pleasure, and a mother can even exclude the father from any management of the property left to the son, and, if the son is under age, appoint another manager. Justinian further enacted that none but orthodox should take any part of an inheritance, and that, if all entitled under a will or on intestacy were heterodox, in the case of clerics the Church, in the case of laymen the Crown, should inherit.

Members of a town council (*decuriones*) had since 535 been obliged, if without any children, to leave three-fourths of their estate to the council : if they had children, legitimate or illegitimate, three-fourths or the whole according to circumstances were to go to such of them as were or became members or wives of members of the council. The law imposing disability for ingratitude applied here also.

A patron, if passed over in his freedman's will, could claim a third (free from legacies and trusts) if there were no children except such as were justly disinherited.

SUCCESSION TO AN INTESTATE. In default of a will duly made and duly accepted by the heirs named or one of them the law provided heirs. The statutable heirs were testator's lawful children (*sui heredes*), and failing these (in old times), his agnates, failing these, the clan (*gens*). Gradually by the praetor's action cognates were also admitted, emancipated children and women other than sisters were no longer excluded, other disabilities were removed and mother and children obtained by statute reciprocal rights of inheritance. The husband or wife claimed only after all blood-relations. This system is found in the Digest, Code, and Institutes. But in 543 and 548 Justinian superseded this system with its multifarious technicalities and ambiguities, and established (but for the orthodox only) a simpler order of succession, which is the more interesting because it largely supplied the frame for the English Statute of Distributions for intestate personalty.

Justinian disregarded distinctions of sex, of inclusion in or emancipation from the family, of agnates and cognates, and allowed in certain cases the share which would have fallen to a deceased person to be taken by his children collectively.

The first claim to succeed was for descendants. Children (and, in default of them, grandchildren) excluded all ascendants and collaterals and took equal shares, whether they sprang from the same marriage or more than one, and whether the marriage was formed by regular settlements or not. A deceased child's children took his or her share among them. Any child who had had from his or her parents dowry or nuptial gift had to bring it into account as part of his or her share. If a parent was alive and had a right of usufruct in the property or part of it, that right remained.

In the next class, that is, when there is no living descendant, come the father and mother and whole brothers and sisters of the deceased. In this case the father does not retain any right of usufruct he may have. If ascendants, not excluded by nearer ascendants, as well as brothers and sisters of the whole blood are found, they all share alike (*per capita*). If a brother or sister has predeceased the intestate, his or her children take collectively his or her share. Of ascendants the nearer is preferred. If there are only ascendants in the same degree, the estate is divided in halves between those on the father's side and those on the mother's.

If there are neither descendants nor ascendants, brothers and sisters are preferred, the whole blood excluding the half-blood, even though the latter be nearer in degree; therefore a nephew or niece of the whole blood excludes brothers and sisters of the half-blood. If there are no brothers or sisters or children of such, either of the whole blood, or half-blood, other relations succeed according to their degree, the nearer excluding the remoter, and those of the same degree sharing *per capita*.

Degrees of relationship were reckoned by the number of births from the one person to the common ancestor added to the number from him to the other person. Thus a nephew or uncle is in the third degree of relationship to me, a second cousin is in the sixth, there being three births from my great-grandfather to me and three also from him to my second cousin.

After all blood-relations are exhausted, the husband or wife would presumably inherit as under the old law before Justinian. A poor widow without dowry was entitled to a fourth of her husband's estate, such fourth not exceeding 100 lbs. gold.

In the case of freedmen dying intestate, children and other descendants have first claim: if there are none, then the patron and his children (531).

If presbyters, deacons, monks, or nuns, die without making a will or leaving relatives, their goods pass to the church or monastery to which they are attached, unless they are freedmen or serfs or decurions, in which cases they pass to the patron or lord or council respectively (434).

In default of any legal claimant the Crown took a deceased's estate.

GIFTS were viewed by Roman Law with considerable suspicion, partly as often made on the spur of the moment without due reflection, partly as liable to exert an improper influence on the donee. In B.C. 204 a law (*Lex Cincia*) was passed which forbad all gifts exceeding a certain value, and required formal execution of gifts within that value, land to be mancipated, goods to be delivered, investments duly transferred, etc. Any gifts contravening the law were revocable by the donor during his life or by will. Gifts between near relatives, either by blood or marriage, were however excepted from the prohibition of the law.

Constantine appears to have repealed this law, and, leaving gifts under 300 *solidi* free, required all gifts above that amount to be described in a written document and recorded in court, and possession to be given publicly before witnesses. In 529–531 Justinian further facilitated gifts. A mere agreement was enough without any stipulation, the presence of witnesses ceased to be necessary, and the fact of the gift was alone required to be recorded in court and that only when its value exceeded 500 *solidi*. Delivery of the object given was, according to Justinian, not so much a confirmation as a necessary consequence of the gift, and was incumbent on the donor and his heirs, especially if it were a gift for charitable purposes. A gift duly made could be revoked by the donor only on clear proof of donee's ingratitude, such as is shewn by insults or attacks on the person or property of the donor, or on non-fulfilment of the conditions of the gift. Remuneration for a service rendered is not a gift within the meaning of these rules.

Gifts between husband and wife, with trifling exceptions, were absolutely void until A.D. 206, and the same rule applied to gifts to either from anyone under the same fatherly power, or from those in whose power they respectively were. But Caracalla by a decree of the Senate made them only voidable. If the donor predeceased the donee and did not repent of the gift, the donee became fully entitled. Gifts from either to increase the marriage settlement were allowable (see above).

Gifts *mortis causa* are only to take effect if the donor die before the donee, and are epigrammatically characterised as something which the donor prefers himself to enjoy rather than the donee, and the donee rather than his heir. Such gifts were valid if made in presence of five witnesses orally or in writing, without any formality and with the effect of a legacy. The *Lex Falcidia* was applied to such gifts by Severus, if the heir had not had his due out of the rest of donor's estate.

Gifts for charitable purposes (*piae causae*) were encouraged by Justinian who (c. 530 and 545) directed that the bishops, whether requested or not or even forbidden by testator, should see that any disposition by will for such purposes was duly carried into effect; the erection of a church should be completed within three years from the time when the inheritance or legacy was available, a house for strangers within a year unless one was hired until the house was built. If this was not done the bishops should take the matter in hand by appointing administrators, the heirs or legatees after such default not being allowed to interfere. The other charitable purposes specially mentioned are houses for aged persons or infants, orphanages, poor-hospitals, and redemption of captives. The bishops are to inspect and if necessary discharge the administrators, bearing in mind the fear of the great God and the fearful day of eternal judgment. All profits from the endowment belong from the first to the charity. Delay after admonition by the bishops made the heirs or legatees who were charged with the charity, liable for double the endowment. Annuities for clergy, monks, nuns, or other charitable bodies were not to be commuted for a single sum, lest it should be spent and the claims of the future be disregarded. The property of the testator was mortgaged for the annuity, unless an agreement was made in writing and duly recorded for setting aside an inalienable rent, larger than the annuity by at least one-fourth and not subject to heavy public dues. If the bishops were slack, possibly being corrupted by the heirs, or others, the metropolitan or archbishop was authorised to interfere, or any citizen might bring an action on the statute and demand the fulfilment of the charity.

If, in order to avoid the *Falcidian Law,* a testator leaving all his property for the redemption of captives, appoints captives to be his heirs, Justinian (531) directed such an appointment to be good and not void for uncertainty. The bishop and church-manager (*oeconomus*) of the testator's domicile had to take up the inheritance without any gain for themselves or the Church. Similar appointments of poor as heirs are valid, and fall, if left uncertain by testator, to the poor-house of the place, or if there are several such to the poorest, or if there be none such, the funds are to be distributed to poor beggars or others in the place.

PROPERTY. The distinctions, which existed under the early Roman Law between land in Italy and land in the provinces with a form of conveyance (*mancipatio*)[1] applicable to the former and not to the latter, disappeared before Justinian. Under him full ownership in all land, wherever situate, was conveyed by delivery actual or symbolical, in accordance with agreement, or at least with the transferor's intention to part with the property. And the same applied to all other corporal objects. Such a distinction between real and personal property, between

---

[1] Mancipation was thus: The parties meet in the presence of no less than five witnesses, all Roman citizens of the age of puberty or upwards. An additional witness called *libripens,* "balance-weigher," holds a bronze balance. The acquirer or purchaser holds a piece of bronze as a symbol of the price, and seizing the thing to be acquired, for instance, a slave, or clod (as symbol of land), asserts it to be his by the law of the Quirites, strikes the balance with the bronze and hands it to the other party or vendor.

land and chattels, as is found in English law, never existed with the Romans either as to transfer of ownership between the living or in succession to the dead. A distinction between movables and immovables is found in some matters, *e.g.*, a title to the former being secured by acquisition on lawful grounds in good faith and uninterrupted possession by the holder and his predecessor in title for three years, whereas title to the latter required like acquisition and ten years' uninterrupted possession if claimant lived in the same province as the possessor, or twenty years when he lived in a different province. Further protection in some cases was given by an additional twenty years' possession: and claims of the Church were by a law of 535 good against one hundred years' adverse possession; but in 541 the period was reduced to forty years.

Rights in things, as distinguished from ownership, were called SERVI-TUDES and were of two classes, according as the benefit of them was attached to persons or to immovables. The principal case of the former was usufruct, *i.e.*, the right of use and enjoyment of profits, corresponding in its main incidents to life tenure. A man might have a usufruct in lands or houses or slaves or herds and even in consumables. Security had to be given to the owner for reasonable treatment and restoration *in specie* or equivalent at the expiry of the usufruct, which was lost not only by death but also by loss of civic status: it could not be transferred to another person. Minor rights of similar character are bare use and habitation.

The second class of servitudes corresponds to English "easements." They were limited rights, appurtenant to certain *praedia* whether farms in the country or houses in towns. They secured to the occupier a limited control over neighbouring houses or lands, which was necessary or at least suitable for the proper use of the dominant farm or house to which they were servient. Rights of way, of leading water, of pasturing cattle, are instances of country servitudes: rights of light and prospect and carrying off water are instances of urban servitudes. They were created usually by grant and were lost by non-user for a period of two years, which was raised by Justinian to ten or twenty years.

EMPHYTEUSIS, *i.e.*, plantation. The practice grew up in imperial times of tracts of country, in many cases waste land, being held by tenants at a fixed rent (usually called *canon, vectigal, pensio*) on the terms that so long as the rent was duly paid the tenant should not be disturbed and could transmit the land to his heirs or sell or pledge it. The owners were usually the State or the Emperor (who had a private domain) or country towns in Italy or in the provinces. The lawyers doubted whether to treat this contract as sale or lease. Zeno, about 480, decreed that it should be regarded as distinct from both, and rest upon the written agreement between lord and tenant. By Justinian's edicts the tenant had to pay without demand the public taxes and produce the receipts and pay the *canon* to the lord, who for three (or in the case of church land, two) years' default could eject him. If rent and receipts were offered and not accepted, the tenant could seal them up and deposit them with the public authority and so be safe against eviction. If eventually the lord did not take them, the tenant could keep them, and pay no more rent till the landlord demanded it, and then be liable only for future rents. As regards improvements, in the absence of express stipulations, the tenant could not sell them to outsiders, until he had offered them to the lord at the price he could get from another, and two months had passed without the lord's accepting. Nor could he alienate the farm to any but suitable persons, *i.e.*, such as were allowed generally to hold on this tenure. The lord had to give admission to the transferee and certify it by letter in his own hand or by declaration before the governor or other public authority, a fee of two per cent. of the price being demandable for such consent.

Edicts of the Emperors were not uncommon, which granted secure possession on some such terms to anyone who cultivated waste lands and was thus in a position to pay the tax upon them. If the lands had been deserted by the owner, he could claim them back only on paying the cultivator his expenses · after two years his right was gone.

OBLIGATIONS. Besides rights which are good against all the world, such as ownership and other rights to particular things, rights good only against particular persons form a most important and perhaps the most notable part of Roman Law. Such are called *obligations* and arise either from contract or from delict (in English usually called "tort"). The detailed classification of these given in the Institutes is in many respects artificial and is not found in the other books of Justinian.

CONTRACTS are voluntary agreements between two or more persons. The Romans required for an agreement which should be enforceable by law some clear basis or ground of obligation. There must be either a transfer of some thing from one of the parties to the other, or a strict form of words accompanying the agreement, or there must be agreed services of one party, usually of both. As the Romans said, the contract must be formed *aut re aut verbis aut consensu*. Otherwise it was a bare agreement (*nudum pactum*), and, though available for defence against a claim, it was not enforceable by suit, except so far as it set forth the details of one of the regular contracts and was concluded in close connexion therewith, or it reaffirmed, by a definite engagement to pay, an already existing debt of promiser's or another (*pecunia constituta*).

It may be convenient to treat first of the most general form. The contract made *verbis* was called "stipulation" and was made by oral procedure between the parties present at the same place. The matter and details of the agreement being stated, the party intending to acquire a right said, according to the original practice, *Spondesne?* " Do you promise? " to which the other replied, *Spondeo*, " I promise." But in later time any other suitable words might be used, *e.g.*, *Dabisne?* " Will you give? " *Dabo*, " I will give." The essential was that the answer should not add to or vary the scope and conditions contained in the questions : the agreement had to be precise. A record in writing was very usual, but not necessary, provided the stipulation could be proved by witnesses. The drawback in stipulation, viz., that it required the stipulator and promiser to meet, was to some extent removed by the use of slaves or children, for they could stipulate (though not promise) on behalf of their master or father, and the fact that they were under his power made the contract at once his contract. A free person *sui juris* could only stipulate for himself, and thus could not act as a mere channel pipe for another. Stipulation however had this great convenience that it was applicable to any kind of agreement, and at once elevated a mere *pactum* into a strict, valid contract. The *pactum* was usually put in writing and the fact of its having been confirmed by a stipulation was added to the record. If a promise was stated, the law presumed it to be in reply to an appropriate question : where consent was recorded, no special form of words was necessary (472). A law of Justinian (531) enacted that such record should not be disputable, whether the stipulation was effected through a slave or by both parties themselves : if it stated that the slave had done it, he should be deemed to have belonged to the party and to have been present : if it stated the latter, the parties should be deemed to have been present in person, unless it was proved by the very clearest evidence (Justinian delights in superlatives) that one of the parties was not in the town on the day named.

A very important contract, resting on a transfer of ownership, was MUTUUM, *i.e.*, loan of money or of corn or any other matters (often called " fungibles ") in which quantity and not identity is regarded, one sum of money being as good as any other equal sum. The lender was entitled to recover the same quantity at the agreed time, but had no implied right to interest unless the debtor made delay. A loan was therefore usually accompanied by a stipulation for interest. Justinian however in 536 enacted that a mere agreement was enough to secure interest to bankers. If no day for payment of a loan was named, the debtor might await creditor's application. Part payment could not be refused. Justinian (531) gave to a debtor on loan as in other cases a right to set off against a creditor's claim any debt clearly due from him.

The rate of INTEREST was limited by law. In Cicero's time and afterwards it was not to exceed 12 per cent. per annum. Justinian forbad *illustres* to ask more than 4 per cent. per annum. Traders were limited to 8 per cent. ; other persons to 6 per cent. But interest on bottomry might go up to 12 or $12\frac{1}{2}$ per cent. ($= \frac{1}{8}$) during the

voyage. Any excess paid was to be reckoned against the principal debt.
Compound interest was forbidden altogether by Justinian, and in
connexion with this the conversion of unpaid interest into principal was
forbidden. And even simple interest ceased so soon as the amount paid
equalled the amount of the principal (so Justinian 535). In loans of
corn, wine, oil, etc., to farmers, Constantine allowed 50 per cent.
interest; Justinian only $\frac{1}{8}$th ($12\frac{1}{2}$ per cent.), and for money lent to
farmers only $\frac{1}{24}$ ($= 4\frac{1}{6}$). He also forbad the land to be pledged to the
lender. In action on a judgment four months were allowed for
payment; after that simple interest at 12 per cent. was allowed.

Any son under his father's power was by a senate's decree of the
Early Empire (Sc. Macedonianum) disabled from borrowing money.
Repayment of any money so borrowed could not be enforced against
either his father or his surety or against himself (if he became
independent), unless he had recognised the debt by part payment. But
the decree did not apply, where the creditor had no ground for knowing
the debtor to be under power, or where a daughter required a dowry, or
where a student was away from home and borrowed to cover usual or
necessary expenses. The fact that the borrower was grown up and
even perhaps in high public office did not prevent the decree's applying.

Other contracts made *re*, involved a transference not of property but
of possession. Such are commodatum, gratuitous loan of something
which is to be returned *in specie*, and depositum, transfer of something
for safekeeping and return on demand or according to agreement. A
third contract under this head was *pignus*, which calls for fuller notice.

Security for debt, etc.   In order to secure a person's performance of
an obligation, two means are commonly in use: (1) giving the promisee
hold over some property of the promiser's; (2) getting a confirmatory
promise from another person: in other words, pledge and surety.

The Romans had three forms of pledge: *fiducia, pignus, hypotheca.*
Fiducia was an old form by which the creditor was made owner (for the
time) of the property: by *pignus* he is made possessor; by *hypotheca* he
is given simply a power of sale in case of default. *Fiducia* went out of
use about the fourth century; it was analogous to and probably the
origin of, our mortgage, the property being duly conveyed to the
promiser, who could, subject to account, take the profits and on default
of payment as agreed, could sell and thus reimburse himself.   A
power of sale was usually made by agreement to accompany *pignus* and
hypotheca. In *pignus* it formed an additional mode of compulsion on
the debtor besides the temporary deprivation of the use of his property:
in *hypotheca* it constituted the essence of the security. *Pignus* was a
very old form and always continued in use: *hypotheca* was no doubt
borrowed from the Greeks, and we first hear of it in Cicero's time. It had
the great convenience for the debtor that he could remain in possession
of the object pledged, and as no physical transfer was required, it could

be applied to all kinds of property, movable and immovable, near or distant, specific or general, corporal or incorporeal (such as investments). And the creditor was not responsible, as he was in the case of *pignus*, for the care and safekeeping of the object. In other respects the law which applied to the one applied to the other. A written contract was not necessary, if the contract could be proved otherwise.

Tacit pledges were recognised in some cases. Thus the law treated as pledged to the lessor for the rent, without any distinct agreement, whatever was brought into a house by the lessee with the intention of its staying there. A lodger's things were deemed to be pledged only for his own rent. In farms the fruits were held to be pledged, but not other things except by agreement. One who supplied money for reconstructing a house in Rome had the house thereby pledged to him; and for taxes or any debt to the Crown (*fiscus*) a person's whole property was so treated: guardians' and curators' property is in the same position as security to their wards; husband's as security to the wife for her dowry (531); and what an heir gets from testator is security to the legatees and trust-heirs; what a fiduciary legatee gets is security to the legatee by trust.

Any clause in a pledge-agreement which provided for forfeiture of the pledged property in default of due payment of the loan (*Lex commissoria*) was forbidden by Constantine. But the right of sale for non-payment of debt was, in the absence of contrary agreement, deemed inherent in pledge. It had however to be exercised with due formality after public notice and the lapse of two years from the time when formal application had been made to the debtor or from the judgment of the Court. Then if no sale was effected, the creditor could after further time and fresh notice petition the Emperor for permission to retain the thing as his own. If the value of the pledge did not equal the amount of the debt, the creditor could proceed against the debtor for the balance; if its value was more, the debtor was entitled to the surplus. Where the creditor was allowed to retain the thing as his own, Justinian allowed a still further period of two years in which the debtor could claim it back on payment of the debt and all creditor's expenses (530).

SURETIES (*fidejussores*) were frequently given and were applicable to any contract, formal or informal, and even to enforce a merely natural obligation, as a debt due from a slave to his master. Sureties were bound by stipulation. If there were more than one, each was liable for the whole for which the debtor was liable, but Hadrian decided that a surety making application for the concession should be sued only for his share, provided another surety was solvent. The creditor had the option of suing the debtor or one of the sureties, and, if not satisfied, then the other; but this was modified by Justinian (535), who enacted that the debtor should be first sued if he were there, and that if he were not, time should be given to the sureties to fetch him; if he could not be produced, then the sureties might be sued, and after that, recourse should be had to the debtor's property. If sureties paid, they had a claim on the debtor for reimbursement and for the transfer to them of any pledge he had given, but could not retain the pledge if debtor offered them the amount of debt and interest. A surety's obligation passed to his heirs.

If a woman gave a guaranty for another person, even for her husband or son or father, so as to make her liable for them, the obligation was invalid. But she was not protected, if the obligation was really for herself, or if she had deceived the creditor or received compensation for her guaranty, or had after two years' interval given a bond or pledge or surety for it. This rule, which dates from the Early Empire (*senatus consultum Velleianum*), was based on the theory that a woman might easily be persuaded to give a promise, when she would not make a present sacrifice. Accordingly she was not prohibited from making gifts. Justinian confirmed and amended the law in 530 by requiring for any valid guaranty by a woman a public document with three witnesses, and in 556 enacted that no woman be put in prison for debt.

The class of contracts which arise CONSENSU, *i.e.*, by the agreement of the parties, without special formalities or transfer of a thing from one to the other, is constituted by Purchase and sale, Hire and lease, Partnership, Mandate.

PURCHASE AND SALE (one thing under two names) is complete when the parties have agreed on the object and the price, or at least agreed to the mode of fixing the price. The agreement may be oral or in writing· if the latter, it must be written or subscribed by the parties; and till that is done, neither party is bound. Whether the contract is oral or written, the intended buyer, if he does not buy, (in the absence of any special agreement on the point) forfeits any earnest money he may have given, and the vendor, if he refuses to complete, has to repay the earnest twofold. (So Justinian 528.) The vendor is bound by the completed contract to warrant to the purchaser quiet and lawful possession but is not bound to make him owner. He must however, unless otherwise agreed, deliver the thing to the purchaser, where it is, and thereby transfer all his own right. From the date of completion of the contract, though delivery has not taken place, the risk and gain pass to the purchaser, but he is not owner until he has paid the price and got delivery, and then only if the vendor was owner, or possession for the due time has perfected the purchaser's title. The vendor is liable to the purchaser on his covenants (*e.g.*, in case of buyer's eviction, for double the value), and also for any serious defects which he has not declared and of which the purchaser was reasonably ignorant.

In case of sale of an immovable Diocletian admitted rescission when the price was much under the value (285). It was probably Justinian who

gave generally a claim for rescission whenever the price was less than half
the real value.   This ground of rescission was later called *laesio enormis*,
and many attempts were made to extend its application.

The contract of LEASE AND HIRE is similar in many respects to that of
purchase and sale.   But the lessee, if evicted, has only his claim against
the lessor on his covenant to guaranty quiet possession, and has no hold
over the land, if sold by his lessor to another.   In letting a farm the
lessor was bound to put it in good repair and supply necessary stabling
and plant: and, if landslip or earthquake or an army of locusts or other
irresistible force does damage, the lessor has to remit proportionably
the current rent.   The like rules held of letting houses, except that plant
was not provided.   The lessee had a good claim on the lessor for any
necessary or useful additions or improvements, and usually could recover
his expenditure or remove them.   He was bound to maintain the leased
property whether farm or house, and to treat it in a proper manner,
cultivating the farm in the usual way.   He could underlet within the
limits of his term ; and the law of the fifth century allowed either lessor or
lessee to throw up the contract within the first year, without any penalty,
unless such had been agreed on.   The usual term of lease was five years,
at least in Italy and Africa; in Egypt one or three years.

Contracts for building a house, carriage of goods, training of a
slave, etc., come under this head, where the locator supplied the site or
other material.   The conductor, who performed the service, was liable
for negligence.

PARTNERSHIP is another contract founded on simple agreement, but
also characterised, like the two last mentioned, by reciprocal services.
It was in fact an agreement between two or more persons to carry on
some business together for common account.   The contributions of the
members and their shares in the result were settled by agreement, and
they were accountable to each other for gains and losses.   Like other
contracts it concerned only the partners : outsiders need know nothing
of it; in any business with them only the acting partner or partners
were responsible.   A partner's heir did not become a partner, except
by a new contract with common consent.   A partnership came to an
end by the death of a partner, or his retirement after due notice, or
when the business or time agreed came to an end.

There was no free development of association into larger companies,
without the express approval of the State.   A company continues to
exist irrespectively of the change or decease of the members, regulates
its own membership and proceedings, has a common chest and a common
representative, holds, acquires and alienates its property as an individual.
In Rome such corporate character and rights were only gradually
granted and recognised, each particular privilege being conceded to this
or that institution or class of institutions as occasion required.

Towns and other civil communities had common property and a

CH. III.

common chest, could manumit their slaves and take legacies and inheritances. They usually acted through a manager; their resolutions required a majority of the quorum, which was two-thirds of the whole number of councillors (*decuriones*). They are said *corpus habere*, "to be a body corporate."

Other associations for burials or for religious or charitable purposes, often combined with social festivities, were allowed to exist with statutes of their own making, if not contrary to the general law. But without express permission they could not have full corporate rights. Guilds or unions of the members of a trade, as bakers, are found with various privileges. Such authorised societies or clubs were often called *collegia* or *sodalitates*. They were modelled more or less on civic corporations: Marcus Aurelius first granted them permission to manumit their slaves.

The large companies for farming the taxes (*publicani*) or working gold or silver mines had the rights of a corporation, but probably not so far as to exclude individual liability for the debts, if the common chest did not suffice.

Mandate differs from the three other contracts, which are based on simple agreement. There are no reciprocal services and no remuneration or common profits. It is gratuitous agency: not the agency of a paid man of business; that would come under the head of hiring. Nor is it like the agency of a slave; that is the use of a chattel by its owner. It is the agency of a friend whose good faith, as well as his credit, is at stake in the matter. The mandatee is liable to the mandator for due performance of the commission he has undertaken, and the mandator is liable to him only for the reimbursement of his expenses in the conduct of the matter.

Similar agency but unauthorised, without any contract, was not uncommon at Rome, when a friend took it upon himself to manage some business for another in the latter's absence and thereby saved him from some loss or even gained him some advantage. The swift process of the law courts in early days seems to have produced and justified friendly interference by third parties, which required and received legal recognition. The person whose affairs had thus been handled had a claim upon the interferer for anything thereby gained, and for compensation for any loss occasioned by such perhaps really ill-advised action or for negligence in the conduct of the business, and was liable to reimburse him for expenses, and relieve him of other burdens he might have incurred on the absentee's behalf. Such actions were said to be *negotiorum gestorum*, "for business done."

But in Rome the usual agent was a slave; for anything acquired by him was thereby *ipso facto* acquired for his master, and for any debt incurred by him his master was liable up to the amount of his slave's *peculium*; and if the business in question was really for the master's account or done on his order the master was liable in full. And though in general when the master was sued on account of his slave (*de peculio*) he had a right to deduct from the *peculium* the amount of any debt due to himself, he had no such right when he was cognisant of the slave's action and had not forbidden it; he could then only claim rateably with other creditors. A son or daughter under power was for these purposes in the same position as a slave.

It was rarely that the Romans allowed a third party who was a freeman and independent to be privy to a contract. The freeman acquired and became liable for himself, and the principals to the contract in case of such an agent had to obtain transfers from him of the rights acquired: they could not themselves sue or be sued on the agent's contract. But two cases were regarded by Roman Law as exceptional. When a person provided a ship and appointed a skipper in charge of it, he was held liable in full for the skipper's contracts in connexion with it, if the person contracting chose to sue him instead of the skipper. And the like liability was enforced, if a man had taken a shop and appointed a manager over it. In both cases the rule held, whether the person appointing or appointed was man or woman, slave or free, of age or under age. The restriction of the owner's liability to the amount of his slave's *peculium* disappeared, and the privity of contract was recognised against the appointer, although the skipper or manager who actually made the contract was a free person acting as mediary. But this recognition was one-sided: the principal did not acquire the right of suing on his skipper's or manager's contract, if the latter were free; he must, usually at least, obtain a transfer of the right of suit from him, the transfer being enforced by suing the skipper or manager as an employee or mandatee.

At one time there was a marked difference between the consensual contract along with most of those arising *re* on the one hand, and on the other hand stipulation and cash-loan (*mutuum*). In actions to enforce the former the judge had a large discretion, and the standard by which he had to guide his decisions or findings was what was fairly to be expected from business men dealing with one another in good faith. In actions to enforce the latter the terms of the bargain were to be observed strictly: the contract was regulated by the words used: the loan was to be repaid punctually in full. Gradually these latter contracts came to be treated similarly to the former so far as their nature permitted, and by Justinian's time the prevalence of equity was assured: the intention of the parties was the universal rule for interpretation of all contracts, and reasonable allowance was made for accidental difficulties in their execution, when there was no evidence of fraud.

Two modes were adopted in classical times for dealing with the engagements or position of parties where the terms and characteristics of a proper contract in due form were not found. One was to treat the matter on the analogy of some contract the incidents of which it appeared to resemble. Thus money paid on the supposition of a debt, which however proved not to have existed, was recoverable, *as if* it had been a loan. Money or anything transferred to another in view of some event which did not take place was recoverable, *as if* paid on a conditional contract, the condition of which had not been fulfilled.

Another mode was for the complainant, instead of pleading a contract, to set forth the facts of the case and invite judgment on the defendant according to the judge's view of what the equity of the case required. Thus barter was not within the legal conception of purchase and sale, for that must always imply a price in money, but it had all other characteristics of a valid contract and was enforced accordingly on a statement of the facts. If a work had to be executed for payment but the amount of payment was left to be settled afterwards, this was not ordinary hire, which is for a definite remuneration, but might well be enforced on reasonable terms.

TRANSFER OF OBLIGATIONS. Before leaving contracts, which are the largest and most important branch of obligations, it is as well to point out that the transfer of an obligation, whether an active obligation, *i.e.* the right to demand, or a passive obligation, *i.e.* the duty to pay or perform, is attended with difficulties not found in the transfer of a physical object, whether land or chattels. An obligation being a relation of two parties with one another only, it seems contrary to its nature for A, who has a claim on B, to insist on payment from C instead; or for D to claim for himself B's payment due to A. With the consent of all parties, the substitution is possible and reasonable, but the arrangement for transfer must be such as to secure D in the payment by B, and to release B from the payment to A. Two methods were in use. At A's bidding D stipulates from B for the debt due to A : B is thereby freed from the debt due to A and becomes bound to D. This was called by the Romans a novation, *i.e.* a renewal of the old debt in another form. Similarly A would stipulate from C for the debt owed by B to A. This being expressly in lieu of the former debt frees B and binds C. These transfers being made by stipulation require the parties to meet. The other method was for A to appoint D to collect the debt from B and keep the proceeds, the suit being carried on in A's name, and the form of the judgment naming D as the person entitled to receive instead of A. Similarly in the other case C would make A his representative to get in B's debt. In practice no doubt matters would rarely come to an actual suit. The method by representation was till 1873 familiar enough in England, a debt being a chose in action and recoverable by transferee only by a suit in the name of the transferor.

Gradually from about the third century it became allowable for the agent in such cases to bring an analogous action in his own name.

DELICTS. The other important class of obligations besides contracts are delicts or torts. They arise from acts which without legal justification injure another's person or family or property or reputation. Such acts, if regarded as likely to be injurious not only to the individual but to the community, become subjects for criminal law; if not so regarded, are subject for private prosecution and compensation. In many cases the injured person had a choice of proceeding against the offender criminally or for private compensation. The tendency in imperial times was to treat criminally the graver cases, especially when accompanied with violence or sacrilege.

The principal classes of delicts were: theft, wrongful damage, and insult (*injuriarum*). Theft is taking or handling with a gainful intention any movable belonging to another without the owner's consent actual or honestly presumed. Usually the theft is secret: if done with violence it is treated with greater severity as robbery (*rapina*). Any use of another's thing other than he has authorised comes under this tort, and not only the thief but anyone giving aid or counsel for a theft, is liable for the same. Not only the owner, but anyone responsible for safekeeping can sue as well as the owner. The penalty was ordinarily twofold the value of the thing stolen, but, if the thief was caught on the spot, fourfold the value. If the offence was committed by a slave the master could avoid the penalty by surrendering the slave to the plaintiff. In early days such a surrender of a son or daughter in their father's power was possible, but probably rare. Robbery was subjected to a penalty of fourfold the value. Cattle-driving was usually punished criminally. Theft from a man by a son or slave under his power was a matter of domestic discipline, not of legal process. Theft by a wife was treated as theft, but the name of the suit was softened into an action for making away with things (*rerum amotarum*).

Wrongful damage rested even till Justinian's time on a statute (*Lex Aquilia*) of early republican date which received characteristic treatment from lawyers' interpretations extending and narrowing its scope. It embraced damage done whether intentionally or accidentally to any slave or animal belonging to another, or indeed to anything, crops, wine, nets, dress, etc., belonging to another, provided it was done by direct physical touch, not in self-defence nor under irresistible force. If the damage was caused by defendant but not by corporal touch, the Romans resorted to the device of allowing an analogous action by setting forth the facts of the case, or by express statement of the analogy. The penalty was in case of death assessed at the highest value which the slave or animal had within a year preceding the death; in case of damage only, the value to the plaintiff within the preceding thirty days. But condemnations under this head of wrongful damage did not involve the infamy which belonged to theft ; that was purposed, this was often the result of mere misfortune. Surrender of a slave who had caused the damage was allowed to free the defendant as in the case of theft. Damage done to a freeman's own body was hardly within the words of the statute; and compensation could be obtained only by an analogous action.

The third class was confined to cases of malicious insult but had a very wide range. It included blows or any violence to plaintiff or his family, abusive language, libellous or scandalous words, indecent soliciting, interference with his public or private rights. Not only the actual perpetrator of the insult, but anyone who procured its doing, was liable. The character of the insult was differently estimated according to the rank of the person insulted and the circumstances of the action. The damages on conviction were, under a law of Sulla which in principle remained till Justinian, assessable by plaintiff subject to the check of the judge. Many of these acts, especially when of an aggravated character, were punished criminally, even by banishment or death.

A fourth class of torts (sometimes called *quasi ex delicto*) makes defendant liable not for his own act but for injury caused by anything being thrown or falling from a room occupied by him near a right of way, or for theft or injury perpetrated in a shop or tavern or stable under his control. The penalty is put at double the estimated damage, except that, if a freeman is hurt, no estimate of damage to a free body was held possible, and the penalty was therefore the amount of medical expenses and loss of work: if he was killed, it was put at fifty guineas (*aurei*).

PROCEDURE. In classical times the parties after summons approached the praetor and asked for the appointment of a *judex* to hear and decide the suit. Instructions proposed by plaintiff and sometimes modified by the praetor at the request of the defendant were agreed to by the parties, who then joined issue, and the formula containing these instructions was sent to the *judex* named. The *judex* heard and decided the case, and, if he found against the defendant, condemned him in a certain sum as damages. But in some few matters the praetor, instead of appointing a *judex* in the ordinary course, kept the whole matter in his own hands. This extraordinary procedure became in Diocletian's time the ordinary procedure, and the praefect or the governor of a province or the *judex* appointed by them heard the case from the first without any special instructions. In the fourth century the case was initiated by a formal notice (*litis denuntiatio*) to the defendant; but in Justinian's time by plaintiff's presenting to the Court a petition (*libellus*) containing his claims on the defendant, who was then summoned by the judge to answer it. If he did not appear, the *judex* after further summons examined and decided the matter in his absence.

Either party before joinder of issue had the right of refusing the *judex* proposed by the governor, etc. Three days were then allowed them to choose an arbitrator, and in case of disagreement the governor or other authority appointed. Jews' suits whether relating to their own superstition or not could be heard by the ordinary tribunals, but by consent they might have the case heard by an arbitrator who was a Jew. Soldiers and officials were not exempt from being sued before the civil tribunals on ordinary matters. Constantine in a constitution of 333 (if genuine) gave either party the right even against the will of the other to have the case transferred to the bishop at any stage before final judgment. But Arcadius in 398 repealed this and required the consent of both parties, so that the bishop was only an arbitrator and his judgment was executed by the ordinary lay officers.

The *judices* were to act on the general law, said Justinian (541), and during their task were not to expect or accept any special instruction for deciding the case. If any application were made to the Emperor, he would decide the matter himself and not refer it to any other *judex*. A *judex* was authorised, if in doubt about the interpretation of a law, to apply to the Emperor.

No suits excepting those touching the Crown (*fiscus*), or public trials were to be extended beyond three years from the commencement of the hearing. When only six months remained of this period, the *judex* was to summon either party, if absent, three times at intervals of ten days, and then to examine and decide the matter, the costs being thrown on the absentee (531).

The courts were open all the year, with the exception of harvest and wine-gathering (sometimes defined as 24 June to 1 August, and 23 August to 15 October), also seven days before and after Easter, also Sundays, Kalends of January, birthdays of Rome and Constantinople birthday and accession of Emperor, Christmas, Epiphany and time of commemoration of the "Apostolical passion" (Pentecost). Neither law proceedings nor theatrical shows were allowed on Sundays ; but Constantine exempted farmers from observance of Sundays. No criminal trials were held in Lent.

Private suits and questions of freedom were to be tried at defendant's place of residence, or of his residence at the date of the contract. So Diocletian (293) following the old rule, *actor rei forum sequatur.* Suits *in rem* or for a *fideicommissum* or respecting possession should be brought where the thing or inheritance is.

Justin (526) forbad any interference with a burial on the ground of a debt due from deceased ; and invalidated all payments, pledges and sureties obtained in these circumstances. Justinian (542) forbad anyone within nine days of a person's death to sue or otherwise molest any of his relatives. Any promise or security obtained during this period was invalid.

PROOF. The person who puts forth a claim or plea has to prove it. The possessor has not to prove his right to possess, but to await proof to the contrary. Thus one who is possessed of freedom can await proof by a claimant of his being his slave. But one who has forcibly carried off or imprisoned another, whom he claims to be his slave, cannot on the ground of this forcible possession throw the burden of proof on his opponent. To prove a purchase it is not enough to produce a document describing the fact, but there must be shewn by witnesses the fact of purchase, the price paid, and possession of the object formally given. To prove relationship, the fact of birth and the parents' marriage, or adoption by them must be shewn: letters between the parties or application for an arbiter to divide the family inheritance are not sufficient.

Persons who have admitted a debt in writing cannot prove payment without a written receipt, unless they produce five unimpeachable witnesses to the payment in their presence. But as a general rule they are not bound by a statement in the document of debt of their having originally received the money, wholly or partly, if they can prove within 30 days after the production of the document that the stated money had not been paid them.

All witnesses must be sworn. One suspected of giving false evidence can be put to the question at once, and, if convicted, can be subjected by the judge hearing the case to the penalty to which the defendant was liable against whom he had given the false evidence. A single witness without other evidence proves nothing, and Constantine enacted (334) that he should not be heard in any suit. All persons (enacted Justinian 527) with like exceptions as in criminal causes are compellable to give evidence. Slaves were sometimes examined under torture.

No judge was to commence the hearing until he had the Scriptures placed before the tribunal, and they were to remain there until judgment. All advocates had to take an oath, touching the Gospels, that they would do what they could for their clients in truth and justice, and resign their case if they found it dishonest (530). Both plaintiff and defendant had to take an oath to their belief in the goodness of their cause (531).

Justinian among other rules respecting documents enacted these:

All persons are compellable to produce documents who are compellable to give evidence. The production is to be in the court, at the expense of the person requiring it. Anyone declining to produce on the ground that he will be injured thereby, must, if this is contested by the other party, make oath of his belief and also that it is not any bribe or fear or favour of someone else that deters him.

All documents were to be headed with year of Emperor, consul, indiction, month and day.

Contracts of sale, exchange and gift (if not such as must be officially recorded), of earnest and compromise and any others arranged to be in writing, were not valid, unless written out fair and subscribed by the parties; if written by a notary, he must complete and sign them and be present himself at their execution by the parties (528 and 536). In 538 it was directed that contracts of loan or deposit or other should, even when written, have at least three witnesses to their completion, and when produced for proof be confirmed by oath of the producer.

In lieu of proof by witnesses or documents, oaths were sometimes resorted to. The judge might propose to one of the parties to support his allegation by an oath, and, if the oath was taken, the judge would naturally decide that point in his favour. But either party might challenge the other, either before trial or in the course of it, to swear to some particular matter, and if the party so challenged swore in the terms of the challenge, the matter would be held to be decided as much as by a judgment, and in any further dispute between the parties or their sureties or persons joined with them the oath if relevant could be pleaded or acted on as decisive. And the same result ensues, if the party to whom the oath is tendered declares his readiness to swear and the other then waives the demand. The party called on to swear may instead of taking the oath retort the demand, and the other party is then in the same position as if the oath had been originally tendered to him. In earlier times probably such tender of oath could be declined in most cases without prejudice, but Justinian apparently makes no restriction, and a defendant for instance to an action for money lent, if plaintiff tendered him an oath whether it was due or not, had no choice except either to take the oath or admit the debt, unless indeed he retorted the tender. Plaintiff, if he accepted the retort, would have first to swear to his own good faith and then could establish his claim by the oath. In all cases the oath, if it is to carry the consequence stated, must not be volunteered, but taken in reply to the challenge and must conform precisely to the terms.

The requirement of an oath was also resorted to in some cases by the judge in order to compel obedience, wrongly refused, to an interlocutory decision. The plaintiff was allowed to fix the damages himself, by an oath of the amount due. This was called *in litem jurare*, "to swear to the disputed claim."

CRIMINAL LAW. The criminal law was put in force either on the magistrate's own initiative or by private persons. Women and soldiers were not admitted as accusers, unless the crime was against themselves, or their near relatives. Anyone desiring to bring an accusation had to specify the date and place of the crime and to give a surety for due prosecution. Laws of Constantine, and Arcadius, retained by Justinian, directed that any servant (*familiaris*) or slave bringing an accusation against his master should be at once put to death before any inquiry into the case or production of witnesses. And the like was enacted (423) in the case of a freedman accusing his patron. Excepted from this rule were cases of adultery, high treason and fraud in the tax-return (*census*). An accuser not proving his case was (373) made subject to the penalty belonging to the crime charged. A like rule of talion was prescribed in some other cases.

CH. III.

A law of 320 prescribed that in all cases, whether a private person or an official was prosecuting, the trial should take place immediately. If accuser were not present or the accused's accomplices were required, they should be sent for at once, and meantime any chains that were put on the accused should be long ones, not close-fitting handcuffs; nor should he be confined in the inmost and darkest prison but enjoy light, and at night, when the guard is doubled, be allowed in the vestibules and more healthy parts of the prison. The judge should take care that the accusers do not bribe the gaolers to keep the accused back from a hearing and starve them: if they do, the officers should be capitally punished. The sexes were to be kept apart (340). Justinian in 529 forbad anyone being imprisoned without an order from the higher magistrates, and directed the bishops to examine once a week into the cause of imprisonment, and to ascertain whether the prisoners were slave or free and whether imprisoned for debt or crime. Debtors were to be let out on bail. if they had no bail they were to have a hearing and be let out on oath, their property being forfeited if they fled. Freemen charged with lesser crimes to be let out on bail, but if the charge were capital and no bail was allowed, imprisonment was not to extend beyond one year. Slaves to be tried within 20 days. The bishops, as ordered by Honorius, had to report any remissness in the magistrates. Private prisons were forbidden altogether by Justinian (529).

The accused was examined by the judge. If a slave was accused, torture was sometimes applied to elicit a confession. In republican times a freeman was not liable to this. Under the Empire the rule was broken, but persons of high rank were exempt, except where the charge was treason (*majestas*) or magical arts.

The judge could compel anyone to give evidence except bishops and high officers and old and sick persons or soldiers or attendants on magistrates at a distance. A private accuser had similar powers, but for a limited number. Defendant could call witnesses, but had no power of compulsion.

Parents and children were not admissible as witnesses against one another, nor were other near relatives; nor freedmen against their patron. Slaves were not admissible to give evidence against their master, except in cases of treason, adultery or fraud on the revenue. As a rule slaves were used as witnesses only in default of others. They were examined, and if their statements were not satisfactory, torture was applied.

If after trial the accused was acquitted, the old practice (retained by Justinian) was for the judge to examine into the conduct of the accuser, and, if he found no reasonable ground for the accusation, to hold him guilty of calumny. For collusion with the accused he might be held guilty of prevarication. Nor was an accuser allowed to withdraw from an accusation once undertaken, especially if the accused had been long in prison or had been subjected to blows or chains. But if the accused consented or had not been harshly treated, withdrawal (*abolitio*) was generally permitted, except on charges of treason or other grave crimes. An accuser, once desisting, could not take the charge up again.

A general indulgence, by which all persons accused (with certain exceptions) were released, was decreed by Constantine in 322 on account of the birth of a son to Crispus. In later years the like indulgence was granted at Easter, and apparently in 385 it was made a standing rule. Persons charged with poisoning, murder, adultery, evil magic, sacrilege or treason, and sometimes other offenders, were excepted.

Most of the legislation on crime goes back to the Republic or to Augustus. The law of treason (*majestas*) is based on a law of the latter. Treason consists in doing anything against the Roman people and includes all assistance to the enemy, attacks on Roman magistrates, intentional injury to the Emperor's statues, collecting for seditious purposes armed men in the city, refusal to leave a province on the appointment of a successor, making false entries in public documents, etc. Abuse or other insult to the Emperor required careful inquiry as to the motive and sanity of the accused; punishment was to await a report to the Emperor. If an accuser failed to establish his charge, he was liable to be examined by torture himself, notwithstanding any privilege from military service, birth or dignity. The punishment for treason was death and forfeiture of property. Conspiracy to compass the death of the Emperor's councillors subjected even the sons of the criminal to incapacity for succession to any inheritance or legacy, and to be reduced to such want that "death would be a comfort and life a punishment" (397).

By a law of Sulla, maintained and developed by the Emperors, murder, magical arts, nocturnal incantations or rites to exert unholy influence over persons, desertion to the enemy, stirring up seditions or tumult, bribing witnesses or judges to act falsely were punished with death in the case of all but the privileged class. So also consulting soothsayers (*haruspices*) or mathematicians respecting the health of the Emperor, introduction of new sects or unknown religions to excite men's minds, forgery or suppression of wills, forgery of seals, coining, melting or mutilating coinage were sometimes punished capitally. Coining was regarded as treason (326).

Constantine (318) forbad under pain of burning any soothsayer from crossing the threshold of another person, even though an old friend, but in the case of magical arts distinguished between those directed against another's safety or chastity, and remedies for disease or country spells against heat or rain upon the crops. Constantius (358) was also severe against all divination, etc. Valentinian (364) forbad all nocturnal religious rites, but relaxed this prohibition on the proconsul of Greece representing that life then would be intolerable.

CH. III.

Adultery could be charged only by the nearest relatives: husband, father, brother, uncle, first cousin. The husband had precedence for sixty days, then the father having the woman in his power, then after the like time outsiders, who however could not accuse her while married, unless the adulterer had first been convicted.

A father was justified in killing his daughter (if in his power) if he caught her in adultery at his or his son-in-law's house, and in killing the adulterer also, but if he killed one and spared the other, he was liable for murder. A husband was justified in killing his wife so caught, but the adulterer only if he was a slave or freedman or pander or player or a condemned criminal. The husband was otherwise bound to repudiate his wife at once. Justinian (542) justified a husband's killing anyone suspected of illicit intercourse with his wife, if, after sending her three warnings supported by evidence of trustworthy persons, he found her conversing with the adulterer in his own or her house or in taverns or suburban places. For making assignations in church the husband after like warnings could send both the wife and man to the bishop for punishment as adulterers according to the laws.

A husband who retained a wife detected in adultery, or compounded for her release, was guilty of pandering. So also was anyone who married a woman convicted of adultery. One accused of adultery and escaping, if he consorted with the woman again, was to be seized by any judge and without further trial to be tortured and killed.

By a law of Augustus (*Lex Julia*) the punishment for adultery was banishment, and for the man, forfeiture of half his property, for the woman, forfeiture of half her dowry and a third of her property. Constantine and Justinian made the punishment death by the sword for the man. Justinian (556) sent the woman into a monastery after being flogged. The like punishments were ordained for *stuprum*, *i.e.*, intercourse with an unmarried woman or widow, who was neither in the relation of concubine nor a person of disreputable life.

Anyone who without agreement with her parents carried off a girl was to be punished capitally, and the girl herself if she consented. A nurse who persuaded her to do so was to have her throat and mouth filled with molten lead. If the girl did not consent, she was still deprived of right of succession to her parents for not having kept within doors or raised the neighbours by her cries. The parents, if they overlooked the matter, were to be banished: other assistants to be punished capitally, slaves to be burnt. So Constantine in 320. Constantius limited the penalty of free persons to death (349). Eventually Justinian punished ravishers and their aiders with death and confiscated their property for the benefit of the injured woman.

PUNISHMENTS were not the same for all persons. Three classes of persons were recognised in Justinian's Digest: *honestiores*, *humiliores* or *tenuiores*, *servi*.

I. The first class contained the imperial senators and their agnatic descendants to the third degree; knights with public horses; soldiers and veterans and their children; decurions. They were not liable to the penalty of death except for parricide or treason or except by an imperial order, nor to the mines or compulsory work or beating. The usual penalty was deportation to an island, in some cases combined with confiscation of part of their property. Deportation involved loss of citizenship.

II. The second class were punished for grave offences by death, more frequently by condemnation to the mines preceded by beating and accompanied with chains. This punishment was usually for life and involved loss of citizenship and property. It formerly involved loss of freedom, but this was abolished by Justinian in 542. Banishment (*relegatio*) might be for life or for a time, and citizenship was not lost.

The death penalty for free persons was usually beheading, in and after second century by sword, not axe; rarely, and only for the gravest offences, crucifying or burning. Beating or torturing to death, strangling and poisoning, were forbidden.

Justinian in 556 enacted that for crimes involving death or banishment the property of the criminals should not be confiscated either to the judges or officials, or, as according to the old law, to the fisc, but should pass to their descendants, or, if there were none, to the ascendants up to the third degree. He also enacted that where the law ordered both hands or both feet to be cut off, one only should be cut, and that joints should not be dislocated. No limb should be cut off for theft, if without violence.

Constantine (318) re-enacted the punishment assigned by old practice to parricide, viz., the criminal to be beaten with rods, sewn up in a sack with a dog, cock, viper and ape, and thrown into a deep sea, if near, or into a river. Justinian retained the law, but confined it to murderers of father, mother and grandfather and grandmother, whereas it had previously been applicable to many other relatives.

III. Slaves were punished for grave crime by beheading, sometimes by crucifying or burning or exposure to wild beasts: for lesser crimes by work in the mines. Flogging was usual in many cases, and regularly preceded capital punishment. Imprisonment was not used as a punishment, but only as security for trial.

Heretics were deprived by Constantine (326) of all privileges given on the ground of religion and were forbidden (396) to occupy any place for worship. In 407 Manichaeans and Donatists were ordered to be treated as criminals; they forfeited all their property to their next of kin (if free from heresy) and were incapable of succession, of giving, of buying and selling, of contracting, of making a will; their slaves were to be held guiltless only if they deserted their masters and served the Catholic Church.

CH. III.

In 428 Manichaeans were to be expelled from their towns, and given over to extreme punishment, and a long list of heretics was forbidden to meet and pray anywhere on Roman soil. In 435 Nestorians, in 455 the followers of Eutyches and Apollinarius were to have their books burnt, and were forbidden to meet and pray. In 527 heretics, Greeks, Jews, and Samaritans were rendered incapable of serving in the army, of holding civil office except in the lower ranks and then without a chance of promotion; and were disabled from suing orthodox Christians for private or public debts. Children of heretics, if themselves free from the disease, might take their legal share of their father's property, and their fathers were to support them and to give dowries to their daughters. In 530 Montanists like other heretics were forbidden to assemble, to baptise, to have Communion, and to receive charitable alms from law courts or churches.

In suits against orthodox, whether both parties or only one be orthodox, heretics and Jews were not good witnesses, but only in suits among themselves. Even this was not applicable to Manichaeans, Montanists, pagans, Samaritans and some others; for they being criminals were incapable of bearing witness in judicial matters; they were however allowed as witnesses to wills and contracts, lest proof should be difficult.

A law of Augustus, confirming analogous republican practice, forbad any Roman citizen who appealed to the Emperor being killed, tortured, beaten or put into chains even by the governor or other high magistrate. This is retained in Justinian's Digest.

Several constitutions at the end of the fourth century (398) were directed against attempts of clergy or monks to prevent due execution of sentences on criminals or debtors.

CHAPTER IV.

GAUL UNDER THE MEROVINGIAN FRANKS.

NARRATIVE OF EVENTS.

At the accession of Clovis, who succeeded his father Childeric about the year 481, the Salian Franks had advanced as far as the Somme. Between the Somme and the Loire the suzerainty of the Roman Empire was still maintained. The various Gallo-Roman cities preserved a certain independence, while a Roman official, by name Syagrius, exercised a kind of protection over them. Syagrius was the son of Aegidius, the former *magister militum*, and he held the command by hereditary right. After the fall of the Roman Empire of the West in 476, he maintained an independent position, having no longer any official superior. Failing any regular title, Gregory of Tours designates him *Rex Romanorum*, and the former Roman official takes on the character of a barbarian king, free from all ties of authority. The seat of his administration was the town of Soissons.

To the south of the Loire began the kingdom of the Visigoths, which reached beyond the Pyrenees and across Spain to the Strait of Gibraltar. The country south of the Durance, that is to say Provence, also formed part of this kingdom. After having long been allies of the Roman Empire the Visigoths had broken the treaties which bound them to Rome; moreover since 476 there was no emperor in Italy, and they occupied these vast territories by right of conquest. Euric, who had been king since 466, had extended his dominions on every side and was quite independent.

In the valley of the Saône and the Rhone, as far as the Durance, the Burgundians had been enlarging their borders. Starting from Savoy, to which Aëtius had confined them, they had extended their possessions little by little, until these now included the town of Langres. In 481 the kingship of Burgundy was shared by two brothers, of whom the elder, Gundobad, had his seat at Vienne, the younger, Godigisel, at Geneva. A third brother, Chilperic, who had reigned at Lyons, had just died. The rumour ran that he had met a violent death, his brothers having had him assassinated in order to seize upon his inheritance.

The Visigoths and Burgundians endeavoured to live at peace with

the Gallo-Romans and to administer their territories wisely. The former
subjects of Rome would willingly have submitted to them in exchange
for the protection which they could afford and the peace which they
could secure; they would willingly have pardoned them for dividing up
their territories; but between the Gallo-Romans and the barbarians
there was one grave subject of dissension. The former had remained
faithful to orthodoxy, the latter were Arians; and although the rulers
were willing to exercise toleration and to maintain friendly relations
with the members of the episcopate, their Gallo-Roman subjects did not
cease to regard them as abettors of heresy, and to desire their fall as
a means to the triumph of the true faith.

To the north of the Burgundian kingdom, the Alemans had made
themselves masters of the territory between the Rhine and the Vosges—
the country which was to be known later as Alsace—and they were
seeking to enlarge their borders by attacking the Gallo-Roman cities to
the west, the Burgundians to the south, and the Ripuarian Franks to the
north-west. They also continued to hold the country on the right bank
of the Rhine which had been known as the *agri decumates*, and they had
established themselves in force upon the shores of the Lake of Constance
and to the east of the Aar. The Ripuarian Franks remained in possession
of a compact State round about Cologne and Trèves, and, near them,
the Thuringians had founded a little State on the left bank of the
Rhine. It should be added that small colonies of barbarians, drawn
from many different tribes, had established themselves here and there
over the whole face of Gaul. Bands of armed barbarians ranged the
country, seeking a home for themselves; Saxon pirates infested the
coasts, and had established themselves in some force at Bayeux.

Such was the general condition of Gaul at the time when Clovis
became king of the Salian Franks. For five years the youthful king—
he was only fifteen at his accession—remained inactive. He seems to have
been held in check by Euric, the king of the Visigoths. But in the year
following the death of Euric, 486, he took up arms and, calling to his
aid other Salian kings, Ragnachar and Chararic, attacked Syagrius.
The two armies came into contact with one another in the neighbourhood
of Soissons. During the battle Chararic held off, awaiting the result of
the struggle. In spite of this defection Clovis was victorious, and
Syagrius had to take refuge with the king of the Visigoths. Alaric II,
who had succeeded Euric. Alaric however surrendered him, on the first
demand of the Frankish king, who thereupon threw him into prison
and had him secretly put to death. After this victory Clovis occupied
the town of Soissons, which thenceforth ranked as one of the capitals of
the kingdom. It is in the neighbourhood of Soissons that we find the
principal *villae* of the Merovingian kings, notably Brennacum (to-day
Berny-Rivière). From Soissons he extended his sway over the cities of
Belgica Secunda of which Rheims is the metropolis, and he entered into

relations with Remi (Remigius), the bishop of this city. Then, gradually, meeting with more or less prolonged resistance, he gained possession of other cities, among them Paris—the defence of which was directed, so the legend runs, by Ste Geneviève—and Verdun-sur-Meuse, which is said to have received honourable terms, thanks to its bishop, Euspicius. Thus, little by little, the dominions of Clovis were extended to the banks of the Loire. In this newly conquered territory Clovis followed a new policy. In occupying Toxandria the Salians had expelled the Gallo-Roman population; here, on the contrary, they left the Gallo-Romans undisturbed and were content to mix with them. The ancient language held its ground, and the Gallo-Romans retained their possessions; there was not even a division of the lands, such as the Visigoths and Burgundians had made. Clovis was no doubt still a pagan, but he respected the Christian religion and shewed an extraordinary deference towards the bishops—that is the only conclusion that can be drawn from the well-known incident of the bowl of Soissons—and the prelates already seemed to see before them a glorious work to be accomplished in the conversion of Clovis to orthodox Christianity.

Not content with bringing the Gallo-Romans under his sway, Clovis waged war also with the barbarian peoples in the neighbourhood of his kingdom. In the year 491 he forced the Thuringians on the left bank of the Rhine to submit to him, and enrolled their warriors among his own troops. He also invited other barbarian auxiliaries to march under his standards—Procopius calls them Ἀρβόρυχοι—as well as the Roman soldiers who had been placed to guard the frontier, and in this way he formed a very strong army.

The fame of Clovis began to spread abroad. Theodoric, king of the Ostrogoths, who had almost completed the conquest of Italy, asked the hand of his sister Albofleda in marriage, and Clovis himself, in 493, espoused a Burgundian princess, Clotilda, daughter of Chilperic, who had died not long before, and niece of the kings Gundobad and Godigisel.

Clotilda was an orthodox Christian and set herself to convert her husband—it would be possible to trace the influence of women in many of those great conversions which have had important political consequences. Half won-over, the king of the Franks allowed his children to be baptised, but he hesitated to abjure for himself the faith of his ancestors. He did not make up his mind until after his first victory over the Alemans.

After his victory at Soissons, Clovis pushed his advance towards the east. The Alemans, already in possession of Alsace, were endeavouring to extend their territories towards the west, across the Vosges. It was inevitable that the two powers should come into collision. The struggle was severe. Clovis succeeded in crossing the Vosges, and, on the banks of the Rhine, probably in the neighbourhood of Strassburg, he defeated his adversaries in a bloody battle (A.D. 496), but was unable to reduce them to subjection. He began to perceive at this time what strength he would gain by embracing Christianity. The bishops, who exercised a very powerful influence, would everywhere declare for him, and would support him in his struggles with the heathen tribes, and even against the barbarians who adhered to the Arian heresy. His wars would then assume the character of wars of religion—crusades, to use the term of later times. It was doubtless from such considerations of policy, rather than from any profound conviction, that he decided to be baptised. The ceremony, to which numerous persons of note were invited, took place at Rheims, whatever some modern historians may say to the contrary. It was celebrated on Christmas day of the year 496. Three thousand Franks went to the font along with their king. This conversion produced a profound and widespread impression. Throughout the whole of Gaul, in the kingdom of the Burgundians as well as that of the Visigoths, orthodox Christians spoke of it with enthusiasm. Avitus, bishop of Vienne, a subject of King Gundobad, wrote to Clovis, king of the Franks: "Your ancestors have opened the way for you to a great destiny; your decision will open the way to a yet greater for your descendants. Your faith is our victory." And he urged him in emphatic language to propagate Catholicism among the barbarian peoples in more distant lands, "which have not yet been corrupted by heretical doctrines." It was quite evident that if the Catholics of the Burgundian and Visigothic kingdoms did not precisely summon Clovis to their aid, they would at least not resist him if he came of his own motion.

Accordingly, four years after his baptism, in the year 500, Clovis commenced operations against the Burgundians. Coming to an understanding with Godigisel, he made war on Gundobad, king of Vienne. He first defeated him near Dijon, and then advanced along the Rhone as far as Avignon. But that was the limit of his success. On Gundobad's promising to pay tribute, Clovis retired. Gundobad, however, not only broke his word, but attacked his brother Godigisel, slew him in a church in Vienne and made himself master of the whole of Burgundy. Thus the attack of Clovis had the consequence of making Gundobad stronger than before. From the year 500 onwards Burgundy enjoyed a period of prosperity. It was at this period that the so-called *Lex Gundobada* and the Roman law of Burgundy were promulgated. Clovis, not being able to subdue Gundobad, notwithstanding the secret support of the orthodox clergy, came to terms with him, and later found him a useful ally in the war with the Visigoths.

If Clovis did not push home his success against the Burgundians, it was doubtless because his own kingdom was menaced by the Alemans. About this time, therefore, he decided to expel that nation from the territories which they occupied; and from 505 to 507 he waged against them a war of extermination. He not only seized the country afterwards known as Alsace, but pursued the Alemans up the right bank of the Rhine and drove them to take refuge in the valley of the upper Rhine (Rhaetia). At this point Theodoric the Great, the king of the Ostrogoths, intervened in favour of the vanquished. Theodoric desired to exercise a kind of hegemony over the barbarian kings and with that view to maintain the balance of power among them. He wrote an eloquent letter to Clovis, in which, while sending him a player on the cither, he begged him to spare the remnant of the Alemans, and declared that he took them under his protection. The Alemans, who were now occupying the high valleys of the Alps, thus passed under the dominion of Theodoric, and paid tribute to him. They formed a kind of buffer-State between the kingdoms of the Franks and the Ostrogoths. We shall see how Witigis, a successor of Theodoric, gave up these remnants of the Alemans to the Franks (536).

As early as 507 Clovis was bending all his energies to the project of wresting from the Visigoths the part of Gaul which they held. The orthodox bishops were now tired of being subject to Arian rulers, and besought the aid of the king of the Franks. Alaric II, who had succeeded Euric in 486, was undoubtedly a tolerant ruler. He gave to the Romans of his dominions an important code of law which is known by the name of the *Breviarium Alarici*; and he allowed the bishops more than once to meet in councils. But being obliged to take severe measures against certain bishops, he was counted a persecutor. Thus, two successive bishops of Tours, Volusianus and Verus, were driven from that see, Ruricius of Limoges was obliged to live in exile at Bordeaux; and all these bickerings made the bishops long for an orthodox ruler. Causes of contention between Franks and Visigoths were not lacking. One difficulty after another arose between the two neighbouring kingdoms. In vain the kings endeavoured to remove them, meeting for this purpose on an island in the Loire near Amboise; in vain Theodoric the Great wrote urging the adversaries to compose their quarrel. He advised Alaric to be prudent and not to stake the fate of his kingdom upon a throw of the dice. He reminded Clovis that the issue of a battle was always uncertain, and threatened to intervene himself if the king of the Franks proceeded to extremities. He invited Gundobad the king of the Burgundians to co-operate with him in maintaining peace. He warned three kings who held the right bank of the Rhine— the kings of the Herulians, the Warnians and the Thuringians—of the ambitions of Clovis. It was too late; the war could not be averted. Beyond question, Clovis was the aggressor. He mustered his troops and made a vigorous speech to them. "It grieves me that these Arians should hold a part of Gaul. Let us march, with the help of God, and reduce their country to subjection." He had with him Chloderic, son of Sigebert, king of the Ripuarian Franks, while Gundobad king of the Burgundians co-operated by advancing upon the

Visigoths from the east. The decisive battle took place at Vouglé, in the neighbourhood of Poitiers (A.D. 507). The Visigoths made a heroic resistance, in which the Arvernians, led by Apollinaris the son of the poet Sidonius, especially distinguished themselves. But the Franks broke down all resistance, and Clovis slew Alaric with his own hand.

After the battle the Salians effected a junction with the Burgundians, and the combined forces advanced on Toulouse and burned that city. Then the conquerors divided their troops into three armies. Clovis subjugated the western part of the country, capturing Eauze, Bazas, Bordeaux and Angoulême; his son Theodoric (Thierry) operated in the central region, and took the cities of Albi, Rodez and Auvergne; Gundobad advanced towards the east, into Septimania, where a bastard son of Alaric II named Gisalic had just had himself proclaimed king, ousting the legitimate son, Amalaric. Soon there remained to the Visigoths, to the north of the Pyrenees, nothing but Provence, with its capital Arles, formerly the residence of the Praetorian Praefect and known as the "little Rome of Gaul" (*Gallula Roma*). The Franks and Burgundians had laid siege to this city when the army of the Ostrogoths came upon the scene. Theodoric had been unable to intervene earlier, for at the beginning of 508 a Byzantine fleet, perhaps at the instigation of Clovis, had landed a force on the shores of Apulia, and the king of the Ostrogoths had had to turn his attention thither. At length, in the summer, he sent an army across the Alps, and its arrival forced the Franks and Burgundians to raise the siege of Arles. His troops occupied the whole of Provence, but instead of restoring this territory to the Visigoths, the Ostrogoths kept it for themselves. Theodoric sent officials to the cities of Provence with orders to treat in a conciliatory fashion this people which had been "restored to the bosom of the Roman Empire." The Ostrogoths did not however content themselves with this success. Their general Ibbas retook Septimania from the Franks and Burgundians, capturing Narbonne, Carcassonne and Nîmes. He left this territory, however, under the rule of Amalaric and rid him of his rival Gisalic. Communication was thus established along the coast of the Mediterranean between the kingdoms of the Ostrogoths and Visigoths.

Nevertheless Clovis gained considerable advantage from the war. If Septimania had eluded his grasp, he had extended his kingdom from the Loire to the Pyrenees. Gundobad alone obtained no profit from the struggle.

Clovis treated with clemency the Gallo-Roman populations whom he had just brought under his dominion. He ordered all clergy, widows, and serfs of the Church, who had been made prisoners by his troops during the campaign, to be set at liberty. There was no new distribution of lands. The Arians, indeed, were required to embrace the orthodox faith, but even their conversion was effected rather by persuasion

than by force. The Arian clergy were allowed to resume their rank
in the hierarchy after a reconciliation by laying on of hands. Their
churches were not destroyed, but after reconsecration were made over to
the use of the orthodox.

On his way back from the war, Clovis in 508 visited the town of
Tours, where he made large gifts to the monastery of St Martin. At
Tours he received from the Emperor of the East, Anastasius, the patent
of consular rank. He was not entitled consul, and his name would be
sought in vain in the consular records; he was an honorary consul,
tanquam consul, as Gregory of Tours quite accurately expresses it.
He at once assumed the insignia of the consulship, with the purple
tunic and mantle of the same colour, and, starting from the church of
St Martin, he made a solemn entry into the town of Tours, and
proceeded to the cathedral of St Gatien, scattering largess as he went.
Clovis was evidently proud of this new honour, which was a proof of
the Emperor's friendship—perhaps he had come to an agreement with
the Emperor directed against Theodoric—but his investiture with the
consulship gave him no new authority. His rights were those of
conquest; they were not dependent on the sanction of the Emperor,
and he continued to govern the Gallo-Romans after 508 as he had
governed them before it. If he wore the Roman insignia at his entry
into Tours, he continued to wear also the crown characteristic of
barbarian kings, and along with the title of honorary consul—translated
in a prologue to the Salic law by Proconsul—he assumed that of
Augustus.

From Tours, Clovis proceeded to Paris where he now established the
seat of his government. The town was admirably situated, lying on an
island in the Seine, at a point about the middle of its course, and not
far from the points at which it receives its two great confluents, the
Marne and the Oise; well placed also for communication with the
northern plain, and with the south of France by way of the Gap of
Poitou. Already the town had overflowed to the left bank, and there
Clovis built a basilica dedicated to the Holy Apostles. This was later
the church of Ste Geneviève, close to what is now the Panthéon. In the
neighbourhood of Paris there sprang up a number of royal *villae*,
Clichy, Rueil, Nogent-sur-Marne, Bonneuil.

Clovis had won great victories; but there were still some Salian
tribes which were ruled over by their own kings, and round about
Cologne lay the kingdom of the Ripuarian Franks. By a series
of assassinations Clovis got rid of the Salian kings, Chararic
and Ragnachar, and the two brothers of the latter, Richar and
Rignomer—the former killed near Mans—and took possession of their
territories. The details which have come down to us of the assassination
of these petty kings are legendary, but that they were murdered would
appear to be the fact. There remained the kingdom of the Ripuarians.

Clovis stirred up Chloderic against his father Sigebert the Lame and then presented himself to the Ripuarians in the character of the avenger of Sigebert. The Ripuarians hailed him with acclamations and accepted him as their king: "Thus day by day God brought low his enemies before him, so that they submitted to him, and increased his kingdom, because he walked before Him with an upright heart and did that which was pleasing in His sight." Such is the singular reflection which closes the narrative of all these murders. Gregory of Tours reproduces it, borrowing it from some traditional source, and the bishop does not seem to have been conscious how singular it was[1].

Clovis died in the year 511, after holding at Orleans a council at which a great number of the bishops of his kingdom were assembled. He had accomplished a really great work. He had conquered nearly the whole of Gaul, excepting the kingdom of Burgundy, Provence and Septimania. By subjugating the Alemans he had extended his authority even to the other side of the Rhine. He had governed this kingdom wisely, relying chiefly on the episcopate for support. He had codified the customary law of the Salian Franks—it is from his reign, between the years 508 and 511, that the first redaction of the Salic law is in all probability to be dated. He may be called with justice the founder of the French nation.

The Merovingians regarded the kingdom as a family inheritance, the sons dividing their father's dominions into portions as nearly equal as possible. This was now done by the sons of Clovis, Theodoric (Thierry), Clodomir, Childebert and Chlotar. Each of them took a share of their father's original kingdom to the north of the Loire, and another share from among his more recent conquests to the south of that river. As their capitals, they chose respectively Rheims, Orleans, Paris and Soissons. Each of the four brothers, urged by covetousness, sought to increase his portion at the expense of his neighbour, and they carried on a contest of intrigue and chicanery. On the death of Clodomir in 524, Childebert and Chlotar murdered his children in order to divide his kingdom between themselves. Two other families were also doomed to extinction. Theodoric died in 534, leaving a very able son Theudibert, the most remarkable among the kings of that period, but he died in 548, and his young son Theodebald fell a victim to precocious debauchery in 555. Childebert died in 558 and of all the descendants of Clovis there now remained only Chlotar I. He fell heir to the whole of the Merovingian dominions, and his power was apparently very great. His son Chramnus rebelled against him and fled to Chonober, count of Brittany, but the father mustered his forces and defeated

---

[1] Greg. Tur. II. 40: Prosternebat *enim* cotidie Deus hostes ejus sub manu ipsius. Loebell, Giesebrecht and others take *enim* in the sense of *but,* as is not uncommon in Gregory. In this case the writer will be marking his disapproval of the murders. God prospered the orthodox king notwithstanding his crimes.

him—"like another Absalom," says Gregory of Tours. Chlotar had him shut up in a hut with his wife and children, and caused it to be set on fire. Afterwards, however, he was overwhelmed with remorse. In vain he sought peace for his soul at the tomb of St Martin of Tours. Struck down by disease he died at his palace of Compiègne, his last words being: "What think ye of the King of Heaven who thus overthrows the kings of earth?" His surviving sons buried him with great pomp in the basilica of St Médard at Soissons (561).

In spite of the fact that during the greater part of this period the kingdom was divided into four parts, it was still regarded as a unity: there was only one Frankish kingdom, *regnum Francorum.* The sons of Clovis had a common task to accomplish in the carrying on of their father's work and the completion of the conquest of Gaul. In this they did not fail. Clovis' expedition against the Burgundians in 500 had miscarried; his sons subjugated that kingdom. Sigismund the son of Gundobad had been converted to the orthodox faith; he restored the great monastery of Agaunum in the Valais, on the spot where St Maurice and his comrades of the Theban legion were slain. He reformed the Church at the great Council of Epaône in 517, where very severe measures were adopted against the Arian heresy. But it was now too late. Sigismund failed to win over the orthodox and he provoked a lively discontent among the Burgundian warriors. The sons of Clovis were not slow to profit by this. Clodomir, Childebert and Chlotar invaded Burgundy in 523, defeated Sigismund in a pitched battle and took him prisoner. He was handed over, with his wife and children, to Clodomir, who had them thrown into a well at St Péravy-la-Colombe near Orleans. And while the Franks were invading the kingdom of Burgundy from the north, Theodoric king of the Ostrogoths, resenting Sigismund's zeal against Arianism, had sent troops from Provence and captured several strong-places to the north of the Durance. Avignon, Cavaillon, Carpentras, Orange and Vaison. Burgundy however regained some strength under the rule of a brother of Sigismund named Godomar, who defeated and slew Clodomir on 25 June 524, at Vézéronce near Vienne. He endeavoured to re-establish some order in his dominions at the assembly of Ambérieux, and his kingdom was thus enabled to prolong its existence until the year 534. At that date Childebert, Chlotar and Theudibert seized Burgundy and divided it between them, each one taking a portion of the country and adding it to his dominions. The kingdom of the Burgundians had existed for nearly a century, not without a certain brilliance. A great legislative work had been accomplished, and among them we find a historian in Marius of Aventicum and a poet in Avitus, whom Milton was to recall in his *Paradise Lost*[1]. For long Burgundy formed

[1] Guizot in his *Histoire de la Civilisation en France*, Vol. II. lect. xviii., cites some parallels tending to shew that Milton was acquainted with the poem of Avitus on

a separate division of the Frankish kingdom, and perhaps even to-day it is possible to recognise among the dwellers on the banks of the Saône and the Rhone certain moral and physical characteristics of the ancient Burgundians seven and a half feet in height, hard-workers but loving pleasure and good wine, and fond of letting their tongues run freely and without reserve.

The sons of Clovis also annexed Provence and the cities to the north of the Durance which the Ostrogoths had occupied. Witigis, who was defending himself with difficulty against the Byzantines, offered them these territories as the price of their neutrality, if they would refrain from siding with Justinian. The Frankish kings divided up Provence (536) as they had divided up Burgundy. They were now masters of the ancient Phocaean colony of Marseilles, with the whole coast-line; at Arles, the old Roman capital of Gaul, they presided over the games in the amphitheatre. Along with Provence, Witigis transferred to the Franks the suzerainty over the Alemans who in 506 had taken refuge in Rhaetia. From this time forward the Franks were masters of the whole of ancient Gaul, with the exception of Septimania which continued to be held by the Visigoths. Time after time did the sons of Clovis attempt to wrest this country from them, but all their expeditions failed for one reason or another. Septimania continued to be united to Spain and shared the fortunes of that country, passing along with it under the domination of the Arabs. It was not until the reign of Pepin that this fair region was incorporated with France.

But if the kingdom of the Franks had on the whole been greatly extended, in one quarter the limits of their dominion had been curtailed. In the course of the sixth century some of the Kelts, driven out of Great Britain by the Anglo-Saxon invasions, themselves invaded the Armorican peninsula, which like the rest of Gaul had been completely Romanised. "They embarked with loud lamentations, and, as the wind swelled their sails, they cried with the Psalmist 'Lord, Thou hast delivered us like sheep to the slaughter, and hast scattered us among the nations.'" Arriving in small separate companies they gained a foothold at the western extremity of the peninsula. Gradually establishing themselves among the original population, before long they ousted it, pushing it further towards the east. The aspect of the Armorican peninsula underwent a rapid change; it lost its earlier name and became known as Brittany, after its new inhabitants. In the western districts the Romanic language disappeared entirely and Keltic took its place; and special saints with unfamiliar names were there held in honour, St Brieuc, St Tutwal, St Malo, St Judicaël. The Britons were divided into three groups, of which each one had its own chief; round about Vannes was

the early ages of the world, of which the first three books, *De Origine Mundi*, *De Peccato Originali* and *De Sententia Dei*, form, as he says, a kind of *Paradise Lost*.

the Bro-Waroch, so called from the name of one of the chiefs; the group of Cornovii, coming from Cornwall, established itself in the west; to the north, from Brest harbour to the river Couesnon extended the Domnonée, the inhabitants of which were natives of Devon. No doubt these various chiefs recognised in theory the suzerainty of the Frankish kings, but they were not appointed by the latter, and were in fact independent. The western extremity of France, the ancient Armorica, was thus separate from the rest of the country; and similarly, between the Gironde and the Pyrenees, the Basques, who belonged to a distinct race and spoke a peculiar dialect, maintained their independence under the rule of their dukes.

Such was the state of the Frankish kingdom proper; but, under the sons of Clovis, Frankish influence extended even over the neighbouring countries. They came in contact with various Germanic peoples and imposed their suzerainty on some of them. Clovis himself had subjugated the Alemans; Theodebald his great-grandson entered into relations with the Bavarians beyond the Lech. Theodoric (Thierry) and Chlotar made war on the Thuringians and destroyed their independence (531). It was from Thuringia that Chlotar took his wife, Radegund, who left him in order to found the famous convent of Ste Croix, at Poitiers. Chlotar even made war upon the Saxons, who inhabited the great plain of northern Germany, and imposed upon them a yearly tribute of 500 cows. Spain and Italy, too, witnessed the warlike exploits of these Frankish princes. From an expedition against Saragossa in 542 Childebert brought back the tunic of St Vincent, and in honour of this relic he founded at the gates of Paris the monastery of St Vincent, later known as St Germain-des-Près. Theudibert made several incursions into Italy. Sometimes posing as a friend of the Ostrogoths, at others as a friend of the Byzantines, he plundered some of the wealthy cities and amassed large spoils. He even made himself master for a time of Liguria, Emilia and Venetia, and had coins minted at Bologna. Indignant because the Emperor added to his titles that of *Francicus*, he even thought of penetrating by way of the valley of the Danube into Thrace, and of appearing in arms before Constantinople. He addressed to Justinian a haughty letter, which has come down to us. So far these sons of Clovis still bear themselves like kings. They had achieved the conquest of Gaul up to the frontiers assigned by nature to that country; they had also turned their arms against Germany, the country of their origin, and had opened up in that direction the pathway of civilisation. Like the ancient Gauls whom they supplanted, they had descended upon Italy, where their incursions created widespread consternation.

To all this the epoch of the grandsons of Clovis presents a striking contrast. The vigorous expansion of the Franks was checked. They failed to wrest Septimania from the Visigoths and make Gaul a united whole. No doubt they made several expeditions against the Lombards of Italy, but these were merely plundering-raids; there were no further conquests. The Merovingians began to turn their warlike ardour against each other; there follows a miserable period of civil war.

Of the four sons of Chlotar I—Charibert, Guntram, Sigebert and Chilperic—who divided their father's kingdom in 561, Charibert the king of Paris early disappeared from the scene, dying in 567. Sigebert king of Metz and Chilperic king of Soissons were bitterly jealous of one another, each constantly endeavouring to filch some fragment of the other's territory. Between these two Guntram king of Orleans and Burgundy adopted a waiting attitude, in order to maintain the balance of power, and giving his aid at the opportune moment to the weaker side to prevent it from being crushed. The rivalry of the two brothers was intensified by that of their wives, which gives to these struggles a peculiarly ruthless character. Sigebert, whose morals were more respectable than those of his brothers, had sent an embassy to Toledo to the king of the Visigoths, Athanagild, to ask the hand of his daughter Brunhild (Brunehaut) in marriage. Brunhild renounced Arianism, professed the Trinitarian faith, and brought to her husband a very large dowry. The marriage was celebrated at Metz with great magnificence. The young poet Fortunatus also, who had just left his home at Treviso, indited an epithalamium in grandiloquent lines into which he dragged all the divinities of Olympus. The new queen was perhaps the only person present who understood these eulogies, for she had been brilliantly educated and spoke Latin excellently. At the half-barbarous court of Sigebert she made a profound impression. The news of this marriage fired Chilperic with envy. He had espoused a somewhat insignificant woman named Audovera, and had afterwards repudiated her in order to live in low debauchery with a serving-woman named Fredegund. But after the marriage of Sigebert, he asked of Athanagild the hand of the latter's eldest daughter, Galswintha. The king of the Visigoths did not dare to refuse. Galswintha came to Soissons, and at first her husband loved her much " because she had brought great treasures." Before long however he went back to his mistress, and one morning Galswintha was found strangled in her bed. Very shortly afterwards the king married Fredegund, and ordered the execution of his first wife Audovera. In this way arose a bitter quarrel between Fredegund and Brunhild, the latter burning to avenge her sister; and it may well be conceived that a peculiarly vindictive and relentless character was thus imparted to the civil war. Almost at the beginning of the struggle Sigebert met his death. He had defeated Chilperic, had conquered the greater part of his kingdom and compelled him to shut himself up in Tournai; he was about to be raised on the shield and proclaimed king at Vitry not far from Arras, when two slaves sent by Fredegund struck him down with poisoned daggers (*scramasaxi*) (575).

The actors left upon the scene, from that time forward, were Chilperic who was now to get back his kingdom, and Brunhild who, after being held prisoner for a time, succeeded after the most romantic adventures in escaping from Rouen and reaching Austrasia, where her son, Childebert II (still a child), had been proclaimed king.

Chilperic is the very type of a Merovingian despot. He had two dominant passions, ambition and greed of gold. He desired to extend his kingdom, he wished to accumulate treasure. He ground down his people with taxes and caused a new assessment to be made. Many of his subjects refused to submit to this increase of taxation, preferring to leave the country and seek an easier life elsewhere. In his capacity as judge he imposed especially heavy fines upon the rich as a means of confiscating their property. He was envious of the great possessions of the Church, complaining that "Our treasury is empty, all our wealth has passed over to the churches; the bishops alone reign, our power is gone, it has been transferred to the bishops of the cities." He therefore pronounced void all wills made in favour of the churches, he even revoked the gifts which his father had left to them. He sold the bishoprics to the highest bidder, and in his reign very few of the clergy attained to the episcopate; rich laymen purchased the priestly office and passed in one day through the various grades of orders. He was at once avaricious and debauched, gourmand and cruel. He delighted in low amours and he made a god of his belly. At the foot of his edicts he inscribes this formula: "Whosoever sets at nought our order shall have his eyes put out."

But with all this he was a man of original ideas. He desired that, contrary to the strict provisions of the Salic law, women should in certain cases be allowed to inherit land. He was no less ready to attack religious dogma than ancient custom. He did not believe that it is necessary to distinguish three Persons in God; he scoffed at the anthropomorphic designations, the Father and the Son, as applied to the Deity. He issued an edict forbidding the Trinity to be named in prayer—the name God was alone to be used. Orthography as well as dogma must bow to his decree. He added to the alphabet four letters, borrowed from the Greek, to represent the long *o*, the "voiceless" *th*, the *œ* and the *w*. It was not the Germanic sounds which he wished to represent more exactly: Chilperic despised the Germanic tongue, and his reform was intended to apply to the Latin. He directed that children were to be taught by the new methods; in ancient manuscripts the writing was to be erased and reinserted with the additional letters. This barbarian king was a devoted admirer of the Roman civilisation; he composed poems in the manner of Sedulius, and wrote hymns which he also set to music. His scepticism regarding the Trinity did not prevent him from being superstitious: he believed in portents, in relics, in sorcerers. He fancied himself able to outwit the Deity. Having sworn, for instance, not to enter Paris without the consent of his brothers, he broke the compact, but to avert misfortune he had a number of the bones of various saints carried in front of his troops. He was a fantastical and violent man, of a strange and complex character; and it is no very flagrant calumny when Gregory of Tours calls him the Nero and the Herod of his time. From all these characteristics it can well be imagined that the struggle which he carried on against Brunhild and her son was fierce and merciless.

He wrested from them a number of towns, among them Poitiers and Tours, and it was thus that Gregory became, to his intense disgust, the subject of this debauched monarch, with whom he was constantly at odds. It may well be supposed that Chilperic had stirred up much wrath and many enmities and it is not surprising that he died by violence. One day as he was returning from Chelles where he had been hunting, a man came close to him and stabbed him twice with a dagger (584). Who his assassin actually was, remained unknown.

While Chilperic succeeded in imposing his authority upon the western Franks in the territories which formed the most recent Frankish conquests—known a little later as Neustria, from the word *niust* "the newest"—Brunhild made strenuous efforts to preserve intact all the prerogatives of the royal power in the eastern region, Austrasia. Exceedingly ambitious, eager to secure her authority by every possible means, it was she who in the name of her son Childebert II (575–596) actually held the reins of power. The great men of the kingdom threw themselves into an embittered struggle against her. Supported by Chilperic and Neustria they refused to give obedience to a woman and a foreigner. Ursio, Bertefried, Guntram-Boso and duke Rauching placed themselves at their head and attacked the adherents of the royal house, chief among whom was Lupus of Champagne. Brunhild tried in vain to separate the combatants; the rebels answered brutally, "Woman, get you gone, let it suffice you to have ruled during your husband's life-time; now it is your son who reigns and it is not under your protection but under ours that the kingdom is placed. Get you hence, or we shall trample you under the hoofs of our horses." By vigorous action, however, the queen succeeded in re-establishing order. She formed an alliance with Guntram king of Burgundy, who at Pompierre adopted his nephew Childebert and recognised him as his heir (577). The pact was renewed ten years later at Andelot (28 November 587). Brunhild got rid of the most turbulent of her nobles by the aid of the assassin's knife; and she suppressed the revolt of Gundobald, a bastard son of Chlotar I, whom the nobles had brought back from Constantinople to set up in opposition to Guntram and Childebert. Besieged in the little town of Comminges situated in a valley of the Pyrenees, Gundobald was forced to surrender, and a Frankish count dashed out his brains with a great stone (585). Finally Brunhild besieged Ursio and Bertefried in a strong castle in Woëvre. The former perished in the flames of the burning castle; the latter took refuge at Verdun in the chapel of the bishop Agericus, but the soldiers tore up the roofing and killed him with the tiles (587). Thus, thanks to the inflexible determination of Brunhild, the Austrasian aristocracy was vanquished. The queen also succeeded in baffling all the plots devised against her and Childebert II by Fredegund, who since 584 had governed Neustria in the name of her infant son Chlotar II. She succeeded so well that when Guntram died on 28 March 593, Childebert was able to enter upon his heritage without the slightest opposition. And when Childebert in turn was carried off by disease while still young, Brunhild's authority was uncontested. Childebert's two sons Theodebert and Theodoric divided his kingdom between them, the former taking Austrasia, and the latter, Burgundy. In reality their grandmother Brunhild continued to rule in their name. Her authority extended over both Austrasia and Burgundy and she imposed the same measures upon both countries. The aristocracy, lay and ecclesiastical, were obliged to conform to her laws. Regarding the royal authority as a trust on behalf of her grandsons, she was determined on leaving it to them intact. She had the satisfaction of seeing her rival Fredegund die in 597; and her grandsons on several occasions defeated Chlotar II, who lost the greater part of his territories.

But the great nobles of Austrasia rose in wrath against her, and Theodebert himself repudiated her tutelage. The incensed Brunhild withdrew to Burgundy, where she continued to rule. There she broke down all resistance, had the patrician Egila put to death, exiled Didier, bishop of Vienne, nominated her followers to every post of emolument, and levied the taxes with the utmost rigour. But she knew that the Burgundian rebels were encouraged by those of Austrasia. It was in Austrasia that she must strike the decisive blow, and in her thirst for power she did not hesitate to set Theodoric against Theodebert and so to provoke a fratricidal struggle. The king of Austrasia was defeated on the banks of the Moselle, in the neighbourhood of Toul, taken to Zülpich and there put to death. Brunhild was now triumphant, but just in the moment of her triumph her grandson Theodoric died (613) in his palace of Metz, at the age of twenty-seven. Breaking with the Merovingian tradition of dividing the kingdom, Brunhild caused the eldest son to be declared sole king, in the hope of reigning in his name. But all the living forces of Austrasia banded themselves together to oppose her ambition. Arnulf, bishop of Metz, and Pepin, the two founders of the Carolingian family, appealed to Chlotar II the son of Fredegund. Brunhild made a magnificent effort to stand up against the storm, but she found herself deserted on all hands, and was taken prisoner on the shores of the Lake of Neuchâtel. Her great-grandsons were killed, or at any rate disappear from history. Brunhild herself was tortured for three days, set upon a camel as a mark of derision, and then tied by her hair, one arm, and one foot, to the tail of a vicious horse, which was then lashed to fury.

CH. IV.

Brunhild is undoubtedly the most forceful figure of this period, and it would be a gross injustice to put her on the same footing with Fredegund. It is true she was exceedingly ambitious and eager for power, but she attempted by means of this power to carry out a policy. She upheld with unrivalled energy the rights of the king against the aristocracy. She treated the Church with firmness but with respect, made gifts to the bishoprics and built a number of abbeys. She entered into relations with Pope Gregory the Great (590–604) who addressed to her a large number of letters, sent her relics, and requested her to take under her protection the estates of the Church of Rome which lay in Gaul. He urged her to reform the Frankish Church, to call councils and to protect Augustine and his companions who were going across the Channel to carry the Gospel to the pagan Anglo-Saxons. But while maintaining these relations Brunhild knew how to control the Frankish Church, as she did the lay aristocracy. She disposed of the episcopal sees at her pleasure, and expelled from his monastery of Luxeuil the abbot Columbanus who had refused to obey her orders. In short in all her conduct Brunhild displayed the qualities of a great statesman.

After Brunhild's death Chlotar II found himself, as Clovis had done before him, sole master of the whole of Gaul. But how different are the two periods! Clovis had been strong in his recent victories, victories due to his own courage and political ability. Chlotar II owed his success not to himself but to the treason of the Austrasian and Burgundian nobles, whom he was consequently obliged to conciliate. In his constitution of 18 October 614, as well as in a *praeceptio* of which the date is unknown, he had to make large concessions to the aristocracy. He proclaimed, under certain restrictions, freedom of episcopal elections, extended the competence of the ecclesiastical courts, and promised to respect wills made by private persons in favour of the Church. He suppressed unjust taxes and pledged himself to choose the counts from the districts they were to administer, which was equivalent to making over this important office to the landed aristocracy. Moreover Chlotar was forced to accord a measure of independence to Austrasia and Burgundy; each of these countries had its own Mayor of the Palace, who was as much the representative of the interests of the local nobles as of those of the king. In 623 he was even obliged to give the Austrasians a king in his young son Dagobert. In the latter's name, Arnulf, bishop of Metz, and Pepin, the Mayor of the Palace, exercised the actual authority. Thus ancient Gaul became once more distinctly divided into three kingdoms: Neustria, Burgundy and Austrasia, having each a distinct character and a separate administration. Already within these kingdoms the local officials, strong in the possession of vast estates, were endeavouring to usurp the royal prerogatives: already these three kingdoms were being parcelled out into seigniories.

Chlotar II's son Dagobert (629–639), however, was still a king in
something more than name.   Although he had a brother Charibert he
succeeded in reigning alone over the whole Frankish kingdom.   He even
subjected it to the authority of a single Mayor of the Palace, by name
Aega.   He made royal progresses through Austrasia, through Neustria
and through Burgundy, sitting in judgment each day, and doing strict
justice without respect of persons.   In Aquitaine he left to his brother
Charibert the administration of the counties of Toulouse, Cahors, Agen,
Périgueux and Saintes, thus making him a kind of warden of the marches
on the Basque frontier.   But on the death of Charibert in 632, he took
over the government of this district also—and up to about 670 Aquitaine
remained under the rule of the Frankish kings.   After that date it
broke away, and the local nobles founded independent dynasties.

Dagobert caused many estates which had been usurped by the
seigniors and the Church to be restored to the royal domain.   He kept
up a luxurious court, which gave, it must be said, anything but a good
example in regard to morals.   He was a patron of the arts and took
great delight in the rich examples of goldsmith's work produced by his
treasurer Eligius (Eloi), whom he afterwards appointed bishop of Noyon.
Many abbeys were founded in his reign.   There was a revival of missionary
activity, too, and St Amandus preached the Gospel to the Basques in
the south and to the inhabitants of Flanders and Hainault in the north.
Throughout the whole of the kingdom the royal authority was paramount.   The duke of the Basques came to court to swear allegiance,
and Judicaël, chief of the Domnonée, was seen at the royal residence at
Clichy.   Dagobert intervened not unsuccessfully in the affairs of the
Visigoths in Spain, and in those of the Lombards in Italy.   He had
also relations with the Empire of Constantinople, taking an oath of
perpetual peace with Heraclius in 631; and the two rulers took
concerted action against the Bulgarian and Slavonic tribes who raided
by turns the Byzantine Empire and the regions of Germany which were
under the suzerainty of the Franks.   Towards the close of his life,
in 634, Dagobert was obliged to give to the Austrasians a king of their
own in the person of his eldest son Sigebert.   Ansegis, son of Arnulf
and of a daughter of Pepin, was appointed Mayor of the Palace and
governed in the name of this child in conjunction with Cunibert, bishop
of Cologne.   In spite of this, when Dagobert died (19 January 639),
in his *villa* at Épinay, men held him to have been a very great prince.
And his fame was to grow still greater owing to the contrast between
his reign and the period which followed it.

This new period, which extends from 639 to 751, is marked by the
lamentable decadence of the Merovingian race.   It is with justice that
the sovereigns who then reigned are known as the *rois fainéants*.   It
was a dynasty of children; they died at the age of 23, 24 or 25, worn
out by precocious debauchery.   They were fathers at sixteen, fifteen and

even at fourteen years, and their children were miserable weaklings. As kings they had only the semblance of power; they remained shut up in their *villae* surrounded by great luxury. Only at long intervals did they go forth, in chariots drawn by oxen. The real authority was thenceforth exercised by the Mayor of the Palace, or by the different mayors who were at the head of the three kingdoms, Neustria, Burgundy and Austrasia, whose separateness became more clearly marked. The mayors made and unmade the kings as interest or caprice prompted; sometimes they exiled them, only to recall them later. Apocryphal Merovingians were often produced who had no connexion with the sacred race. It is useless to make any further reference to these sovereigns, who were nothing but shadows and whose names serve only to date charters. The historian must direct his attention exclusively to the Mayors of the Palace.

Among these mayors the most distinguished were those of Austrasia. They were to make the office hereditary in their family and to found a powerful dynasty which was destined gradually to supplant the Merovingians. The two founders of that dynasty were, as has already been said, Arnulf, bishop of Metz, and Pepin, who had been Mayor of the Palace to the youthful Dagobert when the latter was king of Austrasia only. Both were men of distinguished piety. Arnulf ruled the city of Metz wisely and effected important reforms in the Church. Pepin destined his daughters for the cloister; one of them, Gertrude, founded the abbey of Nivelle in the district now known as Brabant. In this neighbourhood is situated the estate of Landen; whence the designation " of Landen" by which Pepin is distinguished in later documents. Arnulf's son Ansegis, who was Mayor of the Palace to the young Sigebert, married a daughter of Pepin whom the chronicles later call Begga; of this marriage was born the second Pepin, known to historians as Pepin of Heristal.

At first however it seemed probable that the chief representative of the family would be Pepin of Landen's own son Grimoald. For thirteen years, from 643 to 656, he held the office of Mayor of the Palace in Austrasia, while Sigebert continued to bear the title of king. On the death of that prince Grimoald considered himself strong enough to attempt a revolution. He had the locks of Dagobert, the young son of Sigebert, shorn, sent him to an Irish monastery, and had his own son proclaimed king of Austrasia. But the times were not yet ripe for a change of this kind. The Austrasian nobles refused to obey a youth who was not of the blood royal. They rose in revolt and gave up the Mayor of the Palace to the king of Neustria, Clovis II, who had him put to death.

After this tragic event the families of Arnulf and Pepin remained in the background for about twenty-five years. The stage of politics was occupied by two men named Ebroin and Leodegar (Léger) who engaged

in a desperate rivalry.   Ebroin, Mayor of the Palace in Neustria, was
intent on maintaining, for his own advantage, the unity of the Frankish
kingdom and exercising a commanding influence in Austrasia and
Burgundy as well as in Neustria.   His schemes failed first in Austrasia
where he had to acknowledge a king and a Mayor of the Palace,
Wulfoald by name.   In Burgundy Leodegar, bishop of Autun, placed
himself at the head of the nobles.   He was at first successful and
shut up his rival in the monastery of Luxeuil (670).   The principle
was accepted that each country was to keep its own laws and customs,
that no official was to be sent from one country to another, that no one
should aspire to absolute power, and that the post of Mayor of the
Palace should be held by each of the great men in turn.   But Ebroin
was to take a signal vengeance.   Escaping from Luxeuil, he besieged
Leodegar in Autun, and captured the town and the bishop with it.   After
the lapse of a considerable time he caused the prelate to be put to
death.   The Church revered Leodegar as a saint, and many monasteries
were dedicated to him.   Ebroin remained master of Burgundy and
Neustria until at length, in 681, he fell by the dagger of an assassin.

But in the later portion of his life Ebroin had encountered an
obstinate resistance in Austrasia; and now the second Pepin appears
upon the scene.   In Austrasia his authority was almost absolute, and
after the death of Ebroin he kept himself fully informed regarding the
affairs of Neustria and plotted against the successive Mayors of the
Palace in that country.   Finally he took the field against the mayor
Berthar, and gained a decisive victory over him at Tertry on the
Omignon in the neighbourhood of St Quentin (687).   Many historians
have represented this battle as a victory of the Germans of the east over
the Gallo-Romans of the west and have seen in Pepin II's expedition
something in the nature of a second Germanic invasion.   But in point
of fact there were many Germans in Neustria, while a large part of
Austrasia was occupied by Gallo-Romans.   In its capital, Metz, the
Latin tongue—now in process of transformation into the *lingua Romana*—was alone spoken.   The victory of Pepin over Berthar is rather
a victory of the aristocracy over the Merovingian royal house; and in
fact Pepin was to find many supporters among the Neustrian nobles.
Pepin, having won the victory, now proceeded to set up again, for
his own advantage, the power which he had overthrown; in fact,
this battle marks the fall of the Merovingians and the real accession
of the new dynasty, which, from its most illustrious representative,
Charles the Great, was to be known as the Carolingian.   Some chronicles
have this entry: "In the year 687 Pepin began to reign."

The reign of Pepin over this Merovingian kingdom which he had
succeeded in reuniting was not lacking in brilliance.   He defeated the
Frisians, dispossessed them of a portion of their territory, and caused
Christianity to be preached among them.   In this last work he found

CH. IV.

a valuable auxiliary in the Anglo-Saxon Willibrord. Born on the banks of the Humber, Willibrord had gone to Rome to have his mission sanctioned by Pope Sergius I; for the Anglo-Saxons, who had been converted to Christianity by the missionaries of Pope Gregory I, shewed their gratitude by attaching to the papal see the barbarian peoples whom they evangelised. Willibrord founded the see of Utrecht and pointed out the way which Boniface was to follow later on. Pepin also wished to make the Germans on the right bank of the Rhine, who during the recent period of anarchy had cast off their allegiance, recognise again the suzerainty of the Franks. He subjugated the Alemans, and he established once more a member of the noble family of the Agilolfings in the duchy of Bavaria. It was at this period that the church of Salzburg was founded by St Rupert; and about the same time Kilian preached the Gospel in Franconia on the banks of the Main. Pepin protected all these missionaries and cherished the project of assembling councils to reform the Church. From 687 till his death in 714 Pepin II was undisputed master of the whole of Gaul, with the exception of Aquitaine, which alone maintained an independent position.

Pepin II had appointed one grandson (Theodebald) as Mayor of the Palace in Neustria, two others (Arnulf and Hugo)—all under the regency of his widow Plectrude—in Austrasia. But the great men refused to fall in with this arrangement and there ensued a period of anarchy. Charles, an illegitimate son of Pepin, restored order, and was the real executor of his father's policy. His name signifies valiant, bold, and as the continuator of Fredegar remarks, the name fitted the man. He wrested the power from Plectrude and took the title of Mayor of the Palace in his nephew's stead. He defeated the Neustrians at Amblève near Liége (716), at Vincy near Cambrai (717), and again at Soissons, in 719, and forced them to recognise his authority. He made himself master of Burgundy also, and appointed his own *leudes* to the countships and bishoprics of that country. In Aquitaine the duke, Eudo, who had his seat at Toulouse, exercised an independent authority; but Charles obliged him in 719 to acknowledge, at least in name, the suzerainty of the northern Franks. Charles had thus acquired great power, and during some years he even governed without a king. His official title remained the same, Mayor of the Palace, but he was already called, even by his contemporaries, *princeps* or *subregulus*. He presided over the royal court of justice, issued decrees in his own name and had the disposal of every appointment, lay and ecclesiastical; he summoned the assembly of the great men of the kingdom, decided questions of peace and war and held the command of the army. He was king in fact if not in name.

Charles was now to save from a serious danger the realm which he had reunited. The Arabs had conquered Spain in 711; in 720 they had crossed the Pyrenees and seized Septimania, which was a dependency of the kingdom of the Visigoths. Using this as a base they had invaded Gaul. Eudo, duke of Aquitaine, had succeeded, by his able policy, in holding them in check for some years, but in 732 a new *wālī* or governor 'Abd-ar-Raḥmān, belonging to a sect of extreme fanatics, resumed the offensive. Eudo was vanquished on the banks of the Garonne, Bordeaux was taken and its churches burnt, and the Arabs then advanced, by way of the Gap of Poitiers, towards the north. Poitiers resisted their attack, but the basilica of St Hilary, situated outside the walls, was burnt. Without halting, 'Abd-ar-Raḥmān continued his march on Tours, the resting-place of the body of St Martin, which was, as it were, the religious capital of Gaul. Eudo besought the aid of Charles, who hurried up and posted himself at the junction of the Clain and the Vienne. The two armies halted, facing one another, for seven days. Then, on an October Saturday of 732—exactly a hundred years after the death of Mahomet—the battle was joined, and Charles came off victorious. 'Abd-ar-Raḥmān was slain on the field. This battle became extremely celebrated and it is chiefly on account of it that later chronicles give to Charles the surname of *Tudites* or *Martellus* (Charles Martel).

The day of Poitiers marks the turning-point in the fortunes of the Arabs. Harassed during their retirement by Eudo and his Aquitanians, they met with defeat after defeat. But to crown all, at this moment internal dissensions broke out within the Arab Empire. The Ma'ddites regained the ascendancy at the expense of their enemies the Yemenites, but the Berbers in Africa refused to obey the new rulers and rose in revolt. The Arabs, occupied with the suppression of this rebellion, were thenceforth unable to throw powerful armies into Gaul.

Charles proceeded to take the offensive against the Muslims. In 737 he wrested from them the town of Avignon which they had seized, and then attempted the conquest of Septimania, but in spite of strenuous efforts he was unable to effect the capture of Narbonne. He had to content himself with laying waste the country systematically and destroying the fortifications of Agde, Béziers and Maguelonne. He set fire to the amphitheatre at Nîmes, and the marks of the fire are still visible. In 739, the Arabs having attempted a new descent on Provence and even threatened Italy, Charles marched against them once more and drove them out. He allied himself against them with Liutprand, king of the Lombards, who adopted the Frankish ruler according to the Germanic custom.

Charles also completed the subjugation of the barbarian tribes of Germany. He abolished the duchy of Alemannia, intervened in the affairs of Bavaria, made expeditions into Saxony and even, in 738, compelled some of the Saxon tribes to pay tribute. He gave a safe-conduct to Boniface who preached Christianity in Thuringia, in Alemannia and in Bavaria, and constantly befriended the devoted

Anglo-Saxon missionaries.   Boniface, like Willibrord, went to Rome to receive investiture, and the Pope conferred on him successively the titles of missionary, bishop, and archbishop.   It may have been Boniface who brought the papal see into relations with the Carolingians.

The circumstances were as follows.   Liutprand king of the Lombards was anxious to impose his authority on the dukes of Spoleto and Benevento and to wrest from the Byzantine Empire its last remaining possessions in Italy.   He first attacked and defeated Thrasamund, duke of Spoleto, who thereupon took refuge at Rome.   Liutprand demanded from Pope Gregory III the surrender of Thrasamund, and on Gregory's refusal he laid siege to the Eternal City.   The Pope, in distress, sent an embassy to Charles, consisting of the bishop Anastasius and a priest named Sergius, to implore him to deliver the people of Rome from the Lombard oppression.   By these ambassadors he sent to Charles "the keys of the Confession of St Peter," portions of the chains of the Prince of the Apostles and various magnificent gifts.   The "keys" were a kind of decoration which the pontiffs were accustomed to confer on illustrious personages, while the chains were supposed to have miraculous virtues. This embassy impressed the imagination of contemporaries, and the continuator of Fredegar lays much stress on it.   In return for the help which he implored Gregory III offered to renounce the imperial suzerainty and to confer upon the Mayor of the Palace a certain authority over Rome, with the title of Roman Consul.   Gregory III seems to have had a kind of intuition of the great historic change which was afterwards to take place when the popes were to turn away from the Emperor of Byzantium and attach themselves to the king of the Franks.   Charles gave the papal envoys a cordial reception (739) and showered gifts upon the Pope, sending them by the hands of Grimo, abbot of Corbie, and Sigebert, a monk of St Denis.   But that was all.   He could not take sides against Liutprand who had been his ally against the Arabs.   In vain did Gregory write to him in 740 two imploring letters: "I adjure thee in the name of the true and living God, and by the keys of St Peter's Confession which I sent thee, not to prefer the friendship of a king of the Lombards to that of the Prince of the Apostles, but to come quickly to our aid."   Charles turned a deaf ear to this new appeal, and both he and the Pope died not long after.

When he felt his end approaching, Charles divided the kingdom between his sons as if he had been sole master of it.   The eldest, Carloman, received Austrasia, Alemannia and Thuringia, with the suzerainty of Bavaria; the younger, Pepin, had for his share Neustria, Burgundy and Provence, with the suzerainty of Aquitaine.   Not long afterwards (22 October 741), Charles died at Quierzy-sur-Oise and was buried at St Denis.   His grandson, Charles the Great, bore his name and closely resembled him in character; he inherited his great vigour and martial ardour, but he had a higher conception of his

political duty and a wider outlook upon life.   In the *chansons de geste*
the two personages were afterwards confused.

Charles' sons, Carloman and Pepin, rendered some service to France.
They defeated Hunald duke of Aquitaine, the successor of Eudo, and
when Hunald had retired to a monastery in the Île de Rhé they defeated
his son Waifar also.   They took from the Alemans the last vestiges
of their independence.   They forced Odilo duke of Bavaria to give up
to them a portion of his territories—doubtless the Nordgau—and obliged
him to acknowledge their suzerainty.   They made a series of incursions
into Saxony.   But the two brothers were not to govern jointly for long.
In 747 came an unexpected change.   Carloman, fired by religious zeal,
relinquished his throne in order to become a monk.   At Rome, which
was more and more coming to be considered the capital of Western
Europe, he received the priestly vestments from Pope Zachary, and
founded on Mount Soracte a monastery dedicated to St Sylvester, a
name full of significance since at that time the legend was widely current
of the Emperor Constantine's "donation of Italy" to Pope Sylvester.
Carloman had children, whom he had committed to the care of his
brother; but Pepin gradually got them out of the way and drew all
authority into his own hands.

Pepin, now sole Mayor of the Palace, from this time forward aimed
still higher.   He desired the title of king.   For two years a profound
peace had reigned—*et quievit terra a proeliis annis duobus*, says the
chronicler, borrowing the expression from the Book of Joshua.   The
moment seemed propitious for the decisive step.   Pepin proceeded with
great caution.   He was especially desirous of securing the approval
of the highest moral authority of the age.   He sent to Pope Zachary
an embassy consisting of Fulrad, abbot of St Denis, and Burchard,
bishop of Worms, a disciple of St Boniface, and laid before him a question
regarding the kings who still nominally held the royal authority.   The
Pope replied that it would be better that he should be king who held
the reality of power rather than he who only possessed the semblance
of royalty.   Pope Zachary gave a written decision—*auctoritas*—to that
effect.   Armed with this authoritative pronouncement Pepin called
together at Soissons in November 751 an assembly of the Franks.
There he was unanimously chosen king; unlike the Merovingians, therefore, he held his throne by right of election.   But besides this he had
himself, like the Anglo-Saxon kings, consecrated by the bishops, and it
may safely be conjectured that St Boniface presided at the ceremony.
In virtue of this anointing, Pepin, king by election, became also king
"by the Grace of God."   King Childeric was shut up in the monastery
of St Bertin, and the manner of his death is unknown.   The Merovingian
dynasty was ended: a new period opened in the history of France.

CHAPTER V.

GAUL UNDER THE MEROVINGIAN FRANKS.

INSTITUTIONS.

Having narrated in the previous chapter the events of the Merovingian period, we have now to explain what were the institutions of that period, to shew the nature of the constitution and organisation of the Church and describe the various classes of society.

There is one very important general question which arises in regard to the Merovingian institutions. According to certain historians of the Roman school, the Roman institutions were retained after the occupation of Gaul under Clovis. The Merovingian officials, according to these writers, answer to the former Roman officials, the Mayor of the Palace, for instance, representing the former *praepositus sacri cubiculi*; the powers of the king were those formerly exercised by the Roman Emperor; the Germans brought no new institutions into Gaul; after much destruction they adopted the Roman. According to other historians, on the contrary, those who form a Germanic school, all the institutions which we find in the Merovingian period were of Germanic origin; they are the same as those which Tacitus describes to us in the *De Moribus Germanorum*. The Teutons, they assert, not only infused into the decaying Gallo-Roman society the new blood of a young and vigorous stock, but also brought with them from the German forests a whole system of institutions proper to themselves. The historians of both these schools have fallen into exaggeration. On the one hand, in the time of the Roman Empire, Gaul had never had a centralised administration of its own; it was nothing but a diocese (*dioecesis*) governed from Rome. And when Gaul had to provide for its own needs, it became necessary to create a new system of central administration; even the local administration was greatly modified by the necessity of holding the Gallo-Roman population in check, and the number of officials had to be increased. On the other hand, the Germanic institutions which had been suitable for small tribes on the further side of the

Rhine were not fitted to meet the needs of a great State like the Frankish kingdom. A more complicated machinery became necessary. In point of fact the Merovingian institutions form a new system composed of elements partly Roman, partly Germanic; and the powerful influence of Christianity must not be left out of account. These elements were combined in varying proportions according to circumstances, and according to the needs and even the caprices of men. Moreover we must be careful not to think of the institutions as fixed and unchangeable. They are in a state of continual evolution, and those which obtained in Gaul in the time of Charles Martel are strikingly different from those which we find in the time of Clovis. It is the business of the historian to observe and to explain these changes.

During the whole of the Merovingian period the State is ruled by kings. The kingly office is hereditary and the sons succeed the father by an undisputed right. Each son inherits equally, and the kingdom is divided up into as many parts as there are sons. Daughters, who were excluded from possessing land, could not succeed to the kingdom. The people never interfered in the choice of the sovereign. It was only in rare cases that the great men elevated the king, to whom they had given their allegiance, on the shield and carried him round the camp. This was done by the Ripuarians when they put themselves under the rule of Clovis, after the assassination of their king; and again by the nobles of Chilperic's kingdom when they acknowledged Sigebert as their sovereign. In the case of an ordinary succession there was no special ceremony at which the king was invested with authority. Anointing was not practised in the Merovingian period. The kings merely adopted the custom of making, on their accession, a progress through their dominions and imposing an oath of fidelity upon their subjects. This is called *regnum circumire*. Sons who were minors were placed under the guardianship of their nearest relative. At twelve years old they were declared, according to the provisions of the Salic law, to be of age, and were thenceforth supposed to govern in their own name.

The king's official title was *Rex Francorum*, irrespective of the particular part of the country which he ruled. Some epithet such as *gloriosus* or *vir inluster* was usually added. The kings were distinguished by their long hair, and the locks of a prince who was to be deprived of his status were shorn. Chlotar I and Childebert I asked Clotilda whether she would rather see the hair of her grandsons, the sons of Clodomir, cut short, or see them put to death. The lance was also a royal emblem. Guntram presented a lance to Childebert II in token that he recognised him as heir to his dominions. Clovis wore a diadem. All these kings surrounded themselves with great magnificence and sat in state upon a golden throne. When they entered a town they threw money among the crowd, and their subjects greeted them with acclamations in various languages. The king ruled over Franks and

Gallo-Romans alike. He ruled the former by right of birth, in virtue of having sprung from the family to which this privilege appertained; he ruled the latter, not, as has sometimes been suggested, by a delegated authority conferred upon Clovis by the Emperor Anastasius, but by right of conquest. Before long, too, all distinction between Franks and Gallo-Romans disappeared, and the king ruled all his subjects by hereditary right. The power of the king was almost absolute. He caused the ancient customary law of the barbarian peoples to be formulated or revised, as in the case of the Salic law and the laws of the Ripuarians and the Alemans. He did not of course create law; the customs which regulate the relations of men existed prior to the law and it would be difficult to refuse to recognise them. But the king ordered these customs to be formulated, and gave them, when formulated, a new authority. Further, he amended these laws, abrogating provisions which were contrary to the spirit of Christianity or the advance of civilisation. Alongside of the laws peculiar to each of the races he made edicts applicable to all his subjects without exception. The capitularies begin long before the reign of Charles the Great; we have some which go back to the Merovingian period. The king who makes the law is also the supreme judge. He has his own court of justice, and all other courts derive their authority from him. He can even, in virtue of his absolute power, transgress the ordinary rules of justice and order persons who appear to him to be dangerous to be put to death without trial. Childebert II, for example, once invited one of his great men, named Magnovald, to his palace at Metz under the pretext of shewing him some animal hunted by a pack of hounds, and while he was standing at a window enjoying this spectacle the king had him struck down by one of his men with an axe. Anyone who committed a crime by order of the king was declared immune from penalty. The king made war and peace at will, levied taxes at his pleasure, appointed all functionaries and confirmed the election of bishops. All the forces of the State were in his hands. All his orders—they were known as *banni*—must be obeyed; the violation of any of them was punished with the extremely heavy fine of 60 gold *solidi*. All persons belonging to the king's household were protected by a *wergeld* three times as great as ordinary persons of the same class.

Against a despotic use of this power neither the great men nor the people possessed any remedy save that of revolt; and such revolts are frequent in the Merovingian period. No small number of these kings perished by the assassin's knife. One day one of his subjects told king Guntram, "We know where the axe is which cut off the heads of thy brothers, and its edge is still keen; ere long it shall cleave thy skull." At Paris, on another occasion, Guntram assembled the people in a church and addressed them thus: "I adjure you, men and women here present, to remain faithful to me; slay me not as ye slew my brethren. Suffer me to live yet three years that I may bring up my nephews. If I die you will perish also, for you will have no king strong enough to defend you." The government was thus a despotism tempered by assassination.

At the beginning of the Merovingian period there was no council having the right to advise the king and set limits to his power. The assemblies which Tacitus describes disappeared after the invasions. From time to time the great men assembled for a military expedition, and endeavoured to impose their will upon the king. In 556 Chlotar I led an expedition against the Saxons. They tendered their submission, offering him successively the half of their property, their flocks, herds and garments, and finally all they possessed. The king was willing to accept this offer, but his warriors forced their way into his tent and threatened to kill him if he did not lead them against the enemy. He was obliged to yield to their insistence and met with a severe defeat. But that is a case of violent action on the part of an army in revolt, not of advice given by an assembly regularly consulted. Such assemblies do not appear until the close of the Merovingian period, and then as a new creation. The bishops always made a practice of meeting in council, and at these meetings they passed canons which were authoritative for all Christians. During the civil wars the great laymen also began to meet in order to confer upon their common interests, and the bishops took part in these assemblies also. Each of the three kingdoms—*tria regna* as they are called by the chroniclers— had therefore its assemblies of this kind. The sovereign was obliged to reckon with them, and consulted them on general matters. Subsequently when the Carolingians had again united the kingdom, there was only one assembly. It was summoned regularly in the month of March and became known as the field of March—*campus martius*. The great men came thither in arms, and if war was decided on they took the field immediately against the enemy. Before long, however, as the cavalry had great difficulty in finding fodder in March, the assembly was transferred, about the middle of the seventh century, to the month of May, when there was grass for the horses in the meadows, and the *campus martius* became the *campus madius*. Those who were summoned to this assembly brought to the king gifts in money or in kind, which became the principal source of revenue of the State; they tried persons accused of high treason, and before them were promulgated the capitularies. The assembly was thus at once an army, a council and a legal tribunal. The Carolingians made it the most important part of the machinery of government.

The king was aided in the work of administration by numerous officials who both held posts in the royal household and performed administrative functions in the State. We may mention the Referendaries who drew up and signed diplomas in the name of the king; the Counts of the Palace, who directed the procedure before the royal tribunal; the Cubicularies who had charge of the treasuries in which the wealth of the king was laid up; the Seneschals, who managed (among other things) the royal table; the Marshals, who had constables (*comites stabuli*) under their orders, and were Masters of the Horse, etc. Among these officials the foremost place was gradually taken by the Mayor of the Palace, whose office was peculiar to the Merovingian courts. Landed proprietors were in the habit of putting their various domains under the charge of *majores*, mayors; and a *major domus*, placed over these various mayors, supervised all the estates, and all the revenues from them were paid in to him. The Mayor of the Palace was at first the overseer of all the royal estates, and was also charged with maintaining discipline in the royal household. Being always in close relation with the king, he soon acquired political functions. If the king was a minor, it was his duty as *nutricius* to watch over his education. The dukes and counts, who came from time to time to the palace, fell under his authority, and before long he began to send them orders when they were in their administrative districts; and he acquired an influence in their appointment. As the whole of the administration centred in the palace he became in the end the head of the administration. He presided over the royal court of justice and often commanded the army. In the struggle of the great men against the royal house one of the points for which they contended was the right to impose upon the sovereign a mayor of the palace of their choice; and each division of Gaul (Neustria, Burgundy and Austrasia) desired to have its own mayor. We have seen that a single family, descended from Arnulf and Pepin I, succeeded in getting the office of Mayor of the Palace into their own hands and rendered it hereditary. From 687–751 the Mayors of this family were the real rulers of the Frankish kingdom, and in 751 it was strong enough to seize the crown.

The court was frequented by a considerable number of persons. The young sons of the nobles were brought up there, being "commended" to the care of one or other of the great officials of the palace. They there served their apprenticeship to civil or military life, and might look forward to receiving later some important post. The officials engaged in local administration came frequently to the palace to receive instructions. Other great men resided there in the hope of receiving some favour. Besides these laymen, many ecclesiastics were there to be met with, bishops coming from their dioceses, clergy of the royal chapel, clergy in search of a benefice. All these persons were *optimates* of the king, his faithful servants, his *leudes*, that is to say "his people" (*leute*). A distinctive position among them was held by the *autrustiones*, who were the descendants of the Germanic *comites*. They formed the king's body-guard, and usually ate at the royal table. They took an oath to protect the king in all circumstances. They were often sent to defend frontier fortresses, and thus formed a kind of small standing army. They were also charged with important missions.

The kingdom was divided into districts known as *pagi*. In earlier times the *pagi* corresponded to the former Gallo-Roman "cities," but in the northern part of the kingdom their number was increased. At the head of the *pagus* was the count, *comes*—in Teutonic *graf*. The king appointed the counts at his own pleasure, and could choose them from any class of society, sometimes naming a mere freedman. Leudastes, the Count of Tours who quarrelled so violently with Bishop Gregory, had been born on an estate belonging to the royal treasury in the island of Rhé, and had been employed as a slave first in the kitchen, and afterwards in the bakery of King Charibert. Having run away several times he had been marked by having his ears clipped. Charibert's wife had only lately freed him when the king appointed him Count of Tours. The counts were chosen not only from all classes of society, but from the various races of the kingdom. Among those who are known to us there are more Gallo-Romans than Franks. Within his district the count exercised almost every kind of authority. He policed it, and arrested criminals; he held a court of justice, he levied taxes and made disbursements for public purposes, paying over the residue each year into the royal treasury; he executed all the king's commands, and took under his protection the widow and the orphan. He was all-powerful alike for good and ill, and unfortunately the Merovingian counts, greedy of gain and ill-supervised, did chiefly evil: Leudastes of Tours was no isolated exception among them. To assist them in their numerous duties the counts appointed "vicars." The vicar represented the count during his frequent absences; in some cases he administered a part of the district, while the count administered the remainder. Before long there were several vicars to each county and it was regularly subdivided into districts called vicariates. The "hundred-man" (*centenarius*) or *thunginus* of the Salic law was identified with the vicar and the terms became synonymous.

Often it was necessary to concentrate in the hands of a single administrator authority over several counties. In this case the king placed over the counts a duke. The duke was principally a military leader; he commanded the army, and the counts within his jurisdiction had to march under his orders. The duchy did not form a permanent administrative district like the county; it usually disappeared along with the circumstances that gave rise to the appointment. In certain districts however, in Champagne, in Alsace and beyond the Jura on the shores of the Lake of Neuchâtel, there were permanent duchies. In the kingdom of Burgundy we find the title *patricius* as that of an official who governed the part of Provence which was attached to Burgundy, and also appears to have held the chief military command in that kingdom

CH. V.

The official who held the command in that part of Provence, which was a dependency of Austrasia, bore the title of *rector*. These titles were doubtless borrowed from the Ostrogoths, who were the masters of Provence from 508 to 536.

It remains to notice the organisation of justice, finance and the army. The races of Merovingian Gaul were not all under one law. Each race had its own; the principle was that the system of law varied according to the race of the persons who were to be judged. The Gallo-Romans continued to be judged according to the Roman law, especially the compilation made among the Visigoths and known under the name of the *Breviarium Alarici.* As it was in the region south of the Loire that the Gallo-Romans were least mixed with barbarian elements, it was in Aquitaine that the Roman law longest maintained its hold. The Burgundians and the Visigoths had already their own systems of law at the time when their kingdoms were overthrown by the Franks, and the men of these races continued to be judged by these laws throughout the whole of the Merovingian period. The Merovingian kings caused the customary laws of the other barbarian peoples to be preserved in writing. In all probability the earliest redaction of the Salic law goes back to Clovis, and is doubtless to be placed in the last years of his reign, after his victory over the Visigoths, 507–511. We cannot place it earlier, for the following reasons. The Germanic peoples did not use the Latin language until after they had become mixed with the Gallo-Roman population; in the scale of fines the monetary system of *solidi* is used, which only makes its appearance in the Merovingian period; further, the Salic law contains imitations of the Visigothic laws of Euric (466–484); finally, it is evident that the Franks are masters of the Visigoths, since they provide for the case of men dwelling beyond the Loire—*trans Ligerim*—being cited before the tribunals. On the other hand, it is not possible to place the redaction much later, since the law is not yet leavened with the Christian spirit; only in later redactions does Christian influence appear. Similarly, there are incorporated in these later redactions capitularies emanating from the immediate successors of Clovis. The law of the Ripuarians, even in its most ancient portions, is later than the reign of Clovis; that of the Alemans does not appear to be earlier than the commencement of the eighth century, or that of the Bavarians earlier than 744–748. Other laws, like those of the Saxons and Thuringians, were not reduced to writing until the time of Charles the Great. These collections of laws must not be regarded as codes. The subjects are not co-ordinated; there are few rules of civil law; they are chiefly occupied with scales of fines and rules of procedure.

Justice was administered in the smaller cases by the centeniers or vicars, in the more important by the counts. Both classes of officials held regular courts called in Latin *placita*, in Germanic *mall* or *malberg*. The sittings of these courts took place at fixed periods and the dates were known beforehand. The vicars and counts were assisted by freemen known as *rachimburgi* or *boni homines* who sat with the officials, assisted them with their counsels, and intervened in the debates, and it was they who fixed the amount of the fines to be paid by the guilty party. At first the *rachimburgi* varied in number, before long however the presence of seven of them was requisite in order that a judgment might be valid. The *rachimburgi* were notables who gave a portion of their time to the public service; Charles the Great made a far-reaching reform when he substituted for them regular officials trained in legal knowledge, known as *scabini*. The counts also made progresses through their districts, received petitions from their subjects and gave immediate judgment without observing the strict rules of procedure. Above the count's court of justice was the king's. It was held in one of the royal *villae* and presided over by the king, or, later on, by the Mayor of the Palace. The president of the court was assisted by "auditors," more or less numerous according to the importance of the case; these were bishops, counts or other great personages present at the palace. The king could call up before his court any cases that he pleased. He judged regularly the high officials, men placed under his *mundium*, cases of treason and cases in which the royal treasury was interested. He received appeals from the sentences delivered in the count's court. The king's court also exercised jurisdiction in certain matters of beneficence; before it the slave was freed by the ceremony of manumission known as *per denarium*, and married persons made mutual donation of goods. In addition to his regular jurisdiction the king made a practice of travelling through his realm, hearing the complaints of his subjects, and redressing their grievances without waiting for all the delays of legal procedure. The Merovingian legal tribunals endeavoured to introduce some degree of order into a state of society in which crimes were rife, and to substitute the regular action of law for private vengeance and family feud. Unfortunately they did not succeed.

Under the Merovingian kings the system of taxation established by the Romans gradually fell into disuse. This is not difficult to explain when we remember that this fiscal system was extremely complicated, and that the kings had really very little to provide for in the way of disbursements. The officials received no salaries, but had the enjoyment of the revenues of certain *villae* belonging to the royal treasury. When they went on circuit in the service of the king, private persons were obliged to furnish them with food, lodging and means of transport. The army cost the king nothing, for his warriors had to provide their own equipment. The administration of justice was a source of revenue to the king in the shape of the confiscations and fines imposed by the courts. His expenses were limited to the maintenance of his court and the donations made to the great men and the churches, and these expenses were covered by his different revenues, which came chiefly from the royal domains. The kings became possessed of numerous *villae* scattered over the various districts of Gaul, and these properties were constantly augmented by purchases, donations and advantageous exchanges. It is true that at the close of the Merovingian epoch the kings, in order to conciliate the great men, distributed among them a large number of these royal estates, and the treasury became impoverished.

In the second place, the kings levied, at least at the beginning of the period, a number of taxes direct and indirect, which were adaptations of the former Roman imposts. They raised customs dues (*telonea*) on the goods which passed through certain towns, others on goods passing along the high-roads, by a public bridge, or transported by river, and on goods exposed for sale in markets. But these dues were often made over to the churches, abbeys or private persons. Sometimes also the king levied a tax on men who were not of free condition. This was the old *capitatio humana*. Those who were liable to it were inscribed in a public register known as the *polyptychum*. But this impost gradually lost its importance. The queen Bathildis, who lived at the period when Ebroin was Mayor of the Palace, and was herself a former Breton slave, forbade the levying of this tax, because parents killed their children rather than pay for them. The tax became a customary due, of which the incidence was limited to certain persons; traces of it are found in the time of Charles the Great. Similarly the land tax, *capitatio terrena*, brought in less and less. Smitten by fear of the divine wrath Chilperic himself burned the registers in order to win back the favour of God. The *capitatio terrena* came to be limited to certain lands, as the *capitatio humana* was to certain persons. At the end of the Merovingian period it became necessary to create new imposts, and then the warriors were required to bring to the spring assembly gifts nominally voluntary, which soon became compulsory. The minting of coinage was in the earlier part of the period another source of revenue. For a long time the Frankish kings confined themselves to imitating the imperial currency; Theodebert was the first to place his name and effigy on the gold *solidi*. But his example was little followed. Down to the seventh century coinage was minted in Gaul bearing the names of former Emperors like Anastasius, Justin and Justinian, whose types became permanent, or of contemporary Emperors like Heraclius (610–641). From the middle of the seventh century onward we find no coins bearing an effigy. On one side we find simply a man's name —that of the *monetarius*—on the other that of the locality. More than 800 local names are found on the Merovingian coins. Evidently coining had become almost entirely free again; minters, provided with a royal authorisation, went from place to place, converting ingots into specie. Charles the Great however resumed the exclusive right of coining.

The composition of the army varied during the Merovingian period. The army of Clovis with which he conquered Gaul was an army of barbarians, to which some Roman soldiers, encamped in the country, had joined themselves. These Roman troops long preserved their name, their accoutrements, their insignia. Later it seems clear that certain of the barbarian tribes were liable to special military obligations, and in case of military expeditions were the first to take the field. The armies which descended from Gaul upon Italy in the sixth century were principally composed of Burgundian warriors. The Saxons established near Bayeux, the Taifali, whose name is found in the Poitivin district of Tiffauges, were for long distinctly military colonies whose members took the field at the first alarm of war. But soon the Gallo-Romans, too, find a place in the armies. Some of them doubtless asked leave to join an expedition which was likely to bring back spoil; thenceforward their descendants were under obligation to render military service. Others were obliged by the count or the duke to equip themselves, and in this way a precedent was created which bound their descendants. Thus certain free persons, whether Gallo-Romans or barbarians, are subject to the obligation of military service, just as certain persons are subject to the *capitatio humana* and certain lands to the *capitatio terrena*. These persons were obliged to arm themselves and march whenever the king summoned them to do so. But they were rarely all summoned at one time; the king first called on those who lived in the neighbourhood of the scene of war. If it was for an expedition against Germany he summoned the fighting-men of Austrasia, for a war against Brittany he summoned the men of Tours, Poitiers, Bayeux, Le Mans and Angers. All the men thus mustered served at their own expense, and remained on campaign all summer; in winter they returned to their homes, to be recalled, if need were, the following spring. Charles the Great made a great reform in the military organisation. He based the obligation to military service upon property, the principle being that everyone who possessed a certain number of *mansi* was obliged to serve. The number varied from year to year according to the number of fighting-men required.

We thus see how these institutions were incessantly transformed by the influence of circumstances and by human action. Roman and Germanic elements were combined in them in various proportions, and new elements were added to them. The Merovingian institutions thus came to form a new system; and from them arise by a series of transformations the institutions of Charles the Great.

Only the Church, which connects itself with the Gallo-Roman Church, presents an appearance of greater fixity, since the Church claims to hold always the same dogmas and to be founded on stable principles. Nevertheless even the Church underwent an evolution along with the society which it endeavoured to guide. We shall give our attention successively to the secular Church and the religious Orders.

CH. V.

No one could become a member of the secular clergy without the permission of the king. Anyone who desired the clerical office must also give certain guarantees of his moral fitness. His conduct must be upright and pure, and he must possess a certain amount of education. To have married a second time, or to have married a widow, debarred a man from the clerical office, and those who were married must break off all relations with their wives. Clerics were distinguished from laymen by their tonsure, they wore a special costume, the *habitus clericalis*, and they were judged according to the Roman Law. Each cleric was attached to a special church, which he ought not to leave without the written permission of his bishop; the councils impose the severest penalties upon priests wandering at large (*gyrovagi*).

The chief of the clergy was the bishop, who was placed over a diocese—*parochia*, as it was called in the Merovingian period. Theoretically there were as many bishops as there had been *civitates* in Roman Gaul, but the principle was not rigorously carried out. A number of the small cities mentioned in the *Notitia Galliarum* had no bishop in the Merovingian period, for their territory was united to that of a neighbouring city. This was the case in regard to the *civitas Rigomagensium* (Thorame) and the *civitas Salinensium* (Castellane) in the province of the Alpes Maritimae. On the other hand some of the cities were divided up. St Remigius established a bishopric at Laon which was not a Gallo-Roman city. Similarly a bishopric was created at Nevers. Out of the *civitas* of Nîmes were carved the bishoprics of Uzès, Agde and Maguelonne; out of Narbonne that of Carcassonne; out of Nyons that of Belley. This creation of new bishoprics was due to the progress of Christianity. Certain bishoprics which the Merovingian kings created in order to make the boundaries of the dioceses coincide with those of their share of the kingdom—such as that of Melun, formed out of that of Sens, and of Chateaudun, formed out of that of Chartres—had only a transient existence.

Theoretically the bishops were elected by the clergy and people of the city. The election took place in the cathedral, under the presidency of the metropolitan or of a bishop of the province; the faithful acclaimed the candidate of their choice, who immediately took possession of the episcopal chair. But under the Merovingians it is observable that the kings acquire little by little an influence in the elections. The sovereign made known his choice to the electors; in many cases he directly designated the prelate. He might, of course, choose the man most worthy of the post, but usually he was content to be bribed. "At this time," says Gregory of Tours, "that seed of iniquity began to bear fruit that the episcopal office was sold by the kings or bought by the clerics." In face of these pretentions of the monarchy the first councils of the Merovingian period, those of 533 and 538, did not fail to assert the ancient canonical rights. Before long however the bishops saw that they must take things as they were and make the best of them. They were prepared to recognise the intervention of the king as legitimate, while insisting that the king should not sell the episcopate and should observe the canonical regulations. " None shall buy the episcopal dignity for money," runs the pronouncement of the Fifth Council of Orleans, of 549 ; "the bishop shall, with the king's consent and according to the choice of the clergy and the people, be consecrated by the metropolitan and the other bishops of the province." These principles were recalled at the famous council of 614, but without the mention of the king: " On the decease of a bishop there shall be appointed in his place whoever shall have been elected by the metropolitan, the bishops of the province, and the clergy and people of the city, without hindrance and without gift of money." Chlotar II in the edict confirming these canons modified the tenor of this article. While recognising the right of election of the persons interested, he maintained the right of intervention of the prince. " If the elected person is worthy, he shall be consecrated, upon the order of the prince." From that time forward the established procedure was as follows. On the death of a prelate the citizens and the people of the *civitas* assemble, under the presidency of the metropolitan and the other bishops of the province. They choose the successor and make known to the king the act of election—*consensus civium pro episcopatu.* If the king approves, he transmits to the metropolitan the order to consecrate the bishop-elect, and invites the other bishops of the province to be present at the ceremony. If he is dissatisfied with the election, he requests the electors to choose another candidate, and sometimes he himself nominates him.

The power of the bishop was very great. All the clergy of the diocese were under his control, and in the episcopal city a certain number of clerics lived in the bishop's house and ate at his table. Chrodegang, bishop of Metz, laid down about the middle of the eighth century a very strict rule for these clergy, requiring them to live as a community: this was the origin of secular canons. Throughout the whole diocese the bishop reserved to himself certain religious functions. He alone had power to consecrate altars and churches, to bless the holy oils, to confirm the young and to ordain clergy. All other functions he delegated to the archpriests, whose appointment was either made or sanctioned by him. Only these archpriests had the right to baptise, and at the great festivals they alone had the right to say mass. The district under the authority of the archpriest soon came to be considered as a smaller *parochia* within the larger *parochia.* The archpriests were generally placed in the *vici,* the large country-towns. Under them were the clerics who served the oratories of the *villae*; these clerics were presented by the proprietors of the *villae* for institution by the bishop. The bishop was assisted in his work by an archdeacon who exercised oversight among the clergy

CH. V.

and judged contentions arising among them. It was the bishop, too, who administered Church property, and this property was of large extent. Never were donations to the Church more abundant than in the Merovingian period. The benefactors of the Church were, first, the bishops themselves: Bertramn of Mans left to his see thirty-five estates. Then there were the kings, who hoped to atone for their crimes by pious donations, and rich laymen who to provide for the salvation of their souls despoiled their heirs. All property acquired by the Church was, according to the canons of the councils, inalienable. The Church always received and never gave back. In addition to landed property, the Church received from the kings certain financial privileges, such as exemption from customs-dues and market-tax. Often, too, the sovereign made over to the Church the right to levy dues at specified places. Further, since Moses had granted to the tribe of Levi, that is to say to the priests, the right of levying tithes upon the fruits of the earth and the increase of the cattle, the Merovingian Church claimed a similar contribution, and threatened with excommunication anyone who should fail to pay it. The tithe was generally paid by the faithful, but it was not made obligatory by the State. It only acquired that character in the time of Charles the Great. All this property was theoretically in the charge of the bishop of the diocese. He was required to divide it into four parts, one for the maintenance of the bishop and his household, one for the payment of the clergy of his diocese, one for the poor, and one for the building and repair of churches. Little by little, however, property became attached to secondary parishes and even to mere oratories.

The bishop had great influence within his city as well as in the State. In the city he acted as an administrator and carried out works of public utility. Sidonius of Mainz built an embankment along the Rhine, Felix of Nantes straightened the course of the Loire, Didier of Cahors constructed aqueducts. The bishop thus took the place of the former municipal magistrates, whose office had died out; he received the town to govern (*ad gubernandum*); by the end of the Merovingian period certain cities are already episcopal cities. The bishop maintains the cause of his parishioners before the officials of the State, and even before the king himself; he obtains for them alleviation of imposts and all kinds of favours. The bishops' protection was especially extended to a class of persons who formed as it were their clientage—widows, orphans, the poor, slaves, and captives. The poor of the city were formed into a regularly organised body, their names were inscribed on the registers of the Church, and they were known as the *matricularii.*

The bishops and the clergy in general enjoyed important legal privileges. From 614 onwards the clergy could only be judged on criminal charges by their bishops; the bishops themselves could only be cited before councils of the Church. But, still more important, laymen were glad to make the bishop the arbiter of their differences; they knew that they would find in him a judge more just and better instructed than the count. The Church could also give protection to malefactors; the criminal, once he had crossed the sacred threshold, could not be torn thence; it was commonly believed that frightful chastisements had smitten those who attempted to violate the rights of sanctuary.

It would be easy to shew how grossly immoral was the Frankish race—the history of Gregory of Tours is filled with the record of horrible crimes—but at the same time they were profoundly credulous and superstitious. On Sundays, at the sound of the bells, they rushed in crowds to the churches. They frequently received the communion, and it was a terrible punishment to be deprived of it. Apart from the Church services the Franks were constantly at prayer. They believed not only in God but in the saints, whom they continually invoked, and they believed in their intervention in the affairs of this world. They were eager to procure relics, which had healing power. The Church had in its control sacraments, religion, healing virtue, and the bishop held the first place in the Church; he was felt to be invested with supernatural power, and the faithful held him in awe.

Above the bishop was the metropolitan. With a few rare exceptions, the metropolitan had his seat at the chief town of the Roman province. In the course of the fifth century, the province of Vienne was cut in two: there was one metropolitan at Vienne, another at Arles. The latter annexed to his jurisdiction the provinces of the Alpes Maritimae (Embrun) and of Narbonensis II (Aix). Thenceforward twelve metropolitan sees were distinguished: Vienne, Arles, Trèves, Rheims, Lyons (to which was united Besançon), Rouen, Tours, Sens, Bourges, Bordeaux, Eauze and Narbonne. The metropolitan had the right to convoke provincial councils, and presided at them. He exercised a certain oversight over the bishops of the province, and it was to him that it naturally fell to act as judge among them. His title was simply that of bishop: the title archbishop does not appear until quite the end of the Merovingian period. The authority of the metropolitans was subordinate to that of the Frankish Church as a whole, which had as its organs the national councils. These councils were always convoked by the king, who exercised much influence in their deliberations. We have the canons of numerous councils held between 511 and 614, which give us a mass of information regarding ecclesiastical organisation and discipline. These canons are not much concerned with doctrine; they recall the clergy to their duties, safeguard the property of the churches against the covetousness of laymen, and censure pagan customs such as augury and *sortes sanctorum*.

The Frankish Church honoured the Papacy and regarded the bishop of Rome as the successor of St Peter, but the Papacy had no

effective power over this Church, except perhaps in the province of
Arles. Reading the work of Gregory of Tours, which is so full of life
and reflects so exactly the passions and ideas of the time, we do not find
that the Pope plays any part in the narrative. The bishops are appointed without his intervention and they govern their churches without
entering into relations with him. At the end of the sixth century, as
we saw earlier, Gregory the Great maintained an active correspondence
with Brunhild. He gives her advice, and his advice was, without
doubt, listened to with respect. The pope takes no direct action, but
he urges the queen to act. It is not difficult to see however that he
was quite ready to supersede Brunhild in the task of directing the
Frankish Church; he would like to make Candidus, who was the
administrator of the papal patrimony in Provence, a kind of legate
beyond the Alps. There can be no doubt that Gregory I, had he lived,
would have succeeded by his able policy in re-establishing in Gaul the
papal authority as it had been exercised by Leo I before the fall of the
Empire. But after the death of Gregory in 604 relations between
Rome and the Franks became very rare for more than a century.
There are only one or two instances of such relations to which we can
point. Pope Martin I (649–655), for example, requested the sons of
Dagobert to assemble councils in order to combat the Monothelete
heresy, which was supported by the Byzantine Emperors. Relations
were not effectively resumed until the eighth century, but they were then
to have an immense influence upon general history.

We have already seen how, in their opposition to the Emperors of
Constantinople, the popes sought the aid of the Mayors of the Palace,
and how this alliance was concluded. We have also noticed, in passing,
how Boniface brought under the authority of the Holy See the Germanic
races whom he converted to the Christian faith. But, besides this, with
the aid of Carloman and Pepin (after 739), Boniface accomplished another
task. After the death of Dagobert the Frankish Church had fallen
into profound decadence, and Charles Martel had sunk it still lower by
conferring bishoprics and abbeys on rude and ignorant laymen. These
bishops and abbots never wore clerical vestments, but always sword
and baldric. They dissipated the property of the Church and sought
to bequeath their offices to their bastards. For eighty years no
council was called. Every vestige of education and civilisation was in
danger of being swamped. A complete reform of the Church was
necessary in the interests of society itself. To Carloman and Pepin
belongs the merit of having perceived this, and they entrusted this great
work to Boniface. Once more a series of councils was held, in the dominions of Carloman as well as in those of Pepin; there was even a general
council of the whole kingdom in March 745 at Estinnes (Liftinas) in
Hainault. The ecclesiastical hierarchy was restored, measures were
taken against priests of scandalous life; the clergy were encouraged to

become better educated. Above all, this reformed clergy was placed under the authority of the Papacy; the road to Rome became familiar to them. On the one hand there was a political alliance between the popes and the Mayors of the Palace; on the other relations were renewed between the clergy of what had been Gaul and the Papacy. Thus was recovered the idea of Christian unity in one sole Church under the authority of the Pope, as the successor of the apostle Peter.

We have hitherto spoken chiefly of the secular Church, but in even a summary account of the Church of the Merovingian period a place must be found for the monasteries. As early as the fifth century, before the conquest of Clovis, famous abbeys had arisen upon Gallic soil. Such were Ligugé near Poitiers, Marmoutier and St Martin in the territory of Tours, St Honorat on one of the islands of Lerins, St Victor at Marseilles. In the time of Clovis Caesarius founded in the town of Arles one monastery for men and another for women. Under Clovis and his successors monasteries rapidly increased in number. Childebert I founded that of St Vincent, close to the gates of Paris, afterwards to be known as St Germain-des-Près; Chlotar I founded St Médard of Soissons, while Radegund, the Thuringian wife whom he had repudiated, built Ste Croix of Poitiers. To Guntram is due the foundation of St Marcel of Chalon-sur-Saône, and the extension of St Benignus of Dijon. Private persons followed the example of the kings. Aridius, a friend of Gregory of Tours, founded on one of his estates the monastery which from his name was known as St Yrieix. All these monasteries were placed under the charge of the bishop, who visited them and if necessary recalled the monks to their duty. At the head of the household was placed an abbot, generally chosen by the founder or his descendants, but in some cases elected by the community, subject to the bishop's confirmation. Each monastery was independent of the rest, and had a rule—*regula*—of its own, based upon principles borrowed from the early monks in Egypt, from Pachomius, Basil and the writings of Cassian and Caesarius of Arles. The abbeys did not as yet form congregations obeying the same rule. Since they confined themselves to serving as a refuge for souls wounded in the battle of life, they had no influence on the outside world. They were not centres of the religious life radiating an influence beyond the walls of the cloister and exercising a direct action upon the Church.

This type of monastic life was the creation of an Irish monk, Columbanus, who landed on the Continent about the year 585. He settled in the kingdom of Guntram, and established, in the neighbourhood of the Vosges, three monasteries, Annegray, Luxeuil (known in Roman times for its medicinal baths), and Fontaines. These three houses were under his direction and he gave them a common rule, which was distinguished by its extreme severity. Obedience was required of the monk "even unto death," according to the example of Christ, who was faithful to

His Father even unto the death of the cross. The smallest peccadillo, the least negligence in service, was punished with strokes of the rod. The monk must have no possessions; he must never even use the word "my." This rule became common to all the other abbeys which were founded subsequently by Columbanus himself or his disciples. For Columbanus did not remain undisturbed within the walls of Luxeuil. Twice he was torn from his refuge by Brunhild, whose orders he refused to obey. He wandered through Champagne, and under his influence a monastery arose at Rebais and convents for women at Faremoutiers and Jouarre. Later he found his way to the shores of the Lake of Constance in Alemannia where his disciple Gallus founded the monastery which bore his name, St Gall. He ended his days on 23 November 615 in Italy, where the monastery of Bobbio claims him as its founder. Loyal disciples of his had reformed or founded in Gaul a large number of monasteries; in no similar period were so many founded as between the years 610 and 650. We can mention only the most famous—Echternach, Prüm, Etival, Senones, Moyenmoutier, St Mihiel-sur-Meuse, Malmédy and Stavelot. Many of these monasteries received from one hundred to two hundred monks.

All these abbeys obeyed the same rule and were animated by the same spirit; they formed a sort of congregation. In general they declared themselves independent of the bishop—*ad modum Luxovensium*. They chose their abbots and administered their property freely. Moreover these monks did not confine themselves within the walls of their monasteries; they desired to play a part in the Church. St Wandrille claimed that the monks should not merely be allowed to count the years which they spent in the cloister, but those also in which they travelled in the service of God. The disciples of Columbanus were preachers like himself; they proclaimed the necessity of penance, the expiation of every mistake according to a fixed scale, as in the rule of the monastery, and at this time penitentials began to be widely circulated. The sense of sin became very keen among the people, and they multiplied gifts to the Church in order to atone for their transgressions. The monks also became missionaries; each abbey was, so to speak, the head-quarters of a mission. St Gall completed the conversion of the Alemans, Eustasius abbot of Luxeuil converted the heretical Warasci in the neighbourhood of Besançon and went to preach the Gospel in Bavaria. But the very number of these monasteries caused the defects of the rule of Columbanus to be quickly perceived. This rule did not provide for the administration of the monastery; it did not prescribe, hour by hour, the employments of the day; then, again, it was too severe, too crushing, and often reduced men to despair. Now, about a hundred years earlier (c. 529), Benedict of Nursia had given to the monastery of Monte Cassino an admirable rule; this rule was not known in France until after the death of Columbanus and the remarkable growth of monasteries connected with him, but once known its advantages were soon recognised. All the questions which Columbanus had left unsettled here received a practical solution. It regulated the relations of the abbot with the monks and of the monks with one another; it prescribed the employments of the day and the hours to be divided between prayer, manual work and study. Mystical speculations are left aside; there is something of the legal spirit of ancient Rome in these clearly-drawn precepts. The rule of St Benedict at first appeared as a rival alongside of that of St Columbanus; but after the great ecclesiastical reform associated with the name of Boniface it reigned alone; and a little later Louis the son of Charles the Great imposed it (817) upon all the monasteries of his realm. The impetuous torrent which Columbanus had let loose was thus turned into a wide channel, in which its waters could flow calmly.

Merovingian society was composed of remarkably definite gradations, each man having his fixed price, so to speak, marked by the *wergeld*. At the bottom of the scale was the slave. The Germans as well as the Romans had possessed slaves, and their number was increased in the Merovingian period. After a war the prisoners were often reduced to servitude; many of these unfortunates belonged to the Slav race, and the name *slave* gradually took the place of *servus*. There were also slave-dealers who went to seek their human merchandise overseas; young Anglo-Saxons were much sought after on account of their beauty. Then again, a man who could not pay his debts, or a fine inflicted by the courts, fell into servitude; and a freeman who married a slave lost his freedom. Slaves were looked on as chattels; the master could sell them or give them away at his pleasure. Anyone who stole or killed a slave paid a fine of thirty *solidi*, just the same amount as was paid for stealing a horse, and this compensation was paid to the master: the slave was not considered to have any family. Slaves were often very cruelly treated by their masters; Duke Rauching for example made his slaves put out torches by pressing them against their naked legs. The Church however took up their cause; it declared unions between slaves which had been blessed by the priest to be legitimate, and earnestly exhorted masters not to separate husband and wife, parents and children.

Slaves could escape from their condition by enfranchisement. In the Merovingian period there were two kinds of solemn enfranchisement, that *per denarium* before the king, by which the former slave acquired the rights of a Frankish freeman, and that of the Church, by which he became a free Roman. In both cases he was discharged from all obligation towards his former master, but remained in a certain dependence on the king, who fell heir to the property of slaves if they had no children born after their enfranchisement. But usually the slave was simply freed by a written statement to that effect given by the master, and a freedman of this kind, known as *libertus* or *lidus*, remained in a position of close dependence upon his former master. He could, it is true, plead in the courts and enter into binding agreements, but he paid his patron a yearly fee known as the *lidimonium*, and if he died without issue his patron became his heir. The freedman usually retained the land which he had cultivated as a slave, but instead of being a *servilis* holding it became a *lidilis* holding.

On the large estates there was a third class of holding, the *mansi ingenuiles*. These were held by the *coloni*, the descendants of the former Roman *coloni*. Theoretically these *coloni* were free, but they were bound to their holdings; they could not quit them without the permission of the owner, and if they ran away they were brought back by force. But, on the other hand, so long as they paid their rent, they could not be expelled from their holdings and might cultivate them as they chose. They thus form an intermediate class between the slaves who were tied to one place and the freemen, to whom all roads stood open.

The freemen might belong either to the conquering race, the Franks, or the conquered race, the Gallo-Romans; and the two races were under different laws. The Salic law fixes the *wergeld* of a Salian Frank at two hundred *solidi*, that of the Roman at one hundred only. But we must not conclude from this that there was a great gulf fixed between the two races. Where both parties to a case were Gallo-Romans, they were judged according to the Roman law; when a Gallo-Roman was accused by a Frank, judgment was still given according to the Roman law; it was only in a case where a Frank was the defendant that the Salic law was applied, and it is quite natural that this law should be more severe upon the murder of a man of the same race than on that of a Roman. Besides, the further we advance in Merovingian history, the more the two races become intermingled. The Franks admired the Roman civilisation and endeavoured to assimilate it; they learned the common language of Gaul, which was in process of becoming Romanic; they even prided themselves on learning to speak pure Latin. The Gallo-Romans, on their part, adopted the military customs of the barbarians. They frequently gave Germanic names to their children. Both nations were Christian, and the common faith contributed to bring them together.

In theory all these freemen were equal, but little by little distinctions arose among them. In default of a nobility with hereditary privileges, there grew up an aristocracy, *potentes*, *priores*, who exercised a powerful influence. These great men belonged generally to the ancient Gallo-Roman senatorial families, who held vast estates and possessed great wealth. From these families the king chose the great officers of state and the people of the cities chose their bishops; thus there was added to their wealth political power, or the veneration attaching to the sacred office of the priesthood. The Franks who possessed large estates became assimilated to these Roman senators and there thus grew up an aristocracy composed of members of the two races.

In consequence of the troublous times which were the rule in Gaul in the seventh century, the poor and the weak could not depend on the protection of the State, and sought protection from one or other of these powerful personages. They put themselves under his *mundeburdis* as it was called in Germanic; they "commended" themselves to him, according to the expression borrowed from Roman usage, and this expression is suitable enough, for they became in fact clients of these great men. The patron undertook to maintain his clients, to support them in law cases, to further their interests; in return, the client promised to serve his patron on all occasions, to defend him if he were attacked, and to take the field along with him if he attacked anyone else. Each of these great personages had thus under his orders a more or less numerous body of men. To mark these new social conditions new terms were created, or a new sense was given to ancient terms. The protector was called the *senior*; the client was called *vassus*. In the Salic law the term vassal simply meant a slave attached to the personal service of his master; at the close of the Merovingian period it always means one of these voluntary dependents. Those who felt the need of protection could "commend" themselves not only to wealthy private persons but also to royal officers, to the dukes and counts, to the officials of the palace; but above all they could commend themselves to the king himself. In that case the sovereign exercised a double authority over them; first, his public authority as king, and secondly a more special protection, parallel, in so far, to that of the seignior. In time the strength of the king came to depend in large measure on the number of his vassals. The subjection of the individual to the State was replaced by a personal subjection to the king, and the population of the country came to be composed of groups of men bound to one another by personal ties. Thus we find the germs of the feudal system already present in the seventh century.

A time was to come when to this subordination of persons there should be added a subordination of lands. In order to understand this evolution, which was to have so great a historical importance, we must first examine the conditions on which property was held.

With the exception of the towns the soil of Gaul was divided, in the Merovingian period, into large estates, called *villae* or *fundi*. These estates usually bore the name of their original holder; thus the *villae* called Victoriacus had belonged to a man named Victorius, and the modern villages which have descended from these *villae* have kept the old names. Variously transformed according to the district in which they lie, they are known to-day as Vitrac, Vitrec, Vitré, Vitrey or Vitry. Similarly *villae* bearing the name Sabiniacus have become our villages of Savignac, Savignec, Sévigné, Savigneux. Many of these estates, especially in the north and east, changed their names after the invasions, taking the names of their barbarian owners. Thus *Theodonis villa*, Thionville, *Ramberti villare*, Rambervillers, *Arnulfi curtis*, Harcourt, *Bodegiseli vallis*, Bougival near Paris. In the seventh century some estates took the name of the saint to whom the church was dedicated: Dompierre, Dommartin, St Pierre, St Martin. Some *villae* again took their names from some particular variety of trees or plantations; *Roboretum* has become Rouvray, Rouvres; *Rosariae* and *Cannaberiae* have given us the names of our modern villages Rosières and Chennevières. It often happened that through sale, exchange or division among brothers, a *villa* was divided between several owners, but it none the less retained its unity and organisation.

The lands of the *villa* were divided into two portions. One, consisting of the lands lying round about the house of the owner, was farmed directly by him. The other portion was divided up into lots or holdings (*mansi*), of which the owner gave the use to his slaves, his *lidi*, or to freemen; whence comes the distinction between *mansi serviles, lidiles* and *ingenuiles*, of which we have spoken above. Each tenant cultivated his holding for his own profit, but in return for its use was obliged to pay a rent to the owner and to render him certain services. The houses occupied by the tenants were either isolated, in the mountainous districts, or grouped together within a small area. A *villa* was self-sufficing; besides the cultivators there were the workmen who made or repaired the tools and implements. There was a mill and a wine-press which served the whole population of the *villa*, and often there was a forge also. It had its own chapel, of which the priest (often born on the estate) was appointed by the master, with the consent of the bishop. The woods surrounding the *villa* remained in possession of the landowner, but he gave the tenants rights of user. Over all the dwellers on the estate he exercised a seigniorial jurisdiction.

There still existed, no doubt, alongside of the great estates or *villae* a number of small estates belonging to freemen. But these small estates tended to disappear in the course of the seventh century. The fact was that the small proprietors were unable to defend their estates; they had no inducement to sell them, for money would have been of little value to them; accordingly they "commended themselves" to some great man of the neighbourhood, handing over their property to him. He in turn gave them the use of it for life, and thus they were at least certain of occupying it in security until the end of their days. Previously they had held their lands *ex alode* or *de alode parentum*, by inheritance from their ancestors, with the right of using it as they chose; henceforth they held it *per beneficium*, in consequence of a grant made by the great seignior. When agreements of this kind became frequent, two varieties of landed property were distinguished, allodial lands which were held by the owner in person, and "benefices," of which the use was granted by a large proprietor to another person during the lifetime of the latter.

Many circumstances contributed to multiply these benefices. The Church, which had large estates and could not get them all cultivated by its serfs, *lidi* and *coloni*, let parts of them to freemen, who cultivated them, and at the death of the tenant the land returned, in an improved condition, into the hands of the Church. This mode of tenure was already known to the Roman law (*precarium*). It sometimes happened that in exchange for a grant of this kind, the grantee made a gift to the Church of an estate of similar value belonging to himself. Thenceforward he had the usufruct of both estates, that of the Church as well as his own; but at his death the Church took possession of both. The grantee had the advantage during his life of a doubled income, and on his death the Church doubled its property. But it often happened that the Church, which was, as we know, very powerful, received the lands of private persons in the manner described without adding anything of its own, only conceding to the former owner a life-use of the property. Thus in various ways the allodial lands disappeared, and benefices became every day more numerous.

Up to this point we have seen the beneficiaries solicit the benefice and take the initiative in obtaining it. These beneficiaries remained bound by ties of gratitude to their benefactor, they exerted themselves to serve him and marched with him when he went to battle; they were his *vassi*. Before long a man's power was measured by the number of his *vassi*, the army of his clients; and then the great men, in order to increase their clientage, and consequently their influence, began themselves to offer benefices to those whom they desired to attach to themselves and gain as adherents.

The king, or the Mayor of the Palace who replaced him, needed to be able to count on the great men for the wars, whether foreign or civil, in which he engaged. Obligation towards the State was too abstract a conception to be understood, and the mere sense of duty was not strong enough to keep the great men loyal. The king therefore began to distribute lands to these great men. At first he gave them absolutely, but before long these lands were assimilated to the benefices. This evolution took place especially at the time when Charles Martel laid hands upon the property of the Church and distributed it in his own name to his warriors. The property of the Church was inalienable, it could not be given as an absolute possession. The warriors were only the life-tenants of it, and at their death it reverted to the Church. These estates were therefore simply ecclesiastical benefices, granted by the king or the mayor. Once this precedent had been established, estates granted by the king from his own lands were granted on the same conditions, merely for the lifetime of the grantee.

CH. V.

Another great change took place about the same time. One reason why Charles Martel made grants of ecclesiastical property to his warriors was that they had now to support great expense. They served in his armies no longer as foot soldiers but as cavalry, and their equipment was very costly. The revenue of the lands which were granted to them served as an indemnity against the expenses of military service. Thus it came to be considered that the benefice carried with it the obligation of military service. Under Charles the Great, the holders of royal lands were bound to be first at the muster; and before long it was an understood thing that, when a private person who had granted benefices marched to the wars, all his beneficiaries, who were also his vassals, must accompany him. Thus at the end of the Merovingian period the characteristics of the later fief are taking shape. The eleventh century fief is the direct descendant of the eighth century benefice, of which we have just traced the origin.

Another characteristic of the fief is that the holder of it exercises thereon all the powers of the State: he levies taxes, administers justice and summons the men of the fief to follow him to war. Now even in the Merovingian period on some of the great domains the State resigned a portion of its rights to the proprietor or seignior, and thus we find present, from this time onward, all the germs of the feudal system. We have seen how great were the powers of the count and the other royal officials: they often abused these powers, and the proprietors of the great estates complained to the king of their tyranny. In many cases the king listened to their complaints and gave them charters of immunity forbidding all public officials to enter their estates, to claim right of lodging, to try causes, to levy the *fredus* or other impost, or to compel the men to attend the muster of the royal army. Thenceforward the men of this privileged territory had nothing more to do with the agents of the government; the agents of the proprietor took their place; and before long the proprietor himself levied the former state-taxes, judged cases in his private court and regarded it as within his competence to deal with all offences committed upon his domain. He led his men in person to join the royal army, and he was naturally tempted to use them also in the prosecution of his private quarrels. If we remember the extent of some of the domains, which comprised a number of *villae* and were sometimes as large as a modern canton, we see how great was the area which was withdrawn from the authority of the royal officials, if not from that of the king himself. The estates which enjoyed these immunities were veritable seigniories. Alongside of the institutions of the State there had thus arisen another set of institutions which came into collision with the former and brought about the decay of the authority of the State. All the elements of feudalism—commendations, benefices, and immunities —are in existence without its being possible to say that feudalism is as yet constituted, because the elements are not combined into a system.

But before this system came into operation Charles the Great was to re-establish a strong centralised government; he was to make these social forces serve the interests of the State itself, and by his genius was to restore with incomparable brilliancy that Frankish monarchy which at the close of the Merovingian period had seemed likely to disappear.

The Merovingian period as a whole is without doubt a melancholy period. It marks in history what must be called an eclipse of civilisation, and it deserves to be described as a barbaric era. Nevertheless, it must not be imagined that the two hundred and seventy years which it includes were, so to speak, sunk in unbroken gloom. Even in this period it is possible to note some facts concerning industry and commerce, arts and letters.

Industry found refuge chiefly in the country districts, where each estate produced for itself all the supplies necessary to agricultural work and common life. The towns themselves took on a country-like air. The ancient buildings—temples, basilicas, baths—had been destroyed during the invasions and their ruins lay on the ground; the only considerable buildings now erected were churches. A sparse population occupied rather than filled the space surrounded by the half-ruined walls. Many houses had disappeared and wide areas lay vacant; these were turned into fields or vineyards, and thus in the interior of formerly populous cities there were closes and *culturae*. Outside the ramparts there rose, in many cases, a high-walled monastery—a sacred city alongside of the secular city—and these monasteries became new centres of population. Within the decayed cities we nevertheless find, at all events at first, some traces of industry. There is mention in the sixth and seventh centuries of workshops for the manufacture of cloth at Trèves, at Metz and at Rheims. There were also potteries, and numerous specimens of their art have been found in the tombs. The Merovingians had a taste for finely wrought arms, for sword-belt buckles of damascene work, for jewellery and gold-plate. The Merovingian goldsmiths were skilful. Eligius, son of a minter at Limoges, attained by the aid of his art to the highest posts; he became the counsellor of Dagobert and bishop of Noyon. There was also in the Merovingian period a certain amount of commercial activity. The Franks imported from abroad spices, papyrus and silk fabrics. This merchandise was either brought to the ports of Marseilles, Arles and Narbonne, or came by way of the Black Sea and the Danube. In the time of Dagobert a Frankish merchant named Samo went to trade on the banks of the Elbe, and there formed a great Slav kingdom which had its centre in Bohemia, and extended from the Havel to the Styrian Alps. The merchants of the town of Verdun formed an association in the time of Theudibert, about 540. The king aided them by lending them, at the request of the bishop Desiderius, 7000 *aurei*. They were thus enabled to put their business on a sound footing, and in the time of Gregory of Tours the wealth of these merchants was renowned. But commerce was chiefly in the hands of Byzantines and Jews. The Byzantines, who were generally known by the name of Syrians, whether they came from Asia or from Europe, had important trading-stations at Marseilles, at Bordeaux, at Orleans. When in 585 Guntram made his entry into the last-named city he was welcomed with cries of acclamation in the Syriac language. Simeon Stylites conversed with Syrian merchants who had seen Ste Geneviève at Paris. In 591 a Syrian named Eusebius was even appointed bishop of Paris, and gave offices in the Church to his compatriots. The Jews, on their part, formed prosperous colonies. Maintaining friendly relations with their co-religionists in Italy, Spain, and the East, they were able to give a wide extension to their business, and, as the Christian Church forbade the lending of money at interest, all dealing in money, all banking business, was soon in their hands. Five hundred Jews were settled at Clermont-Ferrand; at Marseilles and Narbonne they were more numerous still. The Jew Priscus acted as agent in purchases made by King Chilperic, who held disputations with him concerning the Holy Trinity.

Intellectual culture naturally declined during the Merovingian period. Nevertheless in the sixth century there are still two names which are celebrated in the history of literature, those of the poet Fortunatus and the historian Gregory of Tours. Fortunatus, it is true, was born in Italy and educated in the Schools of Ravenna; but his verses, with their wealth of mythological allusions, pleased the taste of the Frankish lords and the Merovingian kings, of whom he was to some extent a flatterer. He sang the praises of all the monarchs of his period, Charibert, Sigebert and Chilperic; he even lavished on Fredegund his paid panegyrics:

Omnibus excellens meritis Fredegundis opima.

Becoming the adviser of Queen Radegund he settled in her neighbourhood at Poitiers. He there became first priest, and then bishop. It was at this period that he wrote those charming notes in verse, thanking Radegund for the delicacies which she sent him and describing, with a slightly sensual *gourmandise*, the pleasure he derived from a good dinner; but at the same time he finds a more energetic strain in which to deplore the sorrows of Thuringia. And, also doubtless at the request of his patroness, he wrote the fine hymns which the Church still uses in the *Vexilla regis prodeunt* and the *Pange lingua*.

If Fortunatus was the sole poet of the Merovingian period Gregory of Tours is almost the sole historian. In his work, the History of the Franks, this troublous period lives again, with its vices, crimes and passions. The portraits which he gives us of Chilperic, Guntram and Brunhild are painted with extraordinary vividness. His work manifests real literary power. Critics sometimes speak of the *naïveté* of Gregory, but we must not deceive ourselves; this *naïveté* is a matter of deliberate art. Gregory does not of course observe strict grammatical correctness; he is by no means Ciceronian; he writes the language as it was spoken in his day. In a few passages only, where he is obviously writing with conscious effort, he employs rare and poetical expressions, as for example in the account of the baptism of Clovis, in the description of Dijon, in the narrative of his quarrels with Count Leudastes. But to these we prefer those pages where he lets himself go, and writes with his natural vigour, where he slips in malicious reflexions as it were unconsciously, or where he excoriates his adversaries. He has the real gift of story-telling and has justly been called the barbarian Herodotus. After his day all culture disappeared. A vast difference separates him from his continuator, the chronicler who has been named—we do not know for what reason—Fredegar. The chronicle of Fredegar is composed of scraps and fragments from various sources. One of the authors from whom extracts are made writes, "The world is growing old; the keenness of intelligence is becoming blunted in us; no one in the present age can compare with the orators of past times," and this phrase might be applied to the whole of the work. Nevertheless there are still found in Fredegar attempts at portraits of some of the Mayors of the Palace, Bertoald, Protadius, Aega, whereas in the last chronicler of the period, the Neustrian who compiled the *Liber Historiae Francorum*, there is no longer any-thing of that kind; it is a very meagre chronicle of the *rois fainéants*. The lives of the saints, which are still numerous enough, are singularly monotonous; they rarely inform us of any facts and are as like each other as one ecclesiastical image is to another.

A certain number of churches were built during the Merovingian period, such as those of Clermont, Nantes and Lyons, without counting the abbey churches such as St Martin de Tours and St Vincent or St Germain-des-Près at Paris, but of these great buildings no trace remains to us. The only remnants of buildings of this period belong to less important edifices, such as the baptisteries of Riez in Provence and St Jean de Poitiers, the crypt of St Laurent at Grenoble, and of the abbey of Jouarre. The great churches which are known to us from descriptions generally have a nave and two side-aisles with a transept, and are in the form of a Latin cross. At the point of intersection of nave and transept there was a tower, which at first served by way of "Lantern," but afterwards to hang bells in. On the walls were placed numerous inscriptions, sentences taken from the Scriptures, verses in honour of the saints. Pictures recalled to the faithful the history of the saints or scenes from Scripture. Often, instead of pictures the walls, as well as the floor, were covered with mosaic-work in which gold was freely used; a basilica at Toulouse was known for this reason as *la Daurade*. Sculpture in high relief was unknown, even in bas-reliefs the human figure appears very rarely after the sixth century. The artists could no longer even trace the outlines of animals, they drew conventional animals which are difficult to recognise, geometrical designs or roseate and foliate forms.

Some houses which Fortunatus describes to us seem still to have had a fine appearance. Such was the castle built by Nicetius, bishop of Trèves, on a hill overlooking the Moselle. The single entrance gate was commanded by a tower; a mechanical contrivance raised water from the river to turn a mill. This is quite a medieval donjon-keep. There were great houses too at *Bissonnum* and *Vereginis villa*, belonging to the bishop Leontius of Bordeaux, where under porticoes formed by three rows of columns guests could promenade sheltered from rays of the sun. But such dwellings must have been exceptional; the ordinary houses surrounded by the necessary appurtenances must have resembled farms rather than castles. Merovingian art however is mainly represented by the numerous pieces of jewellery which have been discovered, as was mentioned earlier. This art is certainly of Oriental origin: it was practised not among the Franks only, but among the other barbarian peoples of the West, and even here are found the same decorative ornaments.

In art as well as in literature the seventh century and beginning of the eighth are marked by a profound decadence. But just at the period of blackest barbarism the Frankish kingdom came into contact with Italy, the mother of arts and sciences, where the monuments of antiquity were preserved; and with England, where the monks still studied in their cloisters, and where the Venerable Bede had founded a school of worthy disciples. The Anglo-Saxons and the Italians brought to the Franks the treasures they had safely guarded; the Emperor Charles the Great recognised that it belonged to the duties of his office to spread enlightenment, to foster art and literature; and at length, after this night of darkness, there shone forth the brilliance of a true renaissance.

CHAPTER VI.

SPAIN UNDER THE VISIGOTHS.

Of the Gothic kings, it was Euric who really conquered the Iberian peninsula. We cannot indeed exactly determine the extent of his conquests. If we accepted in their literal signification the words of Jordanes, *totas Hispanias*, we should have to believe that Euric ruled over the whole peninsula; but those words are inexact, because we must except not only the Suevic State, but also other territories of the south and centre, which were not conquered by the Visigoths until considerably later. St Isidore, with reference to the campaigns of Euric, uses the words *Hispania superior*, which Hinojosa takes to mean Spain with the exception of Vasconia, Cantabria, and possibly the two *Conventus* of Saragossa and Clunia. Other writers allude to the conquest of districts in the north-east and south-east; and lastly, from the decrees of various councils held between 516 and 546, and from other evidence, we conclude that, near the end of the fifth century, the Visigoths held in Spain practically the whole of the ancient province Tarraconensis with the almost certain exception of part of Vasconia—most of the provinces of Carthaginensis and some portion of Baetica and Lusitania, and Galicia; while the rest of Lusitania remained in the hands of the Sueves, and the Balearic Isles still belonged to the Empire. In Gaul the Visigothic kingdom was bounded on the north-west by the Franks, on the north-east by the kingdom of Syagrius, and on the east by the Burgundians; thus it stretched from the Loire to the Pyrenees, and from the Atlantic to Arles.

International complications immediately confronted the Visigothic king, Alaric II (485–507). They originated in the ambition of the Frankish king, Clovis, whose predecessors had fought against Euric. The first encounter between the two powers was brought about by Clovis' invasion (486) of the kingdom of Syagrius, whom he defeated, and forced to take refuge in Toulouse, under the protection of Alaric. The Frank demanded his surrender. According to Gregory of Tours, Alaric was afraid of incurring the wrath of Clovis, and consented to give up Syagrius. But this docility on the part of Alaric did not deter Clovis from his determination to take possession of as much of Visigothic Gaul as possible. He could rely on a good deal of help from the outcome of his conversion to Catholicism in 496. The clergy and the

Catholic inhabitants of Gaul, both in the Burgundian and in the Visigothic provinces, looked upon Clovis as the leader destined to deliver them from Arian oppression. Even during the reign of Euric, there had been serious disagreement between the Catholic element and the monarch, which had given rise to persecution. The ground was therefore well prepared, and from the evidence of contemporary chroniclers it is clear that Clovis did not fail to take advantage of this inclination on the part of the Catholics, and that he stirred up public opinion in his favour. This led Alaric to adopt rigorous measures in the case of sundry Catholic bishops, whom he banished on the more or less well-founded charge of conspiring with the Franks. In due course Alaric prepared for war. He summoned to arms all his subjects, Visigoths and Gallo-Romans, clergy and laymen, collected sums of money, and when war was imminent (506) he tried to conciliate the Catholic clergy and the Roman element as a whole by the publication of the code which bears his name (the *Breviarium Alarici*), and by other demonstrations of tolerance. The code consisted of passages of Roman Law, which only applied to questions of private legislation among the non-Visigothic population. Theodoric, king of the Ostrogoths, who was related by marriage to Alaric and Clovis, attempted to avert war by personal mediation, to which, at his instigation, were added the entreaties of the Burgundians, Thuringians, Warni and Heruli, old friends of Euric. This mediation, to which Cassiodorus alludes, only served to postpone the crisis.

War broke out in 507. On the part of Clovis it was a war of religion, to free Gaul from the Arian heretics. Yet his policy was not quite so effectual as we might have expected, for a considerable part of Alaric's Catholic subjects fought on his side, displaying great courage. This was the case with the people of Auvergne, who, under the command of Apollinaris, son of the famous bishop Sidonius, formed an important element of the Visigothic army. It was a short campaign. The decisive battle was fought in the Campus Vocladensis, which seems to correspond to Vouillé, near Poitiers, on the banks of the river Clain[1]. The battle proved disastrous to Alaric, who was himself slain by Clovis. As a result of this victory, the Franks possessed themselves of the greater part of Gothic Gaul. At the close of 507, Clovis seized Bordeaux; in the spring of 508, he took Toulouse, where he laid hands on the treasure of Alaric; shortly afterwards, he entered Angoulême. His son Theodoric conquered the country round Albi and Rodez, and the small towns on the Burgundian frontier. Moreover, the dioceses of Eauze, Bazas and Auch were incorporated into the Frankish kingdom. To the Visigoths remained only the district afterwards called Septimania, bounded by the Cevennes, the Rhone and the sea, with its capital at Narbonne.

[1] There is some dispute about the exact site

In addition to this war with the Franks, Alaric had to contend with a rebellion of the Bagaudae of Tarragona, whose chief, Burdurellus, was taken prisoner at Toulouse, and there slain (498). On the death of Alaric, the Visigothic magnates chose for their king his illegitimate son Gisalic, instead of Amalaric, his legitimate heir. Theodoric, the king of the Ostrogoths and grandfather of Amalaric, opposed him by armed intervention, and thus re-established the right of succession to the throne and saved the Visigothic kingdom from total destruction. Gisalic, who is represented by the historians of the period as being very wicked and cowardly, was defeated in the neighbourhood of Narbonne by the Burgundians, at that time the allies of Clovis. He fled to Barcelona, whence he was expelled by the troops of Theodoric. He then took refuge in Africa at the court of the king of the Vandals, who refused to support his claims; afterwards, under the protection of Clovis, he returned to Gaul, and was killed there. Meanwhile, the Burgundians, who had taken possession of Narbonne, combined with the Franks, and besieged Arles: but they were defeated by the army of Theodoric, under command of his general Ibbas, who compelled them to withdraw from Carcassonne. Thus, almost all the cities of the province of Narbonne, including the capital, were reconquered, and the whole of Visigothic Spain was placed in subjection to Theodoric, albeit in the name of Amalaric. The final episode of the war was the raising of the siege of Arles in 510; this city was heroically defended by its inhabitants assisted by the Ostrogothic general Tulum. Shortly afterwards (511) Clovis died, and the city of Rodez reverted to the Visigoths. The part of Provence which Theodoric had conquered remained, for the time being, united to the other territories, but, on the death of Theodoric, it became part of the Ostrogothic kingdom in consequence of a treaty between Amalaric and Theodoric's successor Athalaric.

As regards internal policy, matters were settled on the following terms: Amalaric, a minor, was to be king of the Visigoths, and his grandfather Theodoric acted as his guardian. Indeed, for fifteen years, Theodoric was the real ruler of the kingdom both in Gaul and Spain. Theodoric tried to make his rule agreeable to the Visigoths. He adhered to the system, privileges and customs of the time of Alaric; he remitted taxation in the districts which had been especially impoverished by the war; he supplied Arles with money and provisions, and in order that his troops might not prove a burden to the inhabitants, he sent them corn and gold from Italy. His conduct as a guardian was particularly advantageous to Spain. He there displayed all the wise and vigorous policy which had rendered so illustrious his rule in Italy and which was all the more vital to Spain on account of the immorality and anarchy which had crept into the government during the decline of the Empire. Theodoric recovered for the Crown the exclusive right to coin money, which was being exercised by a few private individuals; he contrived to put an end to the extortions practised by the collectors of taxes and by the administrators of the royal patrimony (*conductores villici*) to the detriment of the State funds. It appears that, in the name of Theodoric, the Peninsula was at one time governed by two officials, viz. Ampelius and Liberius, and at another by one alone, viz. Theudis. Some of the chronicles allude to these officials as *consules*, and it is probable that their authority extended over every branch of the administration. On the death of Theodoric in 526, his ward Amalaric assumed complete royal power over the Visigoths. The Frankish peril, which had hitherto been held at bay by the prestige of the Ostrogoths, still presented a threatening aspect. The sons of Clovis were longing to extend their dominion in Gaul by the conquest of the part occupied by the Visigoths. Amalaric attempted to avert the danger by means of an alliance and, after repeated demands, he succeeded in obtaining the hand of Clotilda, daughter of Clovis; but this marriage, which he had regarded as a means of salvation, supplied the Frankish kings with the very pretext they desired. Amalaric did his utmost to make Clotilda abjure the Catholic Faith and embrace Arianism, and according to Gregory of Tours actually ill-treated her. Clotilda made complaint to her brother Childebert, and he hastened to declare open war in Septimania. Near Narbonne he defeated the army of Amalaric (531); the latter fled, but, according to Jordanes and Isidore, he was shortly afterwards slain by his own soldiers. Childebert took possession of Narbonne, where he joined his sister, and seized considerable treasure.

The position of the Visigoths could hardly have been worse. Without the hope of finding a powerful defender such as Theodoric, they found themselves threatened by the Franks, a nation naturally warlike, and further emboldened by its conquest of Aquitaine. In fact, dating from the defeat of Amalaric, the Visigothic kingdom may be regarded as consisting of Spanish territory, and its capital was then transferred from Gaul to the Iberian peninsula. But they had the good fortune to find a man who was equal to the occasion. This was Theudis the Ostrogoth, who had been governor of Spain in the time of Theodoric, and who had settled in the Peninsula, where he had married a very wealthy Spanish woman, the owner, according to Procopius, of more than 2000 slaves and dependents. When Theudis had been formally elected king, he began to make preparations for the ejection of the Franks, who, in this same year (531), had entered the kingdom by way of Cantabria, and in 532 had annexed a small territory near Béziers. In 533 Childebert joined forces with his brother, Chlotar I, invaded Navarre, took possession of Pampeluna, and marched as far as Saragossa, to which he laid siege. The inhabitants resisted bravely: thus the Visigoths had time to send two armies to their assistance; of these one was commanded by Theudis himself, and the other by his general Theudegesil. At their approach the Franks retreated as far

as the Pyrenees. They were seriously defeated by the army of Theudis;
but Theudegesil, whom they succeeded in bribing, permitted them to
escape, and to bear with them the treasures which they had acquired
during the campaign. Among these was the body of St Vincent, the
martyr, for which they built near Paris a church, that afterwards known
as St Germain-des-Près. After having thus ejected the Franks, Theudis
undertook an expedition to the coast of Africa, which was being conquered
by the army of the Byzantines. By this expedition, made in 543, Theudis
only acquired temporary possession of Ceuta, which was shortly afterwards retaken by the Emperor, for in 544 Justinian alludes to it as his
own. Four years later, in 548, Theudis was assassinated in Seville by
a man who pretended to be mad. His successor, Theudegesil, only
reigned for sixteen months. We know nothing more of him than that
he was a man of immoral conduct, and that in 549 he too was assassinated in Seville.

The fact that the Visigoths possessed Seville does not mean that they
ruled over the whole of Baetica. On the contrary, the greater part of
it was independent, controlled by the Spanish-Roman nobles, who since
the time of Majorian, and even before, had obtained possession of the
country. Agila, the successor of Theudegesil, set himself to conquer
these independent territories; he was defeated before Cordova by the
Andalusians, who slew his son, and possessed themselves of the royal
treasure. This defeat (which the chroniclers regard as a divine punishment
for Agila's profanation of the tomb of St Acisclus), his tyrannical
behaviour and his hostility to the Catholics, who constituted the bulk
of the Spanish population, were turned to account by Athanagild, a
Visigothic noble who had designs on the crown. In order to make sure
of success, he solicited the support of the Emperor Justinian, who sent
him a powerful army under the command of his general Liberius (554).
The Byzantines were probably assisted by the inhabitants of the country
who, on account of their Catholic Faith, were bound to welcome the
imperial forces and the person of Athanagild, concerning whom Isidore
himself states that he was secretly a Catholic. They had, therefore, no
difficulty in possessing themselves of the most important towns on the
coasts of the Mediterranean, more particularly those in the east and
south, *i.e.* the district round Valencia, Murcia and Andalusia. Agila
was defeated near Seville by the combined forces of Athanagild and
Liberius, and withdrew to Mérida, where he was assassinated by his own
followers, who forthwith acknowledged the usurper.

Thus when Athanagild became king in 554, the power of Justinian
in the Peninsula was extensive, for he was not content with playing the
part of helper, but claimed a substantial acknowledgment of his services.
It is probable that Athanagild rewarded him by an offer of territory, but
we have no exact information on the subject, because the text of the treaty
which ensued has not been preserved. But it is certain that Liberius

encroached on the boundaries agreed upon, for he seized all the land lying between the Guadalquivir and the Jucar (going from west to east), together with that between the sea and the mountains of Gibalbin, Ronda, Antequera and Loja, the Picacho de Veleta, the mountains of Jaen, Segura and Alcaraz, the pass of Almansa (in the province now called Albacete), the territories of Villena, Monovar and Villajoyosa (from the south-west and the north-east, following the line of the Penibaetian mountain range, and the continuation on the east which connects it with Ibérica). The situation was all the more serious because to the great military strength of the Eastern Empire was now added the aggregate force of all the Spanish-Roman element in Baetica and Carthaginensis, that is to say, all who had remained independent of the Visigoths, and whom Agila had attempted to subdue. These Spanish-Romans who, by reason of their religion, were opposed to the Visigoths, naturally regarded the rule of Justinian as the prolongation of the Empire whereof they had formed a part until the coming of the Goths. Hence the tradition that the inhabitants of these regions rebelled against the Visigoths and proclaimed Justinian as their sovereign is most probably authentic.

Athanagild did not submit to this treachery, but immediately proceeded to make war on the Byzantines, and established his capital at Toledo, an excellent position from the strategical point of view. He attempted to flatter the Catholics, by means of a benevolent policy, which was intended to estrange them from the Empire. The war lasted for thirteen years, that is, throughout the whole of the reign of Athanagild, who had also to fight against the Franks in order to defend Septimania, which was still in the hands of the Visigoths, and against the Vascons, who were continually struggling for independence. But this perpetual warfare did not prevent Athanagild from strengthening his kingdom from within, or from increasing its prosperity. The fame of his wealth and the splendour of his court; the fame of his two daughters, Brunhild and Galswintha, spread to the neighbouring kingdoms. Two Frankish kings, Sigebert of Austrasia and Chilperic of Neustria, were inspired thereby to seek an alliance with him; the former became the husband of Brunhild and the latter of Galswintha. Of these marriages, and more particularly of the second, which took place in 567 and ended in tragedy, we possess detailed accounts in the chronicle of Gregory of Tours, and in the *Carminum Liber* of Venantius Fortunatus. A few months after the marriage of Galswintha, Athanagild died at Toledo (Nov. or Dec. 567).

The throne remained vacant for several months, until the spring of 568, but we do not know the reason of this. The interregnum came to an end with the accession of Liuwa or Leuwa, a brother of Athanagild, who (why or for what purpose we are unable to say) shared the government with his brother Leovigild or Liuvigild, to whom he entrusted the Spanish part, keeping for himself the territory in Gaul. It has been observed that John of Biclar, a chronicler of the latter part of the sixth century, states that Leovigild obtained *Hispania Citerior*. This phrase seems to confirm what has been said before, that from the beginning of the reign of Athanagild, *Hispania Ulterior*, or the greater part of the districts which belonged to it, was either in the hands of the Byzantines or, at any rate, was not loyal to the Visigoths. This evidence, viewed in connexion with the results of Leovigild's campaigns, shews that several districts of north-western Spain, such as Oviedo, Leon, Palencia, Zamora, Ciudad Rodrigo, etc., were independent, under petty princes or rulers, the majority of whom belonged to the Spanish-Roman nobility: it also shews that the district of Vasconia could only nominally be considered as belonging to the Visigothic kingdom.

To remedy this, Leovigild adopted as a guiding principle the ideal of hegemony in the Peninsula. He began by surrounding himself with all the external pomp which adds so much to the prestige of a sovereign; he adopted the ceremonial of the Emperors and celebrated his proclamation in Toledo by striking gold medals, bearing an effigy of himself in regal vestments. But he did this with a view to his relations towards his subjects, and took care not to arouse the jealousy of the Empire: on the contrary, he made use of it to further his own designs. He revived the former connexion between the Visigothic kings and the Emperors, by communicating to Justin II the news of his election as king, and by acknowledging his authority he made a truce with the Byzantine army in the Peninsula, and persuaded it to join with him in opposing the advance of the Sueves.

We hear very little of the Sueves. Since the year 428, when they had been delivered from their barbarous enemies, the Vandals, they had been trying to obtain possession of the territories formerly occupied by the latter, which extended towards the south-east and south-west of the Peninsula. This attempt at territorial expansion gave rise to constant wars, usually between the Sueves and the Romans, sometimes between the Sueves and the Visigoths, though in some cases the two barbarian powers united. (Thus Theodoric I allied with Rechiarius the Sueve against the Romans, and in 460, Theodoric II with Remismund against Frumar, another petty king of the Sueves.) The consequence of this last alliance was that the Sueves, who were partly Catholics and partly Pagans, were converted to Arianism. In 465, Remismund, with the help of the Visigoths, took possession of Coimbra, and shortly afterwards of Lisbon and Anona. But in 466 Euric put an end to these friendly relations, and in a terrible war, to the horrors of which Idatius refers, he forced the Sueves to fall back on their ancient possessions in the north-west. There is a considerable gap in the history of the Sueves, from 468—in which year the chronicle of Idatius comes to an end, until 550 when Carrarich appears as king.

In the reign of Carrarich, or in that of Theodomir who succeeded him (559–570), this people was converted to Catholicism, through the influence of Martin, bishop of Braga (St Martin). During this same period, the Sueves had again extended their eastern and southern boundaries to the Navia in the province of Asturias, to the Orbigo and the Esla in Leon, to the Douro in the country of the Vettones, to the Coa and the Eljas where they join the Tagus, in the direction of Estremadura (west of Alcántara), and in Lusitania to the Atlantic, by way of Abrantes, Leiria, and Parades.

In 569 Leovigild began his campaign against the Sueves and the independent districts in the north-west. He very quickly took possession of Zamora, Palencia and Leon, but Astorga resisted bravely. Nevertheless, the victories which he had gained sufficed to justify him in striking a new medal in commemoration of them. On this medal Leovigild stamped the bust of the Emperor Justin and applied to himself the adjective *clarissimus*. In 570 we see Leovigild, forgetful of his protestations of submission, attacking the district called Bastania Malagneña (the ancient Bastetania, which extended from Tarifa to Adra) where he defeated the imperial forces. Continuing the war in 571 and 572, he took Medina Sidonia (Asidona) and Cordova with their adjacent territories. These victories moved the Sueves, at that time ruled by King Mir or Miron, who in 570 had succeeded Theodomir and who possibly bore the same name, to make war in their turn. They therefore invaded the country round Plasencia and Coria, Las Hurdes and Batuecas—that is, the valleys of the Jerte, Alagors and Arrago—and afterwards the territory of the Riccones[1].

In 573, whilst Leovigild was preparing to check the advance of the Sueves, he received the news of the death of his brother Liuwa, which left him king of all the Visigothic dominion. Immediately he made his two sons, Hermenegild and Recared, dukes of Narbonne and Toledo, although it is not certain which of the two duchies was given to which. He thus reassured himself in this direction, and, when he had secured the capital, he set forth on a new campaign in which he conquered the district of Sabaria, *i.e.* according to the best geographers, the valley of the Sabor, the province of Braganza, and Torre de Moncorvo, which bordered on the Suevic frontier.

These expeditions were interrupted by internal troubles for which the nobles were responsible. From the political point of view the fundamental fact on which all the history of the Visigoths turns, is the opposition between the nobles and the kings. Of these, the nobles were continually struggling to maintain their predominance, and the right to bestow the crown on any one of their members, while the kings were

---

[1] According to Fernandez Guerra the Riccones occupied the places now known as Jaraicejo, Trujillo, Logrosán and La Conquista, although other historians believe that their territory was nearer to Cantabria and Vasconia.

continually endeavouring to suppress all possible rivals, and to make
the succession to the throne hereditary or at any rate dynastic. Gregory
of Tours states that the kings were in the habit of killing all the males
who were in a position to compete with them for the crown; and the
frequent confiscation of the property of the nobles to which the laws
of the period refer, shews clearly the means to which the kings had
recourse in the struggle. Whether Leovigild exceeded his power by
dividing the kingdom between his two sons (and this is the view taken
by Gregory of Tours); or whether he tried in general to lessen the
authority of the nobles—and perhaps not only that of the Visigothic
nobility, but also of the Spanish-Romans—the result was that the
nobles stirred up several insurrections; first amongst the Cantabri, secondly
amongst the people of Cordova and the Asturians, and thirdly, in
Toledo and Evora, at a time when the Sueves and Byzantines were
planning attacks. Leovigild, undismayed by these manifold dangers,
attended to everything and, by dint of good luck, with the help of
Recared, he succeeded in subduing the rebels. He took Ammaia
(Amaya), the capital of the Cantabri; he obtained possession of
Saldania (Saldaña), the stronghold of the Asturians; he quelled the
insurgents in Toledo and Evora (Aebura Carpetana) and in every case
he sealed his victories with terrible punishments (574).

When he had suppressed these preliminary internal rebellions
Leovigild proceeded to conquer various independent territories in the
provinces of Galicia and Andalusia. The former consisted of the
mountainous district known as Aregenses, situated in what is now the
province of Orense, and of which a certain Aspidius was king. The
Andalusians possessed the whole of the tract of country round the
Orospeda mountains, from the hill of Molaton in the east of the present
province of Albacete, to the Sierra Nevada, passing through the provinces
of Murcia, Almeria and Granada, that is to say, the lands of the
Deiittani, Bastetani and Oretani. In both parts of the country Leovigild
was successful, but his victories, and especially those in the Orospeda
mountains, which bordered on the Byzantine dominion, naturally excited
the jealousy of the imperial governors. In order to check the progress
of Leovigild, now threatening them at such close quarters, they stirred
up fresh strife in the interior of the kingdom, instigating rebellions in
the province of Narbonne, on the coasts of Catalonia and Valencia, and
in the central region of the Ebro. Leovigild, assisted by his son
Recared, also succeeded in suppressing these insurrections; he made
triumphant entries into Narbonne, Saragossa, Loja, Rosas, Tarragona
and Valencia, and punished the rebels with the utmost severity. These
campaigns, and the preceding ones in Galicia and Andalusia, lasted from
575 to 578. A notable incident in them—which, although it had no
connexion with the action of Leovigild, yet to some extent favoured his
designs—was the attack made by the Byzantine general Romanus, son

of the patrician Anagartus, on part of Lusitania, in the direction of
Coimbra and the valley of the Munda (*i.e.* the Mondego), which at that
time was governed by a Suevic duke, who bore the title of king.
Romanus seized this individual, his family and his treasure, and annexed
the district to the Empire. Leovigild took advantage of this reverse
to attack the Suevic frontier in the direction of Galicia, and the Suevic
king Mir or Miron was obliged to sue for peace. The Visigothic
monarch granted him a truce for a short time and meanwhile, in the
district afterwards called Alcarria, he built a fortified city to which he
gave the name of *Recopolis* in honour of Recared. There are still a
few traces of it to be seen.

From 578 to 580, there was a period of external peace, but on the
other hand, these years marked the beginning of a civil war of graver
import than any former one; for, in the first place, this war was
concerned with religion; and in the second, with the rash ambition of
one of Leovigild's own sons. This was Prince Hermenegild; the
struggle originated in the same way as the former contests between the
Visigoths and the Franks. Once more, the cause of it was a Frankish
princess, Ingundis, daughter of Sigebert, king of Austrasia, and of
Brunhild, and therefore niece of Leovigild. In 579 Hermenegild
married her, he being an Arian and she a Catholic. Immediately there
was quarrelling at Court, not between husband and wife, but between
Ingundis and her grandmother, Goisvintha, the widow of Athanagild,
who had married Leovigild. Goisvintha was a zealous Arian and tried
to convert her grand-daughter, first by flattery and afterwards by
threats, ending, according to the chroniclers of the period, in violence.
Nothing could shake the faith of Ingundis, but she made bitter
complaints to the Spanish Catholics and the Franks. To prevent
matters from going further, Leovigild sent his son to govern Seville, one
of the frontier provinces. There Hermenegild found himself in an
atmosphere essentially Catholic, and, at the instigation of his wife
Ingundis and Archbishop Leander, he finally abjured Arianism. The
news of his conversion gave fresh courage to the malcontent Spanish-
Romans in Baetica, and the consequence was that Seville and other
cities rebelled against Leovigild and proclaimed Hermenegild as king.
The latter was rash enough to make the venture and fortified himself in
Seville, with the help of the greater part of the Spanish, and of a few
Visigothic nobles. It has been said that, on this occasion, Hermenegild
did not receive the support of the Catholic clergy. This statement is
possibly exaggerated. It is true that Gregory of Tours, John of Biclar,
and Isidore condemn the revolt and call Hermenegild a usurper; but
this does not mean that, at the time of the rebellion, none of the
clergy took his side. It is only reasonable to infer that he did receive
some support from them. Though uniformity of religion on the Arian
basis may have played an important part in Leovigild's scheme of

government; nevertheless, on this occasion, he did not allow himself to be led away by zeal, or by the irritation which the behaviour of his son must have aroused in him. Hitherto, he had been inconsistent in his treatment of the Catholics. He had frequently persecuted them—for instance, we learn from Isidore of Seville that John of Biclar was in 576 banished to Barcelona for refusing to abjure his religion, and that, for ten years, he was subjected to constant oppression. Again, Leovigild had sometimes flattered the Catholics and complied with their desires. In 579 he adopted a policy of moderation. He sent ambassadors to his son to reduce him to submission, gave orders to his generals to act only on the defensive, and took active measures to prevent the clergy from supporting Hermenegild. The latter did not yield; on the contrary, afraid that his father would take revenge, he sought the assistance of the Byzantines and the Sueves.

Then Leovigild thought of establishing some form of agreement between Catholics and Arians, and convoked a synod, or general meeting of the Arian bishops, at Toledo, in 580. At this synod, it was agreed to modify the form to be used in the adoption of Arianism, substituting reception by the laying on of hands for the second baptism. As John of Biclar says, many Catholics, among whom was Vincent, bishop of Saragossa, accepted the formula and became Arians. Nevertheless, the majority remained faithful to Catholicism. Leovigild attempted to reduce this majority by conversions to Arianism, but when these were not forthcoming, he resorted to persecution. Isidore of Seville in his *Historia* says that the king banished a number of bishops and nobles, that he slew others, confiscated the property of the churches and of private individuals, deprived the Catholic clergy of their privileges, and only succeeded in converting a few priests and laymen.

Meanwhile Hermenegild had strengthened his party by winning over to his cause important cities such as Mérida and Cáceres. He twice defeated Duke Aion, who had been sent against him, and in commemoration of these victories, he coined medals after the manner of his father.

But this serious struggle did not cause the king to neglect his other military duties. In 580, the Vascons rebelled once more, possibly under the influence of the Catholic insurrection in Baetica. In 581 Leovigild went against them in person, and after much trouble succeeded in occupying a great part of Vasconia, and in taking possession of the city of Egessa (Egea-de-los-Caballeros). To clinch his success, he founded the city of Victoriàcus (Vitorià) in a good strategical position. Having thus finished this campaign, Leovigild decided to take energetic action against his rebellious son. To this end, he spent several months of 582 in organising a powerful army, and, as soon as it was assembled, marched against and captured Cáceres and Mérida. Whereupon the troops of Hermenegild retreated as far as the Guadalquivir, taking Seville as their centre of defence.

CH. VI.

Before attacking the city, Leovigild set himself to make the Byzantines withdraw from their alliance with his son, and he ultimately succeeded. According to the chronicle of Gregory of Tours, his success was due partly to motives of political expedience and partly to a gift of 30,000 gold coins. When he had thus secured himself in this direction, Leovigild, in 583, marched on Seville. The first battle was fought before the Castle of Osset (San Juan de Alfarache), which he was not long in taking. Amongst the enemy, he found the Suevic king Miron, whom he compelled to return to Galicia.

The siege of Seville lasted for two years. Hermenegild was not in the city, seeing that he had left it shortly before to go in search of fresh help from the Byzantines. He cannot have been successful, since he took refuge in Cordova, whither Leovigild advanced with the army. Convinced that all resistance was in vain, Hermenegild surrendered and prostrated himself before his father, who stripped him of his royal vestments and banished him to Valencia. Shortly afterwards, for some unknown reason, he caused him to be transferred to Tarragona, and entrusted to Duke Sigisbert, whom he ordered to guard his son closely, for his escape might lead to a fresh civil war. Sigisbert confined the prince in a dungeon, and repeatedly urged him to abjure Catholicism. Hermenegild stubbornly resisted, and was finally killed by Sigisbert (13 April 585). Leovigild is accused of the crime by our earliest authority, the *Dialogues* of Gregory the Great, but the best opinion acquits him of it. Hermenegild was afterwards canonised by the Catholic Church.

Whilst the ambition of Hermenegild was thus ruthlessly cut short, his father's was realised in the destruction of the kingdom of the Sueves. He did not lack a pretext: a noble called Andeca who, since the death of Miron in 583, had usurped the crown, in the following year proclaimed himself king of that people, disputing the rights of Miron's son Eburic or Eboric, the ally of Leovigild, who at once invaded Suevic territory. As Isidore says, "with the utmost rapidity" he struck fear into the hearts of his enemies, completely vanquishing them at Portucale (Oporto) and Bracara (Braga), the only two battles fought during the campaign. Andeca was taken prisoner, forced to receive the tonsure, and banished to Pax Julia (Bejar). In 585, the Suevic kingdom was converted into a Visigothic province. Thus, it only remained for Leovigild to possess himself of the two districts held by the Byzantines —one in the south of Portugal and west of Andalusia, and the other in the province of Carthagena—and to make the political unity of the Peninsula an accomplished fact. But it was not given to him to effect this. He died in 586, at a time when his army, under the command of Recared, was fighting in Septimania against the Franks who had twice again made the murder of Hermenegild a pretext for invading this remnant of Visigothic land. Even during the lifetime of

Leovigild, Guntram, king of Orleans, had made an invasion, and had also sent ships to Galicia to instigate an insurrection of the Sueves. The Franks were driven back by Recared and their ships sunk by the naval forces of Leovigild. After this preliminary struggle Leovigild attempted to make an alliance with Guntram, but the Frankish king rejected all his advances, and for the second time invaded Septimania. Recared was engaged in fighting against him when he received the news of his father's last illness, which caused him to return to Spain. No sooner was Leovigild dead, than Recared was unanimously elected king.

His reign was very unlike that of his predecessor. Leovigild had been essentially warlike, striving for the political unification of the Peninsula. Recared fought only in self-defence against the Franks and Vascons; instead of continuing the conquest of Spain, he made peace with the Byzantines, acknowledged their occupation of certain territories and promised to respect it. Moreover, Leovigild desired uniformity of religion, but on the basis of Arianism, whilst Recared made it his main concern, but on the basis of Catholicism. It is probable that he abandoned the warlike policy of his father, because recent events had convinced him that the greatest danger for the Visigothic kingdom lay in the discord between the Visigothic and the Spanish-Roman elements. He probably realised that the main work before him was to unite these two elements, or at least, to induce them to lay aside their discontent and jealousy. More than one reason has been alleged for the change in the religious point of view. It has been supposed that Leovigild himself turned Catholic shortly before his death, and this view is supported by a passage in Gregory of Tours, but it scarcely suits the nature of the king, as illustrated by the earlier events of his life. There is another statement, connected with the above, which has less documentary evidence to support it. It occurs in the *Dialogues* of Gregory the Great, and is to the effect that Leovigild charged Leander, bishop of Seville, to convert Recared. Lastly, the conjecture that Recared had secretly turned Catholic in his father's lifetime, is not supported by any contemporary documents. We are, therefore, led to suppose that this change on the part of Recared was due to one of the following causes:— (1) Reflection, which had ripened in the knowledge of the real force which the Catholics represented in the Peninsula, superior as they were in number to the Visigoths, possessed of money and property in the land, and connected with the Byzantines. (2) A change of conviction on the part of Recared himself, after his accession to the throne, which was possibly brought about by the preaching of Leander, and also by the example of Hermenegild. (3) A possible combination of both causes.

The facts are:—(1) The execution of Duke Sigisbert, which might have been either the outcome of Recared's affection for his brother Hermenegild, or in punishment of Sigisbert's transgression of his orders; but it is noteworthy that Recared accounted for it by stating that Sigisbert was guilty of conspiracy. (2) The public and formal conversion to Catholicism of the king and his family, which, according to John of Biclar, took place in 587, ten months after Recared had ascended the throne.

The conversion was heralded, first, by a decree which put an end to the persecution of the Catholics, secondly, by the adoption of extraordinary measures with regard to the Gothic prelates and nobles in the provinces entrusted to the king's agents (whom Gregory of Tours calls *nuntios*), and lastly by permission given to the bishops of both religions to hold a meeting, to the end that they might freely discuss their respective dogmas. At the conclusion of this discussion, Recared declared his preference for Catholicism and his conversion thereto, which he ratified with all due formality at the Council held in Toledo (the third of this name) in May 589. There were present at this Council 62 bishops, five metropolitans, the king, his wife, and many nobles, all of whom signed the declaration of faith. Henceforth the Catholic religion became the religion of the Visigothic State. According to John of Biclar, the king exhorted all his subjects to be converted to it.

But the faith of a people cannot be changed at the command of a king, nor could the interests which had grown up in the shadow of the ancient national religion allow themselves to be suddenly swept away. There ensued conspiracies and rebellions on the part of the Arian bishops, the nobles and the people, who adhered to their traditional faith. Goisvintha herself, the queen-mother, who lived for some time longer, Sunna, bishop of Mérida, Athelocus, bishop of Narbonne, Bishop Uldila, several counts, amongst others Segga and Witteric, Duke Argimund, and other persons of importance, made plots and conspired against the life of the king, took up arms, and sought the help of the Frankish king Guntram, who made two incursions into Septimania. On both occasions he was defeated and forced to withdraw. Moreover, Recared succeeded in suppressing all the rebellions of the Arians, punished the instigators, and caused many of the books dealing with that religion to be burnt. Nevertheless, although John of Biclar affirms the contrary, Arianism did not die out among the Visigothic people. It continued to exist until the fall of the Visigothic kingdom; it was the cause of fresh insurrections, and, as we shall see, it was sufficiently strong to produce a temporary reaction.

Recared had still to struggle with the Byzantines, who had renewed their quarrel with the Visigoths. But through the mediation of Pope Gregory I, he made with the Emperor Maurice the treaty to which we have already alluded, whereby it was agreed that each monarch should respect the territory possessed by the other. Lastly, Recared made war on the Vascons, whom Leovigild had driven back to the further side of the Pyrenees, and who were trying, though without success, to regain the land which they had formerly held.

Recared's internal policy of appeasing the Spanish-Roman element manifested itself in another direction. According to Isidore of Seville, Leovigild reformed the primitive legislation of the Visigoths, which dated from the time of Euric, by modifying a few laws, suppressing others which were unnecessary, and adding some which had been omitted from Euric's compilation. Since the text of this reform has not come down to us, we know only that it actually existed[1].

From the tone of approval in which Isidore of Seville tells of the reforms accomplished by Leovigild, it has justly been inferred that they were a decided attempt at conciliation, and that it was intended to proceed with them until the differences between Visigoths and Spanish-Romans had been lessened or suppressed. There is more reason to suppose that Recared worked in this direction, but for this we have no such contemporary evidence as that which refers to Leovigild.

The three monarchs who successively occupied the Visigothic throne after Recared were of no great individual importance, but their history gives proof of the disturbed condition of the country. In fact, Recared's son, Liuwa II, who was elected king on the death of his father and who continued his father's Catholic policy, only reigned for two years. In 603 he was dethroned and slain in an insurrection headed by Count Witteric, who gained the support of the Arian party and attempted to restore the ancient religion of the Gothic people. In 610, in consequence of a reaction on the part of the Catholics, Witteric forfeited his crown and his life. The crown was bestowed on Gundemar, a representative of the nobles. He only reigned for two years, during which time he waged two wars, one with the ever-restless Vascons, and the other with the Byzantines. Both these wars were continued by Sisebut, who succeeded him in 612. He, like Gundemar, was a Catholic and he pursued the militant policy of Leovigild. When he had suppressed the Vascon insurrection, Sisebut marched against the imperial forces, and, in a brief campaign, after defeating their general Asarius in two battles, took possession of all the eastern provinces of the Byzantines, that is to say, of the land between Gibraltar and the Sucro (Jucar). The Emperor Heraclius sued for peace, which Sisebut granted on condition of annexing that province to his kingdom, leaving to the Byzantines only the west, from the Straits to the Algarves.

As concerns internal order, the most important event of Sisebut's reign was the persecution of the Jews. They had lived in the Peninsula in great numbers since the time of the Empire under the protection

---

[1] Professor Gaudenzi alone is of opinion that the fragments of St Germain-des-Près, of which I shall presently speak, form part of it. Professor Ureña maintains that the *leges antiquae* of the compilation made in the time of Receswinth, and the four fragments of Visigothic law found in Manuscript B 32 of the Biblioteca Vallicelliana in Rome are to be attributed to Leovigild. Other scholars believe that they are taken wholly or in part from the code of Euric.

of the laws. The *Lex Romana* of Alaric II had only copied those of
the Roman laws which were least favourable to the Jews. It therefore
preserved the separation of races, counting marriages of Jews and
Christians no better than adultery, and forbade the Jews to hold
Christian slaves or to fill public offices. But it upheld their religious
freedom, the jurisdiction of their judges and the use of Jewish law.
But custom was more favourable to them than law, for mixed marriages
took place in spite of the law, the Jews held public offices, and
bought and circumcised Christian slaves. Recared put the laws in force,
and further commanded to baptise the children of mixed marriages
(Third Council of Toledo). Sisebut went further, and began the
persecution of the Jews. He made two series of regulations on the
subject. One of these, which appears in the *Forum Judicum*, restores
and sharpens the laws of Recared ; the other included an order to
baptise all the Jews, under penalty of banishment and confiscation of
goods[1].

What was the cause of this intolerance ? It has been attributed
to the influence of the clergy ; but against this opinion we must set the
disapproval of Isidore of Seville in his *Historia*, and of the Fourth
Council of Toledo, over which the same prelate presided. Equally
untrustworthy is the statement that these measures were forced upon
Sisebut by the Emperor Heraclius, in the treaty made between them
to which we have already alluded, for there is no text to bear out this
statement, and moreover, the analogous case which Fredegar attributes
to King Dagobert is equally unproved. All that we know for a fact is
that Sisebut adopted the measure without consulting any Council, so
that we must attribute the king's resolution either to his own inclination
(Sisebut's piety led him to write Lives of the Saints, for instance, the
well-known life of St Desiderius), or to the desire of obtaining possession
of property by means of confiscation, or of gaining money from the sale
of dispensations. Such were certainly his motives on other occasions.
Moreover, he claimed religious authority for himself, for he considered
that he was the ecclesiastical head of the bishops, and behaved as such.
It is possible that he was also indirectly influenced by the fact that the
Jews had assisted the Persians and Arabs in their wars against the
Christians of the East. The immediate result of the law was that the
greater part of the Jews received baptism, and that, according to the
Chronicle of Paulus Emilius, only a few thousands (*aliquot millia*) sought
refuge in Gaul. But this effect must have been short-lived, for we know
that, nineteen years later, there were in Spain Jews who had not been
baptised and others who had reverted to their former religion.

---

[1] The existence of this law is proved by contemporary evidence, though it does
not appear in the *Forum Judicum*. From a passage in Isidore of Seville we are led
to suppose that this decree was made during the first year of Sisebut's reign, that is
to say, in 612.

Sisebut died in 621, and was succeeded by his son Recared II who reigned for a few months only. He was followed by Duke Swinthila, who had greatly distinguished himself as a general in the wars of Sisebut. He pursued and completed the military policy of the latter, conquering (629) the Algarves, the last province in the possession of the Byzantines. Thus, with the exception of a few unimportant districts in the north, which had no regular government, such as Vasconia, the Pyrenees of Aragon, and possibly some other places in mountainous parts, whose inhabitants remained independent, the Goths at last succeeded in reducing the country to one united State. Swinthila also fought against the Vascons, and on one occasion defeated them. As a military base for his control over the district, he built the fortress of Oligitum, which some geographers take to be the same as the modern Olite, in the province of Navarre.

If Swinthila had stopped short at this point, he would certainly have retained the good will of his contemporaries, and the epithet of "father of the poor" applied to him by Isidore of Seville; but it is probable that Swinthila was too sure of his power when he ventured to deal with the problems of internal policy, and that his failure affected the judgments passed on him. As a matter of fact, Swinthila did nothing more than what Liuwa and Leovigild had done before him, when he shared the government of the kingdom with members of his own family, namely:—his son Recimir, his wife Theodora, and his brother Geila. Why was Swinthila not permitted to do this, seeing that it had been tolerated in the former kings? Whether he set about it with less caution than his predecessors, or shewed more severity in suppressing the conspiracies, we do not know. The fact is that he not only lost the crown in 631, whilst struggling against the party of a noble called Sisenand, who, with an army of Franks, advanced as far as Saragossa, but that the chroniclers of the period call him a wicked and sensual tyrant. He did not die in battle—his defeat was mainly due to treachery—nor did he lose his freedom. In 633, to judge from a canon of the Fourth Council of Toledo, he was still alive, but of his end we know nothing. The political problem was still unsolved; and we shall see that the kings did not abandon the intention of making the crown hereditary.

Of Sisenand, who reigned for six years, and died in 636, we know nothing more important than that he summoned the Council already referred to, which condemned Swinthila for his "evil deeds" and passed canons relating to the Jews. These canons indicate a change of policy in the clergy, which is all the more interesting, because, as we have said before, the Council had for its president Isidore of Seville. On the one hand, in agreement with the doctrine of this prelate, it censured the use of violent measures to enforce a change of religion (Canon LVII); but, on the other hand, it accepted and sanctioned those conversions which had been brought about through fear in the time of Sisebut. It thus obliged those who had been baptised to continue in their new faith, instead of accepting, in accordance with the views of Isidore, the Constitution of Honorius and Theodosius (416), which permitted the Jews who had become Christians by force and not from religious motives, to revert to their former religion. With regard to the succession to the throne, the principle of free election by the assembly of nobles and bishops was established by Canon LXXV. In accordance with this principle, Chintila was elected king in 636. Nothing of importance occurred during the four years of his reign except the summoning of the fifth and sixth Councils of Toledo. The canons of the first are chiefly concerned with the King, the respect due to his person, and some of his prerogatives, and furnish striking evidence of the uneasiness caused by the ambition of the nobility, who were endeavouring by violent means to wrest the crown from the elected king. The Sixth Council, held in 637, which laid stress on the same subjects, also issued a decree dealing with the Jews (Canon III), which again enacted that all who had not been baptised should be driven out of the kingdom. In order to prevent relapses to their former religion, the king forced them to sign a document (*placitum*) on confession of faith, in which, on the pain of the most terrible curses, they bound themselves to live in accordance with the doctrine and practices of Christianity; and to renounce Jewish customs. Moreover, to enforce this policy, the same canon obliges all future kings to swear that they will not permit the Jews to violate the Catholic Faith, nor countenance their misbelief in any way, nor "actuated by contempt or cupidity" open up the path of prevarication "to those who are hovering on the brink of unbelief."

In 640, despite Canon LXXV of the Fourth Council of Toledo, Chintila was succeeded by his son Tulga, though the outward form of election was observed. This explains why his brief reign was disturbed by conspiracies and insurrections. We do not know for certain whether it was in consequence of his death or through the success of one of these insurrections that in May 642 the throne was occupied by one of the nobles—Chindaswinth, who boldly faced the political problem with energetic measures like those of Leovigild. Thus 700 persons, of whom the greater part were nobles, chosen from amongst those who had taken the most active part in conspiracies or shewn signs of political ambition, or proved themselves dangerous to the king, were slain, or reduced to slavery. Many others contrived to escape, and took refuge in Africa or in Frankish territory, and there they doubtless attempted to stir up fresh insurrections, to which reference is apparently made in one of the canons of the Seventh Council of Toledo, summoned by Chindaswinth in 646. This canon imposed heavy penalties, viz. excommunication for life and confiscation of property, on the rebels or emigrants including the clergy, who should try to obtain the support of foreign countries against their native land ; it also exhorted the monarchs of these countries not to allow the inhabitants of their dominions to conspire against the Visigoths. By this means Chindaswinth achieved his purpose, for, throughout his reign (642–653) there was not a single insurrection. On the other hand, supported by the Catholic clergy, who both from doctrinal and practical points of view had always favoured the principle of hereditary succession to the throne, he in 649 admitted to a share in the government his son Receswinth or Recceswinth, who from that time onwards was virtually king, and succeeded his father in 653, without going through the form of election.

When Chindaswinth died, the rebellious nobles thought that the moment had come to take revenge, and, relying on the general discontent which was due to increased taxation and on the ever-restless Vascons, they rose in arms, and with a large force advanced as far as Saragossa, under the command of a grandee called Froja. Receswinth prepared for war, and ultimately succeeded in defeating them, taking Froja prisoner. But the country must have been profoundly agitated, and the throne threatened by very serious dangers, seeing that Receswinth, instead of taking advantage of his victory to inflict severe punishment on the rebels, and subdue them once for all, came to terms with them, granted an amnesty, promised to reduce the taxes, and yielded the question of election. Hence the significance of the Eighth Council of Toledo, held in 653, at which, after having caused himself to be released from the oath which he had taken to shew himself inexorable towards the rebels, he confirmed the above-mentioned Canon LXXV of the Fourth Council. By this canon it was decreed that, on the death of the King, the assembly of prelates and nobles should elect as his successor a man of high rank, and that the person of their choice should bind himself to maintain the Catholic religion and to prosecute all Jews and heretics. This latter part of the Royal oath is a revival of the anti-Semitic policy. The speech or *tomus regius* read before the Council is very bitter, and proves that in spite of all the preceding measures there was still in Spain a great number of unconverted Jews, or that even those converted still observed the rites of their own religion. The Council refused to take measures against the non-converted, but in 654, the king, on his own account, issued various laws which rendered more intolerable the legal position of the Hebrews of all classes. These laws obliged all Jews who had been baptised to sign a new *placitum,* similar to that of the time of Chintila, which imposed on apostates the penalty of being stoned and burnt alive.

Whilst, in this way, the Visigothic kings were gradually widening the gulf between Jews and Christians, on the other hand they were lessening the differences between the Visigoths and the Spanish-Romans, and just as Recared had arrived at uniformity of religion, so did Chindaswinth and Receswinth aim at uniformity of law. The ground was well prepared, for, on the one hand, the principles of Roman jurisprudence had gradually crept into the Visigothic private law, and on the other, the Councils of Toledo had created a common system of legislation of the utmost importance. A proof of the agreement at which the two legal systems had arrived in some cases is furnished by the Visigothic formulae of the time of Sisebut, found in a manuscript at Oviedo. According to the prevalent opinion of legal historians, this unification was completed by Chindaswinth's abolition of the *Lex Romana* or *Breviarium* of Alaric II, to which the Spanish and Gallo-Romans were subjected, and by the specific repeal of the law of Roman origin which forbade marriage between people of different races, though we know that such marriages did take place, like that of Theudis. The accepted theory has recently been modified by the revised opinion of the critics, which ascribes to Recceswinth the abolition of the *Lex Romana* formerly ascribed to his father[1]. In any case, the reign of Chindaswinth was a period of great legislative activity so far as unification is concerned. This activity found expression in numerous amendments and modifications of the older Visigothic Laws compiled by Recared and Leovigild and in the promulgation of other new ones. Ninety-eight or ninety-nine laws, clearly the work of Chindaswinth, are recorded in the texts which have come down to us, and all of them shew the predominating influence of the Roman system. Moreover, as his son Recceswinth leads us to understand in one of his own laws, Chindaswinth began to make what was in fact a new code. Recceswinth, therefore, did little more than conclude and perfect the work begun by his father, that is to say, he codified the laws which were in force in Spain, in their twofold application, Gothic and Roman. They formed a systematic compilation, which was divided into two books and bore the title of *Liber Judiciorum*, afterwards changed to that of *Liber* or *Forum Judicum*. The date of it is probably 654. Two copies of this *Liber* have been preserved; in the modern amended editions it is known by the name of *Lex Reccesvindiana* (Zeumer). It is a collection of laws made expressly for use in the courts and therefore it omits several provisions referring to legal subjects or branches of the same—for instance a great part of the political law, for as a rule this does not affect the practice of the courts. But the fifteen chapters of Book I, which refer to the law and the legislator, form an exception to this; they are the reflection, and

---

[1] *De remotis alienarum gentium legibus,* II. 1. This law, which occurs in several manuscripts and editions of the Visigothic codes, prohibits the use of the Roman legislation in Spain. Nevertheless, there are some historians (Helferich, Stobbe, Gaudenzi, Ureña) whom this revised opinion does not satisfy, and who consider that the amendment or repeal of the *Lex Romana* is earlier. They go so far as to assert that it was the work of Leovigild and that the law of Recceswinth is nothing more than a ratification of the former decree. Nevertheless, the accepted opinion, of which Zeumer is at present the chief exponent, is still the best supported and the most popular.

in some cases the literal copy of the contemporary doctrinal texts of political philosophy—for instance, of Isidore of Seville. It is probable that Braulio, bishop of Saragossa, was one of the compilers of the new code, if not the chief. Receswinth subsequently made other legal provisions, both in the Councils and outside them.

Receswinth died in 672, after reigning for 23 years. Wamba was elected as his successor. Almost the whole of his reign was spent in warfare. He fought first against the Vascons, who made a fresh rebellion, quickly suppressed; then against a general Paulus who, together with Randsind, duke of Tarragona, Hilderic, count of Nîmes, and Argebald, bishop of Narbonne, had incited all Septimania and part of Tarragona to rebellion; and lastly, against the Muslims. The rebellion of Paulus was promptly quelled and punished, and Wamba recovered possession of Barcelona, Gerona, Narbonne, Agde, Magdalona, Béziers and Nîmes, which had constituted the chief centres of disaffection. The war against the Muslims, who had already obtained temporary possession of North Africa, originated in their invasion of the southern coast of Spain, and in particular of the city of Algeciras. The invaders were driven back, and their fleet was destroyed. The experience gained by Wamba, especially on the occasion of Paulus' rebellion, must have shewn him how necessary it was to strengthen the military organisation of the State, to inspire his people with a warlike spirit, and above all, to enforce compulsory service in the army, which appears to have been evaded by some of the nobles and clergy. This need was met by a law passed in 673, which together with three others bearing on civil and ecclesiastical matters, was added to the code of Receswinth. By this law, all who refused to serve in the army and all deserters were deprived of the power to bear witness. Despite all the prestige which Wamba's victories had procured for him, and the mental energy shewn in all his actions, the fundamental weakness of the Visigothic State, namely, the want of agreement between its political elements, appeared once more, and in 680 Wamba was dethroned in consequence of a conspiracy headed by Erwig, one of the nobles, with the assistance of the metropolitan of Toledo. To preserve himself from a similar fate, Erwig adopted a mild and yielding policy, and sought the help of the clergy. In accordance with this policy, he revoked the severe penalties of Wamba's military law, which had displeased the nobles, and restored its victims their ancient nobility. On the other hand, besides persecuting the partisans of Wamba, Erwig made new laws against the Jews, in order that the *Judaeorum pestis* might be wholly exterminated, subjecting the converts to minute regulations that he might assure himself of their religious faith, and to the non-converted he granted the term of 12 months—from 1 February 681—in which to receive baptism under penalty of banishment, scourging and the loss of all their hair. These laws, although very severe, were milder than those of Receswinth, seeing that they excluded the death-penalty. The Twelfth Council of Toledo accepted them in full.

By the use of similar methods, Erwig induced this Council—summoned within three months of his consecration—not only to sanction his usurpation and accept the false pretext that Wamba had become a monk of his own free will and had charged the metropolitan of Toledo to anoint him (Erwig) as his successor, but also to defame the memory of Wamba, to forbid his restoration, and to proclaim the person of Erwig and his family sacred and inviolable (Council XIII, Canon iv). Erwig was so desirous of ingratiating himself with the dangerous elements of the nation that he pardoned, not only those who had been punished in Wamba's time for their share in the rebellion of Paulus, but also all those who had been branded as traitors during the reign of Chintila, restoring to them the property, titles, and civil rights which they had forfeited (Council XIII). The second canon of the same Council continued this policy; it laid down rules for the protection of the nobles, officials of the palace and free-born men, in their suits, so as to prevent the arbitrary degradation and confiscation of property which the kings were wont to order. But this was not the first time that the Visigothic legislation dealt with this point, and established guarantees of this nature. In 682, Erwig, by means of these laws and others, made a revised edition of the *Liber Judiciorum* or *Judicum*[1].

Before Erwig died in 687, he named as his successor Egica, a relation of Wamba and his own son-in-law; and in November of that year Egica was duly elected king. Notwithstanding the oath which he had taken in the presence of Erwig to protect the family of his predecessor, he at once divorced his wife Cixilona, degraded Erwig's other relations, and punished the nobles who had taken the most prominent part in the conspiracy which deprived Wamba of the throne; on the other hand he favoured the partisans of Wamba, whom Erwig had persecuted. This behaviour naturally led to another rebellion of the unruly section of the Visigothic nobles. In the fifth year of Egica's reign,

---

[1] If we are to judge by the issue of the pretentious edict, which is preserved in Law i. Lib. i. tit. 2 of the *Forum Judicum*, this revised edition was made in order to recast all earlier legislation, and the new laws in order to prevent "the numerous lawsuits and varied interpretations, opposition to the enforcement of the law, and the want of decision and stability in the judgment of the court." In place of all this it was intended to "substitute clearness for uncertainty, utility for harmfulness, mercy for the death-penalty, and to abolish the obscurities, and supply the deficiencies of the law." But, in reality, very little of this was accomplished, for the essential part of the new edition of the *Liber* rests on that of Receswinth, with the exception of a few amendments of earlier laws, and the addition of some new ones, amongst others those referring to the Jews (tit. 3 of Lib. xii), and one bearing on military service (9th, 2nd, Lib. ix). Of the Code of Erwig, three copies have been preserved. These date from the ninth and tenth centuries, the most important being that of the Paris MS. 4418.

a conspiracy was discovered of which Sisebert, metropolitan of Toledo, was the leader. The aim of this conspiracy was to slay the king, his sons, and five of the principal officials of the palace. The metropolitan was deprived of his see, excommunicated and sentenced to exile for life, with the confiscation of all his property.

It seems that, during the reign of Egica, there was another more serious conspiracy, directed, not against the king, but against the Visigothic nation. Egica himself denounced it in the royal *tomus* which he presented to the Seventeenth Council in 694, saying, with reference to the Jews, that, " by their own open confession, it was known, without any shadow of doubt, that the Hebrews in these parts had recently taken counsel with those who dwelt in lands beyond the sea (*i.e.* in Africa), that they might combine with them against the Christians "; and when accused, the same Jews confirmed before the Council the justice of the charge. What was the cause and what the aim of this conspiracy? The cause may very well have been the legislation recently made by Egica with regard to the Jews, which, though very favourable to the converts who made sincere profession of the Christian Faith—seeing that it exempted them from the general taxes (*munera*) and from the special payments made by Jews, allowed them to possess Christian slaves and property, and to trade—was unfavourable to the non-baptised and to those who observed the rites of the Jewish Faith, they being burdened with all the taxes from which the first were exempted. We do not exactly know the aim of the conspiracy, although the understanding with the Africans and what happened later in the reign of Roderick give us reason to believe that it was intended to help the Muslims to make another invasion. The Council, regarding the crime as proved, decreed in the eighth canon[1] that all the Jews in the Peninsula should be reduced to slavery and their goods confiscated; it authorised the Christian slave-owners to whom they were consigned to take possession of their sons at the age of seven, and educate them in the Christian Faith, and eventually marry them to Catholics. This law was not enforced in Visigothic Gaul.

During the reign of Egica, the Visigothic code was revised for the last time (693–694)[2]. After the manner of his predecessors, Egica

---

[1] Afterwards converted into Law xviii. Lib. xii. tit. 2 of the *Forum Judicum.*

[2] To judge from the allusion to this revision in the royal *tomus* presented to the Sixteenth Council, it might be thought that it was an attempt at extensive reform, but it was not so. The revision consisted in a brief amendment of a few of Erwig's laws, and the addition of the new ones made by Egica. The eighteen chapters extracted from *nomo-canon*, referring to points of public law (the election of sovereign, etc.), which appear as an introduction in manuscripts of later date than the seventh century, are attributed by some scholars to Egica, but this view is rejected by others who, like Zeumer, do not even believe that, during the reign of Egica, anything was added to the edition of Erwig but Erwig's own laws. After the time of Egica, possibly after the fall of the Visigothic power, there appeared a new

admitted his son Witiza to a share of the government, entrusting to him the north-west, of which the capital was Tuy ; he also stamped the effigy and name of Witiza, together with his own, on the money which was coined. Witiza was therefore allowed to succeed his father without opposition (701). The reigns of Witiza and the two following kings are very obscure. We have but scanty information, and that distorted with legends and partisan inventions. Thus, Witiza has been represented as the wickedest of kings and as a man addicted to every vice. From the testimony of the anonymous chronicler of the eighth century and of the Arab historians from the ninth century onwards, it appears that he was the exact opposite. A critical examination of the sources shews that he was an energetic and benevolent king.

Witiza began by proclaiming an amnesty, which included the nobles who had been condemned by Egica. This produced an excellent effect, but did not suffice to prevent a fresh rebellion, when Witiza, following the example of his father, admitted his son Achila or Agila to a share in the government, entrusting to him the provinces of Narbonne and Tarragona under the charge of a noble, probably called Rechsind, who may have been a relative. We do not exactly know why this policy did not succeed. The chroniclers tell us little, till we come to Lucas of Tuy, who wrote in the thirteenth century, and is the first to allude to it. But we know that conspiracies were formed, that Witiza was obliged to dissolve some meeting or Council, whose attitude had given cause for uneasiness ; that, according to the evidence of the anonymous Latin chronicler, he quarrelled with Bishop Sindered, a man of exceptional piety, and lastly, that he punished some conspirators, amongst others Theodofred, duke of Cordova, whom he blinded, and Pelagius, another noble, whom he banished. This Pelagius, mentioned in the chronicle of Albelda—of the ninth century—is possibly the son of Fafila, or Fairla, duke of Cantabria—who had been banished from court during the reign of Egica, and who was slain by Witiza himself when governor of the north-west provinces—and therefore most likely Pelagius of Covadonga, who would naturally be opposed to Witiza as the murderer of his father. Witiza managed to escape all these dangers and died a natural death in Toledo at the end of 708 or beginning of 709. Archbishop Roderick, a chronicler of the twelfth century, is the first to relate the legend that Witiza was deposed and blinded. Shortly before his death, the Muslims again invaded the Spanish coast, and were driven back by him. According to Isidore of Pax Julia, Witiza also defeated the Byzantines, who during the reign of Egica had attempted to reconquer some of the cities of southern Spain. Witiza was succeeded by Achila ; he, together with his two brothers, Olmund and Artavasdes, and his uncle, Bishop Oppas (the Don Oppas of the legend), were the males of the family of

edition of the *Forum Judicum,* a work of private initiative, known by the copyists of the eighth and following centuries. It is now known as the *Vulgata.*

the late king. Immediately a revolution broke out, for the nobles refused to acknowledge the new king. They produced a frightful state of confusion, but did not at first succeed in deposing him. Finally, the ringleaders met in council in the spring of 710, and elected Roderick (Ruderico), duke of Baetica. Soon afterwards, Roderick defeated the army of Achila, who, together with his uncle and brothers, fled to Africa, leaving the duke of Baetica in possession of the throne.

The reign of Roderick—the title of Don assigned to him by the later chroniclers is a pure anachronism—is still more legendary than that of Witiza, and partly from the same cause—the false reports spread by political enemies, who were afterwards to be the victors, and partly the Moorish invasion and the fall of the Visigothic kingdom. The last king of the Visigoths is enveloped in legends from his first action as a king (the legend of the Tower of Hercules) until after his death (the legend of the Penance). The most important of all is that known as the legend of Florinda, or La Cava (the harlot), which thoroughly explains the invasion of the Muslims and the cause of their expedition to Spain, which resulted in the destruction of the Visigothic kingdom. We therefore have the story in two forms.

1. The connivance of Julian—whoever he may have been—with the Muslims, in order to effect the conquest of Spain; Julian being actuated by purely political motives, and his daughter having no connexion with the matter.

2. The explanation of Julian's connivance with the Arabs by the insult which he had sustained at the hand of Roderick.

The first Christian writer who mentions the count, and calls him Don Julian—the *Don*, as in the case of Roderick, is an anachronism—is the monk of Silos, who wrote at the beginning of the twelfth century. In our days it is generally admitted that this individual was called (not Julian but) Urban or Olban, and this opinion is supported by the reading of the most ancient text of the anonymous Latin chronicler, and by the Arab historians Tailhan and Codera. There is considerable difference of opinion as to who this Urban was. Some think that he was a Visigoth, others a Byzantine, but all are agreed that he was governor of Ceuta. Neither of these hypotheses can be maintained, because there is no certain evidence that Ceuta then belonged to the Byzantine Empire—still less to the Visigothic kings. Nor can the title *rum* given to Urban by the Arab chroniclers, which might mean a Gothic or Byzantine Christian, be taken in a definite sense. On the other hand, the anonymous Latin chronicler, as also Ibn Khaldūn and Ahmed Anasirí Asalauí, state that Urban "belonged to the land of Africa," to the Berber tribe of the Gomera, that he was a Christian and lord or petty king of Ceuta. Whoever he was, the monk of Silos is the first of the Spanish chroniclers to mention him, and to represent him as taking any part in the conquest of Spain; according to the earlier chroniclers, the only people who helped, or rather were helped by, the Arabs, were the sons of Witiza, whom Roderick had deposed. Hence, the connexion between the person of Urban and the fall of the Visigothic State is now generally held by scholars to be a mere legend, perhaps derived from some Arab historian.

The second element of the legend, viz. the violation of the count's daughter, is even more doubtful. The offence committed by Roderick against the count is also, by some of the early chroniclers, attributed to Witiza, and the later chroniclers are not clear whether it was the daughter or the wife of Julian or Urban. Moreover, the monk of Silos is the first to relate this part of the legend ; and the name of La Cava, by which the count's daughter is now generally known, appears for the first time in the fifteenth century, in the untrustworthy history of Pedro del Corral. Nevertheless, the more cautious of the modern critics do not consider the question as definitely settled.

A third explanation, intermediate between the two, has been set forth by Saavedra, the historian and Arabic scholar, and its main outlines are at present more or less generally accepted. He believes that, even granting that Roderick did commit this offence, it had no connexion with the help given by Julian to the Arabs. According to him, Julian was a Byzantine governor of Ceuta, and received assistance from Witiza in 708, when his city was attacked by the Muslims, and was therefore bound to the Visigothic king by ties of gratitude and possibly of self-interest. On the death of Witiza, when Julian was again attacked by the Arabs, he surrendered to them on condition that, during his lifetime, he might continue to hold the city of Ceuta under the supreme authority of the Caliph. When Achila was deposed by Roderick, he sought help from Julian, who helped him by making a preliminary expedition to Spain, which was not successful. Then the family of Witiza had recourse to the Muslim chiefs, who were more powerful than Julian, and after long negotiations, thanks to his intervention, they succeeded in obtaining the support of the Arab troops of Africa, and thus managed to defeat Roderick. This connexion between the Muslims and the sons of Witiza is confirmed by all the chroniclers, and forms a trustworthy starting-point for the history of the invasion. The final attack was preceded by two purely tentative expeditions, of which the first, that attributed to Julian, was made in 709, and the second, a year later, was controlled by an Arab chief called Tarif, who merely laid waste the country between Tarifa and Algeciras, and did not succeed in obtaining possession of any stronghold.

In 711, a large force of Muslim troops, commanded by Ṭāriḳ, the lieutenant of Mūsā, governor of Mauretania, who was accompanied by the count Julian or Urban of the legend, took the rock of Gibraltar, and the neighbouring cities of Carteya and Algeciras. When the enemy had thus secured places to which they could retreat, they advanced on

Cordova, but were detained on the way by a regiment of the Visigothic army under the command of Bencius, a cousin of Roderick. Although the Arabs defeated Bencius, his resistance enabled the king himself to arrive on the field. At that time Roderick happened to be fighting in the north of Spain against the Franks and the Vascons, whom the partisans of Achila had incited to make a fresh attack. When the Visigothic king saw this new danger, he assembled a powerful army and marched against the invaders, who, according to some historians, also increased their forces to the number of 25,000 men. On 19 July 711, the armies met on the shores of Lake Janda, which lies between the city of Medina Sidonia and the town of Vejer de la Frontera in the province of Cadiz. The river Barbate flows into this lake, and as its Arabic name of Guadibeca was misunderstood by some of the chroniclers, there arose the mistaken belief that the battle was fought on the banks of the river Guadalete. The victory was won by the Arabs, owing to the treachery of part of the Visigothic army, which was won over by the partisans of Achila. Among the traitors, the chroniclers make special mention of Bishop Oppas and Sisebert, referring to the latter as a relation of Witiza. So the king could not prevent Ṭāriḳ from cutting off his retreat and dispersing his army. What became of King Roderick? The most common story in the chroniclers, both Arabic and Spanish, is merely that he disappeared, or that his end is unknown. Only a few state plainly that he perished in the battle of La Janda, and even these disagree as to the details of his death. Saavedra[1] has thus reconstructed the history of Roderick after his defeat of La Janda. The Arabs advanced on Seville and, after another victory, they took Ecija, besieged Cordova, which held out for two months, and entered Toledo. King Roderick rallied his forces in Medina, and went to threaten the capital, which was occupied by Ṭāriḳ. The Arab general asked Mūsā for reinforcements; in 712 the latter came himself with a large army. After taking possession of Seville and other strongholds, he advanced on Mérida, the place which the Muslims had most reason to dread. He besieged this city, which held out for a year, and was finally taken by storm.

At this point, we notice an important change in the accounts given by the chroniclers. Hitherto the invaders had met with but little resistance, and a certain amount of sympathy on the part of the towns-people, who, in some cases, had opened the gates of their cities to the foe. The Arabs had only left small garrisons in the towns which they had conquered, entrusting the protection and government of these towns to the Jews, who naturally welcomed the victorious Arabs. But, after

---

[1] Relying on a text of Rasis in which the king is represented as being present at the battle of Sagiuyne or Segoyuela, and on another text of the chronicle of Albelda (of the ninth century), which states that Roderick reigned for three years, 710–713; also on the definite statement of the Arab historians, that the king took refuge in a place called Assanam or Assuagin.

the taking of Mérida (June 713), a change appears to have set in. Possibly about that time Mūsā, who had seen for himself what the country was like, and what advantages he had gained, disclosed his intention of changing his tactics. The Muslim troops had hitherto acted as auxiliaries of Achila's party, but at this point Mūsā began to regard the victorious Muslims as fighting on behalf of the Caliph. In any case about this time the Visigoths began to offer a general resistance, which first shewed itself in the revolt of Seville. Mūsā sent his son ʿAbd-al-ʿAzīz to suppress it, and he himself advanced as far as the Sierra de Francia, not without giving orders to Ṭāriḳ, who was at Toledo, to come and join him with an army in the wild mountainous country, which extends thence to the Estrella, passing through the Sierra de Gata and forming a means of communication with Portugal. Of one place, Egitania or Igaeditania (Idanha a Vella), we possess money coined by Roderick, possibly in 712. The king of the Visigoths had established himself there. Finally, the combined forces of the Muslims came up with him near the town of Segoyuela in the province of Salamanca. In the battle (September 713) Roderick was defeated, and probably slain. His corpse was perhaps borne by his followers to Vizeu, for if we believe the chronicle of Alfonso III, written in the ninth century by Sebastian of Salamanca, a tomb was there discovered with the inscription: " Hic requiescit Rudericus, rex Gothorum."

Thus ended the rule of the Visigoths, for Mūsā, after the battle of Segoyuela, marched to Toledo, which had revolted on the departure of Ṭāriḳ, and there proclaimed the Caliph as sovereign, dealing the death-blow to the hopes of Achila and his supporters. Achila was obliged to content himself with the recovery of his estates, which had been confiscated by Roderick, and with his residence at Toledo, where he lived in great pomp. His brother Artavasdes established himself at Cordova and assumed the title of count, which he transmitted to Abū Saʿīd, his descendant. Olmund remained in Seville, and Bishop Oppas held the metropolitan see of Toledo. As for Julian, he shortly afterwards followed Mūsā on his journey to Damascus, the capital of the Caliphate, and subsequently returned to Spain ; according to Ibn ʿIyād, the Arab historian, he then established himself in Cordova, where his son, Balacayas, became an apostate, and where his descendants continued to reside. This then is Saavedra's theory.

The end of the Visigothic kingdom of Spain was the natural result of the political divisions and the internal strife which had undermined the State. Since the time of Recared, and even more since that of Chindaswinth, there had been no insuperable difficulty in the amalgamation of the Visigothic and Spanish-Roman elements. In recent times their opposition has been exaggerated ; it has been supposed that the imperfect nature of the fusion effected by the kings betrayed itself in national weakness, that the two racial elements lacked cohesion, and therefore they could not make head against the foreign invaders. But our information proves that they were much more closely united than has generally been supposed. Moreover, the most fruitful cause of antagonism between Visigoths and Romans—the distribution of lands, houses and slaves—was not as widely enforced in the Peninsula as in Gaul, where, nevertheless, it did not prevent the fusion of the two elements. Concerning the way in which this distribution was made in the territories ceded by Honorius to the Visigoths, by the application of the law of tenancy (*de metatis*), contained in the code of Theodosius, we now possess exact information shewing that the distribution did not apply to all the Gallo-Roman *possessores*. With regard to Spain, we know for a fact that the Sueves applied this law, and we have good reason to suppose that, touching the arable land and part of the forests, the Visigoths did the same, after the conquests of Euric, in the districts which they acquired. We have various data in support of this; amongst others, the fact that the laws of *consortes* remained in force. It is also probable that they made distribution of the houses, the slaves engaged to cultivate the fields, and the agricultural implements; but, in any case, the private property of the Spanish-Romans seems to have suffered less than that of their neighbours in Gaul.

Moreover—notwithstanding the statement apparently contained in the military law of Wamba—the fact that, up to the time of Roderick, the Visigoths were constantly engaged in warfare, seems to confute the accusation of effeminacy and military decadence which has been brought against them. The Arabs before they came to Spain had been victorious in other countries where these conditions did not prevail. The fact that they were able to effect the conquest of the Peninsula in the comparatively short space of seven years is due—apart from the prowess of the Muslims —to the political disagreements of the Visigoths, to the indifference of the enslaved classes who found it profitable to submit to the victorious Arabs, to the support of the Jews—the only element really estranged from the bulk of the nation by persecution—and lastly, to the selfishness of some of the nobles—one more proof of the political unsoundness of the State—who preferred their personal advantage to concerted action on behalf of a monarch. The internal history, the history of the Visigothic kingdom, is one long struggle between the nobility and the monarchy. The kings were supported by the clergy in their efforts to consolidate the royal power and transmit it from father to son, while the nobles strove to keep it elective, and held themselves free to depose the elected king by violence. Nevertheless, the kings gained a certain strength, especially those endowed with great personal qualities, such as Leovigild, Chindaswinth, Receswinth and Wamba. The Visigothic king was an absolute monarch, at times despotic, notwithstanding the principle of submission to the law which, from the contemporary works on ecclesiastical politics, passed into the legislation. The king was the chief of the army and the only legislative power. The last is clearly proved by the Councils of Toledo, concerning which there have been so many erroneous opinions.

It is therefore necessary to discuss in some detail the organisation and authority of these Councils. The kings alone were empowered to summon them, they had also the right to appoint the bishops, and to deprive them of their sees, thus exercising in the Catholic Church the power which, in these matters, they had been wont to exercise in the Arian. Their power to summon the Councils is acknowledged in the decrees passed by each of these, with the possible exception of the seventh, which seems to leave the question undecided. On the other hand, the decree of the ninth Council clearly states that the bishops have not the power to assemble except by command of the king. The latter did not issue his summons at regular intervals. The Council was formed of two elements, the clerical and the lay. The first consisted of the bishops, who in varying numbers were present at all the Councils; the vicars, who appeared for the first time at the third Council; the abbots, who began to attend at the eighth; and the archpriest, archdeacon, and precentor of Toledo. The lay element was composed of the officials or nobles of the palace (*optimatibus et senioribus palatii, magnificentissimis ac nobilissimis viris*, etc.), whose presence is attested by the signatures and prefaces to the decrees of all the Councils dealing with civil matters. From these we see that the lay element is absent from the Council held in 597 (which is not numbered), from that summoned by Gundemar, also known as "Gundemar's Ordinance," from the fourteenth and from the seventh, which merely confirmed or re-enacted a law already approved by the lay element at the Royal Council. We are left in doubt as to the presence of the lay element at the following Councils:—the tenth, where the signatures are probably incomplete; the eighteenth, of which there are no decrees in existence; and the third of Saragossa, from which the signatures are missing. As in the case of the ecclesiastics, the number of the nobles varied considerably. We see from the decrees of the twelfth and sixteenth Councils that they were chosen by the king, and we learn from those of the eighth Council that this was in accordance with an ancient custom. What part did the nobles take in the assemblies? Historians are by no means agreed; some hold that they had a voice in the discussion of lay matters only, others that they were nothing more than passive witnesses, or that their presence was a pure formality; again, others believe that they represented the king. Perez Pujol, the most recent historian of Visigothic Spain, has a convincing argument that, in matters wholly or partly lay, the nobles had the same rights to discuss and vote as the ecclesiastical members of the Council. This is the inference drawn from authentic texts of the eighth, tenth, twelfth, thirteenth, seventeenth Councils, and from the sixth, which is conclusive with regard to the vote. The difference between the respective powers of the lay and clerical elements was limited to matters wholly religious, and the right of proposing laws to the king.

With regard to lay matters, the functions of the Councils were of three kinds: (1) *Deliberative*, concerning the methods of government, adoption of new laws, modification or repeal of the old ones, and their codification or compilation. On these points the king consulted the Councils, both in the *tomus regius* which he handed to them at the opening of the Council, and in special communications, such as the one sent to the sixteenth Council (9 May 693). (2) *The right to petition or to initiate legislation*, that is to say, the right to present to the monarch, for approval, such proposals as were not included in these communications or in the *tomus regius*. But only the ecclesiastics were entitled to take this initiative. (3) *Judicial*, that is to say, the power to act as a kind of tribunal in the case of disputes connected with the administration; this tribunal settled the complaints and charges brought by the citizens against the government officials, and possibly also against influential men. In this sense, the Council formed part of the system of the courts. It is not known whether these matters were laid directly before the Council, or whether they first passed through the hands of the king. The discussion concerning the *tomus* and the royal communications was followed by voting, as a result of which the original proposal of the monarch was approved or modified. He frequently entrusted to the Council, not only the adoption of specially important laws, but also the general revision of all the existing laws—as we see from the *tomus regius* of the eighth, twelfth, and sixteenth Councils. This added to the freedom enjoyed by the clergy with regard to legislative initiative (as expressed in the canons of the sixteenth and seventeenth Councils) and furnishes grounds for the very general opinion that the Visigothic monarchy was dominated by the clergy, and was therefore mainly ecclesiastical in character. In the different Visigothic codes, and, consequently, in the most recent versions of the *Liber* or *Forum Judicum*, there is a large proportion of laws made by the Councils on ecclesiastical initiative: further, the political and theological doctrines of the time—of which Isidore of Seville is the chief representative—are reflected at every stage in the legislation, such as the duties of the monarch, the divine origin of power, the distinction drawn between the private means of the monarch and the patrimony of the Crown, etc., and the duty of the State to defend the Church and to punish crimes committed against religion.

The Visigothic legislation was deeply imbued with the spirit of Catholicism. This was due, not only to the piety of the monarchs and upper classes, but also to the superior culture of the clergy, which gave them great authority over Spanish society, and enabled them to defend the principles of justice. Yet we have no right to suppose that, from the time of Recared, the clergy ruled the kings. We have seen that the kings controlled the bishops, that they appointed them, deprived them of their sees, and convoked them, so that they always had the means of checking any encroachment. We know that there were frequent disputes between the Crown and the prelates, that the latter often made conspiracies, headed rebellions, and were in consequence punished by the kings; we also know that for some time there was difference of opinion between the kings and the upper clergy on the subject of the Jews. Lastly, we must not forget that, in legislative matters, not only did the kings issue provisions *motu proprio* without consulting the Councils—there is no lack of examples—but also that, even with regard to the decisions and suggestions of the latter, they always reserved for themselves the right of approval, as we may clearly see from the royal declarations at the eighth, thirteenth, and sixteenth Councils, apart from their general power of confirmation, without which the decrees were not valid. So far as we know, the kings always enforced the decisions of the Councils; and they could well afford to do so. It was a corrupt bargain. The Councils sanctioned the worst acts of hypocritical kings like Erwig, while the kings allowed their theological and political doctrines to creep into the legislation. This appears to be the truth of the matter.

The fall of the Visigothic State did not put an end to Gothic influence in Spain. Like the Roman Empire, the Visigothic rule made a deep impression on the race and on the character of the Spanish people. Portions of Visigothic law were incorporated into their legal constitution: in the sphere of legislation, not only did their principles survive for several centuries, but some of them have come down to the present day, and are amongst those regarded as most essentially Spanish. The *Forum Judicum* remained in force in the Peninsula for centuries; in the thirteenth, as it was still thought indispensable, it was translated into the vernacular—that is, Castilian—and, down to the nineteenth, its laws continued to be quoted in the courts. No sooner was the new monarchy established in Asturias, than it attempted to restore the Visigothic State, seeking for precedents in the latter and claiming to be its successor. This influence is proved by various passages of the chronicles which treat of the Reconquest and by the texts of the laws of Alfonso II, Bermudo II, Alfonso V, and other kings. The word *Goth* survived to denote a Spanish Christian, and, in the sixteenth century, the victorious Spaniards introduced it into America.

It was not only on legislation and politics that the Visigothic influence left its mark. It has now been proved that the Visigothic codes, even in their final and most complete form, by no means included all the legislation which existed in Spain. Apart from the law, and, in many cases, in direct opposition to it, there survived a considerable number of customs, almost all Gothic, which were firmly rooted in the people. These, after an existence which, to the modern observer, seems buried in obscurity—for they are not mentioned in any contemporary document—came to the surface in the legislation of the medieval *Fueros*, which was founded on custom, as soon as the political unity of Visigothic Spain had been destroyed. It has been shewn by several modern scholars who have investigated the subject, such as Pidal, Muñoz, Romero, Ficker, and Hinojosa, that many of these principles or *Fueros* faithfully reflect the ancient Gothic law. Here, then, is a new social factor of medieval Spain, which descends directly from the Visigoths.

Conversely, in matters of social life and culture, the Visigoths were deeply affected by the Byzantine and by the Spanish-Roman element. The Roman spirit first affected them when they came in contact with the Eastern Empire in the third and fourth centuries. Afterwards in Gaul, and still more in Spain, a Western and properly Roman influence produced a much deeper effect, as is shewn by the advance in their legislation. Subsequently the Byzantine influence was revived by the Byzantine conquests in south and south-east Spain (554–629), and also by the constant communication between the Spanish clergy and Constantinople; indeed, we know that many of them visited this city. Some scholars have attempted to trace Byzantine influence in matters juridical, but it is not perceptible either in Visigothic legislation, or in the *formulae* of the sixth century, or in the legal works of Isidore of Seville. On the other hand, the influence of Byzantine art and literature is manifest at every stage in the literary and artistic productions of the period. In the territory in subjection to the Empire, Greek was spoken in its vulgar form, and learned Greek was the language of all educated men. Moreover, Byzantine influence played a considerable part in commerce, which was chiefly carried on by the Carthagena route —this city being the capital of the imperial province—and by the Barcelona route, which followed the course of the Ebro to the coast of Cantabria.

As might have been expected, the Roman-Latin influence was more powerful than the Byzantine. On the whole, the Visigoths conformed to the general system of social organisation which they had found established in Spain. According to this system, property was vested in the hands of a few, and there was great inequality between the classes. Personal and economic liberty was restricted by subjection to the *curia* and the *collegia*. The Visigoths improved the condition of the *curiales*, and lightened the burden of the compulsory guild, which pressed heavily on the workmen and artisans; but, on the other hand, they widened the gulf between the classes, by extending the grades of personal servitude and subjection on the lines followed by the Roman Empire in the fourth century; and these, owing to the weakness of the State, became daily more intolerable. With regard to the economic question of population, the Visigoths reversed the established Roman practice which was mainly municipal, and restored the rural system, which in their hands proved very efficient, as we see from the distribution of the local communities and from the system of local administration, although the Roman scheme of country-houses (*villae*) in some respects coincides with this; they also improved the condition of agriculture. With regard to the family, the Visigoths were less susceptible to Latin influence, inasmuch as they retained the form of the patriarchal family and of the *Sippe*, which found its ultimate expression in solidarity of the clans in matters relating to the family, to property, and to punishment of crime, etc. Nevertheless, here too Roman influence did not fail to produce some effect; in the legislation, at least, it modified the Gothic law in an individualistic sense.

Of the original language, script and literature of the Visigoths, nothing remained. The language left scarcely any trace on the Latin, by which it was almost immediately supplanted in common use. Modern philologists believe that most of the Gothic words—a bare hundred—contained in the Spanish language have not come from the Visigoths, but that they are of more ancient origin, and had crept into vulgar Latin towards the end of the Empire, as a result of the constant intercourse between the Roman soldiers and the Germanic tribes. The Gothic script fell rapidly into disuse in consequence of the spread of Catholicism, and the destruction of many of the Arian books in which it had been used. Although there is evidence that it survived down to the seventh century, there are but few examples of it; documents were generally written in Latin, in the script wrongly termed *Gothic*, which is known to Spanish palaeographers as that of Toledo.

The literature which has come down to us is all in Latin, and the greater part of it deals with matters ecclesiastical. Although amongst the writers and cultured men of the time there were a few laymen, such as the kings Recared, Sisebut, Chindaswinth, and Receswinth, duke Claudius, the counts Bulgaranus and Laurentius, the majority of the historians, poets, theologians, moralists and priests were ecclesiastics; such were Orosius, Dracontius, Idatius, Montanus, St Toribius of Astorga, St Martin of Braga, the Byzantines Licinianus and Severus, Donatus, Braulio, Masona, Julian, Tajon, John of Biclar, etc. The most important of all, the best and most representative exponent of contemporary culture, was Isidore of Seville, whose historical and legal works (*Libri Sententiarum*) and encyclopaedias (*Origines sive Etymologiae*) —the latter were written between 622 and 623—reproduce, in turn, Latin tradition and the doctrines of Christianity. The *Etymologiae* is not only exceedingly valuable from the historical point of view as a storehouse of Latin erudition, but it also exercised considerable influence over Spain and the other Western nations. In Spain, France, and other European countries, there was scarcely a single library belonging to a chapter-house or an abbey, whose catalogue could not boast of a copy of

Isidore's work. Alcuin and Theodulf took their inspiration from it, and for jurists it was long one of the principal sources of information concerning the Roman Law before the time of Justinian.

Of the artistic productions which the Visigoths left behind in Spain, there is not much to be said. In addition to the undoubted Byzantine influence, which, however, did not exactly reveal itself through the medium of Visigothic art, since it had its own province like that of other Western countries, it is possible that the work of the Visigoths shewed other traces of Eastern art. We have much information concerning public buildings—palaces, churches, monasteries and fortifications—built during the Visigothic period, and more especially during the reigns of Leovigild, Recared, Receswinth, etc. But none of these buildings have come down to us in a state of sufficient preservation to enable us to state precisely the characteristic features of the period. The following buildings, or at least some part of them, have been assigned to this period: the churches of San Roman de la Hornija, and San Juan de Baños at Palencia; the church of San Miguel de Tarrasa, and possibly the lower part of Cristo de la Luz at Toledo; the cathedral of San Miguel de Escalada at Leon; Burguillos and San Pedro de Nave, and a few other fragments. It is also thought that there are traces of Visigothic influence in the church of St Germain-des-Près at Paris, which was built in 806 by Theodulf, bishop of Orleans, a native of Spain. But the capitals found at Toledo, Mérida and Cordova, and, above all, the beautiful jewels, votive crowns, crosses and necklaces of gold and precious stones discovered at Guarrazar, Elche, and Antequera, must assuredly be attributed to the Visigoths. We possess numerous Visigothic gold coins, or rather medals struck in commemoration of victories and proclamations, modelled on the Latin and Byzantine types and roughly engraved. They furnish information concerning several kings whose names do not occur in any known document, and who must probably be regarded as usurpers, rebels, or unsuccessful candidates for the throne, such as Tutila or Tudila of Iliberis and Mérida, and Tajita of Acci, who are supposed to belong to the period between Recared I and Sisenand, and Suniefred or Cuniefred, who possibly belongs to the time of Receswinth or Wamba.

CHAPTER VII.

ITALY UNDER THE LOMBARDS.

THE Lombards are mentioned first in the time of Augustus and Tiberius by Velleius Paterculus and Strabo, and a hundred years later by Tacitus. Their first residence was the Bardengau on the left bank of the lower Elbe, and here they were conquered by Tiberius at the time before the battle in the Teutoburgian forest, when the Romans still intended to subdue the whole of Germany. After the deliverance of the inner part of Germany by Arminius, the Lombards were ruled by Marbod, who went over to Arminius and later on brought back to his compatriots Italicus, the son of Arminius, whom the Cherusci had fetched from Rome and then driven away again. They are generally described as a small tribe, the fiercest of all German tribes, and only their bravery enabled them to hold their position between their stronger neighbours. On the whole their habits seem to have been the same as those of all other Germans at the time of Tacitus; some of their laws of a later period shew a certain resemblance to those of their former neighbours by the North Sea. As with all Germans, their kingship is no primitive institution, and whatever tradition tells about it is only fabulous. It is the smallness of their tribe which accounts for their principal quality— the tendency to assimilate the allied or subdued individuals or tribes. Roman influence seems to have touched them only in the slightest degree during the first five centuries of our era. At the time of their wanderings they began to shew differences from their neighbours.

We know nothing about the way the Lombard wanderings took, though tradition says a good deal about them. The extensive farming they practised, consisting more in cattle-breeding than agriculture, and the loose organisation of the tribe made it easy for them to leave their dwelling-places. Perhaps here, as is so often the case, the first motive was need of land, a natural result of the increase of population, while at the same time so small a tribe had no possibility of enlarging its boundaries. A division of Lombards invaded Pannonia with the Marcomanni about the year 165, but were repulsed by the Romans and obliged to return. They did not again reach the old Roman frontier, the Danube, till 300 years later, under a certain king Godeoch,

who occupied the desolated Rugiland after the destruction of their
empire by Odovacar in the year 487. Meanwhile during the
troubles of their wanderings and continual wars the institution of a
constant commander-in-chief in form of kingship seems to have taken
the place of the Tacitean duke who was invested for every single war.
From Rugiland they wandered into the land which was called "Feld"
(in Hungary) but were subdued by the Heruli and forced to pay
tribute. At that time they were probably landlords, leaving the land
to subjected half-freemen (*aldiones*) for culture; we may suppose that
they were at that time strongly influenced by their neighbours, the
Bavarians, and it was then that they adopted Christianity in its Arian
form. But not very long afterwards, during the Franco-Ostrogothic
war in Gaul, the Lombards, under the reign of their king Tato of
the family of Leth, shook off the yoke of the Heruli, who were
allied with Theodoric, succeeded in beating them completely in a battle
somewhere in the Hungarian plain, and entirely destroyed their realm.
The Lombards now had the Gepidae on the south and the Danube on
the west. Tato's nephew and successor, King Vacho, who had married
one daughter to a Frankish king and another to Garibald, duke of
Bavaria, considered himself friend and ally of the Roman Emperor.

When after the death of the last "Lethingian" king his guardian
Audoin had mounted the throne, the Lombards crossed the Danube
and, while the Ostrogothic land was in great confusion, occupied the
south-west of Hungary, and also Noricum, the south of Styria, both
belonging in name to the Roman Empire, but left to them for settlement
by Justinian. In this way they were loosely federated with the Empire,
which paid them subsidies, but was nevertheless troubled by their raids.
They assisted Narses in his decisive expedition to Italy, bringing him
2500 warriors with 3000 armed followers, but the Byzantine soon sent
them back after the deciding battle, seeing how dangerous they were to
friend and foe through their fierceness and want of discipline. Meanwhile
the Lombards and Gepidae, stirred up by the Roman Emperor, were engaged in constant battles and struggles. After Audoin's death his son and
successor Alboin, well known to fable, concluded a league with the Avars,
engaging himself to pay the tenth part of all cattle for their help in war
and, in case of victory, to give up the land of the Gepidae to the Avars.
The latter made their invasion from the north-east, the Lombards
from the north-west. In the decisive battle Kunimund, king of the
Gepidae, was slain by Alboin's hand, the king's daughter taken prisoner
and made queen by Alboin. Part of the Gepidae took flight, another
part surrendered to the Lombards; their realm existed no more, their
land and the few who stayed behind fell under the government of the
Avars, who were now the Lombards' most dangerous neighbours. But
the Lombards renewed their confederacy with them, and left to
them the land they had themselves occupied till then, intending to

conquer for themselves a better and richer land in Italy, which many
of them already knew. At the command of Alboin they assembled on
1 April 568, with family, goods and chattels, with a mixed multitude
of all the subjugated races already assimilated by their people. With
a great number of allies—20,000 Saxons among others—and grouped in
tribes (*fara*) they crossed the Alps under the guidance of Alboin.
About the same time Narses was recalled by Justinian's successor: hence
arose a rumour, reporting that the commander had committed treason,
by calling the Lombards; and this became the saga of Narses.

In spite of the well-organised defensive system which Narses had
established, the Romans seem to have been surprised and made no
attempt at defence. The Lombards overcame the Friulian *limes* with
its castles and, marching into the Venetian plain, took Cividale
(Forum Julii), the first important place that fell into their hands, and
afterwards the residence of the ducal dynasty of the Gisulfings; they
also destroyed the town of Aquileia, whose patriarch fled to Grado,
the later New-Aquileia, with his treasure, part of the population and
of the soldiers. But the imperialists succeeded in holding out in
Padua, Monselice and Mantua, thereby defending the line of the
Po, while Vicenza and Verona fell into Alboin's hands, so that the
important *limes* of Tridentum, which bordered on Bavaria in the north,
was separated from the bulk of the imperial army. On 4 September
569, Alboin entered Milan; the archbishop Honoratus fled to Genoa,
which for two generations remained the asylum of the bishops of Milan.
Ticinum (Pavia) alone offered resistance for a time and could only be
taken after a long siege, during which and afterwards other Lombard
troops scoured the country up to the Alps and took possession of the
land except a few fortifications. Undoubtedly the Lombard bands had
as little idea of systematic attack as the imperialists of systematic
defence: and it seems the latter judged the Lombard invasions to be
like other barbarian invasions, which soon passed away. Alboin himself
seems to have dated his reign in Italy from the time of his occupation
of Milan.

Alboin did not long enjoy his fame. Revolted by her husband's
insolence, who forced her to drink from a cup made of her father
Kunimund's skull, Rosamund conspired with Alboin's foster-brother
Helmechis and a powerful man called Peredeo; the barbarian hero-
king was murdered in his bed (in spring 572). But as Rosamund
could not realise her plan of taking possession of the throne with
Helmechis, against the Lombards' opposition, the two fled to Ravenna,
taking the royal treasure with them. Here the queen wanted to
get rid of her accomplice and marry Longinus, praefect of Italy;
but Helmechis forced her to finish the poison she had given him. So
the praefect could only deliver Alboin's daughter and the treasure to
Constantinople. This is what the saga related, and we can neither

confirm nor contradict its details.   The duke Cleph of the family of Beleos
was now made king by the Lombards at Pavia, but was murdered after
one and a half years' reign (574).   Lombard bands spread further in
middle and southern Italy, but so small was the need of a single leader
that they chose no more kings, but every one of the dukes, 35 in number,
reigned independently in his own district.

These dukes, called *duces* by our authorities, but whose Lombard
titles we do not know, are not to be confounded with the *duces* in the
Tacitean sense.   We must picture them as leaders of a military division
chosen by the king from among the nobles.   Their position changed
naturally, when the Lombard people was no longer on the march, but the
same clans were garrisoned permanently in the same town, as the saga of
Gisulf's appointment in Friuli exemplifies, and occupied permanently the
same district, living on its produce.   These districts generally coincided
with the Roman division in *civitates*, and a walled town formed the
centre.   Probably these towns were at first used as victualling stations,
managed in a more or less regular manner, sometimes perhaps by
imposing payment of a third on the peasants of the district.   But this
could only be considered a transition state, preparing the way for
definite settlement.   The fierce Lombards had not come as federates or
friends like the Goths, but as enemies, and treated the Romans *jure
belli*.

The Roman freeman—the *curialis* who owned a moderate property
in the town or the great landowner in the country—had fled, or had
been killed or enslaved, and only the great mass of working people, the
coloni and the agricultural slaves, had been left on the soil, though
many had perished during the terrors of war.   When the Lombards
began to settle, they divided the land, with all its bondmen, as far
as it had not been entirely devastated, between the free Lombards,
who thereby took the place of the Roman landlords.   The *coloni* were
considered as *aldiones*, as half-freemen, and paid tribute and did predial
service for the Lombards as they had done for the Romans before.   Of
course the possessions of the Catholic Church, which was the Church of
the Roman State, fell under the same lot of division.   The dukes claimed
for themselves all the public land with its traditional duties as well, but
every free Lombard warrior was entitled to part of the booty, and therefore became also a landowner.   In this way the local division in all those
parts which had not been totally devastated, and which were ploughed
again after a time, suffered no change.   The culture was much the same,
with the one difference that the Lombards, having brought great herds
of cattle, especially swine, from Pannonia, attached more importance
within the manor to stock-management and cattle-breeding than the
Romans had done.   The towns and municipal settlements were likewise
unchanged, because the Lombards, who had known stone buildings only
upon Roman soil, accommodated themselves to the conditions of a

higher culture. It is certain that regard was paid to the connexion between the *fara* (clan) in every settlement, but on the other hand it was just the manorial and municipal settlement which entirely destroyed the connexion within the *fara*, so that the rest of the original clan-organisation soon disappeared. Two of the duchies were somewhat different in origin and organisation from those of the north of Italy, the "great duchies" of Spoleto and Benevento. They did not go back to the time of conquest in common, but were founded by independent enterprises of Lombard bands, who had severed from the great mass under command of their chiefs and invaded the land on their own account. They were much larger in extent than one *civitas*, so that here the *civitas* forms a subdivision of the duchy.

In the year 575 or 576 the patrician Baduarius, son-in-law to the Emperor Justin, and his army were entirely beaten by the Lombards. They approached Ravenna, the duke Faroald even occupied for a time Classis, its port, destroyed the Petra Pertusa, which defended the Via Flaminia, and thereby forced the passage of the Apennines. Faroald occupied Nursia, Spoleto and other towns and installed an Arian bishop in Spoleto, which was now the centre of his duchy. Another duke, Zotto, who with his partly heathen bands inundated the province of Samnium and spread terror all around, settled down in Benevento. The connexion between Ravenna and Rome was interrupted at times; even Rome was besieged in the year 579, but the Lombards were obliged to give up the siege as well as that of Naples two years later, because Roman walls, kept in good condition and provided with a sufficient number of defenders, were impregnable to them. During the next years the two dukedoms took a still wider range, limited only by Rome with its surroundings and by Byzantine seaport-towns, which could not be taken from the land side. During the kingless time Benevento and Spoleto grew so strong that they were able to keep up their independence.

In the north of Italy too the incoherent government of the dukes did not permit any uniform action. Even in Alboin's time various troops had detached themselves and pillaged in Gaul, but upon the whole these adventurers had no success against Mummolus, commander-in-chief of the Burgundian king Guntram. The Saxons, who did not want to assimilate with the Lombards and intended to make their way home through the land of the Franks, were likewise beaten in the following years.

But these bands had shewn the way into the neighbouring kingdom to the dukes of North Italy. Some of these marched into the upper valley of the Rhone and were beaten by the Burgundians near Bex (574) and no better did they fare next year, as they were repulsed by Mummolus, after having laid waste the land between the Rhone, the Isère and the Alps. At this time Susa and Aosta, the most important passage over the West Alps, seem to have fallen into the hands of the Franks, and on the other side, a Frankish duke, Chramnichis, advanced from Austrasia into the dukedom of Trent, but was, after a short success, totally defeated with his troops by the duke Evin near Salurn. These conflicts took a dangerous aspect when the Emperor Maurice sent subsidies (50,000 *solidi*) to the young king Childebert of Austrasia in order to drive out the Lombards.

In 584 King Childebert conducted an army against Italy, and so weak had the want of monarchical leading rendered the Lombard dukes that they dared not offer resistance, and sent presents in token of submission. Besides this their force of resistance had been weakened by the treason of some of their fellow-countrymen who were not ashamed of joining the imperialists against their own people. The imperial policy was to combat barbarians with barbarians, and to spend very large sums for this purpose. In this manner they had won over the duke Drocton of Brexillum, a Lombard duke of Suevic family, who succeeded in expelling Faroald from Classis, and other deserters were found as well. Standing in danger of losing all their booty by dispersing their forces, the dukes of West Italy at last resolved to unite again under a king's leading.

They elected Authari the son of Cleph (584), and conceded to him (as we hear), in order to give material foundation to the new kingship, half of their own lands, which were later administered by royal *gastaldi*. The dukedom had, in consequence of the settlements during the last ten years, become quite a different thing from what it had been at the time of Alboin, and also the new kingship was obliged to represent not only the leading power of the army as before but also territorial power.

The king's attempt to strengthen the new central power against the forces of disunion, grown strong during the last period, now formed the most important part of the Lombard State's politics, as it was the king's task to form a really united State. He was no longer satisfied with the dignity of a barbarian chieftain, but aspired to reign lawfully within the territory of the Roman Empire. We see this from the fact that Authari first took up the name Flavius, which all his successors kept, though he was not acknowledged by the Empire, as for instance Theodoric had been.

The Lombards wanted their territory to comprise all Italy, and a legend illustrating the fact tells us that Authari rode into the sea at the south point of Italy, and touched a solitary column, projecting out of the waves, with his spear and called out: "This is to be the boundary of the Lombard realm"; but in reality Authari's task was of a more modest character and limited to the north of Italy. A new attack of the Austrasians failed in consequence of the leaders' disagreements, and as the Exarch Smaragdus felt too weak to offer resistance to the Lombards without their help, Authari managed to conclude an armistice for three years, the first that was concluded between the Lombards and the Empire. Authari seems to have availed himself of this opportunity partly to restore order in North Italy and partly to ensure his boundary in the north, and above all to destroy the Franco-Byzantine league, which threatened the existence of his realm. He therefore betrothed himself to Childebert's sister, but the engagement was soon broken by the Franks when the Frankish imperial and catholic party of Brunhild got the ascendant. Authari however married Theodelinda (588 ?), the Catholic daughter of the Bavarian duke Garibald, who, by her mother, belonged to the old Lombard royal family of the Lethings. The other daughter was married to the mighty duke Evin of Tridentum, and her brother Gundoald was made duke of Asti by Authari. When the Franks, by this time, repeated their invasion of Italy under the leading of a few dukes, they were entirely beaten after a hot battle. Childebert's revenge was prevented by Authari's negotiations with him (589) and by his offer to become even a dependent confederate and pay tribute. Meanwhile, after the armistice had ended, Authari had succeeded in removing the last remnants of imperial power on the northern boundaries of Italy, and had probably also obtained his acknowledgment by the duke of Friuli. Nevertheless his position was much impaired when a new exarch, Romanus, appeared in Ravenna with reinforcements, regained Altinum, Modena and Mantua, and induced the Lombard dukes of the Emilia, as well as the duke of Friuli, to join the imperialists. The negotiations were broken off, and imperialists and Franks planned to destroy the Lombard power by a systematic and simultaneous attack from north and south, and had even agreed already on the distribution of the booty. Twenty Frankish dukes broke forth from the Alps in two divisions, one marching against Milan, the other under the duke Chedinus against Verona, after having broken through the fortification of the frontier and devastated the land all around (summer 590); but no important conflicts took place, because the Lombards retired into their fortifications, fearing the enemy's overwhelming numbers. The exarch came to meet the Franks at Mantua, and intended to march in a line parallel to them against Pavia, to which Authari had drawn back; but this plan was not put into practice, it is said, in consequence of misunderstandings.

The Frankish dukes tried to secure their moveable booty, and Duke Chedinus is said to have concluded an armistice for ten months; but epidemics and famine caused great losses on their way back. After these efforts, which had brought no real success to them, the Franks ceased to invade Italy for more than a century and a half. Authari lived to manage the negotiations for peace which led to a lasting friendship between the Franks and Lombards later on, though only on condition of paying tribute to the Franks—a burden which was, as it seems, not for a long time thrown off by the Lombards. The northern boundary, at all events, was secured, and the Lombards were only threatened from one side, by the Byzantines. But Authari did not live to see the definite treaty of peace; he is said to have been poisoned and died (5 Sept. 590). The result of his active life was the establishment of a kingdom and the Lombard State, though many difficulties still awaited the Lombards from within and without.

Two months after Authari's death, Agilulf, duke of Turin, obtained the crown and married his predecessor's widow, Theodelinda. In May 591 an assembly of Lombards at Milan acknowledged him solemnly, but a number of North Italian dukes had then to be subdued in repeated battles; also Piacenza and Parma were again subjected, and in the latter town the king's son-in-law was established as duke, as the king generally claimed the right to nominate the dukes himself. He ensured the northern boundary by an agreement with the Avars which became a defensive and offensive alliance later on. The time had now come for a systematic attack on the imperialists. The newly-nominated duke of Benevento, Arichis, who had consolidated his duchy by gaining nearly all the territories in South Italy with the exception of a few towns on the coast, had the especial task of marching against Naples and threatening Rome from the south, while Ariulf of Spoleto had already destroyed the land communication between Rome and Ravenna in April 592, and even appeared before Rome in the summer, afterwards turning to the north and taking the castles on the upper Tiber. To be sure, the exarch succeeded in regaining them during the time he was free of Agilulf; but in 593 the king himself advanced southward, occupied Perugia and appeared before Rome. The siege ended in a treaty with Pope Gregory who only wished for peace, but it was not acknowledged by the exarch after the king had marched off; the war did not cease, and the Lombards made constant progress. It was only after the Exarch Romanus' death (596) that, at the pope's instance, the negotiations were renewed seriously; it is true that the new exarch, Callinicus, carried on the war in North Italy, but he concluded an armistice of a year in autumn 598 on the basis of the *status quo* and engaged himself to pay 500 pounds in gold to the Lombard king. The armistice was renewed for the time from spring 600–601 but, when the war was taken up again, the exarch succeeded in making prisoners of the duke of Parma and his wife, Agilulf's daughter; but the Lombard king took Padua, devastated Istria with Slav and Avar troops, conquered the fortified town of Monselice, enforced peace on the rebellious dukes of Friuli and Tridentum and occupied in 603 Cremona and Mantua. The central position of the imperialists at Ravenna appeared to be endangered after the subjugation of all the north of Italy, and the Exarch Smaragdus, who was again sent to Italy after the fall of the Emperor Maurice, hastily concluded a new armistice till 605, and surrendered the king's daughter. Then Agilulf crossed the Apennines once more, occupied Balneum Regis and Orvieto, but in November 605 the imperialists obtained a new armistice at the price of paying a tribute of 12,000 *solidi*. From that time till Agilulf's death and even afterwards, this armistice was continually prolonged. It is true that a definite state of peace, which would have naturally led to a legal partition of the Italian soil, was not effected, though Agilulf's ambassador Stablicianus seems to have entered into negotiations on this subject in Constantinople. Agilulf died in 616 after 25 years of a warlike reign, in which he had expanded and strengthened his empire and obliged the Romans to pay tribute.

To Agilulf his son Adaloald (a minor) followed in name, but Theodelinda exercised the ruling influence on government in his place. While Authari had never allowed Lombard children Catholic baptism, a Catholic chapel had been conceded to Theodelinda at Monza and Adaloald himself was already baptised as a Catholic, though by a schismatic, and Theodelinda, who exchanged occasional letters with Pope Gregory, was schismatic in relation to the Three Chapters. In this way Agilulf had not tolerated the organisation of the Roman Church within the reach of his power, but the schismatic bishop of Aquileia and his schismatic suffragans had taken refuge with the Lombards. Agilulf had also given deserted land in the Apennines at the confluence of the torrent Bobbio and the Trebbia to the Irish monk Columba (Columbanus) who had fled from Gaul, and differed dogmatically from Rome. He also gave permission to lay the foundations of a monastery at Bobbio, but the monks soon turned to orthodoxy after Columbanus' death, and even got a privilege in 628, by which they were exempted from the power of the neighbouring bishop of Tortona. In contrast to the national chiefs, who were still Arian, the government favoured the Catholics or at least the schismatics, and in consequence Roman influence made rapid progress in the Lombard kingdom, favoured partly by the social influence of the Roman subjects, partly by the intercourse with the Roman neighbours, which the long armistices had so well prepared. Nevertheless the peace was once more broken at the beginning of Adaloald's reign between the Exarch Eleutherius and the Lombards under the commander Sundrarius, who owed his training to Agilulf, but this war was ended by another armistice, the exarch consenting to pay a tribute of 500 pounds in gold. In the following years the Roman influence on the king was so great that he was generally said to be either mad or bewitched. Perhaps it was the national party among the Lombards which raised upon the buckler Arioald, the duke of Turin, the husband of Adaloald's sister Gundeberga, and after several combats dethroned King Adaloald, who was then said to have been removed by poison (626). Arioald reigned ten years too, without much change in the course of Lombard politics. He came in conflict with his Catholic wife, who was released from prison by the intervention of the Franks

and allowed Catholic service in a church of John the Baptist at
Pavia.

The alliance which Agilulf had formed with the Avars was dissolved.
They invaded Italy and killed Gisulf, duke of Friuli, with nearly the
whole of his army; his widow perfidiously surrendered Cividale which
was entirely burnt down and the open country was devastated, the
Lombards offering resistance only in the fortified castles at the frontier,
till the Avars turned back to Pannonia after their raid. No help was
to be expected for Friuli at that time from the weak kingdom; but at
last Gisulf's sons escaped from the Avars, and the two eldest, Taso
and Cacco, took the reins of government into their hands. While the
power of the Avars was decreasing, the young dukes in alliance with
Bavarians and Alemans fought successfully against the Slavs, and during
Arioald's reign penetrated victoriously into the valleys of the Alps
perhaps as far as Windisch-Matrei and the valley of the Gail, and
obliged the Slavs to pay tribute. But, at the instigation of Arioald,
it is said, the exarch craftily murdered Taso and Cacco, and their uncle
Grasulf was nominated duke of Friuli while the two younger sons of
Gisulf, Radoald and Grimoald, appealed to the protection of the mighty
duke Arichis of Benevento.

After Arioald's death the nobles in the kingdom elected the duke
Rothari of Brescia, an ardent Arian, who was connected with the former
dynasty by his marriage with the widowed queen Gundeberga. Nevertheless his policy (unlike that of his predecessors in the last twenty years)
was decidedly hostile to the Romans, though he tolerated the gradual
establishment of the Catholic hierarchy in the Lombard kingdom. He
sought to keep order in all internal matters and to raise the king's authority
over the nobles, and to this purpose war against the Byzantines, which
had rested during two decades, was taken up again, in order to strengthen
the king's royal domain by new conquests. He passed the Apennines and
conquered the coast between Luna and the Frankish boundary; he did not
instal dukes here but kept the conquered land under direct royal administration, so that the greatest part of the west of Italy was royal. He
destroyed Oderzo in the east, the last remnant of Roman power on the
Venetian mainland, and smote the Byzantines in a bloody battle on the
borders of the Scultenna not far from the central seat of Roman dominion;
he concluded a suspension of hostilities shortly before his death (652). His
son Rodoald followed him, but was killed after a few months' reign.

More famous even than by his victorious enterprises and by the
saga that attaches itself to the name of "King Rother," Rothari was the
first legislator of the Lombards. Up to that time, the Lombards, like
all barbarian nations, had been ruled by customary laws, handed down
to them verbally by their ancestors. Rothari ordered them to be written
down, published as *Edictus* after having consulted his nobles, and confirmed according to Lombard custom by an assembly of warriors at Pavia

CH. VII.

(22 Nov. 643). Of course it was a territorial law, for only the Lombard, who alone was "folk-free," was subject to Lombard law in the Lombard State, and the fact of its being written down shewed clearly enough that the Lombard State placed itself in the same line with the *respublica* (the Empire) and the other acknowledged States as perfectly equal to them. When Rothari declares the law should protect the poor against the oppressions of the mighty, we can find therein part of the means he employed to keep order in internal matters. The kingship was not only protected by some of the laws of the *Edictus* but also shewed its power by the fact of issuing legal regulations for the whole country, which, if not at once, were at all events after a short time accepted irrevocably from Benevento to Cividale. Its matter is essentially German law, but in the supplements which Rothari's successors added, we can trace alien influence; and, moreover, the form is naturally influenced by Roman patterns. Comparative science of law has proved that Lombard law had the greatest likeness to Saxon, Anglo-Saxon, and Scandinavian law —a proof that the Lombards preserved their law unchanged in essential matters since their departure from the lower Elbe. The *Edictus* is systematically arranged, and treats of crimes against king, state or man, especially compensations for bodily injuries, law of inheritance and family right, and manumission, then obligations and real estate, crimes against property, oath and bail. It can well be called the best juridical codification of barbarian law.

The successor of Rothari's son was Aripert, the son of that duke Gundoald of Asti, who had come from Bavaria with his sister Theodelinda. During the nine years of his reign he, as a Catholic, carried on the traditions of Theodelinda, in opposition to Rothari. He built a Catholic church at Pavia and favoured the Catholic hierarchy, although the assertion of a poem which celebrates the merits of his dynasty about the year 700, that "the good and pious king" abolished the Arian heresy, is probably exaggerated. The bishop of Pavia was converted to Catholicism. A change of policy took place only after his death (661), when his two young sons Godepert in Pavia and Perctarit in Milan, to whom he had left the government, fell out, and Godepert claimed the help of the mighty duke Grimoald of Benevento against his brother. After the death of Arichis, and of his son Ajo, who had perished in a battle against Slav pirates near Sipontum (662), the two sons of Gisulf of Friuli, Radoald and Grimoald, attained the dignity of dukedom consecutively, and energetically maintained their power in several battles against the imperialists. Grimoald, duke of Benevento since 657, now marched into North Italy by the east side of the Apennines against the centre of the Lombard realm, while his subordinate, the count of Capua, marched through Spoleto and Tuscia and joined the duke by Piacenza. Assisted by the treachery of the duke Garibald of Turin, Grimoald seized the reins of government

himself after having killed King Godepert with his sword; Perctarit
had fled from Milan to the Avars and his wife and young son Cunincpert had been sent into exile to Benevento. Grimoald now married
Aripert's daughter, who was already betrothed to him, and legitimated
his power by a later election at Pavia; for the purpose of gaining
firm support he bestowed royal domains in upper Italy on several
of his faithful followers of Benevento. He was the first Lombard
king who united the king's royal domain in the north with Benevento under his actual government.

Mighty as he was, Grimoald had a long struggle for the preservation
of his royal power. Perctarit came back, and seemed to submit himself,
but was soon obliged to fly to the Franks, after the discovery of a
conspiracy between his followers and some disaffected dukes. The intervention of a Frankish army in favour of the banished dynasty had no
success; by stratagem Grimoald contrived to attack them suddenly near
Asti and slew them. In the year 663 the Emperor Constans had landed
at Tarentum, in order to obtain a new base for his hard-pressed empire
by conquests in the West, and the expulsion of the Lombards was
naturally the first condition for this enterprise. The Emperor occupied
Luceria with superior forces, assaulted Acerenza without success, and
then besieged Grimoald's young son Romuald at Benevento. The latter
pledged his sister Gisa in token of submission after having offered resistance bravely; but Grimoald had already reached the river Sangro with a
relieving army, though many Lombards had left him, and young Romuald
did not fulfil his pledge; the Emperor gave up his siege and moved on
to his own city of Naples. This imperial army was said to have been
defeated twice: at all events Constans gave up war against the Lombards
for a time and after a short visit to Rome went on to Sicily, where he was
murdered. Romuald then occupied Tarentum, Brundusium and all the
rest of the imperial dominion on the Adriatic coast of South Italy, with
the exception of Otranto; and Grimoald, after having installed Transamund, a duke of his choice, in Spoleto, again devoted himself to his most
urgent tasks in North Italy, where he found in rebellion the duke Lupus
of Friuli, whom he had left in his place at Pavia. Evidently menaced
by other rebellions as well, the king himself appealed to the Khagan of
the Avars, for help against the duke; Lupus perished in the battle, but
the Avars now prepared to occupy Friuli as conquered land. But, in
spite of the insufficiency of his military forces, Grimoald induced them to
depart, and set up Wechthari, a powerful soldier and the terror of the
Slavs, as duke of Friuli in place of Arnefrit, the son of Lupus, who had
tried to regain his father's inheritance by help of the Slavs, but had
been beaten and killed near Nimis. Grimoald took away Forlì from
the Byzantines and razed to the ground Oderzo, where his brothers had
once been murdered: then he made peace with the Franks, so that
Perctarit did not feel safe any longer in his asylum, and prepared to fly

to England. At this time the mighty king Grimoald died, after having made sure the limits of his realm, and broken the dukes' power, in the ninth year of his reign (671). His eldest son Romuald took his place in the dukedom of Benevento, while the young boy Garibald, his son by Aripert's daughter, inherited the royal crown.

By this time Perctarit returned from his exile and dethroned his nephew Garibald with the help of his numerous followers; he and his dynasty now held the throne for more than 40 years consecutively. He made his son Cunincpert co-regent (680) and entered into friendly terms with Romuald of Benevento, whose son, the younger Grimoald, married Perctarit's daughter. In the south as well as in the north-west Catholicism gained exclusive power, and in Benevento and Pavia many foundations of cloisters spoke of a growing piety, shewn especially by the two princesses. Numerous Lombard bishops had already attended the Roman synod of 680; on the other hand the Three Chapters Schism lasted on in Austria, on the eastern bank of the Adda, in contrast to Neustria westwards, where royalty had taken root more decidedly. The duke Alahis of Tridentum, who had extended his territory northward in the direction of the Bavarians, was too strong for Perctarit and even added the dukedom of Brescia to his own. After Perctarit's death he also occupied Pavia, drove King Cunincpert to a refuge on an isle in the Lake of Como and acted as king, acknowledged by the greater part of the north of Italy. But passing for a heretic and acting recklessly against the Church, he made an enemy of the hierarchy, and Cunincpert was soon able to return to Pavia, protected by their adherents. Between Neustria and Austria on the field of Coronate a battle was fought between them; Alahis fell, and a great part of his followers perished in the flood of the Adda. This was at once a victory of kingdom over dukedom, and orthodoxy over the Three Chapters Schism. An insurrection in Friuli was also subdued; at a synod that had been convoked at the king's request in Pavia (698?) even those bishops of Austria who were still schismatic acknowledged the fifth and sixth oecumenical councils, and thus the unity of Catholic faith was established in Lombard Italy. The only lasting effect of this schism was the division of the patriarchate of Aquileia between the bishops of Grado and of Old-Aquileia, following the civil boundaries between Lombards and Romans. Even before the Roman Church triumphed throughout the whole Lombard realm, after the Emperor Constans' attempt to reconquer what he had lost had failed, and the Bavarian dynasty's traditional policy of peace had replaced Grimoald's belligerent policy—even at that time definite peace had been made between the Empire and the Lombards, thereby placing the Lombard State amid the States which were officially acknowledged by the *respublica*. The acknowledgment of the *status quo*, the limits, which had been fixed by a hundred years of war, formed the basis of peace; and the Lombards renounced any further policy of conquest. This peace seems to have been concluded between 678–681 at Constantinople, and from that time the Lombard bishops, when the pope confirmed their nomination at Rome, swore to provide that "peace, which God loves, be maintained in eternity between the *Respublica* and us, that is, the Lombard people."

Roman influence affected the Lombards in different ways. Intercourse with the half-free Roman subjects had always been a strong force since the beginning of the settlement; the schismatics coming from the Roman Empire had found reception even at a very early period, as had the merchants during the times of armistice, who maintained friendly relations and profited by the great Lombard market; but when definite peace had been made, lasting relations and safe intercourse with the new allies were possible, so that free Romans and above all Catholic clergy established themselves in the lands of their new friends and allies, who also acknowledged their right to be tried by Roman law. Intermarriage must have frequently happened at a very early period, and was furthered by Lombard laws, which considered the freedman and free as equal, so that marriages with freedmen or freedwomen were allowed and very common; after the definite peace even unions between Lombards and women of the Roman Empire were not a rare thing either. As the Lombards were in a small minority, even in their own territory, intermarriage naturally had a marked effect. The adaptation of the reigning people to the Roman culture they had found led the same way. Thus they came to the knowledge of new forms of culture and luxury, which could only be satisfied in the Roman manner, partly by the industry of Roman subjects, partly by booty made in war, and since the peace also by regular imports. Trade and art are of Roman stamp, although the workmanship is decayed and accommodates itself somewhat to barbarian taste. It was only in Italy that the Lombards learnt to erect stone buildings, to construct larger ships and use weapons of metal; their clothing changed similarly and they gradually accepted the vulgar Latin language, especially because all the terms of their new culture belonged to that language, the only written language used, not only for written law, but all other documents which were drawn up by Roman ecclesiastics and notaries following Roman formulae. As their importance grew, the written word gained supremacy in all matters of law. The oldest stories of Lombard history and tradition are also written in Latin, and whatever there was of science, in connexion with the Roman Church, was of course Latin. So the lasting peace, and especially the peace with the Catholic Church, essentially accelerated the process of assimilation in this sphere as well as in all others.

Constitutional development, as well as culture, was conditioned by the fact and manner of settlement. The territorial State develops a centralising kingship in combat with centrifugal forces, and hides the original basis of German freedom. The sept or clan had already lost every economical foundation by the settlement, and we find no traces of the *centena* among the Lombards. Politically the sept recedes as well, but in matters of right it is only gradually superseded by the State. Rothari's legislation endeavours to restrain the feud-right to the sept; high penalties are fixed for the purpose of making the injured choose these instead of feud; guiltless acts are not to lead to feud. The members of the sept intervene as assistants at an oath, as combatants for a woman's right at an ordeal; and the *mundium* of an unmarried woman is due to the members of the sept if she has no nearer family relations. In contrast to these poor remnants of the sept's power, which once had been so great, family-connexion is very powerful, so that even by a disposal a last will was allowed only very late and quite exceptionally. The national assembly, that is the assembly of *arimanni*, still existed, and this as well as the kingship expressed the Lombard unity; but this assembly also was naturally entirely changed by the territorial State, having lost its organic foundations in the septs, and as an assembly comprising all or nearly all warriors was quite impossible considering the territorial extension of the State. In reality it consisted only in the army that was just ready for military operations, the king's attendants and the dukes and nobles present, and, whereas the nobles were actually often summoned to the preparatory council, the assembly of warriors had no possibility of influencing current state affairs and only served to heighten solemnities at a king's election or law-giving. The other element of unity, which had probably been born only in the time of wanderings—the kingship—predominated more and more in comparison; it seems to have been attached to one family at a very early period, and up to the eighth century connexion with the Lethingians was kept up at least by the feminine line; but besides this inherited right, general German custom demanded election, raising upon the buckler, and a solemn act of fealty from the *fideles*. On the other hand, the territorial State and Roman influence soon decided the extent of the king's power, though he called himself *rex gentis Langobardorum*. This influence expresses itself not only in the addition of the Roman name of Flavius and the Roman name of honour, *vir excellentissimus*, but also in the assertion of the king's nearly unlimited power, which is already expressed in Rothari's Edict: "we believe that the hearts of the kings are in the hands of God." The king not only leads the folk in war with all rights implied thereby. As supreme justice and protector of peace, he has his own peace secured by a high penalty, intervenes wherever all other powers make default, is the Lombard State's supreme guardian in a certain sense, and being the State's only representative, no difference is made between his own rights and those of the State. His alone is the right of coinage, since the Lombards—before Rothari even—had learnt the art and use of coining from the Romans; and that the duke of Benevento coined as well as the king only shews how independent he kept himself of the Lombard State.

Opposed to the centralising kingdom is the particular power of the dukes, their different positions varying of course from the *summus dux gentis Langobardorum* down to the duke of a small provincial town in North Italy. But on the whole the dukes endeavoured to found their power on inherited rights, and to exercise in their own territory the same authority which belonged to the king in the whole State, whereas the king claimed for himself the right of nominating the dukes and treated them as his officials. But the foundation of the king's royal domain was especially intended to counterbalance the power of the dukes; the larger this royal domain, the greater was the power of the State. Except those duchies which were in the hands of the royal family, this royal domain is said to have been partly formed by the half of all ducal property, which was given up to Cleph—though this cession can only relate to the dukes of a part of northern Italy—and partly by the conquest of new land, which was not left to the dukes. The whole royal domain has its own royal administration, lying in the hands of the *gastaldi* who are partly royal stewards, partly the king's representatives with competence in matters military and judicial, but being only the king's officials they have, in contrast to the dukes, no independent jurisdiction. In Benevento and Spoleto, where immediate royal power does not reach, the *gastaldi* are officials of the duke in the district of a *civitas*. Subordinated to these *iudices*, that is the dukes and *gastaldi* who generally reside in walled towns and whose office consists in a whole *iudiciaria*, stand the *actores* (*sculdahis*, *centenarius*, *locopositus*) out of town, and these are assisted by *saltarii*, *decani*, etc.

Change of social structure caused a change of power in the Lombard State. Although differences in distribution of the land had always been made in correspondence with a family's rank, and although the *wergeld* was not uniform but varied by habit and *secundum qualitatem personae*, every Lombard was not only warrior but also landlord and lord of the manor. This ruling nation stood in contrast to those who had no political rights, the *coloni* and *aldii* and *massarii* (unfree farmers on holdings), as well as the likewise unfree *ministeriales* of the home-farms and the unfree agricultural assistant labourers; the Lombards only were taken into account politically as well as economically. But this distribution having been made but once, gave no security whatever for a lasting condition; the natural increase of population and the accidental impoverishment of Lombard families, as well as manumissions to complete freedom, created a class of Lombards without land. Part of them worked as tenants, that is small tenants, who took holdings on lease for 29 years, remaining legally free, but losing in social status (*libellarii*); another part may have become merchants, trade developing on account of the definite peace, and so commercial capital stood alongside of land rent. This new state of economic affairs expressed itself also in military service which was varied according to property as early as the eighth century, commercial capital being placed on a par with landed property. A law of 750 dictates cavalry service with coat of mail and horse and complete equipment to all who possess at least seven *casae massariae*; the landlord of at least 40 *iugera* has to follow with one horse, lance and shield; those who possess still less, with shield and bow; a part of the poor was obliged to do predial service in the fields at home. This economic development rendered it possible for the king to form for himself a power independent of its former limitations within the State, creating a central organisation of power by investing the free poor with landed property out of his royal domain. The king, that is the State, at this time of natural economy owed his income to landed property and payments in kind, for instance the different *munera* (*angariae* and *operae*) to preserve public streets and buildings, and different dues, market dues, port dues, which were raised by royal *actores* and were of entirely Roman origin. The royal property was naturally increased by every new conquest, and the *coloni* and slaves paying dues were used as if they were private property; or the king took possession of the land which had been public before the conquest, and let it for pasture for the neighbouring herds.

The royal court lived on the income of the king's landed property, but this court was composed of followers who stood in a special relation of fealty to the king, the *Gasindi*, who on that account were greatly honoured, and had a higher *wergeld* than the other free Lombards. The king entrusted them with all sorts of commissions and delegations, chose all court officers from them, especially the royal marshal (*marpahis*), the majordomus (*stolesaz*), the treasurer (*vesterarius*), the sword-bearer (*spatharius*), the chancellor (*referendarius*). In this manner a special court-nobility developed itself through the king's favour, standing in contrast and competition with the Lombard nobility. But it was also the custom that such *Gasindi* were endowed with land by the king, so that the king's landed estate provided for this new nobility not only indirectly by keeping up the royal household, but also directly. This new institution was only rendered possible by the fact that a considerable part of the population, when the original conditions of the Lombard settlement were changed, was obliged to seek a new subsistence, and found it by the king's favour. On the other hand the king's possessions diminished continually by these donations, so that for him and his adherents it was necessary periodically to gain new land; and this was generally only possible through new conquests, and so the peaceful period of the Bavarian dynasty was followed by a belligerent period.

After Cunincpert's death (700), his young son Liutpert reigned under the wise Ansprand's guardianship. Raginpert, duke of Turin, son of Godepert and nephew of Perctarit, claimed the throne and defeated Ansprand near Novara, eight months after Cunincpert's death. When he died, shortly afterwards, his son and co-regent Aripert (II), after a second battle, took prisoner Liutpert, who had again advanced against Pavia, and sent the duke Rothari of Bergamo, who aspired to the throne, into exile to Turin, where he was killed after a few days. Now Ansprand was also obliged to leave his refuge on Lake Como and fly to the duke Teutpert of Bavaria. Liutpert was killed, Ansprand's eldest son blinded, his wife and daughter mutilated, and only his youngest son Liutprand spared. So the family of Godepert ruined the race of Perctarit. But no change of policy took place. King Aripert II was peaceable and friendly towards the Romans, and even gave back to the pope the patrimony in the Cottian Alps. He was dethroned in the winter of 712, when Ansprand came back to Italy, after nine years of exile, with a Bavarian army. Aripert fled to Pavia and was drowned when trying to swim across the Ticino, burdened with all his treasures. Ansprand was acknowledged as king but only reigned for three months; but on his death-bed he was told that the Lombards had raised his son Liutprand upon the buckler and thereby legitimated his own usurpation as well. He died 13 June 712.

Though Liutprand did not reverse the Lombard State's development during the last hundred and fifty years, he favoured Roman influence within his realm in every way. He left no doubt concerning his orthodoxy and attachment to the Roman faith, while nobody surpassed his generosity towards churches and monasteries, but he still followed the glorious traditions of the victorious kings which had been interrupted after Grimoald, and strictly kept in view his aim of uniting Italy under the Lombard kingdom, although he chose various ways of approaching it in the course of his reign. For this reason he was opposed by the Roman Empire and the dukes of Spoleto and Benevento, who had been nearly independent during the Bavarian dynasty's reign. Mixed up in quarrels about the Bavarian throne through his affinity with the dukes of Bavaria, he advanced the Lombard boundaries to Mais near Meran; for the rest the northern frontier was well defended by his friendship with the Frankish Charles Martel, whose son Pepin he had adopted by shaving of the hair according to an old custom, and to whom he had even brought help against the Saracens in Provence (737–738). In domestic politics he continued his predecessor's legislation, endeavoured to protect his subjects against denial of legal help, and intervened with great energy in administration and jurisdiction by the royal court of justice in Pavia and by special *missi*. His aim was naturally to replace the loose structure of the Lombard State by a series of officials ruled by the king, and one of his most efficient means was to give the preference to the *Gasindi*, and another was to instal relations and other *fideles* in all duchies and bishoprics. His ideal of kingship, which is evident in his laws, already shews a great difference from that of the former Lombard kings and is strongly influenced by Roman and ecclesiastical interpretations.

The time was favourable for an aggressive policy, because Roman Italy, led by the pope, rose in rebellion against the Emperor. Common hostility against the Emperor formed a link between Liutprand and Pope Gregory II for a while, but the pope soon came to see clearly that the king near him was more dangerous than the distant Emperor. As a token of friendship Liutprand, following the pope's admonition, restored to him his confiscated patrimony in the Cottian Alps. For the moment peace was only endangered by the duke Romuald II of Benevento, who attacked the castle of Cumae by surprise; but after the duke of Naples, aided by the pope's militia, had regained the place and killed the garrison, the pope even paid Romuald the indemnification which he had offered for a peaceable evacuation, and thereby won his friendship. Meanwhile the duke Faroald of Spoleto began to move as well; Narni was taken, Liutprand occupied Classis, the port of Ravenna, and carried booty and prisoners away. He gained other successes at the cost of the *respublica*; the frontier castles surrendered to him and so he was able to extend the Lombard boundary to Bologna; Osimo in Pentapolis went over to him as well. Then he turned southwards, and attacked the castle of Sutri by surprise (728); this was too much for the pope; the king approached too nearly his own sphere of action. After Liutprand had been in possession of the castle for one hundred and seventy days, the pope insisted on his "restoring and donating" it to the apostles Peter and Paul. Meanwhile the dukes of Spoleto and Benevento had entered into a league with the pope and defended the frontier of the *ducatus Romae* against the troops of the Emperor. The new exarch Eutychius, who had landed at Naples, did not succeed in making the two dukes desert the league with the pope; his entreaties had no effect on Liutprand till he offered a very important service to the king, placing his own troops at the king's disposal against the independent dukes, so as to take them in the rear and force them to render homage to the king and send hostages in token of their fidelity. The king repaid this service by leading the exarch to Rome, and as the pope could not think of resistance, he again submitted to the Emperor. But the Lombard troops did not enter the imperial town and Liutprand paid homage to the graves of the *Principes apostolorum* whom he had never intended to combat (729). So the Italian revolution brought double success to Liutprand: territorial acquisition of land in the north and the two dukes' formal submission in the south; and at the same time he had appeared as principal arbiter in these differences on Italian soil.

Liutprand's next care was to make the two duchies' formal dependency real and effective. When difficulties arose after the death of Romuald II of Benevento (731-732), on account of the succession, he marched on Benevento, carried away the young duke Gisulf for education, and installed his own nephew Gregorius, relying upon his own sovereign power. Nearly at the same time, after a breach of the league with the exarch, a plot of the Roman *dux* of Perugia against Bologna miscarried, and a Lombard army led by Hildeprand, another nephew of Liutprand, occupied the impregnable town of Ravenna, the centre of the imperial administration.   But the exarch succeeded in regaining the capital by a sudden attack and making Hildeprand prisoner, with help of the navy of the lagoons, against which the Lombards were helpless.   Soon after this misfortune Liutprand seems to have concluded an armistice, on account of which Hildeprand was sent back.   Then Liutprand fell ill at Pavia (735), Hildeprand was proclaimed king by the Lombards, and Liutprand acknowledged him as co-regent after his recovery.   New difficulties arose in Friuli, where the duke Pemmo had covered the Lombard name with fame in different combats with the Slavs and displayed great splendour in his princely court at Cividale; he got entangled in a quarrel with the king's favourite Calistus, whom Liutprand had made patriarch of Aquileia, because the latter wanted to remove his residence from the small town of Cormons to Cividale, and had taken by force the bishop's palace, which the dukes had resigned to the fugitive bishop of Julia Carnica.   Liutprand interceded in the patriarch's favour, dismissed the duke Pemmo and set up in his place his son Ratchis, who proved himself the king's faithful subject.   No king had ever reigned so powerfully.

But now the time had come when Liutprand thought it necessary to deal the death-blow to the Roman Empire in Italy, as soon as the independence of the duke in middle Italy was broken.   This duke, Transamund of Spoleto, had taken the Roman castle Gallese and might have been of great use to the king in barring the communication between Ravenna and Rome, but he preferred to deliver up the castle to the pope Gregory III, engaging himself never to carry arms against him any more. But Liutprand, crossing the Pentapolis, arrived at Spoleto in June 739, and appointed a new duke Hilderic, while Transamund fled to Rome. The king demanded in vain the rebel's delivery before the walls of Rome, took away the castles of Ameria, Horta, Polimartium, and Bleda from the *ducatus Romae*, but then returned to North Italy.   Meanwhile a Roman party in Benevento set up one Godescalc in the duchy in place of the deceased duke Gregorius, without regard to the king's claims.   In the following year (740) Liutprand and Hildeprand attacked Ravenna and laid the exarchate under contribution, and at the same time Lombard bands issuing from the castles devastated the Campagna.   The pope sent an embassy, praying the king to give back these border forts, and also claimed the help of the Lombard bishops by a circular letter.   At the same time the army of the *ducatus Romae*, aided by Benevento, reinstated in Spoleto the duke Transamund, who was accepted with open arms by his own people (Dec. 740).   But even now Transamund did not dare to attack the king and win back to the Romans the four castles, as the pope had wished.   Pope Zacharias, who had followed Gregory at the end of 741, gave up his predecessor's Spoletan policy in consequence, and offered to the king the help of the Roman army against Spoleto, on condition of his promise to restore the four castles. Attacked on two sides (742) Transamund surrendered to the king; then the latter advanced against Benevento, and as Godescalc abandoned his own country and was surrendered before he reached the ship destined to bring him to Constantinople, the king gave back his ancestral duchy to Gisulf who had by now grown up and was faithfully devoted to him. But after he had brought all difficulties in South Italy to an end the pope himself overtook him on his way back in his camp at Terni, reminding him of his promise. The Catholic king received the pope with all customary marks of reverence, and gave him the desired charter concerning the restoration of the four towns. After this several nobles escorted the pope on his return journey, and handed over to him the keys of the surrendered towns, and the parts of the patrimony which had been conquered were also restored to him. In exchange for this the pope concluded an armistice with the king for twenty years in the name of the *ducatus Romae*. In this way the king meant to eliminate one enemy, in order to concentrate all his forces against the other part of the Roman dominion. After having appointed his nephew Agiprand duke of Spoleto, he crossed the Apennines and sent his army against Ravenna at the beginning of the following year (743). The exarch and the archbishop of Ravenna in their desperation begged for the pope's intervention, and the latter actually came to meet the king at Pavia, by way of Ravenna. The king condescended to conclude an armistice, occupying the castle of Caesena and part of the territory of Ravenna meanwhile as a pledge, until the embassy he sent to Constantinople should have concluded a definite peace. We do not know Liutprand's real motives for giving up the attack; but it seems possible that changes of foreign politics, especially with the Franks, as well as sympathy with the Romans within the Lombard realm, nourished by the bishops, joined with personal motives to cause his compliance. Though he had not attained his aim when he died at the beginning of the year 744, he had brought the Lombard State's power to a height which it had never before attained.

Liutprand's former co-regent Hildeprand followed him on the throne, but was not acknowledged everywhere. Transamund returned to Spoleto. Ratchis of Friuli was proclaimed king and Hildeprand dethroned after eight months' monarchy. The imperialists greeted the elevation of Ratchis with joy, and the new king actually concluded peace with Rome for twenty years. In Spoleto he asserted his authority, and Transamund was replaced by a new duke, Lupus. We may judge by the severity of his orders concerning passports, and by his rules against riot that Ratchis was prepared to meet dangers from within and without, and so he tried to increase his party by ample distributions of land to the Church, and

to the Romans, the countrymen of his wife Tassia. He evidently strove
to lessen the disparity between Romans and Lombards. Nevertheless
he saw himself compelled to invade the imperial Pentapolis and besiege
Perugia. But when he desisted from this blockade upon the pope's
personal intervention, the Lombards gave vent to their indignation over
their king's romanising policy. The nobles raised Aistulf, the king's
brave and fierce brother, upon the buckler at Milan (June 749); Ratchis
was forced to abdicate, went to St Peter's on pilgrimage, was accepted as
a monk by the pope, and retired to Monte Cassino.

Aistulf immediately took up again with the greatest energy Liutprand's conquering policy. The donations which Ratchis had made
before Aistulf's elevation were annulled, intercourse with Romans was
forbidden, commerce with a foreign country keenly watched, the frontier
well guarded, and military duty regulated on the basis of the new social
structure. The important towns of Comacchio and Ferrara were occupied
and the Lombard king gave forth a charter as early as 7 July 751 in the
palace of Ravenna, which the last exarch, Eutychius, was said to have
surrendered. The north of Italy was now entirely in the hands of the
Lombards, except the district of the Lagoons and the towns of Istria.
Aistulf turned to central Italy, where Duke Lupus had died, and took
into his own hands the government of Spoleto, the key-city of Rome.
His next assault was of course directed to Rome. He stood before the
walls of Rome in June 752 and received a papal embassy; it is alleged
that he promised peace for forty years but broke the armistice after
four months. His conditions were very hard: tribute paid by the
inhabitants of the *ducatus Romae* and acknowledgment of his sovereignty.
He ordered the abbots of Monte Cassino and San Vincenzo, who had
appeared as the pope's envoys before him, to follow his commands as
Lombard subjects, and return to their monasteries without entering
Rome. The Emperor's embassy, which was conducted to Ravenna by
the pope's brother, only so far succeeded that Aistulf sent an envoy to
Constantinople with proposals that seemed unacceptable, at least to the
pope. But the two envoys returned to Italy without having effected
their object, while the Lombards had taken the castle of Ceccano, which
belonged to the Church. Now Pope Stephen obtained a safe conduct
and at the Emperor's command marched himself to Aistulf's court at
Pavia (autumn 753). The king sent to meet him with orders not
to venture a word about restoring the conquered territory. But the
pope was not to be deterred, and fervently entreated the king to fulfil
the conditions contained in a letter which an imperial envoy had
brought. But it was in vain. Then the Frankish ambassadors, who
had accompanied the pope, intervened and required Aistulf to let the
pope go to Gaul. When the pope, at his next audience, declared
that it was actually his intention to cross the Alps, Aistulf, it is said,
roared with rage like a wild beast. But after vain endeavours to change

the pope's resolution, he was obliged to dismiss him, not daring to detain him by force and expose himself to immediate conflict with the Franks. The pope left Pavia on 5 November. The new Frankish king Pepin was clearly resolved upon interfering in Italy, and Aistulf saw himself face to face with a new situation immediately before reaching the aim he had longed for so fervently.

But all links had not yet been broken off. Pepin sent embassies over the Alps three times in order to induce Aistulf to yield, but in vain. The public feeling among the Frankish nobles was by no means favourable to war, and Aistulf, wishing to profit thereby, sent to Gaul Pepin's brother and former co-regent Carloman, who was now monk in Monte Cassino. While the Frankish army was already advancing, the pope once more sent a letter full of entreaties to Aistulf, and Pepin offered 12,000 *solidi* as recompense for the disputed territories; Aistulf refused with threats and brought the whole of his forces, and the military material he had stored up for his enterprise against Rome, to Susa at the foot of Mont Cenis, awaiting the Franks' attack. He was too impatient however to hold out behind the fortified *clusae*, and attacked the Frankish vanguard by surprise; but not being able to deploy his superior forces in the narrow vale, he was thrown back and was himself very nearly killed; then he concentrated the rest of his army in the fortified city of Pavia, where the main army of the Franks appeared after a few days. But as the Franks shrank from a long siege and the Frankish nobles, who had kept up friendly relations with the Lombards dating perhaps from the time of Charles Martel, tried to mediate, peace was made, Aistulf confirmed the treaty by oath, promising to surrender those territories of Italy he had occupied illegally and to acknowledge formally the Frankish king's sovereignty. He sent forty hostages and made lavish presents to the king and the nobles as recompense for the expenses of war (autumn 754). The pope returned to Rome, accompanied by the Frankish ambassador Fulrad, and Pepin retired over the Alps. But Aistulf did not think of keeping his oath. Of all the towns he only surrendered Narni, and seeing that Pepin did not interfere again, he resolved to put an end to the quarrel by a master stroke. On 1 Jan. 756 a Lombard army again encamped before Rome on the right bank of the Tiber, Aistulf rapidly approached from Spoleto and the Beneventans from the south. With terrible threats, he required the pope's surrender while his bands plundered the Campagna. Pepin's envoy, the abbot Warnehar, fought against the Lombards in full harness and then informed his prince of what he had seen. But Rome's strong walls saved her again; Aistulf gave up the siege after five months and returned to Pavia (5 April) to await a new attack from Pepin when winter was over and the melting snow rendered the passage possible.

The Lombards were once more dispersed by the Franks near the *clusae* of Mont Cenis, and Aistulf again took refuge behind the walls of Pavia. Shut up in this fortress, he again entreated forgiveness and peace of Pepin by the nobles' intervention. The latter granted the rebel life and realm, which he had forfeited. Following the Frankish verdict to which he had appealed, he was obliged to pay as indemnity a third of the great royal hoard and costlier presents than two years before to guarantee his further submission, and engage himself to pay a yearly tribute of 12,000 *solidi*, as the Lombards had once done in the time of Agilulf. He actually now yielded up the towns whose surrender had been stipulated two years earlier and Comacchio besides, and so the same boundaries were re-established which had parted the two territories before Aistulf's accession to the throne. Liutprand's conquests however remained to the Lombard dominion, so that to the great disappointment of pope and emperor the status of the peace made in 680 was not restored. Nevertheless this was the greatest humiliation the Lombard realm had ever suffered for more than a century and a half, since that first league between the Byzantine Emperor and the Franks had been broken. Aistulf's eager policy of attack was crossed by a new factor which had not entered into his predecessor's calculations. The proud king did not long survive his fall. He died in consequence of an accident while hunting (December 756).

After Aistulf's death a grave crisis broke out in the Lombard State. The monk Ratchis left Monte Cassino and was acknowledged as ruler, "servant of Christ and prince of the Lombard people," especially in the north of the Apennines. But Spoleto as well as Benevento detached itself from the kingdom and set up Alboin as duke of Spoleto, who swore an oath of allegiance to the pope and the Frankish king. The duke Desiderius was raised upon the buckler in Tuscany, and as he engaged himself by document and by oath to surrender the towns belonging to the Empire, and to live in peace and friendship with the pope and the Frankish king, the Frankish plenipotentiary in Rome supported him with great energy and the pope prepared the Roman army for his defence. Ratchis then abdicated for the second time. On the pope's demand, Desiderius actually ceded Faenza and Ferrara, but as soon as he felt himself sure on the throne, he entered Spoleto by force without consideration of the pope's wishes, made Duke Alboin prisoner as a rebel, drove away the duke Liutprand of Benevento, who was obliged to take refuge behind the walls of Otranto, and set up Arichis as duke in his place, and gave him his daughter Adelperga to wife. He made a proposal of co-operation against the pope and the duke of Benevento to an imperial embassy which passed by: at the same time he tried to render the pope's connexion with his former allies as difficult as possible, appeared at St Peter's grave in Rome, pretending friendly intentions, and forced the pope to write a letter to Pepin, interceding for the surrender of the Lombard hostages. To be sure the pope recalled this letter by means of the very messenger who brought it, but still Desiderius succeeded in averting a new Frankish intervention, greatly desired by the pope, by making certain concessions, especially in relation to the patrimonies. At his next visit to Rome, Desiderius framed a compact on the Frankish embassies' advice about 763 on the basis of mutual acknowledgment of the *status quo*; and Desiderius promised to come to the pope's aid with all his forces in case of an attack from the Emperor. It was only after Pope Paul's death (767) that new difficulties with Rome arose when a party, hostile to the late government, had raised Constantine to the papal throne, and the defeated party's leader, the *primicerius* Christophorus, claimed the Lombards' help. The defeated party entered Rome by force, led by Lombard troops and the Lombard priest Waldipert, but the Lombard candidate Philip was not able to maintain himself on the papal throne in place of Constantine; Stephen III was elected and Waldipert himself slain by his former adherents (768). Shortly after this failure Desiderius tried to procure the archbishopric of Ravenna for Michael, one of his confidants (769); but Frankish commissioners dismissed him at the pope's wish.

A new combination in foreign politics seemed to change the present situation to the disadvantage of the pope and in favour of Desiderius. Desiderius and Tassilo of Bavaria, both menaced by the Frankish preponderance, had entered into friendly relations, and Tassilo had married Liutperga, daughter of Desiderius. Pepin's widow Bertrada conceived the plan of securing peace by bringing one of her sons into relationship with the Lombard royal family. Notwithstanding the pope's amazement, she crossed the Alps and asked one of Desiderius' daughters in marriage for her son Charles. The betrothal took place under the guarantee of the Frankish nobles and the marriage was accomplished. Meanwhile Bertrada had endeavoured to reassure the pope about her transactions with Desiderius. The latter had evidently renewed his promise to respect the territorial *status quo* and restore the patrimonies which were the private property of the Roman Church. Of course the next consequence was the fall of the anti-Lombard party prevailing in Rome. This was approved of by the pope, who wanted to escape his minister's predominant influence. Desiderius appeared before Rome with military forces, but under pretence of praying at the Apostle's grave and arranging disputed questions. The pope came out to him and received his promise by oath. But a papal chamberlain named Paulus Afiarta, the leader of the Lombard party, raised up within the town a revolt against Christophorus, whereupon the pope maintained that Christophorus and his party conspired against his life. The accused offered resistance within the town, but were betrayed by the Romans, abandoned by the pope, and cruelly killed by Paulus Afiarta and his accomplices. Desiderius did not now want to hear anything more about transactions with the pope. But the Frankish kings seem to have taken offence at his way of acting. Carloman died in Dec. 771, but Charles, who laid claim to the whole Frankish realm without considering Carloman's children, resolved to depart from the last year's policy. He repudiated Desiderius' daughter, well knowing that he made an enemy of the Lombard king by this insult. Carloman's widow Gerberga with her children and followers fled to the Lombard king, who was ready to use them as weapons against Charles. The new pope Hadrian was naturally on the side of Charles, and so the political combination of the time before Bertrada's intervention was re-established. Embassies between the pope and Desiderius had no effect, because the pope did not trust the king's promises, and for fear of losing his hold upon the Frankish king firmly refused to anoint as kings Carloman's children at the wish of Desiderius. Paulus Afiarta and his followers (the Lombard party) were removed and punished, so that the Frankish influence again decided the papal policy.

Meanwhile Desiderius had again occupied Faenza, Ferrara, Comacchio (spring 772), and threatened Ravenna on every side; then he took Sinigaglia, Jesi, Urbino, Gubbio, commanded his troops to attack Bieda and Otricoli, in order to frighten the pope, and marched against Rome with Carloman's children, after having vainly entreated the pope to come to him. The latter made all preparations for defence and raised his forces in Rome, but sent three bishops to the royal camp at Viterbo with a bull, threatening with excommunication the king and all who dared to step upon Roman soil. Desiderius actually broke up his camp and retired; but the answer he made to the Frankish embassies, which appeared in Italy at the pope's wish, in order to become acquainted with the state of things, shews clearly enough that he expected to meet a decisive stroke. He had prepared himself for this moment during the whole time of his reign, trying to ensure the dynasty by the nomination of his son Adalgis as co-regent (759), and to restrain the independence of the dukes, though still attaching them to his person. He had made costly presents to the great monasteries, and endowed them with privileges, and had strengthened his party by new donations of landed property. But nevertheless the Lombard kingdom did not offer united resistance to the Franks. A number of emigrants had already fled to the Franks even before the beginning of the war, and many nobles now left Spoleto and went to Rome. Benevento did not take any part in the war, and after the first failure not only the Spoletan contingents but also a number of towns submitted to the pope voluntarily. Charles only found resistance from the towns where the Lombard kings defended themselves. Treason played a great part in the fall of the Lombard realm, a fact which can be traced even in the sagas. After having refused Charles' last offer, to pay 17,000 *solidi* if he fulfilled the pope's demand, Desiderius put his trust in the strong position near the *clusae* of Susa, which he had fortified. Here, at the Porta d' Italia, he expected Charles, who marched over Mont Cenis, while another corps took its way over the Great St Bernard. But, owing to this circuit, no battle seems to have taken place. Desiderius was obliged to retire to Pavia (Sept. 773) with the warriors who were still faithful to him, while Adalgis sought refuge with Carloman's children behind the fortified walls of Verona, but fled from here also after a time and went into exile at Constantinople. But except at Pavia and Verona Charles found no resistance whatever in the Lombard realm. Verona with Carloman's children surrendered even before Christmas to a detached troop under Charles himself, whereas the siege of Pavia was prolonged to the beginning of June 774, though famine and epidemics raged within the town.

After the capitulation Charles brought Desiderius and his wife to Gaul with the royal treasure, having received homage of the Lombards who had gathered at Pavia, leaving there a Frankish garrison. This was the end of the independent Lombard realm, and Charles dated his succession in this realm from the fall of the royal town of Pavia.

To be sure, the duchy of Benevento in the south had succeeded in keeping its independence throughout all these disasters, and the prince Arichis, Desiderius' son-in-law, considered himself the Lombard king's successor; but, important as this fact has proved for Italian history, the Lombard kingdom had always been rooted in the north. The occasion for its fall was given by the renewal of that combination between the remnants of the *respublica*, now represented by the pope, and the Franks, who had developed into a consolidated power; and the Lombard State had never been equal to these combined forces. A deeper reason lay in the structure of the Lombard State, which had not been able, even in the intervals of peace, to attain any organic unity. The small number of the Lombard people in connexion with their form of settlement, conditioned as it was by the state of affairs in the Roman Empire, had given too great importance from the first to the single local groups and their dukes. Kingship, which had been re-established in the distress of those times, exerted its uniting and centralising power very slowly, and a perfect union had never been accomplished. For the kingdom was founded on its royal domain, and the latter on new conquests of land, with which the king's followers had to be furnished. As was always the case in the medieval State in which agriculture was practised, the warriors who were rewarded in this way did not permanently attach themselves to the king, and thus formed a continual danger to the kingship. The king was continually forced to new conquests and then obliged to give them up again voluntarily, so that even the mightiest rulers made little lasting impression on the State, especially when the possibilities of donations diminished as the Lombard element drew nearer to the Roman. On the other hand, the assimilation with the inhabitants of Italy in race and culture had been rapidly carried out just on account of the smallness of the conquering tribe and the necessary adaptations resulting; and it was not the cultural and racial difference, but rather a difference of organisation, resulting from the land's history and settlement, which separated the three parts of Italy—the kingdom, the ecclesiastical State and Benevento—through more than a thousand years.

CHAPTER VIII.

(A)

IMPERIAL ITALY AND AFRICA: ADMINISTRATION.

WHEN in the year 534 Justinian organised the imperial administration
in Africa, and after the year 540 in Italy, it was not so much his intention
to create a new civil code as to restore in the main the conditions which had
existed before the break in the Roman rule. In Africa this break had been
complete owing to the constitution of the Vandal kingdom. In Italy the
Roman civil administration had remained unaltered, even at the time
when the rule of the Gothic king had superseded the direct imperial
government, and therefore, after the expulsion of the Gothic army
quartered on the land, only the military administration had to be created
completely anew. Maintenance of the continuity, which from an imperial point of view had legally never been broken, and equal rights with
those provinces which had never bowed to the yoke of the barbarians,
are therefore the natural principles upon which Justinian founded his
reorganisation of the West. It was, however, impossible in practice to
ignore altogether the development of the last century. Africa and Italy
had for so many years lived in political independence of each other, that
it was no longer possible to look upon them as a united whole; in
consequence of this, their administration remained entirely separate, as
before. Whereas the *dioecesis* of Africa had been under the rule of the
praefectus praetorio per Italias, until its occupation by the Vandals, it
now received its own *praefectus praetorio,* who took the place of the
former, henceforth superfluous *vicarius Africae,* so that the *praefectus
Italiae* was limited to Italy. Sardinia and Corsica, however, which had
been in the possession of the Vandals and were now won back by
Justinian together with the Vandal kingdom, remained united with
Africa. It was further of decisive importance for Italy that it was no
longer, as before the so-called fall of the West-Roman Empire, ruled by
two emperors with a local division of power, but by one only, and that he
resided in the East. For the consequence was, that the court offices and
central offices proper, such as the *magister officiorum,* the *quaestor,* the
comites sacrarum largitionum, rerum privatarum and *patrimonii,* which
as the highest administrative offices in Italy had been maintained within

the Gothic kingdom parallel with the court offices and central offices at Constantinople, now disappeared in Italy and were amalgamated with the central offices at Constantinople. The same applies to the Senate, which likewise was not a local but an imperial governing body. There was no need to dissolve it; it disappeared from Rome in the natural course of events, for the officials, of whom it was composed at that time, henceforth only existed at Constantinople, the residence of the single emperor.

The principle underlying the bureaucratic administration by which the Empire had been governed since Diocletian, and the details of which had only been developed during the centuries following his reign, remained unchanged: all autonomy was supplanted by a body of imperial functionaries grouped hierarchically, according to their local and practical powers, subject only to the absolute will of the Emperor and appointed by him, chosen from the ranks of the landowners, the only persons who had the right to migrate from their place of origin. They had at their disposal as an auxiliary force a body of officials (*officium*), arranged likewise hierarchically, but drawn from another class of the people. Opposed, however, to the ruling class, which carried out the will of the State by means of the bureaucratic organisation, stood, as the working members of the State, all the rest of the population, tied hereditarily to their class and its organisation, which as far as it existed had only the one object of making its members jointly responsible for the expenses of the State. The principle also of separating the civil from the military power, which had first been completely carried into force by Constantine the Great, though sometimes abandoned by Justinian in the East, was intended by the Emperor to come into full force in the West, as soon as an end had been put to the state of war[1].

While the details of the Italian administration have to be gathered partly from the so-called *Pragmatica sanctio pro petitione Vigilii*, and partly from the remaining sources, chiefly the letters of Pope Gregory, which unfortunately nowhere present a complete picture, the Codex Justinianus (I. 27) contains the statutes of the organisation for the civil and military adjustment within the African *dioecesis*, issued by Justinian in the year 534. These statutes provided that the *praefectus praetorio Africae*, who as a functionary of the highest class and receiving a salary of 100 pounds of gold (about £4500), stood at the head of the civil administration, should have (besides his private cabinet, the *consiliarii* and *cancellarii*, the *grammatici* and *medici*) an official staff of 396 persons, divided into ten *scrinia* and nine *scholae*. Four of the former, who were also the best paid, were entrusted with the financial administration, and one with the exchequer. Beside these there were the *scrinium* of the *primiscrinius* or *subadiuva*, and one each of the *commentariensis* and of the *ab actis*, who conducted the business of the chancery and the

---

[1] To avoid repetition a knowledge of the administration of the Roman Empire is here assumed. It has been described in Vol. I. Ch. II.

archives, and lastly the *scrinium operum* for the Public Works and the *scrinium libellorum* for the Jurisdiction. The *cohortales*, probably assistant clerks, were divided into the *scholae* of *exceptores*, *singularii*, *mittendarii*, *cursores*, *nomenculatores*, *stratores*, *praecones*, *draconarii* and *chartularii*. The sum total of the salaries paid to the staff amounted to 6575 gold *solidi* (a little over £4000), which had to be raised, like the praefect's salary, by the *dioecesis*. Subordinate to the praefect were seven governors, three of whom had the rank of a *consularis* and four that of a *praeses*. It seems that the former—the text is not quite clear —were the governors of the old *provincia proconsularis* (Zeugitana, Carthage), of Byzacena and of Tripolis, whilst the latter, who were of inferior rank, appear to have governed Sardinia, Numidia and the two Mauretanias (Sitifensis and Caesariensis); a staff of 50 clerks was attached to each of them.

For the protection of the *dioecesis*, after peace had eventually been so completely restored that the conquering army and the moveable field-army of the *comitatenses* could be withdrawn, a frontier-army was to be newly enrolled, garrisoned and settled, and to be entrusted to the military commanders of the separate frontier-provinces (*limites*). These were under the *duces* of Tripolitana (in Leptis Magna), of Byzacena (in Capsa or Thelepte, the command of which was afterwards shared with a second *dux* at Hadrumetum), of Numidia (in Constantina), of Mauretania (in Caesarea), and of Sardinia. Whilst these *duces* were to take up a temporary residence in the capitals until the reoccupation of the old frontiers should be complete, a few of the larger forts along the frontier were given into the charge of tribunes. One of these, who was subordinate to the *dux* of Mauretania, was also stationed at Septum to watch the Straits of Gibraltar and to command the battleships there. Each of these *duces* had, besides an *assessor*, a staff of 40 clerks with a number of gentlemen-at-arms, the latter of whom he paid out of his own sufficiently high stipend, handed over to him by the praefect. The *duces*, *viri spectabiles*, *i.e.* officials of the second class, were subordinate in military rank to the commanding *magister militum* of the moment. It is true that this arrangement was quite provisional, for the *limites* were not to be definitely adjusted till the old frontiers had been won back by the Roman arms.

In Italy Justinian's division of provinces can hardly have differed essentially from the old Roman one, which had been accepted by the Ostrogoths. The jurisdiction of the praefect was curtailed not only by the separation of Sardinia and Corsica and by the loss of the two Rhaetias on the northern frontier, but furthermore by the enactment of Justinian, which put Sicily under a special *praetor* of the second class, from whom an appeal passed directly to the *quaestor* of the court at Constantinople. It is doubtful whether the intermediate court of the two *vicarii* (*Italiae* and *urbis Romae*) was maintained under the praefect.

With regard to the provincial governors the *Pragmatica sanctio* ordains that they should be chosen from the inhabitants by the bishops and most distinguished men in each province, but must obtain the sanction of the praefect—a very peculiar regulation, which does not agree with the general bureaucratic principles of the Byzantine administration, and which seems to prove that as early as the middle of the sixth century the position of the provincial governors, like that of the town councils in Italy, was brought very low and considered more of an *onus* than an *honor*. Not long afterwards this regulation was extended to the whole Empire. The special position of the municipal officials of Rome under the *praefectus urbi* together with other privileges of the old imperial capital was maintained, though from the outset this administrative department hardly fitted any better here than elsewhere into the frame of the general administration, and had to be relieved of a number of its former duties.

The defence of the frontiers, temporarily established by Belisarius in Africa, was organised in Italy by Narses, who had restored the natural frontiers of Italy in the north to nearly the dimensions which had been recognised by the Lombards in Gothic times after the cession of Noricum and Pannonia to them. It is probable that the location of the frontier troops was also influenced by the distribution of the garrisons during the Gothic rule. In the east, Forum Julii (Friuli) was the centre of a chain of small fortresses on the southern slope of the Alps, which were connected with the fort of Aguntum (Innichen) by the pass over the Kreuzberg. From this point the valley of the Rienz probably became the frontier. The bishopric of Seben (Brixen) also belonged to the Empire, and further south a chain of forts from Verruca (near Trent) as far as Anagni (Nanó) can be traced. Further west, the Alpine passes were secured by forts at their southern end; thus mention is made of one situated on an island in the Lake of Como, and of another at the outlet of the pass over Mont Cenis at Susa. It is not clear in what manner these *limites*, which had replaced the old *ducatus Rhaetiarum* and the *tractus Italiae circa Alpes* of the *Notitia Dignitatum*, were separated from each other. It appears, however, that some of the troops which had come to Italy under Narses were garrisoned and settled in them, and that certain generals who had served under Narses were placed at the head of these *ducatus*. This would be the easiest explanation for the fact that at a very early date the command over the garrisoned legions in Italy was not held by ordinary *duces*, but by men holding the higher rank of *magister militum*.

Justinian's dispositions had all been made on the assumption that peace would be completely restored throughout the two new sections of the Empire. During the wars of conquest, the Emperor's authorised generals were, in Africa Belisarius, who was *magister militum per orientem*, and in Italy latterly Narses, who, as *patricius* and holder of high court offices, belonged to the highest rank. These had acted without restriction, both in their military and in their civil capacity, subject only to the instructions they received from the Emperor. Procopius calls each alike αὐτοκράτωρ τοῦ πολέμου.

Circumstances, however, allowed neither country any lasting peace; martial law continued as a consequence of the state of war, and neither Africa nor Italy could safely be left without an active army. It became necessary to create and to uphold a supreme authority, to which the civil administration had to be subordinated for military purposes. In Africa a passing attempt was made by Justinian to equip the *praefectus praetorio* with the power of a *magister militum*, but this was an exceptional case. In Africa, as also in Italy, when the Lombards invaded it after the recall of Narses, the rule was to appoint extra-ordinary military commanders, who held a high rank and were superior to the *praefectus*. But when the state of war proved to be chronic, the extraordinary office developed into a regular one. In the year 584 an exarch is mentioned in Italy for the first time, and here as in Africa the title exarch is henceforth commonly applied to the head of the military and civil administration. In this combination of military and civil functions the exarch reminds us of certain exalted provincial governors, whom Justinian, deviating from the general principles of the Roman administration, had already installed in the East. But the exarch is far more than these. Holding, as he does, the highest office in his division of the Empire, he not only belongs to the highest class with the title *excellentissimus*, but he owns also the full title of *patricius*, a distinction not usually shared by the praefect. If the patrician holds a court office it is usual, in official language, to substitute this for the title *patricius*, as for instance *cubicularius et exarchus*, or occasionally *patricius et exarchus*. In ordinary life, when speaking of the exarch in Italy and Africa, only the title *patricius* was used.

The power of the exarch was practically unlimited. Like the Gothic kings, he was the emperor's representative; and as such, like his pre-decessors, *e.g.* Belisarius and Narses, he held absolute command over the active troops temporarily stationed in that part of the Empire, as well as over the frontier legions. At the same time he took a hand, whenever it pleased him, in the civil administration, decided ecclesiastical matters, negotiated with foreign countries and concluded armistices. His power was only limited in time, inasmuch as he might at any moment be recalled by the emperor, and in extent inasmuch as his mandate applied only to a definite part of the Empire. He could there-fore issue decrees, but could neither make laws nor conclude a peace valid for the whole of the Empire. The command of the exarch of Italy extended beyond Italy to the rest of the old *dioecesis* of West Illyricum, and to Dalmatia, which also, since Odovacar's time, had been added to the Italian kingdom. The military system of Sicily, on the other hand, was allowed, at least in later years, to develop independently.

It followed naturally that the exarch, who resided at Ravenna, had at his court, besides an *officium* befitting his rank, a number of advisers and assistants for the miscellaneous branches of his activity. We will only mention here the *consiliarius*, the *cancellarius*, the *maior domus*, the *scholastici* versed in jurisprudence, and in Africa a ὑποστράτηγος with the rank of *patricius*, a representative of the emperor's representative. He was further, like all generals of that time, surrounded by a number of private soldiers, gentlemen-at-arms who held a more distinguished position than soldiers of the regular army. The court of these vice-emperors was in every aspect a copy of the imperial court, and their powerful position makes it conceivable that, when in the middle of the seventh century the centre of the Empire was in distress, the attempt was repeatedly made both from Africa and Italy to replace the emperor by an exarch. It was in this manner that the dynasty of Heraclius attained to the throne.

The consequences of the uninterrupted state of war, caused in Africa by the Berbers and later by the Muslims, and in Italy by the Lombards, of course affected, not only the head of the general administration, but also its organisation and its efficacy. Tripolitana was detached from Africa, probably under the Emperor Maurice, and added to Egypt. Mauretania Sitifensis and the few stations of the Caesariensis which the Empire was able to uphold, were joined together into one province, Mauretania Prima, whilst distant Septum, with the remains of the Byzantine possessions in Spain, became the province Mauretania Secunda. Of still greater importance is the fact that Justinian's plan of restoring the frontiers of the Empire to the extent they had before the Vandal occupation, was never carried out. It even became necessary in several provinces to move back again the line of defence already reached, so that the *duces* did not hold command in the border-lands of their own provinces, but were stationed with their garrisoned legions in the interior. This makes it impossible to define the sphere of local power between the *dux* and the *tribuni* on the one hand, and the *praeses* on the other. The provinces themselves became as it were *limites*. Just as the praefect continued to exist under the exarch, so there existed, at least in the beginning of the seventh century and perhaps even up to the definite loss of Africa, side by side with the *duces*, a number of civil *praesides*, not to speak of the various revenue officers who were employed for the taxation. Naturally the *duces* and the *tribuni* who were appointed by the exarch proved the stronger, and continually extended their powers at the expense of the civil officials. The development, which must have led to the complete suppression of the civil administration, hardly reached its final stage in Africa, because it was forcibly cut short by the Mahometan occupation. It went further in Italy. The Lombards in their onslaught had broken up the whole of the Italian administration in the course of about ten years; attempts to re-establish it failed, and when about the beginning of the seventh century the Empire had accepted the inevitable, it made no further attempt to gain the remote border-lands, but saw its task in trying to secure what remained of the Roman possessions. It had been customary so far for the various army corps, of which some were recruited from the East, to fight in different parts of Italy, led by their *magistri militum* under the superior command of the exarch. The *primus exercitus* was stationed at Ravenna at the immediate disposal of the commander-in-chief. But gradually, and especially when by the repeated truces a certain state of equilibrium had been attained, there were no more reinforcements from the East, except perhaps the regiment of guards for the exarch, and the legions in Italy were stationed at those points which seemed most important for the defence. In the interior of Italy also *ducatus* sprang up in all directions with *duces* or *magistri militum* at their head; everywhere forts were erected and put under the command of a tribune.

By the conquests of Rothari, who seized Liguria, and of Grimoald in the seventh century, as also by those of Liutprand and Aistulf in the eighth century, the frontiers were still further displaced, but as early as the first half of the seventh century the following *ducatus* can be distinguished: Istria and Venetia, both confined to the coast-land and the islands; the exarchate proper (in the narrower sense), the *provincia Ravennatium*, the borders of which lay between Bologna and Modena in the west, along the Po in the north, and from which the *ducatus* of Ferrara was detached in the eighth century; the Pentapolis, *i.e.* the remains of Picenum, with its *dux* residing at Ariminum; the *ducatus* of Perugia, which with its numerous and strong forts covered the most important passes of the Apennines and the Via Flaminia, the only connexion between the remains of the Byzantine possessions in the north, and in particular Ravenna, with Rome; Tuscia to the north of the lower course of the Tiber; Rome and her immediate surroundings, with the forts *in partibus Campaniae* to the south, as far as the valley of the Liris; the *ducatus* of Naples, *i.e.* the coast-towns from Cumae to Amalfi with a part of Liburia (Terra di Lavoro); the *ducatus* of Calabria, consisting of the remains of Apulia and Calabria, Lucania and Bruttium. This division supplanted the old division into provinces, and, when about the middle of the seventh century not only the praefect of Italy, but also the provincial *praesides* disappeared completely, the names of the old provinces continued to be used in ordinary conversation only to define certain parts of Italy. The functions of the *duces* and *praesides* were completely absorbed by the *magistri militum* in the same way as those of the *praefectus praetorio* were absorbed by the exarch. The whole administration had been militarised, and the same status established which in the East under similar conditions appears as the "theme" system.

The civil administration of the State, however, was not only threatened by the military organisations, but also by another factor, the Church, which prepared to occupy the gaps left by the activity of the State, and to enter upon a part of its heritage.   Through means of influence peculiar to herself and not accessible to the State, the Church had in Italy a very special position through her extensive landed property, as also by right of privileges which former emperors, in particular Justinian, had accorded to her.   The legal privileges of the Church went so far, that popes of the sixth century already claimed for the clergy the right to be judged by ecclesiastics only, and its landed property was protected by special laws. The influence of the Church in all matters could only be controlled by the actual power and authority of the State, for the claim of the pope and of the ecclesiastical hierarchy to be the representatives of the *civitas Dei,* and as such superior to worldly authorities, permitted a growth of power to an unlimited extent.

The material foundation for this power was supplied by the immense wealth, of the Roman Church especially, which designated its possessions by preference as *patrimonium pauperum.*   The starting-point for its activity was indeed the care of the poor, a field which had been entirely neglected by the State, but gained importance in proportion to the increasing distress of the times and the insufficiency of the public administration.   The State itself, in fact, not only allowed the bishops an important voice in the election of the provincial governors, but it granted them a certain right of control over all officials, in so far as they were permitted to attend to the complaints of the oppressed population, and to convey them to the magistrates in authority or even to the emperor himself.   Time after time there was intervention, mostly by the popes, and no part of the administration was free from their influence.

The predominance of the ecclesiastical influence over the secular in the civil administration shews itself very clearly in the department of municipal government, for the *curiales,* the remainders of the old πόλις, having lost their autonomy and become mere bearers of burdens, were already doomed.   In Lilybaeum, for instance, the wealthy citizens, manifestly the *curiales,* had made an agreement with the bishop in accordance with which the bishop took over certain of their burdens, and in return a number of estates were transferred to the Church.   At Naples the bishop tried to get possession of the aqueducts and the city gates.   Above all, at Rome the pope extended the range of his power in his own interest and in the interest of the population, who could no longer depend upon the regular working of the public administration. The *Pragmatica sanctio* had guaranteed the maintenance by the State of the public buildings at Rome; nevertheless, in the seventh century the care of the aqueducts as well as the preservation of the city walls passed over to the papal administration.   By this time no more mention is made of the *praefectura urbis,* and when after almost two centuries it appears again in our sources, it has become a pontifical office. The old public distribution of provisions was replaced by the benevolent institutions of the Roman Church, by her diaconates, shelters, hospitals and her magnificent charity organisation, through which money and provisions were dealt out regularly to a large part of the population. The vast granaries of the Roman Church received the corn brought from all the patrimonies, especially from Sicily, for the purpose of feeding a population whose regular sources of income were totally insufficient for their support. The recognised superiority of the papal administration is also illustrated by the fact that the State further felt induced to hand over to the granaries of the Church the revenue paid in kind by Sicily, Sardinia and Corsica and set aside for the provisioning of Rome and its garrison, so that the pope appears in many respects as the emperor's paymaster (*dispensator*). But the pope becomes also the emperor's banker when the funds for the payment of the army are made over to him, so that— for a time at least—the soldiers are paid through his offices. Thus the organs of state administration were one by one rendered superfluous by the development of a well-organised papal central government, whilst the managers of the pontifical estates in the different provinces, the *rectores patrimonii*, who were entrusted with the representation of the pope in all secular matters, had an ever-increasing number of duties heaped upon them.

In proportion as the reinforcements of soldiers from Byzantium failed, Italy had to depend more upon her own resources, *i.e.* upon the soldiers who had been settled in Italy at the time when the inner boundaries were established—evidently in imitation of the old *limitanei*—and upon the native population, which latter being compelled to take its share in the watch-service (*murorum vigiliae*) and obliged to provide for their own up-keep, could soon no longer be distinguished from the former. For example, the *castrum Squillace* was erected on land belonging to the monastery of the same name, and for the allotments conceded to them the soldiers had to pay a ground-rent (*solaticum*) to the monastery. The *castrum Callipolis* had been built within the precincts of a manor owned by the Roman Church, and the *coloni* of the Church themselves formed its garrison. All those who were obliged to do military service in a fort under the command of the tribune formed the *numerus* or *bandus*, and being a corporation had the right to acquire landed property. The inhabitants of Comacchio, for instance, taken collectively, are called *milites*, and only in the large cities, such as Rome or Ravenna, the *milites* do not embrace the entire population. On the other hand we often find the inhabitants of a fort dependent upon a landlord. But though the power of a tribune and that of a landlord were originally derived from entirely different sources, they were naturally brought nearer to each other in the course of their development, for while it became more common for the tribunes to acquire landed property, the landowners grew more military. For the tribune did not only hold the command of a fort, the power of raising part of the taxes, and the jurisdiction over the population within the whole district of the fort, but in addition to this the landed property of the State or of the corporation fell to his share. Thus, the more the armed power assumed the character of a *militia*, the more important it became that the tribunes, who probably continued to pay their nomination-tax or *suffragium* to the exarch, should be chosen from the landlords of the district, like the officers holding command under them in the *numerus*, who are occasionally mentioned, such as the *domesticus*, the *vicarius*, the *loci servator*, and others. Probably in many cases the nomination by the exarch became a mere formality, and certain seigniorial families raised a claim to the tribunate. These local powers, the lords of the manor, who were qualified for the tribunate, formed the actual land-owning military aristocracy, who, by uniting in themselves all the administrative offices of the first order, virtually ruled over Italy, although under the supervision of officials appointed by the central government. Among these local powers were the various churches, the bishoprics, and above all the Roman Church, the estates of which must in many respects have been exempt from the government of the tribunes, much the same as were the *fundi excepti* of the preceding time, so that they existed by the side of the secular tribunes, but not in subjection to them. When in the beginning of the eighth century the *militia* in the town of Ravenna was reorganised, a special division was provided for the Church besides the eleven other *bandi*. About the same time we see the *rector* of the *patrimonium* of Campania leading the soldiers of the Church in a campaign.

The conclusion and spread of this development of local powers formed the social change which led to the great Italian revolt in the first third of the eighth century. The state of anarchy in the centre of the Empire and the dangers by which Constantinople itself was threatened through the advance of Islam, had been a powerful help to the Italian struggle for independence. Different parts of Italy had at various times witnessed risings of the local powers, till the separate discontented forces united in a great opposition movement under the leadership of the pope. This took place when Gregory II boldly withheld the increased tax which Leo the Isaurian, the great organiser of the Byzantine Empire, attempted to raise for the benefit of the central government; and when, in addition to this, the edict against the worship of images and the outbreak of Iconoclasm incited religious passions against the imperial reformer. The first act of the rebels was to expel the exarch and the *duces*, the representatives of the central government, and to replace them by confidential friends of the local powers. At Rome the pope, and at Venice an elected *dux* (doge) took the place of the former authorities. The *dicio*, as it was then called, was by this revolt transferred from the

CH. VIII. (A)

emperor to the local authorities, though they remained in formal adherence to the Empire. This, at least, was the pope's wish, and no emperor set up by the opposition in Italy was generally recognised. The suppression of the revolt resulted in the resumption of the *dicio* by the emperor, and during the next generation Italy was again ruled by his deputies and appointed *duces*. The fact, however, that in consequence of the Italian revolt the local powers had for a number of years been practically independent, could not be undone. Henceforth it was impossible to appoint officials in the place of tribunes. In the local organisation the landed proprietors had gained a complete victory over the bureaucracy, and in this the hereditary principle had prevailed. But the bureaucratic superstructure, by which the emperor exercised his *dicio*, was entirely out of touch with the seigniorial element at its base, and from this resulted—at least as far as North and Central Italy were concerned, where the revolution had temporarily taken a firm hold —the complete and permanent dissolution of the central power of the State.

Not very long after the termination of the Italian revolt there appears at Rome as the highest imperial authority the *patricius et dux Stephanus*. The title of *patricius*, and various other circumstances, indicate that he was no longer subordinate but equal to the exarch of Ravenna, and that Central Italy south of the Apennines had been constituted as an independent province or theme. This division of Byzantine Italy, which had long been geographically prepared, was probably due as much to strategical reasons, *e.g.* the advance of the king of the Lombards, as to any political necessity. Stephanus, however, seems to have been the first and last to bear the new title; after him there appears no other permanent representative of the emperor at Rome. The exarchate proper, comprising the Byzantine possessions north of the Apennines from which the *ducatus* of Rome had been detached, was ruled by the exarch, who resided at Ravenna until King Aistulf took possession of that town (750–751), when only Venice and a part of Istria of the lands north of the Apennines remained under Byzantine rule. All that was left to the Byzantines in the two southernmost peninsulas of Italy was, at a date which cannot be exactly determined, united into a *ducatus* which received the name of Calabria, and retained this name even when the Byzantines had completely evacuated the south-eastern peninsula which had formerly borne this name, and were confined to their forts of the former Bruttium in the south-west. This *ducatus*, which was not linked geographically to the rest of Byzantine Italy, was placed under the command of the *patricius* of Sicily, so that it was separated from Italy in its administration. In the same way the churches of southern Italy were, in consequence of the Italian revolt, detached from Rome and subordinated to the Greek patriarchate at Constantinople. Thus in the second quarter of the eighth century there were in the western part of the Byzantine Empire three themes under patrician governors—the Exarchate, Rome, and Sicily (with Calabria), of which the latter was for the most part Greek in language and culture, whereas the two first were Latin.

After the disappearance of the patrician governor from Rome, the pope took his place and claimed the right to rule directly the city of Rome with her surroundings, and also indirectly the *ducatus* attached to Rome in the north and south as supreme lord of the two *duces*, and to restore more or less the situation which had existed during the Italian revolt. The papal bureaucracy, which had been developed to a certain extent on the model of the Byzantine bureaucracy, took the place of the imperial administration.   In other words, the pope assumed the *dicio* over Rome and the district belonging to it.   Here in times of war and peace he reigned like the exarch before him, negotiated and concluded truces with the Lombards, recognising however the suzerainty of the emperor, whose commands he received through special embassies, and reckoning his dates from the years of the emperor's reign.   At the emperor's command he went to King Aistulf at Pavia, and thence—probably also in accordance with the imperial wishes—crossed the Alps and visited the king of the Franks.   The concessions of Pepin and Charles the Great were called "restitutions," by which was understood that the old boundaries between the Empire and the Lombard kingdom, as they had been recognised before Liutprand's reign, were restored, and the sovereignty of the emperor within these boundaries was legally undisputed.   This is proved by the fact that down to the year 781 the popes reckoned their dates from the years of the emperor's reign.   The dispute between the popes and the Frankish kings on the one side and the emperors on the other arose from the fact that Pepin gave the *dicio* of the restored domains to the pope, and not to the emperor who laid claim to it, so that the pope became the real master in the new Pontifical State and no room was left for a representative of the emperor. Moreover the pope overstepped the limits which had hitherto bounded the sphere of his power, by including in his *dicio* not only the former patrician *ducatus* of Rome but also the exarchate proper.   This gave rise to protracted struggles with the archbishop of Ravenna, who as the exarch's successor assumed the *dicio* north of the Apennines.   It was probably in the year 781 that the new state of affairs was officially recognised and thereby consolidated, by an agreement between Charles and Pope Hadrian on the one side, and the Greek ambassador on the other.   According to this agreement the emperor, or rather the empress-regent Irene, abandoned all claims to the sovereignty over the Pontifical State in favour of the pope.

The emancipation from the *dicio* of the imperial government of those parts of Italy which still remained under Byzantine rule, was carried out in a way analogous to that of the Pontifical State, the only difference being that here the acquisition of the *dicio* was effected by the local powers themselves and not through the interference of a foreign ruler, and that the formal suzerainty of the Empire was maintained for a longer time. In Venice, which about the end of the seventh century had been detached from Istria as a special *ducatus*, circumstances were particularly favourable to the development of the seigniorial local powers as represented by the tribunes, though it is true that after the suppression of the Italian revolt it fell back under the imperial *dicio*, and was again ruled by *duces* or *magistri militum* nominated by the emperor, not by elected chiefs. In the second half of the eighth century, however, after the fall of the exarchate, the bonds of subordination relaxed here as elsewhere, and the nomination of the Doge became more and more an act of mere formality. The Doge was placed in power by that fraction of the tribunicial aristocracy which was for the moment in the ascendancy; by them he was elected and to them he looked for support. He succeeded in making his office lifelong, and sought to legalise his position by soliciting and receiving a court title, as a form of recognition by the emperor at Constantinople. In agreement with the emperor, some Doges even tried to make the power hereditary in their families, chiefly we may suppose in virtue of their extensive landed property and their wealth. Nevertheless, from the time when in his final treaty of peace with Byzantium (812) Charles the Great definitely renounced the conquest of Venice, the suzerainty of the Greek emperor was permanently recognised. This was shewn by the sending of ceremonial embassies whenever a change of sovereign took place at Constantinople, by the appeal for recognition of every new Doge, who probably had to buy his Byzantine title with a high *suffragium*, and by the fact that the Venetian fleet was obliged to lend support to the Byzantines, at least in the West. We also hear otherwise of occasional interference on the part of the Byzantine emperor, though Venice naturally grew more and more independent.

In the south, the *dux* of Naples considered himself the successor of the imperial governor of Campania, and a right of control over him was in fact claimed by the *patricius* of Sicily. The actual holder of the *dicio*, however, was the *dux*, who, while professing adherence to the Greek Empire, often acted in political matters with complete independence, making his office first lifelong and afterwards hereditary. In the first quarter of the ninth century the Byzantine Empire succeeded temporarily in re-establishing a *magister militum* as the real functionary, but in the course of time here as elsewhere the local powers, and at times the bishop, remained victorious, so that the position of Naples resembled in every way that of Venice. It is however true that some other local seigniories, in particular Amalfi and Gaëta, detached themselves from the *ducatus* of Naples and, after a gradual secession from the supreme rule of the *dux* of Naples, exercised the *dicio* independently within their spheres of interest, formally as direct subjects of the Greek emperor, and enjoying equal rights with Naples. At the head of these minor States were *hypatoi* or *praefecti*, who in time also developed dynasties. Thus the Byzantine bureaucracy was supplanted everywhere by local powers who usurped the *dicio*, and of whom some, for instance Venice and the coast towns of southern Italy, acknowledged the emperor's suzerainty, whilst others, like the Pontifical State, refused to do so. The victory of the local powers signified at the same time the universal establishment of the medieval system of seigniorial rule.

(B)

GREGORY THE GREAT.

If the sixth century after Christ was one of the great ages of the world's history, it would not be difficult to claim for Pope Gregory I that he was the greatest man in it. The claim would be contested on behalf of the Emperor Justinian and the monk Benedict of Nursia, if not by many another who influenced the course of affairs; but if the work of medieval leaders of men is to be judged by its results on later ages, Gregory would seem to occupy a position of commanding greatness which is unassailable.

The facts of his life for the fifty years before he became pope are soon told, yet hardly one of them is without significance. He was born in Rome, of a family noble by race and pious by hereditary attachment to the things of God, probably in the year 540. Justinian was Caesar, dwelling at Constantinople, but exercising no slight control over Church and State in Italy. Vigilius was pope and an example of pitiable irresolution in things both sacred and profane. Few could have foreseen in 540 that before the life—not a long one—of the child born to the ancient family of Roman senators and nobles would have closed in a new century, the temporal power of the Papacy would have been securely founded and the power of the Empire and the authority of the Emperor in Italy threatened with a speedy end. In the onrush of barbarian conquest it was not the military success of Justinian's generals which was to be continued under the heirs of his Empire and to secure the position which they had won. They had—in the words of the *Liber Pontificalis*—made all Italy rejoice, but it was the patient diplomacy of a great pope which would preserve the central independence of Christian Rome, between the decaying power of the Byzantines and the extending dukedoms of the Lombard invaders. It would not be preserved for long, it is true; but so firmly was it founded

on the immemorial traditions of the city, and the holy sanctions of
the ecclesiastical rule, that it was destined to survive and emerge into
supremacy when the discordant powers which had threatened it had
passed away. And that this was so was due conspicuously to the
descendant of Pope Felix IV who first saw the light before the sixth
century had run half its course.

Gregory was the son of the *regionarius* Gordianus, a rich nobleman
with a fine house on the Caelian hill who held an office of organisation
connected with the Roman Church. His mother was afterwards ranked
among the saints, and so were two of his father's sisters. He was
brought up in the life of a Christian palace, among the riches of both
worlds, as a saint, says his biographer John the Deacon, among the
saints. In his education none of the learning of the time was neglected,
and it is with the consciousness of a wider knowledge than the stricter
folk of the day would allow that his biographer calls him *arte philo-
sophus*, a student of Divine philosophy, not of the degraded type of
Greek word-splitting which had lingered on at Athens till Justinian
closed the schools ten years or so before Gregory was born. He was taught
grammar, rhetoric, dialectic, after the fashion of the day. He did not
learn Greek then, or even later, though he lived six years in Constantinople. For literary elegance he never cared, and he almost boasted of
the barbarisms of his style. In later life he is found reproaching a
Frankish bishop for expounding grammar, perhaps even for studying it;
but there was more in the reproof than the mere regret for time wasted
that might be more profitably employed not only by a bishop, but, as
he says, by a religious layman: it was the sense of alarm with which the
Christian scholars still regarded a mythology whose morals were by no
means dispossessed from their influence on men. Of Art, on the other
hand, he was not ignorant: towards painting as well as music he was
sympathetic throughout his life. What special training he received
was, there seems no doubt, in law. When boyhood was over, he
emerges into light as praefect of the City of Rome (573), holding what
was at least theoretically the highest office among the citizens, one of
great labour and dignified ostentation, and, even in the decay of the
city's independence, of serious responsibility. That his tenure of office
was distinguished by any special achievement we do not know; but his
leaving it was dramatic and significant. His father was dead: his
mother had gone into a nunnery: he was one of the richest men, as he
was the highest official, in Rome. But the religious training of his early
years had never ceased to dominate his life. Now, at the very time
when political leaders were most needed, and when he was in a position
to win the foremost place among them, he laid aside ambition, put off
his silk and his jewels, gave his father's property for the founding of six
monasteries in Sicily and in charity for the Roman poor, and turned the
great palace on the Caelian hill into a house of monks, entering it

himself as a brother among the rest. For three years he lived in seclusion the religious life, according to the rule, there can be little doubt, of St Benedict, which he often afterwards so warmly eulogised. The chief of the Roman citizens had become a humble monk among monks : it was a contrast typical of the life, set betwixt civilisation and Christianity, barbarism and ascetic devotion, of the early Middle Age.

In the monastery of St Andrew the second part of Gregory's training was accomplished. For three years he was learning all that monasticism could teach him. And first it taught him a keen interest in the evangelisation of the heathen. It was probably at this date (though the evidence is uncertain), when he was one of the most famous personages in Rome, the chief civil ruler of the city who had given up all for the religious life, that his attention was first directed towards the distant isle of Britain. There is no reason to doubt the familiar story told so picturesquely by Bede, a *narratio fidelium* as the earlier Monk of Whitby calls it, that he was walking in the forum when he saw some Anglian lads, probably exposed for sale. He had heard of their coming and desired to see the denizens of a country concerning which Procopius had told the strange tale that thither Gaulish boatmen ferried the souls of the dead by night. Beautiful boys these were, with light complexion and light hair. " Alas," he said, when he was told they were heathens, "that lads so bright should be the slaves of darkness." He asked what was the name of their race. " *Angli*," they told him, and he answered that they had angel faces and should be coheirs of the *angeli* in heaven. They came from Deira : so should they be saved *de ira Dei*. Their king was Aelle : Alleluia should be sung in his land. From that moment Gregory planned to evangelise the English. He obtained the leave of the Pope, Benedict I ; but the punning habit which seemed to have given him the first thought of his mission now intervened to check him in its course. He sat reading, during the rest time on the third day of his journey, and a locust settled on his book, and *locusta* seemed to mean *loco sta* : he should not proceed. So it proved, for messengers from the Pope hurried to command his return, for the people of Rome would not suffer the departure of one whose services to them had been so recent and whose conspicuous self-abnegation seemed to shed a glory on the city of St Peter. The call of the Angles was set aside, but it was not forgotten. Gregory was given to learning, to asceticism, and to active assistance to the papal court.

The learning of his school-days was now continued on more exclusively ecclesiastical lines. In earlier years he had loved to read Augustine and Jerome. He became a deep student of the Bible. Later years, when he can have had little time for close study, shewed that he had become acquainted with the text of the Scriptures in detail more exact than was at all common in his day. What he read he pondered on, and he became a master of that " divine art " of Meditation which was to be so exhaustively developed in the Medieval Church. And to meditation he added vigil and fast till his health was injured for the rest of his life. But the time, as he looked back to it again and again from the troubled world, seemed like a happy shore as seen by the storm-tossed mariner on the waves of a mighty sea. On the sea of public life indeed he was soon about to embark again.

First he was made one of the Seven Deacons who shared with the Pope the governance of Rome, in charge of the seven regions of the city. For such a post few could have been so well fitted as he who had played so conspicuous a part in municipal life. This may have been in 578. In that year Benedict I died; while the city was in throes of plague and flood, and the Lombards were on the point of attack. Pelagius II, the new pope, determined to send to Constantinople, as his resident at the Emperor's court, one who knew so completely the needs and the dangers of old Rome. In the spring of 579 Gregory left Italy as the *apocrisiarius* of the Pope. The six years, or more, during which he resided in the imperial city supplied perhaps the last and most important of the formative influences of his life. Tiberius II was emperor (578–582), Eutychius was patriarch (577–582). The papal envoy was theologian as well as statesman, and he controverted a theory of the latter that the resurrection-body would be impalpable, convincing at least the former so that he put the erroneous treatise in the fire. But while he did not neglect theology, for he also wrote while he was at Constantinople his famous *Moralia*, a commentary on the Book of Job, a very *Corpus* of Divinity in itself, containing also many wise saws and modern instances, he was more continuously and actively employed in studying the magnificent system of imperial government. In a city notorious for the luxury of the nobles and the political independence of the people, where public interest was divided between the controversies of theologians and the games of the hippodrome, he saw how the turbulent life of a fickle and arrogant population was guided, not always wisely, by ecclesiastics, and restrained with extraordinary and imperceptible tact by an army of officials who, when dynasties changed and the throne tottered, preserved the fabric of the imperial constitution through all hazards and gave for centuries the most marvellous example of constitutional organisation amid the confused revolutions of Medieval Europe. As a theologian Gregory made it his business to see and talk with heretics that he might win them to truth, contrary to the example of those among whom he lived, some of whom were "fired by mistaken zeal and imagine they are fighting heretics while indeed they are making heresies." As for his own theological controversies, if he entered upon them charitably he certainly took them seriously: John the Deacon tells that at the end of his dispute with the patriarch Eutychius he took to his bed from exhaustion. In 582 Eutychius was succeeded by a famous ascetic, John "the Faster," a Cappadocian. With him Gregory had no dispute till later days: but the first letter between them that is preserved, written in 590, reads as though their cordiality had never been great.

In the imperial court the papal envoy made many friends: and when Tiberius had chosen Maurice for his successor Gregory had still closer relations with those of Caesar's household. Theoctista, the new Emperor's sister, and Narses, one of his generals, are found later among those to whom he wrote. He was intimate too with other foreign ecclesiastics, visitors like himself at the centre of imperial power, notably with Leander of Seville, afterwards the victorious champion of Catholicism against the Arian Visigoths. Leander and Gregory became close friends: it was Leander who induced Gregory to write his *Moralia*, and he received its dedication. In later years no congratulations on Leander's success were so warm as those of his old companion; though the Spanish prelate was absent in body yet, said Gregory, he was felt to be ever present in the spirit his image impressed upon the heart of his friend. Anastasius, once patriarch of Antioch, also lived in Constantinople, with memories of the theological storm which clouded the last days of Justinian, and he was said to have refuted the Aphthartodocetic opinions which that Emperor probably never held and the edict in favour of them which he certainly never issued. With him also Gregory was on cordial terms.

But from the imperial Court itself the papal *apocrisiarius* could find no support for the cause which he came to advocate. The Lombards had northern Italy at their feet, Pelagius wrote piteously begging for succour. But Maurice looked eastwards rather than towards the West, and as Caesar would not, or could not, help the Pope. When Gregory returned to Rome in 585 he had accomplished nothing. But he had acquired a knowledge of foreign politics, of the routine of imperial administration, and of the great personages of his time, which was invaluable to him.

For five years Gregory remained at Rome as head of his own monastery, and he made it a school of saints, and a home of Biblical study. He himself wrote commentaries on several of the Scriptures, and completed his lectures on the Book of Job which (like the *Magna Moralia*) became almost a popular classic in the Middle Age and proved a storehouse from which very much of later theology was extracted. To him also was entrusted by Pope Pelagius the conclusion of the unhappy controversy of Justinian's day on the Three Chapters; and he set before the bishops of Istria the orthodox creed as Rome and Constantinople had accepted it in a treatise of lucid and masterful reasoning. In 590 Pelagius died and the Roman people insisted that he who had once been their highest official and was now the most eminent of their monks should become their bishop. If he was reluctant to accept it, he yet in the interval before the imperial assent could be obtained shewed himself to be the religious leader that the city needed in its distress.

Rome was swept by the plague: Gregory had himself done his utmost to abate it by sanitary measures: Pelagius himself had been its victim. Now the abbot of St Andrew's organised a demonstration of public penitence, and preached a famous sermon which another Gregory, himself a hearer, and afterwards the great bishop of Tours, statesman and historian, recorded from his lips. As the penitential procession, moving in seven bodies and singing litanies, passed through the streets, death was still busy: in one hour, as the solemn march went on, eighty men fell dead: but at last, said a legend of later days, the Archangel Michael was seen to stand on the cupola of the Mausoleum of Hadrian and to sheathe his flaming sword. So the plague was stayed: and the Castle of Sant' Angelo, with all its long history of romance and crime, bears witness to the memory.

Six months after the death of Pelagius, in August 590, came the sanction of Maurice the Emperor to the choice that had been made of his successor. Gregory, still a deacon, prepared for flight, but he was discovered, taken to St Peter's and consecrated a successor of the Apostle as bishop of Rome. It was on 3 September 590.

It was a ship rotten in every plank and leaking at every seam that he came to captain: so he wrote to his brother of Constantinople. With a real regret did he abandon the Rachel of contemplation for the Leah of active life. Yet if any ecclesiastic was ever fitted for rule, for statesmanship, for practical labour among men, it was Gregory the Great.

If Gregory's most obvious achievements, in the sight of his own time, lay in the region of politics, it must be remembered always that he himself viewed his whole work from the standing-point of a Christian bishop. He sets this before every reader in his *Regulae Pastoralis Liber*, a book which, probably addressed to John of Ravenna, his "brother and fellow-bishop," was welcomed by all who knew him, both clerk and lay, by the Emperor Maurice, who had a Greek translation made of it, as well as by Leander of Seville; and, later on, to read it became part of the necessary erudition of a bishop. Throughout the book there is a sense of tremendous responsibility. The conduct of a prelate, says Gregory, ought to surpass the conduct of the people as a shepherd's life does that of his flock. In his elevation he should deal with high things, and high persons, yet should he not seek to please men, being mindful of the duty of reproof and yet reproving with gentleness. The mind anxious about the management of exterior business is deprived of the sense of wholesome fear; and the soul is flattered with a false promise of good works: there is danger in refusal as well as in acceptance of high places; but most danger lest while earthly pursuits engross the senses of the pastor the dust that is driven by the wind of temptation blind the eyes of the whole Church. The entire treatise shews an intimacy of practical knowledge in regard to men of all classes and of all characters which is evidence how well fitted was the writer for dealing with all sorts and conditions of men. And how he dealt with them may be found out from the fourteen books of his epistles, that wonderful storehouse of Roman religion and diplomacy laid up by the first of the great popes. The register of his letters is known to have been in existence not long after his death. It was known in later years to Bede and Boniface, and formed the basis of the latest collection and arrangement. In this many details of policy may be followed, and the main aims and methods of the great Pope may be studied. Each alike, the treatise and the letters, shews the same ideal of the pastoral office, that it is a work of governance of men to be exercised by those who have intimate knowledge of men's hearts and are skilled in the treatment of their souls. Politics are but a branch of the dealing with men on behalf of God which belongs of obligation to a bishop of Christ's Church. And this thought, almost as much as any necessary assertion of orthodox faith and profession of brotherly kindness, is to be seen in the synodical letter in which he announced to the patriarchs of Constantinople, Antioch, Alexandria and Jerusalem his accession to the Roman bishopric, and his belief in the doctrine of the Four General Councils, as also in that of the more recent Fifth. The practical expression of this ideal in the life of the new Pope could be read by all men who came in contact with him. He lived ascetically, as he had lived in his own monastery, and while nuncio at Constantinople: he surrounded himself with grave and reverend men, dismissing the curled and exquisite fops who had thronged the courts of earlier popes, a gang of self-indulgent scholars and servants obnoxious to the stern man who had not so learned Christ. Of himself the words of his early biographer Paul the Deacon present a vivid picture: "He was never at rest. Always was he busy in taking care for the interests of his people, or in writing some treatise worthy of the Church, or in searching out the hidden things of heaven by the grace of contemplation." His daily audiences, his constant sermons, filled up the burden of his continual correspondence. And all through the fourteen years of his pontificate he struggled against the illnesses which had perhaps their beginning in his ascetic rigours. If his letters breathe a spirit of sternness and make high demands upon men of commonplace intellect and low ideals, there was no one with whom he was more stern, no one before whom he set higher ideals, than himself.

Gregory's policy towards the whole Christian world radiated from the centre. There, at Rome, men could see his life of strict rule: they could see him reconsecrating Arian churches to Catholic use, could hear him preaching, could watch his elaborate measures for the relief of the poor. "Other pontiffs," says his biographer, "gave themselves to building churches and adorning them with gold and silver; but Gregory, while he did not altogether neglect this duty, was entirely

taken up with gaining souls, and all the money he could obtain he was
anxious to give away and bestow upon the poor." He was a practical
ruler first of all and that as a Christian bishop: afterwards he was a
theologian and a statesman. This accounts for the fact that he views
all political questions *sub specie aeternitatis* and shews no interest in any
work of pure learning or scholarship even in Rome itself.

And indeed the practical needs of the time were enough to absorb
the whole thoughts of any man who was set to rule. If in the East the
emperors were fully occupied with wars against Persians and Avars, and
were able to give little heed and no help to the stress of the city from
which their sovereignty took its name, the Papacy, already partly the
representative and partly the rival of the imperial power, was beset on
every side by the barbarian invasion and settlement. Rome itself had
become, for all practical purposes, an isolated and distant part of the
Roman Empire. Imperial power in Italy had dwindled till it was only
a name. But at the ancient centre of the ancient Empire sat, in the
fourteen years from 590, a man of commanding genius, of ceaseless
vigilance and of incessant activity, whose letters covered almost every
political, religious and social interest of his time. His influence as a
great spiritual teacher and a great ruler of men radiated over the whole
Christian world.

The internal cares belonging to the " patrimony of St Peter" were
not light. The estates from which the income was derived were
scattered all over Italy, most largely in Sicily and round Rome, but
also in east and south, beyond the peninsula in Illyricum and Gaul,
in Africa, and in the isles of Corsica and Sardinia. They were administered by a multitude of officials, often with the help of the
imperial administrators. Gregory liked to choose his agents from
among the clergy, and employed priests and even bishops in this secular
service.

All were directly under the orders of the bishop of Rome himself,
and Gregory's letters of appointment contain special provision for the
care of the poor, for the keeping of strict accounts to be sent to Rome,
for the maintenance generally of ecclesiastical interests. Thus the
rectores and *defensores* were often charged with a sort of supervision
which, while it at several points encroached upon the proper province of
the bishop, served to keep the distant and scattered estates in close touch
with the central authority of the Roman see. Thus what was at first
a mere matter of the ownership of property, through its duties and
responsibilities being enjoyed by the greatest bishop of the Church,
tended to become a lordship no less spiritual than material. Even
bishops themselves were under the eye of the Pope's representative, and
that naturally came to mean that sooner or later they would fall under
the jurisdiction of the Pope. For this Gregory's indefatigable care was
largely responsible. We find him within the first eighteen months of

his pontificate writing almost once a month to the *Rector Siciliae*, the subdeacon whom he long employed in positions of trust in different parts of Italy. The letters shew minute care for justice, for the suppression of unjust exactions, for the redress of grievances, as well as for the maintenance of proprietary rights: besides the great landlord, there speaks the great bishop and shepherd of the souls of men. No matter was too small for the Pope's attention, whether it was a safeguard for the interests of a convert from Judaism, a direction as to the disposal of cows and calves, of houses and granaries, or a criticism of the provision for personal needs. "You have sent us," he once wrote, "a miserable horse and five good donkeys. The horse I cannot ride because it is miserable, nor the donkeys, good though they be, because they are donkeys." Different views have been taken of this interesting correspondence between Gregory and his *factor*, but at least it reveals the very close attention which the Pope paid to detail in the oversight of the vast possessions of his see. "As we ought not to allow property belonging to the Church to be lost, so we deem it a breach of law to try to take what belongs to others," are words which might serve as a motto for his relation towards temporal things. With minute care he stopped the abuses which had stained the administration under his predecessors. But above all the Pope endeavoured to shew in practical alms-giving the fervent charity of his heart. John the Deacon tells that there was still preserved, nearly three hundred years later, among the muniments of the Lateran, a large book in which the names of the recipients of his benefactions, in Rome or the suburbs, in the Campagna and on the coast, were set down. In nothing was he more insistent than in the duty of ransoming captives, those taken in the wars and sold as slaves in markets even so far away as Libya. Many letters deal with the subject, convey his exhortations to bishops to join in the work and return thanks for the gifts he had received to help it. Thus did the largest landowner in Italy endeavour to discharge the duties of his trust.

From his administration of the papal patrimony we pass naturally to his policy as a ruler, his dealings with the affairs of the world, as a statesman and as a pope.

As a statesman his first and closest concern was with the Lombards. Already he had been concerned in endeavouring to protect Rome and the parts of Italy still unconquered: that had been the special object of his long embassy at Constantinople. The emperors had given no aid, but the Franks had caused a diversion by thrice attacking the Lombards in flank. But the snake was not killed, hardly scotched; and before Gregory had been long on the throne peace between Franks and Lombards had been made by the new king Agilulf, who had married Theodelinda, the late king's widow, and he turned the thoughts of the Lombards towards the extension of their conquests from imperial Rome.

Still the ancient Empire, dimmed in its glory and with ill-welded traditions from Christian and pagan past, held out in the great cities of Genoa and Naples, of Ravenna and Rome, the two last the centres of government under exarch and pope. At first the danger seemed to come not from the king but from one of the dukes. At Spoleto on the Flaminian Way was settled a Lombard colony of invaders under Ariulf, the outposts of whose territory were almost within sight of Rome; and Gregory when he wrote to his friends at Constantinople declared that he found himself "bishop not of the Romans but of the Lombards, men whose promises are swords and whose grace a pain."

Against "the unspeakable Ariulf" he was ever on the watch. In 591 and 592 he was taking constant precaution, telling the *Magister militum* at Perugia to fall, if need be, on his rear, and bidding the clergy and people of the lesser cities in the neighbourhood to be on their guard and to obey the Pope's representative in all things. Step by step the Lombard duke approached, as yet without active hostility. In July 592 at length he spoke of Ariulf as being close to the city, "slaying and mutilating"; and Arichis, the Lombard duke of Benevento, was at the same time threatening Naples. The Pope himself sent a military commander to the southern city. He bitterly resented the weakness of Romanus the exarch, which prevented him from dealing in martial fashion with the duke of Spoleto. Left helpless, he prepared to make a peace with Ariulf, and in July 592 it seems that a separate agreement was concluded which saved Rome from sack. Paul the Deacon tells that an interview between the Lombard duke and the Roman bishop made the "tyrant" ever after a devoted servant of the Roman Church. "His heart was touched by divine grace, and he perceived that there was so much power in the Pope's words that with humblest courtesy he made satisfaction to the most religious Apostolic bishop." Gregory's statesmanship and charm won a diplomatic victory which preserved Rome from the Lombards.

But indirectly it would seem as if this success laid the city open to another attack. Romanus the exarch was encouraged by it to secure the communications between Ravenna and Rome by a campaign which recovered many cities, including Perugia, from the Lombards. This new activity on the part of the Empire which he may well have deemed moribund aroused Agilulf, the Lombard king, to action. He marched southwards, recaptured Perugia, and put to death Maurisio, a duke of the Lombards, who had surrendered the city to the exarch and now held it for the Empire. Thence he marched to Rome.

Gregory was illustrating Ezekiel, in sombre homily, by the tragic events of his day, the decay of ancient institutions, the devastation of country, the destruction of cities. Daily came news which deepened the gloom of his picture, till at length he closed the book and set himself to defend the city. The defence as before was that of spiritual not material arms. Agilulf met Gregory on the steps of St Peter's, and the weighty wisdom of the prelate gave power to his prayers for the city: they prevailed, the siege was abandoned, and Agilulf went back to Milan, where the letters of Gregory were as familiar to the clergy and as powerful as was his rule in Rome.

Thither came epistles to Theodelinda, the Arian Agilulf's Catholic wife, instructing her in the right belief as to the still unfinished strife about the Three Chapters, and to Constantius the bishop, begging him to negotiate a peace between the Lombards and the Empire.

Peace was impossible so long as the Caesar at Constantinople claimed the lordship of all Italy, and the Lombard barbarian asserted all real power over the peninsula. Nor was Gregory at the time the person to bring the foes together, for in August 593 he had written to the Emperor Maurice in terms of criticism strangely bold and direct. When Maurice was " not yet lord of all " he had been Gregory's own lord, and still the Pope would call himself the unworthy servant of the pious Emperor. But a new edict which forbade a civil servant of the Empire, or a soldier, to become priest or monk, seemed to him a monstrous infringement of individual and religious liberty. By it, he said, the way to heaven would be closed to many, for while there were those who could lead a religious life in a secular dress, yet more there were who unless they forsook all things could in no way attain salvation. What answer would he, who from notary had been made by God first captain, then Caesar, then Emperor, then father of Emperor yet to be, and to whose care the priests of God had been entrusted, make to the divine inquest of the Last Day if not one single soldier was allowed to be converted to the Lord? And Gregory drew a lurid picture of the " end of the ages" which seemed to be at hand, the heavens and the earth aflame and the elements melting with fervent heat, and the Divine Judge ready to appear with the six orders of angels in His train. Yet it is an illustration of the fidelity with which Gregory performed all his secular obligations that he had caused the law against which he so vehemently protested to be published in the usual way.

This was not the only divergence in opinion between the Pope and the imperial Court. Gregory, with all his respect for authority, was at least able to hold his own, and there was for a while at least no breach in the friendly relations with Constantinople. Maurice sent relief to the sufferers from the Lombard invasion, and Gregory lost no opportunity of advising that the separate peace which he had made with Agilulf should be enlarged at least into a general truce. Gregory, *inter gladios Langobardorum*, could appreciate the needs of Italy in a way that was impossible for the distant Augustus. In 595 however the divergence came to a head. The Emperor reviewed the Pope's peace policy in terms of contemptuous condemnation and Gregory answered in one of the most vigorous of all his letters, dated June 595. He resented the imputation

that because he thought that a firm peace could be made, as indeed it
had been made, with Ariulf of Spoleto, he was a fool. Fool indeed was
he to suffer what he suffered in Rome among the swords of the
Lombards; but still he was a servant of the truth, and grave injustice
was it to the priesthood that he should be deemed a liar. On behalf
of all priests he made dignified protest, recalling the action and
words of the great Constantine as a rebuke to his successor in the
Empire. "Where all is uncertain I betake myself to tears and prayers
that Almighty God will rule with His own hand our most pious lord,
and in the terrible judgment will find him free from all offences, and so
cause me to please men that I may not offend against His grace."

How the Emperor received this letter we do not know; but already
there were other causes of dispute between Rome and Constantinople.
His experience had not made the Pope very cordial towards Church
or State in the New Rome. Useful at Constantinople Gregory must
undoubtedly have been, but the fact that he never learned Greek shews
at least that there were limits to his usefulness. The information he
received would often be inadequate, the means of communication with
the people among whom he dwelt incomplete. Official interpreters do
not always represent meanings faithfully. Gregory had to deal most
with the imperial Court, where his ignorance of Greek may not have been
so great a barrier; but, in his relations with the Patriarch, it would
at least serve to prevent any strengthening of the friendship between
Churches which were already beginning to drift apart.

That the Church was under the rule of five patriarchs was a
familiar view, and at least from the time of Vigilius (537–555) it
had been accepted in official language at Rome. Thus Gregory had
announced his own election to the patriarchs of Constantinople,
Alexandria, Jerusalem and Antioch. His letters shew traces of another
theory, that of the three patriarchates, Rome, Antioch and Alexandria,
sharing, as it were, the throne of St Peter. But Constantinople had
long asserted a pre-eminence. Justinian had recognised its precedence
as second of the great sees, superior to all others save Rome, and had
declared the Church of Constantinople to be "the head of all the
churches." In doing this no doubt the Empire had claimed no supreme
or exclusive dignity for the New Rome, nor asserted any indivisible
or unalterable jurisdiction. But what the law recognised had encouraged further expansion of claim. At first the relation between
Constantinople and the elder see was regarded as parallel to that
between the two capitals: they represented not diversity but unity:
as there was one Empire, so there was one Church. When John
the Patriarch accepted the formula of faith drawn up by Pope
Hormisdas he prefixed to it an assertion of the mutual relation: "I
hold the most holy Churches of the old and the new Rome to be one.
I define the see of the Apostle Peter and this of the imperial city to be

one see." From this it was an inevitable step to use titles which Rome used. The pontiff of Constantinople claimed to be oecumenical (οἰκου-μενικός or *universalis*) patriarch.

In 588 Pelagius declared the acts of a synod at Constantinople to be invalid because the patriarch had used the phrase. Very likely Gregory himself had been the adviser of this course. Now in 595 he pursued the protest. John the Faster had written to him and had employed the offensive title " in almost every line." Gregory wrote, as he describes it, " sweetly and humbly admonishing him to amend this appetite for vain glory." He forbade his envoy to communicate with the patriarch till he had abandoned the title. At the same time he repudiated any wish to assume it for himself. " The Council of Chalcedon," he said, " offered the title of *universalis* to the Roman pontiff but he refused to accept it, lest he should seem thereby to derogate from the honour of his brother bishops." He saw indeed that political interests were complicating the ecclesiastical claim. His envoy had been commanded by the Emperor to adjure him to live in peace with the patriarch, who seemed to him to be as hypocritical as he was proud. Then either he must obey the Emperor and encourage the proud man in his vanity, or he must alienate the Emperor, his lord and the natural defender of Rome. He did not hesitate. He wrote to the Emperor, tracing the misfortunes of the Empire to the pride of the clergy. When Europe was given over to the barbarians, with cities ruined, villages thrown down and provinces without inhabitants ; when the husbandman no longer tilled the soil, and the worshippers of idols daily murdered the faithful, the priests who should have abased themselves in sackcloth and ashes sought for themselves empty names and titles novel and profane. Peter was never called Universal Apostle, yet John strove to be Universal Bishop. " I confidently affirm that whosoever calls himself *sacerdos universalis*, or desires to be so called by others, is in his pride a forerunner of Antichrist." What he said to the Emperor he reinforced to the Empress. There should be no peace with the patriarch so long as he claimed this outrageous designation. On the other side the argument became no attitude of aggression, hardly a claim for equality. The patriarchs did not assert that they were above the popes, and they constantly declared that they had no wish to lessen the authority of the other patriarchs. But whatever the Greeks might say, the Latins saw that words represented ideas ; and universality could not be predicated of Constantinople in any sense which was not offensive to the venerable see and city of Rome. The bitterness of the strife abated when John the Faster died on 2 September 595, it may be before Gregory's severe judgment had reached him. Cyriacus, his successor, was a personal friend of the Pope, and a man of no personal pride. Gregory welcomed his accession and thanked the Emperor for his choice. But in spite of friendly letters the claim was not abandoned. The patriarchs continued to use the title of oecumenical bishop, and before a century had passed the popes followed their example.

Gregory saw that the patriarchs of Constantinople were in danger of sinking into mere officials of the State, for with all their lofty position they were in the power of the imperial Court. But the tone in which he addressed them was always distinct from that which he employed towards the lay officials of the Empire. From the beginning of his pontificate he had carefully cultivated relations with the exarchs of Ravenna and of Africa, the praetor of Sicily, the dukes of Naples and Sardinia, the praefect of Illyria, the proconsul of Dalmatia, and with lesser officials rural and urban. His constant letters shew how closely he mingled in their concerns, watched their conduct, approved their industry, advised on their political action, intervened on their behalf or against them at Constantinople. Many of the officials were his close friends; and the Emperor, in spite of the divergence between them, did not cease to give heed to the counsels of one whom he knew to be a wise and honest man.

The maintenance of the imperial power in Italy indeed depended not a little on the great Pope, who yet by his incessant and widespread activity was preparing the way of the ecclesiastical power which should succeed it in the rule of the peninsula. The subdeacon who was his agent at Ravenna, and those who administered the property of the Church in the Campagna or in Sicily, the bishops themselves all over the Empire, reported to Rome and their words were not without effect, and in all the advice which issued from this information Gregory pressed without faltering the authority of the Church: the pope was above the exarch, the Church above the State: if the civil law was invoked to protect the weak, to guide the rulers, to secure the rights of all Christian men, there was behind it the supreme sanction of the law of the Church. It was natural indeed that they should not be distinguished: a wrong against man was a wrong against God. It did not matter whether it was the oppression of a peasant or the pillage of a monastery: iniquity, it was the perpetual cry of the great pontiff, should not go unpunished. And, in a corresponding view to his attitude towards civil justice, Gregory insisted on the privileges of clergy in the law courts; and in the civil courts he is found placing representatives of his own beside the lay judges. Outside the law there was still a wide sphere in which the aid of the State was demanded on behalf of the Church. Governors would bring back schismatics, were congratulated on their victories over heathen, were urged to act against heretics, and to protect and support those who had returned to the faith.

On the other hand he no doubt set plain limits, in his own mind, to his sphere of action and that of the bishops. He constantly told the Italian bishops to observe the rights of the lay courts, not to interfere in the things of the world save when the interests of the poor demanded help. But his own keen sense of justice, his political training, his knowledge of affairs, forbade him to hold his tongue. The Empire, like the Church, was to him a splendid power of holy and heroic tradition : there was ever, he said to an imperial official, this difference between the Roman emperors and the barbarian kings that while the latter governed slaves the former were rulers of free men. To keep this always in the mind of the governing class must have been his aim, and his consolation, when, as he said, the cares of the world pressed so heavily upon him that he was often doubtful whether he was discharging the duties of an earthly official or those of a shepherd of men's souls.

In both capacities his work was continuous and engrossing. Invasion, rapine, insecurity of life and property, made clerk as well as lay lax livers, negligent stewards, cruel and faithless, luxurious and slothful. Against all such Gregory was the perpetual witness.

When Romanus the exarch died, probably in 596, his successor at Ravenna, Callinicus, received a warm welcome from the Pope. For a time there was a lull in the tempest, but still Gregory preached vigilance, to bishop and governor alike, for Italy had not shaken off the terror even if Rome was for the moment outside the area of the storm. Writing in 598 to a lady in Constantinople the Pope was able to assure her that so great was the protection given by St Peter to the city that, without the aid of soldiers, he had "by God's help been preserved for these many years among the swords of the enemy." A truce was made with Agilulf, it seems, in 598 : in 599 this became a general peace in which the Empire through the exarch, and with the active support, though not the signature, of the Pope, came to agreement with Agilulf the Lombard king and with the dukes of Spoleto and Benevento. His letters shew how much this was due to the tact, the wisdom, the patient persistence of Gregory ; and it is certain also that Theodelinda, the Catholic wife of Agilulf, had played no unimportant part in the work of pacification. At Monza remain the relics of this wise queen ; fitly beside the iron crown of the Lombards is the image of the protection that was given by the peace of Church and State, a hen that gathers her chickens under her wings.

The year 599 which dates this peace between the "Christian Republic" and the Lombards marks a definite epoch in the history of Italy. Paul the Deacon in his *History of the Lombards* shews that it was a time of crisis, conquest, and resettlement for Agilulf the king. The letters of Gregory shew that it was for him a period of incessant activity and reassertion of papal authority, while at Rome the city was "so reduced by the languor of various diseases that there are scarce left men enough to guard the walls" and the Pope himself was in the clutch of increasing sickness, often unable to leave his bed for days together. Italy was still swept by pestilence ; and exhaustion as well as political peace gave quiet for some two years.

In 601 the flames of war were rekindled by a rash move on the part of the exarch Callinicus. Agilulf again took up arms, seized Pavia and levelled it to the ground—a fate which the medieval chroniclers century by century record to have befallen the unhappy city. He made alliance with the heathen Avars, and with them ravaged Istria. He passed over northern Italy in a career of conquest: he carried the Lombard frontier forwards to include the valley of the Po. At Ravenna the imperial authority lingered on, and the exarch Callinicus was succeeded by Smaragdus, holding office for a second time. But the reality of power was passing, if it had not already passed, under the incessant energy of Gregory, into the hands of the Pope, who had become the practical ruler of central Italy. It was in the year 603, when the Empire and the Lombards were at war, that Gregory shewed his aloofness from a strife which seems to have left the power of the Church undisturbed, by his rejoicing at the Catholic baptism of Adaloald, the firstborn son of Agilulf the Arian and Theodelinda the Catholic queen. Paul the Deacon indeed says, though he is unsupported by other witness, that Agilulf the father had already accepted the Catholic faith. As his sickness grew the great Pope saw the future less dark than it had been during his life of anxiety. Rome, if impoverished and enfeebled, was securely in the possession of its bishop; and the conflicts which raged over northern and central Italy could hardly end, now that Catholicism was conquering the Lombards, otherwise than in favour of the papal power.

It may well be that this feeling coloured his attitude when news came to him of the revolution at Constantinople in 602. Maurice had long seemed to Gregory, as indeed he had seemed to his people, to be unworthy of the imperial throne. He was timid when he should have been bold, rash when prudence was essential to the safety of the State. His health had broken down, and fits of cowardice alternated with outbursts of frenzied rage. All the tales of him that reached Rome would increase Gregory's dislike and distrust. Already he had rebuked the Caesar to his face, and well he may have thought, when he heard of his deposition and murder by the centurion Phocas, that the warning he had given had been disregarded, and the judgment he had prophesied had come. With Maurice perished his whole family, with whom Gregory had been on terms of affectionate regard. Maurice had been an unwise, perhaps a tyrannical ruler, and certainly he had seemed to the Pope an oppressor of the poor. And he had supported the patriarch in his overweening pretension to be "universal bishop." When Phocas therefore announced his accession, silent no doubt as to the butcheries which accompanied it, and dwelling rather on his orthodoxy and attachment to the Apostolic See, Gregory replied in language of surprising cordiality. The revolution was to him something that came from "the incomprehensible providence of God"; and he trusted that soon he should be comforted by the abundance of rejoicing that the sufferings of the poor had been redressed—" We will rejoice that your benignity and piety are come to the imperial throne." Later letters to Phocas and his wife Leontia breathe the same spirit: of congratulations on the political change: of hope that it will mean relief and liberty for the Empire: of solicitude that the aid which Maurice had long denied might now be given to Italy, trodden down by the barbarian and the heretic. We are shocked as we read Gregory's cordial letters to the brutal murderer of Maurice; but we must remember that the Pope had no representative at Constantinople to tell him what had really happened: all that he may have known was that popular indignation had swept a tyrant from the throne and avenged its injuries on him and his innocent family, and that a soldier had been set up, with all due forms of law, as ruler in his stead. From a bed of suffering he indited these letters to those from whom he might have new hopes of the salvation of Italy. But he wrote as an official of the Church to an official of the State, and he mingled with his formal words of congratulation and the Church's *Gloria in excelsis* no words of personal adulation. Whatever may be the true judgment on Gregory's attitude at this moment, it is obvious that in the change of dynasty he hoped for a better prospect for Italy and knew that more power would come to Rome itself and the Roman bishop.

It is as a Roman and a Roman bishop that Gregory fills the great place he holds in the history of the Middle Age. He was a Roman of the Romans, nurtured on traditions of Rome's imperial greatness, cherishing the memories of pacification and justice, of control and protection. And these, which belonged to " the Republic," he was eager to transfer to the Church. Vague were the claims which the Roman bishops had already put forth in regard to the universal Church. But what all bishops held as inherent in their office, the right of giving advice and administration, was held by the Roman pontiffs to belong especially to the see which was founded in the imperial city. There was a prerogative of the Roman bishop as of the Roman Emperor, and already the one was believed to run parallel to the other. The Pope directly superintended a large part of the Christian world: everywhere he could reprove and exhort with authority, though the authority was often contested. And Gregory's exercise of this power was one of the great moments in the world's history. To the practical assertions of his predecessors he gave a new moral weight, and it was that which carried the claims to victory. Well has it been said by Dean Church that " he so administered the vast undefined powers supposed to be inherent in his see, that they appeared to be indispensable to the order, the good government and the hopes, not of the Church only, but of society." And this success was due not so much to the extent of her claims or the weakness of his competitors, but to the moral force which flowed from his life of intellectual, moral and spiritual power.

We can trace, in different but conspicuous ways, the effect of this force in Africa, in Britain, in Spain and in Gaul, in Istria and Dalmatia, as well as nearer home. In Africa there was a period of revival since the imperial reconquest from the Vandals. For more than half a century the Church, diminished in power no doubt and weakened in its organisation, had been re-established, and Arianism had been successfully extirpated, if we may judge from the silence of the Pope's letters. The imperial officials were ready to accept his advice, or even authority. Side by side with the bishops of Numidia and Carthage, we find Gennadius the exarch extending the influence of the papal see; and appeals to Rome seem to have been recognised and encouraged. On the other hand Gregory was careful to make no practical encroachment on the power of the bishops and even to encourage their independence, while he asserted the supremacy of Rome in uncompromising terms: "I know of no bishop who is not subject to the Apostolic See, when a fault has been committed." His intervention was chiefly invoked in regard to the still surviving Donatism of Numidia. Against the Donatists he endeavoured to encourage the action of both the secular and the ecclesiastical power. "God," he said to the praetorian praefect Pantaleo, "will require at your hand the souls that are lost." In one city even the bishop had allowed a Donatist rival to establish himself; and Church and State alike were willing to let the heretics live undisturbed on the payment of a ransom-rent. To Gregory it seemed that the organisation of the Church was defective and her ministers were slothful.

The primacy in northern Africa, except the proconsular province, where the bishop of Carthage was primate, belonged to the senior bishop, apart from the dignity of his see or the merits of his personal life; and it was claimed that the rule went back to the time of St Peter the Apostle and had been continued ever since. Gregory accepted the historic account of the origin of the African episcopate, as is shewn by a letter to Dominicus, bishop of Carthage. On it he based an impressive demand for stedfast obedience, and he appointed a bishop named Columbus to act as his representative, though he was not formally entitled Vicar Apostolic. A council in 593 received his instructions; but they do not seem to have been carried out. A long correspondence shews the urgency of the need for action against the Donatists, and the difficulty of getting anything done. By the toleration of the imperial government they had been enabled to keep their churches and bishops; they conducted an active propaganda, they secured the rebaptism of many converts. For six years, from 591 to 596, Gregory's letters shew the vehemence of the contest in which he was engaged. In 594 a council at Carthage received an imperial decree stirring Church and State to action; but the State did not abandon its tolerant attitude: still there was great slackness, and Gregory wrote urgently to the Emperor on the subject. It would seem that some measures were taken, and that the law was in some districts enforced; but Donatism if it died down did not become extinct. It was largely through his constant interventions in the matter of heresy that Gregory was able to establish on so firm a basis the papal authority in the exarchate of Africa. He concerned himself no less with the surviving pagans, urging Gennadius to wage war against them " not for the pleasure of shedding blood but with the aim of extending the limits of Christendom, that by the preaching of the faith, the Name of Christ should be honoured among the subject tribes." Constant in urging the secular officials to action, Gregory was still more urgent with the bishops. A continual correspondence was maintained with the African episcopate: everyone who had a grievance applied to him: no important decision was arrived at without his consent. He claimed to defend with unchanged determination "the rights and privileges of Saint Peter." Paul of Numidia applied to him for justice against the Donatists, and the patrician Gennadius, who persecuted him, bishop though he was. With stedfast persistence the Pope insisted on securing the trial of the case himself, and sent the bishop back to Africa assured of the imperial protection. Almost insensibly his persistence and the moral grandeur of his character told on the independence of the imperial officials. They began to listen to his advice, and then to admit his authority; and it was soon hard to distinguish their respect for the man from their obedience to the See. And at the same time, amid the chaos of administrative disorder, the people put their trust in the Church: they took the bishops for their defenders, and most of all the Bishop of Rome. Gregory exercised the authority then bestowed upon him partly through Hilarus, whom he sent to be overseer of the patrimony of the Church, and partly through the Numidian bishop Columbus. If protest was made—as it seems to have been made by a Numidian primate Adeodatus and by Dominicus of Carthage—it was overruled: Rome, said Gregory, was the mother church of Africa, and her authority must be respected. Such a pope was one to make it respected, whether he advised and exhorted in regard to the decay of spiritual life in monasteries, or reproved administrators and judges for unjust exaction of tribute. No better illustration of the way in which the papal claims attained acceptance could be found than is afforded by the history of Africa in the time of Gregory the Great.

While Donatism died hard in Africa, nearer home the controversy of the Three Chapters was not yet concluded. In Istria the Church was in schism, for it had not submitted to the decision of East and West. Gregory invoked (with but small success) the secular arm against Severus, patriarch of Aquileia, and summoned him to Rome. The bishops of the province protested and adjured the Emperor to protect them, professing no obedience to Rome and threatening to acknowledge the ecclesiastical authority of Gaul. Maurice commanded Gregory to stay his hand, which he did very reluctantly. He had long before intervened in the matter as the secretary of Pelagius II: he distrusted the Istrian bishops as schismatics and as assertors of independence, and when he became pope had again addressed them in lucid theological arguments. He received individual submissions, and he used every kind of pressure to heal the schism; but when he died his efforts had not been entirely successful. With Milan too he had similar difficulties. Defective theology was combined with provincial independence in resistance to papal power. In Dalmatia and Illyria other difficulties needed other treatment. An archbishop whose manner of life did not befit his office was rebuked, ironically exhorted, pardoned: when he died a strong attempt was made to fill his place by a man of austere life whom the Pope had long honoured. The attempt was a failure, and a very long and bitter struggle ensued in which Maximus, the imperial candidate, was refused recognition, summoned to trial at Rome and only at last admitted to his see as lawful prelate when he had lain prone in penance at Ravenna, crying "I have sinned against God and the most blessed Pope Gregory." Over Illyria generally, in spite of the creation of Justiniana Prima as a patriarchate by the Emperor who had given it his name, he exercised the power of a patriarch. He forbade the bishops to attend a synod at Constantinople without his leave. He made it plain that Illyria belonged to the West and not to the East.

And in the West he was ever eager to enlarge the boundaries of the Church. Already as a young man he had set his heart on the conversion of the English. As pope he had the means to undertake it. It may be that he planned it, as Bede says, as soon as he came to discharge the office of pontiff, and also, as one of his letters suggests, that he prepared for it by ordering the purchase of English slave boys to be trained in Gaulish monasteries. It was probably in 595 that he first sent forth the monk Augustine and his companions to journey through Gaul to Britain for the conversion of the English. When, daunted by anticipated dangers, the monks sent Augustine back, Gregory ordered him to return as their abbot, and furnished him with letters to the bishops of Gaul, and notably to Vergilius of Arles, the bishop of Aix and the abbot of Lerins, as well as to Theodebert of Austrasia and Theodoric of Burgundy, children of nine and ten, under the guardianship of Brunhild their grandmother. To Brunhild herself, "queen of the Franks," who went with him, he was sure, "in heart and soul," the Pope said that the English nation, by the favour of God, wished to become Christian, and he was sending Augustine and other monks to take thought—in which he bade her help—for their conversion. He considered that the bishops of Gaul had been remiss, in doing nothing for the conversion of those English tribes whom he regarded as their neighbours: but when in 596 he set the new mission in motion, he was able, as his letters shew, to rely upon personal kindness from the queen towards the missionaries and upon the aid of Gaulish priests as interpreters of the barbarous English tongue. The mission was, vaguely, to "the nation of the English," for Gregory knew no difference between the men of Deira and the men of Kent; and Augustine would learn at Paris, if not before, that the wife of Aethelberht of Kent was daughter of a Frankish king.

The tale of the landing, the preaching, and the success will be told elsewhere. Here it belongs only to note that Gregory continued to take the keenest interest in the venture he had planned. He instructed Vergilius of Arles to consecrate Augustine as bishop, and spread over Christendom the news of the great work that was accomplished. To Eulogius, patriarch of Alexandria, he told of the conversion, due, as he said, to their prayers, and he warmly thanked Syagrius, bishop of Autun, and Brunhild for their aid. To Augustine in 601 he sent the pallium, a mark of favour conferred by pope or emperor, not, it would seem, as conferring metropolitan authority, which Augustine had already exercised, but as recognising his position as a special representative of the Roman see. To the queen Berhta, whose somewhat tardy support of the Christian faith in her husband's land he was able now to eulogise and to report even to the Emperor at Constantinople, he wrote words of exhortation to support Augustine, and to Aethelberht her husband admonition and praise with his favourite eschatological reference. To the end Gregory remained the trusted adviser of the Apostle of the English. He sent special reinforcements, with all manner of things, says Bede, needed for public worship and the service of the Church, commending the new missionaries again to the Gaulish bishops and instructing them especially as to the conversion of heathen temples into Christian churches. And he gave a very careful reply, written with characteristic breadth and tact, to the questions which Augustine addressed to him when the difficulties of his work had begun to be felt. The authenticity of these answers, it is true, has been doubted, but the evidence, external as well as internal, appears to be sufficient[1]. The questions related to the support of the mission clergy, the liturgical use of the national Church now formed in England, the co-operation necessary in the consecration of bishops, and to matters touching the moral law about which among a recently heathen nation a special sensitiveness was desirable. Gregory's answers were those of a monk, even of a precisian, but they were also eminently those of a man of affairs and a statesman. "Things," he said, "are not to be loved for the sake of places, but places for the sake of good things," and the claim of Rome herself depended on such an assertion. As a monk he dealt firmly with morals: as a statesman he sketched out the future organisation of the English Church. London

---

[1] See Mason, *Mission of St Augustine*, pp. viii, ix. Ewald does not decide against them.

was to be one metropolitan see, York the other, each with the pallium and with twelve suffragan sees. Neither bishop was to be primate of all England by right, but the senior in consecration was to be the superior, according, it seems, to the custom of the Church in Africa of which he had experience, but restricted as his wisdom shewed to be desirable. It may be that Gregory had already heard of the position of the British Church: if so, he provided for its subjection to a metropolitan. Certainly he judged acutely according to the knowledge he possessed.

The beginnings of the English mission had brought the Pope into closer observation than before with the kings and bishops of peoples but recently converted to the faith. In Austrasia, Neustria and Burgundy reigned a race of kings whose wickedness was but slightly tempered by the Christianity they had accepted. In Spain there was more wisdom and more reality of faith.

From Britain we pass naturally to the country through which Gregory's envoys passed on their way to new spiritual conversion: from Gaul we may pass to Spain. So far did Gregory's interests extend: of his power it may not be possible to speak with so much certainty. In truth the Church in Europe was not yet a centralised body, and local independence was especially prominent among the Franks. Even in doctrine there are traces of divergence, though these were kept in check by a number of local councils which discussed and accepted the theological decisions which came to them from East and West. But the real power resided in the bishops, as administrators, rulers, shepherds of men's souls. Christianity at this period, and notably Frankish Christianity, has been described as a federation of city churches of which each one was a little monarchy in itself. If no one doubted the papal primacy, it was much further away than the arbitrary authority of the kings, and in nothing were the Merovingians more determined than in their control of the Church in their dominions. If in the south the bishop of Arles, as vicar of the Gauls, maintained close relations with the Roman see, the episcopate as a whole held aloof, respectful certainly but not obedient. The Church in Gaul had been engulfed in a barbarian conquest, cut off from Italy, severed from its ancient spiritual ties. The conversion of Clovis gave a new aspect to this separation. The kings assumed a powerful influence over the bishops, and asserted their supremacy in ecclesiastical matters. Whatever may have been the theory, in practice the interference of Rome in Gaul had become difficult, and was consequently infrequent: it had come to be considered unnecessary: the Church of the Franks had outgrown its leading-strings. But in practice? The special privileges of the see of Arles are evidence of a certain submission to the Papacy on the part of the Merovingian kings, though the monarchs were autocrats in matters of religion as well as in affairs of state, and did not encourage resort to the Holy See. It fell to Gregory, here as elsewhere, to inaugurate an era of defined authority.

When he became pope the royal power of the Merovingians was at
its height: in a few years it would totter to its fall, but now the clergy
were submissive and the bishops for the most part the creatures of the
court.   When he died the claims of Rome to supremacy were established,
even if they were not fully admitted.   With Gaul throughout his pontificate he maintained close relations.   Gregory of Tours tells with what
joy his namesake's election was received by the Franks, and from the first
sets himself to tell his doings and sayings with an unusual minuteness.
Within a year of his accession the new Pope was called upon to judge
the bishops of Arles and Marseilles, whom Jewish merchants accused to
him of endeavouring forcibly to convert them: Gregory reproved and
urged the bishops rather to preach and persuade than to coerce.   Again,
he reproved Vergilius of Arles and the bishop of Autun for allowing the
marriage of a nun, commanding them to bring the woman to penitence,
and exhorting them with all authority.   He intervened in the affairs of
monasteries, granting privileges and exemptions in a manner which
shews the nature of the authority he claimed.   By his advice the
difficult questions raised by the insanity of a bishop in the province of
Lyons were settled.   He claimed to judge a Frankish bishop and restore
him to his see, though here he felt it necessary to explain and justify
his conduct to the masterful Brunhild.   He is found reproving the iconoclastic tendencies of Serenus of Marseilles, and ordering him to replace
the images which he has thrown down.   He gave directions as to the
holding of church councils, he advised bishops as to the administration of
their dioceses and the enforcement of ecclesiastical discipline.   His correspondence with bishops and monks was constant, the requests to him to
intervene in the affairs of the Gallican Church were frequent.   Thus
he prepared himself to inaugurate in Gaul a decisive and necessary
reform.

Here he came into direct relations with the kings.   In 595
Childebert of Austrasia applied to him for a recognition of the powers,
as papal representative, of the bishop of Arles—evidence of the survival
of the traditional idea of dependence on the Roman Church.   In granting
the request Gregory took occasion to develop his scheme of ecclesiastical
discipline.   Simony, interference with the election of bishops, the nomination of laymen to the episcopate, were crying evils: and the kings were
responsible for them.   He believed that the Frankish monarchy, the
purity of whose faith shone by comparison with the dark treachery of
other peoples, would rejoice to carry out his wishes; and in the notorious
Brunhild he strangely found a deep religious sense and good dispositions
which should bear fruit in the salvation of men: to her he repeated the
desires which he had expressed to Childebert and urged her to see that
they were carried out.   He applied to her to put down crime, idolatry,
paganism, to prevent the possession by Jews of Christian slaves—with
what success we do not know.   Unsuccessful certainly he was when he

urged Theodoric and Theodobert to restore to the bishop of Turin
the parishes which he had lost during the barbarian invasion and which
the Frankish kings were by no means willing should be under the control
of a foreign bishop. But with Brunhild he seems always to have held
the most cordial relations: she asked his advice and assistance in
matters of religion and politics, in regard to a question of marriage law
and to the relation of the Franks with the Empire in the East. And
throughout his pontificate the attitude of the kings was one of deep
respect, that of the Pope that of father by counsel which easily wore
the cloak of authority.

It was thus that early in his pontificate Gregory warned Childebert
and Brunhild, as he warned Vergilius and the bishops of Childebert's
realm, of the need of instant action against the gross simony which was
eating away the spiritual life of the Church. Young men, evil livers,
laymen snatched from the business or pleasures of the world, were
hurriedly ordained or hurriedly promoted and thrust into the high
places of the Church. In 599 he addressed the bishops of Arles, Autun,
Lyons and Vienne in vigorous protest, laying to their charge at least
the acquiescence which made gross abuses possible. Ready though
he was to submit to lawful exercise of the royal power in nomination,
he utterly forbade the ordination of laymen in high office, as inexcusable
and indefensible. The Church was to be strengthened against the world
by total prohibition of marriage to the clergy and by the summoning of
yearly councils for the confirmation of faith and morals. In the councils
everything was to be condemned which was contrary to the canons; and
two prelates should represent him and inform him of what was done.
The abbot Cyriacus was sent on a special mission, with letters to bishops,
to kings, and to the queen Brunhild, to bring discipline to the Gallican
Church. But the murderous uncertainty of dynastic intrigues set every
obstacle in the way of a reform which might make the bishops less the
creatures of the kings. To Theodoric at one moment thanks were given
for his submission to papal commands, and he was directed to summon
a council. At another a special envoy was sent to indicate and insist
on reform. At another letter after letter in vehement exhortation was
addressed to Brunhild, apparently the real ruler of the distracted realm.
Bishops were again and again reproved, exhorted, reproached. But it is
difficult, perhaps through the scanty nature of the historical materials of
the period, to discover cases of definite submission to the papal authority.
It was asserted with all the moral fervour and all the sagacious prudence
which belonged to the great man who sat in the papal chair. It was not
repudiated by Frankish kings and bishops: rather the assertion was
received with judicious politeness and respect.

But beyond this the evidence does not carry us. That the policy of
the Frankish State was affected, or that the character of the kings, the
ministers of the Crown, or even the bishops, was moulded by the influence

of the Papacy it would be impossible to say. Tyrannous and fratricidal, the Merovingian kings lived their evil lives unchecked by more than a nominal regard for the teaching of Christian moralists. But Gregory's continual interest in the Frankish Church was not in vain. He had established a personal relation with the barbarous kings : he had created a papal vicar in the kingdom of the South : in granting the pallium to the bishop of Autun he had at least suggested a very special authority over the lands of the Gauls : he had claimed that the Roman Church was their mother to whom they applied in time of need. If the practical result was small ; if the Frankish Church maintained a real independence of Rome, and Arles never became a papal vicariate ; yet Frankish monks, priests, poets, as well as bishops and kings, began to look to Rome as patron and guide. Venantius Fortunatus, Columbanus, Gregory of Tours, in their different ways, shew how close was the relation of Gregory the Great to the religion of the Franks.

Brighter was the prospect when Gregory turned from the moral chaos of Gaul to the growing unity of Spain. The Visigothic race had produced a great warrior in Leovigild, whose power, as king of all the Goths, extended from Seville to Nîmes. He obtained for his son Hermenegild Ingundis the daughter of Brunhild (herself the child of Athanagild, Leovigild's predecessor as Visigothic king) and the Frankish king Sigebert. From Gregory's letters we learn a story of martyrdom as to which there is no reason to believe that he was deceived. Ingundis, beset by Arian teachers who had obtained influence over Leovigild, not naturally a persecutor, a tyrant or a fanatic, remained firm in her faith, and when her husband was given rule at Seville she succeeded with the aid of his kinsman Leander, bishop of Seville and friend of Gregory, in converting him to the Catholic belief. War was the result. Leovigild attacked his son, says John of Biclar, for rebellion and tyranny. Hermenegild sought the aid of the Catholic Sueves and " the Greeks "— the imperial garrisons which had remained since the partial reconquest of Spain by Justinian. But Leovigild proved the victor: the Suevic kingdom was extinguished, and Hermenegild was thrown into prison. Ingundis escaped with the Greeks and died at Carthage on her way to Constantinople. " Hermenegild was killed at Tarragona by Sigisbert " is the simple statement of John of Biclar, Catholic bishop of Gerona. Gregory in his *Dialogues* tells the tale more fully. On Easter Eve 585 he was offered communion by an Arian bishop, and when he refused to receive it at his hands he was murdered by the order of his father. He was regarded as a martyr and 13 April was observed throughout all Spain. His blood proved the seed of the faith.

A year later his brother Recared became king and accepted Catholicism. "No wonder," says Gregory, "that he became a preacher of the true faith, for his brother was a martyr, by whose merits he is aided in bringing back many souls to the bosom of God." Nor could this have happened had not Hermenegild the king laid down his life for the truth. So one Visigoth died that many might live. In a great synod at Toledo Recared abjured Arianism, and in May 589 was summoned the council which was to confirm the Catholicism of Spain. Leander preached the sermon which concluded the assembly, and reported to the Pope the orthodox speech of Recared, the acceptance of the creeds and decisions of the four general councils and the enactment of canons to regulate the lives and professions of the now Catholic people. Leander's letter was a veritable song of triumph for a victory to civilisation as well as religion, and as such Gregory accepted it with delight. In later years the Pope corresponded with Recared himself, wisely refraining from mixing himself up in the Visigothic relations with Constantinople, where Athanagild, son of the martyred Hermenegild, was being brought up, but praising him warmly for his devotion, and pointing him, as was his wont, for warning and encouragement, to the day of doom which was always in his own thoughts. To Leander he wrote frequently to the end of his life. He had sent him a pallium, through King Recared, as a recognition of ancient custom and of the merits of both king and prelate. He advised him, as he advised Augustine, in important matters of doctrine and practice. He gave him his *Pastoral Care* and his *Moralia*: and he remained his friend to the end of his life. At the exercise of authority over the Spanish Church Gregory made no attempt. He was content to recognise the great miracle, as he called it to Recared, of the conversion of a people, and to leave to their kings and bishops the direction of their Church. But outside the Gothic dominions his letters dealt with a case, in which he believed that injustice had been done to a bishop of Malaga, with great explicitness and claimed an authority which was judicial and political as well as ecclesiastical. If the documents are genuine, as is probable, they shew that Gregory was prepared not only to use to the full the powers of the Empire, when it was in agreement with him, for the redress of injustice in Church as well as State, but to extend by their means the jurisdiction and authority of the papal see. But equally clear is it that when he did so it was justice he sought to establish, not personal power: Spain for a long while remained to a considerable extent apart from the general current of life in the Western Church.

In June 603 the long agony with which the great Pope had so bravely struggled came to an end. The Romans to whom he had devoted his life paid no immediate honour to his memory: but a legend in later days, based perhaps on a statement of his archdeacon Peter, attributed to him a special inspiration of the Holy Spirit, and gave rise to his representations in art with a dove hovering over his head. His enormous energy had bequeathed to the Church a mass of writings which placed him among her four great doctors and exercised a powerful influence on the theology of the following centuries. For long Gregory was regarded as the great Christian philosopher and moralist, the interpreter of Holy Scripture, the teacher of the rulers of the Church. His sermons, his music, his dogmatic theology and his method of interpretation were for long the models which the Western Church followed unquestioningly. But the historical importance of his life would be as great as it is had he never written a single theological treatise. The influence of his career came from his personal character, the intense power of the active Christianity which radiated from his sick bed as from his throne.

Gregory emerges from the darkness of his age as a figure whom men can plainly see. His letters reveal him as few other heroes of the Middle Age are revealed : hardly any great ecclesiastics save Bernard and Becket are so intimately known. We recognise him as a stern Roman, hating the barbarians as unclean, despising the Greeks as unworthy of their share in the Empire which had sheltered them with its name. He was a passionate advocate of justice between man and man, a guardian of men's rights, a governor set to repress wrong and to preserve the stability of the ancient State. He was eminently practical, as a builder, an administrator, a philanthropist and a patriot. No doubt his fame is due partly to the weakness of his predecessors in the Papacy and partly to the insignificance and wickedness that followed. But his fame is due still more to the real achievement of his life. He gave to the Papacy a policy and a position which were never abandoned or lost.

The primacy of the see of Rome was by him translated into a practical system as well as a theory and a creed. His personal character, and that passion of his for a justice more righteous even than that of the old Roman law, made his claim to hear appeals, to be judge as well as arbiter, seem more than tolerable, even natural and inevitable. In the decay of old civilisation, when the Empire, East and West, could scarce hold its own, there remained in Rome, preserved through all dangers, a centre of Christian authority which could exercise, in the person of Gregory, wisely, loyally, tactfully, the authority which it claimed. Gregory was indeed, as John the Deacon calls him, *Argus luminosissimus*. He could admonish princes, and rebuke tax-gatherers : nothing seemed too small or too great for the exactness of his survey. And, after the example of all great rulers, he founded a tradition of public service which could be passed on even by weak hands and incompetent brains. He made Christian Rome a centre of justice. He gave to the Papacy a policy of attracting to itself the best in the new nations which were struggling for the sovereignty of Italy. If it was impossible for the Empire to fight the barbarians, peace must be made with them, and if peace, a lasting peace. In any case the Church should be their home, and tyranny should be turned into love. This was his ideal for Italian and Lombard alike. And his principles, of even-handed justice, of patriotism, of charity, were the bases on which he endeavoured to erect a fabric of papal supremacy. From his letters, as from a storehouse of political wisdom, there came in time rules in the Canon Law, and powers were claimed far beyond what he had dreamed of. Where he was disinterested lesser men were greedy and encroaching: where he strove to do justice others tried to make despotic laws. All over the Christian world Gregory had taught men to look to the Pope as one who could make peace and ensue it. On this foundation the medieval Papacy was founded. Not long was it contented so to rest.

CHAPTER IX.

THE SUCCESSORS OF JUSTINIAN.

WITH the death of Justinian we enter on a period of transition. The magnificent dream of extending the Roman Empire to its ancient limits seemed all but realised, for by the campaigns of Belisarius and Narses, Africa, Spain and Italy had been recovered. But the triumph had crippled the conqueror: already ruinous overdrafts had anticipated the resources which might have safeguarded the fruits of victory. Rome relaxed her grasp exhausted. Time was ringing out the old and ringing in the new. The next century was to fix in broad outlines the bounds within which for the future the empire was to be contained. Now, if we will, the Roman world becomes Byzantine. The secular struggle with Persia ends in the exaltation of the Cross over the worship of the sacred fire, the Sassanids fall before the Arab enthusiasts, and in the East Constantinople must meet changed conditions and an unexpected foe. In the West, while Spain is lost and but a harassed fraction of Italy remains, the outstanding fact is the settlement of the Slav tribes in the lands south of the Danube and their recognition of the overlordship of the Empire. A new Europe and a new Asia are forming: the period marks at once a climax and a beginning.

During his lifetime Justinian had clothed no colleague with the purple, but he had constantly relied upon Justin's counsel[1], and this nephew's intended succession was indicated by his appointment to the post of *curopalates.* Even on his lonely death-bed the Emperor made no sign, but the senators were agreed. It was their secret that Justinian's days were numbered, and they kept it well, prepared to forestall every rival. Through the long winter night Justin and his consort Sophia, seated at their window, looked over the sea and waited. Before the dawn the message came: the Emperor was dead and the Roman world expected a new monarch. The court poet paints Justin's tears as he refused the throne which the senators offered him—*Ibo paternas tristis in exsequias,*

---

[1] *Nil ille peregit Te (=Justino) sine.* Corippus, *In Laudem Justini,* I. 140.

regalia signa recuso; the formalities satisfied, he was easily overpersuaded, and walked through the silent city to the palace which was closely guarded by the household troops under the future emperor Tiberius (14 Nov. 565). Later, with the purple over his shoulders and wearing the gems which Belisarius had won from the Goths, Justin was raised aloft on the shield as the elect of the army; then the Church gave its approval: crowned with the diadem and blessed by the patriarch, he turned to the senate— during the old age of his uncle much had been neglected, the treasury exhausted and debts unpaid: all Justinian's thought and care had been set upon the world to come: the Empire shall rejoice to find the old wrongs righted under Justin's sway. In the company of Baduarius his son-in-law, newly appointed *curopalates*, and escorted by the senate, the Emperor then entered the circus where gifts were distributed, while the populace acclaimed their chosen ruler. The proceedings appear to have been carefully planned: Justin met the debts of those who had lent money to his uncle, and set free all prisoners. At midday he returned to the palace. The last honours to the dead had yet to be paid; in solemn procession, with candles burning and the choir of virgins answering to the chanting of the priests, the embalmed body of Justinian was borne through mourning crowds to its golden sepulchre in the church of the Twelve Apostles. Forthwith the city gave itself to rejoicing in honour of the Emperor's accession; amidst greenery and decorations, with dance and gaiety, the cloud of Justinian's gloomy closing years was dispelled, while Corippus sang, "The world renews its youth."

The *In Laudem Justini* of this poet laureate is indeed a document of great interest, for it paints the character and policy of Justin as he himself wished them to be portrayed. His conception of his imperial duty was the ideal of the unbending Roman whom nothing could affright. This spirit of exalted self-possession had been shewn at its height when the senate was leader of the State, and it was not without a definite purpose that the rôle of the senate is given marked prominence in the poem of Corippus. Unfortunately for this lofty view of the Empire's task and of the obligations of the nobility, it was precisely in the excessive power of the corrupt aristocracy that the greatest dangers lay. Office was valued as an opportunity for extortion, and riches gained at the expense of the commonwealth secured immunity from punishment. When all the armies of the Empire were engaged in the struggle with Persia, the government was forced to permit the maintenance in the European provinces of bodies of local troops; this was apparently also the case in Egypt, and again and again we see from the pages of John of Nikiou that the command of such military force was employed as an engine of oppression against helpless provincials. An unscrupulous captain would openly defy law and authority, and had no hesitation in pillaging unoffending villagers. While freely admitting that these accounts of the condition of affairs in Egypt hardly justify inferences as to the character of the administration in other parts of the Empire, yet stories related by chroniclers who wrote in the capital suggest that elsewhere also the ordinary course of justice was powerless to prevent an aristocracy of office from pursuing unchecked its own personal advantage. Justin, who scorned to favour either of the popular parties amongst the demes, looked to the nobles to maintain his high standard—and was disappointed. Similar views underlay all his foreign policy: Rome could make no concessions, for concessions were unworthy of the mistress of the world before whom all barbarian tribes must bow in awe. "We will not purchase peace with gold but win it at the sword's point":

> Justini nutu gentes et regna tremescunt,
> Omnia terrificat rigidus vigor...
> —Fastus non patimur.

Here lies the poignant tragedy of his reign. He would have had Rome inspired anew with the high ardours of her early prime; and she sank helpless under the buffets of her foes. For himself his will was that men should write of him:

> Est virtus roburque tibi, praestantior aetas,
> Prudens consilium, stabilis mens, sancta voluntas,

and yet within a few years his attendants, to stay his frenzied violence, were terrifying him, as a nurse her naughty child, with the dread name of a border sheikh upon the Arabian frontier. It is in fact of cardinal importance to realise that Justin at first shared the faith of Shakespeare's Bastard, "Come the three corners of the world in arms, and we shall shock them."

But if this policy were to be realised there must be no internal dissension and the theological strife of Justinian's last years must be set at rest. In concert with John, his courtier patriarch[1], Justin strove long and anxiously for union. John the patrician, on his embassy to Persia, was charged with the reconciliation of the Monophysites; exiled bishops were in due course to return to their sees, and Zechariah, archdeacon and court physician, drew up an edict which should heal the divisions between the friends and foes of the Council of Chalcedon. But the fanaticism of the monks at Callinicum defeated John's diplomacy, and the renewed efforts of the Emperor were rendered fruitless when Jacob Baradaeus refused to accept an invitation to the capital. Justin's temper could no longer brook opposition, and in the seventh year of his reign (571–572) he began in exasperation that fierce persecution of the Monophysites which is depicted for us by one of the sufferers in the pages of John of Ephesus.

---

[1] Cf. J. Haury, "Johannes Malalas identisch mit dem Patriarchen Johannes Scholastikos?" *B. Z.* ix. (1900), pp. 337–356.

Such then were the aims and policy of the new monarch. With the haughty pride of a Roman aristocrat, with his ill-timed obstinacy and imperious self-will, Justin flung defiance at his enemies; and he failed to make good the challenge.

Seven days after his accession he gave audience to Targasiz, an Avar ambassador, who claimed the annual payment which Justinian had granted. Did they not merit a reward, the envoy argued, for driving from Thrace the tribes which had endangered the capital?—would it not indeed be perilous to refuse their request? Plea and threat were alike of no avail. Surrounded by the gorgeous pageantry of a court reception, Justin offered the barbarians the choice of peace or war: tribute he would not pay; it were prodigality to lavish on barbarians the gold which the Empire could ill spare. He met their murmurs with immediate action, shipped the Avars across the strait to Chalcedon, and only after six months dismissed them—three hundred strong—to their homes. For a time indeed the Emperor's proud words appeared to have had their effect, but in truth the Avars were busy in Thuringia waging successful war with the Frankish Sigebert; their revenge for Rome's insult was perforce postponed, and Justin was free to turn his attention to the East.

John Comentiolus, who bore to the Persian court the news of Justinian's death and of his nephew's accession, was given instructions to raise the question of Suania. Under the terms of the Fifty Years' Peace which had been concluded between the two empires in 561, Chosroes had agreed to evacuate Lazica; the Romans contended that Suania was part of Lazica and must also be relinquished. Persia had not admitted this construction of the agreement, and the question still remained undecided. Suania indeed was in itself of no particular value; its importance lay in its strategic situation, for through it the Persians could attack the Roman frontier in Colchis. The possession of Suania would secure Rome's position in the east of the Euxine. The embassy was detained upon its journey and John found that Saracen tribesmen who acknowledged Persia's overlordship had arrived before him at the court of Madain; Justinian had granted them money payments on condition that they should not ravage the Roman frontiers, but these payments Justin had discontinued, contending that they were originally voluntary gifts or that, even if they had been made under a binding engagement, the obligation ceased with the death of the giver. The unwisdom of the dead, even though he were an emperor, could not bind the living, and the days of weakness were now past. The Saracen claims were supported by Chosroes, but the matter was allowed to drop, while the Emperor by his envoy expressed his strong desire for peace with Persia and for the maintenance of the treaty between the two peoples. John casually remarked that, if Lazica was evacuated, Suania by right should also fall to Rome. The king apparently accepted this view, but professed himself bound to refer the question to his ministers. The latter were willing to yield the territory for a price, but added conditions so humiliating to the Empire that John felt himself unable to accept the proposed terms. The king's counsellors in fact sought by diplomatic delays to force Rome to take action in Suania, so that they might then object that the people themselves refused to be subject to the Empire. The plan succeeded, and John foolishly entered into correspondence with the king of Suania. By this intervention Persia had secured a subject for negotiation, and now promised that an ambassador should be sent to Constantinople to discuss the whole situation. Justin disgraced his envoy, and Zich, who, besides bearing the congratulations of Persia, was charged with proposals as to Suania, was stopped at Nisibis. Justin returned thanks for the greetings of Chosroes, but stated that as to any other matters Rome could not admit discussion. On Zich's death Mebodes was sent to Constantinople, and with him came the Saracen chiefs for whom he craved audience. Justin shewed himself so arbitrary and unapproachable that Mebodes, though abandoning his patronage of the Saracens, felt that no course was open to him save to ask for his dismissal. The question of Suania was not debated, and Ambros, the Arab chieftain, gave orders to his brother Camboses to attack Alamoundar, the head of the Saracen tribesmen who were allied to Rome. From the detailed account of these negotiations given by Menander the reader already traces in Justin's overbearing and irritable temper a loss of mental balance and a wilful self-assertion which is almost childish in its unreasoning violence.

Meanwhile the Emperor could not feel secure so long as his cousin Justin, son of the patrician Germanus, was at the head of the forces on the Danube, guarding the passes against the Avars; the general was banished to Alexandria and there assassinated. It seems probable that Justin's masterful wife was mainly responsible for the murder. About the same time Aetherius and Addaeus, senators and patricians, were accused of treason and executed (3 Oct. 566[1]).

In the West the influence of the quaestor of the palace, Anastasius (a native of Africa), would naturally direct the Emperor's attention to that province. Through the praefect Thomas, peace was concluded with the Berber tribesmen and new forts were erected to repel assaults of the barbarians. But these measures were checked[2] by the outbreak of

---

[1] There is some doubt as to the precise date of the murder of Justin. Johannes Biclarensis assigns it to the same year as the conspiracy of Addaeus and Aetherius (*i.e.* 566, in John's reckoning=Ann. 11. Justini) and Evagrius clearly places it before the trial of Addaeus and Aetherius (Evagr. v. 1–3). Theophanes, it would appear wrongly, records it (p. 244, 3) under the year 570.—For the prominent position occupied by Sophia, cf. Warwick Wroth, *Catalogue of the Imperial Byzantine Coins in the British Museum, London* (1908), I. p. xix.

[2] For three subsequent invasions by the Moors in which one praefect and two *magistri militum* were killed, see Joh. Bicl., M.G.H. *Chronica Minora* (ed. Mommsen), II. (1894), p. 212, and Diehl, *L'Afrique byzantine*, pp. 459–460.

hostilities in Europe between the Lombards and the Gepids. In the war which ensued the Lombards gained the advantage, and the Gepids then sought to win the alliance of Justin by the splendour of their gifts. Baduarius, commanding in Scythia and Moesia, received orders to aid Kunimund, and the Roman forces won a victory over Alboin. The latter, looking around for allies in his turn, appealed to Baian, the Khagan of the Avars, who had just concluded a peace with Sigebert. The Lombards, Alboin urged, were fighting not so much against the Gepids as against their ally Justin, who but recently had refused the tribute which Justinian had conceded. Avars and Lombards united would be irresistible: when Scythia and Thrace were won, the way would be open for an attack upon Constantinople. Baian at first declined to listen to the Lombard envoys, but he finally agreed to give his assistance on condition that he should at once receive one-tenth of all the animals belonging to the Lombards, that half the spoil taken should be his, and that to him should fall the whole territory of the conquered Gepids. The latter were accused before Justin by a Lombard embassy of not having kept the promises which had been the price of the Roman alliance; this intervention secured the neutrality of the Emperor.

We know nothing of the struggle save its issue; the Gepids were defeated on the Danube and driven from their territory, while Kunimund was slain. But his grandson Reptilanis carried the royal treasure in safety to Constantinople, while it would seem that the Roman troops occupied Sirmium before the Avars could seize the city. Justin despatched Vitalian, the interpreter, and Komitas as ambassadors to Baian. They were kept in chains while the Avar leader attacked Bonus in Sirmium: this city, Baian claimed, was his by right; it had been in the hands of the Gepids, and should now devolve upon him as spoils of the victory. At the same time he offered conditions of peace which were remarkable for their extreme moderation—he only demanded a silver plate, some gold and a Scythian toga; he would be disgraced before his allies if he went empty-handed away. These terms Bonus and the bishop of Sirmium felt that they had no authority to accept without the Emperor's approval. For answer Baian ordered 10,000 Kotrigur Huns to cross the Save and ravage Dalmatia, while he himself occupied the territory which had formerly belonged to the Gepids. But he was not anxious for war, and there followed a succession of attempts at negotiation; the Roman generals on the frontier were ready to grant the Avar's conditions, but the autocrat in the capital held fast to his doctrinaire conceptions of that which Rome's honour would not allow her to concede. Targitius and Vitalian were sent to Constantinople to demand the surrender of Sirmium, the payment to Baian of sums formerly received from Justinian by the Kotrigur and Utigur Huns who were now tributary to the Avars, and the delivery of the person of Usdibad, a Gepid fugitive. The Emperor met the proposals with high-sounding words and Bonus was bidden to prepare for war. No success can have attended the Roman arms, for in a second embassy Targitius added to his former demands the payment of arrears by the Empire. Bonus was clearly incapable, argued Justin, and Tiberius was accordingly sent to arrange terms. After some military successes, it would seem, he concurred with Apsich in a proposal that land should be furnished by the Romans for Avar settlement, while sons of Avar chieftains should be pledges for the good faith of their fellow-countrymen. Tiberius went to Constantinople to urge the acceptance of these terms, but Justin was not satisfied: let Baian surrender his own sons as hostages, he retorted, and once more despatches to the officers in command ordered vigorous and aggressive action. Tiberius returned to be defeated by the Avars, and when yet another mission reached the palace, the Emperor realised that the honour of Rome must give place to the argument of force. Peace was concluded, and the Avars retired (end of 570?). The course of the negotiations throws into clear relief the views and aims of Justin, while the experience thus gained by Tiberius served to mould his policy as emperor.

For the rest of the reign the East absorbed the whole energy of the State. In order to understand clearly the causes which led to the war with Persia it is necessary to return to the year 568, when Constantinople was visited by an embassy from the Turks. This people, who had only recently made their appearance in Western Asia, had some ten years before overthrown the nation of the Ephthalites and were now themselves the leading power in the vast stretch of country between China and Persia. The western Chinese kingdom was at times their tributary, at other times their ally; with a vision of the possibilities which their geographical position offered they aspired to be the intermediaries through whose hands should pass the commerce of West and East. Naturally enough they first appealed to Persia, but the counsels of a renegade Ephthalite prevailed: the Turks were, he urged, a treacherous people, it would be an evil day for Persia if she accepted their alliance. Dizabul however, Khan of the Western Turks under the suzerainty of the great Mo-kan[1], only relinquished the project when he discovered that the members of a second embassy had been poisoned by Persian treachery. Then it was that his counsellor Maniach advised that envoys should be sent to the Roman capital, the greatest emporium for the silk of China. It was a remarkable proposal; the emperors had often sought to open up a route to the East which would be free from Persia's interference—Justinian, for example, had with this object entered into relations with the Ethiopian court—but no great success had attended their efforts, and now it was a Turk who unfolded a scheme whereby the products of East and West should pass and repass without

---

[1] Silziboulos (Šil-Čybul-baya-qaγan).

entering Persian territory, while the Turks drew boundless wealth as the middlemen between China and Rome. Obviously such a compact would not be acquiesced in by Persia, but Persia was the common foe: Turk and Roman must form an offensive and defensive alliance. Rome was troubled in her European provinces by the raids of Avar tribes and these tribesmen were fugitives from the Turk: Roman and Turk united could free the Empire from the scourge. Such was the project. The attitude of Rome's ministers was one of benevolent interest. They desired information but were unwilling to commit themselves; an embassy was accordingly despatched to assure Dizabul of their friendship, but when the Khan set off upon a campaign against Persia, Zemarchus with the Roman forces began the long march back to Constantinople[1]. On the journey he was forced to alter his route through fear of Persian ambushes in Suania; suspicions were clearly already aroused and it would seem that for a time the negotiations with the Turks were dropped[2]. More than this was needed to induce Chosroes to declare war.

In 571 Persian Armenia revolted and appealed to the Empire. It would seem that Justin had been attempting to force upon his Armenian subjects acceptance of the orthodox Chalcedonian doctrine, and Chosroes in turn, on the advice of the magi, determined to impose the worship of the sacred fire upon the whole of Persarmenia. The Surena with 2000 armed horsemen was sent to Dovin with orders to establish a fire temple in the city. The Catholicos objected that the Armenians, though paying tribute to their Persian overlord, were yet free to practise their own religion. The building of the temple was however begun in spite of protests, but ten thousand armed Armenians implored the Surena to lay the matter before Chosroes, and in face of this force he was compelled to withdraw. Meanwhile, it appears, the Armenians had secured from Justin a promise that they would be welcomed within the boundaries of the Empire, and that religious toleration would be granted them. On the return of the Surena in command of 15,000 men with directions to carry into execution the original design, 20,000 Armenians scattered the Persian forces and killed the Surena, and his severed head was carried to the patrician Justinian who was in readiness on the frontier at Theodosiopolis. At the same time the Iberians, with their king Gorgenes, went over to the Romans. The fugitives were well received; the nobles were given high positions and estates, while the Roman province was excused three years' tribute.

It was just at this time (571–572) that a new payment to Persia fell due under the terms of the peace of 561–562, Chosroes having insisted that

---

[1] The embassy of Zemarchus is dated 572–573 by John of Ephesus, vi. 23.

[2] The later embassy of Valentinus in 575–576 produced no lasting result. On these missions see J. Marquart, "Historische Glossen zu den alttürkischen Inschriften," *Vienna Oriental Journal*, xii. (1898), pp. 157–200.

previous instalments should be paid in advance. Sebocthes arrived (probably early in 572) to remind the Emperor of his obligations. In the judgment of Chosroes it was to Persia's present advantage that the peace should remain unbroken. The disagreeable question of Suania was shelved for the time, and Rome's claims were quietly ignored. Sebocthes preserved a studied silence in relation to the disturbances in Armenia and, when Justin mentioned that country, even appeared willing to recognise the rights of the Christian inhabitants. On dismissal, however, he was warned by the Emperor that if a finger was raised against Armenia it would be regarded as a hostile act. Justin indeed seems to have been anxious to force Persia to take the aggressive. He chose this moment of diplomatic tension to send the *magistrianus* Julian on a mission to Arethas, then reigning in Abyssinia over the Axumite kingdom. The envoy persuaded Arethas to break faith with his Persian suzerain, to send his merchandise through the country of the Homerites by way of the Nile to Egypt and to invade Persian territory. At the head of his Saracens the king made a successful foray and dismissed Julian with costly gifts and high honour[1]. Evidently Justin considered that Chosroes was only waiting until the Roman gold had been safely received, and that he would then declare war on the first favourable opportunity.

The Emperor determined to strike the first blow. The continuance of the peace entailed heavy periodical payments, and throughout his reign Justin was consistently opposed to enriching the Empire's enemies at the expense of the national treasury. Though the subsidies paid to Persia were to be devoted to the upkeep of the northern forts and the guarding of the passes against eastern invaders, it was easy for any unkindly critic to represent them as tribute paid by Rome to her rival[2]. Again Justin had welcomed the Turkish overtures: the power which had overthrown the Ephthalites would, he thought, be a formidable ally in the coming struggle. Further, through the mistakes in diplomacy of his own envoy, Suania had remained subject to Chosroes, and it was now additionally necessary that the country should belong to the Empire, since Persian ambushes rendered insecure the trade route to Turkish territory from which so much was hoped. But above all the capital had been deeply stirred by the oppression of the Armenians · Justin was resolved to champion their cause and, as a Christian monarch, to challenge the persecutor in their defence. When the ambassadors of the Frankish Sigebert returned to Gaul early in 575 they were full of the sufferings of the Armenians; it was to this cause, they told Gregory of Tours, that the war with Persia was due.

---

[1] This invasion is assigned by Theophanes (244–245) to the year 572. On this account cf. G. Hertzsch, *De Scriptoribus Rerum Imp. Tiberii Constantini* (Leipsic, 1882), p. 38.

[2] Cf. the story in John of Ephesus, vi. 23.

CH. IX.

The decisive step was taken in the late summer of 572 when, without warning, Marcianus[1], a first cousin of the Emperor on his mother's side, invaded Arzanene. Justin had given orders for an immediate attack on Nisibis, but precious time was wasted in fruitless negotiations with the Persian *marzpan*, while Chosroes was informed of the danger, Nisibis victualled and the Christians expelled. Very early in 573 Marcianus, at the head of troops raised from Rome's Caucasian allies, won some slight successes, but despatches from the capital insisted on the immediate investment of Nisibis; the army encamped before the city at the end of April 573. The Emperor however, suspecting his cousin's loyalty, appointed Acacius Archelaus[2] as his successor. Although Nisibis was about to capitulate, the new commander on his arrival brutally over-threw the tent and standard of Marcianus, while the general himself with rude violence was hurried away to Dara. The army, thinking itself deserted, fled in wild confusion to Mardes, while Chosroes, who had hastened to relieve Nisibis, now advanced to besiege Dara. At the same time Adarmaanes marched into the defenceless province of Syria, captured Antioch, Apamea and other towns, and rejoined Chosroes with a train of 292,000 prisoners. After an investment of more than five months, on 15 Nov. 573, Dara fell through the negligence or treachery, men said, of John, son of Timostratus. The city had been regarded as impreg-nable; men seeking security in troublous times had made it the treasure house of the Roman East, and the booty of the victors was immense.

On the news of this terrible disaster Justin ordered the shops to be shut and all trade to cease in the capital; he himself never recovered from the shock, but became a hopeless and violent imbecile. It seems that for five years (presumably since 569) Justin had been ailing and suffering from occasional mental weakness, but it was now clear that he was quite in-capable of managing the Empire's affairs. Through the year 574 the Empress in concert with Tiberius, the *comes excubitorum*, carried on the government. They were faced with a difficult problem: Rome had been the aggressor, could she be the first to propose terms of peace? Persia however intervened, and sent a certain Jakobos, who knew both Greek and Persian, to conclude a treaty. Rome, Chosroes argued, could not be further humbled: she must accept the victor's conditions. The letter was sent to the Empress owing to Justin's incapacity, and it was her reply that Zacharias bore to the Persian court[3]. Rome would pay 45,000 *nomismata* (metal value about £25,000) to secure peace for a year in the East, though Armenia was not included in this arrange-ment. If the Emperor recovered, a plenipotentiary should be sent to

[1] Called Martinus in Theoph. 245, 25.

[2] Theophanes of Byzantium is mistaken in thinking that the new commander was Theodore, the son of Justinian.

[3] Evagrius v. 12 (p. 208) must be regarded as a confusion with the later embassy of A.D. 575.

determine all matters in dispute and to end the war. But Justin did
not recover, and by the masterful will of the Empress, Tiberius was
adopted as the Emperor's son and created Caesar in the presence of the
patriarch John and of the officials of the Court (Friday, 7 Dec. 574).
It was a scene which deeply impressed the imagination of contemporary
historians. Justin in a pathetic speech confessed with sincere contrition
his failure, and in this brief interval of unclouded mental vision warned
his successor of the dangers which surrounded the throne.

Tiberius, his position now established, at once busied himself with
the work of reorganisation. His assumption of power marks a change
of policy which is of the highest importance. The new Caesar, himself
by birth a Thracian, had seen service on the Danube, and realised that
from the military standpoint the *intransigeant* imperialism of Justin
was too heroic an ideal for the exhausted Empire. Years before he had
approved of terms of peace which would have given the Avars land on
which to settle within Rome's frontiers. Greek influence was everywhere on the increase; at all costs it was the Greek-speaking Asiatic
provinces which must be defended and retained. Persia was the formidable foe and it was her rivalry which was the dominating factor in the
situation. Tiberius had indeed with practical insight comprehended
Rome's true policy. Syrian chroniclers of a later day rightly appreciated
this: to them Tiberius stands at the head of a new imperial line, they
know him as the first of the Greek emperors. But if in his view the
Empire, though maintaining its hold on such bulwark cities as Sirmium,
was in the future to place no longer its chief reliance on those European
provinces from which he had himself sprung, the administration must
scrupulously abstain from arousing the hostility of the eastern nationali-
ties : religious persecution must cease and it must be unnecessary for his
subjects to seek under a foreign domination a wider tolerance and a more
spacious freedom for the profession of their own faith. The Monophysites
gratefully acknowledged that during his reign they found in the Emperor
a champion against their ecclesiastical oppressors. This was not all :
there are hints in our authorities which suggest that he regarded as ill-
timed the aristocratic sympathies of Justin, and strove to increase the
authority of the popular elements in the State. It is possible that
the demesmen, suppressed by Justinian after the Nika sedition and
cowed by Justin, owed to the policy of Tiberius some of the influence
which they exercised towards the close of the reign of Maurice. Even at
the risk of what might be judged financial improvidence, the autocrat
must strive to win the esteem, if not the affection, of his subjects.
Tiberius forthwith remitted a year's taxation and endeavoured to restore
the ravages which Adarmaanes had inflicted on Syria. At the same
time he began to remodel the army, attracting to the service of the
State sturdy barbarian soldiers wherever such could be found[1].

[1] Is not Theophanes 251, 24 really summarising the Persian war as carried on by

Obviously the immediate question was the state of affairs in the East.   In the spring of 575 Tiberius sent Trajan, quaestor and physician, with the former envoy Zacharias to obtain a cessation of hostilities for three years both in the East and Armenia; if that was not possible, then in the East excluding Armenia.   Persia however insisted that no truce could be granted for any less period than five years, and the ambassadors therefore consented, subject to the approval of the Emperor, to accept a truce of five years in the East alone, Rome undertaking to pay annually 30,000 gold *nomismata*.   These terms Tiberius rejected: he wanted a truce for two years if possible, but in no event would he accept an agreement which would tie his hands for more than three years: by that time he hoped to be able successfully to withstand Persia in the field.   At last Chosroes agreed to a three years' treaty which was only to affect the East and was not to include Armenia. Meanwhile, before the result of the negotiations was known, Justinian, son of the murdered Justin, was appointed general of the East.   Early in the summer, however, Chosroes with unexpected energy marched north and invaded Armenia; Persarmenia returned to its allegiance, and by way of the canton of Bagrevand he advanced into the Roman province and encamped before Theodosiopolis.   This city, the key of Persarmenia and Iberia, he resolved to capture, and thence to proceed to Caesarea, the metropolis of Cappadocia.   The siege, however, was soon abandoned, and near Sebaste the Persians met the Roman army under Justinian, who had now assumed command in Armenia. Personal jealousies paralysed the action of the imperial troops, and the enemy was thus able to capture and burn Melitene.   Then the fortune of war turned.   Chosroes was forced to flee across the Euphrates and, with the Romans in hot pursuit, only escaped with great loss over the mountains of Karcha.   Justinian followed up this advantage by spending the winter on Persian soil.   His troops pillaged and plundered unchecked, and in the spring of 576 he took up his position on the frontier.

The shame of the flight from Melitene was a severe shock to Persian pride, and there seemed every prospect that now at last peace would be concluded.   At Athraelon, near Dara, Mebodes met Rome's envoys John and Peter, patricians and senators, together with Zacharias and Theodore, count of the treasury.   During the negotiations however Tamchosro defeated Justinian in Armenia (576).   Elated by this victory, the Persians withdrew the concessions which they had already made.   Still all through the years 576–577 the plenipotentiaries discussed terms; two points stood in the way of a final settlement: Persia claimed the right

---

Tiberius II and does not εἰς ὄνομα ἴδιον = his position was now legalised, and as Caesar he could raise troops in his own name?   Finlay sees in the passage the creation of a troop of *Buccellarii*.

to punish those Armenian fugitives who in 571 had fled to the Empire, and these Rome absolutely declined to surrender, while Chosroes in turn persisted in his refusal to consider the cession of Dara which Tiberius demanded. In 578, when the three years' truce had all but expired, a new embassy headed by Trajan and Zacharias began the task afresh.

Meanwhile, in 578, to put a stop to the mutual dissensions of the Roman generals Tiberius appointed as commander-in-chief of the eastern troops Maurice, a Cappadocian of Arabissus, descended, it was said, from the aristocracy of old Rome[1], who had formerly served as the Emperor's *notarius* and whom, on becoming Caesar, he had created *comes excubitorum*. With the means supplied to him by Tiberius, Maurice at once began to raise a formidable army; he enrolled men from his own native country, and enlisted recruits from Syria, Iberia, and the province of Hanzit. With these forces he successfully invaded Arzanene, captured the strong fortress of Aphoumon, and carried back with him thousands of Persians and much spoil.

In the autumn of this year (578) Justin, who had temporarily recovered his reason, crowned Tiberius Emperor (26 Sept.) and eight days later, on 4 Oct., his troubled life was ended.

Tiberius now as ever sought military triumphs only as a means to diplomatic ends. In consequence of the victories of the summer he had in his hands numerous important captives, some of them even connexions of the royal house. He at once despatched Zacharias and a general, Theodore by name, giving them full powers to conclude peace and offering to return the prisoners of war. The Emperor professed himself prepared to surrender Iberia and Persarmenia (but not those refugees who had fled to the shelter of the Empire), to evacuate Arzanene and to restore the fortress of Aphoumon, while in return Dara was to be given back to the Empire. Tiberius was desirous of arriving at a speedy agreement, so that the enemy might not gain time for collecting reinforcements. Despite the delay of a counter mission from Persia there was every prospect that Rome's conditions would be accepted, when in the early spring of 579 Chosroes died and was succeeded on the throne by Ormizd. Though the Emperor was willing to offer the same terms, Ormizd procrastinated, while making every effort to provision Dara and Nisibis and to raise fresh levies. At length he definitely refused to surrender Dara and stipulated anew for an annual money payment (summer, 579). The military and diplomatic operations of the years 579–581, though interesting enough in themselves, did not really alter the general position of affairs.

Thus inconclusively dragged on the long hostilities between the rival powers in the East, but in Europe the Avars had grown discontented

---

[1] A later tradition connects him with Armenia: cf. *B. Z.* xix. (1910), p. 549.

with the Empire's subsidies. Targitius was sent in 580 to receive the tribute, but immediately after the envoy's departure Baian started with his rude flotilla down the Danube and, marching over the neck of country between that river and the Save, appeared before Sirmium and there began to construct a bridge. When the Roman general in the neighbouring fortress of Singidunum protested at this violation of the peace the Khagan claimed that his sole aim was to cross the Save in order to march through the territory of the Empire, recross the Danube with the help of the Roman fleet, and thus attack the common enemy, the Slav invaders, who had refused to render to the Avars their annual tribute. Sirmium was without stores of provisions and had no effective garrison. Tiberius had relied upon the continuance of the peace and all his available troops were in Armenia and Mesopotamia. When Baian's ambassador arrived in the capital, the Emperor could only temporise: he himself was preparing an expedition against the Slavs, but for the present he would suggest that the moment was ill-chosen for a campaign, since the Turks were occupying the Chersonese (Bosporos had fallen into their hands in 576) and might shortly advance westward. The Avar envoy was not slow to appreciate the true position, but on the return journey he and the attendant Romans were slain by a band of Slav pillagers—this fact casually mentioned gives us some idea of the condition at this time of the open country-side in the Danubian provinces. Meanwhile Baian had been pressing forward the building of the bridge over the Save, and Solachos, the new Avar ambassador, now threw off the mask and demanded the evacuation of Sirmium. " I would sooner give your master," Tiberius replied, " one of my two daughters to wife than I would of my own free will surrender Sirmium." The Danube and the Save were held by the enemy, and the Emperor had no army, but through Illyria and Dalmatia officers were sent to conduct the defence. On the islands of Casia and Carbonaria Theognis met the Khagan, but negotiations were fruitless. For two years, despite fearful hardships, the city resisted, but the governor was incompetent, and the troops under Theognis inadequate, and at last, some short time before his death, Tiberius, to save the citizens, sacrificed Sirmium. The inhabitants were granted life, but all their possessions were left in the hands of the barbarians, who also exacted the sum of 240,000 *nomismata* as payment for the three years' arrears (580–582) due under the terms of the former agreement which was still to remain in force.

It was during the investment of Sirmium that the Slavs seized their golden hour. They poured over Thrace and Thessaly, scouring the Roman provinces as far as the Long Walls—a flood of murder and of ravage: the black horror of their onset still darkens the pages of John of Ephesus.

In the year which saw the fall of Sirmium (582) Tiberius died. Feeling that his end was near, on 5 Aug. he created Maurice Caesar and gave to him the name of Tiberius[1]; at the same time the Emperor's elder daughter was named Constantina and betrothed to Maurice. Eight days later, before an assemblage of representatives of army, church and people, Tiberius crowned the Caesar Emperor (13 Aug.) and on 14 Aug. 582, in the palace of the Hebdomon, he breathed his last. The marriage of Maurice followed hard on the funeral of his father-in-law. We would gladly have learned more of the policy and aims of Tiberius. We can but dimly divine in him a practical statesman who with sure prescience had seen what was possible of achievement and where the Empire's true future lay. He fought not for conquest but for peace, he struggled to win from Persia a recognition that Rome was her peer, that on a basis of security the Empire might work out its internal union and concentrate its strength around the shores of the eastern Mediterranean. "The sins of men," says the chronicler, "were the reason for his short reign. Men were not worthy of so good an emperor."

"Make your rule my fairest epitaph" were the words of Tiberius to Maurice, and the new monarch undertook his task in a spirit of high seriousness. At his accession Maurice appointed John Mystakon commander-in-chief of the eastern armies, and this position he held until 584, when he was superseded by Philippicus, the Emperor's brother-in-law. The details of the military operations during the years 582–585 cannot be given here it may be sufficient to state that their general result was indecisive—most of the time was spent in the capture or defence of isolated fortresses or in raids upon the enemy's territory[2]. No pitched battle of any importance occurred till 586. Philippicus had met Mebodes at Amida in order to discuss terms of peace, but Persia had demanded a money payment, and such a condition Maurice would not accept. The Roman general, finding that negotiations were useless, led his forces to Mount Izala, and at Solochon the armies engaged. The Persians were led by Kardarigan, while Mebodes commanded on the right wing and Aphraates, a cousin of Kardarigan, on the left. Philippicus was persuaded not to adventure his life in the forefront of the battle, so that the Roman centre was entrusted to Heraclius, the father of the future emperor. Vitalius faced Aphraates, while Wilfred, the praefect of Emesa, and Apsich the Hun opposed Mebodes. On a Sunday morning the engagement began: the right wing routed Aphraates, but was with

---

[1] It would seem that Germanus was also created Caesar but declined the responsibilities which Maurice was prepared to assume.

[2] A short chronological note may however be of service. 582, autumn: John Mystakon commander-in-chief in Armenia: Roman success on Nymphius turned into a rout through jealousy of Kours. 583: Capture of fort of Akbas, near Martyropolis, by Rome. Peace negotiations between Rome and Persia. 584: Marriage of Philippicus to Gordia, sister of Maurice: Philippicus appointed to succeed John in the East. He fortifies Monokarton and ravages country round Nisibis. 585: Philippicus ill: retires to Martyropolis. Stephanus and the Hun Apsich successfully defend Monokarton.

difficulty recalled from its capture of the Persian baggage; the defeated troops now strengthened the enemy's centre and some of the Roman horse were forced to dismount to steady the ranks under Heraclius. But during a desperate hand-to-hand struggle the cavalry charged the Persians and the day was won: the left wing pursued the troops under Mebodes as far as Dara. Philippicus then began the siege of the fortress of Chlomara, but his position was turned by the forces under Kardarigan; a sudden panic seized the Roman commander, who fled precipitately under cover of night to Aphoumon. The enemy, suspecting treachery, advanced with caution, but encountered no resistance, while the seizure of the Roman baggage-train relieved them from threatened starvation. Across the Nymphius by Amida to Mount Izala Philippicus retreated: here the forts were strengthened and the command given to Heraclius, who in late autumn led a pillaging expedition across the Tigris.

The flight of Philippicus may well have been due, at least in part, to a fresh attack of illness, for in 587 he was unable to take the field, and when he started for the capital, Heraclius was left as commander in the East and at once began to restore order and discipline among the Roman troops.

Maurice's well-intentioned passion for economy had led him to issue an order that the soldiers' pay should be reduced by a quarter; Philippicus clearly felt that this was a highly dangerous and inexpedient measure—the army's anger might lead to the proclamation of a rival emperor; he delayed the publication of the edict, and it was probably with a view of explaining the whole situation to his master that, despite his illness, he set out for Constantinople. On his journey, however, he learned that he had been superseded and that Priscus had been appointed commander-in-chief. If Maurice had ceased to trust his brother-in-law let the new general do what he could: Philippicus would no longer stay his hand. From Tarsus he ordered Heraclius to leave the army in the hands of Narses, governor of Constantina, and himself to retire to Armenia; he further directed the publication of the fatal edict.

Early in 588 Priscus arrived in Antioch. The Roman forces were to concentrate in Monokarton; and from Edessa he made his way, accompanied by the bishop of Damascus, towards the camp with the view of celebrating Easter amongst his men. But when the troops came forth to meet him, his haughtiness and failure to observe the customary military usages disgusted the army and at this critical moment a report spread that their pay was to be reduced. A mutiny forced Priscus to take refuge in Constantina, and the fears of Philippicus proved well founded. Germanus, commander in the Lebanon district of Phoenicia, was against his own will proclaimed emperor, though he exacted an oath that the soldiers would not plunder the luckless provincials. A riot at Constantina, where the Emperor's statues were overthrown, drove the fugitive Priscus to Edessa, and thence he was hounded forth to seek shelter in the capital.

Maurice's only course was to reappoint Philippicus to the supreme command in the East, but the army, which had elected its own officers, was not to be thus easily pacified: the troops solemnly swore that they would never receive the nominee of an emperor whom they no longer acknowledged. Meanwhile, as was but natural, Persia seized her opportunity and invested Constantina, but Germanus prevailed upon his men to take action and the city was relieved. The soldiers' resentment was lessened by the skilful diplomacy of Aristobulus, who brought gifts from Constantinople, and Germanus was able to invade Persia with a force of 4000 men. Though checked by Marouzas, he retired in safety to the Nymphius, and at Martyropolis Marouzas was defeated and killed by the united Roman forces: three thousand captives were taken, among them many prominent Persians, while the spoils and standards were sent to Maurice. This was the signal that the army was once more prepared to acknowledge the Emperor, and all would have been well had not Maurice felt it necessary to insist that Philippicus should again be accepted by the troops as their general. This however they refused to do, even when Andreas, captain of the imperial shield-bearers, was sent to them; and only after a year's cessation of hostilities (588–589) was the army, through the personal influence of Gregory, bishop of Antioch, persuaded to obey its former commander (Easter 590). Philippicus did not long enjoy his triumph. About this time Martyropolis fell by treachery into Persian hands, and with the spring of 590[1] the Roman forces marched into Armenia to recover the city. When he failed in this Philippicus was superseded by Comentiolus, and although the latter was unsuccessful, Heraclius won a brilliant victory and captured the enemy's camp.

It is at first sight somewhat surprising that the Persians had remained inactive during the year 589, but we know that they were fully engaged with internal difficulties. The violence of Ormizd had, it seems, caused a dangerous revolt in Khūzistan and Kerman, and in face of this peril Persia accepted an offer of help from the Turks. Once admitted into Khorasan, Shaweh Shah disregarded his promises and advanced southwards in the direction of the capital, but was met by Bahram Cobin, the governor of Media, and was defeated in the mountains of Ghilan. The power of the Turks was broken: they could no longer exact, but were bound to pay, an annual tribute. After this signal success Bahram Cobin undertook an invasion of Roman territory in the Caucasus district; the Persians encountered no resistance, for the imperial forces were concentrated in Armenia. Maurice sent Romanus to engage the enemy in Albania, and in the valley of one of the streams flowing into the Araxes Bahram was so severely worsted that he was in consequence removed from his command by Ormizd. Thus disgraced he determined to seize the

---

[1] This is not the usually accepted chronology. The present writer hopes shortly to support the view here taken in a paper on the literary construction of the history of Theophylactus Simocatta.

crown for himself but veiled his real plan under the pretext of championing the cause of Chosroes, Ormizd's eldest son[1]. At the same time a plot was formed in the palace, and Bahram was forestalled: the conspirators dethroned the king and Chosroes was crowned at Ctesiphon. But after the assassination of Ormizd the new monarch was unable to maintain his position: his troops deserted to Bahram, and he was forced to throw himself upon the mercy of the Emperor. As a helpless fugitive the King of kings arrived at Circesium and craved Rome's protection, offering in return to restore the lost Armenian provinces and to surrender Martyropolis and Dara. Despite the counsels of the senate, Maurice saw in this strange reversal of fortune a chance to terminate a war which was draining the Empire's strength: his resolve to accede to his enemy's request was at once a courageous and a statesmanlike action. He furnished Chosroes with men and money, Narses took command of the troops and John Mystakon marched from Armenia to join the army. The two forces met at Sargana (probably Sirgan, in the plain of Ushnai[2]) and in the neighbourhood of Ganzaca (Takhti-Sulaimān) defeated and put to flight Bahram, while Chosroes recovered his throne without further resistance. The new monarch kept his promises to Rome and surrounded himself with a Roman body-guard (591). By this interposition Maurice had restored the Empire's frontier[3] and had ended the long-drawn struggle in the East.

In 592 therefore he could transport his army into Europe, and was able to employ his whole military force in the Danubian provinces. Maurice himself went with the troops as far as Anchialus, when he was recalled by the presence of a Persian embassy in the capital. The chronology of the next few years is confused and it is impossible to give here a detailed account of the campaigns. Their general object was to maintain the Danube as the frontier line against the Avars and to restrict the forays of the Slavs. In this Priscus met with considerable success, but Peter, Maurice's brother, who superseded him in 597, displayed hopeless incompetency and Priscus was reappointed[4]. In 600 Comentiolus, who was, it would appear, in command against his own will, entered into communications with the Khagan in order to secure the discomfiture of the Roman forces: he was, in fact, anxious to prove that the attempt to defend the northern frontier was labour lost. He ultimately fled headlong to the capital and only the personal interference of the Emperor stifled the inquiry into his treachery. On this

---

[1] There seems no sufficient evidence for the theory that Bahram Cobin relied on a legitimist claim as representing the prae-Sassanid dynasty.

[2] See H. C. Rawlinson, "Memoir on the site of the Atropatenian Ecbatana," *Journal of the Royal Geographical Society* (1840), pp. 71 ff.

[3] See maps by H. Hübschmann in "Die altarmenischen Ortsnamen," *Indogermanische Forschungen*, xvi. (1904), and in Gelzer's *Georgius Cyprius*.

[4] For the siege of Thessalonica in this year, cf. Wroth, *op. cit.* i. p. xxi.

occasion the panic in Constantinople was such that the city guard—the δῆμοι—were sent by Maurice to man the Long Walls[1].

On the return of Comentiolus to the seat of war in the summer of 600, Priscus, in spite of his colleague's inactivity, won a considerable victory, but the autumn of 601 saw Peter once again in command and conducting unsuccessful negotiations for a peace. Towards the close of 602 the outlook was brighter, for conditions had changed in favour of Rome. The Antae had acted as her allies, and when Apsich was sent by the Khagan to punish this defection, numbers of the Avars themselves deserted and joined the forces under Peter. Maurice would seem to have thought that this was the moment to drive home the advantage which fortune offered, for if the soldiers could support themselves at the expense of the enemy, the harassed provincials and the overburdened exchequer might be spared the cost of their maintenance. Orders were sent that the troops were not to return, but should winter beyond the Danube. The army heard the news with consternation . barbarian tribes were ranging over the country on the further side of the river, the cavalry was worn out with the marches of the summer, their booty would purchase them the pleasures of civilised life. The Roman forces mutinied and, disobeying their superiors, crossed the river and reached Palastolum.

Peter withdrew from the camp in despair, but meanwhile the officers had induced their men to face the barbarians once again, and the army had returned to Securisca (near Nikopol). Floods of rain, however, and extreme cold renewed the discontent; eight spokesmen, among whom was Phocas, covered the twenty miles between Peter and the camp and demanded that the army might return home to winter quarters. The commander-in-chief promised to give his answer on the following day: between the rebellious determination of the troops and the imperative despatches of his brother he could see no loophole of escape; of one thing alone he was assured: that day would start a train of ills for Rome. True to his promise he joined his men and to their representatives he read the Emperor's letter. Before the tempest of opposition which this evoked the officers fled, and on the following day, when the soldiers had twice assembled to discuss the situation, Phocas was raised upon a shield and declared their leader. Peter carried the news with all speed to the capital; Maurice disguised his fears and reviewed the troops of the demes. The Blues, on whose support he relied, numbered 900, the Greens 1500. On the refusal of Phocas to receive the Emperor's ambassadors, the demesmen were ordered to man the city walls. Phocas had been chosen as champion of the army, not as emperor: the army had refused allegiance to Maurice personally but not to his house;

[1] It seems probable that in some source hostile to Maurice the treachery of Comentiolus was transferred to the Emperor himself and to this was added the story of the failure to ransom the prisoners. The basis of fact from which the story sprang may perhaps be discerned in Theophylact, *e.g.* p. 247, 18 (edn. de Boor).

accordingly the vacant throne was offered to Theodosius, the Emperor's eldest son, or, should he decline it, to his father-in-law Germanus, both of whom were hunting at the time in the neighbourhood of the capital. They were at once recalled to Constantinople. Germanus, realising that he was suspected of treason, armed his followers and surrounded by a body-guard took refuge in the Cathedral Church. He had won the sympathies of the populace, and when the Emperor attempted to remove him by force from St Sophia, riots broke out in the city, while the troops of the demes deserted their posts on the walls to join in the abuse of Emperor and patriarch. Maurice was denounced as a Marcianist and ribald songs were shouted against him through the streets. The house of the praetorian praefect, Constantine Lardys, was burned to the ground, and at the dead of night, with his wife and children, accompanied by Constantine, the Emperor, disguised as a private citizen, embarked for Asia (22 Nov. 602). A storm carried him out of his course and he only landed with difficulty at the shrine of Autonomus the Martyr; here an attack of gout held him prisoner, while the praetorian praefect was despatched with Theodosius to enlist the sympathy of Chosroes on behalf of his benefactor. The Emperor fled, the Greens determined to espouse the cause of Phocas and rejected the overtures of Germanus, who now made a bid for the crown and was prepared to purchase their support; they feared that, once his end was gained, his well-known partiality for the Blues would reassert itself. The disappointed candidate was driven to acknowledge his rival's claims. Phocas was invited to the Hebdomon (Makrikeui) and thither trooped out the citizens, the senate, and the patriarch. In the church of St John the Baptist the rude half-barbarian centurion was crowned sovereign of the Roman Empire, and entered the capital "in a golden shower" of royal gifts.

But the usurper could not rest while Maurice was alive. On the day following the coronation of his wife Leontia, upon the Asian shore at the harbour of Eutropius five sons of the fallen Emperor were slain before their father's eyes, and then Maurice himself perished, calling upon God and repeating many times "Just art thou, O Lord, and just is thy judgment." From the beach men saw the bodies floating on the waters of the bay, while Lilius brought back to the capital the severed heads, where they were exposed to public view.

Maurice was a realist who suffered from an obstinate prejudice in favour of his own projects and his own nominees; he could diagnose the ills from which the Empire suffered, but did not always choose aright the moment for administering the remedy. He had served a stern apprenticeship in the eastern wars, and saw clearly that while Rome in many of her provinces was fighting for existence, the importance of the leader of armies outweighed that of the civil governor. In some temporary instances Justinian had entrusted to the praefect the duties of a general, and had thus broken through the sharp distinction between the two spheres drawn by the Diocletio-Constantinian reforms. Maurice however did not follow the principle of Justinian's tentative innovations : he chose to give to the military commander a position in the hierarchy of office superior to that of the civil administration, conferring on the old *magistri militum* of Africa and Italy the newly coined title of exarch : this supreme authority was to be the Emperor's vicegerent against Berber and Lombard. It was the first step towards the creation of the system of military themes[1]. It was doubtless also considerations of practical convenience and a recognition of the stubborn logic of facts which led to Maurice's scheme of provincial redistribution. Tripolitana was separated from Africa and joined like its neighbour Cyrenaica to the diocese of Egypt ; Sitifensis and Caesariensis were fused into the single province of Mauretania Prima, while the fortress of Septum and the sorry remnants of Tingitana were united with the imperial possessions in Spain and the Balearic Isles to form the province of Mauretania II, thus solidifying under one government the scattered Roman territories in the extreme West. Similar motives probably determined the new arrangements (after the treaty with Persia in 591) on the Eastern frontier. It was again Maurice the realist who disregarded the counsels of his ministers and made full use of the unique opportunity which the flight of Chosroes offered to the Empire.

In Italy the incursion of the Lombards presented a problem with which the wars on the Danube and in Asia rendered it difficult for Maurice to cope. Frankish promises of help against the invaders were largely illusory, even though the young West-Gothic prince Athanagild was held in Constantinople as a pledge for the fulfilment by his Merovingian kinsfolk of their obligations. It was further unfortunate that the relations between Pope and Emperor were none of the best ; many small disagreements culminated in the dispute concerning the title of oecumenical patriarch which John the Faster had adopted. The contention between Gregory and Maurice has certainly been given a factitious importance by later historians—the over-sensitive Gregory alone seems to have regarded the question as of any vital moment and his successors quietly acquiesced in the use of the offending word—but the disagreement doubtless hampered the Emperor's reforms ; when he endeavoured to prevent soldiers from deserting and retiring into monasteries, the Pope seized on the measure as a new ground of complaint and raised violent protest in the name of the Church.

As general in Asia Maurice had restored the morale of the army, and throughout his life he was always anxious to effect improvements in military matters. He was the first Emperor to realise fully the importance of Armenia as a recruiting ground[2], and it may well be from

[1] See Ch. XIII.

[2] When an Emperor is at great cost transporting men from Armenia to the Danube provinces, is the story probable that he sacrificed thousands of prisoners of war through refusal to pay to the Khagan their ransom?

this fact that late tradition traced his descent from that country. It was just in this sphere of military reform, however, that he displayed his fatal inability to judge the time when he could safely insist on an unpopular measure; his demand that the army should winter beyond the Danube cost him alike throne and life. It was further an all-advised step when Maurice in his later years (598 or 599) reverted, as Justin had done before him, to a policy of religious persecution. By endeavouring to force Chalcedonian orthodoxy on Mesopotamia he effected little save the alienation of his subjects. It was left to Heraclius to follow Tiberius in choosing the better part and endeavouring by conciliation to introduce union amongst the warring parties. But the great blot on the reign of Maurice is his favouritism towards incapable officials; the ability of men like Narses and Priscus had to give place to the incompetency of Peter and the treachery of Comentiolus. Time and again their blunders were overlooked and new distinctions forced upon them. The fear that a victorious general of to-day might be the successful rival of to-morrow gave but a show of justification to this ruinous partiality.

But despite all criticisms Maurice remains a high-minded, conscientious, independent, hard-working ruler, and if other proof of his worth were lacking it is to be found in the universal hatred of his murderer.

Other executions followed those of Maurice and his sons: Comentiolus and Peter were slain, while Alexander dragged Theodosius from the sanctuary of Autonomus and killed both him and the praefect Constantine. Constantina and her three daughters were confined in a private house. Phocas was master of the capital. But elsewhere throughout the Empire men refused to ratify the army's choice: through Anatolia and Cilicia, through the Roman province of Asia and in Palestine, through Illyricum and in Thessalonica civil war was raging[1]: on every side the citizens rose in rebellion against the assassin whom Pope Gregory and the older Rome delighted to honour; even in Constantinople itself a plot hatched by Germanus was only suppressed after a great part of the city had been destroyed by fire. The ex-empress as a result of these disorders was now immured with her daughters in a convent, while Philippicus and Germanus were forced to become priests.

A persistent rumour affirmed that Theodosius was still alive; for a time Phocas himself must have believed the report, for he put to death his agent Alexander; furthermore Chosroes was thus furnished with a fair-sounding pretext for an invasion of the Empire: he came as avenger of Maurice to whom he owed his throne, and as restorer of Maurice's heir. When in the spring of 603 Phocas despatched Lilius to the Persian court to announce his accession, the ambassador was thrown into chains, and in an arrogant letter Chosroes declared war on Rome. About this time[1]

---

[1] Cf. H. Gelzer, *Die Genesis*, etc., pp. 36 ff.

also (603) Narses revolted, seized Edessa and appealed to Persia for support. Germanus, now in command of the eastern army[1], marched to Edessa with orders to recover the city. In the spring of 604 Chosroes led his forces against the Empire, and while part encamped round Dara, he himself made for Edessa to attack the Romans who were themselves besieging Narses. As day broke the Persians fell upon Germanus, who was defeated and eleven days later died of his wounds in Constantina; his men fled in confusion. Chosroes, it would appear, entered Edessa, and (according to the Armenian historian Sebeos) Narses introduced to the Persian king a young man whom he represented to be Theodosius; the pretender was gladly welcomed by Chosroes, who then retired to Dara, where the Romans still resisted the besiegers. On the news of the death of Germanus Phocas realised that all the forces which he could raise were needed for the war in Asia. He increased the annual payments to the Avars, and withdrew the regiments from Thrace (605?). Some of the troops under the command of the eunuch Leontius were ordered to invest Edessa, though Narses soon escaped from this city and reached Hierapolis; the rest of the army marched against Persia, but at Arxamon, between Edessa and Nisibis, Chosroes won a great victory and took numerous captives; about this time, after a year and a half's siege, the walls of Dara were undermined, the fortress captured and the inhabitants massacred. Laden with booty the Persian monarch returned to Ctesiphon, leaving Zongoes in command in Asia. Leontius was disgraced, and Phocas appointed his cousin Domentiolus *curopalates* and general-in-chief. Narses was induced to surrender on condition that no harm should be done to him; Phocas disregarded the oath and Rome's best general was burned alive in the capital.

Meanwhile Armenia was devastated by civil war and Persian invasion: Karin opened its gates to the pretended son of Maurice, and Chosroes established a *marzpan* in Dovin. In the year after the siege of Dara (606) Sahrbarâz and Kardarigan entered Mesopotamia and the country bordering on the frontier of Syria; among the towns which surrendered were Amida and Resaina. In 607 Syria, Palestine and Phoenicia were over-run; in 608 Kardarigan in conjunction, it seems, with Sahîn marched north-west and, while the latter occupied Cappadocia, spending a year (608–609) in Caesarea which was evacuated by the Christians, the former made forays into Paphlagonia and Galatia, penetrating even as far west as Chalcedon. In fact the Roman world at this time fell into a state of anarchy, and passions which had long smouldered burst into flame. Blues and Greens fought out their feuds in the streets of Antioch, Jerusalem and Alexandria, while on every side men easily persuaded themselves that Theodosius yet lived. Even in Constantinople Germanus thought

---

[1] Appointed to supersede Narses shortly before Maurice's death, the Emperor being anxious to meet the objections of Persia.

that he could turn to his own profit the popular belief. Our authorities are unsatisfactory but it would seem that two distinct plots with different aims were set on foot. There was a conspiracy among the highest court officials headed by the praetorian praefect of the East, Theodorus: Elpidius, governor of the imperial arsenal, was willing to supply arms, and Phocas was to be slain in the Hippodrome. Theodorus himself would then be proclaimed emperor. Of this plan Germanus obtained warning, and for his part determined to anticipate the scheme by playing upon the public sympathy for the house of Maurice. While nominally championing the cause of Theodosius, he doubtless intended to secure for himself the supreme power. Through a certain Petronia he entered into communication with Constantina, but Petronia betrayed the secret to Phocas. Under torture Constantina accused Germanus of complicity and he in turn implicated others. The rival plot met with no better success. Anastasius, who had been present at the breakfast council where the project was discussed, repented of his treason and informed the Emperor. On 7 June 605 Phocas wreaked his vengeance on the court officials, and about the same time Germanus, Constantina and her three daughters met their deaths.

Alarms and suspicions haunted the Emperor and terror goaded him to fresh excesses. In 607, it would seem, his daughter Domentzia was married to Priscus, the former general of Maurice, and when the demesmen raised statues to bride and bridegroom, Phocas saw in the act new treason and yet another attempt upon his throne. It was in vain that the authorities pleaded that they were but following long-established custom; it was only popular clamour that saved the demarchs Theophanes and Pamphilus from immediate execution. Even loyalty was proved dangerous, and anxiety for his personal safety made of a son-in-law a secret foe. The capital was full of plague and scarcity and executions: Comentiolus and all the remaining kindred of Maurice fell victims to the panic fear of Phocas. The Greens themselves turned against the Emperor, taunting him in the circus with his debauchery, and setting on fire the public buildings. Phocas retorted by depriving them of all political rights. He looked around for allies: at least he would win the sympathies of the orthodox in the East, as he had from the first enjoyed the support of Rome. Anastasius, Jacobite patriarch of Alexandria, was expelled: Syria and Egypt, he decreed, should choose no ecclesiastical dignitary without his authorisation. Before the common attack, Monophysite Antioch and Alexandria determined to sink their differences. In 608 the patriarchs met in the Syrian capital. The local authorities interfered, but the Jacobite populace was joined by the Jews in their resistance to the imperial troops. The orthodox patriarch was slain and the rioters gained the day. Phocas despatched Cotton and Bonosus, count of the East, to Antioch; with hideous cruelty their mission was accomplished, and the Emperor's authority with difficulty re-established.

Thence Bonosus departed for Jerusalem, where the faction fights of Blues and Greens had spread confusion throughout the city.

The tyrant was still master within the capital, but Africa was preparing the expedition which was to cause his overthrow. In 607, or at latest 608, Heraclius, formerly general of Maurice and now exarch, with his ὑποστράτηγος Gregory, was planning rebellion. The news reached the ears of Priscus, who had learned to fear his father-in-law's animosity, and negotiations were opened between the Senate and the Pentapolis: the aristocracy was ready to give its aid should a liberator reach the capital. Obviously such a promise was of small value, and Heraclius was forced to rely upon his own resources. But he was at this time advanced in life, and to his son Heraclius and to Gregory's son Nicetas was entrusted the execution of the plot. It is only of recent years, through the discovery of the chronicle of John of Nikiou, that we have been able to construct the history of the operations. First Nicetas was to invade Egypt and secure Alexandria, then Heraclius would take ship for Thessalonica, and from this harbour as his base he would direct his attack upon Constantinople.

During the year 608, 3000 men were raised in the Pentapolis, and these, together with Berber troops, were placed under the command of Bonâkis (a spelling which doubtless hides a Roman name) who defeated without difficulty the imperial generals. Leontius, the praefect of Mareotis, was on the side of Heraclius, and the governor of Tripolis arrived with reinforcements. High officials were conspiring to support the rebels in Alexandria itself, when the plot was revealed to Theodore, the imperialist patriarch. When the news reached Phocas he forthwith ordered the praefect of Byzantium to convey fresh troops with all speed to Alexandria and the Delta fortresses, while Bonosus, who was contemplating a seizure of the patriarch of Jerusalem, was summoned to leave the Holy City and to march against Nicetas. On the latter's advance, Alexandria refused to surrender, but resistance was short-lived, and the patriarch and general met their deaths. Treasure, shipping, the island and fortress of Pharos, all fell into the hands of Nicetas[1], while Bonâkis received the submission of many of the Delta towns. At Caesarea, where Bonosus took ship, he heard of the capture of Alexandria, and while his cavalry pursued the land route, his fleet in two divisions sailed up the Nile by the Pelusiac channel and by the main eastern arm of the river. At first Bonosus carried all before him and inflicted a crushing defeat near Manüf on the generals of Heraclius, thereby reconquering the Delta for Phocas, but he was repulsed from Alexandria with heavy loss and suffered so severely in a fresh advance from his base at Nikiou that he was forced to abandon Egypt

---

[1] According to Theophanes the corn-ships of Alexandria were prevented from reaching the capital from 608 onwards.

and to flee through Asia to Constantinople[1]. The imperialist resistance was at an end and the new rule was established in Egypt (apparently end of 609).

We have no certain information as to what the younger Heraclius was doing during the year 609, but it seems not unlikely that it was at this time that he occupied Thessalonica, for here he could draw reinforcements from the European malcontents. It is at least clear that, when he finally[2] started in 610 on his voyage to Constantinople, he gathered supporters from the sea-side towns and from the islands on his route. At the beginning of September, it would seem, he cast anchor at Abydus in Mysia, where he was joined by those whom Phocas had driven into exile. Crossing the Propontis he touched at Heraclea and Selimbria, and at the small island of Calonymus the Church, through the bishop of Cyzicus, blessed his enterprise. On Saturday, 3 Oct., the fleet, with images of the Virgin at the ships' mastheads, sailed under the sea-walls of the capital. But in face of the secret treachery of Priscus and the open desertion of the demesmen of the Green party the cause of Phocas was foredoomed; Heraclius waited upon his ship until the tyrant's own ministers dragged his enemy before him on the morning of 5 Oct. "Is it thus, wretch, that you have governed the State?" asked Heraclius. "Will you govern it any better?" retorted the fallen Emperor. He was forthwith struck down, and his body dismembered and carried through the city. Domentiolus and Leontius, the Syrian minister of finance, shared his fate and their bodies, together with that of Bonosus, were burned in the Ox Forum. In the afternoon of the same day Heraclius was crowned emperor by Sergius the patriarch: people and senate refused to listen to his plea that Priscus should be their monarch: they would not see in their liberator merely the avenger of Maurice, nor suffer him to return whence he came. On the same day Heraclius married Eudocia (as his betrothed, Fabia, daughter of Rogatus of Africa, was re-named) who became at once bride and empress. Three days later, in the Hippodrome, the statue of Phocas was burned and with it the standard of the Blues.

During 610 the Persians had been advancing westwards in the direction of Syria: Callinicum and Circesium had fallen and the Euphrates had been crossed. After his accession Heraclius sent an embassy to Persia: Maurice was now avenged, and peace could be restored between the two empires. Chosroes made no reply to the embassy: he had proved all too conclusively Rome's weakness and was not willing to surrender his advantage. Meanwhile Priscus was appointed general and sent to Cappadocia to undertake the siege of Caesarea, which was at this time in the occupation of the Persians. For

---

[1] For further details see John of Nikiou, and for a map of the Delta cf. Butler, *The Conquest of Egypt*, etc.

[2] Despite Theophanes 296[2], Alexandria probably did not fall till 609. Heraclius probably sailed from Africa in 610.

a year the enemy resisted, but at last, in the late summer of 611, famine drove them to evacuate the city. They cut their way through the Roman troops, inflicting serious loss, and retired to Armenia where they took up winter quarters. In the same year Emesa was lost to the Empire. In 612, on the news that the Persians were once more about to invade Roman territory in force, Heraclius left the capital to confer with Priscus in Caesarea. The general pleaded illness and treated the Emperor with marked coolness and disrespect. His ambitions were thwarted: he had gained nothing by the revolution and objected that the Emperor's place was in Constantinople: it was no duty of his to intermeddle personally with the conduct of the war. For the moment Heraclius had no forces with which to oppose Priscus; he was condemned to inaction and compelled to await his opportunity. In the summer Sahîn led his army to Karin, and reduced Melitene to submission, afterwards joining Sahrbarâz in the district of Dovin. The Persians were masters of Armenia. In 611 Eudocia had given birth to a daughter and in May 612 a son was born, but on 13 Aug. the Empress died. In 613 the Emperor, despite the protests of the Church, married his niece Martina. In the autumn of 612 Nicetas came to Constantinople, doubtless to confer with Heraclius as to the methods which were to be adopted in the government of Egypt. Priscus also made his way to the capital to honour the arrival of the Emperor's cousin, and was invited by Heraclius to act as sponsor at his son's christening which took place, it would seem, on 5 Dec. 612. Here the Emperor charged his general with treason, and forced him to enter a monastery. In Constantinople Priscus could no longer rely on the support of an army and resistance was impossible. Heraclius appealed to the troops then in the capital, and was enthusiastically greeted as their future captain. Nicetas succeeded Priscus as *comes excubitorum*, while the Emperor appointed his brother Theodore *curopalates*; he also induced Philippicus to leave the shelter of a religious house and once more to undertake a military command.

In the following year (613)[1] Heraclius was free to carry out his own plan of campaign: he determined to oppose the enemy on both their lines of attack. Philippicus was to invade Armenia, while he himself and his brother Theodore would check the Persian advance on Syria. The aim of Chosroes was clearly to occupy the Mediterranean coast line. A battle took place under the walls of Antioch, and there, after their army had been strengthened by reinforcements, the Persians succeeded in routing the Greeks: the road was now open for the southward march, and in this year Damascus fell. Further to the north the Roman troops held the defiles which gave access to Cilicia: though at first victorious,

---

[1] This chronology, which is not that adopted by recent authorities, the present writer hopes to justify in a detailed account of the campaigns of Heraclius which will shortly appear in the *United Service Magazine*.

in a second engagement they were put to flight; Cilicia and Tarsus were occupied by the enemy. Meanwhile in Armenia Philippicus had encamped at Valaršapat, but was compelled to beat a hurried retreat before the Persian forces. The Romans were repulsed on every side.

But the worst was not yet: with the year 614 came the overwhelming calamity of the fall of the Holy City. Advancing from Caesarea along the coast the Persians under Sahrbarâz arrived before Jerusalem in the month of April. Negotiations were put an end to by the violence of the circus factions, and the Roman relief force from Jericho, which was summoned by Modestus, was put to flight. The Persians pressed forward the siege, bringing up towers and rams, and finally breaching the walls on the twenty-first day from the investment of the city (? 3 or 5 May 614). For three days the massacre lasted, and the Jews joined the victors in venting their spite on their hated oppressors. We hear of 57,000 killed and 35,000 taken captive. Churches went up in flames, the patriarch Zacharias was carried into Persia and with him, to crown the disaster, went the Holy Cross. At the news Nicetas seems to have hastened to Palestine with all speed, but he could do no more than rescue the holy sponge and the holy lance, and these were despatched for safe custody to the capital. It was true that, when once Jerusalem was in his power, Chosroes was prepared to pursue a policy of conciliation: he deserted his former allies and the Jews were banished from the city, while leave was accorded to rebuild the ruined churches; but this did little to assuage the bitterness of the fact that a Christian empire had not been able to protect its most sacred sanctuary from the violence of the barbarian fire-worshipper.

In 615 the Persians began afresh that occupation of Asia Minor which had been interrupted by the evacuation of Caesarea in 611. When Sahîn marched towards Chalcedon, Philippicus invaded Persia, but the effort to draw off the enemy's forces proved unsuccessful. Asia Minor however was not Syria, and Sahîn realised that his position was insecure. He professed himself ready to consider terms of peace. Heraclius sailed over to the enemy's camp and from his ship carried on negotiations with the Persian general. Olympius, praetorian praefect, Leontius, praefect of the city, and Anastasius, the treasurer of St Sophia, were chosen as ambassadors, while the Senate wrote a letter to the Persian monarch in support of the Emperor's action. But as soon as Sahîn had crossed the frontier, the Roman envoys became prisoners and Chosroes would hear no word of peace.

Thus while Syria was lost to the Empire and while Slavs were ranging at will over the European provinces, Heraclius had to face the overwhelming problem of raising the necessary funds to carry on the war. Even from the scanty records which we possess of this period we can trace the Emperor's efforts towards economy: he reduced the number of the clergy who enjoyed office in the capital, and if any above

this authorised number desired residence in Constantinople, they were to
buy the privilege from the State (612).   Three years later the coins in
which the imperial largess was paid were reduced to half their value.
But in June 617 (?) yet another disaster overtook Heraclius.   The
Khagan of the Avars made overtures for peace, and Athanasius the
patrician and Kosmas the quaestor arranged a meeting between the
Emperor and the barbarian chief at Heraclea.   Splendid religious rites
and a magnificent circus display were to mark the importance of the
occasion, and huge crowds had poured forth from the city gates to be
present at the festivities.   But it was no longer increased money
payments that the Khagan sought: he aimed at nothing less than the
capture of Constantinople.   At a sign from his whip the ambushed
troops burst forth from their hiding-places about the Long Walls.
Heraclius saw his peril. throwing off his purple, with his crown under
his arm, he fled at a gallop to the city and warned its inhabitants.
Over the plain of the Hebdomon and up to the Golden Gate surged
the Avar host: they raided the suburbs, they pillaged the church of
Saints Cosmas and Damian in the Hebdomon, they crossed the Golden
Horn and broke in pieces the holy table in the church of the Archangel.
Fugitives who escaped reported that 270,000 prisoners, men and women,
had been swept away to be settled beyond the Danube, and there was
none to stay the Khagan's march.   In 618 those who were entitled at
the expense of the State to share in the public distribution of loaves
of bread were forced to make a contribution at the rate of three *nomismata*
to the loaf, and a few months later (Aug. 618) the public distribution
was entirely suspended.   Even such a deprivation as this was felt to
be inevitable: the chronicle of events in the capital does not record
any popular outbreak.

It was probably in the spring of 619 that the next step was
taken in the Persian plan of conquest, when Sahrbarâz invaded Egypt.
He advanced by the coast road, capturing Pelusium and spreading
havoc amongst its numerous churches and monasteries.   Babylon, near
Memphis, fell, and thence the Persians, supported by a strong flotilla,
followed the main western branch of the Nile past Nikiou to Alexandria
and began the siege of the Egyptian capital.   All the Emperor's
measures were indeed of little avail when Armenia, Rome's recruiting
ground, was occupied by Persia, and when Sahrbarâz, encamped round
Alexandria, had cut off the supply of Egyptian grain so that the capital
suffered alike from pestilence and scarcity of food.   The sole province
which appeared to offer any hope to the exhausted treasury was Africa,
and here only, it seemed, could an effective army be raised.   It was with
African troops that Nicetas had won Egypt in 609: even now, with
Carthage as a base of operations, the Persians might surely be re-
pelled and Egypt regained.   Thus reasoning, Heraclius prepared to set
sail from Europe (619 ?).   When his determination became known,

Constantinople was in despair; the inhabitants refused to see themselves deserted and the patriarch extracted an oath from the Emperor that he would not leave his capital. The turbulence of New Rome itself seems to have been silenced in this dark hour.

In Egypt Nicetas, despairing of the defence of Alexandria, had fled from the city, and Persians, disguised as fisher-folk, had entered the harbour at dawn with the other fishing-boats, cutting down any who resisted them, and had thrown open the gates to the army of Sahrbarâz (June 619). It did indeed seem that Chosroes was to be the master of the Roman world. About this time too (we do not know the precise year) the Persians, having collected a fleet[1], attacked Constantinople by water: it may well have been that this assault was timed to follow close upon the raid of the Avar horde. But upon the sea at least the Empire asserted its supremacy. The Persians fled, four thousand men perished with their ships, and the enemy did not dare to renew the attempt.

Heraclius realised that in order to carry war into Asia there must at all costs be peace in Europe. He sacrificed his pride and concluded a treaty with the Khagan (619). He raised 200,000 *nomismata* and sent[2] as hostages to the Avars his own bastard son John or Athalarich, his cousin Stephanus, and John the bastard son of Bonus the *magister*. Sergius had forced Heraclius to swear that he would not abandon Constantinople, and the Church now supplied the funds for the new campaign. It agreed to lend at interest its vast wealth in plate that the gold and silver might be minted into money; for this was no ordinary struggle: it was a crusade to rescue from the infidel the Holy City and the Holy Cross. Christian State and Christian Church must join hands against a common foe. While Persian troops overran Asia, penetrating even to Bithynia and the Black Sea, Heraclius made his preparations and studied his plan of campaign. From Africa he had been borne to empire under the protection of the Mother of God, and now it was with a conviction of the religious solemnity of his mission that he withdrew into privacy during the winter of 621 before he challenged the might of the unbeliever. He himself, despite the criticism of his subjects, would lead his forces in the field: in the strength of the God of Battles he would conquer or die.

On 4 April 622 Heraclius held a public communion; on the following day he summoned Sergius the patriarch and Bonus the *magister* together with the senate, the principal officials and the entire populace of the capital. Turning to Sergius, he said: "Into the hands of God and of His Mother and into thine I commend this city and my son." After solemn prayer in the cathedral, the Emperor took the sacred image of the Saviour and bore it from the church in his arms. The troops

---

[1] These may have been Roman ships captured at Tarsus and other harbours at this time occupied by Persia.

[2] So modern historians: but perhaps these hostages were given in 623.

then embarked and in the evening of the same day, 5 April, the fleet set sail. Despite a violent storm on 6 April the Emperor arrived in safety at the small town of Pylae in the Bay of Nicomedia. Thence Heraclius marched "into the region of the themes," *i.e.* in all probability Galatia and perhaps Cappadocia. Here the work of concentration was carried out · the Emperor collected the garrisons and added to their number his new army. In his first campaign the object of Heraclius was to force the Persian troops to withdraw from Asia Minor: he sought to pass the enemy on the flank, to threaten his communications and to appear to be striking at the very heart of his native country. The Persians had occupied the mountains, hoping thus to confine the imperial troops within the Pontic provinces during the winter, but by clever strategy Heraclius turned their position and marched towards Armenia. Sahrbarâz endeavoured to draw the Roman army after him by a raid on Cilicia; but, realising that Heraclius could thus advance unopposed through Armenia into the interior of Persia, he abandoned the project and followed the Emperor. Heraclius at length forced a general engagement and won a signal victory. The Persian camp was captured and Sahrbarâz's army almost entirely destroyed. Rumours of impending trouble with the western barbarians in Europe recalled Heraclius to the capital, and his army went into winter quarters. The Emperor had freed Asia Minor from the invader.

Chosroes now addressed a haughty letter to Heraclius which the Emperor caused to be read before his ministers and the patriarch: the despatch itself was laid before the high altar and all with tears implored the succours of Heaven. In reply to Chosroes Heraclius offered the Persian monarch an alternative: either let him accept conditions of peace, or, should he refuse, the Roman army would forthwith invade his kingdom. On 25 March 623 the Emperor left the capital, and celebrated Easter in Nicomedia on 15 April, awaiting, it would seem, the enemy's answer. Here, in all probability, he learned that Chosroes refused to consider terms and treated with contempt the threat of invasion. Thus (20 April) Heraclius set out on his invasion of Persia, marching into Armenia with all speed by way of Caesarea, where he had ordered his army to assemble[1]. Chosroes had commanded Sahrbarâz to make a raid upon the territory of the Empire, but on the news of the sudden advance of Heraclius he was immediately recalled, and was bidden to join his forces to the newly raised troops under Sahîn. From Caesarea Heraclius proceeded through Karin to Dovin: the Christian capital of the province of Ararat was stormed, and after the capture of Nachčavan he made for Ganzaca (Takhti-Soleïmán), since he heard that Chosroes was here in person at the head of 40,000 men. On the defeat of his guards,

[1] The reader is warned that this paragraph rests upon an interpretation of the authorities which is peculiar to the present writer. This he hopes to justify in his special study (to appear in *B.Z.* June 1912) on the date of the Avar surprise.

however, the Persian king fled before the invaders; the city fell, while
the great temple which sheltered the fire of Ušnasp was reduced to
ruins. Heraclius followed after Chosroes, and sacked many cities on his
march, but did not venture to press the pursuit: before him lay the
enemy's country and the Persian army, while his rear might at any
moment be threatened by the united advance of Sahrbarâz and Sahîn.
Despite opposition, extreme cold, and scarcity of provisions he crossed
the Araxes in safety, carrying some 50,000 prisoners in his train. It
was shrewd policy which dictated their subsequent release; it created
a good impression and, as a result, there were fewer mouths to feed.

It was doubtless primarily as a recruiting ground that Heraclius sought
these Caucasian districts—the home of hardy and warlike mountaineers—
for the sorely harried provinces of Asia Minor were probably in no
condition to supply him with large contingents of troops. This is not
however the place to recount in detail the complicated story of the
operations of the winter of 623 and of the year 624. Sahîn was utterly
discomfited at Tigranokert, but Heraclius was himself forced to retire
into Armenia before the army of Sahrbarâz (winter, 623). With the
spring of 624 we find Lazes, Abasges and Iberians as Roman allies,
though they subsequently deserted the Emperor when disappointed in
their expectations of spoil and plunder. Heraclius was once more unable
to penetrate into Persia, but was occupied in Armenia, marching and
countermarching between forces commanded by Sarablangas, Sahrbarâz
and Sahîn. Sarablangas was slain, and late in the year Van was captured,
and Sahrbarâz surprised in his winter quarters at Arces or Arsissa (at the
N.E. end of Lake Van). The Persian general was all but taken prisoner,
and very few of the garrison, 6000 strong, escaped destruction.

With the new year (625) Heraclius determined to return to the
West, before he once more attempted a direct attack upon Persia. We
can only conjecture the reasons which led him to take this step, but it
would seem probable that the principal inducement was a desire to assert
Roman influence in the south of Asia Minor and in the islands. The
Persians had occupied Cilicia before the capture of Jerusalem; in 623
it would appear that they had made a raid upon Rhodes, had seized the
Roman general and led off the inhabitants as prisoners, while in the
same year we are told that the Slavs had entered Crete. There is some
evidence which points to the conclusion that the Emperor was at this
time very anxious to recover the ground thus lost. There was considerable doubt however as to which route should be pursued—that
through Taranda or that by way of the Taurus chain. The latter was
chosen despite its difficulty, as it was thought that provisions would be
thus more plentiful. From Van the army advanced through Martyropolis
and Amida, where the troops rested. But meanwhile Sahrbarâz, in hot
pursuit, had arrived first at the Euphrates and removed the bridge of
boats. The Emperor however crossed by a ford and reached Samosata

before March was out. As to the precise route which he followed on his march to the Sarus there is considerable dispute[1], but there is no doubt that after a hotly contested engagement on that river Heraclius forced the Persian general to beat a hasty retreat under cover of night. It seems probable that the Emperor remained for a considerable time in this district, but our sources fail us here, and we know only that he ultimately marched to Sebastia, and crossing the Halys spent the winter in that Pontic district where he had left his army at the end of the first campaign.

The following year (626) is memorable for the great siege of the capital by the united hordes of Avars, Bulgars, Slavs and Gepids, acting in concert with a Persian force, which endeavoured to co-operate with them from the Asiatic side of the strait. Sahrbarâz' ill success on the Sarus led Chosroes, we are told, to withdraw from his command 50,000 men and to place them, together with a new army raised indiscriminately from foreigners, citizens and slaves, under the leadership of Sahîn. Sahrbarâz, with the remainder of his army, took up his position at Chalcedon with orders to support the Khagan in his attack on Constantinople. Heraclius in turn divided his forces: part were sent to garrison the capital, part he entrusted to his brother Theodore who was to meet the "Golden Lances" of Sahîn, and the rest the Emperor himself retained. Of Theodore's campaign we know nothing save the result: with the assistance of a timely hail-storm and by the aid of the Virgin he so signally defeated Sahîn that the latter died of mortification. Of the operations in Europe we are better informed. From the moment that Heraclius had left the capital on his crusade against Persia the Khagan had been making vast preparations, in the hope of capturing Constantinople. It was the menace from the Danubian provinces which had recalled Heraclius in the winter of 623, and now at last the Avar host was ready. On Sunday, 29 June, on the festival of St Peter and St Paul, the advance guard, 30,000 strong, reached the suburb of Melanthias and announced that their leader had passed within the circuit of the Long Walls. Early in the year, it seems, Bonus and Sergius had sent the patrician Athanasius as an ambassador to the Avar chief, virtually offering to buy him off at his own terms. But since the spring the walls had been strengthened, reinforcements had arrived from Heraclius and his stirring letters had awakened in the citizens a new spirit of confidence and enthusiasm. Athanasius, who had been kept a prisoner by the Khagan, was now sent from Hadrianople to learn the price at which the capital was prepared to purchase safety. He was amazed at the change in public feeling, but volunteered to carry back the city's proud reply. On 29 July 626 the Avars and the countless forces of their subject tribesmen encamped

---

[1] There are difficulties in accepting the emendations of the text of Theophanes proposed by J. G. C. Anderson, "The Road-System of Eastern Asia Minor," *J. H. S.* xvii. (1897), pp. 33–34.

before New Rome. The full story of the heroic defence cannot be related in this place, but one consideration is too important to be omitted. Had the Romans not been masters of the sea, the issue might well have been less favourable; but the small Slav boats were all sunk or over-turned in the waters of the Golden Horn, while Sahrbarâz at Chalcedon was doomed to remain inactive, for Persia possessed no transports and the Roman fleet made it impossible for the besiegers to carry their allies across the straits. Thus at the very time that the barbarian attack by sea collapsed in hopeless failure, the citizens had repulsed with heavy loss the assault on the land walls which was directed mainly against that section where the depression of the Lycus valley rendered the defences most vulnerable. At length, on the eleventh day after his appearance before Constantinople, the Khagan destroyed by fire his engines of war and withdrew, vowing a speedy return with forces even more overwhelming. As the suburbs of the city and the churches of Saints Cosmas and Damian and St Nicholas went up in flames, men marked that the shrine of the Mother of God in Blachernae remained inviolate: it was but one more token of her power—her power with God, with her Son, and in the general ordering of the world. The preservation of the city was the Virgin's triumph, it was her answer to the prayers of her servants, and with an annual festival the Church celebrated the memory of the great deliverance. Bonus and Sergius had loyally responded to their Emperor's trust[1].

This was indeed the furthest advance of the Avars. They had appeared in the Eastern Alps as early as 595–596, and had formally invested Thessalonica in 597; it would seem that the city was only saved through an outbreak of pestilence amongst the besiegers[2]. After 604 there was no Roman army in the Danube provinces, and in the reign of Phocas and the early years of Heraclius must be placed the ravaging of Dalmatia by Avars and Slavs and the fall of Salonae and other towns. At this time fugitives from Salonae founded the city of Spalato, and those from Epidaurus the settlement which afterwards became Ragusa. A contemporary tells how the Slavs in those dark days of confusion and ravage plundered the greater part of Illyricum, all Thessaly, Epirus, Achaia, the Cyclades and a part of Asia. In another passage the same author relates how Avars and Slavs destroyed the towns in the provinces of Pannonia, Moesia Superior, the two Dacias, Rhodope, Dardania and Praevalis, carrying off the inhabitants into slavery. Fallmerayer's famous contention that the Greek people was virtually exterminated is certainly an exaggeration, though throughout Hellas there must have been Slav forays, and many a barbarian band

---

[1] The date of the composition of the *Hymnus Acathistus* would appear, despite an enormous literature on the subject, to remain still undetermined.

[2] Pestilence had also served the city well when besieged by the Goths. For the siege, cf. W. Wroth, *op. cit.* I. p. xxi.

must have planted itself on Greek soil.   But when all is said, the
remarkable fact remains that while in the Danube provinces Roman
influence was submerged, Hellenism within its native territory asserted
its supremacy over the Slav invader and maintained alike its natural
language and character.   Thus towards the close of our period amongst
the chaos of peoples making good their independence of the Avar overlordship there gradually emerged certain settlements which formed the
nucleus of nations yet to be.   Not that Heraclius invited into the
Empire Croats and Serbs from a mythical Serbia and Croatia somewhere
in the North—Croats and Serbs had already won by force their own
ground within the Roman frontier—but rather he recognised and
legalised their position as vassals of the Empire, and thus took up the
proud task of educating the southern Slavs to receive civilisation and
Christianity.

In 626, while the capital played its part, the Emperor was making
provision for striking a conclusive blow at Persia.   He needed allies and
reinforcements, and he once more sought them among the tribesmen of the
Caucasus.   It is probable that as early as the autumn of 625 he had sent
a certain Andrew as envoy to the Chazars[1], and in 626 a force of 1000
men invaded the valley of the Kur and pillaged Iberia and Eger, so that
Chosroes threatened punishment and talked of withdrawing Sahrbaráz
from the West.   The Chazars even took ship and visited the Emperor,
when mutual vows of friendship were interchanged.   In the early summer
of 627 the nephew of Dzebukhan (Ziebel) ravaged Albania and parts of
Atropatene.   Later in the year (after June 627), envious of the booty
thus won, the Chazar prince took the field in person with his son, and
captured the strongly fortified post of Derbend.   Gashak, who had been
despatched by Persia to organise the defence of the north, was unable to
protect the city of Partav and fled ignominiously.   After these successes
Dzebukhan joined the Emperor (who took ship from Trebizond[2]) in the
siege of Tiflis.   The Chazar chieftain, irritated by a pumpkin caricature
of himself which the inhabitants had displayed upon the walls, was
eager for revenge and refused to abandon the investment of the city,
though he agreed to give the Emperor a large force raised from his
subjects when the Roman army started on the last great campaign in
the autumn of 627[3].

---

[1] The chronology of this paragraph rests in part upon the view that Moses
of Kagankaitukh Kal has effected some transpositions in the apparently contemporary
source which was used by him in this part of his work.

[2] Our sources are agreed that Heraclius went to the Chazar country by ship.
The departure from Trebizond is on conjecture based on Eutychius, ed. Pococke, II.
p. 231.   For a discussion of the authorities, cf. Gerland, *B. Z.* III. pp. 341 ff.

[3] Tiflis subsequently fell: on the peace of 628 Iberia became once more Roman,
and Heraclius set Adarnase I upon the throne; cf. J. Marquart, *Osteuropäische und
ostasiatische Streifzüge*, pp. 400 ff.

Heraclius advanced through Sirak to the Araxes, and, crossing the river, entered the province of Ararat. He now found himself opposed by Râhzâdh, a Persian general who was probably advancing to the relief of Tiflis. But though the Chazar auxiliaries, dismayed by the approach of winter and by the attacks of the Persians, returned to their homes, the Emperor continued his march southward through Her and Zarewand west of the Lake of Urmiyah and reached the province of Atropatene. Pressing forward, he crossed the mountain chain which divides Media from Assyria, arriving at Chnaitha 9 Oct., where he gave his men a week's rest. Râhzâdh had meanwhile reached Ganzaca and thence followed the Emperor across the mountains, suffering severely on his march from scarcity of supplies. By 1 Dec. the Emperor reached the greater Zab and, crossing the river (*i.e.* marching north-west), took up his position at Nineveh. Here (12 Dec.) he won a decisive victory over Râhzâdh. The Persian general himself fell, and his troops, though not completely demoralised, were in no condition to renew the struggle. On 21 Dec. the Emperor learned that the defeated Persians had effected a junction with the reinforcements, 3000 strong, sent from the capital; he continued his southern march, however, crossing the lesser Zab (28 Dec.) and spending Christmas on the estates of the wealthy superintendent of provincial taxation, Iesdem. During the festival, acting on urgent despatches from Chosroes, the Persian army crossed the Zab higher up its course, and thus interposed a barrier between Heraclius and Ctesiphon. The Emperor on his advance found the stream of the Torna (probably the N. arm of the Nahr Wán canal) undefended, while the Persians had retreated so hurriedly that they had not even destroyed the bridge. After the passage of the Torna he reached (1 Jan. 628) Beklal (? Beit-Germa), and there learnt that Chosroes had given up his position on the Berázrúd canal, had deserted Dastagerd and fled to Ctesiphon. Dastagerd was thus occupied without a struggle and three hundred Roman standards were recovered, while the troops were greeted by numbers of those who had been carried prisoners from Edessa, Alexandria and other cities of the Empire. On 7 Jan. Heraclius advanced from Dastagerd towards Ctesiphon, and on 10 Jan. he was only twelve miles from the Nahr Wán; but the Armenians, who had been sent forward to reconnoitre, brought back word that in face of the Persian troops it was impossible to force the passage of the canal. Heraclius after the battle of Nineveh had been, it would seem, ready to make terms, but Chosroes had rejected his overtures. In an enemy's country, with Persian troops in a strong defensive position blocking his path, with his forces in all probability much reduced and with no present opportunity of raising others, knowing that Sahrbaráz was still in command of a Persian army in the West with which he could attack his rear, while the severity of winter, though delayed, was now threatening, Heraclius was compelled to retreat. Chosroes had at least been driven to inglorious flight: the disgrace might well weaken his subjects' loyalty, and any such lessening of the royal prestige could only strengthen the position of the Romans; the Emperor even by his enforced withdrawal might not thereby lose the fruits of victory.   By Shahrizúr he returned to Baneh, and thence over the Zagros chain to Ganzaca, where he arrived 11 March—only just in time, for snow began to fall 24 Feb. and made the mountain roads impassable.

But with the spring no new campaign was necessary; on 3 April 628 an envoy from the Persian court reached Ganzaca announcing the violent death of Chosroes and the accession of his son Siroes; the latter offered to conclude peace, and this proposal Heraclius was willing to accept. On 8 April the embassy left for Ctesiphon, while on the same day the Emperor turned his face homeward and in a despatch to the capital, announcing the end of the struggle, expressed the hope that he would soon see his people again.   It is uncertain what were the precise terms of the peace of 628, but they included the restoration of the Cross and the evacuation of the Empire's territory by the armies of Persia.   It is probable that the Roman frontier was to follow the line agreed upon in the treaty of 591.   These conditions were, it would seem, accepted by Siroes (Feb.—Sept. 628), but Sahrbarâz had never moved from Western Asia since 626 and it was doubtful whether he would comply with such terms.   Thus when the Cross was once more in Roman hands, Heraclius was able to distribute portions of the Holy Wood amongst the more influential Christians of Armenia—a politic prelude to his schemes of church union—but felt it necessary to remain in the East to secure the triumph which he had so hardly won.   After a winter spent at Amida, in the early spring the Emperor journeyed to Jerusalem and (23 March 630) amidst a scene of unbounded religious enthusiasm restored to the Holy City the instrument of the world's salvation. On the feast of St Lazarus (7 April) the news reached Constantinople, and Christendom celebrated a new resurrection from the power of its oppressors; a fragment of the true Cross sent from Jerusalem served but to deepen the city's exultation[1].

Sahrbarâz however refused to withdraw his army from Roman soil, and in June 629 Heraclius met him at Arabissus and purchased his concurrence by a promise to support him with imperial troops in his attempt to secure the Persian throne.   Sahrbarâz marched to Ctesiphon, only to perish after a month's reign, and thus the Empire was freed from the invader.   In September Heraclius returned to the capital and after six years' campaigning enjoyed a well-earned sabbath of repose.   It is an important moment in Roman history: the King of kings, the Empire's only rival, was humbled and Heraclius could now for the first time add

---

[1] This chronology differs widely from that adopted by recent authors (*e.g.* Bolotov and Marr).   A hitherto unnoticed passage in a contemporary document—the Ἐπάνοδος τοῦ λειψάνου τοῦ ἁγίου μάρτυρος Ἀναστασίου ἐκ Περσίδος εἰς τὸ μοναστήριον αὐτοῦ (Acta Martyris Anastasii Persae, ed. Usener, p. 12, 34a)—seems to show that Heraclius did not reach Jerusalem until A.D. 630, whence he travelled to Constantina.

to the imperial style the proud title of βασιλεύς. The restoration of
the Cross suggested the sign which had been given to the great Constantine,
and Africa adopted (629) the first Greek inscription to be found on the
imperial coinage—the motto ἐν τούτῳ νίκα. This may stand for us as
a symbol of the decline of the Latin element within the Empire: from
the reign of Phocas the old Roman names disappear and those of Graeco-
Oriental origin take their place.

With these campaigns the period of the successors of Justinian has
reached its end and a new epoch begins. The great contest between
the Empires has weakened both combatants and has rendered possible
the advance of the invaders from the South. Spain has driven out her
last imperial garrisons, the Lombards are settled in Italy, the Slavs
have permanently occupied the Danubian provinces—Rome's dominions
take a new shape and the statesmen of Constantinople are faced with
fresh problems. Imperialist dreams are past, and for a time there is no
question of expansion: at moments it is a struggle for bare existence.
In his capital the old Emperor, broken in health and harassed by
domestic feuds, watches the peril from the desert spreading over the
lands which his sword had regained and views the ruin of his cherished
plans for a united Empire.

The character of Heraclius has fascinated the minds of historians
from the time of Gibbon to the present day, but surely much of the
riddle rests in our scanty knowledge of the early years of his reign: the
more we know, the more comprehensible does the Emperor become.
At the first Priscus commanded the troops and Priscus was disaffected:
Heraclius was powerless, for he had no army with which to oppose his
mutinous general. With the disappearance of Priscus the Emperor was
faced with the problem of raising men and money from a ruined and
depopulated empire. After the ill-success of his untrained army in 613,
by the loss of Syria and Egypt the richest provinces and even the few
recruiting grounds that remained fell into the enemy's hands. Heraclius
was powerless: the taunt of Phocas must have rung in his ears: "Will
you govern the Empire any better?" Africa appeared the sole way of
escape: among those who knew him and his family he might awake
sacrifice and enthusiasm and obtain the sinews of war. The project
worked wonders—but in other ways than he had schemed. Men were
impressed by the strength of his sincerity and the force of his personality
—more, the Church would lend her wealth. Then came the Khagan's
treachery—the loss of thousands of men who might have been enrolled
in the new regiments which he was raising: the peace with the Avars
and after two more years had been spent in further preparations,
including probably the building of fresh fortifications for the capital
which he was leaving to its own resources, the campaigns against Persia.
At last, through long-continued hardships in the field, through ceaseless
labours that defied ill-health, his physical strength gave way and he

became a prey to disease and nervous fears. Do we really need fine-spun psychological theories to explain the reign with its alternations of failure and success? It may at least be doubted.

Yet it is not in these last years of gloom and suspicion that we would part with Heraclius: we would rather recall in him despite all his limitations the successful general, the unremitting worker for the preservation and unity of the Empire which he had sailed from Africa to save, an enthusiast with the power to inspire others, a practical mystic serving the Lord Christ and the Mother of God—one of the greatest of Rome's Caesars.

CHAPTER X.

MAHOMET AND ISLĀM.

OUR knowledge of Mahomet, his life and his teaching, is derived entirely from documents which have been handed down by Muslims; no contemporary non-Muslim account is extant, and the testimony of later non-Muslim writers has as little claim to consideration as the statements in the Talmud concerning Christ. Among our authorities the Koran, for obvious reasons, occupies the foremost place. The pieces of which it is composed are acknowledged, alike by those who assert and by those who deny its supernatural character, to have been promulgated as divine revelations by the Founder of the religion himself, nor is there any ground for the supposition that the text underwent substantial change in later times. But although the authenticity of the Koran admits of no dispute its interpretation is involved in peculiar difficulties. It was not put together till about two years after Mahomet's death, and the arrangement of the chapters is wholly arbitrary, without regard to subject-matter or chronological sequence. Even a single chapter, as is recognised not only by modern European critics but also by all Muslim theologians of repute, sometimes consists of earlier and later fragments which were combined either by accident or through some mistake as to their import. Such mistakes were all the more likely to occur in consequence of the peculiarly allusive style in which the Koran is written; when it refers to contemporary persons or events, which is often the case, it seldom mentions them in explicit terms, but employs various circumlocutions. Hence it is impossible to explain the book without continually calling in the aid of Muslim tradition, as embodied in the works of theologians and historians, the earliest of whom lived some generations after the time of the Prophet. This literature is of enormous extent, but it contains many unintentional misrepresentations and many deliberate falsehoods. To separate the historical from the unhistorical elements is often difficult and sometimes impossible.

The condition of Arabia in pre-Muslim times is, from the nature of the case, very imperfectly known to us. The great majority of the inhabitants consisted of small nomadic tribes who recognised no authority but that of their own chiefs. The nomads, being wholly ignorant of the art of writing, could leave behind them no permanent records, and as tribes were frequently broken up, in consequence of famine, internal dissensions and other calamities, their oral traditions had little chance of surviving. It was only in a few districts that a settled and comparatively civilised population existed. Wherever such a centre of civilisation was formed, the nomads in the immediate vicinity had a tendency to fall under the influence of their more cultured neighbours, and sometimes tribal confederacies, dignified with the name of "kingdoms," came into being. In early times, by far the most important of these civilised regions was to be found in south-western Arabia, the land of the Sabaeans, or, as it is now called, *Yaman* (*i.e.* the South). The power and prosperity of the Sabaeans, to which innumerable ruins and inscriptions still bear witness, began to decline about the time of Christ and were utterly overthrown, near the beginning of the sixth century, by the inroads of the half-savage Abyssinians. Meanwhile other Arabian kingdoms had arisen in the north, in particular that of the clan called the Ghassān, on the eastern frontier of Palestine, and that of the Lakhm on the Euphrates; the former kingdom was politically subject to the Byzantine Emperors, the latter to the Persians. But about the time when Mahomet came forward as a prophet both of these vassal kingdoms ceased to exist, and for a while there was nowhere within the borders of Arabia any political organisation which deserved to be called a State.

In religious, as in political matters, Arabia presented no appearance of unity. The paganism of the Arabs was in general of a remarkably crude and inartistic kind, with no ritual pomp, no elaborate mythology and, it hardly needs to be said, no tinge of philosophical speculation. The religion of the ancient Sabaeans probably bore a greater resemblance to that of the more advanced nations, but in the time of Mahomet this Sabaean religion was almost wholly forgotten, and the paganism which still survived consisted mainly of certain very primitive rites performed at particular sanctuaries. An Arabian sanctuary was, in some cases, a rudely constructed edifice containing images of the gods or other objects of worship, but often it was nothing more than an open space marked by a sacred tree or a few blocks of stone. Some sanctuaries were frequented only by members of a particular tribe, while others were annually visited by various tribes from far and near. The settled Arabs, as a rule, paid more attention than the nomads to religion, but even in the settled districts there seems to have been a singular lack of religious fervour. The traditional rites were kept up from mere conservatism and with hardly any definite belief as to their meaning. Hence wherever the Arabs came into close contact with a foreign religion, they readily adopted it, at least in name. Arabian communities professing some sort of Christianity were to be found not only on the northern frontier but also at Najrān in the south. Judaised communities were especially numerous in the north-west of the Arabian peninsula, and Zoroastrian communities in the neighbourhood of the Persian Gulf.

Among the centres of Arabian paganism none occupied a more distinguished place than Mecca (in Arabic *Makka*, or sometimes *Bakka*) which, thirteen centuries ago, was a small town situated in a barren valley, about 50 miles from the Red Sea coast. In an open space near the middle of the town stood the local sanctuary, a kind of rectangular hut, known as the *Ka'ba* (*i.e.* Cube), which contained an image of the Meccan god Hubal and various other sacred objects. A large proportion of the Arabian tribes regarded Mecca with exceptional veneration; all the surrounding district was a sacred territory, within which no blood might be shed. Some miles from the town a yearly festival took place and was attended by crowds of pilgrims from all quarters. Recent investigations have proved that this institution, called in Arabic the *Ḥajj*, *i.e.* "festival" or "pilgrimage[1]," originally had no connexion with Mecca itself, and may possibly have been established before Mecca and the Ka'ba had come into existence. However this may be, it is certain that in historical times the pilgrims who attended the festival usually visited the Ka'ba and were treated by the Meccans as their guests; hence the annual Pilgrimage came to be intimately associated with the holy city.

In the sixth century after Christ most of the inhabitants of Mecca belonged to a tribe which bore the name of Ḳuraish. It was well known, however, that the Ḳuraish were recent immigrants. Both the town and the sanctuary had formerly been in the possession of other tribes, but as to the origin of Mecca no credible tradition survived. The Ḳuraish were subdivided into a number of clans, each of which claimed the right of managing its own affairs. On important occasions the chief men of the various clans met to deliberate; but there was no central authority. The sterility of the soil rendered agriculture almost impossible, and the Meccans had long subsisted by trading with distant countries. Every year great caravans were despatched to Syria and returned laden with wares, which the Meccans sold at a large profit to the neighbouring Bedouins. The mercantile population of the town was naturally far superior, in general intelligence and knowledge of the outer world, to the mass of the Arabs. A considerable proportion of the Meccans had learnt the art of writing, but they used it for practical purposes only. Book-learning, as we understand it, was quite unknown to them.

At Mecca, about A.D. 570[2], Mahomet (properly *Muḥammad*) was born. The clan to which he belonged, the Banū Hāshim, is commonly represented by Muslim writers as one of the most distinguished branches

---

[1] A pilgrimage to Mecca which is not performed in connexion with the yearly festival is called *'umra*, *i.e.* "visit," sometimes translated by "lesser pilgrimage."

[2] The evidence clearly shews that the early disciples of the Prophet had no trustworthy information as to the precise year of his birth.

of the Ḳuraish, but the evidence which we possess tends to prove that in pre-Muslim times it occupied quite a subordinate place. Of Mahomet's father, 'Abdallāh, son of 'Abd-al-Muṭṭalib, we know scarcely anything except that he died shortly before the Prophet's birth. Āmina, the mother of Mahomet, died a very few years later, and the orphan boy afterwards lived for a while in the charge of his grandfather, 'Abd-al-Muṭṭalib, who had a numerous family. On the death of 'Abd-al-Muṭṭalib, one of his sons, Abū Ṭālib, undertook the care of Mahomet, who seems to have been treated kindly but to have endured many hardships, since none of his near relatives were wealthy. When he was about 24 years of age he entered the service of an opulent woman, considerably older than himself, named Khadīja. The antecedents and social position of Khadīja are shrouded in some mystery[1], but it is certain that she had been twice married and that at the time when she made the acquaintance of Mahomet she was living at Mecca with several of her children, who were still quite young. Mahomet appears to have succeeded at once in gaining her confidence. She entrusted him with the management of her property, and about the year 594 sent him to Syria on a commercial expedition, which he directed with conspicuous success. On his return he became her husband. For a few years he led the life of a prosperous tradesman; several daughters were born to him and two sons, both of whom died in infancy.

The process whereby Mahomet was led to occupy himself with religious questions and finally to believe in his divine mission is altogether obscure. That the doctrines which he afterwards preached did not arise spontaneously in his mind but were mainly derived from older religions seems obvious. It appears certain, however, that he was wholly unacquainted with religious literature. Whether he ever learnt the Arabic alphabet is a question which has been fiercely debated, both among Muslims and Christians; at all events we know that, in his later years, whenever he wished to record anything in writing he employed a secretary. But the question whether he could read is of little practical importance, since no religious books seem to have existed in Arabic at that period, and that he could read any foreign language is utterly incredible. We are therefore obliged to conclude that his information was derived entirely from oral sources; who his informants were we can only conjecture. At Mecca itself there was apparently no permanent colony of Christians, Jews or Zoroastrians, but isolated adherents of the principal foreign religions doubtless visited the town from time to time[2]. It has often been suggested that Mahomet

---

[1] See Robertson Smith, *Kinship and Marriage in Early Arabia*, 2nd ed. 1903, pp. 289, 290, who supposes that something discreditable has been deliberately concealed.

[2] We learn from the Koran (chaps. xvi. 105, xxv. 5) that the heathen Meccans accused Mahomet of fabricating his revelations out of material supplied by some foreigner, or foreigners—a charge which the Prophet vehemently denies. It may

acquired some knowledge of Christianity during one of his commercial journeys in Syria. This is possible; but it should be remembered that an Arab trader, ignorant both of Aramaic and of Greek, would have great difficulty in obtaining information on religious subjects from Syrian Christians, since those of them who spoke Arabic usually belonged to the most illiterate class. Moreover another and a very important fact has to be taken into consideration. According to Muslim tradition there were about this time, at Mecca and a few other places in western Arabia, certain individuals who had become dissatisfied with the popular paganism, devoted themselves to religious meditation and professed a monotheistic belief. These persons were called Ḥanīfs, a term of which the origin and precise meaning are obscure. The Ḥanīfs did not form a sect, for they had no organisation and, it would seem, little communication with one another. Our information about them is naturally very meagre, being derived, for the most part, from scraps of poetry which they are said to have composed; but the authenticity of these pieces is often doubtful. One of the most celebrated Ḥanīfs was the Meccan Zaid ibn 'Amr, who appears to have died during Mahomet's boyhood. Another was Waraḳa ibn Naufal, a cousin of Khadīja. This man died, at a very advanced age, some years after Mahomet's marriage. The relation in which he stood to the Prophet renders him an object of peculiar interest: it is therefore all the more to be regretted that so little can be ascertained concerning him. According to one tradition, he ended by adopting Christianity, which is possibly true; he is also said to have translated part of the Christian Scriptures into Arabic, which is highly improbable. But vague as is our knowledge of the Ḥanīfs in general and of Waraḳa in particular, we are justified in believing that before Mahomet's birth a movement in the direction of spiritual monotheism had already begun among the Arabs. How far this movement was originally due to Christian and other foreign influences we can scarcely hope to determine. Our acquaintance with Oriental Christianity in the sixth century is almost entirely confined to the great official Churches; the smaller Christian communities, and especially the half-Christian sects, with whom the Arabs were likely to come in contact, have, with rare exceptions, left no literary records.

With regard to the beginning of Mahomet's prophetic career, and the circumstances under which he received his earliest revelations, we possess many legends but very little genuine tradition. All accounts

be added that Muslim legends about the Prophet's intercourse with Christians and Jews, during the earlier part of his life, are open to the gravest suspicion, since nearly all these stories have an apologetic purpose, namely to prove that the Christian or Jew in question *recognised* Mahomet as a prophet by means of some sign, in particular by a mark on the back, which mark is termed "the seal of the prophetic calling."

agree as to the fact that at this period he spent much time in fastings and solitary vigils, a practice which was probably suggested to him by the example of Christian ascetics. He appears to have been naturally of a nervous temperament, with a tendency to hysteria; whether he suffered from epilepsy, as several European writers have believed, may be doubted[1]. In any case he was subject to paroxysms which presented the appearance of a violent fever; these seizures were regarded, both by himself and by his followers, as symptoms of divine inspiration. It is therefore evident that we are here dealing with a psychological problem which no information would enable us to solve.

The Koran (chap. lxxxvii. 6, 7) admits that Mahomet forgot some of the communications made to him by God, and it is possible that even the oldest passages now extant were produced some time after he had become conscious of his divine vocation. One point seems quite clear, namely that during the first few years of his mission he did not come forward as a public preacher but carried on a secret propaganda within the circle of his more intimate companions. Among the earliest converts were his wife Khadīja, his cousin Ali (properly *'Alī*), son of Abū Ṭālib, and Abū Bakr, who did not belong to the Prophet's clan but remained to the last his most trusted friend. The passages of the Koran which can with any probability be assigned to this more private period are few in number and invariably very short. Those which belong to the earlier part of his public career are much more numerous. They deal mainly with three subjects, (1) the unity and attributes of God, (2) the moral duties of mankind, and (3) the coming retribution. Mahomet's monotheism, like that of the later Hebrew prophets, necessarily involves the condemnation of idolatry, but it is to be noted that he nowhere describes the religion of his pagan fellow-countrymen as something wholly false. Though he identifies the one true God with the God of the Jews[2] and the Christians, he at the same time assumes that the heathen have some knowledge of God[3] and even that God is, in some special sense, the God of Mecca. In a very early passage of the Koran (chap. cvi.) the Ḳuraish are

---

[1] The hypothesis of epilepsy is decidedly rejected by De Goeje, "Die Berufung Mohammed's," in *Orientalische Studien* (Nöldeke-Festschrift), Giessen, 1906, I. pp. 1–5.

[2] The term *Raḥmān*, "the Merciful," which is often used in the Koran as synonymous with "God," was unknown to the heathen Meccans and seems to have been borrowed from the Jews. It may be mentioned, however, that this word appears as an epithet of the Deity not only in Jewish literature but also in the inscriptions of the heathen Syrians.

[3] The ancient poets of pagan Arabia frequently speak of "God" (*Allāh*) in a manner which seems to imply that they recognised Him as the supreme Being. How they conceived the relation between this "God" and the various local deities it is impossible to say with any precision. According to the Koran (chap. xvi. 59 ff.) the heathen regarded certain of their goddesses as the "daughters" of Allāh, but it would be unsafe to assume that the heathen themselves used this phrase in a literal sense, since "daughters of God" may mean (as with the Gnostics) nothing more than "female divine beings."

exhorted to worship "the Lord of this house," that is, of the Ka'ba. Hence it is evident that Mahomet considered himself rather as a reformer than as a preacher of an altogether new religion. Similarly in dealing with ethical questions he often implies that the pagan notions of justice, honour and propriety are to some extent valid. Thus, for instance, his repeated denunciations of avarice are quite in the spirit of the ancient Arabs, to whom the "miser" was an object of special abhorrence.

But in contradistinction to the ethical code of the heathen, which was mainly based upon tribal patriotism ('aṣabīya), Mahomet emphasises the universal obligations of morality, and above all the duty of forgiving injuries instead of avenging them. It is in his doctrine of the Judgment and the life to come that he departs most widely from the ordinary beliefs of the time. The heathen Arabs, like other primitive peoples, were familiar with the notion of a ghost, or wraith, which haunts, at least for a while, the resting-place of the dead body; but the idea of a future retribution was quite foreign to their habits of thought. The doctrine of the Resurrection, as it appears in the Koran, seems to be mainly derived from Christianity; that some details were borrowed from Judaism or Zoroastrianism is possible but can scarcely be proved. Mahomet, as we might have expected, conceives the Resurrection after the most crudely materialistic fashion; to him the reconstruction of the physical organism was an essential postulate of the future recompense. The descriptions of the Judgment itself and of the torments of the damned do not differ substantially from those which are found in popular Christian writings of medieval and modern times. On the other hand the delights of Paradise are often painted in colours to which neither Christianity nor Judaism affords any parallel[1]. But what especially characterises the older portions of the Koran is the constant emphasis laid on the nearness of the Resurrection and the Day of Judgment. Although Mahomet nowhere specifies any definite time, and when questioned on this point by his opponents always professed ignorance, it is clear that he lived in daily expectation of the great events which formed the main subject of his preaching. Nor is this at all inconsistent with the fact that some passages of the Koran seem to announce a special calamity which was to befall the Meccans for their unbelief, rather than a world-wide catastrophe. Similarly, it will be remembered, among the early Christians the expectation of the judgment

---

[1] It is remarkable that passages of this sort are almost entirely confined to the earlier chapters, which date from a time when the very notion of rewards and punishments after death was treated by the Meccans with derision, as the Prophet frequently complains. To suppose, with many European writers, that the early converts to Islām were attracted chiefly by the prospect of a material Paradise is therefore altogether unreasonable, since only those who had *on other grounds* accepted Mahomet as a prophet could believe in any Paradise whatsoever.

of the world and the expectation of the overthrow of Jerusalem were sometimes so closely connected as to become indistinguishable.

A great part of the Koran consists of narratives, inserted for purposes of edification. Scarcely any of these can be described as historical; on the other hand, scarcely any is a pure invention of Mahomet's. In almost every case he utilises some legend that he had heard, in order to enforce his doctrines. Thus he repeatedly introduces persons mentioned in the Old Testament and puts into their mouths discourses in favour of monotheism, moral precepts, etc. The opposition which they encountered and the chastisements which overtook their adversaries are likewise described at great length. The allusions to Christ and the early Christian Church present some very curious and hitherto unexplained features. That Christ, or any other being, can be a "son of God" is emphatically denied; at the same time the belief that Christ was born of a virgin is fully accepted, and among the prophets of past ages He occupies a specially prominent place. But of the facts of Christ's life Mahomet appears to have known next to nothing. In one of the later chapters of the Koran (iv. 156) the *Jews* are condemned for asserting that Christ was put to death and the crucifixion is represented as a deceptive appearance. The fact that Christians believed in the Crucifixion is totally ignored, and we may therefore conclude that on this very important point Mahomet's Christian informants held opinions resembling those which are ascribed to the ancient Docetists.

The disciples of the Prophet called themselves *Muslims*, but were usually known by the name of "Sabians" (*Ṣābi'ūn*)[1]. Their organisation and rules of life were at first of a very simple kind. They bound themselves to abstain from idolatry and from certain immoral practices, especially fornication and infanticide. The cult consisted mainly of prayers, according to the formulae prescribed by the Prophet; meetings for this purpose were held at stated times, but always in strict privacy. In order to indicate that the God whom he proclaimed was identical with the God of the Jews, Mahomet commanded his followers to adopt the Jewish practice of praying towards Jerusalem[2]. At this time he appears to have had scarcely any notion of the difference between Judaism and Christianity; consequently he was able to regard both Jews and Christians as his brethren in religion.

[1] The terms *Muslim*, "one who surrenders himself," and *Islam*, "surrender," are commonly explained as denoting "resignation" to the will of God, but it is more likely that they refer primarily to the *deliberate adoption* of a new faith as distinguished from blind conformity to a hereditary cult. The Sabians—a name which, of course, has no connexion with that of the Sabaeans—seem to have been a sect, or group of sects, of the half-Christian, half-heathen type. Why the Muslims were called Sabians is uncertain; probably the nickname was due, as usual, to some accidental point of similarity.

[2] See 1 Kings viii. 29 ff., Dan. vi. 10.

For several years Mahomet continued to preach with little apparent success. His converts were, with rare exceptions, persons of a low class or even foreign slaves, such as Bilāl the Abyssinian. Some members of his own family, in particular his uncle 'Abd-al-'Uzzā, nicknamed Abū Lahab, bitterly opposed him; even his protector Abū Ṭālib remained to the last an unbeliever. It would be a mistake to suppose that the enemies of the new faith were actuated by religious fanaticism. They were, for the most part, simply men of the world who, proud of their social position, objected to recognising the claims of an upstart and dreaded any sweeping change as likely to endanger the material advantages which they derived from the traditional cult. To the majority of the citizens Mahomet appeared a madman; some called him a "poet," an accusation which gave him great pain, for, as the Koran shews, he regarded the poets with peculiar aversion. That he had to endure many affronts was quite natural, but actual violence could not have been employed against him without risk of a blood-feud, which the Meccans were always most anxious to avoid. Those of his disciples, however, who had no relatives to protect them were occasionally treated with cruelty. At length the majority of the converts, finding their position intolerable, fled for refuge to Abyssinia, with the full consent, if not at the express command, of the Prophet. He himself remained at Mecca with a mere handful of followers.

When it became known that the emigrants had been kindly received by the Christian king of Abyssinia, considerable alarm prevailed among the chiefs of the Ḳuraish, lest the Abyssinians, whose devastating invasions were still vividly remembered, should be tempted to intervene on behalf of the persecuted Muslims. Accordingly a deputation was sent from Mecca for the purpose of persuading the king to hand over the fugitives as prisoners; the king, however, refused, whereupon the indignation of Mahomet's enemies was still further excited. The Prophet, reduced to extremities, fell into the error of attempting to overcome opposition by means of a compromise. He went so far as to publish a revelation in which the three principal goddesses of Mecca were recognised as "highly exalted beings whose intercession may be hoped for[1]." For a while the polytheists appeared to be satisfied, and a report that the persecution was at an end caused some of the emigrants to come back from Abyssinia. In the meanwhile the Prophet repented of the concession he had made, and declared that the verse in question had been put into his mouth by Satan. The feud thereupon broke out afresh. To the heathen Meccans Mahomet's conduct on this occasion naturally seemed to convict him of imposture; since, however, he had long been accustomed to regard all his impulses as due to some

[1] The word *gharānīḳ*, here rendered "exalted," is of doubtful meaning: an early Muslim poet uses it as an epithet of chieftains or warriors (*Kitāb-al-Aghānī*, VII. 75. 27 = VIII. 192. 3).

supernatural cause, it is by no means certain that he did not sincerely believe himself to be acting by divine command both when he made the concession and when he withdrew it[1].

It was probably about this time that an important conversion took place, that of Omar ('*Umar*) ibn al-Khaṭṭāb, a young man of no high social position but endowed with extraordinary ability and perseverance. He had at first been vehemently opposed to the new religion, so that his sudden conversion, of which there are several conflicting accounts, attracted all the more notice and doubtless inspired the Muslims with fresh courage. It is said that he set the example of praying publicly, in the neighbourhood of the Ka'ba; at all events from this time onwards the movement assumed a more open character. The chiefs of the Ḳuraish finally determined to adopt the only method of coercion known to them, short of positive violence; they offered to Mahomet's kinsmen, the Banū Hāshim, the choice of declaring him an outlaw or of being themselves excluded from intercourse with the other Meccan clans. Most of the Banū Hāshim were still unbelievers, but such was the sanctity attached to ties of blood that they all, with one or two exceptions, preferred to incur the penalty of social excommunication rather than deliver over Mahomet to his enemies. How long this breach lasted and by what means it was healed is uncertain; probably the manifold inconveniences which it caused to all parties soon brought about a change of public opinion[2].

Very soon after intercourse had been re-established between the Banū Hāshim and their fellow-townsmen, two serious calamities befell Mahomet, the death of his wife Khadīja and that of his protector Abū Ṭālib. There can be little doubt that this double bereavement rendered the Prophet's position at Mecca more precarious; henceforth he began to consider the possibility of finding a home elsewhere. His first attempt was made at a neighbouring town, called Ṭā'if, but he met with so unfavourable a reception that he speedily returned to Mecca, where he succeeded in obtaining a promise of protection from an influential heathen, Muṭ'im ibn 'Adī. For two or three years the Prophet remained in his native city, making, it would seem, scarcely any effort to gain fresh converts among the resident population. His attention was turned chiefly to the pilgrims who visited Mecca or the immediate neighbourhood on the occasion of the yearly festivals. To these motley crowds he used to preach his doctrines, generally encountering

---

[1] That many Muslim authorities consider this story fabulous is only what we might have expected. But it is amazing that it should be rejected by so impartia a historian as Caetani.

[2] It must be admitted that the story of the excommunication of the Banū Hāshim, as related by the principal authorities, presents some very suspicious features; but to conclude, with Caetani, that the whole episode is fictitious would involve still greater difficulties.

indifference or ridicule. There were, however, some exceptions. In A.D. 620 he fell in with some pilgrims from Yathrib and, finding them well-disposed, entered into a series of negotiations which finally brought about a complete change not only in his own fortunes but in the history of the world.

Yathrib, known in subsequent times as Medina[1], was a scattered group of villages rather than a city, situated in a fertile plain about 200 miles to the north of Mecca. Unlike the Meccans, who subsisted by commerce, the people of Medina had, from time immemorial, devoted themselves to agriculture, in particular to the cultivation of the date-palm. Long before the birth of Mahomet, Jewish colonists established themselves at Medina and propagated their religion with such success that by the beginning of the sixth century most of the inhabitants professed Judaism and were regarded as Jews, though they must have been mainly of Arab descent. These Judaised Arabs were divided into several clans, each occupying its own territory. In civilisation, especially in mechanical arts such as metal-working, they were greatly superior to their heathen neighbours, and for a while they dominated the whole district. But in the course of the sixth century, owing to circumstances with which we are imperfectly acquainted, the power of the Jews declined. Much of their territory passed into the hands of two heathen tribes (the Aus and the Khazraj), who in the time of Mahomet formed the bulk of the population. Between these tribes there raged a long and bitter feud. About the year 616 the Aus, with the help of the Jews, inflicted a severe defeat upon the Khazraj; this battle is known in Arabian tradition as the Day of Bu'āth. But the Khazraj, though humbled, were by no means crushed, and during the next few years every one went about in fear of his life. To the more intelligent of the people of Medina the situation must have seemed intolerable; peace was urgently required, yet no authority capable of restoring peace appeared to exist.

Such was the state of affairs when certain influential citizens of Medina became acquainted with Mahomet. Some of them, who through intercourse with Jews had already imbibed monotheistic ideas, were doubtless attracted by his religious teaching; others perhaps, who were indifferent to religion, felt that a stranger claiming to speak with divine authority might be able to effect what they themselves had attempted in vain. In any case, a period of about two years elapsed between their first interview with the Prophet and their final decision to offer him a home in their midst. Meanwhile he had sent to Medina one of his Meccan disciples, Mus'ab ibn 'Umair, to act as his representative and keep him informed of all that passed.

---

[1] In Arabic, *al-Madīna*, "the city," which is an abbreviation of *Madīnat-an-Nabī*, "the city of the Prophet."

In the year 622, on the occasion of the annual pilgrimage, about seventy of the converts from Medina arranged to hold a meeting with Mahomet at midnight a few miles from Mecca. The Prophet went thither in the company of his uncle 'Abbās, who was still an unbeliever[1], but from the heathen public in general the matter was carefully concealed. Mahomet demanded of the Medinese a solemn promise that if he betook himself to their country they would protect him from attack as they would protect their own families. This they all swore to do. As soon as he had secured a place of refuge, the Prophet ordered his Meccan disciples to emigrate to Medina. Attempts were made by the chiefs of the Ḳuraish to prevent the departure of the Muslims, but nearly all succeeded in escaping and reached Medina a few weeks later in small parties. The Prophet himself, with Abū Bakr and Ali, remained behind for a short time, apparently awaiting news as to the manner in which the Emigrants had been received. It is related, on somewhat doubtful authority, that his departure was hastened by a plot to assassinate him in his bed. In any case he left Mecca secretly, accompanied by Abū Bakr, in the summer or early autumn of 622. For a few days they remained hidden in a cave[2] near Mecca, and then proceeded, as rapidly as possible, to Medina. Thus was accomplished the great event known as the Emigration (*hijra*, distorted by Europeans into *hegira*), which forms the starting-point of the Muslim era[3].

On his arrival at Medina the Prophet was welcomed with enthusiasm by a large proportion of the natives; but he did not at once claim the position of a ruler. Those who acknowledged his divine mission could merely promise personal obedience. The people as a whole had not submitted to his authority; they were only his " Helpers" (*Anṣār*), pledged to defend him, for, according to Arabian notions, a guarantee of protection given by one member of a clan binds all the rest. It was by the gradual extension of his personal influence, not in virtue of any formal agreement, that he succeeded in making himself master of the place. The Meccan " Emigrants" (*Muhājirūn*) were, of course, entirely

---

[1] The presence of al-'Abbās at this meeting seems at first difficult to explain, since Mahomet was nominally under the protection of Muṭ'im ibn 'Adī. Probably the Medinese were afraid that they might afterwards be accused of having carried off Mahomet by force, and therefore required that some member of his family should be present to testify that the Prophet's departure was voluntary.

[2] Koran ix. 40.

[3] The Muslim era dates not from the precise moment of the Prophet's emigration but from the beginning of the *Arabian* year in which the Emigration took place, that is to say, from a point about 6 weeks earlier. Unfortunately, in consequence of the careless manner in which the heathen Arabs kept their calendar, it is not certain when the beginning of this year should be placed. According to the ordinary view, the year began on 16 July A.D. 622, and Mahomet arrived at Medina in the latter half of September; but Wellhausen makes the year begin in April.

CH. X.

devoted to him from the first, and formed, so to speak, his body-guard. Many of the Medinese, especially those of the younger generation, were no less zealous in his cause; their principal duty, during the first few months after the Emigration, consisted in housing and feeding the Emigrants. But not a few, even of those who called themselves Muslims, were either hostile or indifferent; the Koran frequently refers to them as the "Hypocrites" (*Munāfikūn*, a term borrowed from the Aethiopic). The most celebrated of these was a certain 'Abdallāh ibn Ubayy, a chief of the Khazraj, who before the arrival of Mahomet had played a very prominent part. The opposition of such persons is to be ascribed mainly to personal jealousy or other worldly motives. More consistent, and hence more formidable, was the enmity of the Jews. It is clear that at first Mahomet confidently reckoned on their support, but he soon discovered his mistake[1]. With rare exceptions they absolutely refused to acknowledge him as a prophet, and thus forced him to become their adversary. Henceforth the antagonism between Islām and Judaism began to shew itself even in externals. This was seen most clearly when, in the second year after the Emigration, Mahomet ordered his disciples to pray towards Mecca instead of praying towards Jerusalem.

The historian Ibn Ishāk has preserved for us the text of an important document which seems to have been drawn up, under the Prophet's direction, at about this time. It may be described as an attempt to settle, at least provisionally, the relations between the various classes into which the people of Medina were divided[2]. All the inhabitants, believers and unbelievers alike, are declared to be a single community (*umma*); the clans remain distinct for certain purposes but are debarred from making war on one another. Should any dispute arise, the matter is to be brought before " God and Mahomet." All are bound to unite for the defence of Medina in case it should be attacked. No one is to conclude an agreement with the Kuraish (*i.e.* the heathen Meccans) or with any ally of the Kuraish.

The establishing of public security at Medina was necessarily the first object which the Prophet had in view; but in addition to this he found himself compelled to supply his own followers with the rudiments of a legal code. At Mecca his teaching had been almost entirely confined to the sphere of faith and personal morality; of external regulations he had seldom had occasion to speak. But as soon as Islām became the

---

[1] Muslim authorities are unanimous in asserting that at this time both the Jews and the Christians were expecting a prophet to appear in Arabia and that precise descriptions of the coming prophet were contained in the Jewish and Christian Scriptures. How this belief first arose among Muslims is not clear, but converts from Judaism and Christianity doubtless did their best to encourage it.

[2] See Wellhausen, "Muhammads Gemeindeordnung von Medina," in *Skizzen und Vorarbeiten,* IV. pp. 67–83.

religion of a political society, the need of positive enactments made itself felt. Hence those parts of the Koran which were produced after the Emigration—amounting to rather more than one-third of the whole book—consist largely of prescriptions as to the details of practice both in religious and secular matters. Systematic legislation was, of course, a thing of which Mahomet could form no idea; he provided for each case as it occurred, not striving after theoretical consistency but freely modifying previous commands in order to suit altered circumstances. That all these contradictory directions were given out as the word of God caused scarcely any embarrassment at the time, for it was assumed that the Deity, like any other despot, may revoke His orders whenever He chooses; but it is needless to say that later generations, who had no trustworthy information as to the dates of the various passages, sometimes found it hard to decide which commands were revoked and which were still in force[1]. In a few cases we are informed by early Muslim authorities that passages of the Koran were not only "revoked" but actually suppressed.

The institutions which assumed a definite form during the years subsequent to the Emigration may be classed under the following heads:—(1) Religious ceremonial, (2) Fiscal and military regulations, (3) Civil and criminal laws.

To the *first* class belong the five obligatory daily prayers, the public service held every Friday, the duty of fasting from sunrise to sunset during the month of Ramaḍān, and the annual Pilgrimage (of which more will be said later). To these may be added the rules of ceremonial purity, the distinctions between lawful and unlawful food (which were largely borrowed from Judaism) and the prohibition of wine-drinking. The rite of circumcision—performed on boys, not, as among the Jews, on infants—prevailed everywhere in heathen Arabia and was retained by the followers of Mahomet; but it is never mentioned in the Koran and does not properly form part of the religion of Islām.

The *second* class includes the payment of "alms," that is, a kind of income-tax levied on all Muslims, originally for the relief of the poor but in later times for the maintenance of the State. Moreover all Muslims capable of bearing arms might, under certain circumstances, be required to serve as soldiers.

The *civil* and *criminal* laws laid down in the Koran are partly based on old Arabian usages and are partly of foreign origin. Slavery and polygamy having existed in Arabia from time immemorial, we may assume, as a matter of course, that Mahomet never thought of abolishing either the one or the other, but he introduced certain restrictions whereby the condition both of slaves and of women was somewhat

---

[1] Treatises on the "revoking" and the "revoked" passages of the Koran (*fi-n-nāsikh wa l-mansūkh*) have been produced by many Muslim theologians.

improved[1]. In particular, he condemned the practice of "inheriting women against their will[2]," that is, of treating widows as chattels to be appropriated by the dead man's heir. He also made every effort to secure the rights of orphans and in general to protect the weak against the strong. The ancient rule of blood-revenge he recognised in principle, but confined it within narrow limits. A startling innovation, from the point of view of the Arabs, was the punishment of fornication by scourging[3]. It may be mentioned that, according to tradition, the Koran once contained a passage which ordered that fornicators should be put to death by stoning ; and Omar, when he was Caliph, is said to have maintained that this law was still in force.

In describing the Prophet's sojourn at Medina, it is necessary to say something of his domestic history, to which several passages of the Koran explicitly refer. Before he left Mecca, he had already taken to himself a second wife, named Sauda, and during the years which followed the number of his wives steadily increased. The most celebrated of them was 'Ā'isha (daughter of Abū Bakr), whose marriage to Mahomet took place a few months after his arrival at Medina; she was then only about nine years old, but in spite of her tender age she rapidly acquired great influence. When, some five years later, she was accused of misconduct, a passage of the Koran was specially revealed for the purpose of clearing her character. The ascendency which she gained during the Prophet's lifetime continued long after his death and enabled her to play a prominent but by no means an honourable part in the politics of that period. In the books of Muslim tradition 'Ā'isha is one of the authorities most frequently cited.

For more than a year after the Emigration Mahomet and his Meccan disciples were in a condition of great economic distress. The attempts which they made to relieve their necessities by means of pillage did not at first prove successful. In these earliest raids the natives of Medina took no part, for the general principle that it is the duty of Muslims to engage in aggressive warfare against unbelievers had not yet been announced. Moreover it is to be noticed that Mahomet did not at once venture to shock the feelings of his countrymen by violating the sanctity of the four sacred months during which, according to ancient custom, no raids were permitted. At length, towards the end of the year 623, he sanctioned an attack, in the sacred month of Rajab, upon a caravan belonging to the Kuraish, at Nakhla near Mecca. The caravan was taken by surprise and the raiders came back with a considerable amount of booty to Medina. But so strongly was this expedition

---

[1] It has often been asserted that Mahomet forbade his followers to have more than four wives at the same time, but the passage of the Koran (chap. iv. 3) which is cited in support of the statement does not necessarily imply any such prohibition.

[2] Koran iv. 23.

[3] Koran xxiv. 2.

condemned by public opinion that the Prophet found it necessary to give out that his orders had been misunderstood.

Two months later his followers achieved their first great victory. A large caravan, laden with rich merchandise, was returning from Syria to Mecca under the leadership of Abū Sufyān, the chief of the Banū Umayya, one of the proudest families among the Ḳuraish. Mahomet determined to waylay it at Badr, a place south-west of Medina, a few miles from the Red Sea coast, and himself set out thither with rather more than 300 armed men, of whom about 80 were Emigrants and the rest Medinese. Abū Sufyān, however, received news of the intended attack, changed his route and despatched a messenger to Mecca asking for help. The Ḳuraish hastily fitted out an expedition consisting of about 900 men, among whom were most of the Meccan aristocracy. While they were on their way northward they learnt that the caravan had succeeded in reaching a point where it was out of danger; some of them therefore returned to Mecca, but the great majority, confident in their superior numbers and equipment, determined to advance, rather, it would seem, with the intention of overawing than of crushing their adversary. The two armies reached Badr almost at the same moment. Mahomet, ignorant of what had happened, was still expecting the caravan; on discovering his mistake he probably saw that a retreat would be extremely perilous, if not impossible, and accordingly resolved to fight[1]. The Meccans, on this occasion, displayed an extraordinary slackness and absence of forethought. They allowed Mahomet to take possession of a well situated in their immediate neighbourhood and thereby to deprive them of their water-supply. Next morning, when they approached the well they found the bulk of Mahomet's army drawn up around it. But even then no general attack was made. One by one, or in small groups, a number of Meccan chieftains came forward and were killed in hand-to-hand combat by champions of the opposite side. Among the slain was one of the most formidable of the Prophet's enemies, Abu-l-Ḥakam, son of Hishām, usually known by the nickname Abū Jahl. Mahomet himself did not take part in the fighting but remained in a small hut which had been erected for him, praying with passionate fervour and trembling violently. At length, about noon, the Meccans, realising that nothing was to be gained by further bloodshed, began to retire. Being much better mounted than their opponents, they were able to escape with a loss of only 70 slain and 70 captured. Of the Muslims 14 had fallen.

Insignificant as this battle may appear from a military point of view,

---

[1] According to the ordinary story, the news of the approach of the army from Mecca had reached Mahomet before he arrived at Badr, but this is expressly denied by our oldest authority (Tabarī, I. 1286. 2 ff.). See F. Buhl, "Ein paar Beiträge zur Kritik der Geschichte Muhammeds" in *Orientalische Studien*, I. pp. 7–22.

the importance of its results can scarcely be exaggerated. Hitherto the enemies of the Prophet had continually taunted him with his inability to perform miracles; now at length it seemed as if a miracle had been wrought. The victory gained at Badr over a greatly superior force is ascribed in the Koran to the intervention of angels, an explanation which, it is needless to say, was unhesitatingly accepted by all Muslims[1]. On his return to Medina, Mahomet ventured on a series of high-handed measures which struck terror into all his opponents. Several persons who had offended him were assassinated by his order. At the same time the Banū Ḳainuḳā', one of the Jewish clans resident at Medina, were banished from the place; their houses and valuables became the property of the Muslims.

Meanwhile the Meccans, irritated by their defeat and fearing for the safety of their caravans, on which they were dependent for the means of subsistence, had determined to make an attack in force. Early in the year 625 an army of about 3000 men, commanded by Abū Sufyān, marched from Mecca and encamped near a hill called Uḥud, a few miles to the north of Medina. A considerable proportion of the Medinese, in particular 'Abdallāh ibn Ubayy, wished to remain on the defensive; but Mahomet, with less than his usual prudence, rejected their advice. Although the force at his disposal scarcely numbered 1000 men, he resolved to make a sortie and assail the Meccans in the rear. At first this bold plan appeared likely to prove successful. He was able to take up a strong position on the slopes of Uḥud, whence the Muslims charged the enemy and drove them back with some loss. But the Meccan horsemen, led by Khālid ibn al-Walīd, succeeded in outflanking the Muslims, who were at once thrown into confusion. Some fled to Medina, while others fought their way back to the hill. Among these latter was Mahomet himself, who for a while remained hidden in a ravine. Meanwhile a rumour that he was slain had spread in the ranks of the Meccans, and for this reason, it would appear, they did not take advantage of their victory. Supposing that they had sufficiently avenged the blood shed at Badr, they made no attempt to attack Medina but prepared to march homewards. Of the Muslims only about 70 men were left dead on the battle-field; one of these was Ḥamza, the Prophet's uncle, a valiant warrior, it is true, but not by any means a model of piety. Hind, the wife of Abū Sufyān and mother of the Caliph Mu'āwiya, had, together with a number of other women, accompanied the Meccan army; remembering that Ḥamza had slain some of her nearest relatives at Badr, she took vengeance on his corpse by tearing his liver with her teeth. Such barbarity was quite unusual among the

---

[1] The historians, citing the testimony of eye-witnesses, supply us with remarkably precise information about the angels who fought at Badr; thus, for instance, they wore white turbans, with the exception of Gabriel, who had a yellow one (Ibn Hishām, p. 450).

Arabs of that period, and it is therefore not to be wondered at that the act of Hind was long afterwards a topic on which the enemies of her posterity loved to dwell.

When the Meccans began to retreat, Mahomet, realising that Medina was no longer in danger, endeavoured to efface the shame of his defeat by a great show of activity. Although he had himself received some slight wounds he marched a few miles in the track of his victorious foes, obviously not with the intention of attacking them but in order to reassure his own followers. This plan attained its object, and there is no reason to suppose that after the battle his influence at Medina was in any way diminished.

A few months later he made a second attack upon the Jews. The Banu-n-Naḍīr, a Jewish clan who owned some of the most valuable palm-gardens in the neighbourhood of Medina, were suspected, rightly or wrongly, of plotting to murder him. He accordingly declared war against them, and after a siege which lasted about three weeks forced them to emigrate to Khaibar, an oasis inhabited chiefly by Jews, about 100 miles north of Medina. The lands of the Banu-n-Naḍīr were partly appropriated by Mahomet and partly divided among the Emigrants, who thus ceased to depend on the charity of the Helpers.

That Mahomet's conduct should have been bitterly resented by the Jewish population of Arabia is quite natural; but on this, as on other occasions, the Jews shewed themselves wholly incapable of combining in order to resist him by force. The utmost that they attempted was to stimulate the enmity of the heathen Meccans and of the neighbouring nomadic tribes. By this time the chiefs of the Ḳuraish had perceived the fruitlessness of their victory at Uḥud and they therefore listened readily to the Jewish emissaries who urged them to make another and a more serious effort. Accordingly, in the year 627, an alliance against Mahomet was formed between the Ḳuraish and a number of Bedouin tribes, of whom the most important were the Fazāra, the Sulaim and the Asad. The combined forces of the Ḳuraish and their allies proceeded to march towards Medina. They are said to have numbered 10,000 men, which is perhaps an exaggerated estimate, but in any case it is certain that they formed an army much larger than that which had fought at Uḥud two years earlier. Meanwhile the Khuzā'a, a tribe who dwelt in the immediate neighbourhood of Mecca, had sent to Mahomet full information as to the impending attack; their conduct was probably due much more to jealousy of the Ḳuraish than to any special sympathy with Islām. By the time the assailants reached Medina the town was well prepared to stand a siege. In most places nothing more was necessary than to erect a few barricades between the houses; but on one side there was a large open space, across which Mahomet caused a trench to be dug. This device, which appears to us so obvious, struck the Arabs with astonishment; by Mahomet's enemies it was denounced as a dishonourable stratagem. Hence this siege is usually called "the Campaign of the Trench." The idea, we are told, was suggested to the Prophet by an emancipated slave of unknown origin, who is celebrated in Muslim tradition under the name of Salmān the Persian; at all events the word applied to the trench (*khandak*) is derived from the Persian language. In digging the trench Mahomet himself took an active part. The implements required for the purpose were mostly supplied by the Kuraiza, the only Jewish clan who still remained at Medina. It is difficult to believe that the Kuraiza regarded Mahomet with friendly feelings, but it would appear that, in spite of the manner in which he had treated their co-religionists, they still considered themselves as bound by their agreement with him; moreover they probably realised that if Medina were taken by storm the hordes of Bedouins would plunder all parties indiscriminately. During the siege the vigilance and discipline of the Muslims contrasted strangely with the disorder which prevailed on the opposite side. The besiegers, in spite of their vastly superior numbers, seem never to have contemplated a real assault. Small troops of cavalry now and then endeavoured to cross the trench but were easily repulsed by a shower of arrows and stones; on the one occasion when some of them succeeded in forcing an entrance they soon found it necessary to retreat. In explanation of these facts it must be remembered that an extreme dread of attacking fortifications, however rudely constructed, has been characteristic of the Arabs, and in particular of the Bedouins, down to the present day.

Though the loss of life on either side was quite insignificant, both the besiegers and the besieged were soon reduced to great straits. The cold and stormy weather severely tried the defenders of the trench, while the Bedouins without suffered greatly from lack of provisions. Accordingly both parties strove hard to bring the siege to an end by means of negotiation. Mahomet's principal object was to detach the Bedouins from their alliance with the Kuraish; the besiegers, on the other hand, sent secret messages to the Kuraiza urging them to violate their agreement with Mahomet. The chief of this Jewish clan, Ka'b ibn Asad, at first indignantly refused to listen to these suggestions, but finally he yielded, and the Kuraiza forthwith assumed so menacing an attitude that the Muslims became seriously alarmed. The Jews, however, did not venture to make an attack; they remained, as usual, shut up in their fortresses, until the Kuraish and their allies, weary of waiting, suddenly raised the siege, which had lasted only a fortnight, and returned to their homes. Thus ended the last attempt, on the part of the Meccan aristocracy, to crush the new religion.

As soon as the besiegers had departed the vengeance of Mahomet naturally fell on the Kuraiza. He did not content himself with pillaging them but, having compelled them to surrender after a brief siege,

offered them the choice of conversion to Islām or death. The heroism
which they displayed on this occasion seems hard to reconcile with
their former timidity; rather than commit apostasy they preferred to
be slain one by one in the market-place of the town. The number of
these martyrs amounted to over six hundred; the women and children
were sold as slaves.

Henceforth the population of Medina was, at least in name, almost
exclusively Muslim; the "Hypocrites" who remained were a small
minority, and though they sometimes angered the Prophet by their
murmurs and intrigues he had no reason to fear them. Accordingly
his policy, which he had at first represented as one of self-defence, now
became avowedly aggressive. Medina was no longer the refuge of a
persecuted sect—it was the seat of a religious despotism which in a few
years subjugated the whole of Arabia. To ordinary Europeans this
development of Islām naturally appears as a mere misuse of religion
for purposes of political aggrandisement; it is, however, necessary to
remember, in judging of Mahomet's conduct, that the communities
which he attacked were not organised States but societies which recognised no permanent bond save that of blood. With the exception of
the Ḳuraish, who inhabited a sacred territory, almost every Arabian
tribe was engaged in perpetual feuds with its neighbours. In founding
a community united solely by religion Mahomet necessarily placed
himself in a position of antagonism to the tribal system, which required
every man to take the part of his fellow-tribesmen against the members
of all other tribes. But Mahomet was very far from being a cosmo-
polite of the modern type. Though his doctrines logically involved the
equality of all races, it probably never occurred to him that it was his
duty to ignore national and tribal distinctions. The authority of the
tribal chiefs was not to be overthrown but it was to be subordinated to
a higher authority, which could be none other than that of the Prophet
himself. Moreover Mahomet's belief in the peculiar sanctity of Mecca
rather increased than diminished during his long exile. Until the House
of God had been purged of idols the main object of the Prophet's
mission was still unattained. To win over Mecca to the true faith
seemed therefore a matter of supreme importance.

The first expedition made for this purpose took place in the year 628.
Shortly before the time of the annual Pilgrimage Mahomet marched
towards Mecca accompanied by several hundreds of his disciples and
taking with him a large number of camels which were marked with
badges, according to ancient Arabian custom, to denote that they were
victims intended for sacrifice. If his aim was to force his way into the
city, he carefully concealed the design, giving out that he and his
followers were coming simply as pilgrims, to do honour to the Meccan
sanctuary. He hoped to convince the Ḳuraish that Islām would not in
any way interfere with the privileges which they had hitherto enjoyed,

and he persuaded himself that they might thereby be induced to recognise his claims. But the memory of the blood shed at his command and especially of the occasion on which he had violated the truce of the sacred months was vividly present to the minds of the Meccans, and they determined on no account to admit him. When he reached Ḥudaibiya, a place within a few hours' march of Mecca, he found his way blocked by an armed force consisting partly of Meccans and partly of their Bedouin allies. A series of negotiations ensued, in the course of which Othman (properly *'Uthmān*) ibn 'Affān went as Mahomet's agent to Mecca; the selection of this man was doubtless due to his being a relative of Abū Sufyān and other influential citizens. During Othman's absence a rumour that he had been murdered spread through the camp of the Muslims, whereupon Mahomet, fearing, or pretending to fear, an attack on the part of the Ḳuraish, assembled his followers under a tree and required from each of them a promise that he would on no account flee, if a conflict took place. To this scene the Koran alludes[1] as one specially pleasing to God; hence in Muslim tradition it is called "the Homage of good pleasure." Almost immediately afterwards Othman returned to Ḥudaibiya, bringing, it would seem, proofs that his mission to Mecca had not been fruitless. The negotiations were accordingly resumed in the Prophet's camp, whither the Ḳuraish sent a certain Suhail ibn 'Amr as their representative. After prolonged discussion a compromise was agreed upon, whereby Mahomet consented to withdraw for that year, while the Ḳuraish, on their part, promised that the year following he and his disciples should be allowed to enter Mecca, without weapons, and remain there for three days. Furthermore both parties were to refrain from hostilities for ten years; during that time no member of the Ḳuraish who was still a minor might join the Muslim community without the permission of his parents or guardians, whereas the sons of Muslims might freely go over to the Ḳuraish.

The terms of this treaty appeared at first so unfavourable to Islām that the more zealous followers of the Prophet, in particular Omar, vehemently protested. Mahomet, however, perceived that the conditions, humiliating as they might seem, would in the end turn to his advantage, and he accordingly adhered to them in spite of the opposition of his too eager disciples. Never was his influence put to so severe a test and never did he achieve a more signal triumph. From the moment when the treaty of Ḥudaibiya was concluded the number of conversions to Islām became larger than ever.

According to the ordinary Muslim tradition, the Prophet about this time took a step which shewed that he contemplated the conversion not only of Arabia but of the world—he despatched messengers to the Byzantine Emperor Heraclius, to the Persian king and to

[1] Chap. xlviii. 18.

various other foreign potentates, summoning them to recognise his divine mission. But the evidence for this story is by no means satisfactory, and the details present so many suspicious features that it may be doubted whether the narrative rests on any real basis.

Soon after his return to Medina, Mahomet set out on an expedition against Khaibar, where the banished Banu-n-Naḍīr had taken refuge. The Jews, as usual, shrank from a conflict in the open plain and shut themselves up in their fortresses, which fell one by one into the hands of the Muslims. The vanquished were compelled to surrender all their wealth, which was very considerable, but they were permitted to remain at Khaibar as cultivators of the soil, on condition that half of the produce should be annually made over to the Muslim authorities. This is the first instance of an arrangement which was afterwards adopted in most parts of the Muslim Empire where the population consisted of non-Muslims.

Early in the year 629 Mahomet, with about 2000 followers, carried out his project of visiting Mecca as a pilgrim, in accordance with the treaty of Ḥudaibiya. For the stipulated three days he was allowed to occupy the sacred city and to perform the traditional ceremonies in the sanctuary. The scene must have been a curious one, never to be repeated—the great preacher of monotheism publicly doing homage at a shrine filled with idols. The sight of Mahomet's power deeply impressed the Meccan aristocracy, and two of the most eminent among them, Khālid ibn al-Walīd and 'Amr ibn al-'Āṣ, took the opportunity of going over to Islām. Both of these men afterwards played a prominent part in the building up of the Muslim Empire.

A few months later Islām for the first time came into conflict with the great Christian power against which it was destined to struggle, with scarcely any intermission, for a period of eight centuries. In the autumn of the year 629 Mahomet despatched a force of 3000 men, commanded by his adopted son Zaid ibn Ḥāritha, to the north-western frontier of Arabia. The reason which most of the historians assign for this expedition is that a messenger sent by the Prophet had been assassinated, a year earlier, by an Arab chieftain named Shuraḥbīl, who owned allegiance to the Byzantine Emperor. But since Ibn Isḥāḳ, the oldest writer who records the expedition, does not allege any pretext for it, the correctness of the aforesaid explanation is at least doubtful. In any case it is difficult to believe that Mahomet contemplated an attack on the Byzantine Empire, for ignorant as he was of foreign countries he must have been aware that an army of 3000 men would be wholly inadequate for such a purpose. When the Muslim force reached the neighbourhood of the Dead Sea, they found themselves, to their great surprise, confronted by a much larger army composed partly of Byzantines and partly of Arabs subject to the Emperor. After some hesitation Zaid ibn Ḥāritha determined to fight. The battle took place at Mu'ta, a village to the east of the Dead Sea. The Muslims fought bravely but were totally defeated; among the slain was their leader Zaid and Ja'far, a first cousin of the Prophet. The recently converted Khālid ibn al-Walīd, who had accompanied the expedition, finally assumed the command and succeeded in bringing back the greater part of the army safely to Medina.

This reverse was quickly followed by a great success in another quarter. The truce of ten years, established by the treaty of Ḥudaibiya, might perhaps have been observed faithfully if the matter had depended solely on the two contracting parties, Mahomet and the Ḳuraish. But each party was in alliance with certain Bedouin tribes, and, as anyone might have foreseen, a feud among the allies was likely to produce a general rupture. In fact the truce had lasted only a year and a half when Mahomet's allies the Khuzā'a were attacked by a small tribe, the Bakr ibn 'Abd-Manāt, who likewise dwelt in the neighbourhood of Mecca and happened to be in alliance with the Ḳuraish. Some members of the Ḳuraish were accused, rightly or wrongly, of assisting the Bakr ibn 'Abd-Manāt, whereupon the Khuzā'a naturally complained to Mahomet that the terms of the treaty had been violated. The Ḳuraish, on their part, sent Abū Sufyān to Medina, in the hope that hostilities might be averted. What passed between Abū Sufyān and Mahomet on this occasion it is, of course, impossible to know with certainty, but it appears highly probable that, as several modern historians have suggested, the ambassador of the Ḳuraish, realising the superiority of the Muslim forces, agreed to facilitate the surrender of Mecca, while the Prophet promised to avoid all unnecessary bloodshed. No sooner had Abū Sufyān returned to his native city than Mahomet collected an army of about 10,000 men, chiefly Bedouins, and marched southwards. But he abstained from declaring war against the Ḳuraish and endeavoured to conceal the real object of his expedition. On the way he was met by his uncle 'Abbās, who at length professed himself a convert to Islām and joined the Prophet's army. About the end of January 630 the Muslims were encamped within sight of Mecca. No one could now doubt what was Mahomet's aim, but very few of the Meccans shewed any inclination to risk their lives in defence of the city. With the exception of a small band who perished in a fruitless skirmish, the citizens, following the advice of Abū Sufyān, threw away their arms, retired into their houses and suffered the conqueror to enter unopposed. Mahomet, on taking possession of the city, at once proclaimed a general amnesty, from which only ten persons were by name excluded[1]; even of these the majority soon obtained pardon. He then proceeded to destroy the idols with which the city abounded; it was even thought

---

[1] It is somewhat remarkable that among the few persons singled out for special vengeance were three female musicians, whose crime consisted in the fact that they had been accustomed to sing songs reflecting on the Prophet's character.

necessary to efface some of the paintings which adorned the interior of
the Kaʻba. A curious legend relates that while this process of purifica-
tion was being carried out one of the Meccan goddesses, called Nāʼila,
suddenly appeared in the form of a black woman and fled away shrieking[1]
—an example of the belief, familiar to us from early Christian literature,
that the pagan deities are devils. But while many of the ancient gods
vanished for ever, one at least remained and in fact has continued to the
present day. A certain black stone, which formed part of the wall of
the Kaʻba, was regarded by the heathen Arabs with extraordinary
veneration; the practice of kissing this object and of stroking it with
the hand was not only tolerated but expressly sanctioned by the Prophet.
That such fetish-worship disgusted some of his own followers appears
evident from a saying ascribed to the Caliph Omar[2]. How far Mahomet's
policy in these matters was due to genuine superstition and how far
to the desire of conciliating the heathen cannot be determined; but it
is certain that a large part of the ancient cult was adopted into Islām
with little change. For this it was necessary to devise some historical
justification; accordingly the Prophet gave out, perhaps in good faith,
that the Meccan sanctuary had been originally founded by Abraham
and that the ceremonial practised in it was a divine institution though
it had been partially corrupted through the perversity of men. The
Meccans, it is needless to say, gladly accepted the theory which tended,
on the whole, to enhance the prestige of their city. Henceforth the
Ḳuraish, who had so long opposed the new religion, were among its
firmest adherents, if not from conviction at least from self-interest.

The news of the capture of Mecca spread a panic among some of the
neighbouring tribes of Bedouins. It is not probable that they were
much influenced by religious feeling, but they dreaded the loss of their
independence. An army was quickly brought together, consisting of
several tribes who bore the collective appellation of Hawāzin; the most
prominent members of the coalition were the Thaḳīf, a tribe to which
the inhabitants of the town of Ṭāʼif belonged[3]. Mahomet at once
marched from Mecca with a much larger force and encountered the
Hawāzin in the valley of Ḥunain. The Muslims, in spite of their
numerical superiority, were at first thrown into confusion by the onslaught of the enemy, and the Prophet himself was in great peril; the
troops from Medina, however, succeeded in turning the tide of battle.
At length the Hawāzin were not only routed but were forced to abandon
their women and children, together with a vast quantity of flocks and
herds which, after the fashion of the Bedouins, they had brought into

---

[1] Wellhausen, *Mohammed in Medina*, p. 341.

[2] "I know that thou art a stone, without power to harm or to help, and had
I not seen the Messenger of God kiss thee I would not kiss thee" (*Bukhārī*,
ed. Krehl, ɪ. p. 406. 1 ff.).

[3] See above, p. 311.

CH. X.

the battle-field. Immediately after the victory Mahomet proceeded to besiege Ṭā'if, but the inhabitants of the town defended it with unusual vigour and the Muslims were soon obliged to retreat. This discomfiture, however, does not seem to have injured the Prophet's cause, for a few days later the majority of the Hawāzin announced their intention of adopting Islām. The new converts received back their wives and children, but the rest of the booty taken at Ḥunain was distributed among the victors. Nor did the people of Ṭā'if long remain faithful to their old religion; after an interval of about half a year they entered into negotiations with the Prophet and finally submitted to his authority.

In the autumn of this year (630) a report reached Medina that a great Byzantine army was advancing into Arabia from the northwest. The report was certainly false; whether Mahomet believed it or merely utilised it as a pretext for a raid it is impossible to say. In any case he collected all his forces and marched with them as far as Tabūk, which is about 300 miles to the north-west of Medina. As no Byzantines appeared to oppose him, the only result of his expedition was the subjugation of some small Jewish and Christian settlements in the north of Arabia. Both Jews and Christians were allowed to retain their property and the right to profess their religion, on condition that they paid a yearly tribute, the amount of which was fixed in each case by a special treaty.

On the occasion of the next annual Pilgrimage, in the spring of 631, Mahomet issued a solemn proclamation, now contained in chap. ix. of the Koran, whereby heathens were thenceforth excluded from participation in the Pilgrimage and the cult of the Ka'ba. The following year the Prophet himself performed the Pilgrimage and finally settled the details of the ceremonies to be observed in connexion with it. During all subsequent ages this institution, notwithstanding its purely heathen origin, continued to be the great bond whereby Muslims of all parties were held together. Such a result could not have been attained by the Koran alone or by any abstract creed however carefully formulated.

Another matter which he undertook to regulate at about the same time was the sacred Calendar. Till then the Arabs, so far as can be ascertained, had reckoned by solar years but by lunar months, that is to say, they followed the practice, which appears to have been common among the Semitic nations, of inserting an intercalary month from time to time so as to adjust the year to the seasons. But as their notions of astronomy were of the crudest sort, much confusion naturally arose. This the Prophet, who was equally ignorant, endeavoured to remedy by announcing, in the name of God, that thenceforth the year was always to consist of twelve lunar months. Accordingly the Muslim year was altogether dissociated from the natural seasons, for which reason the more civilised Muslim nations are obliged to have a civil Calendar, consisting of Persian, Syrian or Coptic months, as the case may be, in addition to the sacred Calendar.

Soon after his return to Medina, Mahomet made preparations for another campaign against the Byzantines, but before the expedition had started he was seized with fever and expired, in the arms of ʿĀʾisha, on Monday, 7 June 632. Of his last utterances there are various accounts, many of which are obvious fabrications designed to support the claims of rival candidates for the Caliphate. That he ever appointed a successor is highly improbable.

It would be vain to attempt an enumeration of the conflicting judgments which have been passed on his character and his work, not only by fanatical devotees and opponents but even by scientific historians. The immense majority of the attacks published in Europe may be safely ignored, since they were made at a time when the most trustworthy sources of information had not yet come to light. During the last two or three generations more favourable estimates have been formed, but it would be a grave mistake to suppose that even at the present day there is anything like a consensus of opinion on this subject among those who are most qualified to judge. One of the greatest Orientalists that ever lived has recently stated that having, in his younger days, planned a work on the history of the early Muslim Empire he was finally deterred from carrying out the scheme by his inability to offer any satisfactory account of the Prophet's character[1]. This example should suffice to inspire diffidence.

In discussing the subject there are two opposite dangers which we must constantly strive to avoid. On the one hand, we should beware of assuming that Mahomet's doctrine and policy were determined solely by his own personal qualities. Much that strikes us as peculiar in his preaching may in reality be due to his Jewish or Christian informants. It is likewise clear that the spread of his religion was largely governed by factors over which he had no control. All the evidence tends to shew that during the first few years of his propaganda he never dreamt of acquiring political power. He strove, it is true, to convert Mecca as a whole[2], and not merely a few individuals, to the true faith; but this was not in view of an earthly kingdom—it was in view of the impending Day of Judgment. Even when at length circumstances placed him in the position of a ruler his authority rested much more on the voluntary co-operation of his followers than on any material resources that were at his command. It has often been suggested in recent times that the religious movement of which Mahomet was the head coincided with a great national movement on the part of the Arabs who, it is said, had

[1] Nöldeke, in the *Wiener Zeitschrift für die Kunde des Morgenlandes*, xxi. p. 298, footnote 3.

[2] On this point see Wellhausen, *Das arabische Reich und sein Sturz*, pp. 2 ff.

already developed, independently of Islām, a sense of their superiority to other races and were eager to overrun the neighbouring countries. On this question it is difficult to pronounce a definite opinion, since nearly all our information about the Arabs of that period comes through Muslim channels.　But in any case there can be no doubt that in the diffusion of Islām the national feelings of the Arabs played a very important part.

On the other hand, we must not fall into the error of ignoring the extraordinary influence exerted by the Prophet over his disciples, an influence which was apparently due quite as much to his moral as to his intellectual qualities.　The confidence which he inspired may seem to us undeserved, but it is only just to acknowledge that he used his immense power much oftener for the purpose of restraining than for the purpose of stimulating fanaticism.

CHAPTER XI.

THE EXPANSION OF THE SARACENS.

GENERAL REMARKS, ASIA, EGYPT.

THE migration of the Teutonic tribes and the expansion of the Saracens form the basis of the history of the Middle Ages. As the migrations laid the foundation for the development of the Western States, the diffusion of the Saracens gave the form which it has kept till our own day to the ancient contrast of East and West. These two movements gave birth to the severance between Christian Europe and the Muslim East, momentous not only throughout the Middle Ages but even to the present day. True, Spain was long included in the Muslim territory, while Eastern Europe and Asia Minor formed part of the Christian sphere, but these later changes simply alter the geographical aspect; the origin of the contrast, affecting universal history, dates back to the seventh century.

The Middle Ages regarded the severance from such a one-sided ecclesiastical and clerical point of view as was bound to obscure the comprehension of historical facts. The popular version of the matter, even among the cultured classes of to-day, is still under the spell of this tradition :—" Inspired by their prophet, the Arab hordes fall upon the Christian nations, to convert them to Islām at the point of the sword. The thread of ancient development is torn completely asunder ; a new civilisation, that of Islām, created by the Arabs, takes the place of the older civilisation of Christianity ; the eastern and western countries are opposed to each other on terms of complete estrangement, reacting on each other only during the period of the crusades." If we look into Arabian sources with this idea before us, we shall find it fully confirmed, for Arabian tradition also took its bearings from the ecclesiastical standpoint, like the tradition of the West ; with one as with the other everything commenced with Mahomet and the expansion of the Arabs ; Mahomet and the first Caliphs made all things anew and substantially created the civilisation of Islām. It is only in recent times that historical research has led away from this line of thought. We recognise now the historical continuity. Islām emerges from its isolation and becomes heir to the Oriental-Hellenistic civilisation. It appears as the last link in a long development of universal history. From the days of Alexander the Great until the time of the Roman emperors the East had been compelled to endure Western conditions and European rule. But as in the days of the earlier emperors the Hellenic spirit was stifled by the embrace of the East, and as the classical world greedily absorbed the cults and religions of the East, an ethnical reaction of the East sets in from the third century onwards and the Semitic element begins to stir beneath the Hellenistic surface. Within the Christian sphere this current shews itself more especially in the territories of the Greek and Aramaic languages, and the difference between the Greek and the Latin Churches is mainly that between Asia and Europe. With the expansion of the Arabs then the East reacquires in the political sphere the independence which had been slowly preparing in the domain of civilisation. Nothing absolutely new therefore arrives from the expansion of the Arabs, not even conditions uncongenial to the West of the Middle Ages; in fact on closer examination we perceive an intimate inner relationship in the world of thought between the Christianity of the Middle Ages and Islām. This fact is moreover not remarkable, for both spheres of culture repose on the same foundation, the Hellenistic-Oriental civilisation of early Christian times. In the territory of the Mediterranean circle conquered by the Arabs this civilisation lived on, but as the empire of the Caliphs thrust its main centre further and further eastward, and annexed more and more the traditions of ancient Persia, the culture of Islām, at first strongly tinged with Hellenism, was bound to assume an ever stronger Oriental character. On the other hand on Western ground the Germanic genius freed itself from this civilisation, which as a foreign import could not thrive there, to develop out of its remnants the typically Western forms of the Middle Ages.

Just as the ecclesiastical conception on the one hand broke the historical continuity, it perceived on the other hand in the expansion of the Arabs nothing but a further extension of the religion of Islām and therefore totally misunderstood the real nature of the movement. It was not the religion of Islām which was by that time disseminated by the sword, but merely the political sovereignty of the Arabs. The acceptance of Islām by others than Arabians was not only not striven for, but was in fact regarded with disfavour. The subdued peoples might peacefully retain their old religions, provided only they paid ample tribute. As on conversion to Islām these payments ceased, at least in the early times such changes of religion were disliked. The circumstance that a few pious men subsequently practised such proselytism, or that the material advantages of apostasy gradually led the population of the conquered countries to Islām, must not blind our eyes to the fact that the movement originated from quite other motives.

The sudden surging forward of the Arabs was only apparently sudden. For centuries previously the Arab migration had been in preparation. It was the last great Semitic migration connected with the economical decline of Arabia. Such a decline is indisputable, even though we may not be disposed to accept all the conclusions which have in recent times been connected with this oft-discussed thesis. Ever since the commencement of our chronology the Arabs had been in fluctuation. South-Arabian tribes were lords of Medina, others also from South Arabia were settled in Syria and Mesopotamia. Legendary information, confirmed however by inscriptions of Southern Arabia, shews that for a long period the conditions of life in the southern part of the Arabian peninsula had been growing worse. With the decline of political power the care of the public waterworks, on which the prosperity of the land more or less depended, also suffered. In short, long before Mahomet Arabia was in a state of unrest, and a slow, uncontrollable infiltration of Arabian tribes and tribal branches had permeated the adjoining civilised lands in Persian as also in Roman territory, where they had met with the descendants of earlier Semitic immigrants to those parts, the Aramaeans, who were already long acclimatised there.

Persia and Byzantium suffered severely from this constant unrest in their border provinces, and both empires had endeavoured to organise the movement and to use it as a fighting medium, the one against the other. The Romans had organised the Syrian Arabs for this purpose under the leadership of princes of the house of Ghassān, the most celebrated of whom even received the title of patrician, while the Sāssānids founded a similar bulwark in Hīra, where the Lakhmites, under Persian sovereignty, lived a princely life, greatly celebrated by Arabian poets. A short-sighted policy, and probably also internal weakness, permitted the ruin of both of these States, which would have offered an almost insuperable barrier to the Islāmitic expansion. The hitherto united dominions of the Ghassānids were subdivided and various governors took the place of the popular Lakhmite princes. Thus the great empires had succeeded in destroying the smaller Arabian States which had grown too powerful, but the tradition remained, according to which the Arabians on the borders might with impunity levy contributions on the neighbouring cultivated countries during the constant wars between Persia and Byzantium. These traditions were assimilated by those Arabs then gradually becoming dependent on Medina, and their procedure was sanctioned and encouraged by the young and rising Caliphate; at first in a wavering, but later in a more and more energetic manner. The expansion of the Saracens is thus the final stage in a process of development extending over centuries. Islām was simply a change in the watchword for which they fought; and thus arose at the same time an organisation which, based on religious and ethnical principles and crowned with unexpected success, was bound to attain an historical importance quite different from that of buffer States like Ḥīra and Ghassān.

Under these circumstances it would be a mistake to regard the Arab migration merely as a religious movement incited by Mahomet. The question may in fact be put whether the whole movement is not conceivable without the intervention of Islām. There can in any case be no question of any zealous impulse towards proselytism. That strong religious tie which at the present time binds together all Muslims, that exclusive religious spirit of the later world of Islām, is at all events not the primary cause of the Arab migration, but merely a consequence of the political and cultural conditions caused by it. The importance of Islām in this direction lies in its masked political character, which the modern world has even in our own time to take into consideration. In the outset Islām meant the supremacy of Medina, but it soon identified itself with Arabianism, *i.e.*, it preached the superiority of the Arabian people generally. This great idea gives an intellectual purport to the restless striving for expansion, and makes a political focus of the great Arabian State of Medina, founded on religion. Hunger and avarice, not religion, are the impelling forces, but religion supplies the essential unity and central power. The expansion of the Saracens' religion, both in point of time and in itself, can only be regarded as of minor import and rather as a political necessity. The movement itself had been on foot long before Islām gave it a party cry and an organisation. Then it was that the minor streams of Arabian nationality, gradually encroaching on the cultivated territory, united with the related elements already resident there and formed that irresistible migratory current which flooded the older kingdoms, and seemed to flood them suddenly.

If the expansion of the Saracens is thus allowed to take its proper place in the entire development of the Middle Ages, a glance at the state of affairs at the time of the prophet's death leads directly to the history of the Arab migration itself.

The death of the prophet is represented by tradition as an event which surprised the whole world and to the faithful seemed impossible, notwithstanding the fact that Mahomet had always confessed himself to be a mortal man. He had, it is true, never taken his eventual decease into consideration, nor had he left a definite code of laws or any instructions regarding his succession. But can we suppose a similar self-deception also among his nearest companions, who must certainly have seen how he was ageing, and must have had him before them in all his human weakness? Can we suppose any delusion in so circumspect a nature as Abū Bakr, or in such a genius for government as Omar? The energetic and wise conduct of both these men and their companion Abū ʿUbaida, immediately after the catastrophe, seems to prove the contrary and their action seems based on well-prepared arrangements. Energetic action was moreover very necessary, for it was a giant task which Mahomet bequeathed to those entrusted with the regulation of his inheritance. At the very outset loomed up the difficulties in the capital itself. The sacred personality of the prophet had succeeded in holding in check the old antipathies within the ranks of the Medina allies (Anṣār) and the continual petty jealousies between these and the Muhājirūn, the companions of his flight from Mecca. But on his death, which for the great majority was sudden and unexpected, these two groups confronted each other, each claiming the right to take up the lead. As soon as the news of the death first reached them the Khazraj, the most numerous tribe of the Anṣār, assembled in the hall (Saḳīfa) of the Banū Sā'ida. Informed of this by the Aus, who feared a revival of the old dissensions, Abū Bakr, Omar and Abū 'Ubaida at once repaired thither and arrived just in time to prevent a split in the community. The hot-blooded Omar wanted to put a stop to it promptly and by energetic means, and would of a certainty have spoiled the whole situation, but at this stage the venerable and awe-inspiring Abū Bakr, the oldest companion of the prophet, intervened and whilst fully recognising the merits of the Anṣār insisted on the election of one of the Ḳuraishite companions of the prophet as leader of the community. He proposed Omar or Abū 'Ubaida. The proposal did not meet with success and the discussion became more and more excited ; suddenly Omar seized the hand of Abū Bakr and rendered homage to him, and others followed his example. In the meantime the hall and adjoining rooms had become filled with people belonging, not to either of the main groups, but to the fluctuating population of Muslim Arabs of the neighbourhood, who had in the preceding years become especially numerous in Medina, and whose main interest was that matters should remain *in statu quo*. These people really turned the scales, and thus Abū Bakr was chosen by a minority and recognised on the following day by the community, though unwillingly, as even tradition is unable to veil, on the part of many. They rendered homage to him as the representative (Khalīfa) of the prophet. The term Caliph was at that time not regarded as a title, but simply as a designation of office ; Omar, the successor of Abū Bakr, is said to have been the first to assume the distinctive title "Commander of the Faithful," Amīr al-Mu'minīn, rendered by the Greek papyri as ἀμιραλμουμνίν.

The election of Abū Bakr was doubtless a fortunate one, but it was regarded in circles closely interested as an inexcusable *coup de main*. Quite apart from the fact that the Anṣār had failed to carry their point and were accordingly in bad humour, the nearer relations of the prophet and their more intimate companions appear to have carried out a policy of obstruction which yielded only to force. Ali, the husband of the prophet's daughter Fāṭima and father of the prophet's grandsons Hasan and Ḥusain, who had previously held the first claim to the supreme position, was suddenly ousted from the front rank. His uncle ʻAbbās and probably also Ṭalḥa and Zubair (two of the earliest converts to Islām) allied themselves with him. Ali was a good swordsman but not a man of cautious action or quick resolve. He and those nearest to him appear to have had no other object in view than to gather around the corpse of the prophet while the fight for the succession was raging without. The news of Abū Bakr's election however roused them at last from their lethargy, and thereupon ensued an act of revenge, shrouded certainly in mystery by Muslim tradition, but which cannot be obliterated; the body of the prophet was secretly buried during the same night below the floor of his death-chamber. It was the custom, after pronouncing the benediction over the coffin, to carry the dead in solemn procession through the town to the cemetery. As however this procession would have simultaneously formed the triumphal entry of the new ruler, the body was disposed of as quickly as possible without the knowledge of Abū Bakr or the other leading companions. Tradition, which represents the old companions as working together in pure friendship and unanimity, has endeavoured with much care to picture these remarkable occurrences as legal. For instance Mahomet is said to have stated previously that prophets should always be buried at the spot where they died. To the modern historian however this episode unveils the strong passions and deep antipathies which divided, not only the Meccans and the Medina faction, but also the nearest companions of the prophet. Abū Bakr's rule was but feebly established, and a dissolution of the young realm would have been inevitable had not the pure instinct of self-preservation forced the opposing parties into unity.

The news of the death appeared to let loose all the centrifugal forces of the new State. According to Muslim accounts all Arabia was already subjected and converted to Islām; and as soon as the news of Mahomet's death was known, many of the tribes seceded from Islām and had to be again subjected in bloody wars and reconverted. This apostasy is termed *Ridda*, a change of belief, a well-known term of the later law of Islām. In reality Mahomet, at the time of his death, had by no means united Arabia, much less had he converted all the country to Islām. Not quite all of what to-day forms the Turkish province of Ḥijāz, that is the central portion of the west coast of Arabia with its corresponding back-country, was in reality politically joined with Medina and Mecca as a united power, and even this was held together more by interest than by religious brotherhood. The tribes of Central Arabia, *e.g.*, the Ghaṭafān, Bāhila, Ṭayyiʾ, Asad, etc., were in a state of somewhat lax dependence on Mahomet and had probably also partially accepted the doctrine of Islām, whilst in the Christian district to the north and in Yamāma, which had its own prophet, and in the south and east of the peninsula Mahomet either had no connexions whatever or had made treaties with single or isolated tribes, *i.e.*, with a weak minority. It was inexplicable to the subsequent historians of the Arabian State that after the death of Mahomet so many wars were necessary on Arabian soil; they accounted for this fact by a *Ridda*, an apostasy, from Islām. The death of the prophet was doubtless a reason for secession to all those who had unwillingly followed Mahomet's lead, or who regarded their contracts as void on his death. The majority of those regarded as secessionists (Ahl ar-Ridda) had however previously never been adherents of the religion, and many had not even belonged to the political State of Islām. It has but recently been recognised that an intelligible history of the expansion of the Arabs is only possible by making these wars against the *Ridda* the starting-point from which the great invasions developed themselves, more from internal necessity than through any wise direction from Medina—undertakings moreover from the enormous extent of which even the optimism of Mahomet would have flinched.

The movement in Arabia had received through the formation of the State of Medina a new and powerful stimulation. Mahomet's campaigns, with their rich booty, had allured many from afar. He had moreover, as a great diplomatist, strengthened the opposition where he could find no direct acknowledgment. His example alone had also its effect. Should not the prophet of the Banū Ḥanīfa, of the Asad, or of the Tamīm be able to do what the Meccan *Nabī* had done? In this way prophetism gained ground in Arabia, *i.e.*, the tension already existing grew until it neared an outburst. The sudden death of Mahomet gave new support to the centrifugal tendencies. The character of the whole movement, as it forces itself on the notice of the historian, was of course hidden from contemporaries. Arabia would have sunk into particularism if the necessity caused by the secession of the Ahl ar-Ridda had not developed in the State of Medina an energy which carried all before it. The fight against the *Ridda* was not a fight against apostates; the objection was not to Islām *per se* but to the tribute which had to be paid to Medina; the fight was for the political supremacy over Arabia; and its natural result was the extension of the dominions of the prophet, not their restoration. With such a distribution of the Arabian element as has been described it was only in the nature of things that the fight must make itself felt moreover beyond the boundaries of Arabia proper.

Only a few of the tribes more nearly connected with Medina recognised the supremacy of Abū Bakr, the others all seceding. Before the news of these secessions reached Medina an expedition, which had been prepared by Mahomet before his death, had already departed for the Syrian border to avenge the defeat at Mu'ta. Medina was therefore quite denuded of troops. A few former allies wished to utilise this precarious position and make a sudden attack on Medina; this however was prevented by Abū Bakr with great energy. Fortunately the expedition returned in time to enable him to capture the camp of the insurgents after a severe battle at Dhu-l-Ḳaṣṣa (Aug.—Sept. 632). Khālid ibn al-Walīd, who had already distinguished himself under Mahomet, was thereupon entrusted with the task of breaking the opposition of the tribes of Central Arabia. Khālid was without doubt a military genius of the first rank. He was somewhat lax in matters of religion and could be as cruel as his master had been before him; but was a brilliant strategist, carefully weighing his chances; yet once his mind was made up, he was endued with an energy and daring before which all had to yield. He is the actual conqueror of the Ridda, and his good generalship secured victory after victory for Islām.

With a force of about 4000 men he again reduced the Ṭayyi' to obedience, and then in rapid succession routed at Buzākha the Asad and Ghaṭafān, who had gathered round a prophet called Ṭalḥa, scoffingly styled by the Muslims Ṭulaiḥa, meaning the little Ṭalḥa. Khālid's success caused fresh troops to flock to his standard. He then at once proceeded further into the territory of the Tamīm, but against the wishes of the Anṣār accompanying him and without the authority of the Caliph. This arbitrary procedure, together with a cruel act of personal revenge which he performed at the last-named place caused his recall; he was however not only exculpated, but a proposal of his was adopted, to strike a heavy blow at the Banū Ḥanīfa in Yamāma. At this place the prophet Maslama was then ruling, and as in the case of Ṭulaiḥa the Muslims sarcastically formed a diminutive of his name and styled him Musailima. According to tradition this Musailima had maintained friendly relations with Mahomet. Be that as it may, certain it is that he was not in any way subject to Medina in either a political or religious sense, but more probably an imitator of his successful colleague Mahomet. In any case his rule was somewhat firmly established, and it cost Khālid a bloody battle to destroy his power. This memorable battle was fought at 'Aḳrabā and was without doubt the bloodiest and most important during the whole of the Ridda war. We are as yet but poorly informed in regard to the chronology of these events, but it may probably be assumed that the battle of 'Aḳrabā was fought about one year after the death of the prophet.

By the side of these great successes of Khālid the campaigns of other generals in Baḥrain, 'Umān, Mahra, Ḥaḍramaut and Yaman are less important. Moreover the earliest subjection of all these lands under the rule of Islām was not carried out by troops specially sent out from Medina; it may even be doubtful if the commanders, with whose names these conquests are associated, were despatched from Medina. It may be that they were only subsequently legalised and that Muhājir ibn Abī Umayya was the first actual delegate of the Caliph. In any case these districts were unsettled for a long time after the Muslim troops had invaded Syria and the 'Irāḳ. Further, the same districts were in less than half a century later almost independent, and later still a focus of heterodox tendencies.

The further march of events is connected, not with these wars but with Khālid's unparalleled succession of victories, and with the complication on the Syrian border. The subjection of Central Arabia to Medina inspired the Arabs of the border districts with a profound respect, but it simultaneously excited the warlike propensities of the most important tribes of Arabia. It would have been an enormous task for the government in Medina to compel all these restless elements, accustomed to marauding excursions, to live side by side in neighbourly peace under the sanctuary of Islām in unfertile Arabia. Within the boundaries of the empire however such fratricidal feuds were henceforth abolished. It was only to be expected that after the withdrawal of Khālid's army a reaction against Medina should seize upon the newly subjected tribes. The necessity of keeping their own victorious troops employed, as also of reconciling the subjected ones to the new conditions, irresistibly compelled an extension of the Islāmitic rule beyond the borders of Arabia. Chronologically the raid on 'Irāḳ (the ancient Babylonia) stands at the commencement of these enterprises. This however was quite a minor affair, and the main attention of the government was directed to Syria.

Before going further, we have to shew that our exposition differs radically from all the usual descriptions of the expansion of the Arabs, not only in our estimates of the sources and events, but also in our chronological arrangement of them. The conquests of the Saracens have in later years been a focus of scientific debate. Through the labours of De Goeje, Wellhausen and Miednikoff a complete revolution in our views has been effected. We have learnt to differentiate the various schools of tradition, of which that of 'Irāḳ, represented by Saif ibn Omar, has produced an historical novel which can hardly be classed as actual history. The reports of the Medina and the Syrian schools are more trustworthy, and a certain amount of reliance may be placed on the Egyptian school, but they all suffer from later harmonising efforts, and also from their revision during the period of the Abbasids, in which it was sought in every way to depreciate the Umayyads. All these traditions are now being collected and critically sifted in the stupendous annals of Leone Caetani. His epoch-making results are utilised in the following paragraphs.

Between Yamāma and the Ḥīra district, which we must regard as a long, narrow strip of country, the North Arabian (Ishmaelite) tribe of Bakr ibn Wā'il led a nomadic existence on the borders of the cultivated country, covered by the protecting marshes of the lower Euphrates, and this tribe was again subdivided into various independent minor groups. They formed part of the restless border tribes against which Ḥīra had been erected as a bulwark. The sub-tribe of the Banū Shaibān especially had brilliant traditions, for it was these people who had won the first and much celebrated victory of the Arabs over Persian regular troops at Dhu Ḳār before the rise of Islām (between 604 and 611). This tribe of the Banū Shaibān and their leader Muthannā ibn Ḥāritha, whose example was followed by the others, induced Khālid and his Muslims to cross the Persian boundary for the first time. That was not a matter of chance, but shews the deep inner connexion of the Saracen expansion with the migration already in being before the rise of Islām. The Shaibān, like all the other components of the Bakr ibn Wā'il, were wholly independent of Medina, and had no intention of becoming Muslims. But when Medina suddenly extended its dominion beyond Yamāma, and all Arabia echoed with the fame of Khālid in warfare, the Bakr found themselves in a dilemma between the rising Arabian great power and their old hereditary enemy, Persia. What could be more obvious than that, simply because they needed a screen for their rear, they should draw the related Muslims into their alliance and with their assistance continue their raids into the cultivated country? Khālid, reckless plunger that he was, seized with avidity this opportunity for fresh deeds of valour. Tradition reports that the chiefs of the Bakr tribes, and of them Muthannā first and foremost, paid a visit to the Caliph Abū Bakr at Medina, professed Islām, and received from Abū Bakr the command to conquer 'Irāḳ in conjunction with Khālid. In reality it is doubtful whether the Caliph even so much as knew of any connexion between Khālid and the Bakr tribes. At the same time it is not improbable that he gave his consent for Khālid to participate in one of the customary raids of the Bakr ibn Wā'il, but the conversion of the head of the tribes was no part of his plan, much less the conversion of the tribes themselves. They certainly from this time onward were in touch with Medina, and regarded themselves as in political alliance with the Muslims; and in the rapid developments of the next few years they were merged in the Caliph's dominions. Abū Bakr did not at first contemplate any systematic occupation of 'Irāḳ, for he was at that time considering an expedition against Syria, which from the point of view of Medina was of infinitely greater importance. Even at that time they desired to have Khālid in Syria; but he had in any case already taken part in the raid of the Banū Shaibān, either with or without the knowledge of the Caliph. How little any conquest of Persia was contemplated is shewn by the fact that the main body of Khālid's troops was ordered home to recruit, and he undertook his first invasion of Persian territory with only about 500 men, certainly well selected troops, and then continued his march further with the same contingent into Syria.

Khālid attracted volunteers of all kinds from Central Arabia, and marched with them westward of the Euphrates to avoid the marshes; at Khaffān he effected a junction with the Bakr under Muthannā; their combined forces amounted in all to only two to three thousand men, but they had fortune on their side. They crossed the fertile land to the north of Hīra unmolested and plundering as they went; Ullais was also put under contribution, and suddenly they appeared before Hīra. The town was well fortified, but the garrison was palpably insufficient for an open battle. And what was the use of resistance within the walls if their rich lands around were to be desolated? Thinking thus they quickly resolved to pay a ransom, especially as the Arabs only demanded the ridiculously small sum of 60,000 *dirhams*. To the Arabs this seemed an enormous booty. Elated with victory they withdrew, and Hīra was thus saved for the time being. It is scarcely conceivable that the payment of this sum was regarded as an annual tribute. After this expedition Khālid marched on with his braves, by command of the Caliph, right through the enemy's territory, appearing in all directions with lightning speed and disappearing again with equal rapidity, from Hīra through Palmyra to Syria where he appeared, suddenly and unexpectedly, under the walls of Damascus. This expedition, so woven round with legendary lore, and apart from that a military masterpiece, shews better than anything else that the conquest of Persia was not premeditated, and that the Muslims were making their main effort in Syria. The raid against Hīra was made at a time of the greatest confusion in Persia, but few months after the accession of Yezdegerd, when the central authority was to some extent restored by his general Rustam. Thereupon a counter-raid was prepared against the plunderers. Muthannā sought help from Medina. This was in the early days of Omar's government, and he granted the request only with a certain amount of reluctance, refusing to spare his best troops from Syria. The combined troops of the Bakr and of Medina were few and badly handled, and in a second expedition they were almost annihilated; in the so-called Bridge battle Muthannā saved with difficulty the remnants of the Muslim army (26 Nov. 634). It was in consequence of this disaster that Omar, a year later (635), was led to a more energetic interference in the conditions of the 'Irāḳ, but even then his actions were somewhat dilatory. Of this it will be necessary to speak later, if only briefly. For a history of the Middle Ages the expansion of the Arabs in Mediterranean territories is of much greater importance.

The Arabian records of these events are not only distorted by lies, but are terribly confused: especially in their chronology. Fortunately we are better informed through some of the Byzantine writers, especially Theophanes. It was not the sagacity of the Caliphs, wanting to conquer the world, that flung the Muslim host on Syria, but the Christian Arabs of the border districts who applied to the powerful organisation of Medina for assistance. We are told very little about the relations between Mahomet and the great tribes of North Arabia, such as the Judhām, Kalb, Ḳuḍā'a, Lakhm, Ghassān; but the defeat of Mu'ta shews that they were enemies of Medina. It was only the expedition

against Tabūk, which had to be subjected two years before the death of
the prophet, that created friendly relations with at least a few of the
tribes on the southern boundary of Palestine. In the war of conquest
the great tribes of the former boundary State of the Ghassānids still
fought on the side of the Byzantines. The tribes to the south of the
Dead Sea however, such as the Judhām and Ḳuḍā'a, who commanded
the route from Medina to Gaza, had every reason for connecting themselves more closely with Medina. Previously they had been in the pay
of the Byzantines, and being moreover Christians, they had no intention
of allying themselves with the Muslims. Soon after the battle of Mu'ta
however, we are informed, the Emperor Heraclius, who at that time was
in great financial difficulties owing to the debt contracted with the
Church for the great Persian war, suspended the yearly subsidies to the
Bedouins on the southern boundary, probably thinking that with
the new political situation he might venture on this economy. At that
time even a far-seeing politician could not have regarded as serious the
organisation of the ever-divided Arabs living in the interior of Arabia.
Judging by the behaviour of the northern tribes, they continued for a
time to be paid. Theophanes even treats the suspension of subsidies as
being in some way the cause of the summoning of the Muslims. Apart
from this may be added that, after the victories of Khālid in Central
Arabia, these border tribes, like the Bakr ibn Wā'il in the East, were led
into a dilemma; as Byzantium withdrew the subsidies from them it was
only natural that they made an alliance with the Muslims to recoup
themselves by plundering raids.

Their suggestion met with the approval of the Caliph, who probably
recognised that the commotion which had been raised must be diverted
in some direction or other. The Medina people themselves, according to
Arabian reports, do not appear to have at first displayed any enthusiasm
for such a risky action; probably they had not forgotten the disaster of
Mu'ta. Nevertheless in the autumn of 633 various small detachments
were sent off into Syria, the first under Yazīd ibn Abī Sufyān, a brother
of the subsequent Caliph Mu'āwiya, the second under Shuraḥbīl ibn
Ḥasana, the third under 'Amr ibn al-'Āṣ. The first two bodies of
troops, probably co-operating most of the time, took the direct track via
Tabūk-Ma'ān; 'Amr marched along the coast via Aila ('Aḳaba); other
smaller companies followed later and pushed forward from the South into
the country east of the Jordan. The first to get engaged in battle was
Yazīd. Approaching from westward he ascended the hills surmounting
the Wādī 'Araba, the great valley south of the Dead Sea, and surprised
several thousands of Byzantine troops under the Patricius of Caesarea,
named Sergius. These were routed and compelled to retire on Gaza;
before reaching this town however they were overtaken (4 Feb. 634) by
the Arabs and annihilated, Sergius also losing his life. After this
success Yazīd again retired beyond the protecting Dead Sea. Shortly

afterwards 'Amr put in an appearance, coming from Aila with fresh
troops, which had been further strengthened on the way by recruits. They
raided the whole of southern Palestine as far as Gaza, and 'Amr in fact
on one occasion pushed forward into the district of Ḳaisārīya (Caesarea).

Upon hearing of these surprising events the Emperor Heraclius who
at that time was still dwelling at Emesa, in northern Syria, concentrated a great army to the south of Damascus, and placed it under the
command of his brother Theodorus. It was unusually difficult for the
Greeks to recognise any plan of attack on the part of the Arabs; these
simply advanced without any definite aim; the leader of each detachment went whithersoever he listed, and whither he conceived the greatest
amount of booty was available. Possibly the troops of Theodorus may
have destroyed a small detachment of the Arabs in the country east of
the Jordan, but in any case they advanced very slowly in a southerly
direction, where the greatest danger threatened, for Jerusalem was
temporarily cut off from the sea, and even Caesarea and Gaza were
threatened. Immediately after this advance Khālid, approaching in
their rear from the Euphrates, suddenly appeared before Damascus
(24 April 634). He remained unmolested, because all available troops
were then on the way to the South. Clever strategist that he was, and
without the selfish greed for plunder of the other leaders, Khālid at once
recognised the precarious position of the Arabs in the southern part
of Palestine. Advancing down the country east of Jordan he succeeded,
probably with the utmost difficulty, in effecting a junction with the
detachments in the South, engaged in their own selfish interests. Finally,
in the Wādī 'Araba, he united with 'Amr and Yazīd, who were retiring
before the approaching Byzantines. This effected, the combined forces
of the Muslims once more advanced against Theodorus, who had occupied
a strong position at Ajnādain, or better Jannābatain, between Jerusalem and Gaza. On 30 July 634 a bloody battle ensued, terminating
in a brilliant victory for the Arabs. Who commanded the Arabs, or
whether in fact they had any commander-in-chief, remains a matter of
doubt, but it is probably not wide of the mark to recognise the actual
victor in Khālid. Hereupon all Palestine lay open to the Arabs, *i.e.*, all
the flat country; the well-fortified towns, even though without large
garrisons, held out for a considerable time longer. The Arabs, who still
regarded themselves as being out on a plundering expedition, probably
spared the resident population less than they did later, when the
systematic occupation took place. Report states that Gaza also fell at this
time, but this simply means that Gaza was laid under contribution in
the same way that Ḥīra had been before. The Patriarch Sophronius of
Jerusalem, in his Christmas sermon at the end of the year 634, describes
in moving terms the doleful condition of the country. Anarchy appears
to have ruled supreme. The Arabs dispersed themselves throughout the
country, and even pushed forward far towards the North; the temporary

appearance of the Arabs before Emesa in January 635 is credibly authenticated by a Syrian source.

During the six months following the battle of Ajnādain the tone of public opinion must have undergone a considerable change. Men of the rank of Khālid and 'Amr could not but perceive that they could not go on with such planless raids; a systematic occupation of the country appeared urgent. In addition to this the Caliph Abū Bakr died soon after the battle of Ajnādain (634) and the energetic far-seeing Omar had been nominated by him as his successor and recognised on all sides without question. This new view was further supported both at the front and at head-quarters by the continued pressing forward of the Arab element from the south of the peninsula; after the termination of the Ridda wars these people, incited by the unparalleled successes of the Medina people, also marched to Syria. These new arrivals did not however arrive in the form of organised troops, but advanced in tribes, bringing their wives and children with them and hoping to find in the new land fertile residential areas. This process is very difficult to record in detail, and doubtless extended over several years. It was only after the battle of the Yarmūk that the Arabs really began seriously to take in hand the administration of the country. But within six months of the battle of Ajnādain there began a much more systematic progress of the Arabs, who were now clearly placed under the supreme command of Khālid. The last troops of Heraclius had now withdrawn to Damascus, the defeated Theodorus had been recalled to Constantinople and the conduct of further operations lay in the hands of Baanes, who concentrated his troops in the beginning of 635 at Fiḥl, a strategically important position situated south of the Sea of Gennesareth and covering the crossing of the Jordan and the route to Damascus. By cutting dykes he endeavoured to prevent the advance of the Arabs. Impressed however probably by their slowly changing conception of the task before them and led by Khālid, the Muslims forced the position at Fiḥl (23 Jan. 635) and immediately afterwards took possession of Baisān (Bethshan). They then pushed forward determinedly towards Damascus. Baanes again opposed their advance at Marj aṣ-Ṣuffar (25 Feb. 635) but was defeated and two weeks later the Muslims were before the gates of Damascus.

The Arabs were not in a position properly to lay siege to the town, for they were quite ignorant of this kind of warfare. They were compelled therefore to endeavour to isolate the town, and so to exasperate the residents as to cause them to compel the garrison to surrender. It was however not until the early autumn (Aug.—Sept.) that the town capitulated, after Heraclius had endeavoured in vain on several occasions to relieve it; in one of the abortive attempts he had however inflicted on the Arabs a rather serious reverse. The capitulation ensued at last palpably through the treachery of the civil authorities, assisted by the Bishop and the tax-collector. After the fall of Damascus the Arabs proceeded to the pacification of the conquered country, without giving further heed to the Byzantines, from whom they did not consider they had anything more to fear. The various leaders operated in Palestine and the country east of the Jordan; Khālid himself pressed forward once more against Emesa, and occupied this place at the close of the year 635. A number of smaller towns hereupon opened their gates to the conquerors whilst the larger fortresses such as Jerusalem, Caesarea and the coastal towns, still held out in hope of rescue by Heraclius.

Heraclius certainly as yet had no intention of giving up the country to the Arabs. He shewed a feverish activity in Antioch and Edessa. Together with the customary Byzantine mercenaries, Armenians and Arabs formed the main body of his new army, which he placed under the command of Theodorus Trithurius, and in which Baanes had the control of an independent division. The relief of Damascus not having been effected, Heraclius permitted the winter months to pass, intending when he was so much the better prepared to take the offensive and strike a crushing blow against the Arabs. In the spring of 636 this new army unexpectedly approached Emesa, where Khālid was on outpost duty. He at once recognised his dangerous position. Hitherto the Arabs had always fought against an inferior Byzantine force, but now they were suddenly opposed by a powerful army which, even after making all allowance for Arab exaggeration, must have amounted to some 50,000 men. Khālid immediately relinquished not only Emesa but even Damascus and caused all the Arab fighting forces to be concentrated at a point between the northern and southern positions of the Arabs in the country east of the Jordan, to the south-east of the deep Yarmūk valley, and to the north of what is now known as Der'āt, a point admirably adapted to his purpose. Here the Arabs were in the most fertile part of Syria, where the most important highways crossed leading to the southern portion of the country east of the Jordan and to Central Palestine; they were moreover protected in the rear by the deeply hollowed valleys of the Yarmūk tributaries. Should they be defeated here a retreat was under all circumstances secured either into the desert or to Medina. The hurried retirement of the Arabs to this district proves how critical affairs appeared to them : against the huge advancing army of the enemy, they could only oppose about 25,000, scarcely half the number.

The Roman army did not approach by way of Damascus but through Coelesyria and across the Jordan, and probably took up their position near Jillīn, the Jillīḳ of the sources. The two armies must have remained confronting each other for a considerable period; the Arabs were waiting for reinforcements, whilst the Byzantine army was hampered by the petty jealousies of its leaders and by insubordination in the ranks. Several battles were fought in which Theodorus appears to have been at the outset defeated and Baanes was then proclaimed emperor by the troops. The Arabian auxiliaries

CH. XI.

deserted, and under all these circumstances the Arabs had no longer cause to fear the numerical superiority of their opponents. They appear to have outflanked the Byzantines from the eastern side, cut their line of communication with Damascus, and by occupying the bridge over the Wādi-r-Ruḳḳād frustrated also their chances of retreat to the westward. Finally they forced them into the angle between the Yarmūk and the Wādi-r-Ruḳḳād. Those who were not killed here plunged down into the steep and deeply cut beds of the rivers, and those of the latter who had finally managed to escape across the rivers to Jakutha were annihilated by the Arabs on the other side, as, by occupying the bridge, they were enabled with ease to cross the Wādi-r-Ruḳḳād. The decisive stroke in these fights, extending over months, happened on 20 Aug. 636. With this terrible defeat of the Byzantines on the Yarmūk the fate of Syria was permanently decided. The last troops of Heraclius, collected with much trouble, had been thus completely destroyed, and the immediate advance of the Arabs on Damascus rendered impossible every attempt to collect others. Thus Damascus was occupied a second time by the Arabs in the autumn of the same year, and this time finally.

The government of Medina had, as we have already seen, attempted for about the space of a year to introduce a systematic occupation of the country in place of the former planless raids. This policy made it necessary that the army of occupation should have a supreme commandant, who should at the same time act as vicegerent of the Caliph. At the outset Khālid, who on account of his qualities had acquired the senior rank, was confirmed in this position, but in the brilliant general there was entirely wanting the diplomatic art of a pacificator attaining his ends by statesmanlike compromises. For this position one of the foremost men of the theocracy was required, an absolute confidant of the Caliph. Omar selected Abū 'Ubaida, one of the oldest and most esteemed of his companions, of whom we know that, for instance at the death of the prophet, he had played an important part. His task in face of the autocratic army-leaders was a difficult one; he arrived in Syria just before the battle of the Yarmūk, but was prudent enough to leave at this critical stage the supreme command for this battle to Khālid, who was so minutely acquainted with the conditions. Thereupon however he himself intervened, distributed the various military commandants throughout the entire land, and then personally advanced, in company with Khālid, towards the North. Baalbek, Emesa, Aleppo, Antioch and the Arabian tribes residing in the north of Syria, put no difficulties in the way of the conquest. The town of Ḳinnasrīn (Kalchis) alone was less easily dealt with. From northern Syria 'Iyāḍ ibn Ghanm was then subsequently detached to the East, and he subjected Mesopotamia (639–646) without meeting with much opposition. To the North, however, the Amanus formed for centuries the more or less constant boundary of the Caliph's dominions.

In the meantime, *i.e.*, in the course of the years 636 and 637, Shurahbīl and Yazīd had finally occupied the remainder of the interior, and most of the towns on the coast. 'Amr was less fortunate, and invested Jerusalem in vain. The stubborn Caesarea also remained for a time closed to the Arabs. It is no matter of chance that just these two strongly Hellenised towns should have held out. Their resistance gives us a clue to explain the rapid successes of the Arabs. The military power of the Emperor was certainly broken, and he lacked both men and money; but it was of much greater moment that everywhere in Syria, where Semites dwelt, the Byzantine rule was so deeply hated that the Arabs were welcomed as deliverers, as soon as there was no need further to fear Heraclius. To cover his enormous debts Heraclius had been compelled to put on the fiscal screw to its utmost tension. In addition to this domestic pressure there was added that of religion; the church policy of Heraclius, the introduction of the Monotheletic Irenicon, became a persecution of Monophysites and Jews. In addition to this religious division there was now further the natural reaction of the Semitic element against the foreign rule of the Greeks. In the Muslims on the other hand the numerous Christian Arab tribes, and even the Aramaeans too, welcomed blood relations; the tribute moreover demanded by the Arabs was not heavy, and finally the Arabs permitted complete religious freedom; in fact, for political reasons, they rather encouraged heterodox tendencies. Thus, after the Arabs had vanquished the tyrants, the land fell peacefully into their own possession. The resistance of Jerusalem and Caesarea affords the test of this theory, for both of these towns were entirely Hellenic and orthodox. Even these towns however were unable to maintain their position for any length of time, and Jerusalem capitulated as early as 638; Caesarea did not fall until October 640 into the hands of Mu'āwiya, and then only through treachery.

Even before the fall of Jerusalem the Caliph Omar had paid a visit to Syria. His appearance there was the result of the policy of occupation followed by Medina. The head-quarters of the Muslim army was at that time still at Jābiya, a little to the north of the Yarmūk battle-field. To this spot Omar summoned all his military commanders, presumably to support Abū 'Ubaida in his difficult task with the authority of the Caliph. Apart from this however it was desired to lay down uniform principles for the treatment of the subjected peoples, *i.e.*, to define the difficult problem which we of modern times call native policy. Further, the disposition of the money coming in and the whole administration needed an initial regulation, or rather sanction. Later tradition considers Omar the founder of the theoretical system of the ideal Muslim State, but incorrectly so, as will be shewn later. At the same time an initial regulation then certainly took place. On the termination of his work of reorganisation Omar visited Jerusalem, proceeding thence on his return journey to Medina. Abū 'Ubaida remained in the country as Omar's representative, but was not destined to remain in office much longer, for in the year 639, when many thousands from the ranks of the victors succumbed to a fearful epidemic of plague, Abū 'Ubaida was also carried off by it, as was also his successor in office, Yazīd, a short time later. Yazīd's brother, Mu'āwiya ibn Abī Sufyān, was then nominated to the succession by Omar, and in him the man appears at the head of Syria who was destined later in his own person to transfer the Caliphate to Damascus, a development which in its slow preparation is as clear as noonday.

The whole course of the Muslim expeditions in 'Irāḳ shews that the policy of the Caliphs was entirely determined by consideration for Syria. After the unfortunate battle of the Bridge not only the government but also the tribes were still more cautious towards 'Irāḳ expeditions. It was only the eager efforts of Muthannā, of the Bakr tribe, that finally succeeded in gaining the sanction of the Caliph to a new raid, and then only after the first conquest of Damascus. But there was a dearth of warriors; none cared much to proceed to 'Irāḳ, and it was only on the grant of special privileges that a few Yamanites consented to prepare for the march. In the meantime the Persians, who for over a year had not followed up their advantage in the battle of the Bridge, had crossed the Euphrates under Mihrān; but Muthannā, with his auxiliaries from Medina, succeeded in defeating them at Buwaib (Oct. or Nov. 635). With his weak forces he could not however think of following up this small victory, and Omar at that time required all available troops for Syria, where the great army of Heraclius was advancing towards the battle of the Yarmūk. It was not until after this latter decisive victory that the Caliph paid greater attention to the 'Irāḳ. Here also the first thing to be done was the despatch of a general representative, or vicegerent, for which position Sa'd ibn Abī Waḳḳāṣ was selected. To get the necessary troops however for an energetic attack was still attended with great difficulty. Sa'd took the whole of the winter 636–637 to assemble a few thousand men around him. Of the Arabian hordes, incited by religious enthusiasm, according to the customary European traditions, we can find but little trace.

In the meantime the Persians, alarmed by their own defeat at Buwaib, and still more by the terrible collapse of the Byzantine rule in Syria, decided to take energetic steps against the Arabs. The administrator of the kingdom, Rustam, assumed the command personally, and crossed the Euphrates. On the borders of the cultivated land, at Ḳādisīya, Sa'd and Rustam stood for a long time facing each other. Of the size of their respective armies we know nothing positive; the Arabs were certainly not more than 5—6000 strong, including Christians and heathens, and the numerical superiority of the Persians cannot have been considerable. More by chance than from any tactical initiative the two armies became engaged in combat, and in one day the Persian army was routed, and its leaders slain (May—June 637).

And now the fertile black land (Sawād) of 'Irāḳ lay open to the Arabs. Conditions exactly similar to those in Syria caused the Aramaic peasants to greet the Arabs as deliverers. Without meeting with any noteworthy opposition the Saracens pushed on as far as the Tigris, whither they were attracted by the rich treasures of the Persian capital Ctesiphon, or as the Arabs called it the "city-complex" or Madā'in. The right bank of the Tigris was abandoned and the floating bridges broken up. A ford having been disclosed to the Arabs the residue of the garrison followed in the wake of Yezdegerd and his court, who immediately after the battle had sought the protection of the Iranian mountains. The city opened its gates and fabulous booty fell into the hands of the Arabs. After a few weeks of quiet and no doubt somewhat barbaric enjoyment, they had again to make one more stand on the fringe of the mountains at Jalūlā; this also ended victoriously for them, and with that the whole of 'Irāḳ was thus in their hands. Here also it was no matter of chance that the expansion of the Arabs first came to a standstill at the mountains, where the line was drawn between the Semitic and the Aryan elements of the population. Only the province of Khūzistān, the ancient Elam, caused some trouble still. Hither the Arabs appear to have proceeded from the south of the marsh district, when the insignificant raids of the boundary tribes there, encouraged by Medina, assumed after the battle of Ḳādisīya a more serious character, starting from the newly founded base at Baṣra. The chief seat of government was not placed at Ctesiphon, but, by express command of the Caliph, at Kūfa (near Ḥīra): and this was developed into a great Arabian military camp, intended to form the main citadel of Muslim Arabianism as against foreign Persian culture. Later the ancient Baṣra attained an independent position alongside of Kūfa. The rivalry of the two places sets its impress both on the politics and on the intellectual life of the following century.

It was not until after these stupendous victories of Yarmūk and Ḳādisīya that the great Arabian migrations assumed their full development, for now even those tribes who were but little disposed to Islām were compelled to wander forth in order to seek their happiness in those cultivated lands which as rumour told them were only to be compared with Paradise itself. Now it was that the momentous change took place to which reference has been made at the outset; now it was that Islām no longer represented dependence on Medina, as it did in the time of Mahomet and Abū Bakr, but from this time forward it represented the ideal of the common universal empire of the Arabs. And at this stage the further expeditions became systematic conquests, in which usually whole tribes participated. A first step in this direction was to round off the empire, combining the Syrian and 'Irāḳ provinces by the conquest of Mesopotamia. The expedition, begun from Syria as a starting-point, was completed from 'Irāķ by the capture of Mauṣil (Mosul) (641).

A systematic conquest of this description was especially called for in regard to 'Irāķ; for this province could not be regarded as secure as long as its recovery might be attempted. And at this juncture a strong reaction against the Arabs actually set in. The opposition which the Baṣrīs in Khūzistān met with, and which only ceased on the conquest of Tustar (641), was probably in connexion with the activity of the fleeing Yezdegerd and his followers, who summoned the whole of the Iranians to battle against the Arabs. The Baṣrīs and troops from Kūfa had already co-operated systematically in Khūzistān, and similar tactics followed now on Persian soil, where the decisive battle was fought in the year 641 at Nihāwand in the neighbourhood of the ancient Ekbatana. The Arabs gained a great victory; the dense garland of praise which legendary lore has woven around it shews how much depended for the Muslims on this victory. But even after this victory the Arabs were not yet masters of the great Median towns, as Hamadhān, Rayy and Ispahān; these were but slowly conquered during the next few years. Here in fact, where they were not greeted as deliverers by kindred Semites, the Arabs had to withstand a stubborn national opposition. Yezdegerd himself certainly caused them no difficulties; after the battle of Nihāwand he had fled further and further away and had finally gone from Istakhr to Marw in Khorāsān. His satrap there was too narrow-minded to support his fallen superior, and in fact he treated him as an enemy, and in 651–652 the deserted and unfortunate potentate appears to have been assassinated.

The Arabs did not reach Khorāsān until the province of Fārs, the actual Persia, was conquered. Fārs could be reached most conveniently from the Persian Gulf. This expedition had therefore been undertaken, with Baḥrain as starting-point, soon after the battle of Ķādisīya. This made the third base of attack, together with Ctesiphon (Kūfa) and Baṣra, from which the Arabs pushed forward into Iran. Later on the conduct of this expedition passed into the hands of the troops coming from Baṣra. But also in Fārs the same stubborn resistance was met with, which was not broken till after the conquest of Istakhr in the year 649–650 by 'Abdallāh ibn 'Āmir. Following this up 'Abdallāh, especially assisted by the Tamīm and Bakr tribes, began in the following year an advance, the first successful one, towards Khorāsān. This first and incomplete conquest of Persia took therefore more than ten years, whilst Syria and 'Irāķ fell in an astonishingly short time into the hands of the Arabs. In Persia Arabianism has never become national, and, whilst a few centuries later the other countries spoke the Arabian tongue, the Persian vernacular and the national traditions were still maintained in Persia. The religion of Islām moreover underwent later in Persia a

development completely differing from the orthodox Islām. Even
to-day Persia is the land of the Shī'a.

By reason of the great conquests in Syria and 'Irāḳ the capital,
Medina, was no longer the centre of the new empire. Byzantine Egypt
lay close by, and from Egypt a reconquest of Syria, even an attack on
Medina itself might be regarded as by no means impossible. Besides
Alexandria the town of Klysma (Ḳulzum, Suez) appears to have been a
strong naval port. Probably all Egypt was then an important base for
the fleet of the Byzantines and one of their principal dockyards; for the
Arabians of the earlier times it decidedly became such, and it appears not
improbable that their conquest of Egypt was connected with the recognition that only the possession of a fleet would ensure the lasting
retention of the new acquisitions, the Syrian coast towns, for instance.
After the fruitless efforts to take Caesarea this recognition was a matter
of course. Apart from this Egypt, a land rich in corn, must have been
a more desirable land for the central government than the distant 'Irāḳ
or Mesopotamia, for we find that soon after the conquest the growing
needs of Medina were supplied by regular imports of corn from Egypt.
It is therefore without doubt a non-historical conception, when an
Arabian source represents Egypt as having been conquered against the
wishes of the Caliph. The conquest of Egypt falls in a period during
which the occupation of new territories was carried out systematically,
instead of by the former more or less casual raids.

How much this undertaking was helped by the conditions in Egypt
at the time was probably scarcely imagined in the Muslim camp. After
the victories of Heraclius a strong Byzantine reaction had followed the
Persian rule, which had lasted about ten years. Heraclius needed money,
as we have already seen, and further, he hoped by means of a formula
of union to put an end to the perpetual sectarian discord between the
Monophysites and their opponents, and thereby to give to the reunited
kingdom one sole church. But the parties were already too strongly
embittered one against the other, and the religious division had already
been connected so closely with the political that the Irenicon remained
without effect. The Monophysite Egyptians probably never understood
the proposed Monothelete compromise at all, and always thought that it
was desired to force the hated Chalcedonian belief on them. It was
certainly no apostle of peace who brought the Irenicon to the Egyptians,
but a grand-inquisitor of the worst type. Soon after the re-occupation
of Egypt Heraclius, in the autumn of 631, sent Cyrus, the former bishop
of Phasis in the Caucasus, to Alexandria as Patriarch, and at the
same time as head of the entire civil administration. In a struggle
extending over ten years this man sought by the severest means to
convert the Coptic Church to the Irenicon; the Coptic form of worship
was forbidden, and its priests and organisations were cruelly persecuted.
As if that were not sufficient the same man, as a support of the financial

administration, was compelled to add considerably to the burden of taxation, in order to assist in paying the debts of the Emperor already referred to. It is no wonder that this dreaded imperial representative and Patriarch appeared to later Coptic tradition to be the veritable Antichrist. Most of all he was blamed for surrendering Egypt to the Muslims. This Cyrus is in fact, if we are not greatly deceived, the actual personage from whom the main traits of the figure of the Muḳauḳis, so surrounded by legendary lore of Muslim tradition, are taken. The problem of the Muḳauḳis is one of the most difficult ones in the whole history of the conquest of Egypt, which is throughout studded with problems. To the Arabians the Muḳauḳis represents the ruler of Egypt, who concludes with them the capitulation treaties. This was however without doubt Cyrus, for numerous other isolated statements in the legend of the Muḳauḳis apply to him, although other historical personages appear to have been confused with him. The study of Coptic tradition first solved the problem in so far as it identified the Muḳauḳis unhesitatingly with Cyrus. Whether in this obscure name a Byzantine title, a nickname, or a designation of descent is hidden, must remain for the present unelucidated.

The conqueror of Egypt was ʿAmr ibn al-ʿĀṣ, already known to us from the Syrian campaign, a man of great personal authority in the theocracy, but by no means a sanctimonious man, and perhaps less a great general, even if he gained his laurels, than an excellent organiser and a Machiavellian politician, with strong traces of heathenism and of genuine Arabian egotism. In December 639 ʿAmr appeared on the eastern boundary, at that time rather denuded of troops, and about a month later conquered Pelusium (Jan. 640) with only 3—4000 men. ʿAmr was unable to venture on a decisive battle until reinforcements to the number of about 5000 had joined him under the leadership of Zubair, the celebrated companion of the prophet. With these he defeated the Byzantines, commanded by the Augustalis Theodorus, in the battle of Heliopolis (July 640), this being followed up quickly by the occupation of one of the suburbs of Babylon, not far distant from the Cairo of to-day. Babylon was not the capital of Egypt, it is true, but owing to its commanding position at the head of the delta leading towards Alexandria it was the most important position in the country, and was correspondingly well fortified. The citadel of Babylon held out accordingly for a considerable time still. Cyrus, who appears to have been besieged there, entered into negotiation with ʿAmr, in spite of rather strong opposition to this course in his own camp, and then quitted Egypt to obtain from the Emperor a ratification of the provisional treaty agreed upon with ʿAmr. Heraclius was incensed to the utmost; and Cyrus was accused of treachery, and banished. Shortly afterwards (11 Feb. 641), the Emperor died. The relief of Babylon now appeared impossible: even before this the most pernicious intrigues with the Muslims had been carried on in Egypt, and now it was plainly to be seen that the death of the Emperor would fan into new life old passions—which in fact actually occurred. During the next few years the idea of any strong advance against the Saracens could not be entertained. Thus the citadel of Babylon capitulated in April 641. Therewith the eastern Delta and Upper Egypt lay in the hands of 'Amr. He thereupon crossed the Nile and, following the western branch of the river, advanced slowly towards Alexandria, capturing on his way the episcopal see of Nikiou, which capitulated on 13 May. Treachery and fear smoothed the way for him, but nevertheless he appears to have met with quite energetic opposition near Alexandria. He was, it is true, able to obtain possession temporarily of the vicinity of the town, but for the time being there could be no idea of subduing the great, strong Alexandria. As to the slow extension of the Muslim power in the remainder of Egypt we are not very well informed.

In the confusion following on the death of Heraclius the war party, represented as regards Egypt by the Augustalis Theodorus, appears to have gained the supremacy in Constantinople; then however, probably at the instigation of the Empress Martina, who was weary of the perpetual wars with the Saracens, Cyrus was again despatched to Egypt to arrange a capitulation with 'Amr under the most favourable conditions. Cyrus returned to Alexandria (14 Sept. 641) and his further policy is not quite clear. In any case, contrary to his former actions, he was most compliant to the Copts, and it is not improbable that he aimed at an Egyptian primacy under Arabian suzerainty. In the autumn, without the knowledge of the Alexandrians, he concluded the definite treaty with 'Amr, in accordance with which the city was to be evacuated by the Greeks not later than 17 Sept. 642, but for a stipulated tribute the residents were guaranteed their personal safety and the safety of their property, together with full freedom in the exercise of their religion. The Patriarch ran some risk of being lynched when this contract first became known, but he then appears to have convinced the people of its expediency. The Greeks quitted the town and it was actually given over to the Saracens at the appointed date. Cyrus did not live to see this, for he died previously (21 March 642). The capital of Egypt having fallen, 'Amr desired also to cover his flank; he therefore undertook in the following winter 642–643 an expedition to the Pentapolis and occupied Barka without striking a blow.

Alexandria was however no more selected as the seat of the new government than Ctesiphon had previously been chosen for this purpose. The policy of the Caliph was to isolate the Arabian element in the foreign land, and the Saracens therefore built for themselves a city of their own, near to the ancient Babylon, on the eastern bank of the Nile, in a similar way to their procedure at Kūfa and Baṣra; their camp was called by the Greeks "φόσσατον," *i.e.*, "the camp," which name was transmuted in the Arabian idiom into "Fūsṭāṭ" (a tent). The list of the various quarters which has been transmitted to us affords a good idea of the tribes taking part in the conquest of Egypt; for the most part they were from South Arabia. We shall not be inaccurate if we date the commencement of Fūsṭāṭ even before the evacuation of Alexandria (642).

The conqueror of Egypt met the same fate as his great Syrian colleague Khālid; Omar did not choose to allow his various lieutenants to become too powerful, unless he was absolutely sure of them. He appears, therefore, shortly before his death to have transferred Upper Egypt as an independent province to 'Abdallāh ibn Sa'd ibn 'Abī Sarḥ. 'Abdallāh was probably more of a financier than a warrior; he remitted more to the central exchequer, but had no personal authority with the troops. After Omar's death Othman placed him also in authority over Lower Egypt, and recalled 'Amr. When however, after the restoration of order in Constantinople, a Byzantine fleet under the command of Manuel suddenly appeared before Alexandria, and the town rose in rebellion (645), 'Abdallāh was helpless. At the instigation of the troops Othman sent back the tried and trusted 'Amr, who in a very short time drove the Byzantines out of the country and retook Alexandria, this time by force, in 646. Immediately after this success however he was compelled again to relinquish the province to 'Abdallāh, as he refused with scorn to retain the military command without the civil administration. Personal enrichment to some extent—and that has always been the principal aim of the heroes of the conquest—was only possible by manipulation of the taxes; and 'Abdallāh was a foster-brother of the Caliph. Still it must be admitted that 'Abdallāh was not without merit, not only in regard to the taxes, but also in the extension of the boundaries. Thus, for instance, he regulated the conditions on the Upper Egyptian border by treaty with the Nubians (April 652), and on the western side he advanced as far as Tripolis. His greatest achievement however was the extension of the fleet.

Here he joined the efforts of Mu'āwiya in Syria, who himself built ships. The main dockyard however appears to have been Alexandria, and in all the great sea-fights we find a co-operation of Egyptian and Syrian vessels. Arabian tradition neglects their maritime expeditions to a surprising extent, but Western sources have always emphasised this feature of the Arabian success in warfare. The intelligence gathered from the papyri during the last few years shews that the care for the building and manning of the fleet was, at all events in Egypt at the end of the seventh century, one of the chief occupations of the administration. Mu'āwiya required the fleet first and foremost against Byzantium, for, as long as the Greeks had command of the sea, no rest might be expected in Syria and as little in Alexandria. The first task for Mu'āwiya was to seize from the Byzantines their naval base, Cyprus, which lay dangerously near. The first marine expedition of the Arabs was against Cyprus in the summer 649, and this was attended with success. Aradus, which lay still nearer to Syria, was not taken till a year later. In 655 Mu'āwiya contemplated an expedition to Constantinople, in which Egyptian ships in considerable numbers took part. On the Lycian coast near Phoenix, the Dhāt aṣ-Ṣawārī of the Arabs, a great battle ensued, the importance of which is clear from the fact that the Byzantines were led in person by the Emperor, Constans II. Either a certain Abu-l-A'war acted as admiral of the Arab fleet, or, according to other reports, the Egyptian governor 'Abdallāh. Trustworthy details are missing; in any case the battle resulted in a catastrophe comparable with the defeat on the Yarmūk. The powerful fleet of the Byzantines, supposed to be 500 ships strong, was completely destroyed, and the Emperor sought refuge in flight. The Arabs however seem also to have sustained losses sufficient to prevent them from following up their victory by advancing on Constantinople. Fortunately for the Byzantines Othman was murdered shortly afterwards, and thereupon began the struggle for the Caliphate which forced Mu'āwiya to conclude an ignominious peace with the Byzantines.

Later on Mu'āwiya took up afresh this expedition against the Byzantines, this time by water, and in Cilicia and Armenia. The Byzantine Armenia had been visited as far back as 642 by an expedition under Ḥabīb ibn Maslama, in connexion with the conquest of Mesopotamia, and its capital Dwin, north of the Araxes, had been temporarily occupied. Later expeditions were less fortunate, as an Armenian chief, Theodore, the ruler of the Reshtunians, organised an energetic resistance, and after his first success was supported by Byzantium with troops, and also by the grant of the title Patricius. Later on Theodore agreed with the Arabs and placed himself under their suzerainty. This caused a reaction of the Byzantine party and thereupon a counter-demonstration of the Arabs, who pushed forward under Ḥabīb as far as the Caucasus. He was supported by a contingent from the conquered land of Persia, which advanced even beyond the Caucasus, but was there destroyed by the Chazars. In Armenia also the Arabs could only hold their own until the beginning of the civil war. After the reunion in the empire sea and land enterprises, such as those already described, formed part of the yearly recurring duties of the government during the whole of the period of the Umayyads, and these enterprises were only discontinued during an occasional peace. From the papyri we know that for the annual summer expeditions (Jaish, κοῦρσον) special war taxes in kind were levied. These regular expeditions were made in the Near East in two directions; on the one hand to the west, to North Africa, and from 711 onwards to Spain, as we shall illustrate more fully in Chapter XII, and on the other hand to the north, embracing Asia Minor and Armenia.

The conquest of Constantinople was of course the goal which was always present to the minds of the Arabs. More than once too they came

very near to the attainment of their plan ; twice under Muʿāwiya, the first
occasion being principally a land expedition under Fadāla, who conquered Chalcedon (668), and from thence in the spring of 669, in
combination with the Caliph's son Yazīd, who had advanced to his help,
besieged Constantinople. These land expeditions were in vain, and
equally so were the regular, so-called seven years' fights between the
fleets of the two powers, these lasting from 674 or even earlier until the
death of Muʿāwiya (680), and taking place immediately before Constantinople where the Arabs had secured for themselves a naval base. When
at a later date, after the termination of the civil wars, the second great
wave of expansion set in under the Caliph Walīd, Constantinople again
appeared attainable to them. The remarkable siege of Constantinople,
which lasted at least a year (716–717), took place, it is true, afterwards
under Walīd's successor, the Caliph Sulaimān. This also ended unsuccessfully for the Arabs. The Arabian boundary remained as before
mainly the Amanus and the Caucasus, and beyond that the limits of
their dominion varied. But all these regular wars are connected in the
closest degree with the internal history of the Byzantine empire, and for
this reason they are treated in detail elsewhere. Saracens in this quarter
came rather early to the frontier which for a considerable time they were
destined not to cross.

The connexion of matters has compelled us whilst reviewing the
relations between the Saracens and the Byzantines to anticipate other
events in the dominions of the Caliphate. We now return to the reign
of the Caliph Omar, under whom and his successor the expansion reached
limits unchanged for a considerable time, for we cannot gain from the
delineation of the mere outward expansion of the Saracens any satisfactory conception of the Arabian migration, which completely meta-
morphosed the political contour of the Mediterranean world. Even the
interest of the student, in the first instance directed to the West, must
not overlook the civil wars in the young Arabian world-empire, for they
are in even greater degree than either Byzantines or Franks responsible
for bringing to a standstill the movement which threatened Europe.
By doing so we at the same time notice the beginnings of Muslim civilisation. If we fail truly to estimate this the continuity postulated at
the commencement of our chapter becomes obscured, and the great
influence of the East on western countries in the Middle Ages remains
incomprehensible.

Omar died at the zenith of his life, unexpectedly struck down in the
midst of his own community by the dagger of a Persian slave (3 Nov.
644). While Abū Bakr had decreed him as his successor simply by will,
because the succession was felt on all sides to be evident, the dying Omar
did not venture to entrust any particular one of his fellow-companions
with the succession. This strict, conscientious and sincerely religious
man did not dare in the face of death to discriminate between the

candidates, all of whom were more or less incompetent. He therefore
nominated a Board of Election (Shūrā), composed of six of the most
respected of his colleagues, with the instruction to select from their midst
the new Caliph. Ali, Othman, Zubair, Ṭalḥa, Sa'd ibn Abī Waḳḳāṣ and
'Abd-ar-Raḥmān ibn 'Auf had now to decide the fate of Islām. After long
hesitation they agreed on Othman, probably because he appeared to be
the weakest and most pliable, and each of them hoped to rule, first
through him and afterwards in succession to him. This choice looks
like a reaction; they had had enough of Omar's energetic and austere
government—for he upheld the autocratic power of the representative of
the prophet, even as against the proudest and most successful generals,
probably less from personal ambition than from religious and political
conviction. They speculated correctly, but they overlooked the fact
that in a race to profit by the weakness of Othman his own family
had a start which could not be overtaken. Othman was however an
Umayyad, *i.e.*, he belonged to the old Mecca aristocracy, who for a long
time were the chief opponents of the prophet, but who, after his victory,
had with fine political instinct seceded to his camp and had even migrated
to Medina, in order to emulate the new religious aristocracy created by
Mahomet. In this they succeeded only too well, for they counted among
them men of remarkable intelligence, with whom the short-sighted in-
triguers, the honest blusterers and the pious unpolitical members of the
circle of Companions could not keep up. They now induced Othman, who
had at once nominated his cousin Marwān ibn al-Ḥakam to be the omnipotent Secretary of State, to fill all the positions of any importance or
of any value with Umayyads or their partisans.

Later on Othman was reproached on all sides with this nepotism,
which caused great discontent throughout the entire empire. To this
discontent there was added an increasing reaction against the system of
finance, founded by Omar and carried on without alteration by Othman.
The lust of booty had led the Arabs out to battle, and the spoils
belonged to them after deduction of the so-called prophet's fifth. But
what was to be done with the enormous landed property which victors in
such small numbers had acquired, and who was to receive the tribute
paid yearly by the subjected peoples? Payment of this money to the
respective conquerors of the individual territories would have been
the most logical method of dealing with it, but with the fluctuations
in the Arabian population this plan would have caused insuperable
difficulties, apart from which it would have been from a statesman's
point of view extremely unwise. Omar therefore founded a state
treasury. The residents of the newly formed military camps received a
fixed stipend; the surplus of the receipts flowed to Medina, where it was
not indeed capitalised but utilised for state pensions, which the Caliph
decreed according to his own judgment to the members of the theocracy,
graduated according to rank and dignity. Under the impartial Omar

this was not disagreeable to any, the more especially as at that time the gains from the booty were still very large. But when under Othman these gains dwindled and became ever smaller, this state treasury appeared to the Arabian provincial tribes as an oppression of the provinces. The nepotism of Othman increased the opposition, and it finally found expression in open revolt. These fanatical partisans were of opinion that Othman was the man against whom the real holy war should be waged. The Kūfa men were first to rebel against the governor nominated by Othman (655); with unaccountable weakness Othman immediately abandoned his representative. The Egyptians were the most energetic in their protest, and started for Medina in April 655 to the number of about 500. The disquiet which was simmering on all sides was secretly fomented by the disappointed Companions in Medina; they were the real plotters who made use of the discontent of the provincials. When after long discussion the Egyptians besieged Othman in his own house these Companions looked on inactively, or at the most excused themselves by a few pretended manœuvres, but in fact they were not displeased when the rebels stormed the house and slew the defenceless old Caliph whilst at prayer (17 June 655).

From this time onward fate took its own course. Among the Medina companions Ali was now doubtless the nearest claimant to the Caliphate, and some even went so far as to render him homage. On the other hand, would he not certainly appear to all the Umayyads, and especially to the powerful governor of Syria, as the murderer of Othman? Mu'āwiya was firmly established in Syria, and was in a position to venture, under this pretext—to him probably more than a pretext—to dispute the Caliphate even with the son-in-law of the prophet. The Umayyads moreover were not the only enemies that Ali had to contend with. His former allies, Zubair and Ṭalḥa, who were at least as much to blame as he, roused the people against him, and this was done even more determinedly by the prophet's widow 'A'isha, who had always been opposed to him. They were supported by the Baṣra tribes, whilst Ali sought support with the Kūfa people. Near Baṣra the quarrel came to a decision, in the so-called Camel battle, which takes its name from the fact that 'A'isha, in accordance with old Arabian custom, was present at the battle in a camel-palanquin, as a sacred sign of war. Ali conquered and 'A'isha's part was played out. Ṭalḥa and Zubair were killed in the fight (9 Dec. 656). Ali was thus master of 'Irāḳ, and Kūfa became his residence.

Hereupon Arabia ceased to be the centre of the empire, and Medina sank to the status of a provincial town, in which piety and easy-going elegance had the necessary quiet for development. The history of Nearer Asia however again resolved itself, as it did before Islām, into the opposition between 'Irāḳ and Syria. The two halves of the empire armed themselves for the fight for supremacy, Muslims against Muslims. At first the better discipline of the Syrians and their higher culture carried the day. The recollection however of the brief political splendour of 'Irāķ formed the basis for a movement which was destined to gain strength, which a century later swept away the rule of the Umayyads. Once more was the capital of the latest Asiatic world-power transferred to Babylon.

After the Camel battle Ali's position was thoroughly favourable, as Mu'āwiya could not take any energetic steps against him so long as Egypt remained on Ali's side. Mu'āwiya's main attention was therefore fixed on Egypt; and in this view he was aided and abetted by 'Amr, the first conqueror of Egypt, who had allied himself with Mu'āwiya in the hope of attaining through him the governorship of Egypt. For that reason he rendered Mu'āwiya most important services in the war against Ali, and as Ali at this juncture advanced against Mu'āwiya a battle extending over several days ensued, after long delay, at Şiffīn on the Syrian border, not far distant from Raķķa (26–27 July 657). Ali's victory appeared certain, when 'Amr conceived the idea of fastening copies of the Koran to the points of the lances and calling on the holy book for a decision. This trick succeeded, and much against his will Ali was forced to yield to the pressure of the pious members of his army. A court of arbitration was thereupon agreed on. Mu'āwiya's confidential representative was of course 'Amr, whilst Ali had forced upon him in a like capacity Abū Mūsā al-Ash'arī, a man by no means thoroughly devoted to him. They had scarcely parted when those same pious members of his army altered their views, and now blamed Ali for having placed men, instead of God and the sword, as judges over him. Several thousand men separated from Ali and entered into a separate camp at Harūrā, whence they were called Harūrites or secessionists, Khārijites. They resisted Ali by force, and he was compelled to cut down most of them at Nahrawān (7 July 658). Later on they split into innumerable small sects and still gave much trouble to Ali and the Umayyads. The sense of independence and the robber-knight ideas of the ancient Arabians lived still in them, but under a religious cloak. Offshoots from these people, the so-called Ibādites, exist even to-day in South Arabia and in East and North Africa.

The information we have as to the result of the court of arbitration is untrustworthy. In any case the clever 'Amr outwitted his coadjudicator by persuading him also to deal with Ali and Mu'āwiya as being on the same footing, whilst of course Ali was the only one who had a Caliphate to lose. Ali appears actually to have been divested of this dignity by decree of the arbitration, but this decision did not induce him to abdicate. This arbitration court was held at Adhruḥ in the year 658. Even more painful for Ali than this failure was the loss of Egypt, which 'Amr shortly afterwards reconquered for himself, and administered until his death more as a viceroy than a governor. No definite decision was brought about between Ali and Mu'āwiya, as their forces were about equally balanced. It was not until July 660 that Mu'āwiya caused himself to be proclaimed Caliph at Jerusalem. Six months later Ali succumbed to the dagger of an assassin (24 Jan. 661). Mu'āwiya had to thank this circumstance for his victory, for Ali's son and successor Hasan came to terms with him in return for an allowance. Herewith began the rule of the Umayyads, and Damascus became the capital of the empire.

This has been rightly termed the Arabian Empire, for it was founded on a national basis, in marked contrast to the subsequent State of the Abbasids, for which Islām served as a foundation. The first Caliphs had striven after a theocracy, but, as all the members of the theocracy were Arabs, an Arabian national empire was created. For a time the migration of the tribes had more weight than religion. We see this most clearly by the fact that no longer the pious companions, but the old Arabian aristocracy, no longer Anṣār and Muhājirūn, but the Arabian tribes of Syria and 'Irāḳ, determined the destinies of the empire. The great expansion however was only able to hold back religion for a time. Religion soon served to give authority to the government in power, but at the same time provided a special motive for all kinds of opposition. That is shewn by the domestic policy of the Umayyad State; in the first place to force the discipline of the State on the ruling class, *i.e.*, the Arabs, without which no successful combined social life was possible, and in the second place it was necessary to regulate their relations with the non-Arabian subordinate class.

The fight for the supremacy in the State, which appeared to the 'Irāḳ after the days of Ali as the rule of the hated Syrians, formed the life-task of all the great Caliphs of the house of Umayya. Mu'āwiya had still most of all the manners of an old Arabian prince; he appeared to the Romaic element simply as the πρωτοσύμβουλος of his governors, σύμβουλοι. In Syria they had been accustomed to such things since the days of the Ghassānids, and to that may be ascribed the better discipline of the Syrian Arabs, who in all respects stood on a higher plane of culture than those of 'Irāḳ. Mu'āwiya was a clever prince, and ruled by wisdom over the tribes, whose naturally selfish rivalries supported the structure of his State like the opposing spans of an arch. His rule was so patriarchal, and his advisers had so much voice in the matter, that some have thought to have found traces of parliamentary government under Mu'āwiya. Nevertheless Mu'āwiya knew quite well how to carry his point for the State, *i.e.*, for himself, though he avoided the absolutist forms and the pomp of later Caliphs. The nepotism of Othman was quite foreign to his rule; although his relatives did not fare badly under him he nevertheless looked after the principles of State in preference to them. He had a brilliant talent for winning important men. On the same principles as the Caliph in Damascus, the Thakifite[1] Ziyād, whom he had adopted as a brother, ruled as an independent viceroy

---

[1] *I.e.* of the tribe of Thaḳīf. See p. 325.

over the eastern half of the kingdom. Muʻāwiya's aspirations in state policy were finally to found a dynasty. He proclaimed his son Yazīd as his successor, although this act was opposed not only to the ancient common law based on usage but also to the mode of election of the theocracy.

On Muʻāwiya's death (18 April 680) Yazīd was accordingly recognised in the West and partially also in ʻIrāḳ. At once a double opposition began to foment; that of the Ali party in ʻIrāḳ, which had already begun to revive under Muʻāwiya, and the theocratic opposition of the Ḥijāz. The endeavour to transfer the central government once more, respectively to ʻIrāḳ and to the Ḥijāz, probably underlay the opposition in both cases. As regards ʻIrāḳ that theory is a certainty, for the families of Kūfa and Baṣra had not forgotten that in Ali's time they had been the masters of the empire. Now however Ali's Shīʻa (party) was thrust into the background by the Syrians. They looked back to Ali, and their ardent desire was a restoration of that golden period for Kūfa. Their enthusiasm for Ali and his kin is therefore nothing more than a glorification of their own special province, of the one and only ʻIrāḳ Caliph. This brilliant period they hoped after the death of the great Muʻāwiya to recover for themselves by selecting Ḥusain, the second son of Ali. Ḥusain complied with the solicitations of the Kūfa people. These however, unsteady and undisciplined as ever, shrank from rebellion and failed him at the last moment. Ḥusain and those remaining faithful to him were cut down at Karbalā (10 Oct. 680). Ali's son had thereby, like others before him, fallen as a martyr to the cause of Shīʻism. Political aspirations slowly assumed a religious tinge. The death of the prophet's grandson in the cause of the Kūfa people, their remorse on that account, their faded hopes, their hatred of the Syrians, and, last but not least, heterodox currents which now began to shew themselves, prepared the way for the great Shiite insurrection a few years later under Mukhtār. Ali is now no longer simply the companion and son-in-law of the prophet, but has become the heir of his prophetic spirit, which then lives on in his sons. The Ali dynasty—so at least say the legitimists—are the only true priestly Imāms, the only legal Caliphs. The struggle for the house of the prophet, for the Banū Hāshim, becomes more and more the watchword of the opposition party, who, after their political overthrow in ʻIrāḳ, removed their sphere of operation to Persia. There however this Arabian legitimism united with Iranian claims, and, in the fight for the Banū Hāshim, the Persians were arrayed against the Arabs. With this war-cry the Abbasids conquered.

Although Ḥusain's expedition to Karbalā had ended in a fiasco, the Umayyads were not destined to get off so lightly against the opposition of the Medina people, an opposition of the old elective theocracy against the new Syrian dynasty. Their opposition candidate was ʻAbdallāh, son of that Zubair who had fallen in the fight against Ali. Yazīd was

compelled to undertake a campaign against the holy cities, which earned
for him the hate of later generations. The matter was however not so
bad as it has been represented, and was moreover a political necessity.
His military commander broke up the resistance of the Medina party in
the battle on the Harra (26 Aug. 683), subsequently besieging the
opposition Caliph in Mecca. Just at this time Yazīd died (11 Nov. 683),
and now the succession became a difficult question. Ibn az-Zubair had the
best chance of being universally recognised, as Yazīd's youthful son and
successor, Muʻāwiya II, a man of no authority, died only a few months
after his father. In Syria too large groups of the people, especially the
members of the Ḳais race, sided with the Zubair party, whilst the Kalb
race, who had been long resident in Syria, and with whom Muʻāwiya had
become related by marriage, allied themselves unreservedly with the
Umayyads. The Kalb knew only too well that the Umayyad rule
meant the supremacy of Syria. And now the question arose, which
branch of the family should rule. Practical necessities and traditional
claims led to the Umayyad party finally selecting on the principle of
seniority a man already known to us, Marwān ibn al-Ḥakam, to be
Caliph. The decisive battle against the Zubair faction took place at
Marj Rāhiṭ in the beginning of 684. The Umayyads were victorious,
and Marwān was proclaimed Caliph in Syria.

The Umayyads had however to pay dearly for this victory, for it
destroyed the fundamental principles of the Arabian Empire. Hate once
generated at Marj Rāhiṭ, the blood-feud there arising was so bitter
that even the ever-growing religious spirit of Islām was unable to make
headway against it. The Arabs had previously been divided into
numerous factions warring against each other, but now the battle of
Marj Rāhiṭ created that ineradicable race hatred between the Ḳais and
Kalb tribes, which spread to other older racial opponents. The Ḳais
were distributed throughout the entire kingdom; the opposition towards
them drove their opponents into the ranks of the Kalb. The political
parties became genealogical branches according to the theory of the
Arabs, which regarded all political relationship from an ethnical standpoint. And now for the first time, not in the remote past, arose that
opposition between the Northern and Southern Arabians which permeated public life, and which only in part coincided with actual racial
descent. Here it was the Ḳais, there the Kalb, and under these party
cries the Arabs tore at each other henceforward throughout the whole
empire, and this purely political and particularist tribal feud undermined
the rule of the Arabs at least as much as their religious political
opposition to the authority of the State, for it was just the authority of
the State itself which was thereby ruined; the governors could no
longer permanently hold aloof from the parties, and finally the Caliphs
themselves were unable to do so. But for the time being the actual
zenith of the dynasty followed these disorders.

Marwān quickly succeeded in conquering Egypt, and then died, leaving a difficult inheritance to his son 'Abd-al-Malik (685–705). Complications with the Byzantines, who had incited the Mardaites, an unconquered mountain tribe in the Amanus, against him, rendered it impossible for him during his first years of office to take energetic steps in 'Irāk. The Zubair faction represented by Zubair's brother Muṣ'ab ruled there nominally. Apart from these however the Shiites had now attained to eminence and had organised a great insurrection under Mukhtār. They defeated an army sent out by 'Abd-al-Malik, but were then themselves defeated by the Zubairite Muṣ'ab. The latter was hindered in his fight against 'Abd-al-Malik by the Khārijites, who offered opposition to any and every form of state government and had developed into an actual scourge. In the decisive battle against 'Abd-al-Malik on the Tigris (690) Muṣ'ab accordingly succumbed to the military and diplomatic superiority of the Syrian Caliph. The opposition Caliph still maintained his resistance in Mecca. 'Abd-al-Malik despatched against him one of his best men, Ḥajjāj, who managed in 692 to put an end both to the Caliphate and to the life of the Zubairite.

This Ḥajjāj became later 'Abd-al-Malik's Ziyād, or almost unrestricted viceroy, of the eastern half of the empire. He exercised the authority of the State in a very energetic manner, and his reward is to be shamefully misrepresented in the historical account given of him by the tradition of 'Irāk, created by those who had been affected by his energetic methods. Ḥajjāj was also a Thakifite. He carried out in 'Irāk what 'Abd-al-Malik endeavoured to do in Syria, namely, the consolidation of the empire. The constitutional principles of the dominions of Islām were, according to tradition, formulated by Omar, but the extent to which tradition ascribes these to him is impossible, for the ten years of his reign, occupied as they were with enormous military expeditions, did not leave him the necessary time and quiet. For this reason later investigators consider that the chief merit must be attributed to Mu'āwiya. Probably however the honours must be divided between Omar, Mu'āwiya and 'Abd-al-Malik, possibly including Hishām. Omar made the Arabs supreme over the taxpaying subjected peoples, and avoided particularism by the introduction of the state treasury. Mu'āwiya placed the Arabian Empire on a dynastic basis and disciplined the tribes by introducing the political in place of the religious state authority. 'Abd-al-Malik however was the first to create the actual Arabian administration, and this was followed under Hishām by the abolition of the agrarian political prerogative of the Arabs, to be discussed later. This process in the economic life was followed under the Abbasids by its extension to politics.

The Arabs were not so foolish as many modern conquerors, who first destroy the administrative organisation which they find in newly conquered foreign countries, and then suddenly stand face to face with insuperable difficulties. In accordance with their fundamental political point of view they left all such matters as they found them, contenting themselves with the punctual payment by the local authorities of the stipulated tribute. How this was collected was a matter of small moment to them. Only the supreme heads of the more important administrative departments were Arabs. All the middle and lower administrative positions were filled by natives as late as the eighth century, and even later. This complicated system was not interfered with until the reign of ʻAbd-al-Malik and his successor Walīd, and then not in the sense of immediately making it Arabian, though it was placed on a bilingual basis by the introduction of Arabic. Arab-Greek documents of this period, from Egypt, have been preserved to us in profusion. But in other matters also the result of the more settled conditions was seen in the changes made by ʻAbd-al-Malik. He is regarded as the founder of the Arabian coinage; true, he accepted here the already existing systems, that is, for the Byzantine districts he renewed the old gold coinage, and for the Persian territories the old silver coinage was adopted. The principal point however seems to be that under this ruler it was first recognised that Omar's fiscal system was untenable, and that both in principle and in form it must cease. Hitherto the Muslims had remained exempt from taxation and the subjected peoples had provided the necessary revenue. At the outset they had forgotten that through the extension of Islām as a religion the number of taxpayers would of necessity become smaller and smaller, so that thereby religion would sap the foundations of the Arabian State. With the foundation of the military camps, which soon grew into large towns, the natives had on the spot a much better source of income than in the country, where the peasants had to pay their quota of tribute. Thus an exodus from the country began, and at the same time the number of converts to Islām increased. As the new believers ceased to be subject to taxes, the result of this process on the state treasury may easily be imagined. At the same time it became thus evident that the form of Omar's regulations was unsuitable, for this exodus from the country simply necessitated an individual treatment of the districts liable to pay duty, and these conditions compelled the Arabs to concern themselves with details. But in doing so the Arabian upper class was of necessity deeply concerned with the construction of the whole system of government. This process commences under ʻAbd-al-Malik. His representative Ḥajjāj sought to avoid the evil consequences for the treasury by including the newly converted believers as liable to taxation, thus deviating from Omar's system.

The increasing settlement of Arabs in the fertile country, which had been liable to tribute whilst in the possession of non-Muslims, had the same result as the change of religion in the subjected peoples. Omar II sought to obviate this by forbidding the sale of such country.   It was not however till later, and probably by degrees, that it was decided, principally under the Caliph Hishām, to alter the principle of taxation, though the alteration is much obscured by tradition.   The tribute, which was principally drawn from the ground tax, was converted into a ground tax pure and simple, and was levied irrespective of creed on all property owners; the tribute intended to demonstrate the dominion of the Arabs was resolved into an individual poll-tax of the old sort, which was only payable by non-Muslims and ceased in the event of conversion. This state of affairs is regarded by tradition as Omar's work, but it is the result of gradual development extending over a century.   This very energetic manner in which the Arabs applied themselves to the adminis-tration commenced with 'Abd-al-Malik and found its termination under the Abbasids.

Under 'Abd-al-Malik and his viceroys, his brother 'Abd-al-'Azīz in Egypt and Ḥajjāj in 'Irāḳ, an executive authority was founded, which, although occasionally shaken by serious revolts, was nevertheless strong, so that his successor Walīd (705–715) was again able to consider the question of an extension of the boundaries.   Under his rule the Arabian Empire attained its greatest expansion; Spain was conquered, and the Arabs penetrated into the Punjab and far into Central Asia, right to the borders of China.   These incursions however do not fall within the range of our present observation.   Under 'Abd-al-Malik and Walīd the empire, and above all Syria, stands on the pinnacle of prosperity; the most stately buildings were erected, such as the Omar Mosque in Jerusalem, and the Umayyad Mosque in Damascus.   Poetry flourished at the brilliant Syrian court, and, guided by Christian learning, Arabian science begins to make its appearance.

Now however the traces of impending collapse begin to appear. It was only with difficulty that Ḥajjāj suppressed a powerful military revolt.   The supremacy of the State could only be maintained in 'Irāḳ with the assistance of Syrian troops.   In the eastern provinces the Ḳais and Kalb wage constant warfare with each other, and the reign of the later Umayyads is occupied in a struggle with these permanently mutinous eastern districts.   Most of the later Umayyads enjoyed but a brief reign, Sulaimān 715–717, Omar II till 720, Yazīd II till 724. Hishām, 724–743, who grappled seriously with the problem of agrarian policy, and secured once again in Khālid al-Ḳasrī a viceroy for the East after the style of Ziyād and Ḥajjāj, was the only one capable of restoring once more a certain amount of quiet.

Thereupon however followed the irretrievable decline of the Umayyad State.   The political opposition of Ḳais and Kalb converted the Caliph into the puppet of inter-tribal feuds; Umayyads fought against Umay-yads.   The rulers succeeded each other in rapid succession.   History records four Umayyad Caliphs in the period of 743 to 744.   It would occupy too much space here to trace all these disturbances. When Marwān II, the last of the Umayyads, a man by no means personally incapable, ascended the throne in the year 744, the game was already lost. Particularism had won the day. The general fight between all parties was however essentially a fight against Syria and the Umayyads. In this cause the new combination, which made its first efforts in the far east, in Khorāsān, attained success. In no other place were the Arabs so intermingled with the subject peoples as here, and here too the religious opposition against the Umayyads was taken up more vigorously than anywhere else. It has already been indicated above that the Shī'a was destined to prevail in Persia. In their fight for the family of the prophet, the Abbasids, under their general Abū Muslim, were victorious, and then, supported by the Persian element, they conquered first the eastern Arabs and subsequently the Syrians. In the year 750 the Umayyad rule was at an end.

The victory of the Abbasids was a victory of the Persians over the Arabs. The subjected classes had slowly raised themselves to a level with the Arabs. When Christians and Persians first accepted Islām it was not possible to include them in the theocracy in any other way than by attaching them as clients (Mawāli) to the Arabian tribal system. They were the better educated and the more highly cultivated of the two races. In the numerous revolts they fought on the side of the Arabs. The contrast between the Arabs and the Mawāli had its cause in the constitution of the State as founded by Omar. The more the Mawāli increased in importance and the more they permeated the Arabian tribes, so the universalistic, *i.e.*, the democratic tendency of Islām was bound in corresponding degree to force its way into wider circles. On the other hand the continuous fights of the Arabian tribes against the authority of the State and against each other led to a dissolution of the political and ethnical conditions under which Islām had caused the preponderance of the Arabian element. Thus grew more and more a tendency to level Arabs and non-Arabs. Both became merged in the term Muslim which even to this day represents for many peoples their nationality. The Persians were much more religious than the Arabs, and they accepted the political ideal of the Shī'a, which was tinged with religion, more than actually religious. This religious movement then swept away the dominion of the Umayyads, and thereby the international empire of the Abbasids took the place of the national Arabian Empire. The Arabian class disappeared and was superseded by a mixed official aristocracy, based no longer on religious merit and noble descent, but on authority delegated by the ruling prince. Thus arose out of the patriarchal kingdom of the Umayyads the absolutist rule of the Abbasids and therewith Persian civilisation made its entrance into Islām. The ancient East had conquered.

CHAPTER XII.

THE EXPANSION OF THE SARACENS (*continued*).

AFRICA AND EUROPE.

WE are dividing the history of the expansion of the Saracens into an Asiatic-Egyptian and an African-European order of development. This division is founded not on outward, but on internal reasons. Even at the present time Islām in Northern Africa presents an appearance quite different from the Islām of Asia and Egypt. The reason for this must be sought in the totally different composition of the population. The Aramaic element of Nearer Asia and Coptic Egypt offered much less resistance to the Arabian nationality and the Arabian language than did the Persian element in Mid-Asia. The Berbers or Moors of Northern Africa take up a middle position between these two; they certainly accepted Islām and Arabian culture, but they remodelled them, and preserved their own nationality in their customs and to a large extent also in their language. Moreover, an encroachment of Islām into Europe in so significant a form as that experienced in the Middle Ages would have been scarcely conceivable without the great masses of the Berbers, who were always on the move. Later too the Saracens of Southern Europe continually appear in political relations with Africa. The history of Islām in Europe is therefore indissolubly connected with its history in Northern Africa, whilst on the other hand it is in reality merely associated with the history of the Eastern Caliphate by a certain community of culture and religion.

The commixture of Arabs and Berbers, which gave the impress to the whole of the Islām of the West, was a slow process. Centuries passed, but in the end Islām has attained what Phoenicians and Romans strove for in vain. These two great colonising nations always settled principally in the towns on the coast, and doubtless assimilated the Berbers crowding round them; in spite however of all the settlements of colonists by Rome, the flat country and especially the hinterland remained in Berber hands. As Mommsen says, the Phoenicians and Romans have been swept away, but the Berbers have remained, like the palm trees and the desert sand. With the destruction of the Roman power the influence of the widespread organisation of the Berber tribes grew and the Byzantine restoration under Justinian was limited by the growth of the Berber element. The exarchs had continually to deal with insurrections of the Berbers, and were probably scarcely able to exercise authority outside the limits of the ever decreasing number of towns held by garrisons which commanded respect. It is therefore clear from the beginning that it was not the Byzantines who made the occupation of Northern Africa difficult for the Arabians, but the Berbers, who in their time of need made common cause with their former tyrants against the new intruder. The Arabs had much trouble to make it clear to the Berbers at the point of the sword that their real interest lay with Islām and not against it. As soon as they had once realised this fact they accepted the Arabs for their leaders and flooded Southern Europe, while in Africa the nascent civilisation of Islām effected an entrance, though it received a Berber national colouring.

The continued occupation of Alexandria called for a screening of the flank by occupying also the adjoining territory of Barḳa[1]. Barḳa was the leading community of the ancient Pentapolis. The rich towns of this group at once experienced the consequence of the occupation of Egypt when the Arabians appeared before them. It has been already mentioned that the Arabs through 'Amr made peace with Barḳa immediately after the occupation of Alexandria. That took place as early as the autumn of the year 642 and the winter thereupon following, under the leadership of 'Uḳba ibn Nāfi', of whom more is yet to be said. The Pentapolis belonged thenceforward permanently to the Empire of Islām, although retaining in the first instance administrative independence. Bordering on Barḳa was the ancient Proconsular Africa, the eastern half of which, lying between the Greater and the Lesser Syrtis, was clearly distinguished by the Arabs under the title of Tripolis, from the northern half, with the capital Carthage, this latter territory being termed by them simply Africa (Ifrīḳīya). After the occupation of Barḳa various raids took place even under 'Amr (642–643), these extending throughout the whole territory of Tripolis, while individual detachments went southward into the desert. There can be little doubt that even at that time 'Uḳba pushed forward as far as Fezzan (Zawīla) and another Amīr of the name of Busr penetrated to the Oasis of Jufra (Waddān). This latter incident took place while 'Amr was besieging Tripolis, which he finally occupied at least temporarily. At the Nafūsa mountains 'Amr turned back, as the Caliph was averse to pushing forward any further. In spite of these successes there was for the time being no question of any permanent settlement of the Arabs westward of Barḳa. 'Uḳba may have undertaken some small isolated expeditions with Barḳa

[1] The following exposition is based on a critical re-examination of the sources of the works of Caudel and Wellhausen.

as a base, but the main fighting forces of Egypt were concentrated round Alexandria, which once more had temporarily fallen into the hands of the Byzantines.

Only after Alexandria had been reconquered and 'Abdallāh ibn Sa'd had become governor of Egypt was a new expedition to the west on a larger scale undertaken under his guidance, probably as early as the end of 647. The Byzantine state authority was now in complete dissolution. The Patricius Gregory of Carthage had revolted the year before, probably because, after the second fall of Alexandria, he considered himself safe from any energetic steps on the part of the Greeks. Nevertheless Carthage itself does not appear to have given him its adhesion, and he based his rule in fact on the Berbers, for which reason he took up his residence in the interior, in the ancient Sufetula, the present Sbeitla. To how small an extent he must have been master of the situation is proved by the fact that he did not even take the field against 'Abdallāh. The latter, with separated detachments, plundered the territory of Tripolis, without being able to take the town itself; one Arab division in fact appears at that time to have penetrated to Ghadames. When 'Abdallāh arrived at the site of the subsequent Ḳairawān he turned and marched on Sbeitla, where he annihilated Gregory's army. The fate of the Patricius himself is uncertain; probably he fell in battle. This battle is also named after 'Aḳūba, a place lying somewhat further to the north. But here again no consolidation of the Arabian rule resulted. A counter attack on the part of the still unconquered towns was to be feared, and 'Abdallāh therefore allowed himself to be persuaded to retire on payment of an enormous sum of money, stated to have been 300 talents. The whole expedition lasted somewhat more than a year (647–648).

Hereupon the confusion following on the assassination of the Caliph Othman brought the expansion for the time being to a standstill. When however Mu'āwiya had asserted his authority and his faithful ally 'Amr had again become master in Egypt, the expeditions towards the west were renewed, and in these 'Amr's nephew, the 'Uḳba ibn Nāfi' above mentioned, appears to have been the moving spirit, operating from Barḳa as a base. Along with him a number of other leaders are mentioned, who undertook small excursions against various Berber tribes and against such towns as the ancient Lepta (660–663). All details are dubious; of the subsequent period too our knowledge is but scanty. Probably after the death of 'Amr Africa was entrusted, at all events temporarily, as a separate province to Mu'āwiya ibn Ḥudaij, the head of Mu'āwiya's Egyptian party in his fight against Othman; this man was sent out directly by the Caliph with a considerable army against the united Byzantines and Berbers, and defeated them. The fortress of Jalūlā was taken by him. Mu'āwiya's expedition was in conjunction with a diversion of the fleet against Sicily, of which more remains to be said. This event may be dated with tolerable accuracy as having occurred in the year 664.

Shortly afterwards 'Uḳba ibn Nāfi' appears to have become the successor of Ibn Ḥudaij. After a brilliant raid through the chain of oases on the northern fringe of the Sahara, where he renewed the Arabian dominion, he undertook in the year 670 an expedition against the so-called Proconsular Africa, where he founded, as an Arabian camp and strategical point of support, on the same lines as Baṣra and Kūfa, Ḳairawān, which became later so famous. Shortly afterwards, at most in a few years, he was recalled.

Under Ibn Ḥudaij and 'Uḳba Africa had grown into a province independent of Egypt; now it was once more attached to Egypt. The new governor-general Maslama ibn Mukhallad sent his freedman Dīnār Abu-l-Muhājir as 'Uḳba's successor. By him 'Uḳba was put in chains; Maslama plainly disapproved 'Uḳba's policy. He had good reason for his disagreement, for 'Uḳba was the type of the arbitrary, reckless leader of the Arabian horsemen; proud as he was, he knew no such thing as compromise, and in his view the Arabs were to conquer by the sword and not by diplomacy; he punished all renegades without mercy. Many Berbers had indeed accepted Islām as long as a contingent of Arabian troops was in their neighbourhood, only to secede as soon as the latter had withdrawn. 'Uḳba treated with impolitic haughtiness the proud leaders of the Berbers who allied themselves with him. His much-renowned raids were displays of bravado without lasting success, but they were in accordance with the taste of Arabian circles and as later on he met his death on one of these expeditions in the far west, his fame was still further enhanced by the martyr's crown. Thus even at the present day Sidi 'Uḳba is a popular saint in Northern Africa. Tested by the judgment of history his less-known successor Dīnār was a much greater man, for it was he who first vigorously opposed the Byzantines and at the same time he was the pioneer in paving the way to an understanding with the Berbers.

After having proved his superior strength, Dīnār appears to have won over the Berbers, especially their leader Kusaila, by conciliatory tactics. With their assistance he proceeded against the Byzantines of Carthage. Though he could not yet take the town he occupied other neighbouring portions of their territory. Thereupon he undertook an advance far to the westward, right away to Tlemcen, which he could do without risk owing to his relations with the Berbers.

In the meantime 'Uḳba had succeeded in obtaining once more from the Caliph Yazīd the supreme command in Northern Africa (681–682). He took revenge on Dīnār by leading him around in chains on all his expeditions. He again formed the main Muslim camp at Ḳairawān, whence Dīnār had removed it, and he approached the Berbers once again with true Arabian haughtiness—in short, in all matters he acted on lines diametrically opposed to those of his predecessor. The result proves the correctness of Dīnār's policy, for the powerful Kusaila incited the Berbers against 'Ukba and fled on the earliest opportunity from his camp. 'Ukba therefore proceeded westwards under much less favourable conditions than Dīnār, and though he advanced beyond Tlemcen to Tangier and appears after crossing the Atlas to have even penetrated right to the Atlantic Ocean, yet on the return journey both he and his prisoner Dīnār were cut down by mutinous Berbers. They could not have been surprised if he had not fancied the whole of the west already conquered, and therefore divided up his army into small detachments. Or it may be that he was no longer able to keep together the troops, who were laden with booty. And thus at Tahūdha, not far from Biskra, he suffered the martyr's death (683). This was the signal for a general rising of the Berbers and the renewal of their co-operation with the Byzantines. The Arabs were compelled to relinquish Africa, and Zuhair ibn Kais, the commandant of Kairawān, led the troops back. Kusaila was enabled to wander unpunished with his bands throughout all Africa. Thus at the time of the death of the Caliph Yazīd the whole of Africa beyond Barka was again lost. This fact further confirms our judgment of the vastly too much celebrated 'Ukba.

'Abd-al-Malik attempted as early as 688–689, if we may believe the unanimous opinion of the Arabs, to restore the Caliph's authority in Africa. He did not wait, as might have been expected, until after the conclusion of the civil war against the opposition Caliph, 'Abdallāh ibn Zubair. This new expedition however, commanded by the same Zuhair, did not proceed against the Byzantines, but against Kusaila, for in all these wars the Byzantine towns managed in a masterly way to make use of the Berbers as a bulwark. First of all Kairawān which had drifted under Berber rule was freed, and then a further advance was made against the Mons Aurasius, Kusaila's base. Kusaila was defeated in a bloody battle and fell, whilst Zuhair's troops penetrated as far as Sicca Veneria, the present Kef, and it may be even further. The energy of the Arabs was however then exhausted. On the return march a fate similar to 'Ukba's overtook Zuhair, and from similar causes. The Byzantines had in fact taken advantage of his absence to attack Barka. Zuhair with a few faithful followers was cut down by them.

Kairawān however remained in the hands of the Arabs and now began from this point outwards the work of the real pacificator, Ḥassān ibn an-Nu'mān, though we do not quite know when the arrangement of the conditions was placed in his hands. As the first Syrian Amīr on African soil he thoroughly understood how to combine severe discipline with astute diplomacy. In all material points he adopted Dīnār's policy. Like Dīnār he recognised in the first instance the Byzantines as his main enemy. As soon as the arrival of the auxiliary troops sent by the Caliph permitted him to do so, he advanced against the still unvanquished Carthage, and conquered it in the summer of 697. Following this up he defeated the united Byzantines and Berbers at

Satfura, to the north-east of Tunis, but without being able to prevent them from again concentrating at Bizerta. In the autumn of the same year certainly the Arabs lost Carthage again to the Patricius Johannes, but his powerful fleet was dispersed in the summer of 698 by a still greater Arabian fleet, and thus the fate of the town was sealed. From this time onward the Arabs were supreme at sea, so that it is by no means the land troops only of Ḥassān which decided the final fate of Northern Africa. In his policy towards the Berbers he was at first not fortunate. A holy prophetess, the so-called Kāhina, had roused the Berber tribes to a united advance and had thus become the successor of Kusaila. On the banks of the little river Nini, not far distant from Bagai, on one of the spurs of Mons Aurasius, she defeated Ḥassān's army, which was driven back as far as Tripolis. But in the long run the Kāhina was not able to maintain her position, and the clever diplomacy of Ḥassān appears also to have won over several tribes and leaders from her circle. Thus Ḥassān's final victory over the Kāhina a few years later at Gafes becomes at the same time the commencement of a fraternisation with the Berbers. It is extremely difficult to fix the chronological sequence of the fights against the Kāhina in regard to the expeditions against Carthage. If they are placed between the two conquests of Carthage, as has been done, then the whole chronological structure falls to pieces; it is therefore the simplest to assume the date of Ḥassān's defeat as occurring only after the final fall of Carthage and to date his victory as about 703. For in the end it was not the land army but the fleet which rendered possible the occupation and retention of the Byzantine coast towns. The peace with the Berbers however led them into the camp of the Arabs and thus too the final fate of such Byzantine towns as might still be holding out was sealed. And now, with Islām as their watchword, heads of certain of the Berber tribes, appointed by the Arabs, advanced against the tribes of the west, who still remained independent. The prospect of booty and land united the former enemies, who were moreover so similar to each other in their whole style of living; the moment now approaches when Africa becomes too confined for this new wave of population, which the influx of Islām has brought to flood level. The latinised and hellenised population of the towns appears to a large extent to have migrated to Spain and Sicily, for in a remarkably short time Latin civilisation disappeared from Northern Africa.

The Arabs only conquered Northern Africa after they had relinquished their first policy of plunder for that of a permanent occupation. The commencement of the new policy was 'Uḳba's foundation of Ḳairawān. By that step however in the first place only the starting-place for the raids was changed. Dīnār was the first seriously to consider the question of not merely plundering the open country but of taking the fortified towns; and in this design his Berber policy was to support him. These plans however could only be carried out when more troops became available for Africa after the restoration of unity in the empire by 'Abd-al-Malik, further when the fleet began also to co-operate, and when simultaneously a clever diplomatist effected the execution of Dīnār's plans in regard to the Berbers in more extended style. This man however was Ḥassān ibn an-Nu'mān.

His policy was continued by Mūsā ibn Nuṣair, who is regarded in history as the actual pacificator of Northern Africa and the conqueror of Spain. Mūsā appears to have assumed office in the year 708, though tradition on the point is rather shaky. The first years of his government were occupied with the subjection of the western Berbers, the latter years being devoted to the conquest of Spain, in which work his freedman and military commander Ṭāriḳ had paved the way for him. The conquest of Spain must be ascribed less to the craving of the Arabs for expansion than to the fact that the newly-subjected tribes of Moors, whom the prospect of booty had lured to the banner of Islām, had to be kept employed. At the seat of the Caliphate these far-reaching enterprises were followed with a certain amount of misgiving.

There certainly was little time available to intervene, for events followed one after the other in precipitate haste, and the frail kingdom of the Goths fell into the hands of the conquerors like a ripe fruit by a windfall. The actual cause is obscure. History tells of disputes in regard to the succession, and that the last king of the Goths, Roderick, who succumbed to the Arabs, was a usurper (cf. Chap. vi). Tradition tells of a certain Count Julian, the Christian ruler of Ceuta, whose daughter had been violated by Roderick, and who therefore led the Arabs and Berbers to Spain to satisfy his vengeance. Few characters in the earlier history of Islām have interested the historians to such an extent as this Julian, of whom it is not definitely known to which nation he belonged and to which sovereignty he owed allegiance. According to the reconstruction of Wellhausen and Codera he was not named Julian at all, but Urban; he was probably of Moorish ancestry and a vassal of the Gothic kings, but all beyond this is pure hypothesis.

Induced apparently by the struggles for the throne in the Gothic kingdom, and probably less with a view to conquer than to plunder, Ṭāriḳ crossed into Spain in the year 711 with 7000 Berbers, who were subsequently supplemented to a total of 12,000, and landed near to the rock which still bears his name. (Gibraltar = Gebel Ṭāriḳ = Mount Ṭāriḳ.) After having collected his troops, Ṭāriḳ appears to have practised highway robbery along the coast from Gibraltar westwards and to have gone around the Laguna de la Janda in the south. King Roderick opposed him in the valley of the Wādī Bekka, nowadays called Salado, between the lake and the town of Medina Sidonia. According to the earliest Spanish tradition the site is also named after the neighbouring Transductine promontory (Cape Spartel).

It was here, not at Vejer (or Jerez) de la Frontera, that the great decisive battle was fought in July 711, in which the Gothic army, thanks to the treachery of Roderick's political enemies, was defeated by Ṭārik's troops. The king himself probably fell in the battle, for he disappeared at all events from this day forward[1].

This great success led to an unexampled triumphal procession, which can only be explained by the fact that the rule of the Goths was deeply hated among the native population. As on Byzantine ground, so here too had political and religious blunders set the various elements of the population at variance, and thus prepared the way for the invasion. The Jews especially, against whom an unscrupulous war of extermination had been waged by the fanatical orthodox section, welcomed the Arabs and Berbers as their deliverers. The towns alone, in which the Gothic knighthood held predominance, offered any effective resistance. Ṭārik must have been very accurately informed of the condition of the country; the authorities represent him as advised in his arrangements for the whole of the further campaign by Julian (Urban). The sequel certainly justified the daring plan of pushing forward to Toledo, the capital of the Gothic kings; the more important cities of the south, *e.g.* Seville, were left to themselves, others, as Malaga and Archidona, were subdued by small detachments; the main body of the army proceeded by Ecija and Cordova to Toledo. It was only at Ecija that Ṭārik met with any vigorous resistance, and at this point a battle ensued, which is described as the most severe and stubborn of the whole campaign. Cordova and Toledo fell by treachery. The aristocracy and the higher ranks of the priesthood did not even await the arrival of the Muslims, but either repaired to places of safety or sought union with the conquerors.

Ṭārik was thus master of the half of Spain by the end of the summer of 711. His unprecedented successes aroused the jealousy of Mūsā, his superior officer and patron, who had remained passively in Northern Africa, because a systematic conquest of Spain was not intended in Ṭārik's expedition—only one of the customary summer raids of the Muslim troops. Ṭārik had however now destroyed the Gothic kingdom. Mūsā nevertheless, desiring for himself the fame and the material advantages attending on the conquest of wealthy Spain, advanced thither also with 18,000 troops in the following spring, and landed in June. Purposely avoiding Ṭārik's tracks, he first of all conquered the towns which still held out, prominent among which were Medina Sidonia, Carmona and Seville. Seville was the intellectual centre of Spain; it had been the seat of government for centuries under the Romans, and under the Goths it had not lost its former splendour. It was only captured after a siege of several months' duration. From the campaign of Mūsā it can be seen that Ṭārik's stratagem had by no means destroyed all resistance, but that the heavy work of the conquest of the

---

[1] Another view is given in Ch. VI. p. 185.

country had to follow the rapid occupation of the capital. The Arabs would scarcely have succeeded in the conquest of Spain without the internal disorders which had preceded their arrival, and the consequent want of discipline and unity. Even as it was, after the fall of Seville, Mūsā still met with obstinate resistance before Mérida, whose impregnable walls resisted all attempts at undermining. The inhabitants however finally recognised their advantage in peacefully surrendering the town (30 June 713). Seville too rose once more in revolt, but was finally subjugated by Mūsā's son, 'Abd-al-'Azīz. It was only after all these successes that Mūsā could enter Toledo, where Ṭāriḳ awaited him.

Mūsā now vented his anger on his too-successful subordinate, but soon afterwards the same fate overtook himself. His letter of recall, signed by the Caliph Walīd (713–714), reached him 15 months after his landing, and but few weeks after his entry into Toledo. The victorious old man slowly made his way overland towards Syria, taking enormous treasures with him. Arabian papyri in the British Museum have preserved various data in regard to the expenses of provisioning his princely train during his temporary stay in Egypt. In Damascus he fell into disfavour and does not again appear in the foreground. His sons too, of whom he had left 'Abd-al-'Azīz as governor in Spain, and the others in Africa, did not long enjoy the fruits of their father's great deeds, for they also were soon either deposed or murdered.

This account of events in the conquest of Spain is chiefly based on Arabian sources, the importance of which, as compared with the certainly valuable Latin historians, has been decidedly undervalued in recent times. According to the latter Mūsā, and not Ṭāriḳ, was the actual conqueror of Spain; they represent Ṭāriḳ as merely the victor in the battle at the Transductine promontory, whilst Mūsā consummated his triumphal march by the conquest of Toledo; of any opposition between Mūsā and Ṭāriḳ there is no mention. Both groups of authorities agree in recording that under Mūsā, or at least by his direction, Saragossa also was taken. Notwithstanding contradictory reports, it is certain that Mūsā did not also cross the Pyrenees.

The crossing of this range did not take place until a few years later (717 or 718), under the leadership of Mūsā's fourth successor, Ḥurr. North of the Pyrenees, in the same way as to the south, the quarrels of the various races offered the Arabs an inducement to invade the country, and with the then prevalent lack of geographical knowledge the seemingly possible idea of reaching Constantinople by land from Gaul may have haunted their brains, for was not the fall of the proud imperial city the ardently desired end and aim of the foreign policy of the Caliphs? The leaders of the expeditions sent out from Spain had however more obvious designs; it was the booty, which might reasonably be looked for in the rich treasures of the convents and churches of Gaul, which lured them onwards. The daring march, which subsequently led to the celebrated defeat of Tours or Poitiers, is directly attributed by the authorities to this lust of booty. The chief officers of the Merovingians were engaged in fighting with the dukes of Aquitaine. While the France of the future was gradually gaining ground in the north in the midst of heated fighting, the dukes of Aquitaine were threatened on all sides. The Duke Eudo of Aquitaine had to sustain the first onslaught of the Arabs, and this was finally broken against Eudo's iron-willed adversary, Charles Martel.

Details of the raids made by Ḥurr are not known. They were continued by his successor Samḥ, who captured Narbonne in 720, and this formed the base of operations for the Spanish attacking forces until 759. The further undertakings of Samḥ however were a failure. He endeavoured to conquer Toulouse in 721 by attacking it with battering rams. But Duke Eudo relieved the distressed town and won a decisive victory. The leader of the Muslims fell in battle. This was the first great success of a Germanic prince over the Muslims, so long accustomed to victory. It was not the last; for the later expeditions of the Muslims were no longer crowned with success; in fact Eudo began to utilise to his own ends the growing difficulties between the Arabs and the Berbers. After a pause the Spanish Amīr 'Abd-ar-Raḥmān prepared to strike a great blow. He proceeded in 732 over the Pyrenees, defeated Duke Eudo between the Garonne and the Dordogne, and followed to the vicinity of Tours, attracted by the church treasures of the town. Here he was met by Charles Martel, whom Eudo had called to his assistance, and was vanquished in the battle of Tours or Poitiers, 732, which lasted several days. Here the complete superiority of the northern temperament over that of the southerners displayed itself. According to the report of the historians the Frankish warriors stood firm as a wall, inflexible as a block of ice. The light cavalry of the Caliphs failed against them. It was however not only the temperament, but also the physical superiority of the Teutons, which asserted itself in any fighting at close quarters, that won the battle. When the Teutons after the last day's fighting, in which the Muslims had lost their leader, wished to renew the struggle, they found that the Arabs had fled. The entire camp, with the whole of the munitions of war, fell into the hands of the victors.

The battle of Tours or Poitiers has often been represented as an event of the first magnitude in the world's history, because after this the penetration of Islām into Western Europe was finally brought to a standstill. The Arabs certainly undertook occasional raids, in regard to which we have but scanty information; they occupied, for instance, Arles and Narbonne, until they were expelled thence by Charles Martel and Pepin. In these expeditions however the Arabs only appear as allies of the grandees of Southern Gaul, who desired with their help to ward off the advance of Charles. The Caliph Hishām, at that time in power, certainly encouraged a vigorous expansion in connexion with his policy of restoration; but the attack of the Saracens was no longer successful, and as early as 759 the Arabs had to relinquish Narbonne, their last base north of the Pyrenees, to Pepin. The Saracen assault was therefore apparently broken by the battle of Tours or Poitiers—but only apparently, for that which might be regarded as cause and effect was but a chronological coincidence. Every movement has its limits, and the migration of the Arabs would not have been enough to place the requisite forces of men in the field for a permanent occupation even of Spain if they had not sought them outside their own limits among the Berbers. By joining the Arabs and conquering Spain for them, the Berbers carried the Saracen movement into another new country, but at the same time they made it heterogeneous, and as an addition to the internal Arabian feuds they created a new one, that between Arabs and Berbers. This strife, still latent during the first years of victory, came to light about the time of the battle of Tours or Poitiers. But a further cause rendered additional Saracen raids into Gaul impossible. In the northern corner of Spain a remnant of the opposition against the penetration of Islām had preserved its independence as a State; year by year this small State grew in size, and in a short time it inserted itself like a wedge between the Arabian magnates and the Pyrenees. On this was founded the legend of St Pelagius, which is treated more fully in another part of this work.

Under these circumstances the expansion of the Muslims came to a natural standstill from internal causes, and the consequences of the battle of Tours or Poitiers must therefore not be exaggerated. The plundering of these towns would decidedly not have resulted in a permanent occupation of Gaul by the Saracens. Their defeat before Constantinople was of vastly greater significance. The fall of Constantinople would have entirely remodelled the history of the East, as in fact it did, seven centuries later.

The battle then of Tours or Poitiers marked the extreme point of advance of the Saracens into Western Europe, but it was not the cause of the sudden stoppage, or rather recess of the movement. That fact lay, as above stated, in the feud between Arabs and Berbers. This strife was bound to be so much the more fatal for the Arabs, as at the same time the discord between Ḳais and Kalb in the East made its influence felt in the West also, and thus broke up the compact unity of the hitherto paramount nationality. The details of this process have little value for the history of the Saracen expansion treated in these chapters. A brief description of the principal events will suffice to explain the other great advance of the Saracens against Mid-Europe (Sicily, Sardinia and South Italy).

The whole of the western portion of the empire of the Caliph, the so-called Maghrib, *i.e.* Northern Africa and Spain, was placed after the completion of the conquest under various governors, who had their seat of government in Ḳairawān. The Spanish sub-prefects however often had an almost independent position. They resided at first at Seville, but shortly afterwards chose as the seat of government Cordova, which was thus destined for centuries to become the brilliant residence of the western Caliphate. Until its secession from the eastern main empire, and in fact for centuries afterwards, the destinies of Spain were united in the closest manner with those of Northern Africa through the Berbers, who were now settled on both sides of the Straits of Gibraltar. Thus it came that Spain, on the outbreak of Berber unrest in Northern Africa, was at once drawn into this fatal movement. The only difference was that in Northern Africa the Berbers were the subjects, who had however expected to attain an equal footing with the Arabs by the adoption of Islām, whilst in Spain the Arabs and Berbers had together conquered a foreign land, whose wealth and territory they divided. At this stage the Arabs committed the great mistake of shewing themselves too ostentatiously as the masters, *i.e.* in Africa they proceeded arrogantly and violently against the proud Berbers, who had cost so much trouble to subdue, whilst in Spain they allotted the Berbers the worst portion of the booty. This caused a first revolt, which was however but partial. The Berber Munusa in Northern Spain declared his independence, and entered into friendly, even family connexions with the Duke Eudo. His call however found but little response among his countrymen, and he was put down with little trouble (729 or 730).

More serious were the developments in Africa. It was at the time of Caliph Hishām, under whom the revision of Omar's system of taxation, which had gradually become a necessity, was enforced more generally and energetically. The bureaucracy which accompanied this revision, and the Asiatic despotism which was gradually creeping in, were nowhere so unsuitable as in the mountain homes of the Berbers, who were only held in check by diplomacy and the prospect of booty. As with the Orientals in general and especially with the Berbers every national or economical opposition easily assumes a religious tinge, so it was in this case too. We have already spoken of the Khārijites, who had detached themselves from Ali after the battle of Ṣiffīn. Their doctrine was that of the absolute sovereignty of the people, who were justified at all times in deposing an unjust Caliph or Imām. We have already indicated that the Umayyads had much trouble with these people. The profession of the doctrine of the Khārijites was one of the most important forms in which the opposition against the growing despotism and the bureaucracy found expression, especially among the old-Arabian circles, just as, among the Persians, this opposition took the form of the Shī'a. With the increasing tension betwixt Umayyad troops and the Berber populace, the Khārijite ideas had an unsuspected spread among the latter. And as the Arabs had now lost their readiness for battle by reason of their tribal feuds, the Berbers ventured, under the Caliph Hishām, openly to secede. After local revolts, which were quickly suppressed, a serious rebellion began in the extreme west. The whole territory of what is now called Morocco within a short period shook off the domination of the Arabs (741). Hishām hereupon sent a powerful army, composed of the best Syrian troops, to Africa, and it was intended that this force should co-operate with the garrisons already there. But the feuds amongst the Arabs themselves more than counter-balanced their better equipment, and in consequence the Berbers won a mighty victory (741) at the river Sebu, or, as the best Latin authority gives it, " super fluvium Nauam," and thus put in doubt the supremacy of the Arabs. Later on numerous fugitives crossed over into Spain and brought new confusion into the confusion there prevailing. But here as there for a short period the authority of Damascus was once more restored. Ḥanẓala ibn Ṣafwān, the new governor, managed by time-honoured methods to prevent common action on the part of the Berbers, and then later vanquished the main body of the Berber troops (742) at Aṣnām, not far from Ḳairawān. His representative, 'Abu-l-Khaṭṭar, then enforced order in Spain. The Berber revolt was thus broken, but it was the Berbers notwithstanding, and not the Arabs, who decided the destinies of the countries. Though the majority returned to Muslim orthodoxy, remnants of the Khārijites have maintained their position in Northern Africa even to the present day, under the name of Ibāḍites.

This peace lasted scarcely three years. Spain arose out of the new tumults as an independent State, for which a period of high prosperity was in prospect. In North Africa too a series of independent States was gradually formed. After the residence of the Caliph had been removed nearer to Central Asia it was probably natural that the Mediter-ranean territories, inhabited by a vigorous population, should begin a separate existence as States. After the fall of the Umayyads the countries to the east of Barḳa, permeated by the Saracen expansion, only occasionally and then only nominally held common cause with the Eastern Empire. The first usurper preserved at least the appearance of dependence. In the year 745 'Abd-ar-Raḥmān ibn Ḥabīb, of the tribe of Fihr, declared himself in Tunis independent of the governor Ḥanẓala, who had conducted the affairs of the Maghrib since the revolt of Ḳairawān. Belonging to a race long tried and approved on African soil, 'Abd-ar-Raḥmān could count on followers by reason of the universal discontent. By a brutal intrigue he compelled Ḥanẓala to leave Africa without drawing the sword. The last of the Umayyads, Marwān, sub-sequently legalised the *de facto* authority of 'Abd-ar-Raḥmān. For this 'Abd-ar-Raḥmān paid a small tribute and named the Caliph in his pulpit prayers, but he was otherwise his own master; and his position was not influenced by the change in the dynasty in the East. When the rule of the Abbasids had become consolidated and it was proposed to make an energetic attack on him from Bagdad, he renounced his obedience to the Abbasids and received fugitive Umayyads as honoured guests in Kairawān (754–755). These Umayyad princes however brought discord into 'Abd-ar-Raḥmān's family, in connexion with which he himself and two of the princes met their deaths. A third prince, 'Abd-ar-Raḥmān ibn Mu'āwiya, forced his way through to Spain and became the founder of the western Caliphate. In Africa the murder of Ibn Ḥabīb led to a general disorganisation and set free all the tendencies towards decentralisation. Independent Berber dynasties arose in the extreme West, as for instance the Banū Midrār in Sijilmāsa (757) and Banū Rustam in Tahert (761), the latter under the banner of the Khārijites; in the nearer West the Arabs on the one hand and the Berbers, who had also separated into parties, on the other, fought for the possession of Kairawān, which did not again acknowledge the authority of the Abbasids until 761, and then only for a short time; the province of Africa, as far as to the border of Algeria, was once more restored, though with disturbances and interruptions, but the whole of the far West remained irretrievably lost.

Here in the far West a third State was soon founded. A descendant of Ali named Idrīs, who had fled from the Abbasids, created for himself, in the year 788, an independent kingdom, which soon extended eastward to beyond the town of Tlemcen. Here again a clever leader managed to unite the Berbers by a religious party-cry. The kingdom of the Idrīsids was the first Shī'ite State founded in the West.

The remainder of the province of Maghrib once so extensive was moreover destined to make itself independent in the last decade of the eighth century. The constant dissensions between the Arab leaders and tribes could no longer be permanently controlled by the governors sent from Bagdad. The Amīr of Mzab (in the back-country of Algeria) Ibrāhīm ibn Aghlab, who had grown up in Africa, and whose father had been the means of reconquering the Mzab, was on the other hand the right man in the right place to restore state authority (800). When he had succeeded in this however he demanded from the Caliph the hereditary investiture in return for payment of a tribute and the customary naming of the Caliph in the pulpit prayers and on the coinage. This amounted to complete independence. Thus arose the dynasty of the Aghlabids of Kairawān, which gave to Africa a series of clever, but also often worthless, rulers. In proportion to the smallness of their kingdom they had a considerable naval force, and thus they became the leaders of the expansion of Islām into Mid-Europe. It was under them that Sicily was conquered.

Before turning however to Sicily, we must still sketch the further destinies of Northern Africa, in as far as it is connected with the history of Islām in Southern Europe. In spite of their brilliant performances

the authority of the Aghlabids was in a tottering state. The diversion
to Sicily of the generals and troops, always inclining towards insubordination, gave them a respite for a considerable time; after lasting
for a century their kingdom was destroyed by the political lack of
discipline of the Berber tribes and by bloody quarrels within the dynasty
itself.

These conditions were cleverly utilised by the Shī'ite opposition,
which just at that time, after many ill-successes in Asia, had pushed
forward into Africa, where the propaganda of the Idrīsids had paved
the way for them. The leader of the movement was named 'Ubaidallāh,
whose descent from Ali is by no means established beyond doubt; the
race itself however was called, after Fātima, the daughter of the Prophet,
the Fāṭimites. When 'Ubaidallāh had become master of the situation
in the year 909, through the fortunate trend of circumstances and
his skill in recruiting, he assumed the cognomen Mahdī, *i.e.* the
directed one, a title in which the old claims of Ali's kinsmen to the
Caliphate found expression. Mahdī founded a new capital, Mahdīya,
and established a State which for centuries held the supremacy in the
eastern Mediterranean. For this end of course the possession of Egypt
was needed, but the acquisition of this was first effected by Mu'izz
(969), Mahdī's third successor, who was the founder of Cairo. The
centre of gravity of the Fāṭimite kingdom was now transferred eastward,
especially when Syria also was conquered. Africa soon attained independence again as a State under Yūsuf Bulukkin, a Berber of the
Ṣanhāja, the governor appointed by the Fāṭimites; Yūsuf founded the
dynasty of the Zīrids (972–1148), alongside of whom the Hammādids
held their ground in the West, and specially in Algeria, from 1107 till
1152. The kingdom of the Idrīsids in Morocco had in the meantime
been split up into a number of petty principalities. The Fāṭimites
however remained the rulers of the eastern territory, and under them
Egypt experienced its most brilliant times, but suffered also its worst
defeat. In 1171 the heir to the Fāṭimite kingdom was Saladin.

We were compelled to give an anticipatory sketch of the history of
North Africa until the commencement of the times of the Crusades, in
order to understand the second great advance of the Saracens against
Sicily and Southern Italy as one connected whole. Incidents from the
standpoint of individual countries, these regular attacks of the Muslims
on Mid-Europe are presented, in the light of universal history, as a
connected movement, which naturally closes with the occupation of
Sicily and also of parts of the Continent. As in Spain, the reaction of
the Christian world follows upon the action of Islām. Just as they
came, so the Muslims are gradually forced back. Here we have to do
with the forward action alone, and though from chance reasons this
took place much later in Sicily and Italy than in Spain or Asia Minor,
yet its description comes notwithstanding within the scope of a general

history of the expansion of the Saracens, for the conquest of Sicily is connected in the most intimate way with the occupation of Northern Africa, and could only succeed after the conditions in the latter territory had somewhat improved. It is the same movement which took the Saracens across the Straits of Gibraltar. The subsequent advance of the world of Islām against Eastern Europe and the occupation of Constantinople by the Turks are in no way connected with the original movement as described here; the events now related below are the last ramification of the Arabian exodus.

As Michele Amari says in his classical work on the Muslims in Sicily, only a glance at the map is needed to shew that Sicily must be involved in continuous war with the Saracens after their occupation of Africa. And yet this same great historian represents the first naval expedition against Sicily not as starting from Africa but from Syria, and that too at a time when the subsequent Caliph Mu'āwiya was still governor of Syria. The strongly contradictory reports about this event may most easily be reconciled by regarding the first appearance of an Arabian fleet in Sicily as taking place under the Caliphate of Mu'āwiya, and connecting it with the expedition of his African governor, Mu'āwiya ibn Ḥudaij, against the Byzantines (664). Arabian tradition also accepts this Ibn Ḥudaij as the leader. It is quite probable that he himself never saw Sicily, but that the raid was made under his orders by his representative, 'Abdallāh ibn Ḳais. It is however quite certain that this naval expedition did not start from Syria but from the Pentapolis (Barḳa); the Syrian fleet had opportunities of booty nearer home; of the Pentapolis however we learn from the papyri that it was an important naval base in the seventh century, and here the fleet operating in the west received recruits from the fleets coming from Egypt. This opportunity serves to point out once again that, with the exception of special occasions the regular war of the Arabs against the Byzantines consisted of individual summer campaigns, which bore the name κούρσοι and took place by water or on land. From this old custom piracy, that terrible scourge of the western Mediterranean, was developed in course of time as the great kingdoms became split up into small states, and the name Corsair is also etymologically related to the word κοῦρσον. The despatch of the fleet by Ibn Ḥudaij was such a κοῦρσον. The booty consisted of captive women and church treasures, images, which according to the Arabian historians Mu'āwiya endeavoured to sell for gold as quickly as possible among the idol-worshipping Indians.

Just as this first expedition against Sicily was connected with the occupation of Northern Africa, so we must not disconnect the occasional raids of the following decades from the ever-increasing use of the fleet in the western seat of war. It can therefore cause no surprise that during the *régime* of the great pacificators of the Berbers, *i.e.* under Ḥassān and Mūsā, war was waged on Sicily more frequently.

At that time also the small island of Pantellaria, the stepping-stone between Africa and Sicily, was occupied by the Arabs, and Sardinia was plundered. It is needless to recount in detail all these numerous piratical expeditions against the islands of the Mediterranean. They were the terror of the residents on the coast, but very little was in reality attained by them. In any case Sicily must have been well defended. But if Syracuse itself could only purchase the retirement of 'Abd-ar-Raḥmān ibn Ḥabīb by payment of tribute (740), and even if this ruler, after acquiring the sovereignty in Northern Africa, attempted to gain Sicily also, these matters were but incidents which had no influence on the course of history. During the second half of the eighth century Sicily was scarcely troubled at all by its tormentors, for, as we have seen, Northern Africa was almost in a state of anarchy.

It was not until after a more powerful State had been formed by the Aghlabids that the expeditions against Sicily were at once renewed. Not only the Aghlabids but also the Idrīsids and even the Spanish Muslims took part in these piratical raids, each as a rule on their own account but occasionally working conjointly. When the Sicilians had perhaps succeeded in completing a treaty with the Aghlabids and looked forward to a period of rest and peace, then the vessels of the Idrīsids would suddenly appear. A large proportion of these expeditions have another connexion, for the raids are episodes in the long fight between the Franks and the Spanish Umayyads, but in the case of many of these sudden attacks we cannot now determine the State to which the Saracens in question belonged. One expedition in the year 813 is specially well known to us, because it advanced far to the northward and even touched on Nice and Civita Vecchia. In the same year or shortly afterwards Reggio also received a first Saracenic visitation. Corsica in particular was in the midst of the fighting, whilst Sardinia was better able to defend itself; the smaller islands, *e.g.* the Pontine group and even Ischia (8–12 Aug. 812), were occasionally attacked—in fact, a revival of the Saracen expansion began. But still great successes could not be recorded, for on the one hand various Saracenic fleets were lost at sea through storms, and on the other hand not only the Byzantines but also Charles the Great took energetic steps to secure their lands against the ravages of the Saracens, though they generally confined themselves to acting on the defensive. As for such a thing as paying the Saracens off in their own coin by undertaking a piratical expedition to Northern Africa, that occurred but once, when the African coast between Utica and Carthage was terrorised by a small Frankish fleet under Count Boniface of Tuscany.

There was no really serious advance of the Saracens against European territory, until the year 827. Acting not on their own initiative, but called in to the assistance of a Christian insurrection, the Aghlabids conquered the rich island of Sicily. By this means an outpost of Islām was pushed forward close to Italy, and it followed as a matter of course that the Saracens became an important factor in the diversified confusion of the States of Central and Southern Italy.

The occasion was a military revolt, such as was of everyday occurrence in Sicily, the "Siberia" of the Byzantine Empire. The details are not clear, but we may probably assume, with Amari, that Euphemius, the leader of the rebels, was compelled to flee from the Byzantine governor, Photeinos. He went to Africa to Ziyādatallāh I, the third prince of the race of Aghlabids, requested help, and promised, after the conquest of the island, to regard himself as Ziyādatallāh's vassal. The latter took counsel with his all-powerful minister, the Ḳāḍī Asad ibn al-Furāt, then seventy years of age, who, as head of the clergy, was leader of the internal policy of the Aghlabids, founded as it was on orthodoxy, and who moreover must be described as a military leader of eminence. The opportunity was favourable, and therefore no delay could be brooked in carrying the religious war to the long-coveted island. Apart from this, no better opportunity could be found to keep the ever-insubordinate Arabs and Berbers employed. Thus the undertaking was resolved on and at once commenced.

The aged Ḳāḍī himself undertook to lead the army, consisting of 11,000 men, which landed at Mazara, defeated Photeinos and advanced to Syracuse. But at this stage of the proceedings a reverse followed. The town was impregnable; an epidemic, to which Asad himself succumbed, broke out among the besieging troops; Euphemius was murdered; the Byzantines sent fresh troops, but Ziyādatallāh was unable to send reinforcements on account of the unrest in Africa. The Africans therefore were compelled to retire on Mazara and Mineo, and it began to appear as if this energetic attempt to conquer the island would fail. The blockaded Africans however were relieved by Spanish co-religionists (829), and then the aspect of affairs was changed. Palermo was conquered in the beginning of September 831 by fresh troops from Africa. The Muslims even began to form connexions with the States on the Continent, of which we shall see more presently. The Byzantines were forced back step by step. For all that, the war lasted over ten years longer before the capture of Messina (probably 843) by the Aghlabid prince, Abu-l-Aghlab Ibrāhīm. Byzantium could no longer help the Sicilians, for all the troops were required in the East. They still held out however at a few points. The apparently impregnable Castrogiovanni, situated on a high sugar-loaf mountain, which even to the present has maintained a remarkably sinister medieval character, did not fall till the year 859, after a long defence, into the hands of 'Abbās ibn al-Faḍl, who had succeeded Ibrāhīm. But the energy of the undisciplined African soldiery did not last beyond this stage, and even before the island was completely conquered the Arabs and Berbers were at daggers drawn and the Saracenic advance appears to have come to a standstill here from the same reasons as in Southern France. The last energetic prince of the house of the Aghlabids, Ibrāhīm II, further succeeded (21 May 878) in capturing and destroying Syracuse. Later on he came himself to Sicily and attacked with brutal cruelty the only Christian communities who were still independent, in the Etna district, and he also destroyed Taormina (902). The conquest of Sicily was thus completed. The re-conquest by the Normans did not begin till 1061.

Ibrāhīm II met his death in the same year before Cosenza, after having carried the religious war across the straits into Calabria. He was not the first Saracen on Italian ground, for immediately after the conquest of Palermo the Aghlabid generals had interfered in the internecine quarrels of the Lombard States in Southern Italy, and thus these Aghlabids had soon become the terror of Southern and Central Italy. Everyone who has travelled along the incomparable coast between Naples and Palermo knows the numerous "Saracen towers," the ruins of the coastguard towers, from which the approach of Sicilian or African fleets had to be announced. Even to-day, in the time of a peaceful, money-bringing invasion of foreigners, there still dwells in the memories of the people occupying this favoured country the recollection of that other invasion of quite other character, the Saracen calamity, which for centuries restricted all healthy development. This forms the final chapter in the spread of Islām into Central Europe. In depicting it we must rely mostly on western sources, as the Arab-Berber robber-States which sprang up in Southern Italy never attained civilisation enough to have literary records, and Sicilian and Eastern writers tell us little about Italy[1].

As in Sicily so in Italy the Saracens did not come without an appeal. For a long time past the Duchy of Benevento had endeavoured to annex the free town of Naples, which was besieged at various times and was compelled to agree to the payment of a tribute, which however was at once suspended whenever any resistance appeared possible. After having unsuccessfully requested Louis the Pious (814–840) to intervene, and having also been unable to find any sufficiently powerful allies in his own neighbourhood, Duke Andreas of Naples turned to the Saracens in Sicily. These availed themselves eagerly of this opportunity to interfere in Italy and in the year 837 they relieved Naples, at that time besieged by Duke Sikard of Benevento. Sikard retired with indignation, but the alliance thus formed by Naples lasted for many a long year to the benefit of both parties. The Duchy of Benevento was a natural enemy to both of them and it could not be otherwise than agreeable to the Neapolitans when, shortly afterwards, Sikard's troops were defeated by Saracens at Brindisi, and the town itself was burnt. In fact Naples even returned the assistance rendered in 837 by helping the Saracens in 842–843 to conquer Messina.

---

[1] The following account utilises the results of Amari and Lokys.

After Sikard's death the Duchy of Benevento was divided into two principalities; Radelchis resided in Benevento and Sikonolf in Salerno, and the two were constantly fighting. This self-destruction on the part of the sole great power of Southern Italy was of course in the highest degree welcome to the Saracens. Sikard died in 839, and immediately afterwards the Saracens of Sicily were once more in Calabria. They even advanced as far as Apulia, and though the conquest of Bari was not at first attained, Taranto fell and was not relieved even with the help of the Venetians, whom the Byzantines had called to their assistance (840). The victorious Muslims pushed forward to the Adriatic, burned Ossero on the island of Cherso, and Ancona, and even appeared temporarily in the neighbourhood of Venice, whose trading ships they captured. In 842 also the Venetians suffered a further defeat. Bari, which was to be the main base of the Saracens for thirty years, had already fallen (probably 841). Radelchis, pressed hard by Sikonolf, had called the masters of Sicily to his assistance, and they had begun by taking Bari from their ally. Radelchis had of course in his distress to accept this with a good grace and come to terms with these strange and unruly allies. The Saracens under the Berber Khalfūn advanced from Bari as a base against Sikonolf, but after a bloody battle they were driven back on Bari, which in the meantime they had converted into a strong fortress. As the Muslims constantly received reinforcements this one victory served Sikonolf but little; and Radelchis too, especially after he had received (in 842), whether he liked it or not, his infidel allies under the leadership of Masar into his capital, Benevento, became the puppet of the Saracens, who ravaged the whole country with their despotism and cruelty—a terrible scourge for friend and foe alike.

In spite of all such misfortunes however Radelchis was of course under the circumstances victorious over his adversary. As Sikonolf could not help himself in any other way, he too sought Saracen allies. He is said to have applied to the Spaniards, whose numerous raids into Provence, Northern Italy and in fact as far afield as Switzerland do not come within the scope of this chapter. It is moreover much more probable that Sikonolf did not draw his auxiliaries directly from the Iberian peninsula, but from Crete, where a Muslim robber-State had been in existence since 826, founded there by Spanish Saracens who had been expelled for mutiny from their country. With these new troops, who were more easily governed, as they had no neighbouring great power on whose support they could calculate, Sikonolf succeeded in defeating his opponent and locking him up in Benevento. He was however unable to take the town owing to difficulties in his own camp, and so everything remained in the same state as before. Masar with his Saracens swept through the whole country, plundering as he went, and undertook expeditions far towards the north.

These advances however of the Saracens, starting from Bari and

Benevento, were not the only raids with which the unfortunate country was infested. The large ports of the western coast were in constant dread of unpleasant surprises, for in the year 845 the Sicilians had chosen Ponza and Ischia as naval bases, to which moreover they soon added Cape Miseno. The towns of Naples, Gaëta, Amalfi and Sorrento formed an alliance for the purpose of mutual defence, as the Duke of Salerno was not in a position to assist them. In the following years the Muslims prepared to deal a severe blow. For a long time Rome with its vast church treasures had tempted them. On 23 Aug. 846, a fleet of 73 vessels, stated to have been manned by 1100 Muslims, appeared before Ostia, and in the early morning of 26 August the Saracens stood before the walls of Rome, where they plundered the quarters of the town lying outside the walls, especially the church of St Peter and the cathedral of St Paul, and they broke open the graves of the apostolic prelates. Unfortunately the information we have respecting this event is extremely scanty and it is moreover distorted by legend, for the very idea of the hordes of the false prophet having ravaged in the capital of Christendom gave a magnificent scope for the imagination of the western world. God himself immediately afterwards seemed to desire to avenge this visitation, for after a few successes before Gaëta, whither the Saracens had withdrawn from Rome, and just when they proposed to return, their entire fleet, conveying all their stolen treasures, was destroyed in a storm (847).

The impression made by these events was enormous. In 847 King Louis II appeared in Southern Italy, defeated the Saracens and conquered Benevento. With the disputing parties there he arranged that they should make common cause against the infidels in Bari and Taranto. This plan was frustrated through the selfish policy of the small States of Southern Italy. Nothing was effected against the continued piratical raids of the Sicilians. It was not until the year 849 when the Saracens planned another great expedition against Rome and collected for this purpose in Sardinia, that the seaports of the western coast united for the defence of Rome. The fleets met before Ostia, and the fight had already begun when the elements waxed tempestuous and the naval battle and the Sicilian fleet came to a sudden and violent end. The Italian fleet was probably also destroyed—information on the point is missing—but the sacred city was rescued. Even now, in the Stanzas of the Vatican, the celebrated picture of this sea fight, painted from sketches by Raphael, recalls this wonderful rescue of Rome.

Even though these naval expeditions were but episodes, the Saracen fortress at Bari was a constant menace to Southern Italy. The successes gained by King Louis had been lost again immediately after his departure, and Bari once more extended its power to Benevento. Louis II, who had in the meantime been crowned as Emperor, was therefore compelled once more to decide on an expedition to the south. On this occasion he advanced on Bari, but was unable to capture it, as his vassal States failed

him at the critical moment.   However he managed to obtain possession
of Benevento for the second time, and he caused the Saracen leader Masar
to be executed (28 May 852).   The Saracen commander-in-chief in
Sicily, 'Abbās ibn al-Faḍl, avenged this deed by plundering and occupying
the Calabrian coast.

The same performance was repeated as after the first departure
of Louis.   Meanwhile Mufarrij ibn Sālim had taken up Khalfūn's
position at Bari.   He took his revenge for past failures by founding an
independent State, declaring his allegiance directly to the Abbasid
Caliph.   His successor assumed the title of Sultan, thus proclaiming his
independence of the Sicilian Amīr.   Little is known of the doings of
these rulers of Bari, who were probably soldier-emperors like the subsequent Mamelukes in Egypt.   The country as far as Central Italy lay
defenceless at their feet, as the troubles in the territory of the old
Duchy of Benevento became greater and greater, and prevented all
defence.   The western historians give the most incredible reports of the
bloodthirstiness of these sultans.   Capua and Naples had to suffer the
most, but the rich monasteries further to the north, as San Vincenzo on
the Volturno, and Monte Cassino, also saw the enemy either within their
walls, or at least before them.

In order to put a stop to this distress the Emperor once more
undertook (866) a great expedition against the Saracens, and finally
forced them back on Bari and Taranto.   In order to subjugate Bari
however a fleet was necessary, and after long negotiations this was
eventually placed at his disposal by the Byzantines.   By co-operation
at this stage the two emperors and their vassals at last succeeded
(2 Feb. 871) in breaking the power of Bari.   On his way to Taranto
however to take this last bulwark from the Muslims the Emperor was
compelled to fall back on Ravenna, and this too through the treachery
of the self-same petty princes, whom he had just rescued from the
severest distress.   At the same time the Saracens appeared once more,
this time on the western coast, and attacked Salerno, pushing forward
also even as far as Capua.   Louis sent help once more, and the Saracens
were defeated at Capua on the Volturno, whereupon they left Italy,
but only to return shortly afterwards with renewed forces.   They did not
meet the Emperor again in the south.   He died in 875 in Northern
Italy, and with his death all his successes appear to have vanished.

At this point Byzantium assumed the moral heritage of the
Carolingian and profited by his deeds.   The further struggle with the
Saracens and their final expulsion from Italy belongs to the great
Byzantine restoration under the Macedonian emperors of the Basilian
dynasty.   A few words only may here be added in regard to the conclusion of the Saracen domination on Italian soil.   With the consent
of the residents the Byzantines, who were up to that time stationed
in Syracuse, had also settled in Bari.   The loss of Syracuse in the

year 878 was certainly a severe blow; Calabria and Taranto were still in the hands of the Muslims, and the Adriatic too was not safe from them. Basil was however the first to succeed in defeating the Saracens at sea, to land in Calabria, conquer Taranto (880) and a few years later to expel the last remnants of the Saracens from Calabria. Thus Southern Italy became once more a portion of the Byzantine Empire. The subsequent attacks of the Saracens in this quarter were no more than episodes, although the coast towns were again occasionally laid under tribute to the Saracens, and the constant strife between Saracens and Byzantines did not in fact cease until the Normans conquered both contending parties.

Through the downfall of Bari, the Saracens' base of attack for Central Italy had naturally been shifted. They came now exclusively from the West. The small Lombard States, rendered shrewd by their experiences in the past, had made a treaty with the Sicilian Saracens, on which account the latter, from 875 onwards, directed their raids principally towards the north, and harassed the pope. In 878 Pope John VIII was even compelled to pay the Saracens a tribute, in order to purchase a short period of rest and quiet. For several years thereafter the Saracens succeeded once again in gaining strong bases on the coast and in the interior, as, for instance, in the mountains to the north of Benevento and on the right bank of the Garigliano at Trajetto. Especially from the latter point they still undertook numerous plundering expeditions through Central Italy up to the gates of Rome; Monte Cassino too, which they had not previously entered, was looted and destroyed in the course of one of these raids. It was not until 915 that, thanks to the initiative of John X, the camp on the Garigliano was destroyed. Thus ended the reign of Islām on Italian soil, though we still hear of many a later piratical excursion.

Owing to the irregular nature of the Saracenic raids in Southern Italy, the events in Sicily and on the mainland have had to be pourtrayed separately, but it is easy to see the inner connexion of the two. The subsequent march of events can be given without further ceremony in connexion with the history of the island. The Muslim command here had been in the meantime changed. On the ruins of the Aghlabid dominion the Fāṭimite Mahdī had founded a new and promising State; the Arabs and Berbers of Sicily seemed apparently to have submitted with a good grace to the new order of things in their native country (910), but the fact soon made itself apparent, that the governor sent by Mahdī was not equal to the situation. The Saracens of Sicily, under the leadership of the Arab Amīr Aḥmad ibn Ḳurhub, thereupon declared their independence and named the Abbasid Caliph instead of the Fāṭimite in their pulpit prayers (913). But such a period of unity, patched up in times of need, between Berbers and Arabs, never lasted long. As early as 916 the Berbers gave up the unfortunate Amīr to the Caliph Mahdī to be cruelly executed, and Sicily became once more a province of the Fāṭimite Empire (917).

Thus strengthened the Fāṭimites again commenced their piratical trips from Africa and Sicily, and the Byzantines purchased peace for their coasts for some time by a treaty with Mahdī. The latter recouped himself for this in the north, by plundering the district of Genoa and the town itself in 934 and 935, at the same time casually honouring Corsica and Sardinia with a visit.

These years were not happy ones for Sicily; one unscrupulous governor drove the Islāmic upper classes to revolt, whilst another subjected them in an unprecedentedly bloody struggle. Thereafter a more favoured time began under the rule of the Arab Ḥasan ibn Ali, who had been entrusted with the governorship by the second Fāṭimite in 948. Ḥasan belonged to a family called Banū abi-l-Ḥusain, and the Fāṭimite to the Kalb; he and his successors and relatives who ruled after him are therefore called the Kalbites, a brilliant dynasty, under whom all the gifts of civilisation began to collect and take shape, which gave later a distinctive character to the Norman culture, and even to that of Frederick II.

The energetic Amīr repressed the particularism which militated against successful development, and thus created the foundations of a well-regulated and more or less independent State. The Fāṭimites were shrewd enough to restrict their choice to members of the race of Banū abi-l-Ḥusain, whenever a new governor was required, without however permitting too much private power to arise by so doing. Closely related members of the family were always employed by the Fāṭimites in Egypt, thus securing themselves against any efforts at independence on the part of the Amīr for the time being. But apart from this the governor had complete freedom, especially since the Fāṭimites had removed their capital to Egypt. In this way the Amīr of Sicily acted as a necessary counterpoise to the Amīr of Ḳairawān. In the foreign policy of the Fāṭimites moreover Sicily played in the long run a more and more important part, especially since the Fāṭimites had become the leading Muslim power in the eastern Mediterranean territory and were engaged in constant struggles with the Byzantines for supremacy. This however can only for the present be briefly touched upon.

Ḥasan ibn Ali reigned until 965. During his rule renewed fights took place in Calabria and Apulia, in fact the Byzantines even ventured on a landing in Sicily, but in the year 965 the Greek fleet was utterly destroyed off Messina. But shortly after, when the conquest of Egypt was impending, the Fāṭimites concluded terms of peace with Byzantium and thus Italy also obtained a period of rest from the Saracens, and an alliance was even made with them temporarily when the movements of the Emperor Otto II began in Lower Italy. In 982 however Otto was seriously defeated by the Saracens at Stilo in the Bay of Taranto.

This strange friendship soon came to an end, and in the decades before and after the year 1000 we come across the Kalbite Amīr again in Southern Italy. In Sicily however the population experienced years of progress and prosperity under intelligent rulers. The general welfare was shewn most completely in the households of the Amīrs. The material prosperity of the Orient of the time, the refined style of living, the rich intellectual life of Court circles in Bagdad, Cordova and Cairo, were also to be met with in Palermo, whose best period corresponds to the reign, unfortunately but too short, of the Amīr Yūsuf (989–998). But immediately after Yūsuf's decease indications began to appear which shewed that the Kalbite dynasty had passed its highest point of excellence. Yūsuf was rendered incapable of holding the reins of government by a stroke and his son Ja'far (998–1019) was not fortunate in his methods. The opposition between Arabs and Berbers, never quite extinct, now started up again. The revolt which followed ended with the expulsion of the Berbers and the execution of a brother of the Amīr, who had led them. Ja'far was however compelled to yield to another revolt, carried out by another brother. Thus weakened inwardly Sicily was no longer able effectively to resist the various hostile naval powers, such as Byzantium and Pisa, which threatened it; and early in the new century the Sicilian fleet suffered various defeats. It was not until the Zīrids allied themselves with the Sicilians that, during its third decade, more extended raids could be undertaken against the Byzantine lands, but these too always ended in defeat.

Added to these defeats there followed, from 1035 onwards, a civil war, which was the beginning of the end of the dynasty and also of the sway of Islām in Sicily. On this occasion the trouble was not between Arabs and Berbers, but was the consequence of the expulsion of the latter. The Berbers had to be replaced by other troops, and these of course cost money, so that the taxes had to be raised. The native population thereupon took up arms. The Amīr Aḥmad at this stage applied to Byzantium for assistance, whilst the rebels, who were led by a brother of the Amīr, called in the help of the Zīrids. The Byzantine general Maniakes, in whose army were numerous Normans, gained battle after battle (1038–1040), but then experienced difficulties with the Normans on account of his bad treatment of them, and also fell out with Stephanos the leader of the Byzantine fleet, so that all the fruits of their victories were lost to the Byzantines (up to 1042). The native population too had in the meantime forced the Zīrids, on account of their licentious behaviour, to return to Africa, so that there would really have been a good field for the revival of the Kalbite rule.

In the course of this general fight, each party against the others, the individual minor magnates and the towns had learned to fight for themselves, so that Sicily emerged from the great war no longer as an undivided State, but as a conglomerate of petty principalities and civic republics, all mutually at variance with each other. One main antagonism was in evidence among these States, the same that had called forth the whole civil war; the opposition between the Arab aristocracy and the natives who had been converted to Islām. The former congregated around Syracuse, the latter at Girgenti and Castrogiovanni. The leader of the Arabs was Ibn ath-Thimna. Being defeated by the opposing party he called the Normans into the country in 1061; these had in the meantime founded a vigorous State on the mainland. The Norman conquest, the details of which are given elsewhere, was completed in 1091.

The rule of Islām in Italy is therewith at an end, the expansion has passed its zenith, and it is now thrown back on Africa. The process lasted a few centuries longer in Spain, but here too Islām remained merely an episode in history. The blessings of culture which were given to the West by its temporary Islāmitic elements are at least as important as the influence of the East during the time of the Crusades. The lasting injuries which the constant Saracen scourge inflicted on Europe must not be exaggerated, for the Saracens did only what every Christian maritime power of that period held to be justifiable. Robbery and a trade in slaves were as legitimate on one side as on the other. As far as their deeds were concerned the opponents were evenly matched. It was only later on that the western land produced from its own inner self a new world, whilst the East has never since attained a higher pitch of excellence than that which immediately followed the Saracen expansion.

CHAPTER XIII.

THE SUCCESSORS OF HERACLIUS TO 717.

BESIDES Constantine, who had been his colleague since 613, Heraclius left four sons by Martina—Theodosius, who was deaf and dumb, Heraclius, who had been crowned in 638, David the Caesar, and Martin the *nobilissimus,* and (though Constantine was twenty-eight and Heraclius only sixteen) he desired by his will that they should enjoy equal rights, while Martina received the honours of an empress and a mother from both. Relying upon this provision, Martina claimed to exercise the practical sovereignty herself: but the people would not permit this, on the ground that a woman could not receive foreign envoys, and compelled her to leave the government to her stepson. Anticipating such a result, Heraclius had entrusted a large sum to the patriarch Pyrrhus for her benefit: but, Philagrius the treasurer having discovered this and informed Constantine, Pyrrhus was forced to surrender it. As the Emperor was suffering from consumption (which caused him to reside at Chalcedon), Philagrius, fearing to be left exposed to Martina's vengeance, persuaded him to send a donative to the soldiers through Valentine the Armenian, the commander of Philagrius' guard, urging them to protect his two sons and maintain their claim to the succession. Valentine however used the money to gain influence for himself; and after Constantine's death (24 May 641) Philagrius was forcibly ordained and banished to Septum (Ceuta), and many of his supporters were flogged, without opposition from the army, though Martina tried to attach it to her son's cause by a further donative in the name of the dead Emperor. But in consequence of her incestuous marriage and her attempt to exclude Constantine from power she was exceedingly unpopular, and by the malevolence of her enemies she was now accused of poisoning him. Valentine, who had either originated this report or used it for his own purpose, placed himself at the head of a military force in Asia, occupied Chalcedon on the pretext that the lives of Constantine's sons were in danger, and sent instructions to the troops in the provinces not to obey Martina, while the Empress brought the army of Thrace to defend the capital. To allay the commotion, Heraclius produced his elder nephew, Heraclius, a boy of ten, to whom he had stood godfather, and, touching the wood of the cross, swore that the children should suffer no harm; he even took the boy to Chalcedon and gave the same assurance to Valentine and his army; but, though Valentine allowed him to return, he refused to lay down his arms. By these acts the Emperor succeeded for a time in gaining the support of the capital. But the country round Chalcedon was covered with vineyards, many of which belonged to the citizens of Constantinople; and, when the vintage came on and the produce was reaped by Valentine's army, they cried loudly for an accommodation, directing their attack against the patriarch Pyrrhus, who was the strongest supporter of Martina and was suspected of having been concerned in the murder of Constantine, and insisting on the coronation of the young Heraclius. The Emperor then went to St Sophia and ordered Pyrrhus to crown his nephew: but the people insisted that according to custom he should do this himself; and they gave the new Augustus the name of Constantine, though to distinguish him from his father he was popularly known as Constans (Sept.). The feeling against Pyrrhus was however still unabated; and, after a mob had vainly sought him in the cathedral, and in revenge desecrated the sanctuary, on the following night he laid his stole on the altar in token of leave-taking (29 Sept.), and after hiding for a time escaped to Africa: and, though he had neither resigned nor been deprived, Paul was ordained to succeed him (Oct.).

Peace was now made, Valentine being appointed Count of the excubitors and receiving a promise that he should not be called to account for the money received from Philagrius, who was recalled from exile, and that his soldiers should receive a donative. The Caesar David was then crowned as a third emperor under the name of Tiberius, and Valentine marched to Cappadocia to act against the Arabs.

The peace was however of short duration. The troops in Cappadocia produced a letter purporting to have been written by Martina to a certain David, in which he was urged to attack Valentine, marry Martina, and depose Constans. Soldiers and people rose against the Empress under the leadership of Theodore the Armenian, who, having seized David in a fortress to which he had fled, cut off his head and had it exhibited all over the eastern provinces. On Theodore's return to Constantinople Martina was by decree of the Senate deprived of her tongue, and Heraclius and Tiberius of their noses, and they were all banished to Rhodes (Dec.). Constans thus became sole emperor.

All this must have been done at the instigation of Valentine, who after unsuccessful operations against the Arabs returned to Constantinople with a guard of 3000 men and forced Constans to give him the rank of Caesar (early in 643): but on strong opposition manifesting itself a compromise was made, whereby he gave up this title, but was made commander of the troops in the capital and gave his daughter in marriage to Constans. Two years later his tyrannical acts led to a popular rising, during which he was seized and beheaded. His military command was given to Theodore (646)[1].

The Arabs first invaded Asia Minor during the commotions of 641. In 642 a plan of Valentine for a combined attack on them was frustrated by his defeat; but Theodore and Procopius penetrated as far as Batnae, and an Armenian force occupied Amida and nearly reached Edessa before they were routed. In 643, Valentine having returned to Constantinople, the enemy again entered Asia Minor, and Arabissus capitulated to 'Umair. In 644 Mu'āwiya, *amīr* of Syria, took and plundered Euchaita; and in 646 after besieging Caesarea for ten days he ravaged the neighbourhood, returned, and forced it to pay tribute, afterwards vainly attacking Amorium. On this expedition he found the Cilician fortresses deserted and left garrisons in them till his return, but in 647 had them destroyed. In 649 Ḥabīb, and in 651 Busr, raided Isauria, and in 651 Sufyān also invaded Roman territory from Germanicea, while in 649 Mu'āwiya placed a fleet on the sea and plundered Constantia in Cyprus, but retreated on the approach of a Roman fleet under Cacorizus the chamberlain.

These were only plundering expeditions: but about 647 Ḥabīb occupied Melitene, Sozopetra, and Adata; and, as the war had gone against the Romans, Constans in 651 sent Procopius to treat for peace with Mu'āwiya (the Caliph Othman was ignored), and a truce was made for two years, the Emperor paying tribute and leaving Gregory, the nephew of Heraclius, as a hostage.

The truce of 651 was hardly more than nominal; for the secession of Armenia led to the Emperor's expedition to that country (652) and to the outbreak of fresh hostilities there, and after the expiration of the armistice the war was renewed on a larger scale than before. Great preparations were made by Mu'āwiya for an attack by sea and land upon Constantinople. He himself, starting from Melitene, took Ancyra and advanced to Dorylaeum (653), destroying all the fortresses on the way. Meanwhile ships were being hastily built at Alexandria, Tripolis, and other places; and in 654 a fleet under Abū'l-A'war after occupying Cyprus pillaged Cos, Crete and Rhodes (where the famous colossus, long since fallen, was broken up and sold to a Jew). But, while the work was going on at Tripolis, two Roman brothers, Mu'āwiya's slaves, liberated the prisoners, and with their help killed the governor and his guard, burnt the ships, and escaped by sea to Roman territory. Mu'āwiya, who was probably recalled by the news of this disaster, did nothing this year beyond taking a fortress near Melitene: but the naval preparations were not given up, and in spring 655 Abū'l-A'war was sent to Phoenix in Lycia, a place celebrated for cypresses, to cut wood for shipbuilding, where he was joined by the Egyptian ships under 'Abdallāh. But the

---

[1] The details and chronology of events after the death of Heraclius are very doubtful.

new naval policy of the Arabs had forced the Romans also to institute a standing fleet; and the invaders were attacked by the Emperor in person, who was accompanied by his brother, Theodosius. In the battle which followed the Arabs were victorious, the Roman fleet being almost destroyed and Constans with difficulty escaping in disguise; but the Arabs, having attained their object, returned. Mu'āwiya at the same time made an expedition by land as far as Caesarea; but in 656 the murder of Othman and the civil war which followed put an end to his schemes, and he was at last glad to buy peace by paying tribute (659). The Emperor used the respite to reduce some Slavonic tribes, some of which he transferred to Asia to assist in the defence against the Arabs.

Constans had crowned his eldest son, Constantine, as Augustus in Apr. 654, and in 659 conferred the same dignity on his two younger sons, Heraclius and Tiberius, and had his brother Theodosius put to death on a charge of conspiracy (659). This made him very unpopular both with the citizens and with the army; he was greeted in the streets with the appellation "Cain," and at last, finding life in Constantinople irksome and perhaps dangerous, although war had again broken out with the Arabs, resolved to leave his capital and devote his attention to restoring the imperial power in the West, for which the disunion among the Lombards after the death of Aripert (661) afforded an obvious opportunity. In 662 he invaded the duchy of Benevento, and took several cities with little or no resistance. He failed indeed before the strong town of Acerenza; but he stormed Luceria, which he razed to the ground, and laid siege to Benevento itself, which was defended by Duke Romuald in person. Here he was met by a vigorous defence, and, having heard that Grimoald was marching to his son's assistance, made terms with the Duke, receiving his sister Gisa as a hostage, and raised the siege. An attempt to attack Capua was foiled by a defeat on the Calor, and he then withdrew to Naples for the winter. In spring (663) he sent the Persian Sapor on a fresh invasion; but he had hardly crossed the frontier when he was met by Romuald at a place called Forinum and severely defeated. Constans then abandoned all thought of reducing the duchy, and, secured against attack by the possession of Gisa, betook himself to Rome, and was met by the Pope and clergy six miles from the city, which he entered on 5 July, the first Emperor who had been seen in the ancient capital for 190 years. He attended service in the principal churches and made offerings, but left a more impressive memorial of his visit by appropriating all the bronze ornaments that he could find, including the tiled roof of the Pantheon. This last with some of the other articles he sent to Constantinople, carrying the rest with him. After a stay of twelve days he returned to Naples, and then went on to Sicily, which was threatened by the Arabs, and settled at Syracuse, where he set himself to organise measures for the defence of Sicily and Africa. For this purpose heavy burdens were laid on his Italian and

Sicilian subjects: but he was so far successful that no further invasion of Sicily was made while he lived, and in Africa, though the patrician Nicephorus is said to have been defeated in 665, no permanent conquest was effected till after his death. From Syracuse he sent for his wife and sons; but, as this foreshadowed a transfer of the seat of government, the citizens, headed by Andrew the chamberlain and the patrician Theodore of Colonia, refused to let them go.

It was not only at Constantinople that Constans was unpopular; and in 668 a plot was formed among those who surrounded him, one of whom, Andrew, son of Troilus, while the Emperor was bathing, poured an unusual quantity of soap over his face so as to blind him, and then killed him by striking him on the head with a silver ewer (15 July). The army proclaimed as emperor an Armenian named Mzhezh, who is said to have been of high character, but seems to have had no other recommendation except good looks, and was reluctant to accept the honour. His elevation found no favour elsewhere, the armies of Italy, Sardinia, and Africa united to overthrow him[1], the rebellion collapsed (Feb. 669)[2], and the assassin Andrew, Mzhezh himself, and his chief adherents suffered death, among them the patrician Justinian, whose young son, Germanus, afterwards patriarch, was mutilated.

Before turning to the eastern war it is necessary to speak of the military and administrative organisation which by a process we cannot trace in detail had been growing up during the reigns of Heraclius and Constans. The co-ordination of civil and military officials instituted by Diocletian had been greatly modified by Justinian, who in many places combined both functions in the hands of one man. From this time the civil governors, where they still existed, gradually became subservient to the military power, and the process was completed by the Persian and Saracen invasions, which made military rule a necessity, while the loss of the eastern provinces caused a new distribution of forces, and therefore new administrative divisions. Hitherto Asia Minor had hardly needed defence; and the only large contingent permanently stationed there was a portion of the *scholae* (guards) under the *magister militum praesentalis* quartered in the north-west, where in a district reaching from Paphlagonia and Galatia to the Hellespont they still remained under the name of *imperiale obsequium* (ὀψίκιον), while their commander bore the title of Count. Of the countries under the *magister militum per Orientem* only Isauria and Cilicia remained; but, as his troops were required to defend southern Asia Minor, they were also quartered in part of Cappadocia and the district to the west of it, but were still known as *Orientales* (ἀνατολικοί). Further west by the Aegean was a section of the Thracian army which had followed Heraclius to the Persian war and were known as *Thracesii*; but these were under the Anatolic general. Armenia and

---

[1] For the alleged expedition of the young Emperor see *Byz. Zeitschr.* XVII. 455.
[2] I infer the date from Michael, p. 437.

Pontus Polemoniacus had been placed by Justinian under a *magister militum per Armeniam*; and these provinces with Helenopontus and part of Cappadocia were still occupied by the Armeniaci. Thrace was still ruled by the successor of Justinian's *praetor*, and the Aegean islands obeyed the commander of the naval forces (*carabisiani*), who took the place of Justinian's *quaestor Justinianus*, and also exercised jurisdiction, at least for some purposes, over most of the south coast of Asia Minor[1]. Each of these divisions was called a theme (θέμα), and the title of the commanders of all except Obsequium was στρατηγός. Illyricum was almost lost; but the Illyrian praefect still ruled in Thessalonica, exercising military as well as civil powers. The provincial governors perhaps remained as minor judicial officers, but the vicars of the dioceses had disappeared. Of the great civil functionaries, the city-praefect, the *magister officiorum* (μάγιστρος), and the quaestor retained their old titles; but the *comes largitionum* was now known as λογοθέτης τοῦ γενικοῦ and the *comes rei privatae* as *sacellarius* (treasurer), while the praefect of the East may have survived under some other title, with greatly reduced functions. The general tendency of these changes was to abolish the dependence of one official on another, and bring them all into direct relation to the Emperor.

In 661 Ḥasan's abdication enabled Muʿāwiya to renew the war. A raid by Ḥabīb in 661 effected nothing; but in 662 the Romans were defeated, and in 663 Busr wintered in the Empire. As Constans had taken the bulk of the Anatolic theme to the West, ʿAbd-ar-Rahmān, son of the celebrated Khālid, could advance in 664 to Colonia (Archelais), where he wintered, and in 665, after failing in an attack on some islands in Lake Caralis, he placed a garrison in Amorium, the head-quarters of the Anatolics, which was forced to capitulate, took Pessinus and, after an unsuccessful attack on another fortified place, Cius, Pergamum, and Smyrna. Having been joined by some of the Slav colonists, he again wintered in Roman territory, and then returned to Emesa, where he soon afterwards died, it is said by poison (666).

In 666 Malik made a raid from Adata and wintered in Roman territory, and in 667 Busr ravaged the district of Hexapolis, west of Melitene, while another force wintered at Antioch in Pisidia: but in 668 the rebellion of Sapor, now general of the Armeniacs, gave an opening for a more dangerous attack. Sapor sent Sergius, one of his subordinates, to ask for the Caliph's support; and on hearing of this the young Constantine, who was ruling in his father's absence, sent Andrew the chamberlain to present gifts to Muʿāwiya and beg him not to countenance rebellion. The two envoys met at the Caliph's court, and Muʿāwiya decided in favour of Sergius, who insulted Andrew by calling him not a man but a eunuch. Andrew returned by the pass of Arabissus on the road to Hexapolis, where Sapor then was, the commandant of

[1] The territorial jurisdiction of the naval στρατηγός was perhaps developed later.

which still held for the Emperor, and having instructed this officer to watch for Sergius and arrest him if he passed that way, went on to a place called Amnesia. Here Sergius was brought as a prisoner, and Andrew avenged the insult to himself by having him mutilated and then hanged. Sapor now advanced to Hadrianopolis in Bithynia; and Muʻāwiya sent Faḍāla to his assistance, while Constantine sent Nicephorus to oppose him. But, while Sapor was riding before the walls, his horse bolted and dashed his head against the gate, which caused his death. His men then returned to their allegiance; and Faḍāla, who had only reached Hexapolis, was obliged to ask for reinforcements, which were sent under Muʻāwiya's son, Yazīd, while a fleet under another Yazīd supported the army. The Arabs advanced to Chalcedon, and in spring 669 crossed to Thrace and attacked Constantinople, which was defended by Constantine (usually known as Pogonatus), now reigning Emperor. No serious siege was however undertaken; and in the summer pestilence and lack of food compelled them to retire: but on their way back they took Amorium, in which a garrison was placed. During the winter however Andrew surprised the town by night in deep snow and slew the Arabs to a man.

In 670 Faḍāla came again by sea to the Propontis and wintered at Cyzicus; and during the years 668–671 other lesser raids took place. In 672 Busr carried off numerous prisoners, and in 673 another great effort was made. A fleet under Mahomet wintered at Smyrna, and another under Ḳais in Lycia, with which an army under Sufyān co-operated, and a colony was settled in Rhodes, while an attack on Constantinople was being planned, to meet which Constantine prepared fireships provided with Greek fire, the invention of the Syrian architect Callinicus. On the arrival of reinforcements the combined fleet appeared before Constantinople in spring 674, and after occupying Cyzicus assailed the city without success from April to September, and returned to Cyzicus for the winter. The same year Faḍāla and ʻAbdallāh wintered in Crete; and other expeditions were made every year without important result: but meanwhile the fleet at Cyzicus attacked Constantinople each year down to 677[1], when the loss in men and ships compelled it to withdraw. On its return it suffered severely from a storm off the Pamphylian coast, what remained of it was attacked by the division of the Roman fleet which from the town of Cibyra in Pamphylia was called Cibyrrhaeotae, and few, if any, ships returned home. This disaster and the Mardaite invasion of Phoenice and Palestine (678) caused Muʻāwiya for the second time to buy peace by paying tribute. The colony in Rhodes was now withdrawn, and the fortress of Camacha on the Euphrates, which the Arabs had after two earlier unsuccessful attempts taken in 679, restored. The garrison in Cyprus was removed by Yazīd, but the island continued to

---

[1] The invitation to the Pope in 678 to send deputies to Constantinople shews that the siege did not last beyond 677.

pay tribute.   The last raid was one in Isauria in the early part of 680.
Peace having been thus secured on the east, the Khan of the Avars and
other barbarian rulers sent presents and made treaties with the Emperor.

Meanwhile a theological controversy which seemed likely to cause a
division between East and West and facilitate usurpations like that of
Mzhezh was demanding the attention of the government.   The disaffection of Egypt and the East arising from the Synod of Chalcedon
had long been a menace to the Empire and had led to Zeno's attempt
to restore union through the Henotikon and the attempt of Justinian
to placate the Monophysites by the condemnation of the Three Chapters;
but in neither case was permanent success attained.   The rapid conquests
of the Persians drew the attention of Heraclius to this state of affairs,
and led him to try a plan suggested by the patriarch Sergius, himself a
Syrian by birth, to whom it had occurred that the Monophysites might
accept the expression "two natures" if satisfied that this did not imply
two operations (ἐνέργειαι).   About 618 accordingly Sergius wrote to the
Egyptian George Arsas, one of the Paulianist section of the Monophysites, adherents of the patriarch Paul of Antioch, deposed in 578,
asking for quotations in support of the doctrine of one operation, and
suggesting a union on this basis.   Further steps in this direction were
however prevented by the Persian occupation of Egypt.   In 622 again
Heraclius during his Armenian campaign conversed with a Monophysite
leader named Paul, to whom he propounded the doctrine of one operation,
but without success.   He then drew up an edict against Paul, which was
sent to Arcadius of Cyprus, in which the doctrine of two operations was
condemned.   In 626, while in Lazica, he discussed the question with
Cyrus, bishop of Phasis, who was doubtful on the point and wrote to
Sergius for information.   Sergius answered his objections and sent him
a copy of a letter of Menas of Constantinople to Pope Vigilius in which
one operation was asserted: by this Cyrus seems to have been satisfied.
Communication with the East having been restored in 628, Sergius sent
the letter of Menas to Theodore, bishop of Faran near Sinai, who expressed his assent.   This correspondence and Menas' letter were then
sent to the Monophysite Paul at Theodosiopolis.

After the recovery of the East the plan of reconciliation was taken
up in earnest.   In 630 or 631 Heraclius met the patriarch Athanasius
at Hierapolis in Syria and promised him the official patriarchate of
Antioch (vacant since 610) if he would accept communion with the
Chalcedonians on the basis of the doctrine of one operation; and to
this he was ready to consent; but, though some Jacobite monasteries,
especially that of Maron in the Lebanon, accepted the union, the
patriarch's death wrecked the scheme (631)[1].   In 631 the Armenian
Catholicus, Ezra, came on the Emperor's invitation to Syria, was

---

[1] So Michael, and Elijah of Nisibis. Cf. Mansi, xi. p. 504, where Athanasius is
distinguished from living heretics. Owsepian's chronology is untenable.

induced to accept the communion of the Chalcedonians, and on his return ratified the union at a synod at Theodosiopolis, but without formally recognising the Synod of Chalcedon. In 632, on the death of the patriarch George, Cyrus was appointed to the see of Alexandria and immediately opened negotiations with the chief Monophysite party in the city, the Theodosians. With these a union was effected by means of nine articles, in which the doctrine of two natures was asserted with a qualification, and one theandric operation maintained, while there was no acceptance of the Synod of Chalcedon or anathema against the Monophysite leaders (3 June 633).

At this point opposition arose. Sophronius, a Palestinian monk, who was then in Alexandria, entreated Cyrus not to make public proclamation of the articles; whereupon Cyrus referred him to Sergius, to whom he gave him a letter. As Sergius was unable to convince Sophronius, who was a man of great influence, the attempt at union seemed likely to cause a new schism: accordingly he agreed to a compromise by which both expressions "one operation" and "two operations" were to be avoided; and Sophronius with a letter of explanation from Sergius returned to Jerusalem, where early in 634 he was chosen patriarch. Sergius meanwhile wrote to Cyrus in the sense of the compromise; but Cyrus, not wishing to undo his own work, did not immediately accept it. Receiving a request from Heraclius at Edessa to send the quotations in support of the doctrine of one operation and one will contained in the letter of Menas, Sergius did so, but suggested that the controversy should cease. He then wrote an account of the affair to Pope Honorius, proposing that both expressions "one operation" and "two operations" should be rejected as stumbling-blocks, but specially reprobating the latter as implying the doctrine of two wills, which he condemned as impious. In answer to this Honorius concurred in the banishment of both expressions, and maintained the doctrine of one will, the advocates of which are generally known as Monotheletes. Sophronius now sent his synodical letter to the patriarchs, in which in accordance with the compact he avoided the expression "two operations," but strongly asserted the doctrine implied in it. This letter Sergius ignored: but Honorius wrote to Sophronius begging him to let the dispute drop; and the messengers of Sophronius said that he would do so if Cyrus would do the same. To him therefore the Pope also sent a request to cease preaching one operation. Sophronius however sent bishop Stephen of Dora to Rome to try to bring the Pope round to his side; but the capture of Jerusalem (637) and his own death, which soon followed, prevented any further action on his part, while in Egypt the abandonment of the doctrine on which the union was built destroyed the union itself, and the violent measures used by Cyrus to enforce conformity made matters worse than before.

The next step on the part of Sergius was to compose the *Ekthesis*, in which the principles contained in the letter to Honorius were put in the shape of a formal confession of faith (636). Heraclius on his return from the East signed this document, and it was posted on the walls of St Sophia (autumn 638). A copy was sent to Cyrus, who received it with veneration, and to Severinus, who had been elected to the papacy after the death of Honorius (Oct.); while a synod at Constantinople threatened spiritual penalties against anyone who asserted either one operation or two operations. This was the last act of Sergius, who died 9 Dec. 638. As Severinus rejected the *Ekthesis*, confirmation of his election was refused, and his emissaries were detained in Constantinople; but on their allowing it to be understood that they would obtain his acceptance permission was given for his consecration, which took place 28 May 640.

Egypt having been cut off by the Arab invasion, the question resolved itself into a contest between Rome and Constantinople. Severinus died two months after his consecration without accepting the *Ekthesis*; and his successor, John IV, wrote to the new patriarch, Pyrrhus, to denounce it: whereupon Heraclius, now at the point of death, in a letter to the Pope disclaimed the responsibility for it, which he threw on Sergius. After his death John wrote to Constantine maintaining the doctrine of two wills, explaining away Honorius' letter, and asking for the removal of the *Ekthesis*. The civil troubles prevented any further steps at the time; but the government of Constans gave the Pope to understand that the *Ekthesis* would be removed (642); and Pope Theodore (consecrated 24 Nov.) wrote to Paul of Constantinople to complain that this had not been done. He further reproached Paul for having taken possession of the see when Pyrrhus had not been formally deposed, and wrote to the Emperor to suggest that Pyrrhus should be tried at Rome. Sergius of Cyprus expressed his adherence in a letter to the Pope (29 May 643): but his strongest support came from Africa, where the exarch Gregory was contemplating rebellion.

The most resolute opponent of Monotheletism was Maximus, archimandrite of Chrysopolis, who had met Sophronius in Africa shortly before the Alexandrine union, and had now again gone thither to stir up opposition to the *Ekthesis*. Here in the presence of Gregory he held a dispute with Pyrrhus (July 645); who, hoping by Gregory's help to obtain restoration, declared himself converted, and having gone to Rome with Maximus, condemned the *Ekthesis* and was received by the Pope with the honours of a patriarch. In 646 several synods were held in Africa; and letters in condemnation of the *Ekthesis* were written to the Pope, the Emperor, and the patriarch, the last being sent through the Pope. Theodore forwarded the African letter with a remonstrance of his own; and Paul answered by an enunciation of the Monothelete doctrine; upon which Theodore declared him deposed.

Gregory rebelled in 647: but in 648 he fell in battle with the Arabs;

and Pyrrhus, having nothing more to hope from the party of Maximus, went to Ravenna and made his peace with the government by recanting his recantation. Theodore then solemnly deposed and anathematised him in St Peter's. Meanwhile, as the *Ekthesis* had only shifted the dispute from operations to wills, Paul made another attempt on the same lines to restore peace. An imperial edict, known as the Type, was at his instigation put forth, by which the *Ekthesis* was abrogated and all controversy on either question forbidden under heavy penalties (648); and, when the papal representatives refused to accept this, they were punished by imprisonment, flogging, or exile.

Theodore died in May 649; and his successor, Martin, who was consecrated without awaiting the imperial confirmation (5 July), immediately held a synod in the Lateran, which asserted the doctrine of two wills, denounced all who maintained one operation or one will, and condemned the *Ekthesis* and the Type, and Sergius, Pyrrhus, Paul, Cyrus, and Theodore of Faran (5–31 Oct.). The synodal acts were sent to the Emperor; and Paul of Thessalonica, who refused to accept the Roman theology, was declared deposed by a letter of the Pope.

Martin by his illegal consecration and flagrant disregard of the edict had defied the Emperor; and the answer of Constans, acting under the advice of Paul, was to send the chamberlain Olympius to Italy as exarch with orders to find out the general disposition towards the Type, and, if it should be favourable, and if the local army supported him, to arrest Martin, whom the Emperor did not recognise as Pope, have the Type read in all the churches, and make the bishops sign it; but, if not, to wait till a stronger force could be collected. Olympius however, observing the state of affairs at Rome, preferred to play the part of Gregory, and accordingly came to an understanding with the Pope and threw off allegiance to the Emperor. Some time afterwards he died in Sicily, whither he had gone to repel an Arab invasion; and after the imperial authority was thus restored in Italy, the new exarch, Theodore Calliopas, entered Rome with an army (15 June 653), and arrested Martin in the Lateran church (17 June) on charges of sending a letter and money to the Arabs and of disrespect to the Virgin (*i.e.* Nestorianism). At midnight on the 18th he was removed from Rome, conveyed to Misenum (1 July) and placed on board ship for Constantinople, which after a short stay in Naxos he reached (17 Sept.). He was kept in prison till 20 Dec., and then brought before the Senate. Being ill from the voyage and the long confinement, he was carried to the court in a litter. The charges of usurpation and disobedience, the real ground of his arrest, were kept in the background, nor do we hear anything more of those made against him at Rome; but he was accused of complicity with Olympius. Next, after the Emperor had been consulted, he was first exposed to the public gaze in the entrance-hall of the building, and then placed in a gallery overlooked by a hall in the palace where Constans

was: here a crowd was allowed to surround him. The treasurer after
again consulting the Emperor finally ordered him to be deprived of his
pontifical head-dress, as not being lawful Pope, and delivered to the
praefect to be beheaded. He was then stripped naked except for one
torn garment and dragged with a chain round his neck over rough
stones to a common prison with a sword in front of him, and thence
to the praefect's praetorium, where he was chained to the jailer: but in
the evening the praefect sent food with an assurance that the sentence
would not be executed, and the chains were removed. The sentence had
in fact been passed in order to frighten him into submission; and after
Paul's death, which shortly followed, unsuccessful attempts were made to
extort a statement that Pyrrhus, who had returned to Constantinople
after his reconciliation and was seeking restoration, had recanted under
compulsion at Rome. Nevertheless Pyrrhus was restored, but died on
Whit Sunday following (1 June 654). As all attempts to induce Martin
to communicate with the clergy of Constantinople were vain, he was on
15 Mar. removed to the house of a scribe, and thence on 11 Apr. to a
ship, in which he was conveyed to Cherson in the Crimea (15 May),
where he remained till his death in Sept. 655, complaining bitterly of
the lack of food and the neglect of his friends at Rome to send supplies.

Martin had however better reason to complain of the fickleness of
the Romans. At the time of his arrest the exarch had ordered the
clergy to elect a new pope; and after a year's resistance they yielded,
and (10 Aug. 654) Eugenius was consecrated to the papacy. The new
Pope sent envoys to Constantinople without a letter; and these communicated with the new patriarch, Peter, under a compromise. It
had been implied in the Type that the expressions "one will" and "two
wills" were both in a sense correct: and, though this doctrine had been
condemned by the synod, the envoys acquiesced in it (655). Peter then
sent a synodical to the Pope in which this principle was stated; but
popular clamour compelled Eugenius to reject it.

Maximus had since 645 been living in Rome; and, as he was
believed to have been the chief instigator of Martin's resistance, it was
thought that, if he could be induced to submit, the cause would be won.
Accordingly an imperial commissioner who had been sent to order
Martin to communicate with Peter tried to persuade Maximus to accept
the Type; and on his refusal he was arrested (653) and conveyed to
Constantinople, where he was brought before the treasurer and Senate
and accused of advising the *magister militum* of Numidia to disobey
the orders of Heraclius to march against the Arabs in Egypt, of
encouraging Gregory's rebellion, of disrespect to the Emperor, and of
anathematising the Type (655). During part of the proceedings the
patriarchs Peter of Constantinople and Macedonius of Antioch, who
resided in the capital, were present, and on Whit Sunday (17 May)

Peter made a special attempt to induce him to accept the compromise which had satisfied the Roman envoys: but, as he refused to yield anything, he was banished to Bizye in Thrace. On 24 Aug. 656 Theodosius, bishop of Caesarea in Bithynia, and two senators came to Bizye with an offer to repeal the Type if he would communicate with the Church of Constantinople; and on this being rejected Theodosius agreed to accept two wills and operations, that is without condemning the other doctrine according to the compromise; and, as Maximus insisted on the Emperor and the patriarch sending a profession of faith to the Pope, Theodosius undertook to try to bring this about. Maximus promised that, if Theodosius were sent to Rome, he would go with him, but refused to accept one will and one operation in any sense. Constans would not concede this, but made another attempt to win Maximus over. On 8 Sept. he was brought with great respect to the monastery of Theodore at Rhegium, and the next day Theodosius and two patricians came and promised him high honours if he would accept the Type. This he also refused, and the patricians assailed him with blows and abuse till persuaded by Theodosius to desist. He was then conveyed under military guard to Selymbria (14 Sept.), and thence to Perberis. Five years later he was brought before a synod at Constantinople, anathematised with Sophronius and Martin, and flogged. He was then deprived of his tongue and right hand, taken to Lazica (8 June 661), and imprisoned. In this exile he died at the age of 82 (13 Aug. 662).

The Armenians had outwardly accepted orthodox communion in 631; but, when Constans in 648 ordered them to receive the Synod of Chalcedon, they in a synod at Dvin openly refused. In 652, the chiefs having invited the Arabs into the country, Constans came with an army and lodged at Dvin in the house of the Catholicus, Nerses, who inclined to the Roman party and from opposition to the chiefs proclaimed the Synod, but had so little support that, when the Emperor returned early in 653, he was forced to go with him and did not return to his see till 658. After his death in 662 no more was heard of the union.

Vitalian, who succeeded Eugenius on 30 July 657, announced his ordination to Constans and sent a synodical to Peter in which he conformed to the Type. Peter in answer wrote a letter in which the numbers "one" and "two" applied to operations and wills were declared immaterial, the Emperor sent presents and renewed the privileges of the Church of Rome, and Vitalian's name was inserted in the diptychs of Constantinople, which did not contain that of any of his predecessors since Honorius. Peter's successor, Thomas (17 Apr. 667–15 Nov. 669) sent no synodical; but for this the Arab attack was afterwards alleged as a reason. The next two patriarchs, John (Nov./Dec. 669–Aug. 675) and Constantine (2 Sept. 675–9 Aug. 677), sent synodicals in which no reference was made to the disputed points; but, Constans being dead,

Vitalian yielded to popular feeling and rejected John's synodical: similarly his successor, Adeodatus (672–676), rejected that of Constantine; and his name was therefore not inserted in the diptychs of Constantinople. Accordingly the next patriarch, Theodore, sent no synodical, and, supported by Macarius of Antioch, urged Constantine IV to have Vitalian's name expunged from the diptychs. The Emperor, not wishing to perpetuate the schism, refused the request and wrote to Pope Donus (676–678), asking him, as the war prevented a general synod, to send deputies to discuss the disputed points with the two patriarchs. When the letter arrived, Donus was dead; and, as his successor, Agatho (678–681), had no intention of sending deputies to confer with Theodore, no answer came, and the Emperor was persuaded to allow Vitalian's name to be struck off. The original purpose of Monotheletism however, the reconciliation of the Monophysites, had been nullified by the Arab conquests; and, as the Pope conceded nothing, Constantine saw that to restore unity he would have to sacrifice the patriarch. Theodore was therefore deposed, and his place taken by George (Nov. or Dec. 679). Agatho then summoned a synod, which met at Rome on 27 Mar. 680, maintained the doctrine of two operations and two wills, condemned Sergius, Pyrrhus, Paul, Peter, Cyrus, and Theodore of Faran, and sent its decree to the Emperor with a long dogmatic letter from Agatho on the model of the *Tome* of Leo. Similar decrees were passed by synods at Milan and at Hatfield in England (17 Sept.). The deputies from Rome, who reached Constantinople on 10 Sept., were also accredited as representatives of the Pope and the synod at the proposed conference: and, peace having now been made, Constantine requested the patriarchs to summon the bishops under their jurisdiction to a synod, which met in the domed hall (*trullus*) of the palace in the presence of the Emperor and the chief officers of state (7 Nov.), and, as representatives of the non-existent patriarchs of Alexandria and Jerusalem were somehow procured, called itself oecumenical. The sittings, of which there were eighteen, continued to 16 Sept. 681; and the synod agreed as well with the Pope in dogmatic matters as that of Chalcedon. The letter of Menas was pronounced spurious, as were also two letters ascribed to Vigilius. Macarius brought forward patristic passages in support of Monotheletism; but they were declared to prove nothing, and quotations were produced on the other side. George now professed himself in agreement with the letters of the Pope and the Roman synod; and at his request Vitalian's name was restored to the diptychs. Macarius on the other hand refused to abandon his Monothelete opinions and was deposed together with his disciple, the archimandrite Stephen, and Theophanes was appointed to succeed him. All the Monothelete leaders mentioned in the Roman decree were then condemned with the addition of Honorius, and their writings ordered to be burnt. An attempt at a compromise made by the presbyter Constantine of Apamea in Syria was

rejected, and those condemned were formally anathematised in spite of
the protest of George against the inclusion of his predecessors in the
anathema: with these Macarius and other living Monotheletes were
joined. A statement of faith was then drawn up, and a letter addressed
to the Pope with a request to confirm the proceedings. Finally an
imperial edict was posted up in the vestibule of St Sophia, which forbade
anyone under severe penalties to teach one will or operation. Macarius
and his followers were banished to Rome, where, with the exception of
two who recanted, they were shut up in separate monasteries. The
papal envoys, who took back with them the synodal Acts and a letter of
the Emperor addressed to the Pope-elect, Leo II, dated 31 Dec., reached
Rome in June 682; and Leo after his consecration (17 Aug.) confirmed
the Acts in a letter to Constantine.

After the peace with the Arabs and the defeat by the Bulgarians in
680, which compelled the Emperor to cede the country north of Haemus,
his chief attention was given to the succession. The ancient practice
had been to divide an emperor's dominions between his sons after his
death: and such a division had been projected by Maurice, but prevented
by his overthrow. After the Arab conquests the reduced size of the
Empire made this practically impossible: and Heraclius therefore arranged
that the only two among his sons who had reached years of discretion
and were not disqualified by any physical defect should reign jointly, a
provision of which we have seen the bad result. Constans went further
and gave the imperial title to all his sons while they were children, and
therefore at his death left three nominal colleagues on the throne: but,
as joint government was impossible, the exercise of the imperial functions
fell to the eldest. This state of affairs quickly led to trouble. The
younger brothers bore the imperial title, and their names appeared upon
coins and in official documents, so that, when Constantine had sons of his
own, the difficulty arose that in case of his death his brother Heraclius,
as senior Emperor, would exclude them from the sovereignty. Accordingly, when his elder son, Justinian, had reached the age of 12, he
deprived his brothers of their titles and cut off their noses (681)[1].
The Anatolic troops soon after their return from Sicily marched to
Chrysopolis and demanded that Heraclius and Tiberius should be given
an equal share of power with their elder brother, saying that, as there
was a Trinity in heaven, there should be a Trinity on earth (681–2).
Constantine pretended to agree and issued a proclamation that all
three should receive equal honour, while he sent Theodore of Colonia
to invite the leaders to come into the city and confer with the
Senate, but, as soon as they were in his power, had them arrested and
hanged; and the troops, deprived of their leaders, retired. Henceforth

---

[1] The last meeting of the synod is dated by the years of all three Emperors, but
the edict of confirmation is in Constantine's name only.

the younger sons of emperors, though they might bear imperial titles, were usually excluded from power and from marriage; and, as the daughters of an emperor who had sons had been excluded from marriage since Theodosius' time, collateral branches, and therefore disputed successions, were avoided; but on the other hand a lasting hereditary succession was made impossible, and the crown lay open to any ambitious man or any nominee of the army—a state of affairs which continued till the system of compulsory celibacy was abolished by the Comneni.

At the beginning of September 685 Constantine died of dysentery, and was succeeded by Justinian[1].

Constantine had taken advantage of the anarchy which followed the death of the Caliph Yazīd (683) to renew the war; and Melitene was destroyed by the Romans, and the Arabs forced to abandon Germanicea. Hence 'Abd-al-Malik on succeeding his father, Marwān, as Caliph in Syria, was compelled to renew the peace by paying a larger tribute (7 July 685). Nevertheless the new Emperor not only sent an army under the Isaurian Leontius to Armenia and the adjacent countries as far as the Caucasus, which, having seceded from the Arabs, had been invaded by the Chazars (687), but sent another to co-operate with the Mardaites in Syria, and Antioch was occupied (688) for a time. Upon this 'Abd-al-Malik, not even yet being in a position to carry on war, again asked for terms, and a truce was made for ten years on the conditions that he should pay the same tribute as before, that Armenia, Iberia, Arzanene, and Atropatene should be ceded, and the tribute of Cyprus divided, and that Justinian should transfer the Mardaites to his own dominions (689). The Emperor then went to Armenia, where he appointed chiefs, took hostages, and received 12,000 Mardaites, whom he settled in different parts of the empire (690). By this step his forces were increased; but the Mardaites would perhaps have been of more use to him in the Caliph's territories.

Justinian had been willing to make peace because he had become involved in a war with the Bulgarians, in which he suffered a defeat (689). During this war however he reduced large numbers of Slavs, whom he settled in the north-west of Asia Minor and organised as a military force under the name of "peculiar people" (λαὸς περιούσιος)[2]: this force is said to have amounted to 30,000 men.

Having made peace with the Bulgarians and strengthened the offensive power of the Empire by the acquisition of Mardaites and Slavs, he sought an opportunity of breaking the peace with the Arabs. He began by a breach of the spirit of the compact by which the tribute of Cyprus had been divided; for he removed a large proportion of the population to

[1] *E.H.R.* xxx. (1915), pp. 50–51.
[2] Deut. xiv. 2, xxvi. 13; Tit. ii. 14.

the Hellespont and other districts in the south and west of Asia Minor
(691): and as Justinian I, whose example he seems always to have had
in mind, had refounded his native town as Nova Justiniana and given it
primatial rights in northern Illyricum, so Justinian II founded the city
of Nea Justinianopolis for the Cypriots in the Hellespont, and the synod
of 691 recognised the metropolitan of Cyprus, now bishop of this city,
as metropolitan of the Hellespont, in prejudice of the rights of Cyzicus,
and enacted that he should enjoy the same independence of the patriarch
as in Cyprus.   Next the Emperor refused to receive the tribute-money
in the new Arabic coinage, on which texts from the Koran were imprinted,
and in spite of the Caliph's protests announced that he would no longer
observe the treaty, and collected forces for an attack.   'Abd-al-Malik,
delivered from his rival 'Abdallāh[1], had no reason to reject the
challenge, and sent his brother Mahomet into Roman territory.   Meanwhile Justinian with a large army, in which the bulk of the Slavs were
included, marched to Sebastopolis, while the Arabs occupied Sebastia.
Between these two places the armies met, and the Arabs went into the
battle with a copy of the treaty displayed instead of a flag (693).
At first victory inclined to the Romans; but, most of the Slavs having
been induced by promises to go over, they were routed; and Justinian
on reaching the district where the Slavs were settled massacred all whom
he could find with their wives and children.   The first result of the
defeat was the loss of Armenia; and in 694 Mahomet with the Slavs
again invaded the Empire and carried off many captives, while an
attempt of the Romans to invade Syria from Germanicea led to another
disastrous overthrow, which forced them to abandon that city, and in
695 Yahya raided the country S.W. of Melitene.

The ex-patriarch Theodore by accepting the new order of things had
escaped condemnation at the synod, and after Constantine's death
induced the new Emperor to deprive George and restore him to the see
(Feb./Mar. 686).   As his restoration would be likely to rouse the Pope's
suspicions, Justinian laid the synodal Acts before the patriarchs of Constantinople and Antioch, the Pope's *responsalis*, such bishops as were in
the city, the chief civil and military officials, and the heads of the civic
factions, obtained their confirmation of them (686)[2], and announced
the fact to Pope John V with an assurance of his intention to maintain
the authority of the synod (17 Feb. 687).

But the mental attitude of East and West differed so much, and
through their different surroundings their practices had become so divergent, that concord could not long be maintained.   Neither the fifth nor the
sixth synod had passed canons; and therefore, though the Arab invasions
had in many ways introduced new conditions which needed regulation,

[1] See Ch. xi.

[2] As John died in Aug. 686, the date of the letter can only be that of the
Emperor's official signature.

CH. XIII.

there were no canons of general obligation later than those of Chalcedon.
Accordingly at the end of 691 a synod was held in the Domed Hall for
the purpose of making canons only.   This synod, generally known as
the Trullan from its place of meeting, or the Quinisext because it completed the task of the fifth and sixth synods, called itself oecumenical:
it was attended by the patriarchs Paul of Constantinople (Jan. 688–
Aug. 694) and George of Antioch, and titular patriarchs of Alexandria
and Jerusalem; and, though the papal legates did not formally take
part in it, Basil of Gortyna claimed to represent the Roman Church.
The assembly drew up a list of existing canons which were to be held
binding, regularised the practice that had grown up with regard to the
Eastern patriarchates by enacting that a bishop should suffer no detriment
because he was prevented by barbarian incursions from going to his see,
laid down rules dealing with the monastic life, the receiving of the
eucharist, and the taking of orders, and condemned some surviving
heathen observances and some practices prevailing in outlying parts of
the Empire such as Armenia and Africa.   If it had done no more, little
would have been heard of it; but in the following points it offended the
Church of Rome.   It accepted all the apostolic canons, whereas the
Roman Church received fifty only, and it laid special stress on the sixty-
fifth, which forbade the Roman practice of fasting on Saturdays in Lent;
following Acts xv. 29, it forbade the eating of flesh that contained
blood; it forbade the representation of Christ as a lamb in pictures;
above all it gave the patriarch of Constantinople equal rights with
the Pope, and in regard to the question of clerical celibacy, on which
the Eastern and Western customs differed, it not only condemned the
practice of compelling men to separate from their wives on taking higher
orders, but declared such separation, except under special circumstances,
to be unlawful.   On the other hand it condemned marriage after ordination to the sub-diaconate and forbade the ordination of men who had
been married twice.   These regulations were described as a compromise;
but in reality they differed little from a confirmation of the Eastern
practice, with a prohibition of irregularities.   Papal legates were present
in Constantinople, and were afterwards induced to sign the Acts; but
Pope Sergius disowned them, and, when urged to sign himself, refused.
Justinian at last ordered him to be arrested and brought to Constantinople; but the army of Italy supported the Pope, and it was only by
his intercession that the imperial commissioner escaped with his life (695).

At the beginning of his reign Justinian was necessarily in the hands
of others; and, as he afterwards devoted his restless energies almost
entirely to foreign and ecclesiastical affairs, the civil administration continued to be conducted by ministers who, as is natural in men who know
that their power is precarious, had little scruple about the means adopted
to extort money.   Of these the most obnoxious were the two finance-
ministers, the treasurer, Stephen, a Persian eunuch, who is said to have

flogged the Emperor's mother, Anastasia, during his absence, and the public logothete (γενικὸς λογοθέτης), Theodotus, an ex-monk, who used to hang men up over fires for purposes of extortion. Such abuses were promoted by the fact that Justinian, as in other matters, so in the love of building followed the model of his namesake, and for these operations large sums were needed; and his unpopularity was increased by the conduct of Stephen, who, acting as superintendent of the works, had the workmen and their overseers tortured or stoned if they did not satisfy him. Further, on one occasion, in spite of the opposition of the patriarch Callinicus, the Emperor pulled down a church to gain room for building, and so made the clergy of the capital his enemies. Again, whereas in earlier times prisons had generally been used to keep persons in custody for a short time, it now became the practice to detain men for long periods in the praetorium by way of punishment; and, though this may often have been a mitigation, the novelty roused hostility, and the existence of many disaffected persons in one place constituted a danger which brought about the Emperor's fall.

Among the prisoners was Leontius, who commanded in Armenia in 687. One night towards the end of 695, after he had been in prison three years, he was suddenly released, named general of Hellas (as this theme is not otherwise known at this time, it was perhaps a temporary commission), supplied with a military train sufficient to fill three cutters, and told to start immediately. Unable to believe in the Emperor's sincerity, he consulted two of his friends, Paul, a monk and astrologer, and Gregory the archimandrite, an ex-military officer, who urged him to strike a blow at once, assuring him of success. Leontius and his small following then went to the praetorium and knocked at the gate, saying that the Emperor was there. The praefect hastily opened the gate and was seized, beaten, and bound hand and foot; and the prisoners, of whom many were soldiers, were released and armed. The whole force then went to the Forum, where Leontius raised the cry, "All Christians to St Sophia!" and sent messengers to do the same all over the city, while a report was spread that Justinian had given orders for a massacre (perhaps of the Blue faction), and that the life of the patriarch was in danger. A great crowd, especially of the Blues, collected in the baptistery of the cathedral, while Leontius with a few followers went to the patriarch and compelled him to come to the baptistery, where he gave his sanction to the rising by the words, "This is the day that the Lord hath made," which the crowd answered by the formula of imprecation, "May the bones of Justinian be dug up!" They then rushed to the circus, to which at daybreak the Emperor, deserted by all, was brought. The people demanded his immediate decapitation; but Leontius was content with cutting off his nose and tongue (not so completely as to prevent him from speaking) and banishing him to Cherson. The multitude then seized Stephen and Theodotus, dragged them by ropes along the main street till they were dead, and burnt their bodies. The Blues proclaimed Leontius emperor, and he was crowned by the patriarch.

As the Arabs were preparing to reconquer Africa, there was little fighting in Asia Minor during Leontius' reign. In 697 the Caliph's son, Walīd, invaded the Empire from Melitene, and the patrician Sergius, who commanded in Lazica, betrayed that country to the Arabs. Further invasions were prevented by a plague and famine; and in 698 the Romans entered the district of Antioch and gained an unimportant victory.

In 697 Leontius sent the whole fleet under John the patrician to recover Africa, which had for the second time fallen into the hands of the Arabs; and John, having expelled the enemy from Carthage and the other fortified towns on the coast, reported his success to the Emperor and remained in Carthage for the winter. But early in 698, when a larger armament arrived from the east, he was unable to withstand it, and, abandoning his conquests, returned for reinforcements. When he reached Crete however, the crews renounced their allegiance and proclaimed Apsimar, *drungarius* (vice-admiral) of the Cibyrrhaeots, emperor under the imperial name of Tiberius. They then sailed to Constantinople, which was suffering from plague, and after a short resistance the besiegers were admitted through the gate of Blachernae at the N.W. corner by the treachery of the custodians, and plundered the capital like a conquered city. Leontius was deprived of his nose and sent to a monastery, and his friends and officers were flogged and banished and their property was confiscated (end of 698).

The new Emperor, as a sailor, gave special attention to the defence of the Empire on the sea side, restoring the sea-wall of Constantinople, and settling the Mardaites on the Pamphylian coast. He further re-peopled Cyprus by sending back the inhabitants whom Justinian had removed (699). Military operations also were conducted with considerable success, which must be ascribed to an innovation which Tiberius immediately after his accession introduced by appointing his brother Heraclius, who as a general shewed himself not unworthy of his name, commander-in-chief of all the Asiatic themes, and charging him with the custody of the Cappadocian frontier. In 701 the Romans made a successful raid as far as Samosata, and in 704 Heraclius killed or captured the whole of an Arab force which was besieging Sisium in Cilicia. On the other hand Walīd raided Roman territory in 699, his brother 'Abdallāh took Theodosiopolis in 700, in 703 Mopsuestia was occupied and Armenia Quarta betrayed to the Arabs, and in 705 the Caliph's son, Maslama, took two fortresses, and a Roman army was defeated in Armenia.

Meanwhile Justinian was living in Cherson, a place which, while acknowledging the supremacy of the Emperor, was not governed by any imperial official, and enjoyed a large measure of republican freedom. Here he made no secret of his intention to seek restoration, and the citizens, fearing the Emperor's vengeance, determined either to kill him or to send him to Constantinople. He had however friends in the town, who informed him of their purpose, and, fleeing to Dora, in the south-east of the Crimea, he asked to be allowed to visit the Khan of the Chazars, who ruled in the neighbourhood. The Khan granted the request, received him with honour, and gave him his sister in marriage, to whom in memory of the wife of Justinian I he gave the name of Theodora. He then settled at Phanagoria.

Tiberius in alarm promised the Khan many gifts if he sent him either Justinian himself or his head; and the Khan, agreeing to this, sent him a guard under pretence of protection, while instructing his representative at Phanagoria and the governor of Bosporus to kill him as soon as orders should be received. Of this Theodora was informed by a slave of the Khan and told Justinian, who sent for the two officials separately and strangled them. Sending Theodora back to her brother, he embarked on a fishing-boat and sailed to Symbolum near Cherson, where he took his friends from the city on board, one of whom bore the Georgian name of Varaz Bakur. He then asked the aid of the Bulgarian ruler, Tervel, promising him liberal gifts and his daughter in marriage. To this he agreed; and, accompanied by Tervel himself and an army of Bulgarians and Slavs, Justinian advanced to Constantinople (705). Here the citizens received him with insults; but after three days he found an entrance with a few followers by an aqueduct, and the defenders, thinking the walls were undermined, were seized with panic and made no resistance. Tiberius fled across the Propontis to Apollonia, but was arrested and brought back, while Heraclius was seized in Thrace and hanged on the walls with his chief officers. Tervel was invited into the city, seated by Justinian's side as Caesar, and dismissed with abundance of presents, while Varaz Bakur was made a proto-patrician and Count of Obsequium. Tiberius and Leontius were exhibited in chains all over the city, and then brought into the circus, where Justinian sat with a foot on the neck of each, while the people, playing on the names "Leontius" and "Apsimar," cried, "Thou hast trodden upon the asp and the basilisk (kinglet), and upon the lion and the dragon hast thou trampled." They were then taken to the amphitheatre and beheaded. Of the rest of Justinian's enemies some were thrown into the sea in sacks, and others invited to a banquet and, when it was over, arrested and hanged or beheaded; but Theodosius the son of Tiberius was spared, and afterwards became celebrated as bishop of Ephesus. Callinicus was blinded and banished to Rome, and Cyrus, a monk of Amastris, made patriarch (706). On the other hand 6000 Arab prisoners were released and sent home. As soon as his throne was secure, Justinian fetched his wife, who had in the meantime borne him a son, whom he named Tiberius and crowned as his colleague.

One of the first objects to which the restored Emperor turned his attention was the establishment of an understanding with Rome as to the Trullan synod. Having learned that coercion was useless, he tried another plan. He sent the Acts to John VII, asking him to hold a synod and confirm the canons which he approved and disallow the rest; but John, fearing to give offence, sent them back as he received them. His second successor, Constantine, however consented to come to Constantinople and discuss the matter (710). Landing seven miles from the capital, he was met and escorted into the city by the child Tiberius and the senators and patriarch; and Justinian, who was then at Nicaea, met him at Nicomedia, and, prostrating himself before him, kissed his feet. A satisfactory compromise (of what nature we do not know) was made, and the Pope returned to Rome (Oct. 711).

In the time of Tiberius the Arabs had never been able to cross the Taurus; but with the removal of Heraclius Asia Minor was again laid open to their ravages. A raid by Hishām the son of 'Abd-al-Malik in 706 produced no results: but in 707 Maslama, accompanied by Maimūn the Mardaite, advanced to Tyana (June). A rash attack by Maimūn cost him his life; and the Caliph Walīd sent reinforcements under his son, 'Abbās. All the winter the Arabs lay before Tyana, which was stoutly defended; and Justinian, who had fallen out with Tervel and required the Asiatic troops in Europe, sent an army mostly of rustics to its relief. The generals however quarrelled, and the rabble was easily routed by the Arabs, who pressed the siege of Tyana until it surrendered (27 Mar. 708). The inhabitants were removed to Arab territory. Maslama then raided the country to the north-east as far as Gazelon near Amasia, while 'Abbās after defeating a Roman force near Dorylaeum, which he took, advanced to Nicomedia and Heraclea Pontica, while a small detachment of his army entered Chrysopolis and burnt the ferry-boats. In 709 Maslama and 'Abbās invaded Isauria, where five fortresses were taken; but at sea the Romans captured the admiral Khālid, whom however Justinian sent to the Caliph, and attacked Damietta in Egypt. In 710 an unimportant raid was made by Walīd's son, 'Abd-al-'Azīz: but in 711 Maslama took Camacha, as well as Taranta and two other fortresses in Hexapolis[1], which was now annexed; and, as Sisium was the same year occupied by Othman, the frontier was advanced to the Sarus. On the other hand a Roman army sent to recover Lazica, where Phasis only remained in Roman hands, after besieging Archaeopolis was compelled to retreat.

After a defeat by the Bulgarians (708) and the restoration of peace, Justinian turned his energies to exacting vengeance from the Chersonites, who had now accepted a Chazar governor. In 710 he collected ships of all kinds, for the equipment of which he raised a special contribution from all the inhabitants of the capital, and sent them to Cherson under the patrician Stephen Asmictus, whose orders were to kill the ruling men

[1] " Khspolis " (Michael, p. 452) is a corruption of Hexapolis.

with all their families and establish Elijah the *spatharius* (military chamberlain) as governor. With him was sent a certain Vardan, who in spite of his Armenian name (probably derived from his mother's family) was son of the patrician Nicephorus of Pergamum who had commanded in Africa and Asia under Constans, and, having been banished to Cephallenia by Tiberius and recalled by Justinian, was to be again exiled to Cherson. The city was unable to resist, the chief magistrate, Zoilus, and forty of his principal colleagues with their families and the Tudun (the Chazar governor), were sent in chains to Justinian, seven others were roasted over a fire, twenty drowned in a boat filled with stones, and the rest beheaded. The children were however spared for slavery; and Justinian, furious at this, ordered the fleet to return (Oct.).

Off Paphlagonia the fleet was almost destroyed by a storm; but he threatened to send another to raze Cherson and the neighbouring places to the ground and kill every living person in them. The citizens then strengthened their defences and obtained the help of the Khan, while Elijah and Vardan made common cause with them. Justinian sent 300 men under George, the public logothete, John the praefect, and Christopher, turmarch of the Thracesii, with orders to replace the Tudun and Zoilus in their positions, and bring Elijah and Vardan to Constantinople (711). The citizens, pretending to accept these terms, admitted the small force; but immediately shut the gates, killed George and John, and handed the rest over to the Chazars, and the Tudun having died on the way, the Chazars avenged him by killing them. The Chersonites then proclaimed Vardan emperor, and he assumed the Greek name of Philippicus. Justinian, more enraged than ever, had Elijah's children killed in their mother's arms and compelled her to marry her negro cook, while he sent another fleet with powerful siege-engines under the patrician Maurus Bessus with the orders which he had before threatened to give. Philippicus fled to the Chazars, and Maurus took two of the towers of the city, but, Chazar reinforcements having arrived, was unable to do more, and, afraid to return, declared for Philippicus and asked the Khan to send him back, which he did on receiving security in money for his safety. The fleet then sailed for Constantinople. Justinian's suspicions had been aroused by the delay; and, thinking himself safer in the territory of the Obsequian theme, commanded by Varaz Bakur, he took with him the troops of that theme, some of the Thracesii, and 3000 Bulgarians sent by Tervel, and, having crossed the Bosporus and left the rest in the plain of Damatrys about ten miles east of Chalcedon, proceeded with the chief officers and the Thracesian contingent to the promontory of Sinope, which the fleet would pass. After a time he saw it sail by, and immediately returned to Damatrys. Meanwhile Philippicus had entered Constantinople without opposition. The Empress Anastasia took the little Tiberius to the church of the Virgin at Blachernae, where he sat with amulets hung round his neck, holding a column of the altar with one hand and a piece of the cross with the other. Maurus and John Struthus the *spatharius* had been sent to kill him; and, when they entered the church, Maurus was delayed by Anastasia's entreaties, but John transferred the amulets to his own neck, laid the piece of the cross on the altar, and carried the child to a postern-gate of the city, and cut his throat. Varaz Bakur, thinking Justinian's cause desperate, had left the army and fled, but he was caught and killed. Elijah was sent with a small force against Justinian himself, whose soldiers on a promise of immunity deserted their master, and Elijah cut off his head and sent it to Philippicus, who sent it to Rome (end of 711).

The new Emperor was a ready and plausible speaker, and had a reputation for mildness; but he was an indolent and dissolute man, who neglected public affairs and squandered the money amassed by his predecessors. Accordingly no better resistance was offered to the Arabs. In 712 Maslama and his nephews, 'Abbās and Marwān, entered Roman territory from Melitene and took Sebastia, Gazelon, and Amasia, whence Marwān advanced to Gangra, while Walīd ibn Hishām took Misthia in Lycaonia and carried off many of the inhabitants of the country. In 713 'Abd-al-'Azīz again raided as far as Gazelon, while Yazīd invaded Isauria, and 'Abbās took Antioch in Pisidia and returned with numerous captives. Meanwhile Philippicus for some unknown reason expelled the Armenians from the Empire, and they were settled by the Arabs in Armenia Quarta and the district of Melitene (712). In Europe also the Bulgarians advanced to the gates of Constantinople (712).

There was however one subject on which Philippicus shewed a misplaced energy. Having been educated by Stephen, the pupil of Macarius, he was a fervent Monothelete, and even before entering the city he ordered the picture of the sixth synod to be removed from the palace and the names of those condemned in it restored to the diptychs. Cyrus, who refused to comply with his wishes, was deposed and confined in a monastery, and a more pliant patriarch found in the deacon John (early in 712), who was supported by two men afterwards celebrated, Germanus of Cyzicus and Andrew of Crete. Shortly afterwards the Acts preserved in the palace were burnt, and a condemnation of the synod and the chief Dithelete bishops was issued, while many prominent men who refused to sign this were exiled. At Rome the document was contemptuously rejected, the Romans retaliated by placing a picture of the sixth synod in St Peter's and abandoning the public use of the Emperor's name; and Peter, who was sent to Rome as duke, was attacked and forced to retire (713).

An emperor without hereditary claim to respect, who could not defend the Empire from invasion and wantonly disturbed the peace of the Church, was not likely to reign long; but the fall of Philippicus was eventually brought about by a plot. A portion of the Obsequian theme, which had been the most closely attached to Justinian, had been brought to Thrace to act against the Bulgarians, whose ravages still continued; and, trusting to the support of these soldiers and of the Green faction, George Buraphus, Count of Obsequium, and the patrician Theodore Myacius, who had been with Justinian at his return from exile, made a conspiracy against the Emperor. After some games in the circus, in which the Greens were victorious, he had given a banquet in the baths of Zeuxippus, returned to the palace and gone to sleep, when an officer of the Obsequian theme and his men rushed in, carried him to the robing room of the Greens, and put out his eyes (3 June 713). The conspirators were however not ready with a new emperor: and, as the other soldiers were not inclined to submit to their dictation, they were unable to gain control of affairs; and on the next day, which was Whit Sunday, Artemius, one of the chief imperial secretaries, was chosen emperor and crowned, taking in memory of the last civilian emperor the name of Anastasius. George and Theodore were requited as they had served Philippicus, being blinded on 10 and 17 June respectively and banished to Thessalonica.

The ecclesiastical policy of the late Emperor was immediately reversed, the sixth synod being proclaimed at the coronation, and the picture soon afterwards restored. Anastasius wrote to assure the Pope of his orthodoxy; and John, who under Philippicus had from fear of offending either Emperor or Pope sent no synodical to Rome, wrote to the Pope to explain that he had always been an adherent of the synod. He therefore retained the see till his death, when he was succeeded by Germanus (11 Aug. 715), who had also abandoned Monotheletism.

Anastasius was a great contrast to his predecessor. A capable man of affairs, he set himself to place the Empire in a state of defence and appoint the best men to civil and military posts: but in the condition to which affairs had been brought by the frenzy of Justinian and the indolence of Philippicus a stronger ruler than this conscientious public servant was needed. In 714 Maslama raided Galatia, 'Abbās took Heraclea (Cybistra) and two other places, and his brother Bishr wintered in Roman territory. On the other hand an Arab general was defeated and killed. In the anarchic state of the Empire however Walīd wished to send out something more than raiding expeditions; and Anastasius, hearing reports of this, sent Daniel the praefect on an embassy with instructions to find out what was going on; and on his reporting that a great expedition was being prepared ordered all who were unable to supply themselves with provisions for three years to leave Constantinople, while he set himself to build ships, fill the granaries, repair the walls, and provide weapons of defence.

In 715 a fleet from Egypt came, as in 655, to Phoenix to cut wood for shipbuilding; and Anastasius chose the fastest ships and ordered them to meet at Rhodes under a certain John, who also held the offices of public logothete and deacon of St Sophia. Some of the Obsequian theme, whom it was probably desired to remove from the neighbourhood of the capital, were sent on board; and, when John gave the order to sail to Phoenix, these refused to obey, cast off allegiance to Anastasius, and killed the admiral. Most of the fleet then dispersed, but the mutineers sailed for Constantinople. On the way they landed at Adramyttium, and, not wishing to be a second time defeated by the absence of a candidate for the throne, chose a tax-collector named Theodosius, whom, though he fled to the hills to escape, they seized and proclaimed emperor. Anastasius, leaving Constantinople in a state of defence, shut himself up in Nicaea, where he could watch the disaffected theme: but the rebels rallied to their cause the whole theme with the Gotho-Greek irregulars of Bithynia, collected merchant-ships of all kinds, and advanced by land and sea to Chrysopolis (Sept.). The fighting lasted six months, after which on the imperial fleet changing its station they crossed to Thrace and were admitted by treachery through the gate of Blachernae. The houses were then pillaged, and the chief officials and the patriarch arrested and sent to Anastasius, who, thinking further resistance useless, surrendered on promise of safety and was allowed to retire as a monk to Thessalonica (5 Mar. 716)[1].

Meanwhile the Arab preparations were going on with none to hinder. Even when the civil war was ended, there was little hope of effectual resistance from the crowned tax-gatherer and his mutinous army; and, if the Empire was to be saved, it was necessary that the government should be in the hands of a soldier. The Obsequian theme, though from its proximity to the capital it had been able to make and unmake emperors, was the smallest of the three Asiatic themes; and the other two were not likely to pay much regard to its puppet-sovereign. The larger of these, the Anatolic, was commanded by Leo of Germanicea, whose family had been removed to Mesembria in Thrace when Germanicea was abandoned. When Justinian returned, Leo met him with 500 sheep and was made a *spatharius*. Afterwards he was sent to urge the Alans of the Caucasus to attack the Abasgi, who were under Arab protection, and in spite of great difficulties he was successful: moreover, though he seemed to be cut off from the Empire, by his courage, presence of mind, and cunning (not always accompanied by good faith) he effected not only his own return but that of 200 stragglers from the army which had invaded Lazica. This exploit made him a marked man, and he was chosen by Anastasius for the command of the Anatolic theme: on that Emperor's overthrow both he and the Armenian Artavazd, who commanded the Armeniacs, refused to recognise Theodosius.

Late in 715 Maslama, who had been appointed to lead the expedition

---

[1] I take Leo's term in the χρονογραφεῖον ascribed to Nicephorus as dating from this time.

against Constantinople, took the Fortress of the Slavs, which commanded the passes of the Taurus, and returned to Epiphania for the winter; and in 716 he sent his lieutenant Sulaimān in advance, intending to follow with a larger army, while Omar was appointed to command the fleet. Sulaimān penetrated without opposition to Amorium, which, as it had then no garrison and was on bad terms with Leo because of his rejection of Theodosius, he expected easily to take. The Arabs moreover knew Leo to be a likely candidate for the crown and hoped to use him as they had used Sapor: accordingly, as Amorium did not immediately fall, they proclaimed him emperor, and the citizens were induced by the hope of escaping capture to do the same. Sulaimān having promised that, if Leo came to discuss terms of peace, he would raise the siege, Leo came with 300 men, and the Arabs surrounded him to prevent his escape; but Leo, who as a native of a town which had only been in Roman hands for ten years since 640 (he was probably born a subject of the Caliph), was well acquainted with the Arab character and could perhaps speak Arabic, induced some officers whom he was entertaining to believe that he would go and see Maslama himself, while he conveyed a message to the citizens to hold out, and finally escaped on the pretext of a hunting expedition. Soon afterwards the Arabs became tired of lying before Amorium and forced Sulaimān to raise the siege; whereupon Leo threw 800 men into the city, removed most of the women and children, and withdrew to the mountains of Pisidia, where he was safe from attack by Maslama, who had now entered Cappadocia and, in hope of gaining Leo's support, refrained from plundering the country. To him Leo sent an envoy to say that he had wished to come and see him, but treachery had deterred him from doing so. From this envoy Maslama heard of the garrisoning of Amorium; but this made him the more desirous of securing Leo; and he promised, if he came, to make satisfactory terms of peace. Leo pretended to agree, but protracted negotiations till Maslama, unable for reasons of commissariat to remain in Anatolic territory, had reached Acroinus (Prymnessus) in the Obsequian district, and then, having previously come to an understanding with Artavazd, to whom he promised his daughter in marriage (which, as he had no son, implied an assurance of the succession), started for Constantinople, while Maslama passed into Asia, where he wintered. The fleet was however less successful, for the Romans landed in Syria and burnt Laodicea, while the Arabs had only reached Cilicia. Meanwhile Leo made his way to Nicomedia, where Theodosius' son, who had been made Augustus, and some of the chief officers of the palace, fell into his power. The Obsequians were unable to organise serious resistance, and Theodosius after consulting the Senate and the patriarch sent Germanus to Leo, and on receiving assurance of safety abdicated. Leo made a formal entry by the Golden Gate and was crowned by the patriarch (25 Mar. 717). Theodosius and his son took orders and ended their days in obscurity.

CHAPTER XIV.

THE EXPANSION OF THE SLAVS.

THE Slavs, numbering at present about one hundred and fifty million souls, form with the Balts (the Letts, Lithuanians, Prussians) the Balto-Slavonic group of the Indo-European family. Their languages have much in common with German on the one hand and with Iranian on the other. The differentiation of Balto-Slavonic into Old Baltic and Old Slavonic, and then of Old Slavonic into the separate Slavonic languages was caused partly by the isolation of the various tribes from one another, and partly by mutual assimilation and the influence of related dialects and unrelated languages. Thus it is not a matter of genealogy only, but is partly due to historical and political developments.

Until lately the place where the Old Balto-Slavonic branched off from the other Indo-European languages and the place of origin of the Slavs were matters of dispute. But in 1908 the Polish botanist Rostafiński put forward from botanical geography evidence from which we can fix the original home of the Balto-Slavs (and consequently that of the Germans too, for the Balts could only have originated in immediate proximity to the Germans). The Balto-Slavs have no expressions for beech (*fagus sylvatica*), larch (*larix europaea*), and yew (*taxus baccata*), but they have a word for hornbeam (*carpinus betulus*). Therefore their original home must have been within the hornbeam zone but outside of the three other tree-zones, that is within the basin of the middle Dnieper (*v.* map). Hence *Polesie*—the marshland traversed by the Pripet, but not south or east of Kiev—must be the original home of the Slavs. The North Europeans (ancestors of the Kelts, Germans, and Balto-Slavs) originally had names for beech and yew, and therefore lived north of the Carpathians and west of a line between Königsberg and Odessa. The ancestors of the Balto-Slavs crossed the beech and yew zone and made their way into Polesie; they then lost the word for beech, while they transferred the word for yew to the sallow (Slav. *iva, salix caprea*) and the black alder (Lithuan. *yèva, rhamnus frangula*), both of which have red wood. It is not likely that the tree-zones have greatly shifted

since, say, B.C. 2000. For while the zones of the beech and yew extend
fairly straight from the Baltic to the Black Sea, the boundary of the
hornbeam forms an extended curve embracing Polesie. The reason for
this curve is the temperate climate of Polesie which results from the
enormous marshes and is favourable to the hornbeam, which cannot
withstand great fluctuations of temperature. And this curve must have
been there before the rise of the Old Balto-Slavonic language, otherwise the Balto-Slavs living without the limit of the beech and yew could
not have possessed a word for the hornbeam. According to a tradition
the Goths in their migration from the Vistula to the Pontus about the
end of the second century A.D. came to a bottomless marshland, obviously
on the upper Niemen and Pripet, where many of them perished. At
that time the impassable morasses of Polesie had already existed for
centuries, though their enormous depths may first have become marshland in historic times owing to the activity of the beaver—which raises
dams of wood in order to maintain a uniform water level; and, as
floating leaves and other remains of plants stuck in the dams, a gradually
thickening layer of peat was formed from them and the land became
continually more marshy. It follows that though the curve of the
hornbeam boundary may have been a little smaller in prehistoric times
than it is now, it cannot have been greater, and there can be no objection
to the argument from the four tree-boundaries.

Polesie—a district rather less than half as large as England—is a
triangle, of which the towns Brest Litovsk, Mohilev, and Kiev are roughly
speaking the apices. It was once a lake having the form of a shallow
dish with raised sides, and before its recent drainage seventy-five per cent.
of it was nothing but marsh, covered to half its extent partly with pine
groves and partly with a mixed forest, but otherwise treeless. The upper
layer consists of peat extending to eighteen feet in depth, and here
and there under the peat is a layer of iron ore about two inches thick.
Enormous morasses traversed by a thick and intricate network of streams
alternate with higher-lying sandy islets. The flow of water is impeded,
because the subsoil is impervious, the gradient of the rivers is slight, and
the bed of the lower Pripet is confined by high banks. The morasses
are covered with reeds and rushes—less often with sweet flags on sandy
ground—the surface of the streams with water-lilies and the like, which
so hinder their flow that they constantly have to change their course.
Between reeds and rushes there are places with reed-grass—and
less often with soft grass—which the peasants mow standing up to
the waist in water, or from a boat. Only the higher-lying places—
small oases difficult to get at—can be cultivated.

The average temperature throughout the year is over 43° Fahr.;
January mean 20° Fahr., July mean $65\frac{7}{10}$° Fahr. The average fall of
moisture is 16–24 inches; depth of snow seven inches at the most; snow
remains not quite three months (from the middle of December nearly

to the middle of March), often only for two or three weeks. The Pripet is frozen from the middle of November to the middle of January; it is navigable for 220 to 300 days. Notwithstanding the soft mild climate, the land is unhealthy: the putrefying marsh develops miasmatic gases causing epidemic lung and throat diseases, and the loathsome elf-lock (*plica polonica*); and the swarms of gnats cause intermittent fever. But since draining, the weakly breed of men and beasts has visibly improved.

This anomalous land has developed a singular people. The present population does not even now reach half a million; so that the entire Old Slav race in Polesie cannot have amounted to more than a few hundred thousand souls. The inhabitants of Polesie are White Russians, but those of the southern tract are black-haired mongoloid Little Russians who emigrated from the South to escape the advance of the Altaian mounted nomads. The White Russian is of middle stature, the recruit being on an average 5 ft. 4 ins. high. (Old skeletons measure 5 ft. 4$\frac{4}{5}$ ins. to 5 ft. 5$\frac{4}{5}$ ins., so that the marsh has had a degenerating effect. In healthier districts outside Polesie the Slavs become taller and stronger; in the sixth century, according to Procopius, they were "all of considerable height and remarkable strength.") Their skin is white, flaxen hair predominates (57 per cent.), their eyes are grey or sky-blue.

According to Procopius the South Slavs were reddish (ὑπέρυθροι), but most of them are now dark and black- or brown-haired, and in large districts we find slavised black-haired Roumanians. Marco Polo (Italian text) calls the Russians *la gente molto bella...e sono bianchi e biondi*, and Ibrāhīm ibn Ya'qūb in the tenth century marks as exceptional the dark and black hair of the Bohemians. This fact is due to an admixture of alien dark races.

The broadest rivers, the greatest seas, the highest mountains, the most terrible deserts can be overcome; the treacherous marsh alone is invincible. Here the inhabitants of two places can see each other and yet be as distant as Europe is from America. Before the drainage many places in Polesie could be reached only by enormous detours, and others were accessible only over the ice in the depth of winter. Thus the Slavs in their original home were divided into small groups which had very little intercourse during the greater part of the year. But in a low grade of civilisation the stranger is an enemy, and they had no kind of political, territorial, or social cohesion. Still later, when they came into contact with the East Romans, they were—according to Procopius— "not ruled by one man but lived from the earliest times in 'democracy,' and so they deliberated in common on all their affairs—good and bad." "Mauricius" attests that they were "kingless and hostile to one another," and never cared to form large bands; in this sense we must understand the further assertion that they were "free and by no means easily moved to let themselves be enslaved or dominated" by their like. The more easily were they enslaved by a foreign yoke: "they yield to the first comer," reports Pseudo-Caesarius. The only organic wholes were formed by small groups of villages—in Polesie sometimes by single villages—under patriarchal government. There could be no thought of social distinctions, as differences of rank did not exist.

Probably the Slavs, like the Germans, had no collective name before they spread from Polesie: for, failing the notion of a State, they had likewise no notion of a people. The name Slavs is correctly Slovêne (sing. Slovênin) and is probably a *nomen topicum*—meaning roughly "inhabitants of *Slovy*"—belonging originally only to one populous tribe[1]. The East Romans came into contact at first with a part of this tribe and thus named all other Slav tribes north of the Danube *Sklawēnoi, Sthlawoi*[2]; nevertheless, for a time they distinguished from them the *Antai* of South Russia who spoke the same language with them.

As with all Indo-Europeans, the Slav family was originally patriarchal; there is no trace of a matriarchate. The marriage bond was first loosened later among the individual Slav peoples under the yoke of the nomads. The wife bought or carried off by force was at first the property of the husband. This was usual from the earliest times, and is still presupposed in certain old ceremonial customs (*e.g.* mock-abduction by previous arrangement). The rich might live in polygamy, but the mass of the people were monogamic. The isolation of the little villages in Polesie made the marriage bond all the closer. The conjugal fidelity of the Slavs was universally marvelled at, and according to "Mauricius," St Boniface, and others, their wives were so extraordinarily honourable that many thought it unseemly to outlive their husbands, and voluntarily put an end to their lives.

Until recently it was generally believed that the ancient Slavs lived in house-communities (*Zadrugas*), that is, that after the father's death the sons did not divide the inheritance, but continued to live together under the direction of a house-elder. The modern Servo-Croatian *Zadrugas* were taken for survivals of Old Slavonic custom; and this seemed more likely, because the White Russians in Polesie—where the original home of the Slavs has just been discovered—also live in *Zadrugas*, and moreover traces of this mode of life remain not only among the other Slav peoples, but even among the German and many other peoples. But the Servian *Zadruga* turned out to be a consequence

---

[1] Hence Slovyene (North Russia, near Novgorod), Slovêne (Bulgaria), Slovintzi (Pomerania), Slovatzi (North Hungary), Sloventzi (Austrian Alps).

[2] Hence comes Arabic-Persian *Çaqlāb*, Latin *Sclaveni, Sclavi*. The Teutons named the Slavs *Vinithôs* or *Vĕnĕthâs*, rendered approximately by Tacitus *Veneti*, late Latin *Venethae, Venedae*, German *Wenden*. Shakhmatov has proved that the Slavs inherited this name from their former rulers, the Keltic *Venedi*, who occupied the district of the Vistula about the third and second centuries B.C. Jordanes harmonised the Teutonic name with the Greek, so that he took *Vinidae* as collective name and *Antes* and *Sclavini* as branch names.

of the originally East-Roman system of taxation—the καπνικόν, hearth-tax—in accordance with which each separate hearth formed the unit of taxation. To be sure the Old Servian laws directed the married son to detach himself from his father, but under the dominion of the Turk he remained—often only outwardly—in the undivided household in order to pay only one hearth-tax as before. But the hearth-tax occurs also among the Altaian conquerors; and it was also not unknown to some Teutonic peoples. As a matter of fact there exists no free people where society is based on the communistic household. *A priori* indeed other causes of its origin are also conceivable: *e.g.* seigniorial prohibition of division, and especially insufficiency of land and over-population after the peasant-holdings have become by successive divisions too small for further subdivision. And of all places this might best be assumed of Polesie—a country so poor in cultivable land. But in the sixth century Procopius states: "They live scattered far apart in wretched huts and very frequently change the place of their dwellings." Communistic households do not exist under such conditions.

The house-community, *Zadruga*, must be distinguished from the Russian village-community (*Mir* or *Obshtchina*) which has also been long regarded as of ancient Slavonic origin. It disposes of the whole of the land and soil of the village, periodically taking possession of all the peasant-holdings and allotting them afresh. But it has been recently found that these village-communities too came into existence very late, in consequence of the capitation-tax introduced by Peter the Great in 1719. For the payment of this tax the villein-village was collectively liable, and, as soon as the number of able-bodied men materially altered through births and deaths, all the land of the village was to be re-distributed in equal parts among the existing inhabitants. These periodical redistributions were not legally established before 1781[1]. They were rightly estimated by Fustel de Coulanges: "Far from being collective ownership, the *Mir* is collective serfdom."

In agriculture and diet the ancient Slavs entirely differed from the Germans. The latter lived chiefly on milk and meat and were cattle-rearers, leaving the agriculture to be done by women, old men, and serfs. But Polesie is entirely unsuited to cattle: milch cows cannot live on reeds and rushes, and grass grows only in oases and gives poor nourishment. Even now, when the marshes have been drained, the peasant's cow is a miserable animal, giving very little milk and chiefly retained for draught purposes. Still more wretched was his horse, and there are hardly any sheep. The pig thrives better, but it does not live in clover, for there is but little sweet calamus and other roots, the nut-giving beech does not grow at all, and the acorn-bearing oak only here and there. According to the Arabian geographer of the ninth century, the Slavs who were subject to a *kumiz*-drinking and therefore mounted-

---

[1] Kovalevsky, *Modern Customs*, pp. 94 f.; Sergyeevich, *Vremia*.

nomad king had only a few pack-horses—only eminent men had riding-horses, and they occupied themselves with swine-rearing as other peoples with sheep. It is therefore evident that the horses belonged not to the Slavs but to their Altaian masters, and that the Slavs in Russia then had no domestic animals except swine. The same is reported by Constantine Porphyrogenitus a hundred years later. "The Rōs (Scandinavian rulers of the Russian Slavs) strive to live at peace with the Patzinaks (mounted nomads of the Pontus steppe) for they buy from them cattle, horses, and sheep...as none of these animals are found in Russia" (*i.e.* in the Russian Slav land). Hence milk as a common article of diet was unknown to the ancient Slavs, so that they had no words of their own for *cattle, heavy plough, milk, curd* and such-like, but had to borrow from German and Altaian sources.

Polesie is rather more favourable to agriculture; though only the dry islets are cultivable. Even now, after the drainage, very little grain is produced. In the enormous sea of forest and marsh the little fields escaped the notice of observers, so that the Arabian geographer could say that the Slavs mostly lived among trees, having no vines and no cornfields. The scantiness of cultivable land forced the Slavs to a very intensive tillage of the soil with the hand-hoe or by yoking themselves to their excellently constructed hook-ploughs. Of course there was no wealth of grain in Polesie itself, but the manna-grass (*glyceria fluitans*), which is sweeter and still more nutritious than millet, grows there wild in abundance in standing water and wet meadows. It was still exported in the nineteenth century, and it probably served the ancient Slavs as food. For clothing and oil, flax and hemp were cultivated.

Polesie was rich in big game—aurochs, elk, wild boar, bear, wolf—and in fur-coated animals—beaver, otter, fox, sable, marten, ermine, squirrel, etc. But imperfect weapons and the difficulty of the country made hunting not very productive, so that there was little game as food. On the other hand, there was all the more fishing, and the natural abundance was increased by damming the flowing water with weirs. Bee-keeping played an important part among all Slav peoples from the earliest times. The intoxicating *Med*, fermented from honey, was to the Slavs what wine and beer are to other peoples.

The isolating marsh hinders intercourse; the White Russian is above all a husbandman and fisherman. Void of all enterprise, he leaves others to trade with the fruits of his labour and they drain him to the last farthing. Drunkenness is his only hateful quality; otherwise he has very attractive traits. He is thrifty almost to avarice, cautious in the management of his affairs, and shews an endurance that harmonises little with his slender physique. He is in no way aggressive but rather dreamy, confiding, not at all malicious, good tempered, not without dignity, very hospitable, and a lover of amusement. The dance, song, and music are his natural element. On summer

evenings the village youths assemble in the streets and often promenade
the whole night long singing in chorus their melancholy lyric songs.
The White Russian has remained true to the ancient Slav character.
According to Procopius, the Slavs were not malignant or villainous,
but harmless and naïve; "Mauricius" says, "They are hardened to heat,
frost, wet, nakedness, and hunger, and are well-disposed to strangers."
According to Adam of Bremen (died 1075) there was no more hospitable
and kindly people than the Slavs of Pomerania. The variety of musical
instruments among the Slavs struck the Arabian geographer of the ninth
century, and all Slav peoples are still very musical.

The bottomless marshes of the Pripet were no sufficient protection
from sudden raids and attacks; in winter the nomads could penetrate
over the ice on their fleet horses far into the land, and in summer the
pirates could use the rivers up to their sources. Defence was hopeless.
This made the Old Slavs exceptionally unwarlike, and shy as the beast
of the forest. In summer, when suddenly attacked, they had to disappear like frogs into the water or into the woods; in winter they
had to take refuge behind the shelter of their numerous stockades.
According to Procopius they fought without armour but with little
shields and darts, some even without coat and cloak and with only an
apron about their loins. But not even this wretched equipment was
really Slavonic; it must have been borrowed from some German
people, probably the warlike Heruli who fought in the same way.

Polesie is a land of exuberant fancy. A remarkable autumnal stillness is peculiar to its sea of marsh, a stillness not disturbed even by
the humming of a gnat and only broken now and then by the gentle
rustling of the rushes. To the fisherman as he glides at night in his
punt over the smooth silver water it is as impressive as its contrast, the
surging of the sea of reeds and the roaring of the forest in the storm-
wind. This produced in the inhabitant an uncontrolled imagination
which made him people the world of nature with spirits. To-day he
still personifies sun, moon, fire, wood, marsh, will-o'-the-wisp, spring
and all else that is perceivable. But joy and sorrow, every illness,
Sunday, every holiday, are also spirits. His house, stable, barn,
threshing-floor have their own goblins, each with wife and children.
To this must be added ancestor-worship. On certain days the father
says at the evening meal "Holy ancestors, we invite you to come to us
and eat of all that God has given to us, in which this house is rich—
Holy ancestors, I pray you come, fly to us." Kneeling with bread and
salt in his hands he prays to the spirit of the house and its wife and
children, beseeching its favour and deliverance from all evil. The Polesian
has only obscure ideas of a future life, but he has most definite knowledge
of the wicked dead and their appearance as werewolves and vampires. So
superstitious is he that he harbours in his mind a copious code of secret
expedients for scaring away all evil spirits, and at every step he is

careful not to provoke a spirit. Still he cannot know everything; this
is possible only for particular wizards of both sexes who have intercourse with the spirits of evil and whose help is sought in need and
richly rewarded.

The world is the work of God, the creator of all good and useful
beings and things, and of the devil who made the mountains, marshes,
beasts of prey, poisonous plants, illnesses, etc. God breathed into man
a good spirit, the devil an evil one. The Polesian is very much in the
dark about the godhead itself: "God knows how many gods there are."
The Christian saints are to him smaller, special gods; thus St Elias is
god of thunder, George of cattle and game, Nicolas of fields, Cosmas
and Damian of smiths. They stroll about in the world amusing themselves by playing all sorts of pranks on mankind. Noteworthy is the
cult of fire, namely of the hearth-fire, which must never be allowed to go
out and is transferred to any newly-occupied house. The White Russian
heathenism (with a very thin varnish of Christianity) goes back to the
earliest Slavs, and clear traces of it are still found among all the Slav
peoples. It is identical with the Shamanism of the Altaians, with this
difference—that what constituted the belief of large masses in Polesie
was among the mounted nomads a Shaman mystery of which the mass
of the people took no notice, observing only the hocus-pocus of the
wizards. The attention of observers was mostly attracted by the fire-
worship, and thus the Arabian geographer of the ninth century calls
both the Slavs and the Altaian-Magyars fire-worshippers. According
to Procopius the Slavs believed in one single chief god, denied Fate,
and worshipped rivers, nymphs, and other δαιμόνια. No traces of
mythology have survived; the later-mentioned gods and their worship
belong to the individual Slav peoples.

Many Slav peoples burned the bodies of the dead, others—among
them the Polesians—buried them. But the burning of bodies must be
attributed to the influence of foreign conquerors, namely the Germans.
As a matter of fact the Norman Rōs likewise burned the bodies of the
dead together with their self-destroyed widows (Ibn Faḍlān), and the
widows of the Heruli also hanged themselves on their husbands' burial-
mounds.

Polesie is still the most backward district of backward Russia. As
a consequence and at the same time as a cause of the slender needs of
the people we see no division of labour. The Slav had to make for
himself his few utensils; and in these, judging by the buried remains
which are very poor in metal articles, he displayed remarkable taste in
form and ornament. He could only supply the external market with
raw products—costly furs, wax, and honey—but it is not likely that
he brought them to the market, for he himself was offered wholesale
as a captured slave.

In our first volume it was shewn how the salt-desert zone of the

Asiatic Background developed the wild mounted nomad.   Here we have a second example of the great natural law that a people is and remains what its land of origin has made it.   Just as the mounted nomad is the son and product of the arid salt-deserts, the Slav is the son and product of the marsh.   The Slav and the mounted nomad, like the lands of their origin, are diametrical extremes, and the murderous irony of fate made them neighbours.   The one was a soft anvil, the other a hammer hard as steel.   A second not less weighty hammer (the Germans) came into play, and the anvil was beaten flat.

Dry and tolerably fertile forest land contains so much cultivable soil that it cannot easily be over-peopled: so here men form societies, and States arise.   But primitive man cannot wrest a foot of land from the marsh; on the contrary, he extends it by making dams, transforming small streams into great fish-ponds.   Thus, as the cultivable oases become smaller, the population huddles closer together.   Dry forest land makes its inhabitants stronger, but the marsh has a degenerating influence.   Forest land, however, is not inexhaustible; when what has been reaped from it is not made up for by dunging, or by allowing it to lie fallow—in short, when the soil is merely worked out—it can no longer support the growing population, and compels migration or expansion at the cost of the neighbourhood.   But the unwarlike inhabitants of the marshland can conquer nothing, and can only spread gradually where they meet with no resistance.   This is upon the whole the difference between the expansion of the Germans and that of the Slavs.   The Germanic migration was eruptive as a volcano, the Slavonic a gradual percolation, like that of a flood rolling slowly forward.   Some Germanic people or other leave their home: in the search for a new home they rouse their neighbours, and they in turn rouse theirs, and so it goes on until a hemisphere is thrown into commotion, strong States fall to pieces, mighty peoples perish, and even the Roman Empire quakes.   And the Slavs?   They have occupied and thickly populated immeasurable regions unnoticed by the annalists, and even now we ask in vain how this could have taken place so noiselessly, and whence have come the countless millions of Slavs.

The occupation by the Slavs of the district surrounding Polesie is prehistoric.   They moved northward after the Baltic peoples had abandoned their original home in the hornbeam zone and retired towards the Baltic Sea; eastward over the Oka and to the sources of the Oskol; southward to Kiev—further southwards they could not maintain themselves permanently, as fifteen centuries ago the grass steppe reached as far as Kiev and consequently served the mounted nomads as a camping ground up to that point.   Towards the south-west the Slavs reached the Carpathians, and in the west they spread across the Vistula.   In the time of the Romans the Vistula was regarded as the eastern frontier of the Germans.

This expanded Slavia has indeed the most manifold varieties of climate and soil, yet it forms a contrast to its little nucleus Polesie, the cradle of the Slavs. The latter scattered the inhabitants and isolated them in small villages, whereas the water-network of all the rest of Russia connects even the most distant peoples. It would indeed be easier to go from Lake Ladoga to the Black Sea than from many a Polesian village to the next.

The whole of Russia forms an enormous plain, so that there is nothing to hinder the icy north winds. The Sea of Azov and the northern part of the Caspian are ice-locked; the winter is terribly cold in the south, and the south winds bring burning hot summer days to the distant north. Thus the climate is everywhere the same and thoroughly continental in its extreme severity. In the northern region of the expanded Slav territory the Valdai hills are the watershed of the Baltic, Black, and Caspian Seas. The river basins of the Lovat, Volga, Don, Dnieper, Dwina are however so entangled and, in consequence of the slight gradients, their streams are navigable so far up-stream, that it is only necessary to drag a boat on land over the low narrow watersheds in order to reach the Black Sea or the Caspian from the Baltic by the Ladoga Sea. Similarly, from the Memel-Niemen basin the Dnieper can be reached, from the Dnieper the Volga or the Don, from the Don the Volga, or the Volga from the Dwina. A thousand years ago Russia was even better watered, but since this time many rivers mentioned by the chroniclers as formerly navigable have been dried up by reckless disforesting. This network of rivers, as if created for primitive commerce, is the most magnificent on the face of the earth, and in spite of its inhospitable climate it would certainly have nurtured the highest civilisation, had not its southern entrances been situated in the grass steppe by the Black and Caspian Seas, the domain of the mounted nomads, the arch-enemies and stiflers of all growing civilisation.

Fifteen hundred years ago the Pontus steppe was still grass steppe as far as the northern limit of the black earth (on the Dnieper as far as Kiev), not till later was it divided by the advance of the forest into a northern tree steppe, and a southern grass steppe zone. The Don divides the Pontus steppe transversely: as a rule one people dwelt west of the Don to the mouth of the Danube, and another east of the Don to the Caucasus. Towards the Caspian Sea the steppe becomes very salt, and in further curving round the Caspian it passes into the Central Asiatic steppe and desert zone, the ancient domain of the mounted nomads. So often as these were stirred by internal commotion, the hordes that were from neolithic times onward driven out sought refuge and a new home in the Pontus steppe. As early as the *Iliad* "mare-milking" (ἱππημολγοί) mounted nomads were known there. At the time of Herodotus the Scythians had dwelt for centuries west of the Don, and the Sarmatae east of it, enjoying a long interval of peace, during which the Asiatic background remained in equilibrium and no new horde broke into the Pontus steppe. The wildness of the Scythians gradually decreased and numerous Greek colonies covered the coasts of the Pontus and the Maeotis (the Sea of Azov), becoming flourishing emporia, especially for an enormous export of grain to Greece. This probably caused the Scythians to transplant wholesale agricultural peoples under their subjection. Herodotus includes various peoples, nomads and husbandmen, evidently not of the same origin, under the name Scythian; the latter sowed grain " not for food, but for sale," and there can be no doubt that among them were Slav nations also.

Into this motley of peoples the Hellenic colonies brought the most promising seeds of culture, and seemed likely to send out a stream of civilisation to the west of Europe, as well as one to the northeast. But the Asiatic nomads were on the move, and the still wild Sarmatae were pushed on from the east, crossed the Don, drove out and in part subjugated the Scythians, and had conquered even the western part of the Pontus steppe before the end of the second century B.C. Amid these storms the Hellenic colonies, and with them the seeds of civilisation, perished. During the second or third century A.D. the Sarmatian hordes were driven out by the German Goths and Heruli. The Gothic dominion lasted over two centuries, and is the only non-nomadic episode in the history of the steppe. The Goths were the most magnificent German people, and their influence on the Slavs must have been enormous. But about 375 the Goths were forced to make way for the Huns ; and the steppe remained in nomad hands for fourteen centuries continuously. In succession came Huns, Bulgars, Avars, Chazars, Magyars, Patzinaks, Cumans, Mongols. Like the *buran*, the furious tempest of the steppe, each of these hordes drove its predecessor in wild flight into the civilised lands of Europe, extirpated the Slavonic peasantry which had settled in the grass steppe, and passed over the tree steppe plundering and murdering so that the Slavs were forced to leave this zone too and to withdraw into the marshes of Polesie. Regular commerce was impossible, for on the banks of the rivers, especially in the dangerous rapids of the Dnieper over which the boats had to be carried on land, the nomad lurked in the tall grass and killed the crews and took their wares. Nevertheless, as the Southerner and the Oriental eagerly sought the raw products of the north—wax, honey, and especially strong slaves and pretty female slaves as well as costly furs—reckless Scandinavian pirate merchants found a rich market for these wares, which they had to take to the Euphrates and elsewhere by the roundabout way of the Dwina to the Volga and the Caspian or by Ladoga and the Volkhov, while the Dnieper route stood open only at times and was always extremely dangerous. The greatness of this plunder-commerce is shewn by the finding of Oriental coins in Russia— 11,077 pieces in one place—Scandinavia, Iceland, Greenland, and wherever else the Northmen went. Quite 100,000 coins have been secured, and many more have been kept secret and melted, or lie still in the bosom of the ground, so that Jacob's estimate—a million—is certainly much too low.

The oldest written history of the Slavs can be shortly summarised— myriads of slave-hunts and the enthralment of entire peoples. The Slav was the most prized of human goods. With increased strength outside his marshy land of origin, hardened to the utmost against all privation, industrious, content with little, good-humoured, and cheerful, he filled the slave markets of Europe, Asia, and Africa. It must be remembered that for every Slavonic slave who reached his destination, at least ten succumbed to inhuman treatment during transport and to the heat of the climate. Indeed, Ibrāhīm (tenth century), himself in all probability a slave-dealer, says: "And the Slavs cannot travel to Lombardy on account of the heat which is fatal to them." Hence their high price.

The Arabian geographer of the ninth century tells us how the Magyars in the Pontus steppe dominated all the Slavs dwelling near them. The Magyars made raids upon the Slavs and took their prisoners along the coast to Kerkh where the Byzantines came to meet them and gave Greek brocades and such wares in exchange for the prisoners. The Slavs had a method of fortification, and their chief resort was the fortresses in winter and the forest in summer. The *Rōs* (Vikings, Norse pirates) lived on an island (probably the old commercial town Ladoga between the Ladoga and Ilmen lakes). They had many towns, and were estimated at 100,000 souls. They made war on the Slavs by ship and took them as prisoners to Khazarān and Bulgār (the emporia of the Chazars and Bulgars on the Volga). The Rōs had no villages, their sole occupation was trading with sable and other skins. A hundred to two hundred of them at a time would come into Slavland and take by force the objects that suited them. Many of the Slavs came to them and became their servants for the sake of safety.

We see then the Slav surrounded on the north by pirates, on the south by mounted nomads, and hunted and harried like the beast of the forest. Jordanes' words, "Instead of in towns they live in marshes and forests," cover the most terrible national martyrdom in the history of the world. The "fortifications"—simple ramparts—mentioned by the Arabian geographer were not impregnable; indeed, the strongest fortifi-cations of Europe and Asia were stormed by the nomads and Northmen. "Mauricius" states: "Settled in places very hard of access, forests, rivers, lakes, they provide their dwellings with several exits with a view to accidents, and they bury everything that is not absolutely necessary.... When they are suddenly attacked they dive under the water, and lying on their backs on the bottom they breathe through a long reed, and thus escape destruction, for the inexperienced take these projecting reeds for natural; but the experienced recognise them by their cut and pierce the body through with them or pull them out, so that the diver must come to the surface if he will not be stifled." As late as 1768 parts of the revolting peasants surrounded by the Polish army rescued themselves from the Dnieper by breathing through reeds for more than half a day.

This terrible existence must have further shattered and dissolved Slavdom, already weakened in Polesie. Even partially regular tillage was impossible in districts exposed to constant attacks. Cornfields would have betrayed them, so that they could only be placed far out of reach. Breeding of horses, oxen or sheep, as well as milk food could not be thought of, for cattle were the most coveted booty of the nomads, and what they did not take would have been carried off by the pirates. Even in their original home the Slavs were limited to grain and fish, and they remained so in their wider home.

Even by the ninth century this encircling of the Slavs by the pirates was very old. The Germanic inhabitants of the Baltic districts made a practice of piracy from the earliest times, and very early land-peoples also appear as masters of the Slavs. As we have already seen, they had been enslaved in pre-Christian times by the Keltic Venedi. The Venedi in course of time became fused with Slavs into one Slavic people, thenceforth called *Wends* by the Germans. The first known of their Germanic conquerors were the Bastarnae who, coming from the lower Oder, were in the third century B.C. already in occupation of the Slav lands north of the Carpathians as far as the mouth of the Danube. According to Polybius and Dio Cassius they were a numerous, daring, bibulous people of powerful stature and terrifying appearance who knew neither agriculture nor navigation, and disdained cattle-rearing because they cared only for warlike pursuits. On their expeditions their wives and children followed the army in wagons, and their horsemen fought with foot-soldiers among them. They fell into various clans and divisions under little kings (*reguli*), one of whom stood at the head as leader of the war-band. But a numerous people without agriculture and cattle-rearing cannot live only on plunder and cannot live alone in a land; it needs another more numerous people of serfs, among whom it settles as a dominating class. But north of the Carpathians such a people could only be the Slavs. Thus arose the oldest known Slavo-Germanic State. The second Germanic people from whose influence the Slavs could not escape was the ferocious Heruli situated by the Black Sea east of the Goths and the Don, for the same weapons and the same burial customs are found among them as among the Slavs. The third people were the Goths.

According to the oldest Gothic tradition (given by Jordanes) King Ermanarich (died 373) overcame the Slavs (Veneti) "who, notwithstanding that they were despised as warriors, nevertheless being strong in numbers attempted at first a stout resistance." His great-nephew

Vinithar attacked the South-Russian Slavs, the Antae, and after one reverse overcame first them and then the Huns, who had come to their help, in two battles, but fell in the third. It is certainly strange that a tribe of the Slavs, who were despised as warriors not only by the Germans but also by the Byzantines, could defeat even in one battle a German leader before whom the Huns themselves recoiled. Still, it is a fact that the Antae were successful warriors, and later in the sixth century possessed the whole region from the Dniester to the Don, which was formerly held by the Goths. It is astonishing that the Byzantine sources of the sixth century distinguish the Antae from all the remaining Slavs, but at the same time emphasise the fact that they spoke the same language. And the name Ἀνται is *not* Slavonic. The military superiority of the Antae is, as Kunik has shewn, to be traced back to a non-Slavonic conquering folk, the Antae, who overcame certain Slav stocks and ruled them long and powerfully as a superior warlike class[1]. This folk then became Slavised, and, as was the case with many such despotisms both German and nomadic, it too fell apart into small States, which however still negotiated common concerns in general meetings, and proceeded as one body in external affairs. We hear the same of the Bastarnae. In the tenth and eleventh centuries we find in the former abodes of the Antae of the Pontus steppe the Slavonic Tiwertzi and Ulichi whose names are equally non-Slavonic. How could they have maintained themselves against the nomads here where they were daily exposed to the inroads of all the Asiatic hordes, if they were pure Slavs without a Germanic or Altaian warrior-stratum?

Still less could the Slavs resist the pressure of foreign conquerors after the Scandinavian Vikings had renewed their attacks. Leaving their families behind them, these appeared at first in small bands of one to two hundred men as well-organised followers (*vaeringjar*) of a sea-king, and always returned home after selling their plunder. At important points on their route they established trading stations, and in the course of time these became fortified settlements surrounded by a subjected Finnish, Baltic, or Slavonic population. Hence a regulated government was developed, no longer exclusively resting on plunder. From the word *vaeringjar* came the name of a people *Varangians*, Βάραγγοι. The Varangians gradually extended their sway over the whole of Russia—over Kiev about the year 855—covered it with originally independent towns (*garðar*)[2], and finally formed these little States into a single empire of the Rōs[3] (Russians). In brief, trading Scandinavian

---

[1] On the other hand, cf. Hruševśkyj, I. pp. 175 ff., 577 ff.

[2] Hence Russia was called by the Scandinavians *Garðariki*, *i.e.* the kingdom of many forts.

[3] This name too is Swedish, for which Esthonian has *Rōts*. In Old Swedish Roþer, Roþin is the name of a strip of coast in Sweden. *Roþsmenn* = rower, seafarer, and this word, like Varangians, became the name of a people.

sea-robbers got possession of the Russian network of waterways, overcame the Finns and Slavs, and the Scandinavian dynasty of the house
of Rurik (= Old Norse: *Hroerekr*) created the powerful Russian State.

As in the North Germano-Slavic, so in the South Nomado-Slavic
States were formed. A nomadic milk-feeding horde dominated a
Slavic vegetarian peasant class. A similar state of affairs lasted till
yesterday in Ferghana, the former Khanate of Khokand, where the
vegetarian Tadjiks languished from the earliest times in the basest
nomadic servitude. The same thing can be also traced back far into
ancient times in East Europe on the western border of the steppe
zone. So we find it as early as Ephorus (fourth century B.C.).

A horde of Sarmatae, the Iazygians, migrated into Central Hungary
where (c. A.D. 337) the serfs of the Sarmatae, the Sarmatae Limigantes,
revolted against their lords, the Sarmatae Arcaragantes or Sarmatae
Liberi, and repulsed them[1]. Here we have a similar double stratum to
that which Ephorus mentions, and because the *Tabula Peutingeriana*
(about the third century A.D.) mentions the Venedi Sarmatae and
the Lupiones Sarmatae next to the pure nomadic wagon-inhabiting
Sarmatae Hamaxobii, Sarmatae Vagi, many assume that these serfs of
the Sarmatae, the Limigantes, were Slavs[2]. The oldest explicit information concerning a Nomado-Slavic State on the lower Danube is to be
found in Pseudo-Caesarius of Nazianzus of the sixth—probably even the
fourth—century A.D., viz. that of the galactophagous Phisōnitae or
Danubians (*Phisōn* according to Marquart is equivalent to *Danubius*)
and the vegetarian Slavs[3].

The best account we have is of the similar *Avaro-Slavic* State. The
dominating Avar nomad class was absorbed as a nation and language
by the subjugated Slavs, but even after the destruction of the Avar
Empire it survived socially with Slav names, as is shewn by the remarkable passage in the Arabian geographer of the ninth century: "The
seat of their prince lies in the middle of the Slav land....This prince
possesses mares, whose milk...is his only food[4]." As mare-milkers he
and the dominating class were mounted nomads and, as the date proves,
of Avar origin. This information alone destroys our former conceptions
of the character of the Slav States north of the middle Danube and the
Carpathians, and compels us to assume that nomadic States extended far
into the territory of the Balts and even as far as the Baltic. The seafarer Wulfstan at the end of the ninth century says of the Eastland
(Prussia, east of the mouth of the Vistula): "Their king and the richest
men drink mares' milk but the poor and the slaves drink mead[5]."

---

[1] Müllenhoff, II. p. 377. [2] Niederk, II. pp. 127 ff.
[3] Müllenhoff, II. p. 367. Peisker, *Beziehungen*, 125 [311].
[4] Harkavy, p. 266. Marquart, p. 463; Tumanskii, p. 135, where the passage
runs: *The food of their princes is milk.*
[5] *Alfred the Great*, by T. Bosworth, p. 22. Adam of Bremen (§ 138) says that

Naturally the activity of the nomads was not uniform over this immense region; it was greater at their base, the steppe, among the South Russian Slavs, of whom in 952 the Emperor Constantine Porphyrogenitus says that *they reared no horses, oxen or sheep*—and consequently must have been vegetarians—although at that time they had already been for a century under the powerful sway of Scandinavian Rōs.

Thus we see how Slavdom was influenced on all sides by plundering peoples. All so-called Slav States of which we have sufficient information turn out to be either Germanic or Altaian foundations. And unless we do violence to all German, Byzantine, and Oriental evidence of the political and military incapacity of the Slavs, we must not represent the remaining Slav States as of Slav origin merely because there is no express statement of their Germanic or Altaian origin. The strongest proof of this is the remarkable fact that all titles of rank in Slavic (except *voyevoda*, duke) are partly from Germanic, partly from Altaian sources.

Between Germanic and Altaic oppressors the Slavs were crushed for centuries; and yet they became the most numerous people of Europe because of the enormous size of their territory and because their tyrants were neither numerous nor united. The robbers could not follow the individual Slavs into the forest thickets and the marshes, so that from them the wastes left by massacre were peopled anew. Besides this, the impetuosity of the two robber-peoples periodically languished. We know this of the Vikings from their activity in Europe. England, France, Spain, Italy suffered terribly from them, but for long intervals they were quiet, and after a single defeat the enemy often did not return for a long time. Their might was also broken from time to time in their own land, and then the afflicted peoples enjoyed a healing respite. This was less the case with Russia, where a few dozen robbers won decisive victories and where the Northmen only had no serious opponents but their like. It was the same with the mounted nomad. His first appearance was terrible beyond description; but his fury exhausted itself on the numerous battle-fields, and when his ranks were thinned he had to call out his Slav serfs to fight on his behalf. Thus he led masses of Slavs into the steppe where they revived and increased until once again a new and vigorous wild horde forced its way in from Asia and repeated the destruction.

The primitive German was as savage in war as the mounted nomad, but far superior in character and capacity for civilisation. The German with one leap into civilisation so to speak from a plunderer becomes a founder of brilliant and well-ordered States, bringing to high perfection the intellectual goods which he has borrowed. On the other hand the

the ancient Prussians ate horse-flesh, and drank the milk of their mares (*kumiz*) to intoxication. Helmold (twelfth century) (*Chronica Slavorum*, I. i.) gives similar information.

lightest breath of civilisation absolutely ruins the mounted nomad. This
enormous contrast shewed itself also in the kind of slavery. The mounted
nomad treated the subjugated peoples like the beasts of the forest which
are hunted and harried for amusement and mere delight in killing.
Himself void of all capacity for civilisation, he stifles all germs of civilisation found among his subjects, outraging their sense of justice by his
lawlessness and licence, and the race itself by the violation of their
women. The German on the other hand treated his serf as a useful
domestic animal which is destroyed only in anger and never wantonly.
He enjoyed a certain autonomy, remaining unmolested after the performance of definite duties. Even the Scandinavian pirates, according
to the Arabian geographer, handled their serfs "well" (from an Oriental
point of view)[1]. It is then no wonder that the Slavs, incapable of
resisting the terrible plundering raids and powerless to give themselves
political organisation, preferred to submit voluntarily to the dominion
of the pirates.

Concerning this the oldest Russian chronicler Pseudo-Nestor states
(under the year 859): "[The Slavs] drove the Varangians over the sea,
and...began to govern themselves, and there was no justice among them,
and clan rose against clan, and there was internal strife between them....
And they said to each other: Let us seek for a prince who can reign
over us and judge what is right. And they went over the sea to the
Varangians, to Russ, for so were these Varangians called....[They] said
to Russ: Our land is large and rich, but there is no order in it; come
ye and rule and reign over us. And three brothers were with their
whole clan, and they took with them all the Russ, and they came at
first to the Sloviens and built the town of Ladoga, and the eldest
Rurik settled in Ladoga....And the Russian land got its name from
these Varangians[2]."

The misery of the Slavs was the salvation of the West. The energy
of the Altaians was exhausted in Eastern Europe, and Germany and
France behind the Slavic breakwater were able freely to develop their
civilisation. Had they possessed such steppes as Hungary or South
Russia, there is no reason to suppose that they would have fared any
better than the Slavs.

The compact Slav settlement of the countries east of the Elbe and
south of the Danube took place between the sixth and seventh centuries.
In their occupation of the German mother-countries between the Elbe
and the Vistula two phases are to be distinguished—one pre-Avar and the

---

[1] This assertion is correct, for (according to the oldest law-book—*Russkaya
Pravda*) the Slav peasants (*smerdi*) under the dominion of the Rōs actually were personally free.

[2] Thomsen, pp. 13 ff. These Germanic *Russ* are to be distinguished from the
modern Slavonic Russians.

other with the force of the Avars behind it. In the first the Slavs reached and perhaps crossed the Riesengebirge, and perhaps already got as far as the middle and lower Oder. In the records of the Germans no trace of it is found, because from the beginning of the fifth, and indeed for the greater part from the end of the third century A.D., the country westward to the Oder and southward to the Riesengebirge was abandoned by its old German inhabitants. The oldest evidence of this is the name Silesia, from the mountain *Slęz'* (Zobtenberg) and the river *Slęza* (little Lohe). *Slęz* (originally *Silengŭ*) leads letter for letter to *Siling*, *Slęza* to *Silingia*, consequently to the German Σιλιγγαι, who according to Ptolemy lived just here. The Slavs must have found Silingians still there and have taken this name from them either before or soon after 406, when they crossed the Rhine and made their way with the Vandals and Sueves to Spain. It must be admitted that the Slavs found everywhere scattered remnants of the Germans, because they merely adapted the German names *Oder, Elbe (Albi), Moldau (Walth ahva)*, etc. to their own mouths (*Odra, Labe, Vltava*). For certain times and in certain districts there was a mixed population, and it is to be particularly noticed that even in the sixth century the Germans, who had long withdrawn to the South, did not admit that the East as far as the Vistula had definitely passed to the Slavs. It had not been conquered from them—only occupied by loose bands of settlers.

From the third to the fifth century the hurricanes of war stirred up by the Goths and the Huns between the Carpathians, the Pontus, and the Danube raged over and around the Slavs. We hear not a word of their share in the fight. Not before the seventh decade of the sixth century did the advance of the Avars to the Elbe disclose the great change which had silently come to pass.

The Avars, like the Huns, must have needed an enormous number of dependent Slavs. The territory by the Pontus left vacant by the withdrawal of the Goths, Heruli, etc. was occupied by Slavs, naturally as serfs to the Huns. The subjugation of the Germans was disastrous to the Huns; they threw off the yoke after Attila's death, and the Hunnish Empire perished, Hungary became German and the Huns withdrew into the Pontus steppe. This steppe was directly afterwards in the hands of Bulgar hordes who controlled numerous Slav tribes. Here between the Dniester and Dnieper in the first half of the sixth century lived the Antae, "the bravest of the Slavs," who constantly joined in the Bulgar plundering raids in the East Roman Empire. In 558 Justinian was successful in instigating against them both the Avars who had suddenly emerged from the Asiatic background. The Avars demanded territory of Justinian but refused the offer of Lower Pannonia—which they would have had to wrest from the fierce Heruli and Lombards—and remained in the Dobrudja, contenting themselves with a yearly tribute for their defeat of the Bulgars and Antae. But when Justinian's successor discontinued the tribute, the Dobrudja was no longer of any value to them. They then turned towards the north-west and suddenly appeared in the Eastern territories of the Frankish kingdom on the Elbe. They could not make their way thither through Hungary as it was occupied by the powerful Gepidae, and thus they had to go through North-Carpathian Slavland and through Bohemia. They must therefore first have subdued these lands. Their base of operations against the Franks in Thuringia is to be sought in Bohemia, where they found excellent summer-pastures in the mountain ring and good winter-quarters in the plains for their herds. It would be misunderstanding the entire nature of the mounted nomads, and of the Avars in particular, to regard these wars with Sigebert the king of the Franks as mere plundering expeditions. In the latter the nomads never confronted the enemy, but went round his positions with marvellous speed, and then charged behind his back. They confronted him or sought him out only when they had to defend their own land. In the first campaign they were defeated, but they won the second, and the consequence was that the North Sueves evacuated the oldest German land between the Elbe and the Oder. Nevertheless, Baian, the Avar Khagan, made peace with Sigebert, as he was attracted elsewhere: the Lombard king Alboin in Pannonia was preparing to wrest Italy from the East Romans, and in order to protect his rear he united himself with Baian against the Gepidae in Hungary and Transylvania. The kingdom of the Gepidae was destroyed, the Lombards made their way to Italy, and in 568 the Avars were complete masters of Hungary with its steppe on the Danube and Theiss so excellent for nomads.

The evacuation of Old Germany by the North Sueves, the destruction of the kingdom of the Gepidae, and the withdrawal of the Lombards to Italy —three co-related events—mark an epoch in the history of the world, for the entire East was abandoned by the Germans to the Avars and their followers the Slavs[1]. Once more the map of Europe was suddenly changed, and from the steppes of Hungary the Avars became the terror of all their neighbours. But they did not give up the territories won from the Germans between the Oder and the Elbe, Saale, Main, Regnitz, Nab, for—as we shall see—a horde of the Avars wintered yearly on the Main and Regnitz till about the year 603, and the Khagan resettled the waste German land as far as the Baltic with Slavs brought there from the first, North-Carpathian, Avar kingdom.

The existence of this first Avar-Slavonic kingdom is proved by the account which the Arabian geographer of the second quarter of the ninth century (before the conquest of Hungary by the Magyars) gives of the mare-milking and therefore Altaic Great King, whose realm lay in the territory of the Slavonic *Dulyebs* or *Volynyans* south-west of Polesie,

[1] Müllenhoff, II. pp. 101 ff. Authorities in Zeuss, *Die Deutschen*, pp. 731 f.

the very people who according to Pseudo-Nestor had been formerly kept
in servitude by the Avars. Bordering on the steppes as they did, they
were from the earliest times a prey to the inhabitants of the steppes.
Before the Avars various nomadic and Germanic peoples were their
masters; and these peoples left behind warlike elements which were
sharply distinguished—even after becoming Slavised—from the subjected
Slav mass. The king was called in Slavic *knez* (from *kŭnęgŭ*), Germanic
kuninga. Further among the Sorb-Serbs the class of the *vićazi-vitezi*
"knights" (from *vitęgŭ*), that is, German vikings; and the numerous
Polish nobility has the German title *szlachta*.

Out of this Germano-Altaio-Slavonic mixture of the Dulyebi-
Volynyane and other Slavonic peoples north of the Carpathians, Baian
created for himself an almost inexhaustible reservoir of men whom he
formed into barriers against the Germans[1] on his western frontiers.
He transplanted a part of the Dulyebi-Volynyane to Pannonia (where
later was the Comitatus *Dudleipa*), another to South Bohemia (the later
countries of *Doudleby* and *Volyň*), a third to the distant north (the island
of *Wollin*) at the mouth of the Oder. Similarly he tore apart the
North-Carpathian Croats (*Khr'vati*) of the upper Vistula and placed them
partly in the Elbe and Saale, where several villages bear their name,
partly in Carantania (pagus *Crauuti*), partly to Pannonia and Dalmatia,
where later independent Croatian States arose; the North-Carpathian
Serbs (*Serbi*) partly on the Saale and the Elbe (later the mighty *Sorbs*),
partly where to-day they are independent in Serbia and Montenegro.
The Slav nations of to-day are therefore not original but a gradual
crystallisation since the sixth century into linguistic units out of the
peoples transplanted by the Avars—a process already completed by the
tenth century[2].

[1] Transplanting of entire nations was customary with the nomads. Thus the
Scythians transplanted many peoples, among them "Assyrians" to the Pontus in
Asia Minor, and "Medes" to the Don. In a similar way the Avars transplanted
Macedonian Slavs to Pannonia, and the Bulgars, after the destruction of the Avar
kingdom by Charles the Great, populated North and South Hungary with Slavs
whom they had captured by regular man-hunts in Macedonia. The Mongols too took
large numbers of Russians, etc. to Hungary, which they had half depopulated, and
these too they destroyed before their own withdrawal thence.

[2] No traces of an earlier intermixture are to be observed in the individual Slav
languages. Even in the tenth century the *Nortabtrezi* of Mecklenburg spoke a
different dialect from the *Osterabtrezi* of South Hungary, and the *Sorbs* on the Saale
and Elbe from the *Serbs* on the Drina. The Nortabtrezi belong with the Sorbs to the
Elbe-Slavonic, the Osterabtrezi with the Serbs to the South-Slavonic language-group,
and all the Slavonic languages form one unbroken chain of languages connected by
transitionary dialects. Hence many Slavists declare that the duplication of these
folk-names is accidental, and that the Slavs in their original home were divided
into the same peoples as at present, who spread unmixed in all directions. But in
our time it is recognised how quickly fragments of a people adopt the language of
their environment, and the historical arguments against a radiating expansion of
the Slavs are admitted by other Slavists.

CH. XIV.

Baian's purpose was probably that of settling the most warlike branches, viz. those dominated by Germans, in the strategically most important places. Thus we see why, for example, the Sorb-Serbs who were controlled by vikings were split up.

The limits of the Avar power are marked by the abode of the Obodritzi in Mecklenburg, the Volynyans at the mouth of the Oder, the Dregovichi in Polesie and in Macedonia, the Milengi in Morea, the Severyans east of the Dnieper and in Moesia, the Serbs and Croats on the Adriatic and on the Saale. Thus the Avar power at one time or another extended from the Baltic to the southern extremity of Greece, from East Tyrol to the river Donetz in Russia, doubtless with very unequal intensity and unequal duration. Only one will, that of the Khagan, could carry through so vast a change—the transplanting of one and the same people partly to the Baltic, partly to the Adriatic, Ionic, and Aegean Seas.

The Khagan could not leave his Slavs without supervision, and therefore he had to maintain among them a standing Avar garrison with wives and children. But the Avars were a nomad people who only camped among the Slavonic peasantry in winter—more than half the year—and during the summer grazed the higher positions and heaths, of course leaving behind a guard over the Slavs, while their army went to battle and plunder[1].

The Slavised Avar nomads long survived the Avar Empire in many Slav lands, and even in the twelfth century we are told by Herbord of the Baltic Slavs of the Island of Rügen (Slav. *Ruiana*): "The men's occupation is either hunting or fishing or cattle rearing. For therein consists their entire wealth as husbandry is only scanty there." Here the nomads had to do without mountain summer-pastures.

Concerning the relation of the Avars to the Slavs, "Fredegar" states that from the earliest times the Wends [here in particular are meant the Slavs of the upper Main and its tributary the Regnitz north and east of Nuremberg] were used by the Huns [Avars] as *befulci*, that is, when the Huns took the field against any people the Wends had to fight in

---

[1] Theophylactus, VI. 2, states (A.D. 591): Three captives were brought before the Emperor Maurice having neither swords nor any other weapon, but only citharas with them. Being questioned they answered that they were Slavs from the coast of the northern ocean [Baltic Sea], whither the Khagan sent envoys with presents to ask for auxiliaries. They brought back as answer to the Khagan that he could expect no help from such a distance—they themselves had been fifteen months on the journey—and their people were absolutely peaceable. They played on the zither because they were unacquainted with weapons, their land produced no iron and therefore they lived there still and peacefully, and as the war trumpet was not understood there they played on the zither. These were obviously spies, but the fiction of their entire harmlessness could only deceive the Emperor when the story of the Khagan's embassy to the Baltic Slavs appeared natural. The whole mystification produced the widespread story of the *dove-like nature of the Slavs*.

front. If they won the Huns advanced to make booty; but if they were defeated they rallied with the support of the Huns. Without these *befulci* the Avars, who were speedy on their marvellously trained horses but helpless and defenceless on foot, could have done little against trained infantry. They therefore had to call out countless, because wretchedly armed, masses of Slav foot-soldiers who, with certain death at the hands of their goaders behind them, charged forward in despair[1]. On the other hand the Avar cavalry formed an incomparable mail-armed force with sword, bow and pickaxe, and even the horses of the leaders were protected by armour. However the Avars were not in themselves numerous enough to supply the necessary reserves for their enormous empire, and with the expansion of their dominion the need for new masses of cavalry grew. This need was supplied by constant reinforcements from other Altaian hordes out of the steppe. Among them the most numerous were the Bulgars. The Khagan's victorious flag, and the prospect of booty, worked irresistibly upon the plundering sons of the steppe.

By the transplantation of Slav peoples to the western borders of his robber-State the Khagan meant to keep in check his neighbours, the Saxons on the lower Elbe, the Franks on the Saale, the Bavarians on the Nab and upper Danube, the Lombards in Italy, while he himself, with his rear protected, was free for plundering raids on the East Roman Empire, in which he employed enormous masses of Slavs as *befulci*. He had no intention of conquering even a part of the Roman Empire and settling it with Slavs, for this was not to his interest; he had land in abundance and he needed the Slavs for his own colonising purposes. He therefore left them the East Roman to pay tribute, and his plundering supplied him further. Nevertheless his procedure was uneconomical. The greater number of the East Romans were partly exterminated and partly carried into slavery. The vacuum thus created was permanently occupied by the Slavs who finally spread almost over the entire Balkan peninsula and even reached Asia Minor. Very exhaustive information about these Avaro-Slavic plundering raids is given in the sources, but it is not definitely known when the Slavs permanently settled there; certainly the greater part not before 602.

In this previously Roman territory the dominating Avar and Bulgar nomad class merged with the Slavonic peasantry into a national organism, and powerful military States of Slav speech arose; but the real holders of power were not the Slavs but the Slavised Altaians, and it is a delusion to think that the Slavs themselves, the Croats, Serbs, (new-) Bulgars, Macedo-Slavs became fit for war in the Avaro-Bulgar school. They remained a peasant folk living—partly to this day—alongside of a nomad shepherd

---

[1] The Mongols in Hungary in 1241 availed themselves of the same aid, driving the captives before them into the fight and against the fortresses, cutting down at once all who recoiled. They did not however put themselves willingly in danger.

class. The domination of the nomads appears most clearly among
the Bulgarian Slavs who to-day are named after their nomadic masters
the Altaian Bulgars. After the destruction of the Avar kingdom by
Charles the Great, the Bulgarian kingdom extended from the Balkans to
the Moravian Carpathians. The Serbs and Croats also founded mighty
States. In the Middle Ages the Slavs of Dalmatia were dreaded pirates,
and even the tiny Slav peoples of Macedonia and Greece kept the Romans
occupied with many wars. But even at the beginning of the seventh
century the commercial town of Saloniki obtained grain from the Thes-
salian Slavs. Led by the Avars, the Slavs pressed into the Peloponnesus,
and the report was long believed that the Avars occupied the Peloponnesus for 218 years so that no Roman durst enter it[1]. According to
Constantine Porphyrogenitus the Croats of the tenth century could put
60,000 horsemen and 100,000 foot into the field. But as the Slavs were
a foot people, such a very strong cavalry must refer to the Avar and
Bulgar ruling class, which at that time stood out clearly from the
Slav peasantry in Dalmatia ; and to this day the name of the Khagan
Baian denotes to the Croat the highest state official, the *Ban, Banus* (in
Constantine : βοάνος), just as the name of Charles the Great—*Karl*—
denotes to all Slavs *Kral*, the king. The Old Serbian State also had
a strong body of cavalry, in connexion with which it must be noted that
numerous nomadic Roumanians with horses and sheep, but without
agriculture and ox-rearing, were, and still are, to be found in Serbia and
the other Balkan countries.

The Roumanians, Slavonic *Vlasi, Vlakhs*, are Romanised Altaians,
probably Avars and Bulgars, for a still older nomad people could not
have survived the wild Bulgar-Avaro-Slavonic storms which raged for
a century over the Balkan peninsula. Like all mounted nomads the
Bulgars and Avars were intent on cattle robbery (*baranta*), and so the
indigenous wandering herdsmen specially suffered, for herds of sheep are
not quick-footed enough to be hidden in time from mounted robbers.
With the loss of his herds the wandering herdsman inevitably perishes as
he cannot acquire new herds, and the acquisition of single animals would
be of no use to him. The vegetarian peasant can better secure himself
since he does not depend on cattle but on the soil, which the robber
cannot destroy, and seed-grain is more easy to obtain than a herd of
cattle.

The nomadic Vlakhs lived along with the peasant peoples of the
Balkan peninsula and gradually adopted their language and became
denationalised for a second time. They further attained to their highest
prosperity as wandering herdsmen in Turkish times, after the fall of the
Slav States effaced the customs barriers with a tithe on the import and
export of sheep and horses ; the herdsmen could thus graze summer and

[1] For the literature *v.* Niederle, *Starožitnosti,* II. p. 210.

winter wherever was convenient for them. We know most about the Old Serbian State, where the Vlakhs constituted an important element and a rich source of income for the sovereign and the other landlords. By them the larger mountain pastures were made the most of and indeed devastated and disforested by the reckless grazing-off of the new growth, by the searing of the grass to freshen the pasturage, and by the peeling of young beech-trees as a substitute for honey to sweeten milk foods[1]. They provided the State with excellent horses, of small stature but hardy, and good cavalry for the army. They managed also the commerce, for it had to be a caravan trade with pack-horses, because most of the mountain ranges run parallel with the sea and were then impassable for wagons. The Vlakhs themselves traded in wool, skins and the famous Vlakhish cheese which had to have a definite weight for Ragusa, and even served as a substitute for money. In return they chiefly brought sea-salt. By this trading the Vlakhs acquired knowledge of the world, and became far superior in experience and shrewdness to the boorish Slav peasant. They grazed the mountain pastures (*planina*) to the height of 5000 ft., from the end of April to the middle of September, and then slowly made their way, often taking two months, to winter on the coasts on account of the mild snowless climate and the salt which splendidly nourishes the sheep. They lived chiefly on milk and cheese. Their chief enemy was the ice when it locked up the grass in early spring. Thousands of sheep then starved and the richest man might become a beggar in a few days. As they had no fixed settlements, they could not easily be enslaved by the landlords, and after payment of the grazing-tax they enjoyed freedom of movement without restraint. They themselves were a heavy burden for the peasantry, especially through their destruction of the cornfields. Thus peasants and herdsmen were in opposition, there was no intermarriage between them, and the State had to regulate the wandering people and to protect the peasants with draconic laws. The Emperor Dušan's law-book of 1349 states: "Where a Vlakh or an Albanian camps in a village district, there another who comes after him shall not camp; if he camps there by force, he shall pay the fighting-fine (100 hyperpyres, that is fifty gold ducats) besides the value of what he has grazed off." Even the Ragusans in Dalmatia, although they were entirely dependent for their trade with the interior on the Vlakh caravans, complained bitterly of the mischief they did when they wintered in Ragusan territories, and finally forbade them to winter there.

All the more must the Avar nomads have oppressed the subjugated Slav peasantry, for here the Avar was master, and the peasant was without rights and protection. The Avar tribes as wandering herdsmen amongst

[1] Roumanian herdsman life described by Ponqueville, *Voyage*, II. pp. 208 ff., 2nd ed. pp. 382 ff. Jireček, *Das Fürstentum Bulgarien*, pp. 181 ff.—The almost universal bareness of the soil on the chalk mountains is much more due to the wandering herdsmen than to the Venetian demand for timber for shipbuilding.

the West Slavs could not graze their herds in connected winter-quarters as in the steppes, because the snow lies deeper and longer in central Europe. Neither had they there, as in Dalmatia, mild coasts rich in salt and free from snow—the best imaginable winter-pasture—and so they had to break up and live scattered in the Slav villages where the peasantry had to store up grain and hay for them during the summer and convert even the villages into suitable cattle-pens. This is pointed to by the very small Slavonic round villages with one single exit, which are common in Bohemia and as far as the Baltic, and which still preserve the character of closable cattle-pens[1].

Compared with the Slavs, the Avar oppressors were very few in number, and could not therefore always master them. Now and then these became restive, and refused obedience. The Khagan, occupied in many distant places, did not always find leisure to chastise them, and thus many Slav tribes gained their liberty.

There were, however, differences among the Avars themselves, who were only held together by the iron hand of the Khagan. They were but a mixed multitude. Where there was a prospect of rich booty they followed him joyfully, but where no treasure allured them—*e.g.* in 602 against the poor but warlike Antae—they simply refused obedience and deserted to the Romans. According to " Mauricius " such desertion was a common event, and it helps to explain why the Khagan did not repeat his victorious marches against the Frankish kingdom till the year 596[2]. Avar hordes were indeed very loosely held together, and some fell away and established small States on the old basis of Slav servitude. The dissolution began as early as 603 in consequence of the successful revolution of a part of the north-west Slavs and the formation of a Slav union under Samo. By this the Avar hordes distributed among the Elbe Slavs between Bohemia and the Baltic were permanently cut off from the main horde in Hungary.

After the dissolution of the great Avar State the Avars and the Bulgars themselves remained as a noble class, which finally became Slavised and nationally absorbed in the subjected peasantry. In Dalmatia as late as the tenth century the Avars were still sharply distinguished from the Croats. The mare-milking grand-prince north of the Carpathians in the ninth century may indeed already have become Slav, but by origin he must have been Avar. Strange was the fate of a Bulgar horde which fled to Dagobert the Frank. The Bavarians

---

[1] Illustrated by Meitzen, *Siedlung*, I. p. 52, II. pp. 259, 362, 450–6, 485, Atlas 87 and explanatory map.

[2] This irruption of the Avars into Thuringia in 596 was due to outside pressure, for since 593 the Avar Slavs in what is now Roumania had been hard pressed by the Romans, and even the Avars' own territory in the Hungarian steppe was threatened. Something very pressing in the north-west of the Avar State must have therefore occurred to compel the Khagan to abandon the south-east and to leave the Slavs there to themselves.

massacred them and only seven hundred escaped with their families under Alciocus into the Marca Winidorum (Carantania), where they lived many years with the Slav prince Walluc. This Alciocus must be identical with the Alzeco who with his entire army—evidently stragglers from Hungary—came peaceably to Italy and received from the Lombard king Grimoald (662–672) extensive waste territory in the Abruzzi mountains north-east of Naples. Although these Bulgars learnt vulgar Latin, at the time of Paulus Diaconus they still retained their mother tongue intact. This is natural, for only when they wintered in Apulia did they find it necessary to use the vulgar Latin of the peasants, while in the summer-pastures on the mountains they were by themselves. It is therefore quite conceivable that their descendants did not forget their original language till much later.

The organisation of the South and West Slavs in the centuries that followed is also Avar and Bulgarian. A number of titles of rank of the Altaians, Bulgars, Avars, Chazars and other West and East Turks (in Chinese Turkestan), Utigurs and Mongols, have survived, and many of these were borrowed early from Iranians and particularly Persians. Many of these titles, some peculiar to the Altaians, some borrowed by them from Iranians, are to be found among the Slavs. At the head of an Altaian empire was the *Khagan* (East Turks, Avars, Chazars, etc.) or *Khan* (Bulgars, Cumans, etc.), and as successors of the Chazar Khagans as conquerors of the Russian Slavs, the first princes of the Scandinavian Varangians-Russ bore the title *Kogan* (in Arabian sources *khāqān Rōs*). The Turkish title *boyla* (Magnate) is found in Bulgar-Slavic and Russian (*bolyarin*). The common Slav word for " Sir," *gospodar*, came from Altaic, where it is a Persian loan-word—Middle Persian *gōspand-dār*, "owner of sheep"—the Altaian masters of the Slavs were indeed shepherds; hence the change in the significance of the word. Of the remaining titles which have come from Altaian into Slav the most important are *župan* (pronounced *zhoopan*) and *pan* (the latter coming from *gŭpanŭ*). Both are to be found in the forms ζουπάν and κοπανός in inscriptions on monuments which the Bulgar khan Omurtag (814–831) had erected to his deceased high officials who bore these titles. Both are obviously Persian loan-words in Altaian, although the original Persian words cannot be restored. The second (*kopan*) occurs among the Patzinaks (χοπόν) also, but *župan* was common to several Altaian peoples in various pronunciations. An important historic criterion is offered by the fact that certain titles of rank are pronounced *yabgu*, *yugur* (Avar), *yopan* (Avar) in Eastern Turkish, but in western dialects *jabgu*, ζούργου (Bulg.), ζουπάν (Bulg.). Among the Slavs whom the Avar khagan Baian had settled on the west front of his Empire, we find on the Elbe and Saale, and then in the Alps and on the Adriatic, *župans*; but in the centre on the Danube in the district of Linz, a *iopan* (pronounced *yopan*) *Physso* is mentioned in the year 777. This means that Baian placed the right wing of his west front against the Saxons and Franks, and the left wing against the Lombards, under Bulgarian *župans*, but the centre against the Bavarians, under Avar *yopans*. How important it was for Baian to settle his western front against the Germans with warlike elements can be seen from the appearance of a second warrior class, that of the Germanic *vikings*, among the Sorbs on the Saale (*vićazi*), and among the Serbo-Croatians in Illyria (*vitezi*). But it is also possible that before the invasion of the Avars this Slav folk dominated by vikings had been subjected by a Bulgarian horde, who set themselves over them as *župans*, somewhere in their home in Transcarpathia, and were then dismembered by Baian, and transplanted together with his *župans* and *vikings* to distant regions.

Before the time of Bulgars and Avars there were still no *župans* among the Slavs with whom the Byzantines came into contact, but Germanic *rīkses*, and not till the year 952 is there a statement by Constantine Porphyrogenitus, "These peoples, Croats, Serbs, have no princes (ἄρχοντας) but *župans* as a kind of elders (ζουπάνους γέροντας) just as the other Slav lands have." In 965 Ibrāhīm ibn Ya'qūb says exactly the same of the "Awbābā" [of Wollin] dwelling on the Baltic at the other end of the Slav world, though he does not actually use the word *župan*. Among the Alpine Slavs (Slovenes) neighbouring on the Croats in South Styria we also meet with a very numerous *župan* class in the fifteenth century under which the common peasantry were placed. Among the Serbians the "zoupanoi gerontes" mentioned by Constantine were the princes of the individual clans, and one of them made himself *grand-župan* (*archon, archezoupanos, megas zoupanos, magnus comes*) of the whole people. Similarly, the independent princes of the Elbe Slavs (not yet subjugated by the Germans) were named by the chroniclers *duces, principes, seniores*, promiscuously; Ibrāhīm calls them the *elders*. After the German subjugation the *seniores = eldesten = supani* of the Elbe Slavs, namely the Sorbs in the modern kingdom of Saxony, were still the highest class of the Slav population, having their possessions in fief, being under feudal law, dispensing justice, and only pledged to serve their lord in war on horseback; thus they came nearer to the German nobility than to the other Slav peasantry. In Mecklenburg, the land of the Obodritzi, the feudal village magistrates—the former *župans*—were expressly reckoned among the vassals of the country. It cannot therefore be doubted that the *župans* of the Elbe Slavs also were *principes, domini*, landlords before their subjugation.

With *župan* is connected *župa* (Slav. *župa*, Lat. *suppa*), that is the district under a *župan*, which among the Serbs was a principality, but among the Slovenes of Lower Styria at the time of the German dominion *župa* denoted only a village district. Here the župans finally dwindled to village-chiefs, and then the word signified their office, *officium suppae* or the *župan* estate. The great Serbian tribal-*župa* and the little

Slovenish village-*župa* formed in a certain sense an economic whole, in that all dwellers in the župa-district possessed right of pasture ; consequently the *župa* was here an undivided grazing-district throughout which the agricultural rotation proceeded as long as there were no permanent fields, and as long as the cornfields opened by clearing or the burning of a piece of forest and again abandoned after their exhaustion became derelict and once more forest-land. In consequence of this general right of use by the inhabitants the word *župa* in Serbia became personified, and signified also the whole of the inhabitants entitled to the right of pasture—and formally of clearing too—the *compastores, conterranei*, so to speak. So long as the Avars were lords in the land, and so long as they remained wandering herdsmen, the requirements of their pasturing and their tyranny were decisive ; the enslaved Slav peasantry could place their fields only where it suited their masters, and there could be no idea of a peasant *right* of clearing. In the Balkan peninsula the nomad shepherds wintered with their herds on sunny snowless sea shores, and for this reason in Dalmatia the word *župa* denotes a sunny land where snow does not fall or where it melts rapidly. Some such districts— standing winter-quarters of the nomads—finally retained the word as their name. Among the Carinthian, Bohemian, and Polish Slavs we find no such *župans* and no such *župas*, for here peasant dynasties arose through peasant revolutions and the *župans* had to give way. But the name itself remained, or was borrowed anew from neighbouring Slavs, and *župan* in Bohemia signified a high state official, and *župa* on the one hand is *beneficium*, and on the other the office connected with it. The members of the highest Bohemian and Polish nobility had the title *pan* (originally *gŭpan*). This word has no connexion with *župan*, but arose from a title *kopan* attested by a Bulgarian inscription as before mentioned.

The Avars and Bulgars naturally tolerated no other *dominus* among the directly dominated Slavs, they were themselves the *župans*, and as *župans* remained as *domini* after the break-up of the Avar Empire, and indeed among the Sorbs and Alpine Slavs, and here and there were very numerous, so that they are to be considered as the Avar and Bulgar dominating class Slavised by the lapse of time, and no longer nationally different from the subject people.

From the conglomeration of Slavs planted by the Avars in the Eastern Alps was formed the people of the Slovenes (Carantani). They extended from the Adriatic Sea to the Danube, and from East Tyrol deep into Hungary. As they had the Avar main horde at hand on the Danube and the Theiss, they were most deeply enslaved. After the destruction of the Avar kingdom by Charles the Great their social organisation appears greatly changed. In Lower Styria south of Cilli as late as the fifteenth century they were under an uncommonly numerous hereditary *župan* class, and even in the smallest hamlet there were one, two, three, or four *župans*. On the other hand, south of this in some districts of Carniola and north of the Drave in Lower Styria (in the *dominium* of *Arnfels*) there was no such župan class at all. There (in Carniola) the village-presidents (also called *župans*) were chosen, but only village-magistrates—likewise called *župans*—appointed for a fixed period of time, by the village peasantry, here (in the Arnfels *dominium*) they were nominated for a certain time by the landlord. In what is now Eastern Carinthia too there was no župan class; the land was ruled by a *peasant duke*.

In the various doomsday books (*Urbar*) we find all the villages belonging to the landlord concerned with a definite statement of the number of the peasant estates, and the enrolled *župans* with all the dues and services. These villages originated at various times, some before and some after the German occupation, and we can determine many which were Old Slavic. Those which were first established by the Germans, even when they were colonised with Slav peasants, are for the most part large and often very regularly and artistically laid out in German fashion, and their dues too are purely German. They cover most of the broad valleys and river plains. The carefully planned villages of the plains are therefore new. In another area of the large districts their origin is uncertain; their nucleus may be old, but they were remodelled, and enlarged by the attachment of new clearings. Yet other districts are so markedly non-German that they must be pre-German. These are not really villages, but tiny hamlets. Large villages were unknown to the early Slavs, and the districts of the Elbe Slavs are thickly set with little villages; the Serbs likewise, for the most part, live in hamlets and isolated farms; the Bohemian and Polish large villages are later foundations after the German fashion, and the large Russian villages were only formed from small villages in modern times.

At the head of almost every village in Lower Styria and Carniola whether large or small, old or new, there is a župan, and even the mayor of Laibach (Slav. *Lyublyana*), the capital of Carniola, bears this title. Thus, since the German occupation, the expression župan covers various meanings among the Slovenes to which the magistrate's office is common, but with different rights and duties. In a Slovene village first established by the Germans—usually large—the *župan* is nothing more than an ordinary magistrate, *judex, magister villae*, living in a farm exempt from taxes, as a rule two hides (*praedia, mansi, hubae*). But in tiny little hamlets of the Tüffer domain, the *župan*—who here too has everywhere two hides (*praedia*)—cannot be a *judex, magister villae*, as he pays tribute, and in certain hamlets he is the only inhabitant, and therefore has no one to preside over. Indeed, in the neighbouring domain, Rann-Lichtenwald, in 1309 there were also villages with two, and in 1448 with even three and four *župans*; two magistrates in a village belonging to one and the same landlord would be absurd. Here the župans considerably increased during the 139 years, and, where there was formerly one, three or four occupied the paternal inheritance either undivided or in divided estates. As they all bore the title, but only one of them could be magistrate of the village, *župan* here signified the member of an hereditary class and not the holder of an office. These *župans* paid far more tribute than the peasants on estates of equal size, the higher taxation consisting in swine, subsidiarily swine-pence—this proves that they had greater rights of pasture than the peasants.

The old Slovene *župan* is a village-magistrate only where there are peasants under him. What was he originally? What he was among the Elbe Slavs (*senior*) and the Serbs (*princeps, dominus*), viz. landlord, as descendant of the Avaro-Bulgar herdsman class. Under the German dominion he lost his former seigniorial character; the Germans seized a considerable part of the territory, especially what was uncultivated, including the wasted plains and valleys, and left what remained to those whom they found there—up to that time nomad župans and their Slav peasants—reckoning two hides (*praedia*) for a župan and one for a peasant. In consequence the župans were so huddled together that they were forced to give up the wandering herdsman life, and as they could no longer keep large herds, they had to adapt themselves to husbandry, contenting themselves with a smaller flock of sheep, and finding compensation in swine-breeding. Their former monopoly in cattle-breeding was also abolished, as under the Germans the peasants also were allowed to engage in cattle-breeding though not to the same extent as the župans. This is shewn by the taxation. The peasants still remained subordinated to the župans, but they were newly distributed among them, with the land, so that a precisely defined number of peasants was allotted to a definite group of župans. Thereupon each group of župans shared the peasantry allotted to them according to a definite principle—evidently hereditary. This follows from the fact that the percentage of župans and peasant hides is repeated in several districts remote from one another, although the individual župans appear so very unequally provided with peasants, some indeed having none at all.

Thus we can see how the German domination forced the former wandering herdsman to become a settled cattle-breeder and little by little a grower of grain, and how the cattle-breeding of these *župans* was preponderant up to late times. Their social position was in earlier times by no means slight: in a list of witnesses (1322) a *župan* was not cited among the peasant witnesses but mentioned before the burghers of Laibach[1]—thus he was at least equal to them in rank. In the thirteenth century in the manorial estates of Tüffer and Lichtenwald one of the village župans acted as Schepho—chief official of a larger administrative district—and this also points to the higher position of a *župan*.

[1] Levec, III. p. 73, or Peisker, *Beziehungen*, 159 [345].

As has been already mentioned, in many districts of Carniola and Styria there was no župan class at all and no permanent župans, but one of the peasants was made village-magistrate—equally called *župan*—from time to time and enjoyed in return a certain remission of dues[1]. But this has nothing to do with the hereditary *župan* of Tüffer and Lichtenwald, where there were settled župans paying large taxes, even four in one and the same village belonging to one and the same landlord.

It will have been seen that a change took place in the signification of the word *župan*, and at the same time a change in the position of the peasant population in general, a change different according to place and time, and further developed and differentiated by the unequal pressure of their lords, by continual colonisation under new conditions, and by the decay and resettlement of entire villages. The unpretending peasant who was entrusted for a time with the office of village-magistrate had as little in common with the old Slovene *župan* as the Frankish horse-boy (*marescallus*) with a great French or German marshal.

While thus the former Avaro-Bulgar herdsman nobility, even if divested of overlordship and turned into a peasantry, maintained itself under the German domination in the sixteenth century in a position distinct from the remaining peasantry and in certain districts of Lower Styria as a numerous hereditary class, it disappeared in the neighbouring province of Carinthia long before the German occupation through revolts of the enslaved peasantry. As we have already seen, these latter had heavy burdens to bear in providing their tormentors with supplies of food and fodder, and giving themselves up to be massacred as *befulci* in countless wars, while the Avar harnessed their wives and daughters like beasts to his wagon, violated them systematically, destroying their family life and indeed reducing their whole existence to the level of brutes. Thus, destitute of all social ties the peasantry revolted; though many risings were stifled in blood before one was successful. And now after ages of servitude a part of the great Slav world was cheered by the sun of a golden freedom, not this time to fade into anarchy. From the midst of the victorious peasantry a prince was chosen to be a just judge and to guarantee the husbandry of the people, and especially the cattle-breeding till then forbidden to them. And that things should ever remain so, a wonderfully ingenious ritual was devised for the installation of each new prince—always a peasant. And as there was as yet no fixed hereditary succession, and a certain time always elapsed before a new prince was installed, the interregnum was provided for by recognition of the eldest member of a certain peasant family as *eo ipso* vicegerent. So tenaciously did the people cling to this ritual that even the splendid German dukes of Carinthia had to humble themselves to assume the

---

[1] Milkowicz, in *Mitteilungen*, II. pp. 23 ff.; Peisker, *Die ältere Sozial- und Wirtschaftsverfassung der Alpenslaven*, IV. pp. 32 f.

ducal throne as peasants. In the year 1286 the ritual—markedly modernised and relaxed—was of the following nature:

For the installation of the duke the oldest member of a certain peasant family, the so-called duke-peasant, had to sit on the "prince's stone" which lies in the Zollfeld near Klagenfurt. The new duke, in a coarse peasant's dress with a staff in his hand and leading a bull and a mare, is conducted by four nobles before the carelessly seated peasant, who has to question those nobles in the Slovene tongue and to find out who the man is, whether he is a just judge, mindful of the country's well-being, of free standing and full of zeal for the Christian faith. This they must swear to. Thereupon the peasant says: "By what right shall he remove me from this my seat?" They answer: "With 60 pfennigs, these two brindled beasts, and the peasant dress which he is wearing; he will also make thy house tax-free." Thereupon the peasant gives the duke a light cuff on the cheek, bids him be a good judge, vacates the seat for him, and takes the beasts. The duke takes his seat upon the stone and swings his drawn sword in all directions. He also takes a drink of fresh water.

The successful revolt of these Slovenes from the Avars took place, as we shall see presently, about 603. The first prince of the Carinthians whose name is known was Walluc (after 641), *dux* in Marca Vinedorum, independent of the Avars as well as of the Bavarians and Lombards. About the year 745 the Avars attempted to subjugate the Carinthians afresh, and their duke, Borut, sought help from the Bavarians. These indeed drove off the Avars but made the Carinthians dependent on the Frankish king, under native princes, of whom the last mentioned is Woinimir in 796; and Arnulf (emperor 896), if not the first, was one of the first German princes who as duke of Carinthia submitted (in 880) to the peasant ceremony.

The peasant revolt was not limited to Carinthia, rather it embraced a great part of the Avar Slavdom from the Alps to the Erzgebirge and the Vistula, for the Bohemian dynasty of the Přemyslids and the Polish dynasty of the Piasts were of peasant origin. The Přemyslids were always conscious of this, and Lutold (died 1112), vassal prince of Znaim (Slav. *Znoyem*), had the chapel which he built there decorated with frescoes which still remain, among them the scene of the election of his ancestor with the hazel-stick, the bast-bag, and bast-shoes. Pulkava, court-chronicler to the Emperor Charles IV, king of Bohemia (1346–1378), states that Přemysl's bast-shoes and bast-bag were "to this day" carefully preserved. "And on the day of the coronation of the Bohemian king, the canons and prelates in procession receive the king that is to be and shew him the bast-shoes and lay the bast-bag on his shoulders so that he may be mindful that he sprang from poverty and may not be presumptuous." This is a poor survival of a more ample ritual which, unlike the Carinthian, had lost all its original

significance, for it did not originate in Prague but was transferred
there after the union of the State of the Lemusi with that of the
Chekhs of Central Bohemia. And it was disagreeable to the later
Přemyslids. King Wenceslas I (1230–1253), who was German in feeling,
was ashamed of his origin, causing his peasant kinsmen to be driven
from Staditzi and giving the village to the Germans. But he does not
seem to have touched the bast relics; the kinsmen appear to have
recovered their heritage, for in the year 1359 the Emperor Charles IV,
as king of Bohemia, declared to the sons of Radosta, co-heirs of Staditzi,
that they and their forefathers had always been free heirs of their
tax-free estates; but as these had not long since been illegally given
away and burdened with taxation by his father, the blind King John
(who fell at Crécy, 1346), Charles IV now restores their rights, but
retains as crown-land the field which Přemysl had once tilled single-
handed (it is to this day called the "king's field") and charges the
petitioners with the care of Přemysl's hazel stock, all the nuts from
which they have to present yearly at the royal table as a memorial of an
event so remarkable.

The peasant origin of the Přemyslids and the Piasts cannot be an
invention of the chroniclers. No high-born dynasty would believe such
a story, rather it would make short work of such blasphemy against its
kingly majesty. The chroniclers merely decked the fact out with the
fruits of their reading in ancient classics, and the Church interpreted it
in the sense of Christian humility.

The peasant prince, Přemysl, was not prince of the whole of Bohemia—
which even much later consisted of several little States—but originally
only of the little people of the Lemusi round Bilin in North-West
Bohemia, in immediate proximity to the Sorb clan Glomachi (German
Daleminzen) in the modern kingdom of Saxony. These Glomachi like
the Lower Styrians remained under *župans*, but their social organisation
was more complicated. Under German domination they fell into the
three classes: (1) *Supani* (Lat. *seniores*, German *eldesten*), (2) *Withasii*
(Slav. *vićazi*) *in equis servientes* (servants on horseback, *esquires*), and
(3) the *Smurdi*, correctly *smrdi*, that is the "*stinkers*," the common
peasant-folk. In addition, there were corresponding to the German
occupation members of German nationality: (4) the *Censuales* (German
lazze), and (5) the *Proprii* (*heyen*). The three Slav classes were under
the special jurisdiction of *župans* with Slavonic as official language.
The Daleminzian *župans* and *smurdi* corresponded to the two Lower
Styrian classes, the *župans* as former *domini* (*seniores*) of Avaro-Bulgar
origin; they were likewise very numerous but their percentage cannot
now be ascertained. On the other hand, the *Withasii* were of Germanic
Norse origin. The Vikings somewhere in Russia must have subjected
the forefathers of the Glomachi, and been transplanted with them by the
Avars after the year 563 to serve as a barrier against the Franks on

the Saale and the Elbe. Had they been later conquerors, they must have stood above the *župans*, but here the *župans* (Avars and Bulgars) were the foremost rank, and therefore the latest conquerors, and at the time of the German domination the *vićazi* took rank next beneath them as feudal peasants liable to cavalry service and standing with the *župans* under feudal law. In West and South Europe too the Vikings on stolen horses were, as is well known, as terrible horsemen on the land as they were pirates by sea.

Thus we find both among the Alp-Slavs and the Slavs on the Elbe a *peasant* State in immediate proximity to *župan* States. Either then the peasant revolution was only successful in places, or the Avars having rallied and enslaved the peasantry of Styria afresh remained there as župans, and then together with the peasantry fell under German dominion. "Fredegar" says: "At this time Samo, a Frank, joined himself with several merchants, went to these Slavs to trade, and accompanied their army against the Avars. He shewed remarkable bravery, an enormous number of Avars fell, he was chosen king, ruled successfully thirty-five years, and beat the Avars in all following wars."

The "Fredegar" compilation incorrectly puts this event under the year 623, for the author of this chapter wrote in 642 or 643, and at that time Samo must have been already dead[1]. If the length of his reign is correctly given, the revolt must have taken place in 605 at the latest. In the year 601 the Avars were depopulated by a disease just as the Khagan had driven Constantinople to such straits that the citizens were making ready to migrate to Chalcedon in Asia Minor. Soon after he was almost destroyed in five defeats at the hands of the Romans in Hungary itself, the heart of Avardom. These plunderers were already face to face with extinction when the Emperor Maurice was dethroned in 602, and were only saved from destruction by the incapacity of his successor Phocas. But their supremacy was now at an end. Samo's revolt thus falls between 602 and 605, most probably in the year 603. Then followed the revolt of the Croats and the Serbs, and finally the Bulgar khan Kubrat on the lower Danube made himself free between 635 and 641.

Of Samo's State only this is certain, that it bordered on Thuringia[2],

---

[1] Schnürer, in *Collectanea friburgensia*, fasc. IX. pp. 113, 233.

[2] Fredegar, pp. 74 f. [631] "it was told to the Frankish king Dagobert that an army of the Wends (Slavs) had broken into *Thuringia*....Then appeared envoys of the [then still free] Saxons before Dagobert....They promised to oppose the Wends and to protect the Frankish territory on the Wend border....[632] Then the Wends at the command of Samo...harried *Thuringia and other provinces*...." This proves that Samo's kingdom bordered on the Thuringian province and did not lie in Bohemia, which lies too far from the Thuringian Gau (*pagus*) for attacks from that quarter (*v.* map). Older historians placed Wogastisburg, one of Samo's strongholds, at Taus (at the foot of the Böhmerwald)—called in older sources *Tugast*—the point at which invaders often entered Bohemia from Bavaria. The Burberg near Kaaden in North-West

and embraced the Main and Redantz (Regnitz) Slavs[1]. Thus it lay in what had been Frankish territory, for Samo himself acknowledged: "The land we inhabit and we ourselves are Dagobert's, yet only in case he will maintain friendship with us." Before the irruption of the Avars into the Frankish kingdom in 562, it extended over the Saale to the Elbe. The Sorbs on the Saale and the Elbe as well as the Slavs on the Main and Regnitz were not transplanted (by the Avars) into this previously Frankish district till later. Thus from this time to the founding of Samo's State scarcely forty-four years elapsed, so that he could not have ceased to be conscious of the fact that his land was really Frankish property. Here, in the country of the Regnitz Slavs, the traces of the wintering of the Avars are to this day effaceable. On the lower Aisch, which flows from the south-west into the Regnitz between Erlangen and Bamberg, broad visages with protruding cheek-bones, deep-set eyes, and black hair are still to be met with.

But the Slavs were originally blue-eyed and fair, and were only black-haired and mongoloid where their women were systematically violated by the Altaian conquerors, and this "Fredegar" attests expressly of Samo's Slavs. The Avars (or Bulgars) must therefore have wintered here also. The same is the case with the Bohemian Slavs, whose black hair struck the traveller Ibrāhīm ibn Ya'qūb in 965 as peculiar. Whether, or how far, Samo's kingdom extended into Bohemia is not known; it is, indeed, improbable that it did so, for even in historic times no State has ever existed on both sides of the Fichtelgebirge and the Böhmerwald. As late as the ninth century several independent Slav clans existed in Bohemia, and they assuredly took part in the Slav revolt against the Avars, for there is as little trace of a *župan* class in Bohemia as in Carinthia. It is therefore to be presumed that the Slav tribes did not proceed singly but in combination against the Avars, and that an ephemeral federation was formed, with Samo at its head. But we have no right to speak of Samo's Empire, and the assumption that his kingdom embraced Carantania, the country of the Alpine Slavs, rests only upon the *Anonymus de conversione Bagariorum et Carantanorum*—a party production of the Salzburg Church directed against the Slav apostle St Methodius, and employing for its own purposes Fredegar's notice of Samo—for the association of Samo with the Carinthian Slavs would prove the latter to be members of the Frankish kingdom, and therefore of the Salzburg diocese.

Bohemia, Czech: *Úhošt̓*, is now proposed. The first suggestion is based on the conjecture *Togastisburg* and is therefore to be rejected, the second overlooks the fact that *Úhošt̓* was then pronounced *Ongošt̓*, so that we ought to find *Ungastisburg* or something similar in Fredegar.

[1] Mention of them does not occur again before 846: "In the land of the Slavs who dwell between Main and Redanz [Slav. *Radnica*] called Moinwinidi and Ratanzwinidi."

The Slav revolts here described were successful only as far as the Erzgebirge (which divides Bohemia from the kingdom of Saxony), for immediately north of this we find the Sorb clans on the Saale and Elbe dominated even after this time by *župans*. In Samo's time the Sorb prince Dervan was subject to the Frankish king. By the successful revolt of the Bohemians, and especially of the Lemusi, the *župans* who dominated the Sorb people were cut off from the main horde of the Khagan in Hungary, so they voluntarily submitted to the Frankish king in order to escape the fate of their clansmen in Bohemia and on the Main-Regnitz. But when Dagobert was defeated by Samo, Dervan fell away from the Franks to Samo, who was well satisfied not to have as enemies the dreaded Sorbs, and let alone their two dominating classes, the Avar *župans* and the Viking *vićazi*. This explains how a *župan* prince could still remain prince under Samo, the deliverer of the peasants. We now see that the whole of Slavdom, with perhaps the sole exception of the North-Russian peoples, was swept along in the Avar tornado. This expansion of the Avar power from the Peloponnesus to the Baltic is not inconceivable, for there were Altaian empires greater still, that of the descendants of Chinghiz-Khan and the kingdom of the Huns, the predecessors of the Avars, which stretched from the Don to the lower Rhine.

The view often put forward, that the Slavs themselves became effective warriors in the cruel Avar school, runs counter to the facts. Neither from the Germans nor from the Romans did they permanently wrest a span of ground; in spite of their enormous expansion their part is purely passive. The German migrations took place under the lead of remarkable and heroic figures; at one time the Germans even gave the Roman Empire its wisest statesmen and most powerful military commanders, but among the millions of Slavs who flooded Germany and the East Roman Empire we do not find the name of even one moderately prominent warrior. Those mentioned by the Byzantine sources, like Khilvud, Dabragezas, Mezamir, Ardagast, Piragast, Musok, cannot be compared with the German army leaders, and also they were obviously not real Slavs, but Slavic descendants of partly Germanic and partly Altaian conquerors. The earliest prominent personality among the Slavs is the Frankish Samo, and the most powerful Slav prince, the Russian Svyatoslav (died 972), was in spite of his Slav name a pure-blooded German, son of Ingvarr and Helga (Slav. *Igor, Olga*) and one of the greatest German heroes in history.

"Mauricius" and other writers describe the Slavs as they must have been in their marshy cradle, without organisation, without military discipline, and consequently quite unsuited for any serious offensive movement. But on the defensive when well led they were excellent in a style which was forced upon them by the continual man-hunts of the pirates and the mounted nomads. Of a military schooling from the Avars there is no trace except that they learned plundering from their tormentors. On the offensive they could do nothing against the Romans, though the Romans likewise could do nothing against the defensive of the Slavs. For example, in 593–4, when the imperial army advanced victoriously over the Danube, it was unwilling to winter in a land where the cold was unbearable and the barbarians were invincible on account of their great numbers. In the defensive power of the Slavs lay also the strength of the Avar-Slav positions on the Baltic, Elbe, and Saale against the Franks even after the fall of the Avar Empire. Only after two and a half centuries of continual warfare did the Germans remain victors.

Considerably more than thirty tiny Slav tribes in the former Old Germania from the Danube to Mecklenburg are mentioned there in four groups[1]. Not one of the groups forms a State, each is only seldom and temporarily united when war threatens, otherwise it is divided into little clans bitterly hostile to one another. Each little clan dwells huddled close together in hamlets and little villages amidst marsh and a dense forest zone through which go roads only passable for pack-horses in dry seasons of the year, provided at the entrance to the forest zone with gates and abattis[2]. And if the enemy forced his way in notwithstanding, the people fled to their numerous earthworks, *civitates*. The Obodritzi in Mecklenburg alone had 53 such *civitates* and the same number of *duces*, and were actually regarded as invincible.

After the time of Charles the Great war with these Slavs was permanent. Thanks to the protection of the mountain range and their peaceful acceptance of Christianity, the Bohemian group maintained itself and finally combined into a powerful Bohemian kingdom. On the other hand the remaining three groups, really some dozen of Lilliputian clans, succumbed to the Germans who always found allies among them, sometimes among the Obodritzi, sometimes among the Lyutitzi. Thus the Elbe Slavs (save some small remnants) were exterminated or Germanised.

---

[1] (1) The Bohemians: Doudlebi, Chekhove (Chekhs), Luchane, Lemusi, Pshovane, Kharvati, Zlichane, etc. (2) The Sorbs east of the Saale and Elbe: Goleshintzi, Nishane, "Selpoli," Lubushane, Lupoglavtzi, Zharovane, Trebovane, Milchane, Susli, Glomachi, etc. (3) The Lyutitzi or Veletove, Wiltzi: Morichane, Sprevane, Brizhane, Stoderane, or Havelane, Ryechane, Ukrane, "Redari," Dolenchane, "Kyzini," Chrezpyenyane, Uznoim, Volini, Rani, etc. from the Sorbs to the Baltic. (4) The Obodritzi: Reregi, Vagri, Polabi, Smolintzi, [G]linyane, Varnovi, Drevane, etc. in Mecklenburg and its vicinity.

[2] The Slav apostle, Otto of Bamberg, on his journey entered "a terrible enormous forest which divides Pomerania and Poland....This wood had not been traversed before by any mortal, except that the Duke [of Poland] in earlier years, before he had conquered the whole of Pomerania,...had cut a way for himself and his army by felling and marking the trees. Following this marking, with great difficulty on account of the enormous snakes and wild beasts,...and on account of the marshes that impeded the vehicles and heavy wagons, we traversed the forest in six days." Herbord, ii. Chap. 10.

And in their despairing and incomparably brave defence they too might have kept off the German colossus could they have reconciled themselves to the Cross, which was made hateful to them by the oppression of the German Government[1]. At the same time it must be clearly noted that they were not aggressors but a thoroughly industrious peasant people. The Avar dominant class which had become Slavised in the course of time was not numerous enough for offence against the German power and the equally invincible Danish vikings; it became much reduced in the continuous defensive wars, and also lost its former ferocity because it was squeezed into narrow tribal bounds, so that it had at last to give up the wandering herdsman life. The Spanish Jew Ibrāhīm ibn Ya'qūb who made a journey in these parts in the year 965 says: "In general the Slavs are intrepid and warlike and were they not at variance among themselves, no people on earth could measure themselves against them. The lands inhabited by them are the most fruitful and richest of all, and they devote themselves zealously to agriculture and other kinds of industry wherein they surpass all northern peoples." According to Herbord, Pomerania had an abundance of honey, wheat, hemp, poppy, vegetables of all kinds, and fruit-trees. Yet the lands between the Elbe and the Vistula are only made fertile by industrious cultivation.

The type of the Slav method of warfare is the powerful Polish leader Boleslav Khrobry (992–1025), who created a kingdom that stretched from the Dnieper to the Elbe, and from the Baltic to the Danube and Theiss. He carried on bloody wars with all his neighbours, especially with the German king Henry II. But Boleslav did not confront the German army in open battle; his strength lay in masterly manœuvring and in the heroic defence of strong positions. "Never—says his unfriendly contemporary Thietmar—have I heard of besieged men who made exertions to defend themselves with greater endurance and more clever circumspection." The sources of Boleslav's strength we know from Ibrāhīm ibn Ya'qūb in the year 965: "The land of Meshko [Boleslav's father] is rich in grain and meat and honey and fields....And he has 3000...warriors, a hundred of whom are a match for a thousand others. And he gives these people clothes and horses and weapons and all that they need. And when a child is born to one of them he at once orders ...a salary to be assigned to the same...and when he reaches full age he

---

[1] Evidence in Schafarik, II. p. 542, Note 2. The heathen Slav looked down upon the Christian as upon a barbarian. "We have nothing in common with you. The laws which we inherited from our fathers we will not give up, we are content with the religion which we have. Among the Christians there are thieves and robbers, whose feet are cut off and eyes poked out; the Christian practises all kinds of crime and punishments upon the Christian. Far from us be such a religion" answered the Pomeranians to Otto of Bamberg. Among them there were no beggars, no locks and keys; they were highly surprised at the fastened chests of the bishop. Their table was always decked with food, and every stranger could enter and satisfy himself. Herbord, II. Chaps. 10, 25, 40.

procures him a wife and pays for him the marriage gift to the maiden's father....And the marriage takes place with the approbation of the king. ...And he is like a tender father to his subjects." This standing army is not native, for it is landless; it consists of foreign mercenaries, evidently Norse vikings.

It is clear that the Polish Slavs, like the Russian, were from the earliest times strongly influenced by the vikings and their plundering raids and settlements. For the vikings who ravaged all the coasts of Europe cannot have left alone the river-mouths of the Baltic. According to Iomsvikinga-saga, in the vicinity of the Slav sea and commercial town Volin (Slav), Winetha (Saxon), Iulin or Iumin (Danish), mentioned by Ibrāhīm and the German chroniclers, the Iomsburg, a sea fort, was built by Danish pirates [about 970], and according to Orderic Vitalis (b. 1075) the German gods Wodan, Thor and Frigg were worshipped in a district of the Lyutitzi at the mouth of the Oder. All three however had also their worship in the Upsala temple among the Swedes.

This viking admixture is clearest among the Baltic Slavs—especially those of the Island of Rügen—and gave them the appearance of a pirate people. Helmold reports that the men of Rügen were [1168] tributary to the Danes, but they revolted, and occupied the rich Danish islands, " and the Danes cannot easily protect themselves from the sudden attacks of the pirates, for there are creeks there in which the Slavs can keep well hidden, and from which they can break out unperceived to attack and plunder the unwary. For the Slavs are particularly strong in sudden surprises. Hence even up to recent times this custom of robbing has such possession of them that they are always ready for maritime enterprises to the entire disregard of the profits of agriculture, for their whole hope and all their wealth depend on their ships. Indeed they do not even trouble themselves much about house-building; rather they fashion for themselves huts of wicker-work, as they only seek shelter at need from storm and rain. As often as war threatens to break out, they thresh all the grain and bury it in holes together with all gold and silver and what precious things they possess; their women and children however they take into their fortified places or at least into the forests, so that nothing remains for the enemy to plunder but the huts, the loss of which they very easily bear. They pay no regard to the attacks of the Danes, indeed they consider it sport to measure themselves against them." We see here a remarkable fusion of the viking pirates, Altaian herdsmen and Slav peasants on the Island of Rügen. But could the most terrible of all pirates, the Danes, who fill the gloomiest pages in British history, here stand helpless before *Slav* pirates? It is more likely that Danish vikings were here opposed by Slavised vikings. So too the Narentanian pirates of Dalmatia, called *Pagani*, seem to be Norse vikings transplanted by the Avars, for here too we find a noble class of *vitezi*.

Giesebrecht excellently characterises the Baltic Slavs: " A mixed race, not seldom fluctuating in sharp contradiction in their belief, law, and customs, the Wends were already a fallen nation when they came into contact with the Franks. Thus from them could proceed much that was energetic as far as it could be carried out by individuals, families, or associations, but nothing that presupposed national unity."

More favourable conditions for a thriving development were obtained by those Slav peoples among whom either the Altaian or the German dominating class destroyed the other. The Russian Slavs with the Varangians whom they absorbed finally reached a national and social harmony, while the Bohemians and a part of the Alpine Slavs overcame their Avar oppressors. But they found it a still harder task to build up their rude freedom into an orderly State. This the Carinthians brilliantly performed, remaining in true freedom without a nobility for a long time. Even under German dominion, under far less favourable conditions, they were an equal match for the Germans of Ditmarschen in Holstein.

As a people who for immemorial ages were deprived of justice and politically broken the Slavs longed only for an ordered legal State. An early example of this is afforded with an objectivity extremely rare among medieval chroniclers by the author of Chapters xlviii and lxviii of the "Fredegar" Chronicle (Chronist B). In Samo's kingdom Frankish merchants were robbed and killed and King Dagobert demanded redress. Samo "only agreed on a reciprocal legal procedure on this and similar disagreements which had arisen on both sides. Hereupon Sycharius in the manner of an arrogant envoy let...fall threats to the effect that Samo and his whole people had to be subject to Dagobert." Samo replied, "The land we inhabit and we ourselves are Dagobert's, yet only in case he will maintain friendship with us." Sycharius: "It is not possible for Christians, the servants of God, to stand in friendship with dogs." Samo: "If you are the servants of God, and we are God's dogs, we are permitted to bite you when you ceaselessly act against his will." This led to Dagobert's crushing defeat at Wogastisburg.

The appeal to law and not to the sword is the basis of Old Slavonic thought and aspiration; the principal task of the Slav princes was to secure a passable administration of justice—the Russian Slavs actually appealed to Norse pirates. The chronicler Cosmas pictures the oldest Bohemian princes as simple judges, and by their memorable ritual the Carinthians hoped to secure the necessary foundation of justice, but this was an ideal not always attainable among a people where no man was willing to subordinate himself to another without an army capable of breaking down resistance. And as the Slavs lacked everything in the remotest way like this, they often became the prey of their warlike neighbours and perished in impotent rebellions to gain the human rights denied them. Mighty Slav States arose indeed, but without the co-operation of the people themselves, whose endeavours were early directed to social questions. This was a favourable soil for social religious dreams of an evangelical way of life, and the Slav temperament reached its greatest perfection in an offshoot of the Hussite movement fanned into flame by the teaching of Wyclif—in the venerable Unity of the Bohemian and Moravian Brethren. This movement was democratic, not communistic—a wonderful theoretic union of human perfection with spiritual purity in the midst of a society saturated with selfishness. Their chief representative, well known in England also, was the founder of the new pedagogy, John Amos Comenius (Komenský), the teacher of the peoples of Europe.

CHAPTER XV.

(A)

KELTIC HEATHENISM IN GAUL.

THE purpose of this chapter is to give a short account of the religion of the Gauls, that is to say the inhabitants of the district bounded by the Rhine, the Pyrenees, the Atlantic and the Mediterranean.

We have to gather our information about this religion from incomplete and vague documents which do not belong to Gaul strictly speaking: that is from the historians of Greece and Rome (Posidonius, Caesar, Strabo, Diodorus, Mela, Lucan, etc.). There are also monuments (bas-reliefs, bronzes, and inscriptions) dating from the time when Gaul already formed part of the Roman Empire, and had been influenced by Rome. Both these sources of information shew us, not the pure and true Gallic religion, but this religion either as it was more or less correctly interpreted by strangers, or more or less transformed by imported beliefs.

Another difficulty arises from the fact that under the term Gallic, the ancients included both the original inhabitants of Gaul and other peoples of quite a different character. There were Aquitanians south of the Garonne, related to the Iberians or Cantabrians of Spain: Ligurians in the Alpine districts, and Germans in the Moselle and Meuse valleys. The rest really belonged to the so-called Gauls, and concerning them two things must be said: first that they fall into two groups, the Kelts between the Marne and the Garonne, who were the earlier settlers, and the Belgae, between the Marne and the Ardennes forest, more recent comers and less civilised. Secondly the Belgae and Kelts, or Gauls as they are sometimes called, do not represent a homogeneous people; but the name must be taken to cover both a very ancient race (usually known as Ligurians) and a smaller group of conquerors or immigrants, who were the Belgae or Kelts proper. This country of Gaul was then composed of as various elements as the *Francia* of the time of Clovis, and each of these groups of peoples doubtless possessed their own gods and rites. Therefore when the Gallic religion is referred to, it must be understood to imply the religion practised in a definite district, and not by a definite race.

Concerning the gods; one type of divinity exists that was probably common to all these peoples, Ligurians, Germans, Gauls and Aquitanians. That is the gods of the soil, or, as the Romans said, *genii loci*, meaning the gods who inhabited the visible and salient features of the earth; such as springs, brooks, lakes, rocks, mountains, forests, trees and bogs. These gods were the most popular, ancient, numerous and varied of all. Each possessed a distinct name, which was at the same time applied to the natural feature, whether it were stream or mountain, over which it presided.

Amongst these divinities, so numerous in Gaul (specially among the non-Gallic peoples on the frontier, such as the Aquitanians, Ligurians and Germans), those that recur most frequently and that seem to have received the greatest share of devotion and fame were connected with springs, streams and rivers. This I believe to be due to the important part played by springs in the economic life of families and villages. They give assurance of life to man and his cattle, and therefore—to quote Pliny the Naturalist—"They create towns and engender gods." Some of these stream-divinities, worshipped in spots destined to become the sites of fair towns, have won a still greater celebrity, as for instance *Nemausus*, the god-fountain or the god of the fountain of the great spring at Nîmes, whose temple was consecrated in later times to Diana; *Divona* the spring of *Burdigala* (Bordeaux) sung by the poet Ausonius, to be discovered to-day in the stream of the Devèze; and *Bibracte*, the spring on Mont Beuvray, the celebrated Bibracte that was the capital city of the Aedui when Caesar fought them. Other Keltic towns which also owe their name and origin to stream-goddesses are *Aventicum* (Avenches in the territory of the Helvetii), and *Arausio* (Orange). Side by side with these must be placed the gods and goddesses of medicinal springs, which were worshipped so devoutly in Roman times, and doubtless also in the time of Gallic independence; such as *Luxovius* at Luxeuil, *Borbo* at Bourbon, and others at Gréoulx, at Luchon, at Dax, at Mont-Dore, etc. In fact it would be necessary to name all the mineral waters of France to complete the list of gods of this description. There were also the deities of rivers, who had their sanctuaries later, sanctuaries rich in every kind of votive offering; of which the most famous in Roman times was that of the Seine springs. Such were the *Dea Sequana* the Seine, *Icaunis* the Yonne, *Matrona* the Marne; while the Classical authors shew that the Rhine was looked upon as a supreme god. Closely related to these divinities, both as regards origin and attributes, were those of lakes and marshes; such as the god of the sacred lake of Toulouse, to whom thousands of ingots of gold and silver, spoils of the Roman proconsuls, were consecrated.

The gods of mountains, or rather of isolated peaks, were perhaps rather less numerous and popular, but were also very powerful. A few of them, by virtue of the majesty of the summit they inhabited, attained (like the Rhine) to the highest rank among the gods. The col of the Puy-de-Dôme, *Dumias*, was accounted one of the greatest deities in Gaul, as were also Ventoux, *Vintur* in Provence, Donon in the Vosges, not to mention lesser heights. Indeed it appears that the true Gauls were more attracted by the worship of mountains than by that of springs.

On the other hand, the Ligurians, Aquitanians and Germans seem to have cared more for that of forests and trees, though this statement must not be taken to refer to anything more definite than a preference for one rather than the other, since all the Gallic peoples were acquainted with the same gods. It is usually possible to distinguish between the gods and goddesses of the whole forest, most plentiful in the North, such as the *Dea Arduenna* of the Ardennes, and the *Deus Vosegus* of the Vosges, and the particular divinities which inhabited a single tree, or a clump of trees; such as the *Deus Fagus* "the god of the beech tree," or the *Deus Sexarbores*, which is the Roman version of the divinity inhabiting a group of six trees. Such gods might be found most frequently in the land of the Aquitanians north of the Pyrenees.

It remains yet to shew in what manner these nature gods were represented and grouped. Sometimes they dwelt in solitude; in which case the stream or mountain only belonged to a single divinity, either male (*e.g. Deus Nemausus*) or female (*e.g. Dea Sequana*). This seems to have been the case specially in regions where Keltic or Iberian influence predominated. Sometimes the mystic properties of a spring were attributed to an indivisible group of gods, most often composed of three, but occasionally of five divinities; called by the Romans "Mothers" or "*Matronae*" or "*Nymphae*" of the spring: for instance *Matres Ubelnae* "the Goddess-Mothers" of the Huveaune (a Provençal spring), but it is clear that the word *Matres* is only the translation of a native word, whose use must have been very ancient. This conception of the gods of springs was general between the Pyrenees and the Rhine, but appeared in a more fully developed form in Provence, the Ligurian districts, and the forest lands bordering on Germany.

It is impossible to attribute to one tribe more than to another the worship of the gods sprung from human life; by which is meant the cult of the dead. We have no trustworthy documentary evidence testifying to this cult before the Roman period. But monuments dedicated to the manes of the departed are as common in every part of Gaul as in Italy and Greece, they shew practically the same formulae, and they bear witness to the same rites and beliefs. Therefore it is safe to attribute to the Gauls or Ligurians that worship of the dead which was an essential element in Greek or Roman life, as Fustel de Coulanges has shewn in *La Cité Antique*.

CH. XV. (A)

Above these local and human deities appear the great gods. In this respect more marked individuality is discernible amongst the different tribes, Kelts, Aquitanians or Ligurians. They gradually gave distinctive characteristics to their superior gods, the more so since these deities were regarded as the protectors and representatives—not of places or men—as were those mentioned above, but of whole nations, states and public societies. Naturally each of these societies, leading its individual life, attributed to its national god or tutelary deities a special character, corresponding to the chief characteristics of its own life. At the same time, in spite of the obvious differences which they display, these superior gods possess certain common features, which serve to recall the existence of the great sovereign and universal deities, older than the grouping of nations.

All the tribes mentioned, whatever their origin may have been, have this in common; that they all believed in the existence of a superior divinity, representing the virtue of the earth, which produces all and reaps all. We find this same divine principle appearing under a multitude of diverse forms in later times, such as the Earth, mother of the god of the Germans, *Dispater*, father of the Gauls, Earth again, from whom the indigenous Britons sprang, *Vesta* or *Herecura* (*Juno Regina*) known to us from the Roman inscriptions in Gaul and Germany; and *Minerva* of the tribes of the South. And if we find later that the Aquitanians of Lectoure and the Kelts of the Viennois and the Three Gauls accepted with enthusiasm the cult of the *Magna Mater* brought to them from the Palatine at Rome and Pessinus in Asia, the explanation lies in the fact that they were accustomed to adore a chthonian divinity of the same nature.

Similarly Gauls, Ligurians and Gallo-Germans worshipped the sun, moon, fire and the stars; and in the more human figures which represented their gods in later times it is possible to see clearly traces of these ancient and primitive beliefs. Thus among the greatest of the Keltic gods was *Taranis* (or *Taranus*) whom Caesar reasonably considered as the equivalent of Jupiter, since his emblems were the thunder-bolt, the S and the wheel of the chariot of the Sun. By his side the same people worshipped *Belenus*, translated Apollo by the Romans, as being more correctly the Sun-god. They also possessed an equivalent for Diana, perhaps in the person of Sirona; while the appearance of stars on various Gallic monuments shews that the cult of the lesser stars was not foreign to them. Above all, these astral or heavenly gods kept their primordial importance among the non-Gallic tribes, the Aquitanians and Ligurians, and among the Gauls in the Belgic district. An examination of the symbols on coins of the period of independence, or the inscriptions of the Roman time, discloses the apparently incontrovertible fact, that in proportion as the Seine is left to the south, and the Ardennes and the Rhine are approached, astral symbols increase on coins, and figures connected with the heavens become more numerous on monuments. For there is no doubt that the symbol of a snake-footed giant supporting a triumphant cavalier, which is so often found in Belgium, may be interpreted as illustrating the episodes in the progress of the seasons or the stars. Also it may be observed that it was this same region that was most notable, in Imperial times, for the worship of the seven days of the week.

The permanent and natural functions of these chthonian and astral gods prolonged their existence and stereotyped their characteristics until the time of the Roman conquest: thus it is easier to speak with certainty of these than of the merely political deities, for their sway was closely connected with the national life of the tribes; as was that of Capitoline Jupiter or Jahveh of the Israelites.

The Kelts, while they formed a federation of cities bearing the same name, owned as their political deity one that the writings of Lucan have made known to us as *Teutates,* and this name itself reminds us of his essential characteristic, which was to identify himself with his people (as did Jahveh with the Israelites), for the root " *teut* " appears to mean something approaching to " national " (*patrius*). It was this god that the Romans, following the example of Caesar, identified with Mercury; though it is probable that any other interpretation would have served equally well: for instance Mars, Saturn or *Dispater,* according as the Classical authors or the worshippers in the Imperial period may have preferred the intellectual, warlike or creative attributes. For like all other national gods of ancient peoples, this deity seems to have been omnipotent. He probably led his people to battle, protected their merchants, taught them all the arts, while he was also the creator of mankind and the founder of the national name, as was Jehovah himself.

Besides this god, but still within the circle of their national deities, the Kelts worshipped *Esus,* who probably came into existence as a duplication or avatar of Teutates. He seems to have possessed the same attributes, though perhaps it is possible to discern in him more definitely and constantly the features of a warrior.

Besides these two, a feminine deity is found, more or less sprung from the earth goddess; she is also at the same time a warlike and intellectual deity, known by the Romans as *Minerva* or *Victoria,* perhaps also the mysterious *Andarta* of certain epigraphic writings. Yet further, there may possibly have been a fourth deity of this nature in the Gallic pantheon, a god of war and labour, of fire and the smithy, identified by the Romans as *Vulcanus.*

If only the tribes bearing the name of Gauls had lived in strict bonds of unity under one government, as did the Carthaginians and Romans, it is probable that the individual characters and special characteristics of the gods might have become permanently fixed. But the Gallic world, like the Greek, was frequently changed by scatterings and quarrels.

CH. XV. (A)

Thus each of the tribes worshipped, conceived of and made combinations of the gods at its own pleasure, until Gaul may be said to have contained as many pantheons as cities; though the same fundamental principles can easily be traced in each.

In this way the Druidical federation which had its centre in the land of the Carnutes, kept as its sovereign gods Teutates and Esus associated with Taranis the thunder-god. Among the Vocontii of Dauphiné the great national divinity appears to have been Andarta, Victory. The Allobroges appear to have consecrated themselves to two military divinities resembling the Roman Mars and Hercules. Perhaps the Arverni, who were for a long time the sovereign people among the Kelts, had with more piety maintained the worship of a single Teutates, to whom they raised the sanctuary that is found consecrated in Roman times to the Latin form of this god, *Mercurius Dumias*.

So far we have only dealt with the Gauls, amongst whom it is possible to discover the existence of political gods, presiding over a great federation or a single city. This type of god is far more difficult to study among the Aquitanians and Ligurians, because their national life was, to a surprising degree, less concentrated, and the tribal system preponderated. Even here, however, we occasionally discover a great god possessing the attributes of Mars, another resembling Hercules, or a third with feminine characteristics. The pacific and creative faculties which caused the Keltic Teutates to resemble Mercury are less clearly marked in the chief gods of this region.

Another cause of the indefiniteness noticeable in the characters of all these gods is the fact that in all probability the Gauls had not yet reached the stage known as anthropomorphism. It must not be understood by this that they completely denied themselves any representation of the gods; for when Julius Caesar speaks of the *simulacra* of their Mercury, or Lucan mentions the *simulacra* of the gods of the Kelto-Ligurian peoples dwelling near Marseilles, they were doubtless thinking of images of the human figure. But these images, not a single one of which has survived for us, can only have been unformed trunks, rough-hewn pillars, a kind of sheath in wood or stone (*arte carent*, said Lucan) analogous to the most ancient *xoana* of the Greeks, without any of the features of a man or those fixed attributes which make it possible to distinguish a Zeus from an Apollo.

The image of the deity was as indefinite as his nature was vague and complex. At the same time, it appears that the religious image was not universally accepted; and that the priests, like those of Latium in the time of Numa, refused to give their authority to representations of the gods.

To the eyes of worshippers the gods were represented rather by emblems than figures, and before the time of Roman influence the Gallic religion was as rich in symbols as it was poor in images. We may study the Gallic coins struck in the second and first centuries B.C., which are the only authentic witness to the period of independence, without finding a single representation of one of the native gods, either full-length or as a bust. On the other hand, attributes, symbols and emblems will be found in abundance, either of the objects which formed the equipment of a god, weapons or utensils, or signs which would be pointless except for the mysterious significance attached to them.

Thus the sign in the form of the letter S, which has given rise to many designs on coins, and to the fabrication of many metal amulets, appears to have been the symbol of Taranis; the same may be said of the wheel or little wheel. The hammer, according to the most reliable theory, was the attribute of Teutates, his changeless weapon.

Further, the gods possessed permanent companions, birds, beasts, trees and animals, which accompanied them during their lives or made manifest their actions. Amongst quadrupeds, the horse appears most often on coins; while of all the birds, the raven most certainly plays the principal part in divine matters in Gaul, as among so many peoples of the ancient world. A chatterer, ever restless with his varied cries, he was manifestly the interpreter of the wishes of the gods on earth, and their permanent oracle.

We are rather better informed on the subject of sacred plants, thanks to some of the writings of Pliny the Naturalist. It must not be forgotten, however, that he wrote more than a century after the loss of Gallic independence, and that the sacred plants had by then been more or less wrested from their divine functions by their transformation into mere magical agents. We know the most important to have been the mistletoe; not mistletoe found in any place, but mistletoe cut from an oak. It owed its great value to several circumstances: mistletoe is very rare on oaks, the oak was the most sacred tree among the Kelts, and the presence of a plant of mistletoe on an oak was therefore a proof that a god had chosen it for his dwelling. Further to explain the potency of mistletoe it must be remembered that its seed is spread by birds, its leaves face the earth, not the sky, and that it displays its perfect greenness at a time when all other vegetation seems dead in the cold winter weather. Thus it is possible that in it the Gauls beheld a symbol of immortality, but Pliny only speaks of it as a remedy for all ills.

Later, under the Roman domination, all these different beings and things comprised in the Gallic religion, gods, animals, plants and emblems, were combined and united to form groups of consecrated images, analogous to those at that time presented by the Graeco-Roman mythology. The sculptors of Roman Gaul continually reproduced and repeated the new conceptions of their belief. We have therefore a type of the thunder-god, clothed more or less like a Jupiter, armed above all with the wheel: a god with a hammer, accompanied by a dog and holding a goblet in his hand: a three-headed god flanked by a serpent with a ram's horn: a horse-god, carried by the snake-footed giant: a goddess seated on a beast of burden (*Epona*, the goddess of horses): a horned god, and many others. But we hesitate before pronouncing these images to be the manifestations of unmixed Keltic thought. At the time when they appeared a century had elapsed since the Gauls had been independent in their thoughts and beliefs; they were no longer under the direction of their priests, and they were ceaselessly open to contact with Greek and Roman imagery, so that they often combined native emblems with copies of foreign symbols; they spoke no more of Teutates, but invoked Mercury in his place. All these images possess a real interest none the less, but it is necessary to guard against attributing to them an undue importance in the history of Gallic religion.

What has been said of religious sculpture is still more true of architecture. All the temples and altars without exception, which were consecrated to Gallic gods, date from the period of the Roman Empire: and by that time the Roman architects and priests had invaded the land with their stereotyped buildings and their customs, the *templum* and *ara*. This does not imply that it is impossible to discover in these constructions a trace of indigenous survivals. Thus a great many temples in Gaul proper are constructed on a square plan (as for instance that of Champlien, in Normandy), and this architectural type is hardly to be found in the Graeco-Roman world, therefore it may possibly recall some sacred customs of the Gauls; but a complete inquiry on these lines has not yet been made. It is certain that in the time of independence, the Gauls possessed sacred places; and a few, like that of the Virgins of the Isle of Sein (in Armorica), must have been complete buildings, with walls and roofs. But these were doubtless made of wood (hence their complete destruction) and they were in the minority among sanctuaries. The majority of consecrated places were simply open spaces limited by ritual, but not by material boundaries; spaces where fragments of the precious metals, destined for the gods, were accumulated. There were also clusters of trees, spaces reserved in the great forests, or even lakes or marshes, like those of Toulouse, which have been mentioned already. When a spring was considered to be holy it is probable that offerings for the god of the place were thrown into the water; the spring was at the same time both god and sanctuary. This theory explains the fact that when sites are excavated the springs often yield the largest crop of surprising discoveries.

All that has been said helps to shew why it is still more difficult to penetrate far in the knowledge of doctrines; that is, the fashion in which the Gauls conceived of the destinies of man, the world, and the gods. But there remain a few indications of their beliefs in these matters, escaped from the total ruin which has befallen their religious poems. Further, it is always possible that the Greeks and Romans have not given a very exact interpretation even of what they were able to learn. At the time when they were writing on Gallic religion there was a fashion prevalent, owing its origin doubtless to Alexandria, of painting the wisdom and philosophy of the barbarians in glowing colours; so that quite possibly they may have endowed the Gallic dogmas with a purity and elevation really quite foreign to them.

The Keltic doctrine most highly praised by these writers is that of the immortality of the soul. They have not explained to us very clearly the nature of this immortality, but it is more than probable (if we examine the equipment of a Gaul in his tomb) that the Kelts imaged the next life as very similar to this, with more pleasures and with greater combats for him who died bravely on the battle-field. This type of immortality is traceable in the beliefs of most barbaric peoples; it has no special mark of nobility, and does not justify the frequent practice of deducing from it any particular glory for the Kelts.

Concerning the world, their religious poems spoke of the struggle between water, earth and fire, of the triumph of the two first-named elements, and of the submergence of all in a future cataclysm. Moreover, the world was later to emerge as victor over destruction. This is a sufficiently childish cosmogony, in which it is possible to trace all the usual elements.

The religious practices of the Gauls do not seem to offer any extraordinary features, either good or bad. Caesar and others tell us that they were the most religious of men, and performed no action without consulting their gods; in this they resembled the Greeks and Romans of primitive times, and if the contemporaries of Augustus were astonished at it, it was merely because at that time it was considered by educated Romans to be good taste to mock at the gods and to act independently of them.

The Gauls must be severely condemned for their human sacrifices, whether of those already sentenced to death, or of innocent persons whom they are said to have enclosed in large wicker hampers. Recently certain modern scholars, too ready perhaps (like the Alexandrians in the time of Posidonius) to admire the Gauls, have tried to deny or excuse these horrible ceremonies. This is only labour lost. We must accept their existence, not forgetting, however, that they were not peculiar to the Gauls, but that the Greeks and Romans themselves had their sacrifices of men and women. The ancients have insisted with equal vehemence on the Keltic practice of divination, and have cited many facts to shew their passion for the art of the diviner, whether by means of birds, entrails of victims, decisions of augurs or dreams. Without doubt the Gauls had essayed all these means for discovering the future, but in this again they took the same course as the Greeks and Romans of earlier times; and if the raven was by them accounted the greatest of soothsaying birds, it held a similar position among the Greeks long before.

With regard to the magical practices of the Gallic world, the ancients have little to tell us. This may simply be due to chance, but possibly the Kelts were really inferior, in this respect, to the Italians and Carthaginians. Various indications (specially the relative scarcity of magical tablets under the emperors) seem to shew that as far as magic is concerned, they were rather imitators than masters.

Perhaps it was in their sacerdotal organisation that the Kelts (they alone can be dealt with in this connexion) shewed most originality; though it is necessary to add that we are only half-informed on the subject.

They called their chief priests *Druids*. This name (whatever its etymology may be) seems to have conveyed a more important meaning to them than did the words *sacerdos* or *pontifex* to the Romans. Nevertheless, the druids were not without some resemblance to the men who bore one or other of these titles at Rome. They also were drawn from the upper class of society; they were selected from the nobles, exactly as the pontifices of primitive Rome were chosen from the patrician ranks. The dignity of druid did not force its holder to withdraw himself from civil and political life. Caesar has told us of an Aeduan druid in his time, Diviciacus by name, who was, perhaps, the chief of all the Gallic druids. He was very rich, wielding great influence both in his own tribe and throughout Gaul, he was probably both married and the father of a family; he was allowed to ride and to wear arms; he accompanied Caesar on his first campaigns, and the Roman proconsul even entrusted the command of a corps of the army to him. His obligations, as a Gaul, do not seem to have differed from those of Caesar as a Roman, and Caesar was *pontifex maximus*.

Two points remain, however, in which the druids do not resemble the priests of Classical antiquity, but rather recall those of the East. First, though each tribe in Gaul had its own druid or druids, all the druids were associated in a permanent federation, like priests of the same cult. Although they were not formally a clergy, they did form a church, like the bishops of the Catholic Church; and this church necessitated both a hierarchy and periodical assemblies.

At the head of the druids was a high-priest, who seems to have held his dignity for life. Since there was an organised hierarchy, the high-priest was succeeded by the man who held the post immediately below his own. If the succession should be disputed by rival claimants of equal rank, a decision was made by means of election, or sometimes by a duel with weapons, standing probably for some kind of divine judgment by the sword.

Every year all the druids of Gaul met in a solemn assembly in the territory of the Carnutes (Chartres and Orleans); this country was chosen because it was considered (and with considerable accuracy) to be the centre of the whole of Gaul. This assembly had at the same time a political, judicial and religious aspect. The druids formed themselves into a tribunal, and judged all cases submitted to their decision;

such as those involving murder, disputed inheritance and boundaries. It is probable that this tribunal came into competition with the jurisdiction of the ordinary magistrates of the cities. The druids pronounced sentences which seem in the main to have consisted of formulae of composition or of excommunication. Those excluded by them from the sacrifices were, said Caesar, treated as scoundrels, and guilty of impiety, and no one dared approach them. It remains to be discovered to what extent this tribunal was attended, its sentences executed and its jurisdiction respected. It may be that in the last century of independence, these druidical assizes were but the survival of very ancient institutions, then falling more and more into desuetude—a form without much meaning. None the less, they are one of the strangest things found in Gaul, and even in the whole of the West.

The second original feature of druidism was that the priests were also the teachers of the Gallic youth. If it were said absolutely that they directed the schools, the expression would be unsuitable. But they gathered round them the young men of the Gallic families, and taught them all that they knew or believed concerning the world, the human soul and the gods. A few of these scholars stayed with their masters until they had reached the age of twenty years; but it is clear that those who were to become priests received the lion's share of attention. Such an institution, making the priests into the educators of the young, is surprising in ancient times, and calls to mind modern conditions. We cannot be certain, however, that in it we have an exceptional phenomenon, for is it not possible that something approaching the druidical teaching may be found in the schools founded in Rome in connexion with the members of the colleges of Augurs and Pontifices?

In all other respects, however, the analogy between druidism and the ancient priesthoods is complete. The druids alone possessed the power of offering sacrifices by the act of presiding at them; they studied philosophy, astronomy and physiology; they wrote (in verse) the annals of their people, as did the pontifices of Rome and the priests of Israel.

The druids were not the only priests of the Gauls. They were the most important, and probably they alone were considered to rank in dignity with the nobles. But they had depending on them a good many subordinate priests who officiated singly, and others who were combined to form a sodality.

The single priests were those who were attached to a sanctuary as a kind of guardian or celebrant of a temple and its god: somewhat resembling the Roman *aedituus*. Among the greater number of tribes they were known as *gutuater*.

The Gauls also possessed priestly confraternities, which seem to have been largely made up of women. The ancient geographers tell us of a few, which were all dedicated to the orgiastic cults, doubtless having a chthonian origin. The most famous was that of the maidens of the Isle of Sein (already mentioned) who foretold the future, and raised or tranquillised storms. The truth of this information has frequently been denied of late, but all ancient religions have confraternities of this kind, all having a similar origin, and all giving rise to, and carrying on, the worship of the Earth-Mother.

Druidism did not disappear with Gallic independence, but it underwent fundamental modifications, which must be mentioned here in order to explain the way in which medieval writers have alluded to it.

The druids, as public high-priests of the Gallic tribes, lost their old place under the Roman domination. They were suppressed, or rather, transformed into *Sacerdotes* according to the Roman custom; and in the *Concilium* of the Three Gauls at Lyons, composed of *Sacerdotes Romae et Augusti* it is possible to trace a Roman interpretation of the druidical assemblies in the land of the Carnutes.

The lower priests, prophets, diviners, sages, guardians of temples and sorcerers, survived in obscurity, carrying on their traditions and sought after by devotees and peasants who were faithful to the old popular cults. Thus it came about that the word druid, which was formerly applied to the sacerdotal aristocracy, was finally used to designate these rustic priests, the last survivals of the national religion. When, therefore, the Latin writers mention druids and druidesses in connexion with mistletoe, remedies and witchcraft, it is probable that they allude to these priests of the uneducated people.

The word druid is found in medieval writings applied to the native priests of Ireland and the so-called Keltic lands. It is difficult to feel sure that the word is there a direct survival, and that the Irish druids really were the authentic descendants of those mentioned by Pliny and Tacitus. In more than one place, the name and the dignity might have been interpolated by a learned writer who had read Caesar and Strabo. But ought this statement to be made general? and further, is it not possible that all druids found in the West in medieval times are the production of literary men? The present writer refrains from expressing an opinion on the subject.

One last question remains in connexion with the druids. Caesar states in his *Commentaries* that their doctrine (*disciplina*) was evolved (*inventa*) in the isle of Britain, from whence it had been taken to Gaul. He adds "those who wish to study it deeply, usually go to the Island, and stay there for a time."

A completely satisfactory explanation of this passage has not yet been given. Perhaps it was simply an invention of the Gallic druids, who wished to invest their doctrine with the attractiveness that belongs to a mystery, and therefore evolved this British origin for it. But perhaps their dogmas and their myths really did spring from the large neighbouring island. In this latter case, two hypotheses must be considered.

In the time of Caesar the British population was composed of two different groups: a minority consisting of conquerors who had come from Gaul, Belgians or Kelts; and a majority consisting of natives. To which of these two races did the druids ascribe the paternity of their intellectual discipline? If to the Gauls, possibly Britain produced a reforming druid, who restored the religious doctrines of the nation to their primitive purity. If to the natives, it may be that an ancient religious community existed on the Island, with foreign rites and teaching, that nevertheless supplied inspiration to the druids.

In either case, one thing seems certain. It is that Britain, the last, in point of date, of the Keltic settlements in Europe, somehow preserved more faithfully than the other countries the religious habits of the common mother-land. It is evident from Caesar that the Britons still respected the most ancient customs of the Gallic race, therefore it is probable that among them religion would have retained the most primitive forms. This may explain why the druids sent their novices there for instruction.

The druids of Gaul, like the pontifices of Rome, were writers. Caesar reiterates his account of their long poems; for to prevent their doctrines from being made known to all, they composed (or had composed) thousands of verses, which they compelled their disciples to learn by heart. These poems dealt with the stars, the gods, the earth and nature; probably also with the origin of the Gallic tribes and the human soul. They were at the same time their books of Genesis and Chronicles. Moral precepts were mixed with or added to this theoretical teaching, the best known being that which taught that death is not to be feared, and that another life is to be expected.

Probably these didactic poems did not exhaust the religious poetry of the Gauls. Their sacred literature seems to have been extraordinarily rich. We find quotations referring to songs of war and victory, also magnificent melodies, hymns in honour of their leaders, and historical poems, often of an epic character, in which facts and supernatural events alternate bewilderingly. The unfortunate fact is that all this is known to us only by the vague allusions to it to be found in the Classical authors.

In connexion with these songs and poems, the word most often used by the ancient writers is *Bardi*, and this was the ordinary term for poet among the Gauls. These *Bardi* must be remembered in considering Gallic religion, for it is possible that they were half priests, half prophets, living in dependence on the druids.

As well as references to druids and Gallic gods, we come across bards in the celebrated Keltic poems of the Middle Ages; and the same question arises in connexion with all these traces of Gallic religion. Do they all come directly and continuously from the past, or are they nothing more than clever reconstructions due to readers of the Classics?

CH. XV. (A)

(B)

KELTIC HEATHENISM IN THE BRITISH ISLES.

Just as the general condition of Britain in Roman times is far more imperfectly known than that of Gaul, so, too, we have but scanty data for painting a complete picture of Keltic heathendom in these islands during the period in question, and that which immediately succeeded it. Such evidence as we find is derived partly from inscriptions, partly from the survival in legend of certain names which are either those of known Keltic deities, or which may be presumed from their forms to have been those of divine beings, partly from the allusions found in legend to heathen practices, and partly from inferences based upon a study of existing folk-lore. A consideration of this evidence leads to the conclusion that the condition of heathenism in Britain was very similar to that of Gaul, except that, in North Britain and Ireland and the less Romanised parts of Southern Britain, there had been less assimilation of the native religion to that of Rome.

In Britain, as in Gaul, the basis of Keltic religion was largely local in character, and rivers, springs, hills and other natural features were regarded as the abodes of gods and goddesses. The belief in fairies and similar beings, as well as in fabulous monsters supposed to inhabit caves, lakes and streams, which comes to view in medieval and modern Keltic folk-lore, is doubtless a continuous survival from the period of heathenism, and certain of the practices connected with regularly recurring festivals, such as the lighting of bonfires, the taking of omens and the like, have probably come down from the same time. The curious reader can find a very full account of these and similar survivals in Sir John Rhŷs's *Celtic Folk-lore*, Campbell's *Tales of the Western Highlands* and Dr Frazer's *Golden Bough*.

Certain of the deities of Britain may have been tribal, and there are reasons for thinking that, in Britain as well as in Gaul, some deities were worshipped by several Keltic tribes, so that these may be regarded as the major deities of the Keltic pantheon. For instance, the name of Lug, a character of Irish legend, and that of Lleu in Welsh legend, are both cognate with the Gaulish Lugus, a god whose wide worship in the Keltic world is attested by the number of places called after his name Lugudunum or Lugdunum (the fortress of Lugus), and it is highly probable that both Lug of Irish legend and Lleu of Welsh legend were once regarded in their respective countries as divine. The Welsh place-names Dinlleu (the fort of Lleu) and Nantlleu (the valley of Lleu) in Carnarvonshire point in the same direction, no less than the ancient British name of Carlisle, Luguvallium (the embankment of Lugus).

A name corresponding to that of the god Segomo of Gaul is found on an Ogam inscription in Ireland—Netta-Segamonas (the Champion of Segamo), and, later, as Nia-Sedhamain (for Seghamain). The Gaulish god Camulos has his British counterpart in the Camalos or Camulos after whom Colchester received its name Camalodunum or Camulodunum. The proper name Camulorigho (in an oblique case) found on an inscription in Anglesey, as well as Camelorigi, which occurs on an inscription at Cheriton in Pembrokeshire, are further evidence that the god Camulos was not unknown in Britain. This is still more probable, since the name of this deity occurs on an inscription at Barhill[1], while the wide range of his worship is suggested by the existence of his name on inscriptions at Salona[2], Rome[3] and Clermont.

It would be unsafe to take the fact that the name of a deity occurs on an inscription in Britain as evidence that the deity in question was worshipped by the natives, since the inscriptions found in Britain are mostly those of soldiers who often paid their vows to the deities of their own lands. At the same time, the area over which certain inscriptions are found makes it highly probable that the deities mentioned on them were worshipped, among other countries, in Britain itself. The following account of the deities mentioned on inscriptions in Britain will suggest not a few instances where this was doubtless the case. The name Aesus, which is probably identical with the Gaulish Esus, occurs once on a British silver coin[4], and this fact makes it not unreasonable to suppose that this god was worshipped in Britain. On an inscription found at Colchester, there is mentioned a god identified with Mercury, called Andescox[5], but of this deity nothing further is known. The name of another god Anextiomarus (a name probably meaning "the great protector") is found, identified with Apollo, on an inscription at South Shields on the Herd sands, south of the mouth of the Tyne, and the beginning of the same name occurs on a stone which is in the Museum at Le Mans. The name Antenociticus is found on an inscription of the second century[6] at Benwell, and Antocus[7] at Housesteads, but the connexion of these gods with Britain is uncertain, as is that of a god Arciaco[8] mentioned on a votive inscription at York. The name Audus[9], identified with Belatucadrus, on an inscription at Scalby Castle, is probably British, and similarly that of Barrex, a god identified with Mars, mentioned on an inscription at Carlisle[10]. A deity, whose name is incomplete (Deo Sancto Bergant...), mentioned on an inscription found at Longwood near Slack (Cambodunum), was not improbably the tribal god of the Brigantes. Another name, Braciaca, identified with Mars on an inscription[11] at Haddon House near Bakewell, was probably that

---

[1] *C.I.L.* vii. 1103. [2] *Ib.* iii. 8671. [3] *Ib.* vi. 46.
[4] Evans, *British Coins*, p. 386. [5] *C.I.L.* vii. 87. [6] *Ib.* vii. 503.
[7] *Ib.* vii. 656. [8] *Ib.* vii. 231. [9] *Ib.* vii. 874.
[10] *Ib.* vii. 925. [11] *Ib.* vii. 176.

of a local British god. At Wardale in Cumberland there occurs on an inscription[1], the name of a god Ceaiius, but the connexions of this name are entirely unknown. At Martlesham in Suffolk, there occurs an undoubtedly Keltic name Corotiacus[2], identified with Mars, and probably a British local god. The name Marriga or Riga, which occurs on an inscription at Malton in Yorkshire[3], is likewise probably that of some local deity identified with Mars. The name Matunus[4], found on an inscription at Elsdon in Northumberland, may be a derivative of the Keltic "matis" (meaning good), and, as it occurs nowhere else, it may well be a local name. There is an inscription, too, at Colchester (c. A.D. 222–235), set up by a Caledonian (Caledo), which mentions a god Medocius, identified with Mars, and clearly this can hardly have been a foreign deity. On the other hand, the name Mounus[5], which occurs on an inscription at Risingham, is probably a contraction of Mogounus, the name of a god who is identified on an inscription at Horberg in Alsace with Grannos and Apollo, and who is probably unconnected with Britain. One of the clearest instances, however, of the occurrence of the name of a British god on an inscription of Roman times, is in the case of the god Nodons or Nodens, whose name is identical with the Irish name Nuada and the Welsh name Nudd. The Irish name Nuada forms the element -nooth in the name Maynooth (the plain of Nuada). The form Nodens or Nodons (in the dative case Nodenti or Nodonti) occurs four times[6] on inscriptions at Lydney Park, a place on the Severn near Gloucester. It is possible that the name Lydney itself comes from a variant of Nodens, or from the name of a cognate deity Lodens, which has given in Welsh the legendary name Lludd. The name Arvalus, which occurs on an inscription at Blackmoorland on Stainmoor, Westmoreland, is most probably the name of a local deity of Brescia, inscribed by a soldier from that region, and there is some doubt, too, as to the British character of Contrebis (identified with Ialonus), though both names are undoubtedly Keltic, found at Lancaster[7] and Overborough[8], inasmuch as Ialonus occurs also on an inscription at Nîmes[9]. The name Contrebis probably means "the god of the joint dwellings," and Ialonus, "the god of the fertile land."

Another Keltic name, found on inscriptions in Britain as well as in Gaul, is that of Condatis ("the joiner together"), identified with Mars, and occurs on an inscription at Piers Bridge, Durham[10] as well as at Chester-le-Street and Allonne, Sarthe, Le Mans. Even when inscriptions were set up in Britain by foreign troops, it must not be too hastily assumed that they paid no deference to local British gods, since the name Mapŏnos, an undoubtedly Keltic name of a British deity, occurs on an inscription[11] found at Ribchester, Durham, for the welfare of

[1] Orelli, 1981.   [2] *C.I.L.* VII. 93[a].   [3] *Ib.* VII. 263[a].   [4] *Ib.* VII. 995.
[5] *Ib.* VII. 997.   [6] *Ib.* VII. 137, 138, 139, 140.   [7] *Ib.* VII. 254.
[8] *Ib.* VII. 290.   [9] *Ib.* XII. 3057 add.   [10] *Ib.* VII. 420.   [11] *Ib.* VII. 218.

Sarmatian troops, and on an inscription[1] found at Ainstable near Armthwaite, Cumberland, erected by Germans, as well as at Hexham, Northumberland[2]. The Geographer of Ravenna[3] mentions a place-name in Britain called Maponi, which was, in full, possibly Maponi fanum. On the Continent the name Maponos occurs only at Bourbonne-les-Bains and Rouen, in both cases as that of a man. The name Mapŏnos meant "the great (or divine) youth," and survived in Welsh legend as that of Mabon. Welsh legend gives his mother's name as Matrŏna (the divine mother), a name identical with that of the original name of the river Marne. In Wales, the name Mabon forms the second element in the place-name Rhiw Fabon (the slope of Mabon), now commonly spelt Ruabon, in Denbighshire. On all the British inscriptions Mapŏnos is identified with Apollo.

It is difficult to be certain whether Mogons, the deity from whom Moguntiacum (Mainz) derives its name, was known to natives of Britain, but the name occurs on inscriptions at Plumptonwall near Old Penrith[4], Netherby[5] and Risingham[6]. In the case of deities of this type the original zone of their worship is not easily discoverable; for example, the name of a god Tullinus occurs on inscriptions at Newington in Kent[7] and Chesterford[8], as well as at Inzino[9] and Heddernheim. There is a similar difficulty in the case of the god Sucellos, whose name occurs on inscriptions at York, Vienne (dep. Isère), Yverdun in Switzerland, Worms, Mainz, and the neighbourhood of Saarburg in Lorraine. It is not impossible that we have here a reference to one of the greater gods of the Keltic pantheon, who was worshipped in Britain as well as in other parts of the Keltic world. It is scarcely possible, again, to doubt the identity with the major Keltic god Teutates of the Toutatis mentioned on inscriptions at Rooky Wood, Hertfordshire[10], Seckau[11] and Rome[12], and of the Tutatis (identified with Cocidius and Mars), mentioned on an inscription at Old Carlisle[13]. It is certain that Cocidius was a British god, and the evidence for the British character of Tutatis appears no less convincing. The name of Cocidius occurs on inscriptions at Lancaster, Old Carlisle, Housesteads, Hardriding, Banksteed near Lanercost Priory, Howgill near Walton, Birdoswald near Bewcastle, Low Wall near Howgill, High Stead between Old Wall and Bleatarn, Old Wall near Carlisle, at a spot between Tarraby and Stanwix, at Netherby, and close to Bewcastle, while it occurs nowhere on the Continent. The name of another deity, Belatucadros, occurs on inscriptions at Whelp Castle near Kirkby Thore in Westmoreland, Brougham Castle, Westmoreland, Plumptonwall near Penrith in Cumberland, Kirkbride in Cumberland, Old Carlisle, Ellenborough, Carvoran, Castlesteads, Scalby

---

[1] *C.I.L.* vii. 332. [2] *Ib.* vii. 1345. [3] 5, 31, p. 436, 20.
[4] *C.I.L.* vii. 320. [5] *Ib.* vii. 958. [6] *Ib.* vii. 996.
[7] *Ib.* vii. 1337, 59. [8] *Ib.* vii. 1337, 60. [9] *Ib.* v. 4914.
[10] *Ib.* vii. 84. [11] *Ib.* iii. 5320. [12] *Ib.* vi. 31182. [13] *Ib.* vii. 335.

Castle, Burgh-by-Sands and Netherby, and its meaning is "brilliant in war." It is remarkable that no inscription in Britain mentions Bĕlĕnos, whose name is found in certain British proper names, such as Cunobelĭnos, the Cymbeline of Shakespeare and the Cynfelyn of the Welsh.

Of inscriptions to grouped goddesses, there are several in Britain dedicated to *Matres*, but only one inscription mentions *Matres Britannae* along with Italian, German and Gaulish "Mothers." The inscription in question[1] is at Winchester. The other grouped goddesses, the Nymphs, that are mentioned on inscriptions, are probably local, and are named on inscribed stones at Great Broughton (*Nymphis et Fontibus*), at Blenkinsop Castle (*Deabus Nymphis*), at Risingham (*Nymphis Venerandis*), and at Nether Croy Farm near Croyhill (*Nymphis*). An inscription dedicated to *Lamiis tribus*, found at Benwell near Newcastle-on-Tyne, also doubtless refers to some local belief. On one inscription found at Chester[2] are the words *Deae Matri*, but unfortunately the inscription is incomplete and we have no further information as to this "Mother-goddess." It is highly probable that the goddess Epona was worshipped in Britain as well as in other parts of the Keltic world, and inscriptions dedicated to her have been found at Carvoran[3], and at Auchindavy near Kirkintulloch[4]. The goddess Brigantia may have been the tribal goddess of the Brigantes, and it is noticeable that her name is identical in form with the Irish Brigit. She is mentioned on an inscription[5], of A.D. 205, at Greetland, and on another inscription[6], at Adel, near Leeds, while, on an inscription[7] in Cumberland, she is called *Dea Nympha Brigantia*. A further inscription[8] of the second century, found at Birrens, near Middleby, reads *Brigantiae sacrum*. An undoubted instance of a local British goddess exists in the case of Sul or Sulis, whence the Roman name Aquae Sulis for Bath, a place whose fame was great, as we learn from Solinus[9], even in Roman times. One inscription found at Bath[10] is of special interest, inasmuch as it refers to the rebuilding of a temple to this goddess. She is further mentioned at Bath on five other inscriptions[11]. There is an inscription dedicated to her at Alzey in Rheinhesse[12], which was probably set up by someone who was grateful to this goddess for restored health. That rivers, too, were worshipped in Britain is attested by the fact that the ancient name of the Mersey or the Ribble was Belīsăma, a name identical with that of a Gaulish goddess. In addition to the foregoing, a goddess Latae or Latis is mentioned on inscriptions at Kirkbampton[13] and Birdoswald[14].

The value of the evidence as to the pre-Christian religion of Britain

[1] *C.I.L.* VII. 5. [2] *Ib.* VII. 168ᵃ. [3] *Ib.* VII. 707.
[4] *Ib.* VII. 1114ᵈ. [5] *Ib.* VII. 200. [6] *Ib.* VII. 203.
[7] *Ib.* VII. 875. [8] *Ib.* VII. 1062. [9] 22, 10. [10] *C.I.L.* VII. 39.
[11] *Ib.* VII. 40, 41, 42, 43, 44. [12] *Ib.* XIII. 6266.
[13] *Ib.* VII. 938. [14] *Ib.* VII. 1348.

and Ireland that is to be obtained from legends and from folk-lore, cannot always be estimated with certainty, but there can be little doubt that many of the characters of both Irish and Welsh legend bear names which once had a religious significance, and that many popular beliefs and customs found in the British Isles go back to pre-Christian times. By the help of Keltic philology several proper names found in legend, such as Mabon and Nudd, to which reference has been made, can be identified with names of deities that occur on inscriptions, or they can be shewn to be similar in formation to certain known types of divine names. For example, -ŏnos and -ŏnā were favourite Keltic terminations for the names of gods and goddesses respectively, and certain Welsh names ending in -on of legendary characters appear from their very structure to have been at one time the names of deities. In addition to Mabon (Mapŏnos) and Modron (Matrŏna), already mentioned, may be adduced Rhiannon (Rēgantŏna), meaning "the divine queen," Teyrnon (Tigernŏnos), "the divine lord," Banon (Banŏna), "the divine lady," Amaethon (Ambactŏnos), "the divine husbandman," Gofannon (Gobannŏnos), "the divine smith." The two latter names suggest the existence among the Kelts of Britain of departmental deities. Certain river-names, too, suggest by their forms that they were of this type, for example, Aeron (Agrŏna), "the goddess of war," Tarannon (Tarannŏnos or Tarannŏna), "the god or goddess of thunder," Ieithon (Iectŏna), "the goddess of speech."

Other legendary names, such as Ler of Irish legend and Llyr of Welsh legend, have meanings which throw light on their original character, for example, "llyr" is used in Welsh poetry for the sea, and there can be little doubt but that the original of both Ler and Llyr was the god of the Irish sea, whose son was the Irish Manannan (the Welsh Manawyddan), the eponymous deity of the Isle of Man. The name Lug, again, of Irish, and Lleu of Welsh legend, is phonetically equivalent to that of Lugus of Gaul, and the meaning of the Welsh word, namely, light, makes it probable that this god had originally some association with the sun or with fire. In Ireland, the legends sometimes speak of certain characters as divine; for example, the goddess Danu or Dana, in the name of the legendary Tuatha Dé Danann (the tribes of the goddess Danu). Similarly, the glossary attributed to Cormac (King-Bishop of Cashel in the ninth century), speaks of the goddess Ana as *mater deorum*, and mentions a goddess Brigit, a poetess and prophetess, worshipped by the poets of ancient Erin. Her father, too, the Dagda, is represented as divine, while her sisters (also called Brigit), were like herself represented as goddesses, the one being patroness of the healing-art, the other of smith-work. There were, also, two Irish war-goddesses, called the Mór-rigu and Bodb Catha. Certain beings belonging to the Tuatha Dé Danann, such as Nuada of the Silver Hand, Ogma, Dian Cecht. Goibniu, Mider and a few others, along with Lug and Ler, appear to have been traditionally raised above the human plane.   Another being who was regarded as divine was the Mac Óc, who was said to have been the son of Dagda the Great and the goddess Boann.

In the lives of the early missionaries of Ireland there are some allusions to the heathenism of the country, and one of the best accounts of this heathenism is to be found in the *Tripartite Life of St Patrick* (trans. by the late Dr Whitley Stokes in *Revue Celtique*, I. p. 260).   This version of St Patrick's life is attributed to St Eleranus of the seventh century.   The passage reads as follows : "Thereafter went Patrick over the water to Mag Slecht, a place wherein was the chief idol of Ireland, to wit, Cenn Cruaich, covered with gold and silver, and twelve other idols about it, covered with brass.   When Patrick saw the idol from the water whose name is Guth-ard (elevated its voice), and when he drew right unto the idol, he raised his hand to put Jesus' crozier upon it, and did not reach it, but it bowed westwards to turn on its right side, for its face was from the south, to wit, to Tara.   And the trace of the crozier abides on its left side still, and yet the crozier moved not from Patrick's hand. And the earth swallowed the twelve other images as far as their heads, and they are thus in sign of the miracle, and he cursed the demon and banished him to hell."   In the *Book of Leinster* (twelfth century) Mag Slecht is said to have been so called because the ancient Irish used to sacrifice there the first-born of their children and of their flocks, in order to secure power and peace in all their tribes, and to obtain milk and corn for the support of their families.   A careful and discriminating study of Keltic legends would reveal no small sediment of pre-Christian thought, just as there are traces of the belief in a "Happy Other-world" and of the rebirth of heroes, in the Irish Voyage of Bran, and non-Christian pictures of another world in the Welsh Annwfn, which a medieval Welsh poem represents as being beneath the earth.   Similarly, the Keltic folk-lore stories of water-bulls, water-horses, water-nymphs, fairies, sprites, and the like give a clue to the way in which Nature was regarded by the Kelts of Britain, as of other lands, before Christianity began its work in these islands.

The contribution of folk-lore research to the study of Keltic Heathendom in Britain is very valuable ; for example, in the account which it gives of such practices as the periodical lighting of bonfires, the customs observed at Lent, May-day, and Harvest time, the vestiges of charms and sacrifices, the observation of omens and the like.   By the use of the comparative method the study of folk-lore may be able to throw not a little light on the significance of the various practices in question.   The evidence from all directions tends to shew that, in Britain and Ireland, as on the Continent, Keltic religion regarded substantially all natural objects as the abodes of divine beings, named and nameless, viewed sometimes collectively and sometimes individually, and it pictured the existence beneath this world of another world, whence many of the blessings of civilisation were derived, and whose inhabitants could enter into various relations, friendly and hostile, with those of this world. There are traces, too, of the conception of local other-worlds, to be found underneath lakes and parts of the sea, while, both in Irish and Welsh legend, there are vestiges of a belief in the blissful conditions of life on certain fabulous islands. In Welsh legend, too, it would appear that the wild country of Northern Britain was regarded as a haunted region. In some Welsh medieval poems there are echoes of a belief that the souls of the departed made their home in the Caledonian forest.

With regard to the priests of Britain and Ireland, we have little direct knowledge, but, though the Irish *drui* may conceivably be a borrowed word from the Gallo-Latin *druida*, it is most probable that it is a native word, and, in any case, the part played by the druids in Irish society as magicians and seers in the legends of Ireland would be their natural part in pre-Christian times. In Welsh society, too, the continuance into fairly recent times of the practice of having recourse to wizards in certain emergencies, points to the antiquity in Welsh life of the institution of the sorcerer. The best description that can be given of Britain and Ireland in the days of their heathendom, is that of countries whose inhabitants could have been seldom free by night or by day from a sense of being haunted, but whose gloom was relieved by visions of happy other-lands, into which the privileged might some day enter. Doubtless, in close conjunction with Keltic heathendom, there was at one time much oral mythology, the fragments of which can now only with difficulty be disentangled from the mass of Keltic medieval and modern folk-lore.

There is one problem upon which no light appears to be available, namely the religious organisation through which was maintained the worship of the major Keltic deities, whose names are found in the British Isles as well as on the Continent, and the distinction, if any, that was made between their worship and that of the minor local deities. All that we know is, from the survival of some of their names, that the tradition of their worship was not entirely lost. At Bath there are remains of a temple dedicated to Sulis, who was identified with Minerva. At Caerwent and Lydney there are also remains of temples, the latter dedicated to a Keltic god, Nodens or Nodons. Near Carrawburgh there was a temple belonging to the British water-goddess Coventina, and at Benwell in a small temple there were found two altars, one to Anociticus and the other to Antenociticus. For an account of these temples the reader is referred to Ward's *Romano-British Buildings and Earthworks* (London, Methuen & Co., 1911).

(C)

GERMANIC HEATHENISM.

Attempts to reconstruct the great edifice of ancient Teutonic religion base themselves on two main sources of information: the Continental and the Scandinavian. English evidence stands midway between the two. With the exception of Tacitus, the Continental writers seldom do more than let fall some chance remark on religious practices, their chief concern being with other matters—in Classical and post-Classical times with the wars of these "barbaric" races, and later, with their conversion to Christianity. We also possess some early laws, and the histories of those tribes fortunate enough to have inspired a medieval chronicler, but the laws date in their present shape from Christian times, and the histories are hardly more sympathetic towards heathen ideas than are the Lives of martyred saints or the edicts of Church Councils. The chief sources from Denmark, Norway and Sweden comprise a great wealth of archaeological information, their early laws, and Saxo's history of the legendary kings of Denmark, written about 1208. It is Iceland which furnishes us with almost all the literary evidence, beginning with the mythological poems of the Older Edda, which can in one sense be termed Icelandic with impunity, in the midst of the conflict as to their origin, since they only reach us from that country. With them may be classed the earlier skaldic poems from the Norwegian court. Then come the Sagas, prose histories of Icelandic families and Norwegian kings, often dealing with events which occurred before the conversion to Christianity about A.D. 1000, but not committed to writing till the twelfth and thirteenth centuries.

Neither source of evidence is perfectly satisfactory. The Scandinavian Sagas, though originating among a people with an extraordinarily keen instinct for historic truth, are far from contemporary with the events they relate. The Continental references to the subject are indeed often contemporary, but they are the observations of alien eyes, and some of them are open to the further objection that the superstitions mentioned may occasionally be mere survivals of the religious legacy of Rome. Fortunately there is more agreement between these two sources than we could have dared to expect, and this common factor in both is the more valuable, since, though one channel of information begins where the other leaves off, they are yet practically independent of one another. While fully admitting that there were extremely wide local divergences in the practices and belief of the various tribes, the following survey of the main features of Germanic heathendom is yet based with some confidence on this common factor, to which a third stratum of evidence, folk-lore, contributes subsidiary testimony. It has seemed best in almost all cases to begin with the fuller, though later, Scandinavian sources, in the light of which it is sometimes possible to interpret the more meagre references of Continental writers.

A problem confronts us at the outset with regard to the position of the two chief gods, Odin and Thor, in Scandinavia. Most of the poetical sources depict Odin as the chief of the gods, as the Allfather of gods and men, while the prose writings contain frequent indications that Thor, the Thunder-god (Anglo-Saxon *Thunor*) stands highest of all in the popular estimation. There can be no doubt that the Sagas are right with regard to their own territory. The frequent occurrence of proper names compounded with Thor (such as Thorolf, Thorstein, etc.) testifies to his importance in Scandinavia, especially as we are told that a name compounded with that of a god was esteemed a safeguard to its bearer. At least one out of every five immigrants to Iceland in heathen times bore a name of which Thor formed part. His is certainly a very ancient cult. His whole equipment is primitive : he is never credited in Scandinavian sources with the possession of a sword, a horse or a coat of mail, but he either walks or drives in a car drawn by goats, and wields the hammer or axe. The sanctity of this symbol appears to date from very remote times : in fact the Museum at Stockholm contains a miniature hammer of amber from the later Stone Age. Another indication of the antiquity of the cult is afforded by Thor's original identity, not only with Jupiter and Zeus, but also with Keltic, Old Prussian and Slavonic thunder-gods. But like these, Thor is much more than a thunder-god. In Scandinavia he is called the Defender of the World, a title which he may have earned in his encounter with the " jötnar." This word usually denotes daemonic beings, but it seems that it may originally have applied to the early non-Aryan inhabitants of Scandinavia, whom the Teutonic settlers drove gradually northwards. We may hazard the conjecture that the Teutonic invasion, which crept forward from the Stone Age till the close of heathen times, was made as it were under the auspices of Thor. He is also the guardian of the land. In Iceland we hear of settlers consecrating their land to Thor, and naming it after him. It is interesting to note that an ancient method of allotting holdings in Sweden was known as the " hammer-partition," while among the Upper Saxons the throwing of a hammer was held to legalise possession of land. But this is probably connected with Thor's guardianship of law and order. The Older Edda represents him as dealing out justice under the great world-ash Yggdrasill. Most of the Scandinavian assemblies began on a Thursday—the day named after Thor—and there seems no doubt that it was he who was invoked under the name of " the almighty god " by those swearing oaths at the Icelandic *Things*. The Russian historian Nestor, of the eleventh century, records that the Scandinavians from Kiev ratified a treaty with the Byzantines by swearing by their god "Perun," the Slavonic Thor. The Frisians attributed their laws to a supernatural being with an axe. Among the Upper Saxons a hammer was the summons to the assembly. In later times in Iceland a small object called "St Olaf's axe" served this purpose. It is likely that this "axe" was originally a "Thor's hammer," for by the irony of fate, many of the attributes of his old enemy Thor attached themselves in popular belief to the sainted king Olaf, who rooted out his worship in Norway. An Icelandic settler invokes him in sea-voyages, and Adam of Bremen states that the Swedes sacrifice to him in famine and in pestilence. As regards disease, we have the further testimony of an Old Norse charm found in an Anglo-Saxon manuscript, which appears to call on Thor to drive away an ailment, and it was until recently a common Swedish practice to mix in the fodder of cattle powder ground from the edge of a "Thor's hammer" or flint axe, to avert disease. It is possible that the miniature T-shaped hammers, often of silver or gold, of which over fifty are to be seen in the Scandinavian museums, were worn to shield the wearer from disease, but the protective functions of Thor were so numerous that the symbols may have served other purposes as well. It has recently been recorded that Manx and Whitby fishermen wear the T-shaped bone from the tongue of a sheep to protect them from drowning; and slaughterers at Berlin wear the same bone suspended from their necks[1]. The appearance of the bearded Thor himself, hammer and all, on a baptismal font in Sweden, has been considered to prove that the hammer was used at the heathen ceremony of naming a child, and we have some ground for supposing that it figured at weddings and at funerals.

Sacrifices to Thor are constantly mentioned, and range from the daily offerings of the Goth Radagaisus in Italy at the beginning of the fifth century to a song in his honour composed in the year 1006 by one of an Icelandic crew starving off the coast of America. It seems probable that the sacrifice at the beginning of all *Things* was to Thor. At one place of assembly in Iceland we hear of a "stone of Thor" on which "men were broken," but human sacrifice is so rarely mentioned in Iceland that the statement is looked upon with suspicion. We must note that Tacitus fails to mention a Germanic Jupiter. It has been suggested that he represents Thor by Hercules.

After the enumeration of the manifold activities of Thor, there seems hardly room for the imposing figure of Odin, and indeed in Scandinavia, besides being the Lord of Valhöll, Odin only presides over war, poetry and magic. Yet in one point he stands nearer to the race of men than Thor, in that he is regarded as the ancestor of most of the royal families of Denmark and of England (where the form of the name is Wodan). It is perhaps hardly correct to speak of Thor and Odin

[1] A. C. Haddon, *Magic and Fetishism*, London, 1906.

as ruling over different social spheres, for Thor numbers earls and
others of high degree among his worshippers, but persons of royal
blood and their followers seem to devote themselves to the worship of
Odin—the cult of a royal ancestor. Nomenclature affords interesting
testimony to some such social division. We have seen what a large
proportion of Norwegian proper names contained " Thor " as a component part, but we do not find any of these borne by a single
Norwegian, Swedish, Danish or English king. Not even among the petty
kings of the period preceding the unification of Norway under King
Harold Fairhair do such names occur. Now we are told that it was just
these petty, often landless, kings who with their followings practised
war as a profession, and it was certainly in Norwegian court circles that
skaldic poetry—an art attributed to Odin—took its origin. If the
position of Odin was at all similar on the Continent, it would be easy
to explain the prominence of this god in all Continental accounts from
Tacitus onwards, for it seems probable that there also each king or prince
was surrounded by a body of warriors devoted to his service, and that
these took the principal part in wars.

In Iceland there is no mention of Odin-worship, though there is one
instance of the " old custom " of throwing a spear over a hostile force, a
rite which originally devoted the enemy to Odin. The existence of the cult
in Norway is vouched for by the custom of drinking a toast consecrated
to him at sacrificial feasts, but we must note that a toast to Odin is only
mentioned at courts. In Sweden, however, Odin is more prominent.
There is a statue of him " like Mars " by the side of Thor in the great
Upsala temple, and the people are said to sacrifice to him in time of war.
A legendary king sacrifices his nine sons to him for long life for himself
—a gift which another story shews it to be within Odin's power to
bestow, if he receives other lives in exchange. It is generally agreed
that he was originally a god of the dead, before he became a god of war,
and it is in the guise of a soul-stealing daemon that he seems to
appear in folk-lore. For Denmark the tales of heroes under Odin's
protection, and the importance of the god in Saxo's stories (where he
sometimes appears himself to demand his victim), form a considerable
body of evidence. Of the Frisians we are told by Alcuin that the island
Walcheren was sacred to a god whom later accounts identify with Mercury.
Mercury is the name under which Odin appears in Tacitus and all Continental writers, and shews that the god must there have borne much the
same character as is ascribed to him in Scandinavian sources, where he is
described as shifty, and full of guile, skilled in magic and runes, and the
inventor of poetry. To judge from the evidence of place-names, his
cult extended as far south as Salzburg. It is also noteworthy that the
Scandinavian account of his equipment, armed only with a javelin,
corresponds to that of the Germans in the time of Tacitus.

An ancient form of sacrifice to Odin in Scandinavia is the gruesome "cutting of the blood-eagle" or removal of the lungs of the victim, of which we hear once or twice, but there seems ground for believing that the usual ritual frequently combined both hanging and stabbing. In fact all those who fell in battle were regarded as sacrifices to Odin. Tacitus tells us that on the eve of the battle between the Chatti and Hermunduri each side dedicated their opponent's army to Mars and to Mercury. By this vow both horses and men, in short everything on the side of the conquered, was given up to destruction. After their victory over the Romans at Arausio (B.C. 105) the Cimbrians hung all their captives and destroyed their spoil. The complete destruction of the legions of Varus, and the total massacre of Britons after an Anglo-Saxon victory, have been suggested as other instances of the same wholesale sacrifice. In some places in Denmark immense masses of heaped up spoil, mostly intentionally damaged, from the fourth century A.D., have been found. These must have been offered as a sacrifice after victory, and have lain undisturbed on the battle-ground owing to a stringent tabu. A dedication of whole armies to Odin is mentioned in later Scandinavian Sagas, where it seems to be connected with the idea that the god needs more warriors in Valhöll.

While Odin and Thor, however inimical to each other they may be, are both regarded as Æsir (gods) in the mythology of the north—in fact Thor is made Odin's son—we are told that Frey and his father Njörd were originally hostages from the "Vanir," a rival race. Certainly their functions in historical times are very different from those of Thor and Odin. Frey, whose name is derived from a word meaning "lord," is only known in Scandinavia. He is a god of fertility, with the usual attributes of such a deity. He is especially honoured by the Swedes, and Adam of Bremen tells us that his statue stood by the side of Thor in the temple of Upsala, that sacrifices are made to him at weddings, and that he grants men peace and pleasure. Tacitus' account of the peaceful, wealth-loving "Suiones" (Swedes) closely corresponds to what we should expect of a nation whose chief god was Frey, and places beyond question the old-established nature of a cult of this kind. In Norway we hear of toasts drunk to Frey and his father Njörd "for prosperity and peace," and a sacrificial feast at the beginning of winter, to secure the same benefits, is associated with Frey in Iceland, where he and Njörd are invoked in legal oaths. A legendary saga relates that Frey, in the company of a priestess who was regarded as his wife, was in the habit of peregrinating the country round Upsala in the autumn, for the purpose of causing plenty. This is the clue which leads us to detect traces of an allied cult on the Continent. The goddess Nerthus, who is worshipped according to Tacitus by seven tribes, apparently in Zeeland (possibly at Naerum, older *Niartharum*), journeys round her island at certain seasons in a covered vehicle. During this time peace prevails, and her presence is celebrated by festivities. The ritual of lustration described by Tacitus is generally regarded as a rain-charm. From the similarity of this cult to that of goddesses of fertility all over Europe, we may assume that Nerthus, like Frey, partook of this character. Amongst other Teutonic races the earliest parallel to her peregrinations is recorded by the Byzantine historian Sozomen, in the fifth century, who states that the Goths lead round a statue in a covered vehicle. From the ninth century we have the item: "concerning the images which they carry about the fields," in a list of prohibited superstitions. But ample evidence for these practices is afforded by the ceremonies, common up to twenty years ago, connected with Plough Monday in England and with Frau Holle in Germany.

It is to be noted that the names Nerthus and Njörd are identical in all but gender, and it seems that in Scandinavia Nerthus has changed her sex and has subsequently been partly ousted by Frey; Njörd, however, still rules over fishery and wealth—two very closely allied ideas among the Norwegians, to whom a sea teeming with fish was quite as important as the fertility of the land. It is just possible that it is Njörd to whom a ninth century Latin poem refers, under the name of Neptune, as a chief god of the Normans. Frey seems also to have partially ousted his sister Freyja. One of the Edda poems is concerned with a certain Ottar, who sacrifices oxen to Freyja, and whom she on one occasion declares to be her husband —a parallel case to that of Frey and the priestess mentioned above, but with the sexes reversed.

Of the numerous other gods mentioned in our sources some may be either tribal deities, or better-known gods under other names. Such are the Frisian god Fosite: the twins whom Tacitus equates with Castor and Pollux, and who are worshipped by the Nahanarvali: the god Saxnot, or Saxneat, forsworn with Wodan and Thunor in an Old Saxon formula for converts, and claimed as an ancestor by the English East Saxon royal family. Other gods, such as Balder and Loki, of whom we only hear in Scandinavia, have been occasionally regarded as mere mythological figureheads. Of the evil-disposed Loki there is indeed no trace of any sort of cult. It has been suggested that he was a Finnish god. Balder is the subject of much controversy, some scholars dismissing him from the rank of deity altogether, while Dr Frazer maintains that the story is a survival of tree worship, and of the ritual sacrifice of the god. In any case the only reference to an actual cult of Balder occurs in a late and doubtful saga. Tyr, who seems to have been a war-god, stands in a different category. It is likely that he had once been an important deity all over Teutonic Europe, though his cult was already overshadowed by that of Odin at the dawn of historical times. Some modern authorities place his cult in close connexion with that of Nerthus—for which view certain local groups of place-names afford support—and regard him as being originally a god of the sky. A reference by Procopius to Ares, in his account of the inhabitants of Thule, and by Jornandes to Mars, both of the sixth century, and both in connexion with human sacrifice, are usually held to indicate Tyr, as is also the important god Mars of Tacitus. The identity of Mars and Tyr is established by glossaries which equate Mars with "Tiw," "Tiig," as in Tuesday. In Scandinavia the word *Tyr* originally means "god," and in compounds is applied to Odin.

There is evidence that Frigg, in Northern mythology Odin's wife, was also widely known among Teutonic nations, but she seems in part to have been ousted from her place by Freyja, and in part to have suffered that general decline which must have overtaken the Germanic goddesses since the time of Tacitus, in whose day female divinities appear to have been in the ascendancy—we think of his Veleda, Isis, Ausinia, Nerthus. It is noteworthy that Bede knows of several important goddesses in England, though all other trace of them has vanished.

One class of female divinities however still held a place in Scandinavian belief at least. It seems likely that the term *dísir*—"(supernatural) female beings"—covered both the valkyries and the norns. The valkyries in the North were Odin's handmaidens in war, and some trace of such beings survives in Anglo-Saxon glossaries, where *wælcyrge* is used to translate "Bellona," "Gorgon," etc., though in the laws the word is merely equivalent to "sorceress." The norns seem to have been hereditary tutelary spirits: they are thought of as causing good or evil fortune to their owner, and appear in dreams to him, frequently in threes, to warn him of impending danger. When there is only one attendant spirit she is called *hamingja*, or "Luck." Such a being appears to the dying Hallfred the Unlucky Poet, and to her the Saga-writer evidently ascribes the ill-luck first of Hallfred and later of his son. It seems possible to discern an original distinction between these beings and the *fylgja* or "associate," which appears as a mere materialisation, as it were, in animal form, of the chief characteristic of its owner;—his soul, perhaps, though it is not the immortal part of him, as it dies on his death. It is probably closely connected with the werewolf beliefs, and that the conception was common to all Teutonic races is indicated by the Song of Roland, which makes Charles the Great dream before Roncesvalles of a fight between a bear and a leopard. The *dísir* are however too capricious to be called guardian spirits. Those of one family, provoked at the coming change of faith, are credited with having killed one of its representatives. We see the reasonableness of the attitude taken up by a would-be convert, who stipulates that the missionary shall guarantee him the mighty archangel Michael as his "attendant angel" (*fylgju-engill*).

All the three sacrifices to *dísir* on record occur in the autumn, and of one it is stated that it took place at night. It is noteworthy that the term *disa-thing* is used as late as 1322 to denote a festival at Upsala. A "*dísar*-hall" appears to be an old name for a temple. From Germany we have a charm which seems rather to invoke the aid of friendly valkyries, *idisi*, than of tutelary spirits, but we find many references to a personified " Luck," the " Fru Sælde," in medieval German poems, and we are told of a poor knight accosted by a gigantic being who declares itself to be his " ill-luck." He shuts it up in a hollow tree and enjoys good fortune ever after.

Northern mythology preserves a memory of three Norns who rule men's destinies, like the Parcae of the Romans, but the words used for Fate—Anglo-Saxon *Wyrd*, Old German *Wurth*, " Weird," literally " that which happens," Old Norse *sköp* or *örlög*, "things shaped" or "laid down of yore"—shew that Fate was not personified, was rather thought of as a force shaping the destinies of the world to unknown ends. It was a mystery ever present to the consciousness of the heathen Germanic races, and their deepest religious conceptions centre round it. The old Greek idea, that a man might unwittingly be forced by a retributive Fate to shameful deeds, never haunted the Northern races, who would have claimed for mankind the completest moral freedom, but in the physical world the decree of Fate was beyond appeal. A man might defy Odin, and even fall upon him with mortal weapons, and gain only a keener tribute of admiration from posterity, but after he had striven to the utmost against all odds, his world required of him that he should accept the ruling of Fate without bitterness, and even, if we read the old tales rightly, with a certain dim recognition of vaster issues at stake than his own death and defeat.

Of ancestor-worship or worship of the dead there are clear traces both in Scandinavia and on the Continent. From Scandinavia we hear how when the god Frey died the Swedes would not burn his body, lest he should leave them, so they buried him in a barrow and sacrificed to him ever after. The case of the quite historical Swedish king Erik, of the ninth century, whom the gods themselves raised to their rank shortly after his death, may also be quoted. Again, a somewhat legendary king Olaf who flourished in South Norway in the first half of the ninth century, is made to say before his death that in his case he does not want people to act as they sometimes do, to sacrifice to dead men in whom they trusted while alive. But after he was buried at Geirstad there was a famine, so they sacrificed to Olaf for plenty and called him the " elf" (*álfr*) of Geirstad. And there was competition for the corpse of the contemporary king Halfdan the Black among the four chief districts of his kingdom : " it was thought that there was a prospect of plenty for whichever got it," and the matter was only settled by dividing the remains into four parts. So much for kings. But ordinary mortals could also enjoy worship after death. An Icelandic source tells us of one Grim, the first settler in the Faroe Islands, who had sacrifices made to him after death. It was the custom at sacrificial feasts to drink to one's dead kinsmen, those who had been buried in barrows. Such toasts are called *minni*, and are paralleled on the Continent by the "drinking to the soul of the dead"

CH. XV. (C)

forbidden by a ninth century Church capitulary. But there is more definite evidence than this. The Norwegian laws expressly forbid worship at barrows, a custom remembered by the saga of the island of Gotland, and Charles the Great forbids burial in them. Almost every Capitulary and Church Council in Germany (though not in England) forbids sacrilege at sepulchres, "laying food and wine on the tumuli of the dead," or partaking of food offered at such places. Among the Saxons, and probably among other tribes, the festival for the dead was celebrated in the autumn. At the beginning of the fifth century the poet Claudian speaks of worship of ancestors among the Getae.

In Iceland some families are said to have believed that after death they entered into a hill, which they accordingly worshipped. In this connexion "elf" is again used, and it seems reasonable to assume that whatever other signification this word may have had later, it must also have meant the spirit of a dead man. Now in Sweden the cult of the forgotten dead may be said to live on to this day, for the peasants still place offerings in the saucer-shaped depressions on some megalithic graves, and here, in heathen times, we find mention of sacrifice to elves, not at a festive gathering, but offered by each household within its own four walls. It took place in the late evening or night, a circumstance which strongly reminds us of Greek sacrifices to "heroes."

There is yet another class of Scandinavian deities, who may be classed as chthonic. These are the *landvættir*, guardian spirits of the land. That they were highly esteemed is evident from the beginning of the Icelandic heathen laws, which enacted that no ship was to approach land with a figure-head on its prow, lest the "landvættir" should be alarmed thereat. In Saxo men are warned not to provoke the guardian gods of a certain place, and that it was perilous to do so transpires from the fear with which a certain spot in Iceland was regarded "because of the landvættir," since a murder had been committed there. The nearest approach to worship of these beings appears in a curious story of the Icelander Egill in Norway, in the year 934. He sets up a horse's head on a stake (a common insult to an enemy) and utters what appears to be a formula: "I turn this mark of contumely against the *landvættir* who inhabit this land, that all of them may go astray: none find nor happen upon her home, till they have driven King Erik and Gunnhild out of the land." It has been suggested that the "Matronae" or "Matres" with German names, monuments to whom were erected by German soldiers in the service of Rome, were guardian spirits of their native land. Northern mythology tells us further of a female daemon of the sea, Rán, who claims the drowned. We know of no direct sacrifices to her, but there are traces of prophylactic sacrifice to some daemonic being of the sea. The Frisians sacrificed human victims before expeditions by sea, as did also the Normans, according to Dudo, though he attributes the sacrifice to Thor. In Norway there are references to the placing of a human victim on the rollers of a ship about to be launched.

Of inanimate objects of worship, besides sacred groves, which will be discussed later, there are sacred springs. Close to the temple at Upsala was a sacred spring, in which we are told that human victims were drowned, and the story should not be too hastily dismissed, since sacred springs are found within the precincts of many old churches all over Germany and England. The occasional practice of Germanic tribes, mentioned by Classical authors, of throwing conquered enemies and valuables into rivers, was probably a recognised form of worship of some god— possibly of Odin. From the frequency of holy springs, wells, and lakes, bearing names compounded with Ás (heathen god), Thor, or Odin, we may assume that they were sometimes sacred to the greater gods, as were probably the sacred salt springs mentioned by Tacitus. On the other hand, Procopius in the sixth century says that the Scandinavians worship, besides other gods, minor spirits in the waters of springs and rivers. Knut's Laws in England, and Church Edicts on the Continent, refer to the worship of rivers and water-wells, and further mention the worship of stones, also known in Scandinavia.

Having now passed in review, however briefly, the chief objects of worship among the Germanic races, it behoves us to consider the manner of that worship. In the North there were three main sacrificial festivals. One, in the autumn, is said to have been "for peace and plenty," the second, at Yule, "for growth," the third, at the approach of summer, was for victory. On the Continent the autumn festival and that at midwinter appear, as in Scandinavia, to have been the most important. We hear very little of a midsummer festival, but its existence is vouched for by the widespread festivities in all Teutonic countries on that day. In Denmark and Sweden special festivals appear to have taken place at Lejre and Upsala respectively every nine years, at which a great number of animals and even men were sacrificed.

The ritual of sacrifice is mainly known to us from the North. The officiating priest fills the sacrificial bowl and reddens the altar with the blood of the victim, scattering some of its contents over the worshippers and the walls of the temple by means of sacrificial twigs. The blood is in fact offered to the gods, or cements a bond between them and the worshippers: the flesh is cooked and eaten. In Scandinavia horses were much valued as sacrifices, so that to eat horse-flesh was regarded as a heathen practice, and Tacitus also knows of sacrifice of horses. Excavations of Icelandic temples, however, reveal a preponderance of the bones of other domestic animals. In England and on the Continent cattle were frequent offerings. Gregory the Great decided to allow the English to eat oxen *ad laudem Dei,* just outside their churches, since they had been accustomed to sacrificing them " to demons." Human sacrifice seems to have persisted in Sweden till quite a late period. In 1026 a little party of Norwegians declared that they narrowly escaped being utilised for that purpose on an expedition to Sweden; and the Saga of the island of Gotland remembers the custom. On the Continent, too, human sacrifice seems to have continued as long as heathenism, and we even hear of an outburst of it among the converted Franks. In Friesland human beings seem frequently to have been sacrificed by drowning. Except perhaps in the last-named country, the victims were almost invariably prisoners taken in war, slaves, or outlaws.

If the sacrifice was a public one—and probably in any case—it was followed by a feast, which lasted till the ale gave out, and no longer. A Norwegian archbishop reveals the importance of the ale even at Christian festivals when he finds it necessary to ordain that a wedding can yet be held, even though there be nothing but whey to celebrate it with, and other Norwegian ecclesiastical ordinances enact that every farmer shall brew so much ale in preparation for the various Church festivals. The drinking itself began with sacrifice in the form of toasts drunk to the gods, and this seems also to have been the case in Germany, for we hear of " drinking wine for the love of the devil." Jonas of Bobbio relates how he found a party of men sitting round an immense vessel of ale, who described themselves as worshipping Wodan. We also hear of an individual in a temple " opima libamina exhibens usque ad vomitum cibo potuque replebatur." Centuries earlier, Tacitus tells us that when the Romans surprised the Germans at a religious festival they cut down an intoxicated foe. It seems that songs and dances were common at such times, and we hear of the wearing of animal masks at Yule and at funeral and memorial feasts[1]. Several other Scandinavian festivals are worthy of notice, such as the " greeting ale " and the " ale of departure." Even when a Norwegian chief is about to flee from the swift vengeance of Harold Fairhair, the " departure ale " has yet to be brewed. Still clearer traces of sacrifice are discernible in the feast, for which the Norwegian laws stipulate, on the occasion of granting rights in the family to an illegitimate son, and also in that made by a slave on his liberation.

During the course of the great Scandinavian festivals, as well as at other times, it appears to have been the custom for private individuals to offer sacrifice for the purpose of propitiation or of learning their future. The means employed in this latter case seem sometimes to have been the sanctified twigs mentioned above. Tacitus knows of divination by twigs and also mentions various other forms of augury. In Friesland the casting of lots seems to have played a particularly important part, and was employed to select men for sacrifices.

We have already had occasion to refer to officiating priests. The

---

[1] Even after the Reformation a Danish bishop finds it necessary to combat the deep-rooted popular belief, that the more the guests drank at a funeral, the better the dead man fared in the other world; and a French traveller says that at such feasts the Danes drink to the souls of the dead, *ce qui leur fait grand bien.*

term, though permissible, is somewhat misleading, as the existence of a special class or caste of priests in Scandinavia is much disputed, and there seems to be considerable divergence on this point among the various Germanic races at different times. In Iceland any leading settler who built or came into possession of a temple officiated in it himself, and was called a *goði* (pl. *goðar*), the connexion of which with *goð* (god) suggests that the priestly function was older than the temporal authority. In Norway the balance of probability seems to lie with the theory that the earls and local chiefs (*hersar*), and probably also the petty kings, each administered the chief temple of his district, perhaps with a *goði* or *gyðja*, priestess (probably of his own family), to help him. In Sweden, where worship was more centralised and systematised, there is some slight evidence for the existence of *goðar*, but it is clear that the king was the high-priest of the people. It is recorded from prehistoric times that when one of their kings failed to sacrifice the people attributed to him a famine which ensued, and sacrificed him " for plenty." As late as the eleventh century they expelled their Christian king for refusal to sacrifice, and the idea of the king's responsibility for bad weather, for instance, can be traced as late as the reign of Gustavus Vasa.

This idea of royal responsibility for national misfortunes is paralleled among the Burgundians in the fourth century. For Denmark the only evidence is the occurrence of the word *goði* on two Runic stones of about the ninth and tenth centuries. In England there must have been a more specialised priestly caste, with disabilities unknown to the Norwegians, for Bede tells us that heathen priests might not bear arms. For the Continent we have extremely little evidence. An Old German glossary translates *cotinc* (formed from *cot*, god), not by *presbyter* but by *tribunus*, and on the other hand the Old German *êwart*, " guardian of law," and the Frisian and Low German *asega, eosega*, " law-sayer," are used to denote "priest"; so we may perhaps assume that the functions of priest were not very highly specialised at the close of heathendom. Tacitus knows of a regular priesthood, whose only administrative function consists in opening public assemblies (probably with a sacrifice, as in Iceland) and in playing some part in their procedure. We hear occasionally of a chief-priest, as among the Northumbrians, and among the Burgundians. Among the latter he was called *sinistus*, and it is worth noting that *sinistans* is the word chosen by Ulfilas for "elders."

Priestesses are rarely mentioned in the North, though they seem to have been common among the Germans of Tacitus' time.

The well-known statement of Tacitus, that the Germani do not confine their gods within walls, but dedicate groves and trees to them, does not seem to have been of universal application even in his own day. But it is quite certain that he is right in the main with regard to the prevalence of grove- and tree-sanctuaries. The frequent occurrence of such place-names as the German Heiligenloh, Heiligenforst, and the

Scandinavian Lund (the latter often compounded with the names of Odin, Thor and Frey) would alone suffice to prove the earlier existence of groves, " grim with ancient religious rites," as Claudian describes them. Of sacred trees, perhaps the most famous was the *robor Jovis* in Hesse. An interesting old Scandinavian proverb, recorded in Iceland, may be quoted here: " One must worship an oak, if one is to live under it." After the erection of a temple the sacred tree may have lived on beside it, and indeed probably conditioned the form of the temple itself. The Icelandic temple, as we know from recent excavations, consisted of a hall, like the hall of the ordinary dwelling-house, and at its further end a smaller building, with slightly rounded corners, which was the real sanctuary, with the altar in the middle and the images of the gods, generally three in number, standing round it. The outer hall, with its sacred pillars and its row of fires down the middle, is thought to have been a later addition for the convenience of worshippers, but the form of the inner building is considered to shew descent from the tree-sanctuary. It has been suggested that the round churches, only found on Germanic territory, are the lineal descendants of the heathen temple, and hence of the tree-sanctuary.

Besides the images, the inner temple contained the sacrificial bowl and twigs, and the sacred ring which the priest wore on his arm at all assemblies, and on which oaths were sworn. Both temple and images appear to have been very highly decorated, sometimes even with gold and silver.

Two other types of sanctuary deserve mention. On the Continent we hear of pillars, apparently called *Irminsûl* (translated *universalis columna*), which may well have been a side-development from the tree-sanctuary. Charles the Great destroyed the most famous of these, in Westphalia. The northern *hörg* is frequently assumed to have been a stone altar or " high place." But the Norwegian laws speak of " making a house and calling it a *hörg*." It is only mentioned in connexion with female deities, or with Njörd, but the occurrence of " Thorsharg" and " Odinsharg" as place-names in Sweden renders it doubtful whether it could have been limited to the use of female (or originally female) deities, at any rate in Sweden. The cognate Old German *haruc* is sometimes translated *lucus* or *nemus*, sometimes only by the vague *fanum*; while the Anglo-Saxon *hearg* seems to be a comprehensive term for any kind of sanctuary, almost corresponding to the Scandinavian *vé*, though this includes *Things*.

In Scandinavia the violater of any sanctuary is called " wolf in holy places," and becomes an outlaw in his own land, though we note that he may be well received in other Scandinavian countries. In Friesland those who broke into a temple to rob it were sacrificed to the god whom they had offended. It is difficult to say how far, on the other hand, the sanctuaries offered a refuge to accused persons and criminals. The abuse

of the right of asylum in medieval churches—many of them only transformed temples—suggests that this was a prominent characteristic of
heathen temples. On the other hand we learn from an Icelandic Saga
that the god Frey would not tolerate the presence of an outlaw even in
the neighbourhood of his temple.

It will now be convenient to consider the funeral customs of the
Teutonic races. Excavations in Scandinavia as well as literary records shew
that towards the close of heathen times the great majority of the dead
were interred in barrows, often in their ships, with some of their valuables,
and occasionally with horses, dogs and other animals. Slaves sometimes
accompany their master or mistress. Leo Diaconus informs us that in
the tenth century the Swedes in the Byzantine Empire used to kill their
captives and burn their bodies with those of their own slain, apparently
with the idea of providing their friends with servants in the next world.
The practice of suttee was not unknown, though very rare. In some
cases everything found in the barrow has been burnt, but inhumation is
the commoner practice. It is noteworthy that weapons are rarely found
in the period preceding about A.D. 500, while after that time, in the
Viking Age, weapons form the most important part of the goods placed
in the grave. It is sometimes shewn in our sources that all these objects,
including the ship, or occasionally a chariot, are provided with the
intention of supplying the dead with what they will need in the next
world, or with the means of getting there.

Besides a few indications of a belief in rebirth, there are no less than
three forms of life after death in Scandinavian belief alone. We will
begin with the most famous, Valhöll (the hall of the slain), where those
who fell in battle feasted and fought into eternity. But when we come
to apply the commonly accepted theory that all those slain in fight passed
into Valhöll, we find it impossible to make it fit the facts as reported to
us. A number of the Edda poems seem to know nothing about Valhöll,
and despatch their mightiest warriors to the dreary abode of Hel, and
the same treatment is frequently meted out in the sagas. The likeliest
explanation seems to be that Valhöll was intimately bound up with the
cult of Odin, which, as we have seen, probably entered into the lives of
a comparatively small class, and was very recent in the North. The
influence of the cult may perhaps be traced in the sudden appearance
of weapons in graves about the fifth century. The great historical
importance of the Valhöll idea lies in the stimulus it gave to desperate
courage in battle. The influence of a similar belief [1] among the Japanese
of our own day was evident in their war with Russia. It was no doubt
belief in some such palace of the dead, only to be reached by those
who died of wounds, which induced the aged among the Heruli to accept
a voluntary death inflicted by stabbing, and it has been shewn that the
formal "marking" of a dying man, mentioned two or three times in

---

[1] Lafcadio Hearn, *Japan, an Interpretation*, p. 507.

the North, is probably a substitute for the older custom of the Heruli in the fifth or sixth century.

Hel answers to the Greek Hades, a shadowy region of which we hear very little in the Sagas, where the word *hel* does indeed frequently occur, but usually merely with the signification of "death."

We have already seen that the conception of a future life spent by the ghost in or near its burial-place was by far the commonest, not only in Scandinavia, but all over Germanic territory. It would not be surprising to find that this, evidently the oldest belief about the dead, was connected with the faith of Thor, and some testimony to that effect is afforded by the inscriptions on a Runic grave-monument in Denmark: "May Thor consecrate these mounds," or in two other cases "these runes." In Sweden we find an inscription which has been translated "Thor give peace." The sign of the hammer occurs on several other monuments, no doubt with a similar force. With regard to the variant of this belief, the "dying into mountains," all the evidence seems to connect it with Thor. In two cases out of the four on record we are explicitly informed that the persons "believed in Thor." In the third case, that of the kinsmen of one Aud, we know no further detail of their religion except in the case of Aud's brother, of whom it is stated that " he believed in Christ, but invoked Thor in voyages and difficulties, and whenever he thought it mattered most."

It is clearly this belief in the continued presence of the dead which caused the widespread worship of them already discussed, and it is this belief, too, which has peopled all Germanic territory with ghosts, whether malignant trolls, slayers of the living, or friendly spirits.

Like all other religions, that of the Germanic peoples was a mass of mixed elements, a jumble of many different stages of culture. Primitive magical rites were no doubt freely practised, and in view of the age-long survival of such rites in rustic festivals and rustic faith, it would be the greatest mistake to belittle their importance in earlier Germanic life. But our sources refer to them so little that we are justified in suspecting the mass of these practices to be already declining into the observances of popular superstition, with possibly nearly as little conscious religious significance as to-day.

There were still traces of an early grim idea of placation by sacrifice: the god of the dead, or the daemonic being who inhabits the sea, demands a human life, and one must be offered that others may be safe. But except for a few legendary instances, we see that the Germanic peoples have progressed so far in corporate sense that the community only offers the lives of those outside its pale—outlaws or captives to whom it knows no obligations. Only in Friesland is there any definite evidence that members of the community were immolated.

But the prevalent idea of sacrifice is a more comfortable one. Gifts are made to the gods, who requite them with favours, an idea which reflects the manners of the time, with its system of gifts and counter-gifts, and which shews that the gods were thought of as recognising a social bond linking them to their worshippers.

The cult of the dead reveals a sense rather of piety than of fear, for we never find that the Scandinavians, at any rate, sank to the placation of evil ghosts by sacrifice. They adopt other, somewhat matter-of-fact precautions against them, such as taking the corpse out through a hole in the wall of the house, burning and scattering the ashes, or decapitating the ghost, though perhaps there never was a prototype in heathen times of the delightfully ironic scene in one of the Icelandic sagas, where the living, ousted from the fireside by the dead, hold a court of law over them and banish them by the verdict of a jury.

On the whole, we are left with the impression that Germanic heathendom was as far from being a religion of dread as it was from the formalism, impregnated with magical ideas, which pervaded the religious system of the Romans. Though the gods could be angry and cause famine and plague and defeat, they were at any rate occasionally the objects of real trust and affection, and their acknowledged favouritism is not imputed to them as injustice. Only near the end of the heathen period do we find any repugnance to the idea of allegiance to non-moral gods.

Perhaps the finest flower of Germanic heathendom should be sought in the period just before its extinction—in the Viking Age, so often accused of godlessness. In the conception of Ragnarök, which fired the imagination of the North, we find the idea of fellowship with the gods: fellowship, not in feasting and victory, but in stress and storm. For the gods too are in the hands of Destiny, of a Fate ever moving towards the end of the world, when they and the armies of the valiant dead together make a vain stand against the race of daemonic beings, monstrous shapes of disorder and destruction, loosed in the shattering of the earth which precedes that Titanic struggle. The great bequests of the heathen Germanic peoples to the new order, their courage, and their ideal of loyalty to a leader, find their highest expression in this vision of preordained defeat.

CHAPTER XVI (A).

THE CONVERSION OF THE KELTS.

(1) ROMAN BRITAIN.

By the British Church is meant the Christian Church which existed in England and Wales, before the foundation of the English Church by Augustine of Canterbury, and after that event to a limited extent in Cornwall, Wales, Cumbria, and Strathclyde.

How, when, where, and by whom was it founded? To these questions no answer is forthcoming. The legends connecting various Apostles, and other scriptural personages, especially Joseph of Arimathaea, with Britain may be dismissed at once. They first appear in very late writings, and have no historical foundations.

We next come to a story which has obtained some considerable credence because it is found in the pages of Bede. It is to the effect that in the year A.D. 156 a British king named Lucius (Lles ap Coel) appealed to Pope Eleutherus to be instructed in the Christian religion, that the application was granted, and that the king and nation were then converted to Christianity. The story first appears in a sixth century recension of the *Liber Pontificalis* at Rome, whence Bede must have borrowed it. It was unknown to the British historian Gildas, and it has no other support. Bede's version of it involves chronological errors, and Professor Harnack has recently driven the last nail into its coffin by his brilliant suggestion or discovery that Lucius was not a British king at all, but king of Birtha (confused with Britannia) in Edessa, a Mesopotamian realm whose sovereign was Lucius Aelius Septimus Megas Abgarus IX[1].

But there is indirect and outside evidence that Christianity had penetrated Britain at the end of the second century. The evidence is patristic in its source, and general in its character. Tertullian writing *c.* 208 speaks of places in Britain inaccessible to the Romans, yet subject to Christ; and Origen writing about thirty years later refers in two passages to the British people having come under the influence of Christianity. But how did they so come? In the absence of precise information, the most probable supposition is that Christianity came through Gaul, between which country and Britain commercial intercourse

[1] *E H. R.* xxii. pp. 767-70.

was active.   There may also have been individual Christians among the
Roman soldiers who were then stationed in Britain.   In fact the almost
universally Latin, or at least non-Keltic names of such British martyrs,
bishops, etc. as have been preserved point to a preponderating Roman
rather than Keltic element in the British Church; though against this
it must also be remembered that, as in the cases of Patricius and
Pelagius, the names known to us may be assumed Christian names
superseding some earlier Keltic names, of which in most cases no record
has come down.   Possibly the British Church consisted at first of
converts to Christianity among the Roman invaders, and of such natives
as came into immediate contact with them, and the native element only
gradually gained ground when the Roman troops were withdrawn.

The known facts are too few for a continuous British Church history
to be built upon them.   The only early British historian, Gildas, *c.* 540,
is the author of a diatribe rather than a history.   Nennius writing in
the ninth century is uncritical, and too far removed from the events
which he records to be relied upon.   Geoffrey of Monmouth writing
in the twelfth century is notoriously untrustworthy and hardly deserves
the name of historian; and all extant Lives of British saints are later
than the Norman Conquest and historically almost valueless.

Yet from these and other sources the following persons and facts
emerge as historical, with probability if not certainty.

(*a*)   Among martyrs: Alban of Verulamium, martyred, as Gildas
asserts, or according to another MS. reading, conjectures, in the persecution of Diocletian.   But as this persecution is not known to have
reached Britain, it is more probable that the persecution in question was
that of Decius in 250–251, or that of Valerian in 259–260.   Bede tells
the story at greater length, and says that the martyrdom took place
at Verulamium, now St Albans.   Both Gildas and Bede evidently quote
from some early but now lost *Passio S. Albani*.   The details may be
unhistorical, as is frequently the case in such *Passiones*, but it would
be unreasonable to doubt the main story, because we have the fifth
century evidence of the Gallican presbyter Constantius who writing a life
of St Germanus describes a visit of Germanus and Lupus to his sepulchre
at St Albans; and the sixth century evidence of a line in the poetry of
the Gaulish Venantius Fortunatus.

(*b*)   Aaron and Julius of Caerleon-upon-Usk.   These two martyrs are
likewise mentioned by Gildas, and though there is no early corroborative
evidence as in the case of St Alban they may be regarded as historical
personages.   Bede's mention, and all later mentions of them, rested upon
the original statement of Gildas, who does not say that they were
martyred at Caerleon-upon-Usk, though this is not unlikely[1].

In the Martyrology of Bede, and in many later Martyrologies and

---

[1] A Marthir or Martyrium of Julius and Aaron is mentioned in a ninth century
charter, *Liber Landavensis*, edit. 1893, p. 225.

Kalendars, 17 Sept. is marked *In Britanniis* [*natale*] *Socratis et Stephani*, and in Baronius' edition of the Roman Martyrology, in 1645, this has grown to *Sanctorum Martyrum Socratis et Stephani*. So 7 Feb. is marked *in Augusta* [= London] *natale Augusti* or *Auguli* episcopi et martyris. There is no early authority for the existence of these saints, and nothing is known of their history.

(c) Among bishops: the existence of the following bishops is known to us:

Three British bishops are recorded to have been present at the Council of Arles in 314. They were:

1. Eborius episcopus de civitate Eboracensi provincia Britannica.
2. Restitutus episcopus de civitate Londinensi provincia supra-scripta.
3. Adelfius episcopus de civitate Colonia Londinensium.

These British sees were fixed in Roman cities, York, London, and Lincoln, if we may suppose that " Londinensium " is a mistake for " Lindumensium." Some however would read " Legionensium " and interpret the word of Caerleon-upon-Usk ; but this suggestion is negatived by the fact that Caerleon never was a Roman colony.

" Eborius " has a suspicious look as the name of a bishop de civitate Eboracensi, but similarity need not here suggest forgery. It is a latinised form of a common Keltic name. There was a bishop Eburius in Ireland in St Bridget's time[1]. They were attended by a priest named Sacerdos, and a deacon named Arminius. Sacerdos has been thought to be a suspicious name for a presbyter, but though we have been unable to find any other instance, it may be pointed out that Priest may be found as a proper name in the clergy list of to-day.

There is no evidence for the suggestion sometimes made that British bishops were present at the Council of Nicaea in 325. The only difficulty in proving a direct negative is the incomplete and unsatisfactory state of the list of signatories.

Athanasius tells us that British bishops were among the more than three hundred bishops who voted in his favour at the Council of Sardica in 345. But he does not mention the names of any of these bishops, or of their sees.

There were British bishops among the four hundred or more who met at the Council of Ariminum in 359. We know this on the authority of Sulpicius Severus, who unfortunately mentions neither the names nor the numbers of these bishops nor of their sees, yet adds that " there were three bishops from Britain who, because they lacked private means, made use of the public bounty, refusing contributions offered to them by the rest." The public bounty refers to the provision for their entertainment (*annonas et cellaria*) which the emperor had ordered to be offered at the public expense.

---

[1] *Acta Sanctorum Hiberniae*, Edinburgh, 1888, col. 66.

(*d*) Another British bishop whose name has come down to us is Riocatus who made two journeys from Britain to Gaul to see Faustus, a Breton and bishop of Riez (died *c.* 492), and carried certain works of Faustus back to Britain.

(*e*) There is extant a book addressed by a British bishop named Fastidius to a widow named Fatalis in the first half of the fifth century. He is mentioned by Gennadius, but his see is not named, *de Viris illustr.* cap. 57. His book *De Vita Christiana* is printed in Migne, *Pat. Lat.* 102, 4.

The only other bishops known to us by name before A.D. 600 are the famous Welsh bishops.

(*f*) There are in existence lists of early British, Welsh, Manx, and Cornish bishops, for the majority of whom no certain evidence can be produced[1]. Some of them, such as St David, first bishop of Menevia, St Dubritius, first bishop of Llandaff, and his immediate successors Teilo and Oudoceus; Kentigern and Asaph, the first two bishops of St Asaph; Daniel, first bishop of Bangor, together with a few less known names on the lists, are historical personages, but these belong to the sixth and seventh century Welsh Church and stand partly outside the period covered by this article.

It must not be forgotten that Patrick and Ninian, bishop of Candida Casa (Whithern), were Britons, but their history belongs rather to Ireland and Scotland than to England. The following facts may be also worth recording as events of the sixth century.

Two bishops of the Britons came from Alba to sanctify St Bridget[2]. Fifty bishops of the Britons of Cell Muine visited St Moedoc of Ferns[3]. These figures indicate that the British episcopate, like that of other parts of the Keltic Church, was monastic and numerous, rather than diocesan and limited in number.

The Keltic saints of Britain like those of Ireland were great travellers. Gildas asserts this. Palladius in his *Historia Lausiaca* speaks of British pilgrims in Syria, and Theodoret writing *c.* 440 speaks of their arrival in the Holy Land. These early independent outside testimonies make it possible to believe many otherwise incredible stories in later *Vitae Sanctorum, e.g.* that David, Teilo, and Padarn went to Jerusalem where David received episcopal consecration, and that the Cornish St Keby (Cuby) made a pilgrimage to the same city. References to British travellers in Rome and Italy cease to excite wonder after this. It does not of course follow that the Jerusalem stories are true, only that they are within the bounds of possibility. The legends are late, and they were probably invented to give independence and prestige to the Keltic episcopate, as compared with the later episcopate of the English Church.

---

[1] These lists may be seen in Stubbs (W.), *Registrum Sacrum Anglicanum*, 2nd edit. Oxford, 1897. Appendix VII.

[2] *Leabhar Breac*, fol. 62 a.   [3] *Ibid.* fol. 81.

There is no serious doubt about the orthodoxy of the British Church. Gildas accuses its clergy of immorality, and of venality, not of heresy. On the other hand testimony to its orthodoxy is plentiful. Athanasius stated that the British Churches had signified by letter to him their adhesion to the Nicene faith. Chrysostom said that "even the British Isles have felt the power of the word, for there too churches and altars have been erected. There too, as on the shores of the Euxine or in the South, men may be heard discussing points in Scripture, with differing voices but not with differing belief, with varying tongues but not with varying faith." Jerome asserted that "Britain in common with Rome, Gaul, Africa, Persia, the East, and India, adores one Christ, observes one rule of faith." Venantius Fortunatus speaks of Britain cherishing the faith, and Wilfrid himself, though openly hostile to the British Church, asserted before a Council held in Rome in 680 that the true Catholic faith prevailed throughout the British, Irish, and Pictish as well as the English race, thus claiming for the whole Keltic Church in these islands what Columbanus claimed for his own Irish Church, when he told Pope Boniface that it was not schismatical or heretical, but that it held the whole Catholic faith[1].

But in defending the orthodoxy of the British Church we must not be supposed to mean that no heretical opinions ever obtained temporary ground, or attracted individuals.

Victricius, bishop of Rouen, came to Britain *c.* 396 at the request of the bishops of North Italy. Nothing is known of the purpose of his journey, except that in his own language it had to do with the making of peace, it has been conjectured, in connexion with the attempted introduction of Arianism, or of some other form of false doctrine. In 429 Germanus, bishop of Auxerre, and Lupus, bishop of Troyes, were sent by a Gallican synod according to Constantius, but by Pope Celestine according to Prosper, to Britain to stem Pelagianism, and in 447 the same Germanus, and Severus, bishop of Trèves, came to Britain for the same purpose. Pelagianism would naturally establish a footing in Britain because Pelagius himself was most probably a Briton by birth, a member of one of those Gaelic families who had crossed from Ireland and settled themselves on the south-western coast of Great Britain[2]. His companion Caelestius, no doubt, was an Irishman, but Faustus of Riez and Fastidius, both semi-Pelagian authors, were the first a Breton, the second British, and the same may be surmised of a certain Agricola,

---

[1] A serious attack on the orthodoxy of the British Church has been recently made by Mr F. C. Conybeare, who seeks to prove that this Church held heretical views about the Trinity, and did not use the Trinitarian formula in the administration of baptism (*Cymmrodorion Transactions*, 1897–8). It is impossible here to follow him point by point; it must suffice to say that he does not seem to have proved his case.

[2] Bury, J. B., *Life of St Patrick*, p. 15.

the son of a Pelagian bishop named Severianus, who taught and spread Pelagianism in Britain, as Prosper tells us *sub an.* 429. Their names have more a Roman than a Keltic sound, but that point cannot be pressed, because Britons frequently assumed a Roman or a Romanised name. But thanks mainly to the Gallican bishops previously referred to all efforts to Pelagianise the British Church were unsuccessful. The last recorded communication between the British Church and Western Christianity took place in 455, in which year, according to an entry in the *Annales Cambriae*, the British Church changed its ancient mode of calculating Easter, and adopted the cycle of 84 years then in use at Rome. This was shortly afterwards exchanged at Rome for the Victorian cycle of 532 years, and that again was changed there in the next century for the Dionysian cycle of 19 years; but neither the Victorian nor the Dionysian cycle was ever adopted in the British Church, which still retained an older Roman cycle.

The archaeological evidence which is forthcoming as to the character and even as to the existence of Christianity in Britain in Roman times is extremely limited; nor is this to be wondered at when we consider the wave of destruction which swept over Britain through the Saxon invasions.

In only one case has a whole church so far survived that we can trace the outline of the building, and measure its dimensions. This church was recently discovered at Silchester (Calleva Atrebatum). It bears a close resemblance to fourth century churches discovered in Italy, Syria, and Africa. Traces of the foundations of a Roman basilica have likewise been found underneath the churches at Reculver and Lyminge in Kent, and at Brixworth in Northamptonshire; but whether those basilicas were used for secular or ecclesiastical purposes is uncertain. The only claim of the above-named churches, and of a few other churches, such as St Martin's at Canterbury, to be regarded as Romano-British, lies in the fact that they have a few stones or bricks of Romano-British date used up a second time in their construction.

Apart from churches the Chi-Rho monogram (☧) has been found in the mosaics, pavements, or building stones of three villas at Frampton in Dorsetshire, Chedworth in Gloucestershire, and Harpole in Northamptonshire; on a silver cup at Corbridge-on-Tyne; on two silver rings from a villa at Fifehead Neville in Dorsetshire; on some bronze fragments at York; on some masses of pewter found in the Thames, on one of which it is associated with A and ω and with the words *spes in deo*; on the bezel of a bronze ring found at Silchester, though the nature of the ornament in this case has been doubted[1]. There was also found at Silchester a fragment of white glass with a fish and a palm roughly scratched upon it.

There are no distinctively Christian inscriptions of a very early date,

[1] *Archaeologia,* LV. p. 429.

CH. XVI (A).

but there are several which suggest a Christian origin by the use of the phrase *plus minus* with reference to the length of a person's life, a phrase often found on early Christian inscriptions abroad ; and there are some pagan altar inscriptions which point to a pagan restoration and a revival after some other influence—possibly the Christian influence—had allowed such altars to fall into neglect or decay.

Archaeological evidence is therefore in itself distinctly weak ; and yet it may be considered sufficiently strong to support facts which are known to us on other and independent grounds ; while further evidence of this kind may be discovered hereafter.

(2) IRELAND.

No exact answer can be given to the question, When was Christianity first introduced into Ireland ?

The popular idea is that it was introduced into Ireland for the first time by St Patrick. This is negatived by the following facts—St Patrick's mission work in Ireland commenced in 432. It is quite true that Patrick as a youth, aged 15–21, had spent six years in captivity in Ireland under a heathen master named Miliucc, 405–411, but it is impossible that at that age and under those conditions he can have done any evangelistic work. Indeed he himself nowhere claims to have done any. In the year before the date of St Patrick's missionary advent to Ireland, that is to say in 431, we find the following distinct statement made in the Chronicle of Prosper of Aquitaine, " Ad Scotos in Christum credentes ordinatur a Papa Celestino Palladius, et primus episcopus mittitur."

This statement must be accepted as historical. There may be some difficulty in interpreting it, but there is no ground whatever for doubting it. Prosper has sometimes been accused of bias ; but bias is one thing, deliberate invention or forgery is another. Nor is there the slightest ground for suggesting that Prosper may have been misinformed. Though not himself a native of Great Britain or Ireland, Prosper belonged to the neighbouring country of Gaul, which he permanently left when he went to Rome in 440, and became secretary to Leo I as bishop of Rome. Prosper was alive in 463, but the exact date of his death is unknown.

If Prosper's statement that there were Christians in Ireland before the arrival there of Palladius were unsupported we should feel bound to accept it ; and we are much more bound to accept it if we find it corroborated by a series of incidents or facts which, if not conclusive singly, have a combined weight in substantiating it.

Before enumerating these facts reference must be made to a passage written by Prosper about six years later. In his *Liber contra Collatorem*, written when Sixtus III was Pope, *i.e.* between 432 and 440, and speaking in praise of that Pope's predecessor Celestine, he says, "et ordinato Scottis episcopo dum Romanam insulam studet servare catholicam fecit etiam barbaram Christianam."

There is no allusion here to the early death of Palladius—the *episcopus* referred to—nor to the failure of his mission; obviously, writing a panegyric on Celestine, it was not to Prosper's purpose to refer to them: nor on the other hand is there any reference to the mission of St Patrick; though, as Prof. Bury has pointed out, if Celestine had sent Patrick, and still more if he had consecrated him, Prosper would almost certainly have referred to the fact, as enhancing the achievements and the reputation of that Pope. The passage is obviously rhetorical and need not be pressed as superseding or cancelling any part of his statement about the mission of Palladius previously quoted.

Its truth is supported by the following statements and allusions, which may be legendary, because the earliest form in which they have come down to us is several centuries later than the events to which they refer, but which may still be true. It is hardly possible to say more of them than this, that if they are true they imply the existence of a pre-Patrician church in Ireland.

Tirechan records that when St Patrick ordained a certain Ailbe as presbyter he shewed him or told him of a wonderful stone altar in the mountain of the children of Ailill[1], to which the *Tripartite Life*, calling Ailbe an archpresbyter, adds that this altar was in a cave, and that there were four glass chalices standing at the four angles of it[2].

In the *Additions to Tirechan's Collections* it is recorded that Bishop Colman at Cluain Cain in Achud (Clonkeen) presented his own church to St Patrick for ever[3].

Tirechan tells a story, also told with unimportant variations by Muirchu Maccu-Machtheni[4], of St Patrick finding a cross (*signaculum crucis Christi*) which had been, through a mistake, erected over a heathen's grave[5].

The *Lives of the Irish Saints* represent some of them, *e.g.* Ailbeus, Ibar, Declan, Ciaran, etc., as older, or as partly older, partly contemporaneous with St Patrick. But these *Lives* are too late in their present form to be accepted as historical, and are only or chiefly valuable for Irish words, and for incidental allusions surviving in them.

The general policy of Loigaire, High King of Ireland, 428–463, who without apparently becoming himself a convert to Christianity was not

---

[1] *Book of Armagh*, fol. 11 b. 1, in Whitley Stokes' *Tripartite Life of St Patrick*, II. p. 313.

[2] *Ibid.* I. p. 95.

[3] *Ibid.* fol. 17 a. 1; *ibid.* II. p. 337.

[4] *Ibid.* fol. 14 a. 1; *ibid.* II. p. 325.

[5] *Ibid.* fol. 8 a. 1; *ibid.* II. p. 295.

CH. XVI (A).

hostile to its promulgation by St Patrick, and the curious policy of the Druids concerning the advent of Patrick, betraying in its language some acquaintance with the ritual of the Christian Church, have been noted as indicating the previous existence of Christianity in Ireland[1].

Pelagius, who must have been born *c.* 370 though the exact date of his birth is unascertained, is known on the authority of St Jerome, and on other grounds, to have been an Irishman, and as such the presumption is in favour of his having been born in Ireland, and of Christian parents; but too much stress must not be laid upon this fact, or supposed fact. Though accepted as a fact by Professor Zimmer, it has been rejected by Professor Bury, who thinks that the evidence points to Pelagius having been born in western Britain[2]. His contemporary and chief disciple, Caelestius, was likewise an Irishman, and probably born in Ireland.

An Irish Christian named Fith, better known under his Latin or Latinised name of Iserninus, was with St Patrick at Auxerre, was ordained there, and also went, though somewhat against his will, when St Patrick went, as a missionary to Ireland[3].

All these facts go to substantiate the statement of Prosper that there were " Scoti in Christum credentes " in Ireland in 431, before the great mission of St Patrick was commenced. But how did they get there? How did Christianity in Ireland originate? To these and such-like questions no certain answer is forthcoming. Although Ireland was never conquered by the Romans, and therefore never became an integral portion of the Roman Empire, as England and the larger part of Great Britain did, yet there are traces of Roman influence in Ireland at a very early date.

Large and not infrequent discoveries of Roman coins in Ireland, ranging from the first to the fifth century, prove that there must have been considerable intercourse during that time between Ireland and Great Britain and the Continent; and some knowledge, possibly some seeds, of Christianity may have been sown by Roman sailors, or merchants, or commercial travellers.

In the third century an Irish tribe, named the Dessi, were driven out of their home in Meath and migrated partly south into Co. Waterford, and partly across the sea to South Wales, where they were permitted to form a settlement, and there are indications that they penetrated into Somerset, Devon, and Cornwall. The Dessi at this

---

[1] *E.g.* by Professor Bury, to whose *Life of St Patrick* the writer of this chapter is much indebted. The wording of the Druids' prophecy will be found there in two forms, pp. 79, 299.

[2] One of St Jerome's expressions is significant, " Progenies Scotticae gentis de Britannorum vicinia." For a complete review of the evidence see *Hermathena*, xxx. p. 26.

[3] *Additions to Tirechan's Collections* in W. Stokes' *Tripartite Life of St Patrick*, ii. p. 343.

time were of course not Christians, but they paved the way, or they formed a highway, by which a century or so later British Christianity may have reached, and probably did reach, Ireland. Irish raids into England and Wales in the course of the fourth century may have brought Christian captives back into Ireland, as one of such raids in the early part of the fifth century brought the captive youth Patrick.

Inhabitants of the south-west of England, whether Brythonic occupiers or Goidelic settlers, establishing and pursuing intercourse with Ireland would naturally land at Muerdea at the mouth of the Vartry near Wicklow, or at some other port on the south-east coast of Ireland, which is the nearest coast of Ireland to that of England; and Christian settlers from Britain would thus influence first of all the south rather than the north of Ireland.

There is an ingenious argument of a philological character which we owe to the keen insight of Professor Zimmer, and which has been explained by him at length in his *Celtic Church in Britain and Ireland*. We can hardly reproduce all the linguistic details here, but a convenient and concise summary of Zimmer's argument has been printed by Professor Bury[1]. It is to this effect. A number of ecclesiastical loan-words assume forms in Irish, which they could not have assumed if they had been borrowed straight from the Latin, and which can only be explained by intermediate Brythonic forms. The presence of these forms in Ireland can, again, be best explained on the supposition that Christianity was introduced into Ireland in the fourth century by Irish-speaking Britons; and the further conjecture arises that the transformation of Brythonic Latin loan-words into Irish equivalents was made in the Irish settlements in western, and especially south-western, Britain, which are thereby indicated as the channel through which the Christian religion was transmitted originally into Ireland.

There is no authority for the legend that the British Ninian laboured in Ireland about the commencement of the fifth century, other than an Irish life existing in the time of Archbishop Ussher, but now lost. Ussher unfortunately does not give its date, or supposed date, but he quotes from it several facts which, if not impossible, do not seem to be at all credible[2]. Yet the story of Ninian's connexion with Ireland gained some footing there, for his name under the affectionate form of *Moenenn* or *Moinenn* or *Monenn*—"my Nynias or Ninian"—is found at 16 Sept. in the Martyrologies of Tallaght, Gorman, Oengus and Donegal.

Though, then, there is sufficient evidence to prove the existence of some Christianity in Ireland before A.D. 432, yet the majority of the population of Ireland at that date was pagan, and the conversion of Ireland to Christianity was mainly though not entirely the work of St Patrick: he is not, therefore, to be robbed of his title of Apostle of the Irish.

---

[1] *Life of St Patrick*, pp. 350–1.
[2] Ussher, *Whole Works*, Dublin, 1847, vi. p. 209.

Pre-Patrician Christianity in Ireland was scanty, sporadic, and apparently unorganised. Exactly when and by whom it was introduced we know not and it is unlikely that we ever shall know. The Roman mission of Palladius in 431 was a failure either through his missionary incapacity, or more probably through his early death, though his death is not recorded; or less probably through his withdrawal from Ireland, according to Scottish legends, to preach the Gospel among the Picts in Scotland, or as is more probable the Pictish population in Dalaradia in the northern part of Ulster, amongst whom he was working, and died before he had spent a whole year in Ireland[1]. Then on learning of the death or departure of Palladius, St Patrick went to Ireland as his successor.

A complete biography of St Patrick cannot be attempted here, but a compressed account of his mission work in Ireland is necessary. It was in the year 432 that Patrick, then in his forty-third year, was consecrated bishop by Germanus, bishop of Auxerre, and started from Gaul for Ireland, fired by a love for that country in which many years before he had spent six years as a captive slave (405–411).

His wise policy was to approach the kings of the petty kingdoms which went to make up Ireland in the fifth century, and among them Loigaire, son of Niall, who in the year of Patrick's arrival in Ireland ranked as High King, with certain rights over all other kings. Tribal loyalty was strong, and if the petty king or chieftain was won over (or even if like king Loigaire he sanctioned the mission without being converted himself), the conversion of his tribe was much facilitated, if not certain to follow.

Landing near Wicklow, Patrick coasted northwards, stopping at the little island afterwards called Inis-patrick, eventually passing up the narrow sea-passage into lake Strangford in that southern part of Dalaradia which is now Co. Down. On the southern shore of this lake he landed, and Dichu the proprietor of that part became his first convert, and granted him, after his return from an ineffectual attempt to convert his old master Miliucc, a site for a Christian establishment at Saul; and in its vicinity Bright, Rathcolpa, Downpatrick also have a legendary connexion with him. Then in Co. Meath, Trim and Dun-shaughlin, both not far from the royal hill of Tara, Uisnech, and Donagh-patrick where Conall, brother of king Loigaire, was converted, are all places associated with the activities of Patrick. Thence he advanced into Ulster, destroying the idol Crom Cruaich in the plain of Slecht, founding churches at Aghanagh, Shancough, Tannach, and Caissel-ire, all in Co. Sligo. Then turning south he founded the church of Aghagower on the confines of Mayo and Galway, not far from the hill Crochan-Aigli (Croagh Patrick), on the summit of which he was believed to have spent forty days and nights in solitude and contemplation.

[1] This is the conclusion of Professor Bury, *Life of St Patrick,* p. 55.

Traces survive of a second journey into Connaught full of interesting incidents, and of a third journey (to be dated thirteen years after Patrick's arrival in Ireland), into the territory of king Amolngaid including the wood of Fochlad, where, according to the most probable interpretation of documents, he had wandered in the days of his early captivity. Here a church was built and a cross set up, in a spot which still bears the local name of Crosspatrick.

The year 444 saw the foundation of Armagh (Ardd Mache) on a small tract of ground assigned to Patrick by Daire, king of Oriel or of one of the tribes of Oriel, at the foot of the hill of Macha, subsequently exchanged for a site on the hill-top.

Traces of Patrick's work in south Ireland are less distinct, but tradition points to his having been there, and he is said to have baptised the sons of Dunlang king of Leinster, those of Natfraich king of Munster, and Crimthann son and successor of Endœ a sub-king, whose residence and territory were on the banks of the river Slaney in Co. Wexford. But Christianity had an earlier footing in the south than in the north of Ireland. Patrick's mission work was therefore less needed there, and his glory clusters rather round northern Armagh than round any place in the south of Ireland.

In 461 Patrick died and was buried at Saul near the mouth of the river Slaney in Co. Down, where he had first landed at the commencement of his missionary enterprise in Ireland.

Subject to the necessary limitations of one man's life and powers, and to the exceptions already described, Patrick was both the converter of Ireland to the Christian religion, and the founder and organiser of the Church in that island. Not that he extinguished heathenism. An ever increasing halo of glory surrounded his memory in later times, until it came to be believed that he converted the whole of Ireland. We are told in a late Life of a saint that "the whole of Hibernia was through him filled with the faith and with the baptism of Christ[1]." But such a sudden and complete conversion of a whole country is unlikely, unnatural, and practically impossible; and there are proofs that paganism survived in Ireland long after St Patrick's time, though the successive steps of its disappearance, and the date of its final extinction cannot be traced or stated with certainty.

Very little light is thrown on this point by the Irish Annals. They are a continuous and somewhat barren record of storms, eclipses, pestilences, battles, murders, famines, and so forth. But there are occasional allusions to charms of a Druidical or heathen nature, which imply either that heathenism was not extinct or that heathen practices continued to exist under the veil of Christianity.

In A.D. 560 at the famous battle of Culdreimne (Cooledrevny) we are told in the *Annals of Ulster* that, "Fraechan, son of Temnan, it was

[1] *Vita Kierani,* quoted in Ussher, *Works,* vi. p. 332.

that made the Druids' *erbe* for Diarmait.　Tuatan, son of Diman...it was that threw overhead the Druids' *erbe*."

The exact meaning of *erbe* is not known, but it was evidently some kind of Druidical charm.

Another mysterious entry made A.D. 738 points in a similar direction: " Fergus Glutt King of Cobha died from the envenomed spittles of evil men."

Later, from the last few years of the eighth century onwards, there are many records of conflicts with the Gentiles; but the reference is in all these cases to the new wave of heathenism which swept over Ireland through the Danish invasions.

Evidence is however forthcoming from other sources.

For example, in the form of baptismal exorcism used in Ireland in the seventh and ninth centuries we find the clause " expelle diabolum *et gentilitatem*," but the last two words have disappeared from the same form as used in Continental and English service-books of the tenth century—in countries where the extinction of paganism had by that time rendered the words obsolete.

The Canon of the Mass in the earliest extant Irish Missal contains a petition that God would accept the offering made "in this church which thy servant hath built to the honour of thy glorious name; and we beseech thee, O Lord, that thou wouldest rescue him and all the people from the worship of idols, and convert them to thee the true God and Father Almighty[1]."

This passage, which has not been found in any other liturgy, tells us of some place in Ireland, probably in Co. Tipperary, where there was still in the ninth century a pagan population among whom some pagan landowner seems to have been at that time sufficiently favourable to Christianity to build a Christian church, although he himself had not yet become a convert.

It is true, as has been already noted, that a fresh inroad of heathenism into Ireland took place through the Danish invasions which began in A.D. 795, and that one of the fleets of their leader Turgesius sailed up the Shannon, which forms the northern boundary of Tipperary; but their paganism was fierce, and it is impossible to think of any Danish settler being sufficiently favourable to Christianity to allow the building of a Christian church at all events within two centuries after the date of their first arrival.

---

[1] The Stowe Missal (ninth century) in *The Liturgy and Ritual of the Celtic Church*, Oxford, 1881, p. 236.

(3) SCOTLAND.

When and by whom and under what circumstances was Christianity first introduced into Scotland? It is not easy to reply to these questions with certainty because of the unsatisfactory character of the later authorities and the scanty character of the earlier authorities on which we have to rely.

Writing *c.* A.D. 208 Tertullian refers to the fact that Christianity had already reached *Britannorum inaccessa Romanis loca*—an expression which must include the north of Scotland, and probably also some of its numerous adjacent islands.

Origen, *c.* 239, speaks of the Christian Church having extended to the boundaries of the world, yet evidently not as all-embracing, for he refers to very many among Britons, Germans, Scythians, and others who had not yet heard the word of the Gospel.

No other Father of the first three centuries refers to Britannia or the Britanni. We turn then to Scottish authorities.

Scotland possesses no early historian at all resembling Bede. The earliest formal history of Scotland is the Chronicle of John of Fordun, who died in 1385, and which takes us up to the reign of David I, inclusive. It was afterwards re-edited and continued from 1153 to 1436 by Walter Bower or Bowmaker, abbot of Inchcolm, a small island in the Firth of Forth, and in that form is generally known as the Scotichronicon. After Fordun come such writers as Andrew of Wyntoun, who between 1420-24 wrote the "orygynale Chronykil of Scotland" from the Creation to 1368; Maurice Buchanan, a cleric in the priory of Pluscarden, a cell of the abbey of Dunfermline, who compiled the *Liber Pluscardensis* in 1461 at the desire of Bothuele, abbot of Dunfermline, which was largely, and especially in the earlier books, a reproduction of the Scotichronicon; Hector Boethius (Boece), 1470–1526, who wrote a history of Scotland in seventeen books (*Scotorum Historiae Libri XVII*). Later Scottish historians need not be enumerated or referred to here.

Now these writers make a definite statement that the inhabitants of Scotland were first converted to Christianity in A.D. 203, in the time of Pope Victor I in the seventh year of the reign of the Emperor Severus. Fordun (lib. II. cap. 35) gives no further details, and the only authority quoted consists of four lines of anonymous Latin poetry which look very much as if they had been composed by himself. Hector Boece, writing later, gives further details of the conversion of Donald I by the missionaries of Pope Victor in 203, the seventh year of Severus.

Now there is no authority for this statement earlier than Fordun, and we can hardly avoid the conclusion that it is a deliberate invention on his part; possibly from a desire that Scotland should not be so very far behind Britain, which claimed to have been converted to Christianity in the second century by Pope Eleutherus in the time of a king Lucius[1].

The statement also stands self-condemned through the anachronisms and the inaccuracies which it contains. There were no Scoti in Scotland in 203, Zephyrinus was then Pope, not Victor, and it was the tenth not the seventh year of the Emperor Severus.

Still there must have been Christians among the soldiers composing the Roman armies of invasion and occupation during, soon after, and even before the reign of Severus. May not some knowledge of Christianity have entered Scotland through them? Unfortunately the traces of Roman occupation in Scotland are extremely scanty. No decorations, emblems, or relics of any kind have been found suggestive of Christianity, and there is not only no proof but there are not the slightest traces of a Romano-Scotic church in the third century. No reliance can be placed on certain statements made to the contrary in the Lives of the Saints. The hagiological literature of Scotland is for the most part very late, and for historical purposes more than usually worthless. With the exception of the two seventh century Lives of St Columba by Cuminius (Cumine) and Adamnan, there is nothing earlier than the Life of St Ninian by Ailred who died in 1166 and two Lives of St Kentigern belonging to the same century, an anonymous and now fragmentary Life written while Herbert was bishop of Glasgow (1147-64), and a Life by Joceline of Furness written during the episcopate of Joceline, bishop of Glasgow (1174-99). All the traditions and legends assigning extremely early dates to certain Scottish saints are without foundation, such as the story in the Aberdeen Breviary which makes St Serf a Christian of the primitive church of Scotland before the arrival of Palladius, whose suffragan he becomes; and the story representing Regulus as bringing relics of St Andrew to Scotland, c. 360. In addition to its purely fictitious details, this latter story antedates the connexion with St Andrew, and the importation of his relics into Scotland, by some four hundred years.

Legends, then, and fiction apart, when was Christianity introduced into Scotland?

In answering this question we have to remember that Scotland as we know it, and as it exists to-day, was not in existence in the earlier centuries of the Christian era. In the seventh century the country which now makes up Scotland comprised four distinct kingdoms.

(1) The English kingdom of Bernicia, extending from the Tyne to the Firth of Forth, with its capital at Bamborough.

(2) The British kingdom of Cumbria, or Cambria, or Strathclyde, extending from the Firth of Clyde on the north, to the river Derwent in

---

[1] For the unhistorical character of this claim, though it has the authority of Bede, see Harnack, *Brief d. brit. Königs Lucius.*

Cumberland, and including the greater part both of that county and of Westmoreland; its capital being the rock of Dumbarton on the Clyde, with the fortress of Alclyde on its summit.

(3) The kingdom of the Picts, north of the Firth of Forth. extending over the northern and eastern districts of that part of Scotland, with its capital near Inverness.

(4) The Scottish kingdom of Dalriada, corresponding very nearly to the modern county of Argyle, with the hill-fort of Dunadd as its capital.

In addition to these four kingdoms there was a central neutral ground corresponding to the modern counties of Stirling and Linlithgow, with a mixed population drawn from all four of the above populations though specially from the first three; and there was a Pictish settlement in Galloway, corresponding to the modern counties of Wigtown and Kirkcudbright, known in Bede's time as the county of the Niduarian Picts. Niduari probably means persons living on the banks or in the neighbourhood of the river Nith, which runs into the Solway Firth between the counties of Kirkcudbright and Dumfries, though the derivation of the word is not certain.

In discussing the introduction of Christianity into these various parts of Scotland we may at once dismiss (1). The history of Bernicia falls more properly under the history of England than under that of Scotland.

(2) The conversion of Strathclyde has been generally ascribed to St Ninian (Nynias) who was engaged in building a stone church at Whithern (*Ad Candidam Casam*) in Galloway at the close of the fourth century, in 397, if we may accept the statement of Ailred that he heard of St Martin's death while the church was in building, and that he dedicated it, when finished, to that saint. But we really know nothing with certainty about St Ninian beyond the scanty account of him given by Bede, for which see below under (3). Bede tells us that he was a Briton—*de natione Britonum*—and it has been generally concluded that he was a Briton of Strathclyde. This seems a very probable inference, though Bede does not say so. If then he was a Cumbrian and not a Welsh or any other Briton, Strathclyde must have been already at least a partially Christian county to have produced this eminent Christian teacher; and the church at Candida Casa was only the first stone church built amongst an already Christian people. But the earlier history of Strathclyde is in any case obscure and, so far as Christianity is concerned, is quite unknown to us. Ailred tells us that Ninian's father was a Christian king, but whether he was inventing facts, or whether he was perpetuating a tradition, or how he obtained his information we know not. At all events it must be remembered that Ailred was separated from Ninian by a gap of over seven centuries. This is not the place to discuss the traces of Ninian's influence and work, or supposed work, in Ireland and the Isle of Man[1].

[1] See p. 505.

CH. XVI (A).

Ninian's time is usually given as *c*. 353–432, but there is no good evidence for the year of either his birth or death.

For about a century afterwards the history of Strathclyde is a blank till we come to St Kentigern or Mungo the great Strathclyde saint, whose life extended from 527 to 612. The latter date is given in the *Annales Cambriae*; the former date rests on the supposition that he was eighty-five years old at his death. For the facts of Kentigern's life we are even worse off than we are for those of the life of Ninian. Unfortunately there is no mention of Kentigern in Bede, and our earliest biographies of him date from the twelfth century, namely, as stated above, an anonymous Life written in the time of Bishop Herbert of Glasgow, who died in 1164, existing only in one early fifteenth century MS. in the British Museum, and a Life by Joceline, a monk of the abbey of Furness in Lancashire, written *c*. 1190 in the lifetime of another Joceline, bishop of Glasgow (1174–99). If we may trust Joceline, Kentigern having been consecrated bishop by a single bishop summoned from Ireland for that purpose, and having fixed his see at Glasgow, practically re-converted Strathclyde to Christianity, the vast majority of its inhabitants having apostatised from the faith since the days of Ninian. This re-conversion included that of the Pictish inhabitants of Galwiethia or Galloway, who had likewise apostatised. He is also credited by Joceline with missionary work in Albania or Alban, which means the eastern districts of Scotland north of the Firth of Forth, and dedications to Kentigern north of the Firth of Forth seem to corroborate Joceline's statement, which however is otherwise unsupported, and cannot be accepted as certainly established: his other statements that Kentigern sent missionaries to the Orkneys, Norway, and Ireland are improbable in the extreme; and it is only the general and inherent difficulty of proving a negative which makes it impossible to refute them.

It may be of interest to add that traces of Strathclyde Christianity coeval with Ninian survive in the names of two, possibly three, bishops engraved on fifth century stones at Kirkmadrine on the bay of Luce, Co. Wigtown, and in the remains of a stone chapel of St Medan, an Irish virgin and a disciple of Ninian, at Kirkmaiden on the same bay.

(3) The Picts. Bede tells us that Ninian converted the southern Picts, *Australes Picti*. It has been thought that these Picts were the Picts of Galloway, the Galwegian or Niduarian Picts, but as Bede describes them as occupying territory within, that is, to the south of, the Mounth, he must refer to the southern portion of the northern Pictish kingdom, which would correspond to the six modern counties of Kincardine, Forfar, Perth, Fife, Kinross, and Clackmannan.

Bede also records the conversion of the northern Picts by St Columba. He gives the date of Columba's arrival in Scotland as 565, but he appears to have landed on and occupied Iona in 563, and in 565 to have crossed the mountain range of Drumalban on his missionary enterprise to the northern Picts. His first arrival in Scotland is dated by other authorities and in the *Annals of Ulster*, the *Annales Cambriae*, and the *Annals of Tighernac* as 562 or 563. Iona[1] was probably assigned to him in the first instance by Conall Mac Comgaill, king of Dalriada, and afterwards confirmed to him by Brude Mac Maelchon, king of the Picts, whom Columba visited at his palace near Inverness, converting both him and his nation to Christianity. Iona was situated between the Pictish and the Dalriadic kingdoms.

We know very few details about this mission work among the northern Picts, which extended over nine years. Neither Bede, nor Adamnan in his *Life of Columba*, which is rather a panegyric than a biography, give us any history of it, but the many churches dedicated to him are a witness to his success, and details of two foundations of Columban churches have been preserved in the *Book of Deer*, viz. Aberdour in Banffshire, and Deer in the district of Buchan.

Columba's activity extended also to many of the small islands adjacent to Scotland, of which next to Iona itself the most important settlements were at Hinba and Tiree; but other islands, including Skye, bear witness to his presence and work by the dedications of their churches.

(4) The Scottish kingdom of Dalriada was founded by a colony from Dalriada in the extreme north of Ireland at the end of the fifth or early in the sixth century: and there can be no reason to doubt that the Dalriadic Irish or Scoti, as they were then called, were a Christian people, and brought their Christianity with them into Scotland *c.* A.D. 490.

Therefore when Columba arrived in Scotland in 563, or 565, he found a Christian people and king in Dalriada, ready to welcome him and to assign Iona to him as his home: and this was the beginning of a new movement which was destined to influence not Scotland only, but England also.

---

[1] More properly *Ioua*. See Fowler's note in his edition of *Adamnan*, p. lxv.

CHAPTER XVI (B).

THE CONVERSION OF THE TEUTONS.

(1) THE ENGLISH

WHEN Teutonic tribes of mixed descent invaded Britain they came as heathen unaffected by Roman Christianity against Keltic tribes partly heathen and partly Christian; the old inhabitants had been Romanised and Christianised in different degrees, varying coastwards and inland, in cities and country, to the south-east and to the west: the invaders moreover covered and at first devastated more land than they could hold, and their own settlement was a long process, varying in length in different districts. The separation of the Britons from the government and influence of Rome had been also slow and reluctant. Hence for many reasons it is hard to generalise about the Christianity with which the Teutonic invaders came into touch. Where this Christianity was not strong or long implanted it tended towards weakness and decay: here and there revivals of heathenism took place: here and there in the long years of Teutonic settlement revivals of Keltic Christianity began. Hence, as time passes on, new vigour of a Keltic and not a Romanised type is found as in Wales among the British: elsewhere the influence of Christianity lessens, and the Britons of some parts, so far from being able to convert the newcomers, keep their own religion more as a custom than as a living force. In either case the result is the same: the invaders are for long years wholly unaffected by the Christianity of the land they are conquering.

Little need be said here of the religion the invaders brought with them: in some points of morals they may have been above some other races and hence the moral code of Christianity might appeal to them, but it is idle to speculate as to elements in their religion which possibly made them readier later on to accept Christian doctrines. Their whole outlook, however, upon the unseen world brought it into close touch with their lives and the fortunes of their race: their religion so far as it was effective was a source of joy in life, and of strength in action, not of fear or weakness. Hence, when they received Christianity, it was with the freedom of sons, not the timidity of slaves, with a ready understanding that its discipline was to strengthen their characters for action. English Christianity was thus marked off from Teutonic Christianity elsewhere by moral differences, slight and not to be over-estimated: moreover, because it started afresh, free from the political and social traditions of the Empire, and because its conditions, in spite of much intercourse with the Continent, were locally more uniform and more insular than elsewhere, its growth took a somewhat peculiar turn. Christianity came to the English from the Papacy, and not from the Empire: it came at one great epoch, and when the Conquest was well under way, rather than by the gradual influence of daily life, as it did with the Teutonic races elsewhere. "The wonderful vitality of imperialist traditions...took no hold here. Escaping this, the English Church was saved from the infection of court-life and corruption...: it escaped the position forced upon the bishops of France as secular officers, defensors and civil magistrates." And this original impulse as described by Stubbs kept on its way in spite of later Frankish influence and inter-course. But at the same time the mission brought with it a larger life and a broader outlook: it is significant that Aethelberht of Kent, the first to accept the new faith, is also the first in the list of kings who put forth laws. Later kings who did the same were also noted for their interest in the Church[1].

The part taken by Gregory the Great, and the impulse he gave to the mission, have been spoken of elsewhere. But it should be noted here as a sign of the responsibility for the whole West felt by the Papal See in face of the barbarian inroads; furthermore the letters of commen-dation given to the missionaries by the Pope to bishops and rulers amongst the Franks opened up more fully lines of connexion already laid down for the future English Church. Two of Gregory's letters would, indeed, suggest that the English had already expressed some wish for missionaries to be sent to them: "it has come to us that the race of the English desires with yearning to be turned to the faith of Christ...but that the bishops in their neighbourhood"—and this apparently applied to the Franks, not solely at any rate to the Welsh—"are negligent." And the Pope (at an uncertain date) had formed a plan for buying English youths "to be given to God in the mon-asteries." This may be taken along with the beautiful tradition current in Northumbria of Gregory's pity for the English boys in the Roman slave-market. But at any rate the time was favourable for a mission owing to the marriage of Aethelberht of Kent, the most powerful English ruler of the time, with Berhta, daughter of Chariberht of Paris; and this Christian queen had taken across to her new home the Frankish bishop Liudhard as her chaplain. But from other indications little seems to have been known in the Rome of that day about the heathen invaders, and the English invasion had cut off the British Christians from inter-course with the Continent.

[1] See Chap. xvii. pp. 548-9.

The mission left Rome early in 596 : during the journey its members wished to return from the perils in front of them, but, encouraged by Gregory's fatherly firmness and knit together by his giving their leader Augustine the authority of an abbot over them, they went on and landed, most probably at Richborough[1], 597. Aethelberht received them kindly, and gave them an interview—in the open air for fear of magic. Augustine—taller than his comrades—led the procession of 40 men (possibly including Frankish interpreters), chanting a Litany as they went, carrying a silver cross and a wooden picture of the crucifixion ; Aethelberht heard them with sympathy, and yet with an open mind. He gave them a home in Canterbury in the later parish of St Alphege : here they could worship in St Martin's church, and they were also allowed to preach freely to the king's subjects. By Whitsuntide the king himself was so far won over as to be baptised—on Whitsunday or its eve, probably at St Martin's church (1 or 2 June 597). The king used no force to lead his subjects after him, but he naturally favoured those who followed him, and soon many were won by the faithful lives of the missionaries, shewn so easily by the common life of a brotherhood. Throughout the story of the Conversion it is indeed to the lives rather than to the preaching of the missionaries that Bede assigns their success, and the tolerance of the English kings in Kent and elsewhere gave them a ready opening. If here and there the missionaries met persecution, it never rose to martyrdom.

According to the Pope's directions, Augustine ought now to be consecrated, and for this purpose he went to Arles, where Vergilius (the usually accurate Bede mistakes the name) consecrated him (16 Nov. 597)[2].

Soon after his return to Kent the new bishop sent off to the Pope by the hands of his presbyter Laurentius and the monk Peter news of

---

[1] See arguments of Professor T. McKenny Hughes (Dissertation III. in Mason's *Mission of St Augustine*) in favour of Richborough : the Canterbury tradition also speaks of Richborough. But other sites, Stonor, or Ebbsfleet, find support. See *e.g.* Pref. to 3rd edn. of Bright's *Early Eng. Ch. Hist.*

[2] The dates usually given for Aethelberht's baptism, and the consecration of Augustine, are connected by Bede. Dates more precise, if less trustworthy, are given by Thorn (late fourteenth century) and by Thomas of Elmham (*R.S.* pp. 78 and 137) following the Canterbury tradition that the baptism took place at Whitsuntide 597 : the consecration is placed 16 Nov. 597. This is apparently founded upon Bede. But Elmham saw the difficulties of these dates. Gregory, *Ep.* VII. 30— to Eulogius of Alexandria (? June 598), speaks of the baptism of many English in the Swale the previous Christmas by Augustine *fratre et coepiscopo*. In 597, 16 Nov. was not on a Sunday, but in 598 it was. I should therefore prefer to place the consecration in 598, disregarding the date of this letter. The Canterbury tradition would hardly be mistaken as to the day, but might be as to the year. Further there would be a natural inclination to shorten the interval between the arrival of Augustine and the king's baptism. It might be, therefore, that the baptism should be placed along with the consecration in 598.

his success, along with a number of questions as to the difficulties he foresaw. We find Boniface in his day doing the same, and we may see in it a common and indeed natural custom rather than a sign of weakness.

The questions and the answers to them only concern us here so far as they shew the special difficulties of the mission and the character of St Augustine. Their importance for the character of the Pope has been shewn elsewhere. But their authenticity has been doubted: some of them are not what might have been expected, *e.g.* those on liturgic selection, and on recognising marriages contracted in heathenism but against Church law. The preface printed in the Epistles but omitted by Bede is more doubtful than the reply itself; and seems intended to explain the chronology of Bede. But the documentary history of the reply and its absence from the registry in Rome—where Boniface in 736 failed to have it found—have also caused suspicion. Yet, considering the ways in which the Epistles as a whole have reached us, this is not in itself sufficient to cause rejection. The arguments that Gregory's answers are not what we should expect, and that the questions concern points all raised afterwards, really cut both ways. The correction (by a later letter sent after the messengers) of a first command (in a letter to Aethelberht) for the destruction of heathen temples[1] would hardly have occurred to a forger, and it therefore carries weight. But the dates and the long interval between the questions (597) and the reply (601) are a little difficult. To heighten the success of Augustine, and to make the mission appear instantaneously successful would come natural to later writers. The later tradition which makes Aethelberht as a second Constantine give up his palace to Augustine as another Sylvester is one indication of such a tendency. If the baptism really took place in 598 the difficulties are less.

The first question relates to the division of the offerings of the faithful between the bishop and his clergy: to this the answer was that the Roman custom was a fourfold division between the bishop, the clergy, the poor and the repair of the churches. But, since Augustine and his companions were monks, they would live in common, so that they would share the offerings in common also. As to the clergy in minor orders they should receive their stipends separately, might live apart and might take wives: but they were bound to obey church rule.

The purely monastic type of mission brought incidentally with it a difference between the systems of division first of offerings, then of systematised tithes, in England, where a fourfold division found no place, and on the Continent, if indeed we can generalise as to the custom observed abroad. Later ecclesiastical regulations and orders

---

[1] *Idolorum cultus insequere, fanorum aedificia everte.* Bede, *H. E.* I. c. 32 (adding date 22 June 601). But is this intended to be more than rhetoric? For cases among Franks see Hauck, *K.G.D.* I. pp. 121–2.

attempted to bring the Frankish system into England, but the English division remained different from the continental.

The second question was why one custom of saying mass should be observed in the Roman Church, and another in the Church of Gaul. The Pope replied that things were not to be loved for the sake of places, but places for the sake of good things: hence what was good in any local custom might be brought into the Church of the English—advice which has been sometimes held to sanction a liturgic freedom not likely to commend itself to the somewhat correct mind of Augustine, and certainly not used by him. Questions as to punishment for thefts from churches and as to the degrees for marriage were perhaps needful in a rough society, and one case mentioned—that of a marriage of a man with his step-mother—presented itself in the case of Aethelberht's successor Eadbald, who took to himself his father's second wife. But as the background to some of these questions there is clearly something of the same social condition which produced the Penitentials of later dates, although it is going too far to ascribe them as a whole to a later day and to Archbishop Theodore as writer.

The sixth and seventh questions dealt with the Episcopate: when asked whether one bishop might consecrate by himself in cases of need, Gregory replied that Augustine, as the only bishop of the Church of England, could do nothing but consecrate alone unless bishops from Gaul chanced to be present. Provision for new sees should, however, be made so that this difficulty should disappear, and then three or four bishops should be present. The seventh question asked how Augustine was to deal with the bishops of Gaul and Britain. Here it may be noted that when elsewhere he spoke of bishops in the neighbourhood of the English Gregory seems to have meant the bishops in Gaul: the British bishops he seems to have ignored. But here he commits them (*Brittanniarum omnes episcopos*) to the care of Augustine (who is, of course, to exercise no authority in Gaul, although he is to be on terms of fellowship with the bishops there), so that "the unlearned may be taught, the weak made stronger by persuasion, and the perverse corrected by authority."

These answers were brought to Augustine by a band of new missionaries, Mellitus, Justus, Paulinus and others, who carried with them sacred vessels, vestments and books, as well as a pall for Augustine. He was to consecrate twelve bishops to be under his jurisdiction as bishop of London. For the city of York a bishop was also to be consecrated, who was, as the districts beyond York gradually received the word of God, also to consecrate twelve bishops under himself as metropolitan. During Augustine's lifetime the Bishop of York was to be subject to him, but afterwards the northern metropolitan was to be independent, and the metropolitan first ordained of the two ruling together was to have precedence. All these bishops were to act together in councils and so on. To Augustine, likewise, Gregory committed all the priests of Britain.

To Mellitus, after he had started, the Pope also sent a later letter (22 June), in which he gave directions about the use of heathen temples; the buildings themselves were not to be destroyed, as he had said before to Aethelberht, but the idols were to be broken and the places purified, altars were to be built, and then the temples were to become churches. Thus the people would keep their old holy places; and rejoicings, like those on the old heathen festivals, were to be allowed them on days of dedication or the nativities of holy martyrs. The church of St Martin at Canterbury had already been given to the mission: on another site, that of an old church once used by Roman Christians, Augustine had built Christ Church, which was to become the mother church of England and the centre of a great monastery: another ruined building—which had been used as a temple—was purified and dedicated as St Pancras, a Roman martyr: outside the city walls the king built a church, St Peter and St Paul, also to be the centre of a monastery, afterwards known, when Laurentius had consecrated it, as St Augustine's, of which Peter was the first abbot. Here the kings and the archbishops were to be buried, and between this monastery and Christ Church a long-lived jealousy arose, which had sometimes great effects upon ecclesiastical politics. In this way Augustine made Canterbury a great Christian centre. If the progress outside Kent was for a long time slow, the tenacity of the Christian hold upon Canterbury itself is also to be noted.

The growth of the mission in new fields and its relations with the British are henceforth the main threads of the history. A meeting with the British bishops and teachers was brought about at Augustine's oak on "the borders of the West Saxons and Hwicce" (either Aust on the Severn, or, less probably, a place near Malmesbury)—a local definition which changed between the days of Augustine and those of Bede. The bishops must have been those of South Wales, and those of Devon and North Wales may have been with them, but the Britons of the West country were now separated from those of Wales by the advance of the West Saxons after Dyrham (577). Augustine urged these bishops to keep catholic unity and join in preaching the Gospel to the English. This task they had not attempted of their own accord: they were still less likely to do it under the new leadership.

There were points of difference between the Roman and British Christians, breaches of uniformity due to a long separation, rather than to original differences, but tending towards difference of spirit, at the very time, moreover, when unity of feeling and of action was most necessary; standing as their observance of Easter shewed outside the general trend of European custom, the British held an attitude towards Rome which had belonged to an earlier day. But these differences, almost

CH. XVI (B).

accidental to begin with, were exaggerated into matters of Christian liberty on the one side, into matters of heresy upon the other. The difference in the date of Easter had been caused by the separation of Britain from the Empire; the British had kept the old cycle of eighty-four years used generally in the West before the English conquest: since the separation Rome—followed gradually by the West— had twice changed to a better cycle, and the last change, moreover, had brought the West into accord with the East[1]. Furthermore Romans and Britons started from a different vernal equinox: 21 March and 25 March respectively; the Britons also kept Easter on the fourteenth of Nisan if that were a Sunday: but the Romans in that case kept it on the Sunday following. There were thus ample differences which would lead to practical discord: but there was no excuse for the charge of Quartodecimanism against the British, for they did not keep the fourteenth of Nisan if it fell on a week-day. There were other differences also; in the tonsure where the Britons (and the Kelts generally) merely shaved the front of the head, whereas the Romans shaved the crown in a circle, and in baptism where the precise difference is unknown. No decision was reached: even the demonstration by Augustine of his gift of miracles—an account of which had reached Rome and caused the Pope to write to him advising humility and self-examination in face of success—was not decisive. The British representatives went back to consult their fellows, and a second meeting—probably in the same place—followed. It is here that Bede places the British story of the way in which upon the advice of a hermit the British discovered the pride of Augustine. But if there was on his side some pride in the older civilisation cherished in the Western capital, there was on the other side the obstinacy of a race long left to itself, and over-jealous of its independence.

At the second conference Augustine—ready to overlook some particulars of British use which were contrary to Western customs—laid down three conditions of union: the same date for Easter; the observance of Roman custom in baptism; and fellowship in missions to the English. But to these conditions the British would not agree, nor would they receive him as their archbishop. It is perhaps well to observe that the difference on these three conditions would have interfered with the attraction of converts. In the eyes of Augustine the mission would appear to have ranked above questions of precedence: the British had not yet overcome their national repugnance to the English, and they saw, what became plainer in later years, that the leadership of the Roman missionaries would be a necessary result from fellowship in work. The growth of bitterness between the races was quickened by the failure of these negotiations.

---

[1] On all these points see the Excursus in Plummer's *Bede*, II. pp. 348 f.

A step forward in organisation was taken when (604) Augustine consecrated Justus to be bishop of Durobrivae, or Rochester in West Kent, and Mellitus to be bishop of London for the East Saxons—whose king Saeberht[1] had become a Christian and was now subject to Kent. Shortly afterwards Augustine died (605), and was followed in his see by Laurentius, who had been already consecrated in his leader's lifetime.

The character of the founder of the line of *papae alterius orbis* has been often sketched in very different colours, and sometimes perhaps with outlines too firm for the material we have at hand. It was long before the enmity between the Britons and English died down, and until it did so the two sides distorted his words and deeds: Britons exaggerated his haughtiness and pride: English exaggerated his firmness in correcting an upstart race. The ordinary view bears marks of both these exaggerations. Disputes between English independence and Papal rule have had a like effect, and incidents in his career have been twisted overmuch to suit a given framework. Our earlier records may not have drawn him exactly as he was: modern writers have certainly taken even greater liberty. He did not rise to the dignity of a Boniface or a Columbanus, but the limits both upwards and downwards of his personality are shewn us by what he did. Unsympathetic yet patient, constructive and systematic he had the genius of his race, he had learnt and could teach the discipline which had trained him, and his personality has been overshadowed by his work.

The rule of Laurentius is known principally for an unsuccessful attempt to reconcile the Irish. An Irish (Scots) bishop Dagan coming among the English would not even eat in the same house with Laurentius and his followers: accordingly Laurentius wrote to "his dearest brothers, the bishops and abbots through all Scotia," pressing unity upon them. But nothing came either of this attempt, or from a like letter to the British, although they may have led to the Canterbury tradition of Laurentius' friendly relations with the British.

Even before the death of Aethelberht—after a long reign of 56 years (616)—the power of Kent had been waning. Raedwald of East Anglia, once a vassal of Kent, who had been baptised at Canterbury, had renounced his allegiance and had tried to combine in some strange way the worship of Christ and of the old gods. In 617 this Raedwald was strong enough to beat even the victorious Aethelfrith king of Northumbria, who had himself beaten the Dalriadic Scots in the North and the Britons at Chester (616)[2]. This latter victory had separated the Britons of Wales from their northern kinsmen, just as the victory of Dyrham (577) had separated them from the south. The

---

[1] Mr W. J. Corbett suggests that Saeberht's name is handed down in Sawbridgeworth (Herts.), a corruption of the Domesday Sabrictesweorthig (cf. Domesday, I. 139 *b*).

[2] For the date see Plummer's *Bede*, II. p. 77. But it is only approximate.

warfare between Raedwald and Aethelfrith had important consequences, both for religion and politics. Edwin, son of Aelle of Deira, was in exile, as his kingdom had been seized on his father's death (588) by Aethelric of Bernicia. Aethelric's son, Aethelfrith, a great warrior against the British, now ruled over both Northern kingdoms, and, to make his dynasty sure, sought the death of his brother-in-law, Edwin, who as babe and youth found shelter first in Wales and then with Raedwald of East Anglia. The East Anglian king refused to give up the fugitive, and in the war which followed he seized Lindsey and then defeated the Bernicians on the ford of the Idle in North Mercia. Aethelfrith was slain, and Edwin gained not only his father's kingdom but also Bernicia.

Aethelberht in Kent had been succeeded by his son Eadbald, who took to himself his father's second wife, thus separating himself from the Christians. In Essex, too, the Christian Saeberht was succeeded by his two sons Saexred and Saeward, who being pagans at heart in the end drove Mellitus away from London. Laurentius was now left alone, for Mellitus and Justus fled to the Franks, and even he was preparing for flight, when a dream delayed him. But before long Eadbald professed Christianity. Justus returned to Rochester, and, in the end, the deaths of Laurentius (619) and his successor Mellitus (624) placed him on the throne of Canterbury (624–627). Mellitus however was not readmitted to London: Kent alone kept its Christianity, but soon the conversion of Northumbria, when Honorius (627–653) was archbishop, brought about a great change.

On Raedwald's death his supremacy passed gradually into the hands of Edwin of Northumbria.

This prince married as his second wife Aethelburga (or Tata), daughter of Aethelberht of Kent, and sister to Eadbald, who was now a Christian. On his marriage he promised his wife liberty for her religion, and even hinted that he might consider the faith for himself. Paulinus, one of the second band of Roman missionaries, went with her to the North, and before he left Canterbury was consecrated bishop by Justus (21 July 625). A year after the marriage Cuichelm king of Wessex sent one Eomer to Edwin to assassinate him, but the devotion of a thegn Lilla, whose name was long remembered, saved Edwin's life; that same night the queen bore him a daughter, Eanfled, the first Northumbrian to be baptised. In double gratitude the king vowed to become a Christian if he defeated his West Saxon foe. When later on he returned home victorious he therefore submitted himself to instruction by Paulinus, and slowly pondered over the new faith. A mysterious vision[1], which he had seen long before at the East Anglian court, when

---

[1] *Oroma gentilis quae viderat ipse supernum, nocte soporata.* (*Carmen de Pontificibus ecclesiae Eboracensis* in Raine: *Historians of the Church of York and its Archbishops, R. S.* i. p. 352.) On the other hand Bede, *H. E.* ii. chap. 12.

a stranger promised him safety and future power, giving him a secret
sign for remembrance, was now recalled to him by Paulinus along with
the secret sign which the messenger in the vision had given him.
Edwin was convinced for himself and called his Witan together in
eastern Deira to debate with Paulinus over the new faith. Hitherto
there had been no sign of life or strength in the English heathenism,
and now Coifi, the chief of the king's priests, shewed its weakness by
his speech: he is the first of his class we meet with, for too much stress
must not be laid on Bede's mention (II. chap. 6) of the "idolatrous
high priests" (*idolatris pontificibus*) who hardened the hearts of the
Londoners against receiving back Mellitus. Bede gives us an account
of the debate, probably from some old tradition, embodying truth but
not to be pressed in detail: Coifi gave his view that the religion they
professed had absolutely no virtue, and no usefulness: he had been its
diligent servant, and had gained no reward. A chieftain spoke next of
more spiritual things: the future life of man seemed dark and mysterious as the night outside might seem to a bird flying through the fire-lit
space where they sat: perchance this new faith could penetrate the
darkness. Coifi thereupon took the lead in profaning and destroying a
neighbouring temple at Goodmanham, by Market Weighton. Afterwards Edwin (12 April 627, Easter day) was baptised at York in the
little wooden church he had built during his preparation for baptism[1].
But after his baptism he built there—in the middle of the old Roman
city, where Severus and Chlorus had died, and whence Constantine had
started on his great career—a nobler church of stone, a material which
marked the beginnings of a new civilisation. This, however, was still
left unfinished when he died, but its site is now covered by the present
crypt.

For six years Paulinus preached and taught both in Bernicia and
Deira, though he left most mark in the latter: from Catterick southwards as far as Campodunum (possibly Slack, near Huddersfield) he
journeyed and sojourned, catechising and baptising, and a church
here, afterwards destroyed by the pagan Mercians, marked his work at
the latter place. In Lindsey also—the north of Lincolnshire, a district
at that time tributary to Northumbria—he taught, and at Lincoln he
built a stone church of beautiful workmanship, in which on the death
of Justus of Canterbury (10 Nov., probably 627) he consecrated as
successor Honorius. In these labours Paulinus was helped by others,
especially by James his deacon, who was not only a man of zeal, but
very skilful in song. When in later days Paulinus fled southwards,
James stayed behind, and around his home near Catterick he taught

---

[1] In Nennius and in the *Annales Cambriae* we find the baptism of Edwin
ascribed to Rhun, the son of Urbgen, but this seems strange in face of what Bede
says, and of the Roman connexions of Paulinus. Most probably it is only a later
Keltic attempt to claim Edwin as a convert won by British efforts.

many to sing in "the Roman or the Canterbury way." This knowledge of music in Yorkshire, which long afterwards caught the notice of Giraldus Cambrensis, was kept alive and furthered by Eddius under Wilfrid and by John (formerly arch-chanter at St Peter's in Rome) under Benedict Biscop. Outside Northumbria, too, the influence of Paulinus worked change. In East Anglia Eorpwald, son of Raedwald (627), was now king, and, by the persuasion of Edwin, was brought, with his territory, to Christianity.

Before long Eorpwald was, however, assassinated by a pagan, and for three years the kingdom fell into idolatry until the accession of his brother Sigebert (630 or 631), who in a time of exile among the Franks had been baptised and more fully taught religion. In the conversion of his kingdom he was greatly helped by Felix, a Burgundian, who had come to Honorius for missionary work in England, had been sent by him to Sigebert, and then placed in Dunwich as bishop for his kingdom (631-647): here there was not only a church built, but a school "after the manner of Kent," in which youths were taught. From quite another part came a fellow-labourer: Fursey from Ireland, the founder of a monastery at Cnobheresburg, often but doubtfully taken to be Burgh Castle near Great Yarmouth, renowned not only for his saintliness but for his mystic experiences and visions; he wandered, as so many of his race did, from a wish to lead the pilgrim life, and like Aidan (with whom Bede instinctively joins him) he was torn in two by the love of mankind, driving him to active work, and by the love of solitude, driving him to the hermit's life.

When his East Anglian monastery was well founded, he handed it over to his brother, Fullan (Faelan), who was a bishop, and the priests Gobban and Dicul. Later, when Penda of Mercia was restoring heathenism, he passed to the land of the Franks and there under Clovis II (638-656) he founded the monastery of Lagny on the Marne. When he was on the point of leaving this new home for a visit to his brethren he died (*c.* 647). His life is significant not only of Keltic restlessness and devotion, but also of the many influences now working on missions: in East Anglia as in the larger field beyond impulses from Rome, Burgundy, Gaul and Ireland all worked together: national and racial antagonisms were overcome by the solvent of Christianity. A new unity was growing up in the West as formerly in the East. What happened in East Anglia, and has been recorded, almost by accident, must have also happened elsewhere.

The energy of Paulinus, backed by the power of Edwin, had wrought so much that the Pope (now Honorius I) carried out the plan of Gregory the Great by sending to Paulinus a pall with the title of archbishop. But the bearers of the gift reached England only to find that Paulinus had fled from the North. Edwin's rule had been effective beyond anything known so far among the English: peace for travellers was enforced, and the king's dignity was shewn in a growing pomp: banners were borne before him not only in war but during peace, and the *tufa* carried before him on his progresses seemed a claim to a power that was either very old or very new. Suddenly this prosperous rule was interrupted by a league between Penda of Mercia, who had gradually grown in power since his accession (626), and Cadwallon of North Wales. In the woodlands of Heathfield, near Doncaster, Edwin was defeated (12 October 633) and slain. York was taken, Deira laid waste: Aethelburga fled with Paulinus, and a time of disorder and paganism "hateful to all good men" began. In Deira Edwin's cousin Osric, in Bernicia Eanfrid, son of Aethelfrith, ruled, and both of them fell from the faith. Within a year Osric was slain in battle against the Welsh who seem to have been holding the land: Eanfrid too was slain when he came to sue for peace from Cadwallon. Eanfrid's brother, Oswald, succeeded, able in war, glorious in peace, and on the Heavenfield, near Chollerford, just north of Hexham, he defeated Cadwallon as he advanced against him from York and slew him on the Deniseburn (635). For a time the northern lands had peace, and Oswald's influence soon reached beyond his own borders. His nearest neighbour, Penda of Mercia, however, more than held his own, and even harried Ecgric, who had succeeded Sigebert in East Anglia: but over the West Saxons Oswald held some kind of influence, which he used to further Christianity. Birinus, according to later tradition a Roman, had gone to Pope Honorius offering himself for missionary service, and after consecration by Asterius, archbishop of Milan, he was sent to Wessex (634): he had meant to work in the inland districts, but in the end stayed near the coast, and so became the apostle of Wessex: the king Cynegils became a Christian; Birinus was consecrated as bishop of Dorchester on Thames (Dorcic), but we know little in detail of his work beyond its results.

When Ecgric was attacked by Penda, Sigebert, recalled from a monastery to lead his former subjects, went to battle armed only with a wand: both he and Ecgric were slain, and Anna, nephew of Raedwald, succeeded. This new king's house was noted for its monastic zeal, and in the number of its saints rivalled the line of Penda. His step-daughter Saethryd and his daughter Aethelburga crossed over to the Franks to the monastery of Brie (Faremoutier-en-Brie): here in a double monastery for both sexes like Whitby (Streoneshalh), favoured by the same dynasty afterwards—both became abbesses. Hither also Ercon-berht of Kent—the first English king to follow Frankish rulers in destroying idols—sent a daughter. An impulse was thus given by the foreign connexion to the growth of monasticism in England: by the middle of the century there were about a dozen houses founded, and through Aethelthryth (Aetheldreda, Audrey) the foundress of Ely, and others, the East Anglian line was foremost in the movement.

CH. XVI (B).

Paulinus, traces of whose work long remained[1], had fled southwards in 633 and there he became, through one of the translations so common in that day, the bishop of Rochester. After his departure the Christianity of Northumbria passed into another phase. In his long exile Oswald had been sheltered among the Scots, and had come to know something of the enthusiasm and learning which made them the best teachers of the day. He had been baptised at Iona, and thither he now sent for a bishop. One was sent, whose name the fine reticence of Bede concealed for a Scots writer some centuries later to supply, but he despaired of the task and went home again. Then Aidan (Aedan), the gentle and devoted, was consecrated bishop and sent (635). After the Scots custom he took his seat on an island, Lindisfarne, or Holy Island, near to the Bernician capital Bamborough. Here there grew up a monastery on the Keltic plan like that of Iona: ruled, however, by Aidan himself, as abbot and bishop, it was also a new and effective missionary centre for Bernicia. Through it Irish (or Scots) influence reached north-eastern England, and changed the land much as it had changed western Scotland. It spread far southwards, but its original home was Iona.

Keltic monasticism, and the work of Columba around Iona, have been described in previous chapters of this work. The eremitic tendency of Keltic monasticism never disappeared, and just as the original monasteries in Ireland itself were mission stations for the tribes among which they were placed, so Iona (originally Hii or Ioua, from which by a mistaken reading Iona has arisen) became a mission station not only for the Dalriadic Scots but for the Picts. Irish monasticism, however, underwent some changes outside Ireland: the love of wandering, the restlessness which Columba " the soldier of the island" shewed by his inability to be idle even for an hour, drove the monks to travel (*pro Christo peregrinari*): on the Continent they aimed at living as strangers: but at Iona Columba and his successors strove to learn the Pictish tongue, and mission work seems to have been esteemed even more highly there than the life of quiet devotion. Learning, however, was never forgotten: not only Columba but his successor Baithene (597–600) copied manuscripts. And where Iona led Lindisfarne followed. But more than all other characteristics the enthusiasm and simplicity of the Irish monks appealed to their hearers and neighbours. Above all it was in Aidan, the apostle of the north, that these spiritual gifts were seen, and on his long preaching tours he won the hearts of all. Oswald himself often went with him as interpreter (from which we may infer that Aidan did not gain the same mastery of language that Columba

---

[1] Traces of respect for the Roman mission are seen in about thirty dedications to St Gregory—mainly old and spread nearly evenly over the country. Kirkdale in Yorkshire and Kirknewton in Northumberland (Plummer's *Bede*, II. p. 105) are the most interesting. See Miss Arnold Forster, *Studies in Church Dedications*, I. p. 308.

did), and as a king Oswald answered to Aidan's ideal: frequent in prayer, fruitful in alms, the first English king to have, or indeed to need, an almoner.

But once again Penda of Mercia broke in: leagued with Cadwalader, successor to Cadwallon, he defeated Oswald at Maserfield (642). Oswald's severed head was rescued and carried off first to Lindisfarne; thence afterwards in St Cuthbert's coffin to Durham, where it was seen in the present generation[1].

In Bernicia Oswald was succeeded by his brother Oswy (Oswiu), but in Deira the old dynastic jealousy revived, and Edwin's kinsman Oswin was chosen king. But Oswy joined the rival houses, for he fetched from Kent Edwin's daughter Eanfled, and made her his queen. Soon afterwards Oswin, who was like Oswald in his goodness and his friendship for Aidan, was betrayed to Oswy at Gilling, and slain (651). Eleven days later Aidan himself died, but his spirit and his work lived on in the school he had made and the disciples he had trained.

In the mere record of events, mainly wars and revolutions, it is easy to overlook the gradual work, the change of character, the growth of civilisation, which had been slowly taking place. The missions from the Continent had brought with them a larger outlook, a wider knowledge of a varied world, and a vision of a vaster unity with an ancient background: the Irish missions had brought deep devotion, spiritual intensity, and the traditions of the great Irish schools. In the north of England these two streams of life were joined, and a rich civilisation was the outcome. Jarrow and Monkwearmouth reached to Iona on the west and to Canterbury on the south, and both Canterbury and Iona stood for a great past. Historic feeling had led Columba to defend the bards[2] for their services to history: Canterbury, by instinct and tradition as well as by training, held to the past, and Bede, like Alcuin later, inherited something from each. Hence come not only his love for religion and order, but also his love of history and historic truth. It was these which helped him to see the growing unity and drove him to record the *Ecclesiastical History of the English Nation*. What he felt in himself answered to the many-sided history with its growing life. We owe him so much for his preservation of details otherwise unknown, for his diligent search after truth, that we are likely to forget his sense of the unity, the common life, which was now growing up out of many elements and from many local beginnings. Bede is the first prophet of English unity, and the first to tell its tale.

The English were now taking their place in civilisation and Christianity. They were soon to be the great missionaries of Europe: they were now able to care for themselves. In 644 Ithamar, the first

---

[1] See A. Plummer, *The Church in Britain before* 1000, I. p. 99. For the battle, see Chap. XVII. in this vol.

[2] Fowler, *Adamnani vita Columbae*, Introd. p. xxi.

Englishman to be "hallowed" as bishop, took the bishop's stool at Rochester: in 647 and 652 Englishmen, first Thomas and then Berctgils (Boniface), became bishops of Dunwich. Honorius at Canterbury died (30 September 653), and after a long vacancy was succeeded by a West Saxon, Frithonas, who took the name of Deusdedit. But in spite of local work and impulses, in spite of gradual change, there was little real unity even of effort, there was still less of organisation. The Roman missionaries had a wider background of civilisation, and were accustomed to larger states with wider interests. They worked for unity, and against the persistence of little states with many narrow policies: to secure civilisation it was necessary to reach larger union. There was already the rich variety of personal character and life: something more was needed now. It was the perception of this lack on the part of the English themselves, and not merely the accident of events, that led to the synod of Whitby and the work of Theodore.

The success of the Scots mission in the north had brought up once more the old differences between the Keltic and Roman Churches: the same difficulty had met Augustine, and the crisis would have come earlier had it not been for the gentle influence of Aidan. When Oswy's bride went northwards she took with her a chaplain Romanus, who kept Easter by the general and Roman rule, whereas the Scots had naturally brought with them their own use. In southern Ireland the Roman Easter had been already adopted (before 634), but the weight of Iona had been thrown strongly upon the other side, so that northern Ireland, Iona and its offshoots, kept to their older usage. Finan, Aidan's successor at Lindisfarne (651–661), had come to Lindisfarne fresh from discussions between the two parties in the Irish monasteries: he found James the deacon, and Ronan, a Scot of continental education and sympathies, urging the Roman use which had now the support of a party at court. Finan was himself a controversialist but he was also more. It was in his days that Peada, son of Penda, and under him king of the Middle Angles (Northamptonshire), married Oswy's daughter, was baptised, and with his father's tacit leave brought Christianity into his sub-kingdom, so influencing Mercia as a whole. The band of missionaries who went to his help from Northumbria was made up of three Northumbrians, including Chad's brother Cedd, and one Scot, Diuma. Diuma became bishop of the Middle Angles and the Mercians after the death of Penda, which took away the last vigorous supporter of heathenism. Under all this turmoil a new generation, with its own point of view, its own work and interests, was growing up. Men who differed from each other were being brought together in peaceful work as well as in controversy. New openings were also being made for work: there was, as Bede tells us, such a scarcity of priests that one bishop—like Diuma—had to be set over two peoples. Diuma was followed by another Scot Ceollach, who left his diocese to return to Iona: then came Trumhere "brought up in the monastic life, English by nation, but ordained bishop by the Scots." Christianity in England was forming a type of its own, moulded by many forces, and the many-sided life, spiritual and intellectual, of Bede's own monastery enabled him to understand this growth.

In Essex Sigebert II (the Good), although still heathen, was a friend of Oswy's and a visitor at his court: in the end he and his attendants were baptised by Finan: the place of baptism was Attewall (? *Ad Murum*, near Newcastle), where Peada was also baptised, and the times of the two baptisms may have been the same[1].

Cedd recalled from Mercia went to Essex as chaplain to this royal convert and after some success in work went home to Lindisfarne for a visit. Here Finan "calling to himself two other bishops for the ministry of ordination"—a sign that the English Church was now passing into more settled life—consecrated him bishop for Essex. As bishop he went back, ordained priests and deacons, built churches at Tilbury and elsewhere, teaching "also the discipline of a life of rule." But his love was divided between the work of his diocese, and the monastic life. Aethelwald of Deira, Oswald's son, who held Deira at some time possibly after the murder of Oswin, was deeply attached to Cedd and his three brothers, one of whom, Celin, was his chaplain. As a place of retreat for the bishop and as a burial-place for the king, a site was chosen "in hills steep and remote, rather hiding places for robbers and homes of wild beasts than habitations for men," and here grew up the famous house of Lastingham[2], where Cedd and after him Chad were abbots. Keltic influence was thus strong. But at the same time we have many signs of a growing unity. Thus we find Oswy of Northumbria and Ecgbert of Kent joining, on the death of Deusdedit of Canterbury (655–664), to choose a successor Wighard, a priest at Canterbury, and send him to Rome for consecration by Vitalian. When part of Essex lapsed into idolatry, Wulfhere of Mercia, who stood over the East Saxon sub-kings Sebbi the Christian and Sighere the heathen, sent his own bishop Iaruman of Mercia to reconvert it (665). Local barriers are thus everywhere overstepped.

The Yellow Pest with all its horrors had caused widespread terror and thrown everything out of gear. The roll of its victims was long. Erconberht king of Kent as well as the archbishop Deusdedit, Tuda bishop at Lindisfarne, the saintly Cedd at Lastingham (where Chad succeeded him): at Melrose the prior Boisil, where also his successor the devoted Cuthbert the missionary of the north all but died. In Essex

---

[1] See Plummer's *Bede*, note, ii. p. 178 : for chronology of Essex, p. 177.

[2] Bede says of the site *quod uocatur Laestingaeu*—with some variations in spelling. This has naturally been taken as Lastingham, but the existence of earlier remains at Kirkdale, with its old church of St Gregory restored under Tostig as Earl of Northumbria, has led antiquarians to place the site there. Kirkdale might be described as in the district, but the evidence is not conclusive.

to the south, and northwards by the Tweed, men turned again to witch-craft and heathen charms. In its mortality and its effects upon society it was somewhat like the later Black Death. Hence the religious and social reconstruction which follows it is all the more significant.

The South Saxons were the last tribe to be brought to Christianity. Wilfrid, whose character was moulded by many forces to be typical of the new age, was chosen, probably through the influence of Alchfrid, Oswy's son, to succeed Tuda. There were few bishops left, and some of those were of Scots consecration. Wilfrid, the eager supporter of continental customs, went to Frankish bishops for consecration. This he received at Compiègne, under ceremonies of unusual pomp, and among the prelates who shared in it was Agilbert (Albert) of Wessex. This bishop, coming originally from the Franks, had worked in Wessex under Coenwalch, until the king grew weary of his " barbarous" speech[1], and invited Wini (also of apparently Frankish ordination) to take the see. Then Agilbert went (663) to Northumbria for a time, after which he went home. Wini's story was unhappy: not many years afterwards he too was driven out of his see, whereupon he "bought" from Wulfhere " for a price" the see of London, and there remained. In all this moral disorder thrown by Bede upon a strange background of miracle and portent can be seen some result of the Pest.

Wilfrid tarried too long among the Franks, for when he reached Northumbria he found Chad placed in his seat. He then retired to his old monastery of Ripon. But in his voyage homewards (spring 666) he had been thrown upon the Sussex coast, and narrowly escaped capture by the barbarians: a wizard standing upon a mound sought to help the wreckers with his charms: he was slain "like Goliath" by a sling, and thus only after a fight did Wilfrid and his company escape. But later on he was to return to Sussex. Meanwhile from Ripon he acted at times as bishop both in Mercia, where along with Wulfhere he founded monasteries such as Oundle, and also in Kent during the vacancy at Canterbury, where as his biographer Eddius tells us he studied the Benedictine rule. Thus he gained something for his native north, and to the south he in turn gave gifts of music, and of crafts, through the singers and the masons who travelled in his train. Even before he worked in Sussex Wilfrid a Northerner was in himself a bond of union between North and South. After 681, when Aethelwalch of Sussex had already become a Christian through the persuasion of Wulfhere, and as we may suppose also of his own queen, Ebba, who came from the Christian district of the Hwicce, Wilfrid began effective work in the almost untouched Sussex. A Scot Dicul had already founded a small monastery at Bosham (Bosanham), but the monks probably lived as

---

[1] See Bede, *H.E.* iii. 7, *barbarae loquellae*. See Plummer's notes, ii. pp. 41 and 146; Bright, *Early Eng. Ch. Hist.* p. 208 note and Freeman, *Life and Letters*, ii. p. 229, who took it to mean Frankish which the king could just understand.

foreigners apart from the people and at any rate had small success. Wilfrid's foundation of Selsey was to have a wider influence. This work of peace is a relief to the ecclesiastical quarrels of Wilfrid's later years. His work in Sussex completed the conversion of the English.

With the Synod of Whitby (664) under Finan's successor Colman and with the coming of Archbishop Theodore (669–690) a new period begins. The wanderings of bishops from see to see, the mingling of missionary effort with more strictly local work, had been even more marked in England than on the Continent. This was not merely a result of Scots or Irish influence; indeed the type of Keltic bishop, non-territorial and with little power, which we know the best, was probably less an original institution than the work of time. There is reason to think that territorial bishops were found in Ireland to begin with[1], and that the later type was due to the same social and ecclesiastical causes which later produced like results in Wales, making the Church pre-eminently monastic, and raising the power of abbots. There were not wanting signs that in the early English Church something the same might have taken place had it not been for the Synod of Whitby and Theodore[2]. After them the work of a bishop becomes more fixed, and its area is limited. But the relative importance of the Synod and of Theodore's rule is sometimes wrongly presented. The Synod with its removal of the obstacle to unity—the difference in Easter—was a striking witness to the need of union and the desire for it. It is not, however, until Theodore comes that the type of bishop is changed: with that the danger from monasticism which threatened England as it later on affected Keltic lands was greatly lessened. What might otherwise have been we can see from the words of Bede in his letter to Ecgbert; from the pretended monasteries, really secular in life and under the control of nobles, great danger threatened and even arose. The Synod of Hertford (673) indeed confirmed those monastic immunities which were now growing up (Canon 3). But its reorganisation of episcopal power prevented this danger being what it would otherwise have been, and the other canons of Hertford enforced a vigorous discipline. In its lasting impression upon the English Church the primacy of Theodore is unique: it summed up the varied past: it was the birthday of a more vigorous and ordered life.

It has become common to weigh the shares of Roman and Keltic missions in the great work thus summed up. The tendency has been to ascribe too much to the charming characters of the northern saints, and to overlook the quiet persistence of the Roman builders. But in striving after a balanced judgment it is possible to place the two parties too distinctly against each other. The generation which came

---

[1] See Bury's *St Patrick*, Appendix 18, p. 375.
[2] For the political effect of church organisation see Chap. xvii.

just before the Synod of Whitby probably made less of the difference than we ourselves do: community of field and community of life was forming a community of type; the English missionaries who later on converted the Teutonic tribes based their work not only upon their own burning zeal but upon the life of monasteries and the care of bishops. These two things were the characteristics of English religious life in the seventh century, and they no less than the new-born religious zeal were due to a long history in which Kelt and Roman bore their part and under which they had grown and drawn together.

(2) GERMANY.

The conversion of the Franks to Christianity, and that too in its orthodox form, has been already dealt with[1]. According to the most probable view of evidence, not quite consistent, and not easy to weigh, Clovis was baptised on Christmas day 496, probably at Rheims[2]. He had however been friendly to Christianity even before his conquest of Syagrius (486), and became naturally more so afterwards. After his conversion, followed by that of many Franks, he was able as an orthodox king to reckon on the help or at least the sympathy of Catholic bishops everywhere: the wars that spread his power took somewhat the character of crusades and for three centuries this remained true of Frankish campaigns against the heathens. Broadly speaking, with the power of the Frankish kings went the power of the Church, although the fellowship between the two was sometimes closer, sometimes looser. As the Frankish power spread into districts less thoroughly Romanised new sees had to be founded, and even in the more settled lands this happened also. But a distinction must be made between the new missionary bishops and the type of bishops already found in the Romanised cities. Up to the settlement under Boniface (Winfrid, Bonifatius) or even later we have a time in which both types appear side by side. As a rule the city bishop owed his appointment to the State: the missionary bishop to the Church. It is not a question of differences between Roman and Keltic clergy, but merely between lands in which Roman traditions survived, and those where missions started quite afresh. What Theodore did for England Boniface was to do for the continental Teutons.

Local differences were many and strong: in Austrasia heathenism was more general to begin with and lived on longer. The Frankish conquests drove together heathens and Christians, and in some places heathenism gained strength: on the whole, the leading families and

---

[1] See Chaps. IV. V.
[2] See Chap. IV. p. 112. For date see Hauck, *K.G.D.* I., later edns, pp. 695 f., Vacandard in *Rev. du Clergé français,* 15 Oct. 1913, pp. 143 f.

the towns were more thoroughly Christianised than the country, which
remained mainly heathen. In some places—like Mainz, Cologne, and
Tongres—Christian communities, sometimes chiefly oriental or foreign,
may have lived on since Roman times and sometimes bishops were left:
in others—like Trier—Christianity was just becoming general when the
Frankish conquest brought in new conditions. Everything depended
upon the centres already gained for Christianity, and across the Rhine
these were few and tended to become fewer. Nearer Italy there were
centres to which Christianity had come from the south, such as Augsburg,
which until about the year 600 was connected with Aquileia. But where
such centres of life were few or Christianity had only begun its growth
the Teutonic invaders could be but little affected by it.

The Keltic missions came to give these new centres, and by a
monastic framework to guard their power. There are some indications
—in the letters of Boniface and elsewhere—that Keltic priests, some of
whom caused him trouble, were more widely spread than we might suppose.
And as Keltic monasteries became stages in systematic pilgrimages to
Rome a steady stream of Christianity was brought to bear upon the
Teutons. The Keltic missionaries were for the most part led to travel
by the wish to live amid new surroundings: they lived among their new
neighbours as strangers, but the evils around them forced them to
become missionaries, and, although Keltic monasticism was ascetic and
rigorous, Keltic monks never feared to plunge into the world and to
play a part there when it seemed good. Frankish Christianity, with its
comparative neglect of penance, seemed to the great missionary Columbanus merely superficial : he stood outside the ordinary Frankish Church :
his altar at Luxeuil was consecrated by an Irish bishop, and he had no
episcopal licence for his foundations. Hence the Keltic monasteries
besides being centres of learning strengthened the tendency already
shewn to exempt monasteries from episcopal control[1]. The difference
about Easter did not of necessity lead to lasting strife, and the
monastic foundations of Columbanus, his comrades and followers, kept
alive upon the Continent the Irish love of learning. As regards the
papal power Keltic tradition and habits belonged to an earlier day when
the papal control had been less effective; this tradition Columbanus
kept and shewed in his defence of the Keltic Easter. But it is a
mistake to take these differences as implying either hostility to the
Papacy or a claim to full independence.

The Keltic monks travelled for the most part in bands of twelve,
but there were other single teachers such as Rupert (Rodbert) a Frank
who towards the end of the seventh century came to Regensburg, the
ducal court of Bavaria, and thence passed into the wild Salzkammergut

---

[1] See Gougaud, *Les Chrétientés Celtiques*, p. 220; Hauck, *K. G. D.* i. pp. 266 and
310. For Columbanus see Chap. v. of this volume. For Severinus, vol. i. p. 425.

with its Roman memories and remains; here a monastery, a nunnery and
a church were planted. A like work was also wrought at Regensburg
by Emmeram, although his first hope had been to preach to the Avars.
These isolated endeavours gave new centres of Christian civilisation, but
in later years few traces of them were left. Work on a larger and more
considered plan was needed. But the life of St Severinus (died 482) in
Noricum (Bavaria) shews how far the influence of a hermit could reach
and how great it could be.

Frisia, with its unknown coasts and wild heathenism, soon began
to attract missionaries. The growth of Christianity here had been due
to the Franks and varied with the state of their church: simony and
careless appointments of bishops had been somewhat checked: the
influence of Columbanus had reached far, not only in the south but
even northwards to the Marne: a new and differently trained generation had grown up, and when the union of the kingdoms under
Chlotar II (613) gave the land rest, the church thus strengthened broke
fresh ground among its neighbours to east and north. Chlotar II had
encouraged Amandus, a hermit of Roman descent from Aquitaine, who
felt himself called by St Peter to distant missions: pilgrimages to Rome
deepened the wish, and after Chlotar had procured his consecration he
worked as a missionary bishop from Ghent as a centre. Hitherto Frisian
merchants had come to the Franks, and Frankish rule had gained
ground upon the borders, but even Maestricht and Noyon, although
bishoprics, were yet partly heathen. Quarrels with King Dagobert, and
banishment for a time (629) turned him to other fields. But both
around Ghent and at Maestricht where he was afterwards bishop (647)
he was unhappy in his work: the enforcement of baptism by royal order
under Dagobert may have been due to his suggestion, and at any rate it
explains his lack of success: spells of work on the Danube, in Carinthia,
at the mouth of the Scheldt and among the Basques varied a strange
career marked by restless energy and much wandering. After his death
a little more ground was gained under the direction of Cunibert of
Cologne, a church was built at Utrecht, and under the well-known
Eligius (bishop of Noyon, 641, and renowned as a silversmith) a better
foundation was laid. But the task was left unfinished until the following
century. Frisia was affected by the changes of Frankish politics.
Christian missions were both too fitful and too disconnected. A general
plan and organisation was needed.

In England, as the letter of Daniel bishop of Winchester to Boniface
(*Ep.* 23) shews, the methods of missions had been carefully thought out,
since the local conditions not only aroused enthusiasm to call forth
missionaries but gave them a training ground for their work. Englishmen were learning at this very time what careful organisation and
ordered work could do. They had felt the benefit of fellowship with
Rome and its traditions while they had still the fresh energy of

younger tribes and growing states. This is the reason why in the eighth century English missionaries take the place of the earlier Kelts.

And the field of labour seemed already fixed for them: they had not forgotten the land from which they had come. Wilfrid landed in Frisia (678) on his way to Rome—in order to avoid the enmity of Ebroin, mayor of the palace—and stayed there a winter because of the friendly welcome by Adelgis the king (who refused to sell his guest) and his people. This was only an episode. Ecgbert, a Northumbrian who was afterwards to go to Iona, who had lived long in Ireland and pledged himself to pilgrimage, was hindered by visions and by storms from a long desired journey to Frisia: in his place he sent a pupil Wicbert who only stayed two years and then went home again. This failure only caused Ecgbert to send another mission of twelve monks. The leader of it, Willibrord, was a Northumbrian whose father Wilgils in old age became a hermit at the Humber's mouth. He had been educated up to the age of twenty at Ripon—Wilfrid's old monastic home—and afterwards in Ireland (*c.* 678). He landed and went to Utrecht, now held by Radbod the Frisian king, who must have regained territory, for Utrecht had formerly been a Frankish town. But Frisia beyond it was lost to the Franks as the result of a war which was just ended and had naturally left ill-will behind it. The defeated Radbod was little likely to favour the faith of his Frankish enemies, and Willibrord saw a chance of securer work under Frankish protection. He therefore journeyed to Pepin, who promised him help for a work which was of interest to both of them. Willibrord shared the enthusiasm of Wilfrid and Boniface for Rome—and indeed others, the Irish Adamnan and Ecgbert for instance, were turning towards Rome and unity. Accordingly Willibrord went to Rome to get consent for his mission, thus beginning the policy which Winfrid afterwards carried out on a larger scale.

Success soon made organisation desirable: the monks elected one Suidbert as their future bishop and he passed across to England to be consecrated there by Wilfrid. But after his return difficulties seem to have arisen and the new bishop left Frisia in order to preach to the Bructeri: a little later we find Pepin, like the earlier kings, taking the organisation into his own hands and sending Willibrord to Rome for consecration (22 Nov. 695) as archbishop of a province to include both Frankish and independent Frisia. Willibrord, who at his consecration took the name of Clement, received the pall at Rome, and from Pepin as his seat Utrecht, where he built a cathedral and a monastery. A native church began, and soon he felt able to devote himself to the Frisians in Radbod's territory since Radbod himself was now friendly to the Franks, and his daughter Theutsind had married Pepin's son Grimoald. But here Willibrord's success was small: Radbod was indifferent although not hostile and Willibrord

CH. XVI (B).

went on further to preach to the Danes. Their country too he left and on his return to Frisia landed on the coast: by venturing to baptise some converts in a holy well he awoke the anger of the heathen and they sought to have him put to death by Radbod. The king however spared his life, but as the hopes of any work among the free Frisians now seemed hopeless he went back to Utrecht. After Pepin's death (16 Dec. 714) the quarrel between his sons enabled Radbod to regain the part of Frisia held by the Franks. The church had gained no real hold among the natives: Willibrord had left, the priests were put to flight, and the land once more under the sway of a heathen king became heathen too. It was now that Winfrid came.

Winfrid was born near Crediton (*c.* 680) of a noble English family: after education first in a monastery at Exeter and then at Nutshall (Nutsall, Netley or Nursling?) he was ordained, and employed in important affairs. But above the claims of learning and the chance of a great career at home he felt the missionary's call to the wild. From London he sailed to Frisia (716): here he stayed for part of a year until on the outbreak of a Frankish war he went back to his West-Saxon monastery. On the death of his old master Winbert the monks wished to make him abbot, but his future work lay plain before him and he refused. He sought letters of commendation from Daniel, bishop of Winchester—a man of much learning and experience to whom Bede owed much information—and with these (718) he went abroad again. But this time passing through Frankland he went to Rome, to visit the threshold of the Apostles. Here he saw Gregory II, and from him he received as "Bonifatius[1] the religious priest"—the name by which he was henceforth known—a letter of commendation (15 May 719). The journey was a common one for an Englishman of the day, but Boniface with his strong wish for missionary work reached Rome when the Papacy was turning towards plans of organisation. Furthermore between him and the Pope a friendship and even a fellowship began.

Taking this new line of organisation under papal guidance Boniface went to Thuringia, where the natives, in new seats, and pressed upon by Franks and Saxons, had partly received and then soon lost Christianity. To win back their leaders was Boniface's new task: the land was disordered in politics and religion alike: heathenism was found side by side with Christianity of strange types. From Thuringia Boniface started for the Frankish court, but on the way he heard of Radbod's death, which might make Frisia a more fruitful field. Already Willibrord, working like Boniface himself under papal sanction, had been consecrated Archbishop of Utrecht, and to his help Boniface now went. When after a three years' stay Willibrord would have had him as

---

[1] For the name see Loofs, *Der Beiname des Apostels der Deutschen, Z.K.G.* (1882), pp. 623-31, and Hauck, *K.G.D.* I. p. 458 n. 1.

coadjutor he pleaded the papal command: he sought leave to depart and passed to Hesse. This was ground more unworked than Thuringia, for the people had kept their older seats and with them their old customs, but it might link Saxony to the Frankish Church. So great was his success—thousands being baptised—that he could soon think of organising a bishopric. He sent a report to Rome and in reply was called thither himself. On his way he probably met[1] Charles Martel, and at Rome he was consecrated (St Andrew's day, 722 or less probably 723). At his consecration he took an oath much like that taken by the suburbicarian bishops, and thus pledged himself to work as a bishop under papal direction. But by a significant change the promise of fidelity to the Eastern Emperor was left out and its place taken by a promise to hold no intercourse with bishops who disobeyed the canons, to work against them and to denounce them to the Pope. The new bishop received letters of commendation to all who could help his work in Germany and especially to Charles Martel. Henceforth Boniface could depend even more than before upon papal direction, help and sympathy: we find him, like St Augustine of Canterbury, sending difficulties to Rome for decision. As he was to build up a church which was suffering from Keltic disorder and Frankish negligence, a collection of canons was a natural papal gift to him.

Boniface now begins a new stage of his work, no longer as a mere missionary pioneer but rather as a missionary statesman in the service of Rome. For his new plans and his new office state support was needed. Backed by a letter from Charles Martel, Boniface went to Hesse to weld together the scattered links of his earlier work. Some twenty years later he wrote to Daniel of Winchester: "Without the patronage of the Prince of the Franks I am able neither to rule the people of the church nor to defend[2] the priests or deacons, the monks or nuns: and I am not powerful enough to hinder the very rites of the pagans and the sacrileges of idols in Germany without his order and the dread of him." The boldness he shewed in felling the sacred oak at Geismar led the heathen to think their gods had lost their power, and from these successes in Hesse Boniface passed to Thuringia. In each district he founded schools of learning and of training for his converts: Amanaburg and Fritzlar in Hesse, Ohrdruff in Thuringia: for women, Tauberbischofsheim, Kitzingen and Ochsenfurt, three foundations near the Main. These were founded before his organisation of Bavaria, and his favourite house Fulda was specially planned to foster Christian civilisation and to be a monastic model. This side of Boniface's work is sometimes overlooked in comparison with his ordering of dioceses, but

---

[1] Hauck, I. pp. 463 n. 3 and 464 n. 1.
[2] *Ep.* 63, p. 329 (Dümmler). The omission of *defendere* in one MS. would make the passage even more emphatic as to the need of state support (as suggested by Browne, *Boniface of Crediton*, p. 62).

CH. XVI (B).

the two were really complementary : on the monastic side he entered
into the heritage of the Keltic monks to whom, when there was no
question of disorder or irregularity, he was by no means an enemy.
At Fulda Sturm, a Bavarian of his own training, ruled : there and elsewhere helpers from England, some of them bound to Boniface by ties of
blood, and all by kinship in devotion, made new homes for themselves :
Burchard, Lul, Denehard, Willibald, Wicbert among the men : Lioba
and Walpurgis among the women.   With England a lively interchange
of letters was kept up : some of his English friends came out to him as
they gradually lost their kinsfolk by death, and others came because of
their love for him.   But in either case they helped to strengthen associations which were of political as well as religious power.   Boniface
himself was strong enough to award praise and blame to English kings ;
he himself, his comrades and his work gave England some hold upon
continental life.

On the death of Gregory II (11 Feb. 731) Gregory III succeeded,
a true successor in his care for Germany.   When Boniface declared to
him that the burden of his growing work was becoming too heavy, the
papal answer was (732) to make him Archbishop, although with no
defined province, so that he could the better call fellow-labourers to his
help.   In the few following years we must probably place much of
Boniface's work in furthering his foundations, and some of his letters
of the time shew him turned to reading and study of questions raised
by his pastoral work.   But about 735 we find him in Bavaria where
once before the duke Theodo and Gregory II had thought of a church
organisation in the interests both of church and duchy.   Hucbert was
now duke under stricter Frankish suzerainty: little had hitherto been
done and Passau was the only see.   In Bavaria Boniface now travelled
and taught.   But his third visit to Rome (probably 738), caused possibly
by his wish to take up once more his old plans for Frisia, now that
the field of Germany was under cultivation, brought a year's break and
rest.   This time Boniface was a great figure both with the Romans and
the pilgrims, so greatly had his renown been spread.

In Bavaria after Hucbert's death (probably 736) Odilo was placed
as duke, a ruler of a different type, less ready to submit to Frankish
direction and a generous patron of the Church.   To Bavaria Boniface
went (739), and now he takes a new position, that of legate of Rome :
his appearance as legate[1] was followed by the meeting of a Synod and
a division of the duchy into four dioceses : Passau (where Vivilo who
had been consecrated at Rome remained), Regensburg, Salzburg and
Freising.   A little later (741) we find Boniface similarly founding another
group of three dioceses for Hesse and Thuringia: Büraburg, near
Fritzlar, for Hesse, Würzburg for southern and Erfurt for northern

---

[1] The change is strongly marked in the letters about Bavaria: see *Epp.* 43, 44,
and 45 (Dümmler): *nostram agentem vicem*, says the Pope of Boniface.

Thuringia. Zacharias who had now (3 Dec. 741) succeeded Gregory III
confirmed this division, although like his predecessor advising caution
against erecting too many sees and so lowering the episcopal standard.
But Boniface's personal inspiration found him able helpers: at Büraburg
an Englishman, Witta, was placed, and at Würzburg another, Burchard,
entered upon the heritage of the Keltic Kilian. The protection of
Charles Martel, even if not too eager, had been of great use: his death
(22 Oct. 741) brought about a change in Boniface's work: henceforth it
was to be for the whole of eastern Frankish territory.

Carloman invited Boniface to come and hold a Synod in Austrasia:
in this way discipline, which had been trampled under foot for some
sixty years, could be restored. Boniface was here faced by conditions
such as he had known in Bavaria. His work in Hesse had already
brought to him opposition from Frankish bishops.

But among the Franks church law was widely disregarded and
Boniface found it hard, as he told Daniel of Winchester, to keep the
oath he had sworn to the Pope. If he was to refrain altogether from
intercourse with offending bishops his work would be impossible. There
was no weakening of his allegiance to the Pope, but a new element,
the Frankish State, was now coming more fully into his life and his plans.
The most striking feature in Boniface's career is the way in which
while never waiting for circumstances he was quick to seize each
circumstance and use it to the utmost good. He never lost sight of
any work he had ever planned and begun: if he turned aside for some
pressing need he wove that special work into his general plan, and with
each new field his outlook broadened.

The new pope Zacharias was a Greek from Calabria, a man of
mildness and yet of diplomatic skill: his tone towards Boniface was
somewhat more commanding than that used by previous popes, and the
explanation may be found in his policy towards the Franks, against
whom he for a time played off the Bavarians and Lombards. Odilo of
Bavaria had probably encouraged Grifo in his revolt against Carloman and
Pepin, and afterwards he began a movement for independence. A papal
envoy is said to have ordered a Frankish army to leave his land[1],
but this did not hinder the defeat of the Bavarian duke. The Nordgau
was separated from his duchy and joined to Austrasia. Neuburg on
the Danube became—possibly through some adaptation of Odilo's plans
—a new bishopric and remained so for some two generations. Eichstädt,
where a monastery had already been founded, was made the seat of
another bishopric for a population of mixed descent.

The projected Council for Austrasia met in a place unknown
(21 April 742)[2], and began the work of reorganisation. Bishops were to

---

[1] See Hodgkin, *Italy and her Invaders*, VII. pp. 100 f. and Hauck, *K.G.D.* I. p. 533.
[2] The date is disputed. Early in 742 seems most likely. See Hauck, *K.G.D.*
I. pp. 518 n. 5 and 520 n. 3; *contra* Loofs who dates it 743.

be consecrated for cities and over them was to be set the archbishop
Boniface, legate (*missus*) of St Peter: councils were to meet yearly:
the moral standard of the priesthood was to be raised, and the priests
were to be subject to the bishops: bishops or priests who were not
known were not to be allowed to minister and heathen customs were to
be put away. In the place given to Boniface it is best to see a restoration of the metropolitan system, and that this was made by royal power
is significant. Not only the bishops of the older and more settled part
of the realm, Cologne and Strassburg, but also those of Würzburg,
Eichstädt, Büraburg and Erfurt, were invited to the Council. To carry
out the reforms laid down was now the work of Boniface. In the next
two years many new bishops were appointed, and (1 March 743) a second
Synod met at Estinnes (Liftinas)[1], and here, by bishops and leading
laymen, the decrees of 742 were confirmed. In 744 (2 March) a Synod
for Neustria met at Soissons, and a new organisation followed for Pepin's
realm also. The archbishoprics of Rheims, Rouen and Sens were to be
restored, and Boniface, who had acted in close friendly if not official touch
with Pepin, asked the Pope to send three palls for them. But before
Zacharias replied (22 June 744) some change was made in the plans and
Grimo of Rouen alone was to have the pall. This change and some
freedom in Boniface's criticism of papal fees and Roman customs made
the Pope a little angry, but we find him none the less (1 May 748)
commending Boniface his "brother, archbishop, legate of the Holy See
and personal representative" to the bishops—expressly named—of both
the eastern and western Franks. And in an earlier letter (5 Nov. 744)
Zacharias even extended the right of free preaching in the province of
Bavaria which was granted by his predecessor. "And not only for
Bavaria, but for the whole province of the Gauls" he was to use the
office of preaching laid upon him by the Pope for reformation and
edification.

The original plan was for Boniface to be Archbishop of Cologne, and
in this position wield even greater power. To this the Pope had agreed.
But when Gewilip was rightly deposed from Mainz, Carloman and Pepin
(perhaps led by enemies of Boniface at court) appointed Boniface his
successor, and so the see of Mainz (which became an archbishopric in
780) as held by a legate and apostle gained a new renown. Cologne
which had probably been an archbishopric in the sixth century became
such again in 785, but the jealousy between the two great cities lingered
on, and echoes even in the letters of Gregory VII.

In the spring of 747 Boniface held his last Synod: one wish of his
was satisfied when the bishops there met decreed their fidelity to Rome.
In the way of reform much had already been done: some unworthy

---

[1] Here again is a difficulty of date 743 or 745. Hahn, *Jahrbuch*, Exc. xiv.
p. 193; *contra* Hauck for 743; see also Hefele-Leclercq, iii. (2), p. 825 (especially
n. 2) sq.

priests had been condemned both by the Franks and at Rome (745): this
last Synod not only regulated metropolitan rights but also the discipline
over priests.   It is clear that the power of the Frankish princes over
the Church counted for much, probably for more than is often allowed.
Boniface had gained both inspiration and experience not only at Rome
but in England before, and he cannot be regarded as a mere emissary
of Roman power extending it over a church free until his day.   The
power of the State was but little affected by the recognition of Rome,
yet Boniface had brought about a union between the two : he did it with
fidelity towards both, but he was the slave of neither.

The anointing of Pepin, after Carloman had withdrawn to a Roman
monastery, is told elsewhere: it took place, 751, under Roman sanction
and by the hand of Boniface.   But there is no reason to make Boniface
the author or inspirer of the deed: he was merely the agent.

The old man, weary with work and longing to rest in the grave at
his beloved Fulda, was preparing for death : the consecration of Lul as
his coadjutor, and then, by papal leave, to be his successor, was a sign of
the coming end.   When Fulda, by an act unusual in the Frankish
Church[1], was placed directly under the Pope, it was a sign of the great
apostle's withdrawal.   He was going back to the dream of his earlier
years.   He would go to Frisia, which had never been far from his
thoughts.   But he knew he was going to his death, for he bade the
faithful Lul send along with him his shroud packed in his box of books.
Lul was to carry out to a perfect end the work in Thuringia, which the
Saxons had lately harried, and he was to finish the partly built church
at Fulda.   In 753 Boniface left, and for two years he worked among
the water-bound washes of the Zuiderzee: when (5 June 754) he was
at Dockum awaiting converts who were to be confirmed a band of savages
attacked him and his followers : they were all slain : the books he had
with him were found and taken to Fulda, and thither also, after
some time at Utrecht, was carried the body of the saint himself there
in the house of his founding, near the middle of his vast field of
toil, the great hero lay at rest.   He had done much to bind together
a growing world and to direct its ways.   His letters, with their eager
interest in the past, with their requests for books, the Scriptures,
commentaries, parts—even particles—of the many works of Bede, with
their Latin verses, traced the outlines of medieval learning, and opened
up channels along which medieval scholarship was long to flow.   The
many activities of his busy life must not hide his great services to learning.
Sometimes when " the vineyard he had dug brought forth only wild
grapes," and disappointments from half-heathen converts and wholly
unworthy priests came thick upon him, he turned to study for rest and

---

[1] Boniface asked for this privilege.   The papal grant, and the royal confirmation,
are alike doubted, but the questions are different.   For the latter see Chap. xviii.
p. 581.

CH. XVI (B).

peace. Even when he was "an old man buffeted by the waves of the German sea," and from dimness of eye could not read the small running hand of the day, he wrote to England for clearly written books. His connexion with England meant much, and when he died Archbishop Cuthbert wrote to Lul that an English synod "lovingly placed him among the splendid and glorious doctors of the faith," and along "with blessed Gregory and Augustine had taken him for their patron saint."

The greatness of his work was seen even more in its endurance than in its variety or its extent. He had visions of what he was to do, and he also saw the lines upon which alone it could be done. The Frankish Empire, the papal supremacy, monastic foundations, ecclesiastical organisation, were perhaps the four greatest features of the medieval world. Each of these was built up by Boniface into the work of his life. He must have seen what each of them would be and would accomplish. But his far-sightedness, his enthusiasm and his wisdom cannot fully explain all he did and all he was. For that we must go to his letters: in them we see his power of friendship, his command of detail, and his breadth of view. In them we see how the great man grew with the very greatness of his work, until the young Englishman with the zeal of his nation's new-found faith upon him became the shaper of the mighty German West.

CHAPTER XVII.

ENGLAND (to c. 800) AND ENGLISH INSTITUTIONS.

It is not surprising that the Venerable Bede, being a Northumbrian, in his Ecclesiastical History completed about 731, just one hundred years after the conversion of Northumbria to Christianity, should regard Edwin of Deira, the king who had brought about the change, as almost the greatest English prince of the seventh century. In his pages Edwin appears as the fifth English king who had won renown by establishing an effective *imperium* over his neighbours, both English and British, and the same view of him is repeated in the Anglo-Saxon Chronicle written two hundred years later, which shews that ninth century tradition reckoned him as the fifth "Bretwalda," a title which seems to mean "the wide-ruler" or over-king. The actual achievements of Edwin's reign, which began in 617 after the defeat of Aethelfrith of Bernicia by Raedwald of East Anglia at the battle of the Idle, shew that the title was not unmerited; for he is credited with subjecting the Isle of Man to his rule, conquering Anglesey from the king of Gwynedd or North Wales, annexing the Southumbrian district of Lindsey and the yet British district of Elmet in South Yorkshire, and even asserting himself along the Thames and waging successful war with the West Saxons. The only English kingdom, according to Bede, which did not bow to him, was Kent, the home of his queen who had induced him to adopt Christianity. His power, however, if striking, was really precarious, and his baptism in 627 soon brought about political difficulties. Other kings had recognised his suzerainty so long as he appeared as the champion of the English against their foes, but his desertion of Wodan made the more conservative of them restive.

The leader of the discontented was Penda, the chief of the Mercians in the Trent valley, and of the "Wreocensaete" or dwellers by the Wrekin, who had settled along the upper Severn and were fast spreading south into Herefordshire. Penda first made his name in 628 by a successful attack on the folk called Hwicce, the branch of the West Saxons who had fixed their seats on the upper tributaries of the Thames, on the Worcestershire Avon and along the lower Severn. A victory at Cirencester made these districts tributary to Mercia and doubled Penda's power, whereupon he came forward as the champion of the old national religion and quickly found himself supported by all those warriors, who hated the new-fangled restrictions which the Christian missionaries threatened to impose in the matters of marriage and private vengeance. The attitude of the heathen chieftains, who probably acted as priests for their several districts and themselves sacrificed and collected temple tolls from their liegemen, like the Icelandic *Godis* of a later time, is not depicted at all clearly by Bede, who had little interest in heathen institutions, but we can gain a fair idea of the shape which their antagonism must have taken if we read the "Christne Saga," which describes a similar struggle between Christ and Wodan in the northern island three hundred and fifty years later[1].

The first folk actually to rise against Edwin's influence were the East Angles, who slew their king Eorpwald for accepting baptism; but the real crisis came in 633, when Penda joined forces with Cadwallon, king of Gwynedd, Edwin's chief British enemy. The rival armies met on the borders of Mercia and Deira somewhere near Doncaster in the woodlands called Heathfield, with the result that Edwin's army was disastrously routed and the "Bretwalda" himself slain.

This fight in Heathfield made the fortune of Mercia. The Deiran supremacy not only disappeared but Bernicia and Deira again fell apart and their leading men apostatised. Cadwallon, eager to regain the North for the British, occupied York, and this forced Paulinus with Edwin's queen to flee to Kent. Penda meantime stepped into Edwin's place as leading king, a fact not emphasised by Bede because of this prince's hostility to Christianity, and created an enlarged Mercia, stretching right across England from the Humber and the Wash on the east to Chester and Hereford on the west.

The provinces of this enlarged state seem to be set out for us in the first section of the so-called "Tribal Hidage," a Mercian document compiled apparently some fifty years later for Penda's successors for revenue purposes. This hidage, or schedule of assessments, indicates that "that which was first called Mercia" comprised in addition to the two Mercian districts, north and south of the Trent, six dependent "maegths" or chieftaincies, namely (1) the land of the Wreocensaete, now Shropshire with parts of Herefordshire, (2) Westerna, a somewhat vague expression which apparently refers to the plain of Cheshire and South Lancashire, (3) the land of the Pecsaete, the dwellers round the Peak and Sheffield, (4) the land of Elmet, which had its centre at Loides[2] (Ledstone near Pontefract) where the road from London to York crossed the river

---

[1] Vígfússon and York Powell, *Origines Islandicae*, I. pp. 309–12, 370–412.

[2] *Loides* has usually been identified with Leeds, but this ignores the fact that in 1066 Leeds was an unimportant village, divided between seven small manors, whereas Ledstone with Kippax at the important crossing of the Aire was the seat of the Earl and the most extensive lay manor of the Elmet district. (Domesday, I. 315 a.)

Aire and which reached north to the Wharfe, (5) Lindsey with the land of Heathfield, and (6) the settlements of the North and South Gyrwe, comprising the fenlands of Holland and the Isle of Ely, perhaps detached from East Anglia. Over these "maegths" as well as in the Mercian homelands the victorious Penda ruled as king; but his influence was also paramount over the sub-kingdom of the Hwicce in Worcestershire and Gloucestershire and over the territories occupied by the Middle Angles (Bede's *Angli Mediterranei*) in Northamptonshire, Bedfordshire and Huntingdonshire. These latter he formed into a second sub-kingdom and entrusted to his son Peada.

The centre of the realm thus constituted was at Tamworth on the Watling Street, and it is clear that, if its parts could only hold together, the new state from its central situation was in a far better position for gaining supremacy over all England than Northumbria had been. The struggle, however, was by no means over; for it was not long before the Northumbrian dynasty recovered from its eclipse and made a determined effort to undo Penda's work.

The new Northumbrian leader was Oswald, one of the sons of Aethelfrith of Bernicia who had been exiled when Edwin of Deira won his kingdom. This prince seized the opportunity afforded by Edwin's death to return to Bernicia, and in 635 signally defeated Cadwallon at Heavenfield near Hexham on the Roman Wall. Upon this he was able not only to reunite Deira to Bernicia, but being a zealous Christian to begin the reconversion of both districts. To effect this he called to his aid, not the exiled Paulinus, but a band of Irish-Scot missionaries from the renowned monastery of Iona on the west coast of Scotland where he had himself learnt Christianity, when in exile. The struggle between the adherents of Christ and Wodan was thus again renewed, but this time not under the auspices of Rome; for the Scots were quite independent of the Papacy and had their own traditions and a peculiar organisation.

The leader of the new mission to Bernicia was Aidan (correctly Aedan), whom Oswald established, not at York amid Roman surroundings, but on the island of Lindisfarne in the North Sea, hard by Bamborough, the Bernician capital. The detailed story of this second attempt to Christianise Northumbria will be found elsewhere; its effect on the newly formed Mercian kingdom is what now concerns us; for Oswald, as a champion of Christ, was bound to attack Penda, even if he had not also felt it his duty to regain for Northumbria its lost political supremacy.

In this enterprise Oswald was not long without allies. The numerous petty chiefs, whom Penda had subdued, were naturally not very heartily on his side. Any overlord, even one who adhered to the old religion, was distasteful to them, and this made it easy to stir up rebels. Besides, notwithstanding Penda's opposition, Christianity was making headway all round him, in East Anglia under Anna who was crowned king in spite of a victorious Mercian invasion, and in Wessex under Cynegils who was converted about this time by an Italian missionary, named Birinus.

These two folk-kings were necessarily Oswald's allies, and if we are to believe Bede, even accepted him as their overlord. At any rate Oswald encouraged Cynegils to set up Birinus as bishop of the West Saxons with his see at Dorchester a few miles below Oxford on the upper Thames, and was himself present as sponsor when Cynegils was baptised. By 640 the allied princes were clearly pressing Penda hard; for Oswald was able to regain Elmet and Lindsey and collect his forces for an attack on the district of "Westerna" round Chester. But here, as it proved, the Christian champion over-reached himself. In this quarter Penda could rely on British help and probably was joined by Cadwalader of Gwynedd. At any rate in 642 he faced Oswald in the north-east corner of Shropshire at the foot of the Welsh hills in the woodlands called Maserfield, and here Oswald was slain and his army destroyed. Penda had his body mutilated, but tradition says that his head was subsequently buried at Lindisfarne, while his arms and his hands were preserved at Bamborough as precious relics of the fight with heathendom. Later he was canonised as St Oswald. The Welsh too preserved his memory, calling the site of the battle Croes Oswallt, while the English called it Oswestry.

The same results followed from the disaster in Maserfield as from Edwin's disaster in Heathfield. Bernicia and Deira again parted company, this time for thirteen years, while Penda retained his position as leading king. Northumbria however did not go back to heathendom, though Penda ravaged it as far as Bamborough. The Irish missionaries had obtained too great a hold on the people to be repudiated, and Aidan did not think of abandoning his flock. In Wessex heathenism had greater success. Cynegils died in 643, and his son Coenwalch, who had married Penda's daughter, succeeded and practised heathen rites. But even here Birinus seems to have maintained a foothold. At any rate Coenwalch soon quarrelled with Penda, and fleeing for refuge to Anna of East Anglia was shortly afterwards baptised by Felix, the missionary bishop of Dunwich. Penda, indeed, as the years went by, must gradually have realised that in spite of his victories he was fighting against the inevitable. In 648 Coenwalch, aided by his kinsman Cuthred, returned to Wessex and openly proclaimed himself a Christian. Peada, too, who had been set over the Midland Angles, was also found among the converts, while missionaries from Lindisfarne headed by Cedd, an Englishman, were invited into Essex by the local chiefs, who had remained heathens ever since the expulsion of Bishop Mellitus in 617.

The prime mover in all this was Oswy, Oswald's younger brother, who after Maserfield had become king of Bernicia and who in 651 tried to regain Deira as well, by putting to death Oswin, a chieftain who was ruling that district with the support of Penda. In this he did not succeed, but it heralded a new struggle in which heathendom had once more to fight for its existence. Penda as usual met the danger with vigour. In 654 he made a savage attack on East Anglia and slew Anna, and the year following collected all his strength to march against Oswy. At first Oswy offered tribute, but Penda refused all terms. His levies, we are told, were organised under thirty different chiefs and included contingents from Wales, East Anglia and Deira. Oswy's forces in comparison were far inferior, but they had the better spirit, some of Penda's allies being half-hearted and some actually treacherous. The collision took place at the ford of the Winwaed, apparently a stream half-way between Doncaster and Ledstone. Here in the district of the Elmetsaete Penda's life-long good fortune deserted him. The Deirans would not fight for him, one of the Welsh contingents took to flight, and in the end Penda himself fell together with the king whom he had recently set up in East Anglia and many of his other vassals.

Oswy's somewhat unexpected victory not only gave him great prestige, but was decisive for the religious destiny of the English. Sussex and much of Wessex and Mercia were still heathen, and Cedd's mission to the men of Essex and Middle Anglia had still much work to do; but from this time onwards active heathen resistance was at an end, for Peada the heir to Mercia already stood for Christianity, and had married Oswy's daughter. It must not be thought that Penda's career had been in vain. He had failed, it is true, to maintain the old religion; but the Mercian State which he had evolved out of a congeries of tiny tribes, was destined to prove permanent, and in spite of Oswy's momentary triumph soon shewed itself able to resist all efforts to bring about its dismemberment. It remained in fact the leading factor in English politics for the next hundred and fifty years.

It may be well at this point to glance at the chief changes from the social and political point of view, which each English tribe underwent as soon as its leaders discarded heathenism. The most far-reaching change of all, next to the introduction of a higher moral standard, is clearly the rise in each kingdom of a small class who could read and write and who had some knowledge of Mediterranean civilisation. The English of all ranks, as pagans, must have lived almost without writing. They were indeed acquainted with the Runic alphabet, and used it for mottoes on weapons and coins, for recording names on gravestones, and now and again for secret messages; but this method of writing was altogether useless for the ordinary needs of civilisation. Here and there, too, there may have been court bards, who may have been capable of reading messages for the kings in the Roman alphabet, but the ordinary chief knew nothing of writing and put nothing on record. Everything that needed to be remembered had to be put in the form of rhythmic verses suitable for chanting to the harp, and all the laws and customs of the tribes were handed down orally by this method. All this now began to change. Wherever the missionaries came, they brought the Roman alphabet with them and were ready to write down and record, at first of course in Latin, but after a few years in the vernacular also, not only accounts of deeds of importance but every-day bargains and contracts. The new learning might be meagre, and the class of writers a small one, but a new epoch had begun. A book ceased to mean a tablet of beechwood and became a book of parchment, and hereafter there was a new leaven ceaselessly at work making for social progress.

Hardly less important politically was the new division set up between clergy and laity, a distinction which dominates all later periods, and which introduced a dualism into the framework of government and society which is now difficult to apprehend in all its subtle bearings. The new class of clergy, the *godcund* estate as opposed to the *woruld-cund* or laity, did not merely step into the places of the priests of heathen days. As already suggested the heathen priests for the most part had not been a class apart, but, like the later *Godis* of Iceland, were probably leading landowners who acted the part of chieftains, judges and priests combined, and enjoyed the right of conducting the sacrifices on national feast-days as an hereditary office appendant to their estates. The edifices, too, which served as temples, if they were like the Icelandic *hovs*, had not been buildings solely devoted to religious uses, but were attached to the big halls of the chieftains used equally for social purposes, so that a sacrifice and a banquet were easily merged together.

The new order of clergy, on the other hand, from the outset did everything they could to mark off their position from that of the heathen priests, asserting themselves to be a caste apart, superior to the lay classes and fenced about by special sanctions definitely recognised by the law. And this in itself led to further developments, causing the bishops to be ever urging on the kings the necessity of recording in writing what the rights were which the clergy were to enjoy, and by what fines and punishments their teaching was to be made effective and their privileges guarded. It thus came about not only that the laws were materially supplemented but that the amendments were put into writing, a step forward in the path of civilisation of the utmost importance. It is true that only one amending code, that for Kent, issued by King Aethelberht, is now extant which dates from the first advent of the missionaries, but there can be no reasonable doubt that similar codes must also have been written down at any rate for Northumbria and East Anglia, as without them the position of the clergy, with no tradition to appeal to, could not have been made secure or their views on morality enforced.

In considering these changes in the laws, it would be unjust to suppose that the work of the bishops was mainly directed to securing the status of their own order. It would be truer to maintain that their aims were revolutionary in every direction. Here, however, only two further points can be touched on.

The first is the solvent effect produced by their teaching on the doctrine, so fundamental to all uncivilised men, of the solidarity of the group of blood relations. Among the English, as among all primitive races, the individual in all his relations in life was in the eyes of the law not so much an independent unit as one of a group of kinsmen. This group the English called a *maegth* (though they also used this expression for a tribe), and those who used Latin a *parentela* or *cognatio*. Any attack made on a free man counted as an attack on the *maegth* to which he belonged and might be resented and avenged by the whole body of *magas* or kinsmen. Conversely, if a free man did any wrong to another he and his kin had to fear the vengeance of all the members of the injured man's *maegth*. Hence there arose everywhere a constant succession of bloodfeuds (*fæhde*), and acts of violence had the most far-reaching consequences lasting sometimes for generations, as one branch of the *maegth* after another took up the feud. Obviously this doctrine was most disastrous to peace and progress and exactly the reverse of all Christian teaching with its insistence on mutual forbearance and on the responsibility of each individual for his own acts. The advent of the new faith accordingly set in train a movement which, bit by bit, if slowly, broke down the idea of the mutually responsible group of kinsmen, or at any rate so altered it as to limit its operations to useful police purposes only.

Secondly, with the change of faith, came the introduction of the English kings to new ideals of what a state should be and of the part a king should play. To missionaries coming from Italy or Gaul, the minute districts ruled by the so-called "kings" can hardly have seemed true states at all. To men familiar with the Merovingian lands, with Austrasia, Neustria or Burgundy, or even with the Lombard duchies in Italy, a state meant an extensive territory, often many hundreds of miles in length and breadth, in which the king claimed autocratic powers and legislated and imposed taxes at will. From the first then, the clergy thought England ought to be treated as a whole, and looked forward to a coalescence of the tribes. Any folk-king strong enough to subject his fellows, any Bretwalda or over-king had their sympathy ; for from such kings alone could they expect adequate protection and endowments. A folk-king, say of West Kent, whose kingdom was so tiny that a day's ride in any direction would bring him to another kingdom, could not afford to give them landed estates; but a " Bretwalda " like Edwin or Penda could, especially as he had the estates of his under-kings to draw on. Inevitably then, if unconsciously, the clergy stood for fewer and larger kingdoms and instilled into the minds of victorious kings ideas which may be called " imperial," encouraging those who gained an *imperium* both to legislate for and to tax their people after the fashion of the Caesars, and at the same time teaching them the methods by which permanent unity might be fostered.

Perhaps the most important political help they could give in this direction was in working out orderly systems for the assessment and collection of tributes. In the Roman Empire before its fall the machinery of taxation had been highly elaborated, and it had been found that the best way to raise a land tax was by assessing it on an artificial partition of the territory to be taxed into a number of equally assessed subdivisions. Each of these districts formed a unit of taxation and each furnished an equal proportion of any tax, though at the same time they might vary largely in area, according as their soil varied in fertility and their population in density. On the Continent, systems of this kind had never been entirely forgotten, at any rate not by the clergy; and so it is not surprising to find that almost immediately after the advent of the missionaries something of this kind, if only in a very rough and ready form, begins to be traceable in England in the shape of the so-called "hide," which is the term applied to equally taxed units of land.

Our main evidence for this, if scanty, is sufficient, and consists in those passages in Bede's history, relating to events that took place in the middle of the seventh century, in which he has occasion to compare different districts one with another. As he wrote in Latin he does not indeed use the vernacular term *higid*, later Latinised into *hida*, but a circumlocution, speaking of the *terra unius familiae*; but this term is always found in English translations of his works translated by *higid*, and so there is no doubt that the two were equivalent. In these passages districts are set before us as reckoned at so many hides; and these hides cannot be units of actual area, as the districts are always spoken of as containing a round number of units, and further the number of units given to them does not vary as their actual size. Most of the hidages given by Bede also have the further peculiarity of being based on a unit of 120, but this ceases to be remarkable, in an artificial assessment scheme, when we remember that the English did not reckon by units of 100, 1000 and 10,000, but like all the Germans by the more practical, because more readily divisible, units of 120, 1200, and 12,000, using what is called a "long hundred" of six score rather than the "Roman hundred" of five score. We are told, for instance, by Bede that the Mercian homeland, in the valley of the Trent, was reckoned at 12,000 hides, Anglesey at 960, the Isle of Man at about 300, Thanet at 600 and the Isle of Wight at 1200. Similarly after the battle of the Winwaed, Oswy makes a thank-offering and devotes 120 hides to the Church, and this appears to have been made up of a dozen scattered estates, each reckoned at 10 hides. This evidence is further backed up by the document already alluded to, the so-called Tribal Hidage which sets before us many more districts and assigns to each a round number of hides. For this list, when analysed, is found, if allowance be made for a slight corruption of the text, to be built up of groups of districts, each group being assessed at a multiple of 12,000 hides.   Further, both in Bede and in the Tribal Hidage and also in the "Song of Beowulf," an English epic that dates from the seventh century, we hear of other districts assessed at 7000 hides; examples are Sussex, Essex, Wreocensaete and Lindsey.   At first this seems to clash with the 12,000 unit, but we get from Bede an explanation when he tells how North Mercia was reckoned at 7000 hides and South Mercia at 5000, thus shewing how a 12,000 hide unit might be divided into approximately, but not exactly, equal moieties.   All this evidence too clearly shews that these assessments were arrived at, not from the bottom by beginning with the assessment of villages, but from the top by assigning units of 12,000 hides to large districts and petty kingdoms and subsequently apportioning the hides to the various component sub-districts.   The introduction of this elaborate system, though it owed something to prior military organisation, must, one would infer, have been largely the work of the clergy, as it could only have been planned by men of education with views as to uniformity and some acquaintance with continental tradition.   The clergy, too, probably benefited by it quite as much as the kings; for they too wanted to raise tolls and church-scots, and had everything to gain by being able to distribute the burden on a definite plan.

It only remains to be said that the main features of this system, when once introduced, remained in force throughout the Anglo-Saxon period, and continued for four hundred years to be the basis on which military and fiscal obligations were distributed, though the actual assessments of particular districts were from time to time modified to suit changed conditions.   The unit of 1200 hides for example was still an important feature of English organisation at the date of the Norman Conquest.   Only a few years before 1066, Worcestershire was reckoned at 1200 hides, Northamptonshire at 3000, Wiltshire at 4800 and so on. It is clear, however, that the hidage unit in many districts was in time considerably enlarged.   The Isle of Wight, for instance, was reckoned at 200 units in 1066, as against 1200 in the time of Bede; East Anglia at 6000 units as against the 30,000 hides given in the Tribal Hidage, and we even know the approximate date when William the Conqueror finally reduced the assessment of Northamptonshire to 1200 hides.

We must now return to the events of 655.   The immediate result of Penda's death was the temporary collapse of Mercia.   Oswy found no one to oppose him and quickly annexed all Mercia north of the Trent as well as Deira and Lindsey.   How far he overran Cheshire or penetrated into the valley of the Severn we do not know; but Bede says that the Mercians submitted to the partition of their province and that Oswy took up the task of converting the country round Penda's capital, appointing Diuma as first bishop of the Mercians.   As for Peada, Penda's heir and Oswy's son-in-law, he is represented as being content with adding the 5000 hides of South Mercia, that is to say Leicestershire, Kesteven and Rutland, to his kingdom of Middle Anglia and as spending his time in making plans for a monastery at Medeshamstede, a site on the edge of the fens overlooking the country of the Gyrwe, well known afterwards as Peterborough.

Meantime in Northumbria the two most important events were the founding of the nunnery of Streaneshalch, afterwards renamed by the Danes Whitby, and the promotion of Oswy's son Alchfrid to be under-king of Deira. With affairs thus settled in the south Oswy next turned his eyes northwards, and according to Bede subdued the greater part of the Picts beyond the Forth. Bede represents him in fact as the greatest of the Northumbrian kings with an *imperium* over all the southern provinces of England as well as over Mercia and the Picts and Scots. This may have been the case in 657; but if so, the quickly won supremacy was short lived, and in the south did not survive beyond the assassination of Peada in 658 and the accession of a more vigorous prince to the headship of Mercia.

The new ruler was Wulfhere, Peada's younger brother and like him a Christian. Elected by some Mercian notables, he came to the throne determined to reconstitute and, if possible, to extend Penda's kingdom. Bede describes the rebellion in a single sentence, merely stating that Oswy's officials were expelled from Mercia; but really the revolt was an event of first-rate importance. For Oswy's overlordship of the Midlands came utterly to an end. So long as he lived, he continued to struggle to regain it, but never with much success; and from this time onwards it grows every year clearer that Northumbria's chance of dominating all England has passed away.

In Wulfhere the Mercians found a leader even abler than Penda, who steadily advanced his frontiers and at the same time thoroughly Christianised his people. On the whole he shunned northern enterprises, his aim being to get control of south-eastern England and even of Sussex, and to hem in Wessex into the south-west. In the latter kingdom considerable progress had followed on Coenwalch's return from exile. Three events deserve mention. These are the assignment about 648 of parts of Berkshire and Wiltshire, reckoned at 3000 hides, to Cuthred, the prince who had helped to restore Coenwalch, a transaction which shews that the assessment system had been applied south of the Thames, the foundation of a second bishopric for Wessex at Winchester, and a successful campaign carried on against the Britons of West Wales. The latter opened with an attack on Somerset, and in 652 a battle occurred near Bath at Bradford-on-Avon; but it was not till 658 that Coenwalch was definitely successful, when a victory at Penn in the forest of Selwood enabled the men of Wiltshire to overrun most of Dorset and to advance the Wessex frontier in Somerset to the banks of the Parrett. Again we only have very meagre accounts of an important event, but it is evident that the settlement of so much new territory must have drawn heavily on the West Saxon population and made them less able than heretofore to withstand Mercian aggression in the Thames valley.

Here then was Wulfhere's opportunity to seize the Chiltern districts. Nor did he lose it. In 661 he advanced out of Middle Anglia, and after capturing Bensington and Dorchester, till then the chief centres of the West Saxons, threw himself across the Thames and laid waste the 3000 hides, known as Ashdown, which Coenwalch had assigned to Cuthred. It would seem that Cuthred was killed; at any rate the West Saxons were completely beaten, and the " Chilternsaete " or dwellers in Oxfordshire and Buckinghamshire, had to accept Wulfhere as their overlord. Their district, reckoned in the Tribal Hidage at 4000 hides, from this time forward may be regarded as Mercian, while the Thames becomes the northern frontier of Wessex and Winchester the chief seat of the West Saxon kings.

A further result of this campaign was seen in the submission of Essex, at this time ruled by a double line of kings, and perhaps divided into two provinces, Essex proper reckoned at 7000 hides and Hendrica to the west of it reckoned at 3500. This was a very substantial gain: for it gave Wulfhere London, even at that day the most important port in England. As might be expected, the Thames did not long set a limit to Wulfhere's ambitions. Using London as a base, he next overran Suthrige, the modern Surrey, and shortly afterwards Sussex. In Surrey after this we hear of Mercian aldermen; but Sussex retained its kings, as Wulfhere found them useful as a counterpoise to the kings at Winchester. Finally we find Wulfhere attacking the Jutes along the valley of the Meon in south-east Hampshire and the Isle of Wight. This brought his arms almost up to Winchester. There is no record however that he attacked the West Saxon capital, but only that he detached the " Meonwaras " and the men of Wight from Wessex and annexed their districts to Sussex. The dates of these events are not exactly known, but clearly they constituted Mercia a power as great as any hitherto established in England. If the title " Bretwalda " means wide ruler, Wulfhere clearly deserves it as much as Oswald or Oswy, and perhaps more so ; for he maintained his supremacy for fourteen years (661–675) and was also quite as zealous as they were to forward the new religion. Examples of his zeal are numerous, as for instance the suppression of heathen temples in Essex in 665, the final foundation of Medeshamstede, and the baptism of Aethelwalch king of Sussex, Wulfhere himself standing as sponsor ; or again the encouragement which he gave to his brother Merewald to found a religious centre for the Hecanas or West Angles which led to the establishment of monasteries at Leominster in Herefordshire and Wenlock in Shropshire.

While Wulfhere was establishing the ascendancy of Mercia an internal struggle of the greatest importance had arisen in Northumbria between those who looked for Christian guidance to Iona and those who looked to Rome. Though the work of evangelising the country had been entirely carried on by the Scots, at first under Aidan of Lindisfarne, and after his death under Finan, there were none the less many clerics in the land who, having travelled abroad, were not content to see the Church cut off from continental sympathy by the peculiarities of the Irish system and the claim of Iona to independence. The leader of this movement was Wilfrid, a young Deiran of noble birth, who after studying at Lindisfarne had journeyed to Rome and finished his education at Lyons. Returning to England in 658, he had become abbot of Stamford in Kesteven, but had retired to Deira when Wulfhere revolted. There from the outset he steadily advocated union with Rome, and winning King Alchfrid's sympathy got himself about 661 appointed abbot of Ripon, a newly founded monastery, in place of Eata, a Lindisfarne monk, who maintained the Iona traditions, especially as to the date of Easter. About the same time Finan died at Lindisfarne, and Colman was sent from Iona to succeed him. In Bernicia the Roman party had another powerful advocate in the person of Oswy's queen, a Kentish princess. She eagerly pushed Wilfrid's cause at court until at last Oswy and his son determined that a synod should be held at Streaneshalch to discuss the matter. This assembly, later known as the Synod of Whitby[1], met early in 664. It consisted of both clergy and laymen, the leaders on either side being Wilfrid and Colman. The test question was as to the proper day for observing Easter. The Scots kept the feast on one day, the Roman churchmen on another. The arguments were lengthy, but the final decision was in favour of Wilfrid; whereupon Colman with the bulk of the Columban clergy decided to leave Lindisfarne and return to Iona. So ended the Irish-Scot mission which for twenty-nine years had been the leading force in civilising northern and central England.

The victory of Wilfrid's party was of great importance in three ways. Firstly it restored the unity of the English Church, bringing all its branches under one leadership, and so made its influence in favour of political unity stronger. Secondly it quickened the spread of civilisation by placing the remoter English provinces under teachers who drew their ideas from lands where the traditions of the Roman Empire were still alive, and where an altogether larger life was lived than among the wilds of the Scottish islands. Lastly it introduced into England a new conception of what a bishop or abbot should be, superseding the homely self-effacing northern missionaries, who despised landed wealth, by more worldly prince-prelates who were by no means satisfied to be only preachers but demanded noble churches and a stately ritual for their flocks and extensive endowments for themselves with a leading share in the direction of secular affairs. It was this aspect of the Burgundian and Frankish Churches that had particularly appealed to Wilfrid, and

[1] See p. 531.

he meant to bring the English Church into line with them, if he could. The opportunity of making a beginning in his own person soon offered itself, owing to the death of Tuda, the bishop who had been placed over Lindisfarne after Colman's withdrawal. To fill the vacancy the Northumbrian princes not unnaturally turned to Wilfrid, and he was quite willing to accept their offer but on the condition that the site of his see should be transferred to York, partly to shew that he was more truly the successor of Paulinus than of Aidan, and partly in imitation of the urban Frankish bishoprics. He further stipulated that he must be consecrated abroad, as he regarded the English bishops as irregularly appointed. He accordingly went to Frankland, and the ceremony took place with great magnificence at Compiègne in presence of twelve Gallican bishops. After this Wilfrid is represented as moving about with a prince's body-guard of one hundred and twenty retainers; but so much state was hardly justified, for he found, on returning to England, that Oswy had quarrelled with his son, that Alchfrid had been driven from Deira and that as a result Oswy was determined not to have his son's friend as bishop of the Northumbrians. Oswy in fact had already appointed another man to Wilfrid's see, in the person of Ceadda, abbot of Lastingham, later known as St Chad. The motive of so anti-Roman a step is not quite clear, but its importance is obvious. It made Wilfrid a bitter opponent of the Northumbrian house and drove him to look towards Mercia. He still remained abbot of Ripon but in 667 we find him performing episcopal functions in Mercia for Wulfhere.

The following year a yet more important step in binding England to civilisation and Roman culture took place when Pope Vitalian helped in filling up the archbishopric of Canterbury and selected for the post, not an energetic Englishman like Wilfrid, but a scholar and born organiser, who was well acquainted at once with Rome and Italy, and with the Greek world of the Byzantine Empire, then without question the most civilised part of Christendom. This remarkable man, called Theodore of Tarsus, from his birthplace in Cilicia, was already sixty-six when he landed in England in 669, and men must have thought that age alone would soon damp his zeal. If so, they were mistaken; for never was an archbishop so strenuous in every sphere, whether as administrator, legislator, counsellor or peacemaker, so that for twenty-one years he kept himself foremost in every English movement, and by his ceaseless activity made the English understand what could be gained from unification and orderly government.

The work which Theodore set himself to do was the thorough organisation of the English Churches upon a centralised system in subjection to Canterbury. Since Augustine's day no archbishop had played any real part outside Kent, and Canterbury had enjoyed only an honorary precedence. Theodore on the contrary regarded all England as his province, and at once set out to visit all its petty kings and make

himself acquainted with their peoples and their needs. In each diocese
he required an acknowledgment of his authority; in York for example
he re-established Wilfrid; and everywhere he inculcated the need of
uniform machinery and ritual.

Condemning the merely missionary types of church organisation as insufficient, he early decided that there ought to be a
greater number of bishops and clergy, a greater number of dioceses and churches, and a substantial landed endowment, if possible,
for each minister of the church, whether priest, monk or prelate, to free
them from the insecurity of dependence on lay charity. The central
feature of this programme was the subdivision of unwieldy dioceses and
the foundation of more mother churches, a somewhat hazardous adventure, as the existing bishops were naturally jealous of any diminution
of their importance. The first step was to get the existing churches
into touch with each other, and make them acknowledge the importance
of uniformity and good discipline. For this purpose Theodore summoned a synod of bishops to meet at Hertford in 673, a memorable
event; for though only four of his six suffragans attended, the meeting
may be regarded as the first attempt in England at a national, as distinct
from a tribal, assembly.

The chief work of the synod, as reported by Bede, was the adoption
of certain canons for the guidance of the bishops, and this was followed
up in 674 by the actual putting into force in East Anglia of the policy
of smaller sees, the bishopric founded by Felix being partitioned and two
new sees created, one at Dunwich for Suffolk and the other at Elmham
for Norfolk.

A good beginning was thus made without opposition; but in his
further progress Theodore soon found himself entangled in the political
rivalries of Mercia and Northumbria and in quarrels connected with
Wilfrid. Theodore had reconciled Oswy and Wilfrid, but in 671 Oswy
died and Northumbria passed to his son Ecgfrith, an ill-fated prince, who
quickly quarrelled with Wilfrid and about 675 reopened the feud with
Mercia by again seizing Lindsey. Both events were made use of by
Theodore, for they furnished him with opportunities for intervening.
To subdivide the see of York had been quite impracticable so long as
Wilfrid had political support; but now Ecgfrith himself came forward
and offered to ignore Wilfrid and further the archbishop's reforms.
Theodore at once announced that though he was willing to let Wilfrid
continue bishop of a reduced see of York, he wished for four moderate-
sized bishoprics in Ecgfrith's dominions, proposing as their seats, in
Bernicia Lindisfarne and Hexham, in Deira York, and in Lindsey
Sidnacaester. Wilfrid obstinately resisted this proposal, declaring that
Theodore had no power to divide his see and that he would appeal
to Rome if any division was forced upon him. Theodore treated the
threat as contumacious, declared Wilfrid deposed, and appointed the

new bishops. Wilfrid replied by sailing for Frisia. In 679 he reached Rome and laid his case before Pope Agatho, being the first English bishop to appeal against his metropolitan to the papal tribunal.

Ecgfrith's attack on Lindsey, delivered about 675, at first was successful, for it coincided with the death of Wulfhere and the accession of Aethelred, his younger brother, to the throne of Mercia. This prince however soon proved himself even more capable than his brother. His first exploit was to overrun Kent and burn Rochester, and by 679 he was quite ready to attack Ecgfrith. No account exists of the campaign, beyond the fact that Aethelred won a decisive victory on the banks of the Trent and would have invaded Deira, had not Theodore suddenly interposed as a mediator, and effected a peace by which Lindsey and perhaps Southern Yorkshire once more passed to Mercia. This was a blow to Northumbrian prestige of such a deadly nature that for the next thirty-five years (679–714) no Northumbrian king dared to attack Mercia, and it was quickly followed by the acceptance of Aethelred's overlordship by Kent which gave him an even greater position than had been enjoyed by Wulfhere.

The part played by Theodore in these developments reveals his farsightedness. It would have been natural if he had seen his interest in preserving the independence of Kent. His policy was just the reverse. He saw that Mercia was the strongest English kingdom, and well able to help in a centralising movement, and so he threw his influence on to Aethelred's side. Hence arose a close connexion between Canterbury and Tamworth, which was to last for over a century.

The first result of this alliance was the erection of three additional Mercian dioceses, the first for the South Mercians and Middle Angles at Leicester, the second for the Hwicce at Worcester, and the third for the southern branch of the Wreocensaete, the Hecana or Magesaete, at Hereford. Even so the mother see at Lichfield remained unwieldy, as it extended over South Lancashire, Cheshire and Shropshire as well as over the lands of the North Mercians in Staffordshire, Derbyshire and Nottinghamshire. Mercia thus obtained five dioceses, for Dorchester was also a Mercian see. The three new sees seem to have been created not simultaneously, but clearly at dates not far off 680, a year made memorable by a second great synod summoned by Theodore to meet at Heathfield to signify the English Church's orthodoxy on the Monothelete question.

Having achieved the reorganisation of northern and central England Theodore might well congratulate himself. Wessex remained undealt with, but he now had fourteen suffragans in place of seven and each had a fairly manageable diocese. The problems which still faced him were the provision of permanent endowments on a sufficient scale and of parish priests and churches. As to the latter, time alone could solve the difficulty and no complete parochial system came into existence for several centuries. Parishes were only slowly evolved as the richer landowners built churches for their estates and most villages had for a long time to be content with the occasional visits of travelling priests. The most that could be done at once was to provide little groups of clerics, living a semi-collegiate life, in monastic cells scattered here and there in each diocese, and let these serve the neighbouring districts. Traces of this system of petty monasteries can probably still be seen in such village names as Kidderminster, Alderminster, Upminster, Southminster and so on, a system very similar to that of the Welsh *clas* but one that ultimately passed away as more churches were built.

With regard to permanent endowments nothing very definite can be said, except that they largely increased under Theodore's auspices, and that it appears to be in his time that the practice of conferring estates on the churches by means of written grants first arose. Bede tells of grants of land in some cases before 670 but of none of any large amount, the largest being Oswy's gift of 120 hides for 12 monastic cells after the battle of the Winwaed, while he definitely says that the Scottish prelates actually refused land in many instances. Wilfrid however had introduced the desire for magnificence, and Theodore encouraged it. More and more we hear of larger gifts, as for instance a gift to Benedict Biscop of 70 hides to found Wearmouth, and a gift to Wilfrid of 87 hides to found Selsey, shortly followed by one of 300 hides in the Isle of Wight. With more frequent gifts came also the need for better means of recording them and rendering them irrevocable; and so arose the use of written conveyances, "Landbooks" as the Saxons called them. These were clearly introduced by the clergy from abroad, being based on Frankish models with formulas drawn from Roman precedents, but no genuine examples can be produced for England before Theodore's time. The earliest specimen in fact that has survived to the present day seems to be a landbook, dated 679, preserved by the monks of Christ Church, Canterbury, by which Lothaire, king of Kent, granted Westanae, that is the western half of Thanet, later known as Monkton, to the abbot of Reculver. Only two or three other examples claim to be of Theodore's time, but few of these are above the suspicion of forgery, and it is clear that it was only after his death that the use of such instruments gradually grew into favour. Even in the case of so old a church as Rochester, its landbooks only begin with a deed dated 735, and altogether there are not more than forty genuine landbooks extant which bear dates earlier than 750.

The later years of Theodore's activity were also a critical period for Wilfrid. As we have seen, he reached Rome in 679, but he did not gain much by his appeal, important as it was as a precedent. Pope Agatho, it is true, issued bulls in his favour, but when he returned to England he was accused of buying them and Ecgfrith put him in prison. Regaining his freedom after nine months, he decided to become a missionary and betook himself to Aethelwalch of Sussex, whose people were still heathen. Here he laboured with great success for five years (681–686), baptising the chief men and founding a monastery at Selsey.   In connexion with this foundation Bede adds the interesting note that there were 250 male and female slaves on the estates which Aethelwalch gave for its endowment, and that Wilfrid gave them their freedom, a significant indication at any rate that a considerable percentage of the English lower orders were excluded from the ranks of the freemen in the seventh century.

Meanwhile a path was opening for Wilfrid's return to Northumbria. On the one hand he became reconciled with Theodore, on the other the Northumbrian king was dead.   After his defeat by Mercia Ecgfrith had turned his attention northwards and had been busy fighting the Picts and Scots.   In 681 he set up a bishopric at Abercorn on the Forth, to minister to the lands he claimed to have subdued, and in 684 he sent a fleet to attack Ireland.   In 685 his raids were even pressed beyond the Tay in pursuit of Bruide the Pictish king; but here he met with disaster, being slain with many of his nobles at Nechtansmere near Forfar. From this date onwards Northumbria distinctly loses its vitality and gradually falls into a chronic state of civil war.   Ecgfrith's successor was Aldfrid, a prince who had spent much of his time in a monastery and who was no fighter.   He was willing to be reconciled to Wilfrid but would not restore him to his old position.   He only offered him the reduced see of York, and the abbacy of Ripon.   With this Wilfrid had to be perforce content, but not whole-heartedly, and he was soon engaged in a new quarrel with Aldfrid over a proposal to create a separate bishopric at Ripon.   This question was just becoming acute when Archbishop Theodore died at the great age of eighty-eight in 690. The absence of his moderating influence soon made itself felt and within two years Wilfrid was again in exile, taking refuge with Aethelred who gave him the monastery of Oundle in Middle Anglia and later made him bishop of Leicester.   The appointment of a new archbishop of Canterbury in 692 in the person of Berctwald, the abbot of Reculver to whom Lothaire had granted Westanae, did nothing to stop the feud, and Wilfrid remained in Mercia for eleven years (691–702).   The most interesting notice we have of him at this epoch implies his attendance in 695 at the translation of the body of St Aethelthryth, the virgin foundress of Ely, formerly Ecgfrith's queen, who in her life had played a considerable part in bringing about his original quarrel in Northumbria.

In reviewing Theodore's achievements, it will be noticed that the only important English kingdom not touched by his activity was Wessex; but here also great changes took place in his later days. These were brought about by the rise to power of Ceadwalla, a young pagan princeling who is first heard of in 684 making an attack on Aethelwalch of Sussex.   For some time before this Wessex had been ruled by a number of petty chieftains, no one branch of the house of Cerdic being able to control the rest, a weakness perhaps due to the loss of the Chilterns to Mercia and to the difficulty of assimilating the recently acquired Keltic provinces of Dorset and Somerset. Ceadwalla had been outlawed in these conflicts and seems to have been in the pay of the Kentish princes when he attacked Aethelwalch. Having slain the Sussex king, he next year turned against Centwine, the leading claimant to the kingship in Wessex, drove him into a monastery and got himself elected king. He followed up these successes by an attack on the Jutes in the Isle of Wight and round Southampton Water— districts which Bede describes as still ruled by their own king and still heathen. Ceadwalla quickly conquered them, and even tried to ex- terminate the Jutes and replace them by West Saxons. His savagery had evidently not been forgotten fifty years later. It is clear, however, that he himself was thinking of becoming a Christian; for as soon as he had the island in his power, he handed over a quarter of it to Bishop Wilfrid, and permitted the advent of Christian missionaries, thus bringing about the fall of the last stronghold of paganism in England.

Having thus secured his position in Wessex, Ceadwalla again attacked Sussex and overran it from end to end, and then pushed on into Kent, designing to set up his brother Mul as an under-king over part of that kingdom. For the moment the design succeeded, and it may well be that, as a result, Surrey was detached from Kent. Mul, however, was not favoured by fortune and shortly met a tragic death by burning. Ceadwalla at once made reprisals; but in the midst of his harryings he was seized with contrition for his deeds and determined to become a Christian definitely, and to abandon his throne and go as a pilgrim to seek baptism from the Pope. He accordingly left England in 688 and, reaching Rome, was baptised by Pope Sergius. He was still only thirty, but died almost immediately afterwards. No reign in Anglo-Saxon history is more bloodthirsty than Ceadwalla's, but his meteoric career had the merit of putting new vigour into the West Saxons, who from this time onwards stand out as far more determined opponents of Mercia than hitherto. Sussex, too, from this date tends to become a vassal of Wessex rather than of Mercia, and so the first move is made towards the distant goal of the ultimate supremacy of the house of Cerdic in England. Ceadwalla was succeeded by Ine, a man of considerable force, who ruled Wessex for thirty-eight years (688–726). The greater part of his reign was devoted to extending his territories. In the east he set up his kinsman Nunna as under-king of Sussex; in the west he encroached year by year on West Wales. Details are lacking, but we may ascribe the conquest of West Somerset to the middle of his reign, Geraint the British king of Danmonia being driven from Taunton. In 710 a fight is mentioned in which Nunna also took part, and, though no results are recorded, an advance into the valley of the Exe may perhaps be presumed, as we find the West Saxons at Crediton near Exeter early in the next reign. Ine's thoughts, however, were not solely bent on war, and the Church found him an active patron and eager to further the principles of Theodore. Among his friends were many notable ecclesiastics, such as Aldhelm, abbot of Malmesbury, the most learned classical scholar in England, Earconwald, bishop of London, the founder of Chertsey Abbey in Surrey and so in some sort Ine's bishop, and Headde, bishop of Winchester. With the approval of men such as these, he pressed forward the endowment of the clergy both by generous grants of land and by formally enacting that the dues called " church-scots" should be compulsory and levied every Martinmas. The extant landbooks, however, which the monks of Glastonbury and Abingdon ascribed to him in later days, can hardly be regarded as genuine.

As his frontiers advanced westwards, the question naturally arose, "Ought the West Saxon see to be divided?" Nothing was done till Headde died in 705. The ideas of Theodore were then taken up and the overgrown diocese split into two. The seat of the new western see, sometimes called Selwoodshire because it comprised Wessex west of Selwood Forest, was fixed at Sherborne and Aldhelm of Malmesbury was consecrated its first bishop, while the reduced see of Winchester was given to Daniel. Some few years later the same principle was applied to Sussex, and Daniel permitted a new bishopric for the South Saxons to be set up at Selsey.

While Wessex was thus developing under Ine, Kent, though subject to Mercia, was not inactive. In Theodore's later years the kingdom had been divided between Lothaire and Eadric, joint rulers, who are remembered for some amending laws supplementing Aethelberht's code. A period of anarchy however followed on Ceadwalla's inroads in 685. This was terminated by the accession of Wihtraed, a particularly devout prince who ruled as Ine's contemporary from 690 to 725 and who is claimed as the first English king to grant general charters of immunity to the churches of his kingdom, thereby freeing their lands from secular and royal dues. Whether Wihtraed's so-called " Privilege" is really a genuine document will probably never be ascertained; but he also issued a code of laws mainly directed to making the status of the clergy clear and definite, which are markedly in favour of the Church.

The example set by Kent was not lost on Ine. Early in his reign he also issued a collection of written laws. As we have them now, they form an appendix to the dooms issued two hundred years later by Alfred, and it is not quite clear how far they have been abbreviated and subjected to revision. None the less they give most valuable evidence for the seventh century, for they seem to present a contrast to the Kentish dooms on many points, and also deal with a larger number of topics. The most interesting sections are perhaps those dealing with the conquered Welsh in Somerset and Dorset. Though it is usual to speak of these laws as codes, it must always be remembered that they are in reality no more than brief amending clauses, dealing only with certain sides of the law, more particularly with the penalties for important crimes, and with the status of the clergy. Family law and the law of property are only scantily touched on, and public institutions, even if alluded to, are never explained, but taken for granted. Moreover, the codes when all put together are extremely brief. Aethelberht's laws, for example, are confined to ninety clauses, and Wihtraed's to twenty-eight, while no laws of this date at all have come down to us from Mercia or Northumbria. It is clear then that any picture of society, which can be deduced from them, must be most imperfect, and that much is left to inference. They have, however, a superiority over similar codes produced by the conquering Germans on the Continent in that they are written in English and so give the native terms for the things of which they speak, whereas the continental codes being in Latin only give approximate equivalents which are often merely mystifying and misleading.

We must now turn back to the affairs of the North. Wilfrid, while in Mercia, had never abandoned his claim to be bishop of undivided Northumbria. In 702 a fresh attempt was made to deal with it, a synod being held at Austerfield on the Idle under the presidency of Archbishop Berctwald. As before, neither Wilfrid nor Aldfrid would give way; the upshot was that, in spite of his age, Wilfrid once more set out for Rome to lay his cause in person before the Pope. In 704, while he was still abroad, Aethelred retired from the throne of Mercia to become a monk at Bardney, and was succeeded by his nephew Coenred; and when Wilfrid returned in 705 with fresh papal letters, he found Aldfrid on his death-bed. Before a synod could meet, the crown of Northumbria passed to a child. This seemed to facilitate a compromise; Wilfrid, however, did not attain his object. He never regained even York and had to be content with the see of Hexham. He lived four years longer and died at Oundle in 709. His death brings to an end the interesting period of Northumbrian history. The northern kingdom from this time onwards is of little account, and its story one long record of faction and decay. The only bright spots in its annals are Bede's literary career at Jarrow and the development of the schools of York, and the only event of permanent importance the conversion of the bishopric of York into an archbishopric. This took place in 735, the year that Bede died, the first archbishop of York being Ecgbert, the prelate who founded the schools and who for thirty-two years devoted himself to their development.

For the whole of the eighth century the Mercian State clearly holds the headship of England. Wessex at first caused some trouble under Ine, and we hear of a fight in 715 at a place usually identified with

Wanborough near Swindon. But Ine was entirely occupied with the
internal affairs of Wessex and Sussex for the last ten years of his reign,
and in 726 he followed the example of Ceadwalla and abdicated, being
filled with a desire to see Rome and die in the neighbourhood of the
popes. Coenred and Ceolred, who occupied the Mercian throne after
Aethelred, may perhaps have feared Ine, but all doubt, as to which
state was supreme, disappeared with the accession of Aethelbald, who
ruled from Tamworth for forty-one years (716–757), only to be succeeded by the still more famous Offa, who ruled for thirty-nine (757–
796). These long reigns are not filled with struggles for supremacy
like those of the seventh century, and lend themselves to briefer
treatment.

Aethelbald's reign is roughly contemporaneous with the career of
Charles Martel, while Offa's extends over a part of the reign of
Charlemagne, with which prince he had friendly relations. Aethelbald
calls himself in his landbooks "King of the Mercians and South Angles";
Offa is addressed by the popes as "King of the English" without qualification. This difference of style pretty well sums up the progress made
in the period, so that at Offa's death it must have seemed to contemporaries that the domination of all England by Mercia was merely a question
of time. As it was, Kent and East Anglia had already been practically
absorbed. In spite of this development these reigns are usually held to
be "an age of little men, of decaying faith and of slumberous inactivity";
but this is hardly the whole truth and arises from the fact that we no
longer have Bede's lively narrative to help us to fill out our picture, our
materials being cut down to the bald statements of the Anglo-Saxon
Chronicle supplemented by a few lives of saints and some two hundred
landbooks, more than half of which are under suspicion of being spurious.
The Chronicle, too, being chiefly concerned with Wessex, gives a quite
inadequate impression of the aims and activities of the leading Mercians.

Aethelbald's reign was clearly favourable to the growth of church
endowments. The earliest Rochester and several of the earlier Worcester
landbooks are ascribed to him. More important, however, than his actual
grants of land, if we can trust it, is his general decree issued in 749, by
which he conceded to all the minsters of his kingdom freedom from all
burdens (*a publicis vectigalibus et ab omnibus oneribus*) excepting only
the duties of repairing bridges and maintaining fortresses. Here we
have an important step towards the encouragement of feudalism; for
clearly this concession does not mean that the peasantry on ecclesiastical
lands are to be free from *vectigal*, but that what has hitherto been paid
to the king will go for the future into the treasuries of the churches.
Thus, as has been well said, the Church got "a grip on those who dwelt
on the land." It should be noticed too that in the grants of this period
little stress is laid upon any consent by the Mercian magnates as a
necessary condition required to make the grants valid. The king declares

himself to be granting his own lands and his own rights. The magnates appear as a rule only in the attesting clauses as *adstipulatores* or witnesses. While Aethelbald was active in supporting the Church, there is also evidence that under him the clergy, led by Archbishop Cuthbert, made strenuous efforts to improve themselves, a synod being held in 747 at Clovesho in which thirty canons were drawn up for the reform of ecclesiastical discipline. These canons no doubt are good evidence that there were abuses needing reform and so bear out to a certain extent the gloomy picture of ecclesiastical decay which Bede has put on record as characteristic of Northumbria in his time. It would, however, be unfair to assume that the decay was as bad in flourishing Mercia as in declining Northumbria; and the acts of this synod point rather to progress and activity. As a warrior Aethelbald does not come much before us. Early in his reign he raided Somerset as far as Somerton on the Parrett, and towards the end of it the West Saxons, led by Cuthred, retaliated by a raid into Oxfordshire as far as Burford, an achievement which the Wessex chronicle makes much of. There seems no real evidence however that this reverse had any permanent effect on the Mercian supremacy. It may have rendered Wessex somewhat more independent, and more hopeful of regaining the Chilterns, but when Offa succeeded to the Mercian throne in 757 there was clearly no question as to his ascendancy in England.

Offa's reign marks the culmination of the power of Mercia. All accounts admit that he was the most powerful of the Mercian kings and easily supreme in England. Among facts that illustrate this are the disappearance of the sub-kings who had hitherto maintained themselves in Essex and in the province of the Hwicce, and the appearance of landbooks in which Offa disposes of estates in Sussex, the kings of Kent and Wessex figuring as consenting vassals among the witnesses. The Kentish men rose against him in 774 at Otford and the men of Wessex in 777 at Bensington; but in both cases only to meet with crushing defeats, and for the rest of his reign he had no further troubles south of the Thames. In 778 he devastated all South Wales and again in 784, and it must be about this period that he ordered the great earthwork to be erected along his western frontier which later ages called Offa's Dyke. This work is still traceable between the Dee and the Wye, and marks, not so much an advance of the Mercians, as a final delimitation of their territory, all beyond it being definitely left subject to Welsh law and custom, even if occupied by the English. Finally, in 793 Offa put the king of the East Angles to death, and annexed his kingdom. On the Continent Offa had considerable renown and Charlemagne even negotiated with him for the hand of one of his daughters for his eldest son. In internal affairs he was also active. For example, he reformed the Anglo-Saxon coinage, introducing a new type of silver penny in imitation of Charles the Great's *denarius,* a type which lasted almost unchanged down to late Plantagenet times, and also a gold coin, called the mancus, copied from the dinars used by the Moors in Spain. He also issued a code of Mercian laws; these are unfortunately lost, but they were utilised by Alfred a century later as a source for his own code. In church matters he is remembered as the founder of St Alban's Abbey (also perhaps of Westminster) and as a liberal benefactor to Canterbury and Worcester, but more especially for his determination to make the Mercian dioceses independent of Canterbury. For this purpose he applied to the Pope to convert the bishopric of Lichfield into an archbishopric. The Archbishop of Canterbury naturally resisted the design, but Hadrian I sent legates to England in 786 to examine the matter, and a synod was held at Chelsea which settled that Higbert of Lichfield should be put in charge of the seven dioceses of Mercia and East Anglia and receive a pallium. In return for this concession Offa promised to give the Pope an annual gift of money, and so inaugurated the tribute known to after ages as Peter's Pence. Offa died in 796, completely master of his realm, but his good fortune did not descend to his only son, a delicate youth called Ecgfrith. This prince only survived his father 141 days, and on his death the crown passed over to his remote kinsman Coenwulf, who once more had to struggle with Kent and who ultimately abandoned Offa's scheme of a separate archbishopric for Mercia in return for the support of the archbishop of Canterbury against the rebels. This concession was undoubtedly a good thing for England, but it marks the beginning of the fall of Mercia.

Before leaving the Mercian period it is natural to ask a few questions as to the social and political organisation of the English in the days of Theodore and up to the close of the eighth century. Can a satisfactory short statement be made about these matters, or must it be admitted that our sources are so scanty and so full of gaps that it is impossible to obtain any definite light on them? The chief difficulty arises from the absence of contemporary laws for either Northumbria, Mercia or East Anglia. Except for a few Mercian landbooks, for Bede's incidental remarks and for the general picture of society presented in lives of such saints as Wilfrid, or in heroic poetry like the Song of Beowulf, apparently composed in Mercia about A.D. 700, we have no contemporary evidence illuminating English institutions north of the Thames. The Kentish laws and those of Ine furnish a fair amount of material for the southern provinces, but can this evidence be assumed to apply to the whole country, especially when we find that there were marked differences between Kent and Wessex? As a rule this question has been answered in the affirmative, and it has been assumed that the main customs of Wessex were also in force in the midlands and the north, while the gaps in the southern evidence have been filled by having recourse to parallel continental practice or to English customs of a later day. It must be admitted that no very sure generalisations can be attained by these methods, and the resulting picture is bound to be marred by mis-conceptions. However, if an outline is to be attempted at all, no other methods are available.

As regards the social organisation the most striking feature revealed by the laws is the great complexity of the class divisions. Society in a petty English kingdom about A.D. 700 did not consist in the main of men on an equal footing with one another, but took the form of an elaborately graded social ladder, each grade above the slaves being distinguished, as in all primitive societies, by its special "wergeld" or money price. In Kent there were four main divisions, *theows, laets, ceorls* and *eorlcund-men,* corresponding to the *servi liberti ingenui* and *nobiles* spoken of by Tacitus when describing the Germans of the first century; but these main classes had many subdivisions, as for instance four grades of bondmen, three of *laets* and four of *eorlcund-men,* while in addition there was the further distinction between the *godcund* and the *woruldcund,* the clergy and the laity, the former having also their own grades. In Wessex there were also four main divisions of the laity but the classification was clearly not the same as in Kent. The four main classes were the *theows,* the *Welshmen,* the *ceorls* and the *gesithcund-men.* Here too there were subdivisions, the laws distinguishing several categories of Welshmen, two of *ceorls* (the *twihynde* and the *sixhynde* classes) and two of *gesithcund-men.* In both kingdoms above the *eorlcund* and *gesithcund* classes, or perhaps forming their highest subdivisions, were the *aethelings.* This grade was composed of the members of the princely kindreds from whom the kings were chosen. These men furnished the bulk of the provincial officials, and from time to time they are seen deposing the kings and breaking up the kingdoms among themselves, each *aetheling* claiming for himself a "shire," that is to say his "share," as a petty principality. It is these *aethelings,* men like Ceadwalla before he seized the crown, who should be regarded as the "nobles" in such petty states as Essex, Sussex, Kent or even Wessex and not the mass of the *eorlcund* or *gesithcund* classes, who were clearly not so much nobles as the equivalent of the knights and squires of later ages. The ordinary *gesithcund-man,* as the name implies, was suited by birth and training to be the companion or "comes" of the *aetheling.* Like the latter, he spent most of his time in war and hunting; but to regard both the leader of a "comitatus" and his "comites" as "nobles" is only confusing.

The upper grades, the "dearly-born" men as they were termed because of their higher "wergelds," were often spoken of in the mass as *eorls,* an expression best translated as the "warriors," whereas all the lower free classes were in a general sense *ceorls* or agriculturists. The most remarkable fact revealed by the laws about the *ceorls,* in the stricter sense of the term, was the inferior status held by the Wessex *ceorls* as compared with the Kentish *ceorls.* It is somewhat difficult to compare their respective "wergelds," for the monetary systems of Kent and Wessex differed; but, whatever the obscurities, it seems to be now agreed that whereas the wergelds of the *eorlcund* and *gesithcund* classes were approximately of equal value, the value of the Wessex *ceorl* was far below that of the Kentish *ceorl*, and little higher than the value of the lowest class of Kentish *laet*. The best way to shew this is to convert the money values given by the laws into terms of livestock, the medium in which the fines were mostly paid. In the case of Wessex this is not a difficult problem. The laws state the amount of the wergeld in Wessex "shillings," and there are passages in Ine's code and also in the later West Saxon laws which indicate that this "shilling" was the equivalent of a "sheep." It seems further that the English reckoned four sheep as the equivalent of one cow. When therefore the laws state that the *twihynde ceorl's* wergeld was 200 shillings, we can interpret the meaning to be that the manslaughter of a *twihynde ceorl* could be atoned for by paying his *maegth* either 200 sheep or 50 cows. In the Kentish laws, on the other hand, we find that the *ceorl's* wergeld was 100 Kentish shillings; but this shilling was at least four times as valuable as the Wessex shilling; many passages in Aethelberht's code shewing that it contained 20 pence, whereas the Wessex shilling most probably contained five. The Kentish shilling was therefore the equivalent, not of a "sheep," but of a "cow"; and accordingly the killing of a Kentish *ceorl* could only be atoned for with 100 cows, or twice the Wessex penalty. The subjoined table, giving the values (*manwyrth*) of the chief grades in cows, shews, better than any description, the differences between Kentish and West Saxon society.

KENT (1 shilling=20d.=1 cow).		WESSEX (1 shilling=5d.=1 sheep).	
aetheling	1500 sh. =1500 cows	aetheling	(not given)
eorlcund	300 sh. = 300 cows	gesithcund or twelf-	
		hynde man	1200 sh. =300 cows
ceorl	100 sh. = 100 cows	sixhynde ceorl	600 sh. =150 cows
laet, 1st grade	80 sh. = 80 cows	Welshman holding	
laet, 2nd grade	60 sh. = 60 cows	5 hides	do. = do.
laet, 3rd grade	40 sh. = 40 cows		
Welshmen (none mentioned)		twihynde ceorl	200 sh. = 50 cows
		Welshman holding	
		1 hide	120 sh. = 30 cows
		do. holding ½ hide	80 sh. = 20 cows
		do. without land	60 sh. = 15 cows

We may next ask, in what relation did the classes stand to each other? It is clear that among men of Teutonic descent the distinctions of rank were for the most part hereditary distinctions. A man was born a *ceorl* or born a *laet*, whereas the gradations recognised among the Welshmen depended on property. It was possible however for an English *ceorl* to acquire a higher rank by accumulating landed property. It is also clear that the lower grades were the dependents or "men" of the upper grades. Everywhere in the laws we meet with the *hlafords* or lords who were entitled to fines called *manbots* if their men were injured, and these lords were lords over freemen as well as over slaves. The peasantry too are put before us as *gafolgeldas* or *tributarii*, that is to say rent-payers, and it is clear that they not only paid tribute to the king, but had also to work for their lords, as well as pay them dues (*gafol*) (Ine, 67). The amount of the work is not recorded, but we may be sure that the warriors and the churches got their lands tilled for them by their men, and for the most part by freemen. A *gesithcund-man* with an estate assessed at 5 hides could not till his land by himself, still less could those with estates assessed at 10 or 20 hides. They worked them by placing lesser freemen upon them, who paid them rents in kind, or services, or both.

Section 70 of Ine's Laws gives an indication of what might be exacted in this way, giving the year's revenue to be derived from a 10 hide estate as 10 vats of honey, 300 loaves, 12 ambers of Welsh ale, 30 ambers of clear ale, 10 sheep, 10 geese, 20 hens, 10 cheeses, an amber of butter, 5 salmon, 20 weighs of hay and 100 eels. We must understand this as the combined render collected by a land agent from many small tenants, some holding no more than a "gyrde" or "yard" of land, that is land assessed at a quarter of a hide, the bulk of them being probably in the position of the *laet* class in Kent. This class, who correspond to the *lazzi* of the Continent, were only as it were half-free; that is to say, they were freemen, but freemen depressed by having alien or servile blood in their ancestry. This affected their status in two ways. Firstly they lacked the protection given by a full *maegth* of free relatives. A freedman, newly freed, as a rule could have had no free relatives, and his descendants only gradually acquired them. At least four generations, or a century, had to pass away before the handi-cap ceased to be felt, and in the interval the support furnished by a *maegth* had to be obtained instead from the *hlaford* to whose family the *laet* owed his freedom. Secondly, such land as a *laet*, or Welshman, held had not been acquired by conquest at the original settlement, but also came from the *hlaford*, and as a consequence was not held freely, but on conditions prescribed by the lord. No doubt it was regarded as heritable, but subject to the goodwill of the lord. In some cases, too, the lord provided a *botl*, or house, for his man as well as the land. These features, it is true, are only mentioned in the Wessex laws, and not in those of Kent; but the low *wergeld* of the Wessex *ceorls* seems easiest explained, if we regard them as originally descended from a class of *laets*, and subsequently raised in status and dignified by a nobler name in consequence of the victorious wars, which had superimposed them on the top of the alien Welsh peasantry among whom they were settled. An exactly parallel change occurred again in England in the ninth century, when the Norsemen conquered eastern England. They too had their *laet* class, called *leysings*, and when these *leysings* settled among the English they were at once raised in status and made to rank as *ceorls*[1].

The political organisation of the petty English states of Theodore's day, or even when Offa was at his zenith, is as difficult to elucidate as the social organisation. Much has to be inferred from later evidence, and many generalisations, which are possibly true for the tenth century, seem to lack authority when applied, as they have been, to the eighth. It is of course clear that all the states had kings, some of them even a dual kingship as in Kent and Essex, and we may also believe that they all possessed some kind of national assembly, known as the *witenagemot* or " meeting of the wise." But when we inquire what part the *witans* played, and how they were composed, little can be asserted with confidence. The lists of witnesses to the landbooks attributed to Aethelbald and Offa are usually supposed to be evidence for the personnel of the Mercian *witan* before A.D. 800; but these records are very difficult material to deal with, while still less confidence can be placed in the landbooks of Wessex or Sussex. What the landbooks shew, if genuine, is that the Mercian *witan* was a very aristocratic and restricted body, comprising the king and the bishops, a few abbots and about a dozen other magnates who are described either as " princes " or " dukes." Even when joined to the Kentish *witan*, the assembly rarely numbered thirty; and except on these occasions there is hardly any evidence of lesser personages than dukes attending. In some Wessex documents the dukes are described as "praefects," and seem to have been seven in number. The Kentish magnates are occasionally described as " comites." The Mercian dukes were clearly *aethelings* set over the various provinces which made up the kingdom, such as Lindsey or Wreocensaete, and many of them were near kinsmen of the king. It is not known whether the kings were expected to summon their *witans* to confer with them regularly, nor can we say how far the kings were really guided by them. They clearly were consulted on the rare occasions when new laws were framed, but it does not follow from this that a strong king submitted to their advice in matters of ordinary administration. Certainly in making grants of land the kings claimed to be dealing with their own property at their own will. In the case of a disputed succession, however, the *witan* played an important part, determining which of the royal kindred should be acknowledged, when the rivals were not prepared to appeal to arms. The king's power must really have depended chiefly on his wealth, and on his prestige as a warrior. If he could keep together and endow an effective retinue and at the same time maintain friendly relations with the bishops, he was probably not much hampered by any organised political system.

If we turn from the central to the provincial institutions, the same want of evidence prevails. We can only dimly imagine what the districts were which had separate dukes; but it is usual to assume that the

[1] Alfred and Guthrum Treaty, A.D. 885.

indications as to the local government of Wessex, which can be gleaned from Ine's laws, may be also applied to Mercia. These laws shew that Wessex was divided into shires, and that each shire had an "alderman" at its head. These officers, the *praefecti* of the Wessex landbooks, were presumably the equivalent of the Mercian dukes. Their duties were to preside in the local assemblies or shiremoots, to maintain order and promote justice, and to lead the forces of their shire in war. Their power, like that of the kings, was dependent on their wealth and on their prestige as military leaders. In theory no doubt they were the king's agents and removable at the king's will, but in practice the aldermanries were not often interfered with, and they tended to become hereditary.

The chief use of the shiremoot was as a court of justice; it appears to have met twice a year and was attended by the *gesithcund-men* and the more important *ceorls*. For small men attendance must have been a burden, for the richer an opportunity for display and for social intercourse. The actual administration of justice was in the hands of those who attended. It was for them to declare the law, and fix what manner of proof should be furnished by the litigants. It was they, rather than the presiding alderman, who must be regarded as the judges. In the language of the time they were the "doomsmen," and they dealt with all cases both criminal and civil. It is obvious that a court of this kind, sitting at long intervals, and not particularly easy of access for the bulk of the inhabitants of a shire, could not have been the only court; for ordinary cases the shires must have been further subdivided, and the courts of these smaller districts must have sat more frequently. Such courts are found in later times sitting once a month, the districts appropriate to them being called "hundreds," and consisting of groups of villages varying in number from two or three to as many as twenty. There is every reason to suppose that these "hundred" divisions existed in England from the first; they are in fact a common feature of all primitive races, but neither the Kentish nor the West Saxon laws have anything to say about them. Traces of them are perhaps seen in the smaller divisions recorded in the Tribal Hidage. We may assume however that only the more important men laid their suits before the shire courts, and that monthly courts of some kind were the really popular courts attended by the mass of the people, the same methods of procedure being used in them as in the higher courts. There is reason to suspect however that, already in Offa's age, some of these smaller courts were no longer under the direct supervision of the alderman or officials appointed by him. Already the greater churches were aiming at special immunities for their estates, and the landbooks bear witness to the readiness of the kings to purchase safety for their souls by freeing the clerical and monastic owners from secular control. In this way the Church took over functions that should have belonged to the king or the alderman, with the result that in many subdistricts the bishops and the abbots rather than any secular authority were practically the controlling officials. For the peasantry in a rude age this may have been a gain, but the outcome was a fusion of the ruler and the landowner which greatly assisted the growth of a system approaching feudalism.

The difficult questions connected with the development of feudal tendencies in the English kingdoms cannot be adequately discussed here for want of space. Not only is the whole subject very complicated, but for a long time past it has formed a topic for controversy, and though some light has been shed upon the darkness, many points still remain obscure. Three problems have been much debated. First, what proportion of the peasantry were free landowners? Secondly, by what stages did the landlord class acquire the right to exact rents and services from their lesser neighbours? and thirdly, how did it come about that military and judicial powers properly belonging to the kings and dukes also fell into the hands of the landowners?

Thirty years ago it used to be supposed, following the current German views as to Teutonic society, that at the outset the bulk of the English peasantry were virtually free landowners, and the problem, which perplexed historians, was how best to account for the rapid decline of their freedom and the rise of landlordism. These views, however, were directly challenged in 1883 by Frederic Seebohm in his treatise on the "English Village Community." This book not only drew a vivid picture of the methods of husbandry employed in Anglo-Saxon times, shewing how tillage was carried on by joint ploughing and how the usual peasant holding or "yardland" was formed of a number of acre and half-acre strips scattered up and down the arable lands of the village and lying intermixed with those of other holdings, but also attempted to trace back all the chief features of medieval serfdom into the earliest periods. In the main he contended, not so much that the English took over a servile system of agriculture ready made from the Romanised Britons, but that dependent tenure and the power of the lord were innate features of all tribal societies, and that consequently the English tribes or "maegths," no less than the tribes of Keltic Wales or Ireland, were at no period within our ken without a considerable percentage of dependent workers. Hence much of the later manorial system and many feudal features should be regarded as present in their villages from their first settlement in England. These views did not command complete assent and were partly challenged by Maitland and other writers, who pointed out many gaps in the chain of argument; but none the less the evidence, marshalled by Seebohm in this book and in two later studies on the characteristics of tribal custom in Northern Europe, entirely revolutionised the whole current of the discussion, so that it is no longer supposed that the marked equality of the yardlands in the English villages can be traced back to a primitive stage of freedom and equality. On the contrary, it is recognised that such equality is much more likely to have been produced and maintained by pressure from above exercised by lords who for their own purposes prevented inequalities arising, such as would naturally spring up within a few years in any free society by the mere application of the Teutonic rule of partible succession among children.

Further discussion has also shewn that, in reality, there were several different types of village community in early England. To begin with, the terms used in the earliest laws for a village vary. In the Kentish laws we find *tun*, *ham* and *wic*, in the West Saxon *weorthig* and *hiwisc*. The former terms survive as English words in the forms "town," "hamlet" and " wick," the latter only in somewhat disguised shapes in suffixes of place-names—for example in Tamworth, Holsworthy, Leintwardine and Hardenhuish. Other terms, not used in the early laws but common enough as suffixes, are *stede*, *hamstede*, *hamtun* and *burh*, the latter being the parent of both " borough" and "bury." Whether differences of type are implied by this wealth of terms is not clear. It has indeed been argued that the suffix " ham" betokens an earlier settlement than the suffix "tun"; but this seems doubtful. As yet no comprehensive study of English place-names has been attempted. The evidence for the divergence of types is really found elsewhere, by studying the plan and structure of the villages as recorded in the maps of the Ordnance Survey. Two divergent types stand out clearly. On the one hand we see villages in which all the homesteads lie clustered together in a single street; these have been termed by Maitland "nucleated villages"; on the other, villages in which the homesteads lie scattered here and there over the village territory. The former is perhaps the most common type, and is especially noticeable in the Thames Valley, in the Eastern Midlands, in Kesteven and Yorkshire, but the latter prevails in Essex and in the south-west. In the Anglo-Saxon landbooks we also have evidence of a third type of village organisation, common in districts where woodlands predominate. In this type an arable head-village had appendant to it a number of woodland members, often lying at a considerable distance and quite detached. The English spoke of these woodlands as "den baere" or "wald baere," or more shortly as "dens." Instances of villages having detached woodlands should perhaps be given, as this type has hardly attracted the attention it deserves. In Middlesex, Fulham and Finchley; in Hertfordshire, Hatfield and Totteridge; in Buckinghamshire, Eton and Hedgerley, or Taplow and Penn; in Berkshire, Ilsley and West Woodhay; in Hampshire, King's Worthy and Pamber, or Micheldever and Durley; in Surrey, Battersea and Penge; in Sussex, Felpham and Fittleworth; Stanmer and Lindfield; Washington and Horsham. In all these pairs the second village named was originally a detached woodland dependent on the other. In the Chilterns, in Kent and in the Weald generally this was the common type of organisation, and it is for this reason that so many of the woodland villages appear to be absent from the Domesday Survey. A "den" might sometimes be fifteen miles away from the head village and even in another county. The system applied also to marshes, heaths and moorlands. Yet another type was the arable village with a number of surrounding "ends," "cots," or "wicks," some of these dependencies being tilled, some only used as pasture farms producing cheeses. It is obvious that no one hypothesis can be imagined which will account for the development of all these varieties of type or for the great differences in the conditions under which the occupying peasants held them. One thing only stands out clearly. In quite early times the basis of the organisation was distinctly aristocratic, and constantly became more so as the kingdoms became consolidated and the relative distance between a king or aetheling and the cultivating peasants became greater. The advent too of the church, as a considerable landowner, only strengthened the aristocratic and feudal tendencies.

Before closing this chapter a few words should perhaps be added on the spread of learning and education among the English, while Mercia was dominant. Something has already been said as to the immediate effect produced by the advent of the first missionaries; it remains to speak of the schools which gave lustre to the seventh and eighth centuries and of the writers trained in them. The most important schools were those of Wearmouth, Canterbury, and York. The first was set up by Benedict Biscop, founder of Wearmouth and Jarrow, who died in 690. He journeyed five times to Rome and each time came back with art treasures and a goodly store of books. These he particularly recommended to the care of his monks on his death-bed. The progress of his school can best be judged by the after career of its most famous pupil, the Venerable Bede. The school of Canterbury owed its efficiency, not to Augustine, but to Hadrian the African abbot, who first recommended Theodore to Pope Vitalian and then accompanied him to England in 669. Like Theodore, Hadrian was well versed in both Latin and Greek, and he also taught verse-making, music, astronomy, arithmetic, and medicine. Pupils soon crowded to the school and many afterwards became famous clerics, for example, John of Beverley; but undoubtedly the most considerable of all from the literary standpoint was Aldhelm, whom we have already spoken of as bishop of Sherborne. For his time Aldhelm's learning was very comprehensive. His extant writings comprise a treatise both in prose and verse on the praise of virginity, which had an immediate success, a collection of one hundred riddles and acrostics, and several remarkable letters, one being addressed to Geraint, the king of Devon, and another to Aldfrid, the king of Northumbria. These writings shew acquaintance with a very extensive literature both Christian and profane, and also a great love for an out-of-the-way vocabulary. A considerable number of scholars took to imitating his style, the most important among them being Hweetberct, abbot of Wearmouth from 716, and Tatwin, a monk of Bredon in Worcestershire, who became archbishop of Canterbury in 731.

Far the greatest and most attractive figure among the scholars of the period is Bede, who was born in 672 and spent his whole life of sixty-three years at Jarrow, never journeying further afield than York. His style is exactly the opposite to that of Aldhelm. It has no eccentricities or affectations, but is always direct, sincere, and simple. Year by year for forty years he worked industriously, producing in turn commentaries on the Scriptures and works on natural history, grammar, and history. For us his historical works are the most important, and of these the greatest and best is the *Ecclesiastical History of the English Nation.* This contains five books. The first is introductory and deals briefly with Christianity in Britain before the advent of Augustine; the other four books deal each with a period of about 33 years, or one generation, and bring the story down to 731. The success of this history was immediate, and copies of it quickly spread over the Continent, so that at his death Bede had secured a European reputation.

Bede's most important pupil was Ecgbert, already mentioned as the first Archbishop of York. To him Bede wrote his last extant letter, dated 5 Nov. 734, pleading for ecclesiastical reforms in Northumbria and denouncing pseudo-monasteries. Ecgbert partly answered this appeal by developing his cathedral school, forming it on the Canterbury model, and here was educated Alcuin, the second English scholar to gain a European reputation in the eighth century. His work, though it throws great lustre on York, was not done in England, but at the court of Charles the Great, with whom he took service. It is a sufficient proof, however, that England in Offa's day had attained to a literary pre-eminence in the West that the great Frankish ruler should have looked to England for a scholar to set over his palace school.

Besides these Latin scholars, there is good evidence that throughout the seventh and eighth centuries there were also many court bards in England who cultivated the art of poetry in English, handing on from generation to generation traditional lays which told of the deeds of the heathen heroes of the past and perhaps composing fresh ones in honour of the English kings and their ancestors. These lays have much in common with the Homeric poems and like them are highly elaborated. Both Aldhelm and Alcuin refer to their existence, but only fragments of them still survive modified to suit Christian ears. The most important example is the Song of Beowulf already referred to. This deals with Danish and Swedish heroes and extends to 3000 lines. English poetry was also cultivated in ruder forms by the common people; for Bede tells us that wherever villagers met for amusement it was customary for the harp to be handed round among the company and for English songs to be sung. A tale is also told of Aldhelm which points in the same direction, how it was his wont to stand on a bridge near Malmesbury and sing songs to the peasants to attract them to church. The best known maker of English Sacred Songs was Caedmon of Whitby.

CHAPTER XVIII.

THE CARLOVINGIAN REVOLUTION AND FRANKISH INTERVENTION IN ITALY.

THE eighth century had hardly entered on its second half when the last of the long-haired Merovingians was thrust from the throne of the Franks, and Pepin the mayor of the palace hailed as king. The change seemed slight, for the new dynasty had served a long apprenticeship. For more than a century the descendants of Clovis had been mere puppets in a king's seat, while the descendants of St Arnulf, though called only Mayors of the Palace or Dukes and Princes of the Franks, had managed, and with vigour and success, the affairs of the realm. Their neighbours, the scoffing Greeks, marvelled at the strange ways of the Franks, whose lord the king needed no quality save birth alone, and all the year through had nothing to do or plan, but only to eat and drink and sleep and stay shut up at home except on one spring day, when he must sit at gaze before his people, while his head servant ruled the State to suit himself. But it was one thing to rule the State and quite another to lay hand upon those sacred titles and prerogatives which the reverence of centuries had reserved for the race of the Salian sea-god; and the house of Arnulf was little likely to forget their kinsman Grimoald who in the seventh century had outraged that reverence by setting his own son upon the throne, and had paid the forfeit with his life and with his child's. Charles Martel (the Hammer), in the last years of his long rule, had found it possible, indeed, to get on with no king at all, dating his documents from the death of the latest do-nothing; but, if he hoped that thus the two sons between whom at his own death he divided Francia like a private farm might enter peacefully upon the fact of kingship without its name, a year of turbulence was enough to teach the sons that to rule the Franks a kingly title must back the kingly power. The shadowy Merovingian whom they dragged forth from obscurity to lend a royal sanction to their acts was doubtless from the first a makeshift. Through their surviving charters, especially those of Pepin, the younger and more statesmanly, who not only appended to his name the proud phrase "to whom the Lord hath entrusted the care of government" but used always the "we" and "our" employed hitherto by royalty alone,

CH. XVIII.

there glimmers already another purpose. But not Pepin himself, even after his brother's abdication left him sole ruler, and when, all turbulence subdued, two years eventless in the annals had confirmed his sway, ventured the final step of revolution without a sanction from a higher power.

To one reared, like Pepin, by the monks of St Denis, and to the prelates who were his advisers, it could hardly be doubtful where such a sanction should be sought. Whatever veneration still attached to ancient blood or custom, Jesus Christ was now the national god of the Franks. "Long live Christ, who loves the Franks," ran the prologue of their Salic Law; "may he guard their realm and fill their princes with the light of his grace." And, if the public law of the Franks knew no procedure for a change of dynasty, the story of another chosen people, grown more familiar than the sagas of German or Roman or Trojan ancestors, told how, when a king once proved unworthy, the God of heaven himself sent his prophet to anoint with oil the subject who should take his throne. Nor could any Frank be at a loss whither to look for such a message from the skies. From the days of Clovis the glory of the Franks had been their Catholic orthodoxy; and to Catholic orthodoxy the mouthpiece of heaven, the vicar of Christ on earth, was the successor of Peter, the bishop of Rome. Since the time when Pope Gregory the Great had by his letters guided the religious policy of Brunhild and her wards there had come, it is true, long interruption to the intimacy of Frankish rulers with the Roman bishop; but, with the rise of the mayors of the palace of the pious line of Arnulf, that intimacy had been resumed. Already to Charles Martel the Pope could plead the gifts of his ancestors and his own to Roman altars; and it was that rude warrior, however unchurchly at times his use of church preferment and church property, who had made possible a reform of the Frankish Church through which it was now, beyond even the dreams of a Gregory the Great, becoming a province of Rome. What, backed by his strong arm, the English zeal of the papal legate Boniface had begun, the sons of Charles had made their personal task. From the first they had turned for guidance to the Pope himself; and when, in 747, Carloman, the elder, laying down all earthly rule for the loftier service of heaven, had with lavish gifts betaken him to the tomb of Peter and under its shadow had chosen for his monastic home the cave which once had sheltered that saintly Pope to whom the despairing Constantine, as men believed, had turned for healing and for baptism, the Frankish pilgrims whose multitude disturbed his peace must have learned afresh the proper oracle for princes in doubt.

It can never be quite certain, indeed, so close were now the relations of the Franks with Rome, that the scruple of conscience which in the autumn of 751 two envoys of Pepin laid before Pope Zacharias—the question whether it were good or no that one man should bear the name

of king while another really ruled—was not of Roman suggestion, or
that the answer had not, in any case, been made sure in advance.
But there were reasons enough why, without prearrangement, the papal
verdict might be safely guessed. It was not Pepin the Frank alone
who ruled while another reigned. For a century that had been as true
of the bishop of Rome; and the Pope not less than the mayor of the
palace needed an ally. Though the nominal sovereign at Rome was
still the Byzantine monarch who called himself Emperor of the Romans,
and though from Constantinople still came imperial edicts and imperial
messengers, the actual control, now that the Lombards had narrowed to
a thread the road from the Exarchate by the Adriatic to the Roman
Duchy by the Mediterranean and now that the Saracens were not only
tasking all the Empire's resources in the East but making hazardous the
sea route to the West, had passed ever more and more into the hands of
the Roman bishop. Even under the law of the Empire his civil functions
were large—the nomination of local officers, the care of public works,
the oversight of administration and of justice, the protection of the poor
and the weak—and what survives of his official correspondence shews how
vigorously these functions were exercised. But the growing poverty of
the public purse, drained by the needs of the imperial court or the greed
of the imperial agents, and on the other hand the vast estates of the
Roman Church, scattered throughout Italy and beyond, whose revenues
made the Roman bishop the richest proprietor in all the West, had
little by little turned his oversight into control. From his own resources
he at need had filled the storehouses, repaired the aqueducts, rebuilt the
walls, salaried the magistrates, paid off the soldiery. At his own instance
he had provisioned the people, ransomed captives, levied troops, bought
off invaders, negotiated with the encroaching Lombards.

This beneficent activity the imperial government had welcomed.
Making the Pope its own banker, it had formally entrusted him with
the supply of the city, with the maintenance of the militia. To him,
as to a Roman magistrate, it addressed its instructions. Meanwhile
the needless civil magnates gradually vanished or became his creatures.
The Roman senate quietly ceased to exist or existed so obscurely that
for a century and a half it ceases to be heard of. The praefect of the
city was the bishop's nominee. Even the military hierarchy, which
elsewhere in Italy was now supplanting the civil, at Rome grew subordinate. The city and its district, separating from the Exarchate, had
indeed become a duchy, and a duke still led its army; but before the
middle of the eighth century the duke was taking his cue, if not his
orders, from the Pope. So long as there remained that slender thread
of road connecting Rome with Ravenna, the Exarch, as imperial
governor of Italy, asserted a shadowy authority over both duke and
Pope; but year by year the Exarch's Adriatic lands narrowed before the
Lombards, and with them his resources and prestige. In 751, a few

months earlier than Pepin's embassy, the Lombards occupied Ravenna itself, and the Exarch was no more. The Roman pontiff was now the unquestioned head of what remained to the Empire in Italy.

Why should there be any question? Who could serve the Empire better than this unsalaried functionary whose duties to heaven seemed an abiding guarantee against the ambitions of earth? And what could the vicar of Peter more desire than thus unhampered to administer his province on behalf of that imperial Rome whose eternal dominion he so often had proclaimed? But imperial Rome did not leave unhampered that spiritual headship for whose sake he had proclaimed her eternal dominion. Neither the rising prestige of the Roman see nor the waning of imperial resources had restrained the emperors from asserting in the West that authority over religious belief and religious practice which they exercised unquestioned in the East. Upon the Roman bishop they had heaped honours and privileges, they had even recognised his primacy in the Church; yet at their will they still convened councils and promulgated or proscribed dogmas, and, when the bishop of Rome presumed to discredit what they declared orthodox, they did not scruple, while their power was adequate, to arrest and depose him or to drag him off to Constantinople for trial and punishment. Their purpose may have been the political one of silencing religious dissension and so ending the quarrels which hazarded the unity of the Empire; but to the successor of Peter the peace and unity of the Empire had worth only for the maintenance and the diffusion of that divinely revealed truth whose responsible custodian he knew himself to be.

When, therefore, in the year 725, the Emperor Leo, having beaten off the besieging Saracens and restored order in his realm, addressed himself to religious reform, and, waiting for no consultation of the Church, forbade the use in worship of pictures and images of the Christ, the Virgin, and the saints—nay, began at once on their destruction—Pope Gregory the Second not only refused obedience, but rallied Italy to his defence against what he proclaimed to Christendom the Emperor's impiety and heresy. And now, after a quarter of a century, though Gregory the Second had been followed in 731 by Gregory the Third, and ten years later he by Zacharias, while on Leo's throne since 740 sat Constantine the Fifth, his son, the schism was still unhealed. The Emperor, after the shipwreck of a fleet sent for the humbling of the rebels, had indeed contented himself with the transfer of Sicily and southern Italy from the jurisdiction of the Pope to that of the Patriarch of Constantinople; and, having thus begun that severance of the Greek south from the Latin north which (helped soon by the unintended flooding of south Italy with religious fugitives from the East) was to endure for centuries, he did not disturb the authority of Rome in the rest of the peninsula. The Pope, on his side, though he laid all Iconoclasts under the Church's ban, opposed the treasonous design to put a rival emperor on the throne, and scrupulously continued to date all his official acts by the sovereign's regnal years. But clearly this was no more than armed neutrality. No emperor could feel safe while religious rebellion had such an example and such a nucleus; and the Pope well knew that it was all over with his own safety and that of Roman orthodoxy the moment they could be attacked without danger of the loss of Italy.

Italian loyalty to Roman leadership there was no room to doubt. The alienation of the Latins from their Byzantine master had grounds older and deeper than their veneration for the pictures of the saints. Their consciousness of different blood and speech had for ages been increased by administrative separateness and by the favoured place of Italy in the imperial system; and, when division of the Empire had brought to her Hellenic neighbours equality of privilege and of prestige, there still remained to Italy the headship of the West. She had welcomed those who in the honoured name of Rome freed her from the Ostrogoth barbarians and heretics; but, when in their hands she found herself sunk to a mere frontier province, the officials of her absentee ruler had soon become unpopular. The growing extortion of the tax-gatherer was sweetened by no pride in the splendours it nourished. The one public boast of Italy, her one surviving claim to leadership, was now the religious pre-eminence of her Roman bishop. His patriarchate over all the West made Rome and Italy still a capital of nations. His primacy, if realised, meant for her a wider queenship. To Italy he was a natural leader. Directly or through her other bishops—nearly all confirmed and consecrated by him and bound to him by oaths of ortho-doxy and of loyalty—he was the patron of all municipal liberties, the defender against all fiscal oppression. And when the imperial court, in its militant Hellenism, used its political power to dictate religious inno-vation, the Roman pontiff became yet more popular as the spokesman of Western conservatism. More than once before the iconoclastic schism had the sympathies of the Italians ranged themselves on the side of the Pope against the Emperor. When that quarrel came it found Italy already in a ferment. Imperial officials on every hand were driven out or put to death, and—what was more significant—their places filled by popular election.

But if, thus sure of popular support, Pope Gregory the Third, as there is reason to believe, already harboured the thought of breaking with the Byzantine authority, a nearer danger stared him in the face. The Empire's Italy was, in fact, but a precarious remnant. There were the Lombards. Already masters of most of the peninsula, they were clearly minded to be masters of it all. The Lombards, of course, were Christians. They had long ceased to be heretics. Against the Icono-clasts they had even lent the Pope their aid. For the vicar of Peter they professed the deepest respect, and their bishops were suffragans of his see. There was no reason to suppose, should they even occupy Rome itself, that they would hamper or abridge the ecclesiastical functions of the Pope. But the Pope well knew what difference lay between a mere Lombard bishop, however venerated, and the all but independent sovereign of the capital of the Christian world. Already the temporal power had cast its spell. Should the Lombard king win Rome, there was much reason to fear that he would make it his own capital. Though orthodox now and deferential, he might not always be deferential or orthodox; and how short the step was from a deferential protector to a dictatorial master papal experience had amply shewn. At Constantinople such a master was quite near enough. The Pope had no mind to exchange King Log for King Stork.

Against the Lombards, therefore, Pope and Emperor made common cause. The Emperor, needing every soldier against his Eastern foes, was only too glad to make the Pope his envoy. The Pope, needing every plea against the eager Lombard, was only too glad to urge the claims of the Empire. But, in spite of papal pleading and imperial claims, the Lombards took town after town. The desperate Pope intrigued with Lombard dukes against the Lombard king. Liutprand turned his arms on Rome itself. Then it was, in 739, that Gregory appealed to Charles the Frank.

It was by no means the first time the Frankish champions of orthodoxy had been called to the aid of Italy against the barbarian; not the first time a Pope was their petitioner. As sons of the Church and allies of the Empire they had crossed the Alps in the sixth century and in the seventh to fight Ostrogoth and Lombard. But the appeal of Gregory was couched in novel terms. Not for the Empire nor for the faith did he now implore protection, but for " the Church of St Peter " and " us his peculiar people"; and as return the Frankish chroniclers record that puzzling offer of allegiance.

The great Frankish " under-king "—so the Pope entitled him—did not lead his host against the Lombard king, his kinsman and ally; but he answered courteously by embassy and gift, he treasured carefully the papal letters, the earliest in that precious file preserved us by his grandson, and it is not impossible that he interceded with the Lombards. In any case, they did not now press on toward Rome; and the mild and tactful Zacharias, who soon succeeded to the papal chair, not only won back by his prayers, for " the blessed Peter, prince of the apostles," the towns seized from the Roman duchy, but staved off the advance of the Lombards upon Ravenna, and before long, when the pious Ratchis succeeded to the throne, he made with him a truce for twenty years. But the persistent Lombards would not so long be cheated of a manifest destiny. Ratchis in 749, retiring like Carloman into monastic life, gave place to the tempestuous Aistulf. By 751, as we have seen, Ravenna was his and the Exarchate had ceased to be. Then came Pepin's conundrum.

The precise terms of Zacharias' reply are not preserved. What is left is only the oral tradition as to its substance. No letter of his can be found among the papal epistles to the Carolings. Errands so momentous often went then by word of mouth; and Pepin's were trusty messengers. One, Bishop Burchard of Würzburg, the new Franconian see so richly endowed by Pepin and by Carloman, was a loyal lieutenant of the legate Boniface, English like him by birth and as his messenger already known at Rome. The other, the Austrasian Fulrad, abbot of St Denis and arch-chaplain of the realm, owed to Pepin both those high preferments and was throughout his life his master's intimate and the Pope's. If their message must in part be guessed at, its outcome is well known. The Merovingian and his son, rejected like Saul and Jonathan, went shorn into the cloister. The aged Boniface, in St Peter's name, anointed king the new David chosen by the Franks.

King Pepin was not ungrateful. That same November of 751 which saw his elevation to the throne saw the capstone put to the organising work of Boniface by the lifting of his see of Mainz to metropolitan authority throughout all Germany, from the mountains to the coast. It saw, too, by papal grant soon royally confirmed (if we may trust two much-disputed documents), his beloved Fulda, his favourite home, the abbey of his heart, raised to a dignity elsewhere unknown in Francia by exemption from all ecclesiastical supervision save the Pope's alone. As coadjutor in the heavy duties of his primacy Pepin gave the old man Lul, best loved of the disciples brought from his English home, and when, even thus stayed, he presently sighed beneath his task, the king released him from his functions to seek among the heathen Frisians the martyr's crown for which he yearned. And Abbot Fulrad, now as royal chaplain the king's minister of public worship, was not forgotten. The earliest of Pepin's surviving royal charters (1 March 752) awards St Denis at Fulrad's prayer a domain long unlawfully withheld; and many another from that year and those which follow bears witness to his constant zeal in the defence of churchly property and rights.

Even as king, indeed, Pepin never gave back into full ownership all those church lands appropriated by his father to the maintenance of a mounted soldiery; but the Church was assured her rents, and the right of the State to make such grants of church lands, though maintained, was carefully restricted. It was doubtless the growing importance of the mounted force, and its dependence on the pasturage of summer, which prompted Pepin early in his reign (755) to change, "for the advantage of the Franks," the time-honoured assembly and muster of the host, the "Field of March," into a "Field of May." The faith itself had still need of swift champions. The Saracens yet had a foothold in Gaul. Septimania, the rich though narrow coastland stretching from Rhone to Pyrenees between the Mediterranean and the Cevennes—the Low Languedoc of later days—was not yet a possession of the Franks. A

CH. XVIII.

remnant of the old realm of the Visigoths and still peopled by their descendants, it had been overrun by the Arab conquerors of Spain, who remained its masters and made it a base for their raids. But in 752 a rising of the Gothic townsmen expelled them from Nîmes and Maguelonne, Agde and Béziers, and offered their land to Pepin. Narbonne alone held out still against the Franks. Gaul thus all but redeemed to Christendom, Pepin in 753 led his host against the rebellious heathen of the north. Crossing the Rhine into the territory of the Saxons and laying it waste to the Weser, he subjected them once more to tribute and this time compelled them to open their doors to the missionaries of Christianity.

But while Pepin had thus been proving in Francia his worth to Church as well as State, there had not been wanting signs that the Church's head might need from him a more personal service. Since early in 752 the soft-spoken Zacharias was no more, and in his place sat Stephen II, a Roman born and of good Roman blood. An orphan, reared from boyhood in the Lateran itself, he was no stranger to its aims and policies. There was need at Rome of Roman pride and Roman self-assertion. Aistulf the Lombard was no man to be wheedled, and his eye was now upon the Roman duchy. From the Alps to the Vulturnus all was now Lombard except this stretch along the western coast. Rome was clearly at his mercy. Already in June the Pope had sent envoys—his brother Paul (later to succeed him as Pope) and another cleric—who made with the Lombard king, as they supposed, a forty years' peace. But it was soon clear that Aistulf counted this no bar to the assertion of his sovereignty. Scarce four months later, claiming jurisdiction over Rome and the towns about it, he demanded an annual poll-tax from their inhabitants. What could it matter to the Roman bishop who was his temporal lord? Stephen, protesting against the breach of faith, shewed his ecclesiastical power by sending as intercessors the abbots of the two most venerated of Lombard monasteries, Monte Cassino and San Vincenzo. The king, in turn, vindicated the royal authority by contumeliously sending them back to their convents. Again and again the Pope had begged for help from Constantinople, and now there appeared, not the soldiery for which he had asked, but, Byzantine-fashion, an imperial envoy—the *silentiarius* John—with letters of instruction for both Pope and king. The Pope obediently sent on the envoy to the king, escorted by a spokesman of his own—again his brother Paul. Aistulf listened to the imperial exhortations, but there his barbarian patience had an end. Yielding nothing, he packed off home the Byzantine functionary, and with him sent a Lombard with counter-propositions of his own; he then turned in rage on Rome, vowing to put every Roman to the sword unless his orders were forthwith obeyed. The Pope went through the idle form of sending by the returning Greek a fresh appeal to the Emperor to

come himself with an army and rescue Italy; he calmed the panic-stricken
Romans by public prayers and processions, himself marching barefoot in
the ranks and carrying on his shoulder the sacred portrait of the Christ
painted by St Luke and the angels; but he had not grown up in the
household of the Gregories without learning of another source of help.
By a returning pilgrim he sent a message to the new king of the
Franks.

That unceasing stream of pilgrims—prelate and prince and humble
sinner—which now from England and the farther isles as well as from
all parts of Francia thronged the roads to the threshold of the apostles
(Carloman to escape their visits had fled from his refuge on Mount
Soracte to the remoter seclusion of Monte Cassino) must have kept
Pepin and his advisers well informed of what was passing in Italy, and
many messages lost to us had doubtless been exchanged by Pope and
king; but what Stephen had next to offer and to ask was to be trusted
to no go-between, not even to his diplomat brother. By the mouth of
the unnamed pilgrim who early in 753 appeared at the court of Pepin
he begged that envoys be sent to summon himself to the Frankish king.
Two other pilgrims—one was this time the abbot of Jumièges—bore
back to the Pope an urgent invitation, assuring him that the requested
envoys should be sent. From the tenor of the Pope's still extant letter
of reply it would appear that by word of mouth a more confidential
message was returned through the abbot and his colleague. The written
one briefly contents itself with pious wishes and with the assurance that
"he who perseveres to the end shall be saved" and shall "receive an
hundred fold and possess eternal life"; and a companion letter which the
Pope, perhaps not unprompted, addressed to "all the leaders of the
Frankish nation" adjures them, without defining what they are wished
to do, to let nothing hinder them from aiding the king to further the
interests of their patron, St Peter, that thus their sins may be wiped out
and the key-bearer of heaven may admit them to eternal life. For the
formal invitation of the Pope and for the sending of the escort the
concurrence of the Frankish folk had been awaited, and it was autumn
before the embassy reached Rome. Meanwhile Aistulf had shewn his
seriousness by taking steps to cut off Rome from southern Italy, and the
Emperor had sent, not troops, but once more the silentiary John, this
time insisting that the Pope himself go with him to beseech the Lombard
for the restoration of the Exarchate. Happily, with the arrival of the
safe-conduct sought from Aistulf, arrived also the Frankish envoys—
Duke Autchar (the Ogier of later legend) and the royal chancellor,
Bishop Chrodegang of Metz, after Boniface the foremost prelate of the
realm.

It was mid-October of 753 when, thus escorted, and in company
with the imperial ambassador, Pope Stephen and a handful of his
official household set out—ostensibly for the Lombard court. King

Aistulf, though notified, did not come to meet them. As they approached Pavia they met only his messengers, who forbade the Pope to plead before their master the cause of the conquered provinces. Defiant of this prohibition, he implored Aistulf to "give back the Lord's sheep," and the silentiary again laid before him an imperial letter; but to all appeals the barbarian was deaf. Then it was that the Frankish ambassadors asked his leave for the Pope to go on with them to Francia, and the pontiff added his own prayer to theirs. In vain the Lombard, gnashing his teeth, sought to dissuade him. A grudging permission was granted and promptly used. The Pope and his escort, leaving a portion of their party to return with the Greek to Rome, were before the end of November safe on Frankish soil. As they issued from the Alps they were met by another duke and by Abbot Fulrad, who guided them across Burgundy to a royal villa near the Marne. While yet many miles away there met them a retinue of nobles headed by the son of Pepin, the young prince Charles, who thus, a lad of eleven, first appears in history. Pepin himself, with all his court, came three miles to receive them. Dismounting and prostrating himself before the Pope, he for some distance humbly marched beside him, leading by the bridle the pontiff's horse (6 Jan. 754).

Such, in brief, is what is told by our one informant, the contemporary biographer of Pope Stephen, of that transalpine journey whose outcome was the temporal sovereignty of the popes, the severance of Latin Christendom from Greek, the Frankish conquest of Italy, the Holy Roman Empire. With the Pope's arrival the Frankish sources, too, take up the tale. Yet only by clever patching can all these together be made to yield a connected story of what was done during the long months of that papal visit—of the Pope's appeal for Frankish aid against the Lombard, of his sojourn through the winter as the guest of Fulrad at St Denis, of the futile embassies for the dissuasion of the Lombard king, of the appearance in Francia of the monk Carloman, sent by his abbot to intercede for the Lombard against the Pope, of a springtide assembly of the Franks and of reluctant consent to a campaign against the Lombard, of an Easter conference of king and Pope and Frankish leaders at the royal villa of Carisiacum (Kiersy, Quierzy), of a great midsummer gathering at St Denis, where in the abbey church Pope Stephen himself in the name of the holy Trinity anointed Pepin afresh, and with him his two sons Charles and Carloman, forbidding under pain of excommunication and interdict that henceforward forever any not sprung from the loins of these thus consecrated by God through the vicar of his apostles be chosen king of the Franks.

Our most explicit account of this coronation, a memorandum jotted down a dozen years later at St Denis by a monkish copyist, adds a detail. Pepin and his sons were anointed not only kings of the Franks but "Patricians of the Romans." Certain it is that this title, though

Pepin himself seems never to have used it, is thenceforward invariably appended to his name and those of his sons in the letters of the Popes. Now, "Patrician" was a Byzantine title—a somewhat nondescript decoration, or title of courtesy, applied by the imperial court to sundry dignitaries (as to the Exarch of Italy and to the Duke of Rome) and not infrequently conferred upon barbarian princes—and there have not been wanting modern scholars who divine from its use that the Pope was in all this the envoy of the Emperor. No intimation of such a thing appears elsewhere in the sources[1]. It is not hard to believe that the Pope may have persuaded the imperial government that his journey into Francia was an expedition in its interest, or that he may even have sought its authority for the gift of the patrician title; it is easy to see that the papal biographer might suppress a fact which by the time he wrote had grown uncomfortable; but, had the Pope in Francia posed as the representative of the Emperor, it is incomprehensible that a function so flattering both to him and to his Frankish hosts should escape all memory. And the title conferred on Pepin was not the familiar one of "Patrician," but the else unknown one "Patrician of the Romans." Precisely what that may have meant has long been a problem; but it could hardly have been aught pleasing to Constantine Copronymus, who had just alienated anew his Italian subjects by an iconoclastic council, whose deference to the religious dictation of the Emperor might excuse almost any treason on the part of Western orthodoxy.

Nor are we at a loss to guess what may have obscured for Pepin the Empire's claim to Italy. For more than two centuries there had been growing current in the West a legend which strangely distorted the history of Church and Empire. Constantine, earliest and greatest of Christian emperors, while yet a pagan and at Rome—so ran the tale in that life of Pope Sylvester which gave it widest vogue—persecuted so cruelly the Christians that indignant Heaven smote him with leprosy. Physicians were in vain. The pagan priests in desperation prescribed a bath in the blood of new-born babes. The babes were brought; but, moved to pity by the mothers' cries, the Emperor preferred to suffer, whereat relenting Heaven, sending in a dream St Peter and St Paul, revealed to him Sylvester as his healer. The Pope was brought from his

---

[1] One document, indeed, were it trustworthy, would more than prove this true: the strange scrap known as the "Pactum Pipini" or "Fragmentum Fantuzzianum." It purports to be the written promise given to the Pope during his visit by Pepin, and opens with an account of the Lombard peril and of the Pope's winning imperial consent and authority for an appeal to the Franks. Unfortunately it exists only in a fifteenth or sixteenth century transcript of a twelfth century copy, and, even if derived from a genuine original, as few critics have believed, is so corrupt in its text and so suspicious in its form that all use of it is hazardous. Even its latest editors (Schnürer and Ulivi, *Das Fragmentum Fantuzzianum*, Freiburg, 1906), though they give a better text and explain away many difficulties, leave ample room for scepticism.

hiding-place on Mount Soracte, disclosed the identity of the gods seen in his dream, and not only cured but converted and baptised him. Thereupon the grateful monarch, proclaiming throughout the Empire his new faith, provided by edict for its safety and support, made all bishops subject to the Pope, even as are all magistrates to the Emperor, and, setting forth to found elsewhere a capital, first laid with his own hands the foundations of St Peter's and the Lateran.

It was doubtless faith in this wild tale which led the rueful Carloman, fain to atone for his own deeds of violence, to choose Sylvester's cave for his retreat and dedicate his convent to that saint. The legend must thereby have gained a wider currency among the Franks; and none could know this better than the papal court. Was it for use with them, and was it now, that there came into existence a document which made the myth a cornerstone of papal power—the so-called Donation of Constantine?

No extant manuscript of that famous forgery is older than the early ninth century, and what most scholars have believed a quotation from it by Pope Hadrian in 778 can possibly be otherwise explained; but minute study of the strange charter's diction seems now to have made sure its origin in the papal chancellery during the third quarter of the eighth century, and startling coincidences of phrase connect it in particular with the documents of Stephen II and of Paul, while to an ever-growing proportion of the students of this period the historical setting in which alone it can be made to fit is that of Stephen's visit to the Franks or of the years which closely follow it[1].

The document makes Constantine first narrate at length the story of his healing, embodying in it an elaborate creed taught him by Pope Sylvester. Then, declaring St Peter and his successors worthy, as Christ's vicars on earth, of power more than imperial, he chooses them as his patrons before God, decrees their supremacy over all the Christian church, relates his building of the Lateran and of St Peter's and St Paul's, and his endowing them " for the enkindling of the lights " with vast

---

[1] The scholars to whom this demonstration is chiefly due are Hauck, Friedrich, and, above all, Scheffer-Boichorst. The first two ascribe it (at least in its final form) to the time of Stephen's visit, the last would connect it rather with Paul; but these two papacies were too continuous to make discrimination easy. Grauert, who ably began this textual criticism, reached a different result; but he has not maintained his position against later students. Whether the Pope was author, accomplice, or victim of the fraud cannot be guessed. Of historical scholarship there is no ground to suspect either Stephen or Paul, and there is reason to believe both dominated by that Christopher who accompanied Stephen into Francia and who soon, and under both Popes, as Primicerius, or chief of the notaries, headed the papal chancellery. During Paul's pontificate Christopher was expressly accused by the Emperor to Pepin of falsifying documents. The latest critics of the Donation—Böhmer, Hartmann, Mayer—all assign it to this period. It is perhaps not without significance that our oldest copy of it is found in a formula-book of St Denis, where it occurs between a letter of Pope Zacharias and one of Pope Stephen.

estates in East and West, grants to the Pope the rank and trappings of an Emperor and to the Roman clergy those of senators, tells how, when Sylvester had refused the Emperor's own crown of gold, Constantine placed upon his head the white tiara and in reverence for St Peter led his horse by the bridle as his groom, and now transfers to him, that the papal headship may forever keep its more than earthly glory, his Roman palace and city and all the provinces and towns of Italy. If this document or the traditions on which it rests were through Fulrad or Chrodegang or the Roman guests familiar to the Frankish king, neither his policy nor his phrases need longer puzzle us.

Even in this life Pepin, like Constantine, needed St Peter's help. The dethroned Merovingians, indeed, had sunk without a ripple, and even while the Pope was on his way to Gaul that turbulent half-brother, Grifo, who had made for Carloman and Pepin such incessant trouble, met death at loyal hands as he was escaping through the Alps from his plotting-place in Aquitaine to a more disquieting plotting-place among the Lombards. But there still was Carloman himself—a gallant prince whose renunciation and monastic vows need bind no longer than the Church should will. There were still his growing sons, committed by him to Pepin's care, but with no rights renounced. Was it in part, perhaps, to vindicate, for himself or for his sons, these rights of the elder line that Carloman had now appeared in Francia as advocate of the Lombard cause? Was his reward, perchance, to be the Lombard's backing of his own princely claims? In any case, what troubled waters these for Lombard fishing! Was the Pope himself only a timelier fisher, and may the reluctance of the Frankish nobles have been due in some part to friends of Carloman and of the Lombard alliance? All this is mere conjecture. But certain it is that Pepin made effective terms with Heaven's spokesman and that the outcome was the papal unction for himself and for his house. Carloman, sick, perhaps with disappointment or chagrin, was detained in a Burgundian monastery, where soon he died. His sons were, like the Merovingians, shorn as monks. Even the fellow-monks whom he had brought with him from Italy were held for years in Frankish durance.

And what did Pepin in return assure the Pope? Stephen's biographer speaks only of an oral promise to obey the Pope and to restore according to his wish the rights and territories of the Roman State[1]. But, when twenty years later the son of Pepin, leaving his

---

[1] "Omnibus eius mandatis et ammonitionibus sese totis nisibus oboedire, et ut illi placitum fuerit exarchatum Ravennae et reipublicae iura seu loca reddere modis omnibus." "Respublica," "respublica Romana," had in Roman usage meant the Empire in general; but the term, which in the papal letters becomes from this time forward "respublica Romanorum," was doubtless vague enough to Frankish ears. Its happy ambiguities and clever use during this period are studied most carefully by Gundlach, in his *Die Entstehung des Kirchenstaates* (Breslau, 1899).

siege of the Lombard capital, went down to Rome for Easter, there was laid before him for confirmation, if we may trust the papal biographer of that later day, a written document, signed at Quierzy during Pope Stephen's visit by Pepin, his sons, and all the Frankish leaders, which pledged to St Peter and to the Pope the whole peninsula of Italy from Parma and Mantua to the borders of Apulia, defining in detail the northern frontier of the tract, and including by express stipulation, not only all the Exarchate "as it was of old time" and the provinces of Venice and Istria, but the island of Corsica and the Lombard duchies of Spoleto and Benevento[1]. May we trust this passage of the *Vita Hadriani*—not only for the fact of a written promise by Pepin and of its confirmation by Charles, but for all the startling contents? This is that "Roman question" about which seas of ink have flowed and still are flowing. For long it was the wont of ultramontane writers to assume both the reality of such a promise and confirmation and the accuracy of this account of it, while with almost equal unanimity those unfriendly to the Papacy or to its temporal power dismissed the one as myth, the other as forgery. But in these later years, now that the temporal power is but a memory, scholars have drawn together[2]. It seems established that the passage, however corrupt, is no interpolation, and that it was written at Rome in 774; and there is a growing faith in its accuracy, even as to the details of Pepin's promise[3]. But how to explain so strange a pact is still a puzzle. Was it, as some have thought, not the main compact between Pope and king, but a scheme of partition for use only in case the Frank invasion should perhaps result in the fall of the Lombard power[4]? Schemes such as this may well have filled the Pope's long Gaulish visit; but for aught but guesswork our sources are

[1] "Civitates et territoria...a Lunis cum insula Corsica, deinde in Suriano, deinde in monte Bardone, id est in Verceto, deinde in Parma, deinde in Regio; et exinde in Mantua atque Monte Silicis, simulque et universum exarchatum Ravennantium, sicut antiquitus erat, atque provincias Venetiarum et Istria; necnon et cunctum ducatum Spolitinum seu Beneventanum." It must of course be remembered that to this barbarous age "seu" meant *and* quite as often as *or*, and that, in general, its Latin is not classical.

[2] Especially since, in 1883, Sickel, reinforcing the earlier arguments of Ficker, established the genuineness of the *Pactum Ludovicianum* of 817, the oldest surviving confirmation of the gift, and since, in 1884, Scheffer-Boichorst and Duchesne demonstrated the contemporaneity of the passage in the *Vita Hadriani*. Duchesne two years later made this demonstration more effective by publishing the first volume of a critical edition of the *Liber Pontificalis*, of which the *Vita* is of course a part.

[3] The *Fragmentum Fantuzzianum*, which purports to be Pepin's *Promissio* itself, has already been described (see p. 585, note). Its list of the territories promised differs in several points from that of the *Vita Hadriani*, though agreeing substantially as to their extent.

[4] This is the solution of Kehr, a scholar long busied with the documents of the popes, and has met with much acceptance. It has been ably supported by Hubert.

too scanty and too crude. The clerics who meagrely penned the deeds of king and Pope were only official scribes, inspired and inspected, who of the deeper planning of their lords perhaps knew little and betray yet less. The papal letters, a more solid support, are mute, of course, during Stephen's visit; and, when they reappear, imperfectly preserved and uncertainly dated, are often but the mask for a wilier diplomacy by oral message. And in this day of the eclipse of culture, when the best trained clerk of convent or of curia groped helplessly for words and for inflections, one can never be quite sure whether what is written is what seemed best worth writing or only what seemed possible to write. Nor may it be forgotten that from the side of Greek or Lombard, great though their stake in the affairs of Italy, we have in all this period not a word.

The Frankish host at last, in the late summer of 754 (possibly the spring of 755), set forth for Italy, taking with it the Pope. Before its start and yet again during the march a fresh attempt was made to scare off or buy off the Lombard from his prey. But neither gold nor threats could move Aistulf from his purpose. Happily for the Franks, the Alpine passes and their Italian approaches had long been in their hands, and now, ere their main army began to climb the Mont Cenis, they learned with joy that Aistulf, routed by their vanguard, whom he had rashly attacked in the mountain defiles, had abandoned his entrenchments in the vale of Susa and sought shelter within the walls of his capital. The Franks, rejoicing in the manifest favour of Heaven, were soon before Pavia; and Aistulf, disheartened, speedily consented to a peace " between the Romans, the Franks, and the Lombards." He acknowledged Pepin as his overlord, and promised to surrender to the Pope Ravenna with all his other conquests. The Pope was sent on, under escort, to Rome; and Pepin, taking hostages, returned to Francia.

But Aistulf soon rued his concessions. Only a single town did he actually give up, and by midwinter of 755–756 he was again ravaging before the gates of Rome. The Pope in panic appealed frantically to his ally. Nay, so great was the emergency that, when the Franks delayed, St Peter himself addressed to Pepin, Charles, and Carloman, and to the clergy, the nobles, and all the armies and people of Francia a startling letter. " I, Peter, apostle of God, who have adopted you as my sons," so runs this strange epistle, duly delivered by messengers from Rome, " do call and exhort you to the defence of this Roman city and the people committed to me by God and the home where after the flesh I repose....And with us our Lady, the mother of God, Mary ever virgin,...doth most solemnly adjure, admonish, and command you.... Give help, then, with all your might, to your brothers, my Roman people,...that, in turn, I, Peter, apostle called of God, granting you my protection in this life and in the day of future judgment, may prepare for you in the kingdom of God tabernacles most bright and glorious and may reward you with the infinite joys of paradise....Suffer not this my Roman city and the people therein dwelling to be longer torn by the Lombard race: so may your bodies and souls not be torn and tortured in everlasting and unquenchable hell fire....Lo, sons most dear, I have warned you: if ye shall swiftly obey, great shall be your reward, and, aided by me, ye shall in this life vanquish all your foes and to old age eat the good things of earth, and shall beyond a doubt enjoy eternal life; but if, as we will not believe, ye shall delay,...know that we, by authority of the holy Trinity and in virtue of the apostolate given me by Christ the Lord, do cut you off, for transgression of our appeal, from the kingdom of God and life eternal[1]."

The Franks delayed no longer. In May they were again upon the march. Aistulf hastened from Rome to meet them; but again he failed to bar their path, and again was shut up in Pavia. It was now, as Pepin drew near the town, that a Greek envoy, who had tried to intercept him on his way, at last came up with him. In honeyed words he claimed for the Empire Ravenna and its Exarchate. But Pepin answered that for no treasure in the world would he rob St Peter of a gift once offered, swearing that for no man's favour had he plunged thus once and again into war, but for love of St Peter and the pardon of his sins. It is the papal biographer who reports his words.

The siege was short. Aistulf, now a convicted rebel, was glad to escape with life and realm by payment of a third of his royal hoard, with pledge of yearly tribute, and by immediate surrender of his conquests. To Abbot Fulrad, as Pepin's deputy, these forthwith were handed over, one by one, from Ravenna, with Comacchio, down the coast to Sinigaglia and over the mountains to Narni; and their keys the abbot bore to Rome, where with the written deed of their donation by his king he laid them on St Peter's tomb.

When the Franks went home, the Exarchate, as Aistulf had found it, was the Pope's. Rome and its duchy, though unnamed by Pepin, were as surely his. But not contentment. Though his lands now stretched from Po to Liris and from sea to sea, the redemption of Italy was but begun. Aistulf's robberies won back, why not Liutprand's? Occasion offered soon. Aistulf was killed by accident while hunting, and his brother Ratchis, without asking leave of the Pope, left the monastery to assume the crown. The outraged Stephen stirred Benevento and Spoleto to revolt, and aided Desiderius, duke of Tuscany, in a struggle for the throne. But this aid had its price: a sworn

---

[1] To count this letter mere rhetoric, as have some, is much to overrate the literary spirit of the age, and—what is more serious—to ignore both the pious fraud so characteristic of the time and the pious credulity on which it safely built. Few scholars now doubt that St Peter's letter was meant to be taken by the Franks as sober revelation. It is by no means improbable that it was penned by the same hand as the Donation of Constantine.

contract bound Desiderius to the surrender of the rest of the towns seized by the Lombards. Abbot Fulrad, who lingered still at Rome, was not only witness to the pact, but with his little troop of Franks took a hand in the enthronement of Desiderius. Perhaps he thought thereby to plight his royal master to enforce the contract; but, though the Lombard, once on his throne, yielded only Faenza and Ferrara, and though Pope Paul, who in that same year (757) succeeded his brother, could extort no more, and filled the ten years of his pontificate with piteous appeals to the "patrician of the Romans" for help against dangers, real or fancied, from Lombard and from Greek, the Frank refrained from further meddling.

Nor was there need of it. Though Desiderius quelled with firm hand the rebels in Spoleto and in Benevento and was not to be cajoled into further "restitutions" to the Pope, and though the Emperor tried intrigue both with Lombard and with Frank, neither assailed Pope Paul with arms. Not even the fiercely contested papal election which in 767 followed his death disturbed the integrity of the Papal State. Pope Stephen III, who in 768 emerged from the turmoil, however he might date his charters by the Emperor's regnal years and report his elevation to the Frank patrician, "his defender next to God," was to all intent as sovereign as they. That so vigorous a ruler and so capable a soldier as Constantine V made no armed attempt to save to his Empire the fair peninsula that gave it birth must doubtless be explained not only by the nearer cares which kept him busy, but by the potent shadow of the Frank; and to that shadow was clearly due the inaction of the Lombard. But the Frank himself, beyond St Peter's gratitude here and hereafter, asked no other meed.

Yet Francia was not without reward. Through the door which war had left ajar culture crept in. "I send you," writes Pope Paul, "all the books which could be found"—and he names the hymn-books and the school-books of his packet, "all written in the Greek tongue," an antiphonal and a responsal, treatises on grammar, geometry, orthography, works of Aristotle and of Dionysius. "I send, too," he adds, "the night-clock"—doubtless an alarm-clock, such as waked the monks to their matins[1]. It is but a glimpse at a traffic which must mainly have found humbler channels. The improving calligraphy of Frankish scribes shews already Roman influence. Bishop Remedius of Rouen

---

[1] Mr Hodgkin thinks "horologium nocturnum" may mean a clock with an illuminated face. The suggestion is tempting, and we remember King Alfred's graduated candles and horn lantern; but the phrase seems to imply something familiar, while illuminated clocks, as Alfred's invention reminds us, were a thing as yet unknown. Bilfinger, the most careful student of the history of time-reckoning and time-pieces, interprets as an alarm-clock the "horologium nocturnum" invented in the ninth century by a Frankish cleric; and Professor Erben of Innsbruck has already suggested this explanation for Pepin's night-clock.

imported from Rome a singing-master for his clergy; and, when the master was called back to head the Roman training-school, sent his monks thither to complete their musical education. Chrodegang of Metz, ever in close touch with Rome, inaugurated the most notable church reform of his day by organising under a discipline akin to the monastic the clergy of his cathedral city. Among the imperial gifts from Constantinople came an organ, the first seen in the West. A more questionable blessing was the advent of Greek theologians: Byzantine envoys debated with papal, before the king and his synod, as to the Trinity and the use of images; and, though they lost the verdict, they must have quickened thought. Nor was the new horizon bounded by Christian lands. The lord of Barcelona and Gerona, Muslim governor of north-eastern Spain, strengthened himself against his Moorish sovereign by acknowledging the Frankish overlordship; and a more distant foe of the Umayyad court of Cordova, the great Caliph Manṣūr, from his new capital of Bagdad, exchanged with Pepin embassies and gifts. It was the beginning of that connexion between the leading power of the Christian West and the leading power of the Muslim East which has proved so perennial, and to the powers of Christian East and Muslim West so costly.

But all this interest in the world at large meant no sacrifice of energy at home. It was precisely the years that fell between or followed the Italian expeditions which saw Pepin most active as a legislator. In four successive synods of his clergy he perfected the work begun by Boniface, but made it clear that in the Frankish Church the crown was still to be supreme. Every spring henceforward all the bishops should gather to the king for synod, and every autumn at his seat in Soissons those clad with metropolitan authority should meet again. Inspection and stern churchly discipline should keep at home and at religious duties priest and monk and nun. All Christians must observe the Sunday rest and worship, and all marriage must be public. "Though at the moment our power does not suffice for everything," runs an introductory clause full of significance for the king's whole character, "yet in some points at least we wish to better what, as we perceive, impedes the Church of God; if later God shall grant us days of peace and leisure, we hope then to restore in all their scope the standards of the saints."

Days of peace proved rare. In 759, having freshly scourged the Saxons to tribute and submission, he "made no campaign, that he might reform domestic affairs within his realm." But in 760 began the task which busied his remaining years—the subjection of Aquitaine. The broad south-west of Gaul, cut off from Neustria by the wide stream of the Loire, from Burgundy by the escarpment of the Cevennes, had not since Roman days fully cast in its fortunes with the rest. When Clovis won it from the Goths he had not sown it with his Franks; and the

Goths, withdrawing into Spain, had left its folk less touched than any other in the west of Europe by Germanic blood and ways. To the chroniclers and even to the laws of Pepin's time they still are "Romans." The race of native dukes which under the later Merovingians had made them almost independent acknowledged Pepin as a suzerain only; and their boldness in harbouring fugitives from his authority and in taxing the Aquitanian estates of Frankish churches had already caused friction and protest when the Frank occupation of Septimania gave rise to war. That this district, so closely knit to Aquitaine before and since, its doorway to the Mediterranean and the highway of its commerce, should pass into the keeping of the Frank was indeed a knell to all their hopes. Duke Waifar had as early as 752 begun to wrest the region from the failing grasp of the Moor, and it was perhaps only to escape his clutches that the Goths of its eastern towns offered themselves to Pepin. This could be borne; but when, in 759, the taking of Narbonne carried to the Pyrenees the Frank frontier, the speedy sequel was the war with Aquitaine.

Pepin did not underrate his foe. Year after year, from 760 to 768, he led against Waifar the whole Frankish host; and, though a brief peace closed the first campaign, the struggle thereafter was to the death. With thoroughness and system, wasting no time in raids, from fortress to fortress, district to district, through Berri, Auvergne, the Limousin, garrisoning and organising as he went, the king relentlessly pushed on. Once desertion and famine forced him to a pause; but there followed a fruitful year—for whose blessings the king, like some American governor or president of modern days, ordained in the autumn a general thanksgiving—and the war went on. By the early summer of 768 the land was wholly overrun, and the death of Waifar ended the brave but hopeless fight. Pepin, himself worn out by the struggle, lived only long enough to enact the statute which should govern the new-won province. By this he fused it with the rest of his kingdom, but left to its people their ancestral laws, guarded them against the extortion of the royal officials, and provided for a local assembly of their magnates which in conference with the deputies of the Crown should have final authority as to all matters, civil and ecclesiastical.

In the palace reared by his son at Ingelheim the fresco devoted to the memory of Pepin pictured him "granting laws to the Aquitanians." It was, indeed, his most lasting work. Though the whole history of Aquitaine betrays her separateness of blood and speech, though still "there is no Frenchman south of Loire," she has never ceased to form with Neustria a single realm. All else—the absorption of Brittany, the conquest of the Saxons, the humbling of Bavaria, whose young duke's desertion had for a moment crippled the war on Aquitaine—Pepin left unfinished to his sons. Between the two, after the bad old fashion of the Franks, he now parted the kingdom. To Charles, the elder, grown a man of twenty-six, fell Austrasia, most of Neustria, the western half of Aquitaine—all, that is, to north and west; to the younger, Carloman, still in his teens, though wedded, all to south and east. Bavaria was assigned to neither: it must first be won.

At St Denis, home of his childhood and his chosen place of sepulture, Pepin died, not yet half through his fifties. His life, though short, was fruitful. Modern scholars are at one in thinking his fame eclipsed unduly by that of his successor. Nearly everything the son accomplished, the father had begun. Vigorous, shrewd, persistent, practical, his own general and his own prime minister, relentless but not cruel, pious but never blindly so, able to plan but able too to wait, Pepin bequeathed to Charles more than a kingdom and a policy. Even for his bodily strength and presence, his power of passion and his length of life, Charlemagne perhaps owed something to the stainless self-control as husband and as father which was Pepin's alone of all his line. How the king looked we have no means of knowing. The legend which caused him in later centuries to be called "the Short" is baseless fable.

CHAPTER XIX.

CONQUESTS AND IMPERIAL CORONATION OF CHARLES THE GREAT.

THE significance of great personalities is nowhere in all history more evident than in the Carlovingian age. Without the work of the great men of the eighth century it is impossible to explain the shaping of the Middle Ages and the theocratic and imperial ideas that governed life in every department. It was Charles the Great, above all, who for centuries gave the direction to the historic development. It is true that imperialism and theocracy in the State were required on general considerations. But their particular form in the West depended very largely on particular individuals.

Charles was born 2 April, probably in the year 742, at some place unknown, and was the eldest son of Pepin the Mayor of the Palace (and afterwards king), and of his wife Bertrada. Shortly before his death in September 768, Pepin had divided the kingdom between his two sons. Charles received Austrasia, Neustria, and half of Aquitania, while Carloman had Burgundy, Provence, Gothia, Alsace, Alemannia, and the other half of Aquitania. The young kings were solemnly enthroned and anointed (9 Oct.) in their respective halves of the kingdom.

We soon hear of disputes between them. We need not assume that Carloman wished to supplant his brother because Charles was born before the marriage of his parents. There is no doubt that Charles was born in lawful wedlock. Unknown personal grounds caused the dispute. When the Aquitanians under Hunald rose against the Frankish rule in the first year of his reign, Carloman refused to help his brother, and Charles reduced the rising by his own power. Bertrada acted as peacemaker, and succeeded in reconciling the brothers. She did more. She passed through Bavaria into Italy to win over the two opponents of the Frankish kingdom, the Bavarian duke Tassilo and the Lombard king Desiderius. The daughter of Desiderius was to be married to Charles, and Gisela the sister of the Frankish kings to the son of the Lombard king. And as Tassilo had married another daughter of Desiderius, and as Frankish emissaries of Sturm, the abbot of Fulda, were working in

Bavaria on behalf of peace, there seemed to be a real bond of union between Francia, Bavaria, and Lombardy.

The old traditions of Frankish policy before the alliance with the Curia seemed to revive. The Pope however had considerable cause for anxiety. When he heard rumours of the proposed marriages he addressed to the two Frankish kings a letter full of passionate hatred against the Lombards and of consternation at a change of Frankish policy. He warned the Franks against an alliance with the Lombards, that stinking people, the source of leprosy, a people that were not recognised amongst civilised nations; and he threatened anathemas if the Papal warnings were disregarded. But when Charles nevertheless brought home his Lombard bride, the Pope accommodated himself to circumstances. He was mollified by the restoration of Patrimonies and in overflowing words besought the blessing of heaven on Charles. Soon the Lombard party even obtained the upper hand in Rome. Desiderius appeared in Rome as the friend of the Pope and overthrew the party that was opposed to the Lombards and friendly to Carloman. In a letter sent to Francia, Stephen praised the Lombard king as his saviour, "his most illustrious son," who at last had restored all the prerogatives of St Peter.

Even if Charles was but little offended at the Pope's opposition to Carloman, such intimate friendship with the Lombards cannot have seemed desirable to him. But all these circumstances were soon radically changed. After a union of one year Charles divorced his Lombard wife. Policy had brought about the marriage, personal wishes of the king, we may surmise, rent the union sharply asunder. Friendship for the Lombards was followed by the bitterest enmity.

There was a further cause. The opposition in Rome increased the estrangement of the royal brothers. Other personal motives may have co-operated. The alienation was so great that Carloman's people urged war. But the sudden death of Carloman (4 Dec. 771) made a complete change in the political situation. Charles seized his brother's portion of the kingdom. There were, it is true, children of Carloman, especially a son, Pepin, who had indisputable rights to the inheritance; but might prevailed over right, and though the enthroning and anointing of Charles took place "with the consent of all the Franks," while the court historians praised the Grace of God because Charles' authority was extended over the whole kingdom without shedding of blood, his disregard of right cannot be denied. Carloman's widow Gerberga had fled with her children and found refuge with Desiderius, now Charles' mortal enemy.

The union of the Frankish dominions under one authority was indispensable for their further development. Not till then did Charles' independent rule begin. The pre-eminence, and at the same time the ruthlessness, of the great ruler had already manifested themselves, but until 771 the softening and restraining influence of his mother had prevailed with him.

Now began the period of vigorous conquest. An empire was founded that embraced all the West German races and extended over wide Romance and Slavic regions and Avar territory—an empire that in consideration and extent might be compared with the West Roman Empire. The real motive in the advance of Carlovingian authority was certainly not religion. It is the secular ideal and the struggle for power which dominate men and nations. The Christian idea was but subordinate. It frequently ennobled, frequently veiled, the desire for power. Later on it had an essential part in the founding of the Empire that brought to a close the development of a universal authority in the West.

The first advance accompanied by immediate success was directed towards Italy for the subjection of the Lombard kingdom. A second was against the Arabs of the Pyrenean Peninsula. This aimed only at an unimportant extension of the Empire on the Spanish border and a closer union of Southern Gaul with the Empire. A third was on the East, in Bavaria and the territory of the Avars. A fourth was on the North and North-east in the territory of the Saxons, the Slavs and the Danes.

The political state of Italy was far from settled in the eighth century. After the collapse of the rule of the Eastern Goths the country had been a province of East Rome, then conquered from the North by the Lombards, and the part lying north-west of the Exarchate of Ravenna and Tuscany was left in possession of the Lombards, and was opposed to the *Respublica Romana*, as Lombard Italy to the Province of Italy. When the vigorous Lombard kingdom, after the time of Liutprand (712–744), aimed at sole rule over all Italy, winning Ravenna with the Exarchate, and the Duchies of Spoleto and Benevento were made dependent, this was regarded as an injury to the *Respublica Romana*. As holder of this political power for the Exarchate of Ravenna and for the people of the whole province of Italy appeared the Roman Bishop. According to law the Eastern Emperor was still lord of the Roman province, he was still (until 772) honoured as sovereign in the Papal documents, and so late as 752 Stephen II had turned to him for help against the Lombards. But political and ecclesiastical circumstances had led more and more to estrangement, and when the Roman Duchy and Rome itself were likely to fall before the advance of Aistulf, Stephen turned to the first Catholic power of the West, to the Frankish king Pepin.

The donation ascribed to Constantine must have been forged in Rome at this time, when the Curia was freeing itself politically from East Rome and as representative of the *Respublica Romana* in the West was desirous of winning what had formerly belonged to the Eastern Empire, and when for this purpose the Curia was obliged to summon the aid of the Franks. Thus old tendencies and views of the Roman Curia were invested with the authority of the Great Emperor Constantine. St Peter is represented as the Vicar of Christ in the world and the Roman bishops as the representatives of the Prince of the Apostles; therefore the Emperor is made to exalt the Chair of Peter above his own secular throne, and in order that the Papal dignity may be honoured with power and glory far above the secular empire, Constantine is made to have conferred upon the Roman bishop the City of Rome and all the provinces, places and towns of Italy and of the West, while he himself removed his capital to the East and erected a residence in Byzantium "because it is not right that the secular Emperor should have authority where the Principality of Priests and the Head of the Christian Religion were established by the Heavenly Emperor."

In the eighth century the Curia put forward for the first time this claim of political sovereignty for the highest office in the Church; and this claim has never since been completely forgotten, though often greatly modified. Pepin satisfied the Curia when Pope Stephen came in person to visit him in France in 754. Pepin presented him with a certain document and promised to procure for him the States of the Church. He twice took the field against the Lombards and won Lombard districts for the Pope. What he promised to bestow we do not know, because the document has not been preserved, and subsequent accounts are not sufficiently circumstantial; but we know that in 754 and 756 Pepin secured for the Curia the possession of the Roman Duchy of Pentapolis and the Exarchate of Ravenna, and that he regarded his promise as thus fulfilled. Pepin was appointed Patricius by the Pope and declared Protector of the Church and her territory. From his Roman Patriciate Pepin inferred a duty to protect, but not a right to rule. His son Charles, on the contrary, managed to change the relation and to transform the obligation of protection into a suzerainty.

After a short vacillation during the first years of the reign of Charles, the Papal policy, under Hadrian (774), the successor of Stephen IV, naturally took its former course of alliance with the Franks and opposition to the Lombards. Circumstances soon became exceedingly threatening. The Pope demanded restoration of church property, but Desiderius marched against Rome, and legates from the Pope hastened over the Alps to implore Frankish help.

Charles acted cautiously. He sent messengers into Italy to ascertain the exact position of affairs, and he made reasonable proposals to Desiderius in order to avoid war. Only when these failed he summoned an Assembly to Geneva, resolved on war and marched over Mont Cenis into Italy, while a second division of his army led by his uncle Bernard chose the road over the Great St Bernard. The defiles of the Italian side had been strongly fortified by Desiderius. Later legends tell of a Lombard minstrel who guided the Franks over the mountains into Italy by secret paths. It is historically certain that Charles caused part of his army to take a circuitous route, while negotiations with Desiderius were renewed, and that this caused Desiderius to give up his position in the defile and withdraw to Pavia, while his son Adalgis with Carloman's widow Gerberga and Charles' nephews sought refuge in the fortress of Verona. Probably about the end of September 773 Charles began the siege of Pavia. An expedition sent thence against Verona obtained the surrender of Gerberga and her sons, of whom no more is heard. Adalgis fled to Constantinople. But Pavia itself held out till the beginning of June 774. The town was ravaged by disease and obliged to surrender. Desiderius with his wife and daughter were taken prisoners, the royal treasure was confiscated, and the Lombard kingdom was at an end.

Before this, however, while the Franks were still besieging Pavia, Charles had taken a journey to Rome. He reached the Eternal City (2 April) and made such an entry as was usually granted to the Greek Exarch and Patrician. The Pope awaited the king in the entrance of St Peter's. Charles approached on foot, kissed each of the steps which led up to the church, embraced the Pope, and entered the church on his right. Together they descended to the grave of St Peter and took an oath of mutual fidelity. After that came an entry into the city itself. On the succeeding days various solemnities were celebrated, and (6 April) the important discussion took place in St Peter's. According to the contemporary Life of Hadrian, the Pope begged and warned Charles to fulfil the promise that had once been given by King Pepin, Charles, Carloman, and the Frankish nobles, on the occasion of the Papal visit to Francia, concerning the bestowal of different towns and districts of the province of Italy. Hereupon Charles caused the document drawn up at Quierzy to be read. He and his nobles assented to everything that was recorded therein and voluntarily and gladly ordered a new document to be drawn up by his chaplain and notary Hitherius, according to the pattern of the former one, and in it he promised to confer on St Peter the same towns and districts within certain limits as described in the document. The boundary begins at Luni, so that Corsica is included. It goes on to Suriano, to Monte Bardone, Parma, Reggio, Mantua, and Monselice. Thus according to the Papal biographer the donation was the Exarchate of Ravenna in its ancient extent, the provinces of Venetia and Istria, and the Duchies of Spoleto and Benevento. The document itself, as he further reports, was attested by Charles with his own hand, and the names of the nobles present were added. Then Charles and his nobles laid the deed first upon the altar, then upon the sepulchre of St Peter, and delivered it to the Pope, taking an oath that they would fulfil all its conditions. A second copy, also written by Hitherius, the king laid with his own hands upon the body of St Peter under the Gospels. A third copy, prepared by the Roman Chancery, Charles took with him.

There can no longer be any doubt that the detailed account in the *Vita Hadriani* of the events of 6 April 774 is correct in the essential particulars. In the most solemn manner Charles then renewed his father's promise. But it is not likely that the contents of the document are always correctly quoted by the biographer of Hadrian, or that Charles bestowed such extensive territories. We hear indeed that the Curia was afterwards not quite satisfied with the performance of the promise of 774, but we never find the Pope asking for so much territory, though we see his utmost hopes quite clearly in the extant Papal correspondence. The Popes had no reason modestly to lay aside demands which in point of law would have had such an excellent foundation as that indicated in the *Vita Hadriani*. Again, the later forged donations by the Frankish rulers in favour of the Curia know absolutely nothing of the immense extent of the promise of the *Vita Hadriani*, nor is there ground for assuming that Charles made a new treaty with the Pope somewhere about 781 and altered the promise of the document of 774 because it was too burdensome. The conclusion therefore seems inevitable that Charles the Great never issued a document of such contents as the Papal book asserts. We must suppose there has been distortion or falsification. Whether the author made these erroneous statements consciously or only through misunderstanding or whether the document was interpolated at the time, is quite unknown. But it seems certain that the donation made in the document which Charles deposited in 774 was not so comprehensive as we read in the Life of Pope Hadrian.

The political conditions of Italy were not finally settled by the conquest of Lombardy. Many difficulties had to be overcome. As early as the end of 775, the Lombard duke Hrodgaud of Friuli rose. A conspiracy of wide ramifications, involving Hildebrand of Spoleto, Arichis of Benevento, and Reginbald of Chiusi, seems to have been threatening. A Greek army under the leadership of Adalgis, the son of Desiderius, was, as some hoped and others feared, to master Rome and restore the ancient Lombard kingdom. But Hrodgaud remained isolated. A quick campaign of Charles in the winter months of 775–6 crushed the rising, and Hrodgaud fell in battle.

Charles' sojourn in the winter of 780–1 simplified the situation in Italy. Charles' second son Pepin was anointed as King of Italy by the Pope, and at the same time Ludwig (Lewis), his four-year-old third son, as King of Aquitania. This step by no means indicates that Charles renounced his own share in the rule of Italy. On the contrary, it was merely a formal concession to the special political needs of Italy, with a view to a stricter control and a closer approximation of the Italian to the Frankish government. The separate kingdom of Italy was not limited to the former Lombard kingdom, for districts were added to it. Such were Istria, which had been conquered by the Franks before 790, and Venetia and Dalmatia, which surrendered towards the end of 805 and belonged to the Empire of Charles the Great till 810, and also Corsica, which was repeatedly defended by the Frankish power against the Saracens in the first twenty years of the ninth century. Outside the

Italian kingdom lay the possessions of the Roman Church, Romania as they were officially called.

Much remained unsettled—the position of the powerful Duchy of Benevento, and above all the relations with the Greeks, who, pushed aside by the events of 774, still plotted against the States of the Church and against the kingdom of the Franks. Sicily, where a Greek *Patricius* was in residence, and South Italy, where their possessions were gradually melting away, gave them a base of operations. Threatened hostilities might still be avoided. The Emperor Leo IV had died suddenly in 780, leaving the Empire to his son Constantine VI, Porphyrogenitus, who was a minor, and for whom the widowed Empress Irene undertook the regency. Irene wished to restore image-worship, and thus come nearer to the Roman Church and to western politics generally. By her command an embassy appeared before Charles to seek the hand of the king's daughter Rotrud for the young Emperor of the East. The betrothal does not seem to have led to any distinct settlement in Italy : on the contrary, the existing conditions were tacitly recognised.

But the continued uncertainty, especially as concerning Benevento, at last made necessary a definite adjustment. Since 758 Arichis, the son-in-law of the dethroned Desiderius, had ruled here, and continued to do so in complete independence after the fall of the Lombard kingdom. With his highly cultured and ambitious consort he desired to make Benevento the centre of an advanced civilisation. He called himself Prince of Benevento, and had himself anointed by the Bishops and set a crown upon his own head, thus seeking to emphasise his sovereign position. The Pope was naturally opposed to this proceeding, for the prosperity and independence of Benevento were a continual danger to him. Charles also, the heir of the Lombard kingdom, could not suffer the rise of a great power in South Italy. The so-called *Annales Einhardi* credibly reports that Charles on his journey to Italy, 786–7, contemplated from the first an attack on Benevento, because he wished to gain the remainder of the Lombard kingdom.

At the beginning of 787, while Charles was waiting in Rome, Romuald the eldest son of Arichis appeared with presents and assurances of peace, hoping to hinder the advance of the Franks towards the South. But the Pope and the Frankish nobles who were present prevailed upon Charles to advance as far as Capua. Arichis, who had shut himself up in the fortress of Salerno, sent a further embassy to make new proposals—that Arichis might be excused from appearing before Charles in person, but that he should give hostages, among them his second son Grimoald, send rich presents and profess his subjection. These proposals were accepted, and Arichis as well as his eldest son Romuald, who had been set at liberty, and the Beneventines took their oath of allegiance before the plenipotentiaries.

This was doubtless a great success, not lessened by the rupture with the Greeks that followed and the breaking off of the betrothal of 781. But difficulties arose when Arichis died (26 Aug. 787) after the death of his eldest son and heir. Then the Beneventines asked for Grimoald the second son of Arichis, whom Charles held as a hostage. But the king hesitated to comply with their wish. Pope Hadrian especially had a share in this decision, for he had informed Charles of the plans of the Greeks to conquer Italy and appoint the duke of Benevento as the Greek *Patricius*, accusing Arichis of treachery and hinting at continued conspiracies of the Beneventines. As a matter of fact there was a Greek embassy at Benevento at the end of 787, trying to effect a great alliance. At different ends of the Empire the forces of opposition were thus arising against Charles at that time. But they did not take concerted action. For there is no evidence that the Beneventines entered into alliance with Tassilo of Bavaria or even with the Avars and Saxons, and indeed it is quite improbable, for otherwise Charles could not so easily have overcome his difficulties.

In the spring of 788, in spite of Papal opposition, Charles at last complied with the wish of the Beneventines and appointed Grimoald duke, first requiring of him a solemn oath to recognise the Frankish supremacy, to place Charles' name in decrees and on coins, and to forbid the Lombards to wear beards. When a Greek army landed in Lower Italy under the Sicilian *Patricius*, perhaps bringing with him Adalgis, son of Desiderius, who had been chosen as a Byzantine vassal prince, the Lombard dukes of Benevento and Spoleto remained faithful to the Frankish cause, joining a small Frankish army and inflicting on the Greeks a decisive defeat in Calabria. The Greek danger was finally removed. No further restoration of Greek rule in Italy was attempted, and from that time Adalgis lived peaceably in Constantinople as a Greek *Patricius*. But the supremacy over Benevento could not be fully maintained. Grimoald soon made himself independent, and later attacks by the Franks had no lasting success.

Through the fall of the Lombard kingdom and the subjugation of Italy by the Franks, the relations of Charles with the Pope necessarily underwent an essential change. On his Easter visit, 774, Charles had given the Pope the solemn assurance that he had not come with his army to Italy to win treasures and make conquests, but to help St Peter to his rights, to exalt the Church of God and to make sure the position of the Pope. But the result of the journey to Rome was that Charles himself laid claim to the rule of the Lombard kingdom. When, after the fall of Pavia, he assumed the title of king of the Lombards and added it to that of king of the Franks, he assumed also the obligations which belonged to his new office. His policy in Italy was the same as that of the Lombard kings before him and of all great rulers of Italy after him —the vigorous ruler of a part striving for the possession of the whole. It was on account of this that the Lombards fell into opposition to the

Pope. Though Charles and the Pope avoided serious conflicts and always worked harmoniously in their endeavour to reduce the Lombard Duchies and to drive the Greek power out of Italy, this was due to the peculiar position of the Frankish king. Charles was not only king of the Lombards but, as *Patricius*, was protector of the Church and her possessions.

Hadrian often reminded Charles of his promise of 774 and demanded its full performance. The Papal claims were only partially satisfied. Thus in 781 Charles promised to see to the restoration of the Patrimonies in the Sabina, but the Pope afterwards demanded in vain the evacuation of the whole territory. So again in 787 a donation of Beneventine towns was promised, also of several Tuscan towns, especially Populonia and Rosellae, but the fulfilment did not perfectly correspond with the Pope's wishes. For when the royal plenipotentiaries handed over to him the episcopal buildings, the monasteries and fiscal estates, and also the keys of the towns, but not sovereign power over the inhabitants, Hadrian complained bitterly. Of what use to him, he asked, was the possession of the town unless he had power over the inhabitants? "He must rule them by royal dispensation, and he was willing to leave them their freedom."

Without doubt all these acquisitions meant for the Roman Curia more than the mere gain of profitable rights. Political rule would secure constitutional privileges. What clearly appears as the leading thought in the forged Donation of Constantine was aimed at by the Popes of the eighth century on a more limited scale—an ecclesiastical State freed from all secular interference. Hadrian and his successors never forgot the thought that no earthly power might govern where the spiritual Head of Christendom had received his seat from the Heavenly Ruler.

Charles was not only king of the Franks and Lombards but he was at the same time, as *Patricius*, protector of the *Respublica Romana*. As successor of the Lombard kings he had to accept somewhat narrower limits, and above all to set absolutely free the districts belonging to the Pope. But as *Patricius* he was entitled to exercise a suzerainty over those territories too. This meant for the Pope and his deputies the enjoyment of profitable rights and immediate authority over the subjects, but for himself the supreme political control.

This was not a process of right but of might. The relations changed gradually. On his first visit in 774, the king asked permission to visit the city of Rome. Later on, such a request was needless. In matters of state, Charles felt himself supreme lord of the Pope and of all Papal possessions. If he asked the Pope to remove abuses which came to light in the Papal territories, or if he laid upon him a command to expel from the Exarchate and Pentapolis the Venetians who carried on trade in men, it was only an application of generally recognised principles. Protection implies sovereignty, and the Protector of the Church became sovereign of the protected territory.

Thus did Charles found a lordship over Italy. The different legal titles which had created it fell more and more into the background, and even the political prerogatives of the Pope became more like the secular authority of other great Churches in Gaul and Italy, which received confirmations of privileges from the State. The Roman Church appears endowed with rich possessions, with great revenues, with important state prerogatives. But over them stood Charles as supreme lord, as the sole true sovereign.

Charles' power meanwhile stretched further beyond Francia and Italy and became more absolute. The patriciate raised the protector of the Church to the position of lord of Christendom and absolute master of the West. That is of course the patriciate not as the Pope bestowed it, but as Charles made it. Later on we shall see how the Frankish monarchy assumed universal and theocratic elements. The Christian theocratic ideas were to justify as it were the violent conquests of Charles. The important point was the acquirement of real power. The great conquests were necessary, if the theocratic Frankish monarchy was to become the Empire of the West.

It was not the relief of the oppressed Christian Spain or the support of political allies but the spread of his power which guided Charles in his wars against the Arabs. At the Diet at Paderborn in 777, Ibn al Arabi, apparently governor of Barcelona and Gerona, asked help from Charles against the Umayyad Caliph of Cordova. The Arabian governor of Barcelona had already in 759 offered to Pepin to recognise Frankish supremacy, and Pepin had formed alliances with the Abbasids the enemies of the Umayyads, and in 765 he had sent ambassadors to Bagdad. The subjugation of Aquitania and Vasconia in the last years of Pepin's reign afforded the basis for further extension of Frankish dominion towards the South.

In the spring of 778 an army summoned from all parts of the Empire marched in two divisions across the Eastern and Western Pyrenees into Spain. It is significant that Charles' first achievement was the siege and capture of Pampeluna, which was inhabited by Christians and belonged to the Christian kingdom of Asturias. No great military successes were gained. Many fortified places recognised Charles' supremacy, but the expected great movement against the Umayyad 'Abd-ar-Rahmān did not take place. Among the Arab opponents of the Caliph of Cordova there was no unanimity. Charles saw that he had been deceived. He advanced as far as Saragossa on the Ebro, and perhaps took temporary possession of the town. Then he turned northwards, and Ibn al Arabi, who bore the blame of the failure of the expedition, was taken back with the army as prisoner. The Christian

Basques of Spain were treated as enemies, and the fortifications of Pampeluna were razed. And as the great army passed through the defiles of the Pyrenees in long columns, unable to open out for any military manœuvres, the rearguard was attacked by the hosts of the Basques and destroyed. In later legends the place is called Roncevalles. Even if the reverse was not in itself important, it was regarded as serious that the attack could not be avenged. And certain heroes among Charles' friends had fallen, the Palgrave Anselm, the Seneschal Eggihard, and above all, Hruodland the Praefect of the Britannic March. Legend however seized upon this event of 15 August 778, and wove around the whole Spanish expedition of Charles, but especially this surprise of Roncevalles, the halo of Christian glory. It exalted the defeat into a catastrophe and made the death of Hruodland the martyrdom of the heroic soldier of God. In the eleventh century these legends took their poetic form in the *Chanson de Roland,* their final form in the pseudo-Turpin, and in the *Rolandslied* of the Pfaffe Conrad of the twelfth century, the most popular form in which they spread over Germany.

The expedition of 778 had completely failed, but the project of a conquest in the South was by no means given up. In the first place, it was necessary to settle the position of Aquitania, which though it was finally conquered, yet had not become Frank. In 781 Charles raised this land with Septimania to a kingdom, and had his son Louis (Ludwig), who was born during the expedition of 778, anointed king of it by the Pope. On the border the boy was invested with arms and placed upon a horse, to hold his solemn entry into his kingdom. Charles wished his son to be brought up as an Aquitanian. He rejoiced later on when the seven-year-old boy appeared at the Diet of Paderborn in the dress of Aquitania with his little mantle and padded hose. But it was not intended that the grave Frankish character should be obliterated or the Frankish dominion over Aquitania in any way shaken. The regents whom Charles appointed in 781, and later Louis himself, only had influence so far as Charles liked. He remained the supreme head, and gave orders in all important matters and even in unimportant matters. It was a political system that answered perfectly. The people of Aquitania, proud of their kingdom, willingly complied with the arrangements of the Empire, and ever proved themselves the readiest to fight the Arabs. In 785 Gerona placed itself voluntarily under Frankish rule. The coast district was won in addition. In 793 there was another advance on the part of the Arabs. It was at that time that the distant enemies of the Franks combined, and political intrigue stretched from Spain to the land of the Saxons and to the Avars. Hishām I, Emir of Cordova, the son of 'Abd-ar-Rahmān, arranged an invasion. Gerona was taken, the Pyrenees were crossed and the Arabian army advanced as far as Narbonne and Carcassonne. A bloody battle was fought against the Margrave William on the river Orbieu, and the Arabs marched back laden with booty.

Soon however the Franks were in a position to make a victorious advance. From Gerona westwards the territory south of the Pyrenees was gradually won and a series of places fortified. In 795 the Spanish March was established. Dissensions among the Muslims and private undertakings of daring adventurers prepared the way for further conquests. In 801 Barcelona was compelled to surrender, and Louis, the king of Aquitania, was hurriedly summoned at the decisive moment, that he might have the credit of taking the proud city. In 806 Pampeluna and Navarre acknowledged the Frankish dominion. Tortosa also, after a long siege, surrendered its keys to Louis in 811, although neither here nor at Saragossa or Huesca was Frankish dominion regularly established. The Spanish March did not reach so far as the Ebro, but only to a line drawn N.N.W. from Barcelona and parallel to the Pyrenees. In 799 the Balearic Islands which in the spring had been ravaged by the Moors, put themselves under Frankish rule, and from that time enjoyed at any rate occasional protection by the Franks.

Bavaria was almost an independent State at the beginning of Charles' reign. After Duke Tassilo had faithlessly deserted the Frankish army in 763, in the middle of the war against Aquitania, the connexion of Bavaria with the Frankish power became looser. It was not that Frankish supremacy was completely renounced. Charles even appears to have exercised influence in the appointment to Bavarian bishoprics. But Tassilo nevertheless acted quite independently, and it is certain that Bavaria did not regularly take part in Charles' warlike undertakings, even if we assume the co-operation of the Bavarian army in the Pyrenean campaign of 778, which is doubtful. When the king and the Pope in 781 demanded that the duke should return to his former allegiance and Tassilo found himself compelled to comply with the demand, his independence was assured, and it was not till his personal safety had been guaranteed by hostages that he appeared at the Mayfield of Worms in 781, to renew the oaths and promises he had formerly made to Pepin, giving twelve nobles as hostages.

This did not bring about good relations. There was soon friction. After 784 there were manifest differences concerning rights in the Etsch districts, but most serious were the different conceptions of the conditions of dependency. Charles deduced from the oath of fidelity an obligation of obedience and services such as the provincial officials of his kingdom were accustomed to render. Tassilo on the other hand understood the subordination as more indefinite, and thought he was not bound to surrender his independence. In 787 the Bavarian duke sought the intervention of the Pope with a view to the restoration of peace with King Charles. Negotiations were opened but came to nothing, because views differed as to the degree of obligations involved in the oaths of fidelity. The Pope, who was entirely the tool of the powerful king, threatened anathemas in case Tassilo did not fulfil Charles' demands. As these were not satisfied, the Franks invaded Bavaria from three sides with an overwhelming force. Tassilo dared not venture a battle. He met the king (3 Oct.) on the plain of the Lech, acknowledged himself vassal and placed the duchy in the hand of the king to receive it back from Charles as a Frankish fief. The Bavarian people were obliged to take an oath of allegiance, and Tassilo had to give as hostages twelve nobles and his own son.

Why the end came nevertheless the next year is not rightly understood. Our information is drawn entirely from Frankish sources. What is reported in the official Annals is not conclusive without confirmation. From them we learn that Tassilo afterwards confessed that he had incited the Avars to make war against the Franks, that he had attempted the lives of the king's vassals in Bavaria, that he had recommended his own people to make secret reservations in taking the oath of allegiance to the king, and had even said that he would rather lose ten sons if he had them than hold to the treaties, that he would rather die than live under them.

The decision came at the Meeting of the Empire which was held at Ingelheim in the summer of 788. Tassilo, who had been invited like other nobles of the Empire, had appeared. He seems to have had no suspicion of what threatened him, and this unsuspecting appearance certainly does not look like guilt. He was immediately arrested, while royal messengers departed for Bavaria to seize the wife, the children, the treasures, and the household of the duke. Then Bavarians appeared as accusers and proved Tassilo's disloyalty. But the charges could not have been very serious, for they had to go back to the *Herisliz* of 763—an incident which must have been regarded as long previously pardoned by the royal declarations of grace in 781 and 787. The meeting, however, so it is reported, unanimously pronounced sentence of death on Tassilo, and only the intervention of Charles procured a mitigation of the sentence. Tassilo was shorn and sent into a monastery as a monk, he and his two sons. His wife also was compelled to take the veil, and they were all immured in different cloisters. But the ceremony of deposition was not yet completed. Six years later, at the Synod of Frankfort of 794, the deposed duke was made to appear, to acknowledge his guilt publicly in the assembly, and to renounce all rights for himself and his successors, in order to obtain the king's pardon and to be received back into his favour and protection. Of this event a report was made in three copies, one for the Palace, one for Tassilo, and one for the Court Chapel.

When we consider all the steps of Tassilo's fall, we easily recognise that he was sacrificed to the policy of the great king of the Franks. They were not acts of justice, they were acts of violence, which were only in appearance connected with any definite process of law.

Suspicious is the use made of the *Herisliz* of 763, which legally must have long been regarded as done with, and even more so is the solemn renunciation before the Synod of 794. Any breach of faith by Tassilo after his homage at the Lech cannot have been very serious.

But even if in his treatment of Tassilo Charles appears to us less as a just judge than as a strong statesman—the part which the last independent duke of Bavaria played in this drama remains pitiful. His deceit and bad faith are only known to us from the official history, but his weakness and political incapacity are shewn by the facts themselves. He did not understand the tasks of his age. During his long rule he favoured and enriched the churches like any Christian prince. But while he furthered the monasteries, he shewed but little understanding for the episcopal organisation with which lay the future. It was precisely this circumstance that immediately sent the leaders of the Church, the Bavarian bishops, over to the enemy when conflict broke out with the powerful Frank. Brave to fight for his hereditary rights and for the political independence of his race, he did not dare, or rather he was unable, to take a comprehensive view of the political situation, and he went unsuspectingly to Ingelheim to be taken prisoner, to be condemned to death, commuted for the life of a monk. Perhaps the result answered to the man's personal wishes, for his hopes and fears were set upon the other world.

Properly speaking, the wide district of Bavaria was not won for the empire of the Franks till 788. After the subjection of the Saxons it was the second great conquest of German territory—a conquest without bloodshed or struggle. This was a fact of immense international importance. It decided that the Bavarian race should share the destinies of the West-German peoples, just as the wars with the Saxons decided those of the North-eastern West-Germans.

The borders of the Frankish kingdom extended over the middle Danube district as far as the Enns, and at the same time over a district of the Slavs already conquered by Tassilo, over Carantania (Carinthia). Before long they were extended still further. For the subjection of the Bavarian kingdom was naturally followed by the struggle against the Avars and the Slavs, the Eastern neighbours of the Bavarians.

The Avars, confused by the Franks with the Huns, to whom they were related as belonging to the Ural-altaic family, had for some centuries come in contact with the Byzantines and Franks. About the end of the sixth century, as we have seen[1], they held a great dominion: but by the end of the eighth century the period of their greatest power was past. They had never risen above the level of barbarian nomads, and the Slavs of the south-east had long thrown off their yoke, and even their own sense of unity was gone. It was remarkable how this uncivilised people sought to make use of the civilised labour of other

[1] Chaps. ix, xiv.

peoples. Agriculture, like all other productive labour, was unknown to them. In the plain between the Danube and the Theiss were situated the "Rings"—the strong circular walls round extensive dwelling-places. According to the assertion of a Frankish warrior—quoted by the Monk of St Gall—the Rings extended as far "as from Zurich to Constance" (therefore about 60 kilometres or nearly 38 miles) and embraced several districts. In these Rings, of which, according to the Monk of St Gall, there were nine, the Avars had heaped their plunder of two centuries.

In 788 the Avars had advanced westward in two divisions, but had been completely defeated near the Danube and in Friuli. In 791 Charles had taken the offensive, not only to acquire rich treasures or to punish the invaders of 788, but to obtain a natural closed frontier towards the East. The Franks advanced as far as the Raab without making a permanent conquest. Their important task in Saxony for a long time hindered new and decisive action. Political alliances began to be formed among those who were at that time threatened by the Frankish sword. The Saracens, the Saxons, and the Avars knew of each other, and Charles' enemies in the north and south counted especially on a successful advance of the Avars. But the Avars lacked endurance. In the year 795 the Margrave Erich of Friuli, supported by the Slav prince Woinimir, advanced over the Danube and took the principal Ring. Large treasures of gold made their way to the Franks, and even if the opinion is scarcely tenable that great changes in prices in the Frankish Empire were the result, still his success was great. In the following year Charles' son Pepin completed the work of conquest. He destroyed the Ring, subdued the Avars, and opened large districts to the preaching of Christianity. In later years small risings had still to be put down, and Frankish blood still flowed in battle against the barbarians. In 811 a Frankish army was sent against Pannonia. But these were only echoes of the past. The Avars themselves are mentioned for the last time in 822. Even in the last years of the eighth century Christianity and colonisation had been introduced among them. The Christian mission was entrusted to the Dioceses of Aquileia, Salzburg, and Passau. The settlement of the middle Danube district began under Charles, that extension of the Germans, *i.e.* of the Bavarian, later also of the Frankish race, which finally embraced the present German Austria and the western districts of Hungary. Under Charles the Danube district about as far as the Leitha and the district of the upper Drave and the Save—the latter as Carantania—were reckoned politically as part of the Empire. The more eastern district, Pannonia, only belonged loosely to the Carlovingian Empire, and in consequence of the long wars it was greatly depopulated.

With Charles ambition and religion worked together. Successes in arms were for him at the same time successes for Christianity.

The ecclesiastical motive was specially strong in the Saxon wars. And the Saxons resisted ecclesiastical subjection as much as political. They struggled with their utmost strength against the Franks for their political freedom and for the imaginary blessings of their national religion.

The Franks had fought against the Saxons even in the sixth century. Chlotar I is said to have laid upon them a tribute of 500 cows, from which Dagobert freed them in 631. In the eighth century, profiting by the weakness of the royal authority, they repeatedly ravaged Frankish territory. The Mayors of the Palace, Charles Martel and his sons, were the first to fight successfully against them. They brought the tribes on the Frankish border into some kind of subjection, and under Pepin the payment of the old annual tribute of 500 cows was regularly demanded. But Christian teaching found no soil. The two Hewalds had paid with their lives for their first attempt to convert their kinsmen. The mission of Willehad was fruitless. The noble work of Utrecht and its school of missions failed in the case of the Saxons.

At the beginning of the reign of Charles the Saxons were in the same state as they are said to have been at the beginning of our era—small independent political communities which only combined temporarily in time of war. The three greater sub-tribes, the Westphalians, the Engers, and the Eastphalians, were not regular political units. The pure morals of the uncorrupted natural peoples still prevailed, but also all the brutality and cruelty of barbarism. The unconditional reverence for the gods and the blind obedience due to supposed utterances of the Divine Will exercised a fatalistic and fanatical influence.

Whether Charles had from the first intended the complete conquest of the whole Saxon territory or whether he was led to it by the force of circumstances, cannot be determined. It is certain that from 775 he aimed at the unconditional surrender of the Saxons.

The first campaign was decided on at the Assembly of the Empire at Worms in the summer of 772. In the territory of the Engers Charles, advancing from the south, took the Eresburg, marched northwards, destroyed the Irminsul, a tall column of wood erected on the Holy Heath which was honoured as the symbolic bearer of the Universe (*universalis columna quasi sustinens omnia*), and finally reached the Weser, where the Engers professed their submission and gave hostages as guarantees of peace. During Charles' absence in Italy in 774 the Saxons made an incursion into Hesse and destroyed Fritzlar, but were quickly driven back. Charles on his return planned radical measures. According to the *Annales Einhardi*, as they are called, he resolved to fight and ravage the faithless Saxons till they accepted Christianity or were utterly destroyed. The Frankish army in 775 marched from the West through the Westphalian country, took the fortress of Sigiburg, and advanced as far as Brunisberg on the Weser. The three Saxon tribes seemed to be entirely conquered, and an unsuccessful rising in 776 only completed the work of conquest. The Eresburg and the Sigiburg were made strong centres of the Frankish power. Carlsburg on the Lippe was built, the people were compelled to accept Christianity and their hostages were trained for Christian propaganda.

From that time Saxony was looked upon as part of the Frankish kingdom, and Charles no longer treated the people as enemies but as rebels. The Westphalian Widukind, the head of the national resistance, had fled to Denmark. In the summer of 777 the annual Assembly was held at Paderborn in the land of the Engers, and the first foundation was laid for the lasting nurture and maintenance of the Christian life, the land being divided into missionary districts and entrusted to the neighbouring bishoprics and great monasteries. Though in the time of the great Spanish campaign in 778, the Saxons made another plundering expedition to the Rhine and as far as Ehrenbreitstein, a detachment of the army that had returned from Spain quickly drove back the rebels, and in the summer campaign of 779 Charles reached the Weser and subdued the three tribes. In the summer of 780 an Assembly was held at Lippspringe at the source of the Lippe, an advance was made to the Elbe and again a new important permanent ecclesiastical arrangement was made. Two years later the Frankish Assembly was again held at Lippspringe. All the Saxons appeared, say the Frankish Annals, only the chief rebel, Widukind, remained away. Charles now went a step further—Saxon nobles were made Frankish counts and the land joined politically to his empire. And at that time apparently those regulations were made which were intended to prevent any rising and to ensure the full acceptance of Christianity under threat of the severest punishment—the *Capitulatio de partibus Saxoniae*.

Any who broke into, robbed or set fire to a church was to be punished with death. Any who from contempt of Christianity ate meat in Lent, any who killed a bishop, priest, or deacon, any who according to heathen custom burnt men as wizards or ate men, any who after heathen rites burned the dead, any who offered human sacrifices, or even any who omitted to be baptised and remained heathen, were to be put to death. Many other ordinances for the maintenance of Christianity and the political authority of the Frankish power were made, and also for the material foundation of Christian churches (surrender of the ownership of land and tithes). Even if there was a mitigation of this unusually severe legislation in the ordinance that the death penalty was to be remitted for those who had fled to a priest and after confession were ready to do penance, yet the law must have been found harsh, and the final Frankish ordinances of the year 782 must have incited to the utmost resistance those who looked on the conquest as only temporary.

When Charles had left the Saxons and had sent a Frankish army to the east in order that with a Saxon levy it might fight against the Sorbs, a general rising broke out under the leadership of Widukind, and when the Frankish army marched against the rebels, it was defeated on the Süntel Hill on the right bank of the Weser. Thereupon Charles himself immediately hastened to Saxony. His appearance gave the upper hand to the party among the Saxons friendly to the Franks and to the Christians. Widukind fled, and the chiefs obeyed the order to deliver up those who had taken part in the rising. Charles however held a strict inquiry, and had 4500 Saxons beheaded on one day at Verden on the Aller—a cruel deed for which we have sufficient historical attestation, though it has been wrongly disputed by some modern authorities.

But Charles had deceived himself as to the effect of these punishments. A general rising of the Saxon people was the result. The campaign of 783, which procured Charles the two victories at Detmold and on the Hase and brought him to the Elbe, was only a passing success. The Frisians also rose. The year 784 was taken up with the warlike undertakings of Charles and his son of the same name. The king remained with his army in Saxony through the winter also in order to undertake raids from the Eresburg, the head-quarters of himself and of his family, and to quell every attempt at a new rising. In the early summer of 785 he marched northwards to Paderborn, held the Frankish Assembly there, and then pressed on into the Bardengau on the left bank of the lower Elbe. All resistance was broken. Friendly overtures were made to Widukind and the other Saxon nobles who had hitherto fought stubbornly against the Franks. At Christmas 785 Widukind with his men appeared at Attigny, was baptised, and allowed to depart as a loyal subject, loaded with rich presents.

The event was looked upon as an important success. A special embassy announced to the Pope the victory of the Christian cause, and by Papal ordinance thanksgivings were offered all over Christendom to celebrate the fortunate ending of the thirteen years' war. But Widukind, the great hero, the most mighty personality in the older Saxon history, lived on in the memory of his people and became the subject of numerous legends. History tells us nothing of his later life, but legend has much to say. The most powerful Saxon families sought to honour him as their ancestor, and the Church and ecclesiastic literature made use of him. His bones worked miracles, his day was celebrated in later centuries, and he was even honoured as a saint.

The year 785 was an epoch in the history of the Saxon wars. Years of peaceful Christianisation followed. And a beginning was made with the episcopal organisation that was still wanting. The Northumbrian Willehad, who had been long working successfully among the Frisians and Saxons as a missionary, was consecrated Bishop of Worms (17 July

787), and the northern districts between the Elbe, the Weser, and Ems were given to him as his diocese. In Bremen he built St Peter's church, which was consecrated (1 Nov. 789) as the see of the first Saxon bishopric. The bishoprics of Verden and Minden must likewise have been founded then or soon afterwards.

The terrible Saxon wars of the first period of Charles' reign had their sequence. In the summer of 792 the Saxon people rose once more against God, the king, and the Christians. This was a national heathen reaction. Perhaps the heavy taxation of which the Church was the cause aroused the wrath of the lower elements of the population. If the easy yoke and the light burden of Christ had been preached to the obstinate Saxons with the same persistence as tithes and hard penances for light sins were exacted, they would not perhaps have shunned baptism—so wrote Alcuin at the time, not without irony. The Saxons sought to enter into alliance with the surrounding heathen, and they turned to the distant Avars. A new period of the struggle began, and at the same time a period of further violent measures to master this obstinate people. In the year 795 Charles for the first time had crowds of hostages sent to Francia. The third part of the population was forcibly deported, reports one group of sources, and the number of exiles is given as 7070. In the years 797, 798, 799 similar measures were taken and at the same time Franks were settled on Saxon soil. In 804 in particular, whole districts of Northern Saxony and Nordalbingia were robbed of their population, *i.e.* the Saxons were dragged away with wives and children. It is certain that no small portion of the Saxon race was at that time removed from its native soil—traces of them are still to be found in later centuries in Frankish and Alemannic regions.

At last the war, which with interruptions had lasted thirty-two years, could be regarded as ended, and the wide German territory as far as the Elbe and further was incorporated permanently into the Frankish Empire. Charles carried out his purpose of either subduing or destroying the Saxons, with wonderful persistence, but at the same time with brutal severity. The Saxons are certainly not to be regarded as stubborn heathens who resisted the blessings of Christian civilisation, but are to be admired as a people of strong purpose defending their national characteristics. But the unavoidable demands of the world's progress could not be resisted. The future belonged, not to the small German states which remained politically isolated: the Saxons had to fall a sacrifice to the great central development which was at that time the ruling factor in the political shaping of the West.

The extension of Frankish rule over Saxony was followed by connexions with the Danes and the Northern Slavs. The court of the Danish king Sigfried was for a long time the centre of Saxon resistance to Charles' Christian propaganda, and it was there that Widukind had always taken refuge. But in 782 the heathen king had sent a friendly embassy to the Franks, though without any wish to make concessions to Christianity. Later also friendly relations are mentioned. In 807 a Danish chieftain submitted. But in 808 King Göttrik marched against the Obodrites who were in alliance with Charles, and when the younger Charles tried to interfere to punish and to help, though he was only able to lay waste districts on the right bank of the Elbe, King Göttrik had a strong wall of defence built, it is supposed from the Treene to the Schlei. In the following year, however, after the failure of attempts at a treaty, Charles caused the fortress of Itzehoe to be built.

In 810 the Danish power seemed to be making a dangerous effort. A Danish fleet of two hundred ships ravaged the Frisian coasts and islands, tribute was laid upon the subjects of the Empire, and King Göttrik, who had remained at home, boasted that he would defeat Charles in open battle and make his entry into Aachen. Charles hastened eastwards with a strong force and took up his head-quarters at Verden, but he had no need to interfere, for Göttrik was assassinated by a follower, and his nephew and successor Hemming quickly made peace. In 811 twelve deputies from the Danes and as many from the Franks met on the Eider, and solemnly swore to keep the agreements that had been made.

Of the Slavs of the north-east, the Obodrites on the lower Elbe, who were nearest to the Franks, always stood on good terms with Charles, while the Wiltzi on the Baltic always remained hostile, and the Sorbs between the Elbe and the Saale were variable. There is evidence of friendly relations with the Obodrites after 780. They probably by that time recognised Charles' suzerainty, but were disinclined to Christianity. They repeatedly took part in the Frankish campaigns, and in 810 Charles appointed their chieftain. In 782 the Sorbs made an unimportant attack on Thuringian territory, in 806 they were defeated by the younger Charles and compelled to submit. But the subsequent building of two fortresses on the right bank of the Elbe, at Magdeburg and at Halle on the Saale, shews that there was no incorporation of the territory of the Sorbs into the Empire. Still less is that the case with the Wiltzi. In 789 Charles undertook a great campaign of conquest. He crossed the Elbe and advanced ravaging as far as the Peene, and the chief Dragowit and the other leaders of the people even took an oath of fidelity, but we can find no trace of permanent subjection or toll, such as Einhard records.

Again there were struggles afterwards. In 806 fortresses were erected against them, and even the submission of 812 was only nominal and transitory. The proper boundary of the Empire on the east, apart from the district of the Nordalbingians, was the Elbe, more to the south the Saale, then the Böhmerwald. For even the land of the Chekhs may not be reckoned as part of the Empire. The passage of Frankish armies did not trouble the Chekhs who were only loosely organised, and the campaigns of the younger Charles in the years 805 and 806 certainly laid the land waste, but there was no lasting submission.

It was a proud Empire, that of the great Charles. From the Pyrenees and the north-eastern part of Spain it stretched to the Eider and the Schlei on the north, from the Atlantic Ocean and the North Sea on the west to the Elbe, the Böhmerwald to the Leitha, the upper Save, and the Adriatic Sea on the east. Further, the whole of North and Central Italy and the greater part of South Italy belonged to him. But his influence extended beyond this. The Slavs and the Avars who dwelt on the east were even reckoned as his and certainly belonged to the sphere of his interests. It is true that the Christian states in Spain and in the British Isles were independent, but even they recognised his friendly superiority. With the Abbasids in Bagdad Charles united against the Umayyads of Spain and against Byzantium. The Caliph is even said to have agreed that the place of the Holy Sepulchre at Jerusalem should be under Charles' authority. Even in the East Charles began to be regarded as the representative of Christian power.

Thus the Frankish king had raised himself above the narrow limits of his nation. His authority had taken a theocratic and universal element. While in the age of Pepin the ecclesiastical idea with its tendencies to universal authority had strengthened the Papacy, and had sought to give the Pope the position of the Roman Emperor in the West, under the reign of Charles all the elements of authority connected with the Church had been serviceable to the Frankish king. The *patricius*, the protector of the Papal possessions, became the protector and patron of the Church generally, and moreover the representative and leader of the spread of Christianity.

This was the necessary result of the forces developed by the needs of the Church itself. If the Christian teaching was to conquer the world, political power must be aimed at along with the spread of the faith. It was precisely in those times of active Christian propaganda that the need of political power was especially felt. The realisation of the theocratic ideal required a dualism: ecclesiastics for the spread of the holy doctrine, laymen to fight for the Faith—at the head of the former, the Pope according to the hierarchical view that had prevailed for centuries, and at the head of the others, the king of the Franks. But the privileges of the actual political power answered the needs of the theocratic idea of that age.

Towards the end of the eighth century a mosaic was placed in the refectory of the Lateran. In it we see St Peter sitting on the throne with the keys in his bosom : on the right and left kneel Pope Leo and King Charles, to the one Peter hands the pallium, to the other the banner of

CH. XIX.

the city of Rome, and the legend runs: "Holy Peter, thou bestowest life on Pope Leo, and victory on King Charles." So was the relation understood in Rome at that time. Two central forces prevailed in Christendom, a spiritual and a secular, the one by spiritual means, the other by might. But how far did the power extend that Peter bestowed with the banner, and how far the power conferred with the pallium? As a matter of fact, the relation of spiritual and secular powers turned out very much to the disadvantage of the former.

The government of Charles did not limit itself to secular matters. Just as the Frankish kings had long been rulers of their Church and as the work of Boniface had done little to alter this, so it was under Charles. The position of governor of the Frankish Church Charles extended over the Church of the West generally. Charles felt himself called to care not only for the external maintenance of Church order, but also for the purity of the faith. Numberless are his measures for the supervision of Church life and the ecclesiastical ordinances. But he also took an active part in the settlement of purely dogmatic questions. As the holy Josiah (so it runs in one capitular) endeavoured to bring back to the service of God the kingdom bestowed upon him by God, so Charles would follow his example. But it is not the Pope who decides what is right and Christian, and then informs Charles. The Pope was not allowed the leading part even in matters of doctrine. On the contrary, Charles took the initiative repeatedly, consulted with his bishops and demanded from the Pope acceptance and execution. His treatment of two questions is specially characteristic.

To deal with Adoptianism, which originated in Spain and greatly stirred the Western Church, Charles caused Synods to be held and to decide under his own presidency. At the Assembly of Frankfort in 794, Elipandus of Toledo and Felix of Urgel were condemned. Charles took a personal interest also in the matter of image-worship. When a council of Nicaea in 787, by the influence of the Empress Irene, re-introduced the worship of images and condemned those who taught otherwise— threatening ecclesiastics with deposition and laymen with outlawry, Charles offered strong opposition to the heretical teaching of Greeks, as he considered it, and caused a learned and comprehensive work, the "Caroline Books" (*Libri Carolini*) to be prepared, perhaps by Alcuin. It is of no further present interest to us that to a great extent the matter dealt with misunderstandings caused by unfortunate renderings of decisions of 787, composed in the Greek language. It is enough that the doctrine of the Greeks was rejected in the sharpest manner and the Pope was required, though he was entirely on the side of the Greeks, to take the side of the Franks and to excommunicate the Greek Emperor as a heretic. Hadrian did not dare directly to repudiate the king's interference in the settlement of questions of doctrine, although he prudently appealed to his primacy, opposed the royal opinion point by point, and defended the Greek view as the orthodox one. Finally, however, he declared himself ready to fulfil the king's wish and to excommunicate the Greek Emperor. He would demand of Constantine the restitution of the Patrimony of Peter, and if the Emperor refused, he would exclude him as an obstinate heretic from Church fellowship. Charles seems to have left this very remarkable proposal unanswered. He simply caused the pseudo-council of Nicaea to be repudiated—and the Pope said nothing.

"This do we praise as a wonderful and special Divine gift," writes Alcuin to Charles, "that thou dost endeavour to keep the Church of Christ inwardly pure and to protect it with as great devotion from the doctrine of the faithless as to defend it outwardly against the plundering of the heathen and to extend it. With these two swords has God's power armed thy right hand and thy left." In the Caroline Books it is declared that by the gift of God he had taken the helm of the Church throughout his dominions, and that the Church had been entrusted to him to steer through the stormy waves of this world. The first letter of Charles to Leo III contains a formal programme of the relation of Pope and king: It is the king's business to defend the Holy Church of God outwardly with arms and inwardly to maintain the Catholic Faith, and it is the business of the Holy Father to support the royal work by his prayers. The "Representative of God who has to protect and govern all the members of God"—so is Charles called—"Lord and Father, King and Priest, the Leader and Guide of all Christians."

These are courtly expressions, but they agree perfectly with the facts. The Frankish kingdom had become a world-empire, *the* Christian Empire of the West. And yet the old fundamental political ideas were still in force—the supreme lord of this power still called himself "King of the Franks and Lombards and *patricius* of the Romans" (*Carolus gratia Dei rex Francorum et Langobardorum ac patricius Romanorum*). Must there not be a change in this respect, must not the increased power find expression in a new title?

It does not appear that Charles definitely sought this, nor does it appear that tendencies of this kind prevailed about Charles. Even in the year 800 Alcuin explained that three powers were the highest in the world—the Papacy in Rome, the Empire in the Second Rome, and the royal dignity of Charles. And the last precedes the others. Charles surpasses all men in power, in wisdom, in dignity, he is appointed by Jesus Christ as Leader of the Christian people. If Alcuin does not wish thereby to set the title of King above that of Emperor, but only to estimate the royal dignity of Charles as higher than that of the Emperor of East Rome, yet so much is clear, that in the eyes of Charles' contemporaries claims to the highest earthly power were compatible with the title of king, and that the monarch in Byzantium, in spite of his title of Emperor, was to be regarded as of less importance than the King Charles. With proud self-consciousness the Franks set themselves on occasion in opposition to the Roman idea of the State. Thus the Prologue to the *Lex Salica*, composed in the eighth century, spoke of the glorious Frankish race that after a victorious struggle had thrown off the hard yoke of the Romans, and after their acceptance of Christianity had enshrined in buildings decked with gold the bodies of the martyrs, burnt and mutilated by the Romans. And in the last decade of the eighth century expressions directly hostile to the Roman Empire were uttered by the confidential friends of Charles. In the Caroline Books the *Imperium Romanum* is characterised as heathen and idolatrous. Here speaks hatred for the East Roman Empire of Constantine and of Irene; but in it there is also seen Augustine's conception of the Roman world-empire as one of the great *civitates terrenae*, and further the idea which the Christian writers had spread, using the interpretation of the dream of Nebuchadnezzar by the Prophet Daniel, the idea that four empires follow one another and that the Roman Empire is the fourth, upon which follows the setting up of the Heavenly Empire, *i.e.* the end of the world. Four *civitates terrenae* and the last of them the Roman Imperium stand in characteristic contrast to the *Civitas Dei*—truly a conception which could hardly lead to the assumption of the Roman Imperial dignity by the Franks.

But on the other hand the Roman Imperial dignity still lived as a universal power in the historical life even of the West. And Byzantium was still looked upon as the head of *one* Roman Empire. It is true that the development of civilisation had brought about a separation of the Christian East and Christian West, complete political separation, and made desirable the limitation of the universal Roman Empire to the West. These were social exigencies which help us to understand the efforts of the Italian Exarchs of the great Emperors for emancipation, including that of the eunuch Eleutherius who in the year 619 marched to Rome to set the West Roman Empire up again and wished to be crowned by the Pope. And then the Pope himself had taken up the idea of Roman Universalism and regarded himself as the sovereign representative of the *Respublica Romana* between Byzantium and the Lombards. Finally the supreme power of Charles had arisen and he had united in himself the power of the kings of the Franks, of the Lombard kings, and of the lord of the *Respublica Romana* and the universalist tendencies which were peculiar to Rome and the Christian Church of the West.

There was great need in the eighth century for a political union of the Christian West. In the Empire of Charles these tendencies were eventually satisfied. But the way to the re-erection of the Western Empire of the Romans was not yet clear, for it contradicted the still recognised position of the Byzantine Emperor as the supreme head of the *Imperium Romanum.* Also in contradiction to it was a deep-seated opposition of the friends of Charles to the Roman imperial idea itself, against the *Imperium Romanum,* the fourth and last of the great world-empires that were founded on the power of the Evil One, and stood in opposition to the Kingdom of God on earth.

There is no doubt that at the end of the eighth century the development of affairs in the West pressed for a certain formal recognition of the universal power of the Frankish king which had prevailed, but the friends of the great monarch did not seek the settlement and could not seek it in the assumption of the Imperial dignity by Charles. The position was still obscure, when the solution came through a spontaneous act of the Pope.

Pope Hadrian I died on Christmas Day 795. The Roman Leo III was elected on the following day, and consecrated on the day after. He did homage to Charles as his overlord. He sent to him the decree of the election with the assurance of fidelity, the keys of the grave of St Peter and the banner of the City of Rome, and he asked for envoys before whom the Romans could take the oath of allegiance. Formerly the Popes had given in their documents the years of the reigns of the Eastern Emperors. Since 772 Hadrian had omitted this, and Leo III reckoned the years of "the Lord Charles, the illustrious King of the Franks and of the Lombards and Patricius of the Romans since he has conquered Italy." Charles answered the Papal message in a manner which expressed the exalted position of the king. Through Angilbert he gave the new spiritual ruler a strict warning to lead an honourable life and to observe the decrees of the Church.

Leo III was hard and cruel, and soon forfeited the sympathies of the Romans. On 25 Apr. 799, when he was taking part in an ordinary procession, a conspiracy broke out. Leo was attacked, torn from his horse, severely treated and sent to the monastery of St Erasmus. During the night he escaped with the help of his chamberlain, being let down the wall by a rope, and hurried to St Peter's, where the two Frankish envoys, the Abbot of Stablo and the Duke of Spoleto, were staying. These on news of the movement in Rome had hastened there with an army. Leo was brought to Spoleto. Soon he was extolled as a martyr on whom the grace of God had wrought miracles. His enemies were said to have destroyed his eyes and torn out his tongue when they attacked him, but during his imprisonment his sight and speech were restored by miracle. And when the two envoys brought him to the land of the Franks to seek help, his triumph was worthy of one on whom the grace of God had so wonderfully lighted, and the people hastened to kiss the feet of the Holy Father. In Paderborn Charles prepared a brilliant reception for the Pope, and Leo was received by the king with kind embraces. But when his Roman opponents, " accursed sons of the devil," also sent messengers to Charles and raised the gravest charges against the Holy Father, accusing him of adultery and perjury, there were not wanting voices round Charles, that Leo should either clear himself by an oath or renounce the Papal dignity. Others, among them especially Abbot Alcuin of Tours, saw in such demands a serious blow to the Papal office itself. This opinion Charles shared. He sent Leo to Rome accompanied by royal envoys, and on 29 Nov. 799 there was a brilliant entry into the City. Then Charles' envoys brought the conspirators to trial. As the serious accusations against Leo could not be proved, the opponents of the Pope were sent as prisoners to Francia; but the investigation caused the Pope many anxious moments, as may be seen from the letters of Angilbert. Rome was not yet pacified, and Charles himself wished to set things in order permanently. In the autumn of 800 he went to Italy, and (24 Nov.) held his solemn entry into Rome. Seven days later the great assembly of Franks and Romans was held in St Peter's to consider the charges brought against the Pope. They agreed to leave it to the Pope to clear himself by an oath voluntarily and without compulsion. It was in that manner they found a way out of the difficulty. No trial of the Pope was to be held, for this must inflict the gravest injury on the Papal office, but yet the suspicions which remained were to be removed. Leo agreed to the proposal, and (23 Dec.) holding the Book of the Gospels, he solemnly declared in the Assembly, that the most gracious and exalted King Charles had come to Rome with his priests and nobles to investigate the charges, and that he himself of his own free will, condemned and compelled by none, at length cleared himself before God of every suspicion.

Never had Charles appeared so manifestly the Lord of Christendom. And just at that time came the legates of the Patriarch of Jerusalem, bringing the keys of the Holy Sepulchre, of the Hill of Calvary and of the City, as well as a banner to testify to the suzerainty of the mighty Charles. Was the ruler of orthodox Christendom to hold for the future only the title of king?

On Christmas Day, as the king rose from prayer before the Confession of St Peter, Pope Leo set a crown upon his head and the whole Roman people there assembled joined in the cry "Hail to Charles the Augustus, crowned of God, the great and peace-bringing Emperor of the Romans." After this cry of homage, the Pope offered him the adoration due to the Byzantine Emperors, and laying aside the title of *patricius*, he was called Emperor and Augustus.

Such is the brief report of the official Frankish Annals. With it agree the statements of the Papal Book, only that there is no mention of the adoration, and a thrice-repeated cry of homage is spoken of. Another account (*Annales Laureshamenses*) tells of deliberations of the Pope, of the assembled Clergy, and of the other Christian people, of deliberations that the Empire was then in the possession of a woman (Irene) at Constantinople, that Charles ought to be called Emperor

because he held Rome, the seat of the Emperors, and that Charles had
yielded to the request of the priests and the whole Christian people and
had accepted the title of Emperor with the coronation by Pope Leo.
Many modern historians have thought that this account makes it
necessary to suppose a previous election by the Roman people. But
the story is worthy of little credit. It abounds in words but is poor
in facts and cannot be set against the harmonious and clear accounts of
the Imperial Annals and of the Papal Book.

The whole proceeding of the Pope, which took Charles entirely by
surprise, is so surely attested that all doubts must be silenced. Even
the question how the people without premeditation could have broken
out into the cries of homage, finds its answer in the fact that the same
Laudes were offered to the *patricius* and hence the cry, only slightly
changed, could very well have been raised on Christmas Day 800,
without previous practice. Einhard however relates in his Life of
Charles, that the new title was at first very unwelcome to the monarch,
and that Charles even said that on this day, although it was a high
Festival, he would not have entered the Church if he had known the
Pope's intention.

Thus we have on the whole a trustworthy account of the proceedings
on Christmas Day 800. From the assured facts we must proceed
to the meaning of the coronation as a matter of law and of general
history.

The spontaneous action of the Pope created the office of Emperor,
and the coronation was looked upon as the decisive act. There was no
election by the people: even the joyous cry offered to the newly crowned
Emperor is not to be regarded as an act of election. The *Laudes* were
only joyful assent to the act which was of itself legally valid. But the
Pope acted as a suddenly inspired organ of God. God Himself crowned
Charles as Emperor through the Pope. This view comes out clearly in
the *Laudes* offered to Charles and it expresses the meaning of the title of
Emperor. The theocratic origin of the office is certain. And this
theocratic element remained. On this basis Charles took his ground
when he himself provided for the succession in 813 and commanded his
son Louis to take the Imperial crown that was resting on the altar
and to put it upon his head—God spoke not through the Pope but
through the Emperor.

It is certain that on the occasion of the coronation of 800 Byzantine precedents played a leading part. The coronation, hitherto
unknown in the West, was due to the fact that since the middle of the
fifth century the Patriarch of Constantinople had been wont to deck the
new Emperor with the crown. The cry of homage goes back to an
older Litany for the *patricius* in connexion with the Byzantine usage,
and in the same way the title of Emperor finds a Byzantine precedent.
But the proceeding of 800 was not an act in accordance with the

Byzantine constitution.   In spite of its resemblances to Greek usages, it was essentially something new.   Historical forces, due to developments in the West and even contrary to Eastern ideas, led to the Western Empire.   The foundation of the Empire in the year 800 sprang not from the soil of the Byzantine constitution, but from disregard of it, and meant a complete break with it.

We must suppose that the thought of the coronation was due to Leo himself or to some one closely connected with him.   At all events this act was, in a certain sense, in sharpest contrast with the Papal ideas of the Donation of Constantine.   For in the latter the most important feature was an Italy independent of the Emperor, but in 800 the Pope himself set the Emperor as the highest secular Lord over his Rome.   He must have been conscious of this difference himself.   But the Pope may have considered that as *patricius* Charles was already supreme, and that his absolute position was already established.   And since the generally prevailing ideas pointed clearly towards the Empire, it might have been regarded as an advantage for the Roman Curia if this last development was due to itself.

No doubt the coronation was intended to express the strongest feeling of gratitude to the powerful King.   But in this Leo deceived himself.   According to accounts which are trustworthy, Charles was displeased at the unexpected event.   It is not easy to understand the reason of his displeasure.   Did he not wish for the crown because he felt himself a German ruler and put the German idea of the State in conscious opposition to Roman absolutism?   Or was it that he did not desire it just at that time because he feared a collision with the Eastern Empire?   Or did he not wish for the crown from the hand of the Pope because he foresaw the latter might build on it a right to crown, and so deduce claims to supremacy?   The later policy of Charles gives many hints for the answer to these questions.   We know that Charles for a long time combined no actual political authority with his position as Emperor, and that he ignored the office in his first division of the Empire in 806.   We also know that he laid the greatest weight on an alliance with Byzantium, and finally that in 813 when he had to arrange for the succession, he allowed no repetition of the precedent of 800, but rejected all co-operation of the Pope.   We must therefore conclude that Charles did not indeed wish to set up the idea of a Germanic priestly kingship against that of the Roman Empire, but that he held fast in 800 to that conception of a Frankish power which had raised him so high.   He was not moved by fear of complications with the East, but he saw that they would arise through this step of the Pope's.   He did not dream of the far-reaching Papal pretensions of a later age, but he did not wish that so important an event as that of 800 should rest on foreign interference.   At the end of the eighth century he had not himself weighed the significance of the change, he had not thought things were ripe for it, he saw in it something inexplicable, something indefinite, which was ground enough for uneasiness and hesitation. Charles certainly did not despise gifts which came to him from heaven, but he wished to ask for them himself, not to receive them unexpectedly through outside intervention.

The coronation came in 800 as a surprise but not as a chance. It sprang entirely from the initiative of the Pope, but it was not a chance idea of Leo's which might as well not have occurred to him. It was rather the outcome of a long chain of events, the result of ordinary historical factors. It had to come, but that it came actually on that Christmas Day and in the manner in which it did, depended on mere chance, purely individual circumstances. Hence the Western Empire did not suddenly bring new elements into the political life of the West. When a modern constitutional historian sees in it a radical constitutional upheaval, when he finds the kingdoms of Charles combined into the united empire and taking their historical form, and yet considers all this to be without constitutional importance, it seems to accord little with the actual circumstances, and even to contradict the clearest assertions of our authorities. We see quite plainly that the new title of Emperor at once took the place of the title of *patricius* which disappeared, while the old title of king on the contrary remained. We must therefore conclude that those offices which before the coronation were connected with the Patriciate are to be looked upon as imperial offices. Even as Charles as *patricius* had been protector of the *Respublica Romana* and supreme in Christendom so was he as Emperor, only that now the monarchical elements were of more significance. As he had been king of the Franks and of the Lombards before 800, so he remained after 800. It is true that the relations of the imperial and the kingly authority were not clearly defined. There was no need, from this point of view, to distinguish the offices which were united in the person of the great monarch. It would not have been possible to draw a sharp line of distinction. Even the duties and rights which originally had certainly belonged to the Patriciate and therefore now belonged to the ruler as Emperor and not as king, were soon combined with the Frankish monarchy.

As "Emperor of the Romans" Charles was crowned, and as master of the *Imperium Romanum* he regarded himself from that time. But was not the seat of the Empire Byzantium? Could two Emperors act side by side? Men asked themselves these questions at the time and the Annals of Lorsch sought to answer them by explaining that the Greeks had no Emperor but only an Empress over them and that therefore the Imperial rank belonged to Charles, the ruler of Rome, the old seat of the Caesars. Charles had taken the office of Roman Emperor in its unlimited universal extent, but he was from the first inclined to allow a limitation. He negotiated with Byzantium and earnestly sought a good understanding. According to the account of a Greek historian, Charles planned a betrothal with the Empress Irene, but the plan fell through owing to the opposition of the powerful *patricius* Aëtius, and during the negotiations the Empress Irene was overthrown in 802.

Charles eagerly sought recognition of his Imperial rank from Irene's successors—from Nicephorus, then from Michael (after 811) and from Leo V (after 813). He went upon the assumption of a division of the *Imperium*, of a peaceful and independent coexistence of the *Imperium Orientale* and of the *Imperium Occidentale*. Not till 810 did he come to a preliminary agreement with Greek agents, whereby he gave up claim to Venice and the towns on the Dalmatian coast, which were even at the beginning of the ninth century occasionally under Frankish rule, and in return was recognised as Emperor by the Greeks. Michael, the successor of Nicephorus, was ready to conclude the treaty, and in the church of Aachen in 812 the Greek ambassadors solemnly saluted Charles as Emperor ($\beta\alpha\sigma\iota\lambda\epsilon\dot{\upsilon}\varsigma$). But Leo V first drew up the Greek document of the treaty and sent envoys with it to Aachen where after Charles' death it was solemnly delivered to Louis. This was the formal step in the creation of the Empire of the West.

The coronation of 800 gave neither a new basis for the monarchical authority nor a new direction for the obligations of the State. In the year 802 an order was issued for a universal renewal of the oath of allegiance, and the religious side of the obligation was emphasised more than before. The theocratic element of the great monarchy was brought to the front. Yet this was nothing new in principle. When in 809 Charles ordered the retention of the *Filioque* in the Creed, in opposition to the action of the Pope, and when the Frankish use as a matter of fact supplanted the Roman, this influence of Charles upon doctrine was not a mere consequence of the coronation. The office of Emperor only became gradually a definite political power, summing up as it were the separate powers of the Frankish ruler and also giving a legal basis for the relation of this absolute authority to the Church of the Pope. When on 6 Feb. 806, to avoid wars of succession, a division of the Empire among the three sons of Charles was arranged in case of his death, the document was sent to the Pope for his signature, and care for the Roman Church was enjoined upon the sons, but nothing was decided about the office of Emperor. A few years later it was looked upon as an office which conferred actual authority and must be reserved for the house of Charles. In September of the year 813 an Assembly was held at Aachen and Charles with his nobles resolved to raise Louis, his only surviving son, to the position of Emperor, while a grandson Bernard, the son of his dead son Pepin, was to be appointed under-king of Italy. In his robes as Emperor, Charles advanced to the altar, knelt in prayer, addressed warning words to his son, caused him to promise fulfilment of all commands, and finally bade Louis take a second crown that was lying upon the altar and place it himself upon his head.

The reign of Charles as Emperor was a period of quiet improvement of great acquisitions. The wars of the earlier period had come to an end, and conquest was over. His magnificent efforts to raise the conditions of social and religious life became apparent. The world power was universally recognised. Far beyond the Christian peoples of the West, Charles enjoyed unconditional respect. In East and West he was looked upon as the head of the Christian Empire, to the Slavs he was so absolutely *the* ruler that his name (as *Kral*) served as an expression for royal authority, just as formerly in the West those of Caesar and Augustus had been chosen to express supreme monarchical power.

On 28 Jan. 814, at 9 o'clock in the morning, Charles died, after an illness of a few days' duration at Aachen, where he had resided by preference during the last years of his reign. He was buried the same day in the Basilica there, and in the manner customary in the West, lying in a closed coffin. Only a later fanciful writer was able to distort this well-attested simple fact. Count Otto of Lomello, one of those who accompanied Otto III on his remarkable visit to the grave of Charles in the year 1000, related, according to the *Chronicum Novaliciense*, that Charles was found sitting on a throne like a living man, with his crown upon his head and his sceptre in his hands, the nails of which had grown through the gloves. Otto III, according to this account, had the robes set in order, the lost portion of the nose replaced by gold and a tooth of the great Dead brought away. It may well be supposed that the awful moment in which the fanciful Otto wished to greet his mighty predecessor in person dazzled the senses of the Count, whose imagination and perhaps the desire for sensation have led astray much learned investigation and popular ideas.

Popular legends soon busied themselves with the person of the Emperor to whom following generations very soon gave the title of the Great. Even in the ninth century all kinds of fables were told about him and the hero became exalted into the superhuman. In the amusing little book of Notker the Stammerer, the Monk of St Gall, anecdotes and popular tales play a part. By that time, two generations after the death of the great king, these tales must have grown very much. In Northern France the legends were specially busy, and the stories of Charles and his Paladins were gathered together in poetic form in the *Chansons de Geste* and later in the *Chanson de Roland*, to travel from France to Germany and to live on in the *Rolandslied*, in the *Willehalm*, and in the Chronicle of the German Emperors of the twelfth century.

Legends had long been developed on the ecclesiastical side. The *Poeta Saxo*, as early as the end of the ninth century, had praised the

Emperor as the Apostle of the land of the Saxons, and the struggle with the Saracens also was praised from this point of view. It is true that Charles could not be regarded as a saint so long as his manner of life was remembered. This caused great trouble to the strict moralist. The monk Wetti for instance represented Charles as suffering terrible punishments in the other world on that account, and Walafridus Strabo, who in the time of Louis turned the *Visio Wettini* into verse, relates that a nun had beheld the tortures of Charles in the fires of Purgatory. But these memories faded, and later it was only the soldier of God, the champion of the faith, the builder of numerous churches, who was remembered. As early as the second half of the tenth century stories were told of a journey of Charles to Jerusalem. In the eleventh century this was generally believed and Charles was extolled as a martyr on account of his many adventures. The picture of the monarch was transformed and his character became that of a Christian ecclesiastic, even that of a monk. The purely ecclesiastical legends about Charles originated in the twelfth century. His life was thought of, not as ascetic, but as holy, and the solemn canonisation in 1165 was the final step in the process.

No authentic portrait of Charles has come down to us, for the equestrian statuette from the Treasury of the Cathedral of Metz, which is now in the Carnevalet Museum at Paris, cannot be proved to be a contemporary representation. The long moustache of the otherwise beardless rider seems rather to belong to Charles the Bald. The first Western Emperor was large in body. The examination of the skeleton in the year 1861 shewed a length of nearly 6 ft. 4 in. But we cannot form a clearer idea of his external appearance, in spite of the excellent description which we owe to Einhard. This faithful counsellor and friend wrote his Life soon after the death of the great Emperor. His picture maintains its great value even though it can be proved to borrow its general, and even its particular, features from the biographies of Suetonius. Einhard made independent observations and drew the portrait of Charles with love and intelligence. We see the old Emperor before us with his majestic form, his round head resting upon a neck somewhat too short and thick, and covered with beautiful white hair, and with his kindly face from which looked the large quick eyes. We learn that much that was not beautiful, such as his too great corpulence, was forgotten on account of the symmetry of his limbs and his harmonious proportions. We learn that in the two last years of his life, when his body had become somewhat weakened through attacks of fever, his old vigorous gait had become a little feeble, owing to the halting of one leg. We hear the Emperor speaking in a curiously high voice, which was in marked contrast with the powerful form of the speaker. We have exact information even about the habits of his daily life, we see how Charles rises in the morning and receives his friends even while dressing, how he discharges the business of government, hears the reports of the Palsgraves, and decides difficult points of law. We learn how he was dressed, how he took hot baths, how fond he was of hunting and how he practised swimming, if possible in company with many others, how he ate much and drank very moderately, how he liked to hear music or to have some book read aloud during his chief meal. We even learn how he took a long rest in the middle of the day in summer, and how the activity of his mind disturbed his rest at night.

Einhard was depicting the monarch in his later years. But the picture does not shew the features of an old man. The vigour of the great king remained unbroken. The whole personality of Charles is made unusually human and brought very near to us by Einhard and by the popular stories of the Monk of St Gall. It is a personality of magic power from which no one can escape, of noble amiability, with a sense of humour, and naturally kind. Tender chords also echoed in this great soul, a deep love for his children, especially for his daughters, and he felt the need of close confidence on the part of his family. But there is not the pure honour of the simple father. His passion is always breaking out, a strong desire, to which the moral ideas of the age could set no limits, an unusually strong inclination for the other sex. And this strong nature, so accustomed to command and to expect obedience, could set no limits to his own desires. There was a remarkable licentiousness in the private life of the Emperor and his court, a want of discipline, immorality even in the eyes of a coarse age, an inclination for freedom and at the same time for what is great. Only he who was himself above rules and ordinances, demands unconditional submission to his will. For the simplicity of his character, his affability and popularity never did harm to his majesty or made him too free. From this great nature there issued a strength which mastered everything. It was a nature full of passion and yet of calm circumspection. Charles never formed important resolutions in his angry moments. He went his way without consideration for the rights or wishes of others, or for individuals of the different peoples, but did so only when he served the purpose of his high mission. This gave his actions invincible strength.

The wideness of his interests and his real understanding for the needs of the people is unique even amongst the greatest in history. His care was given to great things and small, even to the smallest matters—alike to the political, the social, the literary, and to the artistic life of the peoples. Everywhere he made ordinances, everywhere he gave encouragement, everywhere he took a personal part. Everywhere of course as the head of the community, everywhere as a man of action, as an intelligent leader of his people. He was no theorist, no dreamer, not a man of books. Quite pathetic is his endeavour to make himself acquainted with the elements of the culture of the time. In addition to German, he was

master of Latin and understood Greek. But his attempts to acquire
the art of writing had as little success as his endeavour to produce new
ideas in the sphere of Grammar or Chronology. He was no great scholar,
no abstract thinker. And so he shewed himself in his relation to the
Church and to theocratic ideas. In spite of all his interest in questions
of doctrine he had no deep or independent grasp of religious problems.
The teaching of the Church was for him an unassailable truth. From
this he derived his high sense of mission. He placed himself at the
service of theocratic ideas in order to combine them with his quest for
power. This gave his policy an unexpected moral strength. A sense
of the grace of God dominated his work from the very beginning. That
does not mean that he acted as a simple Christian man who is anxious
about the salvation of his soul, but as the Plenipotentiary of God who
has to maintain earthly order in the Christian sense. Necessarily connected with the Christian theocratic idea is all that would strengthen
authority in this world: on this then he seized, and this by virtue of his
naturally strong character he brought to accomplishment.

Charles looked upon his Empire as a Divine State. He felt that he
had been appointed by God as the earthly head of Christians. He read and
loved Augustine's book *de Civitate Dei.* He believed that he had set up
the *Civitas Dei,* in the second empirical sense, which Augustine placed
beside the *Civitas Dei* as the spiritual union of all saints under the
grace of God, as a great earthly organisation for the care of common
earthly needs in a manner pleasing to God, and for the worthy preparation for the better life in the world to come. Augustine, it is true, had
seen the empirical manifestation of the *Civitas Dei* in the universal
Catholic Church. Charles saw no contradiction. For him the ecclesiastical body and the secular were one. He was the head. And while
Augustine placed the Roman Empire as fourth in the order of world-
empires and as a *Civitas Terrena* in opposition to the Kingdom of God,
for Charles this dualism was no more—his *Imperium Romanum* is no
Civitas Terrena, it is identical with the earthly portion of the Church
founded by Christ. The words of Alcuin are significant: Charles rules
the kingdom of eternal peace founded by the Blood of Christ.

The Empire of Charles was intended to realise the Divine Kingdom
upon earth. On the one hand this answered to the great tendencies
which governed the life of the Christian peoples of the West, but on the
other it contradicted them. Government of the world by the laws of
Christ, uniformity of Christian organisation, universalism—these ideals
the new *Imperium Romanum* of Charles seemed to serve. But in the
Christian society there had long prevailed the idea of a Priesthood set
over the laity, the idea of the hierarchical order and of the Papal
Primacy—and these ideas demanded unity and universalism in the sense
that the supreme head of the Society could not be a secular monarch
but only the Bishop of Rome. Hence an imperial universalism could

not finally overcome that of the Curia. Two different currents were perceptible in the Christian-theocratic tendencies towards unity after the year 800, often working together, often against each other. And here it must be observed that the tendencies towards Priestly universal rule are as little to be regarded as specially Roman, as the tendencies towards the Theocratic-christian imperial power as specially German. Rather both were the outcome of a general Western development, and both have as their representatives both the Romance and the Germanic peoples. On the one hand the universal ecclesiastical views necessarily led again and again to a Priestly universal rule, and on the other hand the increasing political needs of the rising Romance and German nations necessarily caused a desire for the independence of the State.

The significance of Charles for the history of the world lies in this, that he transferred the theocratic idea of absolute sovereignty, which had begun to work as a great historical factor in Western history, from the sphere of the Roman Curia to the Frankish State. He prepared the way for the social institutions peculiar to the Middle Ages and at the same time opened the source of unavoidable wars. Of course there were general antecedents for this in the political life of the Franks and of the other Western peoples. But yet it was here that this mighty personality was an independent force.

CHAPTER XX.

FOUNDATIONS OF SOCIETY.

(ORIGINS OF FEUDALISM.)

THE whole period of European history extending roughly from
A.D. 476 to A.D. 1000 appears at first sight as an epoch of chaotic
fermentation in which it is almost impossible to perceive directing
principles and settled institutions. The mere influx of hordes of barbarians was bound to break up the frame of Roman civilisation and to
reduce it to its rudimentary elements. But what made confusion worse
confounded was the fact that the Teutonic, Slavonic, and Turanian
invaders had come with social arrangements of their own which did not
disappear at the mere contact with the Roman world, leaving, as it were,
a clean slate for new beginnings, but survived in a more or less shattered
and modified condition.

And yet when the eye becomes somewhat accustomed to the turmoil
of the dark ages, one cannot but perceive that certain principles and
institutions have had a guiding influence in this checkered Society,
that there is a continuous development from Roman or barbaric roots,
and that there is no other way to explain the course of events during
our period but to trace the working of both these elements of social
life.

One of the principles of concentration which seemed at the outset
to give fair promise of robust growth was kinship. Nature has taken
care to provide the most primitive human beings with ties of relationship
which raise them over individual isolation. Man and wife keep together,
parents rear up their children, and brothers are naturally allied against
strangers. Of course. much depends on the kind of union arising between
man and wife, on the share of each parent in the bringing up of children,
and on the views as to brotherhood and strangers. But before
examining the particular direction taken by these notions in the case of
the Teutonic tribes with whom we are primarily concerned, let us notice
the fact that, whatever shape the idea of kinship may have taken, it was
certainly productive of most important consequences in the arrangement
of early Germanic Society. When Caesar has to tell us about the

occupation of territory by a Germanic tribe he dwells on the fact that the tribal rulers and princes assign land to clans (*gentes*) and kindreds of men who have joined together (*cognationes hominum* qui una coierunt). We need not try to put a very definite meaning on the curious difference indicated by the two terms : it is sufficient for our present purpose to take note of the fact that the idea of kinship lies at the root of both : a Germanic tribe as described by Caesar was composed of clans and clan-like unions. And when Tacitus speaks of the military array of a tribe, he informs us that it was composed of families and kindreds (*familiae et propinquitates*). No wonder we read in the poem of Beowulf that the coward warrior disgraces his whole kindred and that the latter has to share in his punishment.

Like the Roman *gentes*, the Greek γένη, the Keltic clans and septs, the kindreds of the Teutonic tribes were based on *agnatic* relationship, that is on relationship through men, the unmarried women remaining in the family of their fathers or brothers while the married women and their offspring joined the families of their husbands. There are not many traces of an earlier " matriarchal" constitution of Society, except the fact mentioned by Tacitus, that the Teutons considered the maternal uncle with special respect and, indeed, in taking hostages, attributed more importance to that form of relationship than to the tie between father and son. It is not unlikely that this view goes back to a state of affairs when the mother stood regularly under the protection of her brother and her children were brought up by him and not by their father. The mother's kin maintained a certain subsidiary recognition even in later days: it never ceased to be responsible for the woman which came from it, and always afforded her protection in case of grievous ill-treatment by the husband; a protection which in some cases might extend to children. Nevertheless in the ordinary course of affairs, the father's authority was fully recognised and the families and kindreds of the host must have been chiefly composed of agnatic groups bearing distinctive names from real or supposed ancestors and tracing their descent from him through a succession of males. In Norse custom these agnatic relations formed the so-called *bauggildi*, that is the group entitled to receive, and to pay, the armrings of gold constituting the fine for homicide. The payment and reception of fines are, of course, the other side of the protection afforded by the kindred to its members. Not the State but the kindred was primarily appealed to in the case of aggression, and the *maegths, aets, Geschlechter, farae*, or whatever the kindreds were called by different tribes, resorted to private war in order to enforce their claims and to wreak revenge on offenders. It is easy to picture to ourselves the importance of such an institution by the contrast it presents to present social arrangements, but in order to realise fully how complex this system came to be, let us cast a glance at the distribution of fines in one of the Norwegian laws—in the so-called

Frostathingslov regulating the legal customs of the north-western province of Throndhjem[1].

In this *Frostathingslov* we read first in case six marks of gold are adjudged, what everyone shall take and give of the rings (*baugar*). The slayer or the slayer's son shall pay all the rings unless he has '*vissendr*' to help him. The question is, who are called so, and here is the answer. " If the father of the slayer is alive, or his sons or brothers, father's brother or brother's son, cousins or sons of cousins, they are all called ' *vissendr*.' And they are so called because they are sure (*viss*) of paying the fines which are to be paid... (c. 3). The slayer or the slayer's son shall pay to the son of the slain the principal ring of the six marks of gold, namely five marks of weighted silver. The father of the slayer shall pay as much to the father of the dead ; the brother of the slayer shall pay the brother of the dead four marks less two oras ; the father's brothers and the sons of the brother (of the slayer) shall pay to the father's brothers and to the sons of the brother of the slain 20 oras. And the first cousins and their sons...shall pay...13 oras and an ' *örtog*.'..."

By the side of the *bauggildi*, the agnatic group bearing the principal brunt of collisions and claiming the principal compensation payments, appear the *nefgildi*, the personal supporters of the slain, respectively—of the offended man. These are connected with him through his female relations. Together with the *bauggildi* group they would form what was termed a *cognatio* by the Romans, that is the entire circle of kinsmen. The relative importance attached to the two sides of relationship was generally expressed by a surrender of two-thirds of the *wergeld*, the slain man's price, to the father's kin and of one-third to the mother's kin. With mother's kin, however, one would have to reckon also the relations through sisters, aunts, nieces, etc. In fact the *nefgildi* would correspond to what the continental Germans called the *spindle side* of relationship, while the *bauggildi* constituted the *spear side*. For purposes of organisation the *spear side* formed a solid group, while the *spindle side* was divided among several agnatic groups according to the position of the husbands of women supposed to carry the spindles.

The natural advantage of the *bauggildi* or spear kindred found another expression in the fact that in the earlier customary law of Teutonic tribes women were not admitted to inherit land. It was reserved to men as fighting members of the kindred, and the coat of mail went with the land inheritance. (*Lex Angliorum et Werinorum*, 6.) Besides the power of protecting and revenging its members the kindred exercised a number of other functions: it acted as a contracting party in settling marriages with members of other kindreds ; it exercised the right of wardship in regard to minors ; it provided a family tribunal in

---

[1] Though the Norwegian and other Scandinavian laws are late in their present text, they are based on archaic customs, and are commonly used by scholars to ascertain the *principles* of ancient Germanic law.

case of certain grievous offences against unwritten family law, especially in the case of adultery; it supported those of its members who had been economically ruined and were unable to maintain themselves; it had to guarantee to public authorities the good behaviour of its members if they were not otherwise trustworthy.

Altogether the German system of kinship at starting resembled that of Greece and Italy and of the Keltic tribes as a comprehensive arrangement of society on clan-lines. One of the most momentous turning-points in the history of the race consists in the fact that Germanic Commonwealths did not, on the whole, continue to develop in this direction. The natural kindreds were too much broken and mixed up by the migrations, the protracted struggle with the Romans and the confusion of the settlement on conquered soil. There was a loss of that continuity of tradition and comparative isolation which contributed powerfully to shape the tribal arrangements of other Aryan races, more especially of the Kelts of Scotland, Wales and Ireland, and of the Slavs in the Balkan mountains. It is interesting to notice, however, that where the necessary seclusion and continuity of tradition did exist a complicated federation of clans might spring up. The classical case within the region of Germanic settlements is that of the Ditmarschen in Schleswig-Holstein.

"The *propinquitates, parentelae, proximi* (of the Ditmarschen), German *Vründ,* or as they are called in charters from the fourteenth century the *Slachten, Geschlechter* (kindreds), are close associations, the members of which are bound to help each other in private war and revenge, before the courts and in case of economic difficulties. They are very different in size, the largest being that of the Wollermannen who, as Neocorus tells us, were able to send 500 warriors into the field. It happens that the kindreds admit new men after an examination of their worth....Most kindreds originate in voluntary leagues or associations. But the right to membership is inherited by all male descendants. The kindreds (*Geschlechter*) are subdivided accordingly into narrower groups of kinsmen—the *Kluften* and brotherhoods[1]."

Although as a rule the arrangement on lines of relationship declined steadily and rapidly, we witness the existence and operations of kindreds in most Western countries in the earlier centuries of the Middle Ages. The Alemannic Law, for instance, tells us that disputes as to land are carried on by kindreds (*genealogiae*), and a Frankish edict of 571 asserts the right of direct descendants and brothers to inherit land against traditional claims of neighbours which could only have been based on the conception of a kindred owning the land of the township. (*Edictum Chilperici,* 3.) The Burgundians were settled in *farae,* and among the Bavarians five kindreds enjoyed special consideration. In a Bavarian charter of 750 the kindreds of the Agilolfings and of Fagana grant land

[1] Sering, *Erbrecht- und Agrarverfassung in Schleswig-Holstein,* p. 124.

to a bishop of Freising. In these cases the kindreds are represented by certain leaders and their *consortes et participes*[1]. The *maegths* of the Angles and Saxons, the *aets* of the Scandinavians appear often in legal custom and historical narratives, and, in the light of such continental parallels, it seems more than probable (though this has been disputed) that a good number of English place-names containing the suffix *ing* were derived from settlements of kindreds. The Aescingas, Effingas, Getingas, Wocingas, mentioned in Saxon charters in Surrey, as well as numbers of similar names, have left an abiding trace in local nomenclature.

In this way the kindreds did not disappear from the history of Western Europe without leaving many traces, and such traces were most noticeable in the case of noble families keenly interested in tracing their pedigrees and able to keep their cohesion and privileges. But even of the nobility the greater part of them arose through the success of new men and especially through service remunerated by kings and other potentates. As for the rest of the people it became more and more difficult to keep up the neatly framed groups of kinsmen. From being definite organisations the kindreds were diverted into the position of aggregates of persons claiming certain rights and obligations in regard to each other. The complicated *wergeld* protection ceases to be enforceable. A man's life is still taxed at a certain sum, but this sum will be levied under the authority of the government, and this government will try to prevent feuds and even to legislate against the economic ruin in which innocent persons are involved by the misdeeds of their relations.

The same *Frostathingslov*, from which I have quoted a paragraph as to the distribution of rings of *wergeld*, is very much concerned about the disorder and disasters which follow on blood feuds. (*Inledning*, 8): " It is known to all to what extent a perverse custom has prevailed in this country, namely that in the case of a homicide the relatives of the slain try to pick out from the kindred him who is best (for revenge), although he may have been neither wishing, willing nor present, when they do not want to avenge the homicide on the slayer even if they have the means." And in Eadmund I's legislation we find enactments which free the *magas*, the kindred, from all responsibility for the misdeeds of the kinsman, unless they want of their own accord to come to his help in the matter of paying off the fine.

As regards the very important department of landed property, the collective right of kinsmen as to land yields to customs of inheritance which still savour of the original view that individuals only use the land while the kindred is the real owner, but the conception is embodied in a series of consecutive individual claims. In Norway, for instance, *ōdal* land ought to remain in the kindred, but this means that if some possessor wishes to sell it, he has to offer it to the heirs at law for

---

[1] Bitterauf, *Traditionen des Hochstifts Freising*, I. p. 5, quoted by Brunner, *Deutsche Rechtsgeschichte*, XII. p. 117 n. 33.

pre-emption, and that even after a sale to a stranger has been effected the rightful heir may reclaim the land by paying somewhat less than the sum given for it by the outsider.

Let us, however, go back to a time when the social co-operation and defensive alliance of a group of strong men was recognised as a most efficient means of getting on in the world and of meeting possible aggression. People born and bred in a mental atmosphere instinct with such views were not likely to surrender them easily even if circumstances were against their realisation on the basis of natural kinship. Blood relationship is surrounded by artificial associations assimilated to relationship, and acting as its substitutes—by adoption, artificial brotherhood, and voluntary associations of different kinds. The practice of adoption did not attain in Teutonic countries the importance it assumed in India, Greece or Rome. One of the causes of its lesser significance lay in the early predominance of Christianity which prevented Germanic heathendom from developing too powerfully the side of ancestor-worship. But yet we find practices of adoption constantly mentioned in different Teutonic countries. The adopted father became, of course, a patron and leader and, on the other hand, looked to his adopted son for support and efficient help. The ceremony of setting the new child on the parent's knee was a fitting expression of the tie created by adoption. A certain difficulty in the reading of our evidence as to adoption arises, however, from the fact that a "foster-father," as well as a "foster-mother," was sought, not for the sake of protection and lordship, but for providing the material care needed by children under age. The great people of those days were often loth to devote their time and attention to such humble occupations, and a common device was to quarter a boy with a dependent, a churl of some kind, who would have to act as a proper foster-father in rearing the child in the same way as a nurse would do for infants. A curious example of the contrast between the two forms of artificial fatherhood is presented by the Norse Saga of King Hákon, Aethelstan's foster-son. Young Hákon is sent by his father Harald to the court of the powerful ruler of England, King Aethelstan, who receives him kindly and lets him sit on his knee, adopting him thereby as his son. No sooner has the boy sat down on the knee of the monarch of Britain than he claims Aethelstan as Harald's vassal, because he has taken up the duty of a foster-father. In Scandinavian laws adoption in the form of *aetleiding*, admission to the kindred, appears complicated with emancipation from slavery. The unfree man receiving his freedom drinks "emancipation ale" with the members of his new kindred and afterwards steps into a shoe roughly prepared from the hide of an ox's foreleg. This latter ceremony symbolises the coming in of the new member of the kindred into all the rights and privileges of the kinsmen who have admitted him into their midst. The connexion between both sides of this rite—adoption and emancipation—seems to be provided by the frequent recourse to *aetleiding* in the case of sons born to Scandinavian warriors by their unfree concubines. But the ceremonies are characteristic of any kind of adoption bringing new blood and new claimants into a kindred of old standing.

Another form of union constantly occurring in Teutonic Societies was artificial brotherhood. A common practice for starting it was to exchange weapons; sometimes each of the would-be brothers made a cut on his arm or chest and mixed the blood flowing from it with that of his comrade. The newly created tie of brotherhood was usually confirmed by an oath; a historical instance of this variety is presented by the arrangement between Canute and Eadmund Ironside. This kind of artificial relationship lent itself readily to the formation of fresh associations not engrafted on existing kindreds, but carrying the idea of close alliance into the sphere of voluntary unions. We hear of "affratationes" among Lombards, of "hermandades" in Spain, and the English gilds are a species of the same kind. The Anglo-Saxon laws tell us of gilds of wayfarers, who evidently found it necessary to seek mutual support outside the ordinary family groups. In the later centuries of Anglo-Saxon history gilds appear as religious and economic, as well as military institutions, and they are closely akin to Norse associations of the same name.

Here are some paragraphs from the statutes of the thanes gild in Cambridge organised some time in the eleventh century: "That then is first, that each should give oath on the holy relics to the others, before the world, and all should support those who have the greatest right. If any gild-brother die, let all the gildship bring him to where he desired...and let the gild defray half the expenses of the funeral festival after the dead....And if any gild-brother stand in need of his fellows' aid it be made known to his neighbour...and if the neighbour neglect it, let him pay one pound....And if anyone slay a gild-brother, let there be nothing for compensation but eight pounds, but if the slayer scorns to pay the compensation, let the whole gildship avenge their fellow....And if any gild-brother slay a man...and the slain be a twelfe hynde man, let each gild-brother contribute a half-mark for his aid; if the slain be a ceorl two oras; if he be Welsh one ora."

The principles of artificial relationship were easily carried over into the domain of rural husbandry and landed property. A custom with which one has to reckon in all Teutonic countries is the joint household, the large family of grown-up descendants living and working with their father or grandfather. It may also consist of brothers and cousins continuing to manage their affairs in common after the death of the father or grandfather. In the first case the practice implies a reluctance to emancipate grown-up sons and to cut out separate plots for them. In the second case the joint household gives a peculiar cast to Succession. The partners are *Ganerben*, joint heirs, and each has an ideal share in the common household which falls to his children or accrues to his fellows on his death. The *Ganerbschaft* proved an important expedient in order to reconcile the equality of personal rights among co-heirs with the unity of an efficient household. But the existence of the "joint inheritance" was not enforced by law: it resulted from agreement and tradition and could be dissolved at any given moment.

The tenacity and wide diffusion of these unions in practice prove the value of such co-operative societies and the strength of the habits of mind generated by relationship. The same causes operated to give a communal cast to economic associations formed by neighbours or instituted by free agreement among strangers. We cannot generally trace the rural unions of the mark, the township, the *by*, to one or the other definite cause. In some cases they must have grown out of the settlement of natural kindreds; in other instances they were generated by the necessity of combining for the purpose of settling claims of neighbours and arranging the forms of their co-operation; in many cases, again, they were the product of the settlement of colonising associations or military conquerors. But in all these instances the people forming the rural group were accustomed by their traditions of natural or artificial kinship to allow a large share for the requirements of the whole and to combine individual efforts and claims. The contrast between individualism and communalism was not put in an abstract and uncompromising manner. Both principles were combined according to the lie of the land, the density of population, the necessities of defence, the utility of co-operation. In mountain country the settlements would spread, while on flat land they would profit by concentration. Forest clearings would be occupied by farms of scattered pioneers; the wish to present a close front to enemies might produce nucleated villages. At the same time, even in cases of scattered settlements there would be scope left for mutual support and the exercise of rights of commons as to wood and pasture, while in concentrated villages the communalistic features would extend to the allotment regulation and management of agricultural strips. But all these expedients, though suggested by custom, were not in the nature of hard and fast rules, and in the face of strong inducements they were departed from. A new settler joining a rural community of old standing had to be admitted by all the shareholders of the territory, but if he had succeeded in remaining undisturbed for a year and a day or in producing a special licence to migrate from the King, he could not be ousted any more. A householder who had special opportunities as an employer of slaves, freedmen or free tenants, could easily acquire ground for his exclusive use and start on an individualistic basis.

There is ample evidence to shew that in the earlier centuries the

CH. XX.

customs and arrangements of kindreds and of associations resembling them were widely prevalent, while private occupation formed an exception. Matters were greatly changed by the conquest of provinces with numberless Roman estates in full working order and with a vast population accustomed to private ownership and individualistic economy. But it took some time even then to displace old-fashioned habits, and in the northern parts of France, in England, in Germany, and in the Scandinavian countries communalistic features in the treatment of arable and pasture asserted themselves all through the Middle Ages as more consonant with extensive tillage and a complex intermixture of the claims of single householders. The point will have to be examined again in another connexion, but it is material to emphasise at once that the rural arrangements of Teutonic nations were deeply coloured by practices generated during an epoch when relations of kindreds and similar associations were powerful.

The possibility for strong and wealthy men to make good their position as individual owners and magnates was partly derived from a germ existing in every Teutonic household, namely from the power of the ruler of such a household over the inmates of it, both free and unfree. Even a ceorl, that is a common free man, was master in his own house and could claim compensation for the breach of his fence or an infraction of the peace of his home. In the case of the King and other great men the fenced court became a burgh, virtually a fortress. Every ruler of a household, whether small or great, had to keep his sons, slaves and clients in order and was answerable for their misdeeds. On the other hand he was their patron, offered them protection, had to stand by them in case of oppression from outsiders and claimed compensation for any wrong inflicted on them. In this way by the side of the family and of the gild or voluntary association of equals another set of powerful ties was recognised by legal custom and political authority— the relations between a patron and his clients or dependents. The lines of both sets of institutions might coincide, as for instance, when the chieftain of a kindred acted as the head of a great household, or when a gild of warriors joined under the leadership of a famous war-chief. But they might also run across each other and develop independently : there were no means to make everything fit squarely into its place.

The contrast between the permanent arrangements of the tribes and the shifting relations springing from personal subjection and devotion seemed very striking to Roman observers. Tacitus in his tract on the site and usages of Germany describes the institution of the *comitatus*, the following gathered around a chief. While in the tribe the stress is laid on the unconquerable spirit of independence and the lack of discipline of German warriors, in the *comitatus* Tacitus dwells on exactly opposite features. The follower, though of free and perhaps of noble descent, looks up to his chief, fights for his glory, ascribes his own feats of arms to his patron, seems to revel in self-abnegation and dependence. Of course, such authority is acquired and kept up only by brilliant exploits and successful raids, so that if a particular tribe gets slack in these respects, its youths are apt to leave home and to flock abroad around warriors who achieve fame and obtain booty. Thus the *comitatus* appeared chiefly as a school of military prowess and young men entered it as soon as they were deemed fit to receive arms. It was capable of developing into a mighty and permanent political factor. Arminius and Marbod were not merely tribal chiefs but also leaders of military followings, and it is difficult to make out in every instance whether the greater part of a barbaric chieftain's authority was due to his tribal position or to his sway over his followers.

The peculiar features of Germanic social organisation were greatly modified by the conquest of Roman provinces and the formation of extensive states in the interior of Germany and in Scandinavian countries. The loose tribal bonds make way for territorial unions and Kingship arises everywhere as a powerful factor of development. As regards territorial arrangements the *hundred* appears as a characteristic unit in nearly all countries held by Teutonic nations. It seems based on approximate estimates of the number of units of husbandry, of typical free households in a district; each of these households had to contribute equally to the requirements of taxation and of the host, while the heads or representatives of all formed the ordinary popular courts. Such territorial divisions could not, of course, be framed with mathematical regularity and even less could they be kept up in the course of centuries according to definite standards, but the idea of equating territorial units according to the number of households proves deeply rooted and reappears, *e.g.*, in England in the artificial hundreds based on the hundred hides of the Dane law assessment.

By the side of these more or less artificial combinations rose the *Gaue* (*pagi*), or shires, mostly derived from historical origins, as territories settled by tribes or having formed separate commonwealths at some particular time. Such were, for instance, the south-eastern shires of England—Kent, Sussex, Essex, Norfolk, Suffolk, etc.

Roman writers lay stress on the tendency of Germanic nations towards autonomy of the different provinces and subdivisions of the tribe. Caesar says that in time of peace they had no common rulers but that the princes of regions and districts administered justice and settled disputes among their own people. A section of a tribe, a *gau* as it was styled, could sometimes follow its own policy: Ingviomer's *pagus*, *e.g.*, did not join with the rest of the Cherusci in Arminius' war with the Romans. But continual military operations not only forced the tribes to form larger leagues, but also to submit to more concentrated and active authorities. Kingships arose in this connexion and Tacitus tells us that royal power exercised a great influence in modifying the internal organisation of the people. It was hostile to the traditional noble houses which might play the part of dangerous rivals, and it surrounded itself with submissive followers whom it helped to promotion and wealth so that freedmen protected by the King often surpassed men of free and even of noble descent. Tacitus' remarks on the social influence of Kingship are fully borne out by the state of affairs after the Conquest.

It is clear that the occupation of extended territory over which Germanic warriors were more or less dispersed contributed powerfully to strengthen the hands of the King. Without any definite change in the constitution, by the sheer force of distance and the diversion caused by private concerns the King became the real representative of the nation in its collective life. There could be no question of gathering the popular assembly for one of those republican meetings described by Tacitus where Kings and princes appeared as speakers, not as chiefs, and had to persuade their audience instead of giving commands. Thus the popular assemblies of the Franks degenerated into gatherings of the military array which took place once a year in the spring, first in March, later on in May. These meetings were not unimportant as they brought together the King and his folk and offered an occasion for some legislation and a good deal of private intercourse with persons who came from distant parts of the Kingdom. But the assembly was not organised for systematic political action or for regular administrative business. So the King remained the real ruler of his people in peace and war, and the persons he had to reckon with were the princes of his house, the officers of his household, magnates of different kinds, and the clergy. The absence of a definite constitution gave rise to a great deal of violence: indeed violence seems to have been the moving power of government. It impressed people's imagination and even wise rulers could not dispense with it. The famous story of the Soissons chalice is characteristic of the whole course of affairs in Gaul under the Merovingian Kings. Clovis tries to save a precious chalice for the Church after the taking of Soissons and puts it by as an extra share of the loot. A common Frankish soldier, however, does not want to submit to any such privilege and cleaves the chalice with a stroke of his battle-axe. "The King is not to have more than his share," he explains, and Clovis dares not curb his unruly follower in the presence of comrades who evidently would have sympathised with the latter. He bides his time and at the next review cleaves the man's head, in remembrance of the chalice of Soissons.

Everything depended on the personal authority of the King and on his exploits. Theodoric the son of Clovis persuades his army to take part in an expedition against Burgundy. When he plans a campaign against the Thuringians he takes care to incite the wrath of the Franks by describing the misdeeds and offences committed by their enemies. But if the King and the host are not of the same opinion, an unpopular

King is exposed to contumelious treatment. Gregory of Tours tells the story of an altercation between Chlotar I and his host. The Frankish warriors wanted to fight the Saxons while the King urged them to desist from this plan and warned them that if they went to war against his will he would not go with them. Thereupon they waxed wroth and threw themselves on the King, tore up his tent, assailed him with exasperating abuse and threatened to kill him if he did not come with them. He went with them against his wish, and they were beaten. The great means for upholding power under these circumstances was to act with relentless cruelty against enemies or rivals. The annals of Merovingian Gaul are especially notorious in this respect, but they exhibit feelings and moods which are characteristic to some extent of the whole barbaric world of those times. We read in the life of St Didier of Cahors of the wrath of a king who decreed terrible things: some were maimed, others killed, others sent into exile, others again thrown into prison for life[1]. Guntram of Burgundy swore that he would destroy the household of a rebel up to the ninth generation in order to put a stop to the pernicious custom of murdering kings. Sometimes this policy, worthy of wild beasts, achieved its aim of spreading terror, and a tyrant like Chilperic might think that he had it in his power to command anything he wished, *e.g.* to reform the alphabet, to improve the dogma of the Trinity and to impose baptism on all the Jews. But the general result was that when the flush of conquest had passed and the danger of further invasions seemed remote, all the springs and ties which hold and move society gave way. Men ceased to care for the Commonwealth, everyone was intent on his private lust and lucre. These appalling results are ascribed in as many words by Frankish chiefs to this same King Guntram, who swore to exterminate rebels and all their kith and kin. "What shall we do," they said, "when the whole people is affected by vice and everyone finds delectation in iniquity? No one fears the King, no one has any reverence for a duke or a count, and should this state of things displease some of the rulers—seditions rise at once, disturbances begin."

However great the disorder of these lawless times, certain institutional features stand out as the principal means of government. The *comitatus* described above on the strength of the narrative of Tacitus, did not disappear but rather grew in importance after the Conquest. To begin with it encountered on Roman soil a relation which had most probably sprung from the same Germanic root, but had acquired new strength under Imperial rule. I mean the so-called *bucellarii* which appear definitely in the Roman Empire from 395, but are connected with the older practice of employing Germans and other barbarians as guardsmen of the Emperors and of generals. The *bucellarius* was a soldier who

---

[1] *Vita Desiderii Caturcensis,* c. 5, quoted by Waitz, *Deutsche Verfassungsgeschichte,* II. p. 195.

had taken service by private agreement with a military chief. The term is derived from *bucella*, a roll or biscuit of better quality than the ordinary bread provided for the use of soldiers. Thus the very name of these hired warriors implied a privileged treatment. They received their military outfit from their chiefs and on their death this outfit was returned to the commander. Troops of men enlisted on such lines came to play a great part in the wars of the fifth and sixth centuries. Belisarius' best soldiers were private followers of this kind gathered from among warlike barbarian tribes: among others Huns were greatly appreciated as light cavalry. The Visigothic kings also kept troops of *bucellarii* as a regular part of their army. In other Germanic kingdoms we find the followers (*comites*) under different names, but always in similar employment. In fact the different terms afford some indication in regard to what was expected from the follower. They were *gasindi*, *gesith* (*Gesinde*) of their chiefs, that is, servants. The same notion of service was expressed by the German *degen*, the Anglo-Saxon *thegen* (minister), while *hiredma* (A.S.), *hirdr* (Norse), *hzidian* (Russian) point to the fact that the follower was a member of the household of his chief. An expression derived from the tie of mutual fidelity is *antrustio* (Frank. from *trust*—fidelity, protection and troop of confederates). The Danish sources use *vederlag* (Society) while the German lay more stress on the fact that the members of the association are followers (*Gefolge*, cf. A.S. *folgere*, *folgod*).

The relation is generally initiated by two acts: firstly, the submission of the follower to his chief as symbolised by the former stretching out his folded hands which the latter receives in his own; secondly, an oath of fidelity by which the follower promised to support his lord and to be true and faithful to him in every respect. The corresponding duties of the lord were to afford protection to his followers and to keep them well. The Beowulf poem presents a vivid description of the life of a following, a *comitatus*, of this kind—the communion in peace and war, the common feasting in the hall, the moral obligations incurred by the parties to the agreement. It shews also that the *hird* or *gesith* was differentiated into two halves—the elder councillors and the younger fighters (*duguth* and *gogoth*—excellence and youth), exactly in the same way as the "friends" of a Russian chief (*drujina*) were distinguished as the seniors and the juniors. The chief provided the outfit for his followers—horses, swords, coats of mail, shields—but this outfit went back to him on the death of the follower. This is the origin of the *heregeatu* (heriot) of the English followers, so well illustrated by many charters (*e.g.* Earle, *Land Charters*, 223, Will of Abp Aelfric) and by the legislation of Canute. There was no obstacle to the collection of a following by any free warrior; followings are distinctly admitted by Franks, Lombards, Scandinavians and Anglo-Saxons to all who can attract them, and this is characteristic of the rudimentary state of

public law in those times, inasmuch as the holding of armed retainers
who have sworn fidelity to their chief does not agree well with any
properly organised government. As a matter of fact, the keeping of a
following was mostly restricted by economic considerations to powerful
magnates, chieftains and kings. Under ordinary circumstances the
outlay was too great for common free men. But, of course, if there
appeared a prospect of looting or of starting on adventures there was
nothing to prevent famous warriors from collecting a *hird* of their own,
and the Viking raids were to a great extent the results of such private
enterprise.

When tribes settled down and territorial governments were put into
shape, the following became an *instrumentum regni* and the King's
following, his *trustes* or *gesith*, assumed an exceptional importance.
With the Goths of Theodoric and Athalaric the *Sajones* became a body
of officials. The Ostrogothic kings employed them not only as a body-
guard, but as messengers, as revising officers, as commissioners provided
with special powers and not only exempt from ordinary jurisdiction but
sent to control the regular members of the administration. In the same
way the King's thegns of later Anglo-Saxon history become a privileged
official class, without whom no government can be carried on and
who lead in the host, in the Witenagemot and in the moots of the
shires and hundreds. The *huskarls* of the Danish period were in
a similar position. Their service as a fighting body-guard is well ex-
emplified by the battle of Hastings and other events of the eleventh
century; but let us also remember that they were used, among other
things, to collect the *geld*, as may be seen from the story of the two
huskarls of Harthacnut who were killed at Worcester. In England as
well as in France or Italy the situation was much complicated by the
fact that a great number of the followers were settled by their chiefs
on separate estates and thus ceased to be ordinary members of the
chiefs' households. Still a seat in the King's hall along with an estate
of five hides was deemed one of the distinctive privileges of a King's
thegn.

This point raises the question: What means had a government of
those times to carry on its work? In every political organisation there
must be some sources of income to defray expenses, or else the population must be made to provide for necessary contingencies by compulsory
services of different kinds. Where did the governments of Italy, of
France, of England get their money and how were the contributions of
the people towards political organisation collected and administered?
Nowadays these questions would present no difficulties. We are
taught by bitter experience that any effort in the preparation for
war, or in judicial organisation, or in improvement of roads and
sanitary conditions has to be paid for by an increase of taxes and
rates. Therefore it will be rather difficult for us to realise that early

medieval governments had no taxes or rates to speak of at their disposal. The complex and oppressive system of Roman taxation could not be kept up: already in the late years of the Empire its overburdened subjects sought refuge with the barbarians in order to escape from tax collectors. After the downfall of Imperial rule, all the efforts of barbarian kings to maintain systematic taxation were in vain. They called forth insurrections, and even more powerful was a passive resistance in which all persons concerned joined more or less. Taxes broke up into customary payments, and were mixed up in an inextricable manner with rents and profits originating in private ownership.

Here are extracts from two Lombard grants illustrating the confusion between public and private payments and rents. King Aistulf gave some land to the monastery of St Lawrence in Bergamo (A.D. 755) and added the following exemptions from tribute and dues: "Donamus in suprascripta ecclesia omnes scuvias (excubias—repairs of roads and bridges) et utilitates quas homines exinde in puplico habuerunt ad consuetudinem faciendum excepto quando utilitas fuerit ce(n)sus faciendum ubi consuetudinem habuerint, nam ab aliis scuviis et utilitatibus puplicis quieti permaneant[1]." The peasantry on the estates of the said monastery are thus freed from road-making, bridge-making and other public work, although the right to levy a tax (*census*) *where it is customary* is reserved. And here is a fragment from a donation of a certain deacon Gallus: "Ipsa suprascripta casa cum suprascriptis massariis (colonis) ividem resedentem aliut redditum non facias, nec angarias, nec nulla scufias ad ipsa suprascripta Dei Ecclesia, nisi tantum per singulos annos quattuor modia grano, uno animale quale abuerit; pro camissia tremisse uno, una libra cera, uno sistario mel et amplius nulla dationem aut scufia perexsolvant, quia mihi sic actum est[2]." The donor fixed the amount of dues in favour of the monastery according to the custom followed in his own time and exempts expressly the *coloni* of the estate he is granting from all payments and services, except some specified customary rents in kind. The occasional *dationes* and *collectae* which were still levied did not constitute a regular fiscal system, and it may be said that the principal traces of such a system in the earlier Middle Ages are connected with progresses of the King and of Royal officers, who had to be fed and provided with the necessities of life according to a certain customary scale. This is the origin of the so-called *feorms* of rights, of which we hear a good deal in Domesday and in Anglo-Saxon sources. Corresponding arrangements of compulsory hospitality are reported from other places and these could easily be turned into a regular system of provender rents to be levied in the domanial courts of the King.

---

[1] *Monumenta historiae patriae*, XIII. p. 33, 15.
[2] Troya, *Codice diplomatico Langobardo*, IV. pp. 331, 620, A.D. 748.

In the laws of King Ine of Wessex we find the following curious account of the provender rents due from 10 hides of land: 10 casks honey, 300 loaves of bread, 12 buckets of Welsh ale, 30 of clear ale, 2 full grown oxen or 10 wethers, 10 geese, 20 chickens, 10 pieces of cheese, one bucketful of butter, 5 salmon, 20 pounds of fodder and 100 eels (Ine, 70, 1).

The Carlovingian restoration and especially the desperate struggles against the Norsemen compelled the populations of Western Europe to submit to new forms of direct taxation. Of these the most formidable and the best known is the Danegeld; but a detailed account of it must be given elsewhere. But even the Danegeld and the continental impositions corresponding to it were never meant to cover the entire cost of administration. They were chiefly designed to meet extraordinary expenditure, to pay off pirates, to raise heavy contributions of war, etc. In this way the question as to the ordinary means of meeting the requirements of administration has still to be answered. And the answer is clear. The regular administration of medieval States was kept up from the proceeds of crown domains. This point of view is clearly expressed, for instance, in a letter of Bede to Archbishop Ecgbert of York in which the famous historian complains of the reckless squandering of the Kings' estates, while their property should be considered as a fund for the outfit of soldiers and officials. The connexion between landholding and public service was underlined almost to a fault by historical writers until a German scholar, Paul Roth, argued that the Merovingian land charters do not shew any special obligation on the part of the donees and are, in fact, one-sided grants in full property without any agreement as to service attached to them and without any reserved right of confirmation or resumption in favour of the donor. From a technical point of view Roth was quite right: a Merovingian grant does not disclose on the face of it the implied connexion between tenure and service. But the mere fact that such grants of property in land became the regular means of recompensing services to the State is in itself of the greatest consequence. Indeed it may be said that such unconditional grants were more dangerous for the sovereign power in the State than actual *beneficia* with a clearly expressed condition attached to them, because it was impossible to go on remunerating services by grants of estates in full ownership without exhausting the stock in land.

A government proceeding on such lines was sure to be soon confronted by an empty exchequer and no legal means to refill it. But though no juridical condition was formulated, the Frankish or Lombard government never lost sight of the *beneficia* and their holders. The notion that men who had received such *beneficia* were expected to be especially eager in their service to the kings was not only a precept of morals, but led to practical consequences. Officials who had called forth the displeasure of their masters would very likely see their *beneficia* confiscated. In England the confiscation of book-land in case of treason or neglect of military duty was recognised by law. Lombard practice shews another curious expedient for asserting the superior right of the Sovereign in regard to estates granted to followers. They were often given in usufruct without charter so that the donee enjoyed only a matter of fact possession without any legal right and could be ousted at pleasure. As a higher degree of favour this precarious tenure of the estate was exchanged for a regular title to it. Thus the earlier period of medieval life may be characterised by the words— a *régime* based on grants of usufruct and of ownership in land. This fund was nearly exhausted in France towards the end of the first dynasty, and in consequence the monarchy itself was weakened in every respect and the Merovingian rulers had sunk into the state of *rois fainéants*— good-for-nothing kings, while real authority rested with the managers of the privy purse and palace stewards—the *majores domus*.

The national revival occasioned by the necessity to defend Christian Society against the Arabs on one side, and heathen Germans on the other, took the shape of a concentration of power in the hands of the Carlovingian dynasty. And the first thing the new rulers had to do was to replenish the domanial fund and to reorganise the methods of granting estates. In order to acquire the necessary land capital nothing was left but to lay hands on part of the enormous landed property which had been accumulated by the Church. The earlier Carlovingian rulers, more especially Charles Martel, simply appropriated ecclesiastical estates to endow their military retainers. Another device was to quarter soldiers on monasteries and even to appoint officers lay abbots of wealthy ecclesiastical foundations. With Pepin the Short and his brother Carloman these irregular methods savouring of downright pillage were abandoned and a kind of compromise between State and Church was arrived at. We are told that in 751 a "division" of estates took place. Some were given back to the Church, while other lands were registered as "precarious loans" (*precariae verbo regis*) conceded to laymen by ecclesiastical institutions at the request of the King and on condition of the payment of a rent of about one-fifth of the income (*nonae et decimae*) to the owners of the land.

This system was based on the distinct recognition of the superior domain of the Church and on a division of the proceeds between two masters, between the holders of the eminent and of the useful domain, as we might be tempted to put it in conformity with later terminology, although from the point of view of eighth century law the estate of the tenant was not a form of ownership, of *dominium*, at all, but a precarious tenancy. As a matter of custom, however, these tenancies soon grew to be recognised as estates of inheritance conditioned by the performance of certain duties to the King as well as by the payment of rents to the Church. The process described exerted a great deal of influence on the formation of a general doctrine as to *beneficia* in which the conditional character of such donations was emphasised and carried to practical consequences. The Carlovingians worked the administrative apparatus of their empire, as formerly, by means of land-grants, but these grants created definitely conditional tenements. Although as a rule the son succeeded the father as to the "benefice" he was made to ask for a confirmation of his father's estate and might be obliged to pay something for this confirmation. In case of a change in the person of the owner, the superior or senior lord, the practice of resuming the ownership of benefices and of issuing them again under new grants began also to come in. Thus the technical aspect of the practice of feoffment was gradually evolved. In England the process is not characterised by such clearly marked stages, but on the whole the practice of grants of loan-land and book-land followed in the same direction, the form of "loans" being used for constituting tenements which it was especially desirable to retain in the ownership of the lord, while even as to book-land the special obligations of lay holders in regard to the Crown became more and more definitely recognised. Still the final constitution of the doctrine and of the system of fees was effected in England under the influence of French feudalism, as carried over by the Norman Conquest.

This history of tenements conditioned by service is intimately connected with the spread of the relation between lord and follower on one side, with the growth of the economic practice of constituting tenancies on the other. As to followers I shall merely call attention to the convenience of remunerating an armed servant by the grant of a tenement instead of keeping him as a member of the household or paying him wages. The other side of the surrounding conditions requires some further notice. Apart from the incitement towards the creation of tenements which came from the wish to recompense officials and soldiers, there were powerful incitements to the formation of tenancies on lands held by the Church. The teaching of the Church as to good works and salvation was eagerly taken up by the laity, who tried to make amends for all shortcomings and sins by showering gifts on ecclesiastical institutions. It is computed that about one-third of the soil of Gaul belonged to the Church in the Carlovingian epoch. The monastery of Fulda, the famous foundation of Boniface, gathered 15,000 *mansi* in a short time from pious donors. A considerable part of this property came from small people, who tried in this way not only to propitiate God, but also to win protectors in the persons of powerful ecclesiastical lords. A most common expedient in order to guarantee the ownership of a plot to a monastery without losing one's own subsistence was to constitute a so-called *precaria oblata*, that is to grant the land and to receive it back at the same time as a dependent tenement, usually under the condition of paying some nominal rent, for the sake of a recognition of ownership. On the other hand ecclesiastical corporations stood in need of farmers who would undertake the management of scattered portions of property, and it was a common policy for abbots and clerics to concede such dispersed smaller estates or plots to trustworthy men for more or less substantial rents on the strength of so-called *precariae datae*. The expression *beneficium* was in use for such transactions, but it became gradually specialised to denote the tenements of *vassals*, or higher military retainers. There was thus a characteristic tendency to organise land-tenures based on a combination between superior lords or seniors and inferior, dependent tenants.

The same result was reached from yet another point of view, namely through the working of the system of political obligations laid on the citizens. As taxation was undeveloped and had to be represented largely by dues from estates, the demands of the government as expressed in personal services of the subject were very great. The machinery of public institutions was based largely on what has been called *trinoda necessitas*—attendance at the host, repair of bridges and roads, construction of fortresses, and also on the attendance of suitors at the different public courts, more especially at the county and the hundred. Originally it was reckoned in England that one man should serve for one hide: in the Frankish territories the unit of assessment was smaller than the hide, the *mansus* (*Hufe*), roughly corresponding to the English virgate in size, although its value must have been more considerable, at least in Gaul, on account of the more intensive husbandry of the Southern countries. Anyhow it was soon found that owners of single *Hufen* were not of much use to the army while the army service was a crushing burden for them, and we see in all the principal countries of Western Europe attempts to graduate the standards of equipment of the members of the host by combining the poorer men into larger units. The principle of graduated general service is well expressed in Lombard legislation. The second and third clauses of Aistulf's laws subdivide the host into three classes according to equipment. The poorest freemen, characteristically called *arimanni* or *exercitales*—army-men, are bound to attend the host with shield, bow and arrows; the owners of forty *juga* (*jugera* are meant) of land have to appear with spear, shield and horse; the wealthiest whose estates are computed at seven tributary holdings have to attend in a coat of mail, and if they own more landed property have to muster additional soldiers in proper equipment in proportion to their wealth; merchants should have their duties apportioned on a similar scale. A clause of the laws of Liutprand (83) provides that judges and administrative officials should have leave to exempt a certain number of the poorer freemen from personal attendance, on condition that they should help to carry loads for the army with their horses and perform week-work for the officials during their absence in the host.

In one of several capitularies treating of the obligations of men serving in the host Charles the Great lays down the following rules: Let every free man possessed of four settled *mansi* of his own or held of another as a benefice prepare himself and go to the host on his own account either with his senior or with the count. As to the free man having three *mansi* of his own, let one be joined to him who is possessed of one *mansus* and let him help the other in order that he may do service for both. A man having only two *mansi* of his own should be joined to another possessed of two, and let one of them go to the host with the help of the other. Even if a man should only have one *mansus* let three others possessed of the same quantity be joined with him and let them give him help so that he should proceed to the host, while the three others should remain at home.

Even in this mitigated form compulsory service in the host and at the courts proved too heavy a burden for the poorer freemen, who, instead of attending to their own affairs, were driven to serve on protracted expeditions. This meant sheer ruin for the smaller households, and the wish to escape from the harassing demands of the military and administrative machinery led many of these smaller people to surrender their dangerous independence and to place themselves under the protection of lay or clerical magnates. This is one of the roots of the *commendation* in consequence of which the plots of the lower free class shrink apace in favour of the neighbouring great estates. Nor was it the only root. The disruption of the ties of kinship and the insufficiency of ordinary legal protection in those times of violent social struggles and of weak government made it necessary for kinless or broken men to look out for the support of mightier neighbours. And again, all those who had been weakened in the everyday struggle for existence—widows, orphans, men stricken by disease or economic mishaps—could not do better than *commend* themselves to the strong hand of a magnate, although such commendation involved a lessening of private independence and sometimes the loss of land ownership. The various forms of tenant right cropping up in so profuse a manner afforded convenient stages for the gradual descent of the poorer freemen into a condition of clientship, of personal dependence on the "senior."

In this way the most characteristic phenomenon of medieval Society, the great estate or the manor, as they said in England, was being gradually evolved. The most complete instances of such organisations in the ninth century are presented by documents drawn from among the records of Royal and of ecclesiastical administration. Charles the Great's *Capitulare de villis* presents a comprehensive survey of Royal estates which is further illustrated by shorter regulations of the same kind— the *breviaria rerum fiscalium*, the *capitulare de disciplina palatii Aquensis*, etc. The enormous complex of crown domains is seen to consist of three different elements—of home-farms worked under the direct control of stewards (*casae indominicatae, mansioniles*), of tenements held by free men and half-free men (*mansi ingenuiles, lidiles*) and of plots occupied by settled serfs (*mansi serviles*). For purposes of organisation these different *mansi* are sometimes concentrated into *beneficia*, small estates of some 4–10 *mansi*, entrusted to privileged tenants, *vassali*, to whom the *beneficia* have been assigned in remuneration for their services. In other cases a number of *mansi* are put under a steward of the King or Emperor chosen from among his regular servants (*ministeria*). The rents in kind and in money are paid to him from the dependent *mansi*, and various services for tillage, reaping, mowing, threshing, carrying the produce, hedge-making, shearing sheep, and such-like have to be collected and arranged at the central *mansus* with which, as a rule, a home-farm is connected. The *ministeria* are combined in groups under *villae* and these again are congregated around a number of *palatia*, great manors in which the head stewards reside, keep accounts and store the various products of domanial husbandry for direct consumption and for sale. The Royal master and members of his family move from one of the *palatia* to the other with their retinue and consume part of their revenue on the spot. Although the turnover of this economy appears to be very considerable, the home-farms with independent cultivation on a large scale are not common, and there are no *latifundia* in the sense of great plantation estates. The type of combined economy based on the mutual support of a manorial centre and its satellite holdings is the prevalent one, and some of the estates are broken up into small and scattered plots. Another interesting feature consists in the fact, that a second line of subdivisions and groups runs alongside the hierarchy of steward-ships : the peasantry are grouped into tithings and hundreds and these subdivisions are apparently connected with the older personal and territorial arrangement of the population. Altogether the domanial scheme by no means excludes older popular units and institutions. The communities of the Marks, for instance, continue to exist for the purpose of regulating the waste, and in districts with nucleated villages the customary institutions of the townships also live on under the net of the manorial administration.

The formation of great estates went on also on the lands of the Church and the laity : the machinery of their rural administration was shaped more or less on the pattern of the Royal domains. But generally in this case the system was not so complete and the history of its forma-tion is more easy to trace. The possessions of private owners, both lay and clerical, are generally much scattered, having been collected by chance. Even in the fields of every single estate the plots of the lord and of the tenants would lie intermixed. This rendered the growth of home-farms difficult and favoured the imposition of rents coupled with occasional services. The peculiar dualism of manorial authority and township association is especially noticeable on these estates. The practices of the open-field system with compulsory rotation of crops, collective management of pasture and wood, common supervision as of herds, went on as before, only that the usages and regulations of the marks and of the villages were strengthened and complicated by seigniorial authority and perquisites. The *Hufen* (*mansi*) also kept their ground for a long time because, although there was no juridical impediment to their division, the units were kept up as much as possible for economic reasons, as representing self-supporting farms provided with all the necessaries of husbandry in field and wood, in live stock and implements. When divisions took place care was taken that they should follow certain natural fractions of the plough teams and superfluous claimants were either bought out or settled on adjacent cottages. It is impossible to understand medieval society unless we take account of this double aspect of its life.

A description of the medieval manor would be incomplete without a consideration of its bearings in public law. The medieval view of government admitted, and indeed required, that wealth and social influence should be accompanied by political power and public functions. Every householder had some jurisdiction "under his roof-gutter" (*unter der Dachtraufe*) and within the hedge. Personal authority over domestic servants and slaves took, among other things, the shape of criminal and police jurisdiction (*Dienstrecht*). Again the *senior* as the centre of a group of vassals claimed the right to preside over a court composed of these vassals, as his "peers," in order to decide civil suits between them. But the most extensive application of this private view of jurisdiction is to be found in the growth of franchises (*Immunitas, Freiung, Freibezirk*). One of the roots of this system is the condition of Royal domains. Their inhabitants are naturally exempted from ordinary jurisdiction and from common fiscal exactions. They are free from toll and geld or general taxes; in matters of jurisdiction and administration they look primarily to the Royal stewards and not to the ordinary judges and officials of the counties. When a portion of the Royal domain is granted to a subject, its condition is not changed thereby—it keeps its privileges and stands out as a district separate from the surrounding territory. In England especially the condition of "ancient demesne" begins to form itself already before the Norman Conquest. By the side of this institutional root we notice another. As in the later Empire, the government is obliged to have recourse to great landlords in order to carry out its functions of police, justice, military and fiscal authority. Great estates become extra-territorial already under Roman rule in the fourth and fifth centuries, and it would be superfluous to point out how much more the governments of the barbarians stood in need of the help of great landowners. As early as the sixth century we find exemptions *ab introitu judicum*, that is the privilege of landowners to exclude public judges and their subordinate officials from their estates. Civil and afterwards criminal jurisdiction fell necessarily into their hands as a

CH. XX.

consequence of the grant of fines and judicial costs. In the beginning the concession of profitable rights or perquisites of justice may have been especially valued, but the duties of jurisdiction could not be separated from the former: it was out of the question to make one set of people perform the work of judicial administration while another set reaped its profits. From such beginnings the franchises or immunities develop rapidly into a regular and recognised side of landlordship, and with variations in detail the Anglo-Saxon *landrica* follows the same track as the continental *Immunitätsherr*. The different forms of power implied by the franchise are sometimes summed up in quaint, proverbial sentences. A German jingle of this kind speaks of *twinc unde ban* (coercion and command), *glocken klanc unde geschrei* (belfry and summoning of the *posse* of neighbours), *herberge unde atzunge* (lodging and meals to be provided for the representatives of authority), *spruch* (power of magistrate sitting on the bench), *vrevel* (criminal fines), *diup* (keeping and confiscation of stolen goods), *stoc* (prison), *stein* (block). With this may be compared the Anglo-Saxon enumeration—*sac, soc, toll, theam, infangene theof, utfangene theof.*

In one important particular the growth of continental immunity differed materially from the Anglo-Saxon process. It was usually deemed necessary on the Continent to separate the actual exercise of criminal jurisdiction from the right of ecclesiastical estates or districts to claim the franchise. Thus bishoprics and abbeys were bound to appoint special *advocati* (*Vögte*) to exercise the judicial functions in their tribunals, and these offices tended, as everything else in those times, to become hereditary and to assume the nature of benefices. The *Vogt* was a kind of parasitic magnate reared on the proceeds of ecclesiastical immunities.

The general results of the social processes described may be summed up under three heads: (1) a debasement and breaking up of the class of common free men, (2) the rise of a landed aristocracy, (3) the formation of a large and varied mass of half-free people. A characteristic expression of the first of these developments may be noticed in the terms applied to the common people. The quality of the free man is graphically described in a Northern Saga as that of a man who yokes oxen, fits out a plough, constructs a house and builds barns, makes a cart and guides the plough. But the *bonde* (*Bauer*) remained an independent person, conscious of strength and able to stand on his rights only in the North—in Norway and Sweden. In Denmark and England the *bonde*, though as free in the origin, became not only a "husbandman" but a bondman. The Anglo-Saxon *ceorl*, from being the typical free householder sank into the position of a churl sitting on land burdened with rent (*gafol*). The Frankish *villanus*, which ought to designate a member of the township, came to be regarded as a man of vile, low origin and condition. Even *friling* and *liber* occasionally assumed a shade of meaning pointing to the imperfect status of freed men or of persons living under Roman law and not entirely exempt from private authority.

The growth of aristocratic distinctions is reflected during the period under consideration by the figures of the *wergelds*. The Alemannic law already distinguishes between *primi, medii* and *minofledis*; the Lombards speak of *meliorissimi*; the Frankish standard consists in the threefold increase of the *wergeld* for the *antrustiones* of the King; although in this case the privilege was deemed a personal one, the position of the *antrustiones* or *convivae regis* was of indirect importance for their families and its tradition is kept up during Carlovingian times by the *Seniores*. The Anglo-Saxon divisions are even more characteristic. In the Kentish laws the scale of ranks is very gradual—there are subdivisions of *eorls, ceorls* and *laets*. In Wessex society was arranged in three degrees —the men worth two hundred, six hundred and twelve hundred shillings. But the middle class disappears in course of time and the sharp contrast between *twelvehyndemen* and *twyhyndemen* is made the basis for the treaties with the Danes. The *wergelds* cease to be a trustworthy indication of status in the tenth and eleventh centuries, but the general tendency of the social process is sufficiently expressed in them.

The half-free classes are very varied in their origin and social standing. The number of domestic slaves diminished rapidly, partly in consequence of manumissions, and partly because there was a greater need of farmers than of menial servants. Such of the latter as still remained assumed sometimes a privileged position on account of their duties as military retainers and stewards—they formed the group of *ministeriales* from which a part of the continental knightly order traces its origin. The settled serfs (*servi casati*) are assimilated more and more to the *coloni* and the *liti* or *aldiones*. The essence of the position of all these groups is to support the household and the home-farms of their lords by rents and labour services, while at the same time tilling plots of their own. As Tacitus expressed it long ago, the serf of the Germans is like the old *colonus* of Rome; he has his own household and is a tributary of the master in respect of a certain quantity of corn, clothes and live stock. Commended free men and free tenants on a lord's land gravitate, as it were, towards the status of these half-free groups. The mere fact of paying rent and of being a tenant becomes a badge of inferiority. The jurisdictional privileges of the great landowners extend not only over their tenants but also over small neighbours. Altogether, instead of clear distinctions based on birth and personal status we see a variety produced by the tenure of land.

There has been a great deal of controversy as to how far Roman and Germanic influences account for the process described, but it seems impossible to apportion exactly the share of each. It is evident that the disruption of public authority and the aristocratic transformation of

Society were prepared on both sides. The general course of development was especially rapid and complete in those parts of Europe where there was most intermixture between Romance and Germanic elements, especially in the Frankish Empire. Yet England and Scandinavian countries, in spite of their peculiar position, somewhat aside of the main stream, follow processes of their own which also lead to feudalisation. This seems to warrant the conclusion that the coming of feudalism was rather the result of general tendencies than of particular national causes. After the great effort of conquest and invasion, Western European society relapsed into political life on a small scale, into aristocratically constituted local circles.

CHAPTER XXI.

LEGISLATION AND ADMINISTRATION OF CHARLES THE GREAT.

THE State of Charles the Great goes back to the foundation of the empire of the Merovingians. The four hundred years of Frankish rule (500–900) comprise radical changes, it is true, but a definite direction of the development from the first is clearly to be seen. The great Charles is only to be regarded as finishing what the Merovingian Clovis introduced, and the coronation of 800 as concluding a process of formation which began with the baptism of Clovis and with the acceptance of the Catholic Faith on the part of the Frankish people. Always characteristic was the continued and remarkable combination of Roman system and Biblical conceptions with the old German ideas, the rise of ideas of absolute monarchy and the increasing prominence of patriarchal and theocratic principles which changed the character of the State itself.

Not from the initiative of the Frankish people, nor, properly speaking, from its need for expansion, did the great Frankish conquest of the fifth and sixth centuries originate. The people had indeed their share, and the success of the movement depended on the strength and the political capacity of the people themselves, but the empire was none the less the personal foundation of Clovis and the dynasty. Hence we can easily understand that on the one hand German institutions remained, and were even transferred to what was once Roman ground, and that on the other, a powerful influence through Roman systems made itself felt. And, connected with the last, after the acceptance of the Catholic Faith by the Franks, was the influence in increasing degree of ideas which were given through the Bible and the Christian theocratic conception of the world. The growth of the power of the Frankish monarchy is certainly not to be ascribed solely to foreign influences. It is certain that the German monarchy possessed in itself, of its own strength, the capacity for development, and that political circumstances necessitated a great growth of the monarchy in the sixth century. But foreign influences all the same gave the standard in no slight measure, the king stood apart before the political mass, he was inviolable, he was irresponsible, to his word unconditional obedience was due, the idea of high treason finds entrance into the constitution. And these expressly monarchical elements, which were originally strange to the German conceptions of society, never disappeared again in spite of all political changes. As the elevation of the Carlovingians had taken place with the liveliest sympathy of the people or rather of the leaders of the people, a certain participation of the people in the government of the empire was revived in the first half of the eighth century. But no serious deviation of the development of the monarchy in the direction of popular or aristocratic limitation was effected. The characteristic feature of the formation of the Carlovingian State is rather the greater emphasis of the theocratic element. That introduced essentially new influences into the commonwealth, not merely strengthening the power of the kings, but also turning the whole development into new paths.

A principle that had been active from the time of Clovis became in the eighth century dominant: the king derives his authority from God, he appears amid a halo of supernatural glory, but is at the same time bound to definite duties. For God has bestowed the authority in order that the people may be well ruled. An idea of the social body began to be supreme, far surpassing all aims of purely private rule. If the king was in no way head of a body which in itself possessed the constitutional authority, yet he was not simply lord for the sake of lordship. The theocratic element had an ennobling tendency and raised the conception of the commonwealth above the sphere of private rule. Effort for the well-being of mankind was demanded, and the principle *salus publica suprema lex* began to make itself felt.

Moreover, immediately connected with this was the vast extension of the duties which were regarded as lying within the province of the State. Although the idea of the superiority of spiritual power over secular had long been recognised, and although a universal subjection of the world to the Church and its hierarchy ought to have resulted from it, the political development even of the Merovingian period had brought the Church into dependence upon the State. In the Carlovingian period that was entirely the case. The Church had the most prominent place in social life, Church and State ran side by side, the Empire was weighed down with ecclesiastical burdens, but the Church was in the position of Church of the Empire, and the head of the State was at the same time head of the Church. Truly the predominance of the theocratic point of view gave to the Frankish State a new and wide prospect of its rights. Not merely was the object of the State the primitive maintenance of peace at home and of authority abroad, but all questions of the common life were drawn into the domain of the work of the State, everything that concerned the well-being, in the widest sense, of its subjects was to be an object of care to the State, their material as well as their spiritual concerns, questions of this life as well as questions of the future life.

It is not necessary here to say more than that the task of Charles extended beyond the preservation of peace and relations to external powers. In extended degree his care was devoted to economic conditions. The efforts of his predecessors for the promotion of commerce were continued. Measures for the maintenance and erection of bridges and roads were doubtless often undertaken from considerations of national defence, but they were also eminently calculated to serve the purposes of trade. Navigation was to be fostered and rendered safer. It is to be surmised that considerations of intercourse were chiefly taken into account in the magnificent plan for uniting the river-systems of the Rhine and the Danube by a canal between the Rednitz and the Altmühl. Numerous measures enable us to see how much understanding Charles brought to bear upon questions of trade. The numerous ordinances respecting tolls and customs had their origin in the same purpose—fiscal interests were not to be neglected, but yet they were not to be the main consideration—tolls were not to restrict trade. The general prosperity, it may even be said, was really taken into account. Business was indirectly served by manifold regulations for weights and measures, which were aimed against individual caprice and required uniformity. In the same direction point the ordinances respecting the coinage. Coinage was the royal prerogative, and this right was still preserved. Perfect centralisation, it is true, was not yet aimed at, but for some time Charles was thinking of restricting the stamping of money to his places of abode, and although that was not carried out, we find under Charles considerable limitation of places of mintage.

While all these measures were calculated to promote trade, Charles issued direct ordinances with regard to the manner of trade by the restriction of excessive privileges, the prohibition of trade by night, and by regulations for the trade in horses and cattle. The exportation of certain articles was entirely forbidden, especially the exportation of corn in case of failure of the crops. A check was put upon speculation by the decree that corn might not be sold while still growing, or wine before the vintage. Steps were taken against excessive raising of prices, and indeed tariffs of prices were actually issued by the State. All these measures tended to the general well-being, and care was taken for the common interest. How this care on the part of the State began to develop was shewn with special clearness in measures devoted to the relief of the poor. The plague of mendicancy was to be checked, the poorest were to be protected from want. The support of the poor was accordingly delegated by the State to individual rulers, and a kind of general poor relief was required. A decree was actually made that on bishops, abbots, and abbesses a sum of one pound of silver, half a pound, and five *solidi* respectively, should be levied, and definite sums similarly on counts and others. It was thus sought to introduce a poor rate.

Under Charles the activities of the State were enormously extended. In this connexion it is only possible to hint how they turned to the department of intellectual life also, to art and learning, and how Charles aimed at raising the intellectual plane of the laity. As a matter of fact, the official activity of Charles only recognised such limits as the economic ideas of the age laid down.

We observe, under Charles, the first great expansion of the idea of the State itself in the history of the Christian West. It is connected with the increasing prominence of theocratic ideas, while the coronation of 800 was but the visible completion of the long process of development. The theocratic ideas which dominated the Frankish Empire had sprung up previous to 800, and had made the Frankish king the absolute representative of Christian rule in the West. Thus the Empire did not demand any essential change in the relations of people and ruler, for substantially it only established the results of the previous political developments. It is true that special emphasis was laid on duties towards the Church in the new oath of allegiance, which Charles made universal in 802, but this enforced no new idea.

The Theocratic Ideal is a great social force, which exerted influence on the formation of State and society independently of individual circumstances. Charles the Great made it equally serviceable to the State. Universal monarchy was founded with the help of theocratic ideas. But could it endure?

From two sides attempts were necessarily made to break up the Carlovingian universal Empire. In the first place, the theocratic idea demanded unity of social organisation of Christendom. But under the prevalent belief in the superiority of ecclesiastical over secular power, and under the requirements of the strictly hierarchical and monarchical organisation of the Papal Church, Christendom was another unity not under a temporal prince, but under the Pope. Again, opposed to the universal demands of the theocratic idea there stood the particular political needs of the different peoples and races—a second great social force striving for recognition. Before the powerful personality of Charles, those forces which struggled against the theocratic State ruled by a secular prince, were not effective. Under Charles all yielded to the service of the political idea represented by the Frankish monarch. After the death of Charles, however, these restrained forces burst forth again: on the one side the particular needs of the different peoples of the great Empire, on the other that idea of union which desired a predominant position of the Papacy.

That outburst, however, is not our present object. Here we must only indicate that even Charles the Great was not successful in once for all subduing those internal forces hostile to his consolidated State. Further we have to shew how the Carlovingian State sought to solve its increasingly serious problems.

In the centre of the national life stands the king. He represents the nation. His authority is essentially *the* national authority. The fate of that authority involves the fate of the State itself. The Empire doubtless brought about an increase of the external strength of the monarchical position, but not any internal change. Charles already possessed as king all the elements of the power which as emperor he brought to development. The monarchy was hereditary. All male members of the royal house had rights of inheritance; the Empire was to be divided into as many parts as there were claims to satisfy. That was originally the principle of the Frankish monarchy in the sixth century. But in the time of the decadence of the power of the Merovingians it was set aside, the aims of the too powerful aristocracy and the needs of many a district of the Empire for national incorporation withstood it. A selection was made among the members of the royal house. Even the powerful Carlovingians did not represent the principle of chance divisions corresponding to the private circumstances of the royal house. Charles the Great in the year 806 drew up a scheme for the division of his Empire, in case of his death, among his three sons then living, Louis, Pepin, and Charles; but no further division was contemplated. It was intended that only one son—the one whom the people elected—should succeed each of these kings of the divided monarchy. And then the theocratic ideas began to demand a consolidation of political organisation overlooking all individual dynastic claims to supremacy. The ordinance of 813 is the outcome of these tendencies. The death of the sons Pepin and Charles made it possible for Louis to attain the sole monarchy, while Pepin's son Bernard only received Italy as sub-king. But in 813 an ordinance was made for the Empire which continued united, and thus comes before us that tendency to unification which attained supremacy at the very beginning of the reign of Louis only as a result of the ideas which were coming to the front under Charles.

Many of the old Germanic customs are no longer met with under Charles the Great, for instance, the use of the ox-wagon on the occasion of the visit to the great Annual Assembly, and the elevation on the shield, which took place in the Merovingian period when the succession was broken. On the other hand, anointing according to Biblical precedent had been introduced in the Carlovingian age. Just as Pepin in 751 had received the solemn anointing at the hands of Boniface and afterwards of Pope Stephen, so it became afterwards the rule. With the anointing went, under Charles, the coronation. Before 800 there is no certain evidence of such a ceremony in the Frankish Empire, although the Merovingians had already used crown-like diadems as ornaments. After 800 it established itself, and not only emperors, but kings too, were crowned. Originally not necessarily an act to be performed by ecclesiastics, like the anointing, it was soon combined with the anointing and in West Francia, where first a fixed ceremonial was developed, it became from the time of Charles the Bald an integral element of the ceremony, whereas in the Eastern Kingdom, where there is no evidence of a coronation either in the case of Louis the German, or of his sons and Arnulf, it did not perhaps become permanently the custom till after 900. As symbols of monarchical rule we find in addition sceptre and throne, which we may suppose to have first come into use in the Carlovingian time, together with the lance, attested as a royal symbol on the ring of Childeric, and the staff, distinguished at any rate in later times from sceptre and lance.

In the symbols and in the solemnity of the elevation, the change in the royal power is revealed. The spiritual element was placed in the foreground, its divine origin emphasised, and the priesthood played a ruling part. The personality of the monarchy stands forth quite distinct from the populace. The royal title is but simple, originally a continuation of that of the Merovingians, then, independently but from the very beginning, with the significant addition "by the grace of God"—a custom afterwards adopted not merely in the Empire of the Franks but in the whole of the West. The imperial title was exceedingly circumstantial: "Most noble Augustus, crowned of God, great and peace-bringing Emperor, who rules the Roman Empire and who, by the grace of God, is King of the Franks and of the Lombards." Superabundant are the epithets of virtue and exaltation which Charles applied to himself and with which he was saluted. Court ceremonial became the custom, and Byzantine influences served as the model. Whoever approached the Emperor for any official purpose was required to prostrate himself to the ground and kiss the knee and foot of majesty. But all that was a veneer of foreign and external splendour. Underneath is clearly visible the true Germanic character in the conception and accomplishment of national undertakings. The king was guardian of justice and peace. All stood beneath his protection. The king's peace was the general peace of the State, the king's protection covered every member of the State. But together with the general protection which ensured peace for everyone, went a special king's protection which was bestowed on individuals, placing the object of it in closer relation to the king and decreeing severer punishment for every injury to his person.

The subject was bound to unconditional obedience to the king. An oath of allegiance was exacted, a custom not of Roman but of Merovingian origin, which had fallen into disuse, and was re-introduced by Charles the Great. Obedience was, however, claimed from every subject without oath, and disregard of the king's command was severely punished.

The king had the power to issue coercive ordinances and injunctions, he had the power to command, he had the power of the ban. This royal right of the ban is not to be derived from any special priestly or knightly prerogative, but is to be simply regarded as a natural adjunct of the supreme position. It lies in the very nature of kingship to issue coercive commands.

Obedience on the part of the subject flowed from the ordinary obligations of allegiance. Disobedience was disloyalty. Just as disloyalty was differently punished according to the enormity of the offence, even with banishment, confiscation, or death, so, in the same way, disobedience was differently punished, fixed punishments being appointed by law for definite offences, or else the sentence was referred to the monarch's arbitrary power of punishing. The power of the ban possessed by the Frankish kings was not simply the power to order or to forbid under threat of the old fine of sixty shillings. It was on the contrary much further reaching. It demanded obedience on the ground of allegiance, on the ground of the legal principle that the punishment for disloyalty, whatever it be, should light on the disobedient, and that—in so far as special punishments were not already decreed by law—the disobedient might suffer any punishment from the King's Court up to complete outlawry.

If the equivalent fine of sixty shillings was indicated by the king's "ban," that is not to be so understood to mean that disregard of the royal authority was punished by a fine limited to sixty shillings, or that the king could only pursue any who disregarded the royal command with infliction of these definite fines. The fact is rather to be explained in another manner. In the seventh century, and first in the *Lex Ripuaria*, a fine of sixty shillings was fixed by law for definite cases of disobedience to commands issued by authority, not necessarily by the royal authority. This fine, a moderate punishment for disobedience, was further extended in Carlovingian times. The many-sided care of the State for the social life, the growing need for the exaction of punishment by the State more frequently than hitherto, tended to the infliction of the sixty shilling "ban," the usual moderate punishment for disobedience, and in such a way that a trespass was legally explained as transgression of the king's command. So arose the different cases of ban in the eighth and ninth centuries. They originated in the sixty shilling fine of Ripuarian Folklaw which inflicted this fine on disregard of summons to the royal service, but their signification became very different. In the seventh century the sixty shilling punishment was inflicted when a definite ordinance was disregarded, but under Charles the Great if a definite transgression was defined by law as contempt of the king's command. Hence many instances of "ban" under the Carlovingians have nothing to do with disobedience to specific royal ordinances, but on the other hand the sixty shilling fine—the king's ban—was not inflicted at all in processes against contemners of the royal command. But above all it must be clearly understood that the authority of the Frankish king was never limited in such a way as to threaten the contemner of his ordinance with nothing worse than a fine of sixty shillings.

Amongst those who in the first place stood beside the monarch appear the superintendents of the four old court offices, the seneschal, the butler, the marshal, and the chamberlain, who not only performed their official duties in the narrower sense, but could be employed in the most varied capacities in times both of war and peace, as generals, ambassadors, judges amongst others. Then the chief doorkeeper (*Magister ostiariorum*), the quartermaster (*Mansionarius*), the chief huntsman, and less important officials. Of special importance for purely state business was the palsgrave, or rather the palsgraves, for several acted contemporaneously as deputy-presidents of the palace judicial Court, and of course also as ambassadors, generals, and in other similar official capacities.

Besides the judicial Court of the Palace the Chancery was of importance as a court with definite jurisdiction, the court for the preparation of documents. The president was no longer the lay referendary of Merovingian times, but an ecclesiastic, who even in the time of Charles the Great appears to have had no official title, but who was already of great importance and under Louis the Pious rose to much greater importance still. Hitherius, abbot of St Martin at Tours, Abbot Rado of St Vaast, Ercanbald, and Jeremiah, afterwards archbishop of Sens, acted as Charles' presidents of Chancery. Under these, the later chancellors, several deacons and sub-deacons were employed as clerks and notaries. They were all attached to the royal chapel as court chaplains. Chapel, *capella*, was originally the name given to the place where the *cappa* (cloak) of St Martin of Tours was preserved with other treasures, and chaplains were the guardians of these relics. In a derived sense, the body of court ecclesiastics was next designated the chapel. At their head stood the most influential ecclesiastic of the court, the *primicerius* of the chapel, the arch-chaplain, as the title, at first varying, became established under Louis the Pious. The illustrious Abbot Fulrad of St Denis, who had taken so active a part in the elevation of Pepin to the throne, was also arch-chaplain at the beginning of the reign of Charles the Great. To him succeeded Bishop Angilram of Metz and then Archbishop Hildibald of Cologne, who were regarded as the chief advisers of the Emperor, not merely in ecclesiastical, but in other, matters as well.

Chancery and chapel were at first only in so far connected, that many chancery officials were also chaplains and that, as we may suppose, the chapel served also at the same time for the archives. In addition, the arch-chaplain like other high court officials had an active connexion with business dealt with in documents, and hence not unfrequently appears as the one who transmitted to the chancery the order for verification. But that implies no organic connexion between chancery and chapel. Such a connexion was unknown under Charles the Great, and equally so under Louis the Pious. This connexion, so important for later times, was not effected till the time of Louis the German, when the arch-chaplain was placed in charge of the chancery, in 854 temporarily, in 860 permanently.

A court council did not exist in the time of Charles. The monarch summoned at his pleasure those about him and the nobles who were staying at the court, but a council, properly speaking, did not exist. The number of those who, in the wider sense of the word, were courtiers was unusually large. There were staying there the numerous ecclesiastics and scholars, the teachers and pupils of the palace school, the one class those whom the great Emperor had invited from afar, the other those who were living in preparation for the service of Church and State. But there were also numerous knights in attendance, who formed the body-guard of the monarch and were ready to undertake different duties within or without the court. In addition were the different vassals and servants of the courtiers, some free, some not; and also merchants who enjoyed the Emperor's special protection, and who had to supply the needs of the court and its numerous visitors; and moreover the adventurers, the travellers who were trying their fortune, the crowd of beggars, who in the Middle Ages appeared wherever there was active traffic.

Vigorous life was developed at Charles' court. We see there magnificence and genius, but immorality also. For Charles was not particular about the persons he drew round him. He was himself no model, and he suffered the greatest licence in those whom he liked and found useful. As "Holy Emperor" he was addressed, though his life exhibited little holiness. He is so addressed by Alcuin, who also praises the Emperor's beautiful daughter Rotrud as distinguished for her virtues in spite of her having borne a son to Count Roderic of Maine, though not his wife. Charles would not be separated from his daughters, he would not allow their marriage, and he was therefore obliged to accept the consequences. The other daughter Bertha also had two sons by the pious Abbot Angilbert of St Riquier. In fact the court of Charles was a centre of very loose life. It was one of the first acts of the pious Louis to cleanse the court of its foul elements and to issue a strict ordinance to put an end to this dissoluteness. Strictness of morals came, but the magnificence was gone. In truth it was on the personality of the monarch that all depended. The patriarchal tendency predominated, the central official world was in everything dependent on the varying decisions of the monarch himself, it had no independent position or strength. How could the foundation for a lasting absolute monarchy be laid under these circumstances?

Before the activity of the State in the provinces is considered, it is necessary to shew what material resources were available for the monarch and in what manner the individual power of the people for national purposes was put in requisition. Amongst these stand in the first place the revenues from his estates. The Frankish king was the largest landowner in the kingdom. The royal property was continually increased through confiscations, through reversions to the crown for want of heirs, through reclamation of uncultivated territory. Though the king bestowed much land as gift or as fief, which was thereby withdrawn from his own use, what remained was sufficiently important.

On the royal domains also reigned that activity which was found on all large estates and which had developed in connexion with the circumstances of the later Roman Empire but also from the social and economic needs of the German peoples. There was no system of agriculture on a large scale. Only a comparatively small part of the domain was managed by the lord himself (*terra salica, terra indominicata*). The greater part was occupied by dependents, who cultivated for themselves and might work, at any rate in part, on their own account, and were only bound to certain payments and services (*mansi serviles, litiles, ingenuiles*). Charles constituted the management of his estates a definite organisation, which served as a model for the great landowners of later ages. As heads of the different farms held by socage, which served as intermediaries between the land which was cultivated independently and the land held under conditions of service and money payment, appeared sundry *meier* (*maiores*); several of the small farms with their district were united in "deaneries" under a "dean," but of a higher rank were the chief farms, the management of which was entrusted to a *judex*, or as he was generally called later, a *villicus*. A system of lower and chief farms was made. The surplus products were collected on the chief farms in order to be brought, according to definite regulations, to the king's farm, or on the other hand, to be either stored or sold.

Not at the end, but in the very first years of his reign Charles issued for his domains the famous ordinance, the *Capitulare de villis*, in which complete directions were given for all circumstances on the farms, for the use of every kind of farm produce, for book-keeping and accounts, and in which the monarch's active care, even for subordinate matters of agricultural work, is so characteristically shewn. A number of officials of the most different kinds for the cultivation of the royal lands, the *fisci*, both free and not free, come before us; the *juniores* and *ministeriales*, who stood as assistants beside the higher officials, the *judices*. Such were the foresters, the superintendents of the stores (*cellerarii*), the overseers of the studs, the *poledrarii*, and in addition the many artisans, the goldsmiths, the blacksmiths, the shoemakers, cartwrights, saddlers, etc., for whose presence in the districts the *judices* were to make provision and who had received a definite organisation under their own masters. Towards the end of his reign Charles compiled a complete register of the *fisci*, a general inventory of the crown lands.

This was an important work, and fragments of the particulars which it gave have come down to us.

The revenues accruing from the management of these estates certainly formed the most important material foundation of the royal power. But many others were added to these. The king was lord over all land that was not already in private possession. Out of this principle, derived from Roman law, not out of an assumed prerogative of the Frankish king, arose a multitude of privileges which were also of substantial advantage to the royal power. The monarch first exercised authority over large districts so far as they were not settled, next he laid claim to that which was not regarded as appendage to the land itself—animals, rivers, the hidden treasures of the soil which were not agricultural products. Although these privileges were not developed into definite rights—to mountain, salt, and hunting rights—till the age after Charles, yet the beginnings of financial profit are to be found in his day.

By no means inconsiderable were the royal revenues derived from presents from foreigners, from the tribute of subjects, and from plunder taken in war. Through no war, says the historian Einhard, were so great riches acquired as through the subjugation of the Avars. A good part of the immense treasures, it is certain, fell to the king himself. Moreover, the amount of fines must have been considerable, and the count had by law to transmit two-thirds of these receipts to the king's court. The unusual frequency of the punishment of the king's ban, the sixty shilling fine, was owing to the wish to increase the royal revenues. A general money tax, however, was not levied from the subjects. The Roman system of taxes, which the Franks found in Gaul, fell more and more into disuse, and even Charles did not try to extend it. The offering of gifts on the occasion of the great annual assembly, a custom connected with old Germanic practices, was, it is true, maintained, but it did not lead to the development of a tax in the proper sense. It only paved the way for definite imposts where—as in the case of the monasteries—a closer relation of dependence was created, exceeding simple subjection to the State. The king's tribute also, which is more frequently thought of as a due payable by individual freemen, is not to be regarded as a proper tax, and in particular not as a general personal tax. It seems rather to have arisen from a special payment for protection, and in any case it was rendered by many classes of the population, on the ground of special, not general, circumstances of dependence.

The subjects are seen under obligations not to pay taxes but to render service. This is a characteristic element in the national life of that age. The State demanded much, very much from the resources of the individual, in the form not of a tax but of personal service. These services were extraordinarily various. In a certain sense they were unlimited. In the ordinances of Charles reference is made to custom, and the officials are strictly enjoined not to demand services beyond that; but this was only to afford protection against arbitrary acts on the part of the officials and against their making use of obligations to service for their own purposes. This service (*servitium*) embraced obligations of the most different kinds—the boarding, lodging, and forwarding of those travelling or working on state business, the acceptance of duties as envoys, and also co-operation in work, and buildings in the public interest, fortifications, dikes, bridges, and the like. Definite limitations of this obligatory service were not drawn. Varying custom formed the standard and was often the only restriction on the power of the provincial officials who exacted it. But two obligations of the most general kind may be regarded as the most important and probably also as the most oppressive—military and judicial service.

In the time of Charles, when warlike undertakings were frequent, military service must have seemed a heavy burden. It is true that special military regulations are found. In them, mention is made of those to whom crown endowments were given, who were bound to service in war as horsemen, who dwelt scattered over the land and who were always at the disposal of the central authority; and in addition we find troopers, the mounted vassals, on whom royal lands were bestowed, and who were bound to serve as mounted messengers and in the army. But the great mass of freemen remained liable to military service[1]. The organisation of the army even in the time of Charles was doubtless the special care of the upper classes, for the supply of the necessary material of war was entrusted to the nobles capable of furnishing it, and those bound to service already used to assemble under the leadership of their own lords. But nevertheless the principle was maintained that military service is a national duty of the freeman. The service was equal for all in spite of the utterly different positions of those liable. All were obliged to equip and keep themselves. When the call to arms, the *bannitio in hostem*, was raised, all freemen were obliged to obey under the leadership of their lord or the count. The negligent were liable to the severe punishment for disregard of the royal command, the sixty shilling fine, while anyone who left the army without leave was guilty of *herisliz* and lost his life as a traitor.

It was in the king's power to allow modifications in particular cases, in the Merovingian period. The result of the extension of the Empire was that only partial levies were made. The king could therefore take into consideration the needs of different districts, and could spare many classes. The Carlovingians still more than the Merovingians, Charles in particular, sought to lighten the hardships of universal military service. These attempts were attached to older measures, but yet they proceeded

---

[1] Few now hold the opinion of Waitz (*Verfassungsgeschichte*, IV. pp. 533 ff.) that the possession of land was regarded as a condition of military service in Merovingian and Carlovingian times, and that the laws of Charles which neglect this principle are to be regarded as an innovation.

from new principles.   At any rate Charles issued no absolute ordinance, no law which was to furnish a new basis of service.   As in all spheres of social life, so here too Charles contented himself with measures to meet particular cases, with ordinances arising from the needs of the moment, and only valid for certain districts.   His reform of the army took shape through many single rules.   But yet it proceeds from the uniform principle that liability to military service is to be measured by the circumstances of the one liable.   The principle of equal liability of all freemen, dating back to the old German times, was originally founded on the assumption of the fairly equal economic position of the free Germans.   This assumption had long been set aside through the formation of private property and through the immense difference in the possessions of individuals, but the principle of universal equal liability to military service had remained.   Charles now sought to co-ordinate this duty to the altered circumstances.   This was the new and significant point in his regulations.   Those liable to serve were formally classed according to their means, a minimum of property being fixed for full liability.   But, as may easily be understood, in the East, only possessions in land were taken into account, while in the more advanced West, movable goods were also reckoned.   A capitulary issued in 807 for the south Frankish district assumes three hides as the minimum for full personal service, and allows the less wealthy to supply one man for every three hides, but requires contributions for the equipment and maintenance of a warrior even from the possessors of only movable chattels.   In the case of the Saxons another capitulary fixed the standard for furnishing a warrior at six hides when a military undertaking in Spain or against the Avars was in question; at three hides when the campaign was directed against Bohemia; but makes no minimum when the army is to march against the Sorbs.   In a further law, of perhaps general validity, five hides are taken as the unit for computation of liability.   These are all bases, varying in detail, but all proceeding from a uniform principle.   And these principles had a lasting effect which influenced military organisation of succeeding ages outside the limits of the Frankish Empire.   Other judicial reforms tended to the relief of the small man from a heavy and oppressive state duty.

The judicial official, especially the count, summoned the freeman of his *Gau*, or district, to judicial assemblies.   The giving of judgment was universally the business of the people.   Where too frequently used, this summoning of the people to general assemblies pressed very heavily on those in more straitened circumstances.

Charles was the first king who protected the small freeman against too frequent calls.   In different ordinances, he directed that the people should be summoned to judicial assemblies only two or three times in the year, and that at other assemblies, meeting in case of need, only those interested in the case were to appear.   And in all districts of the Empire, and indeed beyond it, these measures led to an institution that lasted for centuries—the unbidden or genuine "Things," the general assemblies, usually held three times a year, of all those liable to serve, which stood in contrast to the bidden "Things," the judicial assemblies, which occurred more frequently and doubtless according to need.

This arrangement of three general assemblies a year for judicial purposes was probably directly connected with the introduction by Charles of the office of judge. In the Merovingian period it was already the custom to choose a select number out of the whole body, who had to propose a verdict, the *Rachinburgi* who presumably were appointed for each case. In connexion with this institution Charles created in the first year of his reign the office of judges (*scabini*). His officials appointed from among the prominent men in the county a somewhat large number, who were officially responsible to the king, and acted as assistants to the count or one of the judges subordinate to the king, and on them rested in the first place the duty of pronouncing judgment. Although there was not the least intention of excluding the purely popular element from the judicial system, yet through the newly created office and its judicial work the possibility was opened of dispensing with further participation of the people in all judicial assemblies, so that popular gatherings should only be summoned three times a year, and yet the administration of justice not be neglected.

Charles' important reform of the judicial system certainly proceeded from the same intention as is to be observed in the military reforms, and indeed generally in Charles' labours—protection for the weak and oppressed. Not that the monarch sought to hinder the great process which was bringing the small freeman more and more into dependence upon a private noble and which in consequence of economic and social conditions was reducing the class of such freemen. But these measures manifest a considerable basis of social and political principle, like those of every executive which considers in a wide sense the well-being of the citizens.

Before we examine more minutely the activities and organ of the State, we must consider the question whether the royal authority was dependent on the co-operation of the people or certain classes of the people, and if so, in what manner.

As a Frankish king, Charles was monarch in the true sense of the word, but he held meetings with people and nobles. Does that then denote a constitutional limitation of the royal powers?

An account is given of national gatherings by Hincmar of Rheims. In his work, *De Ordine Palatii*, he wished to draw a picture of the happy conditions at the court of Charles the Great for the youthful West Frankish king Carloman, the grandson of Charles the Bald, and besides the accounts of men of the older generation, he used a book by Adelhard, abbot of Corvey, on the Order of the Central Government of Charles.

It was the custom, so he relates, for national gatherings to be held not oftener than twice a year—once to arrange affairs of the Empire for the current year, the other time for preliminary deliberations for the following year. In the first all temporal and spiritual nobles took part, but in the other only the higher nobles and selected councillors. Hincmar's account in so far finds confirmation in contemporary records, that authors and documents of the end of the eighth and the beginning of the ninth century speak on the one hand of general national gatherings (*conventus generales, placita generalia*) and on the other of gatherings simply. The latter are assemblies of the nobles of the whole Empire or particular districts, but the former are assemblies of the people under arms, military gatherings, the great general annual meetings, connected with the old Frankish Marchfield.

The Marchfield originated in the Frankish tribal gatherings. It survived all changes of constitution in the sixth and seventh centuries, and maintaining itself at any rate in the Germanic East of the Frankish Empire, it awoke to new life under the Carlovingian mayors of the palace.

Pepin postponed the annual assembly of the army to the 1st of May for military and economic reasons, making it a *Campus Madius* instead of a *Campus Martius*. Charles, however, did not keep to May, but according to need often chose a later date. Of course the great annual gathering had long ceased to be a gathering of all the warriors of the whole Empire. It was a gathering of the levy of the particular time and of the aristocracy. From the Mayfield the army often marched immediately to war, but a Mayfield might be held without any military expedition following, for at the Mayfield business of all kinds was to be discussed. "Let the Mayfield be summoned," so it runs on one occasion, "to treat of the safety of the Fatherland and the well-being of the Franks." But the assembled people were only there to express wishes, to bring forward grievances, and to receive decisions. Only the nobles deliberated with the monarch. In truth, the great annual assembly was not the organ of a constitutional participation of the people themselves. The participation of the people was but a fiction.

Important business was to be performed by king and empire, by king and people in common. This, since the rise of the Carlovingian dynasty, had been a formal principle, and still was so under Charles the Great. But in what manner the people were called to co-operate, who constituted or represented the people, was not laid down. If we may suppose that in the first days of Carlovingian rule the Marchfield or Mayfield was regarded as the organ of popular participation, and that thus a broad popular foundation was desired for the most important decisions of the Empire, yet in course of time that became less and less the case, and, at first perhaps occasionally, but later on generally, it was neglected.

CH. XXI.

Pepin's Law of Succession of 768 and the elevation of Carloman and Charles to the throne took place at small gatherings of nobles, and so did Charles' proclamation as successor of his brother in 771 and the important settlement of the Empire in 806. Even important acts of legislation were not taken in hand at the great annual gatherings, but at assemblies of nobles, for instance the decrees of the *Capitulare Heristallense* of 779, and the incisive rules of the Saxon Law of 797, and perhaps also the comprehensive legislative measures of 802. It was therefore no innovation when under Louis the Pious important laws in the year 816, and the extensive legislation of the year 819, were debated, not at general assemblies of the Empire, but at small meetings of nobles[1]. Without doubt, there was no longer any true participation by the people. Even if it was customary under Charles also to hold a general assembly every year and there to discuss all important affairs of the Empire, especially questions of legislation, yet the monarch was perfectly free to deal with even the most important questions at only a small meeting of nobles.

If we keep these facts in view, we must ask to what purpose was the clumsy institution of the Mayfield? Now that the requirement of the constitution that the people should meet annually to co-operate with the central government was enfeebled, and was now regarded as satisfied if the monarch consulted a considerable number of nobles and took their advice, the sole justification for the perpetuation of the Mayfield lay in military matters; to assemble the army and prepare for a campaign. For this reason, too, Charles chose different dates for holding the May-field, holding it amongst other times in the autumn, just as military needs required. The advantage of holding an annual review of the available forces could not outbalance the heavy sacrifice imposed upon the small man. Even the one very important purpose of affording all classes of the population the opportunity of a personal connexion with the centre of government, was no longer of great weight. Owing to the great extension of the Empire it was no longer possible, and it was besides satisfied by the institution of the king's envoys (*missi dominici*). Thus in the ninth century in times of peace the important reasons for the assembling of the people in arms were lacking. In other words, the Mayfield lost its justification from the moment that war was no longer a regular expression of the life of the State. The Mayfield necessarily disappeared when the great regular military expeditions ceased. This was already the case in the latter years of the reign of Charles the Great and under Louis the Pious. There still occurs for a time the contrast of *placita generalia* and *placita* in the old sense, that is in the sense that by the one was meant the assembly of the people equipped for war, and by the other the meetings of the nobles. But even in the latter part of

---

[1] Cf. the proof in Seeliger, *Volksrecht und Königsrecht*, pp. 336 ff.

the reign of Charles the former no longer took place annually, and instead of the people, only the nobles were summoned.

The transition from the old assembly of the army to the meetings of the nobles was easily and smoothly accomplished in the following manner. The spiritual and temporal nobles who acted at the Mayfields as the representatives of the people were responsible for the carrying out of the royal summons to the great annual gatherings. To them the command was issued to appear fully equipped—*hostiliter*. That implied the mobilisation of the forces as well as the call to the great annual assembly. Inasmuch as the command to the nobles now was to appear in the royal presence not *hostiliter* but *simpliciter*, *i.e.* not with the people under arms but with a simple escort, the change required by circumstances was brought about. The great annual gatherings which in earlier times had been gatherings of the nation under arms (Marchfield, Mayfield), became general meetings of nobles. There still existed a difference between the general and the little assembly, but it meant by this time a distinction between general and special meetings of nobles. And Hincmar, who lived two generations later than Charles, knew, as may easily be understood, only national gatherings of an aristocratic character. He understood the difference between the great and the little assembly in the sense of his own time, namely as between two kinds of meetings of nobles. If he then attributes only pre-liminary deliberations to the smaller gatherings, the composition of which was, as a matter of fact, dependent on the will of the monarch, and ascribes real decisions only to the general meetings of nobles, this arises from his aristocratic conception of the constitution and from his desire to assign to the aristocracy the position of a second independent power beside the monarch. But the age of Charles the Great knew nothing of this.

Thus the genuinely Germanic participation of the people in the government of the State appears strongly repressed under Charles the Great. In the Merovingian period it already seemed occasionally quite subdued, while with the rise of the Germanic dynasty of the Carlovingians it made a vigorous struggle to the front again, but it was really checked by the great personality of Charles and at the same time by the advance of the theocratic element in the monarchical authority. Charles the Great did not bind himself to ask the assent of a national assembly of definite organisation, but transacted the most important state business only at small gatherings of nobles, and thus made any visible limitation of his monarchical power by people or aristocracy illusory, and reduced the participation of the people as a matter of fact to a consultation of those classes of the people whose co-operation seemed to him desirable according to the occasion. At one time he laid the matter before the great annual gathering, at another before a small meeting of nobles, at another before the representatives of the tribe concerned in the new laws. But in spite of this, there remains the peculiar fact that reference is always made to participation by the subjects and that it was clearly regarded as necessary. Thus we can say that the idea of participation by the people was not fully overcome even by the violent effort of the monarchy under Charles the Great. It was greatly hindered, but it lived on to attain new force in favourable circumstances.

Is a similar relation of king and people to be observed in connexion with the formation of Law and with legislation?

Law is formed by custom and legislation. For a long time the formation of Law through custom preponderated among the Germanic peoples. Though many a precept had been given in old times, and many a sage had acted as lawgiver, the systematic development of Law through legislation belongs to a later stage of civilisation, to the time when the Germanic races had come under the influence of the superior Roman civilisation. From the fifth century the Germanic peoples in the mass, the West Goths, the Franks, the Burgundians, the Alemanni, the Bavarians, the Frisians, the Saxons, attained step by step to a written form of their Laws as they came into immediate contact with Roman civilisation. These great systematic codices, called the "Folkrights," were intended for the most part only to formulate the Right already existing among the people, but naturally they frequently advanced consciously or unconsciously to new statutes. And then in the Frankish kingdoms, from the sixth century onwards, appended to the Folkright, came special laws, royal regulations which supplemented or modified the outlines of the Folkright, or dealt with new spheres of law. From the eighth decade of the ninth century these special edicts of the kings, on account of their divisions into smaller sections (*capitula*), were called Capitularies, an expression which has been generally adopted by modern historians. Folkright and Capitularies are the two great sources of the Frankish period which afford information regarding the laws of corporate life on all sides. They are the result of those new demands of a more definite corporate life with common aims, demands which were already arising in the older Merovingian period and reached the summit of their development and their fullest satisfaction through Charles the Great.

In the year 802—so relate the *Annales Laureshamenses*—the Emperor Charles summoned the dukes, counts, and the rest of the people with the legislators, recited and amended the different Folkrights and caused them when so amended to be written down, and issued the rule that the judges should judge only according to the written Law. This account, freed from its exaggerations, agrees with the report of the historian Einhard, " When Charles the Great, after accepting the imperial dignity, observed that there were many defects in the laws of the people and that the Franks have two Laws differing from each other in many points, he intended supplying what was lacking, harmonising what was contradictory, improving what was bad and useless. But of all this he only carried through the addition to the laws of some chapters, and even these incomplete. The still unwritten Laws of all the peoples who were subject to his rule, he caused to be written down." The transmission of the laws entirely confirms the accuracy of these accounts. Numerous manuscripts of the Salic and Ripuarian Folkrights testify that in the Carlovingian period, and apparently at Charles the Great's instigation, steps were taken towards re-writing the old laws, but only verbal improvements were intended, not the removal of clauses that had long ceased to be effective. We know further that Charles caused hitherto unwritten Laws to be written down—perhaps portions of the Frisian Folkright, certainly those of the Saxons, Thuringians, and the Chamavi. The Assembly of Aachen of 802 must be regarded as the scene of these legislative efforts. Hither were summoned those familiar with the Laws of the different tribes in order to procure the material.

But the great Emperor's comprehensive scheme of reform remained unaccomplished, and it was necessary to issue numerous regulations on particular points to correct and to supplement the old copies in order to satisfy the need for a development of the Law. It was through the Capitularies that this was accomplished. They had long been known in the kingdom of the Franks, but under Charles the Great they attained the vast extent to which the remains that have come down to us testify.

Year by year prescripts of every possible kind were issued, decrees which claimed validity either in the whole kingdom or in single districts, rules of a general or special character, explanations of existing regulations of these Laws, supplements to correct conspicuous deficiencies in previous laws, and in addition directions for the state officials in their government.

Are we to separate these laws and ordinances into two groups, according to the difference of the authorities, summoned conformably to the constitution and concerned in their origin, and according to the difference in their contents and the period of their validity? Are we to oppose Folkright to the King's Law?

In the period before the founding of the Frankish Empire the different German tribes had developed their Law mainly according to custom and popularity. To do so was a matter for the people. But when the rule of the Merovingian kings had extended over the different Germanic tribes, this purely popular method began to be disused and another to be followed as well. Although their own hereditary right was to remain to the members of the different tribes and what is called the Principle of Personality was recognised, yet a great change in the tribal Law was unavoidable, due to the Empire and to the royal power representing the Empire. For the Empire laid claim to the supreme power of making laws quite generally and unconditionally. It of course regulated the Right of the people chiefly in reference to the authority of the Empire, but it by no means renounced influence on the laws of the members of the tribe amongst themselves, on penal, legal, and private Law. And so on the one hand stands the Right of the tribe which still continued to be developed in the local courts—the Folkright, while on the other hand are the laws issued by the imperial authority which in a special way supplement the Folkright and develop or often contradict it. These are the King's Law, issuing directly from the king, the creator and upholder of the Empire. In fact two powers take part in the formation of the law— king and people. For the historical understanding of social institutions, it is of interest to seek their different origins, and in the case of many laws it is of importance to determine whether they issued from the judicial consciousness of the people themselves whom they concerned or whether they were dictated by the royal authority. In a certain sense the working of two different forces in the formation of the Law is rightly recognised in the assertion of a legal dualism, in the contrast of Folkright and King's Law[1].

But only in a certain sense. Any deeper systematic distinction is erroneous. Erroneous is the assumption that according to the constitution the king could exercise no influence on the Right of the tribes united in the Empire, and that only in virtue of his Banright, that is, his power of command, essentially contrary to law, did he decree new laws, which as King's Right entered into rivalry and competition with the Folkright. It is erroneous to assume that Folkright is to be understood merely as Customary Right and the King's Right as Right of legislation. Erroneous are all further theories about the constitution founded on this idea. Not by virtue of a power of coercion, but by virtue of the power of making laws inherent in the monarchy did the king influence the development of Law; not only through laws but also through his officials, on occasion of delivery of judgment, did he bring into use new aims of the King's Law. The opinion must be rejected that in the Frankish period, afterwards as before, the people continued to develop their Right by themselves and for themselves according to custom, while the king on the contrary issued ordinances resembling laws and so created a second system of Law in opposition to the Folkright[2].

But another attempt also to systematise the dualism of Folkright and King's Law[3] must be looked upon as unsuccessful, the attempt namely to discover the characteristic difference between Folkright and the King's Law of the Frankish monarchy even in the existing laws

---

[1] This dualism was first, with great clearness, emphasised by Sohm.
[2] This is Sohm's view.
[3] So Boretius, Brunner, Schroeder, and several others.

and to divide the laws into two groups according to their force, and more especially according to the powers responsible for their origin— one group, that of laws approved by the people and formally accepted— laws according to Folkright—and the other group, that of laws issued without any decision of the people—laws according to King's Law. Of such a division the ancient authorities know nothing. An assent to certain laws by the people gathered in the Hundred Court was not constitutionally necessary. Even though the principle was effective that laws were not to be made without the co-operation of those classes for whom they were intended, the summons to a Diet of those concerned was clearly sufficient. For the participation of the people ended with participation of the subjects in Diets. That is the fixed principle of the Frankish State to which all accounts of the legislation of the Frankish kings point.

In connexion with the contrast of Folkright and King's Law, the Carlovingian Capitularies which deal with secular matters, and from which only Capitularies containing ecclesiastical regulations are to be separated, are commonly divided into three groups according to contents, origin, and period of validity: (1) *Capitula legibus addenda*, (2) *Capitula per se scribenda*, (3) *Capitula missorum*. The first are said to contain those decrees which modify or supplement laws of the Folkright; the second to refer to such ordinances as concerned the relation of the subjects to the Empire; the third to be instructions for the king's envoys. The first, according to the usual view, were raised to law by a decision of the people; the second were called into existence on the ground of an agreement of king and Diet and did not claim lasting validity; the third owed their origin to the personal decision of the monarch alone and were of merely temporary validity. The first embrace Folkright; the second King's Law; the third administrative measures.

This favourite differentiation[1] proceeds from modern legal conceptions and reads them into an age that knew nothing of such legal differences, and could not know. When several explanations were necessary at the same time for one Folkright—the *Lex Salica, Ripuaria,* or the *Lex Baiuvariorum,* or when numerous supplements to the *leges* generally were to be issued, it was the custom at the king's court to combine them in special ordinances, in *Capitula legibus addenda.* If, however, there were only a few points of the law in question to be explained, while other legal measures were to be taken at the same time, they were all combined in one ordinance. But of a different origin and of a different validity there is no trace. Whether the penal or judicial clauses occur in a capitulary which simply contains analogous regulations supplementing the rules of a Folkright, or whether they occur in a law referring to matters of a

---

[1] Started by Boretius, adopted by many investigators.

different character, there is no hint of a different origin, and scarcely of a difference in validity, for this was quite independent of the intrinsic significance of the law. That was merely the consequence of a purely external method of legislating applied according to circumstances. It was only applied according to circumstances, for the great mass of extant capitularies shew that the Carlovingians did not and could not know anything of the principles of a threefold division. If we disregard the not very numerous Carlovingian capitularies that can be reckoned as *Capitula legibus addenda,* and if we also disregard those ordinances which are evidently instructions for the king's envoys, there remains the great mass of the capitularies, containing regulations of the most different kinds, judicial and administrative regulations, ordinances for the army, for the administration of justice, for the Church, and in civil matters. That is characteristic of the whole government under Charles the Great—the needs of the moment are satisfied. To the king's court came complaints, requests, inquiries, which were dealt with by the king and councillors or in some cases by the assembled Diet. As ecclesiastical regulations were frequently grouped together in independent ordinances, so occasionally—when the subject required or permitted it— were single groups of secular ordinances: instructions, supplements, or modifications of *leges.* But what had by chance been jointly debated and decided could also just as well be comprehended in a law. This was carried out on no intentional system. Rather, the want of a system was characteristic. Significant is the attempt of the State to provide for the development of the Law by numerous disconnected measures to meet special needs of the moment. There was nothing like a principle of difference between law and prescript, nor even a clear difference between legislation and administration.

Two powers were in operation: King and People. They worked in harmony, they also worked in opposition. A conflict between popular influence and royal influence necessarily manifested itself in the restricted sphere of the Frankish tribe from the moment that the monarchy in its excessive strength arose as a new independent power. But it was seen still more significantly in the districts of those other Germanic tribes which had been brought into subjection by the Frankish king and possessed a copious system of Law independently developed, and which were now to be embraced in the unity of the Frankish Empire. But the conflict of popular and royal influences was not limited to the sphere of legislation. It naturally became prominent in all spheres of corporate life. The consideration of the administration of the provinces under Charles will also shew this—the ancient popular institutions on the one hand, the new desired by the central authority on the other.

The Carlovingian government of the provinces was based upon the system of counties. The whole Empire was divided into districts, at the head of which stood counts, an old institution already known under the Merovingians, but first consistently and fully used by Charles the Great. Thereby a long process was brought to a close, a process of competition between the institutions desired by the Frankish government and the ancient institutions of the different tribes and districts incorporated into the Frankish State. We are often no longer able to recognise what existed before the Frankish conquest, and how it was overcome by institutions of the Frankish kingdom. But there had been a long struggle between the two forces—between the old popular institutions on the one hand, and those proceeding from the Frankish authority on the other. In this sense there was a significant opposition of popular and royal influences, of Folkright and King's Law. Gradually we can observe the advance of what was desired by the central authority.

When the Merovingians conquered Gaul and extended their rule over different tribes of the Germanic East, they did not abolish the national institutions altogether. Just as they left to the different peoples their own Law, so they left them also their national institutions. The tribal authorities largely remained, and were merely brought into a condition of dependence, looser or closer. But the process of centralisation was continued by the Carlovingians and perfected by Charles the Great. The old institution of *Herzog*, or Duke, partly local ruler, partly local official, was set aside—a characteristic piece of internal policy. Duke Tassilo of Bavaria was the last representative of the internal ducal authority. After his deposition in the year 788, the Bavarian district was linked on to the usual Frankish county administration. Only among the Basques in Vasconia and the Bretons in Brittany are the native dukes, in the old Merovingian sense, still to be found, even under Charles. Elsewhere dukes are met with, but not as independent representatives of local popular authority. They are merely officials of the king, furnished with extraordinary military power, to whom—sometimes only temporarily—larger provincial districts were assigned or special full powers on the borders of the Empire. Their office, however, as a regular part of the constitution was unknown under Charles. The provincial division of the land rested upon one indispensable basis—the division into counties.

Naturally, on the introduction of this system, former divisions of the people and land were utilised. In Roman Gaul, the old town districts, the *civitates*, became the Frankish counties, *Gaue* or districts; in the purely German parts, the old divisions of people and land which sometimes corresponded to the old German tribes. How far old divisions were utilised or new ones created is, from the nature of the case, not open to investigation in particular instances. One thing must be clearly kept in mind in all examinations of the territorial division of the Frankish as of the later States—the designation *Gau* (*i.e.* District, Latin *Pagus*) very often refers to the county, but not always. It would be a mistake, though it has often been made, to regard every *Gau* as a future county. *Gau* also occurs from the very beginning as the name of other administrative districts besides those of the county. It occurs moreover as a purely geographical description without reference to a definite administrative district. *Gau* and county were frequently synonymous, but occasionally were different from the beginning.

Under Charles the Great the county is the administrative district simply, the natural base of all state activities. Wherever this system of counties was wanting in Charles' Empire, the imperial authority purposely abstained from a real incorporation of that district into the Empire. We may say definitely that the measure of the realisation of the system of counties shews us the measure of acceptance of the imperial power itself.

The *garafio* (*gerefa, greva*) the Franks had already possessed before the foundation of the Empire. *Comites* were already known in the Merovingian age as powerful officials of the Gaulish *civitates*. For some time *graf* and *comes* stood side by side in the Merovingian kingdom. Not certainly in the same *gau*. The relation is rather to be so understood as that the Roman districts in connexion with older arrangements possessed *comites,* while the purely Frankish districts had *grafs.* The distinction soon disappeared. The *comes* adopted much from the *graf*, the *graf* much from the *comes,* and there arose the single office of *graf* under the Frankish monarchy. The *graf* is the definite organ of royal government in judicial, fiscal, military, and administrative respects.

The usual official title for the *graf* is under Charles the Great the Latin word *comes,* and more rarely the less definite expressions *praefectus, praeses, rector,* and also *consul.*

Charles disposed of the office as he thought fit. No general uniform principle directed the choice of men. Largely it was eminent Franks who were placed in important posts of trust, whether in Francia itself or in conquered districts to maintain the authority of the Empire in face of the native chiefs. Occasionally, however, Charles sought to win the most eminent men of the conquered race to himself by conferring upon them the most important provincial posts, and in this way to render possible the gradual reduction of the new people to an integral part of the Empire. Then again, it is reported to us that he bestowed the office of count on men who were not noble, even upon freedmen. In fact, in the bestowal of offices, only the one principle prevailed, that those were to be placed at the head of the district from whom the best service for the good of the Empire might be expected.

The office was bestowed for life, but of course in case of disloyalty, or even of bad government, it might be withdrawn without hesitation. That Charles always reserved a free hand for himself is testified beyond doubt, and therefore the allusions to the count's owing his office to the grace of God are not so much emphasis of independence as a confession of the humility due to God.

The authority of the count himself was unusually extensive. It embraced everything that concerned the State. The count is the king's representative in his district. Just as the authority of the State manifested itself primarily in military and judicial matters, so also did the activities of the count. The count was the supreme administrator of justice in his district. Usually he had to hold the general assemblies of the *gau*, which, according to the regulations of Charles, brought together all the freemen of the *gau* two or three times a year in what were afterwards called the regular "Things." Difficult law cases, it was specially enjoined by Charles the Great, the count was to determine himself and not to leave to his subordinate officials. In the court of the *centenarius* or subordinate judge, it runs in one law, no man may be condemned to death, loss of freedom, or forfeiture of land or slaves— that was reserved for the count or for the king's envoy. It was not intended that this higher jurisdiction should be restricted to the three great annual "Things," but only that the transfer of the most important cases into the hands of the subordinate officials should be prevented[1]. It was a principle of the constitution that the count was the ordinary judge in the *gau*.

The organisation of the army was also in the hands of the count. By him the levies were led or superintended, and he himself went on campaign with the vassals of his district—one of his most important functions. On him it further rested to summon to the royal service and to exact state requirements from the freemen of the *gau*. He had to represent in himself the special defensive authority of the king, just as he had to see to the general peace. And just as the State in Carlovingian times extended its power in different directions, the powers of the count also, the representative of the State in the *gau*, seem unusually extensive, particularly in the direction of matters of police.

In ecclesiastical affairs, also, the count is to help, as though assistant to the bishop. Just as things secular and spiritual converged in Charles' kingship, so willing co-operation was desired on the part of local bearers of ecclesiastical and secular authority. The counts were directed to be obedient to the bishops and to support them in all things. Rivalry often disturbed the harmony, and Charles caused inquiry to be made how an exact definition of the count's powers in spiritual matters and of the bishop's in secular could be accomplished. But there was never any doubt that bishops and counts were to be equally regarded as important officials of the State. Louis the Pious caused the bishops regularly to make reports concerning the counts, and the counts concerning the bishops, so that he could exercise exact control. Naturally, the count was furnished with the coercive powers indispensable to all rulers. Such power under Charles the Great was so regulated that

[1] Such is the view of Waitz, *Verfassungsgesch.* iv. pp. 381 ff., to which for the most part sufficient attention is not paid.

punishments were even fixed for disobedience to official orders, varying according to the nature of the order, in such a way that the official was allowed to determine a penalty independently of the object of the orders, and graduated according to his personal authority[1]. According to the Alemannic Law the count's "ban" amounted to six shillings, according to the Saxon Capitulary of Charles the Great, for smaller transgressions it was fifteen, and for more serious cases of disobedience sixty shillings. Not till later, when the sixty shilling penalty was more generally used and had become the punishment for disregard of a royal order, was the official who was looked upon as essentially the king's official, the count, regarded as holder of this king's ban.

Only a peculiar form of the system of government by counts, not an abrogation of it, is seen in the organisation of the marches, which may justly be looked on as the personal work of the great Emperor. That the counties situated on the border of the Empire were provided with arrangements for the defence and protection of the Empire is natural. We must distinguish from these border counties the march district proper, the newly conquered border land or else that specially arranged for border defence, provided with numerous fortifications and forming a bulwark before the counties of the Empire itself. So arose under Charles himself, or at any rate at his instance, the Spanish, Breton, Saxon or Danish, Sorbian, Avarian, and Friulian marks. Those at the head of them were called *graf*, also *margrave*, *markherzog*, and by similar titles. Sometimes border counties were in connexion with the marches, and so arose a specially strong power, predominantly military, which obtained for its owner the proud title of *duke*. Thus we can understand when the Monk of St Gall, at the end of the ninth century, relates how on the borders of the Empire Charles departed from the rule that to one person only one county should be assigned.

If we see a thoroughgoing uniformity in the division into counties, and only those districts were freed from it which had not been completely incorporated into the Empire, we cannot trace a similar uniformity in the case of the subordinate officials. Here there were great differences. And that is perfectly intelligible. In the first place, if the Empire laid great weight on the carrying out of the county system and sought to put aside everything that resisted the Frankish arrangements, of course the old popular officials could no longer be left in the lower places. Thus many differences are due to a continuation of the old popular system or to a connexion of it with Frankish arrangements. And moreover districts in private ownership became more and more important, and the officials of the private owners more and more assumed public functions, dispossessed the lower state officials and took their place. Hence, in the dominions of Charles the Great we observe

---

[1] Cf. Seeliger, *Volksrecht und Königsrecht*, pp. 356 ff.

different officials acting in the subordinate positions side by side, and the same official titles occur among those holding different official positions.

The officials working under the counts are for the most part to be divided into three classes: (1) Assistants and representatives of the count not restricted to one part of his district. (2) Superintendents of a subdivision of the county. (3) Different officials of private landowners, local superintendents, or town officials for special, particularly military, matters. In the first group the *missi* of the counts and the " viscounts " can be reckoned, although a definite office of this kind can hardly be assumed. We must rather suppose that a count frequently appointed one of his subordinate officials, a *centenarius* and " vicar " to take his place, but only temporarily, and that in such cases this subordinate appeared as *missus* or " viscount." To the second group belongs above all the *centenarius*, the old Frankish official, who must be identified[1] with the " Thunginus " of the Salic " Volksrecht," the old national judge, who was forced into dependence upon the king's officials, the counts, and restricted to the administration of justice in minor matters, in order to leave the higher entirely to the count. To the *centenarius* corresponds the vicar. It is quite clear that under Charles the Great a division of the counties into centenaries and vicariates was everywhere carried out, at least in the middle and western counties of the Empire. To these subdivisions of the West corresponded the *Goe* of Saxony, and to the Frankish *centenarii* and vicars the Saxon *Gografen*. To the third group belong not only the superintendents of the royal domains called *judices* and other officials of these domains like the *villici*, who later were found everywhere, but above all the tribunes (*tribuni*) and mayors (*scultheti*), who are found in smaller districts as executive officials. *Tribuni* and *sculheti* are, from the first, not names for a uniform lower office but for different, though similar, subordinate officials— there were *sculheti* of the king, the count, the private landowner, and others.

But great as were the differences among the officials in the State, and great as was the concession made to the peculiarities of the different peoples and to different local needs, yet Charles knew how to retain in his own hands perfect control over the whole. Indeed it was characteristic of his government that all who had public duties to perform, or who had to provide for the maintenance of Law and Order even in the smallest districts, were controlled by the State and made responsible to the State. The authority of the State did not draw back before private ownership. It pressed forward everywhere. The counts supervised not only their own subordinates but also the officials of ecclesiastical and secular lords.

---

[1] That is the general older view which H. Brunner has tried to set aside, but in my opinion unsuccessfully. He wishes to make a sharp distinction between the *Centenarius* and the *Thunginus*.

All belonged to the one great organism, to the universal State, in the centre of which stood the monarch himself.

But how could the centre remain in living connexion with distant parts and with the provincial officers? To solve this problem was the task of the *missi dominici*, perhaps the most peculiar of all the Carlovingian institutions.

The summit of the Carlovingian constitution was the organisation of the office of the king's envoys, the *missi dominici*. These were not intended to take the place of the dukes removed by the Carlovingians, nor to be bearers of a provincial authority, but to bring the king's will into the provinces, and to render possible an immediate connexion of the people with the supreme government of the Empire. As in all institutions, so here too Charles made a link with what had long existed, while transforming it into something essentially new. The Merovingians had already employed *missi* in different kinds of state business, military, judicial, administrative, fiscal. But it was always particular and special duty which the *missus* had to perform by the king's commission. In the later Merovingian period this institution fell into disuse, and it was not till the time of the Carlovingian mayors of the palace that it was revived. From the time of Charles Martel occurs the designation *missi discurrentes*. Whether that really signifies that *missi* were sent out to travel over a definite district, to control all officials and supplement their work, and whether the *missi* then possessed full powers generally, cannot be decided. But it was certainly so in the first years in the reign of Charles the Great, who made the *missi discurrentes*, the travelling envoys, a regular institution of the State. From 779 the *missi* appear with the quite general function *ad justitias faciendas, i.e.* to preserve the right in every direction. They acted with the counts, and eventually against them, for the administration of justice; they watched the work of the judges, and themselves held a court; they took steps for the improvement of ecclesiastical affairs with or without the bishop, they inspected the monasteries, and they superintended all officials.

Extensive as were the duties of these *missi* even at the beginning of Charles' reign, and essential as was their work for the organisation of the Empire, yet the whole institution only reached its full development after Charles' coronation as emperor through edicts of the Diet held at Aachen in the year 802[1]. Charles no longer wished, so report the *Annals of Lorsch*, to send out as *missi* vassals who possessed no lands. He appointed rather archbishops, bishops, and abbots, with dukes and counts, in whose case bribery need not be feared.

On broad lines, their duties were characterised generally in a capitulary of 802, the particulars being appended in a long list. The

---

[1] The result of the investigations of Waitz (cf. III. p. 451) remains unshaken, even after the further work of Krause.

whole institution, which had long established itself, now appears raised and made permanent. The Empire was divided into large fixed districts (*missatica, legationes*), perhaps partly already in such a way as is testified for the time of Louis the Pious, or perhaps the *missatica* then corresponded to the metropolitan provinces.

Every year these envoys were sent out, generally two or three together, under Charles frequently an ecclesiastic and a layman. They received instructions, directions arranged in sections respecting their official duties, in which too were included general orders to be communicated to the officials and people of the Missaticum (*capitula missorum*). They had to give a report of their work, as a rule probably at a meeting of the Empire, to make inquiries in case of doubt and to obtain new decisions from the monarch or the meeting. The *missus* was to enter into communication both with the officials and also with the people themselves, for to afford assistance against oppression and violence even of the officials was the most important duty of the royal envoys. For this reason they were required to hold general meetings. According to a decree of Louis the Pious, this general meeting was to take place in the middle of May, but of course in case of need it could be divided into several meetings to be held in different places. Here the bishops, abbots, counts, royal stewards, and representatives of the abbesses had to appear, and every count had to bring with him his vicars, centenars, and three or four of the judges. At these provincial assemblies the envoy sought to obtain disclosures of the affairs of his province through the statements of those dwelling in the gaus, who were bound to truth by oath, and of witnesses of crimes. Abuses were removed, bad officials brought to account or even summoned before the king. That this arrangement already existed under Charles may be taken as proved. In addition to these assemblies, the envoys also held special courts of justice in the different judicial divisions of their provinces. They were, however, not to injure but merely to control and supplement the judicial work of the regular judges, especially the counts. Hence their judicial duties were limited to four months, January, April, July, October, while the remaining months were reserved for the courts of the counts. In each of these four months, Charles ordered courts to be held at different places with the count of the district. At other times the envoys travelled about, inspected churches and monasteries, and everywhere saw that things were in order.

Together with the regular envoys, extraordinary envoys were still used as of old on special missions, whether military, judicial, or ecclesiastical. But no great significance was ever attached to them. The importance of the whole institution rests purely on the regular envoys.

The purpose of the centralisation finds expression in this endeavour to preserve the unity of the whole while justifiable local differences were recognised. Unity was to be in the kingdom. Because the king could not appear everywhere in person, his place was taken by men who were to be regarded as his representatives. Herein lies the essential character of the whole institution—arrangements were made which enabled the king to appear personally active in all parts of the Empire. The fundamental idea of the purely personal and immediate government of the monarch is thus realised. In this peculiarity lay the strength, but at the same time also the weakness, of the institution itself. Its strength shewed itself in the fact that thereby an immense influence of the king was made possible, and all things were quickened from the centre. Its weakness was seen in the excessive dependence for strength on the personality of the monarch, and in the failure of continuous and immediate influence of the royal authority from the moment the central power failed. The institution had no strength of its own, it was absolutely dependent on the circumstances of the court. And when the influence from the centre, which under Charles had been so vigorous and powerful, ceased in the later years of Louis the Pious, the institution of the royal envoys became degenerate. It either ceased entirely or it became territorial and thereby was robbed of its proper and original living principle.

Nothing manifests so clearly the whole inner development of the unified Carlovingian State as the history of the royal envoys. Nothing reveals more surely the peculiar nature of the State than this one institution.

The universal empire of the great Charles could not long outlive its founder. General forces certainly were in existence which assisted the unification, such as the thought of universal unity which proceeded from the ecclesiastical conception and from the Roman Empire. It is true that the genius of Charles made these ideas of unity serviceable to his efforts for power. But he failed to equalise the diverging intellectual and material needs of the different peoples subjected to his rule. And he failed to erect a bureaucracy strong in itself and not absolutely dependent upon the changeable circumstances of the court. A bureaucracy certainly was erected; but a bureaucracy of a peculiar kind, a patriarchal bureaucracy. Such a one has no independent strength of its own, it shares for the most part the fate of the ruling family, and is chiefly supported by the ability of the monarch. If this fails, then the State itself fails. To create anything enduring of this kind was beyond the power even of Charles the Great.

It was not the advance of the feudal system that brought about the early collapse of the Carlovingian Empire. The feudal system only furnished the outer form and the external support for the decomposing tendencies. These had their root in the nature of the social development of the Western peoples themselves, in general factors of their civilisation both material and mental, and also in the personal character of the leaders of the State.

CHAPTER XXII.

THE PAPACY, TO CHARLES THE GREAT.

THE growth of the papal power can be regarded from two standpoints according as we interpret the expression in an earthly or a spiritual sense. Are we to regard the popes as rulers over large domains and at times the most powerful of Italian princes; or are we to look on them as the heads of Western Christendom, the supreme arbiters of religion and morals from Iceland to Sicily, from the Atlantic to the eastern out-skirts of Germany and Hungary? At the beginning of the seventh century they were neither, and by the end of the eleventh they were both. Till 1859 their secular dominion remained unimpaired in extent, and since 1517 they have ceased to exercise undisputed moral authority in Western Christendom. In 1870 the last vestige of their temporal power was wrested from their grasp, yet in the same year they made claims to a spiritual authority which would not have been conceded to them by the Church even when their influence was paramount. Closely interwoven therefore as are the temporal and spiritual powers of the Papacy, they are not identical; and however difficult it may be to separate one from the other, they must be distinguished. Yet in the present case it is necessary to deal with the subject from both aspects, paying special attention to the question of the process of the liberation of the Papacy from influences which might subsequently have controlled or fettered its development.

Gregory the Great is said to have originated the medieval Papacy; and this is in part true, though it took nearly three centuries after his work was done to produce the first of the medieval popes. Nicolas I inaugurated the line of priest-kings of Western Christendom in a truer sense than Gregory I. It is true that the earlier pontiff was far the greater man; but the office he filled was less in the eyes of his con-temporaries; and he was obliged to address kings and princes in a more submissive tone than that employed by Nicolas in the ninth century. Gregory was, in fact, a great subject, possessed of vast estates and considerable wealth, able to exercise a powerful influence on the politics of his age, to arrange treaties and to delimit frontiers. But, though a great noble, he was not a sovereign prince, his lands were estates, not dominions; he spoke to emperors and kings not as their equal but as a subordinate; he even judged them from the standpoint of an inferior. Nicolas I on the other hand was lord paramount in his own dominion, and addressed the princes of Western Europe with the authority of a ruler on earth, vested with spiritual powers which rendered him infinitely their superior. The task before us is to trace how this came about, shewing the successive stages by which the Roman pontiffs asserted their independence of all secular authority. It is this which differentiates the Papacy from every other Christian bishopric, making it both a temporal and a spiritual power, and the accomplishment of this took place between A.D. 604 and 868, though this chapter concludes with the year 800.

The immediate successors of Gregory the Great do not appear to have given much promise of the future eminence of the throne they occupied. The popes of the seventh century succeeded one another with suspicious rapidity, few occupying the See of Rome for more than a few years. Appointed by permission of the Emperor or his representative in Italy, the exarch of Ravenna, the pontiffs submitted themselves to the secular power, and felt its heavy hand whenever they presumed to resist the imperial commands even in matters spiritual; nor was it till the eighth century, when the Lombards were extruding the Greeks, as the imperialists of Constantinople had already begun to be called, from the shores of Italy, that a series of greater popes, more fortunate than their predecessors in the duration of their pontificates, were able to assert and maintain their authority. Then it was that the Lombards, who had captured Ravenna, and extended their influence to the South of Italy and were preparing to occupy the *ducatus Romae*, found themselves confronted by the Roman pontiffs claiming to represent the majesty of the Empire and to seize those prerogatives which, as they maintained, had only been wrested from the hands of the Greeks in order to revert to Rome and its chief priest.

Thus began those extraordinary negotiations between the popes and the Frankish rulers, who with the sanction of St Peter were transformed first into native kings and finally into emperors and legitimate lords of the Roman world. In gratitude for these services the kings of the Franks and emperors of the Romans made over to the See of Rome certain parts of northern and central Italy which had belonged to the Empire in the seventh century.

At the same time, whilst the popes were consolidating their authority over Christendom and their dominion in Italy by diplomacy, their power was being strengthened by the assertion of legal claims to all privileges which the reverence of princes was bestowing upon them. Appeals to the antiquity rather of the imagination than of history attempted to shew that the claims of the Roman See were based on immemorial rights or on the acts of emperors whose names, already half legendary in the West, were bound up with the vanished glories of imperial days. The false decretals and the donation of Constantine were demonstrating that nothing which the popes could receive or demand was beyond their rights, and casting a false glamour of legality over any claims they might choose to make.

In dealing with the strange and wonderful history before us it is remarkable that we meet with comparatively few noteworthy characters or dramatic incidents if we except Charles the Great and his coronation at Rome. Hardly any literature worthy of the name illumines our path, and the verses which have come down to us are sufficient to shew that poetry was a lost art. The revival of civilisation and government under Charles is only remarkable because of the darkness which preceded and followed it, and the two striking features of the age, the rise of Islām and the revival of the Roman Empire in the East after a series of unparalleled disasters, do not come into our purview of events. Despite all this the squalor which surrounds the period is brightened by the presence of great ideals, which men kept in their minds and before their eyes, though they were unable to give them form or substance. The remedy for the anarchy of Western Europe was sought in the ideal which the Roman Empire had left, a unity of government for the human race; and men's eyes were turned to Christian Rome to provide what was so sorely needed. The faith in Jesus Christ went far beyond the Roman law in recognising the unity of mankind; and from it, as embodied in the Roman Church, the inheritor of the city which had been mistress of the world, the Frankish monarchs hoped that a Christian Empire would arise to federate humanity. For centuries successive generations persevered in carrying out this idea; and who can deny that it was a grand and noble one? The rise of the papal power is one of the most important events in modern history because it was inspired by the motive which dominated the best thinkers of the Middle Ages and raised their impotent efforts above the sordid policy of our own day. Even the completeness of their failure does not rob them of the glory of having seen great visions and dreamed splendid dreams.

The rise of the papal power was due alike to the necessity of political independence and to the circumstances which freed the popes from the domination of the emperors in Constantinople and the Lombard conquerors of Italy, and enabled them to secure the assistance of the Franks from beyond the Alps: it was due still more to the disintegration of the Empire of Charles the Great under his unfortunate successors. It will perhaps be of assistance to us if each of these be taken separately. We will therefore discuss (1) the Papacy and the Eastern emperors, (2) the Lombards, (3) the Franks, and the new Western Empire.

(1) Since the outbreak of the Arian dispute the eastern provinces had never known the meaning of religious peace, though the way in which that controversy had ended might have encouraged hopes that similar differences were not incapable of adjustment. Despite the

attempt of Constantius to coerce his subjects to unity in his struggle
with Athanasius and despite the feebler efforts of Valens, the question was
allowed much freedom of debate; and the creed of Nicaea, as explained
by the wisdom of the Cappadocian fathers, was ultimately accepted by
all. But the unfortunate dispute concerning the Two Natures of our
Lord, partly owing to the unscrupulous character of those who engaged in
it, and partly to the mutual jealousies of the great patriarchates of the
East, produced schisms which seriously threatened the peace of the
Empire, and ultimately lost it some of its most important provinces.
In this great dispute Rome twice intervened, first in favour of Cyril in
condemnation of Nestorius, and later in opposition to Dioscorus against
Eutyches. On the latter occasion the pope, Leo the Great, put forward
his famous *Tome*, which the Western Church considered to be a fitting
end to the whole controversy. Not so thought many of the Oriental
Churches; especially those of Egypt and Syria, by whom the proceedings
of the Council of Chalcedon were regarded as an insult to Cyril, the
revered head of the Alexandrian Church. In Constantinople, a city
which gained an evil name for the formidable character of its riots and
seditions, parties were evenly divided between the upholders and opponents
of the Council of Chalcedon, between whom the reigning Emperor
endeavoured often in vain to hold the balance, generally at the cost of
being denounced as a heretic and traitor to the Faith.

Policy seemed to require that the Church should come to some such
agreement as was arrived at in the Arian controversy, during which the
work of the Council of Nicaea, without being repudiated, was somewhat modified and explained. In like manner it was hoped that the
ambiguities of the Council of Chalcedon would be removed by the
conciliatory action of the ecclesiastical authority backed by that of
the Emperor. In the Christian East matters of religion and doctrine
had always been considered to lie within the sphere of the imperial
prerogative, and the Emperor regarded himself as even more than the
clergy responsible for the maintenance of the purity of the faith. But
to the Western ecclesiastics the faith as defined by Leo was not to be
explained but accepted with unquestioning obedience, and any attempt
to reopen the question was an insult to his memory and to the Roman
See. Accordingly, when at the instigation of Acacius of Constantinople,
Zeno sanctioned (481) the Henoticon, or scheme of union with the
Monophysites, the Roman Church broke off all intercourse with that of
Constantinople. Fortunately for the prestige of the popes, Italy was
under the government first of Odovacar and afterwards of Theodoric,
both of whom were barbarians professing Arianism, and no intervention
from Constantinople was possible. Till A.D. 519 the Old and the New
Rome remained in a condition of religious separation, and union was
only brought about by the submission of the Church of the new capital.
With the accession of Justinian (527) and the subjugation of Italy

by the Byzantines (535–553) the Papacy entered upon a series of humiliations which no barbarian ruler had even dreamed of inflicting upon it. The loyalty and submission displayed by the popes is a proof of the awe in which they held the majesty of the Empire.

The attitude of Justinian towards the Roman Church was frankly autocratic: he expected and exacted obedience. For the early part of his reign he favoured the orthodox, whilst his wife, the powerful Empress Theodora, inclined to the Monophysite party. But at her death Justinian inclined to a compromise suggested to him by Theodore Askidas, bishop of Caesarea. Briefly, this was to condemn the writings of three divines specially obnoxious to the Monophysites, whilst otherwise maintaining the dignity of the Fourth General Council. Justinian has been reproached for devoting his time to the study of theology instead of attending to the politics of his empire; but in truth, its tranquillity mainly depended on the theological question, and the Emperor hoped that in condemning Theodore of Mopsuestia, Theodoret's writings against Cyril, and the letter of Ibas to Maris the Persian he would render the settlement at Chalcedon acceptable to his Egyptian and other Monophysite subjects. Such was the political aim of the otherwise uninteresting controversy of the "Three Chapters." That the Roman See would oppose the imperial policy was inevitable, especially as the three writers condemned had been acquitted at Chalcedon, and to doubt the justice of the acts of this council was disloyalty to the memory of Pope Leo. But Justinian was not accustomed to allow his will to be disputed. Pope Vigilius was hurried from Rome to Constantinople and forced to assent to the condemnation of the Chapters at the Fifth General Council (553). Never had a pope, at any rate since the days of Liberius, endured such a humiliation. So fully was this realised in the West that the churches of Illyricum and Istria made the weakness of Vigilius, hampered as he was by the promises exacted by the Empress Theodora as the price of his consecration, the pretext of a schism which lasted for a generation or more.

The disasters which overtook the Eastern Empire in the seventh century might well excuse any attempt to procure ecclesiastical unity. More and more the divisions of the Church were becoming tokens of national rather than religious sympathy. The Monophysite in Egypt believed in One nature in Christ, not because he was a theologian but because he was the natural enemy of the Melchite or Greek Christians who declared that Christ was "in Two Natures." The century had opened with the remarkable successes of the Persians, who seemed to have wrested from the Romans the domination of the East and to have restored their Empire to the extent it had reached in the days of Cambyses. The overthrow of the despicable Phocas (610), however, made way for a monarch who, had he died a few years earlier than he did, would have been comparable to Alexander the Great. Heraclius rolled back the tide of conquest, restored the frontiers of the Empire, recovered the Holy Cross, and humiliated Persia. Is it to be wondered at, therefore, that the victorious Emperor should have made another attempt to reunite the Christians, and have listened to those who suggested that, if it could be acknowledged that in our Lord were two natures—the human and the divine—and but one working energy (ἐνέργεια δραστική), Monophysites would unite with the supporters of Chalcedon? To this Honorius (pope 625–638) was disposed to assent, and in his correspondence he used the term "one will" (*una voluntas*) as applying to the Saviour. Hence the controversy is known as the Monothelete. But the action of Honorius was profoundly unpopular in Rome; and the successes of the Muslims and the loss of Egypt and Syria were regarded as a just punishment of the heresy of Heraclius as expressed in his *Ekthesis.*

The Monothelete controversy was fraught with humiliation for the See of Rome. Constans II (641–668), the brutal grandson of Heraclius, issued his *Type* in favour of Monothelete views; and, because he was opposed by Pope Martin I, he ordered the exarch Theodore Calliopas to seize the recalcitrant pontiff and bring him to Constantinople. There the Roman bishop, after enduring insult and imprisonment, which were unable to break his spirit, was deposed and banished by imperial decree to the Crimea, where he died deserted by his friends, a martyr for the faith as defined by his great predecessor Leo. During the reign of Constantine Pogonatus, in the pontificate of Agatho (678–682), the Roman See obtained some reparation for the insults heaped on Martin. At the Sixth General Council, which met in Constantinople 7 Nov. 680, the Monothelete doctrine was condemned, and with it its supporters, Cyrus, bishop of Alexandria, and two patriarchs of Constantinople, Sergius and Pyrrhus. In addition to these, a unique circumstance in ecclesiastical history, the General Council pronounced Pope Honorius to be anathema *non quidem ut haereticus sed ut haereticorum fautor* Thus the Roman See had to accept the deep humiliation of having one of its occupants pronounced unsound in a matter of faith.

A further insult was still in store for the Papacy. In 692 another council was summoned to Constantinople for the purpose of completing the work of the Sixth Council by drawing up canons of discipline. This Synod, generally known as the Council *in Trullo*, passed its canons and sent them for ratification to Pope Sergius, and on his refusal to acknowledge the work of the Council the Protospatharius was sent to arrest him and he was threatened with the fate of St Martin. The Romans however stood by their bishop and rescued him from the imperial officer.

The last pope to be summoned to Constantinople was Constantine (708–715), who came at the invitation of Justinian II (Rhinotmetus). He was, however, treated with honour by that formidable emperor and returned in safety in 711 to Rome.

We have now reached the period of the last struggle between Constantinople and Rome, due, like the Three Chapters in the days of Justinian I and the Monothelete controversy in the following century, to another amazing display of the strength inherent in the Empire. In the famous " Isaurian " dynasty the Graeco-Roman power, which had been threatened at its very source by the triumphant Caliphs, once more shewed itself the strongest force in the world. Again orthodoxy made overtures of peace to Monophysitism, but in a very different form from those of the sixth and seventh centuries. The schismatic or heretical churches, whether Nestorian or Monophysite, shewed a conservatism greater than that exhibited by the Catholics in maintaining a simplicity in church ornamentation which orthodoxy had long abandoned. The images or pictures, originally introduced, to use the words of John of Damascus, as " books for the unlearned," had not found a place in the Monophysite or Nestorian churches; but among the orthodox had become objects of superstitious reverence. To remove this scandal and to save the Church from the reproach of Jews and Muslims as well as to conciliate the Christians outside its pale, Leo the Isaurian in 726 issued his celebrated edict against the images and inaugurated the Iconoclastic controversy. Since the Monophysites opposed the attempt to represent the human appearance of our Lord as contrary to their doctrine of the loss of his manhood in the infinity of his Godhead, the edict was sure to find favour in their eyes[1].

It is not easy to determine the precise effect of the Iconoclastic decree on the Roman Church. Certainly Leo the Isaurian's reign saw the beginning of the complete abandonment of the exarchate of Ravenna and its dependencies by the Greeks[2]. Letters survive, professedly by Pope Gregory II (715–731) to Leo, denouncing him with the utmost violence and defending the image-worship with as grotesque an ignorance of the Old Testament as of the rules of common courtesy. It is now generally supposed, however, that these two letters are spurious, alien as they are to what we know of the wise and prudent man which Gregory II shewed himself in his other dealings. Nor does there seem to have been any formal breach between the Papacy and Constantinople. Down to the end of the eighth century the popes acknowledged the Emperor.

But the chain was really broken. The Lombards took Ravenna, occupied the Pentapolis and began to threaten the *ducatus Romae*, already a virtually independent state with an army commanded by its Duke, and with the Pope almost acknowledged as the representative of the Emperor. When Ravenna was taken is unknown: the whole history of the period is obscure; all that can be said with certainty is that by

---

[1] The origin of the Iconoclastic controversy will be related in Vol. iv. It may have been partly due to the antagonism between the Asiatic (from which the army was mainly recruited) and the Hellenic elements of the Empire. So Bréhier, *La Querelle des Images* (Paris, 1904).			[2] See *supra*, pp. 231–33.

7 July 751 the exarchate had come to an end and the Greeks were no longer a power in Italy. The Pope had also lost his Sicilian estates which afforded his principal revenue. The experience the Papacy had gained by its connexion with Constantinople was not forgotten, and moulded its subsequent policy. It became evident that to work out its destiny it needed alike freedom and protection—freedom to assert its claims to rule over the conscience of mankind, and protection from the enemies who encompassed the defenceless city.

Neither of these could the Byzantine government afford. The Lombards were pressing closer on Rome, and no prospect of aid from the Emperor was at hand; and in any case it would be too great a price to yield to his demands in matters theological. The aims of the Empire and the East were distinct from those of Rome and the West. In the latter there was practically no great religious difference, and the priests, secure in their monopoly of learning, were unlikely to disturb men's minds by explaining the traditional faith or adapting it to the conditions of the hour. In the more educated East questions of the utmost moment caused serious divisions among clergy and laity alike; nor is it without significance that Pope Agatho had to explain to the Sixth General Council that his delegates were rude and unlettered men who had to live by the labour of their hands. So far then were the rough and ignorant clergy even of Rome removed from their brethren of the East. But, though ignorant of the arts of life, the Roman clergy had one distinct advantage over the more cultured ecclesiastics of Constantinople. They had fought a long and stubborn battle with the barbarian invaders of Italy with no one to come to their aid, and in the struggle they had developed political instincts denied to the servants of a political and spiritual despotism. Thus the popes of the eighth century learned the statecraft with which their successors were to raise the papal power to its highest pitch. From the birth of Christ there is approximately as long an interval backwards to Romulus as forwards to the political severance of Rome from the Empire, and at the latter period the foundations of a world-governing power were as surely laid as when the first king built the walls of Rome.

(2) The Lombard invaders of Italy after a long struggle had succeeded in dispossessing the Empire of all pretence to exercise sovereignty in Italy. They had made their appearance in the year 568 under Alboin, and though Paul the Deacon testifies to the comparative mildness of their rule at first, on the death of Alboin it became intolerable. Two facts are worth bearing in mind, namely that the Lombards are the first invaders of Italy who settled with no sort of imperial sanction—Alaric, Odovacar and Theodoric having all had recognition from the Roman government; and further that under their occupation the theory of a united Italy was abandoned, never to be realised till the nineteenth century. There was further a sort of

undeveloped feudalism in the Lombard settlement by which the kingdom was divided into more or less independent dukedoms, some—like those of Spoleto and Benevento—eventually detaching themselves completely from the king's authority. After the death of Alboin in 573 there were no less than thirty-six dukes each exercising unrestrained the power of a petty tyrant. But anarchical as was the condition of affairs among the Lombards at the close of the sixth century, it was becoming evident that the Byzantine government was powerless to expel them from Italy and even that its abandonment of the peninsula was only a matter of time.

The condition of Byzantine Italy was not altogether dissimilar from that of the Lombard territory. As at Pavia, the capital of the king, so at the exarch's seat at Ravenna, the central authority was at times deplorably weak; and in both cases the "dukes" were practically independent princes. The duke of Naples for example was as little amenable to the exarch as the Lombard dukes of Benevento were to their sovereign. The difficulty was principally one of communication. The Lombards held the country and the Byzantines the coast, and unless the road between Rome and Ravenna could be kept open it was impossible for the exarch to govern, succour, or advise the Pope; and in one case a pope's enthronement had to be deferred for more than a year owing to the difficulty in obtaining confirmation of his election. Hence it was of the utmost importance to keep open the Flaminian way leading from Rome to Ravenna and the coast, and the possession of such places as Perugia was vital to the Romans.

The territory occupied in Italy by the Lombards and the exarchate in Italy respectively, say during the pontificate of Gregory I (590–604), was approximately as follows. The Byzantines on the east coast held Istria on the Adriatic, the islands along the coast already known as Venetia, the marshes around Comacchio and Ferrara, the mouth of the Po where Ravenna is situated, and inland as far as Bologna. Practically from Venetia to Ancona the frontiers of the Empire were the Apennines and the sea. Then came a very debatable territory giving access by way of Perugia to the Roman duchy. Proceeding south-ward, Calabria remained imperial till 675, when Brindisi and Taranto fell into the hands of Romuald, duke of Benevento, and Bruttium and Sicily were held by the Greeks. On the western coast were two duchies, Naples and Rome. The Roman duchy was constantly shrinking owing to the encroachments of the Lombard dukes of Benevento and Spoleto, the latter having pushed his frontier almost to the N.E. wall of the city, his boundary being the old Sabine one formed by the Tiber and the Anio. The rest of Italy was held by the Lombards, the valley of the Po being more directly under the authority of the king, whose capital was Pavia, whilst the three great almost independent duchies were Friuli (*Forum Julii*), north of Venetia, Spoleto, extending from the Pentapolis to the Roman duchy, and Benevento in the south. This partition of Italy was practically recognised by the treaty made, mainly by Pope Gregory I, in 593, but throughout the seventh century the power of the Lombards increased whilst that of the exarchate diminished. It is not necessary for our purpose to trace the progress of the Lombard power till we reach the eighth century when the popes came into sharper conflict with it than they had done since the days of Gregory I.

In the century which intervened between the death of Gregory I and the accession of Gregory II the Lombards had been transformed from Arian heretics into devout Catholics, so that the religious difficulty which parted Roman from Lombard had disappeared. The hostility of the popes to the Lombards was therefore political rather than religious. The cause of it was a feeling, inherent in the Papacy, that any supreme secular power in Italy would be detrimental to its interests. This was natural and not wholly unjustifiable, as the sequel of events tends to shew. The whole spirit of the Roman Church in Italy being anti-national, the predominance of one people was felt to be inconsistent with its ideal of universality. We have seen how sorely tried the patience of the clergy had been by the policy of the Byzantine Caesars; but these, at least in theory, were the rulers of the world. The Lombard kings on the contrary were merely local princes, representative of the two things most detested by the Papacy—nationality and barbarism. An even worse evil was in store should (as was far from unlikely) the Lombard territories become a number of independent dukedoms, for in that case the Pope would be at the mercy not even of a king but of a petty prince like the duke of Spoleto; and Rome itself would be the carcass over which the Lombard chieftains would be constantly quarrelling. The breach between the Lombards and the popes was therefore inevitable directly it was understood that the end of the Byzantine rule in Italy was a mere question of time. Let the monarch and his dukes be never so conciliatory and the Pope never so gracious, their interests were radically dissimilar, and either the Lombard dominion must perish or the Papacy must abandon the very motive of its existence. In one respect the pontiffs had a distinct advantage; they were perfectly indifferent to the fate of the Lombards; whilst these, as Catholics, held the priestly office of the bishops of Rome in the highest honour. The period therefore we are about to survey from Gregory II (715) to the accession of Hadrian I (772) is fraught with the most important consequences, as what happened then gives the clue to the whole secular policy of the Papacy for eleven centuries, from Charles the Great to Napoleon III—a policy which, despite all adverse circumstances, is not yet abandoned.

The somewhat complicated relations of six popes, Gregory II and III, Zacharias, Stephen III, Paul, and Stephen IV, with three Lombard kings, Liutprand, Aistulf, and Desiderius, must now occupy the attention of the reader. Liutprand, the Lombard king, reigned 712–744 and this period is almost covered by the pontificates of the two Gregories (715–741), men of great ability as popes and statesmen. Under Gregory II came the breach with the exarchate not so much on account of the Iconoclastic decrees, which were not promulgated till 726, as of the heavy taxation imposed on Italy by Leo the Isaurian.

The politics of the time are certainly perplexing. First we find the Lombards on the side of the Pope labouring to defeat the dastardly plot to murder Gregory hatched by the exarch Paulus and Marinus, duke of Rome. Next the Pope takes part with the great dukes of Spoleto and Benevento against Liutprand, who is in alliance with the Empire against his vassals. Twice we find the Lombard king advancing into the Roman duchy: on the first occasion withdrawing after presenting Sutrium, which he had captured, to the Pope, on the second, in 729, marching to the very gates of Rome only to find the intrepid Gregory entering his camp in peaceful guise and himself conducted as a suppliant to the tomb of St Peter. Gregory II died in 731, and was succeeded by a Syrian of the same name who occupied the chair of St Peter for ten years. His policy was to play the Empire, Liutprand, and the Lombard dukes against one another, and he entered into an alliance with Spoleto and Benevento against their king. The duchy of Rome was invaded by Liutprand in 739, and Gregory III made the first advances towards the Frankish Charles Martel—a momentous step in the history of the Papacy.

Notwithstanding this, Liutprand was throughout subservient to the papal will, and Gregory's successor, Zacharias, obtained from him several cities which had belonged to the Empire. Thus the principle was recognised at Rome that the territory which the Byzantines had once held justly belonged to the Pope. Liutprand, the great Lombard benefactor of the Papacy, died in 744. In the *Liber Pontificalis* he is called "most wicked," shewing that neither gifts nor piety could avert the papal animosity if a monarch's claims were in conflict with those of St Peter.

It was under the ambitious Aistulf that the mutual hostility of Pope and Lombard came to a head. Despite oaths and treaties made by Liutprand and his successor Ratchis, whom Zacharias' exhortations had induced to exchange the crown for the cowl, the king persisted in the conquest of Ravenna. Instigated by Constantine V (Copronymus), Pope Stephen III made his famous journey first to Pavia, where he remonstrated with Aistulf, and then, when he found his protests of no avail, supported by the Frankish envoys to the Lombards, the undaunted Pope crossed the Alps and met Pepin king of the Franks face to face. By the agreement at Kiersy (754) Ravenna was secured for the Pope. Stephen returned to Rome and died in 757, Aistulf having been killed by a fall from his horse in the previous year.

Now that the Byzantine influence at Rome had almost vanished, we begin to see that the interference of exarch and Emperor in papal affairs had not been wholly an evil. The Roman priesthood, great as were its claims, was not really capable of maintaining itself without the support of some external force. For the last century and more papal elections had been uniformly peaceful: but now that the imperial power was no longer a restraint, this peace was at an end. Paul the brother of Stephen was however elected after a contest with the archdeacon Theophylact, and reigned for ten years (757–767), occupied mainly in disputes with Desiderius the last king of the Lombards, who refused, though constantly prevaricating, to observe the agreement made between Pepin and Aistulf after the Frankish invasion of 755, and to restore (*reddere propria propriis*) to the Roman see the cities he had taken. Passing over the negotiations between the Papacy and Desiderius, we may take notice of some incidents which shew the weakness of the Papacy and the danger which threatened it from the Lombard supremacy. The seizure of the papal chair by Toto duke of Nepi, who placed his brother Constantine in it after the death of Paul, the ejection of Constantine by the *primicerius* Christophorus and his son the *sacellarius* Sergius, the choice of Stephen IV, and the horrors which followed—blindings, imprisonments, murders and other cruelties—shewed the savage lawlessness of the Romans when left to themselves. Next we have Pope Stephen and Desiderius caballing together against the too powerful papal officials Christophorus and his son, their betrayal and cruel treatment, and the rise of Paulus Afiarta, the real ruler of the Church and city in the latter days of Stephen IV. This disgraceful state of things at the time of Stephen's death and the accession of Hadrian I, shewed the impotence of the Romans to govern themselves and of Desiderius and his Lombards to restore order. A new act in the drama of papal history is about to begin, dominated by the majestic figure of Charles the Great.

(3) The Franks who succeeded the Lombards as controllers of the destiny of the Papacy enjoyed the distinction of having been the first of the continental Teutons to embrace the orthodox Faith and the only ones which never held any creed save that of Nicaea. Since the days of Clovis who had borne the title of "patrician" their connexion with the Empire had been particularly friendly: and the Roman pontiffs had seen the wisdom of attaching this powerful and energetic nation to the see of St Peter.

One reason for the amity which existed between the Roman ecclesiastics and the Franks lay in the fact that, unlike other barbarian nations, they were not disposed to migrate from their home in northern Gaul; and—widely as their conquests extended—they never contemplated making Italy the centre of their government. Aachen, Laon, Soissons and Rheims were the cities of the Frankish monarch; and the popes felt they could safely summon so remote a nation to deliver Rome from their enemies and then to retire leaving the sacred city to its ecclesiastical rulers.

A still more remote nation was destined to play its part in the events of the eighth century. The conversion of England, planned by Gregory the Great and begun by Augustine, had gone on apace and in it the Church of Rome had played a most honourable part. The Church of Canterbury already acknowledged as a primatial see, was essentially a Roman outpost, though already it had been presided over by a native born archbishop in the person of Frithonas who took the name of Deusdedit. On his death in 664 another native by name Wighard was elected and sent to Rome to be consecrated by Vitalian (657—672). Wighard was presented to the Pope but died before he could be consecrated, and Vitalian sought earnestly for a suitable successor. Failing to induce the African Hadrian to undertake the office he accepted his nominee Theodore, a native of Tarsus, a man of ripe years and learning to whom the infant Church of the English owes so much. It must not however be supposed that, in thus nominating an occupant of the throne of St Augustine, Vitalian can in any way be reproached for setting a precedent for the interference of his medieval successors in the election of English primates. It was not arrogance which made Vitalian nominate, nor did avarice induce Theodore to accept the charge of the Church in a land so remote and barbarous as Britain, and the whole business is illustrative of the care taken on behalf of the most remote Churches by the Roman see of that age.

The close relation which sprang up between the Papacy and the descendants of Arnulf, a Frankish noble who became bishop of Metz (died 624), who ultimately became the famous royal family known as the Carlovingians, was fostered by our great countryman Boniface, the indefatigable missionary in Germany during the first half of the eighth century. This remarkable man combined the zeal of a missionary with complete devotion to the Roman see; and may almost be compared to some proconsul, who, in the days of Rome's secular glory, spent his life in bringing kingdoms and territories under her conquering sway. A native of Crediton and a monk of Netley near Winchester, Winfrid, for that was his original name, joined his countryman Willibrord in his missionary labours among the Frisians. Full of that zeal which makes him a worthy predecessor of Selwyn and Livingstone, he devoted his chief efforts to the conversion of the heathen. His objective was the Saxon nation beyond the Elbe, for his heart seems to have yearned towards the men of his own race; but he laboured in Thuringia and among the Hessians, and finally with his own hands struck a blow at German heathenism by felling the sacred oak at Geismar. His own country sent willing monks and nuns to aid the great missionary. Monastery after monastery was founded to secure the permanence of his labours and thus to pave the way for Frankish conquest and Roman influence. His devoted labours in the cause of the Gospel were supported by the blessings of the popes and the arms of the Franks; since he was both the pioneer of the see of Rome and of the rising house of Charles Martel. Pope followed pope only to receive fresh testimonies of the loyalty of Boniface and to load him with fresh honours.

In 723 the wise and statesmanlike Gregory II recognised the merits of the ardent Englishman by making him a *regionarius* or bishop without a see. When we remember the perilous times of this Pope, harassed alike by the Iconoclastic emperors, and by the prospect of the ruin of the imperial power in Italy, we cannot fail to compare him with his great predecessor and namesake, who when the Lombards were threatening Rome was carefully planning the conversion of England. That Gregory II could in equally anxious times find leisure to send the Englishman Winfrid, who probably then assumed the name of Bonifatius (the fair speaker), to convert Germany, proves that this Pope was no unworthy successor of St Gregory the Great.

Gregory III raised Boniface to the rank of an archbishop, still without confining his labours to any single city, but the real object in thus honouring the great missionary was to give him authority in Gaul where the disorders of the Church, especially in Neustria, were most serious; and indeed the Roman see seems to have desired a reform of the episcopate even more than missionary extension. Boniface loyally co-operated with the Popes in this object and did his utmost to enlist the support of Charles Martel. During the pontificate of the saintly Zacharias we find Boniface at the height of his influence. Council after Council was held under his presidency: the disorders among the clergy both in Austrasia and Neustria were suppressed, and new sees were founded in far Bavaria. In 743 the see of Mogontiacum (Mainz) was raised to the dignity of an archbishopric and conferred on Boniface, who thus became primate of all Germany. Under Stephen III he won the crown of martyrdom after resigning his see in order to prosecute his missionary labours (755).

Such then is a brief outline of the life of the churchman who did more than anyone to bind together the Austrasian Franks and the Roman see. Boniface began his labours as a devoted servant of the Papacy, but he soon recognised the fact that he could neither continue the missionary labour, so dear to his own heart, nor carry out the reforms in Gaul, on which the popes were resolved, without the help of the great Mayor of the Palace, Charles Martel. But engaged as he was in warlike enterprise, Charles, despite the great victory of Tours (732) which delivered Gaul from the Muslims, has not gone down to posterity as a loyal son of the Church. His followers required rewards for their services, and his enemies kept him actively employed in Gaul. Consequently when in 739 Gregory III appealed for the first time to the Franks to enter Italy in order to deliver the Church of Rome from Liutprand, the most generous "oppressor!" of the Holy See known to history, Charles ignored his request; and he is further accused, not without reason, of having laid hands on the estates of the clergy. A century after his death it was generally believed that he had incurred "that righteous damnation of him by whom the property of the Church has been unjustly taken away."

Charles Martel and Gregory III both died in 741. The next pope was, as we have seen, the saintly Zacharias (741–752) under whom Boniface rose to the summit of his influence. The successors of Charles were his sons Pepin and Carloman. The latter prince was a monk at heart and in 747 retired from the world, and Pepin himself was far more religiously disposed than his father. Consequently the reform of the Church north of the Alps went on apace under Boniface, now Archbishop of Mainz and Primate of Germany.

The time had now come for the house of Arnulf to assume the office the power of which they had so long exercised. Confident in the support of the Church, Pepin inquired of Zacharias whether it would not now be advisable for him to ascend the German throne in place of the last puppet Merovingian Childeric III. How far Boniface took part in the elevation of Pepin as king is much disputed. He had withdrawn much from public life since 747. At any rate in 751 Childeric III was deposed, tonsured and sent into a monastery, and Pepin was solemnly anointed and was *more Francorum elevatus in regno*. Thus at the hands of our great countryman the new Frankish dynasty came into being. It was probably owing to Boniface's influence that Pepin's brother Carloman, Mayor of the Palace in Austrasia, renounced the world and settled in Italy in a monastery on Mount Soracte. Thus the Roman see was continually entering into a closer and closer relationship with the most vigorous of the Teutonic nations of the north, the Austrasian Franks, who aided by their English kinsmen beyond the sea were spreading the Gospel eastward in Europe.

In the short but memorable pontificate of Stephen III (752–757) Pepin laid the foundation of the temporal power of the Roman see in return for his formal recognition by the Pope. Hard pressed by the Lombard Aistulf, Stephen crossed the Alps on a visit to the Frankish king. The pontiff was met by Pepin's son Charles, then a boy of eleven, who brought him to his father at Ponthion. There Pepin promised to "restore" to the Holy See the exarchate of Ravenna and the "rights and territories of the Roman Republic." On 28 July 754 Stephen solemnly anointed and blessed Pepin, his wife Bertrada, and his two sons Charles and Carloman, pronouncing an anathema on the Franks should they ever choose a king from another family. Pepin at the same time received the title of "patrician" with all its undefined liabilities as protector of Rome. In the following year Pepin held a "diet" or *placitum* at Carisiacum (Kiersy or Quierzy) and decided to advance into Italy to win Stephen III his rights from the Lombards. A document was drawn up, which has unfortunately perished, setting forth what territories were to be given to the Pope. This is the "donation of Pepin." Twice did the Frankish army invade Italy—on the first occasion at the Pope's personal request and on the second owing to the receipt of the letter which St Peter himself was believed to have addressed to the king of the Franks. In the end twenty-three cities including Ravenna were surrendered by Aistulf to Stephen III, who, at the time of his death in April 757, had become a sovereign prince. But in gaining territory the Papacy lost independence by becoming too great a prize for any man to win without a struggle. The rest of the history of the eighth century shews that in order to enjoy that which Pepin had bestowed the popes must become dependents of the Franks, who were thus compelled to invade Italy as conquerors to maintain the Papacy which they had enriched.

Paul I, the successor of Stephen, enjoyed a somewhat peaceful pontificate of ten years, A.D. 757–767; but we are able to see that the acquisition of the imperial territory on the shores of the Adriatic had further relaxed the feeble tie which still held the Papacy to Constantinople. Paul had to deal with Constantine V, the most formidable of the Iconoclasts; and he had to protect alike the holy images and the possessions of the Roman Church. In his correspondence with Pepin, the Greeks are styled *nefandissimi*. Once the Church had obtained Ravenna and the cities of Emilia and the Pentapolis there could be no restoration of the exarchate. The political connexion between Rome and Constantinople was practically severed by the donation of Pepin. The king of the Franks died in 768, a year later than Paul; and we enter upon one of the most critical eras of papal history. All on which this chapter has hitherto dwelt: the severance from the imperial authority at Constantinople, the disputes with the Lombards, the alliance with the Franks, the work of Gregory II, Boniface, and Stephen III, culminates in Charles the Great. With his accession we stand at the opening of a new epoch in the history of Western Europe, fraught with important consequences. The theological breach between East and West, the medieval theory of Papacy and Empire, the great strife of secular and spiritual powers, are traceable to the years immediately before us.

In considering the relations between the popes and the Franks during the long reign of Charles the Great it is necessary to bear in mind that, though Pepin by his donation had made the popes into priest-kings, their position was precarious in the extreme. Italy under Lombard rule was in a state of anarchy; and Rome itself was the centre of a barbarism which was intensified by being concealed under the specious name of ecclesiastical government and claimed to represent not only the piety but the civilisation of the West. When we read of kings, dukes, pontiffs, cardinals (first mentioned in the *Liber Pontificalis* at this time), of the senate, of the *exercitus* or *militia*; when modern terms like that of the "unification of Italy" are applied to the policy of a ruler like the Lombard Desiderius, we may lose sight of the fact that under this specious veneer there lay an utterly disintegrated society, characterised by a savagery which could hardly be paralleled by the acknowledged barbarism of many countries north of the Alps. The pontificate of Stephen IV (768–772) is, as has been already hinted, a period of violence and bloodshed: and the events which characterised it are repeated almost exactly not thirty years later in the days of Leo III: for centuries not even the person of a pope was safe in Rome without the protecting hand of some external authority. It is only possible here to allude to the strange story of Stephen IV as related in the *Liber Pontificalis*; and to proceed to a hasty summary of the main events of the reign of Charles the Great.

On Pepin's death the Frankish dominions were divided between his two sons Charles and Carloman. The two brothers speedily became rivals, and the scene of their machinations was Italy. Their mother Bertrada had brought about a nominal reconciliation between her two sons Charles king in Austrasia, and Carloman king in Neustria, and in the interests of peace sought to contract matrimonial alliances with the Lombard monarch Desiderius. With this end in view she visited Italy and persuaded Charles to give up the lady whom he had perhaps irregularly married and to take Desiderata, the daughter of the Lombard king. These projects alarmed Stephen IV, and his letter to Charles and Carloman warning them against an alliance with the detestable Lombards, a race infected with leprosy and naturally repulsive to noble Franks, is one of the most extraordinary in the papal correspondence with the Carlovingian family; and confirms us in the idea that Stephen's passionate weakness of character was one cause of the misfortunes of that unhappy pontiff. But the alliance was short-lived. Charles repudiated his Lombard wife, and on Carloman's death in 771 the widow Gerberga placed herself and her children under the protection of Desiderius—a proof that the two brothers regarded the Lombard as the determining factor in their rivalry for the possession of the whole Frankish realm. The Pope sided with Charles against Gerberga and her children; for Desiderius, no doubt hoping that the Franks were sufficiently divided to leave him alone, had ravaged the newly acquired papal dominions in the exarchate and the Pentapolis.

Stephen died in 772, and was succeeded by two pontiffs who held the Papacy for no less than forty-four years. Hadrian I from 772 to 795 and Leo III from 795 to 816. Never till our own days have two successive pontificates occupied so long a period. Till the days of Pius IX no pope so nearly attained to the traditional years of Peter as Hadrian.

Judged by his actions Hadrian was a man of vigour and ability; and if he shews himself querulous and apprehensive in his correspondence with Charles, it only reveals the extreme difficulty of the situation in which he was often placed. His first act on succeeding Stephen was successfully to repress disorder in Rome. Paulus Afiarta, the evil genius of the late Pope, who had brought about the ruin of Christophorus and Sergius, was sent under arrest to Ravenna, where the archbishop Leo, to Hadrian's indignation, put the unfortunate prisoner to death. In the following year, 773, Charles invaded Italy, defeated Desiderius, and invested his capital of Pavia. In 774 the Frankish king paid his first memorable visit to Rome, and was received with due honour by the Pope and the Roman clergy. Touched by his reception and deeply impressed by his visit to the tomb of the Apostle and to the holy churches of Rome, Charles bestowed on Hadrian all that Pepin had given to the Holy See, and, if we may believe the Roman account, something more. The documentary evidence for the donation of Charles needs separate treatment; but the king is said to have included in his magnificent gift all Italy south of the Po which the Lombards occupied. Charles returned to Pavia after his visit to Rome and completed the conquest of the Lombards. Desiderius was forced to retire into a monastery, to make way for the victorious Frank who was now king of the Lombards and Patrician of Rome.

Thus fell the Lombard kingdom after two centuries of rule in Italy; and it may here be observed that none of the nations which had occupied the territory of the Empire had been able to survive the baneful atmosphere of the ruined Roman world. The Visigoths of Spain, the Vandals in Africa, the Ostrogoths in Italy, the Merovingians of Gaul, had all like the Lombards rapidly degenerated in contact with the ancient civilisation. It was beyond the limits of the Empire that a new and more vigorous life was coming into being. Among the Franks in Austrasia, in the monasteries of Ireland, in Britain—from which all traces of Roman dominion had been swept by the conquering Angles and Saxons, arose the makers of a new world. Columbanus the Keltic monk, Wilfrid the English bishop, Boniface the missionary from Devon, Charles Martel and his illustrious sons and grandson, Alcuin the Yorkshire scholar—nearly all of these hailed from lands which Tertullian had described as *Romanis inaccessa, Christo vero subdita.*

When Charles departed from Italy in 774, Hadrian was left alone to assert his authority over the splendid principality he had acquired from his Frankish benefactors. But only by a strong hand could rights be maintained in those unsettled days; and the Pope was hard pressed on all sides. Not only did the unconquered Lombard duchy of Benevento encroach on his territory in the south; his tenure of the exarchate was threatened by Leo, the ambitious archbishop of Ravenna, who sought independence, and was resolved to seize the cities in his neighbourhood over which the Pope claimed jurisdiction. Hadrian, one of the ablest of the popes, did his best to maintain his authority. His troops defended his frontiers against the Beneventans and even captured

Terracina. But his correspondence with Charles reveals the weakness of
his position. That Hadrian was a great man is certain; and Charles
seems to have recognised in him somewhat of a kindred spirit to his
own; and at the Pope's death the Frankish monarch mourned as for a
lost brother. But in this case his position was less assured than his
ability, and he needed the support of the arms and influence of Charles
in order to maintain it. How truly Hadrian deserves to be classed
among the greatest rulers of the Roman Church, and how precarious
was the situation of a pope in the eighth century, is shewn when we
come to the disastrous commencement of the pontificate of his successor
Leo III.

It is one of the ironies of fate that the pontiff to whose lot it fell to
inaugurate the Middle Ages in Western Europe, by an act second to
none in dramatic circumstances and in its far-reaching consequences,
was not a great ruler like Hadrian, but a man in almost every respect
his inferior. Leo III, the son of Atzuppius and Elizabeth, is described as
a Roman priest of blameless character and abounding charity; but there
is a certain mystery overhanging the early days of his pontificate. If we
may judge from the names of his parents he had not the advantage of
being of noble birth, a matter of the utmost importance in his age; as,
not only was it regarded as one of the chief recommendations for a
bishop, but it gave a man the almost indispensable support of powerful
kinsmen. Hadrian, perhaps the earliest example of papal nepotism,
had given the highest positions in the Roman Church to his relatives,
committing to them the administration of its great wealth and extensive
patrimony. The government of the apostolic Church was vested at this
time in seven officials, who though only in deacon's orders took the
highest rank in the hierarchy under the Pope. The chief of these, the
primicerius notariorum, Paschalis, a nephew of Hadrian, who is also
called the *consiliarius* of the Holy See, with Campulus the *sacellarius* or
treasurer, another relative of the late Pope, evidently cherished deep
resentment against Leo; and on the occasion of the procession of the
greater Litany on 25 April 799 (St Mark's day) they determined to
wreak their vengeance. Joining the procession from the Lateran at the
church of St Laurence, the conspirators took their places beside the
Pope, apologising for not wearing their official *planetae* on the plea of ill-
health. When the procession reached the monastery of SS. Stephen and
Sylvester, a band of ruffians dashed forth and threw Leo to the ground.
Then, with Paschalis standing at his head and Campulus at his feet, an
attempt was made to blind the pontiff and to cut out his tongue. The
wretched Pope was left for a while bleeding in the street, then dragged
into the church of St Sylvester, and imprisoned in the Greek monastery
of St Erasmus on the Coelian Hill.

Strange to say, the outrage seems to have produced no great effect
on the Roman people, and Leo remained a prisoner till he had recovered

from his wounds. Then his partisans rescued him, and though he is said to have been welcomed with enthusiasm in St Peter's he did not again enter the city; but placing himself under the charge of Winichis, duke of Spoleto, retired thither. Thence he betook himself to Charles at Paderborn, was received by the king and assured of his protection, under which he was able to re-enter Rome on 29 Nov. 799. Charles himself was fully occupied the greater part of the following year. In the spring we find him in Neustria looking after the defences of the shores of the Channel, in the summer he is at Tours, visiting Alcuin and bewailing the loss of Queen Liutgardis, in August he is holding a great *placitum* at Mainz; and not till autumn was well advanced did he undertake his memorable expedition to Italy, arriving at Rome on 24 Nov. 800.

He came not so much as a defender of the rights of the Pope as in the capacity of his judge. Leo's fair fame as well as his person had suffered at the hands of his adversaries, and grave though to us mysterious charges were spread abroad concerning him. Alcuin had received from his friend Arno, archbishop of Salzburg, so serious an account of affairs in Rome and of Leo III that he thought it advisable to burn it; and Charles himself does not seem to have held the same opinion of Leo as he had of Hadrian. At any rate on 3 Dec., in the presence of the king, the Roman clergy, and the Frankish nobles, Leo solemnly exculpated himself and took an oath on the gospels that he was guiltless of the crimes laid to his charge. It is particularly important in view of his subsequent action to remember that three weeks before Leo had been in the humiliating position of having publicly to profess his innocence.

Charles was now at the height of his glory; master of Italy and northern Europe, he was regarded as the representative of Christendom. A woman who had sinned foully against her own son occupied the throne of the Eastern Caesars, and the eyes of all men turned to the gigantic Frank whose wars with the surrounding barbarians had been for the defence and propagation of the gospel. The day after Leo had professed his innocence the priest Zacharias arrived from Jerusalem with the Keys of Calvary and of the Holy Sepulchre and the banner of Jerusalem. Leo had already sent him the keys of the tomb of St Peter and Rome recognised him as its Patrician.

On Christmas day Charles clothed himself in the Patrician's robe and went, not as a barbarian king but as the greatest of the nobility of Rome, to the already venerable church of St Peter. Then he knelt in prayer before the "confession" of the Prince of the Apostles, and the Mass began. After the reading of the gospel the Pope took from the altar a most precious crown and placed it upon the head of the kneeling monarch. With one voice the assembled multitude, Frank and Roman, ecclesiastic and warrior, shouted "Carolo piissimo Augusto a Deo coronato magno et pacifico Imperatori Vita et Victoria." The birthday of the Christ was the birthday of the new Roman Empire. "From this moment modern history begins" (Bryce).

The significance of the act has been variously interpreted from the first. In the Lives of the Popes and in the German contemporary annals the papal and the imperial share in the transaction have been respectively magnified. The claims of the Pope to exact obedience from temporal rulers and of the Emperors to regard the Popes as their subjects were based throughout the Middle Ages upon the meaning attached to the coronation and unction of Charles. Without attempting to pronounce judgment on so vexed a topic, we may set forth three points: namely (1) the significance of the proclamation of Charles as Emperor to the world of 800, (2) the effects on the Empire and the Papacy respectively, and (3) ultimate results.

(1) The world understood that the nations of the West, after nearly four centuries of anarchy and decay, still recognised that they belonged to the Roman Empire and were resolved to seek for peace and unity under a single ruler. Charles was no more a Frankish king ruling by his might, but the lawful lord of Christendom. As the Faith represented by the Pope was one, so all temporal authority was centred in the person of the Emperor. Hitherto the Roman in the West had regarded the distant Augustus in Constantinople as his lawful master. But the experience of generations had proved him powerless to protect Italy, and in theory at least in the year 800 there was no Emperor. Irene having usurped the throne of Constantine VI, the allegiance due to the Eastern Caesar could be lawfully transferred to Charles.

(2) By his coronation Charles had obtained an accession neither of territory nor of wealth: but he gained that which he never could have secured by himself. It is difficult for us to understand how great a departure from precedent his coronation was. The one title withheld from the barbarians was that of Emperor. They might master Italy as Ricimer, Odovacar, Theodoric, and the Lombard kings had done. They might be decorated with the titles of consul and patrician like Clovis. They might set up puppet emperors and rule in their name. But never did they presume themselves to assume the imperial title. To acknowledge a barbarian king to be his Emperor, as Leo acknowledged Charles, was unexampled in the annals of the Roman world. This explains the astonishment of Charles when Leo III placed the crown on his head, and accounts for his assurance to Einhard that he never would have entered St Peter's had he suspected the intention of the Pope. The Pope on the other hand had by this act taken the place of the Roman people, of the Senate, and of the Army—in a word of all the powers which had in the past proclaimed an Emperor. That he had done so entirely on his own initiative might have been credible of Hadrian, but scarcely of Leo, whose position was too insecure, and his character not sufficiently established to warrant so bold an action. Without the consent and

approval of the Roman people and the nobles who attended Charles he never could have assumed so mighty a rôle. If the Frank knelt unsuspectingly at his devotions to receive the imperial diadem, we can hardly doubt that Leo's action was the result of a carefully preconceived plan of which many of the spectators were fully cognisant. By it, however, the Papacy gained an advantage which no one then possibly foresaw. Pepin and Charles had delivered the Popes from Greek oppression and Lombard tyranny; they had made them princes in Italy by securing them a kingdom which they held for eleven centuries; and in return the Papacy sanctioned the conversion of the mayors of the palace of Austrasia first into kings and finally into Emperors, but in so doing they laid the foundation of claims which were in later days to shake terribly the earth[1].

(3) The new Empire was essentially the creation of the Western genius. Unlike the older imperial system which made the Emperor, Justinian as truly as Augustus, supreme in matters spiritual as well as temporal, the *régime* inaugurated by Leo III emphasised the Augustinian ideal of the City of God; and, though in theory the Christian State in the Middle Ages was essentially one, there arose a practical dichotomy between the province of the clergy and that of the laity. That these worked sometimes in harmony, sometimes in discord but never in complete unity, was one of the results of the Carlovingians creating the Papal States, and of the Popes calling into being the Empire of the West.

---

[1] The significance of the coronation of Charles is notoriously one of the most disputed points in history. Even the contemporary chronicles, the Frankish and the *Liber Pontificalis*, are completely at variance as to the position of Leo III in regard to Charles. It is evident that there had been ample opportunities for Franks and Romans to confer together on raising Charles to the imperial dignity for at least a year before the coronation. That Charles had been negotiating with the Empress Irene since the imperial throne had been vacated by Constantine VI in 796 is equally certain. This may account for Charles' statement to Einhard. He may well have considered the action of Leo, the Romans and the Franks premature, though the idea of assuming the title of Emperor was not new to him. (See Döllinger, *Historical and Literary Addresses*, iii. Waitz, *Deutsche Verfassungsgeschichte*, iii. p. 175, is one of the few to agree with Döllinger in acknowledging that Charles honestly meant what his biographer records of him.)

Prof. Bury, *Eastern Roman Empire*, 802–867, discusses the coronation from the standpoint of Constantinople.

NOTE. In this chapter Popes Stephen II and Stephen III are called Stephen III and Stephen IV in accordance with the modern official numbering.

LIST OF ABBREVIATIONS.

(1) The following abbreviations are used for titles of periodicals:

AARAB.	Annales de l'Académie royale d'archéologie de Belgique. Antwerp.
AB.	Analecta Bollandiana. Brussels.
ABe.	Archives belges. Liège.
AHR.	American Historical Review. New York and London.
AKKR.	Archiv für katholisches Kirchenrecht. Mainz.
AM.	Annales du Midi. Toulouse.
AMur.	Archivio Muratoriano. Rome.
ASAK.	Anzeiger für schweizerische Alterthumskunde. Zurich.
ASHF.	Annuaire-Bulletin de la Société de l'histoire de France. Paris.
ASI.	Archivio storico italiano. Florence.
ASL.	Archivio storico Lombardo. Milan.
ASRSP.	Archivio della Società romana di storia patria. Rome.
BCRH.	Bulletins de la Commission royale d'histoire. Brussels.
BHisp.	Bulletin hispanique. Bordeaux.
BRAH.	Boletin de la R. Academia de la historia. Madrid.
BZ.	Byzantinische Zeitschrift. Leipsic.
CQR.	Church Quarterly Review. London.
CR.	Classical Review. London.
CRSA.	Comptes rendus des séances de l'Académie des inscriptions et belles-lettres. Paris.
DZG.	Deutsche Zeitschrift für Geschichtswissenschaft. Freiburg-i.-B.
DZKR.	Deutsche Zeitschrift für Kirchenrecht. Leipsic.
EHR.	English Historical Review. London.
FDG.	Forschungen zur deutschen Geschichte.
HJ.	Historisches Jahrbuch. Munich.
Hm.	Hermes. Berlin.
HVJS.	Historische Vierteljahrsschrift. Leipsic.
HZ.	Historische Zeitschrift (von Sybel). Munich and Berlin.
JA.	Journal Asiatique. Paris.
JB.	Jahresberichte der Geschichtswissenschaft im Auftrage der historischen Gesellschaft zu Berlin. 1878 ff. Berlin.
JHS.	Journal of Hellenic Studies. London.
JRAS.	Journal of the Royal Asiatic Society. London.
JRGS.	Journal of the Royal Geographical Society. London.
JSG.	Jahrbuch für schweizerische Geschichte. Zurich.
JTS.	Journal of Theological Studies. London.
MA.	Le moyen âge. Paris.
MIOGF.	Mittheilungen des Instituts für österreichische Geschichtsforschung. Innsbruck.

NAGDG.	Neues Archiv der Gesellschaft für ältere deutsche Geschichtskunde. Hanover and Leipsic.
NRDF.	Nouvelle Revue historique du droit français. Paris.
QFIA.	Quellen und Forschungen aus italianischen Archiven und Bibliotheken. Rome.
RA.	Revue archéologique. Paris.
RBAB.	Revue des bibliothèques et des archives de la Belgique. Brussels.
RBén.	Revue bénédictine. Maredsous.
RCel.	Revue celtique. Paris.
RCHL.	Revue critique d'histoire et de littérature. Paris.
RH.	Revue historique. Paris.
RHD.	Revue d'histoire diplomatique. Paris.
RHE.	Revue d'histoire ecclésiastique. Louvain.
Rhein. Mus.	Rheinisches Museum für Philologie. Frankfurt-a.-M.
RN.	Revue de numismatique. Paris.
ROC.	Revue de l'Orient chrétien. Paris.
RQCA.	Römische Quartalschrift für christliche Altertumskunde und Kirchengeschichte. Rome.
RQH.	Revue des questions historiques. Paris.
RSH.	Revue de synthèse historique. Paris.
RSI.	Rivista storica italiana. Turin.
RSS.	Rivista di scienze storiche. Pavia.
SKAW.	Sitzungsberichte der Kaiserlichen Akademie der Wissenschaften. Vienna. [Phil. hist. Classe.]
SPAW.	Sitzungsberichte der kön. preussischen Akademie der Wissenschaften. Berlin.
SS.	Studi Storici. Pavia.
TQS.	Theologische Quartalschrift. Tübingen.
TRHS.	Transactions of the Royal Historical Society. London.
TSK.	Theologische Studien und Kritiken. Gotha.
VV.	Vizantiiskii Vremenik. St Petersburg.
ZCK.	Zeitschrift für christliche Kunst. Düsseldorf.
ZKG.	Zeitschrift für Kirchengeschichte. Gotha.
ZKT.	Zeitschrift für katholische Theologie. Gotha.
ZR.	Zeitschrift für Rechtsgeschichte. Weimar. 1861–78. Continued as
ZSR.	Zeitschrift der Savigny-Stiftung für Rechtswissenschaft. Weimar. 1830 ff.
ZWT.	Zeitschrift für wissenschaftliche Theologie. Frankfurt-a.-M.

(2) Among other abbreviations used (*see General Bibliography*) are:

AcadIBL.	Académie des Inscriptions et Belles-Lettres.
AcadIP.	Académie Impériale de Pétersbourg.
AllgDB.	Allgemeine deutsche Biographie.
ASBoll.	Acta Sanctorum Bollandiana.
BEC.	Bibliothèque de l'École des chartes.
BGen.	Nouvelle Biographie générale.
BHE.	Bibliothèque de l'École des hautes études.
BUniv.	Biographie universelle.
CIG.	Corpus Inscriptionum Graecarum.
CIL.	Corpus Inscriptionum Latinarum.
CSCO.	Corpus scriptorum christianorum orientalium.
CSEL.	Corpus scriptorum ecclesiasticorum latinorum.
CSHB.	Corpus scriptorum historiae Byzantinae.
DCA.	Dictionary of Christian Antiquities.

DCB.	Dictionary of Christian Biography.
DNB.	Dictionary of National Biography.
EcfrAR.	École française d'Athènes et de Rome. Paris.
EETS.	Early English Text Society.
EncBr.	Encyclopaedia Britannica.
FHG.	Müller's Fragmenta Historicorum Graecorum.
KAW.	Kaiserliche Akademie der Wissenschaften. Vienna.
MGH.	Monumenta Germaniae Historica.
MPG.	Migne's Patrologiae cursus completus. Ser. graeca.
MPL.	Migne's Patrologiae cursus completus. Ser. latina.
PAW.	Königliche preussiche Akademie d. Wissenschaften. Berlin.
RAH.	Real Academia de la Historia. Madrid.
RE³.	Real-Encyklopädie für protestantische Theologie, etc.
RGS.	Royal Geographical Society.
RHS.	Royal Historical Society.
SHF.	Société d'histoire française.

In the case of many other works given in the General Bibliography abbreviations as stated there are used.

Abh.	Abhandlungen.	kais.	kaiserlich.
J.	Journal.	kön.	königlich.
Jahrb.	Jahrbuch.	mem.	memoir.
R.	Review, Revue.	mém.	mémoire.
Viert.	Vierteljahrschrift.	n.s.	new series.
Z.	Zeitschrift.	publ.	publication.
antiq.	antiquarian, antiquaire.	roy.	royal, royale.
coll.	collections.	ser.	series.
hist.	history, historical, historique, historisch.	soc.	society.

GENERAL BIBLIOGRAPHY.

I. DICTIONARIES, BIBLIOGRAPHIES AND GENERAL WORKS OF REFERENCE.

Allgemeine deutsche Biographie (histor. Kommission bei d. kön. Akademie der Wissenschaften zu Munich). Ed. Liliencron, R. von, and Wegele, F. X. Leipsic. 1875–1910. (AllgDB.)

Allgemeine Geschichte in Einzeldarstellungen. Ed. Oncken, W. Berlin. 1879–93. (Series by various writers, *see sub nom.*) (Oncken.)

Bardenhewer, D. Patrologie. Freiburg-i.-B. 1894. Translated by Shahan, T. J. Freiburg-i.-B. and St Louis, Minnesota. 1908.

Bibliothèque de l'École des Chartes. Paris. 1839–1900. (BEC.)

Bibliothèque de l'École des hautes études. Paris. 1839 ff. (BHE.)

Biographie universelle, ancienne et moderne. (Michaud.) Paris. 1854–65. 45 vols. [Greatly improved edn. of earlier work, 1811–28, and supplement, 1832–62.] (B. univ.)

Cabrol, F. Dictionnaire de l'archéologie chrétienne et de la Liturgie. Paris. 1901. 2nd edn., 1907, in progress.

Ceillier, R. Histoire générale des auteurs sacrés et ecclésiastiques. 23 vols. Paris. 1729–63. New edn. 14 vols. in 15. Paris. 1858–69.

Chevalier, C. U. J. Répertoire des sources historiques du moyen âge. Bio-bibliographie. Paris. 1883–8. 2nd rev. edn. 1905–7. Topo-bibliographie. Montbéliard. 1894–1903.

Dahlmann, F. C. and Waitz, G. Quellenkunde der deutschen Geschichte. 7th edn. Leipsic. 1906.

Dictionary of National Biography. Ed. Stephen, L. and Lee, S. 63 vols. and suppt., 3 vols. London. 1885–1901. 2nd edn. 22 vols. 1908–9. (DNB.)

Du Cange, C. du Fresne. Glossarium mediae et infimae Latinitatis. Edns. of Henschel, 7 vols., Paris, 1840–50, and Favre, 10 vols., Niort, 1883–7.

Encyclopædia Britannica. 9th edn. London. 1885–9. Additional vols. (10th edn.) 1902–3. 11th edn. Cambridge. 1911. (EncBr.)

Ersch, J. S. and Gruber, J. G. Allgemeine Encyklopädie der Wissenschaften und Künste. Berlin. 1818–50. (Ersch-Gruber.) (Incomplete.)

Fabricius, J. A. Bibliotheca Graeca sive Notitia Scriptorum Veterum Graecorum. 4th edn. Ed. Harles, G. C. 12 vols. Hamburg. 1790–1809. Index. Leipsic. 1837.

Geschichte der europäischen Staaten. Ed. Heeren, A. H. L. and Ukert, F. A. Hamburg and Gotha. 1819–98. (Series by various writers, *see sub nom.*) (Heeren.) Contin. ed. Lamprecht, K. Allgemeine Staatengeschichte. (Lamprecht.)

Grässe, J. G. T. Lehrbuch einer allgemeinen Litterärgeschichte aller bekannten Völker der Welt von der ältesten bis auf die neueste Zeit. Leipsic. 1837–59. (Vols. I, II. Ancient and Medieval Peoples.)

Gross, C. Sources and Literature of English History from the earliest times to about 1485. London. 1900. 2nd edn. enl. 1915. (Gross.)

Hastings, Jas. Encyclopaedia of Religion and Ethics. London. 1908, in progress.

Herre, P. (Hofmeister, A. and Stübe, R.) Quellenkunde zur Weltgeschichte. Leipsic. 1910.

Herzog, J. J. and Hauck, A. Real-Encyklopädie für protestantische Theologie und Kirche. Gotha. 1896–1909. (RE³.)

Keane, H. G. An Oriental Biographical Dictionary, founded on materials collected by Beal, T. W. New and revised edn. London. 1894.

Lichtenberger, F. Encyclopédie des Sciences religieuses. 13 vols. Paris. 1877–82.

Lorenz, O. Genealogischer Hand- und Schul-Atlas. Best edn. by Devrient, E. Stuttgart and Berlin. 1908.

Molinier, A. Les Sources de l'histoire de France. 5 vols. Paris. 1901–6.

Monod, G. Bibliographie de l'histoire de France jusqu'en 1789. Paris. 1888.

Nouvelle Biographie générale, depuis les temps les plus reculés jusqu'à nos jours, avec les renseignements bibliographiques. Sous la direction de J. Ch. F. Höfer. Paris. 1854–66. 46 vols. in 23. (B. Gén.)

Oudin, Casimir. Commentarius de scriptoribus ecclesiae antiquae illorumque scriptis tam impressis quam manuscriptis adhuc extantibus in celebrioribus Europae Bibliothecis a Bellarmino etc. omissis ad annum MCCCCLX. Frankfurt-a.-M. 1722.

Pauly, A. F. von. Real-Encyklopädie der klassischen Alterthumswissenschaft. Vienna. 1837–52. Ed. Wissowa, G. Stuttgart. 1894–1903. New edn. 1904, in progress. (Pauly-Wissowa.)

Potthast, August. Bibliotheca historica medii aevi. Wegweiser durch die Geschichtswerke des europäischen Mittelalters bis 1500. Berlin. 2nd edn. 2 vols. 1896.

Smith, Wm. and Cheetham, S. Dictionary of Christian Antiquities. 2 vols. London. 1875–80. (DCA.)

Smith, Wm. and Wace, Hy. Dictionary of Christian Biography, Literature, Sects and Doctrines. 4 vols. London. 1877–87. (DCB.)

Storia politica d' Italia. Milan. In progress (written by a society of Professors, *see sub nom.*).

Vacant, A. Dictionnaire de la Théologie. Paris. 1901 ff.

Victoria History of the Counties of England. London. 1900. In progress. (Vict. Co. Hist.)

Waitz. *See* Dahlmann.

Wattenbach, W. Deutschlands Geschichtsquellen im Mittelalter bis zur Mitte des xiii. Jahrhunderts. Berlin. 1858. 7th edn. 2 vols. Stuttgart and Berlin. 1904. Ed. Dummler, E. and Traube, L.

Wetzer, H. J. and Welte, B. Kirchenlexikon oder Encyklopädie der katholischen Theologie. Freiburg-i.-B. 1847–60. 2nd edn. Kaulen, F. 1882–1901. (Wetzer-Kaulen.) French transl. Goschler, J. 26 vols. 1869.

Whitney, J. P. Bibliography of Church History (Historical Assoc. Leaflet 55). London. 1923.

II. ATLASES AND GEOGRAPHY.

Baudrillart-Vogt-Rouzcès. Dictionnaire d'histoire et de géographie ecclésiastique. Paris. 1911.

Droysen, G. Allgemeiner historischer Handatlas. Bielefeld. 1886.

Freeman, E. A. Historical Geography of Europe (with Atlas). London. 1881. 3rd edn. revised and ed. Bury, J. B., 1903.

Kretschmer, K. Historische Geographie von Mitteleuropa. 1904. (In Below's Handbuch, *see* vi *below.*)

Longnon, A. Atlas historique de France depuis César jusqu'à nos jours. Paris. 1885.

Poole, R. L. (ed.). Historical Atlas of Modern Europe. Oxford. 1902.

Saint-Martin. Nouveau dictionnaire de Géographie Universelle. 7 vols. Paris. 1879–95. Supplement by Rousselet, L. 2 vols. 1895–7. (Contains short bibliographies.)

Schrader, F. Atlas de géographie historique. Paris. New edn. 1907.

Spruner-Menke. Hand-Atlas für die Geschichte des Mittelalters und der neueren Zeit. Gotha. 1880. (3rd edn. of Spruner's Hand-Atlas etc. Ed. by Menke, Th.)

(FOR PLACE-NAMES :—)

Bischoff, H. T. and Möller, J. H. Vergleichendes Wörterbuch der alten, mittleren und neuen Geographie. Gotha. 1892.

Brunet, J. C. Manuel du libraire et de l'amateur de livres—Supplément (by Deschamps). Paris. 1870.

Grässe, J. G. T. Orbis Latinus. Dresden. 1861. Ed. Benedict, F. Berlin. 1909. (Vol. I only.)

Martin, C. T. The Record Interpreter. London. 1892. 2nd edn., 1910 (for British Isles).

III. CHRONOLOGY.

Clinton, H. F. Fasti Romani. 2 vols. Oxford. 1845–50. (Clinton, F. R.)

Gams, P. B. Series episcoporum ecclesiae Catholicae (with supplement). Ratisbon. 1873, 1886.

Ginzel, F. K. Handbuch der mathematischen und technischen Chronologie. Vol. I. Leipsic. 1906. Vol. II. 1911.

—— Spezieller Kanon der Sonnen- und Mondfinsternisse für das Landgebiet der klassischen Altertumswissenschaften und den Zeitraum v. 900 vor Chr. bis 600 nach Chr. [18 charts.] Berlin. 1899.

Grotefend, H. Taschenbuch der Zeitrechnung des deutschen Mittelalters und der Neuzeit. 3rd enlarged edn. Hanover. 1910.

—— Zeitrechnung des deutschen Mittelalters und d. Neuzeit. 2 vols. Hanover. 1891–8.

Haddan, A. W. and Stubbs, W. Councils and ecclesiastical documents relating to Great Britain and Ireland. (After Spelman and Wilkins.) 4 vols. Oxford. 1869–78.

Ideler, C. L. Handbuch der mathematischen und technischen Chronologie. 2 vols. Berlin. 1825. New edn. Breslau. 1883.

L'Art de vérifier les dates et les faits historiques. 2ᵉ partie. Depuis la naiss. de J.-C. 3rd edn. Paris. 3 vols. 1783 ff., and other edns. and reprints. Also 4th edn. by Saint-Allais. 1818–19. 18 vols. (Art de v.)

Mas Latrie, J. M. J. L. de. Trésor de chronologie, d'histoire et de géographie pour l'étude des documents du moyen âge. Paris. 1889.

Nicolas, Sir H. N. The Chronology of History. London. Best edn. 1838.

Ritter, Carl. Geographisch-Statistisches Lexicon. 2 vols. Leipsic. 1894–5.

Schram, R. Hilfstafeln für Chronologie. Vienna. 1883. New edn. Kalendario-graphische und chronologische Tafeln. Leipsic. 1908.

Wislicenus, W. F. Astronomische Chronologie. Leipsic. 1895.

Bernheim, Ernst. Lehrbuch der historischen Methode und der Geschichtsphilosophie. Leipsic. (5th and 6th enlarged edn.) 1908. Pp. 312–15.
Grotefend, H. Chronologie *in* vol. I, pp. 267 ff. of Meister, Aloys. Grundriss der Geschichtswissenschaft zur Einführung in das Studium der deutschen Geschichte des Mittelalters und der Neuzeit. Vol. I (1). Leipsic. 1906. Vol. I (2) and II (3). 1907, in progress. (Meister.)

(NUMISMATICS :—)

Cohen, H. (contin. Feuardent). Descriptions des Monnaies frappées sous l'Empire romain communément appelées Médailles impériales. 8 vols. 2nd edn. Paris. 1880–92.
Eckhel, J. H. von. Doctrina Numerorum Veterum. 8 vols. Vienna. 1792–8.
Engel, A. and Serrure, R. Traité de Numismatique du Moyen Âge. 2 vols. Paris. 1891–4.
Head, B. F. Corolla Numismatica. London. 1906.
Keary, C. F. Coinages of Western Europe, Honorius to Charles the Great. London. 1879. 3rd edn. 1894.
Luescher von Ebengreuth, A. Allgemeine Münzkunde und Geldgeschichte des Mittelalters und der neureren Zeit. 1904. (Pt 5 of Below's Handbuch, *see* VI.)
Maurice, J. Numismatique Constantinienne. Iconographie et chronologie, description historique, etc. Vol. I. Paris. 1908, in progress. [Plates.]
Wroth, W. Catalogue of the Imperial Byzantine coins in the British Museum. 2 vols. London. 1908. [Plates.]
—— Catalogue of the coins of the Vandals, Ostrogoths, Lombards, etc. in the British Museum (in preparation).

IV. COLLECTIONS OF SOURCES.

Acta Sanctorum Bollandiana. Brussels. 1643–1770. Paris and Rome. 1866, 1887. Brussels. 1894 ff. (ASBoll.)
Böhmer, J. F. Regesta imperii. 11 vols. (New edn. in several parts by various editors.) Innsbruck. 1877 ff.
    Vol. I. Regesten unter den Karolingern. Ed. Mühlbacher, E. 1908 ff.
    Vol. II. Regesten unter... d. Sächsischen Hause. Ed. Ottenthal, E. von. 1893 ff.
Bouquet. *See* Rerum Gallicarum scriptores.
Camden Society, Publications of the. London. 1838, in progress. (Camden.)
Codex Theodosianus. Gothofred, J. Ed. Marvillius, A. and Ritter, I. D. 6 vols. in 3. Leipsic. 1736–45. Ed. Mommsen, Th. and Meyer, P. M. Berlin. 1905.
Corpus Juris civilis. 3 vol. edn. Berlin. 1884–95.
    Vol. I. Institutiones, ed. Krüger, P. Digesta, ed. Mommsen, T. 11th edn. 1908.
    Vol. II. Codex. Ed. Krüger, P. 8th edn. 1906.
    Vol. III. Novellae. Ed. Schoell, R. and Kroll, W. 1895.
Corpus scriptorum christianorum orientalium. Ed. Chabor, J. B. and others. Paris, Rome and Leipsic. 1903 ff. (CSCO.)
Corpus scriptorum ecclesiasticorum latinorum. Vienna. 1866, in progress. (CSEL.)
Corpus scriptorum Historiae Byzantinae. Bonn. 1828–97. (CSHB.)
Duchesne, L. Fastes épiscopaux de l'ancienne Gaule. Paris. 1894, in progress.

Early English Text Society, Publications of the. (EETS.)

Geschichtschreiber der deutschen Vorzeit etc. *First issue* 1847 ff. in MGH (*see below*). New series. Leipsic. 1884, in progress.

Jaffé, Phil. Regesta pontificum Romanorum ab condita ecclesia ad annum post Christum natum 1198. Berlin. 1851. 2nd edn. Wattenbach, W., Loewenfeld, S., Kaltenbrunner, F., Ewald, P. Leipsic. 1885–8. 2 vols. (Jaffé reg.)

Kehr, P. F. Regesta Pontificum Romanorum, in progress. Vol. ɪ. Rome. ɪɪ. Latium. Berlin. 1906–7.

Liber Pontificalis. 3 vols. Rome. 1724–55. Ed. Duchesne, L. 2 vols. Paris. (Bibl. des écoles d'Athènes et de Rome.) 1886–92. Vol. ɪ to 795. (LP.)

Ed. Mommsen, Th. MGH. Gesta Pontif. Romanorum. 1898.

Liebermann, F. Die Gesetze der Angelsachsen. 2 vols. Halle-a.-S. 1898, 1906.

Mansi, J. D. Sacrorum conciliorum collectio. Florence and Venice. 1759–98. 31 vols. Reprint Martin, J. B. and Petit, L. Paris. 1901, in progress.

Migne, J. P. Patrologiae cursus completus. Series graeca. Paris. 1857–66. 161 vols. in 166. (MPG.)

—— Do. Series latina. 221 vols. Paris. 1844–55. Index, 4 vols. 1862–4. (MPL.)

Monumenta Germaniae Historica. Ed. Pertz, G. H., Mommsen, Th. and others. Hanover. 1826 ff. New edns. in progress. Hanover and Berlin. (MGH.) Index, 1890.

    Auctores Antiquissimi. 14 vols. in many pts. 1876 ff. (Auct. ant.) Vols. ɪx, xɪ, xɪɪɪ form Chronica minora (saec. ɪv, v, vɪ). Ed. Mommsen, Th. 1892–8.

    Deutsche Chroniken (Scriptores qui in vernac. lingua usi sunt). ɪ–vɪ. 1892 ff., in progress.

    Diplomata regum et imperatorum Germaniae: includes Diplom. imperii. 1872. Urkunden d. deutschen Könige und Kaiser. 1879 ff., in progress. Diplomata Karolinorum. ɪ.

    Epistolae. ɪ–vɪ, 1.

    Epistolae saec. xɪɪɪ e regestis pontificum Romanorum. ɪ–ɪɪɪ.

    Geschichtschreiber d. deutschen Vorzeit. *See above.*

    Gesta pontificum Romanorum. ɪ. 1898.

    Leges. ɪ–v. 1835–89. Fol.

    Legum sectiones. ɪ–v. (In several vols. and pts.) 4°. 1883–93.

    Libelli de lite imperatorum et pontificum (saec. xɪ, xɪɪ). ɪ–ɪɪɪ. 1891 ff.

    Libri confraternitatum. 1884.

    Necrologia Germaniae. ɪ, ɪɪ. 1884.

    Poetae Latini medii aevi (Carolingi). ɪ–ɪv, 1. 1881 ff.

    Scriptores. 30 vols. in 31. Fol. 1826–96. (Script.)

    Scriptores rerum Langobardarum et Italicarum. 1878.

    Scriptores rerum Merovingicarum. ɪ–ɪv. 1885–96.

    [Scriptores rerum Germanicarum in usum scholarum. Hanover. 1839 ff. Fresh series. 1890 ff. 8°. Contain editions of many of the above.]

Monumenta historica Britannica. Ed. Petrie, H. and Sharpe, T. London. 1848.

Müller, C. Fragmenta Historicorum Graecorum. 5 vols. Paris. 1841–83 (vol. v, ii, ed. Langlois, V.). (FHG.)

Muratori, L. A. Rerum Italicarum scriptores. Milan. 1723–51. Indices chronolog. Turin. 1885. New edn. Carducci, G. and Fiorini, V. Città di Castello. 1900, in progress.

Patrologia Orientalis. Ed. Graffin, R. and Nau, F. (and others). (7 pts.) Paris. 1903–5. (Patr. Orient.)

Record Commissioners, Publications of the. London. (Rec. Comm.) 1802–69.

Rerum Gallicarum et Franciscarum scriptores. (Recueil des hist. des Gaules et de la France.) Ed. Bouquet, M. and others. 23 vols. 1738–1876. Vols. ɪ–xɪx re-ed. by Delisle, L. 1868–80. New series. 4°. 1899, in progress.

Rolls Series:—Rerum Britannicarum medii aevi scriptores. (Chronicles and Memorials of Great Britain and Ireland during the Middle Ages.) Published under direction of the Master of the Rolls. (Various editors.) London. 1858 ff. (Convenient list in Gross.) (Rolls.)

Selden Society, Publications of the. London. 1888 ff. (Selden.)

Turner, C. H. Ecclesiae Occidentalis monumenta juris antiq. Canonum et conciliorum Graecorum interpret. Latinae. Fasc. i, 1, 2; ii, 1. Oxford. 1899–1907, in progress.

(INSCRIPTIONS:—)

Cagnat, R. Cours d'épigraphie latine. 2nd edn. Paris. 1890.

Corpus Inscriptionum Graecarum. Ed. Böckh, A. and others. Berlin. 1828–77. (For Christian inscriptions cf. vol. iv, part 2, ed. Kirchhoff.) (CIG.)

Corpus Inscriptionum Latinarum. Ed. Mommsen and others. Berlin. 1862, in progress. New edn. 1893, in progress. (CIL.)

Hübner, A. E. Exempla Scripturae epigraphicae Latinae a Caesaris morte ad aet. Justiniani. Berlin. 1884.

Le Blant, E. de. L'épigraphie chrétienne en Gaule et dans l'Afrique romaine. Paris. 1890.

—— Nouveau recueil des inscript. chrét. de la Gaule ant. au 8e siècle. (Coll. des doc. inéd. sur l'hist. de France.) Paris. 1892.

Rossi, G. B. de. Inscriptiones Christianae urbis Romae vii° saeculo antiquiores. Rome. 1857–88. (2 vols. only published.)

V. ORIGINAL WRITERS.

Anglo-Saxon Chronicle. Ed. Plummer, C. 2 vols. Oxford. 1892–9. (Based on Earle.) Best edn. Also ed. Earle, J. Two of the Saxon Chronicles, parallel. Oxford. 1865. Thorpe, B. Rolls ser. 2 vols. London. 1861. Transl. Gomme, E. E. C. (With notes.) London. 1909. Stevenson, J. 1853.

Bede. Historia ecclesiastica gentis anglorum. Ed. Plummer, C. 2 vols. Oxford. 1896. Best edn. Holder, A. Freiburg. 1882. 2nd edn. 1890. Bks iii, iv. Ed. Mayor, J. E. B. and Lumby, J. R. Cambridge. 1878. 3rd edn. 1881, and earlier edns. Transl. Sellar, A. M. (with notes). London. 1907. Gidley, L. Lond. 1870, and earlier translations. Old English version. Ed. with transl. Miller, T. EETS. 1890.

Cedrenus. CSHB. Ed. Bekker, I. 2 vols. 1838–9.

Chronicon Paschale. CSHB. Ed. Dindorf, L. 2 vols. 1832.

Constantine Porphyrogenitus. Opera. 3 vols. CSHB. Ed. Reiske, J. J. 1829–30, 1840.

Einhard (Eginhard). Vita Karoli imperatoris. MGH, script. rer. germ. Ed. Waitz (after Pertz). 4th edn. 1880. Wattenbach, W. (after Jaffé). Berlin. 1876. Transl. Glaister, W. London. 1877.

Evagrius. Historia ecclesiastica. Ed. Bidez, J. and Parmentier, L. In Byzantine texts: ed. Bury, J. B. London. 1898.

Fredegarius. Chronicarum quae dicuntur F. scholastici libri iv. 642 (658). Continuationes to 768. Ed. Krusch, Br. MGH, script. rer. merov. ii.

Gregorius Turonensis. Opera omnia. Ed. Arndt, W., Bonnet, M., Krusch, Br. MGH, script. rer. merov. i.

Isidore of Seville. Historia de Regibus Gothorum, etc. MGH. 1894.

John of Antioch. FHG. iv, v.

Jordanes. De Getarum sive Gothorum origine et rebus gestis (Getica). MGH, auct. ant. v. 1882. Transl. Mierow, C. Princeton. 1908. New Edn. 1915.

Origo gentis Langobardarum. MGH, Leges. iv. 1868.

Paulus Diaconus, historia Langobardarum and Continuationes. MGH, script. rer. Langobard. et Ital. 1878.

Procopius. De Bellis and Historia Arcana. Ed. Haury, J. Leipsic. 1905–6. 3 vols. Ed. Kraschennikov, M. Dorpat. (Iuriev.) 1899. De Bello Persico (2 bks), Vandalico (2 bks) and Gothico (4 bks). CSHB. 1833. Geschicht-schreiber d. d. Vorzeit (*see* iv *above*). 1885. Also Hist. Arcana and de Aedificiis. CSHB. 1838. Trans. Athenian Society, Athens. 1906. Of the buildings of Justinian. (Transl.) Stewart, A. and others. Palest. Pilgrims Text Soc. London. 1886.

Ṭabari. Annals of Ṭabari. Ed. de Goeje. Leyden. 1879–1901.

Tacitus. Germania. Ed. Halm, C. (Teubner). Leipsic. 1877. Furneaux, H. Oxford. 1894.

—— Annales. Ed. Furneaux, H. 2 vols. Oxford. 1884–91. Transl. Ramsay, G. G. 2 vols. London. 1909.

—— Historia. Ed. Spooner, W. A. London. 1891. Transl. Church, A. J. and Brodribb, W. J. Cambridge. 1864.

—— Transl. Annals and Germany. Church and Brodribb. Rev. edn. London. 1877.

Theophanes. Chronographia. Ed. Classen, J. 2 vols. CSHB. 1839–41. de Boor, C. 2 vols. Leipsic. 1883–5.

Zonaras. Annales. CSHB. Ed. Büttner-Wobst, Th. 1897. 3 vols.

VI. MODERN WORKS.

Alzog, J. Universalgeschichte der Kirche. Mainz. 1841. Best edn. 10th by Kraus, F. X. 1882. Transl. (from 9th German edn.) Pabisch, F. J. and Byrne, T. S. Manual of Church History. 4 vols. Dublin. 1895–1900.

Bardenhewer. Patrologie (*see* i).

Baronius, Cæs. Annales Ecclesiastici una cum critica historico-chronologica P. A. Pagii, contin. Raynaldus, O. Ed. Mansi, J. D. Lucca. 34 vols. 1738–46. Apparatus, 1 vol. Index, 4 vols. 1740, 1757–9.

Below, G. von and Meinecke, F. Handbuch der Mittelalterlichen und Neueren Geschichte. Munich and Berlin, in progress. *See below*, Redlich.

Brunner, H. Deutsche Rechtsgeschichte. 2 vols. Leipsic. 1887–92. Vol. i. 2nd edn. 1906.

Bury, J. B. A History of the later Roman Empire from Arcadius to Irene. (395 A.D. to 800 A.D.) 2 vols. London. 1889.

Dahn, F. Urgeschichte der germanischen u. romanischen Völker. 4 vols. Berlin. 1881–9. (ii, 2 of Oncken.)

—— Deutsche Geschichte. Vol. i, pts 1, 2 (to 814), no more pubd. Gotha. 1883–8.

—— Die Könige der Germanen. 12 vols. 1861–1909. Munich (1, 2), Würzburg (3, 4) and Leipsic (5–12).

Dalton, O. M. Byzantine Art and Archaeology. Oxford. 1911.

Diehl, Ch. Études sur l'administration byzantine dans l'Exarchat de Ravenne. (568–751.) Paris. 1888.

—— L'Afrique byzantine, hist. de la domination byzantine en Afrique. (533–709.) Paris. 1896.

Döllinger, J. J. Ignatius von. Geschichte der christl. Kirche. Vol. i. Parts 1, 2 [to A.D. 630]. Landshut. 1833–5. (No more pubd.) Transl. Cox, E. History of the Church. 2 vols. London. 1840–2.

—— Lehrbuch der Kirchengeschichte. (i; ii, 1.) Ratisbon. (2nd improved edn.) 1834. [A shorter work.]

Duchesne, L. Histoire ancienne de l'Église. 4 vols. Paris. 1905 ff., and later edns. Transl. (vol. I) Early Hist. of the Christian Church, etc. from 4th edn. London. 1909.

—— Les Origines du Culte Chrétien. Paris. 1890. 3rd edn. 1903. 4th edn. 1910. Transl. London (from 4th edn.). 1910.

Ebert, A. Allgemeine Geschichte der Litteratur des Mittelalters im Abendland. 3 vols. Leipsic. 1874–87. 2nd edn. of vols. I and II. 1889.

Finlay, G. Ed. Tozer, H. F. History of Greece, B.C. 146 to A.D. 1864. 7 vols. Oxford. 1877.

Fleury, Claude. Histoire ecclésiastique. 20 vols. Paris. 1691–1720. Continued to end of 18th century under Vidal, O. Many editions. [Orig. edn. to 1414. 4 add. vols. by Fl. to 1517, pub. Paris, 1840.] Eng. transl. (to 456). 3 vols. Oxford. 1843–4.

Fustel de Coulanges, N. D. Histoire des Institutions politiques de l'ancienne France. Completed and ed. Jullian, C. 6 vols. Paris. 1888–92. [*See Bibl. to chapter* v (1).]

Gasquet, A. L'empire byzantin et la monarchie franque. Paris. 1888.

Gelzer, H. Abriss der byzantinischen Kaisergeschichte. 2nd edn. Munich. 1897 (in Krumbacher, *see below*).

Gibbon, Edward. The History of the Decline and Fall of the Roman Empire. 1776–81. Ed. in 7 vols. by Bury, J. B. 1896. Latest edn. 1909 ff. (Bury-Gibbon.) [Notes essential especially for chronology.]

Giesebrecht, W. von. Geschichte der deutschen Kaiserzeit. Vols. I–V. Brunswick and Leipsic. 1855–83. I–III (5th edn.). Leipsic. 1881–90. IV (2nd edn.). Brunswick. 1899. VI (ed. Simson, B. von). Leipsic. 1895.

Gieseler, J. C. L. Lehrbuch der Kirchengeschichte. Bonn. 3 vols. 1824 ff. and 6 vols. in 5, 1828–57. Transl. Davidson, S. 5 vols. Edinburgh, 1854, and Cunningham, Text-book of Ecclesiastical History. Philadelphia. 3 vols. 1836.

Gregorovius, F. Geschichte der Stadt Rom im Mittelalter. 8 vols. Stuttgart. 1859–72. (Translated from 4th edition by Miss A. Hamilton. London. 1894–1902. 8 vols. in 13.)

Gwatkin, H. M. The Knowledge of God. (Gifford Lectures.) 2 vols. Edinburgh. 1906.

Harnack, Adolf. Lehrbuch der Dogmengeschichte. Freiburg-i.-B. 1886 ff. Second enlarged edn. 1894–7. 4th edn. 1905 ff. Transl. Buchanan, N. and others. 7 vols. London. 1894–9. *Also* Mitchel, A. London and New York. 1893.

Hartmann, L. M. Geschichte Italiens im Mittelalter. Gotha. 1897 ff., in progress. (Lamprecht.)

Hase, Karl A. Kirchengeschichte auf Grundlage akadem. Vorlesungen. 1885 ff.

—— Kirchengeschichtliche Lehrbuch zunächst für akademischen Vorlesungen. 1834 (frequently reprinted).

Hauck, A. Kirchengeschichte Deutschlands [to 1250]. 5 vols. Leipsic. 1887–1911. 2nd edn. of vols. I, II, III. 1904–6.

Hefele, C. J., contin. Hergenröther, J. A. G. Conciliengeschichte. 9 vols. Freiburg-i.-B. 1855 ff. 2nd edn. 1873 ff. Transl. of vols. I–V [to 800]. History of the Councils of the Church. London. 1871–96. French transl. Delarc, O., new Fr. transl. Leclercq, H. Paris. 1907 ff., in progress.

Hellmann, S. Studien zur Mittelalterlichen Geschichtschreibung. (I.) Gregor von Tours. HZ. Vol. CVII [3rd ser. 11 (1), 1911].

Hergenröther, J. A. G. Handbuch der allgemeinen Kirchengeschichte. 4th edn. Vols. I, II, ed. Kirsch, J. P. Freiburg-i.-B. 1892 ff. French transl. by Belet.

Historia Generale de la España. By members of Real Acad. de la Hist. Madrid. In progress.

Hodgkin, T. Italy and her invaders. 8 vols. Oxford. 1880–99. 2nd edn. Vols.
  ɪ–ɪv in 5. 1892–6.
Kraus, F. X. Ed. Sauer, J. Geschichte der christlichen Kunst. Freiburg-i.-B.
  and St Louis, Minnesota. 1896–1908. 2 vols. in 3.
Krumbacher, K. Gesch. der byzantinischen Litteratur von Justinian bis zum Ende
  des oströmischen Reiches. Munich. 2nd edn. 1897. Ed. Ehrhard, A. and
  Gelzer, H. (Handbuch d. klass. Altertumswissenschaft.)
Kurtz, J. H. Lehrbuch der Kirchengeschichte. Mittau. 1849. 14th edn.
  Ed. Bonwetsch, N. and Tschackert, P. Vols. ɪ, ɪɪ. Leipsic. 1906.
  Transl. from 9th edn. Macpherson, J. Church History. 3 vols. London.
  1888–93.
Langen, Jos. Geschichte der römischen Kirche. 4 vols. ɪ bis zum Pontifikat
  Leos I. Bonn. 1881.
Lavisse, E. (and others). Histoire de France jusqu'à la Révolution. Paris. 1900–11.
Lavisse, Ernest, and Rambaud, Alfred. Histoire générale du ɪvᵉ siècle jusqu'à nos
  jours. 12 vols. Paris. 1893–1900.
Lecky, W. E. H. History of European morals from Augustus to Charlemagne.
  2 vols. London. 1870. [Very superficial.]
Le Nain de Tillemont, L. S. de. Mémoires pour servir à l'histoire ecclésiastique
  des six premiers siècles. 15 vols. Brussels. 1693–1707. 2nd edn. 16 vols.
  Paris. 1701–12.
—— Histoire des Empereurs. 6 vols. 1690–1738.
Loofs, Fr. Leitfaden zum Studium der Dogmengeschichte. Halle. 1889. 2nd
  edn. enlarged, 1900.
Manitius, M. Gesch. der lateinischen Literatur des Mittelalters. Vol. ɪ. Munich.
  1911.
Milman, H. H. History of Latin Christianity. London. 1854–5. Rev. edn.
  9 vols. 1867.
Möller, W. Lehrbuch der Kirchengeschichte. 3 vols. Tübingen. 1892–1900.
  2nd edn. of vol. ɪ [to ᴀ.ᴅ. 600] by Schubert, H. von. Tübingen and Leipsic.
  1902. Transl. Rutherford, A. History of the Christian Church. London.
  1898.
Mommsen, Th. Römisches Staatsrecht. 3 vols. 1873–8. 3rd edn. Leipsic.
  1887–8.
Mosheim, J. L. von. Institutionum historiae ecclesiasticae antiquae et recentioris
  libri 4. 4 vols. Helmstedt. 1755. Transl. Murdock, J., ed. Soames, H.
  1841. Rev. edn. 1850.
Mühlbacher, E. Deutsche Geschichte unter den Karolingern. Stuttgart. 1896.
  (In Zwiedineck-Südenhorst's Bibliothek deutscher Geschichte.)
Müller, K. Kirchengeschichte. Vols. ɪ, ɪɪ. Freiburg-i.-B. 1892.
Neander, August. Allgemeine Geschichte der christlichen Religion und Kirche.
  6 vols. in 11. Hamburg. 1825–52. Transl. Torrey, J. General History
  of the Church. 9 vols. London. 1847–55.
Pargoire, J. L'Église byzantine de 527 à 847. Paris. 1905 (in Bibliothèque de
  l'enseignement de l'hist. ecclésiastique).
Pollock, F. and Maitland, F. W. The history of English Law before Edward I.
  2 vols. Cambridge. 1895. 2nd edn. 1898.
Quentin, H. Les Martyrologes historiques du Moyen Âge. Étude sur la formation
  du martyrologe romain. Paris. 1908. (Études d'hist. des dogmes et d'ancienne
  littérature ecclésiastique.)
Ranke, L. von. Weltgeschichte. 9 vols. Leipsic. 1881–8. Transl. vol. ɪ,
  Prothero, G. W. London. 1884.
Redlich, O. and Erben, W. Urkundenlehre. Pt ɪ. 1907. ɪv, 1 of Below's
  Handbuch (*see above*).

Romano, G. Le dominazioni barbariche in Italia. (395–1024.) [Storia politica d' Italia scritta da una Società di Professori.] Milan. 1909 ff.

Stubbs, Wm. Constitutional history of England. 3 vols. Oxford. 1874. (Frequently reprinted.) French transl. (with notes and studies). Lefebvre, G. and Petit Dutaillis, Ch. Paris. 1907. English transl. of notes etc. Studies and Notes supplementary to Stubbs' Constitutional History. Rhodes, W. E. Manchester. 1908.

Teuffel, W. S. and Schwabe, L. Geschichte der römischen Litteratur. 1891–2. Transl. Warr, G. C. W. 2 vols. London. 1900.

Tillemont. *See* Le Nain de Tillemont.

Waitz, G. Deutsche Verfassungsgeschichte. 8 vols. Kiel. 1863–78. 2nd and 3rd edns. Berlin. 1880–96.

Werminghoff, A. Geschichte der Kirchenverfassung Deutschlands. I. Hanover and Leipsic. 1905.

Zachariae v. Lingenthal, K. E. Gesch. des griechisch-römischen Rechts. Berlin. 3rd edn. 1892.

CHAPTER I.

JUSTINIAN. THE IMPERIAL RESTORATION IN THE WEST.

I. SPECIAL BIBLIOGRAPHY.

In Diehl, Ch. Justinien et la civilisation byzantine au vi⁰ siècle. Paris. 1901.

II. SOURCES.

(a) CONTEMPORARY.

Agathias. Historiarum libri v. CSHB.

Anonymous. περὶ στρατηγικῆς in Köchly, H. and Rüstow, W. Griechische Kriegs-schriftsteller. Vol. II, part 2. Leipsic. 1855.

Cassiodorus. Variarum libri XII. MGH, auct. ant. XII. Ed. Mommsen, Th. 1894.

Corippus. Johannis. MGH, auct. ant. III. Ed. Partsch, J. 1879.

Epistolae merowingici aevi. MGH, epist. III. Ed. Gundlach, W. 1892.

Evagrius. Historia ecclesiastica. *See Gen. Bibl.* v.

Life of Fulgentius of Ruspae. MPL 65.

Hormisdae papae epistolae. MPL 63.

John Lydus. De Magistratibus. Ed. Wünsch. Leipsic. 1903.

Jordanes. Getica, Romana. MGH. *See Gen. Bibl.* v.

Codex Justinianus. Ed. Krüger, G. Berlin. 1884.

Justiniani Novellae. Ed. Zachariae von Lingenthal, K. E. Leipsic. 1881. 2 vols. Ed. Schoell, R. and Kroll, W. Berlin. 1895.

Liber pontificalis. *See Gen. Bibl.* v.

Malalas. Chronicle in CSHB and (for the new fragments) Mommsen, Th. Johannes von Antiochia und Malalas. Hm. VI, 375 sqq.

Marcellinus Comes. MGH, auct. a nt. XI. Ed. Mommsen, Th. 1894.

Peter the patrician. Fragments in Constantine Porphyrogenitus de Cerimoniis. CSHB.

Procopius. De Bellis. Ed. Haury, J. Leipsic. 1905. 2 vols. Historia Arcana. Ed. Haury, J. Leipsic. 1906.

Life of Severus, Patriarch of Antioch. Ed. Kugener, M. A. in Patr. orient. *See Gen. Bibl.* IV. II, fasc. 1 and 3. (Syrian text and Latin translation.)

Life of John of Tella. Ed. Kleyn. Het Leven Johannes van Tella. Leyden. 1882. Ed. Brooks, E. W. CSCO. Vol. XXV. Paris. 1907. (Text and translation.)

Victor Tonnennensis. Chronica. MGH, auct. ant. XI. 1894.

Zacharias the Rhetor. Hist. eccl. Ed. Ahrens, K. and Krüger, G. (German translation.) Leipsic. 1899. Hamilton, F. J. and Brooks, E. W. London. 1899. (English translation.)

(b) LATER.

Agnellus. Liber pontificalis ecclesiae Ravennatis. MGH. 1878.
Cedrenos. Chronicles. *See Gen. Bibl.* v.
Chronicon Paschale. *See Gen. Bibl.* v.
Constantine Porphyrogenitus. De Cerimoniis. *See Gen. Bibl.* v.
Isidore of Seville. Chronicle and de Regibus Gothorum. *See Gen. Bibl.* v.
John of Antioch. *See Gen. Bibl.* v.
Paulus Diaconus. Historia Langobardorum. *See Gen. Bibl.* v.
Theophanes. Chronicle. Ed. de Boor, C. *See Gen. Bibl.* v.
Zonaras. *See Gen. Bibl.* v.

III. MODERN WORKS.

(a) GENERAL.

Bury. Hist. of later Roman Empire. Vol. I. *See Gen. Bibl.* vi.
Delbrück, H. Gesch. der Kriegskunst. Vol. II. Berlin. 1902.
Diehl, Ch. Justinien et la civilisation byzantine au vi^e siècle. Paris. 1901.
Gfrörer, A. F. Kaiser Justinian. (Byzant. Geschichten ii.) Graz. 1874.
Gregorovius. Gesch. der Stadt Rom. Vol. I. *See Gen. Bibl.* vi.
Grisar, H. Gesch. Roms und der Päpste im Mittelalter. Vol. I. Freiburg-i.-B. 1901.
Hartmann. Gesch. Italiens im Mittelalter. Vol. I. *See Gen. Bibl.* vi.
Hertzberg, G. F. Gesch. Griechenlands seit dem Absterben des antiken Lebens.
    Vol. I. Gotha. 1876.
Hesseling, D. C. Byzantium. Haarlem. 1902. French translation. Paris. 1907.
Holmes, W. G. The age of Justinian and Theodora. 2 vols. London. 1905-7.
Invernizzi, P. De rebus gestis Justiniani. Rome. 1783.
Isambert, F. A. Histoire de Justinien. 2 vols. Paris. 1856.
Ludewig, J. P. Vita Justiniani. Halle. 1731.
Ranke. Weltgeschichte. Vol. iv, 2. *See Gen. Bibl.* vi.
Schmidt, L. Gesch. der deutschen Stämme bis zum Ausgang der Völkerwanderung.
    Berlin. 1904-10.
—— Gesch. der Vandalen. Leipsic. 1901.

(b) ON SOURCES.

On John Malalas and John of Antioch:
    Gleye, C. E. Zur Johannes Frage. BZ. 1896. 422.
    Haury, J. Johannes Malalas, identisch mit dem Patriarchen Johannes
        Scholastikos. BZ. 1900. 337.
    Mommsen, Th. Johannes von Antiochia und Malalas. Hm. vi. 1872.
    Patzig, E. Johannes Antiochenus und Johannes Malalas. Leipsic. 1892.
    Sotiriadis, G. Zur Kritik des Johannes von Antiochia. Jahrbuch für
        klassische Philologie. Suppl. xvi. 1888.
On Procopius:
    Brückner. Zur Beurteilung Procopius von Cäsarea. Ansbach. 1896.
    Dahn, F. Prokopius von Cäsarea. Berlin. 1865.
    Haury, J. Prokopiana. Augsburg. 1882.
    —— Zur Beurteilung des Geschichtschreibers Procopius von Cäsarea.
        Munich. 1896.
    Pancenko, B. O tainoi Istorij Prokopija. VV. ii, iii. 1895-6.
    Ranke. Weltgeschichte. iv, 2, p. 235. *See Gen. Bibl.* vi.

(c) Monographs, Biographies, etc.

Benjamin.   De Justiniani aetate quaestiones militares.   Berlin.   1892.
Bryce, J.   Life of Justinian by Theophilus.   EHR.   1887.   p. 657.
Bury, J. B.   The Nika Riot.   JHS.   1897.
Diehl, Ch.   Études sur l'administration byzantine dans l'exarchat de Ravenne.
    See Gen. Bibl. vi.
—— L'Afrique Byzantine.   *See Gen. Bibl.* vi.
—— Ravenne.   Paris.   1903.
Gasquet, A.   L'Empire byzantin et la monarchie franque.   *See Gen. Bibl.* vi.
Gaudenzi, A.   Sui rapporti tra l'Italia e l'impero d'Oriente.   (476–554.)   Bologna.
    1888.
Hartmann, L. M.   Byzant. Verwaltung in Italien.   Leipsic.   1889.
Hodgkin, Th.   Italy and her invaders.   Vols. iii, iv and v.   *See Gen. Bibl.* vi.
Jörs, P.   Die Reichspolitik Kaiser Justinians.   Giessen.   1893.
Kalligas, P.   Περὶ τῆς στάσεως τοῦ Νίκα.   (Μελέται καὶ λόγοι.   Athens.   1882.)
Leclercq, dom H.   L'Afrique Chrétienne.   2 vols.   Paris.   1904.
Martroye, F.   L'Occident à l'époque byzantine.   Goths et Vandales.   Paris.   1904.
Mommsen, Th.   Das römische Militärwesen seit Diocletian.   Hm. xxiv.   1889.
Pflugk-Harttung, J. von.   Belisars Vandalenkrieg.   HZ.   1889.
Rambaud, A.   De byzantino Hippodromo et de circensibus factionibus.   Paris.
    1870.   (Cf. L'Hippodrome à Constantinople.   R. des Deux Mondes, 15 août
    1871.)
Strzygowski, J.   Der Silberschild aus Kertsch.   Petersburg.   1892.
Uspenski, Th.   Partii Tsirka i dimy v Konstantinopolie.   VV.   i.   1894.
Vassilief, A.   O Slavianskom proiskhogdénij Joustiniana.   VV.   i.   1894.
Warwick Wroth.   Catalogue of Byzantine coins.   Vol. i.   *See Gen. Bibl.* iii.

CHAPTER II.

JUSTINIAN'S GOVERNMENT IN THE EAST.

I. SPECIAL BIBLIOGRAPHY.

In Diehl, Ch. Justinien et la civilisation byzantine au vi⁰ siècle. Paris. 1901.

II. SOURCES.

(a) Contemporary.

Agathias. Historiarum libri v. CSHB.

Chronicle of Edessa. Ed. Hallier, L. Texte und Untersuchungen ix, 2. Leipsic. 1893.

CIL. Vols. iii, vi and viii. *See Gen. Bibl.* iv.

Corpus juris civilis. *See Gen. Bibl.* iv.

Cosmas Indicopleustes. Christian topography. MPG 88.

Cyrill of Skythopolis. Life of St Sabas. Ed. Cotelerius. Eccl. Graec. Monumenta. Vol. iii. Paris. 1686.

Evagrius. *See Bibl. c.* i.

Facundus of Hermia. Opera. MPL 67.

Hierocles. Synecdemos. Ed. Burckhardt, A. Leipsic. 1893.

John Lydus. *See Bibl. c.* i.

John of Beith-Aphtonia. Life of Severus. Ed. Kugener, M. A. Patr. Orient. *See Gen. Bibl.* iv. ii, fasc. 3. (Text and French translation.)

John of Ephesus. Historia ecclesiastica. Ed. Schönfelder, J. Die Kirchengeschichte des Johannes von Ephesos. Munich. 1862. Fragments in Land, J. P. N. and Van Douwen, W. J. Commentarii de beatis Orientalibus. Amsterdam. 1889. (Latin translation.) Also in Nau, F. Analyse de la 2⁰ partie inédite de l'Hist. de Jean d'Asie. ROC. 1897. 2. 457.

Justinian. Opera. MPG 86.

Leontius of Byzantium. Opera. MPG 86.

Liber pontificalis. *See Gen. Bibl.* iv.

Liberatus. Breviarium. MPL 68.

Life of Jacobus Baradaeus. In Comm. de beatis Orientalibus. Ed. Land, J. P N. and van Douwen, W. J. Amsterdam. 1889. (Latin translation.)

Life of John of Tella. *See Bibl. c.* i.

Malalas. *See Bibl. c.* i.

Menander. History. Fragments in CSHB and Excerpta de legationibus. Ed. de Boor, C. Berlin. 1905. 2 vols.

Moschus. Pratum spirituale. MPG 87.

Nonnosos. Fragments. CSHB.

Paulus Silentiarius. Description of Saint Sophia. CSHB. Translation in Salzenberg, W. Altchristliche Denkmäler von Constantinopel. Berlin. 1854. And ed. Friedländer, P. Leipsic. 1911.

Pelagii I papae epistolae. MGH. Epist. iii. Ed. Gundlach, W. Berlin. 1892. MPL 69.

Procopius. *See Bibl. c. i.* Also De Aedificiis. *See Gen. Bibl. v.*

Sacrorum conciliorum nova et amplissima collectio. Vols. viii and ix. *See Gen. Bibl. iv.* (Mansi.)

Severus. Letters. Ed. Brooks, E. W. The sixth book of the select letters of Severus. London. 1902–3. 2 vols. (Text and translation.)

—— Homilies. Ed. Duval, R. Patr. Orient. iv, 1. (Text and French translation.)

Theophanes of Byzantium. CSHB.

Victor Tonnennensis. *See Bibl. c. i.*

Vigilii Papae Epistolae. MPL 69.

Zacharias the Rhetor. *See Bibl. c. i.*

—— Life of Severus. *See Bibl. c. i.*

(b) Later.

Bar-Hebraeus. Chronicon Syriacon. Ed. Bedjan, P. Paris. 1890.

—— Chronicon ecclesiasticon. Ed. Abbeloos, J. B. and Lamy, Th. J. (with translation). Louvain. 1872–7. 3 vols.

Cedrenos. *See Gen. Bibl. v.*

Chronicon Paschale. *See Gen. Bibl. v.*

Codinus. De Aedificiis. De S. Sophia. In Scriptores originum Constantino-politanarum. Ed. Preger, Th. Leipsic. 1901.

Constantine the Rhodian. Description des Saints Apôtres. Ed. Legrand, E. et Reinach, Th. Paris. 1896.

John of Antioch. History. FHG. iv and v. *See Gen. Bibl. iv.*

John of Nikiu. Chronicles. Ed. Zotenberg, H. Notices et extraits des MSS. de la Bibliothèque Nationale xxiv, 1. Paris. 1883. JA. 7th series. Vol. xiii. March–April, 1879.

Michael the Syrian. Chronicle. Ed. Chabot. 3 vols. Paris. 1900–10.

Nicolaos Mesarites. Description of the Church of the Apostles. Ed. Heisenberg, A. Die Apostelkirche in Konstantinopel. Leipsic. 1908.

Ṭabari. Ed. Nöldeke, Th. (translation). Leyden. 1879. *See Gen. Bibl. v.*

Theophanes. *See Gen. Bibl.*

Zonaras. Chronicle. CSHB. *See Gen. Bibl. v.* (Vol. iii.)

III. MODERN WRITINGS.

(a) General.

The same as for c. i, and also

Bussell, E. W. The Roman empire. Essays on the constitutional history (81 b.c.–1081 a.d.). London. 1910.

Diehl, Ch. Manuel d'art byzantin. Paris. 1910.

Harnack, A. Dogmengeschichte. *See Gen. Bibl. vi.*

Heyd, W. von. Hist. du commerce du Levant. Trad. Raynaud, F. Vol. i. Leipsic. 1885.

Jireček, K. J. Gesch. der Bulgaren. Prague. 1876.

Pargoire, J. L'Eglise byzantine. *See Gen. Bibl. vi.*

Zachariae von Lingenthal. Gesch. des griechisch-römischen Rechts. *See Gen. Bibl. vi.*

(b) On Sources.

Cosmas :
    Gelzer, H. Kosmas der Indienfahrer. Jahrb. f. prot. Theol. 1883.
John of Ephesus :
    Duchesne, L. Jean d'Asie. Paris. 1892.
Leontius of Byzantium :
    Loofs, F. Leontius von Byzanz. Leipsic. 1887.
    Rügamer, W. Leontius von Byzanz. Würzburg. 1894.
    Junglas. Leontius von Byzanz. Berlin. 1908.
Liber pontificalis :
    Duchesne, L. La nouvelle édition du Liber pontificalis. Mél. de Rome.
    1898.
Procopius of Gaza :
    Seitz, K. Die Schule von Gaza. Heidelberg. 1892.

(c) Monographs, Biographies, etc.

Bellomo, A. Agapeto diacono e la sua scheda regia. Bari. 1906.
Chapot, V. La frontière de l'Euphrate de Pompée à la conquête arabe. Paris.
    1907.
Debidour, A. Théodora. Paris. 1885.
Diehl, Ch. Théodora, impératrice de Byzance. Paris. 1904.
Diekamp. Die origenistischen Streitigkeiten im vi. Jahrh. und das fünfte allge-
    meine Concil. Münster. 1899.
Dillmann, A. Zur Gesch. des Axumitischen Reiches vom iv. bis vi. Jahrh. Abh.
    PAW. 1880.
Duchesne, L. Les missions chrétiennes au sud de l'empire romain. Mél. de Rome.
    1896.
—— Vigile et Pélage. RQH. 1884, ii.
Eustratios. Σευῆρος ὁ μονοφυσίτης. Leipsic. 1894.
Gasquet, A. De l'autorité impériale en matière de religion. Paris. 1879.
Gelzer, H. Die politische und kirchliche Stellung von Byzanz. Leipsic. 1879.
Güterbock. Byzanz und Persien in ihren diplom. Völkerrecht. Beziehungen im
    Zeitalter Justinians. Berlin. 1906.
Hirth, F. China and the Roman Orient. Leipsic. 1885.
Houssaye, H. L'impératrice Théodora. Rev. des deux mondes. 1 Feb. 1885.
Kleyn, H. G. Jacobus Baradaeus. Leyden. 1882.
Knecht. Die Religionspolitik Kaiser Justinians I. Würzburg. 1896.
Labourt, J. Le christianisme dans l'empire perse. Paris. 1904.
Lethaby, W. R. and Swainson, H. The Church of Sancta Sophia. London. 1894.
Mallet, C. E. The Empress Theodora. EHR. ii, p. 1. 1887.
Monnier, H. L'ἐπιβολή. NRDF. 1892.
Nöldeke, Th. Gesch. der Perser und Araber im Zeitalter der Sassaniden. Leyden
    1879.
Peisker, M. Severus von Antiochien. Halle. 1903.
Pfannmüller. Die kirchliche Gesetzgebung Justinians. Berlin. 1902.
Salzenberg, W. Altchristliche Baudenkmäler von Constantinopel. Berlin. 1854.
Strzygowski, J. Die byzant. Wasserbehälter von Constantinopel. Vienna. 1893.
Zachariae von Lingenthal, K. E. Eine Verordnung Justinians über den Seiden-
    handel. Mém. de l'Acad. de Pétersbourg. 1865.

CHAPTER III.

ROMAN LAW.

I. ORIGINAL AUTHORITIES.

Codex Justinianus. Ed. Krüger, P. Berlin. 8th edn. 1906. A full critical edition.

Codex Theodosianus. Ed. Mommsen, Th. Berlin. 1905.

Codex Theodosianus cum commentariis Jacobi Gothofredi. Ed. Ritter, J. D. 6 vols. folio. Leipsic. 1736–45. Valuable chiefly for the rich commentary, indices and glossary.

Corpus juris civilis. 3 vols. Stereotype. Berlin. *See Gen. Bibl.* IV.

Corpus legum ab imperatoribus Romanis ante Justinianum latarum quae extra constitutionum codices supersunt. Ed. Haenel, G., fol. Leipsic. 1857.

Digesta Justiniani. Ed. Mommsen, Th. 2 vols. Berlin. 1870. This is a full critical edition.

Edictum Theodorici Regis. Ed. Bluhme, F. MGH. Legum Sectio I. pp. 145–184.

Fontes juris Romani. (Legal Inscriptions, Praetor's Edict, etc.) First edited by Bruns, C. G., then by Mommsen, Th. 7th edn. by Gradenwitz, O. Tübingen. 1909.

Jus Antejustinianum. Ed. Mommsen, Th., Krüger, P., and Studemund, W. 3 vols. Berlin. Vol. I. Gaius. 5th edn. 1905. Vol. II. Ulpiani Regulae, Pauli Sententiae, etc. 1st edn. 1878. Vol. III. Fragmenta Vaticana, Codices Gregorianus et Hermogenianus, etc. 1890.

Justiniani Institutiones. Ed. Schrader, E. Berlin. 1832. With full explanatory notes.

Justiniani Novellae. Ed. Zachariae von Lingenthal, K. E. 2 vols. Leipsic. 1881.
Abridgements of the Novels were made in the sixth century: the first named in Greek, the second in Latin, viz.:
Theodori Breviarium Novellarum Justiniani. Ed. Zachariae in his Anecdota. Leipsic. 1843.
Juliani Epitome Latina Novellarum Justiniani. Ed. Haenel, G. Leipsic. 1873.

Leges Novellae of Theodosius to Anthemius. Ed. Meyer, P. M., as second volume of Mommsen's Theodosianus. Berlin. 1905.

Lex Burgundionum. Ed. de Salis, L. R. MGH. Legum Sectio I. Tom. II, Pars 1. Hanover. 1892.

Lex Romana Visigothorum. Ed. Haenel, G., fol. Leipsic. 1849.

Syrische Rechtsbücher. Ed. Sachau, E. Vol. I. Berlin. 1907.

Syrisch-Römisches Rechtsbuch aus dem fünften Jahrhundert. Ed. Bruns, C. G. und Sachau, E. Leipsic. 1880.

Textes de droit Romain. Ed. Girard, P. F. 3rd edn. Paris. 1903. (Contains like matter to the above named Fontes jur. Rom. and Jus Antejustinianum, and also Justinian's Institutes.)

II. MODERN WORKS; HISTORICAL AND DOGMATIC.

Bethmann-Hollweg, M. A. von. Der römische Civil-Prozess. 3 vols. Bonn. 1864–6. (Vol. III relates to later Empire.)

Conrat (Cohn), M. Geschichte der Quellen und Literatur des römischen Rechts im früheren Mittelalter. Vol. I. Leipsic. 1891.

Cuq, E. Les Institutions Juridiques des Romains. 2 vols. Paris. 1891–1902. (Justinian and other Imperial Law is at end of vol. II.)

Girard, P. F. Manuel élémentaire de Droit romain. 5th edn. Paris. 1911.

Karlowa, O. Römische Rechtsgeschichte. 2 vols. (not finished). Leipsic. 1885–1901.

Kipp, Th. Gesch. der Quellen des römischen Rechts. 3rd edn. Leipsic. 1909.

Krüger, P. Gesch. der Quellen und Litteratur des römischen Rechts. Leipsic. 1888.

Lenel, O. Das Edictum perpetuum, ein Versuch zu seiner Wiederherstellung. 2nd edn. Leipsic. 1907.

—— Essai de reconstitution de l'Édit Perpétuel. 2 vols. Paris. 1901. Translated from the German first edn. by Peltier, F., with Lenel's assistance.

Maine, H. J. S. Ancient Law. London. 1861. 10th edn. Pollock, F. London. 1906.

Mitteis, L. Reichsrecht und Volksrecht in den Östlichen Provinzen des römischen Kaiserreichs. Leipsic. 1891.

—— Ueber drei neue Handschriften des Syrisch-Römischen Rechtsbuchs. (Aus den Abh. PAW. 1905 (2).) Berlin. 1905.

Mommsen, Th. Gesammelte juristische Schriften. 3 vols. Berlin. 1905–7. Especially vol. II.

Muirhead, J. Historical Introduction to the Private Law of Rome. Edinburgh. 1886. 2nd edn. by Goudy, H. London. 1899.

Müller, C. O. Lehrbuch der Institutionen. Leipsic. 1891.

Pauly-Wissowa. *See Gen. Bibl.* I. Especially Colonat by Seeck in vol. IV; Digesta by Jörs in vol. V.

Roby, H. J. Introduction to Justinian's Digest. Cambridge. 1884.

—— Roman Private Law in times of Cicero and the Antonines. 2 vols. Cambridge. 1902.

Savigny, V. Geschichte des römischen Rechts im Mittelalter. 7 vols. 2nd edn. Heidelberg. 1834–51. Especially vols. I, III and VII.

—— Vermischte Schriften. 5 vols. Berlin. 1850. (Vol. II contains Essays on Roman Colonat and Steuerverfassung.)

Vangerow, V. Lehrbuch des Pandektenrechts. 3 vols. 7th edn. Marburg and Leipsic. 1863–76.

Windscheid, B. Lehrbuch des Pandektenrechts. 3 vols. 7th edn. Frankfurt-a.-M. 1891. Revised by Kipp, Th. 1906.
(The last two books contain copious bibliography.)

Zachariae von Lingenthal, K. E. Gesch. des griechisch-römischen Rechts. *See Gen. Bibl.* VI.

Buckland, W. W. The Roman Law of Slavery. Cambridge. 1908.

Meyer, P. Der römische Concubinat. Leipsic. 1895.

Mommsen, Th. Römisches Strafrecht. Leipsic. 1899.

Morice. English and Roman-Dutch Law. Grahamstown and London. 1905. (Refers to many other books on subject.)

Zeitschrift der Savigny-Stiftung für Rechtsgeschichte; Romanistische Abtheilung Bd. I–XXXI. Weimar. 1880–1910.

Older periodicals and others, less exclusively devoted to Roman Law, are referred to in the treatises named above.

Monographs on every part of Roman Law, and general treatises (Pandekten, Institutiones, etc.), are innumerable, and are also there referred to.

CHAPTER IV.

GAUL UNDER THE MEROVINGIAN FRANKS. (I.)

I. BIBLIOGRAPHIES.

Dahlmann-Waitz. Quellenkunde. *See Gen. Bibl.* IV.
Masslow, O., Sommerfeldt, G. and Quidde, L. Bibliographie zur deutschen Geschichte. 1888–98, Appendix to HVJS, from 1898, Appendix to DZG.
Molinier. Sources de l'hist. de France. *See Gen. Bibl.* I.
Monod. Bibliog. de l'hist. de France. *See Gen. Bibl.* I.
Potthast. Bibliotheca historica. *See Gen. Bibl.* I.
Wattenbach. Deutschlands Geschichtsquellen. *See Gen. Bibl.* IV.

II. CONTEMPORARY DOCUMENTS AND CHRONICLES.

Capitularia regum Francorum, vol. I. Ed. Boretius. MGH.
Chron. Fredegarii. MGH. *See Gen. Bibl.* V.
Concilia aevi Merovingici. Ed. Maasen, F. MGH.
Diplomata, chartae et instrumenta aetatis Merovingicae. Ed. Bréquigny, L. G. O. de, and Pardessus, J. M. 2nd edn. 2 vols. Paris. 1843–9.
Diplomata imperii, vol. I. Ed. Pertz, G. H. MGH. 1872.
Formulae Merovingici et Karolini aevi. Ed. Zeumer, K. MGH.
Gregorius Turonensis, Opera. MGH. *See Gen. Bibl.* V.
Jonas, Vitae sanctorum Columbani, Vedastis, Johannis. Ed. Krusch, Br. Script. rer. germanicarum ad usum scholarum. Leipsic. 1905.
Les diplômes originaux des Mérovingiens, fac-similes phototypiques, avec notices et transcriptions. Lauer, Ph. and Samaran, A. Preface by Prou, M. 2 fasc. Paris. 1908.
Liber historiae Francorum. Ed. Krusch, Br. MGH. Script. rer. merov. II.
Marius Aventicensis, Chronicon. Ed. Mommsen, Th. MGH, auct. ant. XI.
Passiones vitaeque sanctorum aevi merovingici. MGH. Script. rer. merov. II, III, IV, V.
Textes relatifs aux institutions privées et publiques aux époques mérovingienne et carolingienne, publiés par Thévenin, M. Paris. 1887.
Venantius Fortunatus, Opera poetica et pedestria. Ed. Leo, H. and Krusch, Br. MGH, auct. ant. IV.

III. LATER WORKS.

(a) GENERAL.

Bayet, C., Pfister, C. and Kleinclausz, A., in Lavisse, Hist. de France. Vol. II, 1. *See Gen. Bibl.* VI.
Dahn, F. Urgeschichte. Vol. III. *See Gen. Bibl.* VI.
—— Deutsche Geschichte. Vol. I, 1. *See Gen. Bibl.* VI.
—— Könige der Germanen. Vol. VII. *See Gen. Bibl.* VI.
Gutsche, O. and Schultze, W. Deutsche Geschichte von der Urzeit bis zu den Karolingern. 2 vols. Stuttgart. 1894–6.
Havet, J. Questions mérovingiennes. Oeuvres complètes. Vol. I. Paris. 1896.
Hellmann, Sieg. Studien zur mittelalterlichen Geschichtschreibung. I. Gregor von Tours. HZ. Bd. 107, pp. 1–43.

Krusch, Br.   Zur Chronologie der Merowingischen Könige.   FDG.   Vol. xxii (1882).
Kurth, G.   Histoire poétique des Mérovingiens.   Paris.   1893.
Marignan, A.   Études sur la civilisation française.   Vol. i.   La société mérovingienne. Vol. ii.   Le culte des saints sous les Mérovingiens.   Paris.   1899.
Lecoy de la Marche, A.   La fondation de la France du 4ᵉ au 6ᵉ siècle.   Lille.   1893.
Loebell, J. W.   Gregor von Tours und seine Zeit.   2nd edn.   Leipsic.   1869.
Longnon, A.   Géographie de la Gaule au viᵉ siècle.   Paris.   1878.
——   Atlas historique de la France.   *See Gen. Bibl.* ii.
Prou, M.   La Gaule mérovingienne.   Paris.   1897.
Richter, G.   Annalen des fränkischen Reichs im Zeitalter der Merovinger.   Halle. 1873.
Thierry, Aug.   Récits des temps mérovingiens.   6th edn.   2 vols.   Paris.   1856.

(b) SPECIAL WORKS.

Albers, J. H.   König Dagobert in Geschichte, Legende und Sage.   2nd edn. Worms.   1884.
Arbois de Jubainville, H. d'.   Le lieu de baptême de Clovis.   Bulletin de la Soc. des antiq. de France.   1906.
Bonnel, H. E.   Die Anfänge des Karolingischen Hauses.   Berlin.   1866.
Breysig, T.   Jahrbücher des fränkischen Reichs, 714–741.   Leipsic.   1869.
Brosien, H.   Kritische Untersuchungen der Quellen zur Geschichte Dagoberts I. Göttingen.   1868.
Digot, A.   Histoire du royaume d'Austrasie.   4 vols.   Nancy.   1863.
Fauriel, M.   Histoire de la Gaule méridionale sous la domination des conquérants germains.   4 vols.   Paris.   1836.
Gasquet.   L'empire byzantin.   *See Gen. Bibl.* vi.
Gérard, P. A. F.   Histoire des Francs d'Austrasie.   2 vols.   Brussels.   1864.
Hahn, H.   Jahrbücher des fränkischen Reichs, 741–752.   Berlin.   1863.
Hellmann, S.   Studien zur mittelalterlichen Geschichtschreibung: Gregor von Tours.   HZ.   cvii.   1911.
Huguenin, A.   Histoire du royaume mérovingien d'Austrasie.   Paris.   1862.
Junghans, W.   Kritische Untersuchungen zur Geschichte der fränkischen Könige Childerich und Clodovech.   Göttingen.   1857.   French translation by Monod, G.   Paris.   1878.
Krusch, Br.   Chlodovechs Sieg über die Alamannen.   NAGDG.   Vol. xii (1887).
Kurth, G.   Clovis.   2nd edn.   2 vols.   Tours.   1891.
——   Sainte Clotilde.   Paris.   1897.
——   La reine Brunehaut.   RQH.   l (1891).
Lièvre, A. F.   Le lieu de la rencontre des Francs et des Wisigoths sur les bords du Clain en 507.   RH.   lxvi (1898).   (Important.)
Malnory, E.   Saint Césaire d'Arles, évêque d'Arles, 503–543.   Paris.   1894.
Mercier, E.   La bataille de Poitiers (732) et les vraies causes du recul des Arabes. RH.   vii (1878).
Perroud, Cl.   Les origines du premier duché d'Aquitaine.   Paris.   1883.
Pertz, G. H.   Geschichte der Merowingischen Hausmeier.   Hanover.   1819.
Rabanis, J. F.   Les Mérovingiens d'Aquitaine.   Essai historique et critique sur la charte d'Alaon.   Paris.   1856.
Roussel, E.   Le roi Chilpéric.   Annales de l'Est.   xi (1897).
Schubert, H. von.   Die Unterwerfung der Alamannen unter die Franken.   Strassburg.   1884.
Vacandard, E.   Vie de saint Ouen, évêque de Rouen.   Paris.   1902.
Vogel, F.   Chlodwigs Sieg über die Alamannen.   HZ.   lvi (1886).

CHAPTER V.

GAUL UNDER THE MEROVINGIAN FRANKS. (II.)

I. GENERAL.

Besse, J. B. Les moines de l'ancienne France. Période gallo-romaine et méro-
vingienne. Paris. 1906.
Bethmann-Hollweg, M. A. von. Der germanisch-romanische Civilprozess im
Mittelalter. 6 vols. Bonn. 1868–74.
Brunner. Rechtsgeschichte. *See Gen. Bibl.* VI.
—— Forschungen zur Gesch. des deutschen und französischen Rechtes. Stuttgart.
1894.
Duchesne. Fastes épiscopaux. *See Gen. Bibl.* IV.
Esmein, A. Cours d'histoire de droit français. 4th edn. Paris. 1901.
Fahlbeck, P. E. A. La royauté et le droit royal franc. Lund. 1883. French
translation. Bordeaux, 1886.
Fustel de Coulanges, N. D. Histoire des institutions politiques de l'ancienne
France: I. La Gaule romaine; II. L'invasion germanique et la fin de l'empire;
III. La monarchie franque; IV. L'alleu et le domaine rural pendant l'époque
mérovingienne; V. Les origines du système féodal; le bénéfice et le patronat
pendant l'époque mérovingienne; VI. Les transformations de la royauté
pendant l'époque carolingienne. 6 vols. Paris. 1888–92.
—— Recherches sur quelques problèmes d'histoire. Paris. 1885.
—— Nouvelles recherches sur quelques problèmes d'histoire. Paris. 1891.
Glasson, E. Histoire du droit et des institutions de la France. Vols. II and III.
Paris. 1888–9.
Hauck, A. Kirchengeschichte Deutschlands, I. 4th edn. Leipsic. 1904.
Lehuërou, J. M. Histoire des institutions mérovingiennes et du gouvernement des
Mérovingiens jusqu'à l'édit de 615 (*sic*). Paris. 1842.
Löning, E. Geschichte des deutschen Kirchenrechts. Vol. II. Strassburg. 1878.
Montalembert, le comte de. Les moines d'Occident depuis saint Benoît jusqu'à
saint Bernard. 7 vols. Paris. 1860–77.
Pétigny, J. de. Études sur l'histoire, les lois et les institutions de l'époque méro-
vingienne. 2 vols. Paris. 1842–5.
Sickel, W. Die Entstehung der fränkischen Monarchie. Westdeutsche Z. IV
(1885).
Sohm, R. Die fränkische Reichs- und Gerichtsverfassung. Weimar. 1871.
Sybel, H. von. Die Entstehung des deutschen Königthums. 3rd edn. Frankfort
a. M. 1884.
Tardif, J. Études sur les institutions politiques et administratives de la France.
Époque mérovingienne. Paris. 1881.
Vacandard, E. Études de critique et d'histoire religieuse. Paris. 1905.
Viollet, P. Histoire des institutions politiques et administratives de la France.
Vol. I. Paris. 1890.
Waitz, G. Verfassungsgeschichte. Vol. II (2 pts). *See Gen. Bibl.* VI.

II. SPECIAL WORKS.

Barchevitz, V. Das Königsgericht zur Zeit der Merowinger und der Karolinger. Leipsic. 1882.

Beauchet, L. Histoire de l'organisation judiciaire en France. Époque franque. Paris. 1885.

Beaudouin, E. Études sur les origines du régime féodal : la recommandation et la justice seigneuriale. In Annales de l'enseignement supérieur de Grenoble, 1889.

Bernouilli, C. A. Die Heiligen der Merowinger. Tübingen. 1900.

Bonnell, H. De dignitate majoris domus regum Francorum a Romano sacri cubiculi praeposito ducenda. Berlin. 1858.

Bonnet, M. Le latin de Grégoire de Tours. Paris. 1890.

Bréhier, L. Les colonies d'Orientaux en Occident au commencement du moyen-âge. BZ. Vol. xii (1903).

Clemen, P. Merowingische und Karolingische Plastik. Bonner Jahrb. 1892.

Declareuil, O. Les épreuves judiciaires dans le droit franc du ve au viiie siècle. Paris. 1899.

Deloche, M. La trustis et l'antrustionat royal sous les deux premières races. Paris. 1873.

Dippe, O. Gefolgschaft und Huldigung im Reiche der Merowinger. Kiel. 1889.

Engel et Serrure. Traité de numismatique. Vol. i. *See Gen. Bibl.* iii.

Fehr, J. Staat und Kirche im fränkischen Reiche bis auf Karl dem Grossen. Vienna. 1869.

Fournier, M. Essai sur les formes et les effets de l'affranchissement dans le droit gallo-franc. Paris. 1885.

—— Les affranchissements du ve au xiiie siècle, influence de l'église, de la royauté et des particuliers sur la condition des affranchis. RH. Vol. xxii (1883).

Fustel de Coulanges, N. D. De l'analyse des textes historiques. RQH. Vol. xli (1887).

Galy, C. La famille à l'époque mérovingienne. Paris. 1901.

Guilhermoz, P. Essai sur l'origine de la noblesse en France au moyen-âge. Paris. 1902.

Herrmann, E. Das Hausmeieramt, ein echt germanisches Amt. Breslau. 1880.

Hubrich, E. Fränkisches Wahl- und Erbkönigtum zur Merovingerzeit. Königsberg. 1889.

Imbart de la Tour, P. Des immunités commerciales accordées aux églises du viie au ixe siècle. In Études d'histoire du moyen-âge dédiées à Gabriel Monod. Paris. 1896.

—— Les paroisses rurales du ive au ixe siècle. Paris. 1900.

Kurth, G. De la nationalité des comtes francs. In Mélanges Paul Fabre. Paris. 1903.

—— Les ducs et les comtes d'Auvergne au vi^e siècle. Bulletin de l'Acad. roy. de Belgique. Brussels. 1899.

—— Les ducs et les comtes de Touraine au vi^e siècle. *Ibidem.* 1906.

Lesne, E. La propriété ecclésiastique en France aux époques romaine et mérovingienne. Paris. 1910.

Martin, E. Saint Colomban. Paris. 1905.

Monod, G. Études critiques sur les sources de l'époque mérovingienne. Paris. 1872.

—— Les aventures de Sichaire. RH. Vol. xxxi (1886).

Nissl, A. Der Gerichtsstand des Klerus im fränkischen Reiche. Innsbruck. 1886.

Pfister, Ch.   Le duché mérovingien d'Alsace et la légende de sainte Odile.   Paris et Nancy.   1892.

Plath, K.   Die Königspfalzen der Merowinger und Karolinger.   Leipsic.   1892.

Prost, A.   L'immunité.   Études sur l'histoire et le développement de cette institution.   Paris.   1882.

—— La justice privée et l'immunité.   Mém. de la Soc. des antiq.   1886.

Prou, M.   Les monnaies mérovingiennes.   Catalogue des monnaies françaises de la bibliothèque nationale.   Paris.   1892.

—— Examen de quelques passages de Grégoire de Tours relatifs à l'application de la peine de mort.   In Études d'hist. du moyen-âge déd. à G. Monod.   Paris.   1896.

Roloff, G.   Die Umwandlung des fränkischen Heeres von Chlodwig bis Karl den Grossen.   Neue Jahrb. für das klassische Altertum.   Vol. ix (1902).

Roth, P.   Geschichte des Beneficialwesens von den ältesten Zeiten bis ins zehnte Jahrhundert.   Erlangen.   1850.

—— Feudalität und Untertanenverband.   Weimar.   1863.

Schöne, G.   Die Amtsgewalt der fränkischen Majores domus.   Brunswick.   1855.

Sickel, Th.   Beiträge zur Diplomatik.   Vols. i–viii.   SKAW.   1861–82.

Sickel, W.   Die Merowingische Volksversammlung.   MIOGF.   Ergänzungsband, vol. ii (1888).

—— Zur Organisation der Grafschaft im fränkischen Reiche.   *Ibidem.*   Ergänzungsband, vol. iii (1894).

—— Das Wesen des Volksherzogthums.   HZ.   Vol. lii (1884).

—— Die Entstehung der fränkischen Monarchie.   Westdeutsche Z.   iv (1883).

—— Die Privatherrschaften im fränkischen Reiche.   *Ib.*   Vols. xv (1886), xvi (1897).

Vacandard, E.   La scola du palais mérovingien.   RQH.   lxvi (1897).

Weyl, R.   Das fränkische Staatskirchenrecht zur Zeit der Merowinger.   Breslau. 1888.

Wiart, R.   Essai sur la precaria.   Paris.   1894.

Zeumer, K.   Ueber die Beerbung der Freigelassenen durch den Fiskus nach Fränkischem Recht.   FDG.   xxiii (1883).

CHAPTER VI.

SPAIN UNDER THE VISIGOTHS.

I. ORIGINAL DOCUMENTS.

(a) Legal.

Lex Romana Visigothorum. Ed. Haenel, G. Leipsic. 1848. See also Legis romanae Visigothorum fragmenta. Ed. RAH. 1896.

Leges Visigothorum antiquiores. Ed. Zeumer, K. Hanover and Leipsic. 1894. (Contents: Legum codicis Euriciani fragmenta [MS. of St Germain-des-Prés]; Lex visigothorum Reccesvindiana; Chronica Regum visigothorum, added to the MSS. of the Lex visigothorum; Capitula iuris visigothici, from the Holkham MS.; Leges extravagantes.)

Leges Visigothorum. Ed. Zeumer, K. Hanover and Leipsic. 1902. Ex MGH. (Contents: Legum codicis Euriciani fragmenta [MS. of St Germain]; Legum Baiuvariorum, derived from the code of Euric; Liber iudiciorum, of the time of Ervigius; Chronica regum visigothorum; additional laws from MSS. of the years after the fall of the Visigothic kingdom; fragments of the Lex romana visigothorum; Capitula iuris; Acts of councils of Toledo and Tomi et edicta regum selecta.)

Visigothic laws in the MS. of Vallicelliana Library. Ed. in Conrat, Quellen und Literatur des Römischen Rechts. See below, p. 737. And in NRDF. XIII. 1889.

Formulae visigothicae. Ed. Zeumer, K. Hanover and Leipsic. 1886. (Formulae merovingi et Karolini aevi.) Two other new formulae in Gaudenzi, A., Nuove formule di giudizii di Dio. Atti e Memorie della R. Dep. di stor. patria per le prov. di Romagna. 3rd series, vol. III. Bologna. 1885.

(b) Canons.

Collectio canonum Ecclesiae Hispanae. Madrid. 1808. Also: Aguirre, Collectio Maxima Conciliorum Hispaniae. Rome. 1693.

(c) Epigraphics.

Inscriptiones Hispaniae Christianae. Ed. E. Hübner. Berlin. 1872. (The inscriptions discovered after 1872 have been published by F. Fita and other epigraphists in BRAH.)

Le Blant. Inscriptions chrétiennes de la Gaule. See Gen. Bibl. IV.

(d) Numismatics.

Ferreira, Luis Jose. Catalogo da collecção de moedas visigodas. Porto. 1890.

Heiss, A. Description générale des monnaies des rois visigoths d'Espagne. Paris. 1872.

II. CONTEMPORARY AUTHORITIES.

1. Latins. Spanish and French.

Anonimus of Cordoba or Toledo, named erroneously, the Pacense (Isidorus Pacensis). Chronicon. The best edn. that of Tailhan, Anonyme de Cordoue. Paris. 1885. (Is the only contemporary authority for the fall of Visigothic kingdom and of the first years of the Arab conquest.) (611–754.)

Anonimus, continuator of the above. Chronicon. Ed. España sagrada: theatro geograph. hist. de la Iglesia de España. 52 vols. Ed. Florenz, E. and others. Vols. XLVII sqq. Ed. for RAH. Madrid. 1754–1879. (Esp. sagrada.) VI. 3rd edn., pp. 430–41.

Anonimus. Libellus de vitis et miraculis Patrum Emeritensium. (Attributed by Florez to a cleric of Mérida, Paulo.) Ed. Smedt, C. de. Brussels. 1884.

Braulius, Bishop of Saragossa. Liber de Vita B. Aemiliani. Ed. Sandoval, Fundaciones de San Benito. Madrid. 1601. (For the letters of Braulius, see Isidore of Seville.)

Bulgaranus, comes. Epistolae. Ed. Heine. Bibl. anecdotorum. Leipsic. 1848.

Idatii episcopi Chronicon. Ed. Garzon, J. M. and Ram, F. X. de. Brussels. 1845. Another edn. in Esp. sagrada, IV, pp. 345–85, with the addition of a little Idatii Gallaeciae episcopi Chronicon, pp. 420–7. (Special for the first times of the German invasion and the Suevic kingdom.) Also ed. Mommsen, Th., Chron. min. MGH. Spanish translation by M. Macias, in Bol. de la Comis. Mon. Orense.

Isidore of Seville. (St Isidore.) Historia de Regibus Gothorum, Uvandalorum et Suevorum (256–621). Ed. Esp. sagrada. VI, pp. 474–506. A more correct text in St Isidore Opera. Vol. VII. Rome. 1803. (One of the most valuable sources in the part relating to the Goths. The author has used the lost Chronicle of Maximus of Saragossa.)

    Chronicon. Ed. Esp. sagrada, VI, pp. 445–68 and Opera VII.

    De viris illustribus. Ed. Opera. VII.

    Epistolae St Isidori episcopi hispalensis et Braulionis Caesaraugustanis mutuo directae. Ed. Esp. sagrada. XXXI, pp. 318–95. (The letters of Braulius are very interesting for the history, both of institutions and of political events.)

Joannis Biclarensis. Chronicon (567–90). Ed. Esp. sagrada. VI, pp. 375–89. The continuator of J. of Biclara in pp. 422–32. Another edn. in Chronica minora.

Jordanis. De Getarum sive Gothorum origine et rebus gestis. (Getica.) Ed. Mommsen, MGH, auct. ant. v. English translation by Mierow, C. Princeton. 1908. (The value of the work of Jordanis is that it is an extract from the lost History of the Goths, written by Cassiodorus.)

Julianus, Bishop of Toledo. Liber de Historia Galliae, quae temporibus Divae memoriae Principis Uvambae. (Historia Excellentissimi Uvambae Regis.) Esp. sagrada. VI, pp. 534–63.

Martinus Bracarensis. De correctione rusticorum (572–4). Ed. Caspari, C. P. Christiania. 1883. (Interesting for the study of the popular beliefs and superstitions in Gallicia.)

Montani, S. Eugenii III et S. Ildephonsi Opera. Ed. Lorenzana, SS. PP. Toletanorum Opera, I. For the poems of Eugenius, see also MGH (with the poems of Merobaudes, Dracontius and Eugenius).

Paulus Orosius. Historiarum libri VII, adversus Paganos. Ed. Zangemeister, C. Vienna. 1882. (Fourth century and the beginning of the fifth.)

Sisebutus. Epistolae, and Vita vel Passio Sancti Desiderii. Ed. Esp. sagrada.
VII, pp. 309–28 and 328–38.
Tajo, Bishop of Saragossa. Epistola...ad Eugenium episcopum Toletanum.
Ed. Balucio, Miscellaneorum, IV and Esp. sagrada, XXXI, pp. 166–70.

Chronicon Imperialis. (379–455.) MPL. LI.
Fredegarius. Chronicon. (584–652.) *See Gen. Bibl.* v. Hanover. 1889. (This
Chronicle, attributed by Scaliger to an author named Fredegarius, is really
anonymous. Till the year 593 is a complement of the Historia of Gregory
of Tours. Since 593 is the only source for the history of Gaul from the end of
the 6th century to the middle of the 7th.)
Gregorius Turonensis. Historia Francorum. (6th century.) *See Gen. Bibl.* v.
(Two translations in French; one in German.)
Marius Aventicensis. Chronicon. Ed. Arndt. MGH. Chron. min. II. Leipsic.
1875–8.
Prosperus Aquitanus. Chronicon. MPL. LI.
Severus Sulpicius. Chronica. MPL. xx. An Epitoma Chronicorum Severi cogno-
mento Sulpicii, in Esp. sagrada, IV, pp. 431–54.
Sidonius Apollinaris. Epistolarum libri VII and Carmina. Ed. Luetjohann, MGH,
auct. ant. VIII. 1887.

2. ARABS.

Akhbār Majmū'a. (Collection of traditions: 11th century.) Ed. Lafuente
Alcántara, Colec. de obras arábigas. Madrid. 1867.
Anonymous. Fath al-Andalus. (End of the 11th century?) Ed. González, T.
de. Algiers. 1889.
Historical narration added to the Travel of a Moorish ambassador of the 17th
century. Ed. Colec. de obras arábigas, II. Madrid. See Sauvaire, H.
Voyage d'un ambassadeur marocain (1690–1). Paris. 1884.
Ibn 'Abd al-Ḥakam. History of the Conquest of Spain. Göttingen. 1858.
Ibn al-'Idhārī. Al-Bayān al-Mughrib. Ed. Dozy. Leyden. 1848–51. 2 vols.
Partial transl. in Spanish by Fernández y Gonzalez, Historias de Al-Andalus.
Granada. 1860. French transl. with notes by Fagnan, E. 2 vols. Algiers,
1901, 1904.
Ibn al-Ḳūṭīya. Chronicle. Ed. Colec. de obras arábigas, II. (This volume is
unfinished; the translation of Arab text is not printed. Fragments from Ibn
Ḳutaiba may also be read in it.)
Ibn Khaldūn. Histoire des Berbères. Transl. Baron de Slane. Algiers. 1855.
4 vols.
Makḳarī. Translation of P. de Gayangos. The history of the Mohammedan
dynasties in Spain, by Aḥmad ibn Muḥammad al-Makḳarī. London. 1840–3.
(Contents: Ibn Ḳutaiba and other Arab historians.) Another ed. of the
Arab text, Dozy. Leyden. 1855–61.
Rabī' ibn Zaid. (Bishop Recemundus.) Calendar. Ed. Libri, Hist. des sciences
mathématiques en Italie, I. Dozy. Le Calendrier de Cordoue de l'année 961.
Leyden. 1873.
Rasis. Chronicle of the Moor Rasis. (Till 976.) Not the original chronicle, but
a version related by an Arab to a Portuguese cleric. *See* Gayangos. Memoria
sobre la autenticidad de la Crónica llamada del Moro Rasis, in Mem. RAH.
1850. (The most ancient Arabic chronicle relating to Spain.)
Ṭabari. Annales. (10th century.) Transl. Barth, T. Leyden. 1879–89. *See
Gen. Bibl.* v.
Other Arabic chronicles will be found in
Codera, F. Bibliotheca arabico-hispana. Madrid. 1891 ff.

3. GREEKS.

There are some Byzantine historians who can be used as original authorities for Visigothic Spain, as Olympiodorus, Zosimus, Procopius of Cesarea and Priscus of Panion. *See Bibl. c. II.*

III. MODERN WORKS.

1. GENERAL.

Dahn, F. Könige der Germanen. *See Gen. Bibl.* VI.
—— Die äussere Geschichte der Westgothen. Würzburg. 1870.
—— Westgothische Studien. Würzburg. 1874.
—— Bausteine. Berlin. 1879–80.
—— Die Verfassung der Westgothen. 2nd edn. Leipsic. 1885.
—— Urgeschichte. Spanish trans. Barcelona. 1889. *See Gen. Bibl.* VI.
Fernández Guerra, A., Hinojosa, E. de, and la Rada, J. de D. de. Historia de
    España desde la invasión de los pueblos germánicos hasta la ruina de la
    monarquia visigoda. 2 vols. Madrid. 1890. (In Hist. general de España.)
    See Gen. Bibl. VI.
Menéndez y Pelayo, M. Historia de los heterodoxos españoles, I. Madrid. 1879.
Perez Pujol, E. Historia de las instituciones sociales de la España goda. 4 vols.
    Valencia. 1896.

2. ON AUTHORITIES.

Antolin, G. Estudios sobre códices visigodos. BRAH. 1909.
Blázquez, A. La Hitacion de Wamba. Madrid. 1907.
Cipolla, C. Considerazioni sulle Getica di Jordanis e sulle loro relazioni colla
    Historia Getarum di Cassiodoro Senatore. Turin. 1892.
Dahn, F. Prokopius von Caesarea. Ein Beitrag zur Geschichte der Völkerwan-
    derung. Berlin. 1865.
Die Chroniken des Isidorus von Sevilla. FDG. xv. 1885.
Esmein, A. Sur quelques lettres de Sidoine Apollinaire. Rev. gén. du Droit. 1885
Fernández Guerra, A. Libro de Idacio con que se hilvanó la supuesta División de
    Wamba. Madrid. 1878.
Hertzberg, G. F. Die Historien und die Chroniken des Isidorus von Sevilla.
    Göttingen. 1874.
Holder-Egger, O. Ueber die Weltchronik des sogenannten Severus Sulpicius und
    südgallische Annales des 5 Jahrhunderts. Göttingen. 1875.
Jacob, G. Erweiterte Ueberricht über die arabischen und anderen morgenländischen
    Quellen zur deutschen Geschichte bis zum Ausbruch der Kreuzzuge. Berlin.
    1870.
Kaufmann, G. Die Werke des C. Sollius Apollinaris Sidonius als eine Quelle für
    die Geschichte seiner Zeit. Göttingen. 1864.
Krusch, B. Die Chroniken des sogenannten Fredegar. NAGDG. VII, pp. 247–315
    and 431–516.
Kurth, G. Les sources de l'histoire de Clovis dans Grégoire de Tours. Actes du
    Congrès scient. intern. des catholiques. Paris. 1889.
Monod, G. Études critiques sur les sources de l'histoire mérovingienne. Paris.
    1872.
    Preface to the transl. of the work of Junghans.

Saavedra, E. de. La Historia de la ciudad de Alatia. Rev. Hisp.-amer., v. (Relating to the Arabic authorities for the conquest of Spain.) Also, on the subject, the first ch. of the Estudio sobre la invasión de los árabes en España of the same author.

Tailhan, P. La Chronique rimée des derniers rois visigoths de Tolède. Paris. 1884.

See also Prefs. to the editions of primary authorities.

Tardif, J. Extraits et abrégés juridiques des Etymologies d'Isidore de Séville. Paris. 1896.

3. On Documents.

Bluhme. Zur Textcritik des Westgothenrechts. Halle. 1870.

Brunner. Deutsche Rechtsgeschichte, vol. I. *See Gen. Bibl.* VI.

Cárdenas, F. de. Una ley de Teudis desconocida. BRAH. June. 1889.

—— Noticia de una compilación de leyes romanas y visigodas recientamente descubiertas en Inglaterra. Madrid. 1889.

Conrat (Cohn), M. Gesch. der Quellen und Literatur des römischen Rechts im früheren Mittelalter. Leipsic. 1889.

—— Breviarium Alaricianum römisches Recht im fränkischen Reich in systematischer Darstellung. Leipsic. 1903.

Ficker, J. Ueber nähere Verwandschaft zwischen spanisch-gothischen und norwegischisländisches Recht. Innsbruck. 1887.

See on this subject, Maurer, Zur nordgermanischen Rechtsgeschichte. Kritische Viert. für Gesetzgebung und Rechtswissenschaft, XXXI. 1889.

Fita, F. El papa Honorio I y San Braulio de Zaragoza. La ciudad de Dios IV. 1870. (On the *placitum* of the Jews addressed to Chintila.)

Fitting. Ueber einige Rechtsquellen der vorjustinianische spätern Kaiserzeit. ZR. XI. 1873.

Garcia y Garcia, J. Historia de la ley primitiva de los visigodos y descubrimiento de algunos de sus capitulos. Madrid. 1865.

Gaudenzi. Un' antica compilazione di diritto romano e visigoto. Bologna. 1886.

—— Tre nuovi frammenti dell' Editto di Eurico. Riv. ital. per le scienze giuridiche, VI. 1888.

Hinojosa, E. de. Historia general del Derecho español, I. Madrid. 1887.

Lécrivain, C. Remarques sur l'Interpretatio de la Lex Romana Visigothorum. Toulouse. 1889. (From AM. I.)

Stobbe, O. Gesch. der deutschen Rechtsquellen. Brunswick. 1860.

Stouff, L. L'Interpretatio de la loi romaine des Wisigoths dans les formules et les chartes du VIᵉ au XIᵉ siècles. Mélanges Fitting, II. Montpellier. 1908.

Tardif, J. Les leges Wisigothorum. NRDF. XV. 1891.

Ureña, E. de. La legislación gótico hispana. (Leges antiquiores. Liber iudiciorum.) 2nd edn. Madrid. 1906.

Zeumer, K. Geschichte der westgothischen Gesetzgebung. NAGDG. XXIII (1897) und XXVI (1900).

4. Monographs, Biographies and Special Treatises.

Amardel. Les derniers chefs Goths de la Septimanie. Narbonne. 1901.

Bourret, C. L'École chrétienne de Seville sous la monarchie des visigoths. Paris. 1885.

Cañal, C. San Isidoro. Seville. 1897.

Cirot, G. Un nouveau roi visigothique. BHisp. Jan.–Feb. 1899.

Codera, F. El llamado conde D. Julian. Estud. criticos de hist. arábe esp. Saragossa. 1903.

Coello, F.   Vias, poblaciones y ruinas de la provincia de Alava.   Madrid.   1875.

Dozy, R. P. A.   Recherches sur l'histoire et la littérature de l'Espagne pendant le Moyen Age.   3rd edn.   Leyden.   1881.

Fahlbeck, P. E.   La royauté et le droit royal français.   Lund.   1883.

Fernandez Guerra, A.   Caida y ruina del imperio visigótico español.   Madrid. 1883.

——   Deitania y su cátedra episcopal de Begastri.   Madrid.   1879.

——   Las diez ciudades bracarenses nombradas en la inscripcion de Chaves.   Rev. archeologica, II.   Lisbon.   1888.

Fernández y González, F.   Los reyes Acosta y Elier (Agila II) de la Crónica del Moro Rasis.   La España moderna, Nov. 1889.

Fernández y López, M.   El tesoro visigótico de la Capilla.   Seville.   1895.

Fustel de Coulanges.   Histoire des institutions, vol. II.   *See Gen. Bibl.* VI.

Gaudenzi.   Sui rapporti tra l'Italia e l'Impero d'Oriente fra gli anni 476 e 554. Bologna.   1886.

Gómez Moreno, M.   Excursión á través del arco de herradura.   Cultura Española. 1906.

Görres, F.   Katholikenverfolgungen im westgothischen Reiche.   Realencyklop. der christl. Alterthum.   Ed. Kraus, I.   Freiburg.   1882.

Graetz.   Die Westgothische Gesetzgebung in Betreff der Juden.   Breslau.   1857.

Havet, J.   Des partages des terres entre les Romains et les Barbares chez les Burgondes et les Visigoths.   RH. VI.   1878.

Hinojosa, E. de.   Influencia que tuvieron en el Derecho público de su patria y principalmente en el derecho penal, los filósofos y teólogos españoles.   Madrid. 1890.

Lamperez, V.   Historia de la arquitectura cristiana española en la Edad Media.   I. Madrid.   1908.

Lievre, A. F.   Le lieu de rencontre des Francs et des Wisigoths sur le bord du Clain en 507.   RH. LXVI, p. 90.

Mayans y Siscar, G.   Defensa del rey Witiza.   Valencia.   1772.

Menendez Pidal, R.   La penitencia del rey D. Rodrigo.   Origen probable de la legenda.   RCHL.   Jan. 1897.

Pflugk-Harttung, J. v.   Zur Geschichte des Westgothenkönigs Leovigild.   FDG. XXVI.   1886.

Saavedra, E. de.   Estudio sobre la invasión de los árabes en España.   Madrid.   1892.

CHAPTER VII.

ITALY UNDER THE LOMBARDS.

1. DOCUMENTS AND AUTHORITIES.

Leges Langobardorum, ed. Bluhme, MGH, Leges iv—and "correctiores recudi curavit" Bluhme: "Edictus ceteraeque Langobardorum leges cum constitutionibus et pactis principum Beneventanorum" in Fontes iuris Germanici antiqui in usum scholarum ex MGH separatim editi. Hanover. 1869. Ed. Padelletti in Fontes iuris Italici medii aevi. i. Turin. 1877.

Charters and diplomas collected : Troya, Carlo, Codice diplomatico Langobardo dal 568 al 774, 6 vols. Naples. 1852-5. Also local collections of charters.

Authorities collected in MGH. Scriptores rerum Langobardicarum et Italicarum, saec. vi-ix, 1878, especially :

Anonymus, Origo gentis Langobardorum ;
Paulus diaconus, historia Langobardorum, and Continuationes of his work ;
Catalogi regum et ducum Langobardorum.

Cf. the writers cited in the bibl. to cc. viii a, ix, xiii and Gregorius Turonensis and Fredegarius with continuations cited to cc. iv, v, xviii.

Treatise about the language : Bruckner, W., Die Sprache der Langobarden (Quellen und Forschungen zur Deutschen Sprach- u. Culturgeschichte. lxxv. 1895).

2. MODERN WORKS.

(a) GENERAL.

Dahn. Urgeschichte, vol. iv (1889), chap. vii. *See Gen. Bibl.* **vi.**
—— Könige der Germanen, vol. xii: Die Langobarden (1909).
Hartmann, L. M. Geschichte Italiens, *see Gen. Bibl.* vi, vol. ii, 1 (Römer und Langobarden bis zur Theilung Italiens. 1900) and ii, 2 (Die Loslösung Italiens vom Oriente. 1903).
Hodgkin. Italy and her invaders, vol. v (The Lombard invasion) and vi (The Lombard kingdom. 1895). *See Gen. Bibl.* vi.
Leo, H. Geschichte der italienischen Staaten (Heeren). Vol. i. 1829.
Muratori. Vols. iii and iv. *See Gen. Bibl.*
Romano, G. Le dominazioni barbariche in Italia, 395-1024. Libro iii. Milan. 1910. *See Gen. Bibl.* vi.

(b) On Authorities.

Origo and Paulus:

Abel, Otto. P. d. und die übrigen Geschichtschreiber der Langobarden übersetzt. 2nd edn. Leipsic. 1888. (Geschichtschreiber der Deutschen Vorzeit II, 15.)

Bethmann. In Archiv f. ält. deutsche Gesch. x, 335. Mommsen, NAGDG. v, 57.

Dahn, F. Paulus diaconus, I: Des P. d. Leben u. Schriften. Leipsic. 1876.

Jacobi, R. Die Quellen der Langobardengeschichte des P. d. Halle. 1877.

Waitz. NAGDG. v, 421—Schmidt, L., ib. XIII, 391.

Diplomas:

Bresslau, H. Urkundenlehre I, 260.

Chroust, A. Untersuchungen über die Langobardischen Königs- und Herzogsurkunden. Graz. 1888.

Hartmann, L. M. MIOGF. Ergänzungsband VI, 17 and NAGDG. XXV, 615.

(c) Special Treatises.

To §§ 1, 2:

Bluhme. Die gens Langobardorum und ihre Herkunft. Bonn. 1868.

Schmidt, L. Aelteste Geschichte der Langobarden. Leipsic. 1884.

—— Allgemeine Geschichte der germanischen Völker bis zur Mitte des 6. Jahrhunderts (Below's Handbuch, Abth. II, 1909) II, vol. 4. *See Gen. Bibl.* VI.

Wiese. Die aelteste Geschichte der Langobarden. Jena. 1877.

To § 3:

Crivelucci, A. SS. I, 59 and II, 396.

To §§ 4–6:

Pabst. Geschichte des langobardischen Herzogthums in FDG. II. 1862. 405. Cf. below notes to §§ 15–17.

To § 5:

Hirsch, F. Das Herzogthum Benevent. Leipsic. 1871.

Jenny. Geschichte des langobardischen Herzogthums Spoleto. Basel. 1890.

To §§ 6, 7:

Tamassia, N. Langobardi, Franchi e chiesa Romana fino ai tempi di re Liutprando. Bologna. 1888.

To § 12:

Brunner. Deutsche Rechtsgeschichte. *See Gen. Bibl.* VI. I, § 53.

Merkel, J. Geschichte des Langobardenrechts. Berlin. 1850.

Pertile, A. Storia del diritto Italiano. Turin. 1896. I, § 13.

Salvioli, Gius. Manuale di storia del diritto Italiano. 1899. § 35.

To § 13:

Bury. Later Roman Empire. II, bk v, c. VIII. *See Gen. Bibl.*

To § 14:

Meyer, W. Die Spaltung des Patriarchats Aquileia (Abh. d. kön. Gesellschaft d. Wissenschaften zu Göttingen. Phil.-hist. Kl. N. F. II, 6, 1898).

To § 15:

Salvioli, Gius. Contributi alla storia economica d' Italia I: sullo stato e la popolazione d' Italia. (Atti e Memorie dell' Accad. di Palermo.) 1900.

Cipolla, C. Della supposta fusione degli Italiani coi Germani. (Reale Accademia dei Lincei. Rendiconti. Vol. IX, 6–10. Rome. 1901.)

To §§ 16, 17 :

    Hegel, C. Gesch. der Städteverfassung von Italien. I. Leipsic. 1847. c. 3.

    Schupfer, F. Degli ordini sociali e del possesso fondiario appo i Langobardi. SKAW. xxxv, 269, 391. 1860.

    —— Delle istituzioni politiche Langobardiche. Florence. 1863.

    Halban, A. v. Römisches Recht in den germanischen Volksstaaten. 3 vols. Breslau. 1899–1907. Vol. II. Das Reich der Langobarden.

    Cf. Salvioli, Gius., *supra* §§ 116–118 ; Pertile, *supra* §§ 4–9.

To §§ 19–21 :

    Martens, Politische Gesch. des Langobardenreiches unter K. Liutprand. Heidelberg. 1880.

    Monticolo. Le spedizioni di Liutprando nell' Esarcato. ASRSP. xv, 321, 1892.

To §§ 22–26 :

    Cf. the treatises cited below to c. XVIII.

CHAPTER VIII (A).

IMPERIAL ITALY AND AFRICA (ADMINISTRATION).

1. SPECIAL BIBLIOGRAPHIES.

See Diehl, L'Afrique byzantine, and Id. Études sur l'Administration byzantine dans l'Exarchat de Ravenne. *See Gen. Bibl.* vi.

2. AUTHORITIES.

See bibliography to cc. i, ii, vii, ix, xiii, xviii.

3. MODERN WORKS.

Calisse, C.   Il governo dei Bisantini in Italia.   RSI.   1885.

Cohn, H.   Die Stellung der byzantinischen Statthalter in Ober- und Mittelitalien. Berlin.   1889.

Diehl, Ch.   Études sur l'Administration byzantine dans l'Exarchat de Ravenne. *See Gen. Bibl.* vi.

—— L'Afrique byzantine.   *See Gen. Bibl.* vi.

Gregorovius, F.   Gesch. der Stadt Rom im Mittelalter, vol. ii.   *See Gen. Bibl.* vi.

Hartmann, L. M.   Gesch. Italiens, i–iii, 1.   *See Gen. Bibl.* vi.

—— Untersuchungen zur Geschichte der byzantinischen Verwaltung in Italien (540–750).   Leipsic.   1889.

Hegel, C.   Geschichte der Städteverfassung von Italien seit der Zeit der römischen Herrschaft bis zum Ausgang des 12. Jahrhunderts.   Leipsic.   1847.

Hodgkin.   Italy, vols. iv (Imperial Restoration).   v (Lombard invasion).   vi (Lombard kingdom).   vii (Frankish invasion).   *See Gen. Bibl.* vi.

Mommsen, Th.   Die Bewirtschaftung der Kirchengüter unter P. Gregor I (Z. für Sozial- u. Wirtschaftsgeschichte.   i.   1893).

CHAPTER VIII (B).

GREGORY THE GREAT.

I.

Special Bibliography in Bardenhewer, Patrologie. English transl. pp. 655–7. *See Gen. Bibl.* I.

Chevallier. Bio-Bibliographie. 2nd edn. Vol. I. Col. 1870–4. *See ib.*

Potthast. *See ib.*

Short bibliog. in Hartmann, Gesch. Italiens. II. I, c. vi, p. 194. *See ib.*

On the *Letters* references by Bury, J. B. in Bury Gibbon. v. App. (8vo. edn. p. 510.)

II. ORIGINAL AUTHORITIES.

Opera. Ed. Fossiani, P. 6 vols. Rome. 1588–93. Also, among others (see Bardenhewer *above*, p. 655) the Maurist edn. Paris. 1705. Repr. Venice. 1744. MPL 75–9.

> Eng. transl., Select Letters, in Select Library of Nicene and Post Nicene Fathers, *and in* Library of the Fathers of the Holy Catholic Church.

Epistolae. Gregorii I Papae Registrum epistolarum. Ed. Ewald, P. and Hartmann, L. M. MGH. 1887–99.

Jaffé. Regesta Pontificum. I, pp. 143–219. II, p. 738. *See Gen. Bibl.* IV.

Liber Pontificalis. *See ib.*

Bede. Hist. ecclesiastica. *See Gen. Bibl.* v.

Gregory of Tours. *See ib.*

Ildefonsus of Toledo. Libellus de viris illustribus. XIV. MPL 96.

Isidore of Seville. De scriptoribus ecclesiasticis. MPL 83.

Joannes Diaconus. Vita Gregorii. MPL 75.

[Monk of Whitby] *in* Gasquet, A. A Life of Pope Gregory the Great. 1904.

> Ewald, P. Die älteste Biographie Gregors I. (Hist. Aufsätze dem Andenken an G. Waitz gewidmet.) Hanover. 1886.
>
> *See also* Seeley, J. R. Paul Ewald and Pope Gregory I. EHR, III, 295.

Paulus Diaconus. Vita Gregorii. MPL 75. pp. 41–59. *See also* edn. of an Italian MS. by Grisar, H. ZKT, XI. (1887.) 158–73.

—— Hist. Langobard. Ed. Waitz. MGH, script. rer. Lang. 1878.

III. GENERAL MODERN WORKS.

Barmby, J. Gregory the Great (The Fathers for English Readers). London. 1892.

Bassenge, F. E. Die Sendung Augustins zur Bekehrung d. Angelsachsen. Leipsic. 1890.

Benedetti, D. E. S. Gregorio Magno e la schiavitù. Rome. 1904.

Browne, G. F. The Church in these Islands before the coming of Augustine. Four lectures 1894. 2nd edn. London. 1895.

—— Augustine and his companions. London. 1895.

Bury, J. B.   Later Roman Empire.   *See Gen. Bibl.* vi.

Capello, G.   Gregorio I e il suo pontificato.   Saluzzo.   1905.

Carducci, J.   Storia di San Gregorio Magno e del suo tempo.   Rome.   1909.

Church, R. W.   The Letters of Pope Gregory I *in* Miscellaneous Essays.   London. 1888.

Diehl, Ch.   Études sur l'Administration byzantine.   *See Gen. Bibl.* vi.

—— L'Afrique byzantine.   *See ib.*

—— Études byzantines.   Paris.   1905.

Doize, J.   Deux études sur l'administration temporelle du pape Grégoire le Grand. Paris.   1904.

Duchesne, L.   Autonomies ecclésiastiques: Églises séparées.   Paris.   1905.   Transl. The Churches Separated from Rome.   Matthew, A. H.   London.   1907. (Internat. Catholic Library.   Vol. ix.)

Dudden, F. H.   Gregory the Great, his place in history and thought.   2 vols. London.   1905.

Ebert, A.   Allg. Gesch. d. Litteratur.   i.   pp. 542–56.   (For Gregory's writings) *see Gen. Bibl.* vi.

Ewald, P.   Studien zur Ausgabe des Registers Gregors I.   NAGDG.   iii.   (1878.) 433–625.   (Summary of argument in Hodgkin.   *See below.*   Vol. v, c. vii. Note F.   pp. 333–43.)

Gass, W.   Gesch. d. christlichen Ethik.   2 vols.   Berlin.   1881–7.   Vol. i.

Görres, F.   Papst Gregor d. Grosse und Kaiser Phocas.   ZWT.   xliv.   (1901.) 592–602.

Gregorovius.   City of Rome in the Middle Ages.   *See Gen. Bibl.* vi.

Grisar, H.   Roma alla fine del mondo antico.   Rome.   1899.

—— Gesch. Roms und der Päpste im Mittelalter.   Freiburg-i.-B.   1899 ff.   Transl. Hist. of Rome and the Popes in the Middle Ages.   Cappadelta, L.   London. 1911 ff.

—— San Gregorio Magno.   Rome.   1904.

—— Ein Rundgang durch die Patrimonie des hl. Stuhls im Jahr 600.   ZKT.   i. (1877.)   321–60.

—— Verwaltung und Haushalt d. papstl. Patrimonie um d. Jahr 600.   ZKT.   i, 526–63.

—— Der Römische Primat nach der Lehre und Regierungspraxis Gregors des Grossen.   ZKT.   1879 (iii).   655–93.

—— Studien zum Ausgabe des Registers Gregors I.   Ib. pp. 179 sqq.

Hartmann, L. M.   Gesch. Italiens.   *See Gen. Bibl.* vi.

—— Ueber zwei Gregorbriefe.   NAGDG.   xvii.   (1882.)   193–8.

—— Zur Chronologie d. Briefe Gregors I.   Ib. xv.   (1890.)   411–17.   (In reply to Weise, *op. cit.*)

—— Zur Orthographie Papst Gregors I.   Ib. xv.   529–49.

Harnack.   Dogmengesch.   iii, 3, pp. 241 ff.   Or Engl. Transl. v, 262 f.   *See Gen. Bibl.* vi.

Hauck.   Kirchengesch. Deutschlands.   *See Gen. Bibl.* vi.

Hefele.   Conciliengesch.   *See ib.*

Hodgkin.   Italy and her Invaders.   *See ib.*

Holme, L. R.   Extinction of the Christian Churches in North Africa.   London. 1898.

Howarth, H. H.   St Gregory the Great.   London.   1912.

Hutton, W. H.   The influence of Christianity upon national character illustrated by the lines and legends of the English Saints.   London.   Bampton Lectures for 1903.

Kellett, F. W.   Pope Gregory the Great and his relations with Gaul.   London. 1890.

Lampe, F.   Qui fuerint Gregorii Magni Papae temporibus in imperii Byzantini parte occidentale exarche et qualia eorum jura atque officia. Breslau. 1892.

Langen.   Gesch. d. römischen Kirche. *See Gen. Bibl.* vi.

Lau, E. J. T.   Gregor I d. Grosse nach seinem Leben und seiner Lehre geschildert. Leipsic. 1844.

Lavisse, E.   L'entrée en scène de la papauté. R. des Deux Mondes. Dec. 1886.

Leclercq, H.   L'Espagne chrétienne. Paris. 2nd edn. 1906. (Bibl. de l'enseignement de l'hist. ecclés.)

Loofs, Fr.   Leitfaden zum Studium der Dogmengeschichte. pp. 445-53. (4th edn. 1906.)

Malfatti, B.   Imperatori e Pape ai tempi delle signoria dei Franche in Italia. i. Milan. 1876.

Manitius, M.   Gesch. der christ.-latein. Poesie. Stuttgart. 1891. pp. 384-8. [For hymns attributed to Gregory I. *See also:* Dreves, G. M.   Haben wir G. d. Gr. als Hymnendichter anzusehen? TQS. 1907, pp. 548-62 and 1909, pp. 436-45.]

Mann, H. K.   Lives of the Popes in the Early Middle Ages. 8 vols. London. 1902-10.

Menendez Pelayo, M.   Historia de los heterodoxos Españoles. 3 vols. Madrid. 1880-1. Vol. i.

Mommsen, Th.   Zu den Gregorbriefen. NAGDG. xvii. (1892.) 189-92.

—— Die Bewirtschaft d. Kirchengüter unter, etc. Papst Gregor I. Z. für Sozial- u. Wirtschaftsgesch. i. (1893.) pp. 43-59.

Pargoire, J.   L'Église byzantine. *See Gen. Bibl.* vi.

Pingaud, L.   La Politique de Saint Grégoire le Grand. Paris. 1872.

Roger, M.   L'Enseignement des lettres classiques d'Ausone à Alcuin. Paris. 1905.

Schwarzlose, K.   Die Patrimonien d. röm. Kirche bis zur Gründung d. Kirchenstaats. Berlin. 1887.

—— Die Verwaltung und die finanzielle Bedeutung der Patrimonie d. röm. Kirche. ZKG. xi. (1890.) 62-100.

Vaes, M.   La papauté et l'église franque à l'époque de Grégoire le grand. RHE. Juill.-Oct. 1905.

Weise, J.   Italien und die Langobardenherrscher von 568 bis 628. Halle. 1887.

Wisbaum, W.   Die wichtigsten Richtungen und Ziele des Papstes Gregors des Grossen. Cologne. 1884.

Wolfsgruber, C.   Gregor der Grosse. Saulgau. 1890. 2nd edn. Ratisbon. 1897.

—— Die vorpäpstliche Lebensperiode Gregors des Grossen nach seinem Briefe dargestellt. Vienna. 1886.

Wollschack, Th.   Die Verhältnisse Italiens insbesondere der Langobarden nach dem Briefwechsel Gregors I. Horn. 1888.

IV. LITURGY AND PLAINSONG.

(1) Original Material.

The Sacramentary in Muratori, L. A.   Liturgia Romana Vetus. Venice. 1748. [*On which see* Bishop, E.   On some early Manuscripts of the Gregorianum. JTS. iv. 411-26.]

Wilmaert, A.   Un missel Gregorien ancien. RBén. July, 1909. p. 231 sqq. [Account of a palimpsest at Monte Cassino.]

The Antiphonale.   Paléographie Musicale. Solesmes. [Oldest MS.] *And see* Frere, W. H.   Graduale Sarisburiense, a facsimile of a 13th century English Gradual with an Introduction. Plainsong and Medieval Music Soc. London. 1901. And separately, The Sarum Gradual and the Gregorian Antiphonale Missarum. London. 1895. [Excellent index.]

(2) Modern Works.

The Oxford History of Music. Ed. Hadow, W. H. 6 vols. Oxford. 1901 ff.
Vol. I. The Polyphonic Period. Pt. I. Woolridge, H. E. 1901.

Cabrol, F. Dictionnaire. Article on Chant. *See Gen. Bibl.* I.

Caspari, W. Untersuchungen zum Kirchengesang im Alterthum. ZKG. xxvi,
xxvii. (1905–6.) 317–49, 425–46; 52–69.

Duchesne, L. Origines du culte chrétien. *See Gen. Bibl.* vi.

Gastoué, A. Origines du Chant Romain.

Gevaert, F. A. Les Origines du chant liturgique de l'église latine. Ghent. 1890.

—— La mélopée antique dans le chant de l'église latine. Ghent. 1895.

Hohaus, W. Die Bedeutung Gregors des Grossen als liturgischer Schriftsteller.
Pt. I. Primus ordo Romanus. Glatz. 1889.

Morin, G. Les véritables Origines du chant grégorien. Rome and Tournai. 1904.

(À propos du livre de M. Gevaert. Les Origines du chant liturgique de l'église
latine.)

Muratori. Liturgia Romana vetus. 2 vols. Venice. 1748.

Pothier, J. Les Mélodies Grégoriennes.

Probst, F. Die abendländische Messe vom 5ten bis zum 8ten Jahrhundert. Münster-
i.-W. 1896.

—— Die älteste römischen Sakramentarien und Ordines erklärt. Münster-i.-W.
1892.

Vivelli, C. Vom Musiktraktate Gregors des Grossen. Eine Untersuchung über
Gregors Autorschaft u. über den Inhalt der Schrift. Leipsic. 1911.

Wagner, P. Einführung in die Gregorischen Melodien. Ein Handb. d. Choral-
wissenschaft. 2nd edn. Pt. I. Ursprung u. Entwickelung d. liturg. Gesangs-
formen b. z. Ausgange des Mittelalters. Freiburg (Switz.). 1901. Transl. by
Plainsong Soc.

Wilson, H. A. Index to Roman Sacramentaries. Cambridge. 1892.

CHAPTER IX.

THE SUCCESSORS OF JUSTINIAN.

[This Bibliography does not deal with Spain, Italy, the conquests of the Arabs, Monothelitism, the system of military Themes, nor with the literature upon the Hymnus Acathistus. A more complete critical bibliography will be given in the author's forthcoming "Bibliography for the History of the Roman Empire from Anastasius to Heraclius."]

AUTHORITIES.

1. GREEK.

(a) CONTEMPORARY.

Chronicon Paschale. *See Gen. Bibl.* v.

Evagrius. Hist. ecclesiastica. Ed. Bidez, J. and Parmentier, L. *See Gen. Bibl.* v.

George of Pisidia. CSHB. Vol. xix. Ed. Querci. Bonn. 1837.
        Carmina Inedita. Ed. Sternbach, Leo. Wiener Studien. xiii (1891).
           pp. 1–63. xiv (1892). pp. 51–68.

*John of Antioch. FHG, iv, v. 1883–5. *See Gen. Bibl.* iv (Müller). And cf. Mommsen, Th. Bruchstücke des Johannes von Antiochia und des Johannes Malalas. Hm. vi (1871). pp. 323–83.

*John of Epiphania. FHG, iv.

Maurice (?). Artis militaris, lib. xii. Ed. Scheffer, J. Upsala. 1564.

*Menander. FHG, iv.

*Theophanes of Byzantium. Ibid.

Theophylactus Simocatta. Historiae. Ed. Boor, C. de. Leipsic. 1887.

   * For these fragments cf. Excerpta Historica jussu Imp. Constantini Porphyrogeniti confecta ediderunt U. Ph. Boissevain, C. de Boor, Th. Büttner Wobst. Berlin. 1903, etc.

(b) NOVELS.

Jus Graeco-romanum. Ed. Zachariae von Lingenthal. Pars iii. Leipsic. 1857.

(c) LATER.

Cedrenus. *See Gen. Bibl.* v.

Constantine Porphyrogenitus. Opera. *See Gen. Bibl.* v.

George the Sinner or the Monk. Chronicon. Ed. Boor, C. de. 2 vols. Leipsic. 1904.

Glycas. Chronicon. CSHB. Ed. Bekker, I. 1836.

Leo Grammaticus. Chronicon. CSHB. Ed. Bekker, I. 1842.

Μονεμβασίας Χρονικόν. In Lampros, S. P. Ἱστορικὰ μελετήματα: τὸ περὶ κτίσεως Μονεμβασίας Χρονικόν, pp. 97–128, and in N. A. Beēs: Τὸ "περὶ τῆς κτίσεως τῆς Μονεμβασίας" χρονικόν, αἱ πηγαὶ καὶ ἡ ἱστορικὴ σημαντικότης αὐτοῦ. Βυζαντίς ι, pt. 1. (1909.) pp. 57–105.

Nicephorus. Opuscula historica. Leipsic. 1880. Ed. Boor, C. de.

Nicephorus Kallistos Xanthopoulos. MPG 147. 1865.

Suidas. Ed. Bernhardy, G. 2 vols. Halle and Brunswick. 1853.
Theodosius of Melitene. Chronographia. Ed. Tafel, T. L. F. in Monumenta
 Saecularia, etc. Kön. Akad. d. Wissenschaften. Munich. 1859.
Theophanes. Chronographia. Ed. Boor, C. de. *See Gen. Bibl.* **v.**
Zonaras. Annales. CSHB. Vol. III. *See Gen. Bibl.* **v.**

2. LATIN.

Anastasius Bibliothecarius. Historia tripertita. Ed. Boor, C. de. Leipsic. 1885.
Corippus. In Laudem Justini. Ed. Partsch, J. MGH, auct. ant. III. 1879.
 Ed. Petschenig, M. in Berliner Studien für classische Philologie und
 Archäologie: herausgegeben von Ascherson, F. IV. Berlin. 1886.
Fredegarius. Chronicon. *See Gen. Bibl.* **v.**
Gregory of Tours. Historia Francorum. *See Gen. Bibl.* **v.**
Isidore. ⎱ MGH, auct. ant. XI. Chronica Minora. Saec. IV, V, VI, VII.
John of Biclaro.⎰ Vol. II.
Liber Pontificalis. *See Gen. Bibl.* IV.
Paulus Diaconus. Historia Langobardorum. Ed. Bethmann, L. and Waitz, G. *See
 Gen. Bibl.* v.
Thomas Archidiaconus. Historia Salonitana. Ed. Rački, F. Agram (Zagreb).
 1894. Monumenta spectantia historiam Slavorum Meridionalium. Vol. XXVI.
 Scriptores. Vol. III. Jugoslavenska Akademija Znanosti i Umjetnosti.

3. SYRIAC AND OTHER ORIENTAL WRITERS.

Agapius of Hierapolis. The writer could only use the translation by Baron Rosen in
 Zamyetki o lyetopisi Agapiya Manbidzhskago. Zhurnal Ministerstva narodnago
 Prosvyeshcheniya, January, 1884, Part 231, pp. 47–75. But see now Patr.
 Orient. t. VIII, Fasc. 3, where Vasiliev, A. has publ. the text with French
 translation.
Anonymus of Fourmont. Text never pubd. but see précis in Histoire d'une Révolu-
 tion arrivée en Perse dans le sixième siècle. Hist. de l'Acad. IBL. depuis
 1726 jusqu'en 1730. Amsterdam. 1736. Vol. IV, pp. 508–21. And in Hist.
 de l'Acad. IBL. avec les Mémoires de littérature tiréz des Registres de cette
 Académie depuis l'année 1726, etc. Vol. VII. Paris. 1733. pp. 325–33.
Anonymus of Guidi. (See under Chronicles *infra.*) German translation and
 commentary by Nöldeke, Th. Vienna. SKAW. Vol. CXXVIII. 1893.
Bar Hebraeus. Chronicon ecclesiasticum. Edd. Abbeloos, J. B. et Lamy, T. L.
 Louvain. 1872–7.
 Chronicon Syriacum. Edd. Bruns, P. J. et Kirsch, G. G. Leipsic. 1789.
Chronicles. Various Syriac chronicles are edited in CSCO. Scriptores Syri, Ser. III,
 vol. IV. Chronica Minora. Paris. 1903, with Latin translations. Here refe-
 rences to other editions and translations will be found.
Elijah of Nisibis. Baethgen, F. W. A. Fragmente syrischer und arabischer
 Historiker, etc. Abhandlungen für die Kunde des Morgenlandes. VIII. 1884.
 Brooks, E. W. and Chabot, J. B. Edd. with Latin translation. CSCO.
 Scriptores Syri, Ser. III, vol. VII, VIII. Paris. 1910.
 Delaporte, L. J. La Chronographie d'Élie Bar Šinaya métropolitain de
 Nisibe, etc. Paris. 1910.
John of Ephesus. Church History. Part III. Ed. Cureton, W. Oxford. 1853.
 German translation by Schönfelder, J. M. Munich. 1862.
John of Nikiu. Text and translation by Zotenberg, H. in Notices et Extraits
 des MSS. de la Bibliothèque Nationale, Paris, 1883, but should preferably
 be consulted in JA., 7th Series, vol. XIII, March–April, 1879.
Michael the Syrian. Ed. Chabot, J. B. Paris. 1899, etc. With French translation.

Moses of Kalankaitukh.   Historia Albaniae.   Ed. Shahnazarean.   Paris.   1860.
>   Russian translation by Patkanian, K.   Istoriya Agvan Moiseya Kagankatvatsi.
>   St Petersburg.   1861.
Sebeos.   Ed. Mihrdatean, Th. M.   Constantinople.   1851.   Patkanian, K.   St
>   Petersburg.   1879.
>>   French translation by Macler, F.   Histoire d'Héraclius.   Paris.   1904.   (But
>>   note corrections of Labourt, Bulletin critique, xxvi.   1905.   pp. 321-3.)
>>   For the Pseudo-Sebeos cf. id. JA, Series x, vol. vi (1905), pp. 121-55.
Stephen of Taron.   Ed. Shahnazarean, K.   ¦Paris.   1859.   Malkhasean, St.
>   St Petersburg.   1885.   Translation by Gelzer, H. and Burckhardt, A.
>   Scriptores Sacri et Profani.   Fasc. iv.   Leipsic.   1907.
Tabari.   *See Gen. Bibl.* v.   And see Nöldeke, Th. *infra*.
Thomas Ardzruni.   In Brosset, M.   Collection d'historiens arméniens.   Vol. i.
>   St Petersburg.   1874.

4. HOMILIES, SERMONS, LIVES OF SAINTS, ETC.

[See Ehrhard, A. in Krumbacher, K.   Gesch. d. byz. Litteratur.   2nd edn.
Hagiographie, pp. 176 sqq.]
Acta S. Demetrii.   There is no complete or satisfactory text.   See MPG 116.
>   Tougard, A.   De l'histoire profane dans les actes grecs des Bollandistes.   Paris.
>   1874.   And further fragments in the modern literature, infrà.
Acta Martyris Anastasii Persae.   Ed. Usener, H.   Ex libello Universitatis Rhenanae
>   Natalicia Regis Guilelmi III die iii m. Augusti a. mdcccxciv celebranda indicentis.
>   Bonn.
Combefis.   Historia Haeresis Monothelitarum.   Vol. ii.   Paris.   1648.   (pp. 755 sqq.)
>   A contemporary account of the finding of the Virgin's robe.   (Loparev (*v. infra*)
>   has printed the old Slav version and a Russian translation in VV, ii.)
Dmitrivsky, A. A.   Opisanie liturgicheskikh rukopisei khranyashchikhsya v
>   bibliotekakh Pravoslavnago Vostoka.   2 vols.   Kiev.   1895-1901.
Doctrina Jacobi nuper baptizati.   Ed. Bonwetsch, N.   Abhandlungen d. k. Gesell-
>   schaft d. Wiss. zu Göttingen.   Phil.-hist. Klasse.   N. F. xii, No. 3.   Berlin.
>   1910.   Cf. BZ, xx (1911).   pp. 573-8.   (Important for enforced conversion
>   of Jews under Heraclius.)
S. Eutychii Vita.   ASBoll.   April 1.
Georgii Chozebitae confessoris et monachi Vita.   AB.   vii (1888).   pp. 95-144,
>   336-59.   Cf. viii (1889), pp. 209 f. and vii, pp. 360-70.   Miracula B. Mariae
>   Virg. in Choziba.
Hoffmann, J. G. E.   Auszüge aus syrischen Akten persischer Märtyrer.   Vol. vii of
>   Abhandlungen für die Kunde des Morgenlandes.   1880.   (Deutsche Morgen-
>   ländische Gesellschaft.)   And cf. literature quoted in Patr. Orient., ii, 4, p. 409.
Ioannu, Th.   Μνημεῖα ἁγιολογικά.   Venice.   1884.
John the Almsgiver.   Leontios' von Neapolis Leben des Heiligen Johannes des
>   Barmherzigen Erzbischofs von Alexandrien.   Ed. Gelzer, H.   (Sammlung
>   ausgewählter kirchen- und dogmengeschichtlicher Quellenschriften.   Ed.
>   Krüger, G.   Part v.)   Freiburg and Leipsic.   1893.
Maurice.   Histoire de Saint Maurice, empereur des Romains.   Patr. Orient., v, 5,
>   pp. 773-8.   1910.
Miracula Artemii.   In Sbornik grecheskikh neizdannikh bogoslovskikh Tekstov
>   iv-xv vyekov, etc.   Ed. Papadopoulo-Keramevs, A.   St Petersburg.   1909.
Olympiadis Translatio.   AB.   xvi.   (1897.)   pp. 44-51.   Cf. ibid. xv (1896),
>   pp. 402-4.
S. Simeon Junior Stylites.   Ibid. pp. 321-96.
De Symeone Salo.   ASBoll.   July 1.   pp. 120-51.

Theodorus (?). Περὶ τῆς τῶν ἀθέων βαρβάρων καὶ Περσῶν κατὰ τῆς θεοφυλάκτου ταύτης πόλεως μανιώδους κινήσεως καὶ τῆς φιλανθρωπίᾳ τοῦ Θεοῦ διὰ τῆς Θεοτόκου μετ' αἰσχύνης ἐκείνων ἀναχωρήσεως. In Nova Patrum Bibliotheca, VI (Rome, 1853), 2, pp. 423–37, but much better text in Sternbach, L., Rozprawy, etc. (vid. infrà), pp. 297 sqq.

(And on the church festivals commemorating the triumphs of Heraclius see Sergy. Polnuy Myesyatseslov Vostoka. Moscow. 1876. 2nd edition. Vladimir. 1901. Cf. Debolsky, G. Dni Bogosluzheniya pravosl. Kath. Vost. Tserkvi. St Petersburg. 1846. v Maltzew, A. Myesyatseslov pravosl. Kath. Vost. Tserkvi. Berlin. 1900.)

5. WORKS ON THE AUTHORITIES.

Acta S. Demetrii:

Gelzer, H. Die Genesis der byzantinischen Themenverfassung. *See infra.*

Laurent, J. Sur la date des Églises St Démétrius et Ste Sophie à Thessalonique. BZ, IV (1895), pp. 420–34 (where references to the earlier literature are given).

Pernice, A. Sulla Data del Libro II dei Miracula S. Demetrii Martyris. Bessarione. Serie II, vol. II, Ann. VI (1902). Rome. pp. 181–7.

Tafrali, O. Sur la Date de l'Église et des Mosaiques de Saint Démétrius de Salonique. R. Archéologique. 4th Ser. XIII (1909). pp. 83–101.

—— Sur les Réparations faites au VIIᵉ siècle à l'Église de Saint Démétrius de Salonique. RA. 4th Ser. XIV (1909). pp. 380–6.

Uspensky, Th. O vnov otkruituikh mozaikakh v tserkvi Sv. Dimitriya v Soluni. Izvyestiya russkago arkheologicheskago Instituta v Konstantinopolye. XIV (1909). Sofia (Sophiya). pp. 1–61.

Adamek, Otto. Beiträge zur Geschichte des byzantinischen Kaisers Mauricius (582–602). I. Jahresberichte des ersten k. k. Staatsgymnasiums zu Graz 1889–90. II. Ibid. 1890–1.

Agapius of Hierapolis: Vasiliev, A. Agapy Manbidzhsky khristiansky arabsky istorik x vyeka. VV, XI, pp. 574–87 and Avertissement, Patr. Orient., v, 4. 1910.

Anonymus of Fourmont. Baynes, N. H. The Historical Interest of the Anonymus of Fourmont. (Paper to appear shortly.)

Antiochus Strategius:

Kallistos, Archimandrite. Ἀντίοχος Στρατήγιος. Ἅλωσις τῆς Ἱερουσαλὴμ ὑπὸ τῶν Περσῶν τῷ 614. Jerusalem. 1910. From Νέα Σιών.

(And cf. EHR, XXV (1910), where an English translation is given of part of the account.)

Marr, N. Antiokh Stratig. Plyenenie Ierusalima Persami v 614 g. Tekstui i Razuiskaniya po Armyano-gruzinskoi Filologii. IX. St Petersburg. 1909.

Evagrius: Bidez, J. and Parmentier, L. De la place de Nicéphore Kallistos Xanthopoulos dans la tradition manuscrite d'Evagrius. Revue de l'Instruction publique en Belgique, XL (1897), 161–76 (and further literature is referred to in the preface to their edition).

Freund, A. Beiträge zur Antiochenischen und zur Konstantinopolitanischen Stadtchronik. Dissertation. Jena. 1882.

George of Pisidia :
  Hilberg, Isidor. Textkritische Beiträge zu Georgios Pisides. Wiener
    Studien, ix (1887), pp. 207–22.
  Maas, P. Der byzantinische Zwölfsilber. BZ. xii (1903), pp. 278 sqq.
  Sternbach, Leo, in Rozprawy Akademii Umiejętności wydział filologiczny.
    Ser. ii, vol. xv. Cracow. 1900.
Gregory of Tours : Carrière, A. Sur un chapitre de Gregoire de Tours relatif à
    l'histoire d'Orient. BHE. (Sect. hist. et philolog.) Annuaire 1897–8.
    pp. 5–23.
Hertzsch, G. De Scriptoribus rerum imperatoris Tiberii Constantini. Dissertation.
    Leipsic. 1882.
Jeep, L. Quellenuntersuchungen zu den griechischen Kirchenhistorikern. Jahr-
    bücher für classische Philologie. Supplementband xiv (1884), pp. 56–173.
John of Biclaro : Görres, F. Johannes von Biclaro. Theol. Studien und Kritiken
    (1895), pp. 103–35.
John of Ephesus :
  D'yakonov, A. Ioann Ephesky i ego tserkovno-istoricheskie trudui.
    St Petersburg. 1908. (Inaccessible when the chapter was written.)
  Land, J. P. N. Johannes Bischof von Ephesos, etc. Leyden. 1856.
  Smith, R. P. The Third Part of the Ecclesiastical History of John, Bishop
    of Ephesus. Oxford. 1860. (For further references cf. D'yakonov,
    pp. 1, 2.)
Liber Pontificalis : Hartmann, L. M. Fragmente einer italienischen Chronik.
    Festschrift zu Otto Hirschfelds 60ten Geburtstag. Berlin. (1903.) pp. 336–40.
[Maurice ?] Artis militaris lib. xii :
  Aussaresses, F. L'auteur du Strategicon. Revue des Études anciennes, viii
    (1905), pp. 23–40.
  Gyomlay, V. G. Bölcs Leo Taktikája mint magyar történeti kútforrás.
    Budapest. 1902. (Inaccessible to the present writer.)
  Mayer, Ernst. Die dalmatisch-istrische Munizipalverfassung und ihre
    römischen Grundlagen. ZSR, xxiv, xxxvii of ZR. 1903. German-
    istische Abteilung (see pp. 251–5).
  Patrono, C. M. Contro la Paternità imperiale dell' Οὐρβικίου τακτικὰ
    στρατηγικά. Teramo. 1906. (Estratto dalla Rivista Abruzzese di
    Scienze, Lettere ed Arti, xxi.)
  Vari, V. R. Zur Überlieferung mittelgriechischer Taktiker. BZ, xv (1906),
    pp. 47–87.
  Zachariae von Lingenthal, K. E. Wissenschaft und Recht für das Heer, etc.
    BZ, iii (1894), pp. 437–57.
Miracula Artemii : Palmieri, P. A. Testi teologici greci inediti dei secoli iv–xv.
    Rivista storico-critica delle scienze teologiche, vi (1910), pp. 201–16.
  Baynes, N. H. Topographica Constantinopolitana. JHS, xxxi (1911),
    pp. 266–8.
Moses of Kalankaitukh : Manandian, Agop. Beiträge zur albanischen Geschichte.
    Leipsic. Dissertation. 1897. (In this will be found full references to the
    earlier literature on the subject.)
Nicephorus : Burckhardt, A. Der Londoner Codex des Breviarium des Nicephorus.
    BZ, v (1896), pp. 465–77.
Paschal Chronicle : Mercati, G. A Study of the Paschal Chronicle. JTS, vii,
    (1906), pp. 397–412 (cf. ibid. ii (1900), pp. 288–98, vii, pp. 392 sqq.).
Theophanes :
  Boor, C. de. Zur Chronographie des Theophanes. Hm, xxv (1890), pp. 301–7.
  Brooks, E. W. The Chronology of Theophanes, pp. 607–775. BZ, viii
    (1899), pp. 82–97.

Tafel, G. L. F. Theophanis Chronographia. Probe einer neuen kritisch-exegetischen Ausgabe. SKAW, ix (1852).

Theophylactus Simocatta: Bury, J. B. The Chronology of Theophylaktos Simocatta. EHR, iii (1888), pp. 310–5.

Baynes, N. H. The Literary Composition of the History of Theophylactus Simocatta. Ξένια. Hommage International à l'Université nationale de Grèce à l'occasion du soixante-quinzième anniversaire de sa fondation. Athens. 1912. pp. 32–41.

Thomas Archidiaconus: Kršnjavi, I. Zur Historia Salouitana des Thomas Archidiaconus von Spalato. Agram. 1900.

Zonaras: Sauerbrei, P. De Fontibus Zonarae quaestiones selectae. Dissertationes Jenenses, i (1881), pp. 3–82. Leipsic. [Date given on title—1881.]

6. GENERAL WORKS.

Bury, J. B. A History of the Later Roman Empire. *See Gen. Bibl.* vi.

—— The Imperial Administrative System, etc. British Academy. Supplementary Papers i. London. 1911.

Bussell, F. W. The Roman Empire, etc. 2 vols. London. 1910.

Butler, A. J. The Arab Conquest of Egypt and the last thirty years of the Roman Dominion. Oxford. 1902.

Chapot, V. La Frontière de l'Euphrate de Pompée à la Conquête arabe. Bibliothèque EcfrAR. Fasc. 99. 1907.

Diehl, Ch. L'Afrique byzantine. *See Gen. Bibl.* vi.

—— Études byzantines. Paris. 1905.

—— Justinien et la Civilisation byzantine au vi^e siècle. Paris. 1901.

Duval, Rubens. Anciennes Littératures chrétiennes. La Littérature syriaque. 3rd edn. Paris. 1907. (In Bibliothèque de l'enseignement de l'histoire ecclésiastique.)

Finlay, G. History of Greece. *See Gen. Bibl.* vi.

Gasquet, A. L'empire byzantin et la monarchie franque. *See Gen. Bibl.* vi.

Gelzer, H. Abriss der byzantinischen Kaisergeschichte. 2nd edn. 1897. *See Gen. Bibl.* vi.

—— Byzantinische Kulturgeschichte. Tübingen. 1909.

Gelzer, Matthias. Studien zur byzantinischen Verwaltung Ägyptens. Leipsic. 1909. (=Heft xiii of Leipziger Historische Abhandlungen, herausgegeben von E. Brandenburg, etc.)

Gibbon, E. Decline and Fall of the Roman Empire. Ed. Bury. *See Gen. Bibl.* vi.

Grenier, P. L'Empire byzantin. Son évolution sociale et politique. 2 vols. Paris. 1904.

Hertzberg, G. F. Geschichte der Byzantiner, etc. Berlin. 1883. (Oncken.)

Hesseling, D. C. Byzantium. Haarlem. 1902. (French translation, Essai sur la civilisation byzantine. Paris. 1907.)

Heyd, W. von. Histoire du commerce du Levant au moyen-âge. Édition...publiée ...par F. Raynaud. Leipsic. 1885–6.

Holmes, W. G. The Age of Justinian and Theodora. A History of the Sixth Century A.D. 2 vols. London. 1905–7. (Chs i and ii, on the capital and society in the sixth century.)

Labourt, J. Le Christianisme dans l'Empire perse sous la Dynastie sassanide (224–632). 2nd edition. Paris. 1904. (In Bibliothèque de l'enseignement de l'histoire ecclésiastique.)

Lebeau, C. Histoire du Bas-Empire. Ed. de Saint Martin. Paris. 1824–36.

Milne, J. G. A History of Egypt under Roman Rule, etc. London. 1898.

Nöldeke, Th. Tabari. Geschichte der Perser und Araber zur Zeit der Sassaniden etc. Leyden. 1879.

Oman, C. W. C. History of the Art of War: The Middle Ages. London. 1898.

Paparrhegopoulos, K. Ἱστορία τοῦ Ἑλληνικοῦ ἔθνους. Ed. Karolides, P. 4th edn. Athens. 1902–3.

Pargoire, J. L'Église byzantine de 527 à 847. *See Gen. Bibl.* VI.

Rawlinson, G. The Seventh Great Oriental Monarchy. London. 1876.

Scala, R. von. Das Griechentum seit Alexander dem Grossen. In H. F. Helmolt's Weltgeschichte. Vol. V. Leipsic and Vienna. 1904.

Wigram, W. A. An Introduction to the History of the Assyrian Church, etc. London. 1910.

Wroth, W. Imperial Byzantine Coins. *See Gen. Bibl.* III.

7. GEOGRAPHY, TOPOGRAPHY, ETC.

Adonts, N. Armeniya v epokhu Yustiniana. Tekstui i Razuiskaniya po Armyano-gruzinskoi Filologii. XI. St Petersburg. 1908. (Inaccessible to the writer until his work was completed.)

Anderson, J. G. C. The Road System of Eastern Asia Minor with the evidence of Byzantine Campaigns. JHS, XVII (1897), pp. 22–44 (with map).

Bolotov, V. Ekskurs o geographii Egipta. VV, XV (1908), pp. 32–48.

Ebersolt, J. Le Grand Palais de Constantinople. Paris. 1910.

George the Cyprian. Descriptio orbis Romani. Ed. Gelzer, H. Leipsic. 1890. Cf. Bury, J. B. The Roman Empire in 600 A.D. EHR, IX (1894), pp. 315–20.

Hübschmann, H. Die Altarmenischen Ortsnamen. Mit Beiträgen zur historischen Topographie Armeniens und einer Karte. Indogermanische Forschungen, XVI (1904), pp. 197–490.

Kinneir, J. M. Journey through Asia Minor, Armenia and Koordistan in the years 1813, 1814. London. 1818. (With map of the campaigns of Heraclius.)

Lynch, H. F. B. Armenia. 2 vols. London. 1901.

Marquart, J. Osteuropäische und ostasiatische Streifzüge. Ethnologische und historisch-topographische Studien zur Geschichte des 9. und 10. Jahrhunderts. (cir. 840–940.) Leipsic. 1903.

Millingen, A. van. Ἡ ἀληθὴς θέσις τοῦ Ἑβδόμου. ὁ ἐν Κωνστ. Ἑλλ. φιλ. σύλλογος: ἀρχ. ἐπιτρ. παράρτημα τοῦ κ′–κβ′ τόμου (1892), pp. 33–7.

—— Byzantine Constantinople. The Walls of the City and adjoining historical Sites. London. 1899.

Mordtmann, A. Esquisse topographique de Constantinople. Lille. 1892.

Ramsay, Sir W. M. The Historical Geography of Asia Minor. RGS, Supplementary Papers. IV. London. 1890.

Rawlinson, H. C. Notes on a Journey from Tabriz, etc. in October and November 1838. JRGS, X (1840), pp. 1–64. London.

—— Memoir on the Site of the Atropatenian Ecbatana. Ibid., pp. 65–158 (with map).

8. THE SLAV SETTLEMENTS.

[The literature is very large : further references can be found in
Archiv f. Slav. Philologie, Supplementband. Berlin. 1892.
Niederle, L. Slovanské Starožitnosti. Prague. 1902, etc.
Stanojević, St. Vizantija i Srbi, *infra.*
Zagorsky, V. François Rački et la renaissance scientifique et politique de la Croatie, 1828–94. Paris. 1909.]

Bury, J. B. The Treatise de administrando imperio. BZ, XV (1906), pp. 517–77 at pp. 556 sqq.

Fallmerayer, J. P. Fragmente aus dem Orient. 2nd edn. Ed. Thomas, G. M. Stuttgart. 1877.

Gelzer, H. Die Kirchliche Geographie Griechenlands vor dem Slaweneinbruche. ZWT, xxxv (1892), pp. 419–36. (And cf. Die Genesis der byzantinischen Themenverfassung, infrà.)

Grot, C. J. Izvestiya Konstantina Bagryanorodnago o Serbakh i Khorvatakh. St Petersburg. 1880. An extract therefrom : Zur Kritik einer Stelle des Constantin Porphyrogenitus. Archiv für Slav. Phil. v (1881), pp. 390–7, where the older literature is criticised.

Jagić, V. Ein Capitel aus der Geschichte der südslavischen Sprachen. Archiv für Slav. Phil. xvii (1895), pp. 47–87.

Jiriček, C. Gesch. der Serben. (Lamprecht.) 1 Abt. vol. i. Gotha. 1911.
—— Die Romanen in den Städten Dalmatiens während des Mittelalters. Part i. Denkschriften KAW, xlviii. 1902. And see Part 3. Ibid., 1904, pp. 72 sqq. Nachträge und Berichtigungen. (Invaluable.)

Kos, Fr. Iz zgodovine Jugoslovanov v šestem stoletju po Kr. Izvestja Musejskega društva za Kranjsko. Letnik viii (1898). Sešitek 3 to 6. Laibach.

Manojlović, G. Iz sirski pisane "Crkvene povjesti" Joannesa Efeskago. Vjestnik of the Croatian Landesarchiv (1899), pp. 115–20. (Inaccessible to the present writer.)

Nodilo, N. Historija Srednjega Vijeka za Narod Hrvatski i srpski. Knjiga iii. Varvarstvo otima mah nad Bizantijom do Smrti Cara Heraklija. (566–641.) Zagreb. (Agram.) 1905.

Nodilo, S. Pad Solina. Glasnik Matice Dalmatinske. August, 1903, pp. 1–7.

Oblak, V. Eine Bemerkung zur ältesten südslavischen Geschichte. Archiv f. Slav. Phil. xviii (1896), pp. 228–34.

Paparrhegopoulos, K. Σλαυϊκαὶ ἐν ταῖς Ἑλληνικαῖς χώραις ἐποικήσεις. In Ἱστορικαὶ Πραγματεῖαι. Μέρος Α'. ἐν Ἀθήναις. 1858. pp. 261–370.

Rypl, Matthias. Die Beziehungen der Slaven und Avaren zum oströmischen Reiche unter der Regierung des Kaisers Heraklius. Programm der deutschen k. k. Staatsrealschule in Budweis. Budweis. 1888.

Shishmanov, P. D. Slavyanski selishcha v Krit i na drugite gr'tski ostrovi. B'lgarski Pregled God. iv. Kn. iii. June 1897. Sofia. pp. 62–93.

Stanojević, St. Vizantija i Srbi. Knjige Matitse Srpske. Broj 7–8 (1903) and 14–15 (1906). Novy Sad. [Neusatz, Hungary.] (Excellent.)
—— O Juzhnim Slovenima u vi, vii i viii veku. Glas. Srpske kral. Academije. lxxx. (Drugi Razred 47.) Belgrade. 1909. pp. 124–54.

Vasil'ev, A. Slavyane v Gretsii. VV, v (1898), pp. 404–38, 626–70.

9. TURKS, AVARS, ETC.

Bury, J. B. The Turks in the Sixth Century. EHR, xii (1897), pp. 417–26 (and cf. Appendix to vol. v of his edition of Gibbon).

Brosset, M. Histoire de la Georgie. i. St Petersburg. 1849. Additions et éclaircissements 1851. Introduction : Table des Matières, etc. in vol. iii. 1858.

Cahun, L. Introduction à l'Histoire de l'Asie. Paris. 1896.

Drouin, E. Mémoire sur les Huns Ephthalites dans leurs Rapports avec les Rois perses sassanides. Le Muséon, xiv (1895), pp. 73–84, 141–61, 232–47, 277–88. (Here references are given to the earlier literature.)

Hirth, F. Über die chinesischen Quellen zur Kenntnis Centralasiens unter der Herrschaft der Sassaniden etwa in der Zeit 500 bis 650. Vienna Oriental Journal, x (1896), pp. 225–41.

Marquart, J. Zur Chronologie der alt-türkischen Inschriften. Leipsic. 1898.

Marquart, J. Historische Glossen zu den alt-türkischen Inschriften. Vienna Oriental Journal, xii (1898), pp. 157–200.

Parker, E. H. The Origin of the Turks. EHR, xi. 1896. pp. 431–45. (Cf. Academy. Dec. 21, 1895.)

Radlov, W. Die alt-türkischen Inschriften der Mongolei. St Petersburg. 1895. More important is N. F., 1897, with Anhang, Die historische Bedeutung der alt-türkischen Inschriften, by Barthold, W. (The second series (1899) deals with a later period.)

Thomsen, V. Inscriptions de l'Orkhon déchiffrées. Mémoires de la Société Finno-Ougrienne. Suomalais-ugrilaisen seuran toimi tuksia v Helsingfors 1896 and cf. ibid. xii. 1898. Vambéry, H. Noten zu den alt-türkischen Inschriften der Mongolei und Siberiens.

Vailhé, S. Projet d'alliance turco-byzantine au vie siècle. Échos d'Orient, xii (1909), pp. 206–14.

10. VARIOUS MONOGRAPHS.

Amélineau, E. Étude sur le Christianisme en Égypte au viie siècle. (Éloge de Pisentios, évêque de Keft.) Paris. 1887.

—— Monuments pour servir à l'histoire de l'Égypte chrétienne aux iv–viie siècles. Paris. 1895. Mémoires publiés par les Membres de la Mission archéologique française au Caire, iv. Fasc. 2. Paris. 1895.

—— Samuel de Qalamoun. Revue de l'histoire des Religions, xxx (1894), 1–47. Paris.

Aussaresses, F. L'armée byzantine à la Fin du vie siècle d'après le Stratégicon de l'empereur Maurice. Bibliothèque des Universités du Midi. Fasc. xiv. Bordeaux. 1909.

Baynes, N. H. The First Campaign of Heraclius against Persia. EHR, xix (1904), pp. 694–702.

—— The Date of the Avar Surprise. BZ, xxi (1912), pp. 110–23.

—— The Restoration of the Cross at Jerusalem. EHR, xxvii (1912), pp. 287–99.

—— A Critical Study of the Military Operations of the Emperor Heraclius. (To appear shortly in the United Service Magazine.)

—— The Revolt of Bahram Cobin. (To appear shortly.)

Bréhier, L. L'origine des titres impériaux à Byzance. BZ, xv (1906), pp. 161–78.

Bury, J. B. The Naval Policy of the Roman Empire in relation to the Western Provinces, etc. Centenario della Nascità di Michele Amari: Scritti di Filologia, etc. Vol. ii. pp. 21–34. Palermo. 1910.

—— The Constitution of the Later Roman Empire. Creighton Memorial Lecture. Cambridge. 1910.

Christensen, Arthur. L'Empire des Sassanides, Le Peuple, L'État, La Cour. D. Kgl. Danske Vidensk. Selsk. Skrifter, 7 Raekke, historisk og filosofisk Afd. i, 1 Copenhagen. 1907.

Clermont-Ganneau, C. La Prise de Jérusalem par les Perses en 614. Recueil d'Archéologie orientale, ii (1897), pp. 137–60. (English translation: The Taking of Jerusalem by the Persians a.d. 614. Palestine Exploration Fund. Quarterly Statement, Jan. 1898, pp. 36–54.)

Couret, Conte A. La Prise de Jérusalem par les Perses en 614. Orléans. 1896.

—— La Palestine sous les Empereurs Grecs, 326–636. Grenoble. 1869.

Demetriy, A. K voprosu o dogovorakh russkikh s Grekami. VV, ii (1895), pp. 531–50. (Contains a diplomatic study on Menander (Bonn, 359–64): wrongly dated in 628, pp. 535 sqq.)

Drapeyron, L. L'Empereur Héraclius et l'Empire byzantin au VIIᵉ siècle. Paris. 1869 (out of print). And cf. Grande Encyclopédie, vol. XIX, 1894, s.v. Héraclius.

Duckworth, H. T. F. John the Almsgiver. Oxford. 1901.

Duval, R. Histoire d'Édesse. Paris. 1892. (And in JA.)

Εὐαγγελίδης, T. E. Ἡράκλειος ὁ Αὐτοκράτωρ τοῦ Βυζαντίου (575–641 μ. X.) καὶ ἡ κατὰ τὸν ζ' μ. X. αἰῶνα κατάστασις τοῦ Βυζαντιακοῦ κράτους. Odessa. 1903 (written 1893). [The Emperor as national hero of the Greeks.]

Gelzer, H. Die Genesis der byzantinischen Themenverfassung. Abhandlung V of vol. XVIII of Abhandlungen der philologisch-historischen Classe der kön. Sächsischen Gesellschaft der Wissenschaften. Leipsic. 1899. pp. 1–133.

—— Das Verhältnis von Staat und Kirche in Byzanz. Ausgewählte Kleine Schriften. Leipsic. 1907. pp. 57–141 or HZ. Vol. LXXXVI (N. F. L) (1901), pp. 193 sqq.

—— Der Streit über den Titel des ökumenischen Patriarchen. Jahrbuch für protestantische Theologie, XIII (1887), pp. 549–84.

—— Die politische und kirchliche Stellung von Byzanz. Verhandlungen der 33ten Versammlung deutscher Philologen und Schulmänner in Gera. Leipsic. 1879. pp. 32–55.

—— Ein griechischer Volksschriftsteller des 7. Jahrhunderts. Ausgewählte Kleine Schriften. Leipsic. 1907. pp. 1–56 or HZ. N. F. Vol. XXV (1889), pp. 1 sqq.

—— Chalcedon oder Karchedon. Rhein. Mus. N.F. XLVIII (1893), pp. 161–74.

Gerland, E. Die persischen Feldzüge des Kaisers Herakleios. BZ, III (1894), pp. 330–73.

Görres, F. Papst Gregor der Grosse und Kaiser Phokas. ZWT, XLIV. N. F. IX (1901), pp. 592–602.

—— Das Christentum im Sassanidenreich. Ibid. XXXI (1888), pp. 449–68.

—— Die Sassaniden von Shâpûr II bis Chosroes II (310–628) und das Christentum nach den von Georg Hoffmann veröffentlichen syrischen Martyreracten des brit. Museums. Ibid. XXXIX (1896), pp. 443–59.

—— Die byzantinische Abstammung der spanischen Westgoten Könige Erwich und Witiza sowie die Beziehungen des Kaisers Maurikios zur germanischen Welt. BZ, XIX, 1910, pp. 430–9.

Groh, Kurt. Geschichte des oströmischen Kaisers Justin II nebst den Quellen. Leipsic. 1889.

Güterbock, K. Römisch-Armenien und die röm. Satrapieen im vierten bis sechsten Jahrhundert. Eine rechtsgeschichtliche Studie. In Festgabe der juristischen Fakultät zu Königsberg für ihren Senior Johann Theodor Schirmer zum 1 August, 1900, pp. 1–58.

—— Byzanz und Persien in ihren diplomatisch-völkerrechtlichen Beziehungen im Zeitalter Justinians, etc. Berlin. 1906.

Haury, J. Johannes Malalas identisch mit dem Patriarchen Johannes Scholastikos? BZ, IX (1900), pp. 337–56.

Hicks, G B. St Gregory and the Emperor Phocas. The Downside Review, IV (XXIII) (1904), pp. 59–72.

Janin, R. Formation du patriarcat oecuménique de Constantinople. Échos d'Orient, XIII (1910), pp. 135–40, 213–18.

Jorga, N. Der lateinische Westen und der byzantinische Osten in ihren Wechsel-beziehungen während des Mittelalters. Einige Gesichtspunkte. In Studium Lipsiense: Ehrengabe Karl Lamprecht dargebracht, etc. Berlin. 1909. pp. 89–99.

Koch, P. Die byzantinischen Beamtentitel von 400 bis 700. Dissertation. Jena. 1903.

Kraitschek. Der Sturz des Kaisers Mauricius. In Bericht über das Vereinsjahr des akad. Vereins deutscher Historiker in Wien. Vienna (1896), pp. 81–137 (cf. BZ, VII, 188). (Now unobtainable: a copy was courteously presented to the writer by the Society.)

Kretschmann. Die Kämpfe zwischen Heraclius I und Chosroes II. Part 1. Programm. Domschule zu Gustrow. 1875. Part 2. Ibid. 1876.

Kulakovsky, Yu. K istorii Bospora kimmeryskago v kontsye VI, v. VV, III (1896), pp. 1–17.

Loparev, Kh. Staroe svidyetelstvo o Polozhenii rizui Bogoroditsui vo Vlakhernakh v novom istolkovanii prityenitelno k nashestviyu Russkik na Vizantiyu v 860 godu. VV, II (1895), pp. 581–628.

Maspero, J. Φοιδερᾶτοι et Στρατιῶται dans l'Armée byzantine au VIe. Siècle. BZ, XXI (1912), pp. 97–109.

Mordtmann, A. D. Die Chronologie der Sassaniden. 1871.

Mordtmann, A. Οἱ Ἄβαρες καὶ οἱ Πέρσαι πρὸ τῆς Κωνσταντινουπόλεως. ὁ ἐν Κωνστ. Ἑλλ. φιλ. σύλλογος ἀρχ. ἐπιτρ. παράρτημα τοῦ κ'–κβ' τόμου. Constantinople. 1892. pp. 54–60.

Owsepian, G. Die Entstehungsgeschichte des Monothelitismus. Leipsic. 1897. (Suggestive for the chronology of the campaigns of Heraclius.)

Patkanian, K. See Prud'homme, É. *infra*.

Patrono, C. M. Bizantini e Persiani alla Fine del VI Secolo. Florence. 1907. Estratto dal Giornale della Società Asiatica italiana. XX. 1907. pp. 159–277.

—— Studi Bizantini. Dei Conflitti tra l' imperatore Maurizio Tiberio e il Papa Gregorio Magno. Rivista di Storia Antica, N.S. XII (1909), pp. 47–63 (1910), pp. 169–88.

Pernice, A. L' Imperatore Eraclio. Saggio di Storia bizantina. Florence. 1905.

Prud'homme, É. Essai d'une histoire de la dynastie des Sassanides d'après les renseignements fournis par les historiens Arméniens. Par M. K. Patkanian: traduit du russe par M. E. Prud'homme. JA. Series VI. Vol. VII. Feb.–March, 1866, pp. 101–238.

Rhétoré, J. La Prise de Jérusalem par les Perses. R. biblique internationale, VI (1897), pp. 458–63.

Ricci, Seymour de. Proceedings of the Society of Biblical Archaeology, XXIV, 1902, pp. 97–107. A list of the praefects of Egypt.

Siderides, X. A. Ἐπανόρθωσις ἀφηγησέων γεγονότων τινων ἐπὶ αὐτοκράτορος Ἡρακλείου τοῦ Α'. ὁ ἐν Κωνστ. Ἑλλ. φιλ. σύλλογος τόμος κη' (1904), pp. 98–118.

Spintler, R. De Phoca Imperatore Romanorum. Dissertatio historica. Jena. 1905.

Usener, H. De Stephano Alexandrino commentatio. Bonn. 1880.

Uspensky, Th. Partii tsirka i dimui v Konstantinopolye. VV, I (1894), pp. 1–16.

Vailhé, S. Les Juifs et la prise de Jérusalem 614. Échos d'Orient, XII (1909), pp. 15–17.

—— La Prise de Jérusalem par les Perses en 614. ROC, VI (1901), pp. 643–9.

—— Exécution de l'Empereur Maurice à Calamich en 602. Échos d'Orient, XIII (1910), pp. 201–8.

—— Le Titre de patriarche oecuménique avant S. Grégoire le Grand. Ibid. XI (1908), pp. 65–9.

—— S. Grégoire le Grand et le Titre de Patriarche oecuménique. Ibid. pp. 161–71.

Vasilievsky, V. Avarui a ne Russkie. Theodor a ne Georgy: zamyechaniya na statyu Kh. M. Lopareva. VV, III (1896), pp. 83–95.

Wenger, L. Vorbericht über die Münchener byzantinischen Papyri. Sitzungsber d. kön. Bayerischen Akad. d. Wissenschaften. Phil.-phil.-hist. Kl., Abh. 8 Munich. 1911.

CHAPTER X.

MAHOMET AND ISLAM.

I. MUSLIM WORKS.

The Koran. Of the English translations the best are those of Rodwell (1861) and Palmer (1880). Of the innumerable Arabic Commentaries on the Koran the most important is that of Ṭabarī (who died A.D. 923), printed at Cairo in 1901–3.

The Biography of the Prophet by Ibn Isḥāḳ († A.D. 768) in the recension of Ibn Hishām († A.D. 834), edited by Wüstenfeld. (Göttingen. 1858–60.) Of this work there is a very inaccurate and misleading German translation by Weil (1864).

The Book of the Prophet's Campaigns by Wāḳidī († A.D. 823). The first part of this book (about a third of the whole) was edited by A. von Kremer. Calcutta. 1856. The rest of the Arabic text is still unpublished, but there is an abridged German translation by Wellhausen, entitled Muhammed in Medina. Berlin. 1882.

The Biography of the Prophet by Ibn Saʿad († A.D. 845). The earlier portion of this book has been edited by Mittwoch, E. 1905, and by Horovitz, J. 1909, as part of a series entitled Ibn Saʿad, Biographien Muhammeds, seiner Gefährte und der späteren Träger des Islams. [General editor, E. Sachau.] Leyden. 1904 ff. Another portion has been edited, with a German translation, by Wellhausen in his Skizzen und Vorarbeiten, Part IV [see below].

The Annals of Ṭabarī (the author of the above-mentioned Commentary on the Koran), edited by De Goeje and others. Leyden. 1879–1901. A great part of Ṭabarī's account of the Prophet is taken verbatim from Ibn Isḥāḳ.

Among the numerous collections of Traditions the following are the most important:

    (a) The Ṣaḥīḥ of Bukhārī († A.D. 870), edited by Krehl and Juynboll (Leyden. 1861–1908).

    (b) The Ṣaḥīḥ of Muslim († A.D. 875).

    (c) The Musnad of Ibn Ḥanbal († A.D. 855).

The Usd-al-Ghāba of Ibn al-Athīr († A.D. 1234) and the Isāba of Ibn Ḥajar († A.D. 1449), two Biographical Dictionaries containing accounts of the Prophet's contemporaries arranged in alphabetical order.

II. EUROPEAN WORKS.

Those accounts of Mahomet and Islām which were published in Europe before the beginning of the 19th century are now to be regarded simply as literary curiosities. Even if the writers had been strictly impartial—which was seldom the case—the nature of the materials which lay within their reach would have placed them at a great disadvantage. An edition of the Koran, with a Latin translation and a copious "refutation" by Luigi Maracci, appeared at Padua in

1698, but the works of the earlier Muslim commentators and historians, without which the Koran could not be rationally interpreted, remained unknown in Europe for more than a century later. The principal sources whence Gibbon and other European writers drew their information on this subject were the following: (1) A brief historical summary composed by the Christian ecclesiastic Gregory Barhebraeus, also called Abu-l-Faraj or Abul-pharagius († A.D. 1286): (2) another summary by the Muslim annalist Abu-l-Fidā († A.D. 1331): (3) a historical romance of uncertain date falsely ascribed to the historian Wāḳidī.

The older authorities, long neglected and sometimes wholly forgotten by Muslims, have during the last three generations been gradually brought to light by European Arabists. Moreover, researches in other departments, particularly Jewish and Christian Oriental literature, have elucidated certain details which even the best Muslim authorities leave unexplained or explain wrongly. Of the works which embody these results the following are the most important.

Becker, C. H. Christenthum und Islam. Tübingen. 1907. (Religionsgeschichtliche Volksbücher für die deutsche christliche Gegenwart. Ed. Schiele, F. M.)

Buhl, F. Muhammeds Liv. Copenhagen. 1903.

Caetani, L. C. (Principe di Teano). Annali dell' Islam. Vols. I, II. Milan. 1905–7 [by far the fullest statement of the evidence that exists at present].

Goldziher, I. Muhammedanische Studien. (2 pts.) Halle. 1889, 1890.

—— Vorlesungen über den Islam. Heidelberg. 1910.

Grimme, H. Mohammed. Munich. 1904. (Weltgeschichte in Charakterbildern. II. Abth.)

Houtsma, M. T. "Der Islam" in Lehrbuch der Religionsgeschichte. 2 vols. Ed. Chantepie de la Saussaye, R. D. Vol. I, pp. 468–537. Tübingen. 1905.

Lyall, Sir C. J. Article "The words 'Ḥanīf' and 'Muslim,'" JRAS, Oct. 1903, pp. 771–84 [probably the best account of the Ḥanīfs].

Macdonald, D. B. Development of Muslim Theology, Jurisprudence and Constitutional Theory. London. 1903.

Margoliouth, D. S. Mohammed and the Rise of Islam. New York and London. 1905 (Heroes of the Nations series).

Muir, W. The Life of Mahomet. 4 vols. London. 1858–61. Second edn. (abridged). 1877. Third edn. 3 vols. 1894.

—— Mahomet and Islam. London. 1887.

Müller, A. Der Islam im Morgen- und Abendland. Berlin. 1885.

Nöldeke, T. Geschichte des Korans, Göttingen 1860 [new edition, revised by Schwally, Part I, Leipsic 1909]: article "The Koran" in EncBr. 9th edn. vol. XVI, pp. 597–606, republished, with some changes, in his Orientalische Skizzen. Berlin. 1892 [English translation, Sketches from Eastern History. London and Edinburgh. 1892].

Pautz, O. E. A. Muhammeds Lehre von der Offenbarung quellenmässig untersucht. Leipsic. 1898.

Sprenger, A. The Life of Mohammad from original sources [1st Part only published]. Allahabad. 1851.

—— Das Leben und die Lehre des Mohammad. Berlin. 1861–5. Second edn. 1869.

Wellhausen, J. Article "Mohammedanism," Part I, in EncBr. 9th edn. vol. XVI.

—— Skizzen und Vorarbeiten, Part III. Berlin. 1887. Second edn. 1897. Part IV (1889) [specially important for the history of Medina before Islām], Part VI (1899).

—— Das arabische Reich und sein Sturz. Berlin. 1902.

CHAPTERS XI AND XII.

THE EXPANSION OF THE SARACENS.

1. SPECIAL BIBLIOGRAPHIES.

Müller, A. (till 1892), Kuhn, E. (1892–5), and Schermann, L. Orientalische
Bibliographie. Berlin. 1888 ff. annually. (Indispensable.)

Pons Boigues, F. Ensayo Bio-Bibliográfico sobre los Historiadores y Geografos
Arabigo-Españoles. Madrid. 1898.

Playfair, Sir R. L. Supplement to the Bibliography of Algeria. London. 1898.
(Valuable for Northern Africa.)

—— and Brown, Dr R. A Bibliography of Marocco (Supplementary Papers of
RGS). London. 1892.

In connexion with :
  Caetani, L. (P. of Teano). Annali dell' Islam. Milan. 1905 ff. 5 vols. *In
  progress.* (Covers so far the twenty-three first years of Islam. Standard
  work.)
  Arnold, T. W. The Preaching of Islam. Westminster. 1896. (Very full.)

2. ORIGINAL DOCUMENTS, PAPYRI AND INSCRIPTIONS.

Amari, M. I Diplomi Arabi del Archivio Fiorentino. Florence. 1863.

Becker, C. H. Papyri Schott Reinhardt, i. Heidelberg. 1906.

—— Arabische Papyri des Aphroditofundes. Z. für Assyriologie, xx, 68 ff.
Strasburg. 1907.

—— Neue arabische Papyri des Aphroditofundes. Der Islam, ii, 245 ff. Strasburg.
1911.

Bell, H. I. and Crum, W. E. The Aphrodito Papyri, Catalogue of the Greek
Papyri in the British Museum. Vol. iv. London. 1910. (Extremely
important for early administration.)

—— Translations, *see* Der Islam, ii, pp. 269 ff.; 372 ff. ; iii, pp. 132 ff. Strasburg.
1911.

Berchem, M. van. Matériaux pour un Corpus Inscriptionum Arabicarum.
Mémoires de la Mission archéologique française au Caire, xix. 2 vols.
Cairo. 1894 ff.

Cusa, S. I Diplomi Greci ed Arabi di Sicilia. 2 vols. Palermo. 1868.

Karabaček, J. Papyrus Erzherzog Rainer, Führer durch die Ausstellung. Vienna.
1894.

3. AUTHORITIES.

(a) GENERAL HISTORY OF EARLY ISLAM.

Abu Hanīfa al-Dināweri. Kitāb al-Akhbār aṭ-ṭiwāl. Publ. by Guirgass. Leyden.
1888.

Abulfeda. Annales Mulemici. Ed. Adler, J. G. Ch. et Reiskius, J. J. Vols. 1–4.
Copenhagen. 1789.

Al-Suyūṭi. Tarīkh al-Khulafā. Cairo. 1888 [1305].

Balādhurī. Anonyme arabische Chronik, Bd xi, vermutlich das Buch der Verwandtschaft der Adligen. Ed. Ahlwardt, W. Greifswald. 1883.
—— Liber expugnationis regionum. Ed. Goeje, M. J. de. Leyden. 1866. (Important.)
Fragmente syrischer und arabischer Historiker. Ed. Baethgen, F. Abh. für die Kunde des Morgenlandes. viii, No. 3. Leipsic. 1884.
Ibn al-Athīr [Izzal-din Husain ibn al-Athir]. Chronicon. Ed. Tornberg, C. J. 14 vols. Leyden. 1862–76.
—— Usd al-Ghāba fī Ma'rifat al-Ṣaḥāba. 5 vols. Cairo. 1868 [1285].
Ibn Khaldūn. Kitāb al-'ibar. 7 vols. Cairo (Bulāk). 1867 [1284].
—— Les Prolégomènes d'Ibn Khaldoun. 3 vols. Ed. and transl. Slane, MacGuckin de. Paris. 1863–8.
Ibn Khallikān. Vitae illustrium virorum. Ed. Wüstenfeld, F. 13 pts. Göttingen. 1835–50. Translation, Biographical Dictionary, MacGuckin de Slane. 4 vols. Paris. 1842–71. (Oriental Translation Fund.) Revised issue of Vol. iii (1). 1845.
Ibn Sa'ad. Biographien Muhammeds, seiner Gefährte und der späteren Träger des Islams bis zum Jahre 230 der Flucht. *In progress. See Bibl. c. x* (1).
Michael the Syrian. Chronique de Michel le Syrien, patriarche jacobite d'Antioche. (1166–99). Ed. Chabot, J. B. Paris. 1899–1904. (3 vols. in several pts.)
Scriptores Syri, Chronica Minora. CSCO. Ser. iii, vol. 4. 1903–4.
Ṭabari. Annales quos scripsit. Ed. Goeje, M. J. de. 15 vols. Leyden. 1879–1901. (Best source for the history of the Caliphate.) Transl. (French) of a Persian Translation by Zotenberg, H. Vols. 1–4. Paris. 1867–74. And *see* Nöldeke *below.*
Theophanes. Chronographia. Ed. de Boor. *See Gen. Bibl.* v.
Wākidi [Muhammad ibn 'Umar]. History of Muhammed's Campaigns. Ed. Kremer, A. v. Calcutta. 1856.
—— Muhammed in Medina. Transl. Wellhausen, J. Berlin. 1882.
Ya'ḳūbī. Ibn Wadhih qui dicitur al-Ja'qubī. 2 vols. Ed. Houtsma, M. Th. Leyden. 1883.

(b) Egypt.

Abu'l-Mahāsin ibn Tagribardi. Annales 2 vols. Ed. Juynboll, T. G. J. Leyden. 1855–61.
Amélineau, M. E. Fragments Coptes pour servir à l'Histoire de la Conquête de l'Égypte par les Arabes. JA, Oct.—Nov. 1888. pp. 389–409.
El-Kindi. The Ta'rīkhu Miṣr. Ed. Guest, A. G. (Gibb Memorial Fund.) London. 1912.
Eutychius [Saīd b. Batrik]. Contextio gemmarum sive Eutychii Patriarchae Alexandrini Annales. (Arabic and Latin.) Ed. Pococke, E. (Pocockius). 2 vols. Oxford. 1658. Ed. and transl. Cheikho. CSCO, script. Arabici. Ser. iii, vol. vi. 1906.
John of Nikiu. Chronicle. Ed. and transl. (French) Zotenberg, M. H. Paris. 1883. (Indispensable for the study of the Conquest.) *See Bibl. e.* ix, 3.
Maḳrīzī. Kitāb al-mawā'iz wa-l-i'tibār bi-dhikr al-khiṭaṭ wa-l-āthār. 2 vols. Cairo. 1853 (1270). French transl. Casanova, P. Cairo. 1906. (Mém. de l'institut fr. d'archéol. orientale du Caire. Vol. iii.) Livre des admonitions et de l'observation pour l'hist. des quartiers et des monuments d'Égypte.
Severus b. Muḳaffa of Ashmunain. Historia patriarcharum Alexandrinorum. Ed. and transl. Evetts (Patrologia Orientalis, v, 1). Paris. Seybold, C. F. CSCO, script. Arabici. Ser. iii, vol. ix. 1904 ff. (Full of information.)

(c) AFRICA AND SPAIN.

Ajbār Machmuâ. Cronica Anonima del Siglo xi.　Ed. Lafuente y Alcantara, D. Emilio.　(Coleccion de Obras Arábigas, i.)　Madrid.　1867.

Continuationes Isidorianae.　Ed. Mommsen.　MGH. ii. Chron. Min. iv, v, vi, vii.　(Best Latin sources.)

Ibn el-Adhari.　Histoire de l'Afrique et de l'Espagne intitulé al-Bayano 'l-Moghrib.　Ed. Dozy, R. 2 vols.　Leyden.　1848–51.　French transl. Fagnan, E. Algiers.　2 vols.　1901–4.

Ibn Khaldoun.　Histoire des Berbères.　Transl. de Slane.　4 vols.　Algiers. 1852–6.

Makkarī [Aḥmad Ibn Muhammad].　Analectes sur l'Histoire et la Littérature des Árabes d'Espagne.　Ed. Dozy, R. and others.　2 vols.　Leyden.　1855–61.

(d) SICILY AND ITALY.

(*Arabic sources only.*)

Amari, Michele.　Biblioteca Arabo-Sicula ; con appendice.　2 vols.　Leipsic. 1857, 1875.　(Full collection of Arabic sources on Sicily and Southern Italy.)　Italian translation.　2 vols.　Rome.　1880.

Centenario della nascità di Michele Amari.　2 vols.　Palermo.　1910.　(Many valuable additions to the above.)

4. MODERN WORKS.

(a) GENERAL HISTORY OF EARLY ISLAM.

Arnold, T. W.　The Preaching of Islam : a History of the propagation of the Musulman faith.　London.　1896.

Becker, C. H.　Christianity and Islam.　London and New York.　1909.

—— Der Islam als Problem.　(Der Islam, i, 1 ff.)　Strasburg.　1910.

Berchem, Max van.　La propriété territoriale et l'impôt foncier sous les premiers Califes.　Geneva.　1886.

Brockelmann, C.　Geschichte der arabischen Litteratur.　2 vols.　Weimar.　1898.　(Not a real history, but a Catalogus Catalogorum.)

Browne, E. G.　A literary History of Persia from the earliest times until Firdawsi.　London.　1902.

Caetani, L.　Studi di Storia Orientale.　Vol. i.　Milan.　1911.

Codera, Fr.　Limites probables de la conquista arabe en la Corsillera pirenaica.　(BRAH. Vol. xlviii.　1906.　pp. 289–310.)

Gelder, H. D. v.　Moḥtar de valsche Profeet.　Leyden.　1888.

Goeje, M. J. de.　Mémoires sur la Conquête de la Syrie (Mémoires d'Histoire et de Géographie Orientales).　Vol. ii.　Leyden.　1900.

Goldziher, I.　Muhammedanische Studien.　2 vols.　Halle.　1888–90.　(Fundamental.)

Heyd, W.　Histoire du Commerce du Levant au Moyen Age.　Ed. Raynaud, Franç. Furcy.　2 vols.　Leipsic.　1885–6.

Kremer, A. v.　Culturgeschichte des Orients unter den Chalifen.　2 vols.　Vienna.　1875–7.　(To be used critically, but still unique.)

Lammens, Le P. Henri.　Études sur le Règne du Calife Omaiyade Mo'awia Ier.　(Mélanges de la Faculté Orientale, i, ii.)　Beirut.　1906–7.　(Also separately.　Important.)

—— Le Triumvirat d'Aboû Bakr, 'Omar et Aboû 'Obaida.　(Ib. iv, 113 ff.)　Beirut.　1910.

Lane Poole, Stanley. The Mohammedan Dynasties. Westminster. 1894. (Very useful, but not without mistakes.)

Le Strange, G. Palestine under the Moslems (650 to 1500). [A description of Syria and the Holy Land from medieval Arabian geographers.] 1890. (Palestine Exploration Fund.)

Miednikoff, N. A. Palestina ot zavoievasija ieia Arabami do krestovich pochodog, po arabskim istocnikam. 4 vols. St Petersburg. 1897–1907.

Muir, W. Annals of the early Caliphate from original sources. London. 1883.

Müller, A. Der Islam im Morgen- und Abendland. 2 vols. Berlin. 1885. (Standard work.)

Nöldeke, Th. Geschichte der Perser und Araber zur Zeit der Sassaniden. Aus der arabischen Chronik der Tabari übersetzt, etc. Leyden. 1879.

—— Die Ghassänischen Fürsten aus dem Hause Gafna's. Berlin. 1887.

Périer, Jean. Vie d'al-Hadjdjädj ibn Yousof d'après les sources Arabes. Paris. 1904.

Ranke, L. v. Weltgeschichte. v. *See Gen. Bibl.* vi. (Antiquated, but still interesting.)

Rothstein, G. Die Dynastie der Laḥmiden in al-Ḥira. Berlin. 1899.

Snouck Hurgronje, C. Mekka. Leyden. 1888. 2 vols. (Standard work.)

Vloten, G. van. Recherches sur la Domination arabe, le Chiitisme et les Croyances messianiques sous le Khalifat des Omayades. Verhandelingen der Koninklijke Akademie van Wetenschappen te Amsterdam. Afdeeling Letterkunde. Vol. i, 3. Amsterdam. 1894.

—— De Opkomst der Abbasiden in Chorasan. Leyden. 1890.

Weil, G. Geschichte der Chalifen. 5 vols. Mannheim and Stuttgart. 1846–62. (Antiquated, but still indispensable.)

Wellhausen, J. Das arabische Reich und sein Sturz. Berlin. 1902. (First critical history of Omaiyad period.)

—— Die Kämpfe der Araber mit den Romäern in der Zeit der Umaijaden. Nachr. v. d. kön. Gesellschaft d. Wissenschaften zu Göttingen. 1901. Heft 4.

—— Die religiös.-politischen Oppositionsparteien im alten Islam. Abh. der kön. Ges. d. Wiss. Göttingen, Phil.-hist. Kl. N. F. v, 2. Berlin. 1901.

—— Prolegomena zur ältesten Geschichte des Islams. (Skizzen und Vorarbeiten. vi.) Berlin. 1899.

Winckler, Hugo. Arabisch-Semitisch-Orientalisch-Kulturgeschichtlich-mythologische Untersuchung (Mitteilgn. Vorderasiat. Gesellschaft. 1901–4.) Berlin. (Fundamental for the historical conception of the Arab migration.)

Wüstenfeld, F. Vergleichungstabellen der Muhammedanischen und Christlichen Zeitrechnung. Leipsic. 1854.

(*b*) EGYPT.

Becker, C. H. Beiträge zur Geschichte Aegyptens unter dem Islam. Strasburg. 1902–3.

Brooks, E. W. On the chronology of the conquest of Egypt by the Saracens. BZ. 1895. (Important.)

Butler, Alfred J. The Arab conquest of Egypt and the last thirty years of the Roman Dominion. Oxford. 1902. (Valuable.)

Goeje, M. J. de. De Moḳauḳis van Egypte. Études dédiées à Leemans. Leyden. 1885.

Guest, A. R. The foundation of Fustat and the Khittahs of that Town. JRAS. Jan. 1907. London.

Karabaček, J. von. Der Moḳauḳis von Aegypten. Mitt. a. d. Samml. der Papyrus Erzherzog Rainer. 1887. Vol. i, pp. 1–11. (Misleading.)

Lane-Poole, S. A History of Egypt in the Middle Ages. London. 1901. (Accurate, but too short.)

Marcel, T. Égypte depuis la Conquête des Arabes jusqu'à la Domination Française. (Description de l'Égypte, État Moderne.) New edn. Paris. 1877. (Very accurate and still most valuable.)

Quatremère, Ét. Mémoires géographiques et historiques sur l'Égypte et sur quelques contrées voisines. 2 vols. Paris. 1811.

Wüstenfeld, F. Die Statthalter von Aegypten zur Zeit der Chalifen. Göttingen. 1875. (Résumé of sources, but no history.)

(c) NORTHERN AFRICA, SPAIN AND FRANCE.

Caudel, M. Les Premières Invasions Arabes dans l'Afrique du Nord. Paris. 1900. (Very useful; gives new sources.)

Codera, F. Estudios Criticos de Historia árabe española. (Coll. de estudios Árabes. VII.) Saragossa. 1903. (Important.)

—— Narbona, Terona y Barcelona bajo la dominación Musulmana (Anuari del Institut d'Estudis Catalans). Barcelona. 1909–10.

Dozy, R. Histoire des Musulmans d'Espagne, jusqu'à la Conquête de l'Andalousie par les Almoravides. 4 vols. Leyden. 1861. (Standard work.)

—— Recherches sur l'histoire et la littérature de l'Espagne pendant le moyen age. 3rd edn. 2 vols. Leyden and Paris. 1881. (Indispensable.)

Fournel, H. Les Berbers, Étude sur la Conquête de l'Afrique par les Arabes. 2 vols. Paris. 1875–81.

Keller, F. Der Einfall der Sarazenen in die Schweiz. Mitt. d. Antiqu. Ges. in Zürich. xx. Zürich. 1856. (To be used critically.)

Menéndez Pidal, J. Leyendas del ultimo rey Godo (Notas é investigaciones). New edn. Madrid. 1906.

Mercier. Histoire de l'Afrique Septentrionale (Berbérie) depuis les temps les plus reculés jusqu'à la conquête française. 3 vols. Paris, 1888. (Important.)

Reinaud, M. Invasions des Sarrazins en France. Paris. 1836. (Antiquated, but still valuable.)

Roth, W, Okba Ibn Nafi el-Fihri, der Eroberer Nordafrikas. Göttingen. 1859.

Saavedra, Ed. Estudio sobre la Invasion de los Arabes en Espana. Madrid. 1892. (Useful.)

Schwenkow, L. Die lateinisch geschriebenen Quellen zur Geschichte der Eroberung Spaniens durch die Araber. Göttingen. 1894. (Very important.)

Zotenberg, M. H. Invasions des Visigoths et des Arabes en France. Extrait du tome II de l'Histoire générale de Languedoc. Toulouse. 1876.

(d) SICILY AND SOUTHERN ITALY.

Amari, M. Storia dei Musulmani di Sicilia. 4 vols. Florence. 1854–68. (Standard work of prime importance.)

Bianchi-Giovini, A. Sulla dominazione degli Arabi in Italia. Milan. 1846. (Antiquated.)

Brooks, E. W. The Sicilian Expedition of Constantine IV. BZ. XVII.

Chalandon, F. Histoire de la domination normande en Italie et en Sicile. 2 vols. Paris. 1907.

Gay, Jules. L'Italie Méridionale et l'Empire Byzantin depuis l'Avènement de Basile I jusqu'à la prise de Bari par les Normands. Paris. 1904. (Valuable.)

Lokys, G. Die Kämpfe der Araber mit den Karolingern bis zum Tode Ludwigs II. Heidelberger Abh. zur mittleren und neueren Geschichte. Heidelberg. 1906. (Based upon Western sources, very accurate.)

Moscato, G. B. Cronaca dei Musulmani in Calabria, San Lucido. 1902.

Nallino, C. A. Di alcune epigrafi sepolcrali arabe trovate nell' Italia meridionale. (Miscellanea di archeologia, di storia e di filologia dedicata al prof. A. Salinas. Palermo. 1907. pp. 243–53; aggiunte, 417–20.)

Poupardin, R. Études sur l'histoire des principautés lombardes de l'Italie méridionale et de leurs rapports avec l'empire franç. (MA, 2. Ser. x, 1906, pp. 26, 245–74; xi, 1907, pp. 1–25.)

Wenrich, Joannes Georgius. Rerum ab Arabibus in Italia insulisque adjacentibus, Sicilia maxime, Sardinia atque Corsica gestarum commentarii. Leipsic. 1845.

CHAPTER XIII.

THE SUCCESSORS OF HERACLIUS.

1. SPECIAL BIBLIOGRAPHIES.

In Krumbacher's Gesch. d. byzantinischen Litteratur (*see Gen. Bibl.* vi), under each
author and at the end.
Also in Bury's edn. of Gibbon, vol. v, Appendix.
In connexion with the Monothelete controversy : RE³, s.v. Honorius I, Martin I,
Maximus Konfessor, Monotheleten.

2. ORIGINAL DOCUMENTS.

Acta Conciliorum, Mansi, vols. x–xii.   *See Gen. Bibl.* iv.

3. AUTHORITIES.

(*a*) CONTEMPORARY.

Acta S. Demetrii, in ASBoll., Oct. 4 (for the state of Macedonia).
Agatho diaconus.   Epilogus, in Act. Conc. 12, p. 189 (for the reign of Philippicus).
Bede.   Chronicon.   Ed. Mommsen, Th.   MGH, auct. ant. xiii (chron. min.).
Chronicon Maroniticum (Syr.).   Ed. Brooks, E. W., with transl. Latin by Chabot,
J. B.   CSCO.   Chron. Minora 2.   1904.
Epistolae paparum Honorii I, Joannis IV, Theodori, Martini I, Constantini I.
MPL 80, 87, 88.
Liber Pontificalis.   *See Gen. Bibl.* iv.
Liber de Rebus Armeniae.   MPG 127.
Maximus.   Opera.   2 vols.   MPG 90, 91 (including the Acta and the Vita ac
Certamen, the latter a later work).
Passio S. Martini.   MPL 87.
Sebeos.   Historia Heraclii (Arm.).   Ed. Patkanean, K.   St Petersburg.   1879.
French transl.   Macler, F.   Paris.   1904.

(*b*) LATER.

i. *Greek and Latin.*

Anastasius presbyter.   Contra Monophysitas sermo IVus.   In Mai, A.   Script. Vet.
Nova Coll. e Vaticanis codd. ed.   10 vols.   Rome.   1825–38.   Vol. vii, 193.
Cedrenus.   Synopsis Historiarum.   *See Gen. Bibl.* v.
Constantine Porphyrogenitus.   Opera.   *See Gen. Bibl.* v (for the themes, and date
of death of Sergius of Constantinople).
Continuationes Isidorianae Byzantia Arabica et Hispana.   Ed. Mommsen, Th., MGH,
auct. ant. xi.
Georgius Monachus.   Chronicon.   MPG 110 (with the interpolations).   Ed. De Boor, C.
Leipsic.   1904.
Leo Grammaticus (so-called).   Chronographia.   CSHB.
Nicephorus.   Opuscula historica.   Ed. De Boor, C.   Leipsic.   1880.
Παραστάσεις σύντομοι χρονικαί.   Ed. Preger, Th. (Script. Orig. CP, fasc. i).   Leipsic.
1901.
Theodosius Melitenus.   Chronographia.   Ed. Tafel, T. L. F.   Monumenta Saecularia.
Kön. Akad. d. Wissenschaften.   Munich.   1859.
Theophanes.   Chronographia.   *See Gen. Bibl.* v.
Zonaras.   Annales.   *See Gen. Bibl.* v.

ii. *Oriental.*

Balādhurī. Liber expugnationis regionum (Arab.). Ed. De Goeje, M. J. Leyden. 1863. Portions relating to Asia Minor transl. by Brooks, E. W., in JHS 18. 1898.

Chronicon anni 846 (Syr.). Ed. Brooks, E. W., with Latin transl. by Chabot, J. B. CSCO. Chron. Minora 2. 1904.

Dionysius (so-called). Chronicon (Syr.). Ed. and transl. French. Chabot, J. B. BHE 102. 1895. (A work of the year 775.)

Elijah of Nisibis. Opus chronologicum (Syr. and Arab.). Ed. and transl. Latin. Brooks, E. W., and Chabot, J. B. CSCO. 2 vols. 1910.

Ibn al-Athīr. Chronicon perfectissimum (Arab.). Ed. Tornberg, C. J. 14 vols. Leyden. 1851–71. Portions relating to Asia Minor not found in earlier writers transl. by Brooks, E. W., in JHS 18.

John the Catholic. Historia Armeniae (Arm.). Ed. Anon. Jerusalem. 1867. French Transl. Saint-Martin, J. Paris. 1841.

John of Nikiu. Chronicon (Aeth.). Ed. and transl. French. Zotenberg, M. H., in Notices et extraits des MSS. de la Bibl. Nat. 24. Paris. 1883. Also a more faithful translation with notes by the same in JA, 7ᵉ sér. tom. x, p. 451; xii, p. 245; xiii, p. 291. 1877–9. (Transl. of a lost Arabic version of a lost Coptic text.)

Kitāb al-ʿUyūn (Arab.). Ed. De Goeje, M. J., in Fragm. Historicorum Arabicorum 1. Leyden. 1871. Portions relating to Asia Minor not found in earlier writers transl. by Brooks, E. W., in JHS 18, 19. 1898–9.

Leontius. Historia Chalifarum (Arm.). Ed. Ezean, K. St Petersburg. 1887. French transl. Shahnazarean, V. Paris. 1856. Russian transl. Patkanean, K. St Petersburg. 1862.

Makrīzī. Narratio de exped. a Graecis Francisque adv. Dimyatham ab A.C. 708 ad 1222 susceptis (Arab.). Ed. and transl. Latin. Hamaker, H. A. Amsterdam. 1824.

Michael the Syrian. Chronicon (Syr.). Ed. and transl. French. Chabot, J. B. 3 vols. Paris. 1899–1910.

Moses of Kalankaitukh. Historia Albaniae (Arm.). Ed. Shahnazarean, V. Paris. 1860. Ed. Emin. Moscow. 1860. Russian transl. Patkanean, K. St Petersburg. 1861.

Stephen (Asolik) of Taron. Historia Armeniae (Arm.). Ed. Malkhasean, S. St Petersburg. 1885. German transl. Gelzer, H., and Burckhardt, A. Leipsic. 1907.

Ṭabarī. Annales (Arab.). Ed. De Goeje, M. J., etc. 15 vols. Leyden. 1879–1901. Portions relating to Asia Minor translated by Brooks, E. W., in JHS 18. Portions relating to the Sassanid Empire translated into German by Nöldeke, T., Gesch. d. Perser u. Araber. Leyden. 1879.

Yaʿḳūbī (Ibn Wāḍiḥ). Historiae (Arab.). Ed. Houtsma, M. Th. 2 vols. Leyden. 1883. Portions relating to Asia Minor translated by Brooks, E. W., in JHS 18.

4. MODERN WORKS.

(a) GENERAL.

Bury. Later Roman Empire. *See Gen. Bibl.* vi.

DCB, esp. Stokes, G. T. Person of Christ. (Sect. Monotheletism.)

Dulaurier, J. P. L. F. E. Recherches sur la chronologie arménienne. (Bibl. Hist. Arm. pt. i.) Paris. 1859.

Gelzer. Byzant. Geschichte. *See Gen. Bibl.* vi.

Hefele, C. J. Conciliengeschichte. *See Gen. Bibl.* vi.

Lampros, S. P. Ἱστορία τῆς Ἑλλάδος. 3 vols. Athens. 1886–92.

Lebeau, Ch. Histoire du Bas-Empire. 29 vols. Paris. 1757–1817. 2nd edn. Ed. Saint-Martin, J. 21 vols. 1824–36.

Müller, A. Der Islam im Morgen- u. Abendland. 2 vols. (Oncken. Haupt-Abth. ii, Thl. 4.) *See Gen. Bibl.* vi.

Muralt, E. von. Essai de chronographie byzantine...de 395 à 1057. St Petersburg. 1855.

Paparrhegopoulos, K. Ἱστορία τοῦ Ἑλληνικοῦ Ἔθνους. Athens. 1853. 4th edn. Ed. Karolides, P. 5 vols. 1902–3.

Pargoire, J. L'église byzantine. *See Gen. Bibl.* vi.

Ramsay, Sir W. M. The Historical Geography of Asia Minor. RGS. Suppl. Papers, 4. London. 1890.

Ranke, L. von. Weltgeschichte. *See Gen. Bibl.* vi.

RE³. *See Gen. Bibl.* i.

    esp. Krüger, G.   Martin I.
                      Monotheleten.
       Seeberg, R.   Maximus Konfessor.
       Gelzer, H.   Armenien.

Sathas, K. N. Μεσαιωνικὴ Βιβλιοθήκη. 3 vols. Venice. 1872–3 (for the establishment of the Mardaites in the Empire).

Weil, G. Geschichte der Chalifen. 5 vols. Mannheim. 1846–62.

(b) On Authorities.

Acta Demetrii :

    Gelzer, H. Die Genesis d. byzantinischen Themenverfassung. Abh. d. Kön.-Sächs. Ges. d. Wissenschaften, Phil.-hist. Kl. 1899. No. 5.

    Pernice, H. Sulla data del libro ii dei Mirac. S. Dem. Mart. Bessarione, 2ᵉ ser. vol. ii, fasc. lxv, p. 181. 1902.

Arabic authors :

    Brockelmann, C. Gesch. d. arab. Litteratur. 2 vols. and index. Berlin. 1898–1902.

    De Goeje, M. J., and Thatcher, G. W., in EncBr., 11th edn., s.v. Arabia.

Chronicon anni 846 :

    Brooks, E. W. A Syriac Chronicle of the year 846. Z. d. Deutschen Morgenl. Gesellsch. 1897, p. 569.

    —— The sources of Theophanes and the Syriac chroniclers. BZ. 1906. p. 578.

Chronicon Maroniticum :

    Brooks, E. W. The sources of Theophanes, etc. (*see above*).

    Nöldeke, Th. Zur Gesch. d. Araber im 1 Jahrhundert der Hígra aus syrischen Quellen. ZDMG. 1875. p. 82.

"Dionysius" :

    Nau, F. La 4ᵐᵉ partie de la Chron. de D. de T. (review of M. Chabot's edn). Bulletin Critique, 1896, p. 121.

    —— Nouvelle étude sur la Chron. attribuée à D. de T. Ibid., p. 464.

    —— Les auteurs des chron. attr. à D. de T. et à Josué le Stylite. Bull. Crit., 1897, p. 54.

    Nöldeke, Th. Chron. de Denys de Tellmahré (review of M. Chabot's edn). Vienna Oriental Journal, 1896, p. 160.

Elijah of Nisibis :

    Baethgen, F. Fragm. syr. u. arab. Historiker. Abh. für die Kunde des Morgenlandes herausg. v. d. Deutschen Morgenl. Gesellsch. 8. Leipsic. 1884.

Leo, Theodosius, Cedrenus, and the interpolator of George :
De Boor, C.   Die Chronik der Logotheten.   BZ. 1897. p. 233.
Patzig, E.   Leo Grammaticus u. seine Sippe.   BZ." 1894. p. 470.
Serruys, D.   Recherches sur l'Épitomé.   BZ. 1907. p. 1.
Michael and Theophanes:
Brooks, E. W.   The Chronology of Theophanes (607–775).   BZ. 1899. p. 82.
—— The Sources of Theophanes, etc. (*see* under Chron. anni 846).
Nicephorus:
Burckhardt, A.   Der Londoner Codex d. Breviarium des Nik. Patriarcha.
BZ. 1896. p. 465.
Syriac authors:
Duval, R.   La Littérature Syriaque.   (Bibl. de l'enseignement de l'hist. eccl.)
Paris. 1899. 3rd edn. 1907.

(*c*) Monographs and Special Treatises.

Anderson, J. G. C.   The road-system of eastern Asia Minor.   JHS. 1897. p. 22
(With map.)
Brooks, E. W.   Arabic lists of the Byzantine themes.   JHS. 1901. p. 67.   (With
references to Arabic authorities which cannot be given above.)
—— On the lists of the patriarchs of Constantinople from 638 to 715.   BZ. 1897.
p. 33.   (With references to several catalogues of patriarchs which cannot be
included among the authorities above.)
—— The locality of the battle of Sebastopolis.   BZ. 1909. p. 154.
—— The London catalogue of patriarchs of Constantinople.   BZ. 1898. p. 32.
(With text.)
—— The Sicilian expedition of Constantine IV.   BZ. 1908. p. 455.
Bury, J. B.   The naval policy of the Roman Empire in relation to the Western
provinces from the seventh to the ninth century.   (Centenario della nascità
di M. Amari, 2.)   Palermo. 1910.
—— The imperial administrative system in the ninth century, with a revised text of
the Kletorologion of Philotheos. (Brit. Acad. Suppl. Papers, i.) London. 1911.
Diehl, Ch.   L'origine des thèmes dans l'empire byzantin.   (Études d'hist. du
moyen âge déd. à G. Monod.)   Paris. 1896.
Gelzer, H.   Die Genesis d. byz. Themenverfassung.   Abh. d. kön.-Sächs. Ges. d.
Wissenschaften, Phil.-hist. Kl., 1899, No. 5.
Ghazarian, M.   Armenien unter der arabischen Herrschaft bis zur Entstehung des
Bagratidenreiches.   Z. f. arm. Philologie. 1903. p. 149.
Görres, F.   Justinian II u. d. römische Papsttum.   BZ. 1908. p. 432.
Grégoire, H.   La bataille de Sébastopolis.   BZ. 1910. p. 259.   (Correction of art.
by Brooks, *see above.*)
Kaestner, J.   De imperio Constantini III (641–68).   Leipsic. 1907.   (The fullest
account of the reign.)
Kulakovskiy, Y.   K voprosu ob imeni i istorii themy "Opsikiy."   VV, 1904, p. 49.
Michael, E.   Wann ist Papst Martin I bei seiner Exilierung nach Konstantinopel
gekommen?   Z. f. kath. Theol. 1892. p. 375.
Owsepian, G.   Die Entstehungsgesch. d. Monotheletismus nach ihren Quellen
geprüft u. dargestellt.   Leipsic. 1897.
Schenk, K.   Kaiser Leon III.   Halle. 1880.   (With a useful summary of the
preceding period.)
Wellhausen, J.   Die Kämpfe d. Araber mit den Romäern in d. Zeit d. Umaijaiden.
Nachr. v. d. kön. Ges. d. Wissenschaften zu Göttingen, Phil.-hist. Kl.
1901. p. 414.

CHAPTER XIV.

EXPANSION OF THE SLAVS.

I. SPECIAL BIBLIOGRAPHIES.

Bibliografiya, Русская историческая, 1855 ff.   St Petersburg.   1861 ff.
Kołodziejczyk, E.   Bibliografia słowianoznawstwa polskiego.   Cracow.   1911.
Krumbacher, K.   Geschichte der byzantinischen Literatur von Justinian bis zum Ende des oströmischen Reiches.   2nd edition.   Munich.   1897.
Mezhov, V. I.   Указатель книгъ и статей по русской и всеобщей исторіи...за 1800–1854.   Bibliographie des livres et articles russes d'histoire et sciences auxiliaires de 1800–54.   St Petersburg.   1892–3.
Niederle, L.   Slovanské Starožitnosti.   Prague.   1902 ff. (contains for each special subject an exhaustive list of references).
Zíbrt, Č.   Bibliografie české historie.   Prague.   1900 ff.

II. ANCIENT AND MEDIEVAL AUTHORITIES.

Adam of Bremen.   Gesta pontificum Hammenburgensium.   Ed. by Lappenberg, J. M.   1846.   In MGH, SS. vii.
Agathias scholasticus.   De imperio Justiniani, ed. Niebuhr, B. G.   Bonn.   1828. CSHB.   Ed. Dindorf, L. in Historici graeci minores.   Vol. ii.   Leipsic.   1871.
Agnellus abbot of Ravenna.   Liber pontificalis ecclesiae Ravennatis edited by Holder-Egger, O.   1878 in MGH, SS. Rer. Langob.
Alfred the Great.   A description of Europe, and the voyages of Ohthere and Wulfstan, by Bosworth, J.   London.   1855.
Anastasius.   Historia tripartita.   Ed. Boor, C. de.   Leipsic.   1885.
Annales Altahenses, Fuldenses, Laureshamenses, Mettenses, Sangallenses, etc., MGH.   Script. i.
Anonymous Arabian Geographer of the second quarter of the 9th century.   Account of the Northern lands (Russia), excerpted by Bekrī, Gardēzī, Ibn Rusta, Persian Excerpts, Medieval Mahomedan Authorities, *see below*.
Anonymus de Conversione Bagoariorum et Carantanorum.   Ed. Wattenbach. 1854, MGH.   Script. xi.   Ed. Ginzel, J. A., Geschichte der Slawenapostel Cyrill und Method.   Vienna.   1861.   pp. 46 ff.
Anonymus Geographus Bavarus, Descriptio pagorum Slavorum, ed. Zeuss, Die Deutschen, p. 600.   Ed. Schafarik, Slaw. Alterthümer, ii, p. 673.   Ed. Králiček, A.   Der sogenannte bairische Geograph und Mähren (in Z. des Vereins f. d. Gesch. Mährens.   Brünn.   1898, p. 216).   Photographic facsimile in Schiemann, T.   Russland, Polen u. Lievland, i, p. 28 f.
Anonymus Ravennas, Cosmographia.   Ed. Pinder, M. and Parthley, G.   Berlin. 1860.
al Bekrī, "Book of the Kingdoms and Routes" [Excerpts from the Arabian

Geographer]. Ed. and transl. into French by Defrémery, Ch., Fragments de géographes et historiens arabes et persans, relatifs aux anciens peuples du Caucase et de la Russie méridionale, in JA. 4th ser. xiii. 1849. pp. 460-77. Ed. and transl. (Russian) by Kunik, A. and Rosen, Baron W., Извѣстія ал-Векри и другихъ авторовъ о Руси и Славянахъ. St Petersburg. 1878 (Suppl. 2 to Zapiski of the Imp. Acad. (Имп. Академіи Наукъ) xxxii, 1879) and 1903. 2 vols.

Caesarius of Nazianzus, Questions and Answers, MPG. xxxviii. 1862. Also: Müllenhoff, Deutsche Altertumskunde ii 34 f., 367 f. Peisker, Beziehungen, p. 125 [311] f. (on the Danubian Slavs).

Cassiodorus, Variarum epistolarum libri xii. Ed. Mommsen, Th. MGH. Auct. ant. xii.

Cedrenus, Georgius. Historiarum compendium. Ed. Bekker, J. 2 vols. Bonn. 1838-9. CSHB.

Chronica minora saec. iv-vii. Ed. Mommsen, Th. MGH, auct. ant. xi.

Chronicon Paschale. Ed. Dindorf, L. 2 vols. CSHB. 1832.

Constantinus Porphyrogenitus. De thematibus et De administrando imperio. Ed. Bekker, J. CSHB. 1840.

—— Excerpta de legationibus. Ed. Boor, C. de. Berlin. 1903.

Cosmas, canon of Prague. Chronicae Bohemorum libri iii. Ed. Köpke, R. MGH. Script. ix. 1851. p. 35 f. Ed. Emler, J. in Fontes Rerum Bohemicarum. Vol. ii. Prague. 1874. pp. 10-15 (on the Election of the Peasant Přemysl as Prince).

Diocleas Presbyter. Regnum Slavorum. Ed. Črnčić, J. Popa Dukljanina ljetopis....Kraljevica. 1874.

Documenta Historiae Chrvaticae periodum antiquam illustrantia. Ed. Rački, F. Agram. 1877. (Monumenta spectantia historiam Slavorum Meridionalium. Vol. vii.)

Doomsday books ("Urbar") of various manors of Styria and Carniola are mentioned in Milkowicz, Beiträge, Dopsch, Peisker, Sozial- u. Wirtschaftsverfassung, *see below*, p. 782.

Einhardi Vita Karoli Magni Imperatoris. Ed. Waitz. *See Gen. Bibl. v.*

Evagrius. *See Gen. Bibl. v.*

Fredegarius. *See Gen. Bibl. v.*

Gardēzī. Excerpts from the Arabian Geographer. Ed. and transl. into Magyar by Kuun, G. count of, in A Magyar Honfoglalás Kútföi. Budapest. 1900. p. 137 ff. Ed. with Russian translation by Barthold, W., Отчетъ о поѣздкѣ въ среднюю Азію, in Mém. de l'Acad. Imp. des Sciences. St Petersburg. 8th ser. i. 1897.

Gradivo za zgodovino Slovencev v srednjem veku. Ed. Kos, F. Laibach (Lyublyana). 1902 ff.

Gregory the Great, Pope, Epistolae. Ed. Hartmann, L. M. 1887-99. MGH. Epist. i, ii.

Helmold. Chronica Slavorum. Ed. Lappenberg, J. M. and Weiland, L. 1869. MGH. Script. xxi. Ed. Schmeidler, B. Hanover. 1909. (Script. Rer. Germ.)

Herbord. Vita Ottonis episcopi Bambergensis. Ed. Köpke, R. 1868. MGH. xx.

Herodotus. Ed. Sayce, A. H. (Bks. i-iii) and Macan, R. W. London. 1883, 1895-1908. (And other edns.) Transl. Macaulay, G. C. 2 vols. London. 1890. Rawlinson, G. (for notes). London. 1858-60. 4th edn. 1880. Commentary, etc. How, W. W. and Wells, J. 2 vols. Oxford. 1912.

Historia miscella. Ed. Droysen, J. G. 1879. MGH, auct. ant. ii.

Ibn Faḍlān. Ibn Foszlan's und anderer Araber Berichte über die Russen älterer Zeit. Ed. and transl. Frähn, C. M. St Petersburg. 1823. Jacut's Geographisches Wörterbuch. Ed. Wüstenfeld, F. Vol. i. Leipsic. 1866.

Ibn Rusta (or Rosteh, Dasta). "Book of Precious Jewels." (Excerpts from the Arabian Geographer.) Ed. de Goeje, Bibliotheca Geographorum Arabicorum. VII. Lugduni Bat. 1892. Ed. with notes and a Russian translation by Chwolson, D. Извѣстія о Хозарахъ...Ибн Даста. St Petersburg. 1869.

Ibrāhīm ibn Ia'qūb. Reisebericht über die Slawenlande a.d.J. 965. Ed. and comm. by Westberg, F. in Mém. Acad. Imp. des Sciences. St Petersburg. 8th series. Tome III, No. 4. 1898.

Inscriptions of the Bulgar Khans Omortag and Malamer, in Izvyestiya of the Russian Archaeol. Institute in Constantinople (Русскаго Археол. Института). x. Sofia. 1905.

John, abbot of Biclaro. Johannis abbatis monasterii Biclarensis Chronica. Ed. Mommsen, Th. MGH, auct. ant. XI. (Chronica minora II.)

John, abbot of Viktring. Johannis abbatis Victoriensis liber certarum historiarum. Ed. Schneider, F. I. Hanover. 1909. p. 290 ff. (Script. Rer. German.) On Carinthian Peasant Prince.

John, bishop of Ephesus. The third part of the Ecclesiastical History. Transl. Payne Smith. Oxford. 1860. Transl. German by Schönfelder, J. M. Munich. 1862.

Jordanes. De Getharum sive Gothorum origine et rebus gestis. Ed. Mommsen, Th. MGH. Auct. ant. v, pt. II. 1832.

Liber predialis vrborie ecclesie Salzburgensis in Rayn et Lihtenwalde A.D. 1309. In Peisker, Soc.- u. Wirtschaftsverfassung. 1909. *See* p. 782, *below.*

Malalas, Johannes. Chronographia. Ed. Dindorf, L. Bonn. 1831. CSHB.

Marco Polo. The Book of Ser Marco Polo... Yule, H. 2 vols. London. 1871. 2nd edition. 1874. 3rd edition. 1903.

—— Italian version by Ramusio, G. B., Navigationi e viaggi. Venice. 1559. Vol. II. Engl. transl. London. 1625.

Martinus Gallus. Chronicon, in Monumenta Poloniae historica. Ed. Bielowski, A. Vol. I. Lemberg. 1864.

Masudī. Maçoudi, "Les Prairies d'or." Text and French transl. by Barbier de Maynard. Paris. 1861-9. Ed. Charmoy, Mém. Acad. Imp. des Sciences. St Petersburg. 6th ser. II. 1834. The passages relating to the Slavs transl. into German by Marquart, J. Streifzüge. p. 102 f.

"Mauricius." Arriani Tactica et Mauricii Artis militaris libri... Ed. Scheffer, J. Upsala. 1664. pp. 272-90. l. XI, c. 5 (on the Slavs). Reprint by Šafařík, Starožitnosti, II, p. 694 ff. Schafarik, Alterthümer, II, p. 662 ff.

Medieval Mahomedan Authorities on the Peoples of Eastern Europe. Edited and translated into Russian by Harkavy, A. J. Сказанія мусульманскихъ писателей о Славянахъ и Русскихъ. St Petersburg. 1870.

Memoriae Populorum olim ad Danubium, Pontum Euxinum...et inde magis ad Septentriones incolentium, a Scriptoribus Historiae Byzantinae erutae et digestae *by* Stritter, J. G. 4 vols. St Petersburg. 1771-9.

Menander Protector. Historiarum libri VIII. Ed. Müller, C. *See Gen. Bibl.* IV. Ed. Dindorf, L., Hist. Gr. Min. II. Leipsic. 1871.

Michael the Great. Chronique de Michel le Syrien, patriarche jacobite d'Antioche. Ed. et traduite en français par Chabot, J. B. Vol. I. Paris. 1899. Cf. Marquart, J. Streifzüge. p. 480 f.

Miracula Sti Demetrii, in Acta Sanctorum. (Oct.) Vol. IV. Ed. 1866.

Moses of Khorene. Moïse de Corène, Géographie d'après Ptolémée. Texte arménienne trad. en français par Soucry, A. Venice. 1831.

"Nestor." Лѣтопись по Ипатскому списку. St Petersburg. 1871. New edn. 1908.

—— Лѣтопись по Лаврентьевскому списку. St Petersburg. 1879. New edn. 1897.

"Nestor." Transl. (German) by Schlözer, A. L. Несторъ. Russische Annalen. 5 vols. Göttingen. 1802–9.

—— Transl. (French) by Léger, L. Chronique dite de Nestor... Paris. 1884. (Publications de l'école des langues orient. vivantes.)

Ottokars Österreichische Reimchronik. Ed. Seemüller, J. Hanover. 1890. MGH. Deutsche Chroniken. v, p. 265 f. (On Carinthian Peasant Prince.)

Paulus Diaconus. Historia Langobardorum. Ed. Waitz, G. Hanover. 1878. (Script. Rer. Germ.)

Persian Excerpts of the Xth century from the Arabian geographer. Ed. and transl. into Russian by Tumanskii, in Zapiski of the Oriental Series of the Imp. Archaeolog. Society (Восточ. Отдѣл. Имп. Археол. Общества). x. St Petersburg. 1897. p. 121 ff.

Pravda. Русская Правда. Ed. Sergyeevich, V. St Petersburg. 1904.

Priscus. Fragmenta. Ed. Boor, C. de. In Excerpta Historica iussu Imp. Constantini Porph. confecta. Vol. i. Excerpta de legationibus. Pt 2. Berlin. 1903. p. 575 ff.

Procopius of Caesarea. De bello Gothico. Ed. Dindorf, W. Bonn. 1833. (Graece et latine), CSHB. Ed. Comparetti, D. Rome. 1895. Ed. Haury, J. Leipsic. 1905. (Lib. iii, cap. 14, Characterization of the Slavs.)

Ptolemy. Claudius Ptolemaeus, Geographia. Ed. Nobbe, C. F. A. 3 vols. Leipsic. 1843–5. Ed. Müller, C. 2 vols. Paris. 1883 and 1901.

Pulkawa of Radenin, Přibík. Chronicon Bohemiae. Ed. Emler, J. and Gebauer, J., in Fontes Rerum Bohemicarum. Vol. v. Prague. 1893. (Election of the Peasant Přemysl as Prince.)

Rationarium Stirie A.D. 1265–7. Ed. Rauch, A., in Script. Rer. Austriacarum, Vol. ii. Vienna. 1793. p. 114 ff. Ed. Dopsch, A., in Gesamturbare, die landesfürstlichen, der Steiermark (Urbare, Österreichische, part i. Vol. ii). Vienna. 1910.

Regino. Chronicon. Ed. Kurze, F. Hanover. 1890. (Script. Rer. Germ.)

Svod zákonův slovanských... Ed. Jireček, H. Prague. 1880.

Tabula Peutingeriana. Ed. Miller, K. Die Weltkarte des Castorius, genannt die Peutingerische Tafel. Ravensburg. 1888.

Tacitus, C. Cornelius. De Germania. Ed. Furneaux, H. Oxford. 1893. (Cap. 46, on the Venedi.)

Theophanes Confessor. Chronographia. Ed. Boor, C. de. Leipsic. 1883–5.

—— continuatus. Ed. Bekker, J. Bonn. 1838. CSHB.

Theophylactus Simocattes. Historiae. Ed. Boor, C. de. Leipsic. 1887.

Thietmar, bishop of Merseburg. Chronicon. Ed. Kurze, F. Hanover. 1889. (Script. Rer. Germ.)

Thomas, archdeacon of Spalato. Historia pontificum Salonitanorum. Ed. Heinemann, L. 1892. MGH. Script. xxix. Ed. Rački, in Monumenta spect. historiam Slavorum meridionalium. Tom. xxvi. Agram (Zagreb). 1894.

Vincentius Kadłubek. Chronicon Polonorum, in Monumenta Poloniae historica. Ed. by Bielowski, A. Vol. ii. Lemberg. 1872.

Widukind. Rerum gestarum Saxonicarum libri. Ed. Waitz, G. Hanover. 1882. (Script. Rer. Germ.)

William, archbishop of Tyrus. Guillelmi Tyrensis archiepiscopi Historia rerum transmarinarum. ii 17; xx 4. MPL. cci. (On the Serbs.)

Zakonik Стефана Душана. Ed. Novaković, S. 2nd edn. Belgrade. 1898.

III.　MODERN WORKS.

a.　GENERAL.

Archiv für slavische Philologie.　Ed. Jagić, V.　Berlin.　1876 ff.

Balzer, O.　O zadrudze słowiańskiej.　Uwagi i polemika.　Reprint of Kwartalnik Historyczny.　xiii.　1899.

—— Rewizya teoryi o pierwotnem osadnictwie w Polsce.　Reprint of Kwartalnik Historyczny.　xii.　1898.

Below, G. von.　Das kurze Leben einer viel genannten Theorie.　(Über die Lehre vom Ureigentum.)　In Beilage zur "Allgem. Zeitung."　Munich.　1903.　No. 11 and 12.　(On Zadruga and Mir.)

Berneker, E.　Slavisches etymologisches Wörterbuch.　Heidelberg.　1908 ff.　Cf. Vasmer, M., Kritisches und Antikritisches zur neueren slavischen Etymologie, in Rocznik Slawistyczny.　iii.　Cracow.　1910.

Bonnell, E.　Beiträge zur Alterthumskunde Russlands...hauptsächlich aus den Berichten der griechischen und lateinischen Schriftsteller zusammengestellt. St Petersburg.　1897.

Braun, F.　Разысканія въ области готославянскихъ отношеній.　i.　St Petersburg.　1899.

Brückner, A.　Historya a filologia, in Przegląd Historyczny.　iv.　Warsaw.　1907. p. 265 ff.

—— Słowiane i Niemcy, in Biblioteka Warszawska.　1900.

—— Ursitze der Slaven und Deutschen, in Archiv für slavische Philologie.　xxii. 1900.　p. 237 ff.

Budilovich, A. S.　Первобытние Славяне въ ихъ языкѣ, бытѣ и понятіяхъ по даннымъ лексикальнымъ.　Kiev.　1878–82.

Cohn, G.　Gemeinderschaft und Hausgenossenschaft.　Stuttgart.　1898.　Reprint of Z. für vergleichende Rechtswissenschaft.　Vol. xiii.

Florinskii, T. D.　Славянское племя.　Kiev.　1907.　(With 2 maps.　Statistics of present day Slavdom.)

Florinskii, V. M.　Первобытние Славяне по памятникамъ ихъ доисторической жизни.

Florschütz, J.　Utjecaji Turkotatara i Germana na Slavene.　Reprint of Vjesnik, Nastavni, tom. xiv.　Agram.　1906.

Fustel de Coulanges, N. D.　Le problème des origines de la propriété foncière, in RQH.　1889.　Transl. Ashley, W. J.　The Origin of Property in Land. London.　1891.

Hildebrand, R.　Recht und Sitte auf den verschiedenen wirtschaftlichen Kulturstufen.　Jena.　1896.　2nd recast edn.　1907.

Hilferding, A.　Древнейшій періодъ исторіи Славянъ, in Vyestnik Evropy. St Petersburg.　1868.　iv.

Hirt, H.　Die Indogermanen, ihre Verbreitung, Urheimat und Kultur.　2 vols. Strassburg.　1905–7.

Jagić, V.　Verwandtschaftsverhältnisse innerhalb der slavischen Sprachen.　Eine einheitliche slavische Ursprache? (in Archiv für slavische Philologie.　Vol. xix, xx, xxii).　Berlin.　1897 f., 1900.

Janko, J.　Über Berührungen der alten Slawen mit Turkotataren und Germanen vom sprachwissenschaftlichen Standpunkte in "Wörter und Sachen," tom. i. Heidelberg.　1909.

—— O stycích starých Slovanů s Turkotatary a Germány s hlediska jazykozpytného, in Věstník České Akademie.　xvii.　Prague.　1908.

Kadlec, K. Rodinný nedíl čili zádruha v právu slovanském. Prague. 1898.
—— K "Slovu o zádruze." Kritická úvaha o nové theorii J. Peiskera. Prague. 1900. Reprint of Sborník, Národopisný. VI.
—— Rodinný nedíl ve světle dat srovnávacích dějin právních. Brünn (Brno). 1901.
Kętrzyński, W. Germania wielka i Sarmacya nadwiślańska wedlug Kl. Ptolomeusza. Cracow. 1901.
Kossina, G. Die indogermanische Frage archäologisch beantwortet, in Z. für Ethnologie. 1902.
Kovalevsky, M. Marriage among the early Slavs, in Folklore. London. 1890. Dec.
Krček, F. Teorya Peiskera o niewoli prasłowiańskiej w świetle krytyki. Lemberg (Lwów). 1909. Reprint of Kwartalnik Historyczny. XXII.
Krek, G. Einleitung in die slavische Literaturgeschichte. 2nd edn. Graz. 1887.
Lefèvre, A. Germains et Slaves, origines et croyances. Paris. 1903.
Leger, L. La mythologie slave. Paris. 1901.
Lelewel, J. Narody na ziemiach sławiańskich. Posen (Poznań). 1853.
Máchal, J. Bájesloví slovanské. Prague. 1907.
Maciejowski, W. A. Historya prawodawstw słowiańskich. 4 vols. Warsaw. 1832–5. 2nd edition. 1856–68. Transl. German by Buss, F. J. and Nawrocki, M. Slavische Rechtsgeschichte. Stuttgart. 1835–9.
Maretić, T. Slaveni u davnini. Agram. 1889.
Marquart, J. Osteuropäische und ostasiatische Streifzüge. Leipsic. 1903.
Meitzen, A. Siedelung und Agrarwesen der West- und Ostgermanen, der Kelten, Römer, Finnen und Slawen. 3 vols. and Atlas. Berlin. 1895.
Miklosich, F. Etymologisches Wörterbuch der slavischen Sprachen. Vienna. 1886.
Morfill, W. R. Slavonic Literature. London. 1883.
Much, R. Deutsche Stammeskunde. Leipsic. 1900 (in Sammlung Göschen).
—— Die Heimat der Indogermanen im Lichte der urgeschichtlichen Forschung. Berlin. 1902.
Müllenhoff, K. Deutsche Alterthumskunde. 4 vols. Berlin. 1870–98. New and improved edition by Roediger, M. 1890 ff.
Muralt, E. de. Essai de Chronographie Byzantine pour servir à l'examen des annales du Bas-Empire et particulièrement des chronographes slavons de 395–1057. St Petersburg and Leipsic. 1855.
Niederle, L. Обозрѣніе современнаго Славянства. St Petersburg. 1909, in Enciklopediya of Slavonic philology (Славянской Филологіи), ed. Jagić, V. Vol. II. With a map (Statistics of present day Slavdom).
—— O původu Slovanů. Prague. 1896.
—— J. Peiskers neue Grundlagen der slavischen Altertumskunde, in Archiv für slavische Philologie. Vol. XXXI. 1910.
—— Slovanské Starožitnosti. Prague. 1902 ff. Cf. review of Murko, M. in Časopis za zgodovino in narodopisje. Marburg a. Dr. (Maribor). 1906. p. 214 ff.
Peisker, J. Forschungen zur Sozial- und Wirtschaftsgeschichte der Slawen. Graz. 1896–1900 (I. Zur Geschichte des slawischen Pfluges. II. Die altslowenische Župa. III. Die serbische Zadruga). Reprint of Z. für Sozial- u. Wirtschaftsgesch. v and VII.
—— Neue Forschungen zur Sozial- und Wirtschaftsgeschichte der Slawen. I. Die älteren Beziehungen der Slawen zu Turkotataren und Germanen und ihre sozialgeschichtliche Bedeutung. Stuttgart. 1905. Reprint of Viert. f. Sozialu. Wirtschaftsgesch. III.
Pekař, J. K sporu o zádruhu staroslovanskou, in Časopis, Český Historický, tom. VI. Prague. 1900.

Perwolf, J. Славяне, ихъ взаимныя отношенія и связи. Warsaw. 1886.

—— Slavische Völkernamen, in Archiv f. slavische Philologie. vii, viii. Berlin. 1884, 1885.

Pogodin, A. Изъ исторіи славянскихъ передвиженій. St Petersburg. 1901. Cf. Jagić, in Archiv f. slav. Philol. xxiii. 1901. p. 610 ff.

Pypin, A. N. and Spasowicz, V. D. Исторія славянскихъ литературъ. 2nd edition. 2 vols. St Petersburg. 1879–80. German transl. by Pech, T. Geschichte des slavischen Literaturen. Leipsic. 1880–4. French Transl. by Denis, E., Histoire des littératures slaves. i. Boulgares, Serbo-Croates, Yougo-Russes. Paris. 1881.

Rachfall, F. Zur Entstehung des Grundeigentums bei den Slaven, in Jahrb. für Nationalökonomie und Statistik, vol. lxxiv. 1900. p. 202 ff.

Rhamm, K. Ethnographische Beiträge zur germanisch-slawischen Altertumskunde. 3 vols. Brunswick. 1905–8.

Rostafiński, J. O pierwotnych siedzibach i gospodarstwie Słowian w przedhistorycznych czasach, reprint of Sprawozdania Akad. Um. Cracow. 1908. French transl. Les demeures primitives des Slaves et leur économie rurale dans les temps préhistoriques, in Bulletin internat. de l'Acad. des Sciences. Cracow. 1908. With map.

Šafařík, P. J. Slovanské Starožitnosti. Prague. 1837. 2nd edition by Jireček, J. 1862–3. 2 vols. German transl. by Mosig von Aehrenfeld : Schafarik, P. J., Slawische Alterthümer. Leipsic. 1843–4. 2 vols.

—— Über die Abkunft der Slawen. Ofen. 1828.

Schachmatov, A. See Shakhmatov, A.

Schafarik, P. J. See Šafařík, P. J.

Schrader, O. Reallexikon der indogermanischen Altertumskunde. Strasburg. 1901.

Shakhmatov, A. Къ вопросу о финско-келтьскихъ и финско-славянскихъ отношеніяхъ, in Izvyestiya (Bulletin) of the Imp. Acad. St Petersburg. 1911. Nos. 9 and 10.

—— Zu den ältesten slavisch-keltischen Beziehungen. Reprint of Archiv für slavische Philologie, vol. xxxiii. 1911.

Sobyestianskii, J. M. Ученія о національныхъ особенностяхъ характера и юридическаго быта древнихъ Славянъ. Kharkov. 1892.

Surowiecki, W. Siedzenie początku narodów słowiańskich. Warsaw. 1824.

Tomaschek, W. Kritik der ältesten Nachrichten über den skythischen Norden. SKAW. 1888. Phil.-hist. Sect. cxvi.

Vasmer, M. Грекославянскіе этюды. i–iii. In Izvyestiya of the Russian Lang. Sect. of the Imp. Acad. (Отдѣл. Русск. Языка…Имп. Акад.) lxxxvi. St Petersburg. 1909.

Veselovskii, A. N. Изъ исторіи древнихъ германскихъ и славянскихъ передвиженій. St Petersburg. 1900. (Ibid. v.)

Vondrák, V. Vergleichende slavische Grammatik. 2 vols. Göttingen. 1906–8.

Westberg, F. Beiträge zur Klärung orientalischer Quellen über Osteuropa, in Bulletin Acad. Imp. St Petersburg. 5th series. xi. 1899.

—— Къ анализу восточныхъ источниковъ о восточной Европѣ, in Zhurnal of the Ministry of National Instruction. (Министерства Народ. Просв.) St Petersburg. February and March. 1908.

Wojciechowski, T. Chrobacya. Rozbiór starożytności słowiańskich. i. Cracow. 1873.

Zeuss. Die Deutschen und ihre Nachbarstämme. Munich. 1837.

b. SPECIAL.

Ankershofen, G. baron. Handbuch der Geschichte des Herzogthumes Kärnten. Vol. ı. Klagenfurt. 1850.

Bachmann, A. Geschichte Böhmens. Vol. ı. Gotha. 1899.

Barsov, N. P. Очерки русской исторической географіи. Географія Начальной лѣтописи. Warsaw. 1873. 2nd edn. 1885.

Baudouin de Courtenay, J. Резья и Резьяне, in Sbornik, Slavyanskii, ııı. St Petersburg. 1876. (On the Slavs in the Venetian province.)

Beck, C. Ortsnamen der Fränkischen Schweiz. 1907. Ortsnamen des Aischtales und seiner Nachbartäler. 1908. Ortsnamen des Pegnitztales und des Gräfenberg-Erlanger Landes. Nürnberg. 1909. Reviewed by Miedel, J., in Z. für deutsche Mundarten. Berlin. 1908, p. 86 ff.; 1911, p. 83 ff.

—— Über nichtdeutsche Elemente in bayerischen Ortsnamen, ibid. 1911, p. 133 ff. (Expansion of the Slavs in Bavaria.)

Bestuzhev-Ryumin, K. N. Русская исторія. ı. St Petersburg. 1872.

Blauth, J. Osuszenie bagien Polesia. Reprint of Czasopismo techniczne. Lemberg (Lwów). 1899. German transl.: Trockenlegung der Sümpfe in Polesie, in Oesterreichische Monatschrift für den öffentlichen Baudienst. Vienna. 1899. With map.

Bobchev, S. S. Българската челядна задруга. Sofia. 1907. Reprint of Sbornik за народ. умотворения... Том. xxıı.

Bogišić, V. Pravni običaji u Slovena. Agram (Zagreb). 1867.

Bogusławski, W. Dzieje Słowiańszczyzny północno-zachodniéj. 4 vols. Posen (Poznań). 1887-1900.

Bogusławski, W. and Hórnik, M. Historija serbskeho naroda. Bautzen (Budyšin). 1884.

Böttger, H. Diöcesan- und Gaugrenzen Norddeutschlands. 4 vols. Halle. 1875. (Expansion of the Elbe Slavs.)

Bradley, H. The Goths from the earliest times... 4th edition. London. 1898.

Bremer, O. Ethnographie der germanischen Stämme. Strasburg. 1900. In Grundriss der germanischen Philologie. Ed. Paul, H. ııı. 2nd edn.

Bretholz, B. Geschichte Mährens. ı. Brünn. 1893.

Brückner, A. Cywilizacja i język. Szkice z dziejów obyczajowości polskiej. 2nd edn. Warsaw. 1901.

—— O Piaście, in Rozprawy Akad. Um. Cracow. xxxv. 1898.

—— Piast, in Przegląd Historyczny. ıv. Warsaw. 1907. p. 15 ff.

—— O Rusi normańskiej jeszcze słów kilka, in Kwartalnik Historyczny. xxııı. Lemberg. 1909. p. 362 ff.

—— Die slavischen Ansiedlungen in der Altmark und im Magdeburgischen. Leipsic. 1879. (Preisschriften der Jablonowskischen Gesellsch. xxıı.)

—— Geschichte Russlands. Gotha. 1896.

Bruun, Ph. J. Черноморье. Сборникъ изслѣдованій по исторической географіи южной Россіи. 2 vols. Odessa. 1879-80.

Büdinger, M. Oesterreichische Geschichte bis zum Ausgang des 13. Jahrhunderts. ı. Leipsic. 1858.

Bugge, A. Vikingerne. 2 vols. 1904-6. German transl. Hungerland, H. Halle. 1906.

Bujak, F. Studya nad Osadnictwem Małopolski. ı. Cracow. 1905.

Bury, J. B. The Chronological Cycle of the Bulgarians. BZ. xix. 1910. p. 127 ff.

—— History of the Later Roman Empire, a.d. 395–800. 2 vols. London. 1889.

—— The treatise De administrando imperio. BZ. xv. 1906. p. 522 ff.

Caro, J. Geschichte Polens. Gotha. 1863.

Čelakovský, J. Povšechné české dějiny právní. Prague. 1900 ff.

Cervesato, A. Le colonie slave della Grecia, in Pensiero Italiano. Milan. 1896. fasc. 47 f.

Cvijić, J. Антропогеографски проблеми балканскога полуострва, in Zbornik, Etnografski, of the Belgrade Academy. iv.

Czermak, W. Dzieje Polski. i. Vienna. 1906.

Dimitz, A. Geschichte Krains... i. Laibach. 1874.

Dopsch, A. Die ältere Sozial- und Wirtschaftsverfassung der Alpenslawen. Weimar. 1909.

—— Nochmals die ältere Sozial- und Wirtschaftsverfassung der Alpenslawen (Berichtigung). Reprint of Viert. f. Sozial- u. Wirtschaftsgesch. vii. 1909.

Dovnar-Zapol'skii, M. Очеркъ исторіи Кривичской и Дреговичской земель до к. xii. вѣка. Kiev. 1891.

—— Очерки семейственнаго обычнаго права крестьянъ Минской губерніи, in Obozrenie, Etnograficheskoe. 1897. No. 1.

—— Запално-русская сельская община въ xvi. вѣкѣ. St Petersburg. 1897.

Drinov, M. Погледъ врьхъ происхожданіе-то на блъгарскій народъ и начало-то на блъгарска-та исторія. Philippopolis. 1869.

—— Заселеніе балканскаго полуострова Славянами. Moscow. 1873.

Dudík, B. Mährens allgemeine Geschichte. i. Brünn. 1860.

—— Dějiny Moravy. 2nd edn. Vol. i. Prague. 1874.

Dümmler, E. Über die älteste Geschichte der Slaven in Dalmatien (549–928). Vienna. 1856. SKAW. (Phil.-hist.) Vol. xx.

—— Über die südöstlichen Marken der fränkischen Reiches unter den Karolingern, in Archiv für Kunde der österreichischen Geschichtsquellen. x. Vienna. 1853.

Erckert, R. von. Wanderungen und Siedelungen der germanischen Stämme in Mittel-Europa von der ältesten Zeit bis auf Karl den Grossen. Berlin. 1901.

Fallmerayer, J. P. Die Entstehung der heutigen Griechen. Stuttgart. 1835.

—— Fragmente aus dem Orient. ii. Das slavische Element in Griechenland. Stuttgart. 1845.

Filevich, I. P. Исторія древней Руси. Warsaw. 1896.

Fritze, E. Dorfbilder. Meiningen. 1906. (Expansion of the Slavs in Thuringia.)

Gąsiorowska, N. Pierwotne osadnictwo Polski w literaturze wspólczesnej, in Przegląd Historyczny. vii. Warsaw. 1910. p. 353 ff.

Gebauer, J. and Masaryk, T. G. Unechtheit der Königinhofer und Grüneberger Handschrift. Berlin. 1887, in Archiv für slavische Philologie. x, xi.

Gedeonov, S. A. Варяги и Русь, историческое изслѣдованіе. 2 vols. St Petersburg. 1876.

Gerland, E. Neue Quellen zur Geschichte des lateinischen Erzbistums Patras. Leipsic. 1903. (On the Slavs in Greece.)

Gherghel, J. Zur Frage der Urheimat der Rumänen. Vienna. 1910.

Giesebrecht, L. Wendische Geschichten. 3 vols. Berlin. 1843.

Gilferding. See Hilferding.

Goldmann, E. Die Einführung der deutschen Herzogsgeschlechter Kärntens in den slovenischen Stammesverband. Breslau. 1903. Refuted by Puntschart, P. in Göttingische gel. Anzeigen. 1907. p. 82 ff.

Goll, J. Samo und die karant. Slaven. MIOGF. xi. 1890. p. 443 ff.

Golubovskii, P. Печенѣги, Торки и Половцы до нашествія Татаръ. Исторія южно-русскихъ степей.... Kiev. 1884. (History of the Pontus Steppes.)

Groh, K. Kämpfe der Avaren und Langobarden. Halle. 1889.

Grot, K. J. Извѣстія Константина Багрянороднаго о Сербахъ и Хорватахъ и ихъ разселеніи на Балканскомъ полуостровѣ. St Petersburg. 1882, in Zapiski of the Russian Geogr. Soc. Ethnogr. Section. (Имп. Русск. Геогр. Общества по Отдѣл. Этногр.) ix.

Gutschmid, A. von. Kritik der polnischen Urgeschichte des Vincentius Kadłubek, in Archiv für Kunde d. österreichischen Geschichtsquellen. Vol. xvii. Vienna. 1857.

Hampel, J. Altertümer des frühen Mittelalters in Ungarn. Brunswick. 1905.

Hartmann, J. Die Württembergischen Ortsnamen..., in Württembergische Jahrbücher. Stuttgart. 1874. ii. p. 212. (On the Slavs in Württemberg.)

Haxthausen, A. Freiherr von. Die ländliche Verfassung Russlands. Leipsic. 1866.

Herman, O. A magyarok nagy ösfoglalkozása. Budapest. 1909.

Hertzberg, G. F. Geschichte Griechenlands. Gotha. 1876. Vol. i. p. 120 ff. (The Slavs in Greece.)

Heyd, W. Geschichte des Levantehandels im Mittelalter. i. Stuttgart. 1879.

Hilferding, A. Борьба Славянъ съ Нѣмцами на балтійскомъ поморьѣ. St Petersburg. 1861.

—— Исторія балтійскихъ Славянъ. i. Moscow. 1855. 2nd edn. 1874.

Hoops, J. Waldbäume und Kulturpflanzen im germanischen Altertum. Strasburg. 1905.

Hopf, K. Geschichte Griechenlands vom Beginn des Mittelalters. Leipsic. 1867 (in Ersch-Gruber. i. Sect. A—G. Tom. 85–6).

Houdek, V. Der "Heidentempel" in Znaim, seine Geschichte und kunsthistorische Bedeutung. Znaim. 1900. (Old frescoes depicting the election of the peasant Přemysl as Prince.)

Hruševśkyj, A. Пинское Полѣсье. 2 vols. Moscow. 1901, 1903.

Hruševśkyj, M. Анти, in Zapiski. Наук. Товар. Им. Шевченка. xxi. 1898.

—— Історія Украïни-Руси. 2nd edn. i. Lemberg. 1904. German transl., Gesch. des ukrainischen (ruthenischen) Volkes. i. Leipsic. 1906.

Huber, A. Geschichte Österreichs. Vol. i. Gotha. 1885.

Hunfalvy, P. Ethnographie von Ungarn. Budapest. 1877.

Ilovayskii, D. I. Разысканія о началѣ Руси. Moscow. 1876. 2nd edn. 1882. Supplements 1886 and 1902.

Immanuel, F. Die Trockenlegung des Poljesje, in "Globus." Vol. lxvi. 1897. p. 293 ff. With map.

Ivanov, P. Историческія судьбы Волынской земли.... 1895.

Jacob, G. Welche Handelsartikel bezogen die Araber des Mittelalters aus den nordisch-baltischen Ländern? 2nd edn. Berlin. 1891.

—— Die Ortsnamen des Herzogtums Meiningen. Hildburghausen. 1894. (On the Slavs in Thuringia.)

Jagić, V. Ein Kapitel aus der Geschichte der südslavischen Sprachen, in Archiv für slavische Philologie. Vol. xvii. 1895.

—— Zur Entstehungsgeschichte der kirchenslavischen Sprache, in Denkschriften KAW. Phil.-hist. Sekt. Vol. xlvii. 1900.

Jireček, C. J. Geschichte der Bulgaren. Prague. 1876. Translated into Russian by Bruun and Palauzov, with additions and alterations by the Author. Odessa. 1878.

—— Das Fürstentum Bulgarien. Prague. 1891. p. 118 ff. (On the Roumanian shepherds.)

—— Geschichte der Serben. I. Gotha. 1911.

—— Die Romanen in den Städten Dalmatiens während des Mittelalters (in Denkschriften KAW. (Phil.-hist. Sekt.) XLVIII f.). 1902, 1904.

—— Die Wlachen und Maurowlachen, in Sitzungsber. d. kön. Böhmischen Gesellschaft d. Wissensch. Prague. 1879.

Jireček, H. Slovanské právo v Čechách a na Moravě. 2 vols. Prague. 1863 f.

—— Das Recht in Böhmen und Mähren. Prague. 1865.

Jireček, J. and Jireček, H. Entstehen christlicher Reiche im Gebiete des heutigen österreichischen Kaiserstaates vom J. 500 bis 1000. Vienna. 1865.

Jovanović, A. S. Историјски развитак српске задруге. Belgrade. 1896.

Kaemmel, O. Die Anfänge deutschen Lebens in Österreich bis zum Ausgange der Karolingerzeit. Leipsic. 1879.

Kånchov, V. Македония. Етнография и статистика. Sofia. 1900.

Kay, de. The Spreewald and its Wend inhabitants, in Century Monthly Magazine, 1897, February.

Keary, C. F. The Vikings in Western Christendom, A.D. 789 to 883. London. 1891.

Kętrzyński, W. O Słowianach mieszkających niegdyś między Renem a Labą, Salą i granicą czeską. 1899. Reprint of Rozprawy Akademii Um. Cracow. Hist.-phil. sect. II. XV. 1901. With 7 maps. (Expansion of the Slavs west of the Elbe and Saale.)

Keussler, J. Zur Geschichte und Kritik des bäuerlichen Gemeindebesitzes in Russland. 2 vols. Riga. 1876, 1883.

Klyuchevskii, V. Курсъ русской исторіи. I. Moscow. 1906.

Knothe, H. Die Stellung der Gutsunterthanen in der Oberlausitz, in Neues Lausitzisches Magazin. LXI. 1885.

Korsh, F. О нѣкоторыхъ бытовыхъ словахъ, заимствованныхъ древними славянами изъ такъ называемыхъ урало-алтайскихъ языковъ. St Petersburg. 1909. Reprint of Zapiski of the Imp. Russ. Geogr. Society, Ethnogr. Section. (Имп. Русск. Геогр. Общ. по Отдѣл. Этногр.) XXXIV.

—— Опыты объясненія заимствованныхъ словъ въ русскомъ языкѣ. Reprint of Izvyestiya. Имп. Акад. Наукъ. St Petersburg. 1907.

Kos, F. Kdaj so Slovenci prišli v svojo sedanjo domovino? In Izvestja of the Mus. Society for Carniola. (Muzejskega Društva za Kranjsko.) Tom. VI. Lyublyana (Laibach). 1896.

Kotlyarevskii, A. Древности юридическаго быта балтійскихъ Славянъ, in Sbornik of the Russian Language Section of the Imp. Acad. (Отдѣл. Русск. Языка Имп. Акад. Наукъ.) I. St Petersburg. 1895.

Kovačević, L. and Jovanović, L. Историја српского народа. Belgrade. 1893.

Kovalevsky, M. Modern customs and ancient laws of Russia. London. 1891.

Krauss, F. S. Sitte und Brauch der Südslaven. Vienna. 1885.

Krones, F. Zur Geschichte der ältesten, insbesondere deutschen Ansiedlung des steiermärkischen Oberlandes, in Mittheilungen des Hist. Vereines f. Steiermark. Vol. XXVII. Graz. 1879.

—— Die deutsche Besiedelung der östlichen Alpenländer, in Forschungen zur deutschen Landes- u. Volkskunde. V. Stuttgart. 1889.

Krones, F. Handbuch der Geschichte Österreichs...mit besonderer Rücksicht auf die Länder-, Völkerkunde und Culturgeschichte. i, ii. Berlin. 1876 f.

—— Verfassung und Verwaltung der Mark und des Herzogthums Steier von ihren Anfängen bis zur Herrschaft der Habsburger. Graz. 1897. (Forschungen zur Verfassungs- und Verwaltungsgesch. der Steiermark. i.)

Krusch, B. Die Chronicae des sogenannten Fredegar. NAGDG. vii. 1882. (On Samo.)

Kulakovskii, J. Гдѣ зачинается территорія Славянъ по Іордану? (in Zhurnal Министерства Народ. Просв. (Ministry of National Instruction). 1905. iii).

Kunik, A. Die Berufung der schwedischen Rodsen durch die Finnen und Slaven. 2 vols. St Petersburg. 1844–5.

Lamanskii, V. J. О Славянахъ въ Малой Азіи, Африкѣ и Испаніи. St Petersburg. 1859.

Lampros, S. Ἱστορία τῆς Ἑλλάδος. Vol. iii. Athens. 1892.

Landau, G. Der Bauernhof in Thüringen..., in Correspondenzblatt des Gesammt-Vereines der deutschen Geschichts- u. Altertumsvereine. x. Stuttgart. 1862. Jan. (Expansion of the Slavs in Thuringia.)

Lelewel, J. Dzieje Polski. Warsaw. 1829. 7th edition. 1852. French transl. Histoire de Pologne. Paris. 1844. German transl. Geschichte Polens. Leipsic. 1845.

—— Dzieje Litwy i Rusi.... Paris. 1839. 2nd edition. (Poznań) Posen. 1844. French transl. by Rykaczewski, Histoire de Lithuanie et de la Ruthénie jusqu'à leur union définitive avec la Pologne. Paris. 1861.

—— Polska, Dzieje i rzeczy jej rozpatrzywane. 20 vols. Posen. 1854–68.

Leo, F. Die capitatio plebeia und die capitatio humana im römisch-byzantinischen Steuerrecht. Berlin. 1900.

Lessiak, P. Alpendeutsche und Alpenslawen in ihren sprachlichen Beziehungen, in Germanisch-Romanische Monatschrift. ii. Heidelberg. 1910.

Levec, W. Pettauer Studien, in Mitteilungen der Anthropol. Ges. Vienna. Vol. xxviii f., xxxv. 1898 f., 1905. (On the Župans.)

Lippert, J. Sozialgeschichte Böhmens in vorhussitischer Zeit. 2 vols. Prague. 1896 and 1898.

Loserth, J. Die Herrschaft der Langobarden in Böhmen, Mähren und Rugiland. Reprint of MIOGF. ii.

Luchitzkii, I. Сябры и сябринное землевладѣніе въ Малороссіи, in "Vyestnik, Syevernii." 1889, fasc. 1 and 2. Transl. French, Loutchisky, Études sur la propriété communale dans la Petite Russie, in Revue internationale de sociologie. iii. 1895. p. 465 ff. Transl. German, Lutschizky, Zur Geschichte der Grundeigentumsformen in Kleinrussland, in Jahrbuch für Gesetzgebung, Verwaltung u. Volkswirtschaft in Deutschland. xx. 1896. p. 165 ff.

Luschin von Ebengreuth, A. Österreichische Reichsgesch. i. Bamberg. 1895.

—— Grundriss der österreichischen Reichsgeschichte. Bamberg. 1899.

Marković, M. Die serbische Hauskommunion (Zadrůga)... Leipsic. 1903.

Marquart, J. Die nichtslawischen (altbulgarischen) Ausdrücke in der bulgarischen Fürstenliste. Leyden. 1910. Reprint of "T'oung-Pao." Vol. xi.

Meyer, G. Const. Sathas und die Slavenfrage in Griechenland. (Essays und Studien, i.) Strasburg. 1885. p. 117 ff.

Milkowicz, W. Beiträge zur Rechts- und Verfassungsgeschichte Krains. Die Supanei-Verfassung, in Mitteilungen des Museal-Vereins f. Krain. ii, iii. Laibach. 1889 f.

Miller, W. The Balkans: Roumania, Bulgaria, Servia, Montenegro. London. 1896. (Story of the Nations.)

Morfill, W. R. History of Russia. New York. 1902.

Muchar, A. A.   Geschichte des Herzogthums Steiermark.   I.   Grätz.   1844.

Muka, E.   Die Grenzen des sorbischen Sprachgebiets in alter Zeit, in Archiv für slavische Philologie.   xxvi.   1904.

Müllenhoff, K.   Beowulf.   Berlin.   1889.

Müller, J.   Gehört Nordwestdeutschland den Slawen? (in Jahresbericht der Männer v. Morgenstern....   xii.   1909-10.   p. 128 ff.).

Munch, P. A.   Det Norske folks Historia.   2 vols.   1852-5.   German transl. by Claussen, G. F., Das heroische Zeitalter der nordisch-germanischen Völker.   Lubeck.   1854.

Murko, M.   Geschichte der älteren südslawischen Litteraturen.   Leipsic.   1908.

Mutafchiev, P.   Селското землевладѣніе въ Византія.   Sofia.   1910.   Reprint of Sbornik за народ. умотвор.   xxv.

Němeček, O.   Das Reich des Slawenfürsten Samo.   Reprint of xxiii. Jahresbericht d. deutschen Realschule in Mährisch-Ostrau.   1906.

Nerad, F.   Samo a jeho říše, in Zpráva of the Realschule in Telč (Moravia).   1896.

Niederle, L.   Antové, in Věstník Král České Společnosti Nauk.   Prague.   1909.

——   Čechové a Avaři, in Časopis, Český Historický, tom. xv.   Prague.   1909.

——   Michal Syrský a dějiny balkánských Slovanů v vi. stol., in Sborník prací hist. Prague.   1906.

——   K slovanské kolonisaci Malé Asie a Syrie v viii-x. století, in Sbornik по славяновѣдѣнію, tom. ii.   St Petersburg.   1907.

Novaković, S.   Село.   Belgrade.   1891.   In "Glas" of the Servian Acad.   xxiv.   (On the Servian Zadruga.)

Novotný, V.   České dějiny.   Vol. 1.   i.   Prague.   1912.

Olrik, A.   Nordisk Aandsliv i Vikingetid og tidlig Middelalder.—German transl. by Ranisch, W.   Nordisches Geistesleben....   Heidelberg.   1908.

Pajk, M.   Črtice o nekdanjih slovenskih nasedbinah v Gorenji Austriji (in Izvestja Muzejskega Društva za Kranjsko.   vii.) (Lyublyana) Laibach.   1897.

Palacký, F.   Geschichte von Böhmen.   i.   Prague.   1836.   3rd edn.   1864.

Panchenko, V. A.   Крестьянская собственность въ Византіи, in Izvyestiya of the Russian Archaeolog. Institute in Constantinople.   (Русск. Археол. Инстит.)   Tom. ix.

Paparrigopulos, K.   Sur l'établissement de quelques tribus slaves dans le Péloponnèse. Athens.   1843.

——   Σκλαυϊκαὶ ἐν ταῖς Ἑλληνικαῖς χώραις ἐποικήσεις, in his Ἱστορικαὶ πραγματεῖαι. I.   Athens.   1858.

Pavinskii, A.   Полабскіе Славяне.   Историческое изслѣдованіе.   St Petersburg.   1871.

Peisker, J.   Die ältere Sozial- und Wirtschaftsverfassung der Alpenslawen.   Reprint of Viert. f. Soz.- u. Wirtschaftsgesch.   vii.   1909.

——   The Asiatic Background, in Cambridge Medieval History.   Vol. i, c. xii.

——   Die Knechtschaft in Böhmen.   Prague.   1890.

Pekař, J.   O správním rozdělení země České do polovice 13. století, in "Sborník prací historických"....   Prague.   1906.   (On Župan.)

Perwolf, J.   Германизація балтійскихъ Славянъ.   St Petersburg.   1876.

Píč, J.   Starožitnosti země České.   Prague.   1899 ff.

Piekosiński, F.   Ludność wieśniacza w Polsce w dobie piastowskiej.   Cracow.   1896.

Podrecca, C.   Slavia italiana.   Cividale.   1884.

Pogodin, M.   Древняя русская исторія....   i.   Moscow.   1871.

Popowski, J.   Entsumpfungs-Arbeiten in dem Polesie.   Vortrag....   Vienna.   1884.

Potkański, K.   Lachowie i Lechici.   Cracow.   1898, in Rozprawy Akad. Um. Cracow.   (Phil. ser. ii.)   Vol. xii.

Pouqueville, F. Ch. H. L. Voyage dans la Grèce. Vol. II. Paris. 1820. p. 208 ff. 2nd edition. 1826. p. 382 ff. (Manners and customs of the Roumanian Nomad-shepherds.)

Puntschart, P. Herzogseinsetzung und Huldigung in Kärnten. Leipsic. 1899. Reviewed by Wretschko, A. v., in Götting. gel. Anzeigen. 1900. p. 929 ff. See also Puntschart, ibid. 1907. p. 82 ff.

Rački, F. Biela Hrvatska i Biela Srbija, in "Rad" Jugoslavenske Akad. Vol. LII. Agram. 1880.

—— Hrvatska prije XII vieka glede na zemljišni obseg i narod, in "Rad," vol. LVI. 1881.

—— Nutarnje stanje Hrvatske prije XII stoljeća, in "Rad," vol. XCI, XCIX. 1888, 1890.

—— Nacrt jugoslovjenskieh povjestij do IX. stoljetja, in Arkiv za povjestnicu Jugoslavensku. (South Slavonic Hist.) Vol. IV. 1857.

Ralston, W. R. S. Early Russian History. London. 1874.

Rambaud, A. N. Histoire de la Russie. Paris. 1878. New edition. 1900. Engl. transl. of 1st edn. by Lang, L. B. History of Russia. 2 vols. 1879.

Rehman, A. Ziemie dawnej Polski i sąsiednich krajów słowiańskich opisane pod względem fizyczno-geograficznym. 2 vols. Lemberg. 1895–1904.

Röpell, R. Geschichte Polens. I. Hamburg. 1840.

Rösler, R. Romanische Studien. Leipsic. 1871.

—— Über den Zeitpunkt der slawischen Ansiedlungen an der unteren Donau, in SKAW. LXXIII. 1873.

Ross, Denman W. The early history of land-holding among the Germans. London. 1883.

Rossiya. Россія. Полное географическое описаніе нашего отечества, conducted by Semenov, P. P. and Lamanskii, V. J. Vol. IX. St Petersburg. 1905. (Geogr.-ethnographical description of Polesie.)

Rutar, S. Beneška Slovenija. Laibach. 1899.

Samokvasov, D. J. Памятники древняго русскаго права. I. Moscow. 1908.

Schiemann, T. Russland, Polen und Lievland. Vol. I. Berlin. 1886.

Schlüter, O. Siedelungen im nordöstlichen Thüringen. Berlin. 1903. With maps. (On the Slavs in Thuringia.)

Schnürer, G. Die Verfasser der sogenannten Fredegarchronik. Freiburg (Switzerland). 1900, in Collectanea Friburgensia IX. (On the Slav Kingdom of Samo.)

Schönbach, A. E. Der steirische Reimchronist über die Herzogshuldigung in Kärnten, in MIOGF. XXI. Vienna. 1900. p. 518 ff.

Schottin, R. Die Slaven in Thüringen, in Programm of the Gymnasium. Bautzen. 1884.

Sergyeevich, V. Лекціи и изслѣд. по древной исторіи русскаго права. 3rd edition. St Petersburg. 1903.

—— Русскія юридическія древности. 2nd edition. St Petersburg. 1900–3. 3 vols.

—— Время возникновенія крестьянской поземельной общины. St Petersburg. 1908. (Date of origin of the "Mir.")

Seton-Watson, R. W. Racial problems in Hungary, a History of the Slovaks. London. 1909.

Shishmanov, I. Славянски селища въ Критѣ и на другите острови. Sofia. 1897. Reprint of Bŭlgarski Pregled. IV. (On the Slav settlements in the Greek Islands.)

—— Критиченъ прѣгледъ на въпроса за произхода на прабългаритѣ, in Sbornik за народни умотворения. XVI, XVII. Sofia. 1900.

Sieniawski, E. Pogląd na dzieje Słowian zachodniopólnocznych między Łabą (Elbą) a granicami dawnéj Polski.... Gniezno (Gnesen). 1881.

Smiljanić, M.   Die Hirten und Hirtennomaden Süd- und Südostserbiens, in Globus, vol. LXXIV.   No. 4 f.   1898.

Smirnov, J. N.   Очеркъ культурной исторіи южныхъ Славянъ, in Zapiski of the Kazań Univ.   (Ученыя Казан. Университета.)   1900.

Sobolevskii, A. I.   Гдѣ жила Литва? in Izvyestiya.   Имп. Акад. Наукъ.   St Petersburg.   6th ser.   v.   1911.   p. 1051 ff.

Solov'ev, S. M.   Исторія Россіи съ древнѣйшихъ временъ.   I.   Moscow.   1863.

Sozonovich, I.   Славяне въ Морѣѣ, in Izvyestiya of the Warsaw University.   (Варшав. Унив.)   1887.   No. 2.   (On the Slavs in Morea.)

Stanojević, S.   Византија и Срби.   Vol. I.   Балканско полуострво до VII. века.   Vol. II.   Колонизација Словена на Балканском полуострву.   Novi Sad.   1903, 1906 (in Kńige Matice Srpske.   Nos. 7–8, 14–15.)

Szaraniewicz, I.   Kritische Blicke in die Geschichte der Karpaten-Völker.   Lemberg.   1871.

Szujski, J.   Dzieje Polski.   Lwów (Lemberg).   1862.   2nd edition.   1896.

—— Historyi polskiéj treściwie opowiedzianéj ksiąg XII.   Warsaw.   1880.

Tagányi, K.   Geschichte der Feldgemeinschaft in Ungarn.   Reprint of Ungarische Revue.   XV.   1895.

Tappeiner, F.   Zur Anthropologie und Ethnographie der Resianer, in Sitzungsber. d. Anthropolog. Gesellsch.   Vienna.   1895.

Tetzner, F.   Die Slawen in Deutschland.   Brunswick.   1902.

Thomsen, V.   The relations between Ancient Russia and Scandinavia, and the Origin of the Russian State.   Oxford.   1877.

Tomek, W. W.   Dějepis města Prahy.   I.   Prague.   1855.

Truhlář, J.   Zur Beleuchtung des Handschriftenstreites in Böhmen.   Vienna.   1888.   Reprint of MIOGF.   IX.

Uspenskii, F.   Первыя славянскія монархіи на сѣверозападѣ.   St Petersburg.   1872.

Utiešenović, M.   Die Hauskommunionen der Südslaven.   Vienna.   1859.

Vacek, V. F.   Sociální dějiny české doby starší.   Prague.   1905 f.

Vasil'ev, A.   Славяне въ Греціи, in VV, v.   St Petersburg.   1898.   (The Slavs in Greece.)

Vierling, A.   Die slavischen Ansiedlungen in Bayern, in Beiträge zur Anthropologie u. Urgeschichte Bayerns.   XVI.   1905.

Vocel, J. E.   Pravěk země České.   Prague.   1868.

Wachowski, K.   Słowiańszczyzna Zachodnia.   Vol. I.   Warsaw.   1902.

Weinhold, C.   Altnordisches Leben.   Berlin.   1856.

Wlaïnatz, M.   Die agrar-rechtlichen Verhältnisse des mittelalterlichen Serbiens.   Jena.   1903.   (On the Servian Zadruga.)

Yasinskii, A. N.   Очерки и изслѣдованія по соціальной и экономической исторіи Чехіи....   Yuryev (Dorpat).   1901.

—— Паденіе земскаго строя въ чешском государствѣ.   Reprint of Izvyestiya Университетскія.   Kiev.   1895.

Zabyelin, J. E.   Исторія русской жизни съ древн. временъ.   2 vols.   Moscow.   1876–9.   2nd edition.   1908.

Zachariae von Lingenthal, C. E.   Zur Kenntnis des römischen Steuerwesens in der Kaiserzeit, in Mémoires Acad. Imp.   8th ser.   VI.   Pt. 9.   St Petersburg.   1863.   (On the hearth-tax.)

Zhilinskii, I.   Краткій очеркъ Полѣсья....   St Petersburg.   1892.

Županić, N.   Систем историјске антропологије балканских народа.   Belgrade.   1909.   (Reprint of the "Starinar."   Vols. II and III.)

CHAPTER XV (A).

GALLIC RELIGION.

AUTHORITIES (MODERN).

Dottin, G.   La Religion des Celtes.   1906.   (Taken from his Manuel pour servir à l'étude de l'antiquité classique, 1904.)   Paris.

Gaidoz, H.   Article Gaulois in l'Encyclopédie des Sciences Religieuses, vol. v. Paris.   1878.

Keysler, J. G.   Antiquitates selectae Septentrionales et Celticae.   Hanover.   1720.

[Martin, Dom J.]   La Religion des Gaulois.   2 vols.   Paris.   1727.

Reinach, S.   Bronzes figurés de la Gaule romaine.   (Description du Musée de Saint-Germain.)   Paris.   [1894.]

—— Cultes, Mythes et Religions.   Paris.   3 vols.   1904–8.

Renel, Ch.   Les Religions de la Gaule avant le Christianisme.   Paris.   1906.

Rhŷs, J.   Origin and growth of Religion as illustrated by Celtic Heathendom. (Hibbert Lectures, 1886.)   Oxford.   1888.

Roget de Belloguet, D. F. L.   Ethnogénie gauloise.   4 vols.   Paris.   1868.   Vol. iii. Le Génie gaulois.

CHAPTER XV (B).

CELTIC HEATHENDOM IN THE BRITISH ISLES.

AUTHORITIES (MODERN).

Anwyl, E.   Celtic Religion in pre-Christian times.   (Religions ancient and modern.) London.   1906.

—— Celtic Deities.   Transactions of the Gaelic Society of Inverness.   1906.

—— Celtic Goddesses.   Celtic Review.   July, 1906.

Carmichael, A.   Carmina Gadelica : hymns and incantations.   With notes.   2 vols. Edinburgh.   1900.   (Gaelic and English.)

Frazer, J. G.   The Golden Bough.   2nd edn.   3 vols.   London.   1900.

Hastings, J.   Encyclopaedia of Religion and Ethics.   *See Gen. Bibl.* i.   Articles on Celtic religion.

Joyce, P. W.   Social History of Ancient Ireland.   2 vols.   London.   1903.

McCulloch, J. A.   The Religion of the Ancient Celts.   Edinburgh.   1911.

Rhŷs, J.   Origin and growth of Religion as illustrated by Celtic Heathendom. (Hibbert Lectures, 1886.)   Oxford.   1888.

—— Celtic Folk-Lore.   Welsh and Manx.   Oxford.   1901.

CHAPTER XV (c).

GERMANIC HEATHENDOM.

I. SPECIAL BIBLIOGRAPHIES.

Hermannson, Halldór. Islandica I. Bibliography of Icelandic Sagas. 1908.
III. Bibl. of the Sagas of the Kings of Norway. 1910. Ithaca, N.Y.
Jahresbericht über die Erscheinungen auf dem Gebiete der germ. Philologie (Gesell-
schaft für deutsche Philologie, Berlin). Leipzic. 1879 ff. (Contains a section
devoted to notices of works on religion and mythology.)
Potthast, A. Bibliotheca Historica Medii Aevi. *See Gen. Bibl.* I.

II. EVIDENCE.

1. FROM MONUMENTS. INSCRIPTIONS.

Brambach, W. Corp. Inscr. Rhenanarum. (Verein von Alterthumsfreunden im
Rheinlande, Bonn.) Elberfeld. 1867.
Bugge, S. Norges Indskrifter med de ældre Runer. Christiania. 1891 ff.
Corpus Inscriptionum Latinarum. *See Gen. Bibl.* IV.
Stephens, G. Handbook of the Old Northern Runic Monuments. London and
Copenhagen. 1888. (Contains good plates, but the interpretations are unsound.)
Wimmer, L. F. A. De danske Runemindesmærker. Copenhagen. 1895 ff.

2. DOCUMENTARY. LAWS.

(a) Continental.

In MGH, Leges. Especially important are:
Constitutio Childeberti (Ll. I), Capitulatio de partibus Saxoniae (Ll. v), Lex
Frisionum (Ll. III), Indiculus Superstitionum (Ll. I).

(b) English.

Liebermann. Gesetze der Angelsachsen. *See Gen. Bibl.* IV. Vols. I, II, 1.

(c) Scandinavian.

Corpus Juris Sveo-gotorum antiqui. Ed. Schlyter, C. J. 13 vols. Stockholm.
1838–77.
Gutalag och Guta Saga. Ed. Pipping, H. Copenhagen. 1905–7.
Norges Gamle Love indtil 1387. Ed. Keyser, R. and Munch, P. 5 vols. Christiania.
1846–95.

III. AUTHORITIES.

1. CLASSICAL.

Ammianus Marcellinus. Hist. Rom. Ed. Gardthausen, V. 2 vols. Leipsic. 1874–5.
Tacitus. Germania, Annales, Historia. *See Gen. Bibl.*

2. MEDIEVAL.

(a) *Continental.*

(a) *Lives of Missionaries,* in MGH, scriptores, or in MPL, especially:

 Alcuin. Vita Willebrordi. MGH xxiii.
 Altfrid. Vita Liudgeri. MGH ii.
 Ennodius. Vita Antonii. MGH vi.
     Vita S. Columbani. MPL 82.
 Rimbert. Vita Anskarii. MGH ii. MPL 103.
 Walafrid Strabo. Vita S. Galli. MGH ii.
 Willibald. Vita Bonifacii. MGH ii.

(β) *Histories of Germanic tribes or kings,* especially:

 Adam von Bremen. Gesta Hammaburgensis Eccles. ad 1072. MGH vii.
  (Tr. GddV. vi.)
 Agathias. Hist. MPG 88. German transl. Geschichtschreiber der deutschen
  Vorzeit. Vol. iii. *See Gen. Bibl.* iv. (GddV.)
 Chronique dite de Nestor. Tr. Léger, L. Paris. 1884. (Scandinavians in
  Russia.)
 Dudo. De moribus et actis Normannorum i. MPL 141.
 Gregory of Tours. Hist. Francorum. MGH, script. Merov. i, 1. MPL
  71. (Tr. GddV. iv, v.)
 Jordanes. De Origine Actibusque Getarum. *See Gen. Bibl.* v.
 Paulus Diaconus. Hist. Langobardorum. *See Gen. Bibl.* iv. (Tr. GddV. iv.)
 Procopius. De bello Gothico. CSHB, *see Gen. Bibl.* v. Pars ii. 1833.
  3 vols.
 Thietmar von Merseburg. Chronicon. MPL 139. (Tr. GddV. i.)
 Widukind. Res gestae Saxonicae. MPL 137. (Tr. GddV. vi.)

(b) *English.*

Bede. Hist. eccles. gentis Anglorum. Ed. Plummer, C. (Tr. Sellar, A. M.)
See Gen. Bibl. v

(c) *Scandinavian.*

Elder Edda. Sæmundar Edda. Ed. Bugge, S. Christiania. 1867. Engl.
translations: In Corp. Poet. Bor. Ed. Vigfússon, G. and York Powell, F.
2 vols. Oxford. 1883. (Some rearrangement and some dubious readings.) And
also by Bray, O. The Elder or Poetic Edda. Part i. (Viking Club.)
London. 1907. The most trustworthy translation is in German, by H. Gering.
Die Edda. Leipsic. *n.d.*
Prose Edda. Snorri Sturluson, Edda. Ed. Jónsson, Finnur. Copenhagen. 1900.
(Tr. Anderson, R. B. Chicago. 1880.)
Sagas. Largely contained in the following collections:
 Altnordische Saga Bibliothek. Ed. Cederschiöld, G., Gering, H., Mogk, E.
  Halle. 1892 ff.
 Fornaldar Sögur Norðrlanda. Ed. Rafn, C. 3 vols. Copenhagen. 1829–
  30.

Fornmanna Sögur. 12 vols. Copenhagen. 1825–7.

Heimskringla. Jónsson, Finnur. 4 vols. Copenhagen. 1893–1901.

Saxo Grammaticus. Gesta Danorum. Ed. Holder, A. Strasburg. 1886.
(Tr. Elton, O. with Introd. by York Powell, F. London. 1894.)

[Some of the above are translated by Morris, W. and Magnússon, E., in the
Saga Library. 6 vols. London. 1891–1905. Other translations:
"Story of Burnt Njal." 2 vols. Edinburgh. New edn. with abridged
introduction. London. 1900. "Story of Gísli the outlaw." Edinburgh.
1866. Both by G. W. Dasent.]

IV. MODERN WORKS.

(a) GENERAL.

Bugge, S. Studier over de norske Gude- og Heltesagns Oprindelse. I. Christiania.
1881. II. Helgedigtene. Copenhagen. 1896. (Tr. Schofield, W. H.
Home of the Eddic Poems. Grimm Library. London. 1899.) (Attempts,
with great learning and ability, to show that Scandinavian mythology is largely
derived from Christian and classical legends, a now generally discredited theory.)

Chantepie de la Saussaye, P. D. Geschiedenis van den Godsdienst der Germanen.
Haarlem. 1900. English edition, enlarged, tr. Vos, "Religion of the Teutons,"
with bibliography. Boston. 1902. (Gives a good view of the main features of
Germanic religion.)

Craigie, W. Religion of Ancient Scandinavia. London. 1906. (A brief sketch of
Scandinavian cults.)

Golther, W. Handbuch der deutschen Mythologie. Leipsic. 1895. (Influenced
by Bugge.)

Grimm, Jakob. Deutsche Mythologie. 3 vols. Göttingen. 1835. 4th edn.
(Meyer, E. H.) 3 vols. Berlin. 1875–8. (Tr. Stallybrass. 4 vols. London.
1880–8.) (Obsolete in many points, but invaluable for the mass of references
it contains.)

Gummere, F. B. Germanic origins. New York. 1892.

Hayes, C. H. An introduction to the Sources relating to the Germanic Invasions.
(Columbia Univ. Studies in Polit. Science, vol. XXXIII, No. 3. New York. 1909.)

Herrmann, P. Deutsche Mythologie in gemeinverständlicher Darstellung. Leipsic.
1895. And Nordische Mythologie. Leipsic. 1903.

Mannhardt, W. Wald- und Feldkulte. 2 vols. Berlin. 1875–7. New edn.
Berlin. 1904–5.

Maurer, K. Die Bekehrung des Norwegischen Stammes zum Christentum. 2 vols.
Munich. 1855–6.

Meyer, E. H. Germanische Mythologie. Berlin. 1891. (Interpretations doubtful,
but gives a mass of valuable references, especially to ecclesiastical sources.)

Mogk, E. Deutsche Mythologie, in Paul's Grundriss der germanischen Philologie.
Vol. III, pp. 230–406. 2nd edn. 1900. (A valuable treatise, with a section
devoted to sources.)

Olrik, A. Nordisk Aandsliv i Vikingetiden. Copenhagen. 1907. (Tr. into
German by Ranisch, W. Nordisches Geistesleben. Heidelberg. 1908.)

Petersen, H. Om Nordboernes Gudedyrkelse og Gudetro i Hedenold. Copenhagen.
1876. (Tr. into Germ. by Riess. Über den Gottesdienst des Nordens.
Gardelegen. 1882.)

Pfannenschmid, H. Germanische Erntefeste. Hanover. 1878.

Richthofen, K. von. Untersuchungen über die friesische Rechtsgeschichte.
2 vols. Berlin. 1880–2.

Rydberg, V. Undersökningar i germansk Mythologi. 2 vols. Stockholm. 1886–9.
(Vol. I. Tr. Anderson, R. B. Aberdeen. 1889.) (Puts forward many
interesting and ingenious theories, but frequently fails in establishing them.)

(b) On Authorities.

Jónsson, Finnur. Den oldnorske og oldislandske Litteraturshistorie. 3 vols.
Copenhagen. 1894–1902.
Müllenhoff, K. Deutsche Altertumskunde. 5 vols. Berlin. 1870–91. 2nd edn.
Vols. I and II. Berlin. 1890–1906.
Olrik, A. Sakses Oldhistorie. Copenhagen. 1894.
Wattenbach, W. Deutschlands Geschichtsquellen. *See Gen. Bibl.* I.

(c) Monographs and Special Treatises.

Balder:
    Frazer, J. G. The Golden Bough. 2nd edn. III, pp. 236–350. (In 3rd edn.
    in progress pt. VII will be entitled Balder the Beautiful.)
    Kaufmann, Fr. Untersuchungen zur altgermanischen Religionsgeschichte.
    I. Balder. Strassburg. 1902.
Calendar:
    Tille, A. Yule and Christmas. London. 1899.
    Weinhold, K. Über die deutsche Jahrteilung. Kiel. 1862.
Edda:
    Faraday, W. The Edda, I. (Popular Studies in Mythology, etc. No. 12.)
    London. 1902.
    Gering, H. Vollständiges Wörterbuch zu den Liedern der Edda. Halle.
    1901–3.
Eschatology:
    Olrik, A. Om Ragnarök. Aarböger for nordisk Oldkyndighed. XVII.
    Række II, pp. 157–291. Copenhagen. 1902.
Folk-lore:
    Afzelius, A. A. Svenska Folkets Sägo-Häfder. 9 vols. Stockholm.
    1844–62.
    Árnason, Jón. Íslenzkar Þjóðsögur og Æfintyri. 2 vols. Leipsic. 1862–4.
    (Tr. Powell, G. and Magnússon, E. "Icelandic Legends." London.
    1864–6.)
    Asbjörnson, P. C. and Moe, J. Norske Folke-Eventyr. Christiania. 1868.
    Ny Samling. 1871. (Tr. Dasent, G. W. Popular Tales from the Norse.
    Edinburgh. 1859. New edn. 1903.)
    Christensen, E. T. Danske Sagn. 4 vols. Copenhagen. 1891–6.
    Craigie, W. A. Scandinavian Folk-lore. Paisley and London. 1896.
    Hyltén-Cavallius, G. O. Wärend och Wirdarne. 2 vols. Stockholm.
    1864–8.
    Jakobsen, J. Færøiske Folkesagn og Eventyr. Copenhagen. 1897–1901.
    Wuttke, C. Der deutsche Volksglaube der Gegenwart. Hamburg. 1860.
    3rd edn. by Meyer, E. H. Berlin. 1900.
Indiculus Superstitionum:
    Saupe, H. A. Der Indic. Superst. Leipsic. 1891. (Useful references.)
Inscriptions:
    Kaufmann, Fr. Mythologische Zeugnisse aus römischen Inschriften. In
    Beiträge zur Gesch. der deutschen Sprache und Lit. Paul, H. and
    Braune, W. Vols. XV, XVI, XVIII. Halle.
    Much, R. and Grienberger, Th. von. Zeitschrift für deutsches Altertum.
    Vol. XXXV. Berlin. 1891.
Nerthus-Njörðr:
    Chadwick, H. M. Origin of the English Nation. Ch. X. Cambridge.
    1907.

Kock, A. in Z. für deutsche Philologie. Vol. xxviii, pp. 289 ff. Halle. 1896. (Suggests a philological explanation of the change of sex.)

Weinhold, K. Über den Mythus von Wanenkrieg. SPAW. 1890.

Odin:

Chadwick, H. M. The Cult of Othin. London. 1899.

Jónsson, Finnur. Odin og Tor i det 9 og. 10 Århr. Arkiv för nordisk Filologi. N. F. xiii, pp. 219–47. (Lund. 1901.)

Olrik, A. Odinsjægeren i Jylland. Dania, viii, pp. 139–73. Copenhagen. 1901. (Odin in Danish folk-lore.)

Sacrifice :

Mogk, E. Die Menschenopfer bei den Germanen. Abh. der philol.-hist. Klasse der kön. Gesellschaft der Wiss. Bd. xxvii. No. xvii. Leipsic. 1909.

Temples:

Bruun, D. and Jónsson, Finnur. Om Hove og Hoveudgravninger på Island. Aarböger for nord. Oldkyndighed. Række ii. Vol. xxiv. Copenhagen. 1909. (An English abridgment of this valuable article in the Saga Book of the Viking Club. Vol. vii, pp. 25–37. London. 1911.)

Thümmel, A. Der Germanische Tempel. Halle. 1909.

Vigfússon, Sigurðr. Árbók hins íslenzka fornleifafjelags. Reykjavík. 1880-1.

CHAPTER XVI (A).

(1) BRITISH CHRISTIANITY IN ROMAN TIMES.

Refer also to Bibliography of Vol. I c. XIII.

1. ORIGINAL AUTHORITIES.

Gildas. De excidio et conquestu Britanniae. MGH, auct. ant. XIII, 1-85 (1898), and other edns.

Nennius. Historia Brittonum. Ibid. XIII, 111-198 and other edns., and see note to bibl. for c. XLII B in vol. I.

Ussher, J. Britannicarum Ecclesiarum Antiquitates. Dublin. 1639. Ed. El-rington, C. R. Dublin. 1847 ff. and other edns. [Full accounts of the Legends.]

[A *catena* of extracts from early Christian writers will be found in Williams' Christianity in Early Britain (as below): chap. IV, Excursus A.]

2. MODERN WORKS.

Bright, W. Early English Church History. 2nd edn. Oxford. 1888.
—— The Roman See in the early Church. London. 1896. [Includes a chapter on The Celtic Churches in the British Isles.]

Collins, W. E. The Beginnings of English Christianity. London. (S.P.C.K.) Ch. I (on Romano-British Church and Celtic Christianity.)

Gougaud, L. Les Chrétientés Celtiques. Paris. 1911 (cc. I, II, with full bibliography).

Haddan, A. W. Remains. Oxford. 1876. [Includes an article on The Churches of the British Confession.]

Haddan and Stubbs. Councils. *See Gen. Bibl.* III.

Haverfield, F. Early British Christianity in EHR, XI (1896) 417-30.

Loofs, F. Antiquae Britonum Scotorumque Ecclesiae. London. 1882.

Oman, C. England before the Norman Conquest. London. 1910. Ch. X (on Christianity in Britain during the Roman period).

Plummer, A. The Churches in Britain before A.D. 1000. 2 vols. (Library of Historic Theology, ed. Piercy, W. C.) London. 1911-12.

Williams, H. Christianity in Early Britain. Oxford. 1912.

For Wales only:—

Bund, J. W. Willis. The Celtic Church in Wales. London. 1897.

Lloyd, J. E. A History of Wales. London. 1912.

(2) CONVERSION OF IRELAND.

Acta SS. Hiberniae, ex codice Salmanticensi. Ed. de Smedt, C. Edinburgh and London. 1888.

Annals of Ulster, ed. Hennessey, W. M. Dublin. 1887.

Bury, J. B. Life of St Patrick and his place in History. London. 1905.

Haddan, A. W., and Stubbs, W. Councils, etc. Vol. II, pt 2. *See Gen. Bibl.* IV.

Martyrologies of Donegal, ed. Todd, J. H. Dublin. 1864. Gorman and Oengus, ed. Stokes, W. London. 1895 and 1905. Tallaght, ed. Kelly, M. Dublin. 1857.

Plummer, C. Vitae SS. Hiberniae. Oxford. 1910.

Prosper of Aquitaine. Chron. Consular. MPL (cols. 274, 595).

Stokes, G. T. Ireland and the Celtic Church. 2nd edn. London. 1888.

Stokes, Whitley. Tripartite Life of St Patrick. Parts ı and ıı. (Rolls.) 1887.

Ussher, Archbp. Whole Works. Dublin. 1843–64. Esp. vol. vı for Ninian (p. 209), and Vita Kierani (p. 332).

Warren, F. E. The Liturgy and Ritual of the Celtic Church. Oxford. 1881.
(This includes portions of the Stowe Missal, the antiphonary of Bangor and other early Irish Service books.)

Zimmer, H. The Celtic Church in Britain and Ireland. London. 1902.

There are a considerable number of Irish Annals, Martyrologies, and Vitae Sanctorum, now for the most part printed; but they only throw light incidentally on the subject of this chapter, and therefore are not all enumerated here.

There are also large MS. collections of Irish and Latin documents. Of these the earliest and far the most important is the Book of Armagh, in Trinity College, Dublin, of which a complete publication is promised shortly by the Rev. J. Gwynn, D. D.

(3) CONVERSION OF SCOTLAND.

Cummeneus Albus (Cummien). Liber de virtutibus sancti Columbae, printed by Colgan, Trias. Thaum. 321–4. This is mainly incorporated in the next work, which is described in its colophon as "uirtutum libelli Columbae."

Adamnanus. Vita S. Columbae. Ed. Reeves, W., Irish Archaeological and Celtic Society. Dublin. 1857.

Baedae Historia Ecclesiastica, ed. Plummer, C. *See Gen. Bibl.* v.

Breviarium Aberdonense. Edinburgh. 1510. Repr. London, 1854.

Forbes, A. P. Bishop of Brechin. Kalendars of Scottish Saints. Edinburgh. 1887.

Haddan and Stubbs. Councils. Vol. ıı, pt 1.

Harnack, A. Der Brief des britischen Königs Lucius an dem Papst Eleutherus. SPAW. 1904. *See review* in EHR. Oct. 1907.

Pinkerton, J. Lives of the Scottish Saints. Revised and enlarged by Metcalfe, W. M. Paisley. 1889.

Skene, W. F. Celtic Scotland. 3 vols. Edinburgh. 1876–80.

—— Chronicles of the Picts, Chronicles of the Scots, and other early memorials of Scottish history. Scottish Record Society. Edinburgh. 1867.

CHAPTER XVI (B)

I. CONVERSION OF THE ENGLISH.

(*See Bibl. to* VIII (B), *for Gregory the Great. Also see Bibl. to Chap.* XVII.)

A. ORIGINAL SOURCES.

Aldhelm. Opera. Ed. Giles, J. A., in Patres Eccles. Angliae. Oxford. 1844. Also MPL. LXXXIX.

A. S. Chronicle. *See Gen. Bibl.* V.

Bede. Hist. Eccles. *See ib.*

De Pontificibus et Sanctis Ecclesiae Eboracensis Carmen (probably by Alcuin) *in* Historians of the Church of York and its Archbishops. Ed. Raine, J. 1879. Rolls.

Elmham, Thomas of. Historia Monasterii S. Augustini Cantuariensis. Ed. Hardwick, C. 1858. Rolls.

Haddan, A. W. and Stubbs, W. Councils and Ecclesiastical documents relating to Great Britain and Ireland. Vols. I–III (especially III). Oxford. 1869–78.

Thorne, Wm. Chronica de rebus gestis Abbatum S. Augustini Cantuariensis. Ed. Twysden, Roger. *In* Historiae Anglicanae Scriptores X. 1753–2202. London. 1652.

> For extracts and English translations see Mason, A. J., The Mission of St Augustine, etc. *below.*

B. MODERN WORKS.

Bassenge, F. E. Die Sendung Augustins zur Bekehrung der Angelsachsen. Leipsic. 1890.

Bright, Wm. Chapters of Early English Church History. Oxford. 1878. 2nd edn. Oxford. 1897.

Browne, G. F. The Christian Church in these Islands before Augustine. 2nd edn. London. 1895.

—— Augustine and his companions. London. 1895. 2nd edn. 1897.

—— The Conversion of the Heptarchy. London. 1906.

Cabrol, Fernand. L'Angleterre avant les Normands. Paris. 1908 (2nd edn. 1909).

Collins, W. E. The beginnings of English Christianity. London. 1898.

Creighton, C. History of Epidemics in Britain. Cambridge. 1891. Vol. I, p. 4, sqq. (for the Yellow Pest).

Haddan, A. W. Remains. Ed. Forbes, A. P. Oxford and London. 1876.

Hodgkin, Thos. From the earliest times to the Norman Conquest. (The Political History of England. Vol. I. Ed. Hunt, W., and Poole, R. L.) London. 1906.

Holmes, T. S. The Conversion of Wessex. EHR. VII. 437–43.

Hunt, W. A history of the English Church from its foundation to the Norman Conquest. Vol. I. *In* A History of the English Church. Ed. Stephens, W. R. W., and Hunt, W. London. 1899.

Hutton, W. H. The influence of Christianity upon national character illustrated by the lives and legends of the English Saints (Bampton Lectures for 1903). London.

Mason, A. J. The Mission of St Augustine to England according to the original Documents, being a handbook for the thirteenth centenary. Ed. Mason, A. J. (Contains documents with translations into English; also dissertations, historical and liturgical, by various writers.) Cambridge. 1897.

Mommsen, Th. NAGDG. xvii. pp. 390–95. (On authenticity of Gregory's answer to Augustine.)

Oman, C. England before the Norman Conquest. (A History of England in seven volumes. Vol. i. Ed. Oman, C.) London. 1910.

Plummer, A. The Churches in Britain before A.D. 1000. Vols. i, ii. 1911–12. (Library of Historical Theology. Ed. Piercy, W. C.)

Stubbs, W. Constitutional History. *See Gen. Bibl.* vi.

DNB, and Dict. of Eng. Church Hist. Ed. Ollard, S. L. and Crosse, G. London. 1912. For lives of bishops.

II. CONVERSION OF THE GERMANS.

(*See also Bibliographies for Chaps.* iv, v, xviii, *and* xxii.)

Very full Bibliographies in Potthast: in Will's edn. of Böhmer, J. Fr., Regesta Archiepiscoporum Maguntinensium as below, i (pp. ii sqq. for works, and modern literature, pp. xi–xiii): in Wurth, G., St Boniface, as below, and in Hefele-Leclercq (French trans.), iii, pt. 2, 806–7.

Chevalier, W. Répertoire des Sources historiques.

For MS. *see* Potthast, and prefaces to works, also in articles referred to, especially account of MSS. in Levison, W., *as below*.

A. ORIGINAL SOURCES.

(*a*) WORKS OF BONIFACE.

For German translation of works *see* Külb, Ph. H. Sämmtliche Schriften des hl. Bonif. übersetzt. 2 vols. Regensburg. 1859. (Includes Letters, Canons, Lives, etc.)

Ebert. Allg. Gesch. Lit. *See Gen. Bibl.* vi. i. p. 653 for estimate of Boniface's works.

1. *Sermons:*

In Martène et Durand, amplissima collectio. ix, col. 186–218.

Giles, J. A. Bonifacii opera. London. 1834.

Migne. MPL. lxxxix.

[The doubts as to genuineness of sermons expressed by Oudin, Commentarius, i, col. 1789 (*see Gen. Bibl.* i), are now mostly given up.

See Hahn, H. Die angeblichen Predigten des B. *in* FDG. xxiv. 585–625. 1884. And for reply:

Nürnberger, A. Die angebliche Unechtheit der Predigten des h. B. NAGDG. xiv. 109–34 (1888).]

Dicta: Dicta S. Bonifacii. Ed. Nürnberger, A. J. TQS. lxx. pp. 287–96. Tübingen. 1888.

2. *Boniface's Latin Grammar* (significant for his zeal in classical education, as are also the references to Latin verses in Epistles).

Mai, Angelo. Classicorum Auctorum e Vaticanis cod. editorum Tom. vii, pp. 475–548. Rome. 1835.

Du Rieu, W. N. Schedae Vaticanae, etc. Lugd.-Bat. 1860.

See Bursian, K. Die Grammatik des Winfried-Bonifacius. Sitzungsber. d. München Akad. d. Wissenschaften (philos.-philol. Cl.), pp. 457 sqq. 1873.

3. *Poems:*

> *In* Giles and Migne *as above* also MGH. Poetae Latini Aevi Carolini. I.
> pp. 3–23.
>
> Bock, C. P. Eine Reliquie des Apostels der Deutschen. Freibürger
> Diöcesan Archiv. III. pp. 221–72. (For riddles.)

4. *Penitential* (significant for Boniface's relation to the Celtic discipline and his
connexion with England).

> Incompletely (as Poenitentiale St Bonifacii et antiqua confessio theotisca) in
> Martène and Durand (Tom. VII, col. 48), Giles and Migne. Completely
> by Binterim, A. J., in "C Blasci Dissertatio in qua ostenditur, diaconis
> nunquam fuisse permissum administrare sacramentum poenitentiae,"
> Mainz, 1822: also in Binterim, Die vorzuglichsten Denkwürdigkeiten
> der christ.-katholischen Kirche aus den ersten, mittlern und letzten
> Zeiten, vol. v. Mainz. 1825–41. [On the connexion with Egbert's
> Penitential see Nürnberger, A. Zu den handschriftlichen Überlieferung
> der Werke des h. Bonifaz. NAGDG. VIII. pp. 299–325.]

5. *Letters:*

> Ed. Dümmler, E. Epp. S. Bonifatii et Lulli; in Epistolarum Meroving.
> MGH. III. pp. 231–431. Berlin. 1892. (Best edn.)
>
> *Also in* Jaffé, Ph. Mon. Moguntina. Bibliotheca rer. German. III. (A good
> edn.; less useful are the earlier edns. of works of Boniface.) See for
> criticism Loofs, *below.*
>
> Transl. (German). Tangl, M. Briefe des hl. Bonifatius. Gesch. d.
> deutschen Vorzeit. Vol. XCII. Leipsic. 1912.
>
> Kylie, E. English letters of St Boniface. (King's Classics.) London. 1911.
>
> Diekamp, W. Die Wiener Handschrift der Bonifatius Briefe. NAGDG.
> Vol. IX. pp. 9–28. (1884.)

(*b*) Other Sources.

Lives:

> Levison, W. Vitae S. Bonifatii archiepiscopi Moguntini. *In* Script. rer.
> German. 1905. (Best edn., includes all the lives with an admirable
> Preface.)
>
> 1. Willibald. Vita S. Bonifatii. Ed. first by Canisius, H. Antiquae
> Lectionis. IV. Ingolstadt. 1603. Other edns. by
> Pertz. MGH. Script. rer. Merov. II. 331–53. Hanover. 1829. And
> Jaffé, Ph. Mon. Moguntina. pp. 429–71. Bibliotheca rer. German. III.
> Berlin. 1866.
> Nürnberger, A. J. Vita S. Bonif. 27ster Sitzungsber. der wiss. Gesell.
> Philom. Neisse, 1895, and separately, Breslau, 1896.
>
> 2. Vita Bonifatii auctore Radbodo. Ed. first by Henschen, Godef. and
> Papebroch, Dan. ASBoll. for June, I. Antwerp. 1695. Partly
> in Pertz: a fragment in Jaffé, *as above.*
>
> 3. Vita Bonifatii (Passio S. Bon. Ep. et Mart. et sociorum eius). Ed. first
> in ASBoll. *as above.* Partly in Pertz.
>
> 4. Vita auctore Moguntino (Passio S. Bon.). Ed. first in ASBoll. In
> Pertz and Jaffé.
>
> 5. Passio S. Bonifatii Episcopi et sociorum eius. Ed. first by Nürnberger, A.
> Anecdota Bonifatiana. 26ster Sitzungsbericht d. wissen. Gesell. Philo-
> mathie zu Neisse. Neisse. 1892.
>
> 6. Vitae Bon. auctore Othloho libri duo. Ed. first by Surius, Laurentius,
> De probatis SS. historiis. Vol. III. Cologne, 1572: then by Canisius.
> Partly in Pertz and Jaffé.
>
> Böhmer, J. Fr. Regesta Archiepiscoporum Maguntinensium. Bd. I.
> 742?–1160. Edited by Will, Cornelius. Innsbruck. 1877.

For German translations :

Vita Willibaldi, by Simson, B. E. Berlin. 1863. And

Arndt, W. In Geschichte d. d. Vorzeit. 1888.

Lives 1, 2, 3, 4 and 6 are translated in Külb *as above.*

Woelbing, G. Die Mittelalterlichen Lebenschreibungen des Bonifatius ihrem Inhalte nach untersucht, verglichen und erläutert. Jena. 1892. (Dissertation.)

[For articles on *Lives see* Will's edn. of Böhmer's Regesta, *as above,* Potthast, Dahlmann-Waitz and Kurth. *See Gen. Bibl.* I.]

For the general historical sources see Bibliographies to chaps. IV, XVIII and XXII, especially important are MGH, Script. rer. Meroving., Epistolae Meroving., and Concil. aevi Meroving. (Leg. sect. III).

For Columbanus, see Bibl. in Hauck, Kirchengesch. I. 263. *See Gen. Bibl.* VI.

Ionas. Vitae S. Columbani abbatis discipulorumque eius libri duo. Ed. Krusch, B. MGH, Script. rer. Merov. IV. 1902. *See also* Ionas, Vitae Sanctorum Columbani, Vedastis, Johannis. Ed. Krusch, B. in Script. rer. German. Leipsic. 1905.

Gundlach, W. Ueber die Columban-Briefe. NAGDG. Vol. XV. 1890. pp. 499–526.

—— Columbani Epistolae et Carmina *in* MGH, Epistolae III. Berlin. 1892.

Sebass, O. Über Columbas von Luxeuil Klosterregel. Dresden. 1883.

For the predecessors of Boniface see Hauck and RE³. Also Bibliography of Chap. IV. Many Vitae and Passiones *in* MGH, Script. Meroving. Ed. Krusch, B. and Levison, W. Vol. V. Hanover and Leipsic. 1910.

B. MODERN WORKS.

Breysig, Theodor. Jahrbücher des fränk. Reiches. 714–41. Leipsic. 1869.

Browne, G. F. Boniface of Crediton. London. 1910. [Best English account.]

Buss, F. I. von. Winfrid-Bonifacius. Ed. Scherer, R. Graz. 1883.

Cholevius, E. Einfluss Roms auf d. Amtsführung d. Bonifatius. Königsberg. 1887. (Dissertation.)

Dunzelmann. Zur Anordnung der B. Briefe und der frank. Synoden. FDG. Vol. XIII. 1873.

—— Untersuchung über die ersten gehalten Concilien unter Karlmann und Pippin. Göttingen. 1869.

Ebrard, J. H. A. Die Iroschottische Missionskirche des 6, 7 und 8 Jahrhunderts. Gütersloh. 1873.

—— Bonifatius, der Zerstörer des Columbanische Kirchenthums auf dem Festlände. Gütersloh. 1882. (Imagines a "Culdee" Church to have existed on the Continent.)

Festgabe zum Bonifatius-Jubiläum. Fulda. 1905. [Especially Scherer, C. on "Die Codices Bonifatiani in der Landesbibliotek zu Fulda," and Richter, G., "Beiträge zur Geschichte der Grabeskirche des hl. Bonifatius in Fulda."]

Fischer, O. Bonifatius, der Apostel der Deutschen. Paderborn. 1895.

—— D. Legatenamt d. Bonifatius und seine Mission unter d. Sachsen. FDG. XXVI. pp. 640–7.

Förster, H. Zur Bonifaciusfrage. TSK. 1876. pp. 664–703. (A general study.)

Hahn, H. Jahrbücher des fränk. Reichs. 741–52. Berlin. 1863. (Especially Excursus XIV, The Council of Lestines (Estinnes). Exc. XV, The opponents of Boniface in 745. Exc. XVI for Gewilip. Exc. XXI, Boniface and Grifo. For Fulda see Exc. XXVI and Hauck I, 580–3.)

Hahn, H. Bonifaz und Lul. Ihre Angelsächsischen Korrespondenten. Erzbischof
   Luls Leben. Leipsic. 1883. [Excellent on friends of Boniface.]
—— Noch einmal die Briefe und Synoden des B. FDG. Vol. xv. 1875.
Hauck. Kirchengesch. (*See Gen. Bibl.* vi.) Vol. i. [Indispensable: full treatment in
   notes and Excursus of all contested points with references to latest literature.]
Hefele, C. J. Geschichte der Einführung des Christentum in süd-westl. Deutsch-
   land besonders in Württemberg. 1837.
—— Conciliengeschichte. iii. (*See Gen. Bibl.* vi.) (The new French translations
   by Leclercq should always be referred to also. See iii, pt. 2, 815 and 825 ff. for
   Councils and literature on them.)
Holder-Egger, O. Über die Vita Lulli und ihren Verfassen. NAGDG. ix.
   pp. 283–320. (Assigns this interesting life to Lampert of Hersfeld.)
Jaffé, Ph. Zur Chronologie der B. Briefe und Synoden. FDG. Vol. x. 1870.
Köhler, W. Bonifatius in Hessen und das hessische Bistum Buraburg. ZKG.
   Vol. xxv. pp. 197–232. (Excellent for the relations of various parts of
   Boniface's work to each other.)
Körber, G. W. Die Ausbreitung des Christentum in südl. Baden. Heidelberg.
   1878.
Kurth, G. Saint Boniface. Paris. 1902. 2nd edn. (3rd edn. reprinting.)
   [Excellent bibliography.]
—— Histoire poétique des Mérovingiens. Paris. 1893.
Kylie, E. The Conditions of the German Provinces as illustrating the methods of
   St Boniface. JTS. vii. pp. 29 ff. London. 1905–6.
Lechler, Gotthard. Die Bekehrung der Deutschen zu Christo, nach ihrem ge-
   schichtlichen Gäng. TSK. 1876. pp. 520–38.
Loening. Geschichte des deutschen Kirchenrechts. Strassburg. 2 vols. 1878.
Loofs, F. Der Beiname des Apostels der Deutschen nebst ein Mitteilung über
   Bonifatii Ep. 22 bei Jaffé. (MRG, iii.) ZKG. pp. 623–31. 1882. (Argues
   for derivation of name from *fari* not *facere,* and for its assumption at Rome in
   718 or 719.)
—— Der Chronologie der auf die fränk. Synoden des hl. Bonif. bezüglichen
   Briefe der Bonifat. Briefsammlung. Leipsic. 1881.
Müller, J. P. Bonifacius eine kerkhistorische studie. 2 vols. Amsterdam.
   1369–70.
Neander, A. *See Gen. Bibl.* vi.
Nürnberger, A. J. Die Namen Vynfrith Bonifatius. (28 Ber. d. Philomathie zu
   Neisse.) Breslau. 1897.
Oelsner. Jahrbücher des fränkischen Reichs unter König Pippin. Leipsic. 1871.
Pfahler, G. St Bonifacius und seine Zeit. Regensburg. 1880.
Schmidt, H. G. Über d. Ernennung d. Bonifatius zum Metropoliten v. Köln.
   Coepenick. 1899. (Dissertation.)
Seiters, G. Bonifacius der Apostel der Deutschen. Mainz. 1845.
Sepp, B. Zur Chronologie des ersten der fränk. Synoden des viii Jahrhunderts.
   HJ. xxii. 1901.
Tangl, M. Die Todesjahr d. Bonifatius z. d. Verein. f. Hess. G. Neue Folge 27.
Wattenbach, W. Deutschlands Geschichtsquellen. *See Gen. Bibl.* i.
Werminghoff, A. Kirchengesch. *See Gen. Bibl.* vi.
—— NAGDG. xxiv. p. 459 sqq. (On Synod of 742.)
Werner, A. Bonifacius der Apostel der Deutschen und die Romanisierung von
   Mittel-Europa. Leipsic. 1875.
Articles on Boniface (by Werner, A.), and other missionaries *in* RE[3] : *in* EncBr.
   (by Shotwell, J. T.): *in* Lichtenberger's Enc. (by Paumers): in Wetzer-Kaulen
   (by Kessels). *See Gen. Bibl.* i.

CHAPTER XVII.

ENGLAND (to c. 800) AND ENGLISH INSTITUTIONS.

I. SPECIAL BIBLIOGRAPHY.

Gross, C. Sources and Literature of English History. *See Gen. Bibl.* L

II. ORIGINAL DOCUMENTS.

(a) LAWS.

Liebermann, F. Die Gesetze der Angelsachsen. *See Gen. Bibl.* IV.
Thorpe, B. Ancient Laws and Institutes of England, with an English translation of the Saxon. Record Comm. 1840.

(b) ECCLESIASTICAL CANONS.

Haddan, A. W. and Stubbs, W. Councils, etc. *See Gen. Bibl.* III.

(c) LANDBOOKS AND OTHER DIPLOMATA.

Facsimiles of ancient charters in the British Museum. Ed. Bond, E. A. 4 pts. London. 1873–8.
Facsimiles of Anglo-Saxon Manuscripts. Ed. Sandars, W. B. 3 pts. Ordnance Survey Office. Southampton. 1878–84.
Birch, W. de Gray. Cartularium Saxonicum. Vol. I. London. 1885.
Kemble, J. M. Codex diplomaticus aevi Saxonici. Eng. Hist. Soc. 6 vols. London. 1839–48.
Napier, A. S. and Stevenson, W. H. The Crawford Charters: a collection of early charters and documents now in the Bodleian Library. Oxford. 1895. (Anecdota Oxon. IV, 7.)

(d) POETRY ILLUSTRATING SOCIAL CONDITIONS.

Beowulf, a facsimile of the MSS. Ed. Zupitza, J. (EETS.) 1882.
Clark Hall, J. R. Beowulf and the Finnsbury Fragment, a translation into modern English Prose. London. 1911.
Grein, C. W. M. and Wülker, R. P. Bibliothek der angelsächsischen Poesie. Vol. I Cassel. 1881. Widsith, 35 ff. Beowulf, 1944 ff.

III. AUTHORITIES.

(a) CONTEMPORARY.

Alcuin. Alcuini Opera, cura Frobenii. MPL, c, cI.
      Monumenta Alcuiniana, in Bibliotheca Rerum Germanicarum. Ed. Jaffé, Ph. VI. Berlin. 1873.
Aldhelm. Sancti Aldhelmi opera. Ed. Giles, J. A. MPL. LXXXIX.
Anonymous. Vita S. Cuthberti. Ed. Stevenson, J. in Bede's Opera. London. 1838. Written c. A.D. 700, rewritten by Bede c. A.D. 720. Trans. W. Forbes Leith. Edinburgh. 1888.
Bede. Venerabilis Bedae Opera Historica. Ed. Plummer, C. *See Gen. Bibl.* V.
Eddi. Vita Wilfridi Episcopi Eboracensis. Historians of the Church of York. Ed. Raine, J. Vol. I, pp. 1–103. (Rolls.) 1879.
Felix. Vita S. Guthlaci. Ed. Birch, W. de G. Wisbeach. 1881.

(b) LATER.

Anglo-Saxon Chronicle. Ed. Plummer, C. *See Gen. Bibl.* v.
Annales Cambriae. Ed. Phillimore, E. Soc. of Cymmrodorior y Cymmrodor. ix. 141–83. London. 1888.
Annales Lindisfarnenses. Ed. Pertz. MGH. Script. (No. 594.) xix. 502-8.
Faricius. Vita Aldhelmi, in Vita quorumdam Anglo-Saxonum. Ed. Giles, J. A. Caxton Soc. London. 1854.
Simeon of Durham. Historia Dunelmensis Ecclesiae and Historia Regum. Ed. Arnold, T. (Rolls.) 1885.
William of Malmesbury. De gestis pontificorum Anglorum. Ed. Hamilton, N. E. S. D. (Rolls.) 1870.
—— De gestis regum Anglorum. Ed. Stubbs, W. (Rolls.) 1887–9.

IV. MODERN WORKS.

(a) GENERAL.

Bright, W. Chapters of Early English Church History. Vol. iii. Oxford. 1893.
Brown, G. Baldwin. The Arts in Early England. London. 1903. Vol. i. The Life of Saxon England in its Relation to the Arts. Vol. ii. Ecclesiastical Architecture from the conversion of the Saxons to the Norman Conquest.
Cambridge History of English Literature. Ed. Ward, A. W. and Waller, A. R. Vol. i. Cambridge. 1907.
Cunningham, W. The Growth of English Industry and Commerce. 3rd edn. Cambridge.
Green, J. R. The Making of England. London. 1881.
Hodgkin, T. Political History of England to 1066. London. 1906.
Hunt, W. The History of the English Church from its foundation to the Norman Conquest. London. 1899.
Kemble, J. M. The Saxons in England. London. 1849. Ed. Birch, W. de G. 2 vols. 1876.
Lloyd, J. E. History of Wales. 2 vols. London. 1911.
Makower, F. Constitutional History of the Church of England. Berlin. 1894. Trans. Upton. London. 1895.
Maurer, Konrad. Angelsächsische Rechtsverhältnisse, Kritische Überschau der Deutschen Gesetzgebung. Munich. 1853–6. [Corrects Kemble.]
Medley, D. J. A Students Manual of English Constitutional History. 4th edn. Oxford. 1907.
Oman, C. England before the Norman Conquest. London. 1910.
Ramsey, J. H. The Foundations of England. London. 1898.
Social England, by various writers. Ed. Traill, H. D. and Mann, J. S. Illustrated edn. London. 1901.
Stubbs, W. Constitutional History of England. *See Gen. Bibl.* vi. Vol. i. 6th edn. 1897.

(b) SPECIAL TREATISES.

Aronius, Julius. Diplomatische Studien über die älteren angelsächsischen Urkunden [to A.D. 839]. Königsberg. 1883.
Bateson, M. Origin and early history of double Monasteries. TRHS. N.S. xiii. 137–98.
Bönhoff, Leo. Aldhelm von Malmesbury. Dresden. 1804.
Brunner, H. Sippe und Wergeld. ZR. xvi. Germ. Abth. pp. 14–18. (1882.)

Brunner, H. Zur Rechtsgeschichte der römischen und germanischen Urkunde. Vol. I. 149–208. Das angelsächsische Landbuch. Berlin. 1880.

Chadwick, H. M. Studies on Anglo-Saxon Institutions. Cambridge. 1905.

—— The Heroic Age. Cambridge. 1912.

Corbett, W. J. The Tribal Hidage. RHS. Transactions. N.S. XIV. 187–230. London. 1900.

Earle, J. A handbook to the land charters. Oxford. 1888.

Eckenstein, L. Women under Monasticism. London. 1896.

Hahn, H. Bonifaz und Lul, ihre angelsächsischen Korrespondenten. Leipzig. 1883.

Hildebrand, B. E. Anglosachsiska Mynt i Svenska kongliga Mynt kabinettet. Stockholm. 1846. New edn. 1881.

Holdsworth, W. S. A History of English Law. Vol. II. Anglo-Saxon Period. London. 1903.

Jenks, E. The Problem of the Hundred. EHR. XI. 510. (1896.)

Keary, C. F. and Grueber, H. A. A catalogue of English coins in the British Museum. Anglo-Saxon Series. 2 vols. London. 1887–93.

Liebermann, F. Das Englische Gilde im achten Jahrhundert. Archiv für das Studium der neueren Sprachen, 1896. pp. 333–40. Brunswick. 1896.

Maitland, F. W. Domesday Book and Beyond. Cambridge. 1897.

—— Collected Papers. Cambridge. 1911. The Surnames of English Villages. Vol. II. pp. 84–95.

—— The Survival of Archaic Communities. Ibid. II. pp. 313–65.

—— The Laws of the Anglo-Saxons. Ibid. III. pp. 447–73.

Maurer, K. Über das Wesen des ältesten Adels der deutschen Stämme, pp. 123–95. Die Angelsachsen. Munich. 1846.

Meitzen, A. Siedelung und Agrarwesen der Westgermanen und Ostgermanen. 3 vols. and atlas. Berlin. 1895.

Nasse, E. Ueber die mittelalterliche Feldgemeinschaft. Bonn. 1869. Transl. London. 1871.

Pollock, F. and Maitland, F. W. History of English Law. Bk. 2. Ch. VI § 1 on the blood-feud group. *See Gen. Bibl.* VI.

Rhamm, K. Die Grosshufen der Nordgermanen. Brunswick. 1906.

Roeder, F. Die Familie bei den Angelsachsen. Halle. 1899.

Round, J. H. The Settlement of the South and East Saxons, *in* Commune of London. Westminster. 1899.

Searle, W. G. Anglo-Saxon bishops, kings and nobles. Cambridge. 1899.

—— Onomasticon Anglo-Saxonicum. Cambridge. 1897.

Seebohm, F. The English Village Community. London. 1883.

—— The Tribal System in Wales. London. 1895.

—— Tribal Custom in Anglo-Saxon Law. London. 1902.

Stjerna, Knut. Essays on Questions connected with the old English Poem of Beowulf. Trans. by J. R. Clark Hall. Viking Club, extra Series, Vol. III. London. 1912.

Victoria History of the Counties of England. 1900. *In progress.*

Vinogradoff, P. The Growth of the Manor. London. 1905.

—— Folkland. EHR. VIII. pp. 1–17. London. 1893.

Wilda, W. E. Das Strafrecht der Germanen; chap. V on the Anglo-Saxon wergeld. Halle. 1842.

CHAPTER XVIII.

THE CAROLINGIAN REVOLUTION AND FRANK INTERVENTION IN ITALY.

1. SPECIAL BIBLIOGRAPHIES.

Both the authorities and the modern works for this topic may of course be learned from the standard bibliographies of the history of Germany (Dahlmann-Waitz, Quellenkunde, *see Gen. Bibl.* I) and of France (Monod, Bibliographie, *see ib.*); and the authorities are not only enumerated but critically discussed by Wattenbach (*see ib.*), by Molinier (*see ib.*) and by Jacob (Quellenkunde zur deutschen Geschichte, I, Leipsic, 1906, Sammlung Göschen). Mühlbacher opens his Deutsche Geschichte unter den Karolingern (*see Gen. Bibl.* VI) with an admirable introduction on the sources. Useful, too, are the bibliographies prefixed by Diehl to his Études sur l'Administration byzantine dans l'Exarchat de Ravenne (*see ib.*) and by Kleinclausz to his L'Empire carolingien (Paris, 1902). Best of all, and in English, are the paragraphs on "sources" and "guides" prefixed by Hodgkin to the chapters of his Italy and her Invaders (VII, The Frankish Invasions, VIII, The Frankish Empire, *see Gen. Bibl.* VI).

2. ORIGINAL DOCUMENTS.

The documents of the Carolingian sovereigns have been exhaustively calendared by Mühlbacher (Die Regesten des Kaiserreichs unter den Karolingern, 751–918, 2nd edn., completed by Lechner, Innsbruck, 1908—the work is itself a re-edition of Part I of Böhmer's Regesta Imperii), and with such careful attention to the narrative sources as well that it may almost serve as a guide to the whole body of materials. It includes, too, an excellent chapter on "Quellen und Bearbeitungen," and a "Bücher-Register" which enumerates all publications containing Carolingian documents. The older Acta Karolinorum (Vienna, 1867, 2 vols.) of Th. v. Sickel retains worth chiefly for its masterly chapters on Carolingian diplomatic. The documents themselves (the Capitularia, the Concilia, the Diplomata, the Epistolae) may now best be sought in MGH. Even the letters of Boniface and Lull and those of the Popes to the Carolingians are best edited in this great collection. To the Papal documents in general the Regesta Pontificum Romanorum of Jaffé (*see Gen. Bibl.* IV) must still be the guide; though the greater completeness and the topographical arrangement of the Regesta of Kehr (*see ib.*) make it already an invaluable supplement. The documents fundamental to the story of the papal state are gathered by Cenni in his Monumenta dominationis pontificiae (Rome, 1760–1) and Theiner in his Codex diplomaticus dominii temporalis S. Sedis (Rome, 1861–2).

3. AUTHORITIES.

(a) CONTEMPORARY.

Annales. Into the tangled nomenclature of the Carolingian annals, or into the more tangled question of their authorship and interdependence, it is needless here to go. All may be found in the MGH (Script. i–iv, xiii, xx), though important re-editions of one or two (as of the so-called Annales Laurissenses majores and Annales Einhardi, in 1895, by Kurze, under the new title of Annales regni Francorum) must be sought in the subsidiary school series, the Scriptores rerum Germanicarum.

Clausula de Pippini consecratione (or Nota de unctione Pippini). First edition by Mabillon, De re diplomatica (Paris, 1681, 1709, p. 384), then in ASBoll. (June, i, p. 480), now best edited in MGH (Script. xv, p. 1, and with facsimile of a part, Script. rer. Merov. pp. 465, 466), in the notes to Duchesne's ed. of *Liber pontificalis*, i, p. 458, or, with an emendation, in Haller's Die Quellen zur Geschichte der Entstehung des Kirchenstaates (Leipsic, 1907).

Donatio Constantini (Constitutum Constantini). Best edn. Zeumer in the Festgabe für Rudolf von Gneist (Berlin, 1888)—and separately. Reprinted by Mirbt, Quellen zur Geschichte des Papsttums (2nd edn., Tübingen, 1901, p. 35), and Haller, Die Quellen zur Geschichte der Entstehung des Kirchenstaates (p. 241). English transl. by Henderson in Select Historical Documents of the Middle Ages (London, 1892).

Fragmentum Fantuzzianum. Best edn. Schnürer and Ulivi in Das Fragmentum Fantuzzianum, Freibürger Hist. Studien, 1906, ii (Switz.). That the document is genuine is more than doubtful.

Fredegarii continuatores. Best edn. Krusch, Chronicorum quae dicuntur Fredegarii scholastici continuationes, MGH (Script. rer. Merov. ii).

Liber pontificalis. Best edn. Duchesne, L. *See Gen. Bibl.* iv. (The new edition in MGH does not yet reach the seventh century.)

Paulus Diaconus (Warnefridi). Gesta episcoporum Mettensium. Best edn. MGH (Script. ii). The Historia Langobardorum of Paulus breaks off, alas, with the death of Liutprand.

Theophanes. Chronographia. *See Gen. Bibl.* v.

Willibald. Vita Bonifacii. Editions many. Best perhaps those of Pertz (MGH, Script. ii), Jaffé (Bibliotheca rerum Germanicarum, iii), Nürnberger (Breslau, 1895).

In general, the critical and annotated texts of the MGH have put quite out of date, for the work of scholars, the older collections of Muratori and Bouquet, not to mention the earlier editors.

(b) LATER.

Agnellus. Liber pontificalis ecclesiae Ravennatis. (MGH, Script. Langobard.)

Benedictus, monachus S. Andreae in Monte Soracte. Chronicon. (MGH, Script. iii.)

Chronicon Moissiacense. (MGH, Script. i.)

Einhard (Eginhard). Vita Caroli Magni. Best edn. Waitz. *See Gen. Bibl.* v.

Erchanbert. Breviarium regum Francorum. (MGH, Script. ii.)

Gesta episcoporum Neapolitanorum. (MGH, Script. Langobard.)

Extracts from these narrative sources, with the more important of the documentary ones, are collected, so far as they concern the beginning of the papal state, by Haller in his convenient little volume, Die Quellen zur Geschichte der Entstehung des Kirchenstaates (Leipsic, 1907—in the series of Brandenburg, E. and Seeliger, G., Quellensammlung zur deutschen Geschichte).

4. MODERN WORKS.

(a) GENERAL.

AllgDB. Esp. Hahn, H. Pippin der Jüngere.

Arnold, W. Deutsche Geschichte, II: Fränkische Zeit. 2 vols. Gotha. 1881-3.

Baronius, C. Annales ecclesiastici. *See Gen. Bibl.* VI.

Barry, W. The Papal Monarchy, 590-1303. London and New York. 1902. (Story of the Nations series.)

Baxmann, R. Die Politik der Päpste von Gregor I bis auf Gregor VII. 2 vols. Elberfeld. 1868-9.

Binterim, A. J. Pragmatische Geschichte der deutschen Concilien. 2. Aufl. 7 vols. Mainz. 1851-2.

Brunner, H. Deutsche Rechtsgeschichte. *See Gen. Bibl.* VI.

—— Forschungen zur Geschichte des deutschen und französischen Rechtes. Stuttgart. 1894.

—— Grundzüge der deutschen Rechtsgeschichte. 3rd edn. Leipsic. 1908.

Bryce, J. The Holy Roman Empire. New edn. London. 1904.

Bury, J. B. Later Roman Empire. *See Gen. Bibl.* VI.

Dahn, F. Deutsche Geschichte. *See ib.*

—— Die Könige der Germanen. VIII. Die Franken unter den Karolingern. *See ib.*

—— Urgeschichte der germanischen und romanischen Völker. *See ib.*

Dareste, C. Histoire de France. 2nd edn. 9 vols. Paris. 1874-80.

Dopffel, H. Kaisertum und Papstwechsel unter den Karolingern. Freiburg i. B. 1889.

Ellendorf, J. Die Karolinger und die Hierarchie ihrer Zeit. 2 vols. Essen. 1868.

Fauriel, C. Histoire de la Gaule méridionale. 4 vols. Paris. 1836.

Fehr, J. Staat und Kirche im fränkischen Reiche bis auf Karl dem Grossen. Vienna. 1869.

Ficker, J. Forschungen zur Reichs- und Rechtsgeschichte Italiens. 4 vols. Innsbruck. 1868-74.

Finlay, G. History of the Byzantine Empire, 716-1057. Edinburgh. 1856.

Freeman, E. A. Western Europe in the Eighth Century and Onward. London. 1904.

Fustel de Coulanges, N. D. Histoire des Institutions politiques de l'ancienne France. *See Gen. Bibl.* VI.

Gebhardt, B., and others. Handbuch der deutschen Geschichte. 4th edn. 2 vols. Stuttgart. 1910.

Gibbon, E. Decline and Fall. Ed. Bury, J. B. *See ib.*

Giesebrecht, W. v. Geschichte der deutschen Kaiserzeit. *See Gen. Bibl.* VI.

Graf, A. Roma nella memoria e nelle immaginazioni del Medio Evo. 2 vols. Turin. 1882-3.

Greenwood, T. Cathedra Petri. 6 vols. London. 1856-72.

Gregorovius, F. Geschichte der Stadt Rom. *See Gen. Bibl.* VI.

Halphen, L. Études sur l'administration de Rome au 'Moyen-Âge (751-1252) Paris. 1907. BHE.

Hartmann, L. M. Geschichte Italiens im Mittelalter. *See Gen. Bibl.* VI. (Important.)

Hauck, A. Kirchengeschichte Deutschlands. *See ib.*

Hefele, C. J. Conciliengeschichte. *See ib.*

Heimbucher, M. Die Papstwahlen unter den Karolingern. Augsburg. 1889.

Henderson, E. F.   History of Germany in the Middle Ages.   London.   1894.
—— Short History of Germany.   New York.   1902.
Hertzberg, G. F.   Geschichte der Byzantiner.   Berlin.   1883.   (Oncken II, 7.)
Heusler, A.   Deutsche Verfassungsgeschichte.   Leipsic.   1905.
Hodgkin, T.   Italy and her Invaders.   *See Gen. Bibl.* VI.   (The fullest and best
    treatment in English.)
Kaufmann, G.   Deutsche Geschichte bis auf Karl den Grossen.   2 vols.   Leipsic.
    1880–1.
Kitchin, G. W.   History of France.   3rd edn.   3 vols.   Oxford.   1892–4.
Kleinclausz, A.   L'Empire Carolingien, ses origines et ses transformations.   Paris.
    1902.
Kurth, G.   Les Origines de la Civilisation moderne.   5th edn.   2 vols.   Brussels.
    1903.
Lamprecht, K.   Deutsche Geschichte.   12 vols.   Berlin.   1891–1909.
Langen, J.   Geschichte der römischen Kirche von Leo I bis Nikolaus I.   Gotha.
    1885.
Lavisse, E.   Études sur l'Histoire d'Allemagne.   (R. des Deux Mondes, 1885–7.)
        Esp. L'Entrée en Scène de la Papauté (vol. LXXVIII, p. 842).
            La Conquête de la Germanie par l'Église romaine (vol. LXXX, p. 878).
            La Fondation du Saint-Empire (vol. LXXXVII, p. 357).
—— , and others.   Histoire de France.   *See Gen. Bibl.* VI.
        Esp. II, pp. 257–79: Kleinclausz, A.   Charles Martel et Pépin le Bref.
—— , and Rambaud, A.   Histoire générale de l'Europe.   *See Gen. Bibl.* VI.
        Esp. I, ch. V: Lavisse, E.   Formation du Pouvoir pontifical.
            ch. VI: Berthelot, A.   Avènement de la Maison carolingienne.
Lehuërou, J. M.   Histoire des Institutions carolingiennes.   Paris.   1843.
Lindner, Th.   Geschichte des deutschen Volkes.   2 vols.   Stuttgart.   1894.
—— Weltgeschichte seit der Völkerwanderung.   (*In progress.*)   Stuttgart.   1901 ff.
Longnon, A.   Atlas historique de la France.   *See Gen. Bibl.* II.
Lorenz, O.   Papstwahl und Kaiserthum.   Berlin.   1874.
Malfatti, B.   Imperatori e Papi ai tempi della signoria dei Franchi in Italia.
    2 vols.   (No more published.)   Milan.   1876.
Mann, H. K.   The Lives of the Popes in the Early Middle Ages.   (*In progress.*)
    London.   1902–.
Mansi, J. D.   Concilia.   31 vols.   Florence.   1757–98.
Martin, H.   Histoire de France.   4th edn.   Paris.   1855–60.
Milman, H. H.   History of Latin Christianity.   *See Gen. Bibl.* VI.
Mühlbacher, E.   Deutsche Geschichte unter den Karolingern.   *See Gen. Bibl.* VI.
    (The best German narrative history of this period.)
Muratori, L. A.   Annali d' Italia.   12 vols.   Milan.   1744–9.
Niehues, B.   Geschichte des Verhältnisses zwischen Kaisertum und Papsttum im
    Mittelalter.   I.   2nd edn.   Münster.   1877.
Nitzsch, K. W.   Geschichte des deutschen Volkes bis [1555].   3 vols.   Leipsic.   1883–5.
Perry, W. C.   The Franks.   London.   1857.
Pflugk-Harttung, J. v.   Geschichte des Mittelalters [bis auf Karl den Grossen].
    Berlin.   1889.   (IV, 1, of the Allgemeine Weltgeschichte of Flathe and others.)
Ranke, L. v.   Weltgeschichte.   *See Gen. Bibl.* VI.
Rettberg, F. W.   Kirchengeschichte Deutschlands.   2 vols.   Göttingen.   1846.
Reumont, A. v.   Geschichte der Stadt Rom.   3 vols.   Berlin.   1867–70.
Richter, G., and Kohl, H.   Annalen des fränkischen Reichs im Zeitalter der
    Karolinger.   2 vols.   Halle.   1885–7.
Schröder, R.   Lehrbuch der deutschen Rechtsgeschichte.   5th edn.   Leipsic.   1907.
Schulte, J. F. v.   Lehrbuch der deutschen Reichs- und Rechtsgeschichte.   5th edn.
    Stuttgart.   1881.

Schwarzlose, K. Der Bilderstreit. Gotha. 1890.

Sugenheim, S. Geschichte der Entstehung und Ausbildung des Kirchenstaats. Leipsic. 1854.

Villari, P. Le invasioni barbariche in Italia. Milan. 1901. Eng. transl. 2 vols. London. 1902.

Waitz, G. Deutsche Verfassungsgeschichte. Vols. iii, iv, Die Karolingische Zeit. 2nd edn. *See Gen. Bibl.* vi.

Warnkönig, L. A., and Gerard, P. A. F. Histoire des Carolingiens. Brussels. 1862.

(*b*) On Authorities.

Annales:
> To the older literature (down to 1887) of the endless controversy over the Carolingian annals the excursus of Horst Kohl, Ueber den gegenwärtigen Stand der Annalenfrage (in Richter and Kohl, Annalen des fränkischen Reichs im Zeitalter der Karolinger, ii) may serve as an adequate introduction; and the later literature is enumerated and discussed by Monod, Études critiques sur les sources de l'histoire carolingienne (Paris, 1898), and by Molinier, i, Wattenbach and Jacob (*see above*, p. 801).

Donationes:
> On the so-called Donation of Constantine the most important critical studies are

Bayet, C. La fausse Donation de Constantin. (In the Annuaire de la Faculté des Lettres de Lyon, and separately, Paris, 1884.)

Böhmer, H. Konstantinische Schenkung. RE³, xi, 1902.

Brunner, H. Das Constitutum Constantini. (In the Festgabe für R. v. Gneist, and separately, Berlin, 1888.)

Döllinger, I. v. Constantin und Silvester.—Die Schenkung Constantins. (In his Die Papst-Fabeln des Mittelalters. Munich, 1863; 2nd edn. 1890. Eng. transl., London, 1871; New York, 1872.)

Duchesne, L. Constantin et Saint Silvestre. *Liber pontificalis*, i, introduction.

Friedrich, J. Die Konstantinische Schenkung. Nördlingen. 1889.

Grauert, H. Die Konstantinische Schenkung. HJ. 1882–4.

Hauck, A. Zur Donatio Constantini. (Z. für kirchliche Wissenschaft, 1888, p. 201.)

Krüger, G. Zur Frage nach der Entstehungszeit der Konstantinischen Schenkung. Theologische Literaturzeitung, 1889, pp. 429, 455.

Langen, J. Entstehung und Tendenz der Konstantinischen Schenkungs-Urkunde. HZ. 1883. l, p. 413.

Löning, E. Die Entstehung der Konstantinischen Schenkungs-Urkunde. (HZ, 1890, lxv, p. 193.)

Martens, W. Die falsche General-Konzession Konstantins des Grossen. Munich. 1889.

Mayer, E. Die Schenkungen Constantins und Pipins. (DZKR, also Tübingen, 1904.)

Scheffer-Boichorst, P. Neuere Forschungen über die konstantinische Schenkung. (MIOGF, 1889, 1890, x, p. 302, xi, p. 128. Reprinted in Gesammelte Schriften, i, 1904.)

Weiland, L. Die Konstantinische Schenkung. (1888. DZKR. xxii, pp. 137, 185.)

The older literature (to 1887) on the question of the Carolingian donations—the so-called "Roman question"—is in part enumerated and appraised by Horst Kohl in his excursus Ueber die Schenkungen der Karolinger an die Päpste (in Richter and Kohl, *see above*). To the studies he discusses must be added, above all, Duchesne's (*see above*), and the later contributions of Kehr and Hubert. Since 1880, when the discussion became more acute, the most important special studies are:

Funk, F. X. Die Schenkungen der Karolinger. (TQS, 1882, p. 603.)

Genelin, P. Das Schenkuugsversprechen und die Schenkung Pippins. Vienna. 1880.

Kehr, P. Die sogenannte Karolingische Schenkung von 774. (HZ, 1893, LXX, p. 385.) And cf. his reviews of Schnürer and Lindner in the Göttingische gelehrten Anzeigen, 1895, p. 694. 1896, p. 128.)

Lamprecht, K. Die römische Frage. Leipsic. 1889.

Lindner, T. Die sogenannten Schenkungen Pippins, Karls des Grossen und Ottos I. Stuttgart. 1896.

Martens, W. Beleuchtung der neuesten Controversen über die römische Frage. Munich. 1898.

—— Die römische Frage. Stuttgart. 1881.

—— Neue Erörterungen über die römische Frage. Stuttgart. 1882.

Niehues, B. Die Schenkungen der Karolinger. (HJ, 1881, pp. 76, 201.)

Sackur, E. Die Promissio Pippins vom Jahre 754 und ihre Erneuerung durch Karl den Grossen. (MIOGF, 1895, p. 385.) Die Promissio von Kiersy. (Ib., 1898, p. 55.)

Scheffer-Boichorst, P. Pippins und Karls d. G. Schenkungsversprechen. (MIOGF, 1884, p. 193, repr. in Gesammelte Schriften, I.)

Sickel, T. Das Privilegium Otto I. Innsbruck. 1883. (Of high importance for these donations, though dealing primarily with a later document which rests on them.)

Sybel, H. v. Die Schenkungen der Karolinger an die Päpste. (HZ, 1880, XLIV, p. 47, reprinted in Kleine historische Schriften, III. 1880.)

Also Mayer, E. above. It goes without saying that these donations are also discussed, often in minute detail, by many of the general works already named, and by all the monographs on the rise of the papal state or on the relations of the Popes with the Carolingians.

Fragmentum Fantuzzianum:

This, as what purports to be Pippin's donation itself, is of course discussed, if only to be contemptuously dismissed, by all the studies just named. Apart from brief reviews, the attempt of Schnürer to restore its text and vindicate its genuineness has as yet received small attention. For what has been said and what its editor has to urge in reply see Schnürer, G., Zum Streit um das Fragmentum Fantuzzianum, HJ, 1903, p. 30.

Fredegarii continuatores:

The best discussion of the worth of these may be found in the Jahrbücher of Breysig, Hahn, and Oelsner (see below), and in the article of their editor, Krusch, Die Chronicae des sogenannten Fredegar, NAGDG, 1882 (see pp. 495–515).

Liber pontificalis:

Duchesne, L. Étude sur le Liber pontificalis. Paris. 1877. (I, 1 of the Bibl. EcfrAR.) And articles in RQH, XXVI, XXIX and Mélanges d'Archéologie IV, and especially introd. to edn. of *Liber pontificalis*.

Fournier, P. Le Liber pontificalis. RQH, XLI.

Grisar, H. Der Liber pontificalis. ZKT, XI, XII.

Schnürer, G. Der Verfasser der Vita Stephani II im Liber pontificalis. HJ, 1890, p. 425.

(c) Monographs, Biographies and Special Treatises.

Abel, S. Der Untergang des Langobardenreiches in Italien. Göttingen. 1859.

Armbrust, L. Die Territorialpolitik der Päpste, 500–800. Göttingen. 1885.

Bayet, C. Remarques sur le caractère et les conséquences du voyage d'Étienne III en France. (RH, 1882, xx, p. 88.)

—— Les élections pontificales sous les Carolingiens, 757–885. (RH, 1884, xxiv, p. 49.)

Bladé, J. F. Fin du premier duché d'Aquitaine. (Annales de la Faculté des Lettres de Bordeaux. 1892, pp. 145, 235.)

Brackmann, A. Patrimonium Petri. In RE³.

Bréhier, L. La Querelle des Images. Paris. 1904.

Crivellucci, A. Delle Origini dello Stato pontificio. (SS. 1902–5. x, xi, xiv.)

Diehl, C. Études etc. *See above*, p. 801. (This, with Hartmann's confirming and supplementing researches, is fundamental for Byzantine Italy.)

Dorr, R. De bellis Francorum cum Arabibus usque ad obitum Karoli Magni. Königsberg. 1861.

Drapeyron, L. Essai sur le caractère de la lutte de l'Aquitaine et de l'Austrasie. Compte-rendu of the French Acad. des Sciences morales et politiques, 1875–6. civ, p. 807, cv, p. 247, cvi, p. 813; and separately, Paris, 1877.

Dubruel, M. Fulrad, abbé de Saint-Denis. Paris. 1902.

Duchesne, L. Les premiers temps de l'État Pontifical. 2nd edn. Paris. 1904. (A scholarly but popular narrative.)

Dünzelmann, E. Ueber die ersten unter Karlmann und Pippin gehaltenen Konzilien. Göttingen. 1869.

Eiten, G. Das Unterkönigtum im Reiche der Merovinger und Karolinger. Heidelberg. 1907.

Erben, W. Pippin's Nachtglocke. Beiblatt of the Allgemeine Zeitung, 1904.

Fischer, O. Bonifatius. Leipsic. 1881.

Freeman, E. A. The Patriciate of Pippin. EHR, 1889, p. 684.

Gasquet, A. L'Empire byzantin et la Monarchie franque. *See Gen. Bibl.* vi.

—— Le Royaume lombarde : ses relations avec l'Empire grec et avec les Francs. (RH, 1886, xxxiii, p. 58.)

Gay, J. L'État Pontifical, les Byzantins et les Lombards sur le Littoral campanien. Mélanges d'Archéologie, 1901, p. 487.

Göpfert, A. Lullus. Leipsic. 1880. (Thesis.)

Gundlach, W. Die Entstehung des Kirchenstaates. Breslau, 1899. (Heft 59 of Gierke's Untersuchungen.)

Hahn, H. Bonifaz und Lul. Leipsic. 1883.

—— Jahrbücher des fränkischen Reichs, 741–52. Berlin. 1863. (Thorough.)

—— Pippin der Jüngere. AllgDB. (Excellent.) Hahn is doubtless, too, the author of the valuable pages on this period in Gebhardt's Handbuch d. deutschen Geschichte.

Hamel, H. Untersuchungen zur älteren Territorialgeschichte des Kirchenstaates. Göttingen. 1899.

Hartmann, L. M. Untersuchungen zur Geschichte der byzantinischen Verwaltung in Italien. Leipsic. 1889. (To 750.)

Heinemann, L. v. Der Patriciat der deutschen Könige. Halle. 1888.

Hellmann, S. Die Heiraten der Karolinger. (In the Festgabe for Heigel, Munich, 1903, p. 1.)

Heuser, F. Bonifacius und der Staatsstreich Pipins im Jahre 752. Cassel. 1869. (Programme.)

Hubert, H. Étude sur la Formation des États de l'Église. RH, 1899, lxix, pp. 1, 241.

Jung, J.　Organisationen Italiens von Augustus bis auf Karl d. Gr.　MIOGF, Erganzungsband v, p. 1.

Kehr, P.　Ueber die Chronologie der Briefe Papst Pauls I.　Nachrichten of the Göttingen Academy, 1896, p. 103.　For his studies on the Carolingian donations see above.

Kemmerich, M.　Die Porträts deutscher Kaiser und Könige bis auf Rudolf von Habsburg.　NAGDG, 1908, p. 461.

Knaake, E.　Aistulf.　Tilsit.　1890.

Kroeber, A.　Partage du Royaume des Francs entre Charlemagne et Carloman. BEC, 1856, p. 341.

Kurth, G.　Saint-Boniface.　Paris.　1902.

Lilienfein, H.　Die Anschauungen von Staat und Kirche im Reich der Karolinger. Heidelberg.　1902.　(Heidelberger Abhandlungen, i.)

Löbell, J. W.　De causis regni Francorum ab Merowingis ad Carolingos translati. Born.　1844.

Lombard, A.　Constantin V.　(740–75.)　Paris.　1902.

Oelsner, L.　Jahrbücher des fränkischen Reichs unter König Pippin.　Leipsic. 1871.　(Still the most careful study of Pippin's reign in detail.)

Ohr, W.　Der karolingische Gottesstaat.　Leipsic.　1902.

Pfahler, P.　Bonifacius und die Thronbesteigung Pippins.　TQS, 1879, p. 92.

—— S. Bonifacius und seine Zeit.　Ratisbon.　1880.

Pinton, P.　Le donazioni barbariche ai papi.　Rome.　1890.

Scharpff, F. A.　Die Entstehung des Kirchenstaates.　Freiburg i. B.　1860.

Schnürer, G.　Die Entstehung des Kirchenstaates.　Cologne.　1894.

Sickel, W.　Die Verträge der Päpste mit den Karolingern.　DZG, 1894, p. 301 : 1895, p. 1.

—— Kirchenstaat und Karolinger.　HZ, 1900. lxxxiv.　p. 385.

Tangl, M.　Das Testament Fulrads.　NAGDG, 1907, p. 167.

Thelen, H.　Die Verhandlungen König Pippins und Papst Stephans II.　Oberhausen. 1881.　(Thesis.)

Werner, A.　Bonifacius und die Romanisirung von Mitteleuropa.　Leipsic.　1875.

Weyl, R.　Die Beziehungen des Papstthums zum fränkischen Staats- und Kirchenrecht unter den Karolingern.　Breslau.　1892.　(Heft 40 of Gierke's Untersuchungen.)

CHAPTER XIX.

CONQUESTS AND IMPERIAL CORONATION OF CHARLES THE GREAT.

I. ORIGINAL AUTHORITIES.

Annales Laurinenses majores (741–829). Revision in the *Annales Einhardi* (741–801). Ed. Pertz, G. MGH, Script. I. New edn: Annales regni Francorum, qui dicuntur Ann. Laur. maj. et Einhardi. Ed. Kurze, F. (Script. rer. Germ.). See *Gen. Bibl.* IV.

Annales Laureshamenses 703–803. Ed. Pertz, MGH, Script. I.

Einhardi Vita Karoli Magni. Ed. Pertz, *ib.* II, and Script. rer. Germ. v, ed. Waitz. 1905.

Liber pontificalis. Duchesne, L. II, 1892. See *Gen. Bibl.* IV. (Vita Hadriani; Vita Leonis III.)

Monachus Sangallensis (Notker Bulbulus), De gestis Karoli Magni (MGH, Script. II).

Mühlbacher, E. Die Regesten des Kaiserreichs unter den Karolingern (751–918). 2nd edn. Innsbruck. 1908.

—— Die Urkunden der Karolinger, I. (MGH, Diplomata.) 1906.

II. MODERN WORKS.

Abel, S. and Simson, B. Jahrbücher des fränkischen Reichs unter Karl dem Grossen. 2nd edn. 1888. II. Leipsic. 1883.

Döllinger, J. Das Kaisertum Karls d. Gr. und seiner Nachfolger. (Münchener Histor. Jahrbuch, 1865, and Akademische Vorträge, III. Munich. 1891.)

Hartmann, L. M. Geschichte Italiens im Mittelalter. II, 2, III, 1. *See Gen. Bibl.* VI.

Hauck, A. Kirchengeschichte Deutschlands. II. 2nd edn. Leipsic. 1900. *See ib.*

Hodgkin, Th. Italy and her invaders. VIII. (The Frankish Empire 774–814.) *See ib.*

Kleinclausz, A. L'Empire Carolingien, ses origines et ses transformations. Paris. 1902.

Lilienfein, H. Die Anschauungen von Staat und Kirche im Reich der Karolinger. Heidelberg. 1902.

Mühlbacher, E. Deutsche Geschichte unter den Karolingern. *See Gen. Bibl.* VI.

Ohr, W. Die Kaiserkrönung Karls d. Gr. Tübingen. 1903.

Rauschen, G. Die Legende Karls d. Gr. im 11. und 12. Jahrhundert. Leipsic. 1890.

CHAPTER XX.

FOUNDATIONS OF SOCIETY.

I. CHRONICLES AND LAWS.

Tacitus. De origine situ moribus ac populis Germanorum liber. *See Gen. Bibl.* v.
Caesar. Commentarii de bello Gallico. Ed. Kübler, B. Teubner. Leipsic. 1893.
Gregorius Turonensis. *See Gen. Bibl.* v. (Vol. i.) 1884–5.
Baeda Venerabilis. *See ib.*
Anglo-Saxon Chronicle. *See ib.*
Paulus Diaconus. Historia Langobardorum. *See ib.*
Einhard. Vita Karoli imperatoris. *See ib.*

Birch, W. de Gray. Cartularium Saxonicum : Charters relating to Anglo-Saxon history. London. 1883.
Earle, J. A hand-book to the land-charters and other Saxonic documents. Oxford. 1888.
Kemble, J. M. Codex diplomaticus aevi Saxonici. 6 vols. London. 1839–48.
Liebermann, F. Die Gesetze der Angelsachsen. *See Gen. Bibl.* iv.
Thorpe, B. Diplomatarium Anglicum aevi Saxonici. English charters from 605 to William the Conqueror. London. 1865.

Leges Alamannorum, Baiuwariorum, Burgundionum, Langobardorum, Saxonum. Lex Ribuaria. MGH. iii–v. 1863–89.
Lex Salica : the ten texts with the glosses, and the Lex emendata, synoptically ed. by Hessels, J. H. ; with notes by Kern, H. Dublin. 1880.
Leges Visigothorum. Ed. Zeumer, K. MGH. Legum sect. i.
Capitularia regum Francorum. Ed. Boretius, A. 2 vols. MGH. Legum sect. ii.
Formulae Merowingici et Karolini aevi. Ed. K. Zeumer. MGH. Legum sect. v.
Pardessus, J. M. Diplomata, chartae, epistolae, leges aliaque instrumenta ad res Gallo-Francicas spectantia. 2 vols. Paris. 1843–9.
Rozière, E. de. Recueil général des formules usitées dans l'empire des Francs du Ve au Xe siècles. 3 pts. Paris. 1859–71.
Monumenta historiae patriae. Vol. xiii. Codex diplomaticus Langobardiae. Turin. 1873.
Bitterauf, Th. Traditionen des Hochstifts Freising. Munich. 1905.
Mühlbacher, E. Diplomata. MGH. Diplomata i. 1906.
Guérard, B. Polyptique de l'abbé Irminon. Paris. 1836.
—— Explication du Capitulare de villis. Paris. 1857, and BEC. 3rd ser. Vol. iv.

Norges gamle love indtil 1387. Keyser, R. and Munch, P. A. Vols. i and v. Christiania. 1846–85.
Corpus juris Sveo-Gotorum antiqui. Ed. Collin and Schlyter. Stockholm and Lund. 13 vols. 1827–77.

II. MODERN WORKS.

Amira, K. v. Grundriss des germanischen Rechts. (Grundriss der germanischen Philologie, ed. Paul, H. Vol. II.) Strassburg. 1897.
—— Nordgermanisches Obligationenrecht. 2 vols. Leipsic. 1882–95.
Arnold, W. Deutsche Geschichte. 2 vols. Gotha. 1881–3.
Brunner, H. Deutsche Rechtsgeschichte. *See Gen. Bibl.* VI.
—— Zur Rechtsgeschichte der römischen und germanischen Urkunde. Berlin. 1880.
—— Forschungen zur Geschichte des deutschen und französischen Rechts. Stuttgart. 1894.
Bugge, A. Die Wikinger. German transl. by Hungerland, H. Halle a. S. 1906.
Chadwick, H. M. Studies on Anglo-Saxon institutions. Cambridge. 1905.
—— The origin of the English nation. Cambridge. 1907.
Dahn, F. Die Könige der Germanen. *See Gen. Bibl.* VI.
Delbrück, H. Geschichte der Kriegskunst im Rahmen d. politischen Geschichte. Vols. 1–3. 1900 ff. in progress. 2nd edn. 1908 ff.
Deloche, M. La trustis et l'antrustion royal sous les deux premières races. Paris. 1873.
Dopsch, A. Die Wirtschaftsentwickelung der Karolingerzeit, vornehmlich in Deutschland. Vol. I. Weimar. 1912.
Flach, J. Les origines de l'ancienne France. 3 vols. Paris. 1886–1904.
Fustel de Coulanges, N. D. Histoire des institutions politiques de l'ancienne France. *See Gen. Bibl.* VI.
Gierke, O. Das deutsche Genossenschaftsrecht. 3 vols. Berlin. 1868–81.
Grimm, L. J. Deutsche Rechtsalterthümer. 4th edn. 2 vols. Leipsic. 1899.
Guilhiermoz, P. Essai sur l'origine de la noblesse en France au moyen âge. Paris. 1902.
Hartmann, L. M. Geschichte Italiens im Mittelalter. *See Gen. Bibl.* VI.
Hildebrand, H. Sveriges Medeltid. Kulturhistorisk Skildring. Vols. I–III. Stockholm. 1879–98 and 1903.
Inama-Sternegg, K. T. v. Deutsche Wirtschaftsgeschichte. 3 vols. Leipsic. 1879–1901.
Kaufmann, G. Deutsche Geschichte bis auf Karl den Grossen. 2 vols. Leipsic. 1880–1.
Kemble, J. M. The Saxons in England. New edn. 2 vols. London. 1876.
Kötzschke, R. Wirtschaftsgeschichte bis zum 17. Jahrhundert. Münster.
Kröll, M. L'immunité franque. Paris. 1911.
Lamprecht, K. Deutsches Wirtschaftsleben im Mittelalter. 4 vols. Leipsic. 1885–6.
Lavisse, E. Histoire de France. *See Gen. Bibl.* VI. Vols. I–III.
Maitland, F. W. Domesday Book and beyond. Cambridge. 1897.
Maurer, G. L. v. Geschichte der Frohnhöfe, Bauernhöfe u. Hofverfassung in Deutschland. 4 vols. Erlangen. 1862.
Meister, A. Deutsche Verfassungsgeschichte des Mittelalters. (Grundriss der Geschichtswissenschaft, Meister. *See Gen. Bibl.* III. Vol. II.)
Meitzen, A. Siedelung und Agrarwesen der Westgermanen und Ostgermanen. 3 vols. and Atlas. Berlin. 1895.
Müllenhoff, K. Deutsche Altertumskunde. 5 vols. Berlin. 1870–1900. 1–3. Ed. Roediger, M. 1891–1908.
Pabst. Geschichte der langobardischen Herzogthums. (FDG, II, p. 405.)

Pappenheim, M.   Die altdänischen Schutzgilden.   Breslau.   1885.
—— Über kunstliche Verwandtschaft in germanischen Rechte.   ZSR.   xxix.
    Weimar.   1903.
Pertile, A.   Storia del diritto italiano.   6 vols. and Index.   Padua.   1873-87.
    2nd edn. by Giudice, P. del.   Turin.   1891-1903.
Rhamm, K.   Die Grosshufen der Nordgermanen.   Brunswick.   1906.   (Ethno-
    graphische Beiträge zur germanisch-slavischen Altertumskunde.   1906 ff. in
    progress.   Pt. 1.)
Rietschel, S.   Untersuchungen zur Geschichte der germanischen Hundertschaft.
    ZSR.   xxviii.   1907.
Roth, P.   Geschichte des Beneficialwesens.   Erlangen.   1850.
—— Feudalität und Unterthanverband.   Weimar.   1863.
Schroeder, R.   Lehrbuch der deutschen Rechtsgeschichte.   Leipsic.   1889.
Schupfer, F.   Delle istituzioni politiche longobardiche libri due.   Florence.   1863.
Schwerin, C. Freiherr v.   Die altgermanische Hundertschaft.   Breslau.   1907.
Seebohm, F.   The English village community examined in its relation to the
    manorial and tribal system.   3rd edn.   London.   1884.
—— Tribal custom in Anglo-Saxon law.   London.   1902.
Seeliger, G.   Die soziale und politische Bedeutung der Grundherrschaft im früheren
    Mittelalter.   Leipsic.   1903.
Sohm, R.   Die altdeutsche Reichs- und Gerichtsverfassung.   Weimar.   1871.
Steenstrup, J. C. H. R.   Normannerne.   4 vols.   Copenhagen.   1876-82.   French
    transl. of vol. i.   Beaurepaire, E. de.   Études préliminaires pour servir à
    l'histoire des Normands.   Caen.   1880.
Steenstrup, J. J. S., Erslev, K. and others.   Danmarks Riges Historie.   Copenhagen.
    6 vols.   1896-1907.   Vol. i.
Stubbs, W.   The constitutional history of England.   *See Gen. Bibl.* vi.
Vinogradoff, P.   The growth of the manor.   London.   1905.
—— Romanistische Einflüsse im angelsachischen Recht: das Buchland.   (Mélanges
    Fitting.   Vol. ii.)   Montpellier.   1908.
Viollet, P.   Droit public.   Histoire des institutions politiques et administratives de
    la France.   3 vols.   Paris.   1888-1903.
Waitz, G.   Deutsche Verfassungsgeschichte.   *See Gen. Bibl.* vi.   Vols. i-iv.
Wietersheim, E. v.   Geschichte der Völkerwanderung.   2nd edn.   2 vols.   Leipsic.
    1880-1.

CHAPTER XXI.

LEGISLATION AND ADMINISTRATION OF CHARLES THE GREAT.

I. ORIGINAL AUTHORITIES.

Mühlbacher, E.   Die Regesten des Kaiserreichs unter den Karolingern, 751–918. 2nd edn.   Innsbruck.   1908.

Urkunden der Karolinger (Diplomata Karolinorum) ɪ.   Ed. Mühlbacher, E.   MGH. 1906.

Capitularia regum Francorum.   MGH.   Legum sect. ɪɪ.   Vol. ɪ.   Ed. Boretius, A. 1883.   Vol. ɪɪ.   Ed. Boretius, A. et Krause, V.   1897.

Lex Francorum Chamavorum ; Lex Frisionum ; Lex Saxonum ; Lex Angliorum et Werinorum h.e. Thuringorum.   MGH.   Leges ɪɪɪ, v.   1863, 1875.

Concilia aevi Karolini.   ɪ.   Ed. Werminghoff, A.   MGH.   Legum sect. ɪɪɪ. Concilia, vol. ɪɪ.   1906, 1908.

Hincmarus.   De ordine palatii.   Ed. Krause, V.   Capitularia ɪɪ, pp. 517 sqq. Fontes iuris Germanici antiqui.   Hanover.   1894.

II. MODERN WORKS.

Boretius, A.   Beiträge zur Capitularienkritik.   Leipsic.   1874.

Brunner, H.   Deutsche Rechtsgeschichte.   See Gen. Bibl. vɪ.

Dahn, F.   Könige der Germanen.   See ib.   Vol. vɪɪɪ, 2–6.

Fustel de Coulanges, N.D.   Histoire des institutions politiques.   See ib.   Vol. vɪ. (Les transformations de la royauté, par C. Jullien.)

Krause, V.   Geschichte des Instituts der Missi Dominici.   Innsbruck.   1890. MIOGF.   xɪ.

Seeliger, G.   Die Kapitularien der Karolinger.   Munich.   1893.

—— Volksrecht und Königsrecht.   HVJS.   ɪ.   1898.

—— Juristische Konstruktion und Geschichtswissenschaft.   HVJS.   vɪɪ.   1904.

Sohm, R.   Die fränkische Reichs- und Gerichtsverfassung.   Weimar.   1871.

Waitz, G.   Deutsche Verfassungsgeschichte, ɪɪ, ɪɪɪ, ɪv.   See Gen. Bibl. vɪ.

CHAPTER XXII.

GROWTH OF THE PAPAL POWER.

I. ORIGINAL DOCUMENTS.

Capitularia regum Francorum. Ed. Boretius. 1883. MGH, Leg. Sect. ii, vol. i.
Concilia aevi Karolini. i, ed. Werninghoff, A. and ii, pp. 816–31. (Acta Spuria)
  MGH, Leg. iii, ii, 1 and 2. 1906–8.
Epistolae Merov. et Karol. aevi. i–iii. MGH, Epist. iii–v. 1892–9. (1) Boniface:
  Lul: Codex Carolinus. Popes Gregory II—Stephen III. (2) Alcuin: Charles
  the Great: Elipantus: Paulus Diaconus: Paulus Aquileiensis, etc. (3) Leo III:
  Einhard: etc.
Liber Censuum de l'Église romaine. Ed. Fabre, P. Paris. 1905.
Liber Diurnus Romanorum Pontificorum. Ed. Sickel, Th. v. 1839.
Regesta Pontificorum Romanorum. Ital. Pontificia i–iii. Roma: Etruria. Ed.
  Kehr, P. F. Berlin. 1906–8.
Regesten d. Kaiserreiches unter d. Karolingern 751–918. Ed. Böhmer, J. Fr.,
  Mühlbacher, E. i, 1–3. 2nd edn. by Lechner, J. Innsbruck. 1908.
Urkunden Pippins, Karlmanns, u. Karls d. Grossen. Ed. Mühlbacher, E. 1906.
  MGH, Diplom. Karol. i.

II. ORIGINAL AUTHORITIES.

Annales et Chronica...et Historiae Aevi Karol. MGH, Script. i, ii.
Fragmentum Fantuzzianum. Schnürer, G. E. and Ulivi, D. Freiburg. 1906.
Liber Pontificalis, ed. Duchesne, L. See Gen. Bibl. iv. Ed. Mommsen, Th.
  MGH, Gest. Pont. Rom. i. 1898 (based on Duchesne's edn.).
Paulus Diaconus: Historia Romana. MGH, auct. ant. ii. 1879.
Poetae Lat. aev. Karol. Ed. Dümmler i and ii (pp. 687–98). MGH. 1881–4.
Script. rer. Langobard. et Ital. saec. vi–ix. Ed. Waitz. MGH. 1878.

III. CRITICA.

Duchesne, L. Études sur le liber Pontificalis. Paris. 1887.
Fabre, P. Études sur le Liber Censuum. Paris. 1892.
Sickel, W. R. v. Die Vita Hadriani Nonantuli u. d. Diurnus Handschrift. NAGDG.
  xviii, 107–33.
Sickel, W. Nouveaux Éclaircissements sur la première édition du Diurnus. [Ap.
  Mélanges Jean Havet.] Paris. 1895.

IV. MODERN WORKS.

1. GENERAL.

Bury, J. B.   The Later Roman Empire.   *See Gen. Bibl.* vi.

Dahn, F.   Könige d. Germanen.   *See ib.*

Gibbon, E.   The Decline and Fall of the Roman Empire.   Ed. Bury, J. B.
  See ib.

[Gosselin, J. E.]   Pouvoir du Pape au moyen âge, ou recherches historiques sur
  l'origine de la souveraineté temporelle du Saint Siège.   Par M *****, Directeur
  au Séminaire de Saint-Sulpice.   Paris.   Lyons.   1845.   New edn. augmented.
  (Identified as by Gosselin, J. E.)   Tr. Kelly, M.   The Power of the Popes in
  the Middle Ages.   3 vols.   London.   1853.

Gregorovius.   Hist. of City of Rome in Middle Ages.   *See Gen. Bibl.* vi.

Grisar, H.   Geschichte Roms und der Päpste in Mittelalter.   History of Rome
  and the Popes in the Middle Ages.   Tr. Cappadella, L.   Vols. i, ii.   London.
  1911-12.

Hartmann, L. M.   Untersuchungen z. Geschichte d. byzantinischen Verwaltung in
  Italien.   (540-750.)   Leipsic.   1889.

——— Geschichte Italiens im Mittelalter.   Vols. i-iii.   *See Gen. Bibl.* vi.

Hauck, A.   Kirchengeschichte Deutschlands.   Vols. i and ii.   *See ib.*

Hefele, C. J.   Conciliengeschichte.   *See ib.*

Hergenrother, J.   Handbuch d. Kirchengeschichte.   Vol. ii.   *See ib.* (pp. 4-197).

Hodgkin, T.   Italy and her Invaders.   *See ib.*

Mann, H. K.   Lives of the Popes in the Early Middle Ages.   Vols. i and ii.
  London.   1906.

Milman, H. H.   Hist. of Latin Christianity.   *See Gen. Bibl.* vi.

RE³, articles in.   *See Gen. Bibl.* i.

Wright, R. H.   The "Sancta Respublica Romana."   A.D. 395-888.   2nd edn.
  London.   1891.

2. THE CAROLINGIAN PERIOD.

Abel, S. and Simson, B.   Jahrbücher d. fränk. Reiches unter Karl d. Gr.   Leipsic.
  1866-83.

Bartelli, V.   La polizia ecclesiastica n. legislazione carolin.   Rome.   1899.

Bartolini.   Di S. Zaccaria Papa.   Ratisbon.   1879.

Bréhier, L.   La Querelle des Images.   Paris.   1904.

Brunengo, G.   Il patriciato Romano di Carlomagno.   Prato.   1893.   [First edn.
  1864-6.]

Crivellucci, A. D.   Origini d. Stato Pontificio.   SS.   1901-5.

Dahmen, J.   Das Pontifikat Gregory II's.   Düsseldorf.   1888.

Davis, H. W. C.   Charlemagne [Heroes of the Nations].   New York.   1900.

Döllinger, I. von.   Fables respecting the Popes of the Middle Ages.   (For
  Gregory II, etc.,) tr. Plummer, A.   London.   1871.

Dove.   Corsica u. Sardinien in d. Schenkungen an d. Päpste.   Sitzb. Akad.
  München.   Philos.-Phil. Klasse, 1894.   183-238.

Duchesne, L.   Les premiers temps de l'État Pontifical.   Paris.   1898.   2nd edn.
  1904.   The beginnings of the Temporal Power of the Popes.   754-1073.
  London.   1908.

Fabre, P.   De patrimoniis ecclesiae usque ad aetatem Carolinorum.   Lille.   1892.

Freeman, E. A.   Western Europe in the Eighth Century.   London.   1904.

Gay, J. L'État Pontifical, les Byzantins, les Lombards, etc. [Hadrian I—
John VIII.] Mélanges d'Archéol. et Hist. xxi, 487 sqq. 1901.

Genelin, P. Das Schenkungsversprechen u. d. Schenkung Pippins. Vienna.
1880.

Grashof, O. Der Patriciat d. deutschen Kaiser nach seine Bedeutung u. Geschichte.
AKKR. xli, 193 sqq. 1878 etc. xlii, 209 sqq.

Gundlach, W. Entstehung d. Kirchenstaates u. d. kuriale Begriff d. "respublica
Romanorum." Breslau. 1899.

Haller, J. D. Quellen z. Geschichte d. Entstehung d. Kirchenstaat. Leipsic.
1907.

Halphen, L. Étude sur l'administration de Rome au Moyen Age. (757–1282.)
Paris. 1907.

Hubert, H. Étude sur la formation des États de l'Église. [Reprint.] Paris. 1899.

Kehr, P. Die sogenannt. Karoling. Schenkung v. 774, HZ, 70 (N. F. 34),
pp. 358–442.

Ketterer, J. A. Karl d. Grosse u. die Kirche. München. 1898.

Kühl, O. Der Verkehr Karls mit Papst Hadrian. Königsberg. 1879.

Langen, J. Gesch. d. röm. Kirche. *See Gen. Bibl.* vi.

Lilienfein, H. Die Anschauungen v. Staat u. Kirche im Reich d. Karolinger.
Heidelberg. 1902.

Lindner, Th. Die sogenannt. Schenkungen Pippins, Karls d. G., u. Ottos I an d.
Papst. Stuttgart. 1896.

Martens, M. (i) Die röm. Frage unter Pippin u. Karl d. Gr. Stuttgart. 1881.
(ii) Neue Erörterungen üb. d. röm. Frage, etc. Stuttgart. 1882. (iii)
Beleuchtung d. neuest. Kontroversien üb. d. röm. Frage. Munich. 1897.

Mayer, E. D. Schenkungen Konstantins u. Pippins. Tübingen. 1904, and in
DZKR. iii. Folge 14. 1–69.

Miley, J. History of the Papal States. 3 vols. London. 1850.

Oelsner, L. Jahrbücher d. fränkischen Reiches unter K. Pippin. Leipsic. 1871.

Ohr, W. Der Karoling. Gottesstaat in Theorie u. Praxis. Leipsic. 1902.

Sackur, E. Die Promissio Pippins v. J. 754 u. ihre Erneuerung durch Karl d. Gr.
MIOGF. 385–425.

Schaube, A. Z. Verständigung üb. d. Schenkungsversprechen v. Kiersy u. Rom.
HZ, 72, ii, 193–212.

Scheffer-Boichorst, P. Pippins u. Karls d. Gr. Schenkungsversprechen. [Gesam-
melte Schriften, i, 63–86. Reprinted from MIOGF.] Berlin. 1903.

Schnürer, G. Die Entstehung des Kirchenstaates. Cologne. 1894.

Servière, J. de la. Charlemagne et l'Église. Paris. 1904.

Sickel, W. Kirchenstaat u. Karolinger. HZ (N.F.). 48, 385 sqq.

—— Die Verträge der Päpste unter der Karolingern u. d. neue Kaisertum. DZG.
xi, 301–50. xii, 1–43.

—— Review of Ottolenghi, "Dignità imperiale di C. M." in Göttingische Gelehrte
Anzeigen. 1897. pp. 833 sqq.

Sybel, H. v. Die Schenkungen d. Karolinger an d. Päpste. HZ (N.F.) viii, 47–85;
or in Kleine Hist. Schrift. iii. 1885. Cf. criticisms by Niehues (HJ, ii, 76–99
and 201–41) and G. Hueffer (HJ, ii, 242–53).

Thelen, H. Zur Lösung d. Streitfrage üb. d. Verhandlungen K. Pippins u. Papst
Stephens II zu Ponthion, etc. Oberhausen. 1881.

Vitelleschi, F. Nobili. Storia civile e polit. di Papato d. imp. Theodosio a
Carlomagno. 2 vols. Bologna. 1900–2.

Wattenbach, W. Geschichte des Römischen Papstthums. Berlin. 2nd edn. 1876.

Werminghoff. Kirchenverfassung. Vol. ii. *See Gen. Bibl.* vi.

Weyl, R. D. Beziehungen d. Papstthums z. fränkischen Staats- u. Kirchenrecht
unter d. Karolingern. Breslau. 1892.

3. Coronation of Charles the Great.

Döllinger, J. J. I. von. Das Kaisertum Karls d. Gr. und seiner Nachfolger. HJ. 1865 repr. 1891. Munich. Transl. Warre, M. The Empire of Charles the Great and his Successors. No. 3 of Historical and Literary Addresses by J. I. v. Döllinger. London. 1894. [See Dahlmann-Waitz no. 977.]

Hampe, K. Zur Kaiserkrönung Karls d. Gr. ZKG. 26. 4. 465 sqq.

Ohr, N. Die Ovationstheorie u. d. Kaiserkrönung etc. *Ib.* 26. 2. 190 sqq.

—— La Leggendaria Elezione d. Carlo Magno a Imperatore. Rome. 1903.

Sackur, E. Ein römisch. Majestätsprozess u. d. Kaiserkrönung etc. HZ. 87 (N.F. 51). 385 sqq.

Sickel, W. D. Kaiserwahl Karls d. Gr. MIOGF. 20, 1 sqq.

Walther, J. D. Zeremoniell bei d. Kaiserkrönung etc. Theol. Liter. Blatt. 27. 337 sqq.

CHRONOLOGICAL TABLE

OF

LEADING EVENTS MENTIONED IN THIS VOLUME

314 Council of Arles.
410 Sack of Rome by Alaric.
429 Mission of Germanus and Lupus to Britain.
430 Death of Augustine.
432–461 St Patrick in Ireland.
449 Traditional date of Hengest and Horsa.
451 Battle of the Mauriac Plain.
  Council of Chalcedon.
455 Sack of Rome by the Vandals.
431–511 Reign of Clovis.
482 The *Henoticon* of Zeno.
493 Traditional date of Cerdic.
493–526 Reign of Theodoric in Italy.
506 Issue of the *Breviarium Alarici*.
507 Battle of the *Campus Vogladensis*.
511 Division of the Frankish kingdom by the sons of Clovis.
518 Justin I Emperor.
527–565 Reign of Justinian.
529 The Schools of Athens closed.
532 The *Nika* riot.
  Building of St Sophia begun.
533 Issue of the *Digest*.
  Conquest of Africa by Belisarius.
534 Frankish conquest of the Burgundians.
535–553 The Gothic War.
537–538 The great siege of Rome by the Goths.
540 Capture of Ravenna by Belisarius.
541 Abolition of the Consulships.
543 Death of Theodora.
552 Battle of Taginae.
553 Battle of the Lactarian Mount.
  Fifth General Council.
554 Conquest of Southern Spain by the Imperial forces.
558 The Huns before Constantinople.
560–616 Reign of Aethelberht in Kent.
561 Division of the Frankish kingdom by the sons of Chlotar I.
565 Justin II Emperor.
568 Invasion of Italy by the Lombards.
c. 570 Birth of Mahomet.

575 Assassination of Sigebert.
578 Tiberius II Emperor.
582 Maurice Emperor.
584 Assassination of Chilperic.
589 Conversion of the Visigoths. Third Council of Toledo.
590 Agilulf king of the Lombards.
590–603 Pontificate of Gregory the Great.
591 Chosroes restored by Maurice.
594 Death of Gregory of Tours.
597 Landing of Augustine in Thanet.
　　 Death of Columba.
602 Phocas Emperor.
610 Heraclius Emperor.
613 Reunion of the Frankish kingdom under Chlotar II.
614 Capture of Jerusalem by the Persians.
622 Flight of Mahomet to Medina.
625–638 Pope Honorius.
626 Siege of Constantinople by Persians and Avars.
627 Baptism of Edwin of Deira.
　　 Battle of Nineveh.
628 Peace with Persia.
629 Expulsion of Byzantines from Spain.
632 Death of Mahomet. Abū Bakr Caliph.
633 Battle of Heathfield.
634 Mission of Birinus in Wessex.
　　 Omar Caliph.
635–642 Reign of Oswald in Northumbria.
636 Battle of the Yarmūk.
637 Battle of Ḳādisīya.
638 Capture of Jerusalem by the Arabs.
　　 Issue of the *Ekthesis*.
640 Invasion of Egypt by the Arabs.
641 Constantine III Emperor.
　　 Constans II Emperor.
　　 Battle of Nihāwand.
642 Chindaswinth king in Spain.
　　 Battle of Maserfield.
642–671 Oswy king in Northumbria.
644 Othman Caliph.
647 Final capture of Alexandria by the Arabs.
648 Issue of the *Type*.
653 Mu'āwiya reaches Dorylaeum.
　　 Arrest of Pope Martin.
655 Battle of the Winwaed.
　　 Ali Caliph—Civil war.
659 Mercian Revolt.
661 Mu'āwiya Caliph.
663 Constans in Rome.
664 Synod of Whitby.
668 Constantine IV Emperor.
669–690 Episcopate of Theodore at Canterbury.
671–685 Ecgfrith in Northumbria.
673 Synod of Hertford.
673–677 Saracen attacks on Constantinople.

680 Synod of Heathfield.
    Murder of Ḥusain at Karbalá.
685 Battle of Nechtansmere.
    Justinian II Emperor.
637 Battle of Tertry.
638 Baptism and death of Ceadwalla.
688–726 Ine king in Wessex.
692 The Trullan Council.
695 Leontius Emperor.
697 Final capture of Carthage by the Saracens.
698 Tiberius (Apsimar) Emperor.
705 Justinian II restored.
709 Death of Wilfrid.
711 Philippicus Emperor.
    Battle of La Janda. Saracen conquest of Spain.
712–744 Liutprand king of the Lombards.
713 Anastasius II Emperor.
715–731 Pope Gregory II.
716 Theodosius III Emperor.
716–757 Aethelbald king in Mercia.
717 Battle of Vincy.
717–741 Leo III Emperor.
723 Boniface consecrated a bishop.
725 Beginning of the Iconoclast Controversy.
727 The Italian Revolt.
731–741 Pope Gregory III.
731 End of Bede's *History*.
732 Battle of Tours.
734 Bede's Letter to Ecgbert.
739 Embassy of Gregory III to Charles Martel.
741–752 Pope Zacharias.
741–775 Constantine V Emperor.
743 Boniface archbishop of Mainz.
749 Aistulf king of the Lombards.
750 Fall of the Umayyads.
751–768 Pepin king.
754–756 Frankish Interventions in Italy.
755 Death of Boniface.
    'Abd-ar-Raḥmān I founds an independent dynasty in Spain.
756 Desiderius king of the Lombards.
757–796 Offa king in Mercia.
759 Pepin's conquest of Septimania.
768–771 Charles and Carloman.
771–814 Charles alone.
772–795 Pope Hadrian I.
772–804 Saxon Wars.
774 End of the Lombard kingdom.
778 Roncevalles.
787 Second Council of Nicaea.
    Submission of Benevento.
    Deposition of Tassilo.
787–802 Archbishopric of Lichfield.
794 Diet of Frankfort.
795 Capture of the Avar Ring.

795–816 Pope Leo III.
799 Outrage on Pope Leo (25 Mar.).
800 Arrival of Charles at Rome (24 Nov.).
The Imperial Coronation (25 Dec.).
807–811 Danish Wars.
811 Completion of the Spanish March.
814 Death of Charles (28 Jan.).
831 Saracen conquest of Palermo.
846 Saracen attack on Rome.
859 Saracen conquest of Sicily completed.
871 Capture of Bari from the Saracens.
909–1171 Fāṭimites in Egypt.
915 Saracens driven from the Garigliano.
1033–1040 Campaigns of Maniakes in Sicily.
1061–1091 Norman conquest of Sicily.

INDEX

Ariminum, Council of, 498

Arioald, Duke of Turin, made king of the Lombards, 202 ; and Friuli, 203

Aripert, King of the Lombards, favours the Catholics, 204; daughter of, marries Grimoald, 205; 394

Aripert II, King of the Lombards, destroys the descendants of Perctarit, 210 sq. ; pro-Roman policy, 211

Aristobulus, suppresses the disloyalty of the troops, 279

Aristotle, works of, sent by Pope Paul into Francia, 591

Arles, besieged by Franks, 114, 161; 118 ; seat of a metropolitan, 145; monasteries at, 147; trade of, 155 ; 159; Arabs take, 374 ; Augustine consecrated at, 516

Arles, Bishops of. *See* Caesarius, Vergilius

Arles, Council of, British bishops present at, 498

Arles, province of, and the Papacy, 146, 256, 258 sq.

Armagh (Ardd Mache), founded, 507

Armenia, 7; rivalry of Persia and Rome in, 28 sqq.; *magister militum* appointed for, 32; Justinian's forts in, 33; 35, 39; Monophysites in, 44 sq.; Roman law in, 58; disturbances in, 270 sq.; not mentioned in the treaty, 272; Persians invade, 274; 276, 278 sqq.; Maurice raises recruits in, 283; civil war in, 285; Persians supreme in, 289 sqq.; Persians driven from, 293; 294, 299; Saracens invade, 353, 393; military rule in, 395 sq.; Justinian II in, 406; taken by Arabs, 407; 408 sq.; Romans defeated in, 410

Armenia Quarta, betrayed to the Arabs, 410; Armenians settled in, 414

Armeniaci, the, 396, 416

Armenians, in the imperial army, 11, 343; religious persecution of, 270 sq.; 298; and religious controversy, 403 ; expelled from the Empire, 414

Arminius, chief of the Cherusci, 194, 639

Arminius, deacon, attends British bishops at Council of Arles, 498

Armorica, 118 sq., 466

Armthwaite, 475

Arnefrit, son of Lupus of Friuli, tries to regain the duchy, 205 ; killed, *ib.*

Arnfels, 446

Arno, Archbishop of Salzburg, writes to Alcuin about Leo III, 704

Arnulf, Emperor, as duke of Carinthia, 449; 660

Arnulf, St, Bishop of Metz, resists Brunhild, 123; rules in Austrasia, 124, 126, 136, 575 sq. ; 697, 699

Arnulf, grandson of Pepin II, Mayor of the Palace in Austrasia, 128

Arrago, River, 166

Arras, 120

Art, poverty of in Gaul, 157 sq.; of the Visigoths in Spain, 193 ; Lombardic, 207; Christian, in Britain, 501

Artavasdes, son of Witiza, driven from Spain, 182 sq.; helped by Arabs, 185 sq.; re-established at Cordova, 186

Artavazd, commander of the Armeniacs, refuses to recognise Theodosius III, 416; comes to terms with Leo, 417

Arvalus, god, 474

Arvernians (Arverni), the, at the battle of Vouglé, 114; 464

Arxamon, victory of Chosroes II at, 285

Arzanene, invaded by Marcianus, 272 ; invaded by Maurice, 275; ceded, 406

Ás, god, 489

Asad, Bedouin tribe, 319, 334 sq.; defeated, 336

Asad ibn al-Furāt, leads attack on Sicily, 382

Asaph, Bishop of St Asaph's, 499

Asarius, Byzantine general, defeated by Visigoths, 173

Ashdown, laid waste, 553

Asia, continent, 28, 30 sqq., 42; religious persecution in, 44; 50, 156, 263; Turks in the west of, 269; 283, 292, 330; Arab expansion in, ch. xi. *passim*, 365; 377; the Shī'ites in, 379; 429, 433

Asia, province of, 284; Slavs ravage, 296; Sahrbarâz in, 295, 299; 391, 417

Asia Minor, importance of, to Empire, 27; revival of Monophysitism in, 46; flight of Maurice to, 282; the Persians in, 290, 292; Heraclius recovers, 293; 294, 329, 353, 379; Arabs in, 393 sqq., 412; Slavs settled in, 406; 407, 410, 413, 437 *note*, 439, 451, 462

Asnām, Berbers defeated at, 377

Aspidius, King of Aregenses, 167

Assanam (Assuagin), Roderick said to have taken refuge at, 185 *note*

Assyria, 298

Assyrians, 437 *note*

Asterius, Archbishop of Milan, consecrates Birinus, 525

Asti, defeat of Frankish army near, 205

Asti, Duke of. *See* Gundoald

Astorga, resists Leovigild's attack, 166

Asturians, the, in insurrection, 167

Asturias, province, 166, 190; Christian kingdom of, conquered by Charles the Great, 604

Athalaric, grandson of Theodoric, king of the Ostrogoths in Italy, 10; death, 14; 161, 643

Athanagild, King of Visigoths in Spain, helped by Justinian, 19, 163; marriages of daughters to Frankish kings, 120; made king, 163 ; at war with Byzantines, 164; prosperous rule, *ib.*; death, *ib.*; 165, 259; brought up at Constantinople, 260, 283

Athanasius, St, Bishop of Alexandria, cited, 498, 500; 688

Athanasius, Patriarch, and the religious controversy, 398

Athanasius, patrician, 291 ; ambassador to the Avars, 295

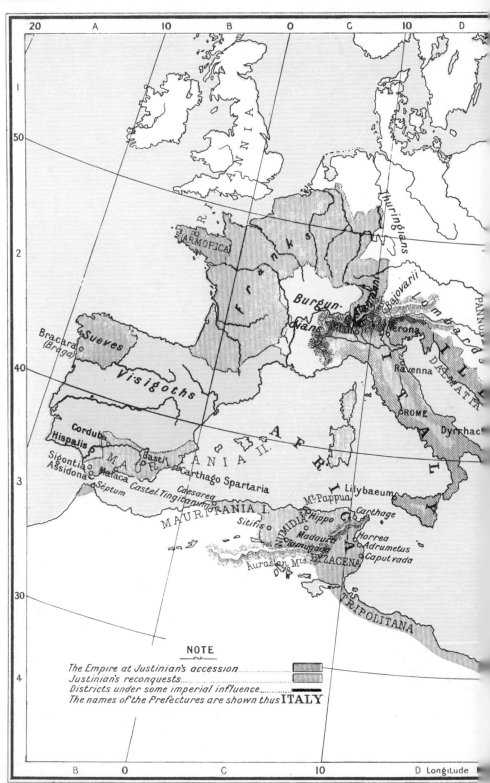

NOTE

The Empire at Justinian's accession..............
Justinian's reconquests..............
Districts under some imperial influence..............
The names of the Prefectures are shown thus **ITALY**

Map 15

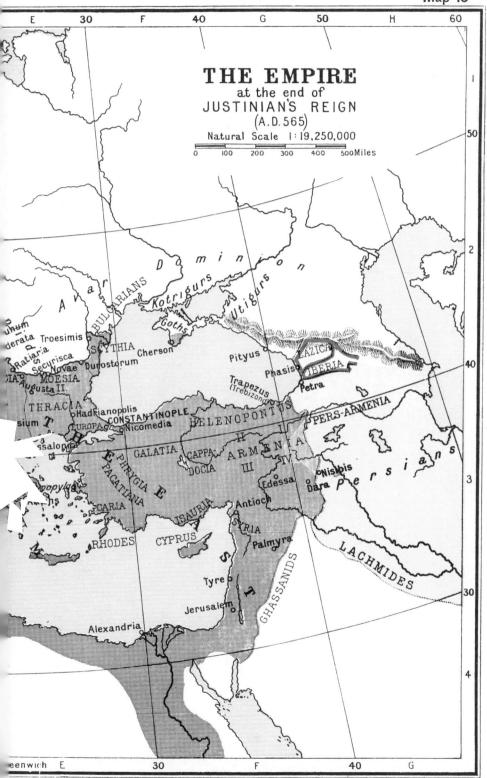

THE EMPIRE
at the end of
JUSTINIAN'S REIGN
(A.D.565)
Natural Scale 1:19,250,000

0   100   200   300   400   500 Miles

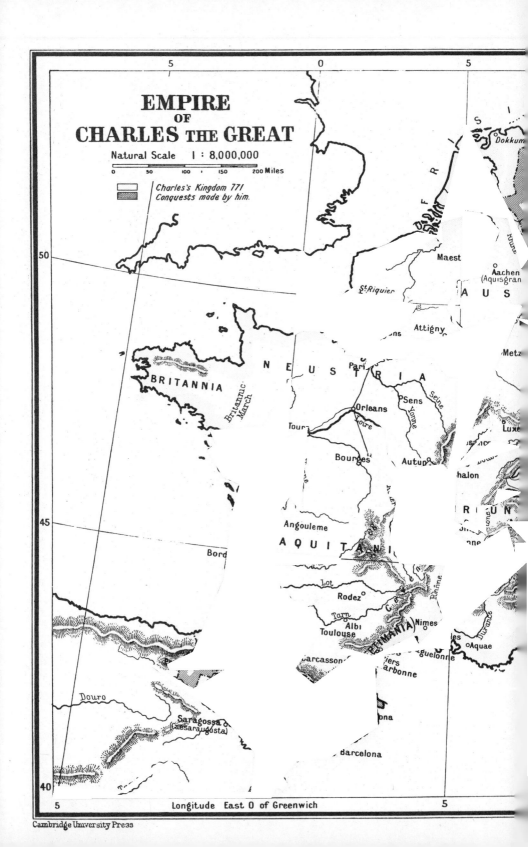

EMPIRE
OF
CHARLES THE GREAT

Natural Scale   1 : 8,000,000

0   50   100   150   200 Miles

Charles's Kingdom 771
Conquests made by him.

5   0   5

Dokkum

FR

S

Maest

Aachen
(Aquisgran

AUS

St Riquier

Attigny

ns

Metz

N E U S T R I A

Pari

Sens

Seine

Orleans

Yonne

Luxe

Tour

Loire

Bourges

Autun

Chalon

50

45

BRITANNIA

Britannic
March

R U N

Angouleme

nne

AQUITANI

Bord

Lot

Rodez

Rhône

Tarn

Albi

Toulouse

SEMANTA

Nimes

Carcasson

es

Aquae

Barbonne

guelonne

Douro

P

Saragossa
(Caesaraugusta)

ona

40

Barcelona

5   0   5

Longitude   East 0 of Greenwich

Cambridge University Press

Map 16

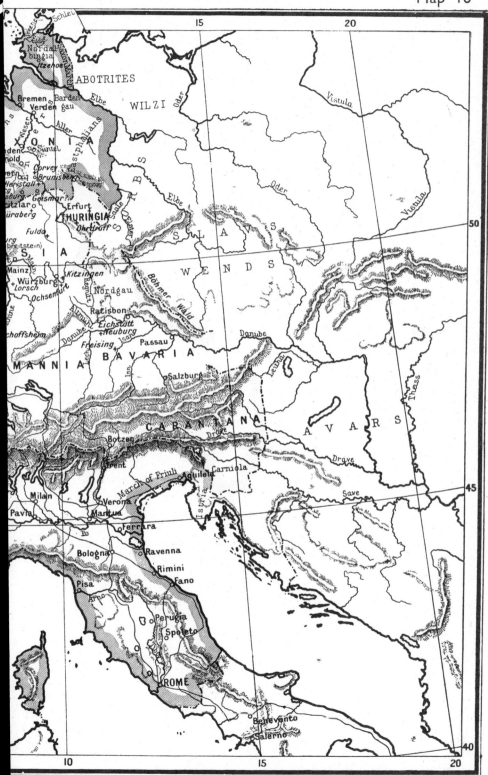

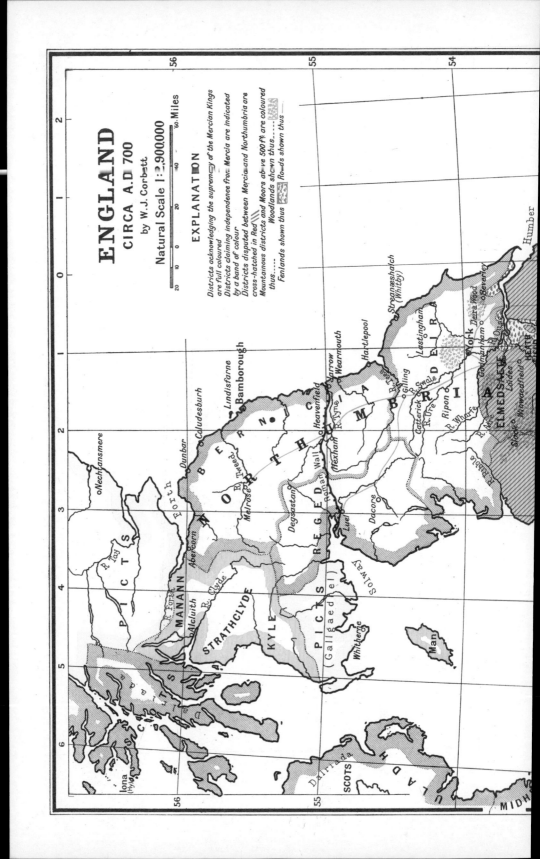

ENGLAND

CIRCA A.D. 700

by W.J. Corbett.

Natural Scale 1:2,900000

20 10 0 20 40 60. Miles

EXPLANATION

Districts acknowledging the supremacy of the Mercian Kings are full coloured
Districts claiming independence from Mercia are indicated by a band of colour
Districts disputed between Mercia and Northumbria are cross-hatched in Red
Mountainous districts and Moors above 500 ft. are coloured thus
Woodlands shown thus
Fenlands shown thus
Roads shown thus

Map 17

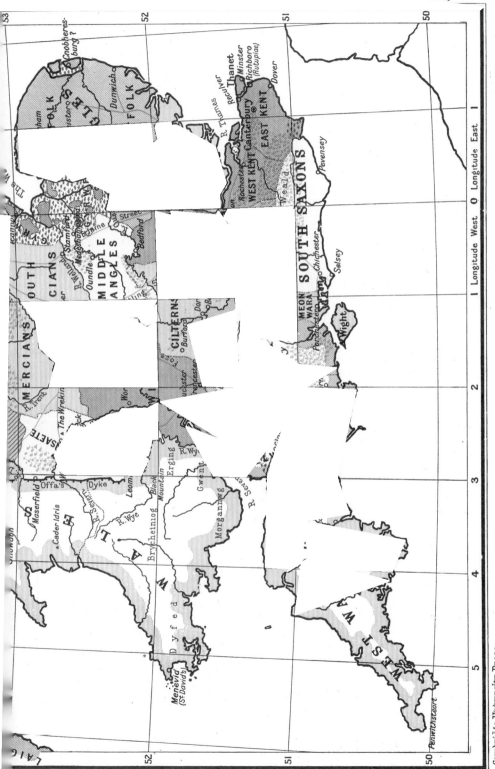

Cambridge University Press

MAP 18
The Eastern Frontier
of
The Empire

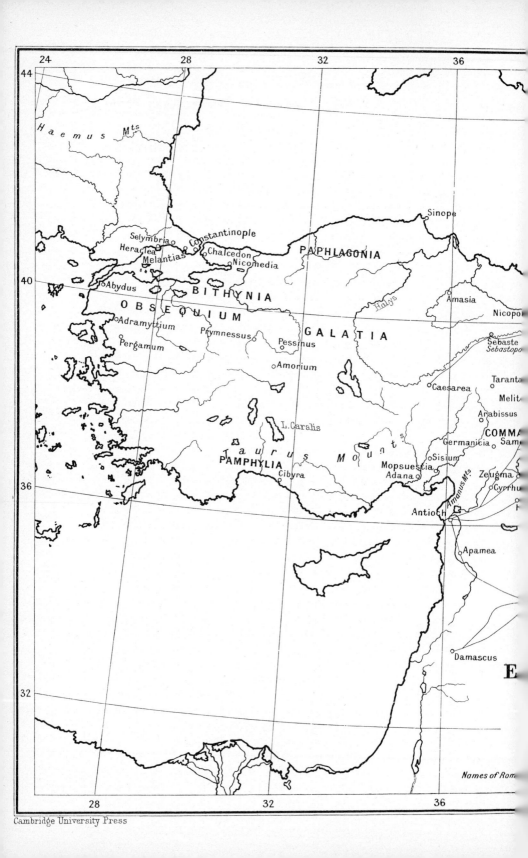

Map 18

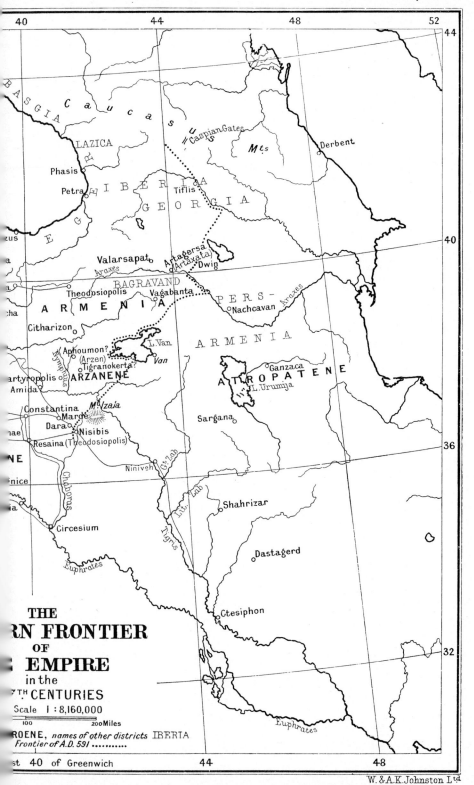

40   44   48   52   44

BASGIA

Caucasus

LAZICA

Phasis

Petra

IBERIA

GEORGIA

Caspian Gates

Mts

Derbent

Tiflis

40

Valarsapat

Artagersa
(Artaxata)

Dwig

Araxes

BAGRAVAND

Theodosiopolis

Vagabanta

PERS-

ARMENIA

Nachcavan

Araxes

Citharizon

L.Van

ARMENIA

Aphoumon?
(Arzen)

Van

Tigranokerta?

ARZANENE

Ganzaca

ATROPATENE

L.Urumija

Nymphius

Martyropolis

Amida?

Constantina

Marde

Dara

Nisibis

Resaina (Theodosiopolis)

M. Izala

Sargana

Niniveh

Gt. Zab

36

Chaboras

Lit. Zab

Shahrizar

Circesium

Tigris

Dastagerd

Euphrates

Ctesiphon

32

THE
RN FRONTIER
OF
EMPIRE
in the
7TH CENTURIES

Scale 1 : 8,160,000

100   200 Miles

ROENE, *names of other districts* IBERIA
Frontier of A.D. 591 ....

st 40 of Greenwich   44   48

W.&A.K.Johnston Ltd

Map 19

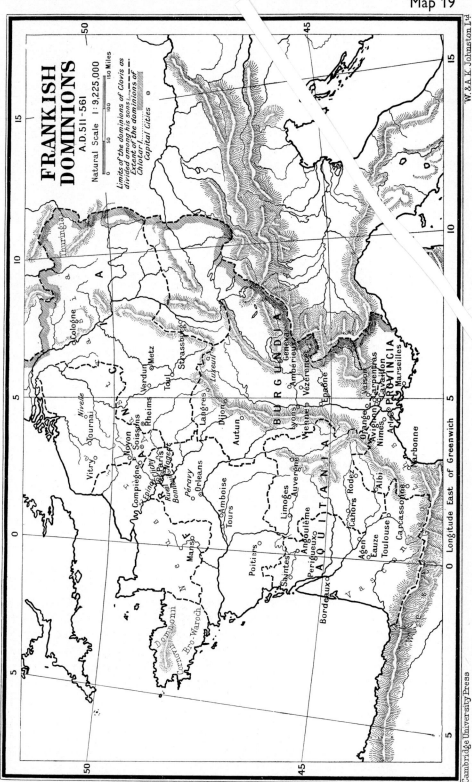

FRANKISH
DOMINIONS
A.D. 511 – 561
Natural Scale 1 : 9,225,000
0   50   100   150 Miles

Limits of the dominions of Clovis as
divided among his sons
Extent of the dominions of
Chlotar I
Capital Cities

Cambridge University Press
W. & A.K. Johnston Ltd.

Map 20

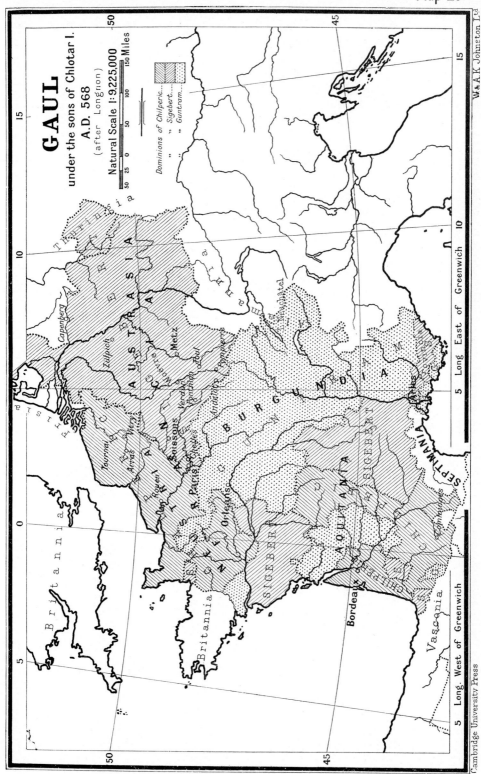

GAUL
under the sons of Chlotar I.
A.D. 568
(after Longnon)

Natural Scale 1:9,225,000

150 Miles

Dominions of Chilperic......
" " Sigebert......
" " Guntram......

Cambridge University Press

W. & A. K. Johnston Ltd

MAP 21
Spain
to illustrate the
Visigothic Era

Map 21

SPAIN
to illustrate the
VISIGOTHIC ERA

Natural Scale 1 : 4,800,000

Provinces are shown according to modern divisions

SPAIN
at the time of the
VISIGOTHIC INVASION

W.&A.K. Johnston Ltd

MAP 22
Italy
under the Lombards

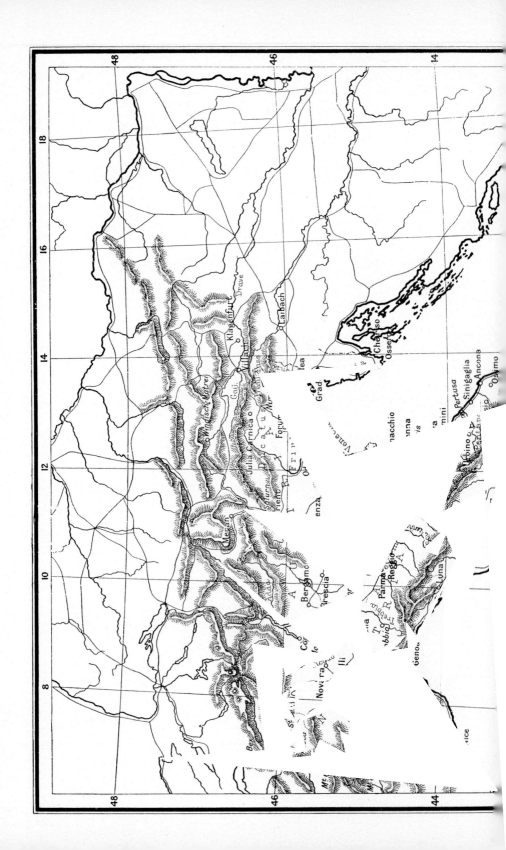

Map 22

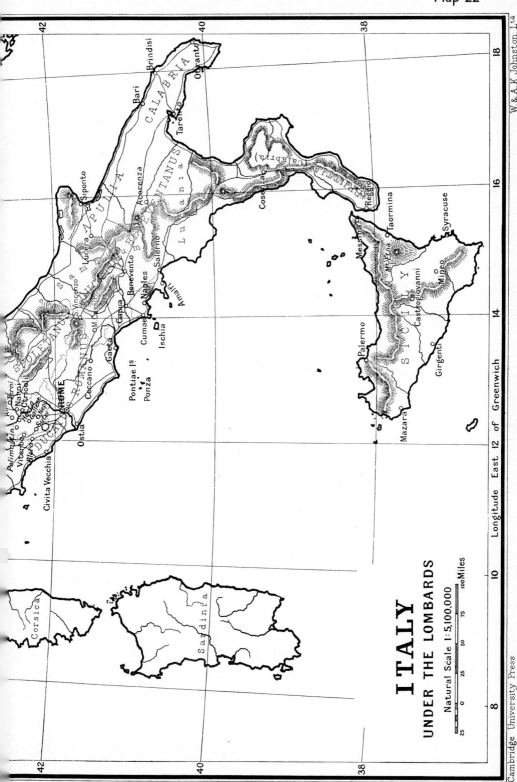

ITALY
UNDER THE LOMBARDS

Natural Scale 1:5,100,000

100 Miles

25 0 25 50 75

Cambridge University Press

W & A.K Johnston. L^td

MAP 23
Arabia
and
Egypt

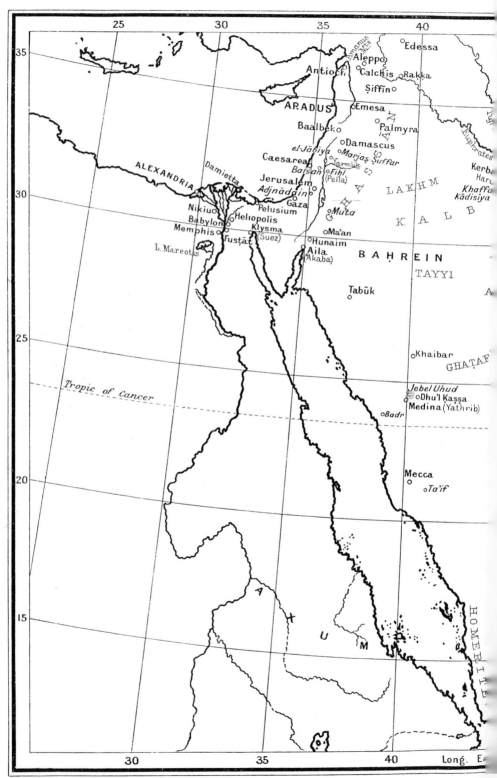

Map 23

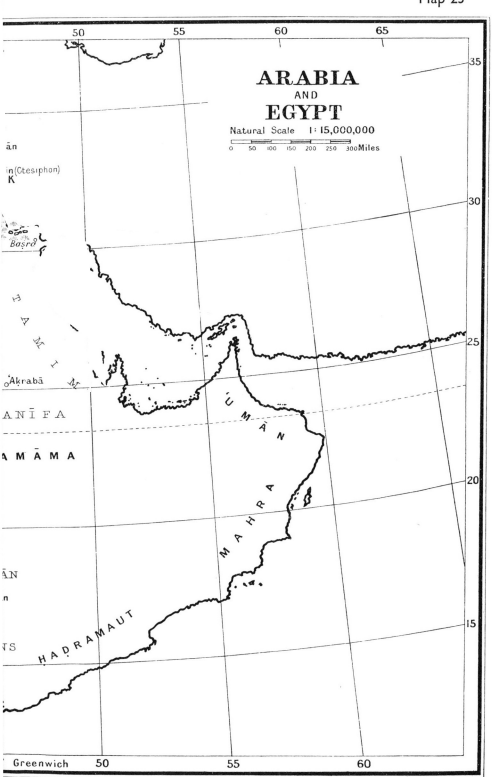

ARABIA
AND
EGYPT

Natural Scale 1: 15,000,000

0   50   100   150   200   250   300 Miles

35

30

25

20

15

ān

in (Ctesiphon)
K

Baṣra

ᴴ

ᴬ
ᴹ
ᴵ

ₒAḳrabā

ANĪFA

AMĀMA

ʿUMĀN

MAHRA

ĀN
n

HADRAMAUT
TS

Greenwich   50   55   60

50   55   60   65

MAP 24
The Caliphate
under Hārūn-er-Rashīd

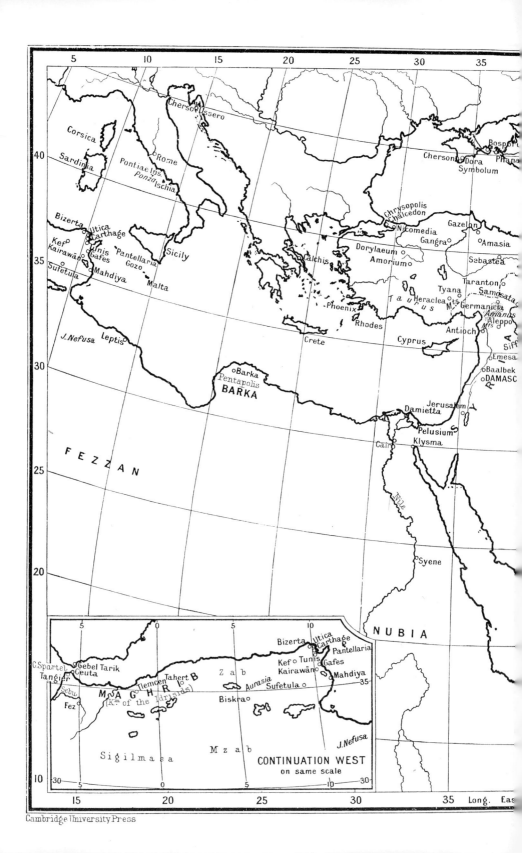

Map 24

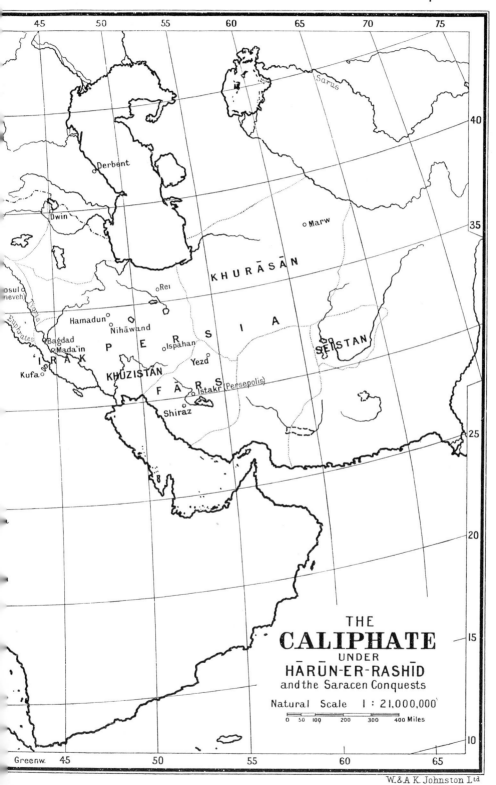

THE
CALIPHATE
UNDER
HĀRŪN-ER-RASHĪD
and the Saracen Conquests

Natural Scale 1 : 21,000,000

0   50   100   200   300   400 Miles

W.&A.K. Johnston Lᵗᵈ

Map 25

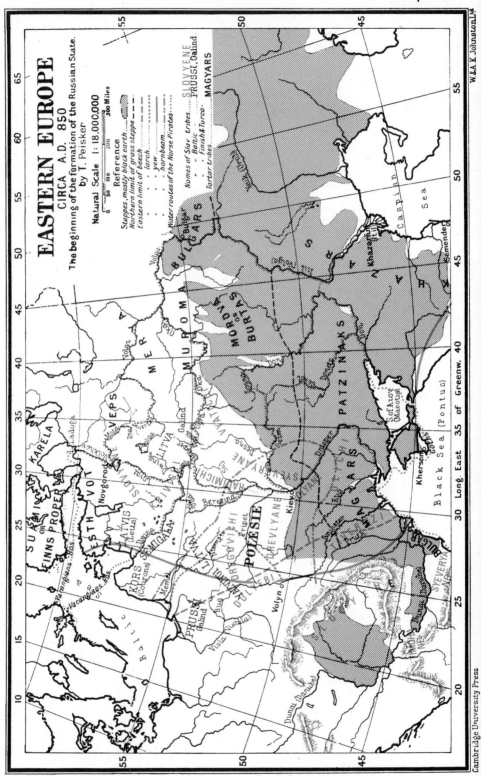

EASTERN EUROPE
CIRCA A.D. 850
The beginning of the formation of the Russian State.
by T. Peisker

Natural Scale 1:18,000,000

0   50   100   200   300 Miles

Reference

Steppes, mostly black earth.........
Northern limit of grass steppe.........
Eastern limit of beech.........
„ „ larch.........
„ „ yew.........
„ „ hornbeam.........
Water routes of the Norse Pirates.........

Names of Slav. tribes.....SLOVYENE
„ „ Baltic „ .....PRUSSI, Galind.
„ „ Finish&Turco- „ .....
Tartar tribes.........MAGYARS

W.&A.K.Johnston Ltd

MAP 26
The Western Front
of
Slavdom

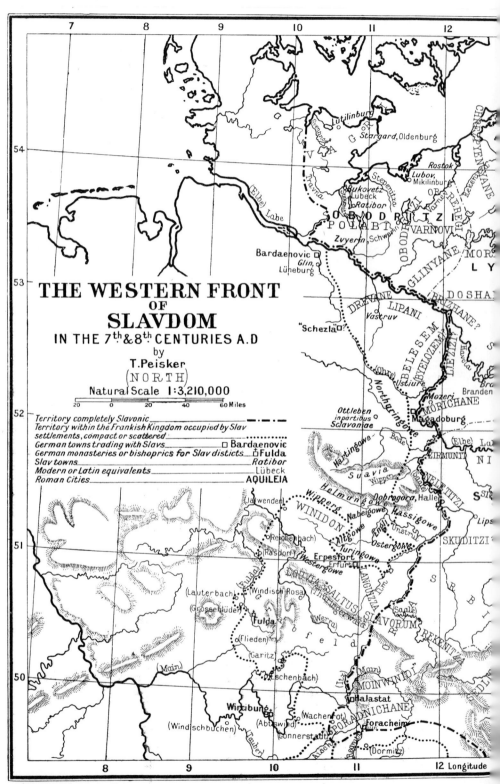

THE WESTERN FRONT
OF
SLAVDOM
IN THE 7ᵗʰ & 8ᵗʰ CENTURIES A.D
by
T.Peisker
(NORTH)
Natural Scale 1:3,210,000

20   0   20   40   60 Miles

Territory completely Slavonic _____ – – – –
Territory within the Frankish Kingdom occupied by Slav
settlements, compact or scattered _____ ....
German towns trading with Slavs _____ □ Bardaenovic
German monasteries or bishoprics for Slav disticts _ ⏥Fulda
Slav towns _____ Ratibor
Modern or Latin equivalents _____ Lübeck
Roman Cities _____ **AQUILEIA**

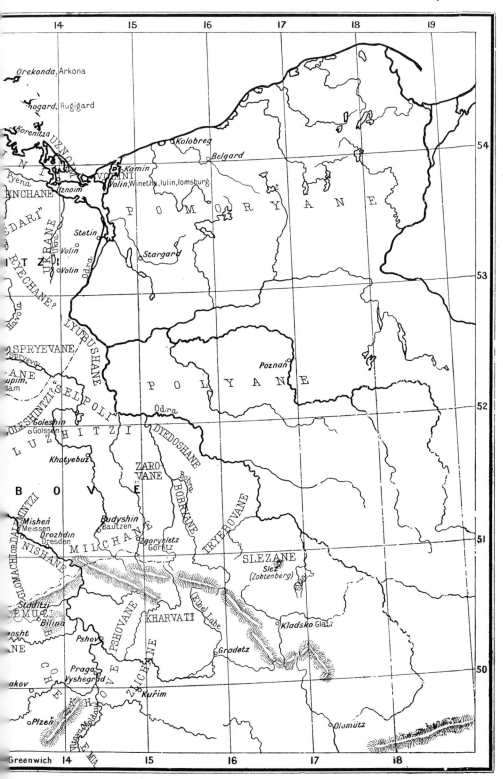

Orekonda, Arkona

hogard, Rugigard

Korenitza

UZNOY

N

Byena

RENCHANE

EDARI"

I T Z

RYECHANE?

SPRYEVANE
Spryevo

ANE
upim,
lam

OLESHINTZI SELPOLI

L U Z H I T Z I

B O V E

HINTZI

Mishen
Meissen

Drozhdin
Dresden

NISHANE

SIOMACHI DALE

Stadtitz

EMUZI

Bilina

osht

NE

Kolobreg

Belgard

Kamin

VOLINI

Iznoim

Volin, Winetha, Iulin, Iomsburg

Stetin

Odra

Volin

Volin

Stargard

UKRANE

LYUBUSHANE

P O M O R Y A N E

P O L Y A N E

Poznań

Odra

Goleshin
Golssen

Khotyebuz

ZARO-
VANE

DYEDOSHANE

Bobra

BOBRANE

Budyshin
Bautzen

Zgoryeletz
Görlitz

M I L C H A N E

TRYEBOVANE

SLEZANE

Slez
(Zobtenberg)

Slez

KHARVATI

Elbe Labe

Kladsko Glatz

CHO

Pshov

PSHOVANE

ZICHNE

Gradetz

Praga
Vyshegrad

akov

Plzeň

Kuřim

Olomütz

EMJA

Mlada

54

53

52

51

50

MAP 26 b
The Western Front
of
Slavdom

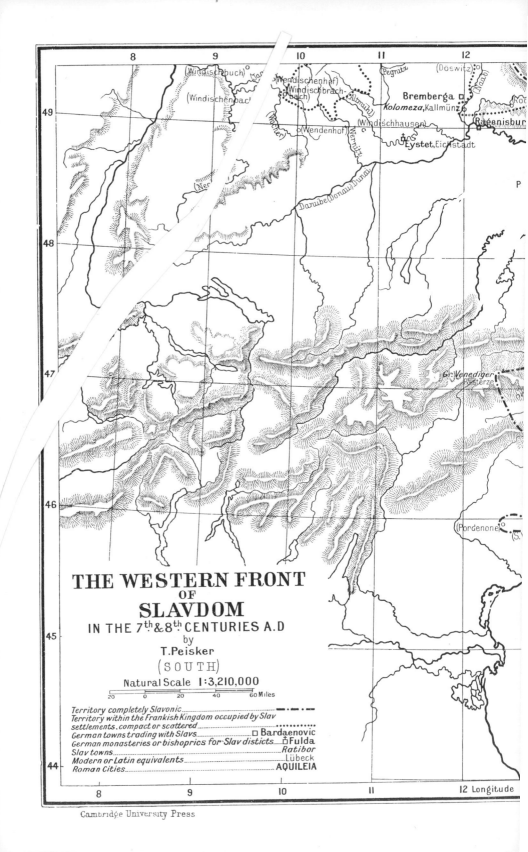

THE WESTERN FRONT
OF
SLAVDOM
IN THE 7th & 8th CENTURIES A.D
by
T. Peisker
(S O U T H)

Natural Scale 1:3,210,000

20   0   20   40   60 Miles

Territory completely Slavonic	—·—·—·—
Territory within the Frankish Kingdom occupied by Slav settlements, compact or scattered	··········
German towns trading with Slavs	□ Bardaenovic
German monasteries or bishoprics for Slav disticts	☐ Fulda
Slav towns	Ratibor
Modern or Latin equivalents	Lübeck
Roman Cities	AQUILEIA

Cambridge University Press

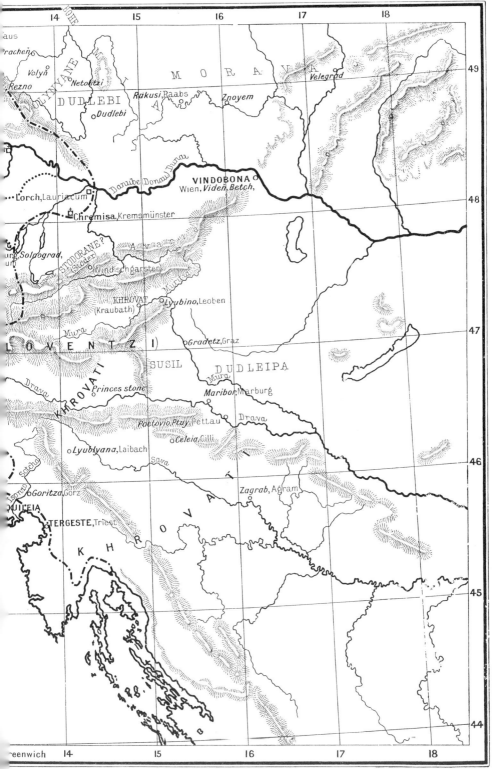

MAP 27
Scotland and Ireland
to illustrate
The Conversion of the Celts

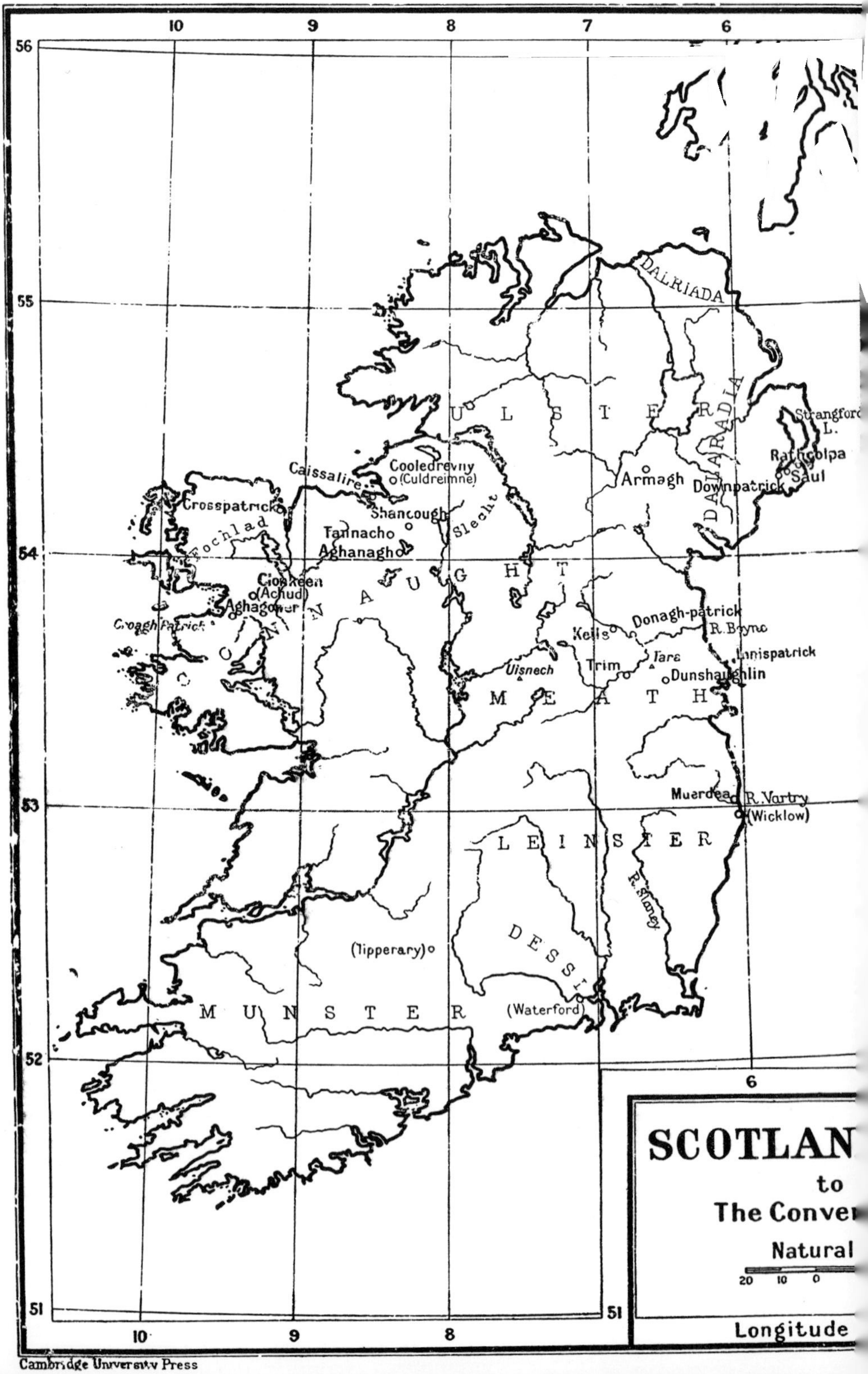
SCOTLAN
to
The Conve
Natural
Longitude
DALRIADA
DALARADIA
ULSTER
CONNAUGHT
MEATH
LEINSTER
MUNSTER
DESSI
Strangford L.
Rathcolpa
Saul
Downpatrick
Armagh
Cooledrevny
(Culdreimne)
Caissalire
Crosspatrick
Fochlad
Shancough
Slecht
Tamnacho
Aghanagh
Cloonkeen
(Achud)
Aghagower
Croagh Patrick
Donagh-patrick
R. Boyne
Keils
Tara
Inispatrick
Uisnech
Trim
Dunshaughlin
Muerdea
R. Vartry
(Wicklow)
R. Slaney
(Tipperary)
(Waterford)
56
55
54
53
52
51
10
9
8
7
6
20
10
0
Cambridge University Press

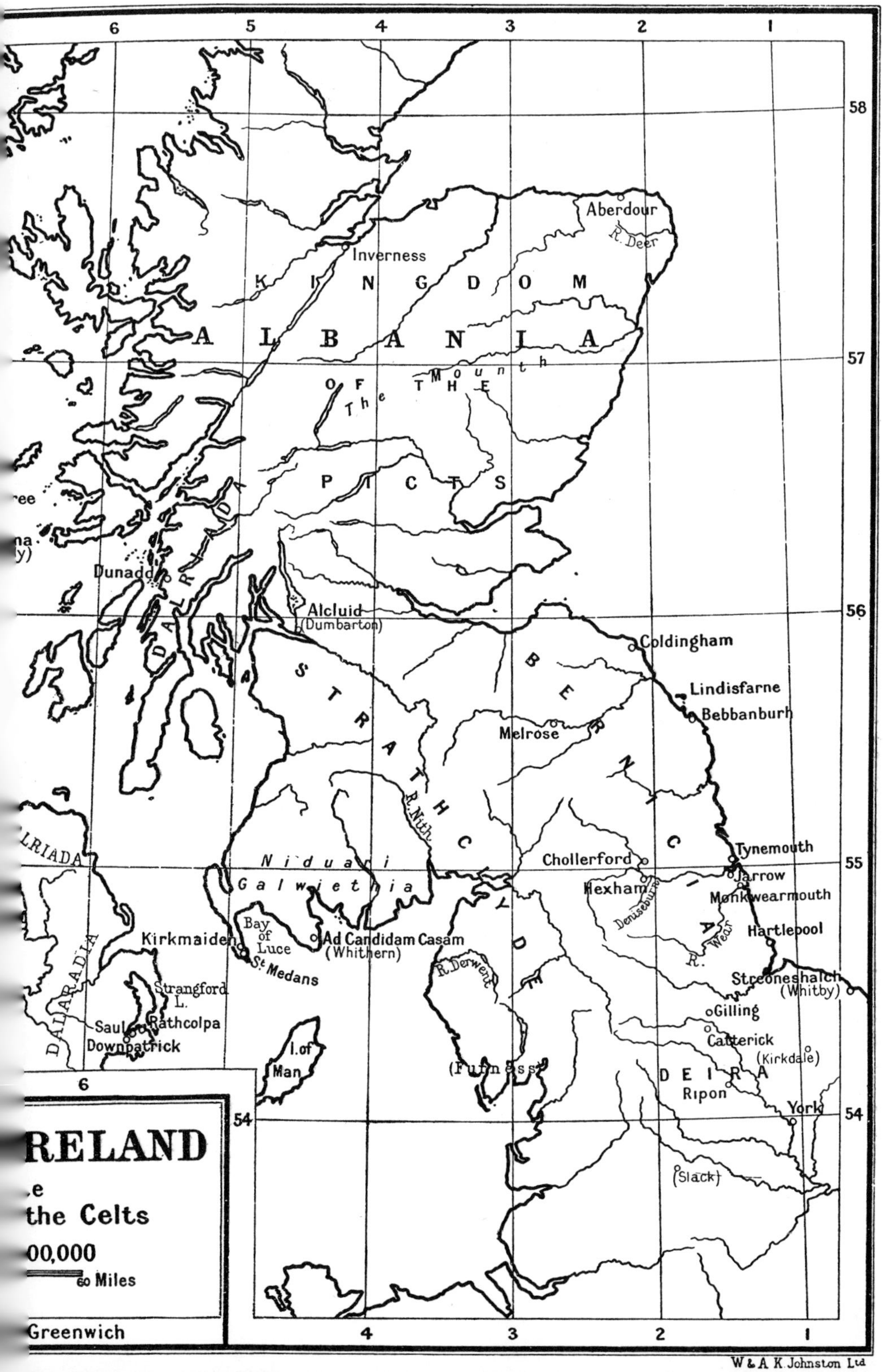
6
5
4
3
2
1
58
57
56
55
54
Aberdour
R. Deer
Inverness
KINGDOM
ALBANIA
OF THE
The Mounth
PICTS
Dunadd
DALRIADA
Alcluid
(Dumbarton)
STRATHCLYDE
BERNICIA
Coldingham
Lindisfarne
Bebbanburh
Melrose
R. Nith
Niduari
Galwiethia
Chollerford
Tynemouth
Jarrow
Monkwearmouth
Hexham
Deniseburn
R. Wear
Hartlepool
Streoneshalch
(Whitby)
Kirkmaiden
Bay of Luce
Ad Candidam Casam
(Whithern)
St Medans
R. Derwent
Gilling
Catterick
(Kirkdale)
DEIRA
Ripon
York
(Slack)
(Furness)
I. of Man
Strangford L.
Saul
Rathcolpa
Downpatrick
DALARADIA
LRIADA
ree
na
y)
RELAND
e
the Celts
00,000
60 Miles
Greenwich
W & A K. Johnston Ltd